PHILOSOPHY FOR A NEW GENERATION

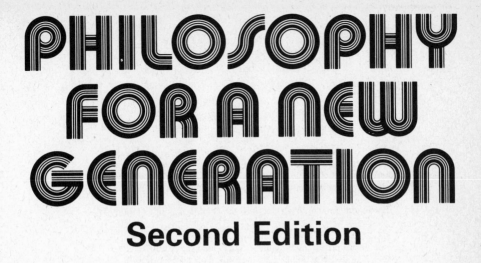

PHILOSOPHY FOR A NEW GENERATION

Second Edition

A. K. Bierman
San Francisco State College

James A. Gould
University of South Florida

The Macmillan Company, New York

Credits and Acknowledgments

Scholarly credits and permission acknowledgments may be found at the bottom of the page on which an essay begins. What immediately follows here are credits to companies who required that their acknowledgments be given on the copyright page.

From *Revolution as Theatre* by Robert Brustein. Copyright © 1971 by Robert Brustein. Reprinted by permission of LIVERIGHT, New York.

Reprinted by permission of Charles Scribner's Sons from *The Life of Reason*, pages 89-103, by George Santayana. Copyright 1953 Daniel M. Cory.

"Justice Through Revolution" is reprinted by permission of Charles Scribner's Sons from *Moral Man and Immoral Society* by Reinhold Niebuhr. Copyright 1932 Charles Scribner's Sons; renewal copyright © 1960 Reinhold Niebuhr.

Reprinted by permission of Charles Scribner's Sons from *Racism and the Christian Understanding of Man*, pages 19-30, 36-38, 86, and 114, by George D. Kelsey. Copyright © 1965 George D. Kelsey.

Reprinted by permission of Charles Scribner's Sons from *Oriental Philosophies*, pages 52-63, by John M. Koller. Copyright © 1970 Charles Scribner's Sons.

In memory of my union brothers Al Anderson, Sidney Zink, Chuck Tyner, Paul Hayner, Ernesto Lombardi, and Floyd Cave, who, while they were in the world, were also of it.

A. K. B.

For Arthur K. Bierman, whose successful fights for the unions and against HUAC were inspirations for the old and new generations alike.

J. A. G.

In part, the problems of philosophy are unchanging; in part, they vary from age to age, according to the special characteristics of human life and thought at the time; and in the best philosophers of every age these two parts are so interwoven that the permanent problems appear sub specie saeculi, *and the special problems of the age* sub specie aeternitatis.

R. G. Collingwood
The Idea of History

Preface to the Second Edition

We are gratified by the reception that the first edition of this book has received. Apparently, many professors in philosophy, humanities, religion, and even English felt that it was time to widen the scope of the "acceptable" literature and confront college and university classes with current issues.

The spirit of the first edition lives even more so in this second edition. We think it is highly improved because we have had a chance to see new literature and to take a wider and more critical look at the old literature. Also, users of the first edition have given us excellent suggestions for improvements, and we have happily incorporated many of them—to the point that this second edition is virtually a cooperative effort. Perhaps this acknowledgment partially justifies our belief that this is the best anthology of its kind available.

This edition is larger by nine essays; and thirty-four of the seventy-two essays (almost one half) are new to this edition. All the introductions are new, with the exception of the first one, although it has been modified.

The greatest changes are the addition of a chapter relating metaphysics to ecology (Chapter Eight) and the deletion of the chapter on technology (Chapter VII of the first edition). However, we have retained Marx's essay for another chapter in the book. The chapter on the self (Chapter Seven, "In Search of Self and Identity") is the one most changed. It is now much less traditionally Western. The chapter includes some essays on Eastern thought, about which students are avid but not always well informed; we have also added essays on alienation and on the self's social environment.

The section "Love and Sex" (fourth section of Chapter Three) has been almost completely changed, with greater emphasis on concepts. The same holds true for the section "Violence" (second section in Chapter Four). To the chapter "Third World Liberation" (Chapter Six), we have added essays on Chicanos, Chinese, and women's liberation.

Some of the traditional authors added are Peter Kropotkin, Josiah Royce, and Immanuel Kant. Among the contemporary authors added are Isaiah Berlin, George Santayana, R. G. Collingwood, Alfred Whitehead, and Jean-Paul Sartre.

Students new to philosophy are always somewhat apprehensive about what will go on in a philosophy class, its being new to them because few high schools offer philosophy courses. Likewise, some professors who have never used anthologies are often apprehensive about how the book can be fitted to their more familiar curriculum. They may not be certain how they can actually use it in their classes. To reassure instructors that the goals to be achieved with this book are both familiar and desirable, we list below twelve kinds of aims students can expect to satisfy with the use of this anthology.

1. Philosophy gets its momentum from argument. The book's essays are saturated with arguments. From these, the student will learn to identify arguments, to evaluate and counter them, and to state arguments of his own.

2. The student will learn how to relate arguments to one another and learn to

appreciate what persistent, sustained thought on a topic is. Robert Audi's essay (second section of Chapter Four) is a particularly good example of close, related reasoning.

3. By reading philosophical essays and by carefully analyzing them, the student will learn how to state his own views more clearly and completely and in a more organized way.

4. He will be able to improve his ability to justify and defend his views once they are clearly and completely stated. Learning how to handle arguments goes hand in hand with organizing his thoughts and data and with anticipating objections that others will have. For instance, the student may think himself a moral relativist. Can he state what that is? And how can he justify that belief if he also believes that racism is wrong for everyone?

5. He will improve his skills in asking productive, interesting questions. For example, in thinking about revolution, what questions should he ask that when answered will constitute a good theory of or defensible opinion about revolution or will advance his understanding of or yield a fresh angle on revolution?

6. The student will learn what a philosophical problem is as distinguished from a question. A problem exists when two opposing views can be defended by arguments that are apparently equally plausible. As an example of two initially equally plausible arguments, consult the introduction to Chapter Five, where we treat Socrates' argument from the *Crito* and a counterargument.

7. By reason of clear statement and sustained argument, the student will be able to see the bearing that various aspects of life, often compartmentalized, have on each other. One instance of this occurs in Chapter Eight, where Alfred Whitehead's essay relates science, nature, poetry, history, morals, and metaphysics.

8. Once launched on relating various aspects of life and with his skills for argument well in hand, the student can begin to formulate an ideology. On the notion of ideology, see the introduction to Chapter One.

9. Many of the essays in this book give classic, influential, abiding arguments and answers to familiar problems and questions. The proofs for the existence of God in Chapter Nine are good examples of this, as are many essays in the chapter on morality (Chapter Three). Learning of these classic formulations will help the student gain historical understanding and perspective on his civilization.

10. When he and his friends are rapping about something, his conversations will be improved by philosophy because he will be able to keep on the track and make the talk productive, thus reducing the customary aimlessness, perhaps inconclusiveness, of such sessions.

11. The student will learn how to clarify his concepts. For example, how would he define "racism"? He can take a look at George Kelsey's essay (in Chapter Six) after trying to define it for himself. Or, he may consider the concept of "love." Everyone uses the word; does it have several meanings or only one? If several, are any of them related? And how do the definitions of it relate to morals, for example?

12. Because philosophy is essentially a dialogue, with a philosopher usually stating his views in opposition to someone else's, the student has to learn to locate his opponent's key arguments and to state his position fairly in order to make his own view worthy. The history of Western philosophy can be seen as a continuing dialogue, thinkers refining philosophies by a series of arguments, ripostes,

refinements, and defenses with and against each other, then the cycle beginning anew with arguments, ripostes, and so on. It is as rewarding, absorbing, and exciting an activity as any person can engage in.

There are some people who have helped make this a better book—and we warmly thank you, Robert A. Dyal, Robert Zaslow, Steward Shaw, Ron Hirschbein, Algis Michunas, Donald Wells, Frank Young, Jesus Contreras, Don Sherburne, and Melvyn Hornick, for your selfless and generous aid. We have to especially thank L. H. Grunebaum for his extensive balanced assessments; Jack Pitt, who has an elegant taste combined with an ordered mind (a perfect combination for a publisher's reader); and Charles Smith, who was our philosophy editor at Macmillan and who must be the most omnivorous reader in the hemisphere.

And who are those nice women floating in a Fellini atmosphere? Susan B. and Jeanette G., of course. M' ladies, thank you.

A. K. B.
J. A. G.

Preface to the First Edition

There are so many excellent introductory philosophy books available that we owe philosophy students and instructors a justification for adding another one. We would not have presumed to edit the book if it were to be only a variation on a familiar theme. On the contrary, we have tried to produce a book that will fill an obvious gap in the literature. There is at present no philosophy anthology that meets the rising student and faculty demand for "relevance." Although "relevance" is a word that has been so tirelessly repeated that it has become tiresome, the hunger for relevance is not tiresome, and we shall probably not be spared the repetition of "relevance" until the demand is met. This anthology is designed for students of philosophy living in the 1970's.

In selecting material for this book, we kept the following in mind:

1. We tried to identify the fields of human interest and endeavor that are of high moment to young people today. These fields determined the choice of chapters.

2. We kept in mind the fact that most students who take an introductory course in philosophy will not take another or will take at most one other. Consequently, this anthology is not designed as an introduction solely for students who will major in philosophy.

3. Although philosophy is not a literary subject, it is a field in which, like any other, good writing promotes comprehension. For this reason, the writing merits of a piece had to be as prominent as its philosophical merits before it was accepted by us.

4. The essays were chosen with an eye for stimulating class discussion and for helping the student to improve his own philosophizing. This anthology is a survey neither of the great philosophers in history nor of the problems that have occupied the interest of prominent modern philosophers or well-known ancient philosophers.

5. We have been very concerned that philosophy not degenerate into a static, fusty exhibit in some mausoleum of ideas. One way of avoiding that is to spur a two-way influence between the practical and the intellectual worlds. We have been partial to essays that stimulate that influence.

Since the scope of the material that we have made eligible for selection is wider than is customary, we cannot pretend to have looked at all of it nor always to have picked the best available on a given topic. If this book merits subsequent editions, they will be improved by comments, references, and recommendations from teachers and students. We welcome your communications.

Many people have already given us generously of their time, their very life substance, and in gratitude we hereby acknowledge their help. Among those who gave us advice on selections are Jack Alexis, Anatole Anton, L. W. Beals, Russell Kahl, Mike Lerner, Jacob Needleman, Roberto Rivera, Peter Radcliff, and Eric Solomon.

Rudolph Weingartner set a high standard for publishers' readers by his measured assessment and fruitful suggestions. He escorted us back to the book, prepared for an improved effort.

Priscilla Johnson, Judy Barkan, and Rider Cooey, please accept our thanks for helping us wrestle a recalcitrant manuscript into a civil state.

A. K. B.
J. A. G.

Contents

TEN   Flight from Meaninglessness

INTRODUCTION: THE FIRE AND THE STONE

Howe canne won gett on sanss fylosoufee? Porley.

—Fanebius Perlyng

Anyone who believes the statement "Not everyone philosophizes" is one who takes the "high road" to philosophy. When he comes to number the philosophers, he would think of Socrates, Plato, Aristotle, Alfarabi, Spinoza, Hume, Locke, Kant, Hegel, Bradley, Wittgenstein, Russell, Moore, and Carnap. These are honored names. According to the high road, one who has no knowledge of philosophers like these knows little or nothing of philosophy.

So, what should we say of two men in a bar arguing whether a man, Tristan, who knew his death was near, is to be considered a suicide because he subsequently cut off his oxygen supply in order to provide his heart for a transplant? Are they philosophizing or not? They are not famous philosophers, perhaps only famous drinkers. One man says Tristan is a suicide because by his own hand he brought on his death by casting off his oxygen supply. The other avers Tristan is no suicide, because he died of natural causes; under oxygen he had only an artificial life. The first rejoins that it would not be suicide if a man severed his oxygen supply accidentally, but in this case it was a deliberate act calculated to end his life; hence, suicide. Intent is all. To this, the second replies that since by his act Tristan gave another person prolonged life, Tristan is not to be considered a suicide but a donor. To call him a suicide is to condemn him; we should praise him instead, and because of that it is morally wrong to call him a suicide. The bartender keeps a discreet silence throughout, but when they leave, he remarks to the remaining customers, "Those two guys are always philosophizing." That is the "low road."

In this anthology we take both the low road and the high road. Philosophy is not something that occurs only in the books of great philosophers. It occurs whenever and wherever men ponder, discuss, or argue over the use, application, limits, or meaning of important ideas. The two men in the bar were arguing about the application of the idea of suicide to the man who cut off his oxygen supply; suicide is an important idea; therefore, the two men were philosophizing.

1

The low road to philosophy is a broader, more generous way. We have all traveled the low road. For anyone editing an anthology, the decision to include the low road as well as the high road broadens the scope of his choice. He is no longer confined to making selections from historically great philosophers or from contemporary, famous, or fashionable ones.

This is a consequence that we, the editors, sought, for it freed us to choose material about ideas that are more directly and obviously important to you. We believe that an introductory philosophy course should begin where you are rather than where past thinkers were. This does not mean that past philosophers or contemporary professional philosophers have nothing relevant to say about the ideas you are interested in. They often do, and some of their works are included in this anthology, but we believe that you will profit most from them if you start philosophizing from where you are and think your way to where they were or are.

When we say that philosophy is concerned with "important ideas," we introduce an element into our definition of philosophy that is subject to variance. An idea that is important to one man may not be important to another; an idea may be important to many people at one time and not at another; what may be important to healthy, young people may not be important to sick, old people; and so forth. We must not assume uncritically that there is an unchanging stock of ideas with which philosophy always has, is now, and always will be concerned. That gives one the impression that philosophy endures because it possesses the unchanging permanence of stone.

We could make a case that philosophy is more like fire than like stone. The stock of ideas with which philosophers have wrestled has continually changed; this stock has been as restless as flame. And like fire, philosophy's continued existence is assured only if it is fed fresh fuel. The universe of ideas is not static. Notice how delightfully archaic is the discussion between Mr. Square and Mr. Thwackum, the philosopher and the divine, respectively, in Henry Fielding's *Tom Jones* (Book III, Chapter III):

After this short introduction, the reader will be pleased to remember that the parson had concluded his speech with a triumphant question, to which he had apprehended no answer, viz., Can any honour exist independent of religion?

To this Square answered, that it was impossible to discourse philosophically concerning words till their meaning was first established: that there were scarce any two words of a more vague and uncertain signification than the two he had mentioned, for that there were almost as many different opinions concerning honour as concerning religion. "But," says he, "if by honour you mean the true natural beauty of virtue, I will maintain it may exist independent of any religion whatever. Nay," added he, "you yourself will allow it may exist independent of all but one: so will a Mahometan, a Jew, and all the maintainers of all the different sects in the world."

Thwackum replied, this was arguing with the usual malice of all the enemies of the true Church. . . . When I mention religion I mean the Christian religion; and not the Christian religion, but the Protestant religion; and not only the Protestant religion, but the Church of England.

Fielding may have raised the question in order to take a sly poke at Thwackum-type divines, but still it is not the kind of question that is likely to have been raised by you or your friends, either in jest or in earnest. The idea of honor is not in vogue at this time; we rarely see or discuss it. It was a prominent idea during the days of chivalry. Now there is an air of nostalgia about it: we think of World War I and von Richthofen and other aces when we think of honor. It may be popular again some day.

Here are some of the outmoded ideas that were once an important part of the stock-in-trade of professional philosophers: perfection, forgiveness, soul, substance, love, innocence, sin, fate, harmony, sublimity, conation, wisdom, authority, will, novelty, analysis, imagination, evolution, the artificial, ideals, dignity, friendship, passion, power, spirit, judgment, intuition, happiness, charity, adultery, obedience, simony, slavery, and immortality.

Why do the ideas that concern philosophers change? There are several explanations. To claim that ideas float in and out of the modish stock just as hemlines and necklines float up and down with the fashion is to make philosophical change appear too arbitrary. Still, there is some truth in it—a truth that should not be harshly condemned. Some people think fashion changes are frivolous and that the people who are influenced by them are weak-willed, wasteful conformists. Yet in a visit to an art museum, these same people will look at several paintings, instead of devoting all their time to one, no matter how "great" it may be. Why? Because they have got all they want out of the picture, are bored looking at it, are curious about the next one, or want to refresh their lagging spirit. The same reasons can be given for approving fashion changes—and for approving philosophical changes.

Changing social and political conditions also explain why some ideas gain importance and others lose it. Consider the effects of the civil rights movement. The ideas of equality, justice, prejudice, discrimination, segregation, and civil disobedience came to the fore. The wave of activism in the colleges and universities has cast up the ideas of participation, freedom, radicalism, relevance, revolution, power, respect, involvement, repression, and confrontation. The hippie and drug culture levitated, perhaps only momentarily, the ideas of love, religion, meditation, leisure, community, festival, tribe, and identity. Opposition to the Vietnam War has revived the ideas of pacifism, conscience and the law, dissent, and imperialism. Black militancy has spotlighted the ideas of oppression, violence, race, and rights.

We are living in a time of social ferment; changes are occurring at a dizzying pace. This has radically altered the stock of ideas with which we comprehend and advocate social change. Although most of the ideas we listed have never been totally eliminated from professional philosophers' stock of ideas, neither have most of them been of central concern. If the social changes that have made them prominent do not subside too soon, these ideas will in time receive greater attention from the professional philosophers. However, that does not dictate that we should wait to philosophize about them; because they are important, we are bound to philosophize about them—now. This anthology is designed to recognize the resurgence of these ideas, the need to philosophize about them, and the value of relating previous philosophizing to the newly prominent ideas.

It is difficult for anyone to get excited about ideas they think unimportant. To force you to "ponder, discuss, or argue over" ideas that are unimportant to you is to force you into juiceless exercises. Perhaps that would introduce you to a history of philosophical doctrines, but it would not help you learn to philosophize—and there is nothing sweeter, more satisfying, or more exhilarating when it is important to *you*.

Social change is not the only kind of change that shakes up our stock of ideas; technological and scientific change also does this. The idea of death has become prominent with the advent of heart transplants. The "pill" challenges our idea of right insofar as it bears on sexual conduct. New "bugging" devices make us anxious enough to think again about the idea of privacy. A Leningrad professor discovered a drug, phenigama, which combats the effect of "mechanization" of industrial work; the idea of social engineering, made so notorious by Aldous Huxley in *Brave New World,* is here! Soma has arrived.

The technologically possible prospect of preserving our bodies indefinitely by sudden freezing and of subsequently reviving them by thawing jeopardizes our idea of mortality, of wills and inheritance, and of divorce (one might just freeze himself until the spouse passes away). Although all these conceptual cramps may be uncomfortable, they at least make us rethink some ideas we had taken for granted.

Our concept of man as a unique, thinking, rational creature has been a source of pride to us. Thinking is man's glory, but the emergence of sophisticated computers that "calculate," "remember," "design" other computers, "follow" directions, and "communicate" casts a shadow on that pride. If machines can do all that, aren't they thinking? Can it be that man is only a supersophisticated machine? Our advances in technology have made us question our concept of man.

Automation has already made us think anew about the ideas of work, labor, and leisure. Since these ideas are not isolated, thinking about and discussing them pull other ideas into our current stock. For example, the shifting amount of work we will do in our life in ratio to the amount of leisure we will have makes a thoughtful person reassess his idea of education. Is a college education to be designed primarily to prepare us for work or for leisure?

So far, our main emphasis has been on matters that support the fire image of philosophy. We have taken the side of Heracleitus, the ancient Greek philosopher who thought that all things in the universe were in motion. "You cannot step twice into the same river," he said. Of the four elements that Greek cosmologists thought the world might be composed (earth, air, fire, and water), Heracleitus thought it to be fire. Fire symbolizes ceaseless change. If philosophy is like fire, then its incessant change continually introduces new ideas to philosophize about. In this case, nothing of past philosophy is relevant to the present or future; you cannot step twice into the same philosophy!

This is an extreme doctrine, although in part true. Its opposite extreme is the stone image of philosophy. Parmenides, another ancient Greek philosopher, claimed that there is no motion in the universe. If philosophy is like stone, then its stock of ideas does not change.

Our anthology represents a compromise. Philosophy is in part like fire and in part like stone. After all, there are some ideas that have formed an unchanging core in the stock of ideas. Philosophers have long and steadily contended with the concepts of good, truth, knowledge, evil, mind, matter, quality, quantity, and ideas. The fire part of philosophy led us to incorporate some essays outside the "classical" corpus, and the stone part led us to select some "classical" material; the compromise led us to relate classical material to current issues. The pedagogical justification for our stand is stated very nicely by William Paley in the preface to *The Principles of Moral and Political Philosophy* (1785, first edition):

An experience of nine years in the office of a public tutor in one of the universities, and in that department of education to which these chapters relate, afforded me frequent occasion to observe, that in discoursing to young minds upon topics of morality, it required much more pains to make them perceive the difficulty, than to understand the solution: that, unless the subject was so drawn up to a point, as to exhibit the full force of an object, or the exact place of a doubt, before any explanation was entered upon—in other words, unless some curiosity was excited before it was attempted to be satisfied, the labour of the teacher was lost. When information was not desired, it was seldom, I found, retained. I have made this observation my guide in the following work: that is, upon each occasion I have endeavored, before I suffered myself to proceed in the disquisition, to put the reader in complete possession of the question; and to do it in the way I thought most likely to stir up his doubts and solicitude about it.

The New Generation

One of the central problems for student movements today is the absence of any theory of society that does justice to the new world in which we of the most industrialized nations live.

—Kenneth Keniston

INTRODUCTION

"The new generation" is a phrase that has been made prominent by journalists. Presumably, the phrase clusters young people into an identifiable group: one that shares an age or a hair style or a type of clothes. This description may satisfy advertisers, hair stylists, or garment manufacturers, but by themselves such features do not confer enough value on the group to justify the wide public attention the group has received.

Is the group tagged "the new generation" of sufficient social significance to justify all the hullabaloo—and further study? Seldom has a group been invested with more socially significant features by high-minded journalists than has the new generation. For proof, it suffices to mention Charles A. Reich's paean to "Consciousness III" in his *The Greening of America;* or Jean-François Revel's celebration of "the Woodstock nation" in his *Without Marx or Jesus*. Reich, Revel, and other journalists have claimed that the views of the new generation have revolutionized and will revolutionize the culture of the United States.

Since a cultural revolution could not have occurred without revolutionaries, there must exist people who share socially significant views and who supply the reality lying beneath "the new generation." But who belongs to the new generation? What social views do you have to share to become a member? Being under thirty or wearing long hair or hang-loose clothes is not enough. Not all of these people share social views.

Let us say that if there is a new generation, it is composed of young persons who share an ideology. And let us also say that an ideology is an idea system that contains at least five components: (1) it describes the present state of the culture; (2) it lists the changed conditions of life; (3) it criticizes the present state of the culture; (4) it projects an ideal culture to replace the present one,

7

the ideal culture being better suited to the changed conditions of life; and (5) it formulates a theory of the dynamics of culture, that is, it has a theory of how to change a culture.

If Kenneth Keniston, in the first essay in this chapter, is correct when he says that "what protesting students throughout the world share is a mood more than an ideology or a program . . .," then a new generation does not exist. Where there is no shared ideology, there is no new generation.

This does not mean, however, that young people need to be trapped by history; they can make history by becoming a new generation, by developing a common ideology. This anthology supplies intellectual material that young people who want to formulate or develop an ideology should ponder, discuss, and argue. The fires of time are burning, and we must salvage the rocks from the past in order to reassemble the foundations of our culture.

To expand somewhat on the ideological task that confronts students who would construct a new generation, we should consider the five components of an ideology at a little more length.

1. *Describing the culture.* The concept of culture is neither clear nor precise. Even the most superficial examination of the definitions you encounter in anthropology books, where you are most likely to find professional accounts of culture, reveals a spectrum of ideas about culture. Many of the terms used to define culture are as vague as the term "culture" itself. Yet, there is enough agreement on some categories of culture to outline fruitfully what a description of a culture should contain. Of course, the list of descriptive categories we discuss here is not complete, but it is long enough to help you get started thinking about culture.

To learn about culture, you must ascertain what the members' *values* are and the hierarchical order in which they place those values. You must also learn which values are *end* values, such as happiness, and which are *means* values, such as work. Values break down into several subcategories, such as personal, moral, economic, political, social, and esthetic values. Within the subcategory of moral value, for example, you must learn something about such allied machinery as the culture's moral concepts, emotions, heroes, judgments, reasoning, and customs.

You can uncover the values held by people sharing a culture by asking them questions, but perhaps a more reliable way is to study their *institutions.* The nature of a culture's institutions is determined in great part by the values held within the culture. This requires examination of the culture's educational, political, economic, production, religious, familial, legal, military, leisure, and communications institutions.

To understand a culture, you must also know something of its *epistemic*, that is, knowledge, equipment. This requires learning the language and something of the language's structure, mastering the culture's concepts, identifying what it knows how to do (its skills and crafts), tracing the extent of its science and technology, and determining its method of gaining knowledge. You can appreciate the importance of a culture's epistemic equipment by reflecting on the enormous cultural change that occurred as a result of Galileo's insistence that the best way to gain knowledge is by experimentation and observation, or by induction. He revolted against the medieval scholar's reliance on an Aristotelian method that emphasized deduction. Consequently, the rapid advance of science and technology was spurred by Galileo's epistemic revolution.

Different cultures may have different views of the *nature of man*. A Judeo-Christian culture holds that man is essentially prone to evil and sin, whereas a Platonic culture holds that man always strives for the good. These differing attitudes toward the moral nature of man have a profound influence on the way a culture views the functions of law and government. The Judeo-Christian culture uses government and law to curb and restrict man's ever present tendencies toward evil. The Platonic culture views government and law as means to fulfill man's potential for good. A culture that holds that man is metaphysically a material, animal being will support different institutions from one that believes man to have an immortal soul. For instance, Russia has its "atheistic" communism and its mechanistic, Pavlovian concept of man. And the United States is critical of these.

Further insight into a culture is gained with identifying which class holds the *power*. In one culture, the priestly class may hold the power, in another it may rest with the landed gentry, and in yet another power may be wielded by those who own the means of industrial production. To understand the nature and source of priestly power, one is forced to examine a culture's religious institutions. To understand the nature and source of the producers' power, one has to examine a culture's economic institutions. Obviously, the culture categories are not isolated from each other; a complete understanding of one cannot be gained without learning its relationships to the others.

Then, too, a culture's *Weltanschauung*, its world outlook, is important. Today, we are witnessing a shift in our attitude toward our cosmic environment. Western science and technology have helped us master many of nature's forces, and we have not hesitated to subject the earth to destruction or pollution in order to make it serve us. Now, however, young people have shifted to a more Oriental and Indian *Weltanschauung*, revering the cosmos and seeing it as an ally rather than as an adversary. They see nature as something to be nurtured rather than subdued. Creation myths have been replaced by evolutionary biology, with its emphasis on a continually developing life line. This, in turn, has altered the West's theory of the nature of man, demoting man from being the darling of the gods to merely being the latest animal brought to the fore by nature. The emotionally unsettling effect that the evolutionary revolution had on nine-teenth-century and early twentieth-century people is hard for young people to appreciate; but, it is not difficult to understand the impact that a changed *Weltanschauung* has made on our culture's theory of the nature of man.

In sum, describing a culture is not easy. It requires careful, analytic thought. After you have done this and have arrived at what you feel is a complete description of the culture, you are ready for the next step.

2. *Listing the changed conditions of life.* Cultural revolution is a sharp change in at least one of the cultural categories that we discussed, with resultant changes in the other categories. Given that a culture is transmitted from an older to a younger generation, we expect that a younger generation learning its lessons well would repeat, and, so, preserve the older generation's culture. We would not expect a cultural revolution unless the younger generation experiences changed conditions of life that make the inherited culture unsuitable.

Cultural changes may occur because of deliberate, thoughtful response to changed conditions of life; however, many, if not most, cultural changes take place without forethought. They just happen, much as rocks break away from their cliffs to fall into the valley below. These cultural "happenings" differ from "deliberate" cultural changes in that we make deliberate changes because they are what we want; we see them as desirable, perhaps because they fit the changed conditions of life. Cultural happenings, on the other hand, occur whether or not we want them. Even though some of these happenings may be undesirable, we are saddled with them once they happen. Deliberate cultural changes are to be preferred to cultural happenings because they maximize our chance of getting what we want.

Consider the following cultural changes, listed in the order of importance given them by a student in a philosophy class: (1) greater sexual freedom, (2) the use of mind-expanding drugs, (3) the decrease of power and influence of organized religion and the increase of new forms of religious expression for Western man, (4) a greater number of educated people, (5) a movement away from accumulation of material goods and toward a general re-evaluation of the values of a materialistic society, (6) the politicalization of Third World people, (7) rapid technological advance, (8) an increased tendency to re-examine the value of established moral codes, and (9) a widening distrust in the credibility of government and authority.

How many of these changes are deliberate and how many are happenings? How many of them are desirable? Which of them are due to changed conditions of life? Is the greater sexual freedom due to the altered conditions of our medical knowledge and technology? Is sexual freedom greater than before because it is better suited to this altered condition of life? Is there a point beyond which we should not expand our technological capabilities? Can technology alter the conditions of life so much that other parts of our culture will not be able to stand the shock of the drastic change? These are the kinds of questions responsible framers of a new ideology must answer, and with strong reasons and facts to support their answers.

3. *Criticizing the current culture.* At this point in the book, we shall not say much about this component because the bulk of the three essays in this chapter try to characterize the new generation's criticism of the current and past culture of the United States. However, through our foregoing discussion of ideology, we have tried to give you a perspective in which you can view these essays. It suffices to say that the essays are mainly concerned with the criticism and projection components of ideology.

4. *Projecting an ideal culture.* **Kenneth Keniston*** (first essay† in this chapter) contends that we are witnessing two youthful revolts or a fusion of them. One of them is an extension of the older, industrial revolution, and the other is a postindustrial revolution. The first, he claims, projects social, economic, and political ideals; the second projects personal, experiential, and communal ideals. The existence of two revolutions sets the stage for tension and conflict. Previously

---

* So the reader may easily find the discussion of a particular essay or author in the introduction for the chapter or section that contains the author's essay, the author's name is printed in boldface where the discussion of him or his essay begins. When a chapter is divided into sections, boldface is used only in the section introductions.

† In this book, the word "chapter" refers to the largest divisions of the book. The word "essay" (although on occasion it may actually be excerpts from a larger work) refers to the individual reading selections included in the book. In some chapters, essays are grouped into "sections" (for example, Chapter Two is divided into four sections, the first of which is "Relativism").

in our discussion, we made some theoretical assumptions that you may have already challenged. We assumed that there is one United States culture to be described and that there is one new generation. We wrote as if every United States citizen were a homogenized culture product when, in fact, the United States contains a large number of cultures. Of course, it is possible that these are not subcultures of a single, all-encompassing master culture. We wrote also as if there were a single revolutionary mood, if not a single budding ideology, shared by long-haired, hang-loose people under thirty.

We suggest that, in reading Keniston, who introduces the notion that there are two ideologies, in reading **G. David Garson** (second essay of this chapter), who expands on the continuing industrial revolution, and in reading **Fred Davis** (last essay of this chapter), who expands on the postindustrial revolution, you consider the possibility that we have two incompatible ideologies and, thus, two new generations. These two generations may make different and conflicting criticisms and project different and conflicting ideals.

Consider the industrial revolutionists' ideal of redistributing the world's wealth to achieve a more equitable balance. They would bulldoze some money off the mountains of our wealth into the valleys of poverty below. This requires increasing our productivity, unless we are simply to give from what we already have. At the same time, the postindustrial revolutionists' ideal is to curtail technology because of the depersonalization and materialization with which it has stained our culture. In short, one revolution seems committed to increasing technology and the other to decreasing it. Faced with incompatible revolutions, one must (1) select one and reject the other, (2) alter both so that they can be fused, or (3) frame an ideology distinct from either of them. In any case, there is some thinking to be done.

5. *Formulating a theory of culture dynamics.* We pointed out earlier that changes in one aspect of culture will effect changes in another. We gave several examples, one being the effect on our theory of the nature of man that was made when the West's *Weltanschauung* shifted from creation myth to evolutionary biology. We also suggested that deliberately induced cultural change is preferable to cultural happenings.

Suppose, now, that you have described your society, that you have a criticism, and that you have projected an ideal culture that will fit with changed conditions of life that you have identified. To achieve your ideal culture, you must know how to bring about the cultural revolution. If your theory of the culture dynamics is accurate, you will know how to do this.

Vice-President Spiro Agnew has a theory of culture dynamics. He believes that if we could restore the family institution, this would affect all the other aspects of culture and repair the cultural ruptures that he and many middle Americans deplore. It is not clear how the restoration of familial relations would, for instance, turn the United States from a warlike to a peaceful nation and tame the tiger's heart in our military institutions, but, then, perhaps that's why it is not a very good theory. Others think that a return to the teachings of Jesus Christ will restore the moral fiber of Americans: once we strengthen our moral muscles, we will recover the traditional work ethic that once made our culture great.

Marx has become an attractive theoretician for many young Americans chiefly because he offers one of the few thoughtful, detailed, plausible accounts of culture dynamics. Of the several descriptive categories we singled out, Marx thought that the key category was the economic one. A culture, he claimed, is determined by a society's mode of production; change it, and changes in the other categories follow. A new generation thinker that wants cultural change knows he has to locate the spring of power that will nurture change or dry into desuetude. Many young thinkers are grateful to Marx for uncovering the spring. Armed with this piece of intelligence, they try to expose the contradictions in our society, one of which is the contradiction between capitalism and democracy. They argue that, on one hand, our culture clasps democracy to its bosom; the United States is popularly thought to be a democracy; power supposedly is equally distributed among the voters, who select their governmental representatives because they hold the views they do. On the other hand, they argue, the culture embraces capitalism; capitalism endorses unequal wealth; and unequal wealth implies unequal power because money is the key factor in electing governmental representatives; therefore, power does not lie with all the people but only with some people, namely, the people who control the money. Thus, a contradiction exists between American democracy and American capitalism. One implies equal power, the other implies unequal power. Cultural change in favor of true democracy requires the elimination of capitalism.

In summary, we have suggested that a new generation does not yet exist because there is no shared ideology among young people; that young intellectuals may yet forge an ideology and so make a new generation; that an ideology has five components to which thinkers must address themselves; that the three essays in this chapter attempt to lay bare the main ideological thrusts; and that the essays concentrate on two ideological components, criticisms of the present culture and projections of an ideal culture.

How the New Generation Got That Way

Kenneth Keniston

Kenneth Keniston (1930-   ) teaches psychology at Yale Medical School and is the author of many articles on the new generation. Among his works are *Young Radicals* (1968) and *The Uncommitted: Alienated Youth in American Society* (1965).

The recent events at Harvard are the culmination of a long year of unprecedented student unrest in the advanced nations of the world. We have learned to expect students in underdeveloped countries to lead unruly demonstrations against the status quo, but what is new, unexpected and upsetting to many is that an apparently similar mood is sweeping across America, France, Germany, Italy and even Eastern European nations like Czechoslovakia and Poland. Furthermore, the revolts occur, not at the most backward universities, but at the most distinguished, liberal and enlightened—Berkeley, the Sorbonne, Tokyo, Columbia, the Free University of Berlin, Rome and now Harvard.

This development has taken almost everyone by surprise. The American public is clearly puzzled, frightened and often outraged by the behavior of its most privileged youth. The scholarly world, including many who have devoted their lives to the study of student protest, has been caught off guard as well. For many years, American analysts of student movements have been busy demonstrating that "it can't happen here." Student political activity abroad has been seen as a reaction to modernization, industrialization and the demise of traditional or tribal societies. In an already modern, industrialized, detribalized and "stable" nation like America, it was argued, student protests are naturally absent.

Another explanation has tied student protests abroad to bad living conditions in some universities and to the unemployability of their graduates. Student revolts, it was argued, spring partly from the misery of student life in countries like India and Indonesia. Students who must live in penury and squalor naturally turn against their universities and societies. And if, as in many developing nations, hundreds of thousands of university graduates can find no work commensurate with their skills, the chances for student militancy are further increased.

These arguments helped explain the "silent generation" of the nineteen-fifties and the absence of protest, during that period, in American universities, where students are often "indulged" with good living conditions, close student-faculty contact and considerable freedom of speech. And they helped explain why "superemployable" American college graduates, especially the much-sought-after ones from colleges like Columbia and Harvard, seemed so contented with their lot.

But such arguments do not help us understand today's noisy, angry and militant

Source: "You Have to Grow Up in Scarsdale to Know How Bad Things Really Are," *The New York Times,* April 27, 1969. © 1969 by The New York Times Company. Reprinted by permission.

students in the advanced countries. Nor do they explain why students who enjoy the greatest advantages—those at leading universities—are often found in the revolts. As a result, several new interpretations of student protest are currently being put forward, interpretations that ultimately form part of what Richard Poirier has termed "the war against the young."

Many reactions to student unrest, of course, spring primarily from fear, anger, confusion or envy, rather than from theoretical analysis. Governor Wallace's attacks on student "anarchists" and other "pin-headed intellectuals" for example, were hardly coherent explanations of protest. Many of the bills aimed at punishing student protesters being proposed in Congress and state legislatures reflect similar feelings of anger and outrage. Similarly, the presumption that student unrest *must* be part of an international conspiracy is based on emotion rather than fact. Even George F. Kennan's recent discussion of the American student left is essentially a moral condemnation of "revolting students," rather than an effort to explain their behavior.

If we turn to more thoughtful analyses of the current student mood, we find two general theories gaining widespread acceptance. The first, articulately expressed by Lewis S. Feuer in his recent book on student movements, "The Conflict of Generations," might be termed the "Oedipal Rebellion" interpretation. The second, cogently stated by Zbigniew Brzezinski and Daniel Bell, can be called the theory of "Historical Irrelevance."

The explanation of Oedipal Rebellion sees the underlying force in all student revolts as blind, unconscious Oedipal hatred of fathers and the older generation. Feuer, for example, finds in all student movements an inevitable tendency toward violence and a combination of "regicide, parricide and suicide." A decline in respect for the authority of the older generation is needed to trigger a student movement, but the force behind it comes from "obscure" and "unconscious" forces in the child's early life, including both intense death wishes against his father and the enormous guilt and self-hatred that such wishes inspire in the child.

The idealism of student movements is thus, in many respects, only a "front" for the latent subconscious destructiveness and self-destructiveness of underlying motivations. Even the expressed desire of these movements to help the poor and exploited is explained psychoanalytically by Feuer: Empathy for the disadvantaged is traced to "traumatic" encounters with parental bigotry in the students' childhoods, when their parents forbade them to play with children of other races or lower social classes. The identification of today's new left with blacks is thus interpreted as an unconscious effort to "abreact and undo this original trauma."

There are two basic problems with the Oedipal Rebellion theory, however. First, although it uses psychoanalytic terms, it is bad psychoanalysis. The real psychoanalytic account insists that the Oedipus complex is universal in all normally developing children. To point to this complex in explaining student rebellion is, therefore, like pointing to the fact that all children learn to walk. Since both characteristics are said to be universal, neither helps us understand why, at some historical moments, students are restive and rebellious, while at others they are not. Second, the theory does not help us explain why some students (especially those from middle-class, affluent and idealistic families) are most inclined to rebel, while others (especially those from working-class and deprived families) are less so.

In order really to explain anything, the Oedipal Rebellion hypothesis would have to be modified to point to an unusually *severe* Oedipus complex, involving especially *intense* and unresolved unconscious feelings of father-hatred in student rebels. But much is now known about the lives and backgrounds of these rebels—at least those in the United States—and this evidence does not support even the modified theory. On the contrary, it indicates that most student protesters are relatively *close* to their parents, that the values they profess are usually the ones they learned at the family dinner table, and that their parents tend to be highly educated, liberal or left-wing and politically active.

Furthermore, psychological studies of student radicals indicate that they are no more neurotic, suicidal, enraged or disturbed than are non-radicals. Indeed, more studies find them to be rather more integrated, self-accepting and "advanced," in a psychological sense, than their politically inactive contemporaries. In general, research on American student rebels supports a "Generational Solidarity" (or chip-off-the-old-block) theory, rather than one of Oedipal Rebellion.

The second theory of student revolt now being advanced asserts that they are a reaction against "historical irrelevance." Rebellion springs from the unconscious awareness of some students that society has left them and their values behind. According to this view, the ultimate causes of student dissent are sociological rather than psychological. They lie in fundamental changes in the nature of the advanced societies—especially, in the change from industrial to post-industrial society. The student revolution is seen not as a true revolution, but as a counterrevolution—what Daniel Bell has called "the guttering last gasp of a romanticism soured by rancor and impotence."

This theory assumes that we are moving rapidly into a new age in which technology will dominate, an age whose real rulers will be men like computer experts, systems analysts and technobureaucrats. Students who are attached to outmoded and obsolescent values like humanism and romanticism unconsciously feel they have no place in this post-industrial world. When they rebel they are like the Luddites of the past—workers who smashed machines to protest the inevitable industrial revolution. Today's student revolt reflects what Brzezinski terms "an unconscious realization that they [the rebels] are themselves becoming historically obsolete"; it is nothing but the "death rattle of the historical irrelevants."

This theory is also inadequate. It assumes that the shape of the future is already technologically determined, and that protesting students unconsciously "know" that it will offer them no real reward, honor or power. But the idea that the future can be accurately predicted is open to fundamental objection. Every past attempt at prophecy has turned out to be grievously incorrect. Extrapolations from the past, while sometimes useful in the short run, are usually fundamentally wrong in the long run, especially when they attempt to predict the quality of human life, the nature of political and social organization, international relations or the shape of future culture.

The future is, of course, made by men. Technology is not an inevitable master of man and history, but merely provides the possibility of applying scientific knowledge to specific problems. Men may identify with it or refuse to, use it or be used by it for good or evil, apply it humanely or destructively. Thus, there is no real evidence that student protest will emerge as the "death rattle of the historical irrelevants." It could equally well be the "first spark of a new historical era." No one today can be sure of the outcome, and people who feel certain that the future will bring the obsolescence and death of those whom they dislike are often merely expressing their fond hope.

The fact that today's students invoke "old" humanistic and romantic ideas in no way proves that student protests are a "last gasp" of a dying order. Quite the contrary: *All* revolutions draw upon older values and visions. Many of the ideals of the French Revolution, for example, originated in Periclean Athens. Revolutions do not occur because new ideas suddenly develop, but because a new generation begins to take *old* ideas seriously—not merely as interesting theoretical views, but as the basis for political action and social change. Until recently, the humanistic vision of human fulfillment and the romantic vision of an expressive, imaginative and passionate life were taken seriously only by small aristocratic or Bohemian groups. The fact that they are today taken as real goals by millions of students in many nations does not mean that these students are "counterrevolutionaries," but merely that their ideas follow the pattern of every major revolution.

Indeed, today's student rebels are rarely opposed to technology *per se*. On the contrary, they take the high technology of their societies completely for granted, and concern themselves with it very little. What they *are* opposed to is, in essence, the worship of Technology, the tendency to treat people as "inputs" or "outputs" of a technological system, the subordination of human needs to technological programs. The essential conflict between the minority of students who make up the student revolt and the existing order is a conflict over the future direction of technological society, not a counterrevolutionary protest against technology.

In short, both the Oedipal Rebellion and the Historical Irrelevance theories are what students would call "put-downs." If we accept either, we are encouraged not to listen to protests, or to explain them away or reject them as either the "acting out" of destructive Oedipal feelings or the blind reaction of an obsolescent group to the awareness of its obsolescence. But if, as I have argued, neither of these theories is adequate to explain the current "wave" of student protest here and abroad, how can we understand it?

One factor often cited to explain student unrest is the large number of people in the world under 30—today the critical dividing line between generations. But this explanation alone, like the theories just discussed, is not adequate, for in all historical eras the vast portion of the population has always been under 30. Indeed, in primitive societies most people die before they reach that age. If chronological youth alone was enough to insure rebellion, the advanced societies—where a greater proportion of the population reaches old age than ever before in history—should be the *least* revolutionary, and primitive societies the *most*. This is not the case.

More relevant factors are the relationship of those under 30 to the established institutions of society (that is, whether they are engaged in them or not); and the opportunities that society provides for their continuing intellectual, ethical and emotional development. In both cases the present situation in the advanced nations is without precedent.

Philippe Aries, in his remarkable book, "Centuries of Childhood," points out that, until the end of the Middle Ages, no separate stage of childhood was recognized in Western societies. Infancy ended at approximately 6 or 7, whereupon most children were integrated into adult life, treated as small men and women and expected to work as junior partners of the adult world. Only later was childhood recognized as a separate stage of life, and our own century is the first to "guarantee" it by requiring universal primary education.

The recognition of adolescence as a stage of life is of even more recent origin, the product of the 19th and 20th centuries. Only as industrial societies became prosperous enough to defer adult work until after puberty could they create institutions—like widespread secondary-school education—that would extend adolescence to virtually all young people. Recognition of adolescence also arose from the vocational and psychological requirements of these societies, which needed much higher levels of training and psychological development than could be guaranteed through primary education alone. There is, in general, an intimate relationship between the way a society defines the stages of life and its economic, political and social characteristics.

Today, in more developed nations, we are beginning to witness the recognition of still another stage of life. Like childhood and adolescence, it was initially granted only to a small minority, but is now being extended to an ever-larger group. I will call this the stage of "youth," and by that I mean both a further phase of disengagement from society and the period of psychological development that intervenes between adolescence and adulthood. This stage, which continues into the 20's and sometimes into the 30's, provides opportunities for intellectual, emotional and moral development that were never afforded to any other large group in history. In the student revolts, we are seeing one result of this advance.

I call the extension of youth an advance advisedly. Attendance at a college or university is a major part of this extension, and there is growing evidence that this is, other things being equal, a good thing for the student. Put in an oversimplified phrase, it tends to free him—to free him from swallowing unexamined the assumptions of the past, to free him from the superstitions of his childhood, to free him to express his feelings more openly and to free him from irrational bondage to authority.

I do not mean to suggest, of course, that all college graduates are free and liberated spirits, unencumbered by irrationality, superstition, authoritarianism or blind adherence to tradition. But these findings do indicate that our colleges, far from cranking out only machinelike robots who will provide skilled manpower for the economy, are also producing an increasing number of highly critical citizens— young men and women who have the opportunity, the leisure, the affluence and the educational resources to continue their development beyond the point where most people in the past were required to stop it.

So, one part of what we are seeing on campuses throughout the world is not a reflection of how bad higher education is, but rather of its extraordinary accomplishments. Even the moral righteousness of the student rebels, a quality both endearing and infuriating to their elders, must be judged at least partially a consequence of the privilege of an extended youth; for a prolonged development, we know, encourages the individual to elaborate a more personal, less purely conventional sense of ethics.

What the advanced nations have done is to create their own critics on a mass basis—that is, to create an ever-larger group of young people who take the highest values of their societies as their own, who internalize these values and identify them with their own best selves, and who are willing to struggle to implement them. At the same time, the extension of youth has lessened the personal risks of dissent: These young people have been freed from the requirements of work, gainful employment and even marriage, which permits them to criticize their society from a protected position of disengagement.

But the mere prolongation of development need not automatically lead to unrest. To be sure, we have granted to millions the opportunity to examine their societies, to compare them with their values and to come to a reasoned judgment of the existing order. But why should their judgment today be so unenthusiastic?

What protesting students throughout the world share is a mood more than an ideology or a program, a mood that says the existing system—the power structure—is hypocritical, unworthy of respect, outmoded and in urgent need of reform. In addition, students everywhere speak of repression, manipulation and authoritarianism. (This is paradoxical, considering the apparently great freedoms given them in many nations. In America, for example, those who complain most loudly about being suffocated by the subtle tyranny of the Establishment usually attend the institutions where student freedom is greatest.) Around this general mood, specific complaints arrange themselves as symptoms of what students often call the "exhaustion of the existing society."

To understand this phenomenon we must recognize that, since the Second World War, some societies have indeed begun to move past the industrial era into a new world that is post-industrial, technological, post-modern, post-historic or, in Brzezinski's term, "technectronic." In Western Europe, the United States, Canada and Japan, the first contours of this new society are already apparent. And, in many other less-developed countries, middle-class professionals (whose children become activists) often live in post-industrial enclaves within pre-industrial societies. Whatever we call the post-industrial world, it has demonstrated that, for the first time, man can produce more than enough to meet his material needs.

This accomplishment is admittedly blemished by enormous problems of economic distribution in the advanced nations, and it is in terrifying contrast to the overwhelming poverty of the Third World. Nevertheless, it is clear that what might be called "the problem of production" *can,* in principle, be solved. If all members of American society, for example, do not have enough material goods, it is because the system of distribution is flawed. The same is true, or will soon be true, in many other nations that are approaching advanced states of industrialization. Characteristically, these nations, along with the most technological, are those where student unrest has recently been most prominent.

The transition from industrial to post-industrial society brings with it a major shift in social emphases and values. Industrializing and industrial societies tend to be oriented toward solving the problem of production. An industrial ethic—sometimes Protestant, sometimes Socialist, sometimes Communist—tends to emphasize psychological qualities like self-discipline, delay of gratification, achievement-orientation and a strong emphasis on economic success and productivity. The social, political and economic institutions of these societies tend to be organized in a way that is consistent with the goal of increasing production. And industrial societies tend to apply relatively uniform standards, to reward achievement rather than status acquired by birth, to emphasize emotional neutrality ("coolness") and rationality in work and public life.

The emergence of post-industrial societies, however, means that growing numbers of the young are brought up in family environments where abundance, relative economic security, political freedom and affluence are simply facts of life, not goals to be striven for. To such people the psychological imperatives, social institutions and cultural values of the industrial ethic seem largely outdated and irrelevant to their own lives.

Once it has been demonstrated that a society *can* produce enough for all of its members, at least some of the young turn to other goals: for example, trying to make sure that society *does* produce enough and distributes it fairly, or searching for ways to live meaningfully with the goods and the leisure they *already* have. The problem is that our society has, in some realm, exceeded its earlier targets. Lacking new ones, it has become exhausted by its success.

When the values of industrial society become devitalized, the elite sectors of youth—the most affluent, intelligent, privileged and so on—come to feel that they live in institutions whose demands lack moral authority or, in the current jargon, "credibility." Today, the moral imperative and urgency behind production, acquisition, materialism and abundance has been lost.

Furthermore, with the lack of moral legitimacy felt in "the System," the least request for loyalty, restraint or conformity by its representatives—for example, by college presidents and deans—can easily be seen as a moral outrage, an authoritarian repression, a manipulative effort to "co-opt" students into joining the Establishment and an exercise in "illegitimate authority" that must be resisted. From this conception springs at least part of the students' vague sense of oppression. And, indeed, perhaps their peculiar feeling of suffocation arises ultimately from living in societies without vital ethical claims.

Given such a situation, it does not take a clear-cut issue to trigger a major protest. I doubt, for example, that college and university administrators are in fact *more* hypocritical and dishonest than they were in the past. American intervention in Vietnam, while many of us find it unjust and cruel, is not inherently *more* outrageous than other similar imperialistic interventions by America and other nations within the last century. And the position of blacks in this country, although disastrously and unjustifiably disadvantaged, is, in some economic and legal respects, better than ever before. Similarly, the conditions for students in America have never been as good, especially, as I have noted, at those élite colleges where student protests are most common.

But this is *precisely* the point: It is *because* so many of the *other* problems of American society seem to have been resolved, or to be resolvable in principle, that students now react with new indignations to old problems, turn to new goals and propose radical reforms.

So far I have emphasized the moral exhaustion of the old order and the fact that, for the children of post-industrial affluence, the once-revolutionary claims of the industrial society have lost much of their validity. I now want to argue that we are witnessing on the campuses of the world a fusion of *two revolutions* with distinct historical origins. One is a continuation of the old and familiar revolution of the industrial society, the liberal-democratic-egalitarian revolution that started in America and France at the turn of the 18th century and spread to virtually every nation in the world. (Not completed in any of them, its contemporary American form is, above all, to be found in the increased militancy of blacks.) The other is the new revolution, the post-industrial one, which seeks to define new goals relevant to the 20th and 21st centuries.

In its social and political aspects, the first revolution has been one of universalization, to use the sociologist's awkward term. It has involved the progressive extension to more and more people of economic, political and social rights, privileges and opportunities originally available only to the aristocracy, then to the middle class, and now in America to the relatively affluent white working class. It is, in many respects, a *quantitative* revolution. That is, it concerns itself less with the quality of life than with the amount of political freedom, the quantity and distribution of goods or the amount and level of injustice.

As the United States approaches the targets of the first revolution, on which this society was built, to be poor shifts from being an unfortunate fact of life to being an outrage. And, for the many who have never experienced poverty, discrimination, exploitation or oppression, even to *witness* the existence of these evils in the lives of others suddenly becomes intolerable. In our own time the impatience to complete the first revolution has grown apace, and we find less willingness to compromise, wait and forgive among the young, especially among those who now take the values of the old revolution for granted—seeing them not as goals, but as *rights*.

A subtle change has thus occurred. What used to be utopian ideals—like equality, abundance and freedom from discrimination—have now become demands, inalienable rights upon which one can insist without brooking any compromise. It is noteworthy that in today's student confrontations no one requests anything. Students present their "demands."

So, on the one hand, we see a growing impatience to complete the first revolution. But, on the other, there is a newer revolution concerned with newer issues, a revolution that is less social, economic or political than psychological, historical and cultural. It is less concerned with the quantities of things than with their qualities, and it judges the virtually complete liberal revolution and finds it still wanting.

"You have to have grown up in Scarsdale to know how bad things really are," said one radical student. This comment would probably sound arrogant, heartless and insensitive to a poor black, much less to a citizen of the Third World. But he meant something important by it. He meant that *even* in the Scarsdales of America with their affluence, their upper-middle-class security and abundance, their well-fed, well-heeled children and their excellent schools, something is wrong. Economic affluence does not guarantee a feeling of personal fulfillment; political freedom does not always yield an inner sense of liberation and cultural freedom; social justice and equality may leave one with a feeling that something is missing in life. "No to the consumer society!" shouted the bourgeois students of the Sorbonne during May and June of 1968—a cry that understandably alienated French workers, for whom affluence and the consumer society are still central goals.

What, then, are the targets of the new revolution? As is often noted, students themselves don't know. They speak vaguely of "a society that has never existed," of "new values," of a "more humane world," of "liberation" in some psychological, cultural and historical sense. Their rhetoric is largely negative; they are stronger in opposition than in proposals for reform; their diagnoses often seem accurate, but their prescriptions are vague; and they are far more articulate in urging the immediate completion of the first revolution than in defining the goals of the second. Thus, we can only indirectly discern trends that point to the still-undefined targets of the new revolution.

What are these trends and targets?

First, there is a revulsion against the notion of quantity, particularly economic quantity and materialism, and a turn toward concepts of quality. One of the most delightful slogans of the French student revolt was, "Long live the passionate revolution of creative intelligence!" In a sense, the achievement of abundance may allow millions of contemporary men and women to examine, as only a few artists and madmen have examined in the past, the quality, joyfulness and zestfulness of experience. The "expansion of consciousness"; the stress on the expressive, the aesthetic and the creative; the emphasis on imagination, direct perception and fantasy—all are part of the effort to enhance the quality of this experience.

Another goal of the new revolution involves a revolt against uniformity, equalization, standardization and homogenization—not against technology itself, but against the "technologization of man." At times, this revolt approaches anarchic quaintness, but it has a positive core as well—the demand that individuals be appreciated, not because of their similarities or despite their differences, but because they *are* different, diverse, unique and noninterchangeable. This attitude is evident in many areas: for example, the insistence upon a cultivation of personal idiosyncrasy, mannerism and unique aptitude. Intellectually, it is expressed in the rejection of the melting-pot and consensus-politics view of American life in favor of a post-homogeneous America in which cultural diversity and conflict are underlined rather than denied.

The new revolution also involves a continuing struggle against psychological or institutional closure or rigidity in any form, even the rigidity of a definite adult role. Positively, it extols the virtues of openness, motion and continuing human development. What Robert J. Lifton has termed the protean style is clearly in evidence. There is emerging a concept of a lifetime of personal change, of an adulthood of continuing self-transformation, of an adaptability and an openness to the revolutionary modern world that will enable the individual to remain "with it," psychologically youthful and on top of the present.

Another characteristic is the revolt against centralized power and the complementary demand for participation. What is demanded is not merely the consent of the governed, but the involvement of the governed. "Participatory democracy" summarizes this aspiration, but it extends far beyond the phrase and the rudimentary social forms that have sprung up around it. It extends to the demand for relevance in education—that is, for a chance for the student to participate in his own educational experience in a way that involves all of his faculties, emotional and moral as well as intellectual. The demand for "student power" (or, in Europe, "co-determination") is an aspect of the same theme: At Nanterre, Columbia, Frankfurt and Harvard, students increasingly seek to participate in making the policies of their universities.

This demand for participation is also embodied in the new ethic of "meaningful human relationships," in which individuals confront each other without masks, pretenses and games. They "relate" to each other as unique and irreplaceable human beings, and develop new forms of relationships from which all participants will grow.

In distinguishing between the old and the new revolutions, and in attempting to define the targets of the new, I am, of course, making distinctions that students themselves rarely make. In any one situation the two revolutions are joined and fused, if not confused. For example, the Harvard students' demand for "restructuring the university" is essentially the second revolution's demand for participation; but their demand for an end to university "exploitation" of the surrounding community is tied to the more traditional goals of the first revolution. In most radical groups there is a range of opinion that starts with the issues of the first (racism, imperialism, exploitation, war) and runs to the concerns of the second (experiential education, new life styles, meaningful participation, consciousness-expansion, relatedness, encounter and community). The first revolution is personified by Maoist-oriented Progressive Labor party factions within the student left, while the second is represented by hippies, the "acid left," and the Yippies. In any individual, and in all student movements, these revolutions co-exist in uneasy and often abrasive tension.

Furthermore, one of the central problems for student movements today is the absence of any theory of society that does justice to the new world in which we of the most industrialized nations live. In their search for rational critiques of present societies, students turn to theories like Marxism that are intricately bound up with the old revolution.

Such theories make the ending of economic exploitation, the achievement of social justice, the abolition of racial discrimination and the development of political participation and freedom central, but they rarely deal adequately with the issues of the second revolution. Students inevitably try to adapt the rhetoric of the first to the problems of the second, using concepts that are often blatantly inadequate to today's world.

Even the concept of "revolution" itself is so heavily laden with images of political, economic and social upheaval that it hardly seems to characterize the equally radical but more social-psychological and cultural transformations involved in the new revolution. One student, recognizing this, called the changes occurring in his California student group, "too radical to be called a revolution." Students are thus often misled by their borrowed vocabulary, but most adults are even more confused, and many are quickly led to the mistaken conclusion that today's student revolt is nothing more than a repetition of Communism's in the past.

Failure to distinguish between the old and new revolutions also makes it impossible to consider the critical question of how compatible they are with each other. Does it make sense—or is it morally right—for today's affluent American students to seek imagination, self-actualization, individuality, openness and relevance when most of the world and many in America live in deprivation, oppression and misery?

The fact that the first revolution is "completed" in Scarsdale does not mean that it is (or soon will be) in Harlem or Appalachia—to say nothing of Bogotá or Calcutta. For many children of the second revolution, the meaning of life may be found in completing the first—that is, in extending to others the "rights" they have always taken for granted.

For others the second revolution will not wait; the question, "What lies beyond affluence?" demands an answer now. Thus, although we may deem it self-indulgent to pursue the goals of the new revolution in a world where so much misery exists, the fact is that in the advanced nations it is upon us, and we must at least learn to recognize it.

Finally, beneath my analysis lies an assumption I had best make explicit. Many student critics argue that their societies have failed miserably. My argument, a more historical one perhaps, suggests that our problem is not only that industrial societies have failed to keep all their promises, but that they have succeeded in some ways beyond all expectations. Abundance was once a distant dream, to be postponed to a hereafter of milk and honey; today, most Americans are affluent. Universal mass education was once a Utopian goal; today in America almost the entire population completes high school, and almost half enters colleges and universities.

The notion that individuals might be free, en masse, to continue their psychological, intellectual, moral and cognitive development through their teens and into their 20's would have been laughed out of court in any century other than our own; today, that opportunity is open to millions of young Americans. Student unrest is a reflection, not only of the failures, but of the extraordinary successes of the liberal-industrial revolution. It therefore occurs in the nations and in the colleges where, according to traditional standards, conditions are best.

But for many of today's students who have never experienced anything but affluence, political freedom and social equality, the old vision is dead or dying. It may inspire bitterness and outrage when it is not achieved, but it no longer animates or guides. In place of it, students (and many who are not students) are searching for a new vision, a new set of values, a new set of targets appropriate to the post-industrial era—a myth, an ideology of a set of goals that will concern itself with the quality of life and answer the question, "Beyond freedom and affluence, what?"

What characterizes student unrest in the developed nations is this peculiar mixture of the old and the new, the urgent need to fulfill the promises of the past and, at the same time, to define the possibilities of the future.

New Generation Ideologies
G. David Garson

G. David Garson (1943-   ) was active in SDS (Students for a Democratic Society) activities at Princeton University during his undergraduate days, 1961-1965. He now teaches at Tufts University, where he is an assistant professor of political science.

CHANGES IN IDEOLOGY: THE FIFTIES AND THE SIXTIES

World War Two left Americans with a new toughness of mind. As neutralist and collectivist nations rejected American forms of democracy and economy abroad, Americans abandoned older ideologies and found comfort in the new formulations of "social science" with its vision of pluralism and consensus in domestic affairs and its foreign policy of deterrence and containment. Sociologists like Raymond Aron and Daniel Bell proclaimed "an end to ideology" and an "exhaustion of political

Source: "The Ideology of the New Student Left," in Julian Foster and Durward Long (eds.), Protest: Student Activism in America (New York: William Morrow, 1970), pp. 184-200. Reprinted with omissions by permission of William Morrow and Company, Inc. Copyright © 1970 by Julian Foster and Durward Long. This paper describes development through 1968, prior to the emergence of Progressive Labor and the Weathermen as dominant groups within SDS in 1969.

ideas in the 1950's."[1] Seymour Martin Lipset wrote that "The characteristic pattern of stable Western democracies in the mid-twentieth century is that they are in a post-politics phase—that is, there is relatively little difference between the democratic left and right."[2] And in fact many Americans could see little difference between the party of Eisenhower and the party of Stevenson.

The 1960's were different. Within a decade, the young intellectuals of the 1950's had become part of the "old left" or "establishment." What had happened? In part, there was a realization that the decade of the 1950's had over-reacted against Depression ideological themes; and race, poverty, and even imperialism were "rediscovered" as important social problems. Encouraged by legitimization of social grievances by various authorities, social movements began to develop in these problem areas. But there was also a growing awareness of the inadequacy of the liberal theories of the 1950's: containment and deterrence had become too closely identified with the sterile ideology of "anti-communism," whereby America justified its worldwide reactionary alliances. Similarly, pluralism had developed into a rationale for the tolerance of defective institutions, for inaction, and for the anarchic fragmentation of power among public groups and private enterprise. The "politics of consensus" did not explain the sense of powerlessness and the deep cynicism toward government felt by large segments of the American people. On the academic side, the "scientific" pursuit of social studies had not produced its promised fruit in the "real world," but instead was leading its students into ever more labyrinthine scholasticism.

Moreover, a new generation had arisen which had never known the ideological factionalism of the 1930's or the McCarthyite intimidation of the early 1950's. These young people saw the increasing American abundance not as a reason for political quietism, but as a compelling justification of their demands for social goals too long deferred as "utopian." In turn, this attitude was related to the development of a distinctive material youth culture in the late 1950's and early 1960's.[3] America could now "afford" to be radical. Indeed, in the face of relative abundance, the lack of concerted action to fulfill the American promise of equality, opportunity, and democracy seemed hypocritical.

.   .   .

Where others saw only the integration demands of the civil rights movement, the new student left, born as a by-product of that movement, saw a broad social lesson being taught. If America had betrayed her promise on so fundamental a question as civil rights, might not other areas also be in need of reexamination and revision? The lesson involved the need for rededication to earlier ideals of democracy which, as Bachrach has described, had come to find themselves in new and threatening contexts.[4]

[1] See Daniel Bell, *The End of Ideology* (New York, The Free Press, 1960), and Raymond Aron, *The Opium of the Intellectuals* (New York, W. W. Norton, 1958).

[2] For a discussion of this point, see Seymour Martin Lipset, *Political Man* (Garden City, N.Y., Doubleday, 1960), Chapter 13, "An End of Ideology."

[3] G. David Garson, "Collective Violence: On the History and Theory of American Disturbances, 1863-1963," unpublished doctoral dissertation, Department of Government, Harvard University, 1968. For an anthology of the new student left, see Mitchell Cohen and Dennis Hale (eds.), *The New Student Left* (Boston, Beacon Press, 1968).

[4] Peter Bachrach, *The Theory of Democratic Elitism: A Critique* (Boston, Little, Brown, and Company, 1967), Chapter 7.

As the lessons of the black revolution confronted the older themes of abundance and pragmatism that were the legacy of the 1950's, two reactions seemed to emerge. The dominant reaction, ignoring that lesson, adopted an increasingly cynical and callous pragmatism which rationalized tokenism in civil rights, endorsed brutal warfare in Vietnam, denied the poor representation on the agencies which dominated their lives, and remained indifferent to students' own demands for a voice in their universities. To the Left and their host of qualified sympathizers, this view seemed born of inertia and despair, carried by men who had given up hope of real social change. An increasingly influential group of intellectuals and activists, in a minority reaction, adopted a truly American radical ideology.[5] In America, as elsewhere, an apathetic majority stood between the two, in crossfire.

DIFFERENTIATION IN IDEOLOGY: THE NEW LEFT AND LIBERALISM

1. The Explication of Values. The first task of the new left was to make their values explicit. This continuing task was begun formally with the framing of the "Port Huron Statement" by the 1962 convention of the Students for a Democratic Society. This statement focused on the need for maintaining an individualistic community in the face of an increasingly bureaucratized society marked by undemocratic, hierarchical authority and by the relentless, undiscriminating enforcement of rules for the sake of rule enforcement.

"We regard men," they wrote, "as infinitely precious and possessed of unfulfilled capacities for reason, freedom, and love." These values were seen threatened by the corruption of political terms by earlier ideologies—by the "establishment's" reference to their adherents as "the free world" or by the Marxists' use of the term "the people's democracies" to denote their followers. According to the movement's view, individualistic values were threatened by a widespread desire to be "toughminded," which, the radicals said, meant "to have no serious aspirations." They were threatened by the routinized use of military violence by liberal-conservative leaders and as significantly by the rise of giant, impersonal corporations and bureaucracies which brought "the depersonalization that reduces human beings to the status of things."

The first stage of differentiation from liberalism involved the assertion of values in tension with contemporary trends. In the context of these trends, the radicals asserted that "Human relationships should involve fraternity and honesty" and that "work should involve incentives worthier than money or survival." With this emphasis on the individual went an emphasis on fraternity and community. "Politics," the Port Huron Statement read, "has a function of bringing people out of isolation and into community." Moreover, "as a social system, we seek the establishment of a democracy of individual participation." They rejected the evaluation raised in voting studies that a decrease in apathy need mean an undesirable increase in political instability. On the contrary, radicals took the reverse view.

By themselves, these concerns were not new, and from a cynical point of view

---

[5] See Staughton Lynd, *The Intellectual Origins of American Radicalism* (New York, Pantheon Books, 1968).

they might be considered naïve. Others, including many of the "old left," chose to dismiss them as a mere fashion or style. There was much in the way of flair to support this view. In the early period, for example, letters among members might be signed "Love . . . ." Yet if style were all that the radical ideology implied, the new left would not have distinguished itself from other humanitarian ideologies.

2. On the Concept of Freedom. Ideology, of course, was not born full-blown, but rather emerged gradually. The new left clearly realized that it was rejecting the older ideologies of the "establishment" liberals and Marxists, but it was at first necessary to be vague about what was to be substituted. It seemed originally that a general radical orientation with love and commitment was enough, and that things could be "played by ear." Tom Hayden, a president of SDS and community organizer in Newark, New Jersey, wrote in 1961 that "The radical program is simply the radical style as it attempts to change the practical life."[6]

Already in 1962, however, the SDS Port Huron Statement insisted that "a new left must transform modern complexity into issues that can be understood and felt close-up by every human being."[7] "Vision" was the word chosen to describe this need, and "style" was de-emphasized. As the SDS chapter organizer's handbook noted, "values alone, though vitally important, are not sufficient. In order to build a political program a clear understanding and analysis of contemporary life is also required."[8] What, however, was to be the content of "vision"?

The most important aspect of "vision" was raised in the SDS constitution, which described the organization as one which

maintains a vision of a democratic society, where at all levels the people have control of the decisions which affect them and the resources on which they are dependent. It seeks a relevance through the continual focus on realities and on the programs necessary to effect change at the most basic levels of economic, political and social organization. It feels the urgency to put forward a radical, democratic program. . . .[9]

This linking of freedom and democracy, repeated in the Port Huron Statement and later documents, was used as a prime point differentiating the new left from liberalism.

Freedom has meant many things. To Grotius it had meant simply not being imprisoned.[10] To Hobbes it had consisted in the state of being uncoerced and unopposed.[11] To Rousseau it was acting in accord with one's "rational will."[12] The theory of liberal pluralism, in contrast, rejected the Rousseauan and other "internal" conceptions of freedom as not adequately facing the problem of coercion. Freedom for the pluralists was not delineated by acting as one thought right, or as acting unopposed, but was defined by the degree of choice the more or

[6] Tom Hayden, "Letter to the New Left," mimeographed letter, Ann Arbor, Mich., SDS, 1961.

[7] The "Port Huron Statement," Cohen and Hale, *op. cit.*

[8] SDS Organizers Handbook, published by the Students for a Democratic Society.

[9] *Constitution of the Students for a Democratic Society.*

[10] Hugo Grotius, *The Encyclopedia of Philosophy*, trans. by Gustov Emil Miller (New York, Philosophical Library, 1955).

[11] Thomas Hobbes, *The Leviathan, or the Matter, Form and Power of a Commonwealth, Ecclesiastical and Civil*, London, 1651.

[12] Jean Jacques Rousseau, "The Social Contract," in Alan P. Grimes and Robert H. Horwitz (eds.), *Modern Political Ideologies* (New York, Oxford University Press, 1959), pp. 20-33.

less coercive institutions of society allowed to the individual. Freedom was said to lie in the interstices of choice between undemocratic and coercive institutions. Freedom was the choice between factories, between products, between schools. Freedom was pluralism because pluralism was choice.

The "establishment" conception of freedom, even in its sophisticated forms, seemed deficient to the new radical community, as it had to certain sections of the "old left." They too rejected the internal concepts of freedom which suggested that one could be "free" by one's behavior and thoughts regardless of the coerciveness of the environment. In their view, freedom involved more than plurality of choice. It involved power. The choice between similar factories did not seem to be the essence of freedom, nor did students accept their supposed "right" to select universities as the most important aspect of their freedom.

Liberty was viewed by the radicals as the right to live under conditions one had helped to set. Democracy and freedom were seen as realistic ideals yet to be achieved, the substance of which involved far more than the forms of elections and suggestion boxes. To be free, students needed a real voice in their universities, workers in their factories, the poor in their neighborhoods, and even doctors in their medical associations. Here SDS was accepting its heritage as the offshoot of the League for Industrial Democracy, but the new ideology left its nominal parent behind as SDS became a formally independent association.

Thus new left ideology came to revolve around four components: freedom and democracy on the one hand, and the preciousness of the individual and of community on the other. Each component reinforces the others. It maintains that there is no real freedom without democracy in all of America's institutions and that there is no real community without a high value placed on the dignity of the individual. Asserting that no real democracy exists without community, the new left argues that community provides the basis for a consensus of discussion rather than one of manipulation.

3. On the Nature of Democratic Institutions. To the reliance on expertise by the "establishment" the new left countered:

We oppose, too, the doctrine of human incompetence. . . . We see little reason why men cannot meet with increasing skill the complexities and responsibilities of their situation, if society is organized not for minority participation but for majority participation in decision-making. . . . Personal links between man and man are needed, especially to go beyond the partial and fragmentary bonds of function that bind men only as worker to worker, employer to employee, teacher to student. . . . [13]

Levels of participation needed to be raised greatly. "The people," a 1965 paper held, "through democratic channels [and] community organizations can and must give guidance to and set priorities for the technocrat, the planner." [14] Such community organizations were not, of course, to be confined to official boards and councils. Another 1965 paper argued, "Today in the United States there does not exist a democracy in the sense that democracy implies freedom for the individual. . . . Today, increasingly our news, our ideology in general, is fed to us through

[13] From the "Port Huron Statement," published in Cohen and Hale, *op. cit.,* pp. 12-13.
[14] Anonymous, "Reflection on a Radical Movement," mimeographed paper, Ann Arbor, Mich., 1965.

impersonal media which allow us no chance for response, no means for intelligent interrogation."[15]

In spite of what sociologists taught about kinship associations and voluntary groups, the tremendous increase in scale that accompanied the rise of Keynesian government and corporate economy had injected an undeniable "mass" character into American life. This was a new development which eroded the reality and perhaps even the future possibility of "substantive democracy." The widespread feeling of inadequacy of community motivated men to search for new communion in churches, unions, suburbs, and all manner of voluntary associations. But these too were plainly inadequate substitutes. Radicals believed that the democratization of information by modern mass media tended to consolidate opinion behind decisions which had already been made. Isolated individuals and families listening to television in their own homes and apartments seemed incapable of coming to decisions based on discussion. The "democratic process" which was the foundation of freedom necessitated a confrontation of views, a personal interchange and discussion; in short, democracy necessitated participation in decision-making institutions in order to be "substantive." It is on this basis that the new left concern for counter-institutions such as community unions and free universities is to be interpreted.

"Democracy," "freedom," "individualism," and "community" were all words found in liberal ideology; in the radical interpretation, however, their connection was made apparent, giving them a new meaning and vitality. For radicals, a free society would democratize all institutions. Academic life, for example, was seen in these terms: "In the 'mass-producing' of men into machines, freedom is the loser. Although the student is usually free to choose between various course offerings, he has little freedom to determine what will be offered. . . . The student's recognition of his subordinate status stems not from a respect for his professor's intellect, but, simply stated, from an acquiescence to authority."

An extreme statement of this concern was articulated by Lee Webb and Paul Booth:

The America which we face denies democracy—it is a nation in which crucial economic decisions which affect us all are made by corporate managers and bankers, in which millions of people are dependent on the indulgence of public welfare systems over which they have no control, in which the decisions of war and peace are made by a clique of advisers and experts. Can this be a democracy? We understand democracy to be that system of rule in which the people make the decisions that affect their lives. . . . In America, community is practically non-existent. In its absence, the only result of an individual's recognition of the root of his problem is frustration born of isolation.[16]

In the tangled complexity of modern industrial society, where everything causes everything else, or so it seems, the first function of ideology is to break into the ring (sphere?) of causation and identify a place where analysis should begin. The economic factors of production had seemed the most pressing area of concern in the Depression years, and ideology of bread-and-butter unionism focused attention on

---

[15] Anonymous, "S.D.S.: Present and Future," mimeographed paper, Ann Arbor, Mich., 1965.

[16] Lee Webb and Paul Booth, "The Anti-War Movement: From Protest to Radical Politics," mimeographed paper, Ann Arbor, Mich., SDS, n.d.

this area by its very structure. In the incomplete but relative abundance of the 1960's, the point to begin analysis seemed to lie in the interrelationships among freedom and democracy, individualism and community institutions. Initial evaluations of social phenomena seemed most relevant if viewed in these terms rather than in terms of "equilibrium," "pluralism," or "consensus." The challenge was to build or point the way toward the kind of democratic institutions demanded by radical ideology but now lacking in American society.

4. The Connection Between Liberals and Corporate Managers. In various publications, the radicals argued that the widespread sense of powerlessness and isolation was itself strengthening the power of elites and undermining democracy. That is, the very alienation and apathy of most citizens magnified the power of existing decision-makers and in turn made participation seem even more futile. Moreover, the process of fragmentation which was at the heart of pluralist ideology (and which was accepted by the new left with serious qualifications) implied not only the break-up of pyramidal elite control of cities as political units grew more complex, but implied as well the breaking up of community solidarity and the disintegration of community itself. To the extent that citizens were apathetic, power was vested in the hands of more (local level) or less (national level) fragmented but nevertheless entrenched elites. The loss of a sense of community (or the failure to achieve it in the first place) meant the absence of a sense of power and a will to participate. The abdication of popular power was the basis of elite power. The new radicals came to understand that elitism and pluralism were two sides to the same coin, a notion foreign to liberal ideologists.

"Liberal corporatism" was the name given to the form elitism took in America. In part, this was a renaming of the "establishment" ideologists as corporate liberals. In a November, 1965, speech at the second massive march on Washington to protest the war in Vietnam, SDS President Carl Oglesby discussed "Liberalism and the Corporate State." In that speech he said:

Seven months ago at the April March on Washington Paul Potter, the President of Students for a Democratic Society, stood in approximately this spot and said we must name the system that creates and sustains the war in Vietnam—name it, describe it, analyze it, understand it, and change it.

The original commitment in Vietnam was made by President Truman, a mainstream liberal. It was seconded by President Eisenhower, a moderate liberal. It was intensified by President Kennedy, a flaming liberal. Think of the men who now engineer that war ... Bundy, McNamara, Rusk, Lodge, Goldberg, the President himself. They are not moral monsters. They are all liberals. ...

... the anti-communist ideology ... depicts our presence in other lands not as coercion, but as protection. It allows us to say that our napalm in Vietnam is only another aspect of our humanitarian love like those exorcisms of the Middle Ages that so often killed the patient. ... This is the action of corporate liberalism. It performs for the corporate state a function quite like what the Church once performed for the feudal state. It seeks to justify its burdens and protect it from change.[1 7]

The dichotomy was posed: "corporatism or humanism, which? It has come to that." Were the "establishment" ideologists self-declared liberals? They were. Were they active in the movements for change—civil rights, power for the dispossessed,

[1 7] Carl Oglesby, "Let Us Shape the Future," published in Cohen and Hale, *op cit.,* pp. 312-321.

anti-imperialism, student representation? They were not. Did they defend governmental policy in these and other areas? They did. From the perspective of the new left, "corporate liberalism" seemed an undebatable description of these older ideologists.

For the new left, the corporate state was not free. It could not be because its institutions were undemocratic.

The fact is that a reasoned case may be made to suggest that modern industrial society faces problems so complex as to render our traditional democratic procedures no longer workable as they were in the past, and historic conceptions of civil and political liberty no longer viable. . . . It isn't enough to talk of changing human nature, nor is it particularly rewarding to concentrate on original sin. There must be an institutional change, for the problem is the problem of power. To be explicit, huge private collectives must be brought under effective control, i.e., rendered fully responsible to society. That there is no pat method for achieving this end does not eliminate its necessity.[18]

Similarly, Kim Moody argued that "The gigantic corporations that are the basis of our present system are authoritarian in essence. . . . The 'democratization of change,' which we are all agreed is a goal, is the most consistent with an economy that has its main units under democratic management."[19] Robb Burlage's "The American Planned Economy: A Critique" also called attention to the "private government" of business.[20] The decisions of businessmen no longer seemed private, and the liberal techniques of control did not seem effective, much less democratic.

Liberalism, in its defense of corporate America, argued that unions and government countervailed business. But as Burlage noted, "The federal government's powers are chiefly in a frozen tax system, marginal regulatory prerogatives as often regulated by the industries as by the commissions, and subsidy policies which all contribute to rather than countervail the corporation economy."[21] The elites that ruled private government in the pluralist system seemed to gain at least as much power through influence over government as they lost to it by regulation by government. Nothing less than the democratization of private government in some form could be consistent with the ideology of the new left and with their definition of freedom.

. . .

The ideology of the new student left differs from that of liberalism primarily in its assertion of the immediate relevance of democratic practices for all institutions, and in its rejection of current modes of participation as inadequate. It is differentiated from liberalism in tactics primarily by its rejection of a strategy of working within the Democratic Party and in coalition with old-line liberal institutions, including trade unions.

. . .

If the original purpose of the new left was to revitalize discussion of domestic and foreign policy and to catalyze change in a thousand expected and unexpected

---

[18] Anonymous, "A Letter to Young Democrats," mimeographed paper, SDS, 1964.

[19] Kimberly Moody, "American Capitalism," mimeographed paper, Ann Arbor, Mich., SDS, n.d.

[20] Robb Burlage, "The American Planned Economy: A Critique," mimeographed paper, SDS, n.d.

[21] *Ibid.*

places, it seems to have done that. If its purpose was to democratize the corporate state, we may understand that what we have treated here as the history of the new left is but a series of preliminary skirmishes in what may be a long period of creative development.

The Life Style of the New Generation

Fred Davis

Fred Davis (1925-   ), professor of sociology at the University of California Medical Center in San Francisco, is studying the interaction of Haight-Ashbury's hippie community with the larger San Francisco community. He is the author of *Passage Through Crisis: A Study of Polio Victims and Their Families* (1963).

And thus in love we have declared the purpose of our hearts plainly, without flatterie, expecting love, and the same sincerity from you, without grumbling, or quarreling, being Creatures of your own image and mould, intending no other matter herein, but to observe the Law of righteous action, endeavoring to shut out of the Creation, and the cursed thing, called Particular Propriety, which is the cause of all wares, bloudshed, theft, and enslaving Laws, that hold the people under miserie.

Signed for and in behalf of all the poor oppressed people of England, and the whole world.
— Gerrard Winstanley and others
June 1, 1649

This quotation is from the leader of the Diggers, a millenarian sect of communistic persuasion that arose in England at the time of Oliver Cromwell. . . .
. . . What distinguishes the Diggers—an amorphous, shifting, and sometimes contentious amalgam of ex-political radicals, psychedelic mystics, Ghandians, and Brechtian avant-garde thespians—from the area's "ordinary" hippies is their ideological brio, articulateness, good works, and flair for the dramatic event. (Some are even rumored to be over 30.) In the eyes of many Hashbury ["Haight-Ashbury"] hippies, therefore, the Diggers symbolize what is best, what is most persuasive and purposive, about the surrounding, more variegated hippie sub-culture—just as, for certain radical social critics of the American scene, the hippies are expressing, albeit elliptically, what is best about a seemingly ever-broader segment of American youth: its openness to new experience, puncturing of cant, rejection of bureaucratic regimentation, aversion to violence, and identification with the exploited and disadvantaged. That this is not the whole story barely needs saying. Along with the poetry and flowers, the melancholy smile at passing and

Source: "Why All of Us May Be Hippies Some Day," *TRANS-action* (now *Society*), December 1967, pp. 10-18. Copyright © December, 1967, by TRANS-action, Inc., New Brunswick, New Jersey.

ecstatic clasp at greeting, there is also the panicky incoherence of the bad LSD trip, the malnutrition, a startling rise in V.D. and hepatitis, a seemingly phobic reaction to elementary practices of hygiene and sanitation, and—perhaps most disturbing in the long run—a casualness about the comings and goings of human relationships that must verge on the grossly irresponsible.

But, then, social movements—particularly of this expressive-religious variety—are rarely of a piece, and it would be unfortunate if social scientists, rather than inquiring into the genesis, meaning, and future of the hippie movement, too soon joined ranks (as many are likely to, in any case) with solid burghers in an orgy of research into the "pathology" of it all: the ubiquitous drug use (mainly marihuana and LSD, often amphetamines, rarely heroin or other opiates), the easy attitudes toward sex ("If two people are attracted to each other, what better way of showing it than to make love?"), and the mocking hostility toward the middle-class values of pleasure-deferral, material success, and—ultimately—the whole mass-media-glamorized round of chic, deodorized, appliance-glutted suburban existence.

THE HIP SCENE IS THE MESSAGE

Clearly despite whatever real or imagined "pathology" middle-class spokesmen are ready to assign to the hippies, it is the middle-class scheme of life that young hippies are reacting against, even though in their ranks are to be found some youth of working-class origin who have never enjoyed the affluence that their peers now so heartily decry. To adulterate somewhat the slogan of Marshall McLuhan, one of the few non-orientalized intellectuals whom hippies bother to read at all, *the hip scene is the message*, not the elements whence it derives or the meanings that can be assigned to it verbally. (Interestingly, this fusion of disparate classes does not appear to include any significant number of the Negro youths who reside with their families in the integrated Haight-Ashbury district or in the adjoining Negro ghetto, the Fillmore district. By and large, Negroes view with bewilderment and ridicule the white hippies who flaunt, to the extent of begging on the streets, their rejection of what the Negroes have had scant opportunity to attain. What more revealing symbol of the Negro riots in our nation's cities than the carting off of looted TV sets, refrigerators, and washing machines? After all, aren't these things what America is all about?)

But granting that the hippie scene is a reaction to middle-class values, can the understanding of any social movement—particularly one that just in the process of its formation is so fecund of new art forms, new styles of dress and demeanor, and (most of all) new ethical bases for human relationships—ever be wholly reduced to its reactive aspect? As Ralph Ellison has eloquently observed in his critique of the standard sociological explanation of the American Negro's situation, a people's distinctive way of life is never solely a reaction to the dominant social forces that have oppressed, excluded, or alienated them from the larger society. The cumulative process of reaction and counterreaction, in its historical unfolding, creates its own ground for the emergence of new symbols, meanings, purposes, and social discoveries, none of which are ever wholly contained in embryo, as it were, in the conditions that elicited the reaction. It is, therefore, less with an eye toward explaining "how it came to be" than toward explaining what it may betoken of life in the future society that I now want to examine certain facets of the Hashbury hippie subculture. (Of course, very similar youth movements, subcultures, and settlements are found nowadays in many parts of the affluent Western world—Berkeley's Telegraph Avenue teeny-boppers; Los Angeles' Sunset Strippers; New York's East Village hippies; London's mods; Amsterdam's Provos; and the summer *Wandervogel* from all over Europe who chalk the pavement of Copenhagen's main shopping street, the Stroget, and sun themselves on the steps of Stockholm's Philharmonic Hall. What is culturally significant about the Haight-Ashbury hippies is, I would hazard, in general significant about these others as well, with—to be sure—certain qualifications. Indeed, a certain marvelous irony attaches itself to the fact that perhaps the only genuine cross-national culture found in the world today builds on the rag-tag of beards, bare feet, bedrolls, and beads, not on the cultural-exchange programs of governments and universities, or tourism, or—least of all—ladies' clubs' invocations for sympathetic understanding of one's foreign neighbors.)

What I wish to suggest here is that there is, as Max Weber would have put it, an *elective affinity* between prominent styles and themes in the hippie subculture and certain incipient problems of identity, work, and leisure that loom ominously as Western industrial society moves into an epoch of accelerated cybernation, staggering material abundance, and historically-unprecedented mass opportunities for creative leisure and enrichment of the human personality. This is not to say that the latter are the *hidden causes* or tangible *motivating forces* of the former. Rather, the point is that the hippies, in their collective, yet radical, break with the constraints of our present society, are—whether they know it or not (some clearly do intuit a connection)—already rehearsing *in vivo* a number of possible cultural solutions to central life problems posed by the emerging society of the future. While other students of contemporary youth culture could no doubt cite many additional emerging problems to which the hippie subculture is, willy-nilly, addressing itself (marriage and family organization, the character of friendship and personal loyalties, the forms of political participation), space and the kind of observations I have been able to make require that I confine myself to three: the problems of *compulsive consumption,* of *passive spectatorship,* and of the *time-scale of experience.*

COMPULSIVE CONSUMPTION

What working attitude is man to adopt toward the potential glut of consumer goods that the new technology will make available to virtually all members of the future society? Until now, modern capitalist society's traditional response to short-term conditions of overproduction has been to generate—through government manipulation of fiscal devices—greater purchasing power for discretionary consumption. At the same time, the aim has been to cultivate the acquisitive impulse—largely through mass advertising, annual styling changes, and planned obsolescence—so that, in the economist's terminology, a high level of aggregate demand could be sustained. Fortunately, given the great backlog of old material wants and the technologically-based creation of new wants, these means have, for the most part, worked comparatively well—both for advancing (albeit unequally) the mass standard of living and for ensuring a reasonably high rate of return to capital.

But, as Walter Weisskopf, Robert Heilbroner, and other economists have wondered, will these means prove adequate for an automated future society in which the mere production of goods and services might easily outstrip man's desire for them, or his capacity to consume them in satisfying ways? Massive problems of air pollution, traffic congestion, and waste disposal aside, is there no psychological limit to the number of automobiles, TV sets, freezers, and dishwashers that even a zealous consumer can aspire to, much less make psychic room for in his life space? The specter that haunts post-industrial man is that of a near worker-less economy in which most men are constrained, through a variety of economic and political sanctions, to frantically purchase and assiduously use up the cornucopia of consumer goods that a robot-staffed factory system (but one still harnessed to capitalism's rationale of pecuniary profit) regurgitates upon the populace. As far back as the late 1940s sociologists like David Riesman were already pointing to the many moral paradoxes of work, leisure, and interpersonal relations posed by a then only nascent society of capitalist mass abundance. How much more perplexing the paradoxes if, using current technological trends, we extrapolate to the year 2000?

Hippies, originating mainly in the middle classes, have been nurtured at the boards of consumer abundance. Spared their parents' vivid memories of economic depression and material want, however, they now, with what to their elders seems like insulting abandon, declare unshamefacedly that the very quest for "the good things of life" and all that this entails—the latest model, the third car, the monthly credit payments, the right house in the right neighborhood—are a "bad bag." In phrases redolent of nearly all utopian thought of the past, they proclaim that happiness and a meaningful life are not to be found in things, but in the cultivation of the self and by an intensive exploration of inner sensibilities with like-minded others.

Extreme as this antimaterialistic stance may seem, and despite its probable tempering should hippie communities develop as a stable feature on the American landscape, it nonetheless points a way to a solution of the problem of material glut; to wit, the simple demonstration of the ability to live on less, thereby calming the acquisitive frenzy that would have to be sustained, and even accelerated, if the present scheme of capitalist production and distribution were to remain unchanged. Besides such establishments as the Diggers' Free Store, gleanings of this attitude are even evident in the street panhandling that so many hippies engage in. Unlike the street beggars of old, there is little that is obsequious or deferential about their manner. On the contrary, their approach is one of easy, sometimes condescending casualness, as if to say, "You've got more than enough to spare, I need it, so let's not make a degrading charity scene out of my asking you." The story is told in the Haight-Ashbury of the patronizing tourist who, upon being approached for a dime by a hippie girl in her late teens, took the occasion to deliver a small speech on how delighted he would be to give it to her—provided she first told him what she needed it for. Without blinking an eye she replied, "It's my menstrual period and that's how much a sanitary napkin costs."

PASSIVE SPECTATORSHIP

As social historians are forever reminding us, modern man has—since the beginnings of the industrial revolution—become increasingly a spectator and less a participant. Less and less does he, for example, create or play music, engage in sports, dance or sing; instead he watches professionally-trained others, vastly more accomplished than himself, perform their acts while he, perhaps, indulges in Mitty-like fantasies of hidden graces and talents. Although this bald statement of the spectator thesis has been challenged in recent years by certain social researchers—statistics are cited of the growing numbers taking guitar lessons, buying fishing equipment, and painting on Sunday—there can be little doubt that "doing" kinds of expressive pursuits, particularly of the collective type, no longer bear the same *integral* relationship to daily life that they once did, or still do in primitive societies. The mere change in how they come to be perceived, from what one does in the ordinary course of life to one's "hobbies," is in itself of profound historical significance. Along with this, the virtuoso standards that once were the exclusive property of small aristocratic elites, rather than being undermined by the oft-cited revolutions in mass communications and mass education, have so diffused through the class structure as to even cause the gifted amateur *at play* to apologize for his efforts with some such remark as, "I only play at it." In short, the cult of professionalism, in the arts as elsewhere, has been institutionalized so intensively in Western society that the ordinary man's sense of expressive adequacy and competence has progressively atrophied. This is especially true of the college-educated, urban middle classes, which—newly exposed to the lofty aesthetic standards of high culture—stand in reverent, if passive, awe of them.

Again, the problem of excessive spectatorship has not proved particularly acute until now, inasmuch as most men have had other time-consuming demands to fill their lives with, chiefly work and family life, leavened by occasional vacations and mass-produced amusements. But what of the future when, according to such social prognosticators as Robert Theobald and Donald Michael, all (except a relatively small cadre of professionals and managers) will be faced with a surfeit of leisure time? Will the mere extension of passive spectatorship and the professional's monopoly of expressive pursuits be a satisfactory solution?

Here, too, hippies are opening up new avenues of collective response to life issues posed by a changing socio-technological environment. They are doing so by rejecting those virtuoso standards that stifle participation in high culture; by substituting an extravagantly eclectic (and, according to traditional aestheticians, reckless) admixture of materials, styles, and motifs from a great diversity of past and present human cultures, and, most of all, by insisting that every man can find immediate expressive fulfillment provided he lets the socially-suppressed spirit within him ascend into vibrant consciousness. The manifesto is: All men are artists, and who cares that some are better at it than others; we can all have fun! Hence, the deceptively crude antisophistication of hippie art forms, which are, perhaps, only an apparent reversion to primitivism. One has only to encounter the lurid *art nouveau* contortions of the hippie posters and their Beardsleyan exoticism, or the mad melange of hippie street costume—Greek-sandaled feet peeking beneath harem pantaloons encased in a fringed American Indian suede jacket, topped by pastel floral decorations about the face—or the sitar-whining cacophony of the folk-rock band, to know immediately that one is in the presence of *expressiveness* for its own sake.

In more mundane ways, too, the same readiness to let go, to participate, to create and perform without script or forethought is everywhere evident in the Hashbury. Two youths seat themselves on the sidewalk or in a store entranceway; bent beer can in hand, one begins scratching a bongo-like rhythm on the pavement while the other tattoos a bell-like accompaniment by striking a stick on an empty bottle. Soon they are joined, one by one, by a tambourinist, a harmonica player, a penny-whistler or recorder player, and, of course, the ubiquitous guitarist. A small crowd collects and, at the fringes, some blanket-bedecked boys and girls begin twirling about in movements vaguely resembling a Hindu dance. The wailing, rhythmic beating and dancing, alternately rising to peaks of intensity and subsiding, may last for as little as five minutes or as long as an hour, players and dancers joining in and dropping out as whim moves them. At some point—almost any—a mood takes hold that "the happening is over"; participants and onlookers disperse as casually as they had collected.

Analogous scenes of "participation unbound" are to be observed almost every night of the week (twice on Sunday) at the hippies' Parnassus, the Fillmore Auditorium, where a succession of name folk-rock bands, each more deafening than the one before, follow one another in hour-long sessions. Here, amidst the electric guitars, the electric organs, and the constantly metamorphizing show of lights, one can see the gainly and the graceless, the sylph bodies and rude stompers, the crooked and straight—all, of whatever condition or talent, *dance* as the flickering of a strobe light reduces their figures in silhouette to egalitarian spastic bursts. The recognition dawns that this, at last, is dancing of utterly free form, devoid of fixed sequence or step, open to all and calling for no Friday after-school classes at Miss Martha's or expensive lessons from Arthur Murray. The sole requisite is to tune in, take heart, and let go. What follows must be "beautiful" (a favorite hippie word) because it is *you* who are doing and feeling, not another to whom you have surrendered the muse.

As with folk-rock dancing, so (theoretically, at least) with music, poetry, painting, pottery, and the other arts and crafts: expression over performance, impulse over product. Whether the "straight world" will in time heed this message of the hippies is, to be sure, problematical. Also, given the lavish financial rewards and prestige heaped upon more talented hippie artists by a youth-dominated entertainment market, it is conceivable that high standards of professional performance will develop here as well (listen to the more recent Beatles' recordings), thus engendering perhaps as great a participative gulf between artist and audience as already exists in the established arts. Despite the vagaries of forecasting, however, the hippies—as of now, at least—are responding to the incipient plenitude of leisure in ways far removed from the baleful visions of a Huxley or an Orwell.

THE TIME-SCALE OF EXPERIENCE

In every society, certain activities are required to complete various tasks and to achieve various goals. These activities form a sequence—they may be of short duration and simple linkage (boiling an egg); long duration and complex linkage (preparing for a profession); or a variety of intermediate combinations (planting and harvesting a crop). And the activity sequences needed to complete valued tasks and to achieve valued goals in a society largely determine how the people in that society will subjectively experience *time*.

The distinctive temporal bent of industrial society has been toward the second of these arrangements, long duration and complex linkage. As regards the subjective experience of time, this has meant what the anthropologist Florence Kluckhohn has termed a strong "future orientation" on the part of Western man, a quality of sensibility that radically distinguishes him from his peasant and tribal forebears. The major activities that fill the better part of his life acquire their meaning less from the pleasure they may or may not give at the moment than from their perceived relevance to some imagined future state of being or affairs, be it salvation, career achievement, material success, or the realization of a more perfect social order. Deprived of the pursuit of these temporally distant, complexly modulated goals, we would feel that life, as the man in the street puts it, is without meaning.

This subjective conception of time and experience is, of course, admirably suited to the needs of post-18th century industrial society, needs that include a stable labor force; work discipline; slow and regular accumulation of capital with which to plan and launch new investments and to expand; and long, arduous years of training to provide certain people with the high levels of skill necessary in so many professions and technical fields. If Western man had proved unable to defer present gratifications for future rewards (that is, if he had not been a future-oriented being), nothing resembling our present civilization, as Freud noted, could have come to pass.

Yet, paradoxically, it is the advanced technology of computers and servo-mechanisms, not to overlook nuclear warfare, that industrial civilization has carried us to that is raising grave doubts concerning this temporal ordering of affairs, this optimistic, pleasure-deferring, and magically rationalistic faith in converting present effort to future payoff. Why prepare, if there will be so few satisfying jobs to prepare for? Why defer, if there will be a superabundance of inexpensively-produced goods to choose from? Why plan, if all plans can disintegrate into nuclear dust?

Premature or exaggerated as these questions may seem, they are being asked, especially by young people. And merely to ask them is to prompt a radical shift in time-perspective—from what *will be* to what *is,* from future promise to present fulfillment, from the mundane discounting of present feeling and mood to a sharpened awareness of their contours and their possibilities for instant alteration. Broadly, it is to invest present experience with a new cognitive status and importance: a lust to extract from the living moment its full sensory and emotional potential. For if the present is no longer to be held hostage to the future, what other course than to ravish it at the very instant of its apprehension?

There is much about the hippie subculture that already betokens this alteration of time-perspective and concomitant reconstitution of the experienced self. Hippie argot—some of it new, much of it borrowed with slight connotative changes from the Negro, jazz, homosexual, and addict subcultures—is markedly skewed toward words and phrases in the active present tense: "happening," "where it's at," "turn on," "freak out," "grooving," "mind-blowing," "be-in," "cop out," "split," "drop acid" ..., "put on," "uptight" ..., "trip out" .... The very concept of a happening signifies immediacy: Events are to be actively engaged in, improvised upon, and dramatically exploited for their own sake, with little thought about their origins, duration, or consequences. Thus, almost anything—from a massive be-in in Golden Gate Park to ingesting LSD to a casual street conversation to sitting solitarily under a tree—is approached with a heightened awareness of its happening potential. Similarly, the vogue among Hashbury hippies for astrology, tarot cards, I Ching, and other forms of thaumaturgic prophecy (a hippie conversation is as likely to begin with "What's your birthday?" as "What's your name?") seems to be an attempt to denude the future of its temporal integrity—its unknowability and slow unfoldingness—by fusing it indiscriminately with present dispositions and sensations. The hippie's structureless round-of-day ("hanging loose"), his disdain for appointments, schedules, and straight society's compulsive parceling out of minutes and hours, are all implicated in his intense reverence for the possibilities of the present and uninterest in the future. Few wear watches, and as a colleague who has made a close participant-observer study of one group of hippies remarked, "None of them ever seems to know what time it is."

It is, perhaps, from this vantage point that the widespread use of drugs by hippies acquires its cultural significance, above and beyond the fact that drugs are easily available in the subculture or that their use (especially LSD) has come to symbolize a distinctive badge of membership in that culture. Denied by our Protestant-Judaic heritage the psychological means for experiencing the moment intensively, for parlaying sensation and exoticizing mundane consciousness, the hippie uses drugs where untutored imagination fails. Drugs impart to the present—or so it is alleged by the hippie psychedelic religionists—an aura of aliveness, a sense of union with fellow man and nature, which—we have been taught—can be apprehended, if not in the afterlife that few modern men still believe in, then only after the deepest reflection and self-knowledge induced by protracted experience.

A topic of lively debate among hippie intellectuals is whether drugs represent but a transitory phase of the hippie subculture to be discarded once other, more self-generating, means are discovered by its members for extracting consummatory meaning from present time, or whether drugs are the *sine qua non* of the subculture. Whatever the case, the hippies' experiment with ways to recast our notions of time and experience is deserving of close attention.

THE HIPPIES' FUTURE

As of this writing [1967], it is by no means certain that Haight-Ashbury's "new community," as hippie spokesmen like to call it, can survive much beyond early 1968. [As of now, 1972, it is alive and well in the Haight-Ashbury and relating fruitfully with the straight culture still resident there and in the hills surrounding the district. — Eds.]

It has not, therefore, been solely the impact of sheer numbers that has subjected the new community to a difficult struggle for survival. A variety of forces, internal and external, appear to have conjoined to crush it. To begin with, there is the hippies' notorious, near-anarchic aversion to sustained and organized effort toward reaching some goal. Every man "does his own thing for as long as he likes" until another thing comes along to distract or delight him, whereupon the hippie ethos enjoins him to drop the first thing. (Shades of the early, utopian Karl Marx: ". . . in the communist society it [will be] possible for me to do this today and that tomorrow, to hunt in the morning, to fish in the afternoon, to raise cattle in the evening, to be a critic after dinner, just as I feel at the moment, without ever being a hunter, fisherman, herdsman, or critic." From *The German Ideology*.) Even with such groups as the Diggers, projects are abandoned almost as soon as they are begun. Perhaps there is some ultimate wisdom to "doing one's own thing"; it was, however, hardly a practical way to receive a flock of kinsmen.

But though Haight-Ashbury's hippie community has passed from the scene, the roots upon which it feeds run deep in our culture. These are not only of the long-term socio-historic kind I have touched on here, but of a distinctly contemporary character as well, the pain and moral duplicity of our Vietnam involvement being a prominent wellspring of hippie alienation. As the pressures mount on middle-class youth for ever greater scholastic achievement (soon a graduate degree may be mandatory for middle-class status, as a high-school diploma was in the 1940s), as the years of adolescent dependence are further prolonged, and as the accelerated pace of technological change aggravates the normal social tendency to intergenerational conflict, an increasing number of young people can be expected to drop out, or opt out, and drift into the hippie subculture. It is difficult to foresee how long they will remain there and what the consequences for later stages of their careers will be, inasmuch as insufficient time has passed for even a single age cohort of hippies to make the transition from early to middle adulthood. However, even among those youths who "remain in" conventional society in some formal sense, a very large number can be expected to hover so close to the margins of hippie subculture as to have their attitudes and outlooks substantially modified. Indeed, it is probably through some such muted, gradual, and indirect process of social conversion that the hippie subculture will make a lasting impact on American society, if it is to have any at all.

At the same time, the hippie rebellion gives partial, as yet ambiguous, evidence of a massiveness, a universality, and a density of existential texture, all of which promise to transcend the narrowly-segregated confines of age, occupation, and residence that characterized most bohemias of the past (Greenwich Village, Bloomsbury, the Left Bank). Some hippie visionaries already compare the movement to Christianity sweeping the Roman Empire. We cannot predict how far the movement can go toward enveloping the larger society, and whether as it develops it will—as have nearly all successful social movements—significantly compromise the visions that animate it with the practices of the reigning institutional system. Much depends on the state of future social discontent, particularly within the middle classes, and on the viable political options governments have for assuaging this discontent. Judging, however, from the social upheavals and mass violence of recent decades, such options are, perhaps inevitably, scarce indeed. Just possibly, then, by opting out and making their own kind of cultural waves, the hippies are telling us more than we can now imagine about our future selves.

Suggested Readings

1. Deloria, Vine, *We Talk, You Listen* (New York: Macmillan, 1970). Although mainly about the American Indian, this book has some excellent discussions about the hippies.

2. Flacks, Richard E., "The Liberated Generation: An Exploration of the Roots of Student Protest," *Journal of Social Issues,* Vol. 23 (1967), 52-75.
3. Oglesby, Carl, "The Idea of the New Left," *New Left Reader* (New York: Grove Press, 1969), pp. 1-19.
4. Reich, Charles A., *The Greening of America* (New York: Random House, 1970).
5. Revel, Jean-François, *Without Marx or Jesus* (New York: Doubleday, 1971).
6. Wolf, Leonard, *Voices of the Love Generation* (Boston: Little, Brown, 1968). Interviews with the leading figures of the Haight-Ashbury hippie movement.

Philosophy and Ideology of the University

Whatever the differences between art and discursive reason, they share a common enterprise: they cultivate the human spirit, which is the capacity of man to transcend his present context for the sake of a more comprehensive, articulate, and worthy vision of himself. That vision, in all its forms, is culture, which it is the obligation of the University to honor and protect.

—Richard Lichtman

INTRODUCTION

For most students, their years at college mark both an end and a beginning. They signify an *end* to childhood, to close parental supervision and school control, to an existence made *for* them and not *by* them; they also signify the *beginning* of a life that is theirs to make, to the heady delights of self-government.

If a college education is to be a prelude to mature life, the student must keep in mind a conception of the kind of life he wants to lead. The kind of life he projects for himself not only should but does influence his notion of a college education. For example, if he envisions his future primarily in terms of employment, he will see his college education as a means to acquire a marketable skill or as a preparation for professional, postgraduate training.

We suggest, therefore, that in thinking about your university education, you place it in the perspective of the rest of your life as you now desire and imagine you will want it to be in all its fullness and that you so shape your college education that it will enable you to create such a perspective for yourself.

"Fine phrases for a fine day," some students may say, "but our day has not come. We do not yet have enough control over the university to 'so shape' our education, valid as your point may be. It is indeed our life and no one can dream what our life is to be for us, but control by others is precisely the ordure we have inherited from colleges and universities dominated by pedantic, stuffy, fawning, and feckless administrators and staffed by a frightened, ambitious, and powerless faculty."

From the other side of the lectern, **Robert Brustein** (whose essay is the second in this chapter) replies, "the faculty member functions not to represent the student's interests in relation to the administration, but rather to communicate knowledge from one who knows to one who doesn't. . . . The idea—so central to scholarship—that there is an inherited body of knowledge to be transmitted from one generation to another—loses favor because it puts the student in an [to him] unacceptably subordinate position, with the result that the learning process gives way to a general free-for-all in which one man's opinion is as good as another's."

To which the student may respond, "Professor, you would grant control of the university to those who possess authority. And you would give authority to those who possess some vague, undefined thing you call an 'inherited body of knowledge.' But your analysis lives in a halfway house. Control over the university does not rests in the hands of those who possess the 'inherited body of knowledge.' It rests with those who are conduits for and those who supply the money. It rests with the governing boards for private colleges and with the legislature and governor for public colleges; they get their money from business, taxes, and federal grants. What gets taught and who teaches it are determined ultimately by the money handlers and suppliers. They determine what part of 'the inherited body of knowledge' gets taught, researched, or written about."

The dialectic about control over and authority in university education begins with this intellectual confrontation. Regardless of who in fact now has control, who should have control? If it is said that those who have authority should have control, we then ask, Who has the authority? Several legitimate claims to authority seem to conflict: On the one hand, the students have the authority vested in them because only they can dream their dreams of life; and since education is a prelude to their vision, the nature of that education should be composed by them. On the other hand, the university is a seat of learning, and the faculty, having the authority of knowledge, should control the university. On still another hand, the people who supply the money—the taxpayers, the producers, and the government—have the authority to expect that the university return their investment by serving their interests; consequently, the money suppliers should control the university.

Philosophy often begins when we are jogged by a set of contrary or contradictory positions, each of which has a plausible claim to our assent. In the present instance, there are three contrary claims about the proper location of authority and, subsequently, of university control. Philosophers, young and old, when faced with such a situation, either show that there really is no conflict, show that there is a way of making the positions compatible, or adduce arguments that decide the issue in favor of one over the others. Brustein and **Spiro Agnew** (first essay in this chapter) present arguments on this issue that will provide you the spark to begin your philosophizing.

The essays in this chapter address themselves to some other philosophic issues concerning the university. These include the relevance of the curriculum; the autonomy of the university; the extent of university involvement in the social and political life of the community; the proper function or functions of colleges and universities; and the nature of a liberal education.

Relevance is a sacred concept that should stimulate philosophizing when it butts up against another sacred concept, namely, objectivity. At first glance, it appears commonplace to state, "The university should be a place where the search for truth is as objective as man can make it, and it also should be an institution where the truth sought after should be relevant to its members and the society that it serves." However, if we pry up the surface of this statement, another contradiction quickly scrambles out.

Consider the following arguments designed to expose a contradiction between relevance and objectivity: Objectivity requires disinterestedness because to be objective one should be impartial; impartiality, in turn, requires purging our subjective bias while we search for truth; to be without bias requires that our personal interests be set aside when we gather data, draw conclusions, and make judgments. Relevance, on the other hand, requires interestedness because in choosing topics for our investigation we have to make value judgments; to make value judgments, we must decide what is of value to us; those things are of value to us that are relevant to our personal interests, our subjective desires, our wants. Thus, relevance and objectivity appear to be contradictory because relevance is essentially tied to interestedness, whereas objectivity is essentially tied to disinterestedness.

Again, when faced with such a situation, philosophers young and old either have to show that there really is no contradiction, show that there is a way of making the positions compatible, or adduce arguments that decide the issue in favor of one over the other. Agnew and **Louis Kattsoff** (whose essay is the last in this chapter) provide arguments you will meet in thinking your way through this issue.

If you think your way very far into the relevance-objectivity issue, you will inevitably confront the concept of university autonomy. Although most of the public thinks that relevance is a demand students have made of their college education, it is seldom noted that American colleges have long aimed toward relevance. This point is made dramatically by **Richard Lichtman** (whose essay is fourth in this chapter) when he contrasts John Stuart Mill's conception of the university with Clark Kerr's. The American university has moved to serve short-run utility; Kerr points out that its curriculum and departments historically have developed as service institutions to agriculture, industry, government, and the military. The university has thus become highly relevant in the last century, but it has become relevant only to some dominant parts of our polity. The students' demand for relevance is not, therefore, a new, radical, unprecedented demand that has been laid on the universities; rather, it is a demand that the university become relevant to what many students see as their neglected interests.

We can understand how this fresh relevance demand is related to the autonomy of the university by noting that some believe the university can turn to serve neglected interests only if it severs itself from service to agriculture, industry, and government. In other words, the university can serve the neglected interests only by asserting its autonomy, by refusing to be the slave of the old interests.

In tracing the connection between relevance and autonomy, we appear to have uncovered a conflict within the concept of relevance itself. It appears that the university must either be relevant to the interests of utility or to the neglected interests of students and that it cannot serve both interests simultaneously.

This idea of inner conflict within relevance can be sharpened by elaborating on a conception of "neglected interests." This conception lies at the heart of the essays of both Lichtman and **Cardinal Newman** (third essay in this chapter). Neither Lichtman nor Newman assert that a university should serve short-run, practical, technological, service interests. Reason should not be exhausted in solving technical problems. Rather, reason should, in Lichtman's words, be set free to "cultivate the human spirit" and help man articulate a "worthy vision of himself." Reason's autonomy, according to Lichtman, is possible only if the university is autonomous from industry, agriculture, and government. Perhaps students will detect their conception of "neglected interests" in Lichtman's remarks: In the multiversity the student "is never required to state the relevance of one area of understanding for another, nor relate their distinct methodologies and insights in coherent, synthetic connection. It is assumed that the summation of individually correct answers will produce something more than fragmented understanding."

Newman mercilessly attacks any conception of the function of the university that would make it serve utility. In his essay, he attempts to explicate the notion of a "liberal education," as opposed to a "servile" utilitarian one. We are all acquainted with the phrase "liberal arts," but not as many have tried to understand its meaning. Newman tries to characterize a vision of a kind of life that will help us compose a prelude called "Liberal education." He thinks of this prelude as an education in which the student "apprehends the great outlines of knowledge, the principles on which it rests, the scale of its parts, its lights and its shades, its great points and its little, as he otherwise cannot apprehend them. Hence it is that his education is called 'Liberal.' A habit of mind is formed which lasts through life, of which the attributes are freedom, equitableness, calmness, moderation, and wisdom; or what in a former Discourse I have ventured to call a philosophical habit."

Notice how closely webbed are the concepts of authority, control, relevance, autonomy, liberal education, and the function of the university. It is typical of philosophizing that thinking hard about one concept entails finding its compatible relations to other concepts.

A couple of cautionary remarks about "function of the university" before we bring this introduction to a close. First, it is philosophically naive to think that "To educate the youth" is an answer to "What is the function of a college?" Educate for what? Of all the things that could be taught, what should be taught? Who is to determine what should be taught? How is it to be taught? Second, it is perilous to let habit force on you the singular, "function," when the plural, "functions," might be more appropriately used: "What are the *functions* of a college?"

Here are several functions that have been proposed for the university at one time or another: (1) improve students' chances for economic success by granting vocational degrees and offering occupational preparation; (2) provide the opportunity to acquire the style and poise of a lady or gentleman, helping to civilize our social jungle; (3) train manpower for the continued technological advancement of our and others' societies, helping to create a material utopia; (4)

give students the chance for intellectual advancement so they may gain personal satisfaction and attain an unfragmented understanding of the universe and its parts; (5) preserve and transmit learning and knowledge from one generation to another and provide the stimulus and means for the discovery of new knowledge; (6) teach students the foundations and outer reaches of morality and responsibility and instill maturity into its votaries; (7) prepare students to be effective citizen participants in a democratic society; and (8) prepare students for a rewarding life in a world with an increasing amount of leisure.

Are there, do you think, any arguments that can be given that would demonstrate that any one or more of the above functions we have listed is not a proper function of the university? If you could show that two of them are incompatible, that would be one kind of demonstration. Of course, you would still have to decide which of them, if either, is a proper function of the university. And for that, you would need a positive argument. As you may have noticed, philosophizing proceeds by argument. Through arguments we have exposed some apparent contradictions that you may harbor in your thought between authorities differently conceived; between relevance and objectivity; within relevance itself; and between a "liberal" and a "servile" education. To escape these apparent contradictions requires further arguments.

The Demand for Relevance

Spiro Agnew

Spiro T. Agnew (1918-   ) was chief executive of Baltimore County, Maryland, 1962-1967; governor of Maryland, 1967-1969; and Vice-President of the United States during the Nixon Administration.

As another fall comes to the campus, American colleges and universities are being hard-pressed—from within and without—to define the role they will play in our country's future.

No one, it seems, is willing to suggest that they return to teaching students to think and to learn. As controversial as that might seem—"non-relevant" would be the term for it in today's vernacular—I herewith propose it.

In other words, let's restore the Ivory Tower and the classical education that has been the bedrock of our civilization. And let's cease the endless pyramiding of irrelevant electives that give the student only "what he wants" and thus ill equip him for the demanding and competitive adult life he is about to enter.

We need more of the mental discipline that produces scholarship and the moral discipline that restores order and allows scholarship to be pursued.

Source: Speech given September 27, 1970, and entered into the *Congressional Record*, September 29, 1970.

Now, before I am tagged a Neanderthal who would disrupt or destroy the processes of education, or stifle dissent on the part of young people, let me assure the reader that that is not my purpose. Please examine the whole argument.

First, some basic beliefs:

I believe that the current generation of young people has demonstrated that it is one of the most concerned generations in our history. But, while lauding their compassion and their motives to achieve justice and progress, I disagree whole-heartedly with their methods. I fear that, as far as their college education is concerned, they are losing valuable time.

I also believe that young people should involve themselves in politics and government—but not at the expense of those on the campus who are there to learn and acquire a bona fide education. The serious students of today cannot concentrate for the shouts of "Action now!"

There is no better way to achieve "Action now" on social and environmental problems than to run for public office or work actively for the election of someone who shares your beliefs. But I do not think that colleges should suspend their classes while this takes place; and students who are so inclined might do well to engage in such activity on their own time, even if it means removing themselves from college and getting a job.

Finally, I believe that the educated person who has had some practical working experience is much better equipped to solve the problems of this society than a classroom of students, no matter how brilliant they may be.

The problem of pollution is far more likely to be solved by the working scientist than by some present-day agitator or his well-intentioned follower from the campus who stridently draws attention to it but offers no solution.

Working with the scientist will be the businessman who, before he began making a profit, studied humanities that now guide him to the realization that there is more to life than profit-making; the government official who won election by gaining the respect and confidence of his constituents instead of screaming obscenities at them; and the worker who builds rather than destroys.

That is who will solve the problem.

I do not mean that there is not a major role to be played by the academic community, but its contribution must come from the research laboratory, the classroom and the library, rather than the street. Above all, its contribution must be the education of those who tomorrow must come to grips with these problems and further speed their solution.

.   .   .

It is in this last-mentioned, real purpose of college that I feel many of our institutions are falling down today. One of the reasons is they have lost sight of the traditional, time-honored purpose of education.

Our colleges and universities have the same responsibility as the many who have preceded them—to build upon the knowledge of mankind accumulated through the centuries, and to pass this on to their students.

It is their duty and their obligation to preserve and broaden the intellectual heritage of our nation and to educate the future leaders of this country and the world.

They cannot fulfill this role—either for the seven million young people now enrolled on our campuses or the millions more who will soon follow—if they retreat from the basic goals of higher education to become emotionally "involved" with government on issues and problems.

Let us examine for a moment the question of "relevance," this modern trend of yielding to student demands for courses that concern themselves with the major political and social issues of the day. Our major universities now offer such subjects as racial conflict, urban problems, alienation of youth, equality of women, and air pollution, to name just a few. They are, in effect, courses in current events.

My feelings about these were well expressed by Bayard Rustin, the civil rights pioneer and Executive Director of the Philip Randolph Institute, when he commented on widely publicized demands for black-oriented subjects and separate cultural centers on campus.

"Everyone knows that education for the Negro is inferior," Mr. Rustin said. "Bring them to the University with the understanding that they must have the remedial work they require. The easy way out is to let them have black courses and their own dormitories and give them degrees . . . .

"What in hell are soul courses worth in the real world? No one gives a damn if you've taken soul courses. They want to know if you can do mathematics and write a correct sentence."

The same thing can be said of practically all so-called "relevant" courses which deal only with current problems out of context. The information gained from such courses will be, for the most part, out of date—irrelevant, if you will—before the student gets out of college or soon thereafter.

It should be the purpose of the college course to teach method and character on the basis of factual information accumulated over the centuries.

Most "relevant" courses, as far as I have been able to perceive, do not give the student the historical perspective that is necessary in making sound judgments. Even in those where the historical background is considered, it is being considered for a special purpose. The student is aware of what he is looking for. This is not what I have always understood to be the broadening experience we normally think of as the purpose of higher education.

In the traditional history course the student learned a body of material, the immediate value of which he did not know. And he was able to make independent judgments, one way or the other, because he was not already committed to a particular viewpoint on a current issue.

That is not so in the "relevant" courses. The material is controversial; the student is more often than not a partisan, an advocate. He may learn persuasion—important, to be sure—but he will hardly be in the best position to learn accurate observation and disinterested analysis.

Yet, this is precisely what college should teach. In everything that is read or learned, what matters are the qualities of character and mind that we retain long after the concrete means to their acquisition have vanished.

The mental qualities to which I refer are the ability to observe accurately, analyze appropriately, and propose solutions to problems that are perceived.

These abilities are hard to acquire in any circumstance, almost impossible where the task is impeded by partisan emotions. Emotional commitment to the material at hand is pleasant; it renders the burdens light by stirring our emotions.

But pleasure and ease are not the goals of college courses. They can be useful, indeed, but for a college course they must be regarded not as goals, but as means. The goals toward which such courses should aim are precisely the abilities which I have mentioned. In my opinion, these goals can most effectively be reached by utilizing material that is not exclusively "hot" or currently controversial.

Such a regimen requires discipline, precisely because it is not easy. Whether this discipline comes from without or within matters little. But come it must, and I believe it is the college's duty to inspire it and nurture it.

The modern trend to let students follow their noses, to "do their own thing," is an irresponsible policy in higher education. This used to be what you did in your spare time. It is becoming a part of the curriculum at many institutions. The courses multiply yearly.

What if the student likes nothing but rock music and New Left cinema? If he can find a few others who feel the same way and organize an assault on the administration building, should he be given these courses?

And after a four-year, heavy diet of such courses, are we going to pronounce him Bachelor of Arts and say to all the world, "This is an educated man!"?

I do not want to indicate here that I do not think there are many matters of legitimate concern to students and reforms that are needed in all of our educational institutions. There are. But the "do your own thing" syndrome is the weakest part of the argument. It has no place in a college curriculum.

There are those who will argue that method can be learned on any material. But as I have said, the purpose of college is not only to learn method; it is also to acquire certain traits of character. In this regard, it very clearly matters what the student reads. I, for one, am not ready to substitute Allen Ginsberg for Shakespeare or Milton.

There is a difference between what is historically significant and what is currently "relevant," and it should be reflected in the sense of values we apply to college courses. The time allowed for education is limited and precious. It should be used wisely. And the faculty, not the students, are the best judges of how it should be filled.

As for the character-building aspect of education, all of us want our children to acquaint themselves with the lofty ideals and noble character that are part of our heritage. It inspires them to reach beyond themselves.

I asked a student once why he studied history, and he told me that it gave him hope, it stimulated him to rise above the petty details of his life. When he felt small—a tiny speck in a world of three billion people—he could draw inspiration from the success of the great leaders of our republic and our world, who also overcame a myriad of problems to succeed. And they came across as individual, real men.

The advocates of relevance insist that the current events themselves are of primary importance, rather than the context in which they exist. This is reminiscent of the old professor who demands that we learn all the "footnotes" of Hamlet rather than its timeless message. What place does this emphasis on the acquisition of details for their own sake have in college education?

Problems are not new in the world. They are always changing. What some may see as a big problem today may well be gone tomorrow. The student must concern himself with acquiring that which will serve him for the next 40 or 50 years, right down to the day he dies. Some of our problems which we think so new and so momentous are as old as man. There was air pollution in the London of Samuel Johnson, and there was noise pollution in the Rome of Juvenal.

While we have added immeasurably to those problems, we also are moving toward conquering them for the first time in history. The country is concerned. Action must follow.

But again I say, if the pollution problem of today is to be solved, it will be solved by those who are educated and experienced, not by those students who have nothing to offer but their concern.

The Case for Professionalism
Robert Brustein

Robert Brustein (1927-   ) is dean of Yale Drama School and is a well-known drama critic. Among his books are *Theatre of Revolt* (1964), *Seasons of Discontent* (1965), and *Third Theatre* (1969).

In such a state of society [a state of democratic anarchy], the master fears and flatters his scholars, and the scholars despise their masters and tutors; young and old are alike; and the young man is on a level with the old, and is ready to compete with him in word and deed; and old men condescend to the young and are full of pleasantry and gaiety; they are loth to be thought morose and authoritative, and therefore they adopt the manners of the young. . . .
—Plato, The Republic, *Book VIII*

Among the many valuable things on the verge of disintegration in contemporary America is the concept of professionalism—by which I mean to suggest a condition determined by training, experience, skill, and achievement (by remuneration, too, but this is secondary). In our intensely Romantic age, where so many activities are being politicalized and objective judgments are continually colliding with subjective demands, the amateur is exalted as a kind of democratic culture hero, subject to no standards or restrictions. This development has been of concern to me because of its impact upon my immediate areas of interest—the theater and theater training—but its consequences can be seen everywhere, most conspicuously in the field of liberal education. If the amateur is coequal—and some would say, superior—to the professional, then the student is coequal or superior to the professor, and "the young man," as Plato puts it in his discourse on the conditions that lead to tyranny, "is on a level with the old, and is ready to compete with him in word and deed."

As recently as five years ago, this proposition would have seemed remote; today, it has virtually become established dogma, and its implementation is absorbing much of the energy of the young. Although student unrest was originally stimulated, and rightly so, by such external issues as the war in Vietnam and the social grievances of the blacks and the poor, it is now more often aroused over internal issues of power and influence in the university itself. Making an analogy between democratic political systems and the university structure, students begin by demanding a representative voice in the "decisions that affect our lives," including questions of faculty tenure, curriculum changes, grading, and academic discipline. As universities begin to grant some of these demands, thus tacitly accepting the analogy, the demands escalate to the point where students are now insisting on a voice in electing the university president, a role in choosing the faculty, and even a place on the board of trustees.

I do not wish to comment here on the validity of individual student demands—certainly, a student role in university affairs is both practical and desirable, as long as that role remains advisory. Nor will I take the time to repeat the familiar litany of admiration for the current student generation—it has, to my mind, already been sufficiently praised, even overpraised, since for all its intrinsic passion, intelligence, and commitment, the proportion of serious, gifted, hard-working students remains about what it always was (if not actually dwindling for reasons I hope soon to develop). I do want, however, to examine the analogy which is now helping to politicize the university, and scholarship itself, because it seems to me full of falsehood.

Clearly, it is absurd to identify electoral with educational institutions. To compare the state with the academy is to assume that the primary function of the university is to govern and to rule. While the relationship between the administration and the faculty does have certain political overtones, the faculty and administration can no more be considered the elected representatives of the student body than the students—who were admitted after voluntary application on a selective and competitive basis—can be considered freeborn citizens of a democratic state; the relationship between teacher and student is strictly tutorial. Thus, the faculty member functions not to represent the student's interests in relation to the administration, but rather to communicate knowledge from one who knows to one who doesn't. That the reasoning behind this analogy has not been more frequently questioned indicates the extent to which some teachers are refusing to exercise their roles as professionals. During a time when all authority is being radically questioned, faculty members are becoming more reluctant to accept the responsibility of their wisdom and experience and are, therefore, often willing to abandon their authoritative position in order to placate the young.

The issue of authority is a crucial one here, and once again we can see how the concept of professionalism is being vitiated by false analogies. Because *some* authority is cruel, callow, or indifferent (notably the government in its treatment of certain urgent issues of the day), the Platonic *idea* of authority comes under attack. Because some faculty members are remote and pedantic, the credentials of distinguished scholars, artists, and intellectuals are ignored or rejected, and anyone taking charge of a classroom or a seminar is open to charges of "authoritarianism." This explains the hostility of many students towards the lecture course—where an "authority" communicates the fruits of his research, elaborating on unclear points when prodded by student questioning (still a valuable pedagogical technique, especially for beginning students, along with seminars and tutorials). Preferred to this, and therefore replacing it in some departments, is the discussion group or "bull session," where the student's opinion about the material receives more attention than the material itself, if indeed the material is still being treated. The idea—so central to scholarship—that there is an inherited body of knowledge to be transmitted from one generation to another—loses favor because it puts the student in an unacceptably subordinate position, with the result that the learning process gives way to a general free-for-all in which one man's opinion is as good as another's.

The problem is exacerbated in the humanities and social sciences with their more subjective criteria of judgment; one hardly senses the same difficulties in the clinical sciences. It is unlikely (though anything is possible these days) that medical students will insist on making a diagnosis through majority vote, or that students entering surgery will refuse anaesthesia because they want to participate in decisions that affect their lives and, therefore, demand to choose the surgeon's instruments or tell him where to cut. Obviously, some forms of authority are still respected, and some professionals remain untouched by the incursions of the amateur. In liberal education, however, where the development of the individual assumes such weight and importance, the subordination of mind to material is often looked on as some kind of repression. One begins to understand the current loss of interest in the past, which offers a literature and history verified to some extent by time, and the passionate concern with the immediate present, whose works still remain to be objectively evaluated. When one's educational concerns are contemporary, the material can be subordinated to one's own interests, whether political or aesthetic, as the contemporary literary journalist is often more occupied with his own ideas than with the book he reviews.

Allied to this problem, and compounding it, is the problem of the black students, who are sometimes inclined to reject the customary university curriculum as "irrelevant" to their interests, largely because of its orientation towards "white" culture and history. In its place, they demand courses dealing with the history and achievements of the black man, both in Africa and America. Wherever history or anthropology departments have failed to provide appropriate courses, this is a serious omission and should be rectified: such an omission is an insult not only to black culture but to scholarship itself. But when black students begin clamoring for courses in black law, black business, black medicine, or black theater, then the university is in danger of becoming the instrument of community hopes and aspirations rather than the repository of an already achieved culture. It is only one more step before the university is asked to serve propaganda purposes, usually of an activist nature: a recent course, demanded by black law students at Yale, was to be called something like "white capitalist exploitation of the black ghetto poor."

On the one hand, the demand for "relevance" is an effort to make the university undertake the reparations that society should be paying. On the other, it is a form of solipsism, among both black students and white. And such solipsism is a serious threat to that "disinterestedness" that Matthew Arnold claimed to be the legitimate function of the scholar and the critic. The proper study of mankind becomes contemporary or future man; and the student focuses not on the outside world, past or present, so much as on a parochial corner of his own immediate needs. But this is childish, in addition to being Romantic, reflecting as it does the student's unwillingness to examine or conceive a world beyond the self. And here, the university seems to be paying a debt not of its own making—a debt incurred in the permissive home and the progressive school, where knowledge was usually of considerably less importance than self-expression.

In the schools, particularly, techniques of education always seemed to take precedence over the material to be communicated; lessons in democracy were frequently substituted for training in subjects; and everyone learned to be concerned citizens, often at the sacrifice of a solid education. I remember applying for a position many years ago in such a school. I was prepared to teach English literature, but was told no such subject was being offered. Instead, the students had a course called *Core,* which was meant to provide the essence of literature, history, civics, and the like. The students sat together at a round table to dramatize their essential equality with their instructor, the instructor—or rather, the coordinator, as he was called—remained completely unobtrusive, and instead of determining answers by investigation or the teacher's authority, they were decided upon by majority vote. I took my leave in haste, convinced that I was witnessing democracy totally misunderstood. That misunderstanding has invaded our institutions of higher learning.

For the scholastic habits of childhood and adolescence are now being extended into adulthood. The graduates of the *Core* course, and courses like it, are concentrating on the development of their "life styles," chafing against restrictions of all kinds (words like "coercion" and "co-option" are the current jargon), and demanding that all courses be geared to their personal requirements and individual interests. But this is not at all the function of the university. As Paul Goodman has observed, in *The Community of Scholars*, when you teach the child, you teach the person; when you teach the adolescent, you teach the subject through the person; *but when you teach the adult, you teach the subject.* Behind Goodman's observation lies the assumption that the university student is, or should already be, a developed personality, that he comes to the academy not to investigate his "life style" but to absorb what knowledge he can, and that he is, therefore, preparing himself, through study, research, and contemplation, to enter the community of professional scholars. In resisting this notion, some students reveal their desire to maintain the conditions of childhood, to preserve the liberty they enjoyed in their homes and secondary schools, to extend the privileges of a child- and youth-oriented culture into their mature years. They wish to remain amateurs.

One can see why Goodman has concluded that many of the university young do not deserve the name of students: they are creating conditions in which it is becoming virtually impossible to do intellectual work. In turning their political wrath from the social world, which is in serious need of reform (partly because of a breakdown in professionalism), to the academic world, which still has considerable value as a learning institution, they have determined, on the one hand, that society will remain as venal, as corrupt, as retrogressive as ever, and, on the other hand, that the university will no longer be able to proceed with the work of free inquiry for which it was founded. As an added irony, students, despite their professed distaste for the bureaucratic administration of the university, are now helping to construct—through the insane proliferation of student-faculty committees—a far vaster network of bureaucracy than ever before existed. This, added to their continual meetings, confrontations, and demonstrations—not to mention occupations and sit-ins—is leaving precious little time or energy either for their intellectual development or for that of the faculty. As a result, attendance at classes has dropped drastically; exams are frequently skipped and papers and reports are either late, under-researched, or permanently postponed. That the university needs improvement goes without saying. And students have been very helpful in breaking down its excesses of impersonality and attempting to sever its ties with the military-industrial complex. But students need improvement too, which they are hardly receiving through all this self-righteous bustle over power. That students should pay so much attention to this activity creates an even more serious problem: the specter of an ignorant, uninformed group of graduates or dropouts who (when they finally leave the academic sanctuary) are incompetent to deal with society's real evils or to function properly in professions they have chosen to enter.

It is often observed that the word *amateur* comes from the Latin verb, to love—presumably because the amateur is motivated by passion rather than money.

Today's amateur, however, seems to love not his subject but himself. And his assault on authority—on the application of professional standards in judgment of his intellectual development—is a strategy to keep this self-love unalloyed. The permanent dream of this nation, a dream still to be realized, has been a dream of equal opportunity—the right of each man to discover wherein he might excel. But this is quite different from that sentimental egalitarianism which assumes that each man excels in everything. There is no blinking the fact that some people are brighter than others, some more beautiful, some more gifted. Any other conclusion is a degradation of the democratic dogma and promises a bleak future if universally insisted on—a future of monochromatic amateurism in which everybody has opinions, few have facts, nobody has an idea.

The Idea of the University
Cardinal Newman

Cardinal John Henry Newman (1801-1890) was a well-known English Catholic theologian and is the author of *Idea of a University* and *Apologia pro vita sua.* He led the Tractarian movement, which criticized the bishops and priests of the Church of England.

A University may be considered with reference either to its Students or to its Studies, and the principle, that all Knowledge is a whole and the separate Sciences parts of one, which I have hitherto been using in behalf of its studies, is equally important when we direct our attention to its students. Now then I turn to the students, and shall consider the education which, by virtue of this principle, a University will give them; and thus I shall be introduced, Gentlemen, to the second question, which I proposed to discuss, viz., whether and in what sense its teaching, viewed relatively to the taught, carries the attribute of Utility along with it.

I

I have said that all branches of knowledge are connected together, because the subject-matter of knowledge is intimately united in itself, as being the acts and the

Source: The Idea of the University (1880).

work of the Creator. Hence it is that the Sciences, into which our knowledge may be said to be cast, have multiple bearings one on another, and an internal sympathy, and admit, or rather demand, comparison and adjustment. They complete, correct, balance each other. This consideration, if well-founded, must be taken into account, not only as regards the attainment of truth, which is their common end, but as regards the influence which they exercise upon those whose education consists in the study of them. I have said already, that to give undue prominence to one is to be unjust to another; to neglect or supersede these is to divert those from their proper object. It is to unsettle the boundary lines between science and science, to disturb their action, to destroy the harmony which binds them together. Such a proceeding will have a corresponding effect when introduced into a place of education. There is no science but tells a different tale, when viewed as a portion of a whole, from what it is likely to suggest when taken by itself, without the safeguard, as I may call it, of others.

.   .   .

It is a great point then to enlarge the range of studies which a University professes, even for the sake of the students; and, though they cannot pursue every subject which is open to them, they will be the gainers by living among those and under those who represent the whole circle. This I conceive to be the advantage of a seat of universal learning, considered as a place of education. An assemblage of learned men, zealous for their own sciences, and rivals of each other, are brought, by familiar intercourse and for the sake of intellectual peace, to adjust together the claims and relations of their respective subjects of investigation. They learn to respect, to consult, to aid each other. Thus is created a pure and clear atmosphere of thought, which the student also breathes, though in his own case he only pursues a few sciences out of the multitude. He profits by an intellectual tradition, which is independent of particular teachers, which guides him in his choice of subjects, and duly interprets for him those which he chooses. He apprehends the great outlines of knowledge, the principles on which it rests, the scale of its parts, its lights and its shades, its great points and its little, as he otherwise cannot apprehend them. Hence it is that his education is called "Liberal." A habit of mind is formed which lasts through life, of which the attributes are freedom, equitableness, calmness, moderation, and wisdom; or what in a former Discourse I have ventured to call a philosophical habit. This then I would assign as the special fruit of the education furnished at a University, as contrasted with other places of teaching or modes of teaching. This is the main purpose of a University in its treatment of its students.

And now the question is asked me, What is the *use* of it? and my answer will constitute the main subject of the Discourses which are to follow.

II

Cautious and practical thinkers, I say will ask of me, what, after all, is the gain of this Philosophy, of which I make such account, and from which I promise so much. Even supposing it to enable us to exercise the degree of trust exactly due to every science respectively, and to estimate precisely the value of every truth which is anywhere to be found, how are we better for this master view of things, which I have been extolling? Does it not reverse the principle of the division of labour? will practical objects be obtained better or worse by its cultivation? to what then does it lead? where does it end? what does it do? how does it profit? what does it promise? Particular sciences are respectively the basis of definite arts, which carry on to results tangible and beneficial the truths which are the subjects of the knowledge attained; what is the Art of this science of sciences? what is the fruit of such a Philosophy? what are we proposing to effect, what inducements do we hold out to the Catholic community, when we set about the enterprise of founding a University?

I am asked what is the end of University Education, and of the Liberal or Philosophical Knowledge which I conceive it to impart: I answer, that what I have already said has been sufficient to show that it has a very tangible, real, and sufficient end, though the end cannot be divided from that knowledge itself. Knowledge is capable of being its own end. Such is the constitution of the human mind, that any kind of knowledge, if it be really such, is its own reward. And if this is true of all knowledge, it is true also of that special Philosophy, which I have made to consist in a comprehensive view of truth in all its branches, of the relations of science to science, of their mutual bearings, and their respective values. What the worth of such an acquirement is, compared with other objects which we seek, wealth or power or honour or the conveniences and comforts of life,—I do not profess here to discuss; but I would maintain, and mean to show, that it is an object, in its own nature so really and undeniably good, as to be the compensation of a great deal of thought in the compassing, and a great deal of trouble in the attaining.

Now, when I say that Knowledge is, not merely a means to something beyond it, or the preliminary of certain arts into which it naturally resolves, but an end sufficient to rest in and to pursue for its own sake, surely I am uttering no paradox, for I am stating what is both intelligible in itself, and has ever been the common judgment of philosophers and the ordinary feeling of mankind. I am saying what at least the public opinion of this day ought to be slow to deny, considering how much we have heard of late years, in opposition to Religion, of entertaining, curious, and various knowledge. I am but saying what whole volumes have been written to illustrate, viz., by a "selection from the records of Philosophy, Literature, and Art, in all ages and countries, of a body of examples, to show how the most unpropitious circumstances have been unable to conquer an ardent desire for the acquisition of knowledge."[1] That further advantages accrue to us and redound to others by its possession, over and above what it is in itself, I am very far indeed from denying; but, independent of these, we are satisfying a direct need of our nature in its very acquisition, and, whereas our nature, unlike that of the inferior creation, does not at once reach its perfection, but depends, in order to it, on a number of external aids and appliances, Knowledge, as one of the principal of these, is valuable for what its very presence in us does for us after the manner of a habit, even though it be turned to no further account, nor subserve any direct end.

III

Hence it is that Cicero, in enumerating the various heads of mental excellence, lays down the pursuit of Knowledge for its own sake, as the first of them. "This pertains most of all to human nature," he says, "for we are all of us drawn to the

[1] *Pursuit of Knowledge under Difficulties*, Introd.

pursuit of Knowledge, in which to excel we consider excellent, whereas to mistake, to err, to be ignorant, to be deceived, is both an evil and a disgrace."[2] And he considers Knowledge the very first object to which we are attracted, after the supply of our physical wants. After the calls and duties of our animal existence, as they may be termed, as regards ourselves, our family, and our neighbours, follows, he tells us, "the search after truth. Accordingly, as soon as we escape from the pressure of necessary cares, forthwith we desire to see, to hear, and to learn; and consider the knowledge of what is hidden or is wonderful a condition of our happiness."

IV

...It is common to speak of "*Liberal* knowledge," of the "*Liberal* arts and studies," and of a "*Liberal* education," as the especial characteristic or property of a University and of a gentleman; what is really meant by the word? Now, first, in its grammatical sense it is opposed to *servile;* and by "servile work" is understood, as our catechisms inform us, bodily labour, mechanical employment, and the like, in which the mind has little or no part. Parallel to such servile works are those arts, if they deserve the name, of which the poet speaks, which owe their origin and their method to hazard, not to skill; as, for instance, the practice and operations of an empiric. As far as this contrast may be considered as a guide into the meaning of the word, liberal education and liberal pursuits are exercises of mind, of reason, of reflection.

But we want something more for its explanation, for there are bodily exercises which are liberal, and mental exercises which are not so. For instance, in ancient times the practitioners in medicine were commonly slaves; yet it was an art as intellectual in its nature, in spite of the pretence, fraud, and quackery with which it might then, as now, be debased, as it was heavenly in its aim. And so in like manner, we contrast a liberal education with a commercial education or a professional; yet no one can deny that commerce and the professions afford scope for the highest and most diversified powers of mind. There is then a great variety of intellectual exercises, which are not technically called "liberal"; on the other hand, I say, there are exercises of the body which do receive that appellation. Such, for instance, was the palaestra, in ancient times; such the Olympic games, in which strength and dexterity of body as well as of mind gained the prize. In Xenophon we read of the young Persian nobility being taught to ride on horseback and to speak the truth; both being among the accomplishments of a gentleman. War, too, however rough a profession, has even been accounted liberal, unless in cases when it becomes heroic, which would introduce us to another subject.

Now comparing these instances together, we shall have no difficulty in determining the principle of this apparent variation in the application of the term which I am examining. Manly games, or games of skill, or military prowess, though bodily, are, it seems, accounted liberal; on the other hand, what is merely professional, though highly intellectual, nay, though liberal in comparison of trade and manual labour, is not simply called liberal, and mercantile occupations are not

[2] Cicer. *Offic.* init.

liberal at all. Why this distinction? because that alone is liberal knowledge, which stands on its own pretensions, which is independent of sequel, expects no complement, refuses to be *informed* (as it is called) by any end, or absorbed into any art, in order duly to present itself to our contemplation. The most ordinary pursuits have this specific character, if they are self-sufficient and complete; the highest lose it, when they minister to something beyond them. It is absurd to balance, in point of worth and importance, a treatise on reducing fractures with a game of cricket or a fox-chase; yet of the two the bodily exercise has that quality which we call "liberal," and the intellectual has it not. And so of the learned professions altogether, considered merely as professions; although one of them be the most popularly beneficial, and another the most politically important, and the third the most intimately divine of all human pursuits, yet the very greatness of their end, the health of the body, or of the commonwealth, or of the soul, diminishes, not increases, their claim to the appellation "liberal," and that still more, if they are cut down to the strict exigencies of that end. If, for instance, Theology, instead of being cultivated as a contemplation, be limited to the purposes of the pulpit or be represented by the catechism, it loses,—not its usefulness, not its divine character, not its meritoriousness (rather it gains a claim upon these titles by such charitable condescension),—but it does lose the particular attribute which I am illustrating; just as a face worn by tears and fasting loses its beauty, or a labourer's hand loses its delicateness;—for Theology thus exercised is not simple knowledge, but rather is an art or a business making use of Theology. And thus it appears that even what is supernatural need not be liberal, nor need a hero be a gentleman, for the plain reason that one idea is not another idea. And in like manner the Baconian Philosophy, by using its physical sciences in the service of man, does thereby transfer them from the order of Liberal Pursuits to, I do not say the inferior, but the distinct class of the Useful. And, to take a different instance, hence again, as is evident, whenever personal gain is the motive, still more distinctive an effect has it upon the character of a given pursuit; thus racing, which was a liberal exercise in Greece, forfeits its rank in times like these, so far as it is made the occasion of gambling.

All that I have been now saying is summed up in a few characteristic words of the great Philosopher. "Of possessions," he says, "those rather are useful, which bear fruit; those *liberal, which tend to enjoyment.* By fruitful, I mean, which yield revenue; by enjoyable, where *nothing accrues of consequence beyond the using.*"[3]

V

...I consider, then, that I am chargeable with no paradox, when I speak of a Knowledge which is its own end, when I call it liberal knowledge, or a gentleman's knowledge, when I educate for it, and make it the scope of a University. And still less am I incurring such a charge, when I make this acquisition consist, not in Knowledge in a vague and ordinary sense, but in that Knowledge which I have especially called Philosophy or, in an extended sense of the word, Science; for whatever claims Knowledge has to be considered as a good, these it has in a higher degree when it is viewed not vaguely, not popularly, but precisely and transcen-

[3] Arist. *Rhet.* i. 5

dently as Philosophy. Knowledge, I say, is then especially liberal, or sufficient for itself, apart from every external and ulterior object, when and so far as it is philosophical, and this I proceed to show.

VI

Now bear with me, Gentlemen, if what I am about to say, has at first sight a fanciful appearance. Philosophy, then, or Science, is related to Knowledge in this way:—Knowledge is called by the name of Science or Philosophy, when it is acted upon, informed, or if I may use a strong figure, impregnated by Reason. Reason is the principle of that intrinsic fecundity of Knowledge, which, to those who possess it, is its especial value, and which dispenses with the necessity of their looking abroad for any end to rest upon external to itself. . . . You see, then, here are two methods of Education; the end of the one is to be philosophical, of the other to be mechanical; the one rises towards general ideas, the other is exhausted upon what is particular and external. Let me not be thought to deny the necessity, or to decry the benefit, of such attention to what is particular and practical, as belongs to the useful or mechanical arts; life could not go on without them; we owe our daily welfare to them; their exercise is the duty of the many, and we owe to the many a debt of gratitude for fulfilling that duty. I only say that Knowledge, in proportion as it tends more and more to be particular, ceases to be Knowledge. . . . The principle of real dignity in Knowledge, its worth, its desirableness, considered irrespectively of its results, is this germ within it of a scientific or a philosophical process. This is how it comes to be an end in itself; this is why it admits of being called Liberal. Not to know the relative disposition of things is the state of slaves or children; to have mapped out the universe is the boast, or at least the ambition, of Philosophy.

Moreover, such knowledge is not a mere extrinsic or accidental advantage, which is ours to-day and another's to-morrow, which may be got up from a book, and easily forgotten again, which we can command or communicate at our pleasure, which we can borrow for the occasion, carry about in our hand, and take into the market; it is an acquired illumination, it is a habit, a personal possession and an inward endowment. . . .

VII

It may be objected then, that, when we profess to seek Knowledge for some end or other beyond itself, whatever it may be, we speak intelligibly; but that, whatever men may have said, however obstinately the idea may have kept its ground from age to age, still it is simply unmeaning to say that we seek Knowledge for its own sake, and for nothing else; for that it ever leads to something beyond itself, which therefore is its end, and the cause why it is desirable;—moreover, that this end is twofold, either of this world or of the next; that all knowledge is cultivated either for secular objects or for eternal, that if it is directed to secular objects, it is called Useful Knowledge, if to eternal, Religious or Christian Knowledge; . . . This they [the practitioners of this view] have professed on the one hand; and on the other, they have utterly failed in their professions, so as ever to make themselves a proverb among men, and a laughing-stock both to the grave and the dissipated portion of mankind, in consequence of them. Thus they have furnished against themselves both the ground and the means of their own exposure, without any trouble at all to any one else. In a word, from the time that Athens was the University of the world, what has Philosophy taught men, but to promise without practising, and to aspire without attaining? What has the deep and lofty thought of its disciples ended in but eloquent words? Nay, what has its teaching ever meditated, when it was boldest in its remedies for human ill, beyond charming us to sleep by its lessons, that we might feel nothing at all? like some melodious air, or rather like those strong and transporting perfumes, which at first spread their sweetness over every thing they touch, but in a little while do but offend in proportion as they once pleased us? Did Philosophy support Cicero under the disfavour of the fickle populace, or nerve Seneca to oppose an imperial tyrant? It abandoned Brutus, as he sorrowfully confessed, in his greatest need, and it forced Cato, as his panegyrist strangely boasts, into the false position of defying heaven. How few can be counted among its professors, who, like Polemo, were thereby converted from a profligate course, or, like Anaxagoras, thought the world well lost in exchange for its possession? The philosopher in *Rasselas* taught a superhuman doctrine, and then succumbed without an effort to a trial of human affection.

"He discoursed," we are told, "with great energy on the government of the passions. His look was venerable, his action graceful, his pronunciation clear, and his diction elegant. He showed, with great strength of sentiment and variety of illustration, that human nature is degraded and debased, when the lower faculties predominate over the higher. He communicated the various precepts given, from time to time, for the conquest of passion, and displayed the happiness of those who had obtained the important victory, after which man is no longer the slave of fear, nor the fool of hope. . . . He enumerated many examples of heroes immovable by pain or pleasure, who looked with indifference on those modes or accidents to which the vulgar give the names of good and evil."

Rasselas in a few days found the philosopher in a room half darkened, with his eyes misty, and his face pale. "Sir," said he, "you have come at a time when all human friendship is useless; what I suffer cannot be remedied, what I have lost cannot be supplied. My daughter, my only daughter, from whose tenderness I expected all the comforts of my age, died last night of a fever." "Sir," said the prince, "mortality is an event by which a wise man can never be surprised: we know that death is always near, and it should therefore always be expected." "Young man," answered the philosopher, "you speak like one who has never felt the pangs of separation." "Have you, then, forgot the precept," said Rasselas, "which you so powerfully enforced? . . . consider that external things are naturally variable, but truth and reason are always the same." "What comfort," said the mourner, "can truth and reason afford me? Of what effect are they now, but to tell me that my daughter will not be restored?"

VIII

Better, far better, to make no professions, you will say, than to cheat others with what we are not, and to scandalize them with what we are. The sensualist, or the man of the world, at any rate is not the victim of fine words, but pursues a reality and gains it. The Philosophy of Utility, you will say, Gentlemen, has at least done its work; and I grant it,—it aimed low, but it has fulfilled its aim. If that man of great intellect [Francis Bacon] who has been its Prophet in the conduct of life played false to his own professions, he was not bound by his philosophy to be true to his friend or faithful in his trust. . . . His is simply a Method whereby bodily discomforts and temporal wants are to be most effectually removed from the greatest number; and already, before it has shown any signs of exhaustion, the gifts of nature, in their most artificial shapes and luxurious profusion and diversity, from all quarters of the earth, are, it is undeniable, by its means brought even to our doors, and we rejoice in them.

IX

Useful Knowledge then, I grant, has done its work; and Liberal Knowledge as certainly has not done its work,—that is, supposing, as the objectors assume, its direct end, like Religious Knowledge, is to make men better; but this I will not for an instant allow, and, unless I allow it, those objectors have said nothing to the purpose. . . . Knowledge is one thing, virtue is another; good sense is not conscience, refinement is not humility, nor is largeness and justness of view faith. Philosophy, however enlightened, however profound, gives no command over the passions, no influential motives, no vivifying principles. Liberal Education makes not the Christian, not the Catholic, but the gentleman. It is well to be a gentleman, it is well to have a cultivated intellect, a delicate taste, a candid, equitable, dispassionate mind, a noble and courteous bearing in the conduct of life;—these are the connatural qualities of a large knowledge; they are the objects of a University; I am advocating, I shall illustrate and insist upon them; but still, I repeat, they are no guarantee for sanctity or even for conscientiousness, they may attach to the man of the world, to the profligate, to the heartless,—pleasant, alas, and attractive as he shows when decked out in them. Taken by themselves, they do but seem to be what they are detected by close observers, and on the long run; and hence it is that they are popularly accused of pretence and hypocrisy, not, I repeat, from their own fault, but because their professors and their admirers persist in taking them for what they are not, and are officious in arrogating for them a praise to which they have no claim. Quarry the granite rock with razors, or moor the vessel with a thread of silk; then may you hope with such keen and delicate instruments as human knowledge and human reason to contend against those giants, the passion and the pride of man.

The University: Mask for Privilege?
Richard Lichtman

Richard Lichtman (1935-   ) was a fellow-in-residence at the Center for the Study of Democratic Institutions and taught philosophy at the University of California at Santa Barbara and Berkeley. In addition, he has written a number of articles published in journals.

Nothing can better illustrate the collapse of reason as an independent, critical agent in our society than a comparison of the remarks of two observers, separated by one hundred years, on the nature of a university education. In the middle of the nineteenth century one of its astutest critics noted:

The proper function of a University in national education is tolerably well understood. At least there is a tolerably general agreement about what a University is not.

It is not a place of professional education. Universities are not intended to teach the knowledge required to fit men for some special mode of gaining their livelihood. Their object is not to make skillful lawyers, or physicians, or engineers, but capable and cultivated human beings. It is very right that there should be public facilities for the study of professions. . . . But these things are no part of what every generation owes to the next, as that on which its civilization and worth will principally depend. They are needed only by a comparative few . . . and even those few do not require them until after their education . . . has been completed. . . . Men are men before they are lawyers, or physicians, or merchants, or manufacturers, and if you will make them capable and sensible men, they will make themselves capable and sensible lawyers or physicians.

What professional men should carry away with them from a University, is not professional knowledge, but that which should direct the use of their professional knowledge, and bring the light of general culture to illuminate the technicalities of a special pursuit. . . . And doubtless . . . the crown and consummation of a liberal education . . . [is that the pupil be taught] to methodize his knowledge; to look at every separate part of it in its relation to the other parts, and to the whole . . . observing how all knowledge is connected, how we ascend to one branch by means of another, how the higher modifies the lower and the lower helps us to understand the higher . . . combining the partial glimpses which he has obtained of the field of human knowledge at different points, into a general map . . . of the entire region.

This view has given way in our time to a very different conception:

The University . . . once was an integrated community. . . . It had a single purpose. . . . The conversation was in common.

This community chose to destroy itself. It became larger. It became heterogeneous. It came to talk in many tongues. . . . With the rise of science over the past century, more and bigger laboratories have been required. . . . The pressure of population, the explosion of books, the scientific revolution . . . all press for size beyond the limits of the face-to-face and mouth-to-ear community.

Knowledge has expanded and expanded, from theology and philosophy and law and

Source: Reprinted, with permission, from the January 1968 issue of *The Center Magazine*, a publication of the Center for the Study of Democratic Institutions in Santa Barbara, California.

medicine and accounting to the whole range of humanities, the social sciences and the sciences and the professions. More knowledge has resulted from and led to more and more research on a larger and larger scale. Research has led to service for government and industry and agriculture . . . all of this is natural. None of it can be reversed. . . . Small intellectual communities can exist and serve a purpose, but they run against the logic of their times.

The campus has evolved consistently with society. It has been pulled outward to society and pulled to pieces internally. The campus consistent with society has served as a good introduction to society—to bigness, to specialization, to diffusion of interests.

The welfare-state university, or multi-university, developed particularly in the United States to provide something for nearly everybody—for farmers, for the minor and newer professions, for the general citizen who wanted to satisfy his curiosity. . . . It made the welfare of society in nearly all its aspects a part of its concern . . . the University has served many masters in many ways.

The University and segments of industry are becoming more and more alike. As the University becomes tied to the world of work, the professor—at least in the natural and some of the social sciences—takes on the characteristics of an entrepreneur. . . . The two worlds are merging physically. . . . [The University is] a mechanism held together by administrative rules and powered by money.

The first of these comments is from John Stuart Mill; the second, from Clark Kerr, until recently President of the University of California.

I have quoted them at length because they illuminate one of the great transitions of the modern age—the decline of autonomous, rational criticism, and the rise of what Professor Herbert Marcuse entitled "one-dimensional man."

They represent the early and terminal stages in the development of centralized, bureaucratic economic power—extended now to such a point that it is able to absorb what was once proclaimed to be a transcendent center of analysis and judgment.

We need not romanticize Mill's age, nor pretend that the university students of whom he spoke acted in radical concert to revise the foundations of their time. They were, in their own way, as readily absorbed into the hierarchy of domestic civil service and foreign imperialism as students of our own society are absorbed into comparable institutions. Of crucial significance is that the very ideal of autonomy has been denied and that those who speak for higher education in this country come increasingly to derive their definition of purpose from the existing agencies of established power.

The pronouncements of Mill and Clark Kerr differ in several significant ways. The first stresses coherence, the second fragmentation; the first is exclusionary, the second is ready to incorporate any interest that society urges upon it; the first distinguishes between higher and lower knowledge, while the second distributes its emphasis in accordance with available financial support. Of greatest importance, perhaps, is that the older view regards itself as bound by intrinsic canons of culture, while the current conception accommodates and molds itself to prevailing trends.

The first view holds to an ideal of transcendence while the second is grossly imminent in its time. For contemporary doctrine, the ancient tension between what the world is and what it might become has all but vanished. The current perspective is an apologia, a celebration, an ideological consecration of this most lovely of all possible worlds—in short, a consenting academy.

This conclusion follows directly from Mr. Kerr's own analysis, for if the University performs all the functions that society imposes upon it, it will in due course most ably fulfill the predominant function every social system requires for its very existence—the justification of its established structure of power and privilege, the masking or idealization of its deficiencies, and the discrediting of dissent.

The history of all previous societies reveals to us a group of men whose primary function was to legitimate established authority. Our own time is only notable for the special urgency it imposes on the task. There are various domestic and international reasons for this development.

The first concerns the growing complexity of our technological order and its encompassing social organizations. The requirements of intelligence become more exact and the skills needed for managerial and bureaucratic roles more demanding. Accompanying these economic developments is the parallel transformation of the society from one concerned primarily with the manipulation of material things to one concerned with the manipulation of individuals. The role of physical labor declines and the role of intellectual skills and personal services is augmented in a growing white-collar stratum.

There is a change in emphasis in the industrial system from force to persuasion, a growth of public relations, managerial counseling, and mass advertising; in short, an extensive shift from production to consumption and from overt authority to covert ideological inducement.

Second, the development of a mass society tied less to specific locations and cultural traditions than to the common mass media for the formation of their life styles produces a populace eager to be formed and potentially dangerous to the status quo if it is not adequately standardized.

Again, the growing education level and sophistication of some sectors of the population make it necessary to mollify the possible dissent of those who might discover flaws in the social façade. But, paradoxically, the development of education facilitates this enterprise, for there are some deceptions which only a semi-educated man could be expected to believe or sacrifice his life for.

But the most important internal need for ideology grows from the slowly developing awareness of the discrepancy between what this social system has the power to provide its members and what it actually makes available to them. Technological resources are adequate to provide a very high level of material welfare to the entire population if the control over these facilities can be made to pass progressively from the hands of a self-authenticating business autocracy to the authority of the people as a whole.

Venerable arguments for the necessity of social injustice, class privilege, physical and cultural deprivation, and the dehumanization of labor are being corroded by the potentialities of abundance. Those who hold power in this system, then, are forced to construct elaborate theories to justify persisting misery. Here, the aid of the University can prove extremely valuable.

But there are two additional motives for illusion which derive from the international position of the United States today. Both stem from the fact of America's predominant economic power and expansiveness in the world, from its dominance over foreign economies on a global scale, and from the need generated by its productive system for subservient foreign nations to act as the suppliers of its resources and the outlets for its dislocations.

The two challenges come from the Soviet Union and China on the one hand, and from the underdeveloped third of the world on the other. The first are threats because they reject capitalistic values and compete with us in the world for economic power. The second set of nations is even more disquieting, however, for they are seeking their self-liberation at the precise moment at which the United States has emerged unmistakably as the world's dominant imperialist power. But we are not prepared to grant them control of their own industrial development, and our counter-effort is an attempt to destroy their movement toward economic autonomy through financial pressure when possible, and military intervention when necessary.

The growing division between what the world is and what it might become is the primary force behind the intensification of ancient ideological functions.

The consequence of these various internal and external pressures is that the United States is urgently compelled to disarm radical dissent and insure the performance of roles necessary to continued international hostility.

Those in power recognize the importance of domestic consensus to achieve these ends. The educational views of men like Mr. Kerr, which stress the need for molding reason to the pattern of contemporary power, appear conveniently to facilitate economic and military service and the soothing of discontent.

A University patterned after Mill's ideal could not possibly perform this task, but the contemporary University performs it masterfully. Approximately 75 per cent of the research budget of the University derives from Federal contracts, and, as Mr. Kerr notes: "Expenditures have been largely restricted to the physical and bio-medical sciences, and to engineering, with only 3 per cent for the social sciences and hardly any support for the humanities."

This distribution is defended on the grounds that it represents the national interest and the flow of money after "the most exciting new ideas." What we are being offered here is a new version of the invisible hand in which Gresham's Law is inverted to the effect that good money always drives out bad money and produces just that balance which promotes the public good.

The Federal funding of the University is only one of the media through which the pattern of society is impressed on higher education, but it exemplifies the defects transmitted through all the available media. The most crucial of these corruptions is the destruction of the internal community of the University and its replacement by a series of fragmented and isolated departmental structures without common speech, common imagination, or common purpose.

Mill's conception of a university as a place in which the student was taught to "methodize his knowledge; to look at every separate part of it in its relation to the other parts, and to the whole," is not only all but nonexistent in the current academic world, it is increasingly difficult for a growing number of educators to understand. Mr. James A. Perkins, President of Cornell, for example, has suggested that the conflict between research and scholarship might be reconciled by simply abandoning liberal education and beginning the process of specialization at matriculation. . . .

The causes of the diffusion of the University need be noted solely for the light they throw on the nature of the disintegration involved. The reason most intrinsic to the University is the fact that knowledge has been growing at a very rapid rate, making it continually more difficult for any one thinker to grasp the whole domain. But this in itself would not produce the fragmentation which occurs (since it is not the case that everything known must be taught by a university) except for the presence of other factors.

First, there is a tendency to refinement in specialized roles which seems to occur in all advanced technological societies. Next, there are the distinctly American elaborations of this theme. One derives from the anti-intellectualism of our life with its distrust of achievement for its own sake and consequent insistence that thought subserve specific ends and redeem itself through the practical results of concrete actions. To this must be added the sense of many intellectuals that if they cannot alter the shape of massive, unresponsive social power they can at least derive some satisfaction by serving it.

In this mood reason gives up the claim to direct social change. It settles instead for the immediate rewards of technical manipulation and becomes an efficient means to ends beyond its power or judgment.

The tendency is strengthened by a widespread assumption that in America the good life has already been achieved in a system of democratic, corporate pluralism. The quest of the ages having been completed, there is nothing more for reason to do but maintain the current structure and make the necessary minor corrections. This tendency is supported by the loose, casual patterning of American life, the laissez-faire climate of American political and economic history, and the general conviction that the pursuit of private, local ends will miraculously produce a public good.

It is not that public life is devoid of integration and rational planning. Industrial firms plan to the limits of their ability, and the foresight of some oligopolies and international cartels is undoubtedly extensive. But these plans are made and the activities coordinated for the sake of individual corporate ends, not for the sake of the polity as a whole. Nothing displays such technical intelligence and ingenuity as an automated factory and produces such irrational dislocation in the lives of men who are unemployed through this human achievement. The sense of the whole system is of rationality defeating its own humane requirements.

As Mr. Kerr has led us to expect, this pattern of sporadic rationality in conflict with its own potential achievement is found within the structure of the University. There, education is defined mechanically as the piling up of specific skills and bits of information, as a mound is constructed out of the piling up of individual grains of sand. The student is never required to state the relevance of one area of understanding for another, nor relate their distinctive methodologies and insights in coherent, synthetic connection. It is assumed that the summation of individually correct answers will produce something more than fragmented understanding.

The center of this disruptive environment is the individual department, where men competing for recognition establish small empires under a mutual security agreement that insures each the safety of his own domain. This safety is further enhanced against the forays of others by increasingly narrowing the limits of one's investigation until the subject is so esoteric that each individual can rightly claim to be the only living authority in the field.

Such a systematic fragmenting of knowledge cannot be corrected by the simple insertion into the curriculum of a few interdisciplinary courses. If the teachers of these courses have to win departmental approval, they are likely to come under the wrath of specialists who rightly see in the man of vision a threat to their insular success. Furthermore, as the current system prevails, the continued existence of comprehensive teachers is more and more problematical.

The immediate result is that the University is more and more populated by scholar-researchers who more closely resemble idiot-savants than men of wisdom;

students find it more and more difficult to gain some comprehensive vision of themselves as world historical beings.

. . .

In the University the teacher retreats before the onslaught of the research technologists and knowledge diffusers. Every university maintains a house Negro or two—a professor whose advancement has been based predominantly upon his power as a teacher and who is dragged out on ceremonial occasions to silence the critic. But for every such anachronism there are one hundred practitioners of the conventions who have scrambled to respectability over a mass of journals and anthologies. The teacher who embodies a vision, whose life manifests in its own activity the content of his teaching art, is vanishing from sight.

What the current generation of students discovers immediately in those who profess to teach them is an almost impassable chasm between the nature of their intellectual pronouncements and the content of their lives. This is one of the grounds of the charge of irrelevance in education and one of the main reasons for student disaffection. Nor is it a defect that can be remedied without transforming the University, and that would in turn require the radical reconstruction of the society in which the University exists.

As William Arrowsmith has commented,

At present the universities are as uncongenial to teaching as the Mojave Desert to a clutch of Druid priests. If you want to restore a Druid priesthood, you cannot do it by offering prizes for Druid-of-the-year. If you want Druids, you must grow forests. There is no other way of setting about it.

If it is in fact true that the University has become a service adjunct to prevailing social powers, it should not be surprising that so much of its activity is taken up in the intense cultivation of disinterested intelligence. There is a clue to this process in one of the works of the German aesthetician Wilhelm Worringer. In his book, *Abstraction and Empathy* . . ., he identifies naturalism with a feeling of confidence in the external world, and particularly the organic, living world. The experience of naturalistic art is held to depend on the subject's identification with organic forms as exemplified in his own existence. Abstract art, on the contrary, is traced to a feeling of anguish and confusion in face of the complexity and instability of living beings; it is viewed as an attempt to flee this realm of dissolution for the sanctity of abstract order.

A great deal of contemporary research appears to be similarly motivated. If it is not immediately useful to established power it tends to withdraw and place between itself and the anxieties and responsibilities of the world what Bullough called "aesthetic distance" and what W. H. Auden referred to as "lecturing on Navigation while the ship is going down."

The University can accommodate itself to national power in one of two ways—overtly or covertly, through subservience or indifference, through the performance of assigned tasks, or the distraction and trivialization of potentially critical thought.

For subservience we can do no better than the introduction to Seymour Martin Lipset's *Political Man.* . . . We discover there a number of astounding things: "that the United States [is] a nation in which leftist values predominate"; that "the values of liberty and equality become institutionalized within America to a greater extent than in other nations"; that "the values of socialism and Americanism are similar"; that, economic systems apart, Herbert Hoover, Andrew Carnegie, and John D. Rockefeller "advocated the same set of social relations among men" as Marx, Engels, and Lenin; that democratic regimes are characterized by an underlying desire to avoid war.

The key to this innovative reconstruction of history is provided in the last chapter of the volume, wherein we are informed that

... the fundamental political problems of the industrial revolution have been solved: the workers have achieved industrial and political citizenship; the conservatives have accepted the welfare state; and the democratic left has recognized that an increase in over-all state power carries with it more dangers to freedom than solutions for economic problems.

How good it must be to see the world as sociologists see it—devoid of economic exploitation, of Iran, Guatemala, the Dominican Republic, and Vietnam; devoid of poverty, injustice, and brutalized technology. History may yet record these sweet reflections less as a hymn to quietude than as the last muffled cry of the ostrich as its mouth fills up with sand. . . .

The fragmented intellect lives in comparative safety and quiet in the security of its own conceptual enclave. Here, it sets barriers against reason and the world. One social scientist tells us:

... science achieves its unparalleled powers by the continuous breakdown of its problem into smaller units and refinements of methods made possible by this division. On the other hand, so deeply entrenched is the humanistic supposition that "to see a man at all one must see him whole" that not even the continuous work on the dikes of their separate disciplines by academicians can keep social thought flowing in its prescribed channels without continuous leakage into and from others. (Don Martindale, Functionalism in the Social Sciences. American Academy of Political and Social Sciences: 1960.)

.   .   .

No reading of the future could have prescribed to American educators the choice they should have made for the American University—this choice was dependent upon the values, principles, and limited wisdom they brought to their understanding of history. What we are really being told in these fragments is that the American educator chose to capitulate to one of the tendencies of his time, that he agreed to relinquish his rational autonomy, and that, having made this specific decision, he is now incapable of regarding himself as anything more than the medium through which the course of the future blindly passes. But this logic unmasks the myth of neutrality, for the choice of passivity, the commitment to subservience, produced the observer's sense that he is the mere conductor of an irreversible process.

The same loss of rational autonomy and moral responsibility which underlies the division between thought and action is the source, too, of the dichotomies of fact and value, means and ends.

The prevailing credo of contemporary social inquiry limits reason to an analysis of those means which will lead most efficiently to given ends; reason is strictly precluded from passing judgment on the ends themselves. The value of the exercise is said to lie in the accumulation of stores of neutral knowledge, useful for whatever ends we intend to employ them.

The significance of this position is that it places reason and technological expertise at the disposal of prevailing power. The thinker who has abdicated responsibility for the purpose of his life by placing control over his actions in powers beyond his authority has made himself a hostage to the times. Having relinquished his claim to normative reason, he is without mooring in the world. The tides of current times, degenerate as they may be, will sweep the uncommitted in their course.

We are witness to the spectacle of men of small imagination, limited in comprehension to diminishing areas of inquiry, lacking the capacity to note the import of their activity for the more pervasive aspects of human enterprise, subservient to an establishment that does not hesitate to use them for the most inhuman and obnoxious ends—men of technical reason, as skilled at killing as at healing, progressively unconcerned with the distinction, and unaware that value resides anywhere but in technique itself. So, crippled reason pays obeisance to power, and the faculty in man most apt to nurture life becomes the instrument of violence and death.

The consequence of fragmentation and of a division in the life of reason is the destruction of human autonomy. The University is thickly populated by cynical or silent men. In response to the compartmentalization of intelligence, pseudo-syntheses appear—unified visions of social man, built on the crudest model of physics or animal psychology. A widespread behaviorism appears in social thought, grounded in a methodology derived third-hand from a defunct philosophy. Quality, uniqueness, creativity, and the moral dimension of existence fall before a reductive insistence upon measurement, qualification, and restrictive processes of infinitely tedious and irrelevant observation. The view of man which emerges is ahistorical, atomistic, mechanical, disjunctive, and, again, ostensibly neutral.

.   .   .

We come at last to the scholarship of civility: devoid of passion, lacking love or outrage, irrelevant to the agency of man. "The advancement of learning at the expense of man," Nietzsche wrote, "is the most pernicious thing in the world."

Exactly what is the moral obligation of the University as a corporate body? It is no use telling us now, as we were told recently by Richard Hofstadter, that while individual members of the University may voice conviction, the University as a public institution is bound to strict neutrality. Mr. Kerr has demolished that argument for all time. It is no less neutral to oppose society than to support it, to refuse a place to military service than to credit it.

Neutrality is only conceivable with isolation. Nothing in the public realm can fail, at specific points, to aid or undermine established power. Man's existence is only possible through action, which requires the selection of choices and the foreclosure of others. One cannot, in all instances, avoid choice; the only hope is to choose responsibly, in light of the largest understanding and the most humane commitment.

As the University is rooted in the world, it must, at given moments, choose a public course. The liberal contention that the University should refrain from criticism is an expression of "preferential neutralism," a transparently hypocritical device for the maintenance of continued service.

Of course, it is not the corporate function of the University to speak to every public issue, nor even to the vast majority of prevailing social concerns. The fundamental purpose of the University does not encompass any specific policy in regard to most contemporary matters. In its public pronouncement and corporate activity, the University should refrain from endorsing particular views in the overwhelming number of cases. But when the University's support is solicited by established agencies of power, it must decide if the services requested of it violate its defining purpose, and reject them if they do. And so, it is also obligated to protest when society has undertaken to violate, in regard either to the University itself or to humanity at large, values that the University is specifically charged to honor.

To discover the public function of a University, one must begin with its internal imperative—the gathering of a community of scholars in devotion to disinterested knowledge. Such, at least, is the traditional wisdom. But it is not adequate to our time.

John Stuart Mill wrote for an age in which the distinction between pure and applied research was largely valid. The man of science could pursue his theory in the general expectation that it would not be employed to endanger mankind. Today the distinction between pure and applied science is disappearing with the growth of a state power so imperious and technologically competent that it can transform the most esoteric knowledge into techniques of terror.

Science has itself contributed to the creation of that state machinery which now makes the enterprise of science hazardous. It has done so because it has lacked responsibility for its growth. It is too late now to fall back on the platitudes of academic freedom; no biochemist can be sure that in pursuing the structure of an enzyme he is not perfecting a lethal form of warfare. This government will have to be disarmed before the clear and present danger now subverting thought can be dissolved. Until men of knowledge act to change the world, they cannot claim the unrestricted right to understand it.

But what is the obligation of those members of the University whose knowledge cannot be technologized? To answer this question, we must answer another. What is the true nature of the University?

The University is the institutionalized embodiment of the life of the dialogue; that is, of communal inquiry. Dialogue is rooted in the fact that men are imperfect and perfectible. Comprehensive knowledge is not given to man in an instant. It is the elaboration of history. Nor is it given to any single man; it is the cooperative achievement of a human community. Dialogue cannot be perfected unless it is free, and the basis of rational freedom is the self-determination of imperfect reason by its own ideal. It is freeing because it liberates intelligence from matter that is extraneous or destructive of its inherent purpose—knowledge.

A mind in pursuit of knowledge is one in which the various facets of awareness are active, cumulative, and mutually relevant, wherein observation, inference, imagination, and evaluative judgment inform each other in a cumulative achievement. It is a process which depends upon creativity—the capacity to construct new alternatives. To this end the University cultivates the arts, whose function is not merely to act as a critical interpreter of experience, but to manifest to us, through concrete works, those ideal possibilities of existence of which we were previously unaware. Whatever the differences between art and discursive reason, they share a common enterprise: they cultivate the human spirit, which is the capacity of man to transcend his present context for the sake of a more comprehensive, articulate, and worthy vision of himself. That vision, in all its forms, is culture, which it is the obligation of the University to honor and protect.

The peculiar alienation of the intellectual leads him to pursue culture as an abstract end. He becomes blind to the simple fact that there is no knowledge independent of the "knowings" of individual men, nor any realm of art or science separate from the creations of actual, concrete human beings. What the University is meant to house and celebrate is not a detached domain of lifeless categories, but the spiritual existence of man, in which those categories live and take their meaning.

What is the obligation of the University in a world in which one nation is reducing the people of another to the most primitive functions of its existence; when the very rudiments of civilization are being extinguished and the orders of life upon which reason grows are being destroyed by systematic violence? In such circumstances it is the obligation of the University to rebel against the violation of man and align itself in public witness with humanity.

Today, the University is required to condemn the government of the United States for its barbaric crusade against the life and spirit of the people of Vietnam. A university that will not speak for man, whatever tasks it continues to perform, has ceased to be a human enterprise.

The University can deny its times because, like any human agency, it is not wholly absorbed in its social context. It has a special capacity to transcend its social constraints because it embodies a tradition of intellectual diversity and articulate criticism and because, of all human functions, thought is the most difficult to curtail. But while the University is uniquely promising, it is also uniquely threatened by the pressures of ideology to which we have already referred. The University is in constant tension between its ideal critical capacity and the powers of secular service that delimit its hope. Therefore, while the protest movement is centered in the University, the activity of protest is not central to the University.

It is possible to act to change the world because we are not totally imminent in it; but it is necessary for us to change the world because we do not very much transcend it. Here is the point of truth in the conception of the multiversity. The sheer understanding that society is corrupt does not place one outside corruption. For we do not experience social existence at a distance; we ingest it. The act by which the University affirms its humanity and denies American barbarism does not constitute the cure of the University.

It may be, as Hegel has noted, that the hand that inflicts the wound is the hand that cures it. But it does so only through an anguished labor. One cannot throw off all he has been made in the density of the social world with a simple shrug of the understanding. Plato knew this truth two thousand years ago. We are still bound by it. The University has been molded by current powers and we have been formed and malformed in our turn. The alienation of society has become our apathy and fragmentation; its anti-intellectualism and glorification of technology, our play at neutralism is an inversion of ends and means; its crude devotion to wealth and power, our imbalance and intellectual prostitution.

To reconstitute one's self is for a man to remake the world in which he is defined. To know what we might become is not a simple act of the intellect; it requires that we engage in such committed action as can destroy the deforming boundaries of our lives. So, action and thought require each other, inform each other, and complete each other. The obligation imposed on the intellectual, as it is imposed on any one man, is not merely to speak against the world but to re-fashion it.

It is not a violation of the purpose of a university that some part of its activity serve society; but the University must determine through its own critical agency that the society it is to serve is a place in which the spirit of man may be nurtured and advanced.

The University is at this moment an ideological institution, a mask for systematic dominance and privilege. But as Marx noted: "The call for men to abandon their illusions about their condition is a call for men to abandon a condition which requires illusion." A free and human community of scholars can only flourish when the multitudinous communities of the exploited, the wretched, and the brutalized peoples of the earth have broken the bonds of their subservience and established themselves as men of full stature. To participate in the projection and the making of that world is the responsibility of the intellectual.

The University as a Weapon
Louis Kattsoff

Louis O. Kattsoff (1908-   ) is professor of philosophy at Boston College. He is also the author of many books, including *Philosophy of Mathematics* (1948), *Physical Science and Physical Reality* (1957), and *Making Moral Decisions* (1965)

It was Lenin, I believe, who insisted that every aspect of society was a weapon in the class struggle. This would naturally include the university, which is the foundation of and source where new ideas and outlooks are created. Here in the university new knowledge is discovered that could be put to good use in the creation of a new social and economic order. It is imperative, therefore, for those universities that do not align themselves with the revolutionary movement to be either captured or destroyed. They should be captured if at all possible since this would give the revolution a fertile source from which partisans could be created who see the world from the point of view of the new ideology and thus would be more sincere and aggressive in their struggle to obtain dominant political power, thereby gaining the control of the organs of government.

The past, and not too distant past, has seen this strategy practiced in the Soviet Union and in Nazi Germany. One need but recall the New Soviet Encyclopedia, and the books on German Physics by a Nobel prize winner, P. Lenard, as well as the periodical *Deutsche Mathematik*. It is perhaps not too surprising that students were among the most violent adherents of Communism and Fascism in both its German and Italian forms.

Especially subject to such an interpretation were and are the disciplines of Sociology, History, and Psychology, as well as the arts, both lively and still. The aim of university education from this point of view is the production of adherents

Source: *Journal of Social Philosophy*, Vol. 2 (Fall 1971), 10-14. Reprinted by permission of the author.

to the cause and loyalty to the Party. True, in many of the university studies one cannot afford to go too far in this direction, since there is always the need for information independent of ideology for the sake of industry, the war machines, the treatment of disease, and so on. But the professors must be first and foremost ideologically sound. This means that they must be prepared to abandon their bourgeois objectivity and make the facts fit their ideology. The Lysenko affair was a case in point, as well as the manifesto of the German professors in support of Hitler, and more specifically some of the writings of Heidegger. In short, the university must be a weapon in the class struggle, whatever classes were involved, either economic or racial. Furthermore, a basic tenet of this outlook was the acceptance of the proposition that the university was indeed such a weapon.

Fundamental to the doctrine that the university is to be a weapon in the class struggle both to produce partisans and to provide ideological arguments is the historical evidence that universities have indeed been weapons in the hands of the power elite for the preservation of the existing power structure. This historical evidence is based on fact. The time was when the university produced those people of the higher classes who were to go into government, the military, or the Church. One can refer to the ideological treatise of Plato, *The Republic*, to the more recent writings of the British philosopher Bradley, or for that matter to the books of Hegel. The extent to which the universities are agencies for the preservation of existing social structures is evidenced even more strongly today in the current rush to universities to help solve the problems of an ailing society. University professors are involved in political movements, in applying their expertise to housing problems, to racial problems, etc., all in the interest of preserving the existing social structure. Nor does this neglect the fact that many of the professors as well as their students are in active protest engaging in peaceful as well as violent deeds which are directed against government policy. These professors as well as their students are motivated by one of two directly opposed aims. On the one hand, there is the group that believes in the capture or destruction of the university for the sake of their own particular ideology, while on the other hand, there are those who feel that the existing order will go down in flames if the course on which the present order is embarked is not altered. Both of these groups believe that the university is somehow a weapon to be used for their own aggrandizement. They argue that since the university is already an instrument in the social struggle, why not accept that fact and proceed accordingly? If, they insist, the university is already in politics up to its ears, why not simply make it more effective in the struggle for "truly moral aims"? Thus runs the persuasive verbiage.

The result is that in recent years the American university has seen not merely students and professors exercising their political rights, but also political and social declarations in the name of the university. Universities declared their opposition to the war in Viet Nam, to the teaching of military science courses, and so on. The struggle for the minds and loyalties of the student and professor goes on to the detriment of scholarly work.

It is time now to make an evaluation of the sentence: "Universities are weapons in the class struggle."

To say that something is a weapon means many things. Chiefly, it signifies that which is used to attain some end. That end may be self-protection, or the destruction of one's enemy. In short, a weapon is an instrument that is used in some sort of combat. Furthermore, anything may be used as a weapon no matter what its proper function. We may use a knife that is ordinarily used to cut bread as a weapon or we may use a chair as a weapon. In point of fact, one may even use other people as weapons to attain one's ends. We have long heard that ideas are weapons, and they may be used either to mislead or to inform, depending upon circumstances. Apparently there is no inconsistency in saying that anything may be a weapon. We conclude, therefore, that whether anything is or is not a weapon depends upon the purpose for which it is used and not upon its intrinsic nature.

Since the characteristic of being a weapon is a function of the purpose of the user and since in any combat the chief and paramount objective is to win the war or battle, it follows that the weapon may be destroyed if its destruction will lead to victory. Actually the weapon may be modified in any fashion that the user finds appropriate in order to make it more effective in that struggle. No weapon is valued for its sake or for its contribution to any other goal except that of victory in the struggle.

The statement "universities are weapons in the class struggle" accepts implicitly that there is a class struggle in which all people are engaged and that, furthermore, there is no other criterion of effectiveness or of value other than victory. Moreover, it also assumes that it is not possible for any university to be above the class struggle any more than labor-unions, or industry, or even moral codes. The university is essentially and intrinsically involved in that struggle. Perhaps it would be better to say that the people (students, faculty and administration) are immersed in the class struggle and what they do as members of the university must be and is an essential part of that struggle. The interesting thing is that even if that statement were true, the fact remains that any society must have universities or their equivalent if they are not to remain static and in imminent danger of extinction. The implications of this will become evident later.

We must consider another aspect of the problem. If we accept the proposition that a university is a weapon, then it follows, as I have remarked earlier, that the university must either be captured or destroyed if it is a university under the control of the enemy. Most revolutionaries will admit that the university may be a very effective weapon and cannot be left in the hands of one's opponent. In consequence, the work of a university must be hampered at the very least, but it would be better still to gain control of that university and use it as a weapon turned against those who constructed it. Since it would be foolish and naive to deny that a class struggle is constantly in progress, and that a university is a social institution and therefore cannot escape being touched by this struggle, all these considerations have the appearance of being indubitable truths. The appearance of being overwhelmingly true is bolstered by the way the universities are used by the ruling powers in any society. This, however, will become less evident when we analyze the actual university in action and not merely class-struggle ideology.

In a broad sense the function of the university is said to be to educate youth. In actual fact the structure of the modern university, as well as that of universities all through the ages since their inception, indicates that this is but one facet of the working of a university. Every modern university has three types of colleges. There is the undergraduate school variously known as the College of Arts and Sciences or the School of Liberal Arts, etc. Already at this level, although the emphasis is on "education," the three main activities of a university are clearly visible: 1) imparting the acquired knowledge already in possession of scholars and libraries, 2) preparing youth for later work in the professions, industry or teaching and

3) critically evaluating the ideas of the past and present as regards man, his world and his knowledge. No university worthy of its name fails to attempt to inculcate in its undergraduates some training in the critical analysis of ideas as such. The importance of training in philosophical analysis is rarely if ever denied by those who understand the true workings of a university. From Plato's Academy to contemporary Oxford the analysis and criticism of ideas is beyond question an essential activity. In fact, many engineering schools as well as technological institutes provide for some training in this area.

The second aspect of the modern university is revealed in the professional schools, where the emphasis is on turning out youth equipped to do the work of the society. Here too there is strong emphasis on the evaluation of ideas, but chiefly to encourage innovation.

Finally, there is the graduate school, where the emphasis is on the discovery of new knowledge. The goal of the graduate is "to make a contribution to knowledge." True, in many cases the training at the graduate level is for the purpose of gathering the latest knowledge in many areas for the greater efficiency in the world of business and economics. But the main function of graduate work centers around a severe criticism of existing knowledge and information. Especially at the graduate level the logical analysis of ideologies, whether they be social, economic, metaphysical, or scientific, is the paramount occupation of the student.

It is evident, therefore, that graduate work has two main functions: 1) the critical evaluation of ideas, and 2) the discovery of new knowledge. Neither of these functions is advanced unless the individual who is engaged in them can do so without bias or prejudgment influencing the direction of his thinking. This is even more the case for the professor who is engaged in the teaching and directing of research on the fringes of human knowledge. The discussions of the role of theoretical constructs by scientists and philosophers have amply demonstrated both the kind of theoretical structure that is used in the ongoing work of the scientist and in ideological criticism and the dangers of an absolutely accepted set of presuppositions. The danger is the greater, the more passionate the adherence to any set of presuppositions, no matter what their origin. Thus the university loses its fundamental characteristic as a university when it adopts a particular set of solutions as ultimate ones. When this happens, criticism becomes either a search for compatibility with the solutions or else an attack upon the credibility of the evidence advanced in support of the new ideas, or an attack upon the loyalty of the person who advances new concepts that may go counter to the proposed solutions. If, therefore, a university is to remain a place where logical criticism and the search for new knowledge are to be unhampered by any sort of social or political pressures, it must always adopt an attitude of objectivity towards the problems it confronts even if by doing so it gives the appearance of "fiddling while Rome burns."

All of this adds up to the following conclusions: No university can afford to be a weapon in any class struggle or in any political struggle, no matter what is involved. This is difficult because people do get involved in struggles for things they consider indispensible for a decent existence. And it becomes doubly difficult when the very existence of the university as a free institution is involved. It is perhaps only under such extreme circumstances that some loosening of the restrictions that I have discussed may be tolerated.

In any case, to return to our theme, whenever the university is regarded as a weapon, it is considered as a weapon to achieve certain aims. It is considered to have as one of its functions the justification of the aims of those who see and use it as a weapon. By becoming a means for the defense of the aims of the struggle and a means of acquiring adherents to the cause, the university then lays itself open to attacks from all sides of the struggle.

If the minds of men are to be kept free to seek the truth wherever the search may lead, it becomes of prime importance to see to it that the university is *not* made a weapon nor an instrument for the aggrandisement of any particular nation, state or class. In these days of intense and often bitter struggle, it is doubly important to preserve the autonomy of the universities. Political manifestos, involving the solution of social or political problems, in so far as they deny the objectivity of the academician must not be accepted as a function of the university.

None of this means that the university may not study social and political problems of society. These problems may very well fit into the research activities of the university, the professor or his students. But such problems when studied by university persons must be approached with the tools peculiar to the academic profession and with the attitudes of objectivity that such studies deserve when done in a university context. As for the solutions of the problems, one of the major tasks of the university person is to try to define what will indeed constitute a solution. Despite popular opinion to the contrary, what constitutes a solution to a problem is not always evident. As for those who feel they do know what constitutes a solution to some social or political problem, it is to be hoped that they will approach the solution with the knowledge and wisdom provided by the store of information gathered by objective studies done by the universities.

It is evident that what has been said implies a sharp separation between those who gather the facts and advance our knowledge and those who go forth and endeavor to apply the results of the search for knowledge. The difference is that between an Einstein and a von Braun, between Aristotle the philosopher and Aristotle the politician, or between Woodrow Wilson the professor and Woodrow Wilson the president. Clearly, the same man can perform the two functions, but not in the same capacity. The maxim should be "When in the university do as the university does, and when in the realm of social and political activity do as the social and political activists do."

All the above was argued from the point of view of one who accepts as a fundamental premise that there is such a thing as true statements and that they depend not on the desires of those who seek them but on some objective fact or facts. The second assumption is that the university is the instrument designed by society to further the search for that truth. Such a theory of truth and the function of a university rests upon a realistic philosophy and is more easily achieved in the natural sciences. In fact, one could argue that the development of the natural sciences gave impetus to the acceptance of this theory of truth. However, the rapid expansion of our knowledge of the structure of human societies coincident with and perhaps the cause of the rise of the social sciences has brought it about that the number of those who would deny both premises has multiplied.

.   .   .

The implications of the second challenge to the function of a university as a context for the untrammelled search for truth are perhaps even more serious. If it is granted that the university is rather an instrument for the preservation of the status quo and the existing power structure, then clearly anyone who challenges the existing power structure or the status quo must gain control of if not destroy the universities of the existing society. Nor does it become surprising under this definition that the struggle takes the form of disruption of the normal process of the university, not as a challenge to merely the existing curriculum but to the very fact of such a university. The objection to the university must from this point of view reach into the very courses taught. The courses must be orientated to the inculcation of basic ideological definition and dogma. Hence, the curriculum is challenged as well as the political orientation of the professors teaching. Deviation cannot be allowed until the university becomes an instrument in the hands of the new power structure and the new status quo for their own preservation. But then again these words may sound as if I were arguing against such a definition of the function of a university; I suppose this cannot be helped, since I do believe this to be basically detrimental and also (but not, therefore) fallacious. Again, from a non-philosophical basis there seems to be no compelling reason why one cannot on emotive or propagandistic terms adopt this definition of the function of a university and accept all the consequences in the name of being politically "realistic." But as before, one must recognize that the same kind of disagreement arises when we speak about philosophic systems. There are those who insist that philosophic systems are themselves only ideological substructures for the justification of a given social structure, and one needs to indoctrinate people to accept that ideology that best serves one's struggle for power. The dangers of emotive and persuasive language in the elaboration of philosophic systems has been well-known to philosophers, especially in recent years under the influence of the linguistic analyses emanating from the British empiricists through the now classic tradition of logical positivism and linguistic analysis.

All of this relativistic surrender to emotive and ideological adherence to superficial incitement to social and political revolution is based on the results of an uncritical acceptance of ideologies instead of a belief in and support of the concept of exact truth or, perhaps better, approximations to the truth based on empirical evidence as well as theoretical models and not merely interpretations.

Fundamentally we must see that the present crisis in our universities is at bottom a struggle to the death between two diametrically opposed views of the nature of the university in the modern world.

The outcome will determine whether we are to have a philosophic basis for our universities or an ideological one.

Suggested Readings

1. Becker, Howard S. (ed.), *Campus Power Struggle* (Chicago: Aldine, 1970).
2. Foster, Julian, and Long, Durward (eds.), *Protest!* (New York: William Morrow, 1970).
3. Grant, Joanne, *Confrontation on Campus* (New York: New American Library, 1969).

4. Graubard, Stephen R., and Ballotti, Geno A. (eds.), *The Embattled University* (New York: George Braziller, 1970).

5. Wallerstein, Immanuel, and Starr, Paul (eds.), *The University Crisis Reader*, Vol. 1 (New York: Vintage Books, 1971).

6. Weaver, Gary R., and Weaver, James H. (eds.), *The University and Revolution* (Englewood Cliffs, N.J.: Prentice-Hall, 1969).

Morality: Old and New

The search for the New Morality is the search for new directions, not the repudiation of direction.

—Charles Ketcham

INTRODUCTION

Children have morals: they don't think they should pinch their little brother, even though they occasionally do; they don't think it's right to snitch on their pal; and they generally realize they ought to obey their Mommy and Daddy. Adults also have morals: a person is supposed to keep his promises; it is wrong to commit adultery; a parent shouldn't favor one child over the others; husbands should take turns with their wives in doing the dishes and changing the baby. Hence, it is possible to have morals without being moral.

What makes thinking about morals interesting—and absolutely necessary—is the fact that everybody has morals but that not everyone's morals are compatible with each other; moreover, any one person may have morals that are not internally compatible, and he often does not know how to make them compatible. Incompatible morals, whether in a given person or in a society, present us with a philosophical question that is of life-and-death importance, not one of merely intellectual import. Although persons do not always act in accord with their morals, they often do; when they do act on the basis of their morals and their morals are incompatible, the result is conflict in action. The selection service board that thinks it is immoral to resist the draft operation and the conscientious objector who believes it is immoral to cooperate with the draft operation are in active conflict when they each act in accord with their morals. The outcome may be a life-and-death matter.

The philosophical question asked by someone aware of the reality and consequences of incompatible morals is this: Is there a rational means of making incompatible morals compatible, whether the incompatibility is between two or more persons' morals or within a single person's morals?

There are nonrational means for dealing with incompatible morals. An extreme way is to kill the person whose morals are incompatible with yours—or for him to kill you. Another way is to exercise enough threat backed by enough power to frighten the other person into silence or to deter him from acting in accord with his morals. A typical way of handling internally incompatible morals is to practice hypocrisy; you can mouth two incompatible pieces of morals but intend to act in accord with only one of them. If, however, these nonrational means for dealing with incompatible morals are highly unsatisfactory to you, then you will likely think it desirable to ascertain if it is possible to give an affirmative answer to the philosophical question we have posed (that is, find out if it is possible to deal with incompatible morals by rational means).

We take it, then, that we have made a case for seriously philosophizing about morals for those who share our desire to avoid bloody means of dealing with incompatible morals. Our philosophic aim is to think our way past unreflective acceptance of a set of incompatible morals to a moral system that we can all share. Such a moral system should have at least three properties: (1) No part of the morals within a moral system may be incompatible with any other part; that is, the morals should be consistent with each other. (2) The set should be comprehensive; it should be a system that contains maxims covering every moral situation and that provides a way of generating whatever morals might be needed later. (3) The set should be integrated; every part of the system should be related to every other part either directly or indirectly.

Unless a set of morals is integrated, we will be unable to determine if the set is internally compatible. Compatibility is a desirable relation between morals; unless each part of the set is related to every other part, we will not be able to detect if each part is compatible with every other part. Suppose one's moral set contains two maxims, that one should not commit adultery and that one should repay his loans. Are they compatible or not? We could show that they are compatible by showing that they are indirectly related to each other by each being related in the same way directly to a third thing. The argument might go like this: Adultery is breaking a promise of fidelity; not repaying a loan is breaking a promise to repay; since both maxims are instances of the maxim that one should keep his promises and since the promise maxim is self-consistent, the adultery maxim and the loan maxim are compatible. Here, knowing that the adultery and loan maxims are compatibly integrated with the promise maxim, we are able to produce an argument showing that they are compatible with each other.

It is worthwhile to observe that one of the features of a set of morals that enables us to integrate it into a system is a difference in the generality of the maxims. In our example, the promise maxim is more general than either the adultery maxim or the loan maxim. One way of proceeding to construct a moral system is to maximize the use of generality. If we hypothesize that there is a set of morals of the lowest generality, say level one, then they might be grouped under another set of higher generality, say level two, and so forth, until, finally, there is a single maxim of the highest generality under which they all are grouped. They would be integrated because each would be indirectly related to every other because each is grouped finally under one and the same highest generality maxim. We find that moral philosophers have indeed tried to construct moral systems with this technique. Utilitarianism is an example; it proposes a single, highest-level maxim: We ought to do that which will produce the greatest good for the greatest number.

Comprehensiveness is a necessary property of a set of morals if it is to be a system of morals, because without this, neither of the other two criteria can be met. If a maxim for some moral situation is not included, then we will not have related a needed maxim to other maxims in the system, and, hence, the set will not have been integrated. And if it is not integrated, it cannot be determined whether the missing maxim is or is not *compatibly* related to the maxims within the set.

So far we have distinguished between morals and a moral system; we have shown why we want philosophically to advance from morals to a moral system; we have indicated that an acceptable moral system has at least three properties, namely, consistency, comprehensiveness, and integration; and we have explained how the varying generality of moral maxims helps to integrate them into a system.

We wish to distinguish also a moral system from an ethical theory. A moral system is a set of moral maxims of varying generality with at least the three properties we have talked about. An ethical theory is a theory *about* morals and *about* a moral system or systems. It consists of reasoned answers to such questions as: Is there a single set of moral maxims that has the three system properties we talked about above? Or are there several possible moral systems? If there are several moral systems, is it possible to evaluate rationally and choose from among them? Suppose we have two moral systems, each with a single, different, highest generality maxim—is there a rational way of choosing one of them? You already have been thinking about ethical theory because our discussion of the properties of a moral system is a discussion about morals and a moral system.

Answers to these ethical theory questions have popularly been divided into two kinds, conventionally labeled "relativistic" and "absolutistic." The first section in this chapter contains essays that deal with relativism and, by implication, absolutism also, because it is an opposite of relativism.

Before turning to relativism, we briefly remind you that a central ingredient of a culture is its morals. Constructing a new generation ideology is impossible without constructing a system of morals, which in turn leads us to think about ethical theory.

RELATIVISM

Could it be brought home to people that there is no absolute standard in morality, they would perhaps be somewhat more tolerant in their judgments, and more apt to listen to the voice of reason.

—Edward Westermarck

Classically, relativism has seemed to many a plausible ethical theory because of two facts. One of them is that incompatible morals exist that we frequently fail to harmonize rationally. The other is that morals vary between cultures.

Edward A. Westermarck, author of *The Origin and Development of the Moral Ideas* (from which the second essay in this section is taken), a two-volume, 1,400-page examination of the various morals found in a large number of cultures, held a relativistic ethical theory. Notice that his opening remarks explain why he began his extensive investigation of morals: He "was once discussing with some friends the point how far a bad man ought to be treated with kindness. The opinions were divided, and, in spite of much deliberation, unanimity could not be attained." Westermarck was baffled by his and his friends' failure to deal rationally with incompatibility.

Why should continuing failure to harmonize incompatible morals lead us to a relativistic theory of ethics? Obviously, the failure to find a rational way of dealing with incompatibility does not prove that no rational solution exists; the most that it proves is that we simply have not found the rational solution. You are probably familiar with the difficulty of finding the proof for geometrical or algebraic theorems; but you do not conclude out of your despair that there is no proof. Westermarck realizes he can't establish relativism in this negative way; he knows that he must generate an ethical theory that demonstrates that no rational way of resolving the incompatibility of morals exists. Hence, the burden of his essay.

We can build some background for understanding Westermarck's positive theory by reflecting on what a rational solution to incompatibility would be. Morals is not the only place where incompatibility occurs; it occurs also in science and mathematics. When two incompatible scientific opinions are put forward, we assume that not both of them are true. We also assume that truth is relative only to the facts, not to person, time, place, culture, or circumstance. A factual statement is true or false regardless of who stated it or regardless of the culture in which the person who stated it lives. And we assume, further, that we agree on the means of discovering the facts and that these means of discovery are uniform for almost everyone. That there are, for example, ten people in a room can be discovered because we share the technique of counting, because we agree on what are and what are not persons, and because normal eyes have uniform capabilities.

In essence, Westermarck's proof that there can be no rational means for resolving incompatible morals rests on the claim that "there can be no moral truth in the sense in which this term is generally understood. The ultimate reason for this is that the moral concepts are based upon emotions and that the contents of emotion fall entirely outside the category of truth." The means we use to settle incompatible scientific claims are, therefore, not applicable to incompatible moral maxims, because the former have a truth property whereas the latter do not. Whether Westermarck's explanation of why incompatibility disputes between moralists is beyond the pale of objective, rational solution is satisfactory, we leave to your philosophical investigations.

We mentioned that the fact that morals vary from culture to culture is another reason that some people have assented to relativistic ethical theory. Variability of morals itself is often mistaken for relativism. The two must be distinguished. Why should sheer variability of morals lead us to say that there is no rational way for people to construct a single moral system on which they can agree? In the last essay of this section, **Carl Wellman** addresses himself to the distinction between variability and ethical relativism and shows that the variability of morals alone does not establish the case for a relativistic ethical theory. He shows this of several varying moral ingredients that he considers in turn; these include mores, social institutions, human nature, acts, goals, value experiences, moral emotions (compare Westermarck's essay in this section), moral concepts, moral judgments, and moral reasoning.

Students too often unreflectively assent to relativism. We suggest that before you claim yourself a relativist that you ask yourself if you really believe that a moral system forbidding racism cannot rationally be shown to be preferable to a system that permits or encourages it; or ask yourself if you really believe that the Nazi extermination of Jews was justified in Germany, or some other place, but not in the United States.

Some of you may wish to hold off committing yourself to a relativistic ethical theory because you feel something has gone wrong if you have to acknowledge that there is no rational way to show racism is wrong, if you have to acknowledge that there is no rational way to choose between two such contrary maxims as "People should not practice racism" and "People may (should) practice racism."

For those who wish to avoid being rushed into a relativistic ethical theory, here is some tactical advice: Always lengthen the maxim rather than force an incompatibility. We will not use racism as an example of this tactical advice because it is too complicated. You can use our tactical advice when you get to George D. Kelsey's essay on racism in Chapter Six (second essay of the first section). Consider, instead, a short frugality maxim: "People should be frugal with their money." Suppose you are a fund raiser for families left destitute by a flood and suppose a rich lady turns down your fund appeal because she believes in the frugality maxim and claims to be an ethical absolutist. One tactic for dealing with the rich lady is to say that the frugality maxim may be true for her but that as far as the flooded families are concerned it is false. Using that tactic backs you into moral incompatibility, which leaves you with an apparent relativism: The frugality maxim is as false for one person as it is true for another. The rich lady can stand on her absolutist principles and continue to refuse you funds because "you young relativists don't appreciate good old-fashioned virtues."

A better tactic is to avoid an incompatibility confrontation; instead, you can point out that frugality is indeed a virtue but that the short frugality maxim states only a half-truth. A fuller truth is captured by the longer frugality maxim: "Poor people should be frugal with their money." So far, no argument. And there is an even longer frugality maxim that fits the rich lady: "Rich people should not be frugal with their money if it can be used to benefit some other person or persons." In making the frugality maxim longer, you are adding further conditions to which the virtue of frugality is relative; this has the logical effect of avoiding incompatibility because the frugality maxim about poor people is perfectly compatible with the one about rich people. But, in adding conditions, you do not thereby concede to relativism. The rich lady cannot refuse you on absolutist principles alone because you are no longer caught in the relativism she opposes on ethical theory grounds. By using the longer-maxim tactic, you force her to consider the moral issues rather than ethical theory issues. This is good because you force her into choosing between rational moral options or arbitrary refusal; you do not leave her with the lone option of dismissing you as a relativist with whom there is no point rationally discussing the matter.

Charles B. Ketcham (first essay in this section) brings two things forcefully home to us. First, that we do not have to travel to meet the challenge of variable sets of morals; we have them right here at home as we witness the pangs of a new generation morals aborning. Such pangs always attend the beginnings of a new ideology, which you have a duty to help generate and systematize. Second, a moral system is not set in concrete; it may change. This is why we said earlier when talking about the comprehensiveness of a moral system that the system should provide a means of adding moral maxims and maintaining its consistency. Ketcham writes at times as if we need moral change because the old morality is absolutistic and should be replaced by the new morality that is relativistic or contextualistic. Be careful when reading him to keep in mind that Ketcham may be confusing a moral system, now changing, with an ethical theory. Absolutism and relativism are kinds of ethical theory, and it may indeed be true that we are witnessing a shift in the intellectuals' and in the masses' allegiance from absolutism to relativism; but this is not the same shift that is involved in moving from an older morals to a new morals.

Toward the New Morality
Charles B. Ketcham

Charles B. Ketcham (1928-   ) is professor of religion at Alleghany College. He was a Fulbright scholar and was a fellow at the Harvard Divinity School. He has lectured at Drew University and Union Theological Seminary. Among his books are *The Search for a Meaningful Existence* (1968) and *Faith and Freedom* (1969).

Because the humanist revolution in thought, expression, and act has been so widespread, the effects are everywhere noticeable. One cannot be exposed daily to our new art forms, new literary forms, new musical expressions, and new theologies and philosophies without being profoundly concerned about and affected by the radical changes they present and symbolize. Though one may reject many of these changes as immature, incomprehensible, irrational, or just plain phony, they have made an impressive impact on our society and, for that matter, on the world. Our electronics revolution—radio, films, television, computers—has only served to intensify and accelerate this impact by making possible and accessible an audio-visual exposure to these radical changes. We are, according to Marshall McLuhan, tribalizing the world.

The theologian Paul Tillich puts the end of the nineteenth century at World War I, but this event is not just the end of that century. It is, Tillich rightly claims, the end of one era and the beginning of another. Surely the course of our study thus far substantiates such a judgment. The whole fabric of our culture is being worked over by some very visible weavers, and it is difficult to establish at this point whether they are merely patching or actually re-weaving a whole new cloth. Consequently, what has been celebrated recently under the simplistic banner of "The New Morality" tends to be a representative mixture of destruction and reformation.

With the ending of an era comes the collapse of old standards, old values, old norms—in short, the old morality. In our own situation, when Absolutes are called into question, when Form itself is questioned, the result is an accelerated deterioration of traditional moral standards which have been variously labeled "the Victorian ethic," "the Protestant ethic," "middle class values," "the American way," and so on. Stability, particularly in terms of predictability, has disappeared. We no longer know what is "right" for us to do as individuals or as a nation. For example, the ethical principles and simple, straight-forward injunctions once thought central and adequate for the national ideal—liberty, justice, equality, freedom of press, freedom of speech, freedom of opportunity—have crumbled under the pressures of the complexities of twentieth-century life. One can no longer realistically expect that all emergent nations will have the American form of democracy any more than one can realistically respond to a Wilsonian plea to "make the world safe for democracy." What we now know is that no one nation can totally and effectively control its own destiny, let alone the destiny of the world. *Pax Americana* may be a glorious wish, but it is certainly not a realistic picture of the political realities of the late twentieth century.

Since discovering that we as Americans have not cornered or monopolized the truth market and have had to compete with other viable political and economic systems, our self-righteousness and our assurance have been shaken. Our national posture has gradually sagged into an expediency relative to self-interest, as the struggle in South-East Asia indicates. The traditional words, though still used, are all too often not attempts at redefinition but, rather, totem terms invoked by confused or frightened citizens in the desperate hope that sheer repetition of the words themselves will somehow re-establish the power of the principle; or such words are often calculated cliches in the mouths of some "superpatriots," politicians and laymen alike, who want to justify injustice and their own self-interests. The growing "credibility gap" (as a two-way gap) between the government and the people is the result. Such civil sickness can only increase, with dissident groups of all kinds becoming increasingly self-seeking and militant, if the loss of national integrity continues. The growing polarities in America over the issues of race and war are evidence of such a trend.

Other examples of the moral confusion of this transition period are not hard to find. We no longer know what is "right" for us to do about the relations among labor, management, and government. The interests of all three are so interlocking that any deviation can cause a national crisis. The old rules about hard work and honest bargaining just do not apply: one cannot bargain with the boss or "catch his eye" when one's point of contact is a management time study or a union quota system; individual unions and industries must abandon much local bargaining for "industry-wide" sessions; labor and management together must now face a government which not only controls and limits their activities to a degree but, in some cases, even becomes a competitor; the government can no longer simply concern itself with domestic issues, for foreign markets and common markets make economics a world problem. So the economic problem and its accompanying moral dilemmas become acute. The coal miner in West Virginia feels the impact of the world, but his credit is still calculated by the local grocery store.

We no longer know what is "right" to do about the problems of interpersonal relations, particularly in the area of sex. Education, population problems, the "pill," and loss of the sacramental nature of marriage all have eaten away at the traditional cultural patterns. Taboos once observed for no other reason than that they were "right and proper" for generations cannot persuade or convince the contemporary questioning mind. Extravagant theological threats ("God will make you impotent!") no longer strike fear into hearts of teenagers or anyone else. Social ostracism for, or legal restraint of, so-called "deviant behavior" is no longer an unavoidable threat. The fear of pregnancy has been removed from sexual intercourse so that this physical expression of "love" has been freed from the moral restraints of responsible paternity or maternity. The questions then are posed: "Why not love with the body as completely as with the heart?" and "Must such physical love necessarily be confined to marriage?" In an age of transition when new values are being established, the emotional, physical, and spiritual strains of the existing value void are often tragically evident in broken hearts, broken homes, and broken lives. Loss of authority has left a legacy of anxiety. The search for the New Morality is the search for new directions, not the repudiation of direction.

The citation of these three areas of acute moral concern as examples is enough to suggest the complexity of the problem. Old patterns are either inadequate or discarded, and, without new expressions, genuine confusion ensues. Some people courageously cling to the old values, the proverbial "good old days," terrified at what might happen if they abandoned them. Others courageously search for new patterns, new values which would provide a meaningful life, frightened that their experimentation may bring irremedial tragedy rather than fulfillment. Still others simply exploit the confusion to gratify their own self-interests, confident that there are no values other than one's own.

When one hears the term "New Morality," one is apt to find reference to any one of the above three possibilities, but particularly the latter two. The very last alternative, however, is representative of the ethics of nihilism and offers little that is constructive for us to consider. It is certainly not an expression of what we have termed the New Humanism.

The "New Morality" has been a catch-all phrase for all activity deviating from pre-World-War-I ethical norms. Yet it should be clearly understood that the breakdown of traditional standards we are witnessing about us, the seemingly inevitable disenchantment and frustration which results when the basis for a once-meaningful life has been threatened, is really only the prelude to the New Morality. But if there is to be a genuine New Morality, it will have to emerge not from the least common denominator of such moral decadence, but rather from some understanding of the implication, the contours, the nature of the New Humanism. Chaos alone can never be the matrix for spontaneous generation. Passive acceptance of the destructive forces at work in society is not the rôle of the New Humanist. What is urgently needed is the thoughtful creation of new and significant value structures. Until this affirmative response is made, the moral dilemma in which we find ourselves can only be intensified.

Before going further, terminology ought to be clarified. Normally the word "morality" is used to describe the value designation inherent or assumed in any specific human act or generally accepted custom. By contrast, the word "ethics" usually denotes a rational system of values which is both prescriptive and adjudicative. Thus to call an act "immoral" or "unethical" is really to misuse both terms. What we mean when we misuse such terms is quite clear: it is *not* that the act has no value at all; it is rather that the act is wrong or harmful either according to custom (morality) or according to system (ethics). Much of the confused talk about the New Morality reveals such a misunderstanding of these basic terms. What most people mean by the search for the New Morality is the search for a New Ethic. However, I have retained the term New Morality not only because of its popular acceptance but, more importantly, for the fact that we are discussing not so much an ethic as an ethos, a context, within which several ethical systems may coexist.

If the New Humanism, in both its secular and religious forms, is to give rise to a New Morality, then it should be possible to determine, on the basis of our study, some of the directions or contours of that morality. Taking as normative the ambiguity we have observed governing all human existence, capacities, and relationships, the New Morality should expect no exemption from such a limitation.

Our understanding of *Being* in terms of self-awareness is limited and elusive; our knowledge of God through the *I-Thou* encounter is private and hidden; our relationship to others is limited by the degree of our authenticity as well as theirs; our information about the physical world is provisional as well as being an apparent one-way rational appropriation; and all these relationships are further limited by the time-fullness of *Being* in which we all participate here-and-now.

Under these circumstances, any New Morality must reflect such limitations in its rejection of absolute prescriptive ends—*the* Good, *the* Right, *the* Truth, *the* Kingdom—as well as absolute prescriptive laws—"obey the government without question," "obey the Bible without question," "obey the parent without question." Any expression of these goals or laws as absolutely inviolable would not only falsely deny the reality of ambiguity but would also establish a priority of abstract principle or law over self, an error Western tradition has made all too often. In the New Humanist's understanding of integrity, there are times when my integrity, or truth of *Being,* is contrary to, or cannot be limited to, the world of objectively verifiable facts, *i.e.,* I do not always tell the medical patient of his condition, or my hostess of her indigestible meal.

But having acknowledged this, one must immediately affirm that life can be *reasonably* lived only if goals or ends or standards such as "the good," "the right," "the truth," "the kingdom," are provisionally accepted; and that chaos can be averted in an inescapably social world only if one does, for example, intelligently obey the government and/or does imaginatively follow the ethical insights of Scripture.

The difference, of course, is immediately evident, for under these latter conditions such goals and laws become *authoritative for our lives but do not function as Absolutes.* Times, insights, and contexts change and, therefore, so must laws, means, and ends. I must so live in the condition of freedom that my authenticity as a self may be maintained even at the risk of defying the existing external authorities. This is not to plead for anarchy but for the constant reevaluation and restatement of that penultimate authority which would permit a continuous authentic expression of self and society. Such is my responsibility to the continuing demands of ambiguity.

The instances of civil disobedience in the American civil rights struggle are a case in point. As opposed to the anarchy and lawlessness of the ghetto riots, civil disobedience challenges the authority and effective justice of the existing laws by the deliberate violation of such laws and the self-surrender of the violators to the government. Such action brings the inadequacy of the laws or customs in question to the attention of society, and a fitting reform can be made. However, when such reforms prove empty or resulting legislation is powerless to enforce the reform, then more serious disobedience, even violence, can result—as we see in the urban riots. Human desperation does not recognize the authority of abstract Absolutes; pleas for sanity at such times appear to the desperate only as rejection, a banishment to futility and meaningless existence.

It is not at all amiss to note here that democracy as a form of government is structured on the reality of ambiguity as a human condition. The three-branch structure of the U.S. Government serves to preserve and honor that ambiguity so that an absolute rule can never be established while responsible authority is always maintained. This recognition of human limitation is reflected in Reinhold Niebuhr's celebrated dictum from *The Children of Light and the Children of Darkness:*

"Man's capacity for justice makes democracy possible; but man's inclination to injustice makes democracy necessary."[1] Ambiguity as a human condition of *Being* must be reflected in the condition of social and political organization.

As priorities change, so do my actions and so do those of all men. Thus the picture of human society is continuously being refocused. All men need to act in such a way that personal and public responsibilities, personal and public actions do not countermand each other. To ignore public responsibility (the world of *It*) is to end with anarchy; to ignore personal responsibility (the world of *Thou*) is to end with dehumanizing conformity. The answer is not merely compromise, for compromise implies that there is some unifying identity between the nature of the *It* world and the nature of the *Thou* world. But this is simply not the case. The "laws, principles, and ends" peculiar to society and the physical world are not those "laws, principles, and ends" peculiar to my personal life. The former we characterized by impersonally ordered relations, the latter by freedom, spontaneity, and decision.

If ambiguity, as evidence in the New Humanism, is normative for the New Morality, then it follows that some form of contextual ethic will emerge. The very fact that such divergent contemporary thinkers as Joseph Fletcher, Karl Barth, Joseph Sitler, Paul Lehmann, and H. Richard Niebuhr all propose some form of contextual ethic is reason enough to take seriously such a contention.

The "contextual ethic" obviously receives its name from the fact that ethical decisions are determined by assessing the context, the various forces—social, political, physical, economic, intellectual, spiritual—past, present, and future, which impose themselves upon us in our deliberations prior to or during any "value" decision. But to describe such an ethic is not to justify its use. A contextual ethic suggests itself as one natural expression for the New Humanism because it does take the ambiguity of existence into account; because it is totally inclusive of all those factors, deliberative and active, which constitute *Being*-in-the-world-here-and-now whether such *Being* is secular or religious; and because we note that the very process of decision-making involves all these factors—attention to our total self within its total orientation of meaning.

It follows, then, that although we acknowledge our dependence upon historical guidance, precedent, and wisdom, no one standard or set of standards can be final for a contextual ethic which tries to take into account all the limiting factors involved in any given new context. In each decision one must ask, "What am I trying to achieve?" "What is known?" "What are the limits?" "What are the priorities?" "What will be the response to my decision?" "What act will, in fact, give the fullest expression to *Being?*" In any given situation, therefore, what we expect from one man we might not expect from another who is politically more powerful, or another better educated, or yet another who is mentally retarded. Likewise, the patterns of response and reward for the twentieth-century American are likely to be quite different from those of a contemporary man of a less advanced culture, though variations within any given culture complex are apt to be limited because of the focus of common forces.

[1] Reinhold Niebuhr, *The Children of Light and the Children of Darkness,* Nisbet and Company, Ltd., London, p. vi.

For some Cassandras the loss of absolute standards, principles, and goals can result only in destructive forces being indiscriminately released against an idyllic heritage. Yet "The backward look behind the assurance/Of recorded history, the backward half-look/Over the shoulder" does not, as Mr. T. S. Eliot reminds us in "The Dry Salvages," convince most of us of the unqualified sanctity of the past. The inhumanity of human behavior seems to be the expression more of allegiance to nonhuman Absolutes than of authentic response to the nature of *Being*—as God or man. Certainly the last fifty years of war, suffering, and growing disenchantment with Absolute demands have served to strengthen this conviction. This is not to resurrect the "noble savage" of Rousseau. It *is* to bring into question the assumption in Western thought that morality and ethics can be meaningfully expressed only with the context of, and as reflections of, an Absolute. One of the things which contemporary interest in the New Humanism seems to be displaying is a growing belief that metaphysical Absolutes such as *the* Good, *the* Truth, *the* Beautiful have really hampered man's free and open expression of *Being*—whether that be in art, music, literature, or morality—and that health can only be achieved when the *I-Thou* and *I-It* can time-fully express themselves. We cannot avoid the ambiguities of human existence, and we are tragically misled if we believe that some ethical system can resolve them for us. Our present "sickness unto death" certainly is no witness for those who deprecate this contemporary revolution in the name of past holiness or of moral perfectionism.

For the contextual ethic, the ambiguities involved are both its strength and limitation. One of the finest of the contextualists, H. Richard Niebuhr, brings this sharply into focus: decisions "are made, it appears, on the basis of relative insight and faith, but they are not relativistic. They are individual decisions, but not individualistic. They are made in freedom, but not in independence; they are made in the moment, but are not nonhistorical."[2] Each of these qualifications deserves further explication.

Niebuhr indicates that the decisions which we reach are relative in four ways: First, they are relative to our limited fragmentary knowledge—as anyone who has contemplated marriage, tried to discipline children effectively, or endeavored constructively to criticize government policy on international affairs surely knows. Second, decisions are relative to the extent of our belief and unbelief—as anyone recognizes who has hedged his commitments to God or man with mental reservations, hidden alternatives, or flight insurance. Third, decisions are relative to our historical and social context—as any first-generation American, any Vista or Peace Corps volunteer, or any Depression-age father and his hippie-age child dazedly admit. Finally, decisions are made relative to the values of our time—as most Victorians admit, gazing wonderingly at the guiltless sexual freedom of the present generation. Niebuhr makes these qualifications about our relative decisions within the Christian heritage, but as already indicated, such qualifications could equally well apply to secular humanism, though "belief" in such a case would be understood in terms of the affirmation of *Being* rather than faith in God.

The reason my decisions are individual but not individualistic is that my individuality is the result of my involvement, the *I-Thou* encounter. I can only know myself in terms of my social context; therefore I can act only out of that

[2] H. Richard Niebuhr, *Christ and Culture,* Harper & Row, Incorporated, New York, p. 234.

context. While I am responsible for my deliberate act, I am not equally responsible for my cultural context. If I display signs of prejudice, it is in part a response to existing elements in my society by which I have been conditioned. Anyone who has tried to overcome a sectional or racial prejudice knows with what difficulty and with how many relapses such a victory is won. If I am an advocate for new sexual mores, or for a radically New Humanism, these must be defined and explained in terms of traditional expression, even if that amounts to a disavowal of that older tradition. Anyone who recognizes the statement, "I know the words you're using but I can't understand what you're saying" is aware of the problem. The individualistic decision simply does not exist; the reality of the here-and-now in which I live involves me with my contemporaries and links me to the past and to the future. But the confusion persists because the linkage is ambiguous; it is not simply the expression of some efficient cause.

My decisions are made in freedom but not in independence because of similar ambiguities. The reason that I use to come to a decision is not only fragmented and partial, it is also schooled by my society, my historical position, and my cultural stance. The time-full limitation of my existence brings my known, historical life continuously into contact with the unknown and the not-yet, so that I am continually impelled to be that which is new, even if it be only a new interpretation of the old. Both authentic and inauthentic acts express my freedom now in terms of my continuity with the past and my dependence upon my cultural conditioning. The freedom of the twentieth-century technocrat is quite different from the freedom of the early twentieth-century industrialist. Ford Motor Company can no longer be the private domain of Henry Ford, yet the corporation's freedom to affect the economic health of the United States is far greater than Henry Ford I ever dreamed.

That decisions are made *now,* but are at the same time not nonhistorical, has been discussed before. The time-fulness of existence not only ensures that meaningfulness is now, it also assures us that one aspect of that meaningfulness is the continuity with past meaningful moments out of which our understanding (ambiguous as that is) of *this* moment arises. Again, the time-fulness of existence assures us that though our decision is *now,* that *now* will have a continuous influence upon future decisions. The commitment I make on my wedding day is part of the now-commitment I must continue making one, ten, or thirty-seven years later.

In each of these aspects of decision, one thing becomes clear: there is no such thing as the guaranteed, absolute, or final "right" decision, as any parent can affirm without analytical justification. Any decision is in some significant part a leap into the unknown, a commitment beyond proof or evidence for which we can only prepare ourselves as responsibly as possible. For the secularist, this means a responsibility to self in terms of *Being;* for the religionist, it means a responsibility to self and to God. In either case, the self is involved in his community of encounter.

In the United States, certain laws govern legalized abortion. Defiance has arisen in the form of a general disregard for the law, with one exception: the *official* Roman Catholic community. For Roman Catholics, the issue revolves about the Church's belief that "life" begins not at birth but at conception. Abortion is therefore the arbitrary taking of a life intended by God—to any Catholic, of course, a heinous sin. The act of abortion is not simply defiance of the State; it is defiance of God. Consequently, there is no pressure for change from official quarters.

For some Catholics, the majority of Protestants, and secularists, however, the situation is different. These groups recognize neither the "natural law" tradition nor any other authoritative or definitive ruling about prenatal life. Other human factors have assumed greater importance. Arguments in favor of abortion usually begin by the loaded question: "Would it not be more humane to end the existence of a foetus which has been damaged by thalidomide or German measles?" Why bring a disfigured, handicapped, or retarded child into the world when it is unnecessary, and cruel for the child? Such arguments are persuasive, but the ethical-legal problem becomes more subtle and more difficult when one anticipates a normal pregnancy.

Many concerned people believe that the life of an unwanted child is jeopardized from the beginning. If, as many child psychologists maintain, the basic attitude of the child toward the world is framed, if not fixed, within the first six months of its life, there is little weight to the counterargument that the unwanted child could win its way into the hearts of recalcitrant parents, if indeed it has "parents" to win. To believe this is to romanticize child-care in the first place, and to ignore the clinical evidence of "disturbed children" who are conditioned by such tension-situations in the second place. It might also be the case that the physical or mental health of the mother would be endangered by pregnancy and birth, a situation for which abortion is the obvious solution. Fortunately, some parts of the world already acknowledge this condition as reason enough for the operation. Or it may be the case that the two people involved in the conception are truly not in love and should not be married. Perhaps they are simply too young for marriage. Must placing the child up for adoption be the only way out?

These and a host of similar "humane" considerations compel people to seek out an illegal abortionist who, for several hundred dollars or more, "takes care of things." If one is not convinced that the official Roman Catholic position concerning the beginning of "life" can be maintained, then the case for possible abortion can be reasonably argued in terms of the merits surrounding each individual situation, so that the result may truly represent that affirmation of life characteristic of the New Humanism. If life is here-and-now, and life is threatened by a pregnancy which is determined deleterious to those involved, then one hopes that laws (which are to protect life) will enable abortion to occur. To deny it categorically under any conditions other than those official Roman Catholicism has established, would seem far too restrictive and punitive. If the reason for denial is that the participants were "bad" or irresponsible and should pay for their folly, then such a primitive denial is not responsive—and, perhaps psychologically irresponsible—to the situation and is possibly sadistic. Nor should abortion be denied because then "everyone would do it"—as though it were done for a lark at lunchtime break. No one who has agonized over the decision, had the standard "dilation and curettage," experienced the emotional strain, and paid the bill, believes it to be so inconsequential.

The above arguments are incomplete, oversimplified, and themselves riddled with ambiguity; but they do at least give some sense of the dilemmas that many people face. Such dilemmas, in turn, provide motivation for action, both legal and illegal, which could change the laws of a nation. The price of such change is high; but the price of no change is higher. It cannot be otherwise for life characterized by ambiguity, for meaning dependent upon encounter here-and-now.

The change in cultural myths or ethos, e.g., the change from a rural mentality to an urban mentality in America, is even more complicated, more risky, more costly, and more lengthy. The technical and financial crises in the major cities of the world are only one phase of the great human problem caused by the change. Politicians whose responsibility it is to administer city governments know the problems in terms of power, representation, and financial apportionments on the local, state, and federal levels. But we all know that there are poignant human problems involving poverty, waste, exploitation, hunger, and so forth, where the risk of the search for meaning has become worth the risk of defiance. . . . Money cannot buy peace for long and can never provide meaning. The recent organization of militant poverty groups, of Black Power groups, and their concomitant refusal of Establishment help and Establishment dollars are all evidences of the colossal struggle going on in the United States. One can only hope, in spite of grave doubts, that reforms will come quickly and reasonably enough that the risk for meaning will not necessitate any greater acts of defiance. Such is the tension of cultural ambiguity which necessarily and continuously juxtaposes one's responsibilities to the *It* and *Thou* worlds.

The change in faith and belief is even more traumatic, for here the point of our orientation, the very center of meaning, is shaken. Despite the fact that we recognize and know the ambiguity of belief, we resist such changes with great tenacity. The change in belief means not only a change in our understanding of *Being* or God, but also a consequent change in our own identity. Is it any wonder, then, that men and women of the older generations, set in their religious ways, become the conservatives of the community? Superior wisdom does not make them so adamant; their fear of change, loss of power, loss of understanding, and loss of meaning does. Is it any wonder that the recent innovations initiated by the Second Vatican Council and by the theological turmoil within Protestantism have produced powerful reactions among all churchmen, laymen and clergy alike? For some, the changes are signs of apostasy—sin in its most subtle form; for others, these changes signal the rebirth without which Christianity is a quaint cultural curiosity. Not since the reformation itself has the Church experienced such change. It is our privilege and peril to live in an age when the need for meaning has produced radical reforms. But, radical reforms in religious expression take generations for effective assimilation. Meanwhile, they occasion profound spiritual anxiety which is often expressed as massive resistance to change.

We are concerned here with all of these changes. We are engaged in a genuine search for a new sense of our humanity and a more relevant morality. The old lights have gone out; the old gods have died; the old ways are inadequate. Life lived meaningfully in the *now,* in terms of our *Being* or in terms of our God, is beginning to emerge, but the patterns are not yet distinct. What is distinct, however, is the overall pattern which includes the presence of the ambiguity of encounter. It is something like this that I believe E. E. Cummings had in mind when he wrote:

> are world's collapsing? any was a glove
> but i'm and you are actual either hand
> is when for sale? forever is to give
> and on forever's very now we stand[3]

[3] E. E. Cummings, "what freedom's not some under's mere above," *100 Selected Poems,* Grove Press, Inc., New York, p. 84.

Thus the delicate balance is sought between structure and freedom, stability and change. As in any fragile human situation, too much weight on one side brings a compensatory reaction to restore the ambiguity necessary for free and meaningful human existence. The danger is that the compensation will be excessive: too much structure brings too much indeterminism; too much objectivity results in too much subjectivism; too much order invites too much chaos. The times in which we live, on all the levels we have discussed, exhibit such contending forces as indeterminism, subjectivism, and irrationality. But, in the gradual emergence of the New Humanism, order and reason will again begin to reassert their authority hopefully, creatively, freely, and affirmatively, yet never absolutely. The awareness of ambiguity adds a new dimension to our understanding of our responsibility for life here-and-now.

The Relativity of Ethics
Edward A. Westermarck

Edward A. Westermarck (1862-1939) is the Danish author of *The Origin and Development of the Moral Ideas* (1924-1926) and was a leading ethical relativist.

The main object of this book [from which this essay is taken] will perhaps be best explained by a few words concerning its origin.

Its author was once discussing with some friends the point how far a bad man ought to be treated with kindness. The opinions were divided, and, in spite of much deliberation, unanimity could not be attained. It seemed strange that the disagreement should be so radical, and the question arose, Whence this diversity of opinion? Is it due to defective knowledge, or has it a merely sentimental origin? And the problem gradually expanded. Why do the moral ideas in general differ so greatly? And, on the other hand, why is there in many cases such a wide agreement? Nay, why are there any moral ideas at all?

Since then many years have passed, spent by the author in trying to find an answer to these questions. The present work is the result of his researches and thoughts.

The first part of it will comprise a study of the moral concepts: right, wrong, duty, justice, virtue, merit, &c. Such a study will be found to require an examination into the moral emotions, their nature and origin, as also into the relations between these emotions and the various moral concepts. There will then be a discussion of the phenomena to which such concepts are applied—the subjects of moral judgments. The general character of these phenomena will be scrutinised, and an answer sought to the question why facts of a certain type are matters of

Source: *The Origin and Development of the Moral Ideas*, 1924-1926, Intro. and Ch. 1. Reprinted with permission of the estate of E. A. Westermarck.

moral concern, while other facts are not. Finally, the most important of these phenomena will be classified, and the moral ideas relating to each class will be stated, and, so far as possible, explained.

An investigation of this kind cannot be confined to feelings and ideas prevalent in any particular society or at any particular stage of civilisation. Its subject-matter is the moral consciousness of mankind at large. It consequently involves the survey of an unusually rich and varied field of research—psychological, ethnographical, historical, juridical, theological. In the present state of our knowledge, when monographs on most of the subjects involved are wanting, I presume that such an undertaking is, strictly speaking, too big for any man; at any rate it is so for the writer of this book. Nothing like completeness can be aimed at. Hypotheses of varying degrees of probability must only too often be resorted to. Even the certainty of the statements on which conclusions are based is not always beyond a doubt. But though fully conscious of the many defects of his attempt, the author nevertheless ventures to think himself justified in placing it before the public. It seems to him that one of the most important objects of human speculation cannot be left in its present state of obscurity; that at least a glimpse of light must be thrown upon it by researches which have extended over some fifteen years; and that the main principles underlying the various customs of mankind may be arrived at even without subjecting these customs to such a full and minute treatment as would be required of an anthropological monograph.

Possibly this essay, in spite of its theoretical character, may even be of some practical use. Though rooted in the emotional side of our nature, our moral opinions are in a large measure amenable to reason. Now in every society the traditional notions as to what is good or bad, obligatory or indifferent, are commonly accepted by the majority of people without further reflection. By tracing them to their source it will be found that not a few of these notions have their origin in sentimental likings and antipathies, to which a scrutinising and enlightened judge can attach little importance; whilst, on the other hand, he must account blameable many an act and omission which public opinion, out of thoughtlessness, treats with indifference. It will, moreover, appear that a moral estimate often survives the cause from which it sprang. And no unprejudiced person can help changing his views if he be persuaded that they have no foundation in existing facts.

CHAPTER I: THE EMOTIONAL ORIGIN OF MORAL JUDGMENTS

That the moral concepts are ultimately based on emotions either of indignation or approval, is a fact which a certain school of thinkers have in vain attempted to deny. The terms which embody these concepts must originally have been used—indeed they still constantly are so used—as direct expressions of such emotions with reference to the phenomena which evoked them. Men pronounced certain acts to be good or bad on account of the emotions those acts aroused in their minds, just as they called sunshine warm and ice cold on account of certain sensations which they experienced, and as they named a thing pleasant or painful because they felt pleasure or pain. But to attribute a quality to a thing is never the same as merely to state the existence of a particular sensation or feeling in the mind which perceives it. Such an attribution must mean that the thing, under certain circumstances, makes a certain impression on the mind. By calling an object warm or pleasant, a person asserts that it is apt to produce in him a sensation of heat or a feeling of pleasure. Similarly, to name an act good or bad, ultimately implies that it is apt to give rise to an emotion of approval or disapproval in him who pronounces the judgment. Whilst not affirming the actual existence of any specific emotion in the mind of the person judging or of anybody else, the predicate of a moral judgment attributes to the subject a tendency to arouse an emotion. The moral concepts, then, are essentially generalisations of tendencies in certain phenomena to call forth moral emotions.

However, as is frequently the case with general terms, these concepts are mentioned without any distinct idea of their contents. The relation in which many of them stand to the moral emotions is complicated; the use of them is often vague; and ethical theorisers, instead of subjecting them to a careful analysis, have done their best to increase the confusion by adapting the meaning of the terms to fit their theories. Very commonly, in the definition of the goodness or badness of acts, reference is made, not to their tendencies to evoke emotions of approval or indignation, but to the causes of these tendencies, that is, to those qualities in the acts which call forth moral emotions. Thus, because good acts generally produce pleasure and bad acts pain, goodness and badness have been identified with the tendencies of acts to produce pleasure or pain. The following statement of Sir James Stephen is a clearly expressed instance of this confusion, so common among utilitarians: "Speaking generally, the acts which are called right do promote or are supposed to promote general happiness, and the acts which are called wrong do diminish or are supposed to diminish it. I say, therefore, that this is what the words 'right' and 'wrong' mean, just as the words 'up' and 'down' mean that which points from or towards the earth's centre of gravity, though they are used by millions who have not the least notion of the fact that such is their meaning, and though they were used for centuries and millenniums before any one was or even could be aware of it."[1] So, too, Bentham maintained that words like "ought," "right," and "wrong" have no meaning unless interpreted in accordance with the principle of utility;[2] and James Mill was of the opinion that "the very morality" of the act lies, not in the sentiments raised in the breast of him who perceives or contemplates it, but in "the consequences of the act, good or evil, and their being within the intention of the agent."[3] He adds that a rational assertor of the principle of utility approves of an action "because it is good," and calls it good "because it conduces to happiness."[4] This, however, is to invert the sequence of the facts, since, properly speaking, an act is called good because it is approved of, and is approved of by an utilitarian in so far as it conduces to happiness.

Such confusion of terms cannot affect the real meaning of the moral concepts. It is true that he who holds that "actions are right in proportion as they tend to promote happiness, wrong as they tend to produce the reverse of happiness,"[5] may, by a merely intellectual process, pass judgment on the moral character of particular acts; but, if he is an utilitarian from conviction, his first principle, at least, has an

---

[1] Stephen, *Liberty, Equality, Fraternity*, p. 338.
[2] Bentham, *Principles of Morals and Legislation*, p. 4.
[3] James Mill, *Fragment on Mackintosh*, pp. 5, 376.
[4] *Ibid.* p. 368.
[5] Stuart Mill, *Utilitarianism*, p. 9 *sq.*

emotional origin. The case is similar with many of the moral judgments ordinarily passed by men. They are applications of some accepted general rule: conformity or non-conformity to the rule decides the rightness or wrongness of the act judged. But whether the rule be the result of a person's independent deductions, or be based upon authority, human or divine, the fact that his moral consciousness recognises it as valid implies that it has an emotional sanction in his own mind.

Whilst the import of the predicate of a moral judgment may thus in every case be traced back to an emotion in him who pronounces the judgment, it is generally assumed to possess the character of universality or "objectivity" as well. The statement that an act is good or bad does not merely refer to an individual emotion; as will be shown subsequently, it always has reference to an emotion of a more public character. Very often it even implies some vague assumption that the act must be recognised as good or bad by everybody who possesses a sufficient knowledge of the case and of all attendant circumstances, and who has a "sufficiently developed" moral consciousness. We are not willing to admit that our moral convictions are a mere matter of taste, and we are inclined to regard convictions differing from our own as errors. This characteristic of our moral judgments has been adduced as an argument against the emotionalist theory of moral origins, and has led to the belief that the moral concepts represent qualities which are discerned by reason.

Cudworth, Clarke, Price, and Reid are names which recall to our mind a theory according to which the morality of actions is perceived by the intellect, just as are number, diversity, causation, proportion. "Morality is eternal and immutable," says Richard Price. "Right and wrong, it appears, denote what actions are. Now whatever any thing is, that it is, not by will, or decree, or power, but by nature and necessity. Whatever a triangle or circle is, that it is unchangeably and eternally. . . . The same is to be said of right and wrong, of moral good and evil, as far as they express real characters of actions. They must immutably and necessarily belong to those actions of which they are truly affirmed."[6] And as having a real existence outside the mind, they can only be discerned by the understanding. It is true that this discernment is accompanied with an emotion: "Some impressions of pleasure or pain, satisfaction or disgust, generally attend our perceptions of virtue and vice. But these are merely their effects and concomitants, and not the perceptions themselves, which ought no more to be confounded with them, than a particular truth (like that for which Pythagoras offered a hecatomb) ought to be confounded with the pleasure that may attend the discovery of it."[7]

According to another doctrine, the moral predicates, though not regarded as expressions of "theoretical" truth, nevertheless derive all their import from reason—from "practical" or "moral" reason, as it is variously called. Thus Professor Sidgwick holds that the fundamental notions represented by the word "ought" or "right," which moral judgments contain expressly or by implication, are essentially different from all notions representing facts of physical or psychical experience, and he refers such judgments to the "reason," understood as a faculty of cognition. By this he implies "that what ought to be is a possible object of knowledge, *i.e.*, that what I judge ought to be, must, unless I am in error, be similarly judged by all rational beings who judge truly of the matter." The moral judgments contain moral

---

[6] Price, *Review of the Principal Questions in Morals*, pp. 63, 74 *sq.*
[7] *Ibid*. p. 63.

truths, and "cannot legitimately be interpreted as judgments respecting the present or future existence of human feelings or any facts of the sensible world."[8]

Yet our tendency to objectivise the moral judgments is not sufficient ground for referring them to the province of reason. If, in this respect, there is a difference between these judgments and others that are rooted in the subjective sphere of experience, it is, largely, a difference in degree rather than in kind. The aesthetic judgments, which indisputably have an emotional origin, also lay claim to a certain amount of "objectivity." By saying of a piece of music that it is beautiful, we do not merely mean that it gives ourselves aesthetic enjoyment, but we make a latent assumption that it must have a similar effect upon everybody who is sufficiently musical to appreciate it. This objectivity ascribed to judgments which have a merely subjective origin springs in the first place from the similarity of the mental constitution of men, and, generally speaking, the tendency to regard them as objective is greater in proportion as the impressions vary less in each particular case. If "there is no disputing of tastes," that is because taste is so extremely variable; and yet even in this instance we recognise a certain "objective" standard by speaking of a "bad" and a "good" taste. On the other hand, if the appearance of objectivity in the moral judgments is so illusive as to make it seem necessary to refer them to reason, that is partly on account of the comparatively uniform nature of the moral consciousness.

Society is the school in which men learn to distinguish between right and wrong. The headmaster is Custom, and the lessons are the same for all. The first moral judgments were pronounced by public opinion; public indignation and public approval are the prototypes of the moral emotions. As regards questions of morality, there was, in early society, practically no difference of opinion; hence a character of universality, or objectivity, was from the very beginning attached to all moral judgments. And when, with advancing civilisation, this unanimity was to some extent disturbed by individuals venturing to dissent from the opinions of the majority, the disagreement was largely due to facts which in no way affected the moral principle, but had reference only to its application.

Most people follow a very simple method in judging of an act. Particular modes of conduct have their traditional labels, many of which are learnt with language itself; and the moral judgment commonly consists simply in labelling the act according to certain obvious characteristics which it presents in common with others belonging to the same group. But a conscientious and intelligent judge proceeds in a different manner. He carefully examines all the details connected with the act, the external and internal conditions under which it was performed, its consequences, its motive; and, since the moral estimate in a large measure depends upon the regard paid to these circumstances, his judgment may differ greatly from that of the man in the street, even though the moral standard which they apply be exactly the same. But to acquire a full insight into all the details which are apt to influence the moral value of an act is in many cases anything but easy, and this naturally increases the disagreement. There is thus in every advanced society a diversity of opinion regarding the moral value of certain modes of conduct which results from circumstances of a purely intellectual character—from the knowledge or ignorance of positive facts—and involves no discord in principle.

Now it has been assumed by the advocates of various ethical theories that all the

---

[8] Sidgwick, *Methods of Ethics,* pp. 25, 33 *sq.*

differences of moral ideas originate in this way, and that there is some ultimate standard which must be recognised as authoritative by everybody who understands it rightly. According to Bentham, the rectitude of utilitarianism has been contested only by those who have not known their own meaning: "When a man attempts to combat the principle of utility . . . his arguments, if they prove anything, prove not that the principle is wrong, but that, according to the applications he supposes to be made of it, it is misapplied."[9] Mr. Spencer, to whom good conduct is that "which conduces to life in each and all," believes that he has the support of "the true moral consciousness," or "moral consciousness proper," which, whether in harmony or in conflict with the "pro-ethical" sentiment, is vaguely or distinctly recognised as the rightful ruler.[10] Samuel Clarke, the intuitionist, again, is of the opinion that if a man endowed with reason denies the eternal and necessary moral differences of things, it is the very same "as if a man that has the use of his sight, should at the same time that he beholds the sun, deny that there is any such thing as light in the world; or as if a man that understands Geometry or Arithmetic should deny the most obvious and known proportions of lines or numbers."[11] In short, all disagreement as to questions of morals is attributed to ignorance or misunderstanding.

The influence of intellectual considerations upon moral judgments is certainly immense. We shall find that the evolution of the moral consciousness to a large extent consists in its development from the unreflecting to the reflecting, from the unenlightened to the enlightened. All higher emotions are determined by cognitions; they arise from "the presentation of determinate objective conditions";[12] and moral enlightenment implies a true and comprehensive presentation of those objective conditions by which the moral emotions, according to their very nature, are determined. Morality may thus in a much higher degree than, for instance, beauty be a subject of instruction and of profitable discussion, in which persuasion is carried by the representation of existing data. But although in this way many differences may be accorded, there are points in which unanimity cannot be reached even by the most accurate presentation of facts or the subtlest process of reasoning.

Whilst certain phenomena will almost of necessity arouse similar moral emotions in every mind which perceives them clearly, there are others with which the case is different. The emotional constitution of man does not present the same uniformity as the human intellect. Certain cognitions inspire fear in nearly every breast; but there are brave men and cowards in the world, independently of the accuracy with which they realise impending danger. Some cases of suffering can hardly fail to awaken compassion in the most pitiless heart; but the sympathetic dispositions of men vary greatly, both in regard to the beings with whose sufferings they are ready to sympathise, and with reference to the intensity of the emotion. The same holds good for the moral emotions. The existing diversity of opinion as to the rights of different classes of men, and of the lower animals, which springs from emotional differences, may no doubt be modified by a clearer insight into certain facts, but no perfect agreement can be expected as long as the conditions under which the emotional dispositions are formed remain unchanged. Whilst an enlightened mind *must* recognize the complete or relative irresponsibility of an animal, a child, or a

[9] Bentham, *Principles of Morals and Legislation*, p. 4 *sq.*

[10] Spencer, *Principles of Ethics*, i. 45, 337 *sq.*

[11] Clarke, *Discourse concerning the Unchangeable Obligations of Natural Religion*, p. 179.

[12] Marshall, *Pain, Pleasure, and Aesthetics*, p. 83.

madman, and *must* be influenced in its moral judgment by the motives of an act—no intellectual enlightenment, no scrutiny of facts, can decide how far the interests of the lower animals should be regarded when conflicting with those of men, or how far a person is bound, or allowed, to promote the welfare of his nation, or his own welfare, at the cost of that of other nations or other individuals. Professor Sidgwick's well-known moral axiom, "I ought not to prefer my own lesser good to the greater good of another,"[13] would, if explained to a Fuegian or a Hottentot, be regarded by him, not as self-evident, but as simply absurd; nor can it claim general acceptance even among ourselves. Who is that "Another" to whose greater good I ought not to prefer my own lesser good? A fellow-countryman, a savage, a criminal, a bird, a fish—all without distinction? It will, perhaps, be argued that on this, and on all other points of morals, there would be general agreement, if only the moral consciousness of men were sufficiently developed.[14] But then, when speaking of a "sufficiently developed" moral consciousness (beyond insistence upon a full insight into governing facts of each case), we practically mean nothing else than agreement with our own moral convictions. The expression is faulty and deceptive, because, if intended to mean anything more, it presupposes an objectivity of the moral judgments which they do not possess, and at the same time seems to be proving what it presupposes. We may speak of an intellect as sufficiently developed to grasp a certain truth, because truth is objective; but it is not proved to be objective by the fact that it is recognised as true by a "sufficiently developed" intellect. The objectivity of truth lies in the recognition of facts as true by all who understand them *fully*, whilst the appeal to a *sufficient* knowledge assumes their objectivity. To the verdict of a perfect intellect, that is, an intellect which knows everything existing, all would submit; but we can form no idea of a moral consciousness which could lay claim to a similar authority. If the believers in an all-good God, who has revealed his will to mankind, maintain that they in this revelation possess a perfect moral standard, and that, consequently, what is in accordance with such a standard must be objectively right, it may be asked what they mean by an "all-good" God. And in their attempt to answer this question, they would inevitably have to assume the objectivity they wanted to prove.

The error we commit by attributing objectivity to moral estimates becomes particularly conspicuous when we consider that these estimates have not only a certain quality, but a certain quantity. There are different degrees of badness and goodness, a duty may be more or less stringent, a merit may be smaller or greater.[15] These quantitative differences are due to the emotional origin of all moral concepts. Emotions vary in intensity almost indefinitely, and the moral emotions form no exception to this rule. Indeed, it may be fairly doubted whether the same mode of conduct ever arouses exactly the same degree of indignation or approval in any two individuals. Many of these differences are of course too subtle to be manifested in the moral judgment; but very frequently the intensity of the emotion is indicated by special words, or by the way in which the judgment is pronounced. It should be noticed, however, that the quantity of the estimate

[13] Sidgwick, *op. cit.* p. 383.

[14] This, in fact, was the explanation given by Professor Sidgwick himself in a conversation which I had with him regarding his moral axioms.

[15] It will be shown in a following chapter why there are no degrees of rightness. This concept implies accordance with the moral law. The adjective "right" means that duty is fulfilled.

expressed in a moral predicate is not identical with the intensity of the moral emotion which a certain mode of conduct arouses on a special occasion. We are liable to feel more indignant if an injury is committed before our eyes than if we read of it in a newspaper, and yet we admit that the degree of wrongness is in both cases the same. The quantity of moral estimates is determined by the intensity of the emotions which their objects tend to evoke under exactly similar external circumstances.

Besides the relative uniformity of moral opinions, there is another circumstance which tempts us to objectivise moral judgments, namely, the authority which, rightly or wrongly, is ascribed to moral rules. From our earliest childhood we are taught that certain acts *are* right and that others *are* wrong. Owing to their exceptional importance for human welfare, the facts of the moral consciousness are emphasised in a much higher degree than any other subjective facts. We are allowed to have our private opinions about the beauty of things, but we are not so readily allowed to have our private opinions about right and wrong. The moral rules which are prevalent in the society to which we belong are supported by appeals not only to human, but to divine, authority, and to call in question their validity is to rebel against religion as well as against public opinion. Thus the belief in a moral order of the world has taken hardly less firm hold of the human mind than the belief in a natural order of things. And the moral law has retained its authoritativeness even when the appeal to an external authority has been regarded as inadequate. It filled Kant with the same awe as the star-spangled firmament. According to Butler, conscience is "a faculty in kind and in nature supreme over all others, and which bears its own authority of being so."[16] Its supremacy is said to be "felt and tacitly acknowledged by the worst no less than by the best of men."[17] Adam Smith calls the moral faculties the "viceregents of God within us," who "never fail to punish the violation of them by the torments of inward shame and self-condemnation; and, on the contrary, always reward obedience with tranquillity of mind, with contentment, and self-satisfaction."[18] Even Hutcheson, who raises the question why the moral sense should not vary in different men as the palate does, considers it "to be naturally destined to command all the other powers."[19]

Authority is an ambiguous word. It may indicate knowledge of truth, and it may indicate a rightful power to command obedience. The authoritativeness attributed to the moral law has often reference to both kinds of authority. The moral lawgiver lays down his rules in order that they should be obeyed, and they are authoritative in so far as they have to be obeyed. But he is also believed to know what is right and wrong, and his commands are regarded as expressions of moral truths. As we have seen, however, this latter kind of authority involves a false assumption as to the nature of the moral predicates, and it cannot be justly inferred from the power to command.

In spite of all this, however, the supreme authority assigned to the moral law is not altogether an illusion. It really exists in the minds of the best, and is nominally acknowledged by the many. By this I do not refer to the universal admission that the moral law, whether obeyed or not, ought under all circumstances to be obeyed; for this is the same as to say that what ought to be ought to be. But it is recognised,

[16] Butler, 'Sermon II.—Upon Human Nature,' in *Analogy of Religion, &c.* p. 403.
[17] Dugald Stewart, *Philosophy of the Active and Moral Powers of Man,* i. 302.
[18] Adam Smith, *Theory of Moral Sentiments,* p. 235.
[19] Ziegler, *Social Ethics,* p. 103.

in theory at least, that morality, either alone or in connection with religion, possesses a higher value than anything else; that rightness and goodness are preferable to all other kinds of mental superiority, as well as of physical excellence. If this theory is not more commonly acted upon, that is due to its being, in most people, much less the outcome of their own feelings than of instruction from the outside. It is ultimately traceable to some great teacher whose own mind was ruled by the idea of moral perfection, and whose words became sacred on account of his supreme wisdom, like Confucius or Buddha,[20] or on religious grounds, like Jesus. The authority of the moral law is thus only an expression of a strongly developed, overruling moral consciousness. It can hardly, as Mr. Sidgwick maintains, be said to "depend upon" the conception of the objectivity of duty.[21] On the contrary, it must be regarded as a cause of this conception—not only, as has already been pointed out, where it is traceable to some external authority, but where it results from the strength of the individual's own moral emotions. As clearness and distinctness of the conception of an object easily produce the belief in its truth, so the intensity of a moral emotion makes him who feels it disposed to objectivise the moral estimate to which it gives rise, in other words, to assign to it universal validity. The enthusiast is more likely than anybody else to regard his judgments as true, and so is the moral enthusiast with reference to his moral judgments. The intensity of his emotions makes him the victim of an illusion.

The presumed objectivity of moral judgments thus being a chimera, there can be no moral truth in the sense in which this term is generally understood. The ultimate reason for this is that the moral concepts are based upon emotions, and that the contents of an emotion fall entirely outside the category of truth. But it may be true or not that we have a certain emotion, it may be true or not that a given mode of conduct has a tendency to evoke in us moral indignation or moral approval. Hence a moral judgment is true or false according as its subject has or has not that tendency which the predicate attributes to it. If I say that it is wrong to resist evil, and yet resistance to evil has no tendency whatever to call forth in me an emotion of moral disapproval, then my judgment is false.

If there are no general moral truths, the object of scientific ethics cannot be to fix rules for human conduct, the aim of all science being the discovery of some truth. It has been said by Bentham and others that moral principles cannot be proved because they are first principles which are used to prove everything else.[22] But the real reason for their being inaccessible to demonstration is that, owing to their very nature, they can never be true. If the word "Ethics," then, is to be used as the name for a science, the object of that science can only be to study the moral consciousness as a fact.[23]

Ethical subjectivism is commonly held to be a dangerous doctrine, destructive to morality, opening the door to all sorts of libertinism. If that which appears to each

[20] Besides the ideal king, the personification of Power and Justice, another ideal has played an important part in the formation of early Buddhist ideas regarding their Master. . . . It was the ideal of a perfectly Wise Man, the personification of Wisdom, the Buddha." (Rhys Davids, *Hibbert Lectures on Some Points in the History of Buddhism*, p. 141).

[21] Sidgwick, *op. cit.* p. 104.

[22] Bentham, *Principles of Morals and Legislation*, p. 4. Höffding, *Etik*, p. 43.

[23] *Cf.* Simmel, *Einleitung in die Moralwissenschaft*, i. p. iii. *sq.*; Westermarck, 'Normative und psychologische Ethik,' in *Dritter Internationaler Congress für Psychologie in München*, p. 428 *sqq.*

man as right or good stands for that which is right or good; if he is allowed to make his own law, or to make no law at all; then, it is said, everybody has the natural right to follow his caprice and inclinations, and to hinder him from doing so is an infringement on his rights, a constraint with which no one is bound to comply provided that he has the power to evade it. This inference was long ago drawn from the teaching of the Sophists,[24] and it will no doubt be still repeated as an argument against any theorist who dares to assert that nothing can be said to be truly right or wrong.

To this argument may, first, be objected that a scientific theory is not invalidated by the mere fact that it is likely to cause mischief. The unfortunate circumstance that there do exist dangerous things in the world proves that something may be dangerous and yet true. Another question is whether any scientific truth really is mischievous on the whole, although it may cause much discomfort to certain people. I venture to believe that this, at any rate, is not the case with that form of ethical subjectivism which I am here advocating. The charge brought against the Sophists does not at all apply to it. I do not even subscribe to that beautiful modern sophism which admits every man's conscience to be an infallible guide. If we had to recognise, or rather if we did recognise, as right everything which is held to be right by anybody, savage or Christian, criminal or saint, morality would really suffer a serious loss. But we do not, and we cannot, do so. My moral judgments are my own judgments; they spring from my own moral consciousness; they judge of the conduct of other men not from their point of view, but from mine, not with primary reference to their opinions about right and wrong, but with reference to my own. Most of us indeed admit that, when judging of an act, we also ought to take into consideration the moral conviction of the agent, and the agreement or disagreement between his doing and his idea of what he ought to do. But although we hold it to be wrong of a person to act against his conscience, we may at the same time blame him for having such a conscience as he has. Ethical subjectivism covers all such cases. It certainly does not allow everybody to follow his own inclinations; nor does it lend sanction to arbitrariness and caprice. Our moral consciousness belongs to our mental constitution, which we cannot change as we please. We approve and we disapprove because we cannot do otherwise. Can we help feeling pain when the fire burns us? Can we help sympathising with our friends? Are these phenomena less necessary, less powerful in their consequences, because they fall within the subjective sphere of experience? So, too, why should the moral law command less obedience because it forms part of our own nature?

Far from being a danger, ethical subjectivism seems to me more likely to be an acquisition for moral practice. Could it be brought home to people that there is no absolute standard in morality, they would perhaps be somewhat more tolerant in their judgments, and more apt to listen to the voice of reason. If the right has an objective existence, the moral consciousness has certainly been playing at blindman's buff ever since it was born, and will continue to do so until the extinction of the human race. But who does admit this? The popular mind is always inclined to believe that it possesses the knowledge of what *is* right and wrong, and to regard public opinion as the reliable guide of conduct. We have, to be sure, no reason to regret that there are men who rebel against the established rules of

[24] Zeller, *History of Greek Philosophy*, ii. 475.

morality; it is more deplorable that the rebels are so few, and that, consequently, the old rules change so slowly. Far above the vulgar idea that the right is a settled something to which everybody has to adjust his opinions, rises the conviction that it has its existence in each individual mind, capable of any expansion, proclaiming its own right to exist, if needs be, venturing to make a stand against the whole world. Such a conviction makes for progress.

The Ethical Implications of Cultural Relativity

Carl Wellman

Carl Wellman (1926-   ) teaches at Washington University in St. Louis and is the author of *The Language of Ethics* (1961) and numerous journal articles.

It is often thought that the discoveries of anthropology have revolutionary implications for ethics. Readers of Sumner, Benedict, and Herskovits are apt to come away with the impression that the only moral obligation is to conform to one's society, that polygamy is as good as monogamy, or that no ethical judgment can be rationally justified. While these anthropologists might complain that they are being misinterpreted, they would not deny that their real intent is to challenge the traditional view of morals. Even the anthropologist whose scientific training has made him skeptical of sweeping generalities and wary of philosophical entanglements is inclined to believe that the scientific study of cultures has undermined the belief in ethical absolutes of any kind.

Just what has been discovered that forces us to revise our ethics? Science has shown that certain things that were once thought to be absolute are actually relative to culture. Something is relative to culture when it varies with and is causally determined by culture. Clearly, nothing can be both relative to culture and absolute, for to be absolute is to be fixed and invariable, independent of man and the same for all men.

Exactly which things are relative and in what degree is a question still being debated by cultural anthropologists. Important as this question is, I do not propose to discuss it. It is the empirical scientists who must tell us which things vary from culture to culture and to what extent each is causally determined by its culture. It is not for me to question the findings of the anthropologists in this area. Instead, let me turn to the philosophical problem of the implications of cultural relativity. Assuming for the moment that cultural relativity is a fact, what follows for ethics?

What follows depends in part upon just what turns out to be relative. Anthropologists are apt to use the word "values" to refer indiscriminately to the

Source: *Journal of Philosophy*, Vol. 60, No. 7 (1963), 169-184. Reprinted by permission of the Journal and the author.

things which have value, the characteristics which give these things their value, the attitudes of the persons who value these things, and the judgments of those people that these things have value. Similarly, one finds it hard to be sure whether "morals" refers to the mores of a people, the set of principles an observer might formulate after observing their conduct, the practical beliefs the people themselves entertain, or the way they feel about certain kinds of conduct. Until such ambiguities are cleared up, one hardly knows what is being asserted when it is claimed that "values" or "morals" are relative.

It seems to me there are at least ten quite different things of interest to the ethicist that the anthropologist might discover to be relative to culture: mores, social institutions, human nature, acts, goals, value experiences, moral emotions, moral concepts, moral judgments, and moral reasoning. Since I can hardly discuss all the ethical conclusions that various writers have tried to draw from these different facts of cultural relativity, what I propose to do is to examine critically the reasoning by which one ethical conclusion might be derived from each of them.

I

It has long been recognized that mores are relative to culture. Mores are those customs which are enforced by social pressure. They are established patterns of action to which the individual is expected to conform and from which he deviates only at the risk of disapproval and punishment. It seems clear that mores vary from society to society and that the mores of any given society depend upon its culture. What does this imply for ethics?

The conclusion most frequently drawn is that what is right in one society may be wrong in another. For example, although it would be wrong for one of us to kill his aged parents, this very act is right for an Eskimo. This is because our mores are different from those of Eskimo society, and it is the mores that make an act right or wrong.

Let us grant, for the sake of discussion, that different societies do have different mores. Why should we grant that the mores make an act right or wrong? It has been claimed that this is true by definition. "Right" simply means according to the mores, and "wrong" means in violation of the mores. There is something to be said for this analysis of our concepts of right and wrong. It seems to explain both the imperativeness and the impersonality of obligation.

The "ought" seems to tell one what to do and yet to be more than the command of any individual; perhaps its bindingness lies in the demands of society. Attractive as this interpretation appears at first glance, I cannot accept it. It can be shown that no naturalistic analysis of the meaning of ethical words is adequate. In addition, this particular analysis is objectionable in that it makes it self-contradictory to say that any customary way of acting is wrong. No doubt, social reformers are often confused, but they are not always inconsistent.

If the view that the mores make an act right or wrong is not true by definition, it amounts to the moral principle that one ought always to conform to the mores of his society. None of the ways in which this principle is usually supported is adequate. (a) Any society unconsciously develops those mores which are conducive to survival and well-being under its special circumstances. Each individual ought to obey the mores of his society because this is the best way to promote the good life for the members of that society. I admit that there is a tendency for any society to develop those mores which fit its special circumstances, but I doubt that this is more than a tendency. There is room for reform in most societies, and this is particularly true when conditions are changing for one reason or another. (b) One ought to obey the mores of his society because disobedience would tend to destroy those mores. Without mores any society would lapse into a state of anarchy that would be intolerable for its members. It seems to me that this argument deserves to be taken seriously, but it does not prove that one ought always to obey the mores of his society. What it does show is that one ought generally to obey the mores of his society and that whenever he considers disobedience, he should give due weight to the effects of his example upon social stability. (c) One ought to obey the mores of his society because disobedience tends to undermine their existence. It is important to preserve the mores, not simply to avoid anarchy, but because it is their mores which give shape and meaning to the life of any people. I grant that the individual does tend to think of his life in terms of the mores of his group and that anything which disrupts those mores tends to rob his life of significance. But once again, all this shows is that one should conform to the mores of his society on the whole. Although there is some obligation to conformity, this is not the only nor the most important obligation on the member of any society.

Therefore, it does not seem to me that one can properly say that the mores make an act right or wrong. One cannot define the meaning of these ethical words in terms of the mores, nor can one maintain the ethical principle that one ought always to obey the mores of his society. If the mores do not make acts right or wrong, the fact that different societies have different mores does not imply that the same kind of act can be right in one society and wrong in another.

II

Cultural relativity seems to apply to institutions as well as to mores. A social institution is a type of organization; it involves a pattern of activity in which two or more people play recognized roles. The family, the church, the government, the liberal arts college, the bridge club are all social institutions. Institutions can be classified more or less specifically. Thus monogamy, polygamy, and polyandry are specific institutions which fall under the generic institution of the family. Since the specific form an institution takes seems to vary from society to society depending upon the culture of that society, let us grant that social institutions are relative to culture. What does this imply for ethics?

A conclusion that is sometimes drawn is that we should never try to adopt an institution from another society or seek to impose one of our institutions upon another people. The main argument for this view is that each institution is an expression of the total culture of which it is a part. To try to take an institution out of its cultural environment is sure to maim or even kill it; to try to bring an institution into an alien culture is likely to disorganize and even destroy that cultural pattern. Thus the attempt to transport an institution from one society to another will fail to achieve its intended result and will produce many unintended and socially undesirable effects.

No doubt the attempt to import or export a social institution is often a dismal failure. The transported institution becomes a mere caricature of its former self, and the society into which it is introduced becomes demoralized or even destroyed. Extreme caution is certainly necessary. But is it not incautious to conclude that the attempt will always fail? The most glaring examples of cultural demoralization and destruction, such as the intervention of the white man in Africa, have involved much more than the imposition of one or two institutions. Moreover, some institutions may be less alien to a given culture than others. If so, there might be some institutions that the society could adopt with only minor modifications. In fact, societies seem to have been borrowing from one another for centuries. While the effects of this borrowing have often been bad, they have not always been totally destructive or even grossly demoralizing. Occasionally they may have been beneficial. It seems unnecessary to conclude that we should never import or export an institution from the fact that social institutions are culturally relative.

III

Another thing which may be relative to culture is human nature. As soon as one ponders the differences between the Chinese aristocrat and the Australian bushman, the American tycoon and the Indian yogi, one finds it hard to believe that there is anything basic to human nature which is shared by all men. And reflection upon the profound effects of enculturation easily leads one to the conclusion that what a man is depends upon the society in which he has been brought up. Therefore, let us assume that human nature is culturally relative and see what this implies.

This seems to imply that no kind of action, moral character, or social institution is made inevitable by human nature. This conclusion is important because it cuts the ground out from under one popular type of justification in ethics. For example, capitalism is sometimes defended as an ideal on the grounds that this is the only economic system that is possible in the light of man's greedy and competitive nature. Or it might be claimed that adultery is permissible because the ideal of marital fidelity runs counter to man's innate drives or instincts. If there is no fixed human nature, such arguments are left without any basis.

One may wonder, however, whether the only alternatives are an entirely fixed and an entirely plastic human nature. It might be that enculturation could mold a human being but only within certain limits. These limits might exist either because certain parts of human nature are not at all plastic or because all parts are only moderately plastic. For example, it might turn out that the need for food and the tendency to grow in a certain way cannot be modified at all by enculturation, or it might turn out that every element in human nature can be modified in some ways but not in others. In either case, what a man becomes would depend partly upon enculturation and partly upon the nature of the organism being enculturated.

Thus cultural relativity may be a matter of degree. Before we can decide just what follows from the fact that human nature is relative to culture, we must know how far and in what ways it is relative. If there are certain limits to the plasticity of human nature, these do rule out some kinds of action, character, or institution. But anthropology indicates that within any such limits a great many alternatives remain. Human nature may make eating inevitable, but what we eat and when we eat and how we eat is up to us. At least we can say that to the degree that human nature is relative to culture no kind of action, moral character, or social institution is made possible by human nature.

IV

It has been claimed that acts are also relative to culture. This is to say that the same general type of action may take on specific differences when performed in different societies because those societies have different cultures. For example, it is one thing for one of us to kill his aged parent; it is quite a different thing for an Eskimo to do such an act. One difference lies in the consequences of these two acts. In our society, disposing of old and useless parents merely allows one to live in greater luxury; to an Eskimo this act may mean the difference between barely adequate subsistence and malnutrition for himself and his family. What are we to make of this fact that the nature of an act is culturally relative?

One possible conclusion is that the same kind of act may be right in one society and wrong in another. This presupposes that the rightness of an act depends upon its consequences and that its consequences may vary from society to society. Since I accept these presuppositions, I agree that the rightness or wrongness of an act is relative to its social context.

It is important, however, to distinguish this conclusion from two others with which it is often confused. To say that the rightness of an act is relative to the society in which it is performed is not to say that exactly the same sort of act can be both right and wrong. It is because the social context makes the acts different in kind that one can be right while the other is wrong. Compare an act of infanticide in our society with an act of infanticide in some South Seas society. Are these two acts the same or different? They are of the same kind inasmuch as both are acts of killing an infant. On the other hand, they are different in that such an act may be necessary to preserve the balance between family size and food resources in the South Seas while this is not the case in our society. These two acts are generically similar but specifically different; that is, they belong to different species of the same genus. Therefore, the conclusion that the same kind of act may be right in one society and wrong in another does not amount to saying that two acts which are precisely the same in every respect may differ in rightness or wrongness.

Neither is this conclusion to be confused with the view that acts are made right or wrong by the mores of society. No doubt our society disapproves of infanticide and some South Seas societies approve of it, but it is not *this* which makes infanticide wrong for us and right for them. If infanticide is wrong for us and right for them, it is because acts of infanticide have very different consequences in our society and in theirs, not because the practice is discouraged here and customary there.

V

The goals that individuals or groups aim for also seem relative to culture. What objects people select as goals varies from society to society depending upon the cultures of those societies. One group may strive for social prestige and the accumulation of great wealth, another may aim at easy comfort and the avoidance of any danger, a third may seek military glory and the conquest of other peoples. What follows from this fact of cultural relativity?

This fact is often taken as a basis for arguing that it is impossible to compare the value of acts, institutions, or total ways of life belonging to different societies. The argument rests on the assumptions that acts, institutions, and ways of life are means directed at certain ends, that means can be evaluated only in terms of their ends, and that ends are incommensurable with respect to value.

Granted these assumptions, the argument seems a good one, but I doubt that ends are really incommensurable. It seems to me that we can recognize that certain ends are more worth while than others, for example that pleasure is intrinsically better than pain. I may be mistaken, but until this has been shown, the conclusion that it is impossible to compare the value of acts, institutions, or ways of life belonging to different societies has not been established.

VI

People from different societies apparently experience the same object or situation in quite different ways depending upon the cultural differences between their societies. The satisfying experience that a cultured Chinese might derive from eating bird's nest soup would be diametrically opposed to the experience I would undergo if I forced myself to gulp down my helping of that exotic dish out of politeness. Again, an experience which I would greatly value, sitting in the bleachers watching the Red Sox clinch the pennant, would be nothing but a boring observation of meaningless motions accompanied by the sensations of scorching sun, trickling sweat, and unyielding benches to a Hottentot visitor. In large measure the nature of any experience is determined by the process of enculturation that the experiencer has undergone. Thus, value experiences are also relative to culture.

It might seem to follow that the same experience could be good to one person and bad to another, but this is just what does *not* follow. The difference in value stems from the fact that, although confronted with similar objects or situations, the two people have very different experiences. The nature of a person's experience depends upon the kind of person he has become through the process of enculturation as much as upon the external stimulus. It would be a mistake to conclude that qualitatively identical experiences are good to me and bad to the Hottentot. Although he and I are in the same ballpark watching the same game, we are having very different experiences.

What one should conclude is that the same kind of object or situation can have different values to people from different societies. This follows from the fact that the nature of a person's experience depends in large measure upon the way in which he has been enculturated, together with the assumption that the value of any object or situation depends upon its effects on experience. Since my ethical view is that the value of objects and situations is derived from their impact upon experience, I accept the conclusion that the same kind of object or situation can have very different values to people who come from different cultures.

VII

It appears that moral emotions are also relative to culture. What a person desires, approves, or feels guilty about seems to vary from society to society depending upon the cultural differences between those societies. What does the fact that moral emotions are culturally relative imply for ethics?

One possible conclusion would be that the same kind of act or person can be morally good in one society and morally bad in another. This is supposed to follow from the fact that the same kind of act or person can be approved in one society and disapproved in another together with the view that to be morally good or bad is simply to be approved or disapproved.

That infanticide is approved in certain South Seas societies and disapproved in ours need not be doubted. That infanticide constitutes exactly the same kind of act in the two societies is, as we have seen, more dubious. But even if it did, I would not accept the conclusion in question; for I would not admit that the moral value of any act or person depends upon whether it is approved or disapproved. That the grounds for moral evaluation lie outside the moral emotions can be seen by the fact that it always makes sense to ask someone *why* he approves or disapproves of something. If approving or disapproving made its object morally good or bad, there would be no need of such justification. Thus, the fact that moral emotions are culturally relative does not prove that identical acts or persons can be morally good in one society and morally bad in another.

VIII

Both linguistic and psychological studies have suggested that people living in different societies conceptualize their experience in different ways. Probably, moral concepts vary from society to society depending upon the cultural backgrounds from which they arise. The ancient Greek thought of virtue quite differently from the modern American; the Christian conception of obligation is probably absent from the mind of the African who has escaped the influence of any missionary. What are we to conclude from the fact that moral concepts are relative to culture?

The obvious implication appears to be that people of different cultural backgrounds are almost sure to disagree on any ethical question. Obvious as it may seem, this is not implied at all. In fact, people using different concepts could never disagree, for disagreement presupposes that both parties are thinking in the same terms. For one thing, on what question are they supposed to be disagreeing? If each person is using his own set of concepts, each person formulates his own question in his own terms. And if the two persons do not have any common set of ethical concepts there is no way for formulating a single question that will be intelligible to both of them. Again, in what sense do their respective answers disagree? When an American says that Poland is undemocratic and a Russian insists that it is a fine example of democracy, it appears that they are disagreeing. No doubt they do disagree in many ways, but not in their utterances. Their statements are quite compatible, for they are using the word "democracy" in different senses. Similarly, people of different cultures would only seem to disagree if they attached different concepts to their ethical words.

The proper conclusion to draw is that any comparison between the ethical views of the members of different cultures can be only partial. As long as each view is stated only in its own terms, there can be no comparison between them; comparison becomes possible only when they are stated in the same set of concepts. But if the sets of concepts are not identical, any translation of one view into the language of the other or of both into some neutral language will be approximate at best. Even where something approaching adequate translation is possible, some of the meaning will be lost or something will be added that was not in the original concept. For this reason, any claim that the ethical views of people in different societies are either identical or contradictory is likely to tell only part of the story. To some extent, at least, the ethics of different cultures are incommensurate.

IX

The aspect of cultural relativity most often emphasized is that pertaining to moral judgments. Objects that the members of one society think to be good are considered bad by another group; acts considered wrong in one society are thought of as right in another. Moreover, these differences in judgments of value and obligation seem to reflect cultural differences between the respective societies. There is a great deal of evidence to suggest that ethical judgments are relative to culture.

To many anthropologists and philosophers it is a corollary of this fact that one of a set of contrary ethical judgments is no more valid than another, or, put positively, that all ethical judgments are equally valid. Unfortunately, there is a crucial ambiguity lurking in this epistemological thicket. Ethical judgments might have equal validity either because all are valid or because none are: similarly, one ethical judgment might be no more valid than another either because both are equally valid or because both are equally lacking in validity. Since these two interpretations are quite different, let us consider them separately.

On the first interpretation, the conclusion to be drawn from the fact that ethical judgments are relative to culture is that every moral judgment is valid for the society in which it is made. Instead of denying the objective validity of ethical judgments, this view affirms it, but in a qualified form which will allow for the variations in ethical belief.

There seem to be three main ways of defending this position. (a) Ethical judgments have objective validity because it is possible to justify them rationally. However, this validity is limited to a given society because the premises used in such justification are those which are agreed upon in that society. Since there are no universally accepted premises, no universal validity is possible. I would wish to deny that justification is real if it is limited in this way. If all our reasoning really does rest on certain premises which can be rejected by others without error, then we must give up the claim to objective validity. When I claim validity for ethical judgments, I intend to claim more than that it is possible to support them with logical arguments; I also claim that it is incorrect to deny the premises of such arguments. (b) Any ethical judgment is an expression of a total pattern of culture. Hence it is possible to justify any single judgment in terms of its coherence with the total cultural configuration of the judger. But one cannot justify the culture as a whole, for it is not part of a more inclusive pattern. Therefore, ethical judgments have objective validity, but only in terms of a given cultural pattern. I would make the same objection to this view as to the preceding one. Since it allows justification to rest upon an arbitrary foundation, it is inadequate to support any significant claim to objective validity. (c) Any ethical judgment has objective validity because it is an expression of a moral code. The validity of a moral code rests on the fact that without conformity to a common code social cohesion breaks down, leading to disastrous results. Since any given moral code provides cohesion for one and only one society, each ethical judgment has validity for a single society. There are at least two difficulties with this defense of objectivity. Surely one could deny some ethical judgments without destroying the entire moral code they reflect; not every judgment could be shown to be essential to social stability. Moreover, the argument seems to rest on the ethical judgment that one ought not to contribute to the breakdown of social stability. How is this judgment to be shown to be valid? One must either appeal to some other basis of validity or argue in a circle. None of these arguments to show that every moral judgment is valid for the society in which it is made is adequate.

On the second interpretation, the conclusion to be drawn from the fact that moral judgments are relative to culture is that moral judgments have no objective validity. This amounts to saying that the distinction between true and false, correct and incorrect, does not apply to such judgments. This conclusion obviously does not follow simply from the fact that people disagree about ethical questions. We do not deny the objective validity of scientific judgments either on the grounds that different scientists propose alternative theories or on the grounds that the members of some societies hold fast to many unscientific beliefs.

Why, then, does the fact that moral judgments are relative to culture imply that they have no objective validity? (a) Individuals make different ethical judgments because they judge in terms of different frames of reference, and they adopt these frames of reference uncritically from their cultures. Since ethical judgments are the product of enculturation rather than reasoning, they cannot claim rational justification. I do not find this argument convincing, for it seems to confuse the origin of a judgment with its justification. The causes of a judgment are one thing; the reasons for or against it are another. It remains to be shown that any information about what causes us to judge as we do has any bearing on the question of whether or not our judgments are correct. (b) It is impossible to settle ethical questions by using the scientific method. Therefore, there is no objective way to show that one ethical judgment is any more correct than another, and, in the absence of any method of establishing the claim to objective validity, it makes no sense to continue to make the claim. I will concede that, if there is no rational method of establishing ethical judgments, then we might as well give up the claim to objective validity. And if the scientific method is restricted to the testing of hypotheses by checking the predictions they imply against the results of observation and experiment, it does seem to be inapplicable to ethical questions. What I will not concede is the tacit assumption that the scientific method is the only method of establishing the truth. Observation and experimentation do not figure prominently in the method used by mathematicians. I even wonder whether the person who concludes that ethical judgments have no objective validity can establish *this* conclusion by using the scientific method. The fact that ethical judgments cannot be established scientifically does not by itself prove that they cannot be established by any method of reasoning. (c) There might be some method of settling ethical disputes, but it could not be a method of reasoning. Any possible reasoning would have to rest upon certain premises. Since the members of different societies start from different premises, there is no basis for argument that does not beg the question. I suspect, however, that we have been looking for our premises in the wrong place. The model of deduction tempts us to search for very general premises from which all our more specific judgments can be deduced.

Unfortunately, it is just in this area of universal moral principles that disagreement seems most frequent and irremedial. But suppose that these ethical generalizations are themselves inductions based upon particular moral judgments. Then we could argue for or against them in terms of relatively specific ethical judgments and the factual judgments that are in turn relevant to these. Until this possibility is explored further, we need not admit that there is no adequate basis for ethical reasoning. Thus it appears that none of these refutations of the objective validity of ethical judgments is really conclusive.

The fact that ethical judgments are relative to culture is often taken to prove that no ethical judgment can claim to be any more valid than any of its contraries. I have tried to show that on neither of the two possible interpretations of this conclusion does the conclusion necessarily follow from the fact of cultural relativity.

X

Finally, moral reasoning might turn out to be relative to culture. When some ethical statement is denied or even questioned, the person who made the statement is apt to leap to its defense. He attempts to justify his statement by producing reasons to support it. But speakers from different societies tend to justify their statements in different ways. The difference in their reasoning may be of two kinds. Either their reasoning may rest on different assumptions or they may draw inferences in a different manner. That is, the arguments they advance may either start from different premises or obey different logics. We can ignore the former case here; for it boils down to a difference in their judgments, and we have discussed that at length in the preceding section. Instead let us assume that people who belong to different societies tend to draw their moral conclusions according to different logics depending upon their respective cultures. What difference would it make if moral reasoning were thus culturally relative?

The most interesting conclusion that might be drawn from the fact that moral reasoning is relative to culture is that it has no objective validity. The claim to objective validity is empty where it cannot be substantiated. But how could one justify the claim that any given kind of moral reasoning is valid? To appeal to the same kind of reasoning would be circular. To appeal to some other kind of reasoning would not be sufficient to justify this kind; for each kind of reasoning involves principles of inference which go beyond, and therefore cannot be justified by appealing to, any other kind.

I find this line of argument inconclusive for several reasons. First, it is not clear that a given kind of reasoning cannot be justified by appealing to a different kind of reasoning. In fact, this seems to be a fairly common practice in logic. Various forms of syllogistic arguments can be shown to be valid by reducing them to arguments of the form Barbara. Again, a logician will sometimes justify certain rules for natural deduction by an involved logical argument which does not itself use these same rules. Second, in what sense is it impossible to show another person that my moral arguments are valid? I can show him that the various moral arguments I advance conform to the principles of my logic. If he does not accept these principles, he will remain unconvinced. This may show that I cannot persuade him that my arguments are valid, but does it show that I have not proved that they are? It is not obvious that persuading a person and proving a point are identical. Third, is the claim to objective validity always empty in the absence of any justification for it? Perhaps some reasoning is ultimate in that it requires no further justification. To assume the opposite seems to lead to an infinite regress. If every valid justification stands in need of further justification, no amount of justification would ever be sufficient.

I do not claim to have established the objective validity of moral reasoning. I am not even sure how that validity might be established or even whether it needs to be established. All I have been trying to do is to suggest that such validity is not ruled out by the fact, if it is a fact, that moral reasoning is relative to culture.

No doubt the reader will wish to challenge my acceptance or rejection of this or that particular conclusion. Quite apart from such specific ethical questions, however, there are certain over-all logical conclusions which seem to me inevitable. (1) What conclusions one can legitimately draw from the facts of cultural relativity will depend upon *which* facts one starts from. It is worth distinguishing between the relativity of mores, social institutions, human nature, acts, goals, value experiences, moral emotions, moral concepts, moral judgments, and moral reasoning; for each of these has different implications for ethics. (2) By themselves the facts of cultural relativity do not imply anything for ethics. Any argument that is both interesting and valid requires additional premises. Thus it is only in conjunction with certain statements that go beyond anthropology that the findings of anthropology have any bearing at all on ethics. (3) What conclusions one should draw will obviously depend upon which of these additional premises one accepts. Therefore, one's ethical and epistemological theory will determine the significance one will attach to cultural relativity. (4) Before we can criticize or even understand the arguments by which ethical conclusions are derived from the facts of such relativity, we must make these additional premises explicit and see what can be said for or against them. My main purpose in this paper has been to make a start in this complicated yet crucial task.

Suggested Readings

1. "Is Ethical Relativity Necessary? A Symposium," *Proceedings of the Aristotelian Society*, Supp. Vol. 17, London (1938).
2. Rader, Melvin, *Ethics and Society* (New York: Holt, 1950), Ch. 5.
3. Savery, B., "Relativity Versus Absolutism in Value-Theory," *The Journal of Philosophy*, Vol. 34 (Feb. 18, 1937), 85–93.
4. Stace, Walter, *The Concept of Morals* (New York: Macmillan, 1937), Chs. 1, 2. One of the best discussions.

HEDONISM AND BEYOND

What is it that makes us take an interest in persons? ... It is our capacity for understanding, evoking our response of reverence or love.

—*H. A. Hodges*

Earlier, in the introduction to this chapter, we pointed out that we can use the difference in generality of moral maxims to help systematize our morals. We illustrated this with the promise maxim; because the maxim "One should keep his promises" is more general than either of two instances of it (practicing fidelity to one's spouse and paying off one's loans), it enables us to integrate the two less general maxims. Now, as a prelude to the introduction of another issue in ethical theory, we will discuss other examples of the use of generality in trying to systematize morals.

Think of a maxim we learned as children, "You should divide the dessert evenly," and of a maxim attaining wider currency day by day, "Husbands and wives should take turns doing dishes (and other chores)." These are maxims of lower generality than "You should act fairly," which covers the other two.

The two relatively general maxims about promise keeping and acting fairly are not as general as it is possible for moral maxims to be. Just as they are more general than other maxims, so there are maxims more general than they. Logically, however, there must be a most general maxim, the highest maxim on the moral maxim pyramid. It seems as if the most general maxim would be "You should do that which is right," because no moral concept dealing with acts is more general than "right" is, except "wrong," which is equally general.

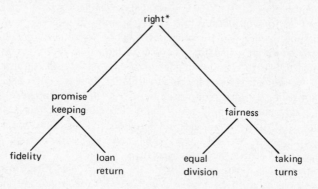

"Right" and "wrong" are the moral concepts we use to talk about human acts. "Good" and "bad" are also moral words; we use them to talk about

---

* Nothing is implied here about the number of levels nor about whether between the levels shown there are other levels.

experiences, human character, and things and their properties and relations. "Good" and "bad," too, are the most general of another set of concepts.

It has been claimed that having enough food to eat and having the respect of others are instances of the relatively more general good of satisfying our needs, in this instance, psychological and physical needs, and that obtaining an education and being free to make our own decisions are instances of the relatively more general good of realizing our human potentiality. Satisfying our needs and realizing our human potential are, in turn, instances of the most general concept of "good" itself.

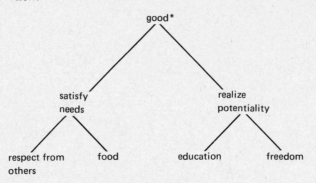

We can raise, now, another ethical theory question: What is the relation between the two general concepts the "right" and the "good"?

Jeremy Bentham, author of the first essay in this section, gave an answer that is called "utilitarianism." For Bentham, the rightness of an act depended on the goodness of its consequences, depended on the utility of the act in producing a balance of good over bad and producing a greater balance of good over bad than any other act possible under the circumstances. According to this theory, "good" is the primary moral concept and "right" is derivative from "good."

An act that we perform may have good consequences for some persons and bad consequences for others. Ratting on your Weathermen cell may have good consequences for you because the "feds" promise to give you immunity, but it has bad consequences for the other members of your cell. Which consequences are we to count in calculating the utility of ratting? Bentham thinks that in calculating the rightness or wrongness of an act we should count the act's good and bad consequences for every person affected; he was a "universal" utilitarian. Universal utilitarianism is contrasted with "egoistic" utilitarianism; the egoistic version claims that the only good and bad consequences that are pertinent in computing the utility of an act are the good and bad that will accrue to the computer himself. According to the universalist, the ratting was wrong; according to the egoist, the ratting was right.

In our culture, we tend to disapprove of ratting, snitching, informing, and betraying. We tend to be loyal to and to exact loyalty from our immediate friends and associates; our morality resembles or, perhaps, is a gang morality. As children we tended to form gangs as a sort of protective agency against parents, teachers, and other adults; we saw that our gang was our mutual-interest group

---

* Nothing is implied here about the number of levels nor about whether between the levels shown there are other levels.

and, in calculating the utility of ratting on our gang, we generally counted the consequences to ourselves and our fellow gang members and did not count the consequences to people who were not in the gang. Children and gangsters are somewhat limited universal utilitarians, "gang utilitarians." People who carry this morality into adulthood carry a gang morality with them.

Bentham was opposed to a gang utilitarianism, although it does move a step away from egoistic utilitarianism. We might ask why we should feel a greater loyalty to our gang than to humanity. Suppose a Weatherman changes his views. He finds that acts of terrorism and violence are producing bad consequences for people outside his Weathermen cell, and, further, he changes from a limited to a universal utilitarianism. Then, considering the consequences for everybody affected, he finds that the only morally right act for him to perform is to rat on his fellow Weathermen. If you have some reservations about morally condemning ratting, snitching, informing, and betraying and hold a utilitarian ethical theory, then you should produce an argument showing why limited utilitarianism is better than universal utilitarianism, an argument explaining why we should feel a greater loyalty to our fellow gang members than to humanity. Gangs are not necessarily small groups of people. Might they not be as large as nations? And isn't patriotism a form of gang loyalty?

Another ethical theory question is this: What and how many things are good? A utilitarian claims to base the rightness of acts on the goodness of their consequences. It is obvious that the utilitarian must address himself to distinguishing good consequences from bad ones. In answering this question, thinkers generally presuppose a distinction between something being good as a means and something being good in itself. For example, money seems good only as a means, whereas happiness seems to be good in itself; we don't wish to attain happiness because it is a means to something else. The ethical theory question can then be rephrased as: What and how many things are good in themselves?

Bentham believes that there is one and only one thing that is good in itself, namely, "pleasure, and what comes to the same thing, immunity from pain." A person who holds this view of the good is called a "hedonist."

We suggest that your ethical theory ruminations about hedonism not be clouded by popular moral conceptions of hedonists. The popular conception of the hedonist is of one who smacks of the libertine, the daring, the self-indulgent, one who is a finicky connoisseur, or one who is an aged, tired pleasure seeker punished with characterless wrinkles. Yet, two of the most famous ethical theory hedonists do not fit this description. Epicurus was the most abstemious of men, and Bentham was a righteous crusader. "Hedonism" is often used as an epithet, as if its chief use were not to describe but to deride moral opponents. The new generation looks on the older, middle-class generation as overachievers, gluttonous for more gadgets, machines, travel, appliances, and clothes with which to pleasure themselves while stuffing the values of community, identity, honesty, openness, and love under their Oriental rugs. The older generation looks on the hippies as underachievers who seek unearned leisure, drugs, free sex, irresponsible lives, and a goalless existence in order to maximize their selfish pleasure search while flushing vocation, cleanliness, regulations, and respect for the law down a Haight-Ashbury street drain. Can we expect to find virtue in the bosom of pleasure when hedonism has such a notorious reputation? Read Bentham before deciding.

H. A. Hodges, in the second essay of this section, calls attention to the kind of criticism that existentialists, among others, level against utilitarianism. Hodges defends the good sense of utilitarians in espousing the primacy of good over right; he prefers them to intuitionists who, by reflecting on maxims without regard to their consequences, claim to be able to assess maxims and rules by the self-evident light of reason. (See the essay by W. D. Ross in the next section.) Still, Hodges believes with the existentialists that the utilitarians' conception of the moral life is too narrow. Morals, Hodges believes, are concerned with relationships between humans, of which there are many kinds, and believes that utilitarians concentrate on a single kind of relationship, that of beneficence.

Beneficence is a relationship, fitting enough for associates in a common enterprise, but is inadequate, for example, as a relationship between friends, and it fails to characterize the close relationship we experience in fellowship. Hodges says, "What I chiefly want of my friend or neighbour is not to receive actual benefits from him, but to know that I have his good will, that he regards me with a friendliness which I can freely reciprocate.... This good will is a kind of being-for-other." Hodges, then, while not rejecting hedonistic utilitarianism, suggests that we go beyond it in order to achieve a fuller moral life.

Utility, Pleasure, and the Good

Jeremy Bentham

Jeremy Bentham (1748-1832) was the leading figure in the early phase of the British Utilitarian Movement in philosophy and politics. He was primarily interested in legal reform and constantly sought a philosophical basis for the reforms he advocated. In this connection he wrote highly influential works on the theory of law and on ethics.

OF THE PRINCIPLE OF UTILITY

I. Nature has placed mankind under the governance of two sovereign masters, *pain* and *pleasure*. It is for them alone to point out what we ought to do, as well as to determine what we shall do. On the one hand the standard of right and wrong, on the other the chain of causes and effects, are fastened to their throne. They govern us in all we do, in all we say, in all we think: every effort we can make to throw off our subjection will serve but to demonstrate and confirm it. In words a man may pretend to abjure their empire; but in reality he will remain subject to it all the while. The *principle of utility* recognises this subjection, and assumes it for the foundation of that system, the object of which is to rear the fabric of felicity by the hands of reason and of law. Systems which attempt to question it, deal in sounds instead of sense, in caprice instead of reason, in darkness instead of light.

Source: An Introduction to the Principles of Morals and Legislation (1780).

But enough of metaphor and declamation: it is not by such means that moral science is to be improved.

II. The principle of utility is the foundation of the present work: it will be proper therefore at the outset to give an explicit and determinate account of what is meant by it. By the principle of utility is meant that principle which approves or disapproves of every action whatsoever, according to the tendency which it appears to have to augment or diminish the happiness of the party whose interest is in question: or, what is the same thing in other words, to promote or to oppose that happiness. I say of every action whatsoever; and therefore not only of every action of a private individual, but of every measure of government.

III. By utility is meant that property in any object, whereby it tends to produce benefit, advantage, pleasure, good, or happiness (all this in the present case comes to the same thing) or (what comes again to the same thing) to prevent the happening of mischief, pain, evil, or unhappiness to the party whose interest is considered: if that party be the community in general, then the happiness of the community: if a particular individual, then the happiness of that individual.

IV. The interest of the community is one of the most general expressions that can occur in the phraseology of morals: no wonder that the meaning of it is often lost. When it has a meaning, it is this. The community is a fictitious *body,* composed of the individual persons who are considered as constituting as it were its *members.* The interest of the community then is, what?—the sum of the interests of the several members who compose it.

V. It is in vain to talk of the interest of the community, without understanding what is the interest of the individual. A thing is said to promote the interest, or to be *for* the interest, of an individual, when it tends to add to the sum total of his pleasures: or, what comes to the same thing, to diminish the sum total of his pains.

VI. An action then may be said to be conformable to the principle of utility, or, for shortness sake, to utility (meaning with respect to the community at large) when the tendency it has to augment the happiness of the community is greater than any it has to diminish it.

VII. A measure of government (which is but a particular kind of action, performed by a particular person or persons) may be said to be conformable to or dictated by the principle of utility, when in like manner the tendency which it has to augment the happiness of the community is greater than any which it has to diminish it.

VIII. When an action, or in particular a measure of government, is supposed by a man to be conformable to the principle of utility, it may be convenient, for the purposes of discourse to imagine a kind of law or dictate, called a law or dictate of utility: and to speak of the action in question, as being conformable to such law or dictate.

IX. A man may be said to be a partizan of the principle of utility, when the approbation or disapprobation he annexes to any action, or to any measure, is determined by and proportioned to the tendency which he conceives it to have to augment or to diminish the happiness of the community: or in other words, to its conformity or unconformity to the laws or dictates of utility.

X. Of an action that is conformable to the principle of utility one may always say either that it is one that ought to be done, or at least that it is not one that ought not to be done. One may say also, that it is right it should be done; at least that it is not wrong it should be done: that it is a right action; at least that it is not a wrong action. When thus interpreted, the words *ought*, and *right* and *wrong*, and others of that stamp, have a meaning: when otherwise, they have none.

XI. Has the rectitude of this principle been ever formally contested? It should seem that it had, by those who have not known what they are meaning. Is it susceptible of any direct proof? It should seem not: for that which is used to prove every thing else, cannot itself be proved: a chain of proofs must have their commencement somewhere. To give such a proof is as impossible as it is needless.

XII. Not that there is or ever has been that human creature breathing, however stupid or perverse, who has not on many, perhaps on most occasions of his life, deferred to it. By the natural constitution of the human frame, on most occasions of their lives men in general embrace this principle, without thinking of it: if not for the ordering of their own actions, yet for the trying of their own actions, as well as of those of other men. There have been, at the same time, not many, perhaps, even of the most intelligent, who have been disposed to embrace it purely and without reserve. There are even few who have not taken some occasion or other to quarrel with it, either on account of their not understanding always how to apply it, or on account of some prejudice or other which they were afraid to examine into, or could not bear to part with. For such is the stuff that man is made of: in principle and in practise, in a right track and in a wrong one, the rarest of all human qualities is consistency.

XIII. When a man attempts to combat the principle of utility, it is with reasons drawn, without his being aware of it, from that very principle itself. His arguments, if they prove any thing, prove not that the principle is *wrong*, but that, according to the applications he supposes to be made of it, it is *misapplied*. Is it possible for a man to move the earth? Yes; but he must first find out another earth to stand upon.

XIV. To disprove the propriety of it by arguments is impossible; but, from the causes that have been mentioned, or from some confused or partial view of it, a man may happen to be disposed not to relish it. Where this is the case, if he thinks the settling of his opinions on such a subject worth the trouble, let him take the following steps, and at length, perhaps, he may come to reconcile himself to it.

1. Let him settle with himself, whether he would wish to discard this principle altogether; if so, let him consider what it is that all his reasonings (in matters of politics especially) can amount to?

2. If we would, let him settle with himself, whether he would judge and act without any principle, or whether there is any other he would judge and act by?

3. If there be, let him examine and satisfy himself whether the principle he thinks he has found is really any separate intelligible principle; or whether it be not a mere principle in words, a kind of phrase, which at bottom expresses neither more nor less than the mere averment of his own unfounded sentiments; that is, what in another person he might be apt to call caprice?

4. If he is inclined to think that his own approbation and disapprobation, annexed to the idea of an act, without any regard to its consequences, is a sufficient foundation for him to judge and act upon, let him ask himself whether his sentiment is to be a standard of right and wrong, with respect to every other man, or whether every man's sentiment has the same privilege of being a standard to itself?

5. In the first case, let him ask himself whether his principle is not despotical, and hostile to all the rest of the human race?

6. In the second case, whether it is not anarchial, and whether at this rate there are not as many different standards of right and wrong as there are men? and whether even to the same man, the same thing, which is right to-day, may not (without the least change in its nature) be wrong to-morrow? and whether the same thing is not right and wrong in the same place at the same time? and in either case, whether all argument is not at an end? and whether, when two men have said, "I like this," and "I don't like it," they can (upon such principle) have anything more to say?

7. If he should have said to himself, No: for that the sentiment which he proposes as a standard must be grounded on reflection, let him say on what particulars the reflection is to turn? If on particulars having relation to the utility of the act, then let him say whether this is not deserting his own principle and borrowing assistance from that very one in opposition to which he sets it up: or if not on those particulars, on what other particulars?

8. If he should be for compounding the matter, and adopting his own principle in part, and the principle of utility in part, let him say how far he will adopt it?

9. When he has settled with himself where he will stop, then let him ask himself how he justifies to himself adopting it so far? and why he will not adopt it any farther?

10. Admitting any other principle than the principle of utility to be a right principle, a principle that it is right for a man to pursue; admitting (what is not true) that the word *right* can have a meaning without reference to utility, let him say whether there is any such thing as a *motive* that a man can have to pursue the dictates of it: if there is, let him say what that motive is, and how it is to be distinguished from those which enforce the dictates of utility: if not, then lastly let him say what it is this other principle can be good for?

OF THE FOUR SANCTIONS OR SOURCES OF PAIN AND PLEASURE

I. It has been shown that the happiness of the individuals, of whom a community is composed, that is, their pleasures and their security, is the end and the sole end which the legislator ought to have in view: the sole standard, in conformity to which each individual ought, as far as depends upon the legislator, to be *made* to fashion his behaviour. But whether it be this or any thing else that is to be *done*, there is nothing by which a man can ultimately be *made* to do it, but either pain or pleasure. Having taken a general view of these two grand objects (*viz.* pleasure, and what comes to the same thing, immunity from pain) in the character of *final* causes; it will be necessary to take a view of pleasure and pain itself, in the character of *efficient* causes or means.

II. There are four distinguishable sources from which pleasure and pain are in use to flow: considered separately, they may be termed the *physical*, the *political*, the *moral*, and the *religious*: and inasmuch as the pleasures and pains belonging to each of them are capable of giving a binding force to any law or rule of conduct, they may all of them be termed *sanctions*.

III. If it be in the present life, and from the ordinary course of nature, not purposely modified by the interposition of the will of any human being, nor by any extraordinary interposition of any superior invisible being, that the pleasure or the pain takes place or is expected, it may be said to issue from or to belong to the *physical sanction.*

IV. If at the hands of a *particular* person or set of persons in the community, who under names correspondent to that of *judge*, are chosen for the particular purpose of dispensing it, according to the will of the sovereign or supreme ruling power in the state, it may be said to issue from the *political sanction.*

V. If at the hands of such *chance* persons in the community, as the party in question may happen in the course of his life to have concerns with, according to each man's spontaneous disposition, and not according to any settled or concerted rule, it may be said to issue from the *moral* or *popular sanction.*

VI. If from the immediate hand of a superior invisible being, either in the present life, or in a future, it may be said to issue from the *religious sanction.*

VII. Pleasures or pains which may be expected to issue from the *physical, political,* or *moral* sanctions, must all of them be expected to be experienced, if ever, in the *present* life: those which may be expected to issue from the *religious* sanction, may be expected to be experienced either in the *present* life or in a *future.*

VIII. Those which can be experienced in the present life, can of course be no others than such as human nature in the course of the present life is susceptible of: and from each of these sources may flow all the pleasures or pains of which, in the course of the present life, human nature is susceptible. With regard to these then (with which alone we have in this place any concern) those of them which belong to any one of those sanctions, differ not ultimately in kind from those which belong to any one of the other three: the only difference there is among them lies in the circumstances that accompany their production. A suffering which befalls a man in the natural and spontaneous course of things, shall be styled, for instance, a *calamity;* in which case, if it be supposed to befall him through any imprudence of his, it may be styled a punishment issuing from the physical sanction. Now this same suffering, if inflicted by the law, will be what is commonly called a *punishment;* if incurred for want of any friendly assistance, which the misconduct, or supposed misconduct, of the sufferer has occasioned to be withholden, a punishment issuing from the *moral* sanction; if through the immediate interposition of a particular providence, a punishment issuing from the religious sanction.

IX. A man's goods, or his person, are consumed by fire. If this happened to him by what is called an accident, it was a calamity: if by reason of his own imprudence (for instance, from his neglecting to put his candle out) it may be styled a punishment of the physical sanction: if it happened to him by the sentence of the political magistrate, a punishment belonging to the political sanction; that is, what is commonly called a punishment: if for want of any assistance which his *neighbour* withheld from him out of some dislike to his *moral* character, a punishment of the *moral* sanction: if by an immediate act of *God's* displeasure, manifested on account of some *sin* committed by him, or through any distraction of mind, occasioned by the dread of such displeasure, a punishment of the *religious* sanction.

X. As to such of the pleasures and pains belonging to the religious sanction, as regard a future life, of what kind these may be we cannot know. These lie not open to our observation. During the present life they are matter only of expectation: and, whether that expectation be derived from natural or revealed religion, the particular kind of pleasure or pain, if it be different from all those which lie open to our observation, is what we can have no idea of. The best ideas we can obtain of such pains and pleasures are altogether unliquidated in point of quality. In what other respects our ideas of them *may* be liquidated will be considered in another place.

XI. Of these four sanctions the physical is altogether, we may observe, the ground-work of the political and the moral: so is it also of the religious, in as far as the latter bears relation to the present life. It is included in each of those other three. This may operate in any case (that is, any of the pains or pleasures belonging to it may operate) independently of *them:* none of *them* can operate but by means of this. In a word, the powers of nature may operate of themselves; but neither the magistrate, nor men at large, *can* operate, nor is God in the case in question *supposed* to operate, but through the powers of nature.

XII. For these four objects, which in their nature have so much in common, it seemed of use to find a common name. It seemed of use, in the first place, for the convenience of giving a name to certain pleasures and pains, for which a name equally characteristic could hardly otherwise have been found: in the second place, for the sake of holding up the efficacy of certain moral forces, the influence of which is apt not to be sufficiently attended to. Does the political sanction exert an influence over the conduct of mankind? The moral, the religious sanctions do so too. In every inch of his career are the operations of the political magistrate liable to be aided or impeded by these two foreign powers: who, one or other of them, or both, are sure to be either his rivals or his allies. Does it happen to him to leave them out in his calculations? he will be sure almost to find himself mistaken in the result. Of all this we shall find abundant proofs in the sequel of this work. It behoves him, therefore, to have them continually before his eyes; and that under such a name as exhibits the relation they bear to his own purposes and designs.

VALUE OF A LOT OF PLEASURE OR PAIN, HOW TO BE MEASURED

I. Pleasures then, and the avoidance of pains, are the *ends* which the legislator has in view: it behoves him therefore to understand their *value.* Pleasures and pains are the *instruments* he has to work with: it behoves him therefore to understand their force, which is again, in other words, their value.

II. To a person considered *by himself,* the value of a pleasure or pain considered *by itself,* will be greater or less, according to the four following circumstances: [1]

1. Its *intensity*.
2. Its *duration*.

---

[1] These circumstances have since been denominated *elements* or *dimensions* of *value* in a pleasure or a pain.

Not long after the publication of the first edition, the following memoriter verses were framed, in the view of lodging more effectually, in the memory, these points, on which the whole fabric of morals and legislation may be seen to rest.

> Intense, long, certain, speedy, fruitful, pure—
> Such marks in *pleasures* and in *pains* endure.
> Such pleasures seek if *private* be thy end:
> If it be *public*, wide let them *extend*.
> Such *pains* avoid, whichever be thy view:
> If pains *must* come, let them *extend* to few.

3. Its *certainty* or *uncertainty*.

4. Its *propinquity* or *remoteness*.

III. These are the circumstances which are to be considered in estimating a pleasure or a pain considered each of them by itself. But when the value of any pleasure or pain is considered for the purpose of estimating the tendency of any *act* by which it is produced, there are two other circumstances to be taken into the account; these are,

5. Its *fecundity*, or the chance it has of being followed by sensations of the *same* kind: that is, pleasures, if it be a pleasure: pains, if it be a pain.

6. Its *purity*, or the chance it has of *not* being followed by sensations of the *opposite* kind: that is, pains, if it be a pleasure: pleasure, if it be a pain.

These two last, however, are in strictness scarcely to be deemed properties of the pleasure or the pain itself; they are not, therefore, in strictness to be taken into the account of the value of that pleasure or that pain. They are in strictness to be deemed properties only of the act, or other event, by which such pleasure or pain has been produced; and accordingly are only to be taken into the account of the tendency of such act or such event.

IV. To a *number* of persons, with reference to each of whom the value of a pleasure or a pain is considered, it will be greater or less, according to seven circumstances: to wit, the six preceding ones; *viz.*

1. Its *intensity*.

2. Its *duration*.

3. Its *certainty* or *uncertainty*.

4. Its *propinquity* or *remoteness*.

5. Its *fecundity*.

6. Its *purity*.

And one other; to wit:

7. Its *extent*; that is, the number of persons to whom it *extends*; or (in other words) who are affected by it.

V. To take an exact account then of the general tendency of any act, by which the interests of a community are affected, proceed as follows. Begin with any one person of those whose interests seem most immediately to be affected by it: and take an account,

1. Of the value of each distinguishable *pleasure* which appears to be produced by it in the *first* instance.

2. Of the value of each *pain* which appears to be produced by it in the *first* instance.

3. Of the value of each pleasure which appears to be produced by it *after* the first. This constitutes the *fecundity* of the first *pleasure* and the *impurity* of the first *pain*.

4. Of the value of each *pain* which appears to be produced by it after the first. This constitutes the *fecundity* of the first *pain*, and the *impurity* of the first pleasure.

5. Sum up all the values of all the *pleasures* on the one side, and those of all the pains on the other. The balance, if it be on the side of pleasure, will give the *good* tendency of the act upon the whole, with respect to the interests of that *individual* person; if on the side of pain, the *bad* tendency of it upon the whole.

6. Take an account of the *number* of persons whose interests appear to be concerned; and repeat the above process with respect to each. *Sum up* the numbers

expressive of the degrees of *good* tendency, which the act has, with respect to each individual, in regard to whom the tendency of it is *good* upon the whole: do this again with respect to each individual, in regard to whom the tendency of it is *good* upon the whole: do this again with respect to each individual, in regard to whom the tendency of it is *bad* upon the whole. Take the *balance*; which, if on the side of *pleasure*, will give the general *good tendency* of the act, with respect to the total number or community of individuals concerned; if on the side of pain, the general *evil tendency*, with respect to the same community.

VI. It is not to be expected that this process should be strictly pursued previously to every moral judgment, or to every legislative or judicial operation. It may, however, be always kept in view: and as near as the process actually pursued on these occasions approaches to it, so near will such process approach to the character of an exact one.

VII. The same process is alike applicable to pleasure and pain, in whatever shape they appear: and by whatever denomination they are distinguished: to pleasure, whether it be called *good* (which is properly the cause or instrument of pleasure) or *profit* (which is distant pleasure, or the cause or instrument of distant pleasure) or *convenience*, or *advantage, benefit, emolument, happiness*, and so forth: to pain, whether it be called *evil* (which corresponds to *good*) or *mischief*, or *inconvenience*, or *disadvantage*, or *loss*, or *unhappiness*, and so forth.

VIII. Nor is this a novel and unwarranted, any more than it is a useless theory. In all this there is nothing but what the practice of mankind, wheresoever they have a clear view of their own interest, is perfectly conformable to. An article of property, and estate in land, for instance, is valuable, on what account? On account of the pleasures of all kinds which it enables a man to produce, and what comes to the same thing the pains of all kinds which it enables him to avert. But the value of such an article of property is universally understood to rise or fall according to the length or shortness of the time which a man had in it: the certainty or uncertainty of its coming into possession: and the nearness or remoteness of the time at which, if at all, it is to come into possession. As to the *intensity* of the pleasures which a man may derive from it, this is never thought of, because it depends upon the use which each particular person may come to make of it; which cannot be estimated till the particular pleasures he may come to derive from it, or the particular pains he may come to exclude by means of it, are brought to view. For the same reason, neither does he think of the *fecundity* or *purity* of those pleasures.

Thus much for pleasure and pain, happiness and unhappiness, in *general*.

A Critique of Utilitarianism

H. A. Hodges

H. A. Hodges (1905-   ), M.A., D. Phil., is a professor of philosophy at the University of Reading. Among his books are *Wilhelm Dilthey, an Introduction* (1969), and *The Philosophy of Wilhelm Dilthey* (1952).

Martin Buber and the philosophers who are known as "existentialists" are at one, despite all differences, in believing that what may be called "personal existence" is of the greatest practical concern to mankind. From this starting-point it is possible to move out in various directions. One might proceed to religious questions, or to that kind of metaphysical speculation whose motive is religious rather than logical. Professor D. M. Mackinnon has chosen to keep the discussion on the more accessible plane of traditional moral theory, and his contention is that the personalist writers have a contribution to make to moral theory which ought not to be neglected. I agree with him, and shall have little to say but to restate what I think is his fundamental contention from my own point of view.

Professor Mackinnon begins his paper with a discussion of utilitarianism and an exposure of its weakness. I should like to begin with a recognition of its merits; for it may be held that, by contrast with the intuitionist approach to moral theory which is current in some quarters, utilitarianism has at least its heart in the right place, though its head is muddled.

The charge against intuitionism is that, though it begins in a perfectly legitimate way, it stops short before coming to the heart of the subject. No doubt it is largely a matter of personal choice whether moral philosophy should begin by considering our sense of duty or by examining the idea of the good. No doubt real discoveries have been made in both ways. In particular, the exercise of analysing our sense of duty may sharpen our use of terms and our awareness of moral issues in a way that is both informative and beneficial. It may also lead to over-subtlety, and when we pass from the formulation and codification of commonly agreed moral judgments to the consideration of fictitious cases, as the enquiry usually leads us to do, it is easy to feel that the character of our thinking changes, and what began as an empirical enquiry into what the moral consciousness asserts is transformed into a profitless exercise of fancy. All that the intuitionist ethic can usefully do is to report what the moral consciousness of most people, in that society to which the philosopher writing it belongs, has to say on those questions on which it has reached a judgment at all. It can tell us what the moral judgment of our contemporaries says we ought to do. But, if we ourselves have reached a certain level of critical awareness, it cannot thereby convince us that we ought to do it. For, even if we share the moral consciousness of our contemporaries, and our own intuitive judgments are the same as theirs, yet by the very fact of being philosophers we are surely committed to calling these intuitions in question.

Source: "Things and Persons." Reprinted from *Proceedings of the Aristotelian Society,* Supp. Vol. 22, by courtesy of the Editor of the Aristotelian Society. © 1948 The Aristotelian Society.

We are used to being told that the question "Why should I do my duty?" is one which no one who understands the terms can ask. It needs little courage to call this bluff. No doubt if X is what I ought to do, I ought to do X. The question, however, is whether anything is really meant by saying that I "ought" to do anything, and whether this idea of "ought" really signifies anything for which a reasonably-ordered life could find a place. The classic tradition of moral philosophy has always held that the idea of "ought" is not primary and irreducible, and that judgments containing it can be derived from more ultimate judgments concerning what is "good"; while it has also commonly been held that these in turn can be reduced to propositions about the nature of man and the world, together with expressions of, or propositions about, human desires and purposes. What I ought to do, in short, depends on what it would be best that I should do, and that in turn depends on what I am and what other things and people are, and what we all most constantly desire. To me it seems that, if duty does not in fact rest on this foundation, it hangs in the air; in that case I do not know what it means and I do not recognise its claim over me.

Now, on this point utilitarianism is clear-sighted. Its *Leitmotif* is that laid down by Bentham in his attack on natural law, that there is nothing in *a priori** principles which cannot be better stated as an induction from experience, and that there is no means of distinguishing true principles from irrational prejudices except by applying this test. Utilitarianism also makes the point that principles, whether *a priori* or empirically grounded, are general and abstract, and that the concrete reality to which they refer and for whose sake they are formulated is the lives of human beings, their satisfactions and their frustrations. That is why the utilitarian philosophy did, in actual history, become the theoretical basis of a great reforming movement whose impetus is not yet spent. Wherever it is taken for granted that the object of law and government is the public good, and wherever moral codes and taboos are criticised from the standpoint of their effect in liberating or frustrating the energies of men, the utilitarian principle is at work. It is the principle that people matter, and that moral principles as well as public institutions are there only to serve the people.

If we are clear about this great merit of utilitarianism, we can go on to recognise its manifold faults in detail. These, or the worst of them, can be summed up in the Diltheian complaint that utilitarianism is not true to its own purposes. As [Wilhelm] Dilthey brings against 19th-century empiricism the charge that it is not empirical enough (*Empirie und nicht Empirismus*† is his slogan), so he brings against utilitarianism the charge that it is not really concrete, that it merely substitutes one sort of abstraction for another. He claims to "trump utilitarianism", to "show that it is a construction from above downwards", and to "defend the concrete realities of the moral impulses against abstract principles". Yet it was not his contention that there are no principles, or that moral judgments cannot be analysed and reduced to their ultimate elements. In moral theory, he says, as in aesthetics and educational theory, there are "all-pervading universally-valid rules". They express the impact of social forces upon the conduct of the individual. No one can get on in the social system if he does not fit in to the various very subtle but unavoidable relationships which that system involves. There are laws which

* [Independent of experience.—Eds.]
† [Experience and not empiricism.—Eds.]

state that certain kinds of conduct tend to bring certain kinds of results; and on these are based imperatives which tell people how, in the interests of society and in their own, they had better behave. The point is that the utilitarians enormously oversimplified the situation, and their version of the principles at work was superficial and unreal.

There are passages in Professor Mackinnon's paper where he seems to say that the reality of moral life cannot be expressed in general terms at all, and that no principles can be laid down for our guidance in this sphere. If this were really so, it would seem to mean that there is no such thing as moral philosophy, but only an art of intuitive perception in moral issues. This would agree well enough with the literary form of Kierkegaard's work and that of other existentialists, but it would confirm the suspicion with which the professional philosopher is apt to regard them. I do not see how a philosophical conference can embrace Professor Mackinnon's views unless their real meaning is something less than this, unless he really means to say, not that there are no principles, but that they are very various and very complex, and that any attempt to explain the moral life in terms of one or two principles of high generality, or to resolve a particular moral issue in that way, will fail to do justice to the demands of the concrete situation. If that is all he means, he joins the long succession of those who have protested against abstract moral theories in the name of life itself, and I go with him in the protest. I would even concede that the moral life is so complex that it is questionable whether any moral theory will be able to do justice to it; the same is, I think, undoubtedly true of aesthetic experience. But the moral of this seems to be not that we should plunge ourselves into the psychological profundities of French or Danish philosophical journalism, but that we should heed Dilthey's call to moral philosophers to explore the diversity as well as the unity of the moral life.

To return to utilitarianism. In its hedonistic form it was wrong as to the real object of human desire. That is a psychological error, and we may leave the psychologists to deal with it; that is their business. But utilitarianism was wrong also in its conception of the relation between action and the end of action. For it worked throughout on the assumption that the end in view, the good which is sought, is something distinct from the action, whose result it is, and which is itself therefore a mere means to this end. It follows from this that the way to judge an action is not by any quality inherent in it, but by its consequences. Yet common experience shows, and Aristotle long ago pointed out, that we often perform actions for their own sake, the satisfaction lying in the action itself and not in its consequences. More, it is often the case that we find satisfaction neither in the outcome of an action nor in the inherent quality of the action itself, but in the place which it holds in a scheme of life and conduct, its relation to other actions in a whole which is felt to be good as a whole. The real value lies, as Mr. [H. W. B.] Joseph put it, in a "form of life". The recognition of these facts takes us away beyond utilitarianism, but it takes us further along the same road, towards an honest consultation of experience.

The next stage will take us beyond Mr. Joseph's formula also, though not, I am sure, beyond his real meaning. For to speak of a "form of life" is to say something which might apply to the conduct of an individual taken in isolation. It implies a coherence in his actions, but this coherence might be contained within his personal existence, his own physical, psychological, and mental development, and his relations with other people and the physical world might be only means to this. But few of us will agree that this is in fact the moral good as conceived by ourselves or by the vast majority of our fellow-men. The relations with an external surrounding reality, which find expression in my actions, are themselves full of significance for me and an important part of my happiness or unhappiness, a principal element in the quality of my life, lies in my consciousness of these relations. My interactions with the physical object in manual work, the regard I must pay to the properties of the materials I work with, and the sense of fruitful co-ordination when my efforts and the natural qualities of the object work together—the similar sense of purposeful collaboration or exhilarating opposition in my relations with physical objects in play—the sense of another life with which I have dealings in my relations with plants and still more with animals—and above all the recognition of a human being like myself, an *alter ego* who regards me as I regard him, and who impinges on me not only by automatic reactions but also and chiefly by conscious purposes and deliberate actions towards me—these relationships and the consciousness of them form a part of human life which is of central importance for our psychological health and our happiness. They are a happy hunting ground for the poets. A more rarefied kind of relationship, but not less real, is that between the human mind and that which confronts it, the object which the scientist explains or the artist contemplates, the living being or the human personality which the psychologist explains, the poet contemplates and portrays, or the historian understands and records. Philosophy makes a big mistake if it confines its interest in logic, in aesthetics, or in ethics to the processes which go on within the thinking, contemplating, or deliberating mind, or the formal principles by which these processes are or should be guided, and overlooks the interplay between subject and object which is the very meaning of all these spheres of activity. But for ethics it is only the relationships with human beings which are of prime concern. In our intercourse with nature, important though it may be to us in many ways, we rarely seem to find moral questions coming up, whereas our relations with human beings seem to be the very province in which such questions are at home.

What is the fundamental relation which we desire to find between ourselves and other human beings, or between other human beings in our entourage? As Professor Mackinnon says, it is not merely beneficence. To think of the right relation between human beings as one in which each is the beneficiary of the rest is to fall far short of the truth. Indeed, it is common experience that when A does something for B, B values the action not primarily for itself, but for the evidence which he takes it to be of A's attitude towards him, and this attitude itself is what B chiefly prizes. Aristotle says in the *Poetics* that the plot of a play is more important than the characterisation, because it is in acting and being acted upon that we are happy or the reverse. However this may be in drama (and it is questionable whether modern drama is as true to this canon as the drama known to Aristotle was), it seems to be quite untrue in human relationships. What I chiefly want of my friend or neighbour is not to receive actual benefits from him, but to know that I have his good will, that he regards me with a friendliness which I can freely reciprocate. It is true that friendliness cannot exist without creating a disposition to serve one's friends. It is true also that we all depend in a great degree upon services rendered by one to another. Still I think it is true that we value such services even more for the good will to which they testify than for their inherent utility.

This good will is a kind of being-for-other. It is the "disponibility" of which Professor Mackinnon speaks. What its expression in conduct may be will depend on the circumstances in which A and B are brought together, the nature and duration of the contacts between them. And I believe that mankind has always recognised certain broad distinctions between types of contact and relationship, assigning to each type the kind of behaviour which is considered to be the appropriate expression of good will in that relation. The *dharma* of Indian thought and the "natural law" of mediaeval European thought are at bottom systems of judgments of this kind. And since the main types of human relationship are constant, while the accidental circumstances in which they have to be worked out are open to change, we find quite naturally that there are variations within the main departments of moral teaching: for instance, the *dharma* concerning host and guest is different in a society where there are no inns from what it is in modern Britain, and the law concerning the suppliant in Homeric society bears obvious relations to the prevailing state of insecurity in those days.

It is interesting to distinguish and describe the main types of relationship and the types of conduct which we expect of one another in them. In itself this is a sociological question, but it is not without importance for ethics, because it seems as if different types of moral theory arise from taking one or other of the main types of relationship as the norm for all. We may distinguish, among others, three interesting types of relationship.

(1) Between *strangers:* I mean that relation which arises between people who meet casually on a single occasion, *e.g.* fellow-travellers in a train, or a shopkeeper and a strange customer, or a man who has lost his way and the passer-by whom he accosts. Here there is no necessary affinity of character between the parties, no permanent common purpose, no important degree of intimacy, but merely the accident of being thrown together on this one occasion. It is the thinnest relation possible between men; yet even here the obligations of courtesy and helpfulness are generally recognised.

(2) Between *associates:* This is the relation set up by co-operation in fulfilment of a common purpose. Such common purposes can be of very various kinds and degrees of importance, and the associations resulting from them may be short-lived or long-lived and may make greater or lesser demands on the associates. In each case, however, their association rests not upon personal attraction or devotion, but upon the common purpose, and each associate has other interests and purposes which stand outside the scope of the association. When these conflict with the common purpose, they act as disruptive forces, and the association has to defend itself againt them by organisation, or at least by creating a public opinion and a spirit of loyalty. The association-relationship therefore involves a rough balance of interests between the associates, which is commonly called justice; and this is the sphere in which that conception is especially at home.

(3) Between *fellows:* I give this name to the relationship based on an affinity felt by one person for another, which depends rather on what they both are than on particular assignable interests which they share. The affinity may be of various kinds, and may give rise to various relations extending through the different levels of friendship to the deepest levels of love and intimacy. When a relationship has to be organised or reduced to rule, it has sunk from a fellowship to a mere association. The governing principle of fellowship is love, in one of the senses of that very ambiguous word, and this is the peculiar sphere of love in human relationships. (It should be said, however, that the word "love" is used by some people, where Kant

would say "respect", to describe that mutual disponibility which underlies all the types of relationship, and of which the specific virtues are so many variants.)

This analysis leads me to a further conjecture as to what Professor Mackinnon means by those passages in which he emphasises the complexity of personal relationships and the difficulty (he says impossibility) of expressing them in terms of general formulæ. The Kantian ethic, with its emphasis on equality and no exceptions before the law, seems to be an excellent analysis of the distinctive nature of associate morality. It and other rigoristic theories of the same type go wrong, it seems, not in their analysis of associate morality itself, but in offering this as an account of morality *sans phrase*. They give no account of the distinctive nature of fellowship morality, and that is why they are often felt to be "cold" and inhuman. The existentialists, on the other hand, and personalists like Buber, represent historically a protest against the advance of collectivism and against collectivist social theories like those of Hegel and Marx. Their metaphysical and metapsychological speculations are to be seen as symptoms of an individuality driven to introspection and at the same time to an intensive cultivation of the most intimate human relationships, and it is therefore natural that they should have had something to tell us about that sphere of life which I have called fellowship. If there is any sphere of life which may seem to go easily into a formula, it is surely that of association with its governing principle, justice. If there is a sphere whose complexity defies analysis and whose very essence lies in delicate adjustments between unique individuals, it is surely that of fellowship. But if the disciple of Buber makes this a rule for the whole of moral theory, is he not as much out of balance in his own way as was Kant?

Now, what is it that underlies this interest in persons, whose manifestations are so various, but which seems in its unity and its diversity to be a main clue to the moral life? It depends on two factors, of which one is cognitive and the other is not so.

The cognitive factor is our understanding of one another. I use the word "understanding" here with the full meaning which has been given to it by Dilthey and his followers. I know what it is to be a man. I know it intimately, from within, because I am a man, and I not only have experiences like other men, but can reflect on them. I have some vague idea also of what it must be to be a horse, though in detail I cannot understand the horse with anything like the fulness or accuracy with which I understand a man like myself. I have no idea at all of what it is to be a stone; indeed, I am not sure that the question has any definite meaning. But the understanding which I have of human life like my own is not merely, as Dilthey maintains, the epistemological foundation of the *Geisteswissenschaften**; it is also the cognitive side of the foundation on which morality rests. It brings me into the presence of other human beings not merely as animals of the same species as myself, but as beings who have thoughts and feelings and purposes. These thoughts and feelings and purposes of theirs, so far as I become aware of them, awaken responses in me, and I know too that my own thoughts, feelings, and purposes, so far as I give them expression, evoke responses in other people. On this foundation rests the possibility of all those relationships which are distinctively human.

But this alone does not suffice to determine the character of these relationships.

*[Nonexact sciences—humanities.—Eds.]

It is conceivable that I might understand other persons quite correctly and profoundly, and yet remain indifferent to what I know of them. This does not in fact normally happen; only a disease of mind or body, or an intolerable load of work or suffering, or a hard ascesis long practised, can bring me to a state of such indifference. Dilthey observes that understanding and appreciation, though logically distinguishable, are in real life inseparable. And the love or reverence for other persons, which animates my conduct so far as it is moral, is an appreciative attitude, made up of affective and volitional elements, and not a form of cognition. And therefore there is and can be, in my consciousness, no reason for it. It is one of those "passions" whose "slave" reason "is and ought only to be". Nor can I give a reason to anyone else, to persuade him to adopt this attitude if he does not do so already. All I can do, in argument with one who denies my moral judgments, is to try to show him that he does in fact love his fellow men, and that in thinking he does not he is under an illusion.

Professor Mackinnon ends his paper with two questions which he says confront the present-day moralist. What can we now say to his two questions?

(1) "What exactly is it to be a person?" This reads more like a metaphysical question than an ethical one, and we may perhaps feel inclined to rule it out of order in this context. Should he not rather ask "What is it that makes us take an interest in persons?" The answer to this has just been given. It is our capacity for understanding, evoking our response of reverence or love. But this is something about us, the subjects who respect persons, not about the persons whom we respect. The answer is more psychological than metaphysical.

(2) "How does one authenticate the claim that one is inclined to make for characteristically personal existence?" That is, I suppose, "How can we show that persons are important?" Answer: We cannot, if "showing" means giving a reason over and above the fact that we are what we are and we love and reverence what we love and reverence. Of course, it is conceivable that someone might give a metaphysical or a biological account of what *causes* us to respond in this way to our own kind, but that would not be a *reason* why we *should*.

There is, however, a third question which might be asked, a question of real practical importance, and it is this: "How can we prevent the sense of the importance of persons from being overlaid and stifled by other motives and interests?" The danger has always been there; for the moral consciousness has never been the sole system of motives operating in man. It is perhaps more serious today than it has been for some centuries on account of the pressures which social history is bringing to bear and the changes in our outlook which are in process of taking place. It is certain that the power-cult which stands at the centre of many modern movements is incompatible with the reverence for persons which has been Mackinnon's theme and mine. It is probable that the intellectual habits associated with scientific work are, if not incompatible with this reverence, at least inimical to it. These forces, relatively new in man's history, are in process of bringing about changes in his ways of thinking and living which we cannot see to their end. Those who do not wish to let morality as hitherto known go by default must ask themselves what forces they can put into the field against those which are making the drift. It seems unlikely that an answer will be found quickly and easily, if it is found at all.

Suggested Readings

Psychological Hedonism

1. Broad, Charlie D., *Five Types of Ethical Theory* (New York: Harcourt, 1954), Ch. 1, "Famous Criticism."
2. Duncker, K., "Pleasure, Emotion, and Striving," *Philosophy and Phenomenological Research,* Vol. 1 (1940), 391-430.
3. Young, P. T., "The Role of Hedonic Processes in the Organization of Behavior," *Psychological Review,* Vol. 59 (1952), 249-262.

Ethical Hedonism

1. Ewing, A. C., *Ethics* (London: English Universities Press, 1953), Ch. 3.
2. Hill, Thomas English, *Contemporary Ethical Theories* (New York: Macmillan, 1950), Ch. 12, "Hedonistic and Related Theories."
3. Moore, G. E., *Ethics* (New York: Oxford, 1949), Chs. 1-2.
4. Sidgwick, Henry, *Methods of Ethics* (London: Macmillan & Co., Ltd. 1922), Bk. 3, Ch. 14.

RULES AND SITUATIONS

It is the shamefulness of vice, not its harmfulness (to the agent himself) that must be emphasized above all. For unless the dignity of virtue is exalted above everything else in actions, then the concept of duty itself vanishes and dissolves into mere pragmatic precepts, since man's consciousness of his nobility then disappears and he is for sale and can be bought for a price that seductive inclinations offer him.

—Immanuel Kant

A rather forbidding name, "deontologists," has been given to the thinkers who disagree with Bentham and other utilitarians and who believe, instead, that the concept of "right" cannot be derived from the concept of "good." The first two essays in this section are by two of the greatest and best-known deontologists, **Immanuel Kant** and **W. D. Ross.**

Ross raises an ethical theory question when he asks, "What makes right acts right?" Given that we have constructed some moral system composed of compatible, comprehensive, integrated maxims, with the most general maxim, "You should do what is right," covering all the rest, and given that every act that is an instance of a maxim in the system, being an instance also of the most general maxim, is an act that is right, we can raise the ethical theory question that Ross raises: All right, every act falling under the maxim is right, but what makes the act right?

"What makes right acts right?" is an ethical theory question, not a moral question, because it cannot be answered with anything in the moral system. Consider some questions that can be answered within a moral system. Suppose someone asks what makes it right that husbands and wives take turns doing the dishes. We can answer, "Because it is an instance of the maxim that we ought to treat people fairly." They can then ask what makes fair treatment right, and we can reply, "Because it is an instance of the maxim that we should deal justly with people." They then may ask what makes dealing justly with people right, and we, moving ever upward in the moral maxim pyramid, finally reach the top and say, "Because it is an instance of doing what is right." If our questioner persists and asks, "What makes doing what is right right?", what are we to answer? Being at the top of the moral maxim pyramid, we have no other maxim to appeal to as we did when we were asked the earlier questions. We cannot appeal to anything within the system because, apparently, we have run out of system.

Because the utilitarians have an ethical theory that holds "right" to be derived from "good," they claim they can answer the question with a maxim: What makes right acts right is that they are instances of the maxim "You should do what produces a balance of good over bad." They get this maxim by transforming the general maxim "You should do what is right" by substituting for the phrase "what is right" the phrase "what produces a balance of good over bad." To them, the phrases mean the same thing.

It is this substitution that deontologists such as Ross and Kant deny can be made. We shall not recount the arguments that Ross gives for his position. You can read them for yourself. But there is a possible confusion we should alert you to.

Do not confuse a moral issue with an ethical theory issue. "You should do what produces a balance of good over bad" is one thing considered as a moral maxim and another thing considered as an answer to the ethical theory question "What makes right acts right?" Deontologists do not reject it as moral maxim but do reject it as an answer to Ross's ethical theory question. They reject it, for one reason, because they think it is possible to ask, "What makes an act in accord with the maxim 'You should do what produces a balance of good over bad' right?" If we can ask that ethical theory question about the utilitarian maxim itself, then we cannot give that maxim as an answer to the ethical theory question "What makes right acts right?" without being circular. It is just another maxim about which Ross can ask his question. The ethical theory question is *about* the maxims; therefore, you cannot use one of the maxims themselves to answer the question. Do not fall into that confusion.

The answer to Ross's question is not of mere theoretical interest. It has great practical import. Different answers to Ross's question will produce different life styles because the answers will sanction different moral systems, some of them incompatible with each other. Suppose someone is an egoistic utilitarian, and suppose he thinks that what makes right acts right is their being to the advantage of the agent. In considering what maxims he is going to include in his system, he will have to exclude the universal utilitarian maxim "You should do what produces a balance of good over bad *regardless of whose good or bad it is.*" Since acts in accord with that maxim are not always to the agent's advantage, acts done in accord with it cannot always be right; hence, it should not be included in the egoist's moral system. The racist in a racist society may find that it is to his advantage to be a racist. An egoistic utilitarian answer to "What makes right acts right?" would sanction his racism. If you think racism is wrong, then you must give a different answer to Ross's question than the egoist gives.

According to the deontologists, turning to universal utilitarianism to answer the racist is unsatisfactory. Your appeal to the racist to include in his calculations the bad that happens to the victims of racism as well as the good that happens to him will be met with the following question from him: "What makes acts with a balance of good consequences, considering all persons affected, right?" Perhaps your desire for an answer will motivate you to read Ross with some interest.

There is another, somewhat more emotionally stirring, aspect to deontology that Kant emphasized. Kant was intensely, unremittingly interested in urging man to moral nobility. Earlier, in discussing the moral use of "good," we said that one of the things that is morally good is human character. For Kant, the only thing unqualifiedly morally good is a good moral character; a man has a good moral character only if he has a good will. A person has a good will if he acts in accord with moral maxims out of a sense of duty; he is then worthy of moral praise; he has achieved moral nobility because he is doing what is right solely becasue it is right. A person who acts in accord with moral maxims because it is to his advantage deserves no moral praise; he is acting prudentially, not morally. Acting prudentially is not acting from a free will; it is drifing on the tide of one's inclinations. A man who returns a lost wallet because he will get a reward does not deserve praise. Kant takes a deontological position on ethical theory because he believes the concepts of moral praise and moral nobility exclude actions to secure good consequences for ourselves from the category of moral actions.

Kant says, "A man's fulfillment of his duty is the universal and sole condition of his worthiness to be happy, and his fulfillment of duty is one with his worthiness to be happy." Whereas a utilitarian advises us to act so as to increase happiness, Kant enjoins us to so act that we will be worthy of happiness. This is putting right before good with an admirable purity. Kant realizes that this is difficult doctrine to follow and tries to show us how we can get people to follow it, by outlining a moral catechism. Maybe the deontologists' doctrine will seem less difficult to realize after you read his pupil-teacher dialogue.

So far in this introduction, we have called attention to three issues raised by deontologists: (1) Ross's emphasis on the primacy of right over good; (2) the clarification that we cannot answer the ethical theory question "What makes right acts right?" with a moral maxim; and (3) Kant's insistence that doing our duty for duty's sake is necessary to achieve moral nobility.

There is a fourth issue we can raise about the deontologists' ethical theory. This is a question about the extent to which moral maxims constitute the whole of our morality.

Some people claim that what distinguishes human life from other forms of life is that humans can and do follow rules and also claim that part of what distinguishes one human culture from another is a difference in their sets of maxims. Animals do not have morality because they do not and cannot follow rules. This puts the concept of the rule, or maxims, at the center of human morality and culture.

Apart from the claim that rules are definitive of human culture, we also recognize their importance for the stability of culture. We have to be able to anticipate each other's actions in order to carry on a cooperative life. Action in accord with stable maxims makes this anticipation possible and provides a morally ordered culture.

Suppose we grant that without stable maxims there would be no moral order. We may now pass to a pair of related questions: To what extent may we identify the moral life with a life prescribed by a particular set of maxims? And do we at present have all the maxims we shall ever need?

In the third essay in this section, **Joseph Fletcher** apparently wishes to deny that the whole of moral life lies in merely conforming with maxims. For him, an exclusively maxim-oriented morality implies a rigidity that makes it impossible to do the right thing in every moral situation we find ourselves in. This "No" answer to our first question may seem plausible to him because he takes too simple a view of the relation of rules to moral decisions: One and the same contemplated act may fall under two or more different maxims; we have no automatic, mechanical procedure to apply that will dictate the correct maxim under which we are to act; hence, maxim selection always requires judgment adapted to the circumstances. For example, a person may hold to a maxim that one should not undergo abortion and also to a maxim that one should not bring malformed children into the world. The agony of moral decision arises in having to choose the maxim we think has priority. Neither Ross nor other deontologists deny that there are such situations.

Even if Fletcher conceded that a rule moralist such as Ross could satisfactorily answer Fletcher's rigidity criticism, Fletcher would still answer "No" to the first question because he would answer "No" to the second question. Fletcher apparently believes that no set of moral maxims can ever be complete; hence, a set of maxims can never wholly prescribe our moral life. Moral rules must always be supplemented by love. The crabbed restraints of legalistic codes are too inflexible to meet the demands of new situations. No form of life constructed solely on moral maxims can be a moral life.

We said, "Fletcher *apparently* believes that no set of moral maxims can ever be complete" because his manner of speaking about love should make us cautious. He says "ethics has only one norm or principle or law (call it what you will) that is binding and unexceptionable . . . the summary commandment to love God and the neighbor." If Fletcher says that a set of moral rules must always be supplemented by love and then speaks of love in rule-sounding terms, it appears that he has simply said that no set of rules is complete if it does not include a "love rule."

On the other hand, if this love rule does not specify what acts we are to perform, then it lacks the quality needed to be a maxim. In this event, we can legitimately ask how love can complete the moral system if it is too vague to add as a maxim.

Learning Moral Rules

Immanuel Kant

Immanuel Kant (1724-1804) is recognized as one of the greatest philosophers of all times. All of his well-ordered life was spent in Königsberg, East Prussia, where he was a professor of philosophy. In *The Critique of Pure Reason* (1781), Kant developed his Critical Philosophy, an ingenious synthesis of rationalism and empiricism. He believed it to be a revolution in the theory of knowledge as significant as that of Copernicus in astronomy. Kant made significant and highly original contributions to cosmology, ethics, aesthetics, jurisprudence, and the philosophy of religion as well as to theory of knowledge.

Although virtue cannot be based on anthropological knowledge drawn from experience, the very concept of virtue implies that virtue must be acquired (that it is not innate). For man's capacity for moral action would not be virtue were it not produced by the *strength* of his resolution struggling with such powerful inclinations to the contrary. Virtue is the product of pure practical reason, in so far as reason, aware of its supremacy (on grounds of freedom), wins ascendancy over the inclinations.

That virtue can and must be *learned* follows directly from the fact that it is not innate. The theory of virtue is, therefore, a *doctrine*. But one does not, merely by the theory of how one should behave in keeping with the concept of virtue, acquire the strength to put the rule into practice. Hence the Stoics [in denying that virtue can be learned] meant only that virtue cannot be *learned* through the mere presentation of duty or through admonitions, but must rather be cultivated (by discipline) and *practiced* by being put to the proof of combat with the inner enemy in man; for one *cannot* straightway do all that one *wills* to do, without having first tried and practiced one's strength. But the *resolution* to practice virtue must be made all at once and in its entirety, since the intention (*animus*) of surrendering at times to vice, in order gradually to break away from it, would in itself be impure and even immoral. Consequently this attitude could also produce no virtue (in so far as virtue is based on a single principle).

Now as for the doctrinal method (and *methodic* treatment is essential to any scientific doctrine—otherwise the exposition of it would be chaotic), this too must be systematic and not fragmentary if the doctrine of virtue is to present itself as a science.—But the doctrine can be delivered either in a *lecture*, as when all those to whom it is directed are a mere audience, or by the method of *questioning*, in which the teacher asks his pupil what he wants to teach him. And this method of questioning is, in turn, divided into the method of *dialogue* and that of *catechism*, depending on whether the teacher addresses his questions to the pupil's *reason* or merely to his *memory*. For if the teacher wants to question his pupil's reason, he

Source: Doctrine of Virtue, Part II, *Metaphysics of Morals.* Copyright © 1964 by Mary J. Gregor. Reprinted by permission of Harper & Row, Publishers, Inc.

must do this in a dialogue in which teacher and pupil reciprocally question and answer each other. The teacher, by his questions, guides the pupil's thinking merely by presenting him with situations in which his disposition for certain concepts will develop (the teacher is the midwife of the pupil's thoughts). The pupil, who thus sees that he is able to think for himself, provides, by his questions about obscurities or doubts in the propositions admitted, occasion for the *teacher* to *learn* how to question skilfully, according to the saying *docendo discimus*.—(For logic has not yet taken sufficiently to heart its task of furnishing us with rules as to the appropriate way of searching for things: that is to say, logic should not limit itself to giving rules for *determinant* judgments but should also provide rules for *preparatory* judgments, by which one is led to conceptions. Such a doctrine can be a guide even to the mathematician in his inventions, and moreover he often makes use of it.)

For the still untrained pupil the first and most essential *doctrinal* instrument of the theory of virtue is a moral *catechism*. This must precede the religious catechism. It cannot be interwoven, as a mere interpolation, in the teachings of religion but must rather be presented separately, as a self-subsistent whole. For it is only by pure moral principles that the transition from the doctrine of virtue to religion can be made, since otherwise the avowals of religion would be impure.—For their own part, even the worthiest and most eminent theologians have hesitated to draw up a catechism for statutory religion which they would personally answer for, although one would have thought this the least that could be expected from the vast treasury of their learning.

But a *moral* catechism, the basic teaching of the doctrine of virtue, involves no such scruple or difficulty since, so far as its content is concerned, it can be developed from ordinary human reason and, so far as its form is concerned, it needs only to be adapted to the didactic rules appropriate to the earliest instruction. The formal principle of such instruction does not, however, permit Socratic *dialogue* as the method of teaching, since the pupil has no idea what questions to ask; and so the teacher alone does the questioning. But the answer which he methodically draws from the pupil's reason must be written down and preserved in precise terms which cannot easily be altered, and so be committed to the pupil's *memory*. In this way the *catechetical method* differs from both the *dogmatic method* (in which only the teacher speaks) and the *method of dialogue* (in which both teacher and pupil question and answer each other).

The *experimental* (technical) means to the formation of virtue is *good example* on the part of the teacher (his exemplary conduct) and *cautionary* example in others. For, to the as yet unformed human being, imitation is what first determines him to embrace the maxims that he afterwards makes his own.—To become conditioned to something is to establish a permanent inclination apart from any maxim, by the often repeated satisfaction of that inclination; it is a mechanism of sense rather than a principle of thought (and one that is easier to *make* than to *break* after it has been acquired).—As for the power of *examples* (good or bad) which can be held up to the propensity for imitation or presented as warnings, what is given to us by others can establish no maxim of virtue. For a maxim of virtue consists precisely in the subjective autonomy of each man's practical reason, and so implies that the law itself, not the conduct of other men, serves as one's motive. Thus the teacher will not tell his pupil "Take an example from that good (orderly, diligent) boy!" For this would only cause the pupil to hate that boy, who puts him in an unfavorable light. Good example (exemplary conduct) should not serve as a model but only as a proof that it is really possible to act in accordance with duty. Thus it is not comparison with any other man whatsoever (with men as they are), but comparison with the Idea of humanity (with what man ought to be) and so with the law, that must serve as the constant standard of the teacher's instruction.

Note
Fragments of a Moral Catechism

The teacher questions the pupil's reason about what he wants to teach him; and should the pupil sometimes not know how to answer the question, the teacher, guiding his reason, suggests the answer.

1. Teacher: What is your greatest, in fact your whole, desire in life?
   Pupil: (is silent)
   Teacher: That everything should always go the way you want it to.
2. Teacher: What do we call such a state?
   Pupil: (is silent)
   Teacher: We call it *happiness* (continuous well-being, enjoyment of life, complete contentment with one's state).
3. Teacher: Now, if it were up to you to dispose of all the happiness in the world, would you keep it all for yourself or would you share it with your fellow-men?
   Pupil: I would share it with others and make them happy and contented too.
4. Teacher: Now that shows that you have a good enough *heart;* but let us see whether you show good *understanding* along with it.—Would you really give the lazy fellow a soft cushion so that he could pass away his life in sweet idleness? Or would you see to it that the drunkard is never short of wine and whatever else he needs to get drunk? Would you give the swindler a charming air and manner to dupe other people? And would you give the brutal man audacity and strong fists so that he could crush other people? Each of these things is a means that somebody wants in order to be happy in his own way.
   Pupil: No, I would not.
5. Teacher: You see, then, that if you had all happiness in your hands and, along with it, the best will, you still would not straightway give it to anyone who put out his hand for it; instead you would first try to find out to what extent each is *worthy* of happiness.—But as for yourself, would you at least have no scruples about first giving yourself everything that you count in your happiness?
   Pupil: I would have none.
   Teacher: But doesn't it occur to you to ask, again, whether you yourself are worthy of happiness?
   Pupil: Of course.
   Teacher: Now, the force in you that strives only toward happiness is *inclination;* but the power that limits your inclination to the condition of your first being worthy of happiness is your *reason;* and your power to restrain and overcome your inclination by your reason is the freedom of your will.
6. Teacher: As to how you should set about participating in happiness and also becoming at least not unworthy of it, the rule and instruction in this lies in

your *reason* alone. This means that you need not learn this rule for your conduct from experience or be taught it by other men. Your own reason teaches you what you have to do and directly commands it. For example, suppose a situation in which you could get a great benefit for yourself or your friends by making up a little lie that would harm no one: what does your reason say about it?

Pupil: That I ought not to lie, no matter how great the benefits to myself and my friend might be. Lying is *base* and makes a man *unworthy* of happiness.—Here we find an unconditional necessitation through a command (or prohibition) of reason, which I must obey; and in the face of it all my inclinations must be silent.

Teacher: What do we call this necessity, which reason lays directly upon a man, of acting in conformity with a law of reason?

Pupil: It is called *duty*.

Teacher: So a man's fulfillment of his duty is the universal and sole condition of his worthiness to be happy, and his fulfillment of duty is one with his worthiness to be happy.

7. Teacher: But even if we are conscious of a good and active will in us, by virtue of which we consider ourselves worthy (or at least not unworthy) of happiness, can we base on this the sure hope of participating in happiness?

Pupil: No, not merely on this. For it is not always within our power to make ourselves happy, and the course of nature does not of itself conform with merit. Our happiness in life (our welfare in general) depends, rather, on circumstances that, by and large, are not under man's control. So our happiness always remains a mere wish which cannot become a hope unless some other power is added.

8. Teacher: Has reason, in fact, grounds for admitting the reality of such a power, which apportions happiness according to man's merit or guilt—a power ordering the whole of nature and ruling the world with supreme wisdom?

Pupil: Yes. For we see in the works of nature, which we can judge, a wisdom so widespread and profound that we can explain it to ourselves only by the ineffably great art of a creator of the world. And from this we have cause, when we turn to the moral order, which is the highest adornment of the world, to expect there a rule no less wise. In other words, we have cause to hold that if we do not make ourselves *unworthy of happiness* by violating our duty, we can also hope to *share* in happiness.

In this catechism, which must be carried through all the articles of virtue and vice, the greatest care must be taken *not* to base the command of duty on the fact that it is actually observed by the men it is supposed to obligate nor even on the advantage or detriment to others flowing from it. It must rather be based quite purely on the moral principle, and only casual mention should be made of advantage and detriment, as of an adjunct which could really be dispensed with but which is serviceable, as a mere instrument, for the taste of those who are weak by nature. It is the *shamefulness* of vice, not its *harmfulness* (to the agent himself), that must be emphasized above all. For unless the dignity of virtue is exalted above everything else in actions, then the concept of duty itself vanishes and dissolves into mere pragmatic precepts, since man's consciousness of his own nobility then disappears and he is for sale and can be bought for a price that the seductive inclinations offer him.

Now, when this is wisely and carefully developed out of man's own reason, with regard for the differences in age, sex, and position which he gradually encounters, then at the end there must be something more—something that moves the soul inwardly and puts man in a position such that he can look upon himself only with the greatest wonder at the original disposition dwelling in him, the impression of which is never erased. When at the end of his instruction he once more, by way of summary, recounts his duties in their order (recapitulates them); and when, in the case of each of them, his attention is drawn to the fact that none of the pains, hardships, and sufferings of life—not even the threat of death—which may befall him because he attends faithfully to his duty can make him lose his consciousness of being their master and superior to them all; then it is time for the question: what is it in you that can be trusted to enter into combat with all the powers of nature in you and around you and, if they come into conflict with your moral principles, to conquer them? Although the answer to this question completely surpasses the power of speculative reason, the question arises of itself. And if he takes it to heart, the very incomprehensibility of this self-knowledge must produce an exaltation in his soul which only inspires it the more to keep its duty holy, the more it is assailed.

In this catechetical instruction in morality it would be most helpful to the pupil's moral development to raise some casuistical questions in the analysis of every duty and to let the assembled children put their reason to the test of how each would go about resolving the tricky problem put before him. The advantage of this is not only that, as a method of *cultivating reason,* casuistry is most suitable to the capacity of the undeveloped (since questions about duty can be decided far more easily than speculative questions), and so is the most appropriate way to sharpen the reason of young people in general. Its advantage lies especially in the fact that it is natural for man to *love* a subject which he has, by his own handling, brought to a science (in which he is now proficient); and so, by this sort of practice, the pupil is drawn unwittingly to an *interest* in morality.

But it is of foremost importance in this instruction not to present the moral catechism mixed with the religious one (to combine them into one) or, what is worse yet, to let it follow upon the religious catechism. On the contrary, the pupil must always be brought to a clear insight into the moral catechism, which should be presented with the greatest diligence and completeness. For otherwise the religion that the pupil afterwards professes will be nothing but hypocrisy: he will embrace duties out of fear and feign an interest in them which is not in his heart.

SECTION II. ETHICAL ASCETIC

The rules for practicing virtue (*exercitiorum virtutis*) aim at a frame of mind that is *brave* and *cheerful* in the observance of duty (*animus strenuus et hilaris*). For in order to overcome the obstacles with which it has to contend, virtue must collect all its strength and at the same time sacrifice many of the pleasures of life, the loss of which can well make the mind morose and surly at times. But what we do cheerlessly and merely as compulsory service has no intrinsic value for us, and so also if we attend to our duty in this way; we do not love it but rather shirk as much as we can the occasion for practicing it.

The cultivation of virtue, *i.e.* moral *asceticism,* takes as its motto for the vigorous, spirited, and courageous practice of virtue the *Stoic* saying: accustom yourself *to bear* the contingent ills of life and *to do without* the equally superfluous pleasures (*assuesce incommodis et desuesce commoditatibus vitae*). It is a kind of *hygiene* that man should practice to keep himself morally *healthy*. But health is only the *negative* side of well-being: it cannot itself be felt. Something must be added to it—something which, though it is purely moral, offers a pleasant enjoyment of life—and this is the habitually cheerful heart, as the virtuous *Epicurus* conceived it. For who should have more cause for a cheerful spirit, without finding it his duty to acquire such a frame of mind and make it habitual, than the man who is aware of no intentional transgression in himself and is secured against falling into such a transgression (*hic murus aheneus esto etc., Horat.*)? On the other hand, monastic asceticism, which, out of superstitious fear or hypocritical self-loathing, goes to work with self-torture and crucifixion of the flesh, does not aim at virtue but rather at fantastic atonement; it inflicts self-punishment and, instead of requiring moral *repentance* for a fault (that is, repentance with a view to self-improvement) insists on *penance* for it. But a self-chosen and self-inflicted punishment is a contradiction (because punishment must always be inflicted by another person); moreover, it cannot produce the cheerfulness that accompanies virtue, but much rather brings with it secret hatred for virtue's command.—Ethical gymnastic, therefore, consists only in combatting the impulses of nature to the extent that we are able to master them when a situation comes up in which they threaten morality; hence it is a combat which gives us courage and makes us cheerful in the consciousness of our restored freedom. To *repent* of something and to impose a *penance* on oneself (for example, a fast) not from hygienic but from pious considerations are, morally considered, two very different precautionary measures. To repent of a past transgression when we recall it is inevitable and, in fact, we even have a duty not to let this recollection atrophy; but self-punishment, which is cheerless, morose, and surly, makes virtue itself hated and drives away its followers. Hence the training (discipline) which man exercises on himself can become meritorious and exemplary only by the cheerfulness that accompanies it.

Duties and the Right

W. D. Ross

William David Ross (1877-   ) was born in Scotland and educated in the Edinburgh and Oxford Universities. He taught for many years at Oxford and served as its vice-chancellor. He is the author of important works in the history of philosophy and is the editor of the Oxford edition of Aristotle, Ross having translated the *Ethics* and *Metaphysics* himself. In *The Right and the Good* (1930) and *Foundations of Ethics* (1939), he presents his own theory of ethics.

The real point at issue between hedonism and utilitarianism on the one hand and their opponents on the other is not whether "right" means "productive of so and so"; for it cannot with any plausibility be maintained that it does. The point at issue is that to which we now pass, viz. whether there is any general character which makes right acts right, and if so, what it is. Among the main historical attempts to state a single characteristic of all right actions which is the foundation of their rightness are those made by egoism and utilitarianism. But I do not propose to discuss these, not because the subject is unimportant, but because it has been dealt with so often and so well already, and because there has come to be so much agreement among moral philosophers that neither of these theories is satisfactory. A much more attractive theory has been put forward by Professor [G. E.] Moore: that what makes actions right is that they are productive of more *good* than could have been produced by any other action open to the agent.[1]

This theory is in fact the culmination of all the attempts to base rightness on productivity of some sort of result. The first form this attempt takes is the attempt to base rightness on conduciveness to the advantage or pleasure of the agent. This theory comes to grief over the fact, which stares us in the face, that a great part of duty consists in an observance of the rights and a furtherance of the interests of others, whatever the cost to ourselves may be. Plato and others may be right in holding that a regard for the rights of others never in the long run involves a loss of happiness for the agent, that "the just life profits a man." But this, even if true, is irrelevant to the rightness of the act. As soon as a man does an action *because* he thinks he will promote his own interests thereby, he is acting not from a sense of its rightness but from self-interest.

To the egoistic theory, hedonistic utilitarianism supplies a much-needed amendment. It points out correctly that the fact that a certain pleasure will be enjoyed by the agent is no reason why he *ought* to bring it into being rather than an equal or greater pleasure to be enjoyed by another, though, human nature being what it is, it makes it not unlikely that he *will* try to bring it into being. But

Source: The Right and the Good (Oxford: Clarendon, 1930), pp. 16-20, 29-33, 41-44. Reprinted by permission of the Clarendon Press, Oxford.

[1] I take the theory which, as I have tried to show, seems to be put forward in *Ethics* rather than the earlier and less plausible theory put forward in *Principia Ethica*.

hedonistic utilitarianism in its turn needs a correction. On reflection it seems clear that pleasure is not the only thing in life that we think good in itself, that for instance we think the possession of a good character, or an intelligent understanding of the world, as good or better. A great advance is made by the substitution of "productive of the greatest good" for "productive of the greatest pleasure."

Not only is this theory more attractive than hedonistic utilitarianism, but its logical relation to that theory is such that the latter could not be true unless *it* were true, while it might be true though hedonistic utilitarianism were not. It is in fact one of the logical bases of hedonistic utilitarianism. For the view that what produces the maximum pleasure is right has for its bases the views (1) that what produces the maximum good is right, and (2) that pleasure is the only thing good in itself. If they were not assuming that what produces the maximum *good* is right, the utilitarians' attempt to show that pleasure is the only thing good in itself, which is in fact the point they take most pains to establish, would have been quite irrelevant to their attempt to prove that only what produces the maximum *pleasure* is right. If, therefore, it can be shown that productivity of the maximum good is not what makes all right actions right, we shall *a fortiori** have refuted hedonistic utilitarianism.

When a plain man fulfils a promise because he thinks he ought to do so, it seems clear that he does so with no thought of its total consequences, still less with any opinion that these are likely to be the best possible. He thinks in fact much more of the past than of the future. What makes him think it right to act in a certain way is the fact that he has promised to do so—that and, usually, nothing more. That his act will produce the best possible consequences is not his reason for calling it right. What lends colour to the theory we are examining, then, is not the actions (which form probably a great majority of our actions) in which some such reflections as "I have promised" is the only reason we give ourselves for thinking a certain action right, but the exceptional cases in which the consequences of fulfilling a promise (for instance) would be so disastrous to others that we judge it right not to do so. It must of course be admitted that such cases exist. If I have promised to meet a friend at a particular time for some trivial purpose, I should certainly think myself justified in breaking my engagement if by doing so I could prevent a serious accident or bring relief to the victims of one. And the supporters of the view we are examining hold that my thinking so is due to my thinking that I shall bring more good into existence by the one action than by the other. A different account may, however, be given of the matter, an account which will, I believe, show itself to be the true one. It may be said that besides the duty of fulfilling promises, I have and recognize a duty of relieving distress,[2] and that when I think it right to do the latter at the cost of not doing the former, it is not because I think I shall produce more good thereby but because I think it the duty which is in the circumstances more of a duty. This account surely corresponds much more closely with what we really think in such a situation. If, so far as I can see, I could bring equal amounts of good into being by fulfilling my promise and by helping some one to whom I had made no promise, I should not hesitate to regard the former as my duty. Yet on the view that what is right is right because it is productive of the most good, I should not so regard it.

---

* [With stronger reason.—Eds.]

[2] These are not, strictly speaking, duties, but things that tend to be our duty, or *prima facie* duties. Cf. pp. 19-20, *The Right and the Good*.

There are two theories, each in its way simple, that offer a solution of such cases of conscience. One is the view of Kant, that there are certain duties of perfect obligation, such as those of fulfilling promises, of paying debts, of telling the truth, which admit of no exception whatever in favour of duties of imperfect obligation, such as that of relieving distress. The other is the view of, for instance, Professor Moore and Dr. [H.] Rashdall, that there is only the duty of producing good, and that all "conflicts of duties" should be resolved by asking "by which action will most good be produced?" But it is more important that our theory fit the facts than that it be simple, and the account we have given above corresponds (it seems to me) better than either of the simpler theories with what we really think, viz. that normally promise-keeping, for example, should come before benevolence, but that when and only when the good to be produced by the benevolent act is very great and the promise comparatively trivial, the act of benevolence becomes our duty.

In fact the theory of "ideal utilitarianism," if I may for brevity refer so to the theory of Professor Moore, seems to simplify unduly our relations to our fellows. It says, in effect, that the only morally significant relation in which my neighbors stand to me is that of being possible beneficiaries by my action.[3] They do stand in this relation to me, and this relation is morally significant. But they may also stand to me in the relation of promisee to promiser, of creditor to debtor, of wife to husband, of child to parent, of friend to friend, of fellow countryman to fellow countryman, and the like; and each of these relations is the foundation of a *prima facie* duty, which is more or less incumbent on me according to the circumstance of the case. When I am in a situation, as perhaps I always am, in which more than one of these *prima facie* duties is incumbent on me, what I have to do is to study the situation as fully as I can until I form the considered opinion (it is never more) that in the circumstances one of them is more incumbent than any other; then I am bound to think that to do this *prima facie* duty is my duty *sans phrase* in the situation.

I suggest "*prima facie* duty" or "conditional duty" as a brief way of referring to the characteristic (quite distinct from that of being a duty proper) which an act has, in virtue of being of a certain kind (e.g. the keeping of a promise), of being an act which would be a duty proper if it were not at the same time of another kind which is morally significant. Whether an act is a duty proper or actual duty depends on *all* the morally significant kinds it is an instance of.

It is necessary to say something by way of clearing up the relation between *prima facie* duties and the actual or absolute duty to do one particular act in particular circumstances. If, as almost all moralists except Kant are agreed, and as most plain men think, it is sometimes right to tell a lie or to break a promise, it must be maintained that there is a difference between *prima facie* duty and actual or absolute duty. When we think ourselves justified in breaking, and indeed morally obliged to break, a promise, in order to relieve some one's distress, we do not for a moment cease to recognize a *prima facie* duty to keep our promise, and this leads us to feel, not indeed shame or repentance, but certainly compunction, for behaving as we do; we recognize, further, that it is our duty to make up somehow to the promisee for the breaking of the promise. We have to distinguish from the characteristic of being our duty that of tending to be our duty. Any act that we do

[3] Some will think it, apart from other considerations, a sufficient refutation of this view to point out that I also stand in that relation to myself, so that for this view the distinction of oneself from others is morally insignificant.

contains various elements in virtue of which it falls under various categories. In virtue of being the breaking of a promise, for instance, it tends to be wrong; in virtue of being an instance of relieving distress it tends to be right. Tendency to be one's duty may be called a parti-resultant attribute, i.e., one which belongs to an act in virtue of some one component in its nature. *Being* one's duty is a toti-resultant attribute, one which belongs to an act in virtue of its whole nature and of nothing less than this. This distinction between parti-resultant and toti-resultant attributes is one which we shall meet in another context also.

Something should be said of the relation between our apprehension of the *prima facie* rightness of certain types of act and our mental attitude towards particular acts. It is proper to use the word "apprehension" in the former case and not in the latter. That an act, *qua* fulfilling a promise, or *qua* effecting a just distribution of good, or *qua* returning services rendered, or *qua* promoting the good of others, or *qua* promoting the virtue or insight of the agent, is *prima facie* right, is self-evident; not in the sense that it is evident from the beginning of our lives, or as soon as we attend to the proposition for the first time, but in the sense that when we have reached sufficient mental maturity and have given sufficient attention to the proposition it is evident without any need of proof, or of evidence beyond itself. It is self-evident just as a mathematical axiom, or the validity of a form of inference, is evident. The moral order expressed in these propositions is just as much part of the fundamental nature of the universe (and, we may add, of any possible universe in which there were moral agents at all) as is the spatial or numerical structure expressed in the axioms of geometry or arithmetic. In our confidence that these propositions are true there is involved the same trust in our reason that is involved in our confidence in mathematics; and we should have no justification for trusting it in the latter sphere and distrusting it in the former. In both cases we are dealing with propositions that cannot be proved, but that just as certainly need no proof.

Our judgements about our actual duty in concrete situations have none of the certainty that attaches to our recognition of the general principles of duty. A statement is certain, i.e. is an expression of knowledge, only in one or other of two cases: when it is either self-evident, or a valid conclusion from self-evident premises. And our judgements about our particular duties have neither of these characters. (1) They are not self-evident. Where a possible act is seen to have two characteristics, in virtue of one of which it is *prima facie* right, and in virtue of the other *prima facie* wrong, we are (I think) well aware that we are not certain whether we ought or ought not to do it; that whether we do it or not, we are taking a moral risk. We come in the long run, after consideration, to think one duty more pressing than the other, but we do not feel certain that it is so. And though we do not always recognize that a possible act has two such characteristics, and though there *may* be cases in which it has not, we are never certain that any particular possible act has not, and therefore never certain that it is right, nor certain that it is wrong. For, to go no further in the analysis, it is enough to point out that any particular act will in all probability in the course of time contribute to the bringing about of good or of evil for many human beings, and thus have a *prima facie* rightness or wrongness of which we know nothing. (2) Again, our judgements about our particular duties are not logical conclusions from self-evident premises. The only possible premises would be the general principles stating their *prima facie* rightness or wrongness *qua* having the different characteristics they do have; and even if we could (as we cannot) apprehend the extent to which an act will tend on the one hand, for example, to bring about advantages for our benefactors, and on the other hand to bring about disadvantages for fellow men who are not our benefactors, there is no principle by which we can draw the conclusion that it is on the whole right or on the whole wrong. In this respect the judgement as to the rightness of a particular act is just like the judgement as to the beauty of a particular natural object or work of art. A poem is, for instance, in respect of certain qualities beautiful and in respect of certain others not beautiful; and our judgement as to the degree of beauty it possesses on the whole is never reached by logical reasoning from the apprehension of its particular beauties or particular defects. Both in this and in the moral case we have more or less probable opinions which are not logically justified conclusions from the general principles that are recognised as self-evident.

There is therefore much truth in the description of the right act as a fortunate act. If we cannot be certain that it is right, it is our good fortune if the act we do is the right act. This consideration does not, however, make the doing of our duty a mere matter of chance. There is a parallel here between the doing of duty and the doing of what will be to our personal advantage. We never *know* what act will in the long run be to our advantage. Yet it is certain that we are more likely in general to secure our advantage if we estimate to the best of our ability the probable tendencies of our actions in this respect, than if we act on caprice. And similarly we are more likely to do our duty if we reflect to the best of our ability on the *prima facie* rightness or wrongness of various possible acts in virtue of the characteristics we perceive them to have, than if we act without reflection. With this greater likelihood we must be content.

The general principles of duty are obviously not self-evident from the beginning of our lives. How do they come to be so? The answer is that they come to be self-evident to us just as mathematical axioms do. We find by experience that this couple of matches and that couple make four matches, that this couple of balls on a wire and that couple make four balls; and by reflection on these and similar discoveries we come to see that it is of the nature of two and two to make four. In a precisely similar way, we see the *prima facie* rightness of an act which would be the fulfilment of a particular promise, and of another which would be the fulfilment of another promise, and when we have reached sufficient maturity to think in general terms, we apprehend *prima facie* rightness to belong to the nature of any fulfilment of promise. What comes first in time is the apprehension of the self-evident *prima facie* rightness of an individual act of a particular type. From this we come by reflection to apprehend the self-evident general principle of *prima facie* duty. From this, too, perhaps along with the apprehension of the self-evident *prima facie* rightness of the same act in virtue of its having another characteristic as well, and perhaps in spite of the apprehension of its *prima facie* wrongness in virtue of its having some third characteristic, we come to believe something not self-evident at all, but an object of probable opinion, viz. that this particular act is (not *prima facie* but) actually right.

It is worth while to try to state more definitely the nature of the acts that are right. We may try to state first what (if anything) is the universal nature of *all* acts that are right. It is obvious that any of the acts that we do has countless effects, directly or indirectly, on countless people, and the probability is that any act, however right it be, will have adverse effects (though these may be very trivial) on some innocent people. Similarly, any wrong act will probably have beneficial effects on some deserving people. Every act therefore, viewed in some aspects, will be *prima facie* right, and viewed in others, *prima facie* wrong, and right acts can be distinguished from wrong acts only as being those which, of all those possible for the agent in the circumstances, have the greatest balance of *prima facie* rightness, in those respects in which they are *prima facie* right, over their *prima facie* wrongness, in those respects in which they are *prima facie* wrong—*prima facie* rightness and wrongness being understood in the sense previously explained. For the estimation of the comparative stringency of these *prima facie* obligations no general rules can, so far as I can see, be laid down. We can only say that a great deal of stringency belongs to the duties of "perfect obligation"—the duties of keeping our promises, of repairing wrongs we have done, and of returning the equivalent of services we have received. For the rest, $\dot{\epsilon}v \ \tau\hat{\eta} \ a\iota\sigma\theta\acute{\eta}\sigma\epsilon\iota \ \acute{\eta} \ \kappa\rho\iota\sigma\iota\varsigma.$[4] This sense of our particular duty in particular circumstances, preceded and informed by the fullest reflection we can bestow on the act in all its bearings, is highly fallible, but it is the only guide we have to our duty.

When we turn to consider the nature of individual right acts, the first point to which attention should be called is that any act may be correctly described in an indefinite, and in principle infinite, number of ways. An act is the production of a change in the state of affairs (if we ignore, for simplicity's sake, the comparatively few cases in which it is the maintenance of an existing state of affairs; cases which, I think, raise no special difficulty). Now, the only changes we can *directly* produce are changes in our own bodies or in our own minds. But these are not, as such, what as a rule we think it our duty to produce. Consider some comparatively simple act, such as telling the truth or fulfilling a promise. In the first case what I produce directly is movements of my vocal organs. But what I think it my duty to produce is a true view in some one else's mind about some fact, and between my movement of my vocal organs and this result there intervenes a series of physical events and events in his mind. Again, in the second case, I may have promised, for instance, to return a book to a friend. I may be able, by a series of movements of my legs and hands, to place it in his hands. But what I am just as likely to do, and to think I have done my duty in doing, is to send it by a messenger or to hand it to his servant or to send it by post; and in each of these cases what I *do* directly is worthless in itself and is connected by a series of intermediate links with what I have promised to return to him. This being so, it *seems* as if what I *do* has no obligatoriness in itself and as if one or other of three accounts should be given of the matter, each of which makes rightness not belong to what I do, considered in its own nature.

(1) One of them would be that what is obligatory is not *doing* anything in the natural sense of producing any change in the state of affairs, but *aiming at* something—at, for instance, my friend's reception of the book. But this account will not do. For (*a*) to aim at something is to act from a motive consisting of the wish to bring that thing about. But we have seen that motive never forms part of the content of our duty; if anything is certain about morals, that, I think, is certain. And (*b*) if I have promised to return the book to my friend, I obviously do not fulfil my promise and do my duty merely by aiming at his receiving the book; I must see that he actually receives it. (2) A more plausible account is that which says I must do that which is likely to produce the result. But this account is open to the

---

[4] "The decision rests with perception." Arist. *Nic. Eth.* 1109 b 23, 1126b 4.

second of these objections, and probably also to the first. For in the first place, however likely my act may seem, even on careful consideration, and even however likely it may in fact be, to produce the result, if it does not produce it, I have not done what I promised to do, i.e. have not done my duty. And secondly, when it is said that I ought to do what is likely to produce the result, what is *probably* meant is that I ought to do a certain thing as a result of the wish to produce a certain result, and of the thought that my act is likely to produce it; and this again introduces motive into the content of duty. (3) Much the most plausible of the three accounts is that which says, "I ought to do that which will actually produce a certain result." This escapes objection (*b*). Whether it escapes objection (*a*) or not depends on what exactly is meant. If it is meant that I ought to do a certain thing from the wish to produce a certain result and the thought that it will do so, the account is still open to objection (*a*). But if it is meant simply that I ought to do a certain thing, and that the reason why I ought to do it is that it will produce a certain result, objection (*a*) is avoided. Now this account in its second form is that which utilitarianism gives. It says what is right is certain acts, not certain acts motivated in a certain way; and it says that acts are never right by their own nature but by virtue of the goodness of their actual results. And this account is, I think, clearly nearer the truth than one which makes the rightness of an act depend on the goodness of either the *intended* or the *likely* results.

Nevertheless, this account appears not to be the true one. For it implies that what we consider right or our duty is what we do *directly*. It is this, e.g. the packing up and posting of the book, that derives its moral significance not from its own nature but from its consequences. But this is *not* what we should describe, strictly, as our duty; our duty is to fulfil our promise, i.e. to put the book into our friend's possession. This we consider obligatory in its own nature, just because it is a fulfilment of promise, and not because of *its* consequences. But, it might be replied by the utilitarian, I do not do this; I only do something that leads up to this, and what I do has no moral significance in itself but only because of its consequences. In answer to this, however, we may point out that a cause produces not only its immediate, but also its remote consequences, and the latter no less than the former. I, therefore, not only produce the immediate movements of parts of my body but also my friend's reception of the book, which results from these. Or, if this be objected to on the grounds that I can hardly be said to have produced my friend's reception of the book when I have packed and posted it, owing to the time that has still to elapse before he receives it, and that to say I have produced the result hardly does justice to the part played by the Post Office, we may at least say that I have *secured* my friend's reception of the book. What I do is as truly describable in this way as by saying that it is the packing and posting of a book. (It is equally truly describable in many other ways; e.g. I have provided a few moments' employment for Post Office officials. But this is irrelevant to the argument.) And if we ask ourselves whether it is *qua* the packing and posting of a book, or *qua* the securing of my friend's getting what I have promised to return to him, that my action is right, it is clear that it is in the second capacity that it is right; and in this capacity, the only capacity in which it is right, it is right by its own nature and not because of its consequences.

The New Religious Morality

Joseph Fletcher

Joseph F. Fletcher (1905-   ), formerly dean of St. Paul's Cathedral, Cincinnati, is professor of social ethics, Episcopal Theological School. He is both a lecturer and an author. Among his books are *Moral Responsibility* (1967), *Morals and Medicine* (1960), and *Situation Ethics* (1966).

There are at bottom only three alternative routes or approaches to follow in making moral decisions. They are: (1) the legalistic; (2) the antinomian, the opposite extreme—i.e., a lawless or unprincipled approach; and (3) the situational. All three have played their part in the history of Western morals, legalism being by far the most common and persistent. Just as legalism triumphed among the Jews after the exile, so, in spite of Jesus' and Paul's revolt against it, it has managed to dominate Christianity constantly from very early days. As we shall be seeing, in many real-life situations legalism demonstrates what Henry Miller, in a shrewd phrase, calls "the immorality of morality."[1]

There is an old joke which serves our purposes. A rich man asked a lovely young woman if she would sleep the night with him. She said, "No." He then asked if she would do it for $100,000? She said, "Yes!" He then asked, "$10,000?" She replied, "Well, yes, I would." His next question was, "How about $500?" Her indignant "What do you think I am?" was met by the answer, "We have already established *that*. Now we are haggling over the price." Does any girl who has "relations" (what a funny way to use the word) outside marriage automatically become a prostitute? Is it always, regardless of what she accomplishes for herself or others—is it *always* wrong? Is extramarital sex inherently evil, or can it be a good thing in some situations? Does everybody have his price, and if so, does that mean we are immoral and ethically weak? Let's see if we can find some help in answering these questions.

APPROACHES TO DECISION-MAKING

Legalism

With this approach one enters into every decision-making situation encumbered with a whole apparatus of prefabricated rules and regulations. Not just the spirit but the letter of the law reigns. Its principles, codified in rules, are not merely guidelines or maxims to illuminate the situation; they are *directives* to be followed. Solutions are preset, and you can "look them up" in a book—a Bible or a confessor's manual.

Source: Situation Ethics (Philadelphia: Westminster Press, 1966). Copyright © 1966, W. L. Jenkins, The Westminster Press. Used by permission.

[1] *Stand Still Like the Hummingbird* (New Directions, 1962), pp. 92-96.

Judaism, Catholicism, Protestantism—all major Western religious traditions have been legalistic. In morals as in doctrine they have kept to a spelled-out, "systematic" orthodoxy. The ancient Jews, especially under the post-exilic Maccabean and Pharisaic leadership, lived by the law or Torah, and its oral tradition (halakah).[2] It was a code of 613 (or 621) precepts, amplified by an increasingly complicated mass of Mishnaic interpretations and applications.

Statutory and code law inevitably piles up, ruling upon ruling, because the complications of life and the claims of mercy and compassion combine—even with code legalists—to accumulate an elaborate system of exceptions and compromise, in the form of rules for breaking the rules! It leads to that tricky and tortuous now-you-see-it, now-you-don't business of interpretation that the rabbis called pilpul—a hairsplitting and logic-chopping study of the letter of the law, pyramiding from codes (e.g., the Covenant and Holiness) to Pentateuch to Midrash and Mishna to Talmud. It was a tragic death to the prophets' "pathos" (sharing God's loving concern) and "ethos" (living by love as *norm*, not program). With the prophets it had been a question of sensitively seeking "an understanding of *the situation*."[3]

Any web thus woven sooner or later chokes its weavers. Reformed and even Conservative Jews have been driven to disentangle themselves from it. Only Orthodoxy is still in its coils. Something of the same pilpul and formalistic complication may be seen in Christian history. With Catholics it has taken the form of a fairly ingenious moral theology that, as its twists and involutions have increased, resorts more and more to a casuistry that appears (as, to its credit, it does) to evade the very "laws" of right and wrong laid down in its textbooks and manuals. Love, even with the most stiff-necked of system builders, continues to plead mercy's cause and to win at least partial release from law's cold abstractions. Casuistry is the homage paid by legalism to the love of persons, and to realism about life's relativities.

Protestantism has rarely constructed such intricate codes and systems of law, but what it has gained by its simplicity it has lost through its rigidity, its puritanical insistence on moral rules.[4] In fact, the very lack of a casuistry and its complexity, once people are committed to *even the bare principle* of legalistic morality of law ethics, is itself evidence of their blindness to the factors of doubt and perplexity. They have lost touch with the headaches and heartbreaks of life.

What can be worse, no casuistry at all may reveal a punishing and sadistic use of law to hurt people instead of helping them. How else explain burning at the stake in the Middle Ages for homosexuals (death, in the Old Testament)? Even today imprisonment up to sixty years is the penalty in one state for those who were actually consenting adults, without seduction or public disorder! This is really unavoidable whenever law instead of love is put first. The "puritan" type is a well-known example of it. But even if the legalist is truly *sorry* that the law requires unloving or disastrous decisions, he still cries, "*Fiat justitia, ruat caelum!*" (Do the "right" even if the sky falls down). He is the man Mark Twain called "a good man in the worst sense of the word."

The Christian situation ethicist agrees with Bertrand Russell and his implied

---

[2] The prophetic J tradition gave way to the E-D tradition, with its precepts and laws.

[3] Abraham J. Heschel, *The Prophets* (Harper & Row, Publishers, Inc., 1962), pp. 225, 307-315.

[4] There are, however, atypical works such as Richard Baxter, *Christian Directory* (1673), and William Ames (Amesius), *De conscientia, eius jure et Casibus* (1632).

judgment, "To this day Christians think an adulterer more wicked than a politician who takes bribes, although the latter probably does a thousand times as much harm."[5] And he thoroughly rejects Cardinal Newman's view: "The Church holds that it were better for sun and moon to drop from heaven, for the earth to fail, and for all the many millions who are upon it to die of starvation in extremest agony ... than that one soul, I will not say should be lost, but should commit one single venial sin."[6]

A Mrs. X was convicted (later cleared in appellate court) of impairing the morals of her minor daughter. She had tried to teach the child chastity, but at thirteen the girl bore the first of three unwanted, neglected babies. Her mother then had said, "If you persist in acting this way, at least be sure the boy wears something!" On this evidence she was convicted and sentenced. The combined forces of "secular" law and legalistic puritanism had tried to prevent loving help to the girl, her bastard victims, and the social agencies trying to help her. Situation ethics would have praised that woman; it would not have pilloried her.

In the language of classical ethics and jurisprudence, the more statutory the law, the greater the need of equity. For, as statutes are applied to actual situations, something has to give; some latitude is necessary for doubtful or perplexed consciences. Inexorably questions arise as to whether in a particular case the law truly applies (doubt), or as to which of several more or less conflicting laws is to be followed (perplexity). The effort to deal with these questions helpfully, even though hamstrung and corseted by rules and "sacred" principles, is what casuistry is. When a law ethic listens to love at all, it tries to rise above its legalism; paradoxically enough, the development of Catholic casuistry is powerful evidence of less legalism in the Catholic fold than the Protestant.

Legalism in the Christian tradition has taken two forms. In the Catholic line it has been a matter of legalistic *reason,* based on nature or natural law. These moralists have tended to adumbrate their ethical rules by applying human reason to the facts of nature, both human and subhuman, and to the lessons of historical experience. By this procedure they claim to have adduced universally agreed and therefore valid "natural" moral laws. Protestant moralists have followed the same adductive and deductive tactics. They have taken Scripture and done with it what the Catholics do with nature. Their Scriptural moral law is, they argue, based on the words and sayings of the Law and the Prophets, the evangelists and apostles of the Bible. It is a matter of legalistic *revelation.* One is rationalistic, the other Biblicistic; one natural, the other Scriptural. But both are legalistic.

Even though Catholic moralists deal also with "revealed law" (e.g., "the divine positive law of the Ten Commandments") and Protestants have tried to use reason in interpreting the sayings of the Bible (hermeneutics), still both by and large have been committed to the doctrines of law ethics.

Antinomianism

Over against legalism, as a sort of polar opposite, we can put antinomianism. This is the approach with which one enters into the decision-making situation armed with no principles or maxims whatsoever, to say nothing of *rules.* In every

[5] *Why I Am Not a Christian* (Simon and Schuster, Inc. 1957), p. 33.
[6] J. H. Newman, *Certain Difficulties Felt by Anglicans in Catholic Teaching* (Longmans, Green & Co., Inc., 1918), p. 190.

"existential moment" or "unique" situation, it declares, one must rely upon the situation of itself, *there and then,* to provide its ethical solution.

The term "antinomianism" (literally, "against law") was used first by Luther to describe Johannes Agricola's views. The ethical concept has cropped up here and there, as among some Anabaptists, some sects of English Puritanism, and some of Wesley's followers. The concept is certainly at issue in I Corinthians (e.g., ch. 6:12-20). Paul had to struggle with two primitive forms of it among the Hellenistic Jew-Christians whom he visited. They took his attacks on law morality too naïvely and too literally.

One form was libertinism—the belief that by grace, by the new life in Christ and salvation by faith, law or rules no longer applied to Christians. Their ultimate happy fate was now assured, and it mattered no more *what* they did. (Whoring, incest, drunkenness, and the like are what they did, therefore! This explains the warning in I Peter 2:16, "Live as free men, yet without using your freedom as a pretext for evil; but live as servants of God." This license led by inevitable reaction to an increase of legalism, especially in sex ethics, under which Christians still suffer today.) The other form, less pretentious and more enduring, was a Gnostic claim to special knowledge, so that neither principles nor rules were needed any longer even as guidelines and direction pointers. They would just *know* what was right when they needed to know. They had, they claimed, a superconscience. It is this second "gnostic" form of the approach which is under examination here.

While legalists are preoccupied with law and its stipulations, the Gnostics are so flatly opposed to law—even in principle—that their moral decisions are random, unpredictable, erratic, quite anomalous. Making moral decisions is a matter of spontaneity; it is literally unprincipled, purely *ad hoc* and casual. They follow no forecastable course from one situation to another. They are, exactly, anarchic—i.e., without a rule. They are not only "unbound by the chains of law" but actually sheer extemporizers, impromptu and intellectually irresponsible. They not only cast the old Torah aside; they even cease to think seriously and *care-fully* about the demands of love as it has been shown in Christ, the love norm itself. The baby goes out with the bath water!

This was the issue Paul fought over with the antinomians at Corinth and Ephesus. They were repudiating all law, as such, and all principles, relying in all moral action choices solely upon guidance in the situation. Some were what he called *pneumatikoi,* spirit-possessed. They claimed that *their* guidance came from outside themselves, by the Holy Spirit. Of what use are principles and laws when you can depend on the Holy Spirit? It was a kind of special-providence idea; a version of the inspiration theory of conscience.[7] Other antinomians claimed, and still do, that their guidance comes from within themselves, as a sort of built-in radarlike "faculty," a translegal or clairvoyant conscience as promised in Jer. 31:31-34, written "upon their hearts." This second and more common form of Gnostic antinomianism, found among both Christians and non-Christians, is close to the intuition theory or faculty theory of conscience.[8]

Perhaps a good example of the guidance idea in today's scene is Moral Re-Armament. It has a doctrine of special providence and daily guidance by "spiritual power" to right and wrong actions and causes. Its basic doctrines were

[7] See warnings in Eph. 6:12; I Tim. 4:1.
[8] See note 22, Chapter II [of *Situation Ethics*].

first worked out under the leadership of Frank Buchman in the twenties, when it was called "The First Century Christian Fellowship." It has won to itself, not so surprisingly, even the French Catholic existentialist philosopher, Gabriel Marcel.[9]

In its present form, with its wealthy clientele, it is a "sawdust trail in a dinner jacket." Part of its ideology, understandably, is the perfectionist notion that "members of the fellowship" can achieve and should live by *absolute* purity (sexual!), *absolute* truth, *absolute* unselfishness, and *absolute* love. Its separation of love from unselfishness is as puzzling as its call for "absolute" virtue and perfectionism and is as pretentious. But after all, if we have the power of the Spirit to tell us daily in a special way *what* the good is, surely we can expect to *do* it "absolutely"! Curiously, the Moral Re-Armament ethic is of the kind one would logically expect to find in the Holiness and Pentecostal movements, and yet, in spite of their self-styled pneumatic character, they are for the most part quite legalistic morally—not antinomian about their ethics at all.

Another version of antinomianism, on the whole much subtler philosophically and perhaps more admirable, is the ethics of existentialism. Sartre speaks of "nausea," which is our anxious experience of the *incoherence* of reality. For him any belief in coherence (such as the Christian doctrine of the unity of God's creation and his Lordship over history) is "bad faith." In every movement of moral choice or decision "we have no excuses behind us and no justification before us." Sartre refuses to admit to any *generally* valid principles at all, nothing even ordinarily valid, to say nothing of universal *laws*.[10] Simone de Beauvoir in *The Ethics of Ambiguity* cannot quite bring herself to accept either "the contingent absurdity of the discontinuous" or "the rationalistic necessity of the continuous," proving herself to be less sturdily existentialist than Sartre, but she admits that the real world is after all "bare and incoherent."[11] She shrinks from a candid antinomianism. But the plain fact is that her ontology—her idea of basic reality—is, like Sartre's, one of radical discontinuity, so that there can be no connective tissue between one situation or moment of experience and another. There is no fabric or web of life, hence no basis for generalizing moral principles *or* laws. Every situation has only its particularity!

On this view, of course, the existentialists rightly reject even all principles, all "generally valid" ethical norms or axioms, as well as all rules or laws or precepts that legalistically absolutize (idolize) such general principles. Radical discontinuity in one's theory of being forces the "absolute particularity" of *tout comprendre, tout pardonner*. Sartre is at least honest and tough-minded. In the absence of any faith in love as the norm and in any God as the norm-giver, he says resolutely: "Ontology itself cannot formulate ethical precepts. It is concerned solely with what is, and we cannot possibly derive imperatives from ontology's indicatives."[12] He is, on this score at least, entirely correct!

Situationism

A third approach, in between legalism and antinomian unprincipledness, is situation ethics. (To jump from one polarity to the other would be only to go from the frying pan to the fire.) The situationist enters into every decision-making

---

[9] Cf. Gabriel Marcel, *Fresh Hope for the World* (Longmans, Green & Co., Inc., 1960); see also Tom Driberg, *The Mystery of Moral Re-Armament* (Alfred A. Knopf, Inc., 1965).

[10] Jean-Paul Sartre, *Existentialism*, tr. by B. Frechtman (Philosophical Library, Inc., 1947).

[11] (Philosophical Library, Inc., 1948), pp. 44, 122.

[12] *Being and Nothingness*, tr. by Hazel Barnes (Philosophical Library, Inc., 1956), p. 625.

situation fully armed with the ethical maxims of his community and its heritage, and he treats them with respect as illuminators of his problems. Just the same, he is prepared in any situation to compromise them or set them aside *in the situation* if love seems better served by doing so.

Situation ethics goes part of the way with natural law, by accepting reason as the instrument of moral judgment, while rejecting the notion that the good is "given" in the nature of things, objectively. It goes part of the way with Scriptural law by accepting revelation as the source of the norm while rejecting all "revealed" norms or laws but the one command—to love God and the neighbor. The situationist follows a moral law or violates it according to love's need. For example, "Almsgiving is a good thing *if* . . . ." The situationist never says, "Almsgiving is a good thing. Period!" His decisions are hypothetical, not categorical. Only the commandment to love is categorically good. "Owe no one anything, except to love one another." (Rom. 13:8) If help to an indigent only pauperizes and degrades him, the situationist refuses a handout and finds some other way. He makes no law out of Jesus' "Give to every one who begs from you." It is only one step from that kind of Biblicist literalism to the kind that causes women in certain sects to refuse blood transfusions even if death results—even if they are carrying a quickened fetus that will be lost too. The legalist says that even if he tells a man escaped from an asylum where his intended victim is, if he finds and murders him, at least only one sin has been committed (murder), not two (lying as well)!

As Brunner puts it, "The basis of the Divine Command is always the same, but its content varies with varying circumstances." Therefore, the "error of casuistry does not lie in the fact that it indicates the infinite variety of forms which the Command of love may assume; its error consists in deducing particular laws from a universal law . . . as though all could be arranged beforehand. . . . Love, however, is free from all this predefinition."[13] We might say, from the situationist's perspective, that it is possible to derive general "principles" from whatever is the one and only universal law (*agapē* for Christians, something else for others), but not laws or rules. We cannot milk universals from a universal!

William Temple put it this way: "Universal obligation attaches not to particular judgments of conscience but to conscientiousness. What acts are right may depend on circumstances . . . but there is an absolute obligation to will whatever may on each occasion be right."[14] Our obligation is relative to the situation, but obligation *in* the situation is absolute. We are only "obliged" to tell the truth, for example, if the situation calls for it; if a murderer asks us his victim's whereabouts, our duty might be to lie. There is in situation ethics an absolute element and an element of calculation, as Alexander Miller once pointed out.[15] But it would be better to say it has an absolute *norm* and a calculating method. There is weight in the old saying that what is needed is "faith, hope, and clarity." We have to find out what is "fitting" to be truly ethical, to use H. R. Niebuhr's word for it in his *The Responsible Self.*[16] Situation ethics aims at a contextual appropriateness—not the "good" or the "right" but the *fitting.*

A cartoon in a fundamentalist magazine once showed Moses scowling, holding

[13] *The Divine Imperative*, tr. by Olive Wyon (The Westminster Press, 1947), pp. 132 ff.
[14] *Nature, Man and God* (The Macmillan Company, 1934), p. 405.
[15] *The Renewal of Man* (Doubleday & Company, Inc., 1955), p. 44.
[16] (Harper & Row, Publishers, Inc., 1963), pp. 60-61. Precedents are Samuel Clarke, *Unchangeable Obligations of Natural Religion* (London, 1706), and A. C. Ewing, *The Definition of the Good* (The Macmillan Company, 1947).

his stone tablet with its graven laws, all ten, and an eager stonecutter saying to him, "Aaron said perhaps you'd let us reduce them to 'Act responsibly in love.' " This was meant as a dig at the situationists and the new morality, but the legalist humor in it merely states exactly what situation ethics calls for! With Dietrich Bonhoeffer we say, "Principles are only tools in God's hands, soon to be thrown away as unserviceable."[17]

One competent situationist, speaking to students, explained the position this way. Rules are "like 'Punt on fourth down,' or 'Take a pitch when the count is three balls.' These rules are part of the wise player's know-how, and distinguish him from the novice. But they are not unbreakable. The best players are those who know when to ignore them. In the game of bridge, for example, there is a useful rule which says 'Second hand low.' But have you ever played with anyone who followed the rule slavishly? You say to him (in exasperation), 'Partner, why didn't you play your ace? We could have set the hand.'And he replies, unperturbed, 'Second hand low!' What is wrong? The same thing that was wrong when Kant gave information to the murderer. He forgot the purpose of the game. . . . He no longer thought of winning the hand, but of being able to justify himself by invoking the rule."[18]

This practical temper of the activist or *verb*-minded decision maker, versus contemplative *noun*-mindedness, is a major Biblical rather than Hellenistic trait. In Abraham Heschel's view, "The insistence upon generalization at the price of a total disregard of the particular and concrete is something which would be alien to prophetic thinking. Prophetic words are never detached from the concrete, historic situation. Theirs is not a timeless, abstract message; it always refers to an actual situation. The general is given in the particular and the verification of the abstract is in the concrete."[19] A "leap of faith" is an action decision rather than a leap of thought, for a man's faith is a hypothesis that he takes seriously enough to act on and live by.

There are various names for this approach: situationism, contextualism, occasionalism, circumstantialism, even actualism. These labels indicate, of course, that the core of the ethic they describe is a healthy and primary awareness that "circumstances alter cases"—i.e., that in actual problems of conscience the situational variables are to be weighed as heavily as the normative or "general" constants.

The situational factors are so primary that we may even say "circumstances alter rules and principles." It is said that when Gertrude Stein lay dying she declared, "It is better to ask questions than to give answers, even good answers." This is the temper of situation ethics. It is empirical, fact-minded, data conscious, inquiring. It is antimoralistic as well as antilegalistic, for it is sensitive to variety and complexity. It is neither simplistic nor perfectionistic. It is "casuistry" (case-based) in a constructive and nonpejorative sense of the word. We should perhaps call it "neocasuistry." Like classical casuistry, it is case-focused and concrete, concerned to bring Christian imperatives into practical operation. But unlike classical casuistry, this neocasuistry repudiates any attempt to anticipate or prescribe real-life decisions in their existential particularity. It works with two guidelines

[17] *Ethics*, tr. by N. H. Smith (The Macmillan Company, 1955), p. 8.
[18] E. LaB. Cherbonnier, unpublished address, Trinity College, December 14, 1964.
[19] *God in Search of Man: A Philosophy of Judaism* (Farrar, Strauss & Cudahy, Inc., 1956), p. 204.

from Paul: "The written code kills, but the Spirit gives life" (II Cor. 3:6), and "For the whole law is fulfilled in one word, 'You shall love your neighbor as yourself' " (Gal. 5:14).

In the words of Millar Burrows' finding in Biblical theology: "He who makes the law his standard is obligated to perform all its precepts, for to break one commandment is to break the law. He who lives by faith and love is not judged on that basis, but by a standard infinitely higher and at the same time more attainable."[20] This is why Msgr. Pietro Palazzini (Secretary of the Sacred Congregation of the Council) freely acknowledges that situation ethics "must not be understood as an escape from the heavy burden of moral integrity. For, though its advocates truly deny the absolute value of universal norms, some are motivated by the belief that in this manner they are better safeguarding the eminent sovereignty of God."[21]

As we shall see, *Christian* situation ethics has only one norm or principle or law (call it what you will) that is binding and unexceptionable, always good and right regardless of the circumstances. That is "love"—the *agapē* of the summary commandment to love God and the neighbor.[22] Everything else without exception, all laws and rules and principles and ideals and norms, are only *contingent*, only valid *if they happen* to serve love in any situation. Christian situation ethics is not a system or program of living according to a code, but an effort to relate love to a world of relativities through a casuistry obedient to love. It is the strategy of love. This strategy denies that there are, as Sophocles thought, any unwritten immutable laws of heaven, agreeing with Bultmann that all such notions are idolatrous and a demonic pretension.[23]

In non-Christian situation ethics some other highest good or *summum bonum* will, of course, take love's place as the one and only standard—such as self-realization in the ethics of Aristotle. But the *Christian* is neighbor-centered first and last. Love is for people, not for principles; i.e., it is personal—and therefore when the impersonal universal conflicts with the personal particular, the latter prevails in situation ethics. Because of its mediating position, prepared to act on moral laws or in spite of them, the antinomians will call situationists soft legalists, and legalists will call them cryptoantinomians.

LOVE HAS NO EQUALS

In its very marrow, Christian ethics is a situation ethic. The new morality, the emerging contemporary Christian conscience, separates Christian conduct from rigid creeds and rigid codes. Some of its critics, both Protestant and Catholic, seem to fear that by dropping codes it will drop its Christian commitment.[24] What it does is to treat all rules and principles and "virtues" (that is to say, all

[20] *An Outline of Biblical Theology* (The Westminster Press, 1946), pp. 163-164.

[21] Article, "Morality, Situation," in *Dictionary of Moral Theology*, ed. by Francesco Cardinal Roberti and Msgr. Pietro Palazzini (The Newman Press, 1962), pp. 800-802.

[22] Matt. 5:43-48 and ch. 22:34-40; Luke 6:27-28; 10:25-28 and vs. 29-37; Mark 12:28-34; Gal. 5:14; Rom. 13:8-10; etc.

[23] Rudolf Bultmann, *Essays Philosophical and Theological* (The Macmillan Company, 1955), pp. 22, 154.

[24] C. B. Eavey, *Principles of Christian Ethics* (Zondervan Publishing House, 1958), p. 246; Kenneth Moore, O. Carm., *American Ecclesiastical Review*, Vol. 135 (1956), pp. 29-38.

"universals") as love's servants and subordinates, to be quickly kicked out of the house if they forget their place and try to take over. Ayn Rand, the egoist and jungle-ethic writer, tersely describes the love ethic (except that it does not teach us to *scorn* a whore, only to help and redeem her): "A morality which teaches you to scorn a whore who gives her body indiscriminately to all men—this same morality demands that you surrender your soul to promiscuous love for all comers."[25]

Augustine was right to make love the source principle, the hinge principle upon which all other "virtues" hang, whether "cardinal" (natural) or "theological" (revealed). Love is not one virtue among others, one principle among equals, not even a *primus inter pares.* * One theologian, Robert Gleason, S.J., in a full-dress attack on situation ethics, threw down the gauntlet most lucidly (and how different a challenge from that of Ayn Rand!) by asserting, "While the motive of love is a noble one, it is not in Christian tradition to present it as the exclusive motive for moral action."[26] This succinctly challenges the view that love has a monopoly control. It flies directly in the face of Paul's "single saying" in Gal. 5:14 and the conclusion of his hymn to love, I Cor., ch. 13. But what else can the man of law do, trapped as he is in his intrinsic rights and wrongs and his collections and systems of virtues and absolutes?

To illustrate what legalism does in the civil order, we might recall what happened a few years ago in an English court. The law reads that a marriage must be validated ("consummated") by sexual union. In the case before it, it found that a young wife had conceived a son by means of A.I.H. (artificial insemination from her husband) because he was suffering a temporary erectile failure, subsequently corrected. The court was faithful to its law, and ruled that the little boy was conceived out of wedlock, i.e., that the child was a bastard, the mother an adulteress or fornicator, the wife husbandless when her child was born, the father without a son and heir, and the child an outlaw. All of this even though their child was seed of their seed, flesh of their flesh!

Augustine was right again, as situationists see it, to reduce the whole Christian ethic to the single maxim, *Dilige et quod vis, fac* (Love with care and *then* what you will, do). It was not, by the way, *Ama et fac quod vis* (Love with desire and do what you please)![27] It was not antinomianism.

Christian love is not desire. *Agapē* is giving love—non-reciprocal, neighbor-regarding—"neighbor" meaning "everybody," even an enemy (Luke 6:32-35). It is usually distinguished from friendship love (*philia*) and romantic love (*erōs*), both of which are selective and exclusive. Erotic love and philic love have their proper place in our human affairs but they are not what is meant by *agapē*, agapeic love or "Christian love." Erotic and philic love are emotional, but the effective principle of Christian love is *will*, disposition; it is an *attitude*, not a feeling.

Situationists welcome the German label for this conception, *Gesinnungs-ethik,* † an attitudinal ethic rather than a legal one. "Have this mind among yourselves, which you have in Christ Jesus" (Phil. 2:5), and *then*, as Augustine says, whatever

---

[25] *Atlas Shrugged* (Random House, Inc., 1957), p. 1033.

* [First among his equals.—Eds.]

[26] "Situational Morality," *Thought*, Vol. 32 (1957), pp. 533-558.

[27] *Ep. Joan.*, vii. 5, in J. P. Migne, *Patralogiae cursus completus, series Latina* (Paris: Garnier Fr., 1864), Vol. 35, col. 2033. "*Semel ergo breve praeceptum tibi praecipitur, Dilige, et quod vis fac.*"

† [Conscience ethic.—Eds.]

you do will be right! The mind of him whom Bonhoeffer called "the Man for others" is to be for others, for neighbors. *That* is *agapē*.

What a difference it makes when love, understood agapeically, is boss; when love is the only norm. How free and therefore responsible we are! The natural law moralists, just to cite an example of legalism, are trapped into cheating on love or even into altogether denying love's demands, in the matter of sterilizations. In the name of a "natural law" of procreation they have to prohibit obstetricians from tying off the tubes of a cardiac mother in delivery, for whom another pregnancy is a mortal danger. In the name of a "natural law" of secrecy they have been known to admonish a doctor to withhold from an innocent girl the fact that she is about to marry a syphilitic man. No such cut-and-dried, coldly predetermined (prejudiced) position could or would be taken by a situationist.

At this juncture we might do well to look at the question whether a situationist can agree with legalism's effort to *force* people to be good. The answer is, of course, that "it all depends." It seems impossible to see any sound reason for most of such attempts to legislate morality. Yet there was a lot of furious surprise in a California city recently when the police found a wife-swapping club and learned there were *no laws* to stop it. The District Attorney saw no cause to be alarmed, even so. "Wife-swapping just doesn't violate any section of the penal code." It is doubtful that love's cause is helped by any of the sex laws that try to dictate sexual practices for consenting adults.

The triple terrors of infection, conception, and detection, which once scared people into "Christian" sex relations (marital monopoly), have pretty well become obsolete through medicine and urbanism. There is less and less cause, on the basis of situation ethics, for the opinion that people should abide by, or pretend to, an ideal or standard that is not their own. It may well be, especially with the young, that situationists should advise continence or chastity for practical expedient reasons, but that is a situational, not a legalistic approach.

THE END OF IDEOLOGY

Political and social establishments feel safer when buttressed by an ethical establishment, a fixed code. In some circles there is a growing hunger for law; it can be seen in cultural conformism, and in the lust for both political and theological orthodoxy. Like the existentialists to an extent, situationists are in revolt against the cultural stodginess of "respectable" and traditional ethics. They rebel against the reigning ethics of American middle-class culture because of its high-flown moral laws on the one hand and its evasive shilly-shallying on the other; it is often and acutely described as "the leap from Sunday to Monday."

Nothing in the world causes so much conflict of conscience as the continual, conventional payment of lip service to moral "laws" that are constantly flouted in practice because they are too petty or too rigid to fit the facts of life. Many people prefer to fit reality to rules rather than to fit rules to reality. Legalism always bears down hard on the need for order, putting its premium on obedience to law, even statutory law. It would, if it could, immobilize Martin Luther King and the sit-in demonstrators or civil rights protesters, whereas situation ethics gives high-order value to freedom, and to that *responsibility* for free decision which is the obverse side of the coin of freedom.

In ethics as in politics we can see that ideology has come to a dead end. Doctrinaire by-the-book theory and practice is too confining, too narrow. "The point is," says Daniel Bell, "that ideologists are terrible simplifiers. Ideology makes it unnecessary for people to confront individual issues in individual situations. One simply turns to the ideological vending machine, and out comes the prepared formula."[28] Substitute "law" for ideology in Bell's statement and we have the nub of the matter. A committee set up by the late President Kennedy to deal with questions of business ethics, of which the writer of this book was a member, got nowhere at all because it was code-minded, wrote a code to cover all business, and found itself possessed of nothing but platitudes.

For real decision-making, freedom is required, an open-ended approach to situations. Imagine the plight of an obstetrician who believed he must always respirate every baby he delivered, no matter how monstrously deformed! A century ago Thomas Huxley rather thought he would prefer being accurate and correct as a moral decision maker, even if he had to be as mechanical as a clock wound up for the day, than assume the burden of mistakes entailed by freedom. What an irony to compare his opinion to Tik-Tok's in *The Wizard of Oz!* There the mechanical man had the special grace of always doing "what he was wound up to do," but he wanted instead to be *human*. And what did he lack? Freedom to choose.

No wonder that Jesus, in the language of a French Catholic moralist whose concern is contemporary, "reacted particularly against code morality and against casuistry," and that his "attitude toward code morality [was] purely and simply one of reaction."[29] Modern Christians ought not to be naïve enough to accept any other view of Jesus' ethic than the situational one. When Edmund Wilson ran his famous article in *The New Yorker* some ten years ago on the Dead Sea Scrolls, he made quite a splash by saying that Jesus' teaching was a copy of the Essenes' teaching at the Qumran community.[30] Actually, the quickest way to expose the error in all such uncritical comparisons is simply to point out that the legalism and code rule of the Qumran sect put even the Pharisees to shame, whereas Jesus boldly rejected all such legalisms.

As we know, for many people, sex is so much a moral problem, largely due to the repressive effects of legalism, that in newspapers and popular parlance the term "morals charge" always means a sex complaint! "Her morals are not very high" means her sex life is rather looser than the mores allow. Yet we find nothing in the teachings of Jesus about the ethics of sex, except adultery and an absolute condemnation of divorce—a correlative matter. He said nothing about birth control, large or small families, childlessness, homosexuality, masturbation, fornication or premarital intercourse, sterilization, artificial insemination, abortion, sex play, petting, and courtship. Whether any form of sex (hetero, homo, or auto) is good or evil depends on whether love is fully served.

The Christian ethic is not interested in reluctant virgins and technical chastity. What sex probably needs more than anything is a good airing, demythologizing it and getting rid of its mystique-laden and occult accretions, which come from romanticism on the one hand and puritanism on the other. People are learning that we can have sex without love, and love without sex; that baby-making can be (and

---

[28] *The End of Ideology: On the Exhaustion of Political Ideas in the Fifties*, new rev. ed. (Collier Books, 1962), p. 17.

[29] J. LeClercq, *Christ and the Modern Conscience*, pp. 59, 61.

[30] Republished as *The Scrolls from the Dead Sea* (Oxford University Press, 1955).

often ought to be) separated from love-making. It is, indeed, for re-creation as well as for procreation. But if people do not believe it is wrong to have sex relations outside marriage, it isn't, unless they hurt themselves, their partners, or others. This is, of course, a very big "unless" and gives reason to many to abstain altogether except within the full mutual commitment of marriage. The civil lawmakers are rapidly ridding their books of statutes making unmarried sex a crime between consenting adults. All situationists would agree with Mrs. Patrick Campbell's remark that they can do what they want "as long as they don't do it in the street and frighten the horses."

Situation ethics always suspects prescriptive law of falsifying life and dwarfing moral stature, whether it be the Scripture legalism of Biblicist Protestants and Mohammedans or the nature legalism (natural law) of the Catholics and disciples of Confucius. One American theologian has complained that situation ethics fails to realize that people are unwilling to grapple with what he calls "paradoxical ambiguities"—that they want something more definite and exact than ethical relativism offers. Of course; they want the Grand Inquisitor. T. S. Eliot was right to say that people cannot bear too much reality. But there is no escape for them. To learn love's sensitive tactics, such people are going to have to put away their childish rules.

REFLECTION AND REPLY

The old morality with its classical absolutes and universals is a form of Pharisaism. Its purpose is to follow the law (moral norms), even though staying as close to love as possible. The new morality, for which situation ethics is the appropriate method, follows love (freedom to put human need before anything else), staying as close to law as possible yet departing as far from it as need be. Jesus taught this situationist kind of freedom from moral law. He held that morals were made for man, not man for morals.

In *The Shaking of the Foundations,* Tillich said of Jesus: "The burden he wants to take from us is the burden of religion. It is the yoke of law, imposed on the people of his time by the religious leaders, the wise and the understanding, as he calls them in their own words—the Scribes and Pharisees, as they are usually called. Those who labor and are heavy laden are those who are sighing under the yoke of the religious law. And he will give them the power to overcome religion and law; the yoke he gives them is a 'new being' above religion." Tillich should have completed his last sentence "and moral laws."

The conflict between Jesus and the orthodox Jews was not "theological" in the sense of differences about doctrine. It was ethical. He spearheaded a *moral* revolt. He was a Jew, not a Christian—but a Jew whose morality was centered on love instead of law. Then Paul took up his cause and theologized it by adding to Jesus' new moral teaching a new teaching about who this Jesus was. He preached a faith about Jesus, not the faith of Jesus. Later, among the Greeks converted by Paul, there were some who wanted to follow a third ethical line, i.e., ignore law altogether. These were the "God-directed" who denied that they needed moral guidelines of any kind. Most of the Christians, however, soon forgot Jesus' bid for freedom and slid back into the legalism he threw out. One recalls the young Nazi's devout cry before World War II: "We Germans are so happy. We are free from freedom."

Here we have the three primary models for ethical strategy: legalism, situationism and extemporism. Our language may change but the shape of the problem stays much the same. We may be more sophisticated conceptually, but the argument is still the old one, in modern dress. One critic has asked whether a codeless love is the only alternative to a loveless code. The reply must be a clear Yes.

I confess that the main thrust of *Situation Ethics* was against legalism. This was because almost all people in our Western culture, especially Christians, are and have been legalistic. They hang on to certain eternally invariable rules of conduct as absolutely valid and universally obliging regardless of the situation. They think there are some things (allegedly learned directly from God) that are always right or always wrong. Yet the recent hippies' ethics, a hang-loose-baby ethics in wild reaction, and its sophisticated support by existentialist writers and philosophers may soon become influential enough to call for a second corrective treatise, aimed in *their* direction.

The thing to note is that situation ethics is in the middle, between moral law and ethical extemporism. One is bound by its principles, the other has none. (Professionals speak of "rules ethics" and "act ethics.") Situation ethics is a victim of polarization—the easiest and silliest of tools used by those who oversimplify life's relativity and fluidity.

If you refuse to give intrinsic validity to moral principles, you are assumed to have none. Even my German publisher, before I knew what he was up to, retitled *Situation Ethics* as *Moral ohne Normen?** The old morality's advocates (Catholic and Protestant) see the new morality camp as cryptoantinomian, while the non-principled and "way out" spontaneists see them as soft legalists. The *via media* is a dangerous path, and I suppose we really are, in some degree, fifth columnists in both of the polar camps. We cannot absolutize both love and law, and the New Testament makes it perfectly clear which one to choose.

Suggested Readings

1. Andelson, Robert, "Some Fundamental Inconsistencies in Fletcher's *Situation Ethics,*" *Personalist* (Summer 1970), 332-337.
2. Broad, C. D., *Five Types of Ethical Theory* (New York: Harcourt, 1930), Ch. 5, "Exposition and Criticism."
3. King, J. Charles, "The Inadequacy of Situation Ethics," *The Thomist,* Vol. 34, No. 3 (July 1970).
4. McCloskey, H. J., "Ross and the Concept of Prima Facie Duty," *Australasian Journal of Philosophy* (1963).
5. Paton, H. J., *The Categorical Imperative* (Chicago: University of Chicago Press), 1948.

* [Morals Without Rules—Eds.]

LOVE AND SEX

Whatever circumstances pave the way, love does not itself appear until a sexual affinity is declared. . . . The glance of an ideal love is terrible and glorious, foreboding death and immortality together.

—George Santayana

Considering how much the subject of love dominates our fiction, poetry, song, dance, theater, and sleeping and waking thoughts, it is astonishing to realize the paucity of philosophical literature on love. It is true that love has been given the metaphysical role of holding the world together and impelling change within it; the biblical sense of "to know" a sexual partner hints punningly at the epistemological secrets of love; the "heart that has its reasons" supposedly defies the logical rationality of our mind and bespeaks a deeper rationality; religion and theology have celebrated the cosmic dimensions of godly love. Despite these philosophical excursions into the domain of love, the bulk of the discussion about love has been contributed by fringe philosophers, the philosophs—philosophically minded littérateurs, historians, psychologists, and sensationalists.

As the essays in this section reflect, the main part of sober philosophical thought about love—professional and popular—has focused on its moral aspects. In the last essay in this section, **Ronald Dworkin** says that "for most people the heart of morality is a sexual code, and if the ordinary man's views on fornication, adultery, sadism, exhibitionism and the other staples of pornography are not moral positions, it is hard to imagine any beliefs he is likely to have that are." Certainly, the most frequently cited evidence that the young are in cultural, moral revolt is their supposed "sexual revolution." Perhaps popular moral thought's preoccupation with sex is accounted for by the ascetic strain in Judeo-Christian religion, its practitioners feeling bound to contend anew with each generation of adolescents and their insatiable sexual hungers. No one in our culture can have failed to entertain the thought that the relation between morality and sex is, starkly and bluntly, one of war.

The origin of the ascetic strain is not to be attributed solely to pursemouth Puritanism, for the satiation of heterosexual hungers may result in children. These children are not gladly disposed of, generally. Because we have a moral obligation to care for, love, nurture, and educate our children, society may properly insist that sexual satisfaction take place within a social structure that is designed to encourage and facilitate fulfillment of our obligations to our children; hence, Judeo-Christian morality has tried to channel the sexual act into occasions within a family institution licensed by marriage.

As has often been claimed, it may very well be that the technological advances in contraception and the legality of abortion rob the ascetic strain of its rationale.

This might then betoken for some an era of ceasefire between morality and sex. It could be thought that each person is now free to choose his own sexual practices without interference from moralists. This, however, would be a rash conclusion. Except perhaps for masturbation, the sexual act involves at least one other person; as long as our act affects someone else, it is properly subject to moral consideration. It may not be as rash to conclude that we should loosen the legal restrictions on sexual relations once the ascetic strain is removed. It may be morally defensible to remove legal restrictions on "consenting adults," although this has been challenged by Lord Devlin, for one; Devlin's arguments are given and critically discussed in Dworkin's essay in this section.

The move toward complete moral liberty in sexual relations upon removal of the ascetic strain might be seen to be rash if you consider morality in a positive as well as in a negative way. Too often, people think of a moral system as a negative device, as a set of maxims that consists exclusively of "Thou shalt nots." It is possible to think of a moral system as containing positive maxims as well, having the purpose of recommending practices that enable a person to humanize himself and others and to secure values that would be lost without the recommended practices. For example, marriage need not be thought of as a mere negative device for curbing sexual freedom; it can also be thought of as an institution that provides for the positive values growing out of a stable family situation.

Suppose, however, that we grant, for purposes of argument, that legalized marriage is a disposable institution. We might then ask what we will put in its place as a mediator between morality and sex. The candidate most often suggested is love; persons who love one another often believe their love is the true and sufficient pledge that sanctions sexual reciprocity. For them, legalized marriage is an empty formality. From this viewpoint, love holds morality in one hand and sex in the other.

If love is to play a mediating role, then, it must be construed in such a way that it partakes of both a moral and a sexual character. One philosophical interest in love is directed toward discovery of the region where morality, love, and sex overlap.

Perhaps the most perspicuous way to approach this philosophical issue is to distinguish between three senses of "love" and to note how they take different positions on a cone of love. In his essay in the previous section, Joseph Fletcher distinguished three kinds of love: *agapē, philia,* and *erōs.* Agapeic love is nonreciprocal and directed toward every other person. It is the love we feel toward everyone else simply because they are human; agapeic love is positioned at the wide end of the cone of love. Philic love is reciprocal and is the love we have for friends; this is a more personal love and is enriched by the close commerce we enjoy with one another. Philic love is positioned closer to the nose of the cone, being directed toward fewer persons.

At the very nose of the cone lies erotic love. It requires maximum reciprocity; it is concentrated more exclusively on a single person than either agapeic or philic love. In the introduction to this section, we are concerned with erotic love, and, unless we indicate to the contrary, "love" will refer to erotic love.

That erotic love overlaps with morality could be shown if it could be shown that agapeic and philic love contain moral ingredients and differ from erotic love not in kind but only in degree. It could be shown that agapeic, philic, and erotic love are similar in kind if they could be shown to contain common moral ingredients. We proceed to show this.

Agapeic love is extended to every person; even the most wretched, cunning, scheming, ugly human has a claim on our moral regard simply because he is human; built into agapeic love is respect for humanity. This same respect typically is part of erotic love. The lover respects the lover. The person who is unsure of his own endowments is nagged by the thought that his lover feels pity rather than love for him. Pity, unlike love, is fed by low estimation; love, unlike pity, is fed by respectful estimation. It appears, then, that erotic love contains, as do agapeic and philic love, at least the moral ingredient of human respect. Having this moral ingredient in common shows these loves do not differ in kind, which, in turn, shows that erotic love and morality overlap.

Doubt about this overlap could come if one confuses erotic love with sexual encounters. That the two are distinct can easily be shown by considering that sexual conquest is frequently attended by disrespect for the conquered. Since victorious disrespect and the respect ingredient in erotic love are contrary, purely sexual excitement and erotic love are contrary and, so, distinct.

Further evidence for the overlap between morality and love can be gathered from the observation that agapeic love contains the moral ingredient of concern for the welfare of others; and so does philic love to an even more intense degree, although philic love is focussed on a fewer number of persons; because erotic love is accompanied by a desire for the welfare of the beloved, erotic love is different only in extent and degree from agapeic and philic love, each containing this same moral factor. It could, further, be speculated that every moral ingredient of agapeic love is contained in philic love, and that every moral ingredient of philic love is contained in erotic love; naturally, the closer we move to the nose of the love cone, the denser become the moral ingredients.

In the first essay in this section, **Rollo May** reports that, despite our immense sexual freedom as contrasted with Victorian repression, his patients' internalized anxiety and guilt have increased. He suggests that this increase may be due to an increase of sexual indulgence without love. Were we to follow up our notion that love and morality overlap, the loss of love in sexual relations implies the loss of the moral element in sexual relations. Without the moral element, what is to distinguish human sexual relations from animal coupling? Perhaps the reported anxiety and guilt are intimations that humans have abandoned their humanity in abandoning the moral ingredient that erotic love carries. The recovery of sexual health may depend upon the recovery of erotic love with its moral factors. When reading May, we suggest that you ask yourself to what extent the five values of sexual love that he sketches depend upon such a love with its moral constituents.

If we suppose that sex and morality overlap by virtue of the mediation of erotic love, an interesting philosophical question arises when we ask about the relation of sexual morality to the rest of morality. **Agnes Heller**, in this section's third essay, writes from a Marxist viewpoint. For her, property is an alienating feature of society: a society that fosters property relations and values tends to foster inequality in marital relations and to diminish the reciprocity of sexual courtesies. In a socialist society, as she conceives it, sexual morality is not isolated from other moral ideals. She says that "in the relation between the sexes the same factors—and only those factors—impair universal values which are detrimental to all other aspects of morality. Breaking the will of another person, deliberate misleading (lies), regarding the other person simply as a tool, ruining other people's lives, lack of reciprocity, and inequality, these are the attitudes and acts in contacts between the sexes which violate the universal generic values most irreparably. But obviously they do not offend against the special ethics of sex morality only, for they also violate the properties of the species in every other aspect of human relations." Heller goes on to elaborate the nature of sexual morality in a society that has no alienation, stating six features central to that future morality.

One way to look at the encyclical of **Pope Paul VI** (the second essay in this section) in contrast to Heller's essay is to consider how much his viewpoint on sexual morality is influenced by his emphasis on the procreative function of sex. This emphasis leads him to favor the formation of sexual morality in such a way that its primary imperative is to fit favorably to the morality of marriage and family; he acknowledges in his opening remarks that contracepted sexual relations do have a bearing on such moral issues as demography, economics, and education, but for him they do not carry the determinative weight for sexual ethics that the divinely instituted procreative function does. Whatever view of sexual relations is favored, however, it is clear that May, Heller, and Pope Paul agree that a philosophical discussion of sexual morality should take place within a perspective that includes all of morality.

So far in the introduction to this section, we have dwelled on the overlap between love and morality, taking it for granted that there is an overlap between love and sex. It should not take any argument to establish that one of the features distinguishing erotic love from philic and agapeic love is the presence of sexual attraction and encounter in the former and its absence, usually, in the latter. Offering the intimacy of our body to our lover is the special token we grant as an expression of our erotic love; promiscuity generally stands in moral disfavor because with its practice intimacy ceases to be a special act; the promiscuous person, according to conventional morality, comes full-bodied but empty-handed. **George Santayana** (fourth essay in this section) draws the distinction between erotic love and other loves elegantly: "What Aristotle calls friendships of utility, pleasure, or virtue, all resting on common interests of some impersonal sort, are far from possessing the quality of love, its thrill, flutter, and absolute sway over happiness and misery ... it is still a deep and dumb affinity, an inexplicable emotion seizing the heart, an influence organizing the world, like a luminous crystal, about one magic point."

Although Santayana finds that erotic love has an animal basis, he presents more "than half the truth" by pointing out that it has an ideal object. As a naturalistic philosopher, he finds that all our ideals are developments of natural passions or functions. The special role he finds "Reason" to have is the elaboration and articulation of these passions and functions that transform them into ideal goods. According to him, the transformation of the sexual instinct into erotic love is not accomplished by moral elaborations alone. "It would be mere sophistry to pretend, for instance, that love is or should be nothing but a moral bond, the sympathy of two kindred spirits or the union of two lives. For such an effect no passion would be needed, as none is needed to perceive beauty or to feel pleasure." You will enjoy Santayana's stylish playing on the chords of romantic, erotic love. He, unlike most serious philosophers, does not observe what appears to have been a powerful injunction: That whereof their couch has told, thereof must their quills be silent.

Sex, Love, and Identity
Rollo May

Rollo May (1909-   ) received his B.A. at Oberlin. Alfred Adler was his teacher. He received his Ph.D. at Columbia University. He is best known for developing the idea of existential psychology with its emphasis upon the here-and-now problems. He is concerned with identity crisis rather than with libido, with the fear of death more than with the birth trauma. His most well-known books are *Existential Psychology* (1961), *Love and Will* (1969), and *Man's Search for Himself* (1953).

There are several strange and interesting dilemmas in which we find ourselves with respect to sex and love in our culture. When psychoanalysis was born in Victorian times half a century ago, repression of sexual impulses, feelings, and drives was the accepted mode. It was not nice to feel sexual, one would not talk about sex in polite company, and an aura of sanctifying repulsiveness surrounded the whole topic. Freud was right in pointing out the varied neurotic symptoms to which this repression of sex gave birth.

Then, in the 1920s, a radical change occurred almost overnight. The belief became a militant conviction in liberal circles that the opposite of repression—sex education, freedom of talking, feeling, and expression—would have healthy effects, and was obviously the only stand for the enlightened person. According to Max Lerner, our society shifted from acting as though sex did not exist to placing the most emphasis on sex of any society since the Roman.

Partly as a result of this radical change, we therapists rarely get nowadays in our offices patients who exhibit repression of sex in the pre-World War I Freudian sense. In fact we find just the opposite in the people who come for help: a great deal of talk about sex, a great deal of sexual activity, practically no one complaining of any cultural prohibitions over his going to bed as often or with as many partners as he wishes.

But what our patients *do* complain of is lack of feeling and passion—so much sex and so little meaning or even fun in it! Whereas the Victorian person didn't want anyone to know that he or she had sexual feelings, now we are ashamed if we do not. Before 1910 if you called a lady "sexy," you insulted her; nowadays the lady accepts the adjective as a prized compliment. Our patients often have problems of impotence or frigidity, but they struggle desperately not to let anyone know they *don't* feel sexually. The Victorian nice man or woman was guilty if he or she did perform sexually; now we are guilty if we *don't*.

One dilemma, therefore, is that enlightenment has not at all solved the sexual problems in our culture. To be sure, there are important positive results of the new enlightenment, chiefly in increased freedom for the individual. And some external problems are eased—sexual knowledge can be bought in any bookstore, contraception is available almost everywhere outside Boston, and external societal anxiety

Source: "Antidotes for the New Puritanism," *The Saturday Review,* March 26, 1966. Reprinted by permission of the author.

has lessened. *But internalized anxiety and guilt have increased.* And in some ways, these are more morbid, harder to handle, and impose a heavier burden upon the individual man and woman than external anxiety and guilt.

A second dilemma is that the new emphasis on technique in sex and love-making backfires. It often seems to me that there is an inverse relationship between the number of how-to-do-it books perused by a person, or rolling off the presses in a society, and the amount of sexual passion or even pleasure experienced by the persons involved. Nothing is wrong with technique as such, in playing golf or acting or making love. But the emphasis beyond a certain point on technique in sex makes for a mechanistic attitude toward love-making, and goes along with alienation, feelings of loneliness, and depersonalization.

The third dilemma I propose is that our highly vaunted sexual freedom has turned out to be a new form of puritanism. I define puritanism as a state of alienation from the body, separation of emotion from reason, and use of the body as a machine. These were the elements of moralistic puritanism in Victorian times; industrialism expressed these same characteristics of puritanism in economic guise. Our modern sexual attitudes have a new content, namely, full sexual expression, but in the same old puritan form—alienation from the body and feeling, and exploitation of the body as though it were a machine.

In our new puritanism bad health is equated with sin. Sin used to be "to give in to one's sexual desires"; now it is "not to have full sexual expression." A woman used to be guilty if she went to bed with a man; now she feels vaguely guilty if after a certain number of dates she still refrains. And her partner, who is always completely enlightened—or at least pretends to be—refuses to allay her guilt and does not get overtly angry at her sin of "morbid repression," her refusal to "give." This, of course, makes her "no" all the more guilt-producing for her.

All this means, of course, that people have to learn to perform sexually but at the same time not to let themselves go in passion or unseemly commitment—which latter may be interpreted as exerting an unhealthy demand on the partner. *The Victorian person sought to have love without falling into sex; the modern person seeks to have sex without falling into love.*

Recently I amused myself by drawing an impressionistic picture of the attitude of the contemporary enlightened person toward sex and love. I call it the portrait of the new sophisticate:

The new sophisticate is not castrated by society but, like Origen, is self-castrated. Sex and the body are for him not something to be and live out, but tools to be cultivated like a TV announcer's voice. And like all genuine Puritans (very passionate men underneath), the new sophisticate does it by devoting himself passionately to the moral principle of dispersing all passion, loving everybody until love has no power left to scare anyone. He is deathly afraid of his passions unless they are kept under leash, and the theory of total expression is precisely his leash. His dogma of liberty is his repression; and his principle of full libidinal health, full sexual satisfaction, are his puritanism and amount to the same thing as his New England forefathers' denial of sex. The first Puritans repressed sex and were passionate; our new man represses passion and is sexual. Both have the purpose of holding back the body, both are ways of trying to make nature a slave. The modern man's rigid principle of full freedom is not freedom at all but a new straitjacket, in some ways as compulsive as the old. He does all this because he is afraid of his body and his compassionate roots in nature, afraid of the soil and his procreative power. He is our latter-day Baconian devoted to gaining power over nature, gaining knowledge in order to get more power. And you gain power over sexuality (like working the slave until all zest for revolt is squeezed out of him) precisely by the role of full expression. Sex becomes our tool like the caveman's wheel, crowbar, or adz. Sex, the new machine, the Machina Ultima.

It is not surprising that, confronted by these dilemmas, people become more and more concerned about the technical, mechanical aspects of the sexual act. The questions typically asked about the act of love-making are not whether there was passion or meaning or even pleasure, but how well did one perform. Even the sexologists, whose attitude is generally the more the merrier, are raising their eyebrows these days about the anxious overemphasis on achieving the orgasm and the great importance attached to "satisfying" the partner. The man makes a point of asking the woman if she "made it," or is she "all right," or uses some other such euphemism for an experience for which obviously no euphemism is possible. We men are reminded by Simone de Beauvoir and other women who try to interpret the love act to us, that this is the last thing in the world a woman wants to be asked at that moment.

I often get the impression, amid the male flexing of sexual biceps, that men are in training to become sexual athletes. But what is the great prize of the game? Now it is well known in psychotherapeutic circles that the overconcern with potency is generally a compensation for feelings of impotence. Men and women both are struggling to prove their sexual power. Another motive of the game is to overcome their own solitariness. A third motive is often the desperate endeavor to escape feelings of emptiness and the threat of apathy: they pant and quiver to find an answering quiver in someone else's body to prove their own is not dead. Out of an ancient conceit we call this love.

The struggle to find an identity is also a central motive in acting out these sexual roles—a goal preset in woman as well as men, as Betty Friedan in *The Feminine Mystique* made clear. The point I wish to emphasize here is the connection between this dilemma about potency and the tendency in our society for us to become machines or ledger books even in bed. A psychiatrist colleague of mine tells me that one of his patients brought in the following dream. "I was in bed with my wife. Between us was my accountant. He was going to make love to my wife. Somehow it seemed all right."

Along with the overemphasis upon mechanism there goes, understandably enough, a lessening of passion and of feeling itself, which seems to take the form of a kind of anaesthesia in people who otherwise can perform the mechanical aspects of the sexual act very capably. This is one reason we therapists get a good number of patients these days with problems of impotence, frigidity, and simple lack of feeling in the sexual act. We psychiatrists often hear the disappointed refrain, "We made love, but it wasn't much good."

Sex is the "last frontier," David Riesman meaningfully wrote fifteen years ago in *The Lonely Crowd*. Gerald Sykes in the same vein spoke of sex as the "last green thing." It is surely true that the zest, adventure, the discovering of vast new areas of feeling and passion in one's self, the trying out of one's power to arouse feelings in others—these are indeed "frontier experiences." They are normally present as part of the psycho-sexual development of every individual, and the young person rightly gets a validation of himself from such experiences. Sex in our society did in fact have this power in the several recent decades since the 1920s, when almost every other activity was becoming "other-directed," jaded, emptied of zest and adventure.

But for various reasons—one of them being that sex had to carry by itself the weight for the validation of the personality on practically all other levels as well—the frontier freshness and newness and challenge of sex were more and more lost. We are now living in the post-Riesman age, and are experiencing the difficult implications of the "other-directed," radar behavior. The "last frontier" has become a teeming Las Vegas and no frontier at all.

Young people can no longer get a bootlegged feeling of personal identity out of the sexual revolt, since there is nothing left to revolt against. A study of drug addiction among young people, published recently in the *New York Times*, reports the young people are saying that the revolt against parents and society, the "kick" of feeling their own "oats" which they used to get from sex, they now have to get from drugs. It is not surprising that for many youngsters what used to be called lovemaking is now so often experienced as a futile "panting palm to palm," in Aldous Huxley's predictive phrase, and that they tell us that it is hard for them to understand what the poets were talking about.

Nothing to revolt against, did I say? Well, there is obviously one thing left to revolt against, and that is sex itself. The frontier, the establishing of identity, can be, and not infrequently is for the young people, a revolt against sexuality entirely. A modern Lysistrata in robot's dress is rumbling at the gates of our cities, or if not rumbling, at least hovering. As sex becomes more machine-like, with passion irrelevant and then even pleasure diminishing, the problem comes full circle, and we find, *mirabile dictu*, a progression from an *anaesthetic* attitude to an *antiseptic* one. Sexual contact itself then tends to be avoided. The sexual revolution comes finally back on itself not with a bang but a whimper.

This is another and surely least constructive aspect of the new puritanism: it returns, finally, to an ascetic attitude. This is said graphically in a charming limerick that seems to have sprung up on some sophisticated campus:

> *The word has come down from the Dean,*
> *That with the aid of the teaching machine,*
> > *King Oedipus Rex*
> > *Could have learned about sex*
> *Without ever touching the Queen.*

What are the sources of these dilemmas? Perhaps if we can get some idea of what went wrong, we shall rediscover values in sex and love that will have genuine relevance for our age.

The essential element, I propose, in the dilemmas we have been discussing is the *banalization of sex and love.* Does not the tendency to make sex and love banal and vapid run through our whole culture? The plethora of books on the subject have one thing in common—they oversimplify sex and love, treating the topic like a combination of learning to play tennis and buying life insurance.

I have said above, describing the modern sophisticated man's dilemmas about sex, that he castrates himself "because he is afraid of his body, afraid of his compassionate roots in nature, afraid of the soil and his procreative powers." That is to say, something much more potent is going on in sexuality than one would gather from the oversimplified books on sex and love—something that still has the power to scare people. I believe banalization serves as a defense against this anxiety.

The widespread tendency among young people to "go steady"—premature monogamy, as it has been called—is an egregious illustration of our point. In my frequent visits to different college campuses for lectures, I have discussed this phenomenon with students, and something like the following seems to be going on. In our insecure age when all values are in flux, at least "the steady" is steady. Always having a date with the same fellow or girl on Saturday night, dancing with this same person through the entire party at college dances, always knowing this one is available, allays the anxiety of aloneness. But it also gets boring. This leads naturally enough to early sexuality: sex at least is something we can do when we run out of conversation—which happens often when the partners have not developed enough in their own right to be interesting very long to each other as persons. It is a strange fact in our society that what goes into building a relationship—the sharing of tastes, fantasies, dreams, hopes for the future and fears from the past—seem to make people more shy and vulnerable than going to bed with each other. They are more wary of the tenderness that goes with psychological and spiritual nakedness than they are of the physical nakedness in sexual intimacy.

Now substituting premature sexuality for a meaningful intimate relationship relieves the young person's anxiety, but at the price of by-passing opportunity for further development. It seems that going steady, paradoxically, is related to promiscuity. I define "promiscuity" with Webster as the indiscriminate practice of sexuality whether with one person or a number: sex is indiscriminate when used in the service of security, or to fill up an emotional vacuum. But promiscuity is a lonely and alienating business. This loneliness becomes one of the pushes toward early marriage. Grasping each other in marriage gives a kind of security—a legal and social security at least—which temporarily allays loneliness, but at the price of haunting dread of a boring marital future. *Each step in this pattern has within it the banalization of sex and love.*

Now the question rarely asked is, are not these young people—possibly wiser in their innocence than their culture in its sophistication—fleeing from some anxiety that is only too real? I propose that what scares them, like what scares our "new sophisticate," is an element in sex and love which is almost universally repressed in our culture, namely the *tragic, daimonic element.*

By "daimonic"—which I hasten to say does not refer to little "demons"—I mean the natural element within an individual, such as the erotic drive, which has the power to take over the whole person. The erotic urge pushes toward a general physiological aim, namely sexual release. But it can push the individual into all kinds of relationships without relation to the totality of his self.

But the potentially destructive effects of the daimonic are only the reverse side of the person's constructive vitality, his passion and other potentially creative activities. The Greeks used the term "daimon" to describe the inspired urges of the poet. Socrates, indeed, speaks of his "daimon" as his conscience. When this power goes awry—when one element takes over the total personality and drives the person into disintegrative behavior—it becomes "demon possession," the historical term for psychosis. The daimonic can be either creative or destructive, but either way it certainly is the opposite to banalization. The repression of the daimonic, tragic aspects of sex and love is directly related to their banalization in our culture.

The daimonic is present in all nature as blind, ambiguous power. But only in man does it become allied with the tragic. For tragedy is the self-conscious, personal realization of being in the power of one element; thus the Greeks defined tragedy as "inordinate desire," "pride," "reaching beyond just boundaries." We have only to call to mind Romeo and Juliet, Abelard and Héloïse, Tristan and Isolde, Helen of Troy, to see the power of sexual love to seize a man and woman, lift them up into a whirlwind that defies rational control and may destroy not only themselves but others at the same time. These stories are told over and over again in Western classic literature, and passed down from generation to generation, for they come from a depth of human experience in sexual love that is profoundly significant. It is a level largely unmentioned in our day, much to the impoverishment of our talk and writing about sex and love.

If we are to overcome banalization, we must take sex and love on several different dimensions at once. Consider, as an analogy, Mozart's music. In some portions of his music, Mozart is engaged in elegant play. In other portions his music comes to us as pure sensuous pleasure, giving us a sheer delight. But in other portions, like the death music at the end of *Don Giovanni,* Mozart is profoundly shaking: we are gripped by fate and the daimonic as the inescapable tragedy rises before us. If Mozart had only the first element, play, he would sooner or later be banal and boring. If he presented only pure sensuality, he would become cloying; or if only the fire and death music, his creations would be too heavy. He is great because he writes on all three dimensions; and he must be listened to on all these levels at once.

Sexuality and love similarly have these three dimensions. Sex not only can be play, but probably an element of sheer play should be fairly regularly present. By this token, casual relationships in sex may have their gratification or meaning in the sharing of pleasure, tenderness, and so on. But if one's whole pattern and attitude toward sex is only casual, then sooner or later the playing itself becomes boring. The same is true about sensuality, obviously an element in any gratifying sex: if it has to carry the whole weight of the relationship, it becomes cloying. If sex is only sensuality, you sooner or later turn against sex itself. The third element, the daimonic and tragic, we emphasized here because that is the one almost wholly repressed in our culture, a fact that has much to do with the banalization of sex and love in our day. In a book like Erich Fromm's *Art of Loving*, for example, the daimonic, tragic element is completely missing.

An appreciation of the tragic and daimonic side of sex and love can help us not only to avoid oversimplification but to love better. Let me illustrate the constructive use of the daimonic. Every person, as a separate individual, experiences aloneness and strives to overcome his loneliness, this striving usually being some kind of love. Sexuality and love require self-assertion: if the person is not to some extent an individual in his own right, he will not only have nothing to give, nothing to relate with, but will be unable to assert himself and therefore unable to be genuinely part of the relationship. Both the man and woman need self-assertion in order to breach the separateness and make some kind of union with each other. Thus there is truth in the vernacular expressions about needing to "let oneself go" and "give oneself over" to the sexual act—or to any creative experience for that matter.

The psychotherapist Dr. Otto Rank once remarked in his latter years of practice that practically all the women who came to him had problems because their husbands were not assertive enough. Despite the oversimplified sound of this sentence, it contains a telling point: our effete cultivation of sex can make us so intellectual and detached about it that the simple power of the act evaporates, and we lose—and this loss is especially serious for women—the important elemental pleasure of "being taken," being "carried away." But the self-assertive power must be integrated with the other aspects of one's own personality, and with the total person of the mate; otherwise it becomes daimonic in the destructive sense.

Let us now summarize some values, potential and actual, in sexual love. There is, first, the overall value of enrichment and fulfilment of personality. This comes from expansion of one's awareness of one's self, one's feelings, one's experience of his capacity to give sexual pleasure and other feelings to the other person, and achieve thereby an expansion of meaning in interpersonal relationship. This fulfilment carries us beyond what we are at any given moment; I become in a literal sense more than I was. The most powerful symbol imaginable for this fulfilment is procreation—the possibility that a new being may be conceived and born. The "birth," however, can and does refer at the same time to the birth of new aspects of one's self.

Tenderness is a second value, a tenderness that is much more than indicated in that most unpoetic of all words, "togetherness." The experience of tenderness comes out of the fact that the two persons, longing as all individuals do to overcome the separateness and isolation to which we are all heir because we are individuals, can participate in a relationship that for the moment is not two isolated selves but a union. In this kind of sexual intercourse, the lover often does not know whether a particular sensation of delight is felt by him or by his loved one—and it doesn't make any difference anyway. A sharing takes place which is a new gestalt, a new being, a new field of magnetic force. A gratifying sexual relationship thus has the gestalt of a painting—the various parts, the colors, feelings, forms, united to become a new whole.

There is the third value which occurs ideally at the moment of climax in sexual intercourse. This is the point when the lovers are carried not only beyond their personal isolation, but when a shift in consciousness seems to occur that unites them also with nature. In Hemingway's novel *For Whom the Bell Tolls*, the older woman, Pilar, waits for the hero, Robert Jordan, and the girl he loves when they have gone ahead into the mountain to make love; and when they return, she asks, "Did the earth move?" The shaking of the earth seems to be a normal part of the momentary loss of awareness of the self and the surging up of a sudden consciousness that includes the "earth" as well. There is an accelerating experience of touch, contact, union to the point where for a moment the awareness of separateness is lost, blotted out in a cosmic feeling of oneness with nature. I do not wish this to sound too "ideal," for I think it is a quality, however subtle, in all love-making except the most depersonalized sort. And I also do not wish it to sound simply "mystic," for despite limitations in our awareness, I think it is an inseparable part of actual experience in the love act.

This leads us immediately to the fourth value, sex and love as the affirmation of the self. Despite the fact that many people in our culture use sex to get a short-circuited, ersatz sense of identity, sexual love can and ought to provide a sound and meaningful way to the sense of personal identity. We emerge from love-making normally with renewed vitality, a vitality which comes not from triumph or proof of one's strength but from the expansion of awareness. Probably in love-making there is always some element of sadness—as, to use our previous analogy, there is in practically all music no matter how joyful—in the reminder that we have not succeeded absolutely in losing our separateness, nor is the infantile hope that we could recover the womb made into reality, and even our increased self-awareness can also be a poignant reminder that none of us ever overcomes his loneliness completely. But by one's replenished sense of one's own significance in the love act he can accept these unavoidable human limitations.

A final value inheres in the curious phenomenon in love-making: that to be able to give to the other person is essential to one's own full pleasure in the act. This sounds like a banal moralism in our age of mechanization of sex and "release of tension" in sexual objects. But it is not sentimentality but a point which anyone can confirm in his own experience in the love act, that to give is essential to one's own pleasure. Many patients in psychotherapy find themselves discovering, generally with some surprise, that something is missing if they cannot "do something for," give something to the partner—the normal expression of which is the giving in the act of intercourse itself. Just as giving is essential to one's own full pleasure, the ability to receive is necessary in the love interrelationship also. If you cannot receive, your giving will be a domination of the partner. Conversely, if you cannot give, your receiving will leave you empty. The paradox is demonstrably true that the person who can only receive becomes empty, for he is unable actively to appropriate and make his own what he receives. I speak, thus, not of receiving as a passive phenomenon, but of *active receiving:* one knows he is receiving, feels it, absorbs it into his own experience whether he verbally acknowledges it or not, and is grateful for it.

Encyclical on Birth Control
Pope Paul VI

Pope Paul VI (1896-   ) became pope in 1964 upon the death of Pope John XXIII. His conservative position is evident in his famous encyclical on birth control (1968), which follows.

1. The most serious duty of transmitting human life, for which married persons are the free and responsible collaborators of God the Creator, has always been a source of great joys to them even if sometimes accompanied by not a few difficulties and by distress.

At all times the fulfilment of this duty has posed grave problems to the conscience of married persons, but with the recent evolution of society changes have taken place that give rise to new questions which the church could not ignore, having to do with a matter which so closely touches upon the life and happiness of men.

Source: Humanae Vitae (Human Life). Reprinted from *The New York Times*, August 1, 1968.

2. The changes which have taken place are in fact noteworthy and of varied kind. In the first place, there is the rapid demographic development. Fear is shown by many that world population is growing more rapidly than the available resources, with growing distress to many families and developing countries, so that the temptation for authorities to counter this danger with radical measures is great. Moreover, working and lodging conditions, as well as increased exigencies both in the economic field and in that of education, often make the proper education of an elevated number of children difficult today.

A change is also seen both in the manner of considering the person of woman and her place in society, and in the value to be attributed to conjugal love in marriage, and also in the appreciation to be made of the meaning of conjugal acts in relation to that love.

Finally and above all, man has made stupendous progress in the domination and rational organization of the forces of nature, such that he tends to extend this domination to his own total being: to the body, to physical life, to social life and even to the laws which regulate the transmission of life.

3. This new state of things gives rise to new questions. Granted the conditions of life today, and granted the meaning which conjugal relations have with respect to the harmony between husband and wife and to their mutual fidelity, would not a revision of the ethical norms in force up to now seem to be advisable, especially when it is considered that they cannot be observed without sacrifices, sometimes heroic sacrifices?

And again: by extending to this field the application of the so-called "principle of totality," could it not be admitted that the intention of a less abundant but more rationalized fecundity might transform a materially sterilizing intervention into a licit and wise control of birth? Could it not be admitted, that is, that the finality of procreation pertains to the ensemble of conjugal life, rather than to its single acts? It is also asked, whether, in view of the increased sense of responsibility of modern man, the moment has not come for him to entrust to his reason and his will, rather than to the biological rhythms of his organism, the task of regulating birth.

4. Such questions require from the teaching authority of the church a new and deeper reflection upon the principles of the normal teaching on marriage: a teaching founded on the natural law, illuminated and enriched by divine revelation.

No believer will wish to deny that the teaching authority of the church is competent to interpret even the natural moral law. It is, in fact, indisputable. As our predecessors have many times declared, that Jesus Christ, when communicating to Peter and to the Apostles His divine authority and sending them to teach all nations His commandments, constituted them as guardians and authentic interpreters of all the moral law, not only, that is, of the law of the gospel, but also of the natural law, which is also an expression of the will of God, the faithful fulfillment of which is equally necessary for salvation.

Conformably to this mission of hers, the church has always provided—and even more amply in recent times—a coherent teaching concerning both the nature of marriage and the correct use of conjugal rights and the duties of husband and wife.

A TOTAL VISION OF MAN

7. The problem of birth, like every other problem regarding human life, is to be considered, beyond partial perspectives—whether of the biological or psychological, demographic or sociological orders—in the light of an integral vision of man and of his vocation, not only his natural and earthly, but also his supernatural and eternal vocation. And since, in the attempt to justify artificial methods of birth control, many have appealed to the demands both of conjugal love and of "responsible parenthood," it is good to state very precisely the true concept of these two great realities of married life, referring principally to what was recently set forth in this regard, and in a highly authoritative form, by the Second Vatican Council in its pastoral constitution *Gaudium et Spes.*

CONJUGAL LOVE

8. Conjugal love reveals its true nature and nobility when it is considered in its supreme origin, God, who is love, "the Father, from whom every family in heaven and on earth is named."

Marriage is not, then, the effect of chance or the product of evolution or unconscious natural forces; it is the wise institution of the Creator to realize in mankind his design of love. By means of the reciprocal personal gift of self, proper and exclusive to them, husband and wife tend toward the communion of their beings in view of mutual personal perfection to collaborate with God in the generation and education of new lives.

9. Under this light, there clearly appear the characteristic marks and demands of conjugal love, and it is of supreme importance to have an exact idea of these.

This love is first of all fully human, that is to say, of the senses and of the spirit at the same time. It is not, then, a simple transport of instinct and sentiment, but also, and principally, an act of the free will, intended to endure and to grow by means of the joys and sorrows of daily life, in such a way that husband and wife become only one heart and only one soul, and together attain their human perfection.

Then this love is total; that is to say, it is a very special form of personal friendship, in which husband and wife generously share everything without undue reservations or selfish calculations. Whoever truly loves his marriage partner loves not only for what he receives, but for the partner's self, rejoicing that he can enrich his partner with the gift of himself.

Again, this love is faithful and exclusive until death. Thus in fact do bride and groom conceive it to be on the day when they freely and in full awareness assume the duty of the marriage bond.

A fidelity, this, which can sometimes be difficult, but is always possible, always noble and meritorious, as no one can deny. The example of so many married persons down through the centuries shows not only that fidelity is according to the nature of marriage but also that it is a source of profound and lasting happiness.

And finally, this love is fecund, for it is not exhausted by the communion between husband and wife, but is destined to continue, raising up new lives.

"Marriage and conjugal love are by their nature ordained toward the begetting and educating of children. Children are really the supreme gift of marriage and contribute very substantially to the welfare of their parents."

RESPONSIBLE PARENTHOOD

10. Hence conjugal love requires in husband and wife an awareness of their mission of "responsible parenthood," which today is rightly much insisted upon, and which also must be exactly understood. Consequently it is to be considered under different aspects which are legitimate and connected with one another.

In relation to the biological processes, responsible parenthood means the knowledge and respect of their functions; human intellect discovers in the power of giving life biological laws which are part of the human person.

In relation to the tendencies of instinct or passion, responsible parenthood means that necessary dominion which reason and will must exercise over them.

In relation to physical, economic, psychological and social conditions, responsible parenthood is exercised, either by the deliberate and generous decision to raise a numerous family, or by the decision, made for grave motives and with due respect for the moral law, to avoid for the time being, or even for an indeterminate period, a new birth.

Responsible parenthood also and above all implies a more profound relationship to the moral order established by God, of which a right conscience is the faithful interpreter. The responsible exercise of parenthood implies, therefore, that husband and wife recognize fully their own duties toward God, toward themselves, toward the family and toward society, in a correct hierarchy of values.

In the task of transmitting life, therefore, they are not free to proceed completely at will, as if they could determine in a wholly autonomous way the honest path to follow; but they must conform their activity to the creative intention of God, expressed in the very nature of marriage and of its acts, and manifested by the constant teaching of the church.

RESPECT FOR THE NATURE AND PURPOSES OF THE MARRIAGE ACT

11. These acts, by which husband and wife are united in chaste intimacy and by means of which human life is transmitted, are "noble and worthy," and they do not cease to be lawful if, for causes independent of the will of husband and wife, they are foreseen to be infecund, since they always remain ordained toward expressing and consolidating their union. In fact, as experience bears witness, not every conjugal act is followed by a new life. God has wisely disposed natural laws and rhythms of fecundity which, of themselves, cause a separation in the succession of births. Nonetheless the church, calling men back to the observance of the norms of the natural law, as interpreted by her constant doctrine, teaches that each and every marriage act must remain open to the transmission of life.

TWO INSEPARABLE ASPECTS: UNION AND PROCREATION

12. That teaching, often set forth by the Magisterium, is founded upon the inseparable connection, willed by God and unable to be broken by man on his own initiative, between the two meanings of the conjugal act: the unitive meaning and the procreative meaning. Indeed, by its intimate structure, the conjugal act, while

most closely uniting husband and wife, capacitates them for the generation of new lives, according to laws inscribed in the very being of man and of woman. By safeguarding both these essential aspects, the unitive and the procreative, the conjugal act preserves in its fullness the sense of true mutual love and its ordination toward man's most high calling to parenthood. We believe that the men of our day are particularly capable of seizing the deeply reasonable and human character of this fundamental principle.

FAITHFULNESS TO GOD'S DESIGN

13. It is in fact justly observed that a conjugal act imposed upon one's partner without regard for his or her condition and lawful desires is not a true act of love, and therefore denies an exigency or right moral order in the relationship between husband and wife. Hence, one who reflects well must also recognize that a reciprocal act of love, which jeopardizes the responsibility to transmit life which God the Creator, according to particular laws, inserted therein, is in contradiction with the design constitutive of marriage, and with the will of the author of life. To use this divine gift, destroying, even if only partially, its meaning and its purposes, is to contradict the nature both of man and of woman and of their most intimate relationship, and therefore it is to contradict also the plan of God and His will.

On the other hand, to make use of the gift of conjugal love while respecting the laws of the generative process means to acknowledge oneself not to be the arbiter of the sources of human life, but rather the minister of the design established by the Creator. In fact, just as man does not have unlimited dominion over his body in general, so also, with particular reason, he has no such dominion over his creative faculties as such, because of their intrinsic ordination toward raising up life, of which God is the principle. "Human life is sacred," Pope John XXIII recalled; "from its very inception it reveals the creating hand of God."

ILLICIT WAYS OF REGULATING BIRTH

14. In conformity with these landmarks in the human and Christian vision of marriage, we must once again declare that the direct interruption of the generative process already begun, and, above all, directly willed and procured abortion, even if for therapeutic reasons, are to be absolutely excluded as licit means of regulating birth.

Equally to be excluded, as the teaching authority of the church has frequently declared, is direct sterilization, whether perpetual or temporary, whether of the man or of the woman. Similarly excluded is every action which, either in anticipation of the conjugal act or in its accomplishment, or in the development of its natural consequences, proposes, whether as an end or as a means, to render procreation impossible.

To justify conjugal acts made intentionally infecund, one cannot invoke as valid reasons the lesser evil, or the fact that such acts would constitute a whole together with the fecund acts already performed or to follow later, and hence would share in one and the same moral goodness. In truth, if it is sometimes licit to tolerate a lesser evil in order to avoid a greater evil or to promote a greater good, it is not licit, even for the gravest reasons, to do evil so that good may follow therefrom; that is, to make into the object of a positive act of the will something which is intrinsically disorder and hence unworthy of the human person, even when the intention is to safeguard or promote individual, family or social well-being.

Consequently it is an error to think that a conjugal act which is deliberately made infecund and so is intrinsically dishonest could be made honest and right by the ensemble of a fecund conjugal life.

LICITNESS OF THERAPEUTIC MEANS

15. The church, on the contrary, does not at all consider illicit the use of those therapeutic means truly necessary to cure diseases of the organism, even if an impediment to procreation, which may be foreseen, should result therefrom, provided such impediment is not, for whatever motive, directly willed.

LICITNESS OF RECOURSE TO INFECUND PERIODS

16. To this teaching of the church on conjugal morals, the objection is made today, as we observed earlier, that it is the prerogative of the human intellect to dominate the energies offered by irrational nature and to orientate them toward an end conformable to the good of man. Now, some may ask: In the present case, is it not reasonable in many circumstances to have recourse to artificial birth control if, thereby, we secure the harmony and peace of the family, and better conditions for the education of the children already born? To this question it is necessary to reply with clarity: The church is the first to praise and recommend the intervention of intelligence in a function which so closely associates the rational creature with his Creator, but she affirms that must be one with respect for the order established by God.

If, then, there are serious motives to space out births, which derive from the physical or psychological conditions of husband and wife, or from external conditions, the church teaches that it is then licit to take into account the natural rhythms immanent in the generative functions, for the use of marriage in the infecund periods only, and this way to regulate birth without offending the moral principles which have been recalled earlier.

The church is coherent with herself when she considers recourse to the infecund periods to be licit, while at the same time condemning, as being always illicit, the use of means directly contrary to fecundation, even if such use is inspired by reasons which may appear honest and serious. In reality, there are essential differences between the two cases: in the former, the married couple make legitimate use of a natural disposition; in the latter, they impede the development of natural processes. It is true that, in the one and the other case, the married couple are concordant in the positive will of avoiding children for plausible reasons, seeking the certainty that offspring will not arrive; but it is also true that only in the former case are they able to renounce the use of marriage in the fecund periods when, for just motives, procreation is not desirable, while making use of it during infecund periods to manifest their affection and to safeguard their mutual fidelity. By so doing, they give proof of a truly and integrally honest love.

GRAVE CONSEQUENCES OF METHODS OF ARTIFICIAL BIRTH CONTROL

17. Upright men can even better convince themselves of the solid grounds on which the teaching of the church in this field is based, if they care to reflect upon the consequences of methods of artificial birth control. Let them consider, first of all, how wide and easy a road would thus be opened up toward conjugal infidelity and the general lowering of morality. Not much experience is needed in order to know human weakness, and to understand that men—especially the young, who are so vulnerable on this point—have need of encouragement to be faithful to the moral law, so that they must not be offered some easy means of eluding its observance. It is also to be feared that the man, growing used to the employment of anticonceptive practices, may finally lose respect for the woman and, no longer caring for her physical and psychological equilibrium, may come to the point of considering her as a mere instrument of selfish enjoyment, and no longer as his respected and beloved companion.

Let it be considered also that a dangerous weapon would thus be placed in the hands of those public authorities who take no heed of moral exigencies. Who could blame a government for applying to the solution of the problems of the community those means acknowledged to be licit for married couples in the solution of a family problem? Who will stop rulers from favoring, from even imposing upon their peoples, if they were to consider it necessary, the method of contraception which they judge to be most efficacious? In such a way men, wishing to avoid individual, family or social difficulties encountered in the observance of the divine law, would reach the point of placing at the mercy of the intervention of public authorities the most personal and most reserved sector of conjugal intimacy.

Consequently, if the mission of generating life is not to be exposed to the arbitrary will of men, one must necessarily recognize insurmountable limits to the possibility of man's domination over his own body and its functions; limits which no man, whether a private individual or one invested with authority, may licitly surpass. And such limits cannot be determined otherwise than by the respect due to the integrity of the human organism and its functions, according to the principles recalled earlier.

The Future Relations of the Sexes
Agnes Heller

Agnes Heller, former assistant to Professor G. Lukacs, a Hungarian critic-philosopher, is on the staff of the Sociological Research Group of the Hungarian Academy of Science. Among her works are *The Theory of Rational Selfishness, The Sociology of Morality or the Morals of Sociology,* and *Social Role and Prejudice.*

It is, for several reasons, impossible to foretell the future of sex and family relations, chiefly because sex and family relations form an integral part of the conditions of social contact and consequently cannot be analysed in isolation. The only way to approach the question is to ask what type of sexual and family relations can be expected if we assume a certain definite set of social relations to prevail in the future. Second, it is not easy to make predictions even on the basis of the future state of social relations. Today more than ever before, mankind is facing several different social alternatives. It depends on human decision, actions and practices which of these alternatives are actually realized. Thus we cannot answer our question merely by the extrapolation of current social trends. What, then, can we do? Taking as our point of departure the given conditions and potential of present society, in its economic, political and social dimensions, we can describe the optimal and least desirable variants of social development and predict the probable development of sexual and family relations under the optimal and least desirable variants.

Such a description itself naturally involves some choice. It is on the basis of our values and our attitude in social conflicts (the two being integrated in practice) that we choose a future for ourselves. The writer of these lines—a Marxist—has chosen a Communist future for herself, which implies a definite attitude to the values mankind has developed to date. Thus, in speaking about the future of sexual and family relations, we will henceforward outline them in the context of a developing Communist society, this being the value system we have chosen, since for us it incorporates the optimal realization of the potential of our times. It does not mean that we exclude a less desirable, or even a repugnant solution, nor that we would exclude the treatment of such a pessimistic possibility from Marxist theory and analysis. What it does mean, however, is that the solutions possible in the perspective of communism remain our yardstick in judging the future of sexual and family relations. Below—partly for reasons of space—we shall deal mainly with the optimum possibility.

The great variability of sexual and moral rules and customs was already well known during the Renaissance. During the Age of Enlightenment the rules of sexual morality were cited as a commonplace example of the changing and incidental character of mores. Beyond variability, we are here primarily interested in the

Source: "On the Future of Relations Between the Sexes, *International Social Science Journal*, Vol. 21, No. 4 (1969), 535-544. Reproduced with permission of UNESCO.

following questions: First, are there amongst widely variable moral customs certain inherent values which appear to be constant since a definite period in history, and if so which can be regarded as universal human values, that is, as factors in the development of the "generic essence" (Marx)? Further, which point beyond themselves in a positive manner? Second, what is the significance and function of sexual mores generally, and what makes them specific within the entire complex of moral customs? The answers to these questions have a far-reaching influence on the concepts we form about the sexual and family relations of the future.

Before the evolution of civilization—of class societies—sexual customs were more variable than after the emergence of class societies. There is no space here to analyse the reason for this phenomenon. Let us point out, however, that this apparent richness conceals real poverty; it actually expresses the social fusion of the tribal world. It is an aspect of the lack of universality and of individuality. In fact only a single one of the values more or less formulated in primitive societies and adapted under civilization with bearing on sexual relations is still operative: the incest taboo. With the passage of time, this norm became instinctive: members of the same family—at least as the social norm—do not even desire each other. By this norm, mankind socially regulated and codified its interests as a species. Thus, the first universal (that is, historically permanent) value to apply to sexual relations was born not merely as a result of natural selection, but by social provision—and this is true even if man was not clearly aware of what he was doing. This was how the process which Marx called "pushing back natural frontiers" (*Zurückweichung der Naturschranken*) started in relation to the sex instinct, a process which, as we shall see, has been very limited in this case.

Beginning with the development of civilization—and to repeat: historically this coincides with the birth of class societies—the variability of moral ethics assumed new forms in the field of sexual contacts. In this way a certain variability developed between different classes and strata within the same society. At the same time the institution of marriage based on private property came into being, together with the social inequality of men and women in sexual and family relations. The influence of private property in sexual and family relations developed permanent characteristics—to be found in every existing structure of customs—which, despite their persistence, do not represent universal human values, for they are rooted in the process of alienation. Alienation is the discrepancy between human essence and existence, the development of the material powers of mankind at the cost of the depletion of the human essence of individuals, and of entire social classes and strata. This is given manifold expression in the trends of sexual relations—in different forms at different historical periods. A common permanent feature—which, by the way, does not only affect family relations—characteristic of every alienated social structuration, is that, under private ownership, life is oriented towards possessions. Only what is in our possession can be regarded as really ours. In this way, the desire for possession becomes a basic drive and motivation, not only in relation to objects, but also to persons. If a person is my property, he or she cannot belong to anyone else, just like my land, my flock, my factory, or my house. Accordingly, the relationship between men and women is also permeated by motives of possession. To avoid any misunderstanding, let me clarify that the drive for possession dominant in sexual and family relations is not to be confused with the aspiration, prevalent in every love relationship, that the person I desire, whom I love, should be "mine." If for no other reason, confusion should be avoided because the "instinct" of possession is independent of desire and emotion. The man avenges the wife "guilty" of adultery and her "seducer" even if he never loved and desired her, simply because she is "his." It is part of one's "honour" not to be deprived of anything that has been one's property, regardless of whether one needs it or not, regardless of the degree of one's need for the object or person. It should be added, of course, that the attitude of wanting to gain possession is closely interwoven even with the desire that the loved or desired person be one's own. The motivation of possession becomes overpowering in this relationship, too, and profoundly influences the desire itself. It is part of male prestige to possess as many women as possible, and this is further enhanced if the women in question are "difficult"; on the other hand, the prestige of women depends on the number—and no less, the social rank—of their suitors and admirers.

Within class society it is generally not human being who confronts human being, but a person occupying one position in the division of labour with one filling another. People are only equal if their position in the division of labour (within the social hierarchy) is similar. This is an equality of unequals, for its basis is not equal human substance or value. Of course, substantial equality is possible even between people similarly situated on the social scale; or, in other words, meaningful relations based on equality are possible even under conditions of alienation. But in the vast majority of cases they are possible under these conditions only between the same sex, in the first place among male friends. The relationship of people of different sexes is—as we said before—by definition unequal. Above all, the woman is judged not on the basis of her own place in the division of labour but according to her father's or husband's position. Only the nineteenth and twentieth centuries brought some change in this field, though not a significant one. Sexual relations are thus condemned to be relations between unequal people, and in this way reflect the alienation of the properties of the species (*Substanz der Gattung*).

This inequality is evident in every aspect of the relations between the sexes. It is reflected in the sexual aspect, for the reciprocity of sexual pleasure is an expressly universal aim only in exceptional periods. It is obvious morally, for what is permissible for the man is forbidden for the woman. It is to be seen in the intellectual and legal fields as well—in the latter it is most clearly demonstrated by the different legal positions of men and women within the family. The subjective aspect of alienation is the silent acceptance of this inequality, rebellions against which usually break out at times of universal social revolutions or as a consequence thereof (during the Renaissance, the Age of Enlightenment, early Romanticism, Utopian Socialism, and later parallel with the spread of Marxism).

Universal social alienation extends to sexual relations in other ways too: through the mediation of the alienation of morality. Attitudes centred on property presuppose a particularist personality, an individual who strives, primarily, to maintain himself under given conditions, even against others if need be, an individual in whom emotions relating merely to his own person—such as envy and jealousy, vanity and selfishness—become dominant, the kind of person unable to look at himself objectively, from a distance, but uncritically identifying himself with his own emotions and interests. Morality develops along with the genesis of the particularist personality, and its function is to regulate particularist ambitions, subordinating them to more universal social requirements and interests. Moral imperatives do not merely remain external—indeed, they would not be moral if they did so. The individual internalizes them, adopts them as part of his internal make-up and code, some internalizing more, others less, depending on the person. Conscience as an "internal judge" is the form in which the "external judge"—public moral judgment and opinion—appears within the personality.

Obviously, morals play an exceptionally important role even in their alienated form in the humanization of mankind, and of the relation between the sexes. Similarly, it is evident that the antagonism between moral norms and individual particularist drives does at least as much to conserve particularism as to humanize it.

Here we are only examining sexual relations. The norms of sex morality also only partly humanize the individual, while on the other hand, they keep alive the opposition between particularist efforts and moral norms (which may also be particularist). The desire for possession, jealousy and selfishness are not eliminated, but merely redirected to areas where they do not conflict—or only very slightly—with social norms. For instance, a man who cannot beat up his superior can find compensation in beating up his wife. Several varieties of sadism and masochism, on record as sexual perversions, are basically nothing more than an outlet for a particularist desire for possession within the permitted framework. (This, of course, applies not only to sex: let us just think of the sadism of war; against the enemy anything is permitted.)

In regard to morality and the relations between the sexes, there is, however, a special problem which should be treated separately. When we mentioned how the incest taboo developed even before the birth of civilization, we also said that this is a manifestation of pushing back natural barriers. In the relationship between the sexes the driving back of natural barriers however appears theoretically in a different form than in all other forms of human contact, simply because it is the only human relationship based on biological (natural) instinct. True, nutrition is also a biological drive, but one for which human contact is of only subordinate importance. On the other hand, the natural instinct at work in the relations between mother and baby is by definition (by nature) one of unequals. In the relations between a mother and her adult children, the natural barriers become less and less effective. Today grown-up children usually "pick" their mothers on the basis of social and ethical judgment, or in other words shape their relations with their mother independently of the kinship bond. And the mother does the same with her adult children. The sex instinct, on the contrary, is an absolute and uneliminable foundation for contact between the sexes. It cannot be driven back, only humanized.

This is the genesis of the special function of moral alienation in the regulation of the relationship between the sexes. The fact is that moral norms either humanize or suppress the sex instinct—there is no third alternative. It is to Freud's everlasting credit that he recognized the antagonism between moral norms and the sex instinct, and all the aberrations caused by the suppression of the sex instinct. Since Freud, however, regarded alienated social relations as the permanent human state, he did not think of the second alternative: the possibility of humanization. And yet several aspects of this alternative were already evident in the prehistory of mankind.

In the humanization of the contact between the sexes and, inseparably, in the simple suppression of the sex instinct, Christianity played a distinctive role, having been for over a thousand years the dominant ideology governing morality. This is where the double function of alienated morality can be most clearly observed. Let us look at humanization first. Christianity accepted and proclaimed (though only as a tendency and an ideology) the equality of women, at least before God. Women are the equals of men in the congregation and, although excluded from the priesthood, can become saints. The moral norms are also the same for both men and women: virginity is a virtue, and adultery a sin for both. (That this morality was not valid in practice, is a different story.) Without this ideological equality, modern love, *amour passion,* would not have come into being.

However, Christian ethics display a peculiar paradox in respect to sexual relations. In Antiquity the degree of humanization in the contact between the sexes reflected the prevailing level of moral development. The Christian world, however, produced the opposite relation as well: the stronger the power of morality, the more suppressed was sex, regarded even ideologically as something "bestial." Although sex itself was permissible (for it serves reproduction of the race), erotic enjoyment, taking pleasure in sex, and especially the cult of pleasure were sins accompanied by guilt feelings. Bourgeois ethics took over Christian ethics at least partly in this respect (primarily affecting women), yet on the other hand—in actual opposition to Christianity—adopted the inequality of the sexes as an ideological principle. Monogamy became openly associated with the brothel.

Consequently, it is by no means fortuitous that the so-called "sexual revolution" is one of the chief manifestations of rebellion against bourgeois ethics. "The sexual revolution" has already had several waves, but never one so sweeping as that experienced today in the Western European student movements. Of course, this is not a unified movement, but one in which several tendencies meet. We can nevertheless distinguish two main trends. One of these turns everything always practised in periods of dissolution of moral norms into an ideological principle; it identifies man with the particularist individual and demands his absolute sexual satisfaction. This is how sexual perversions—and primarily the very sado-masochism of whose clearly particularist character we have already spoken—become ideals. For us, however, the other trend is the more interesting. Its adherents regard the sexual revolution as one way to end alienation—and this is, indeed, what they are looking for. They do not merely declare the right of all human beings to pleasure (the ideology has been provided by Marcuse's *Eros and Civilization*), but consciously believe in the equality of men and women in the relation between the sexes. Moreover they want to eliminate from this relation one of the principal manifestations of alienation, namely the motive of possession. Those pursuing this search through the sexual revolution are probing for a humanized society even if their theory and practice incorporate a great deal of naïvete and even absurdity.

We have already mentioned that forms of humanized relations between the sexes appear even under conditions of alienation, though only exceptionally. Most important is the development of individual love and the demand, which has been imperative for some time, that marriage be based on love. It also includes cultured eroticism, the camaraderie and friendship (the two not being the same) of the couple. Also under this heading falls self-education to overcome the instinct of possession—including self-training to combat jealousy—of which life and literature show many examples. (We are thinking of the *Diary* of Chernishevsky, whose battle against jealousy formed an important element in his total revolutionary attitude.)

Of course, all positive elements pointing towards the development of the species can assume inhuman forms and may in other respects be destructive. This holds even for comradeship and friendship, for Lady Macbeth's comradely identification with her husband sets no good moral example. This kind of moral degradation often goes hand in hand with individual love, too. Love as a passion often virtually sweeps away all the obstacles (including living people) in its way. Here, however, it is not passion itself which is at fault, but prior judgments and a system of prejudices rooted in the human psyche which places obstacles in the way of passion (for instance, reasons of state, as in Racine's *Bérénice,* or the possessive nature of the passion, as in his *Phaedra*). Nor is love independent in other respects from the social and human framework in which it arises: people generally fall in love with persons who can promote their interests. In a class society love crosses social boundaries and classes only exceptionally. This is exemplified in Shaw's play *Widower's Houses.* Love relations are inseparable from financial relations both in prostitution and in marriage, where the woman is generally maintained. And, in the twentieth century, love became a social custom, part of "good manners," and in a certain sense "obligatory." The mass media manipulate love just as much as they manipulate sex (cf. the film *Marty*).

Of course, the depth or superficiality of love is only one manifestation of the depth or shallowness of human essence. The relative prevalence of passionate love coincides historically with the development of human subjectivity in its positive sense, with the birth of modern bourgeois individualism (modern love poetry is the finest expression of the change). The more substantial an individual (emotionally, ethically and culturally), the more substantial the love of which he is capable. The more depleted, the more alienated, a person, the less meaningful, the more superficial and incidental his love.

Nevertheless, we cannot consider the cult of love (and within it of sex) in the twentieth century merely a result of manipulation. The fact is that in a world in which community ties loosen and break, in which the individual is lonely and defenceless, love (and sex) is the only direct and personal human relationship in which one individual finds another. Even the poorest love preserves something of the joy of discovering another person, and reduces or dissolves—though only temporarily—the sense of loneliness and isolation, building a bridge from soul to soul. Thus, even the most commercial relationship between the sexes expresses something of human essence and contributes something to its preservation.

Let us now say a few words about the problem of so-called "sex morality." We raise the question again: is the existence of a separate "sex morality" a lasting value? Our answer is a definite "no." It is no because the existence of all partial or restricted moralities (and this applies not only to sex morality, but similarly to "business morals" or "political morals") is an expression of moral alienation. A large part of public opinion still holds that whatever is contrary to the prevalent sexual mores is "immoral." Moreover, the term "immorality" is often used to cover the violation of the customary rules governing sex. If, on the other hand, we examine the problem from the point of view of the development of the properties of the species—and here already the problem of future trends appears—it becomes clear that in the relation between the sexes the same factors—and only those factors—impair universal values which are detrimental to all other aspects of morality. Breaking the will of another person, deliberate misleading (lies), regarding the other person simply as a tool, ruining other people's lives, lack of reciprocity, and inequality, these are the attitudes and acts in contacts between the sexes which violate the universal generic values most irreparably. But obviously they do not offend against the special ethics of sex morality only, for they also violate the properties of the species in every other aspect of human relations.

Our first assertion in regard to the future then is that the special system of ethics governing "sex morality" will disappear, and contact between the sexes will be judged by the same moral criteria which apply to any other field of human relations.

As we said, we presuppose the kind of future society in which there is no alienation, and in this connexion foresee the ending of alienation in the relation between the sexes, as in all other domains yet analysed.

What is our image of these relations? What can we say about them prospectively?

First of all, the social inequality of men and women will cease. Naturally we do not mean by this the ending of all kinds of inequality, since the inequality of human beings cannot be eliminated in any other respects either. And by the ending of social inequality we do not only mean that social position, and the chances of a start in life will be equal, but also that the differences in traits and characteristics which seem "natural" because we have grown used to them over thousands of years, but which are still results of the social division of labor will be reduced and gradually disappear. Amongst these are the inequality of men and women in sexual enjoyment and in choosing a partner, in intellectual efforts and accomplishments, and also in such emotional and moral attributes as the "natural" hardness and rationality of man and the "natural" softness and emotionality of women, etc.

Since life in general will no longer be centered on property, possessiveness will disappear from the relations between the sexes. The other person will no longer be a prestige object, a trophy, or a means to an end. In the relationship of genuinely free people, the other person is always a goal in himself. Nothing but the termination of the need on one side can end a relationship, just as nothing but reciprocated need for the other person can bring it into existence. Clearly this will not eliminate grief. One-sided or unequal desire and love will always remain a source of pain and sometimes even of tragedy. But the trauma deriving from the frustrated drive for possession will disappear. When one loses a partner, personal loss alone will cause the pain, and not hurt vanity or injured "honour," the feeling that "my property has been taken from me." There will no longer be any catastrophies arising from a distinct "sex morality," just as there will be no sin, and no guilt feelings springing from the supposed transgression of a distinct sex code. Thus, disappointment in love will become a pain worthy of man.

In a non-alienated world where the main drive is no longer for property, persons will no longer be particularistic. Individual personality, which has been only an exception, will become socially typical. Moral norms will no longer confront a person steeped in particularism as something alien. The personality will be able to follow its specific gifts (natural abilities, talents and emotions) in the direction of valid choices, to humanize its impulses instead of suppressing them.

We have seen that this is of special significance in sexuality, where the natural barriers cannot be gradually driven back, but either must be suppressed or humanized. The individual person need no longer suppress his physical desires, if these desires themselves become humanized. We have already mentioned the criteria of humanness: equality, reciprocity, free choice and approaching others as ends in themselves. Thus, even a merely sexual attraction can be entirely human if it fulfils these criteria, just as today even the most "spiritual" love can be inhuman if it does not meet them. The line between what is human and inhuman is therefore not drawn where traditional morality (chiefly Christian) defines the limit, not between the "merely" physical and the "spiritual."

If we say that all human beings will be individuals capable of humanizing their emotions, we certainly do not mean that everyone will love or desire equally and with equal intensity. Quite the opposite. Everybody humanizes his drives on the basis of the above criteria, and these drives can be widely different. But fully developed individuals do not need the rules of "sexual morality" to direct their drives along a human course. Every person knows best what relationship or relationships are most suitable for him. We have already mentioned that, before the development of civilization, extraordinary variability characterized the relations between the sexes. This variability developed within the framework of clans and tribes and in this way was not bound to any universality. In the society of the future such variability will return, but this time individually; in this way it will be characterized by the greatest universality, with the individual pattern directly embodying the universality of the human species.

To this point, we have only discussed the wealth of types in relations between the sexes. Now their depth should also be mentioned. As we have seen, the depth, the meaningfulness of relations between the sexes depends directly on the general depth and substance of human beings. The richer the emotional, moral and intellectual culture, the more universal the warmth of emotions, the richer and more profound the emotional and intellectual relations will become in contact between the sexes.

Without a doubt, the perspective we have outlined implies the disappearance of alienated, monogamous marriage. (By alienated marriage we mean marriage based on property. Its monogamous version is that which for long officially sanctioned the cohabitation of a man and woman for life.) The dissolution of monogamous marriage is something we are already witnessing in this day and age; this is a *factum brutum* today. The mere dissolution of monogamy, however, does not at all mean that new and more worthy relations necessarily develop. To achieve this, a social movement must clearly develop which leads to the liquidation of all forms of alienation. Until real equality of men and women has been achieved, the dissolution of monogamy implies, at least transitionally, greater disadvantages for women. Until a new organic human community has come into being, the dissolution of monogamy makes loneliness explicit—and in this way more distressing—even if it does not increase it.

We regard the dissolution of alienated monogamous marriage, despite its painful conflicts, as a process which points ahead to a better future over the longer range. It reduces the role of ownership and financial relations in cohabitation and in extramarital sexual relations, while also reducing prostitution (this holds particularly for socialist societies). True, as long as there is "spontaneously evolved (*naturwüchsig*) division of labor" (Marx), property and monetary considerations cannot be eliminated from the relation between the sexes. But the motivational force of these factors can, and does, diminish. Nineteenth century Marxists (Engels, Bebel) foresaw and approved this aspect of the dissolution of alienated monogamy. What Engels and Bebel did not foresee were the conflicts and contradictions concomitant with such dissolution, for they regarded socialism as a kind of society made up of close communities, right from the moment of its inception.

We have stressed repeatedly that the people of the future will choose the pattern and depth of their relations individually, without being bound and their impulses suppressed by the taboos of sex morality. This certainly does not mean, however, that the actor himself can ever be the only and chief judge of his deeds. Even the most advanced person may make false decisions, which are opposed to universal value judgements, or can act on occasion against his human substance; moreover, there will never be a time when every person is equally advanced. Consequently there will continue to be a judge and judgement, and this will be the public opinion of communities built on equal and free human relations. This public opinion, however, will differ from all types of public judgements to date in not being founded on particularistic norms hostile to the individual and based merely on custom. It will judge on the basis of the individual case and situation, and the only relevant criterion will be whether a given decision offended against the general values at the given level of development of the species, and whether it might have been possible—and if so at what price—for the individual to refrain from violating them. Thus the judgement of public opinion will not have the effect of suppressing individual impulses but of humanizing them.

Fourier, and in his wake Marx, said that the degree of the humanization of a society can be gauged by the relations between men and women. Here we have sketched a perspective in which a humanized society makes possible humanized relationships between men and women, the first such case in the history of mankind. We do not deny, however (in fact we pointed it out at the beginning), that there is also the possibility of another perspective. In a world ruled by manipulation, everything that today points in the direction of the development of values can have an opposite, undesirable, outcome. Thus, the dissolution of monogamy or the "sexual revolution" can not only herald a more humane future, but can also be the precursor of a decline of those values mankind has progressively created. The individual manipulated on the basis of his particularist motives may sink lower in his relationship with the opposite sex than the ascetic who suppresses his instincts, or the libertine who, blindly and completely unconcerned for others, follows the bidding of his passions. The pseudo-scientific and literary dishing-up of sex life, its "expert" and at the same time conformist teaching based on the appeal of "everybody's doing it" degrades sexuality more than the most tormenting guilt feelings over secret eroticism. (To avoid any possible misunderstanding, these remarks are not directed against sex instruction!) In fact, this sort of manipulation erodes individuality, the very quality which is most valuable in the relation between the sexes, whether in sexuality, eroticism or love.

When we make our choice in social conflicts, we are at the same time making a choice as to the future of the relation between the sexes. We choose the free and equal—and certainly individual—relations of the sexes, relations cleansed of the drive for possession and rich, deep and meaningful in every aspect of human life.

Love

George Santayana

George Santayana (1863-1952), one of the most famous American philosophers, taught at Harvard University for many years. He is the author of more than twenty books, including *The Life of Reason* (1905), *Realms of Being* (1925-1940), and *Skepticism and Animal Faith* (1923).

The conscious quality of this passion differs so much in various races and individuals, and at various points in the same life, that no account of it will ever satisfy everybody.[1] Poets and novelists never tire of depicting it anew; but although the experience they tell of is fresh and unparalleled in every individual, their rendering suffers, on the whole, from a great monotony. Love's gesture and symptoms are noted and unvarying; its vocabulary is poor and worn. Even a poet, therefore, can give of love but a meagre expression, while the philosopher, who renounces dramatic representation, is condemned to be avowedly inadequate. Love, to the lover, is a noble and immense inspiration; to the naturalist it is a thin veil and prelude to the self-assertion of lust. This opposition has prevented philosophers from doing justice to the subject. Two things need to be admitted by anyone who would not go wholly astray in such speculation: one, that love has an animal basis; the other, that it has an ideal object. Since these two propositions have usually been thought contradictory, no writer has ventured to present more than half the truth, and that half out of its true relations.

Plato, who gave eloquent expression to the ideal burden of the passion, and divined its political and cosmic message, passed over its natural history with a few mythical fancies; and Schopenhauer, into whose system a naturalistic treatment would have fitted so easily, allowed his metaphysics to carry him at this point into verbal inanities; while, of course, like all profane writers on the subject, he failed to appreciate the oracles which Plato had delivered. In popular feeling, where sentiment and observation must both make themselves felt somehow or other, the tendency is to imagine that love is an absolute, non-natural energy which, for some unknown reason, or for none at all, lights upon particular persons, and rests there eternally, as on its ultimate goal. In other words, it makes the origin of love divine and its object natural: which is the exact opposite of the truth. If it were once seen, however, that every ideal expresses some natural function, and that no natural function is incapable, in its free exercise, of evolving some ideal and finding justification in an inherent operation like life or thought, then the philosophy of love should not prove permanently barren. For love is a brilliant illustration of a principle everywhere discoverable: namely, that human reason lives by turning the

Source: The Life of Reason (New York: Scribner's, 1954), pp. 89-103. Reprinted by permission of Charles Scribner's Sons. Copyright 1953 Daniel M. Cory.

[1] The wide uses of the English word love add to the difficulty. I shall take the liberty of limiting the term here to imaginative passion, to being in love, excluding all other ways of loving.

friction of material forces into the light of ideal goods. There can be no philosophic interest in disguising the animal basis of love, or in denying its spiritual sublimations, since all life is animal in its origin and spiritual in its possible fruits.

Plastic matter, in transmitting its organization, takes various courses which it is the part of natural history to describe. Even after reproduction has become sexual, it will offer no basis for love if it does not require a union of the two parent bodies. Did germinal substances, unconsciously diffused, meet by chance in the external medium and unite there, it is obvious that whatever obsessions or pleasures maturity might bring, they would not have the quality which men call love. But when an individual of the opposite sex must be met with, recognized, and pursued, and must prove responsive, then each is haunted by the possible other. Each feels in a generic way the presence and attraction of his fellows; he vibrates to their touch, he dreams of their image, he is restless and wistful if alone. When the vague need that solicits him is met by the presence of a possible mate, it is extraordinarily kindled. Then, if it reaches fruition, it subsides immediately, and after an interval, perhaps, of stupor and vital recuperation, the animal regains his independence, his peace, and his impartial curiosity. You might think him on the way to becoming intelligent; but the renewed nutrition and cravings of the sexual machinery soon engross his attention again; all his sprightly indifference vanishes before nature's categorical imperative. That fierce and turbid pleasure, by which his obedience is rewarded, hastens his dissolution; every day the ensuing lassitude and emptiness give him a clearer premonition of death. It is not figuratively only that his soul has passed into his offspring. The vocation to produce them was a chief part of his being, and when that function is sufficiently fulfilled he is superfluous in the world and becomes partly superfluous even to himself. The confines of his dream are narrowed. He moves apathetically and dies forlorn.

Some echo of the vital rhythm which pervades not merely the generations of animals, but the seasons and the stars, emerges sometimes in consciousness; on reaching the tropics in the mortal ecliptic, which the human individual may touch many times without much change in his outer fortunes, the soul may occasionally divine that it is passing through a supreme crisis. Passion, when vehement, may bring atavistic sentiments. When love is absolute it feels a profound impulse to welcome death, and even, by a transcendental confusion, to evoke the end of the universe.[2] The human soul reverts at such a moment to what an ephemeral insect might feel, buzzing till it finds its mate in the noon. Its whole destiny was wooing, and, that mission accomplished, it sings its *Nunc dimittis*, renouncing heartily all irrelevant things, now that the one fated and all-satisfying good has been achieved. Where parental instincts exist also, nature soon shifts her loom: a milder impulse succeeds, and a satisfaction of a gentler sort follows in the birth of children. The transcendental illusion is here corrected, and it is seen that the extinction the lovers

---

[2] One example, among a thousand, is the cry of Siegfried and Brünhilde in Wagner:

> Lachend lass' uns verderben
> Lachend zu Grunde geh'n.
> Fahr hin, Walhall's
> Leuchtende Welt! . . .
> Leb' wohl, pragende
> Götter Pracht!
> Ende in Wonne,
> Du ewig Geschlecht!

had accepted needed not to be complete. The death they welcomed was not without its little resurrection. The feeble worm they had generated bore their immortality within it.

The varieties of sexual economy are many and to each may correspond, for all we know, a special sentiment. Sometimes the union established is intermittent; sometimes it crowns the end of life and dissolves it altogether; sometimes it remains, while it lasts, monogamous; sometimes the sexual and social alertness is constant in the male, only periodic in the female. Sometimes the group established for procreation endures throughout the seasons, and from year to year; sometimes the males herd together, as if normally they preferred their own society, until the time of rut comes, when war arises between them for the possession of what they have just discovered to be the fair.

A naturalist not ashamed to indulge his poetic imagination might easily paint for us the drama of these diverse loves. It suffices for our purpose to observe that the varying passions and duties which life can contain depend upon the organic functions of the animal. A fish incapable of coition, absolved from all care for its young, which it never sees or never distinguishes from the casual swimmers darting across its path, such a fish, being without social faculties or calls to cooperation, cannot have the instincts, perceptions, or emotions which belong to social beings. A male of some higher species that feels only once a year the sudden solicitations of love cannot be sentimental in all the four seasons: his headlong passion, exhausted upon its present object and dismissed at once without remainder, leaves his senses perfectly free and colorless to scrutinize his residual world. Whatever further fears or desires may haunt him will have nothing mystical or sentimental about them. He will be a man of business all the year round, and a lover only on May-day. A female that does not suffice for the rearing of her young will expect and normally receive her mate's aid long after the pleasures of love are forgotten by him. Disinterested fidelity on his part will then be her right and his duty. But a female that, once pregnant, needs, like the hen, no further cooperation on the male's part will turn from him at once with absolute indifference to brood perpetually on her eggs, undisturbed by the least sense of solitude or jealousy. And the chicks that at first follow her and find shelter under her wings will soon be forgotten also and relegated to the mechanical landscape. There is no pain in the timely snapping of the dearest bonds where society has not become a permanent organism, and perpetual friendship is not one of its possible modes.

Transcendent and ideal passions may well judge themselves to have an incomparable dignity. Yet that dignity is hardly more than what every passion, were it articulate, would assign to itself and to its objects. The dumbness of a passion may accordingly, from one point of view, be called the index of its baseness; for if it cannot ally itself with ideas its affinities can hardly lie in the rational mind nor its advocates be among the poets. But if we listen to the master-passion itself rather than to the loquacious arts it may have enlisted in its service, we shall understand that it is not self-condemned because it is silent, nor an anomaly in nature because inharmonious with human life. The fish's heartlessness is his virtue, the male bee's lasciviousness is his vocation; and if these functions were retrenched or encumbered in order to assimilate them to human excellence they would be merely dislocated. We should not produce virtue where there was vice, but defeat a possible arrangement which would have had its own vitality and order.

Animal love is a marvellous force; and while it issues in acts that may be followed by a revulsion of feeling, it yet deserves a more sympathetic treatment than art and morals have known how to accord it. Erotic poets, to hide their want of ability to make the dumb passion speak, have played feebly with veiled insinuations and comic effects: while more serious sonneteers have harped exclusively on secondary and somewhat literary emotions, abstractly conjugating the verb to love. Lucretius, in spite of his didactic turns, has been on this subject, too, the most ingenuous and magnificent of poets, although he chose to confine his description to the external history of sexual desire. It is a pity that he did not turn, with his sublime sincerity, to the inner side of it also, and write the drama of the awakened senses, the poignant suasion of beauty, when it clouds the brain, and makes the conventional earth, seen through that bright haze, seem a sorry fable. Western poets should not have despised what the Orientals, in their fugitive stanzas, seem often to have sung most exquisitely: the joy of gazing on the beloved, of following or being followed, of tacit understandings and avowals, of flight together into some solitude to people it with those ineffable confidences which so naturally follow the outward proofs of love. All this makes the brightest page of many a life, the only bright page in the thin biography of many a human animal; while if the beasts could speak they would give us, no doubt, endless versions of the only joy in which, as we may fancy, the blood of the universe flows consciously through their hearts.

The darkness which conventionally covers this passion is one of the saddest consequences of Adam's fall. It was a terrible misfortune in man's development that he should not have been able to acquire the higher functions without deranging the lower. Why should the depths of his being be thus polluted and the most delightful of nature's mysteries be an occasion not for communion with her, as it should have remained, but for depravity and sorrow?

This question, asked in moral perplexity, admits of a scientific answer. Man, in becoming more complex, becomes less stably organized. His sexual instinct, instead of being intermittent, but violent and boldly declared, becomes practically constant, but is entangled in many cross-currents of desire, in many other equally imperfect adaptations of structure to various ends. Indulgence in any impulse can then easily become excessive and thwart the rest; for it may be aroused artificially and maintained from without, so that in turn it disturbs its neighbors. Sometimes the sexual instinct may be stimulated out of season by example, by a too wakeful fancy, by language, by pride—for all these forces are now working in the same field and intermingling their suggestions. At the same time the same instinct may derange others, and make them fail at their proper and pressing occasions.

In consequence of such derangements, reflection and public opinion will come to condemn what in itself was perfectly innocent. The corruption of a given instinct by others and of others by it, becomes the ground for long attempts to suppress or enslave it. With the haste and formalism natural to language and to law, external and arbitrary limits are set to its operation. As no inward adjustment can possibly correspond to these conventional barriers and compartments of life, a war between nature and morality breaks out both in society and in each particular bosom—a war in which every victory is a sorrow and every defeat a dishonor. As one instinct after another becomes furious or disorganized, cowardly or criminal, under these artificial restrictions, the public and private conscience turns against it all its forces, necessarily without much nice discrimination; the frank passions of youth are met with a grimace of horror on all sides, with *rumores senum severiorum,** with an insistence on reticence and hypocrisy. Such suppression is favorable to corruption: the fancy with a sort of idiotic ingenuity comes to supply the place of experience; and nature is rendered vicious and overlaid with pruriency, artifice, and the love of novelty. Hereupon the authorities that rule in such matters naturally redouble their vigilance and exaggerate their reasonable censure: chastity begins to seem essentially holy and perpetual virginity ends by becoming an absolute ideal. Thus the disorder in man's life and disposition, when grown intolerable, leads him to condemn the very elements out of which order might have been constituted, and to mistake his total confusion for his total depravity.

Banished from the open day, covered with mockery, and publicly ignored, this necessary pleasure flourishes none the less in dark places and in the secret soul. Its familiar presence there, its intimate habitation in what is most oneself, helps to cut the world in two and to separate the inner from the outer life. In that mysticism which cannot disguise its erotic affinities, this disruption reaches an absolute and theoretic form; but in many a youth little suspected of mysticism it produces estrangement from the conventional moralizing world, which he instinctively regards as artificial and alien. It prepares him for excursions into a private fairy-land in which unthought-of joys will blossom amid friendlier magic forces. The truly good then seems to be the fantastic, the sensuous, the prodigally unreal. He gladly forgets the dreary world he lives in to listen for a thousand and one nights to his dreams.

To brood on such an Elysium is a likely prelude and fertile preparation for romantic passion. When the passion takes form, it calls fancy back from its loose reveries and fixes it upon a single object. Then the ideal seems at last to have been brought down to earth. Its embodiment has been discovered amongst the children of men. Imagination narrows her range. Instead of all sorts of flatteries to sense and improbable delicious adventures, the lover imagines but a single joy. Even if he dreads no physical betrayal, he suffers from terror and morbid sensitiveness at every hint of mental estrangement.

This attachment is often the more absorbing the more unaccountable it seems; and as in hypnotism the subject is dead to all influences but that of the operator, so in love the heart surrenders itself entirely to the one being that has known how to touch it. That being is not selected; it is recognized and obeyed. Pre-arranged reactions in the system respond to whatever stimulus, at a propitious moment, happens to break through and arouse them pervasively. Nature has opened various avenues to that passion in whose successful operation she has so much at stake. Sometimes the magic influence asserts itself suddenly, sometimes gently and unawares. One approach, which in poetry has usurped more than its share of attention, is through beauty; another, less glorious, but often more efficacious, through surprised sense and premonitions of pleasure; a third through social sympathy and moral affinities. Contemplation, sense, and association are none of them the essence nor even the seed of love; but any of them may be its soil and supply it with a propitious background. It would be mere sophistry to pretend, for instance, that love is or should be nothing but a moral bond, the sympathy of two kindred spirits or the union of two lives. For such an effect no passion would be needed, as none is needed to perceive beauty or to feel pleasure.

*[With the talk of harsh old men.—Eds.]

What Aristotle calls friendships of utility, pleasure, or virtue, all resting on common interests of some impersonal sort, are far from possessing the quality of love, its thrill, flutter, and absolute sway over happiness and misery. But it may well fall to such influences to awaken or feed the passion where it actually arises. Whatever circumstances pave the way, love does not itself appear until a sexual affinity is declared. When a woman, for instance, contemplating marriage, asks herself whether she really loves her suitor or merely accepts him, the test is the possibility of awakening a sexual affinity. For this reason women of the world often love their husbands more truly than they did their lovers, because marriage has evoked an elementary feeling which before lay smothered under a heap of coquetries, vanities, and conventions.

Man, on the contrary, is polygamous by instinct, although often kept faithful by habit no less than by duty. If his fancy is left free, it is apt to wander. We observe this in romantic passion no less than in a life of mere gallantry and pleasure. Sentimental illusions may become a habit, and the shorter the dream is, the more often it is repeated, so that any susceptible poet may find that he, like Alfred de Musset, "must love incessantly, who once has loved." Love is indeed much less exacting than it thinks itself. Nine-tenths of its cause are in the lover, for one-tenth that may be in the object. Were the latter not accidentally at hand, an almost identical passion would probably have been felt for someone else; for although with acquaintance the quality of an attachment naturally adapts itself to the person loved, and makes that person its standard and ideal, the first assault and mysterious glow of the passion is much the same for every object. What really affects the character of love is the lover's temperament, age, and experience. The objects that appeal to each man reveal his nature; but those unparalleled virtues and that unique divinity which the lover discovers there are reflections of his own adoration, things that ecstasy is very cunning in. He loves what he imagines and worships what he creates.

Those who do not consider these matters so curiously may feel that to refer love in this way chiefly to inner processes is at once ignominious and fantastic. But nothing could be more natural; the soul accurately renders, in this experience, what is going on in the body and in the race. Nature had a problem to solve in sexual reproduction which would have daunted a less ruthless experimenter. She had to bring together automatically, and at the dictation, as they felt, of their irresponsible wills, just the creatures that by uniting might reproduce the species. The complete sexual reaction had to be woven together out of many incomplete reactions to various stimuli, reactions not specifically sexual. The outer senses had to be engaged, and many secondary characters found in bodies had to be used to attract attention, until the deeper instinctive response should have time to gather itself together and assert itself openly. Many mechanical preformations and reflexes must conspire to constitute a determinate instinct. We name this instinct after its ultimate function, looking forward to the uses we observe it to have; and it seems to us in consequence an inexplicable anomaly that many a time the instinct is set in motion when its alleged purpose cannot be fulfilled; as when love appears prematurely or too late, or fixes upon a creature of the wrong age or sex. These anomalies show us how nature is built up and, far from being inexplicable, are hints that tend to make everything clear, when once a verbal and mythical philosophy has been abandoned.

Responses which we may call sexual in view of results to which they may ultimately lead are thus often quite independent, and exist before they are drawn into the vortex of a complete and actually generative act. External stimulus and present idea will consequently be altogether inadequate to explain the profound upheaval which may ensue, if, as we say, we actually fall in love. That the senses should be played upon is nothing, if no deeper reaction is aroused. All depends on the juncture at which, so to speak, the sexual circuit is completed and the emotional currents begin to circulate. Whatever object, at such a critical moment, fills the field of consciousness becomes a signal and associate for the whole sexual mood. It is breathlessly devoured in that pause and concentration of attention, that rearrangement of the soul, which love is conceived in; and the whole new life which that image is engulfed in is foolishly supposed to be its effect. For the image is in consciousness, but not the profound predispositions which gave it place and power.

This association between passion and its signals may be merely momentary, or it may be perpetual: a Don Juan and a Dante are both genuine lovers. In a gay society the gallant addresses every woman as if she charmed him, and perhaps actually finds any kind of beauty, or mere femininity anywhere, a sufficient spur to his desire. These momentary fascinations are not necessarily false: they may for an instant be quite absorbing and irresistible; they may genuinely suffuse the whole mind. Such mercurial fire will indeed require a certain imaginative temperament; and there are many persons who, short of a life-long domestic attachment, can conceive of nothing but sordid vice. But even an inconstant flame may burn brightly, if the soul is naturally combustible. Indeed these sparks and glints of passion, just because they come and vary so quickly, offer admirable illustrations of it, in which it may be viewed, so to speak, under the microscope and in its formative stage.

Thus Plato did not hesitate to make the love of all wines, under whatever guise, excuse, or occasion, the test of a true taste for wine and an unfeigned adoration of Bacchus; and, like Lucretius after him, he wittily compiled a list of names, by which the lover will flatter the most opposite qualities, if they only succeed in arousing his inclination. To be omnivorous is one pole of true love: to be exclusive is the other. A man whose heart, if I may say so, lies deeper, hidden under a thicker coat of mail, will have less play of fancy, and will be far from finding every charm charming, or every sort of beauty a stimulus to love. Yet he may not be less prone to the tender passion, and when once smitten may be so penetrated by an unimagined tenderness and joy, that he will declare himself incapable of ever loving again, and may actually be so. Having no rivals and a deeper soil, love can ripen better in such a constant spirit; it will not waste itself in a continual patter of little pleasures and illusions. But unless the passion of it is to die down, it must somehow assert its universality: what it loses in diversity it must gain in applicability. It must become a principle of action and an influence coloring everything that is dreamt of; otherwise it would have lost its dignity and sunk into a dead memory or a domestic bond.

True love, it used to be said, is love at first sight. Manners have much to do with such incidents, and the race which happens to set, at a given time, the fashion in literature makes its temperament public and exercises a sort of contagion over all men's fancies. If women are rarely seen and ordinarily not to be spoken to; if all imagination has to build upon is a furtive glance or casual motion, people fall in love at first sight. For they must fall in love somehow, and any stimulus is enough if none more powerful is forthcoming. When society, on the contrary, allows constant and easy intercourse between the sexes, a first impression, if not reinforced, will soon be hidden and obliterated by others. Acquaintance becomes necessary for love when it is necessary for memory. But what makes true love is not the information conveyed by acquaintance, not any circumstantial charms that may be therein discovered: it is still a deep and dumb instinctive affinity, an inexplicable emotion seizing the heart, an influence organizing the world, like a luminous crystal, about one magic point. So that although love seldom springs up suddenly in these days into anything like a full-blown passion, it is sight, it is presence, that makes in time a conquest over the heart; for all virtues, sympathies, confidences will fail to move a man to tenderness and to worship, unless a poignant effluence from the object envelop him, so that he begins to walk, as it were, in a dream.

Not to believe in love is a great sign of dulness. There are some people so indirect and lumbering that they think all real affection must rest on circumstantial evidence. But a finely constituted being is sensitive to its deepest affinities. This is precisely what refinement consists in, that we may feel in things immediate and infinitesimal a sure premonition of things ultimate and important. Fine senses vibrate at once to harmonies which it may take long to verify; so sight is finer than touch, and thought than sensation. Well-bred instinct meets reason half-way, and is prepared for the consonances that may follow. Beautiful things, when taste is formed, are obviously and unaccountably beautiful. The grounds we may bring ourselves to assign for our preferences are discovered by analysing those preferences, and articulate judgments follow upon emotions which they ought to express, but which they sometimes sophisticate. So, too, the reasons we give for love either express what it feels or else are insincere, attempting to justify at the bar of reason and convention something which is far more primitive than they and underlies them both. True instinct can dispense with such excuses. It appeals to the event and is justified by the response which nature makes to it. It is, of course, far from infallible; it cannot dominate circumstances, and has no discursive knowledge; but it is presumably true, and what it foreknows is always essentially possible. Unrealizable it may indeed be in the jumbled context of this world, where the Fates, like an absent-minded printer, seldom allow a single line to stand perfect and unmarred.

The profoundest affinities are those most readily felt, and though a thousand later considerations may overlay and override them, they remain a background and standard for all happiness. If we trace them out we succeed. If we put them by, although in other respects we may call ourselves happy, we inwardly know that we have dismissed the ideal, and all that was essentially possible has not been realized. Love in that case still owns a hidden and potential object, and we sanctify, perhaps, whatever kindnesses or partialities we indulge in by a secret loyalty to something impersonal and unseen. Such reserve, such religion, would not have been necessary had things responded to our first expectations. We might then have identified the ideal with the object that happened to call it forth. The Life of Reason might have been led instinctively, and we might have been guided by nature herself into the ways of peace.

As it is, circumstances, false steps, or the mere lapse of time, force us to shuffle our affections and take them as they come, or as we are suffered to indulge them. Every real object must cease to be what it seemed, and none could ever be what the whole soul desired. Yet what the soul desires is nothing arbitrary. Life is no objectless dream, but continually embodies, with varying success, the potentialities it contains and that prompt desire. Everything that satisfies at all, even if partially and for an instant, justifies aspiration and rewards it. Existence, however, cannot be arrested; and only the transmissible forms of things can endure, to match the transmissible faculties which living beings hand down to one another. The ideal is accordingly significant, perpetual, and as constant as the nature it expresses; but it can never itself exist, nor can its particular embodiments endure.

Love is accordingly only half an illusion; the lover, but not his love, is deceived. His madness, as Plato taught, is divine; for though it be folly to identify the idol with the god, faith in the god is inwardly justified. That egregious idolatry may therefore be interpreted ideally and give a symbolic scope worthy of its natural causes and of the mystery it comes to celebrate. The lover knows much more about absolute good and universal beauty than any logician or theologian, unless the latter, too, be lovers in disguise. Logical universals are terms in discourse, without vital ideality, while traditional gods are at best natural existences, more or less indifferent facts. What the lover comes upon, on the contrary, is truly persuasive, and witnesses to itself, so that he worships from the heart and upholds what he worships. That the true object is no natural being, but an ideal form essentially eternal and capable of endless embodiments, is far from abolishing its worth; on the contrary, this fact makes love ideally relevant to generation, by which the human soul and body may be for ever renewed, and at the same time makes it a thing for large thoughts to be focussed upon, a thing representing all rational aims.

Whenever this ideality is absent and a lover sees nothing in his mistress but what everyone else may find in her, loving her honestly in her unvarnished and accidental person, there is a friendly and humorous affection, admirable in itself, but no passion or bewitchment of love; she is a member of his group, not a spirit in his pantheon. Such an affection may be altogether what it should be; it may bring a happiness all the more stable because the heart is quite whole, and no divine shaft has pierced it. It is hard to stanch wounds inflicted by a god. The glance of an ideal love is terrible and glorious, foreboding death and immortality together. Love is a true natural religion; it has a visible cult, it is kindled by natural beauties and bows to the best symbol it may find for its hope; it sanctifies a natural mystery; and, finally, when understood, it recognizes that what it worshipped under a figure was truly the principle of all good.

The loftiest edifices need the deepest foundations. Love would never take so high a flight unless it sprung from something profound and elementary. It is accordingly most truly love when it is irresistible and fatal. The substance of all passion, if we could gather it together, would be the basis of all ideals, to which all goods would have to refer. Love actually accomplishes something of the sort; being primordial it underlies other demands, and can be wholly satisfied only by a happiness which is ultimate and comprehensive. Lovers are vividly aware of this fact: their ideal, apparently so inarticulate, seems to them to include everything. It shares the mystical quality of all primitive life. Sophisticated people can hardly understand how vague experience is at bottom, and how truly that vagueness supports whatever clearness is afterward attained. In truth, all spiritual interests are supported by animal life; in this the generative function is fundamental; and it is therefore no paradox, but something altogether fitting, that if that function realized all it comprises. nothing human would remain outside. Such an ultimate fulfilment would differ, of course, from a first satisfaction, just as all that reproduction reproduces differs from the reproductive function itself, and vastly exceeds it. All organs and activities which are inherited, in a sense, grow out of the reproductive process and serve to clothe it; so that when the generative energy is awakened all that can ever be is virtually called up and, so to speak, made consciously potential; and love yearns for the universe of values.

This secret is gradually revealed to those who are inwardly attentive and allow love to teach them something. A man who has truly loved, though he may come to recognize the thousand incidental illusions into which love may have led him, will not recant its essential faith. He will keep his sense for the ideal and his power to worship. In fortunate cases love may glide imperceptibly into settled domestic affections, giving them henceforth a touch of ideality; for when love dies in the odor of sanctity people venerate his relics. In other cases allegiance to the ideal may appear more sullenly, breaking out in whims, or in little sentimental practices which might seem half-conventional. Again it may inspire a religious conversion, charitable works, or even artistic labors. In all these ways people attempt more or less seriously to lead the Life of Reason, expressing outwardly allegiance to whatever in their minds has come to stand for the ideal. The machinery which serves reproduction thus finds kindred but higher uses, as every organ does in a liberal life; and what Plato called a desire for birth in beauty may be sublimated even more, until it yearns for an ideal immortality in a transfigured world, a world made worthy of that love which its children have so often lavished on it in their dreams.

Homosexuality and Pornography
Ronald Dworkin

Ronald Dworkin (1931-   ) was a professor of law at the Yale University law school until the fall of 1969, at which time he left Yale to succeed H. L. A. Hart as professor of jurisprudence at Oxford University. Dworkin has written a number of important essays in the field of legal philosophy.

There are two chief arguments [in Lord Devlin's book, *The Enforcement of Morals*]. The first is set out in structured form in the Maccabaean Lecture. It argues from society's right to protect its own existence. The second, a quite different and much more important argument, develops in disjointed form through various essays. It argues from the majority's right to follow its own moral convictions in defending its social environment from change it opposes. I shall consider these two arguments in turn, but the second at greater length.

Source: "Lord Devlin and the Enforcement of Morals," *The Yale Law Journal,* Vol. 75. Reprinted by permission of The Yale Law Journal Company and Fred B. Rothman & Company.

THE FIRST ARGUMENT: SOCIETY'S RIGHT
TO PROTECT ITSELF

The first argument—and the argument which has received by far the major part of the critics' attention—is this.[1]

(1) In a modern society there are a variety of moral principles which some men adopt for their own guidance and do not attempt to impose upon others. There are also moral standards which the majority places beyond toleration and imposes upon those who dissent. For us, the dictates of particular religion are an example of the former class, and the practice of monogamy an example of the latter. A society cannot survive unless some standards are of the second class, because some moral conformity is essential to its life. Every society has a right to preserve its own existence, and therefore the right to insist on some such conformity.

(2) If society has such a right, then it has the right to use the institutions and sanctions of its criminal law to enforce the right—"[S]ociety may use the law to preserve morality in the same way it uses it to safeguard anything else if it is essential to its existence."[2] Just as society may use its law to prevent treason, it may use it to prevent a corruption of that conformity which ties it together.

(3) But society's right to punish immorality by law should not necessarily be exercised against every sort and on every occasion of immorality—we must recognize the impact and the importance of some restraining principles. There are several of these, but the most important is that there "must be toleration of the maximum individual freedom that is consistent with the integrity of society."[3] These restraining principles, taken together, require that we exercise caution in concluding that a practice is considered profoundly immoral. The law should stay its hand if it detects any uneasiness or halfheartedness or latent toleration in society's condemnation of the practice. But none of these restraining principles apply, and hence society is free to enforce its rights, when public feeling is high, enduring and relentless, when, in Lord Devlin's phrase, it rises to "intolerance, indignation and disgust."[4] Hence the summary conclusion about homosexuality: if it is genuinely regarded as an abominable vice, society's right to eradicate it cannot be denied.

We must guard against a possible, indeed tempting, misconception of this argument. It does not depend upon any assumption that when the vast bulk of a community thinks a practice is immoral they are likely right. What Lord Devlin thinks is at stake, when our public morality is challenged, is the very survival of society, and he believes that society is entitled to preserve itself without vouching for the morality that holds it together.

Is this argument sound? Professor H. L. A. Hart, responding to its appearance at the heart of the Maccabaean Lecture,[5] thought that it rested upon a confused conception of what a society is. If one holds anything like a conventional notion of a society, he said, it is absurd to suggest that every practice the society views as profoundly immoral and disgusting threatens its survival. This is as silly as arguing that society's existence is threatened by the death of one of its members or the

---

[1] It is developed chiefly in Devlin, *The Enforcement of Morals*, pp. 7-25.

[2] *Ibid.*, p. 11.

[3] *Ibid.*, p. 16.

[4] *Ibid.*, p. 17.

[5] H. L. A. Hart, *Law, Liberty and Morality* (1963), p. 51.

birth of another, and Lord Devlin, he reminds us, offers nothing by way of evidence to support any such claim. But if one adopts an artificial definition of a society, such that a society consists of that particular complex of moral ideas and attitudes which its members happen to hold at a particular moment in time, it is intolerable that each such moral status quo should have the right to preserve its precarious existence by force. So, Professor Hart argued, Lord Devlin's argument fails whether a conventional or an artificial sense of "society" is taken.

Lord Devlin replies to Professor Hart in a new and lengthy footnote. After summarizing Hart's criticism he comments, "I do not assert that *any* deviation from a society's shared morality threatens its existence any more than I assert that *any* subversive activity threatens its existence. I assert that they are both activities which are capable in their nature of threatening the existence of society so that neither can be put beyond the law."[6] This reply exposes a serious flaw in the architecture of the argument.

In short, the argument involves an intellectual sleight of hand. At the second step, public outrage is presented as a threshold criterion, merely placing the practice in a category which the law is not forbidden to regulate. But offstage, somewhere in the transition to the third step, this threshold criterion becomes itself a dispositive affirmative reason for action, so that when it is clearly met the law may proceed without more. The power of this manoeuvre is proved by the passage on homosexuality. Lord Devlin concludes that if our society hates homosexuality enough it is justified in outlawing it, and forcing human beings to choose between the miseries of frustration and persecution, because of the danger the practice presents to society's existence. He manages this conclusion without offering evidence that homosexuality presents any danger at all to society's existence, beyond the naked claim that all "deviations from a society's shared morality . . . are capable in their nature of threatening the existence of society" and so "cannot be put beyond the law."[7]

THE SECOND ARGUMENT: SOCIETY'S RIGHT TO FOLLOW ITS OWN LIGHTS

We are therefore justified in setting aside the first argument and turning to the second. My reconstruction includes making a great deal explicit which I believe implicit, and so involves some risk of distortion, but I take the second argument to be this:[8]

(1) If those who have homosexual desires freely indulged them, our social environment would change. What the changes would be cannot be calculated with any precision, but it is plausible to suppose, for example, that the position of the family, as the assumed and natural institution around which the educational, economic and recreational arrangements of men center, would be undermined, and the further ramifications of that would be great. We are too sophisticated to suppose that the effects of an increase in homosexuality would be confined to those who participate in the practice alone, just as we are too sophisticated to suppose that

---

[6] Devlin, p. 13.

[7] Devlin, p. 13, n.1.

[8] Most of the argument appears in Devlin, chapters V, VI and VII. See also an article published after the book: *Law and Morality,* 1 Manitoba L.S.J. 243 (1964-65).

prices and wages affect only those who negotiate them. The environment in which we and our children must live is determined, among other things, by patterns and relationships formed privately by others than ourselves.

(2) This in itself does not give society the right to prohibit homosexual practices. We cannot conserve every custom we like by jailing those who do not want to preserve it. But it means that our legislators must inevitably decide some moral issues. They must decide whether the institutions which seem threatened are sufficiently valuable to protect at the cost of human freedom. And they must decide whether the practices which threaten that institution are immoral, for if they are then the freedom of an individual to pursue them counts for less. We do not need so strong a justification, in terms of the social importance of the institutions being protected, if we are confident that no one has a moral right to do what we want to prohibit. We need less of a case, that is, to abridge someone's freedom to lie, cheat or drive recklessly, than his freedom to choose his own jobs or to price his own goods. This does not claim that immorality is sufficient to make conduct criminal; it argues, rather, that on occasion it is necessary.

(3) But how shall a legislator decide whether homosexual acts are immoral? Science can give no answer, and a legislator can no longer properly turn to organized religion. If it happens, however, that the vast bulk of the community is agreed upon an answer, even though a small minority of educated men may dissent, the legislator has a duty to act on the consensus. He has such a duty for two closely connected reasons: (a) In the last analysis the decision must rest on some article of moral faith, and in a democracy this sort of issue, above all others, must be settled in accordance with democratic principles. (b) It is, after all, the community which acts when the threats and sanctions of the criminal law are brought to bear. The community must take the moral responsibility, and it must therefore act on its own lights—that is, on the moral faith of its members.

This, as I understand it, is Lord Devlin's second argument. It is complex, and almost every component invites analysis and challenge. Some readers will dissent from its central assumption, that a change in social institutions is the sort of harm a society is entitled to protect itself against. Others who do not take this strong position (perhaps because they approve of laws which are designed to protect economic institutions) will nevertheless feel that society is not entitled to act, however immoral the practice, unless the threatened harm to an institution is demonstrable and imminent rather than speculative. Still others will challenge the thesis that the morality or immorality of an act ought even to count in determining whether to make it criminal (though they would no doubt admit that it does count under present practice), and others still will argue that even in a democracy legislators have the duty to decide moral questions for themselves, and must not refer such issues to the community at large. I do not propose to argue now for or against any of these positions. I want instead to consider whether Lord Devlin's conclusions are valid on his own terms, on the assumption, that is, that society does have a right to protect its central and valued social institutions against conduct which the vast bulk of its members disapproves on moral principle.

I shall argue that his conclusions are not valid, even on these terms, because he misunderstands what it is to disapprove on moral principle. I might say a cautionary word about the argument I shall present. It will consist in part of reminders that certain types of moral language (terms like "prejudice" and "moral position," for example) have standard uses in moral argument. My purpose is not to settle issues of political morality by the fiat of a dictionary, but to exhibit what I believe to be mistakes in Lord Devlin's moral sociology. I shall try to show that our conventional moral practices are more complex and more structured than he takes them to be, and that he consequently misunderstands what it means to say that the criminal law should be drawn from public morality. This is a popular and appealing thesis, and it lies near the core not only of Lord Devlin's, but of many other, theories about law and morals. It is crucial that its implications be understood.

THE CONCEPT OF A MORAL POSITION

We might start with the fact that terms like "moral position" and "moral conviction" function in our conventional morality as terms of justification and criticism, as well as of description. It is true that we sometimes speak of a group's "morals," or "morality," or "moral beliefs," or "moral positions," or "moral convictions," in what might be called an anthropological sense, meaning to refer to whatever attitudes the group displays about the propriety of human conduct, qualities or goals. We say, in this sense, that the morality of Nazi Germany was based on prejudice, or was irrational. But we also use some of these terms, particularly "moral position" and "moral conviction," in a discriminatory sense, to contrast the positions they describe with prejudices, rationalizations, matters of personal aversion or taste, arbitrary stands, and the like. One use—perhaps the most characteristic use—of this discriminatory sense is to offer a limited but important sort of justification for an act, when the moral issues surrounding that act are unclear or in dispute.

Suppose I tell you that I propose to vote against a man running for a public office of trust because I know him to be a homosexual and because I believe that homosexuality is profoundly immoral. If you disagree that homosexuality is immoral, you may accuse me of being about to cast my vote unfairly, acting on prejudice or out of a personal repugnance which is irrelevant to the moral issue. I might then try to convert you to my position on homosexuality, but if I fail in this I shall still want to convince you of what you and I will both take to be a separate point—that my vote was based upon a moral position, in the discriminatory sense, even though one which differs from yours. I shall want to persuade you of this, because if I do I am entitled to expect that you will alter your opinion of me and of what I am about to do. Your judgment of my character will be different—you might still think me eccentric (or puritanical or unsophisticated) but these are types of character and not faults of character. Your judgment of my act will also be different, in this respect. You will admit that so long as I hold my moral position, I have a moral right to vote against the homosexual, because I have a right (indeed a duty) to vote my own convictions. You would not admit such a right (or duty) if you were still persuaded that I was acting out of a prejudice or a personal taste.

It is this feature of conventional morality that animates Lord Devlin's argument that society has the right to follow its own lights. We must therefore examine that discriminatory concept of a moral position more closely, and we can do so by pursuing our imaginary conversation. What must I do to convince you that my position is a moral position?

(a) I must produce some reasons for it. This is not to say that I have to articulate a moral principle I am following or a general moral theory to which I subscribe. Very few people can do either, and the ability to hold a moral position is not limited to those who can. My reason need not be a principle or theory at all. It must only point out some aspect or feature of homosexuality which moves me to regard it as immoral: the fact that the Bible forbids it, for example, or that one who practices homosexuality becomes unfit for marriage and parenthood. Of course, any such reason would presuppose my acceptance of some general principle or theory, but I need not be able to state what it is, or realize that I am relying upon it.

Not every reason I might give will do, however. Some will be excluded by general criteria stipulating sorts of reasons which do not count. We might take note of four of the most important such criteria:

(i) If I tell you that homosexuals are morally inferior because they do not have heterosexual desires, and so are not "real men," you would reject that reason as showing one type of prejudice. Prejudices, in general, are postures of judgment that take into account considerations our conventions exclude. . . . Thus a man whose moral judgments about Jews, or Negroes, or Southerners, or women, or effeminate men are based on his belief that any member of these classes automatically deserves less respect, without regard to anything he himself has done, is said to be prejudiced against that group.

(ii) If I base my view about homosexuals on a personal emotional reaction ("they make me sick") you would reject that reason as well. We distinguish moral positions from emotional reactions, not because moral positions are supposed to be unemotional or dispassionate—quite the reverse is true—but because the moral position is supposed to justify the emotional reaction, and not vice versa. . . .

(iii) If I base my position on a proposition of fact ("homosexual acts are physically debilitating") which is not only false, but is so implausible that it challenges the minimal standards of evidence and argument I generally accept and impose upon others, then you would regard my belief, even though sincere, as a form of rationalization, and disqualify my reason on that ground. (Rationalization is a complex concept, and also includes, as we shall see, the production of reasons which suggest general theories I do not accept.)

(iv) If I can argue for my own position only by citing the beliefs of others ("everyone knows homosexuality is a sin") you will conclude that I am parroting and not relying on a moral conviction of my own. With the possible (though complex) exception of a deity, there is no moral authority to which I can appeal and so automatically make my position a moral one. I must have my own reasons, though of course I may have been taught these reasons by others.

No doubt many readers will disagree with these thumbnail sketches of prejudice, mere emotional reaction, rationalization and parroting. Some may have their own theories of what these are. I want to emphasize now only that these are distinct concepts, whatever the details of the differences might be, and that they have a role in deciding whether to treat another's position as a moral conviction. They are not merely epithets to be pasted on positions we strongly dislike.

(b) Suppose I do produce a reason which is not disqualified on one of these (or on similar) grounds. That reason will presuppose some general moral principle or theory, even though I may not be able to state that principle or theory, and do not have it in mind when I speak. If I offer, as my reason, the fact that the Bible forbids homosexual acts, or that homosexual acts make it less likely that the actor will marry and raise children, I suggest that I accept the theory my reason presupposes, and you will not be satisfied that my position is a moral one if you believe that I do not. It may be a question of my sincerity—do I in fact believe that the injunctions of the Bible are morally binding as such, or that all men have a duty to procreate? Sincerity is not, however, the only issue, for consistency is also in point. I may believe that I accept one of these general positions, and be wrong, because my other beliefs, and my own conduct on other occasions, may be inconsistent with it. I may reject certain Biblical injunctions, or I may hold that men have a right to remain bachelors if they please or use contraceptives all their lives.

. . .

(c) But do I really have to have a reason to make my position a matter of moral conviction? Most men think that acts which cause unnecessary suffering, or break a serious promise with no excuse, are immoral, and yet they could give no reason for these beliefs. They feel that no reason is necessary, because they take it as axiomatic or self-evident that these are immoral acts. It seems contrary to common sense to deny that a position held in this way can be a moral position.

Yet there is an important difference between believing that one's position is self-evident and just not having a reason for one's position. The former presupposes a positive belief that no further reason is necessary, that the immorality of the act in question does not depend upon its social effects, or its effects on the character of the actor, or its proscription by a deity, or anything else, but follows from the nature of the act itself. The claim that a particular position is axiomatic, in other words, does supply a reason of a special sort, namely that the act is immoral in and of itself, and this special reason, like the others we considered, may be inconsistent with more general theories I hold.

. . .

(d) This anatomy of our argument could be continued, but it is already long enough to justify some conclusions. If the issue between us is whether my views on homosexuality amount to a moral position, and hence whether I am entitled to vote against a homosexual on that ground, I cannot settle the issue simply by reporting my feelings. You will want to consider the reasons I can produce to support my belief, and whether my other views and behavior are consistent with the theories these reasons presuppose. You will have, of course, to apply your own understanding, which may differ in detail from mine, of what a prejudice or a rationalization is, for example, and of when one view is inconsistent with another. You and I may end in disagreement over whether my position is a moral one, partly because one is less likely to recognize these illegitimate grounds in himself than in others.

We must avoid the sceptical fallacy of passing from these facts to the conclusion that there is no such thing as a prejudice or a rationalization or an inconsistency, or that these terms mean merely that the one who uses them strongly dislikes the positions he describes this way. That would be like arguing that because different people have different understandings of what jealousy is, and can in good faith disagree about whether one of them is jealous, there is no such thing as jealousy, and one who says another is jealous merely means he dislikes him very much.

LORD DEVLIN'S MORALITY

We may now return to Lord Devlin's second argument. He argues that when legislators must decide a moral issue (as by his hypothesis they must when a practice threatens a valued social arrangement), they must follow any consensus of moral position which the community at large has reached, because this is required by the democratic principle, and because a community is entitled to follow its own lights. The argument would have some plausibility if Lord Devlin meant, in speaking of the moral consensus of the community, those positions which are moral positions in the discriminatory sense we have been exploring.

But he means nothing of the sort. His definition of a moral position shows he is using it in what I called the anthropological sense. The ordinary man whose opinions we must enforce, he says, ". . . is not expected to reason about anything and his judgment may be largely a matter of feeling."[9] "If the reasonable man believes," he adds, "that a practice is immoral and believes also—no matter whether the belief is right or wrong, so be it that it is honest and dispassionate—that no right-minded member of his society could think otherwise, then for the purpose of the law it is immoral."[10] Elsewhere he quotes with approval Dean Rostow's attribution to him of the view that "the common morality of a society at any time is a blend of custom and conviction, of reason and feeling, of experience and prejudice."[11] His sense of what a moral conviction is emerges most clearly of all from the famous remark about homosexuals. If the ordinary man regards homosexuality "as a vice so abominable that its mere presence is an offence,"[12] this demonstrates for him that the ordinary man's feelings about homosexuals are a matter of moral conviction.[13]

His conclusions fail because they depend upon using "moral position" in this anthropological sense. Even if it is true that most men think homosexuality an abominable vice and cannot tolerate its presence, it remains possible that this common opinion is a compound of prejudice (resting on the assumption that homosexuals are morally inferior creatures because they are effeminate), rationalization (based on assumptions of fact so unsupported that they challenge the community's own standards of rationality), and personal aversion (representing no conviction but merely blind hate rising from unacknowledged self-suspicion). It remains possible that the ordinary man could produce no reason for his view, but would simply parrot his neighbor who in turn parrots him, or that he would produce a reason which presupposes a general moral position he could not sincerely

9 Devlin, 15.
10 Ibid., pp. 22-23.
11 Rostow, The Enforcement of Morals, 1960 Camb. L.J. 174, 197; reprinted in E. V. Rostow, The Sovereign Prerogative 45, 78 (1962). Quoted in Devlin 95.
12 Ibid., p. 17.
13 In the preface (Ibid., p. viii) Lord Devlin acknowledges that the language of the original lecture might have placed "too much emphasis on feeling and too little on reason," and he states that the legislator is entitled to disregard "irrational" beliefs. He gives as an example of the latter the belief that homosexuality causes earthquakes, and asserts that the exclusion of irrationality "is usually an easy and comparatively unimportant process." I think it fair to conclude that this is all Lord Devlin would allow him to exclude. If I am wrong, and Lord Devlin would ask him to exclude prejudices, personal aversions, arbitrary stands and the rest as well, he should have said so, and attempted to work some of these distinctions out. If he had, his conclusions would have been different and would no doubt have met with a different reaction.

or consistently claim to hold. If so, the principles of democracy we follow do not call for the enforcement of the consensus, for the belief that prejudices, personal aversions and rationalizations do not justify restricting another's freedom itself occupies a critical and fundamental position in our popular morality. Nor would the bulk of the community then be entitled to follow its own lights, for the community does not extend that privilege to one who acts on the basis of prejudice, rationalization, or personal aversion. Indeed, the distinction between these and moral convictions, in the discriminatory sense, exists largely to mark off the former as the sort of positions one is not entitled to pursue.

A conscientious legislator who is told a moral consensus exists must test the credentials of that consensus. He cannot, of course, examine the beliefs or behavior of individual citizens; he cannot hold hearings on the Clapham omnibus. That is not the point.

POSTSCRIPT ON PORNOGRAPHY

I have been discussing homosexuality because that is Lord Devlin's example. I should like to say a word about pornography, if only because it is, for the time being, more in the American legal headlines than homosexuality. This current attention is due to the Supreme Court's decision and opinions in three recent cases: *Ginzburg, Mishkin* and *Fanny Hill.*[14] In two of these, convictions (and jail sentences) for the distribution of pornography were upheld, and in the third, while the Court reversed a state ban on an allegedly obscene novel, three justices dissented.

Two of the cases involved review of state procedures for constitutionality, and the third the interpretation and application of a federal statute. The Court therefore had to pass on the constitutional question of how far a state or the nation may legally restrict the publication of erotic literature, and on questions of statutory construction. But each decision nevertheless raises issues of political principle of the sort we have been considering.

A majority of the Court adheres to the constitutional test laid down some years ago in *Roth.*[15] As that test now stands, a book is obscene, and as such not protected by the first amendment, if: "(a) the dominant theme of the material taken as a whole appeals to a prurient interest in sex; (b) the material is patently offensive because it affronts contemporary community standards relating to the description or representation of sexual matters; and (c) the material is utterly without redeeming social value."[16] We might put the question of political principle this way: What gives the federal government, or any state, the moral right to prohibit the publication of books which are obscene under the *Roth* test?

Justice Brennan's opinion in *Mishkin* floated one answer: erotic literature, he said, incites some readers to crime. If this is true, if in a significant number of such cases the same readers would not have been incited to the same crime by other stimuli, and if the problem cannot effectively be handled in other ways, this might give society a warrant to ban these books. But these are at least speculative

---

[14] Ginzburg v. United States, 383 U.S. 463 (1966); Mishkin v. New York, 383 U.S. 502 (1966); Memoirs v. Massachusetts (Fanny Hill), 383 U.S. 413 (1966).

[15] Roth v. United States, 354 U.S. 476 (1957).

[16] Memoirs v. Massachusetts (Fanny Hill), 383 U.S. 413, 418 (1966).

hypotheses, and in any event they are not pertinent to a case like *Ginzburg*, in which the Court based its decision not on the obscene character of the publications themselves, but on the fact that they were presented to the public as salacious rather than enlightening. Can any other justification be given for the prohibition of obscene books?

An argument like Lord Devlin's second argument can be constructed, and many of those who feel society is entitled to ban pornography are in fact moved by some such argument. It might take this form:

(1) If we permit obscene books freely to be sold, to be delivered as it were with the morning milk, the whole tone of the community will eventually change. That which is now thought filthy and vulgar in speech and dress, and in public behavior, will become acceptable. A public which could enjoy pornography legally would soon settle for nothing very much tamer, and all forms of popular culture would inevitably move closer to the salacious. We have seen these forces at work already—the same relaxations in our legal attitudes which enabled books like *Tropic of Cancer* to be published have already had an effect on what we find in movies and magazines, on beaches and on the city streets. Perhaps we must pay that price for what many critics plausibly consider works of art, but we need not pay what would be a far greater price for trash—mass-manufactured for profit only.

(2) It is not a sufficient answer to say that social practices will not change unless the majority willingly participates in the change. Social corruption works through media and forces quite beyond the control of the mass of the people, indeed quite beyond the control of any conscious design at all. Of course, pornography attracts while it repels, and at some point in the deterioration of community standards the majority will not object to further deterioration, but that is a mark of the corruption's success, not proof that there has been no corruption. It is precisely that possibility which makes it imperative that we enforce our standards while we still have them. This is an example—it is not the only one of our wishing the law to protect us from ourselves.

(3) Banning pornography abridges the freedom of authors, publishers, and would-be readers. But if what they want to do is immoral, we are entitled to protect ourselves at that cost. Thus we are presented with a moral issue: does one have a moral right to publish or to read "hard-core" pornography which can claim no value or virtue beyond its erotic effect? This moral issue should not be solved by fiat, nor by self-appointed ethical tutors, but by submission to the public. The public at present believes that hard-core pornography is immoral, that those who produce it are panderers, and that the protection of the community's sexual and related mores is sufficiently important to justify restricting their freedom.

But surely it is crucial to this argument, whatever else one might think of it, that the consensus described in the last sentence be a consensus of moral conviction. If it should turn out that the ordinary man's dislike of pornographers is a matter of taste, or an arbitrary stand, the argument would fail because these are not satisfactory reasons for abridging freedom.

It will strike many readers as paradoxical even to raise the question whether the average man's views on pornography are moral convictions. For most people the heart of morality is a sexual code, and if the ordinary man's views on fornication, adultery, sadism, exhibitionism and the other staples of pornography are not moral positions, it is hard to imagine any beliefs he is likely to have that are. But writing and reading about these adventures is not the same as performing in them, and one may be able to give reasons for condemning the practices (that they cause pain, or are sacrilegious, or insulting, or cause public annoyance) which do not extend to producing or savoring fantasies about them.

Those who claim a consensus of moral conviction on pornography must provide evidence that this exists. They must provide moral reasons or arguments which the average member of society might sincerely and consistently advance in the manner we have been describing. Perhaps this can be done, but it is no substitute simply to report that the ordinary man—within or without the jury box—turns his thumb down on the whole business.

Suggested Readings

1. de Beauvoir, Simone, *The Second Sex* (New York: Knopf, 1953).
2. Fromm, Eric, *The Art of Loving* (New York: Harper, 1956).
3. Morgan, Douglas, *Love: Plato, the Bible, and Freud* (Englewood Cliffs, N.J.: Prentice-Hall, 1964).
4. Russell, Bertrand, *Marriage and Morals* (New York: Liveright, 1957).
5. Schneider, Isidor (ed.), *The World of Love*, 2 vols. (New York: George Braziller, 1964).

Political Flux:
Freedom, Violence,
and Revolution

Historically the best way of regarding the substance of liberty in the modern period as well as in the mediaeval is to realize that the new elements which enter into its composition at any given time have almost invariably been rationalizations of particular demands from some class or race or creed which have sought a place in the sun denied to them.

—Harold J. Laski

INTRODUCTION

No adult alive today with even cursory knowledge of current events, at home or abroad, can have failed to note the recurring co-occurrence of the three concepts freedom (or liberty), violence, and revolution. It is no accident that they co-occur. They are intimately related.

Revolution, whatever else it may mean, is an event that shifts the power relations in some social unit. A different group of people either have or share the power after the revolution than had or shared it before the revolution. The new power group is the revolutionaries; they seized power because prior to the revolution those who were in power exercised it in such a way that the revolutionaries were denied the liberty to do something, such as vote, own property, or run their own government. Revolution by its very nature is an attempt to acquire the power that will give men the liberty to do something hitherto effectively denied them. That is why the demand for freedom or liberty occurs with revolution.

As John Locke pointed out, "Great mistakes in the ruling part, many wrong and inconvenient laws, and all the slips of human frailty will be borne by the people without mutiny or murmur." The people are not prone to change their lot by revolution; they adapt to circumstances even if harsh and inequitable, preferring to make do with what they have rather than risk the loss of even that as defeated revolutionaries. Revolutions occur only when some part of the people are aggravated to desperation. Those in power may recognize this desperation, but because their lot will be so radically changed by revolution, they are reluctant to give up the power they hold. Further, if those in power have consented to or designed the conditions that led to desperation, their judgment is so faulty that they are incapable of voluntarily sharing their power in order to preclude a revolution. Consequently, those who seek liberty through acquiring power are left with no choice but to acquire that power forcibly.

One man's force is another's violence. The forcible acquisition of power entails breaking laws and defying authority. Those in power who use the laws to suppress the revolutionaries define revolutionary forces as violence because it is outside their laws. The revolutionaries, on the other hand, no longer recognize the laws as valid and, appealing to moral rights, justify their actions as legitimate force used in pursuit of freedom and deny the appellation of violence.

The empirical fact that men are reluctant to give up or share their power necessitates the use of force, which gets defined as violence. This is why revolution, freedom, and violence co-occur.

Thoughtful people who live in a time of political flux must address themselves to the concepts of revolution, freedom, and violence. The self that bobs aimlessly, thoughtlessly, without intellectual direction on the sea of political flux will be blown randomly by whatever wind prevails at the moment.

FREEDOM

The object of this Essay ["On Liberty"] is to assert one very simple principle . . . that the sole end for which mankind are warranted, individually or collectively, in interfering with the liberty of action of any of their number, is self-protection.
—John Stuart Mill

The essays in this section are concerned with moral and political freedom; those in the second section of Chapter Eight are concerned with metaphysical freedom, freedom of the will.

To be morally or politically free is to be able to do something without having to defy or resist constraints imposed by legally constituted authorities or social customs. There does not seem to be much disagreement about political and moral freedom being good; however, there is disagreement about which specific freedoms are good. Many United States citizens believe that countries not providing for a two-party political system are not free, whereas people in socialist countries believe that those who live in capitalist economies are enslaved. There is also disagreement about who should have what freedoms.

Is freedom good as a means, as an end, or as both? Nothing is good as only an end except some final or ultimate end. Because men often wish to be free in order to be happy and do not wish to be happy in order to be free, it appears that freedom is not good solely as an end. But happiness is not the only ultimate end that men have proposed. They have also proposed that full development of our potentialities is man's ultimate end. Once again, since men believe they require freedom as a means to develop their potentialities, it appears that freedom is not an ultimate end. Still, there is a sense in which men wish to attain humanhood: they wish to become responsible moral and political agents; they do not want to be slaves or political children. Insofar as attaining full humanhood is an end, freedom or self-determination being a constituent of such humanhood, freedom, too, is an end. Depending on the circumstances of one's life, being a free, moral agent may be the ultimate end that men desire, even knowing full well that unhappiness may result from this status. Indeed, Adam and Eve, on one interpretation of the Fall, preferred exercising freedom to retaining the bliss of Eden. John Stuart Mill posed the alternative rather colorfully, asking if you would rather be Socrates dissatisfied or a pig satisfied. Many would choose to be Socrates; this involves the freedom to determine the course of one's own life and is part of the magic of being Socrates, even dissatisfied.

The question about freedom being good solely as an end appears to be answerable only in relation to a kind of life with its values organized around some ultimate end.

Generally, people think of freedom as valuable both as an end and as a means. It is possible to think of something as both because below an ultimate end are subsidiary ends that may also be means: a person may strive for money as a means of getting an education; education is his end and that education may also be considered a means to attaining the end of developing his potentials. Freedom in the abstract does not lend itself to being considered both a means and an end as easily as it does to being considered only an end. For the dual role, it is more suitable to consider the substance of freedom, to consider specific freedoms. Thus, men may revolt in order to gain the end of freedom of speech; freedom of speech can be considered also a means of determining the wisest political course, which, in turn, is a means to a better social life, and so on. Once we consider freedom in terms of specific freedoms and consider those freedoms as means, then, since something that is an effective means in one situation may not be an effective means in another situation, some specific freedom may not always be valuable as a means.

It is easy to show that less specifically formulated freedom is disvaluable. "Doing your own thing" is subject to restrictions. There is a juvenile appeal to the phrase, but reading the first essay in this section, by **Garrett Hardin**, should dispel any hasty conclusion that the phrase says either the first or last thing about freedom. Hardin seeks to show that "doing your own thing" by adding one more cow to the herd eating the grass on the town commons is inconsistent with maintaining the land as a sufficient provider and leads to tragedy; he also seeks to show that "doing your own thing" by polluting at will was once a tolerable freedom but is so no longer; and he also proposes that there may be a time when we will have to curtail the freedom to reproduce. Spaceship earth, if it is to be maintained as a life source, will not be a theater for survival unless we remove some freedoms. Some freedoms have now become disvaluable.

Suppose Hardin's thesis is correct. Suppose that we are willing to concede that there is a distinction to be made between freedom and license. Immediately, another interesting question arises: Is there a way of deciding which liberties are to be allowed and which are to be denied? This is the question to which **John Stuart Mill** addresses himself in the second essay in this section.

Mill was an eloquent defender of nineteenth-century liberal individualism. To him the political state is an unwanted albatross to be miniaturized to the maximum extent; essentially, the state is seen by Mill as a referee; the state has little positive that it can contribute beyond insuring that each individual in the pursuit of his good does not harm others. Says Mill, "The only freedom which deserves the name, is that of pursuing our own good in our own way, so long as we do not attempt to deprive others of theirs, or impede their efforts to obtain it." Mill cannot abide any further regulation of the individual by society because it tends "to compel people to conform to its notions of personal as of social excellence." Underlying Mill's position is a very high regard for being unique in as many respects as possible.

One challenge to Mill's criterion for determining the extent of regulation by the authorities could come from the proponents of other valuable subsidiary ends. Equality and justice, too, are subsidiary end values. Suppose someone were to argue that Mill's criterion leads to great inequality; after all, men are not of equal capabilities in earning a living. Is a person of great capability to be allowed the freedom of exercising his capabilities without restraint? In competing with the person of lesser capability, the man of great capability will, all other things being equal, acquire a greater share of the world's limited goods and, so, deprive and perhaps even starve the latter. Supposing that a person believes in equal sharing of the world's goods or at least believes that justice requires giving a decent portion to every person and suppose that equality and justice are more valuable subsidiary ends than freedom, then he would have to conclude that Mill's limit criterion is too loose.

This argument can be put in a more contemporary vein. Many have-nots, in agreement with the United Nations' statement of human rights, think that liberalism's traditional political rights are only a partial list of rights; they believe that people also have rights to such things as food, shelter, education, and occupation. The have-nots are pressing for new human rights to be added to those that Anglo-American liberalism has advocated. In their view, a society that is satisfied with maintaining the rights to free speech, assembly, and due process to the neglect of maintaining the rights to food and shelter is in need of reform or revolution.

This argument sometimes distinguishes between negative and positive freedom, liberalism's goals being considered negative and the UN's being considered positive. **Isaiah Berlin**, in this section's third essay, distinguishes between these two kinds of liberty. Berlin's method of distinguishing them does not seem satisfactory. For him the positive conception of liberty is "freedom to" (freedom to lead some prescribed form of life), whereas the negative conception of liberty is "freedom from." But, "freedom from" and "freedom to" can be used as alternative ways of saying the same thing. For example, "freedom to speak" can also be stated as "freedom from censorship." To make the distinction more satisfactorily requires using the three interlinked concepts of liberty, rights, and obligation. Once we have done that, we can see more clearly the difference between "liberal rights and freedom" and "UN rights and freedom."

Negative Freedom. If some person, Black, has negative freedom, then Black has a negative right. There are no moral or legal restrictions on Black's acting in some specified way. He has, for instance, a legal right to free speech.

If Black has a right, it is a right against some other person, White, and White has a negative obligation to Black.

Suppose Black's right is free speech, then White has an obligation *not* to interfere with Black's act of speaking.

Positive Freedom. If Black has positive freedom, then he has some socially approved need, goal, or ideal.

If Black has such a goal, then he has a positive right to demand White's cooperation. That is, White has a positive obligation to Black.

Suppose Black's goal is equal education. Then White has an obligation to act in cooperation with Black.

In more schematic form:

Black's negative freedom leads to Black's right leads to White's obligation not to act.

Black's positive freedom leads to Black's right leads to White's obligation to act cooperatively.

Negative freedom obliges the other person's not acting and positive freedom obliges the other person's acting.

Liberal freedoms, such as the freedom of speech, assembly, and the vote, are negative freedoms; they imply rights that prohibit acts of interference. UN freedoms, such as freedom from starvation or freedom to obtain a fair portion of the world's food, freedom from exposure or freedom to take possession of shelter, and freedom from ignorance or freedom to participate in educational activities, are positive freedoms; they imply rights that place an obligation to cooperate in obtaining, taking, and participating.

Berlin warns against the direction in which positive freedom has been steered by Platonic and Hegelian thinkers. Positive freedom, he warns, often turns into disguised coercion. We suggest that you read the essays by Ernesto Che Guevara and Wang Tao-ming in Chapter Six; they address themselves directly to this issue. Guevara is aware that "capitalist spokesmen" believe that the "period of building socialism upon which we have embarked is characterized by the extinction of the individual for the state." Guevara tries to answer the liberal criticism and tries to outline a new relation between the individual and his freedoms and the state.

In this section's last essay, **Kate Millet** shows how complicated social conditions can obscure the myriad means that men have to keep women in a subordinate position. She shows how sexual politics define a status, role, and temperament for women to such an extent that many women do not even realize that they need liberation. For an acid criticism of people who try to compare the status of

women with the status of black people in our society, we suggest that you read
Linda La Rue's essay in Chapter Six. We also recommend as a further
development of the topic of freedom that you read Lerone Bennett's essay,
which also is in Chapter Six.

The Tragedy of the Commons and the Limits of Freedom

Garrett Hardin

Garrett Hardin (1921-   ) teaches at the University of California at Santa
Barbara, where he is professor of biology. He is the author of *Biology: Its Principles
and Implications* (1966), a collection of readings, and is editor of *Population,
Evolution, and Birth Control* (1964) and *Nature and Man's Fate* (1959).

WHAT SHALL WE MAXIMIZE?

Population, as Malthus said, naturally tends to grow "geometrically," or, as we
would now say, exponentially. In a finite world this means that the per capita share
of the world's goods must steadily decrease. Is ours a finite world?

A fair defense can be put forward for the view that the world is infinite; or that
we do not know that it is not. But, in terms of the practical problems that we must
face in the next few generations with the foreseeable technology, it is clear that we
will greatly increase human misery if we do not, during the immediate future, assume
that the world available to the terrestrial human population is finite. "Space" is no
escape.[1]

A finite world can support only a finite population; therefore, population
growth must eventually equal zero. (The case of perpetual wide fluctuations above
and below zero is a trivial variant that need not be discussed.) When this condition
is met, what will be the situation of mankind? Specifically, can Bentham's goal of
"the greatest good for the greatest number" be realized?

No—for two reasons, each sufficient by itself. The first is a theoretical one. It is
not mathematically possible to maximize for two (or more) variables at the same
time. This was clearly stated by von Neumann and Morgenstern,[2] but the principle
is implicit in the theory of partial differential equations, dating back at least to
D'Alembert (1717-1783).

Source: "The Tragedy of the Commons," *Science,* Vol. 162 (December 13, 1968), 1243-1248.
Copyright 1968 by the American Association for the Advancement of Science. Reprinted by
permission of *Science* and the author.

[1] Garrett Hardin, *Journal of Heredity,* Vol. 50 (1959), p. 68; S. von Hoerner, *Science,* Vol.
137 (1962), p. 18.

[2] J. von Neumann and O. Morgenstern, *Theory of Games and Economic Behavior*
(Princeton, N.J.: Princeton University Press, 1947), p. 11.

The second reason springs directly from biological facts. To live, any organism must have a source of energy (for example, food). This energy is utilized for two purposes: mere maintenance and work. For man, maintenance of life requires about 1600 kilo-calories a day ("maintenance calories"). Anything that he does over and above merely staying alive will be defined as work, and is supported by "work calories" which he takes in. Work calories are used not only for what we call work in common speech; they are also required for all forms of enjoyment, from swimming and automobile racing to playing music and writing poetry. If our goal is to maximize population it is obvious what we must do: We must make the work calories per person approach as close to zero as possible. No gourmet meals, no vacations, no sports, no music, no literature, no art. . . . I think that everyone will grant, without argument or proof, that maximizing population does not maximize goods. Bentham's goal is impossible.

We can make little progress in working toward optimum population size until we explicitly exorcize the spirit of Adam Smith in the field of practical demography. In economic affairs, *The Wealth of Nations* (1776) popularized the "invisible hand," the idea that an individual who "intends only his own gain," is, as it were, "led by an invisible hand to promote . . . the public interest."[3] Adam Smith did not assert that this was invariably true, and perhaps neither did any of his followers. But he contributed to a dominant tendency of thought that has ever since interfered with positive action based on rational analysis, namely, the tendency to assume that decisions reached individually will, in fact, be the best decisions for an entire society. If this assumption is correct it justifies the continuance of our present policy of laissez-faire in reproduction. If it is correct we can assume that men will control their individual fecundity so as to produce the optimum population. If the assumption is not correct, we need to reexamine our individual freedoms to see which ones are defensible.

TRAGEDY OF FREEDOM IN A COMMONS

The rebuttal to the invisible hand in population control is to be found in a scenario first sketched in a little-known pamphlet[4] in 1833 by a mathematical amateur named William Forster Lloyd (1794-1852). We may well call it "the tragedy of the commons," using the word "tragedy" as the philosopher Whitehead used it:[5] "The essence of dramatic tragedy is not unhappiness. It resides in the solemnity of the remorseless working of things." He then goes on to say, "This inevitableness of destiny can only be illustrated in terms of human life by incidents which in fact involve unhappiness. For it is only by them that the futility of escape can be made evident in the drama."

The tragedy of the commons develops in this way. Picture a pasture open to all. It is to be expected that each herdsman will try to keep as many cattle as possible

[3] Adam Smith, *The Wealth of Nations* (New York: Modern Library, 1937), p. 423.
[4] William Forster Lloyd, *Two Lectures on the Checks to Population* (Oxford: Oxford University Press, 1833), reprinted (in part) in *Population, Evolution, and Birth Control*, Garrett Hardin, ed. (San Francisco: Freeman, 1964), p. 37.
[5] Alfred North Whitehead, *Science and the Modern World* (New York: Mentor Books, 1948), p. 17.

on the commons. Such an arrangement may work reasonably satisfactorily for centuries because tribal wars, poaching, and disease keep the numbers of both man and beast well below the carrying capacity of the land. Finally, however, comes the day of reckoning, that is, the day when the long-desired goal of social stability becomes a reality. At this point, the inherent logic of the commons remorselessly generates tragedy.

As a rational being, each herdsman seeks to maximize his gain. Explicitly or implicitly, more or less consciously, he asks: "What is the utility *to me* of adding one more animal to my herd?" This utility has one negative and one positive component.

1. The positive component is a function of the increment of one animal. Since the herdsman receives all the proceeds from the sale of the additional animal, the positive utility is nearly +1.
2. The negative component is a function of the additional overgrazing created by one more animal. Since, however, the effects of overgrazing are shared by all the herdsmen, the negative utility for any particular decision-making herdsman is only a fraction of −1.

Adding together the component partial utilities, the rational herdsman concludes that the only sensible course for him to pursue is to add another animal to his herd. And another; and another. . . . But this is the conclusion reached by each and every rational herdsman sharing a commons. Therein is the tragedy. Each man is locked into a system that compels him to increase his herd without limit—in a world that is limited. Ruin is the destination toward which all men rush, each pursuing his own best interest in a society that believes in the freedom of the commons. Freedom in a commons brings ruin to all.

.   .   .

POLLUTION

In a reverse way, the tragedy of the commons reappears in problems of pollution. Here it is not a question of taking something out of the commons, but of putting something in—sewage, or chemical, radioactive, and heat wastes into water; noxious and dangerous fumes into the air; and distracting and unpleasant advertising signs into the line of sight. The calculations of utility are much the same as before. The rational man finds that his share of the cost of the wastes he discharges into the commons is less than the cost of purifying his wastes before releasing them. Since this is true for everyone, we are locked into a system of "fouling our own nest," so long as we behave only as independent, rational, free-enterprisers.

.   .   .

The pollution problem is a consequence of population. It did not much matter how a lonely American frontiersman disposed of his waste. "Flowing water purifies itself every 10 miles," my grandfather used to say, and the myth was near enough to the truth when he was a boy, for there were not too many people. But as population became denser, the natural chemical and biological recycling processes became overloaded, calling for a redefinition of property rights.

HOW TO LEGISLATE TEMPERANCE?

Analysis of the pollution problem as a function of population density uncovers a not generally recognized principle of morality, namely: *the morality of an act is a function of the state of the system at the time it is performed.*[6] Using the commons as a cesspool does not harm the general public under frontier conditions, because there is no public; the same behavior in a metropolis is unbearable. A hundred and fifty years ago a plainsman could kill an American bison, cut out only the tongue for his dinner, and discard the rest of the animal. He was not in any important sense being wasteful. Today, with only a few thousand bison left, we would be appalled at such behavior.

That morality is system-sensitive escaped the attention of most codifiers of ethics in the past. "Thou shalt not . . ." is the form of traditional ethical directives which make no allowance for particular circumstances. The laws of our society follow the pattern of ancient ethics, and therefore are poorly suited to governing a complex, crowded, changeable world. Our epicyclic solution is to augment statutory law with administrative law. Since it is practically impossible to spell out all the conditions under which it is safe to burn trash in the back yard or to run an automobile without smog-control, by law we delegate the details to bureaus. The result is administrative law, which is rightly feared for an ancient reason—*Quis custodiet ipsos custodes?*—"Who shall watch the watchers themselves?" John Adams said that we must have "a government of laws and not men." Bureau administrators, trying to evaluate the morality of acts in the total system, are singularly liable to corruption, producing a government by men, not laws.

FREEDOM TO BREED IS INTOLERABLE

The tragedy of the commons is involved in population problems in another way. In a world governed solely by the principle of "dog eat dog"—if indeed there ever was such a world—how many children a family had would not be a matter of public concern. Parents who bred too exuberantly would leave fewer descendants, not more, because they would be unable to care adequately for their children. David Lack and others have found that such a negative feedback demonstrably controls the fecundity of birds.[7] But men are not birds, and have not acted like them for millenniums, at least.

If each human family were dependent only on its own resources; *if* the children of improvident parents starved to death; *if*, thus, overbreeding brought its own "punishment" to the germ line—*then* there would be no public interest in controlling the breeding of families. But our society is deeply committed to the welfare state,[8] and hence is confronted with another aspect of the tragedy of the commons.

In a welfare state, how shall we deal with the family, the religion, the race, or the class (or indeed any distinguishable and cohesive group) that adopts

---

[6] J. Fletcher, *Situation Ethics* (Philadelphia: Westminster, 1966).
[7] David Lack, *The Natural Regulation of Animal Numbers* (Oxford: Clarendon Press, 1954).
[8] H. Girvetz, *From Wealth to Welfare* (Stanford, Calif.: Stanford University Press, 1950).

overbreeding as a policy to secure its own aggrandizement?[9] To couple the concept of freedom to breed with the belief that everyone born has an equal right to the commons is to lock the world into a tragic course of action.

Unfortunately this is just the course of action that is being pursued by the United Nations. In late 1967, some 30 nations agreed to the following:[10]

The Universal Declaration of Human Rights describes the family as the natural and fundamental unit of society. It follows that any choice and decision with regard to the size of the family must irrevocably rest with the family itself, and cannot be made by anyone else.

.   .   .

CONSCIENCE IS SELF-ELIMINATING

It is a mistake to think that we can control the breeding of mankind in the long run by an appeal to conscience. Charles Galton Darwin made this point when he spoke on the centennial of the publication of his grandfather's great book. The argument is straightforward and Darwinian.

People vary. Confronted with appeals to limit breeding, some people will undoubtedly respond to the plea more than others. Those who have more children will produce a larger fraction of the next generation than those with more susceptible consciences. The difference will be accentuated, generation by generation.

In C. G. Darwin's words: "It may well be that it would take hundreds of generations for the progenitive instinct to develop in this way, but if it should do so, nature would have taken her revenge, and the variety *Homo contracipiens* would become extinct and would be replaced by the variety *Homo progenitivus.*"[11]

.   .   .

PATHOGENIC EFFECTS OF CONSCIENCE

The long-term disadvantage of an appeal to conscience should be enough to condemn it; but it has serious short-term disadvantages as well. If we ask a man who is exploiting a commons to desist "in the name of conscience," what are we saying to him? What does he hear?—not only at the moment but also in the wee small hours of the night when, half asleep, he remembers not merely the words we used but also the nonverbal communication cues we gave him unawares? Sooner or later, consciously or subconsciously, he senses that he has received two communications, and that they are contradictory: (1) (intended communication) "If you don't do as we ask, we will openly condemn you for not acting like a responsible citizen"; (2) (the unintended communication) "If you *do* behave as we ask, we will secretly condemn you for a simpleton who can be shamed into standing aside while the rest of us exploit the commons."

.   .   .

[9] Garrett Hardin, *Perspectives in Biological Medicine*, Vol. 6 (1963), p. 366.

[10] U Thant, *International Planned Parenthood News*, No. 168 (Feb. 1968), p. 3.

[11] *Evolution After Darwin*, Vol. 2, S. Tax, ed. (Chicago: University of Chicago Press, 1960), p. 469.

MUTUAL COERCION MUTUALLY AGREED UPON

The social arrangements that produce responsibility are arrangements that create coercion, of some sort. Consider bank-robbing. The man who takes money from a bank acts as if the bank were a commons. How do we prevent such action? Certainly not by trying to control his behavior solely by a verbal appeal to his sense of responsibility. Rather than rely on propaganda we follow Frankel's lead and insist that a bank is not a commons; we seek the definite social arrangements that will keep it from becoming a commons. That we thereby infringe on the freedom of would-be robbers we neither deny nor regret.

The morality of bank-robbing is particularly easy to understand because we accept complete prohibition of this activity. We are willing to say "Thou shalt not rob banks," without providing for exceptions. But temperance also can be created by coercion. Taxing is a good coercive device. To keep downtown shoppers temperate in their use of parking space we introduce parking meters for short periods, and traffic fines for longer ones. We need not actually forbid a citizen to park as long as he wants to; we need merely make it increasingly expensive for him to do so. Not prohibition, but carefully biased options are what we offer him. A Madison Avenue man might call this persuasion; I prefer the greater candor of the word coercion.

Coercion is a dirty word to most liberals now, but it need not forever be so. As with the four-letter words, its dirtiness can be cleansed away by exposure to the light, by saying it over and over without apology or embarrassment. To many, the word coercion implies arbitrary decisions of distant and irresponsible bureaucrats; but this is not a necessary part of its meaning. The only kind of coercion I recommend is mutual coercion, mutually agreed upon by the majority of the people affected.

To say that we mutually agree to coercion is not to say that we are required to enjoy it, or even pretend we enjoy it. Who enjoys taxes? We all grumble about them. But we accept compulsory taxes because we recognize that voluntary taxes would favor the conscienceless. We institute and (grumblingly) support taxes and other coercive devices to escape the horror of the commons.

RECOGNITION OF NECESSITY

Perhaps the simplest summary of this analysis of man's population problems is this: the commons, if justifiable at all, is justifiable only under conditions of low-population density. As the human population has increased, the commons has had to be abandoned in one aspect after another.

First we abandoned the commons in food gathering, enclosing farm land and restricting pastures and hunting and fishing areas. These restrictions are still not complete throughout the world.

Somewhat later we saw that the commons as a place for waste disposal would also have to be abandoned. Restrictions on the disposal of domestic sewage are widely accepted in the Western world; we are still struggling to close the commons to pollution by automobiles, factories, insecticide sprayers, fertilizing operations, and atomic energy installations.

In a still more embryonic state is our recognition of the evils of the commons in matters of pleasure. There is almost no restriction on the propagation of sound waves in the public medium. The shopping public is assaulted with mindless music, without its consent. Our government is paying out billions of dollars to create supersonic transport which will disturb 50,000 people for every one person who is whisked from coast to coast 3 hours faster. Advertisers muddy the airwaves of radio and television and pollute the view of travelers. We are a long way from outlawing the commons in matters of pleasure. Is this because our Puritan inheritance makes us view pleasure as something of a sin, and pain (that is, the pollution of advertising) as the sign of virtue?

Every new enclosure of the commons involves the infringement of somebody's personal liberty. Infringements made in the distant past are accepted because no contemporary complains of a loss. It is the newly proposed infringements that we vigorously oppose; cries of "rights" and "freedom" fill the air. But what does "freedom" mean? When men mutually agreed to pass laws against robbing, mankind became more free, not less so. Individuals locked into the logic of the commons are free only to bring on universal ruin; once they see the necessity of mutual coercion, they become free to pursue other goals. I believe it was Hegel who said, "Freedom is the recognition of necessity."

The most important aspect of necessity that we must now recognize, is the necessity of abandoning the commons in breeding. No technical solution can rescue us from the misery of overpopulation. Freedom to breed will bring ruin to all. At the moment, to avoid hard decisions many of us are tempted to propagandize for conscience and responsible parenthood. The temptation must be resisted, because an appeal to independently acting consciences selects for the disappearance of all conscience in the long run, and an increase in anxiety in the short.

The only way we can preserve and nurture other and more precious freedoms is by relinquishing the freedom to breed, and that very soon. "Freedom is the recognition of necessity"—and it is the role of education to reveal to all the necessity of abandoning the freedom to breed. Only so, can we put an end to this aspect of the tragedy of the commons.

The Tyranny of the Majority
John Stuart Mill

John Stuart Mill (1806-1873) was a very influential British philosopher in the nineteenth century. His major works include *On Liberty* (1859), *Considerations on Representative Government* (1861), *Utilitarianism* (1863), and *The Subjection of Women* (1869).

The subject of this essay is not the so-called liberty of the will, so unfortunately opposed to the misnamed doctrine of philosophical necessity; but civil, or social liberty: the nature and limits of the power which can be legitimately exercised by society over the individual. A question seldom stated and hardly ever discussed in general terms, but which profoundly influences the practical controversies of the age by its latent presence, and is likely soon to make itself recognized as the vital question of the future. It is so far from being new, that, in a certain sense, it has divided mankind almost from the remotest ages; but in the stage of progress into which the more civilized portions of the species have now entered, it presents itself under new conditions, and requires a different and more fundamental treatment.

The struggle between liberty and authority is the most conspicuous feature in the portions of history with which we are earliest familiar, particularly in that of Greece, Rome, and England. But in old times this contest was between subjects, or some classes of subjects, and the government. By liberty, was meant protection against the tyranny of the political rulers. The rulers were conceived (except in some of the popular governments of Greece) as in a necessarily antagonistic position to the people whom they ruled. They consisted of a governing One, or a governing tribe or caste, who derived their authority from inheritance or conquest, who, at all events, did not hold it at the pleasure of the governed, and whose supremacy men did not venture, perhaps did not desire, to contest, whatever precautions might be taken against its oppressive exercise. Their power was regarded as necessary, but also as highly dangerous; as a weapon which they would attempt to use against their subjects, no less than against external enemies. To prevent the weaker members of the community from being preyed upon by innumerable vultures, it was needful that there should be an animal of prey stronger than the rest, commissioned to keep them down. But as the king of the vultures would be no less bent upon preying on the flock than any of the minor harpies, it was indispensable to be in a perpetual attitude of defense against his beak and claws. The aim, therefore, of patriots was to set limits to the power which the ruler should be suffered to exercise over the community; and this limitation was what they meant by liberty. It was attempted in two ways. First, by obtaining a recognition of certain immunities, called political liberties or rights, which it was to be regarded as a breach of duty in the ruler to infringe, and which if he did infringe, specific resistance, or general rebellion, was held to be justifiable. A second, and generally a later expedient, was the establishment of constitutional checks, by

Source: On Liberty (1859).

which the consent of the community, or of a body of some sort, supposed to represent its interests, was made a necessary condition to some of the more important acts of the governing power. To the first of these modes of limitation, the ruling power, in most European countries, was compelled, more or less, to submit. It was not so with the second; and, to attain this, or when already in some degree possessed, to attain it more completely, became everywhere the principal object of the lovers of liberty. And so long as mankind were content to combat one enemy by another, and to be ruled by a master, on condition of being guaranteed more or less efficaciously against his tyranny, they did not carry their aspirations beyond this point.

A time, however, came, in the progress of human affairs, when men ceased to think it a necessity of nature that their governors should be an independent power, opposed in interest to themselves. It appeared to them much better that the various magistrates of the State should be their tenants or delegates, revocable at their pleasure. In that way alone, it seemed, could they have complete security that the powers of government would never be abused to their disadvantage. By degrees this new demand for elective and temporary rulers became the prominent object of the exertions of the popular party, wherever any such party existed; and superseded, to a considerable extent, the previous efforts to limit the power of rulers. As the struggle proceeded for making the ruling power emanate from the periodical choice of the ruled, some persons began to think that too much importance had been attached to the limitation of the power itself. *That* (it might seem) was a resource against rulers whose interests were habitually opposed to those of the people. What was now wanted was, that the rulers should be identified with the people; that their interest and will should be the interest and will of the nation. The nation did not need to be protected against its own will. There was no fear of its tyrannizing over itself. Let the rulers be effectually responsible to it, promptly removable by it, and it could afford to trust them with power of which it could itself dictate the use to be made. Their power was but the nation's own power, concentrated, and in a form convenient for exercise. This mode of thought, or rather perhaps of feeling, was common among the last generation of European liberalism, in the Continental section of which it still apparently predominates. Those who admit any limit to what a government may do, except in the case of such governments as they think ought not to exist, stand out as brilliant exceptions among the political thinkers of the Continent. A similar tone of sentiment might by this time have been prevalent in our own country, if the circumstances which for a time encouraged it had continued unaltered.

But in political and philosophical theories, as well as in persons, success discloses faults and infirmities which failure might have concealed from observation. The notion that the people have no need to limit their power over themselves, might seem axiomatic when popular government was a thing only dreamed about, or read of as having existed at some distant period of the past. Neither was that notion necessarily disturbed by such temporary aberrations as those of the French Revolution, the worst of which were the work of a usurping few, and which, in any case, belonged not to the permanent working of popular institutions, but to a sudden and convulsive outbreak against monarchical and aristocratic despotism. In time, however, a democratic republic came to occupy a large portion of the earth's surface, and made itself felt as one of the most powerful members of the community of nations; and elective and responsible government became subject to the observations and criticisms which wait upon a great existing fact. It was now perceived that such phrases as "self-government," and the "power of the people over themselves," do not express the true state of the case. The "people" who exercise the power are not always the same people with those over whom it is exercised; and the "self-government" spoken of is not the government of each by himself, but of each by all the rest. The will of the people, moreover, practically means the will of the most numerous or the most active *part* of the people; the majority, or those who succeed in making themselves accepted as the majority: the people, consequently *may* desire to oppress a part of their number, and precautions are as much needed against this as against any other abuse of power. The limitation, therefore, of the power of government over individuals loses none of its importance when the holders of power are regularly accountable to the community, that is, to the strongest party therein. This view of things, recommending itself equally to the intelligence of thinkers and to the inclination of those important classes in European society to whose real or supposed interests democracy is adverse, has had no difficulty in establishing itself; and in political speculations "the tyranny of the majority" is now generally included among the evils against which society requires to be on its guard.

Like other tyrannies, the tyranny of the majority was at first, and is still vulgarly, held in dread chiefly as operating through the acts of the public authorities. But reflecting persons perceived that when society is itself the tyrant—society collectively over the separate individuals who compose it—its means of tyrannizing are not restricted to the acts which it may do by the hands of its political functionaries. Society can and does execute its own mandates; and if it issues wrong mandates instead of right, or any mandates at all in things with which it ought not to meddle, it practices a social tyranny more formidable than many kinds of political oppression, since, though not usually upheld by such extreme penalties, it leaves fewer means of escape, penetrating much more deeply into the details of life, and enslaving the soul itself. Protection, therefore, against the tyranny of the magistrate is not enough: there needs protection also against the tyranny of the prevailing opinion and feeling; against the tendency of society to impose, by other means than civil penalties, its own ideas and practices as rules of conduct on those who dissent from them; to fetter the development, and if possible, prevent the formation, of any individuality not in harmony with its ways, and compels all characters to fashion themselves upon the model of its own. There is a limit to the legitimate interference of collective opinion with individual independence; and to find that limit, and maintain it against encroachment, is as indispensable to a good condition of human affairs, as protection against political despotism.

But though this proposition is not likely to be contested in general terms, the practical question, where to place the limit—how to make the fitting adjustment between individual independence and social control—is a subject on which nearly everything remains to be done. All that makes existence valuable to anyone, depends on the enforcement of restraints upon the actions of other people. Some rules of conduct, therefore, must be imposed, by law in the first place, and by opinion on many things which are not fit subjects for the operation of law. What these rules should be is the principal question in human affairs; but if we except a few of the most obvious cases, it is one of those which least progress has been made in resolving. No two ages, and scarcely any two countries, have decided it alike; and the decision of one age or country is a wonder to another. Yet the people of any given age and country no more suspect any difficulty in it, than if it were a subject on which mankind had always been agreed. The rules which obtain among themselves appear to them self-evident and self-justifying. This all but universal illusion is one of the examples of the magical influence of custom, which is not only, as the proverb says, a second nature, but is continually mistaken for the first. The effect of custom, in preventing any misgiving respecting the rules of conduct which mankind impose on one another, is all the more complete because the subject is one on which it is not generally considered necessary that reasons should be given, either by one person to others or by each to himself. People are accustomed to believe, and have been encouraged in the belief by some who aspire to the character of philosophers, that their feelings, on subjects of this nature, are better than reasons, and render reasons unnecessary. The practical principle which guides them to their opinions on the regulation of human conduct, is the feeling in each person's mind that everybody should be required to act as he, and those with whom he sympathizes, would like them to act. No one, indeed, acknowledges to himself that his standard of judgment is his own liking; but an opinion on a point of conduct, not supported by reasons, can only count as one person's preference; and if the reasons, when given, are a mere appeal to a similar preference felt by other people, it is still only many people's liking instead of one. To an ordinary man, however, his own preference, thus supported, is not only a prefectly satisfactory reason, but the only one he generally has for any of his notions of morality, taste, or propriety, which are not expressly written in his religious creed; and his chief guide in the interpretation even of that. Men's opinions, accordingly, on what is laudable or blamable, are affected by all the multifarious causes which influence their wishes in regard to the conduct of others, and which are as numerous as those which determine their wishes on any other subject. Sometimes their reason, at other times their prejudices or superstitions; often their social affections, not seldom their antisocial ones, their envy or jealousy, their arrogance or contemptuousness: but most commonly their desires or fears for themselves—their legitimate or illegitimate self-interest. Wherever there is an ascendant class, a large portion of the morality of the country emanates from its class interests, and its feelings of class superiority. The morality between Spartans and Helots, between planters and Negroes, between princes and subjects, between nobles and roturiers, between men and women, has been for the most part the creation of these class interests and feelings; and the sentiments thus generated react in turn upon the moral feelings of the members of the ascendant class, in their relations among themselves. Where, on the other hand, a class, formerly ascendant, has lost its ascendancy, or where its ascendancy is unpopular, the prevailing moral sentiments frequently bear the impress of an impatient dislike of superiority. Another grand determining principle of the rules of conduct, both in act and forbearance, which have been enforced by law or opinion, has been the servility of mankind towards the supposed preferences or aversions of their temporal masters or of their gods. This servility, though essentially selfish, is not hypocrisy; it gives rise to perfectly genuine sentiments of abhorrence; it made men burn magicians and heretics. Among so many baser influences, the general and obvious interests of society have of course had a share, and a large one, in the direction of the moral sentiments; less, however, as a matter of reason, and on their own account, than as a consequence of the sympathies and antipathies which grew out of them; and sympathies and antipathies which had little or nothing to do with the interests of society, have made themselves felt in the establishment of moralities with quite as great force.

The likings and dislikings of society, or of some powerful portion of it, are thus the main thing which has practically determined the rules laid down for general observance, under the penalties of law or opinion. And in general, those who have been in advance of society in thought and feeling, have left this condition of things unassailed in principle, however they may have come into conflict with it in some of its details. They have occupied themselves rather in inquiring what things society ought to like or dislike, than in questioning whether its likings or dislikings should be a law to individuals. They preferred endeavoring to alter the feelings of mankind on the particular points on which they were themselves heretical, rather than make common cause in defense of freedom, with heretics generally. . . . The great writers to whom the world owes what religious liberty it possesses, have mostly asserted freedom of conscience as an indefeasible right, and denied absolutely that a human being is accountable to others for his religious belief. Yet so natural to mankind is intolerance in whatever they really care about, that religious freedom has hardly anywhere been practically realized, except where religious indifference, which dislikes to have its peace disturbed by theological quarrels, has added its weight to the scale. In the minds of almost all religious persons, even in the most tolerant countries, the duty of toleration is admitted with tacit reserves. One person will bear with dissent in matters of church government, but not of dogma; another can tolerate everybody, short of a Papist or a Unitarian; another everyone who believes in revealed religion; a few extend their charity a little further, but stop at the belief in a God and in a future state. Wherever the sentiment of the majority is still genuine and intense, it is found to have abated little of its claim to be obeyed.

In England, from the peculiar circumstances of our political history, though the yoke of opinion is perhaps heavier, that of law is lighter, than in most other countries of Europe; and there is considerable jealousy of direct interference, by the legislative or the executive power, with private conduct; not so much from any just regard for the independence of the individual, as from the still subsisting habit of looking on the government as representing an opposite interest to the public. The majority have not yet learnt to feel the power of the government their power, or its opinions their opinions. When they do so, individual liberty will probably be as much exposed to invasion from the government, as it already is from public opinion. But, as yet, there is a considerable amount of feeling ready to be called forth against any attempt of the law to control individuals in things in which they have not hitherto been accustomed to be controlled by it; and this with very little discrimination as to whether the matter is, or is not, within the legitimate sphere of legal control; insomuch that the feeling, highly salutary on the whole, is perhaps quite as often misplaced as well grounded in the particular instances of its application. There is, in fact, no recognized principle by which the propriety or impropriety of government interference is customarily tested. People decide according to their personal preferences. Some, whenever they see any good to be done, or evil to be remedied, would willingly instigate the government to undertake the business; while others prefer to bear almost any amount of social evil, rather than add one to the departments of human interests amenable to governmental control. And men range themselves on one or the other side in any particular case, according to this general direction of their sentiments; or according to the degree of interests which they feel in the particular thing which it is proposed that the government should do, or according to the belief they entertain that the government would, or would not, do it in the manner they prefer; but very rarely on account of any opinion to which they consistently adhere, as to what things are fit to be done by a government. . . .

The object of this essay is to assert one very simple principle, as entitled to govern absolutely the dealings of society with the individual in the way of compulsion and control, whether the means used be physical force in the form of legal penalties, or the moral coercion of public opinion. That principle is, that the sole end for which mankind are warranted, individually or collectively, in interfering with the liberty of action of any of their number, is self-protection. That the only purpose for which power can be rightfully exercised over any member of a civilized community, against his will, is to prevent harm to others. His own good, either physical or moral, is not a sufficient warrant. He cannot rightfully be compelled to do or forbear because it will be better for him to do so, because it will make him happier, because, in the opinions of others, to do so would be wise, or even right. These are good reasons for remonstrating with him, or reasoning with him, or persuading him, or entreating him, but not for compelling him, or visiting him with any evil in case he do otherwise. To justify that, the conduct from which it is desired to deter him must be calculated to produce evil to someone else. The only part of the conduct of anyone, for which he is amenable to society, is that which concerns others. In the part which merely concerns himself, his independence is, of right, absolute. Over himself, over his own body and mind, the individual is sovereign.

It is perhaps hardly necessary to say that this doctrine is meant to apply only to human beings in the maturity of their faculties. . . . Those who are still in a state to require being taken care of by others, must be protected against their own actions as well as against external injury. . . . Liberty, as a principle, has no application to any state of things anterior to the time when mankind have become capable of being improved by free and equal discussion. Until then, there is nothing for them but implicit obedience to an Akbar or a Charlemagne, if they are so fortunate as to find one. But as soon as mankind have attained the capacity of being guided to their own improvement by conviction or persuasion . . ., compulsion, either in the direct form or in that of pains and penalties for non-compliance, is no longer admissible as a means to their own good, and justifiable only for the security of others.

It is proper to state that I forego any advantage which could be derived to my argument from the idea of abstract right, as a thing independent of utility. I regard utility as the ultimate appeal on all ethical questions; but it must be utility in the largest sense, grounded on the permanent interests of a man as a progressive being. Those interests, I contend, authorized the subjection of individual spontaneity to external control, only in respect to those actions of each which concern the interest of other people. If anyone does an act hurtful to others, there is a *prima facie* case for punishing him, by law, or, where legal penalties are not safely applicable, by general disapprobation. There are also many positive acts for the benefit of others, which he may rightfully be compelled to perform: such as to give evidence in a court of justice; to bear his fair share in the common defense, or in any other joint work necessary to the interest of the society of which he enjoys the protection; and to perform certain acts of individual beneficence, such as saving a fellow-creature's life, or interposing to protect the defenseless against ill-usage, things which whenever it is obviously a man's duty to do, he may rightfully be made responsible to society for not doing. A person may cause evil to others not only by his actions but by his inaction, and in either case he is justly accountable to them for the injury. The latter case, it is true, requires a much more cautious exercise of compulsion than the former. To make anyone answerable for doing evil to others is the rule; to make him answerable for not preventing evil is, comparatively speaking, the exception. Yet there are many cases clear enough and grave enough to justify that exception. In all things which regard the external relations of the individual, he is *de jure* amenable to those whose interests are concerned, and, if need be, to society as their protector. There are often good reasons for not holding him to the responsibility; but these reasons must arise from the special expediencies of the case: either because it is a kind of case in which he is on the whole likely to act better, when left to his own discretion, than when controlled in any way in which society have it in their power to control him; or because the attempt to exercise control would produce other evils, greater than those which it would prevent. When such reasons as these preclude the enforcement of responsibility, the conscience of the agent himself should step into the vacant judgment seat, and protect those interests of others which have no external protection; judging himself all the more rigidly, because the case does not admit of his being made accountable to the judgment of his fellow-creatures.

But there is a sphere of action in which society, as distinguished from the individual, has, if any, only an indirect interest; comprehending all that portion of a person's life and conduct which affects only himself, or if it also affects others, only with their free, voluntary, and undeceived consent and participation. When I say only himself, I mean directly, and in the first instance; for whatever affects himself, may affect others through himself; and the objection which may be grounded on this contingency, will receive consideration in the sequel. This, then, is the appropriate region of human liberty. It comprises, *first*, the inward domain of consciousness; demanding liberty of conscience in the most comprehensive sense; liberty of thought and feeling; absolute freedom of opinion and sentiment on all subjects, practical or speculative, scientific, moral, or theological. The liberty of expressing and publishing opinions may seem to fall under a different principle, since it belongs to that part of the conduct of an individual which concerns other people; but, being almost of as much importance as the liberty of thought itself, and resting in great part on the same reasons, is practically inseparable from it. *Secondly*, the principle requires liberty of tastes and pursuits; of framing the plan of our life to suit our own character; of doing as we like, subject to such consequences as may follow: without impediment from our fellow-creatures, so long as what we do does not harm them, even though they should think our conduct foolish, perverse, or wrong. *Thirdly*, from this liberty of each individual, follows the liberty, within the same limits, of combination among individuals; freedom to unite, for any purpose not involving harm to others: the persons combining being supposed to be of full age, and not forced or deceived.

No society in which these liberties are not, on the whole, respected, is free, whatever may be its form of government; and none is completely free in which they do not exist absolute and unqualified. The only freedom which deserves the name, is that of pursuing our own good in our own way, so long as we do not attempt to deprive others of theirs, or impede their efforts to obtain it. Each is the proper guardian of his own health, whether bodily, or mental and spiritual. Mankind are greater gainers by suffering each other to live as seems good to themselves, than by compelling each to live as seems good to the rest.

.   .   .

OF THE LIBERTY OF THOUGHT AND DISCUSSION

The time, it is to be hoped, is gone by, when any defence would be necessary of the "liberty of the press" as one of the securities against corrupt or tyrannical government. No argument, we may suppose, can now be needed, against permitting a legislature or an executive, not identified in interest with the people, to prescribe opinions to them, and determine what doctrines or what arguments they shall be allowed to hear. This aspect of the question, besides, has been so often and so triumphantly enforced by preceding writers, that it need not be specially insisted on in this place. Though the law of England, on the subject of the press, is as servile to this day as it was in the time of the Tudors, there is little danger of its being actually put in force against political discussion, except during some temporary panic, when fear of insurrection drives ministers and judges from their propriety; and, speaking generally, it is not, in constitutional countries, to be apprehended, that the government, whether completely responsible to the people or not, will often attempt to control the expression of opinion, except when in doing so it makes itself the organ of the general intolerance of the public. Let us suppose, therefore, that the government is entirely at one with the people, and never thinks of exerting any power of coercion unless in agreement with what it conceives to be their voice. But I deny the right of the people to exercise such coercion, either by themselves or by their government. The power itself is illegitimate. The best government has no more title to it than the worst. It is as noxious, or more noxious, when exerted in accordance with public opinion, than when in opposition to it. If all mankind minus one, were of one opinion, and only one person were of the contrary opinion, mankind would be no more justified in silencing that one person, than he, if he had the power, would be justified in silencing mankind. Were an opinion a personal possession of no value except to the owner; if to be obstructed in the enjoyment of it were simply a private injury, it would make some difference whether the injury was inflicted only on a few persons or on many. But the peculiar evil of silencing the expression of an opinion is, that it is robbing the human race; posterity as well as the existing generation; those who dissent from the opinion, still more than those who hold it. If the opinion is right, they are deprived of the opportunity of exchanging error for truth: if wrong, they lose, what is almost as great a benefit, the clearer perception and livelier impression of truth, produced by its collision with error.

Two Concepts of Liberty
Isaiah Berlin

Sir Isaiah Berlin (1909-   ) is president of Wolfson College, Oxford. From 1957 to 1967, he was Chichele Professor of social and political theory at Oxford University. Among his major works are *The Hedgehog and the Fox* (1953), *Two Concepts of Liberty* (1958), and *Studies in the Philosophy of History* (1968).

To coerce a man is to deprive him of freedom—freedom from what? Almost every moralist in human history has praised freedom. Like happiness and goodness, like nature and reality, the meaning of this term is so porous that there is little interpretation that it seems able to resist. I do not propose to discuss either the history or the more than two hundred senses of this protean word recorded by historians of ideas. I propose to examine no more than two of these senses—but those central ones, with a great deal of human history behind them, and, I dare say, still to come. The first of these political senses of freedom or liberty (I shall use both words to mean the same), which (following much precedent) I shall call the "negative" sense, is involved in the answer to the question "What is the area within which the subject—a person or group of persons—is or should be left to do or be what he is able to do or be, without interference by other persons?" The second, which I shall call the positive sense, is involved in the answer to the question "What, or who, is the source of control or interference that can determine someone to do, or be, this rather than that?" The two questions are clearly different, even though the answers to them may overlap.

THE NOTION OF "NEGATIVE" FREEDOM

I am normally said to be free to the degree to which no man or body of men interferes with my activity. Political liberty in this sense is simply the area within which a man can act unobstructed by others. If I am prevented by others from doing what I could otherwise do, I am to that degree unfree; and if this area is contracted by other men beyond a certain minimum, I can be described as being coerced, or, it may be, enslaved. Coercion is not, however, a term that covers every form of inability. If I say that I am unable to jump more than ten feet in the air, or cannot read because I am blind, or cannot understand the darker pages of Hegel, it would be eccentric to say that I am to that degree enslaved or coerced. Coercion implies the deliberate interference of other human beings within the area in which I could otherwise act. You lack political liberty or freedom only if you are prevented from attaining a goal by human beings.[1] Mere incapacity to attain a goal is not lack

Source: Four Essays on Liberty (Oxford: Clarendon, 1969). By permission of the Clarendon Press, Oxford.

[1] I do not, of course, mean to imply the truth of the converse.

of political freedom.[2] This is brought out by the use of such modern expressions as "economic freedom" and its counterpart, "economic slavery." It is argued, very plausibly, that if a man is too poor to afford something on which there is no legal ban—a loaf of bread, a journey round the world, recourse to the law courts—he is as little free to have it as he would be if it were forbidden him by law. If my poverty were a kind of disease, which prevented me from buying bread, or paying for the journey round the world or getting my case heard, as lameness prevents me from running, this inability would not naturally be described as a lack of freedom, least of all political freedom. It is only because I believe that my inability to get a given thing is due to the fact that other human beings have made arrangements whereby I am, whereas others are not, prevented from having enough money with which to pay for it, that I think myself a victim of coercion or slavery. In other words, this use of the term depends on a particular social and economic theory about the causes of my poverty or weakness. If my lack of material means is due to my lack of mental or physical capacity, then I begin to speak of being deprived of freedom (and not simply about poverty) only if I accept the theory.[3] If, in addition, I believe that I am being kept in want by a specific arrangement which I consider unjust or unfair, I speak of economic slavery or oppression. "The nature of things does not madden us, only ill will does," said Rousseau. The criterion of oppression is the part that I believe to be played by other human beings, directly or indirectly, with or without the intention of doing so in frustrating my wishes. By being free in this sense I mean not being interfered with by others. The wider the area of non-interference the wider my freedom.

This is what the classical English political philosophers meant when they used this word.[4] They disagreed about how wide the area could or should be. They supposed that it could not, as things were, be unlimited, because if it were, it would entail a state in which all men could boundlessly interfere with all other men; and this kind of 'natural' freedom would lead to social chaos in which men's minimum needs would not be satisfied; or else the liberties of the weak would be suppressed by the strong. Because they perceived that human purposes and activities do not automatically harmonize with one another, and because (whatever their official doctrines) they put high value on other goals, such as justice, or happiness, or culture, or security, or varying degrees of equality, they were prepared to curtail freedom in the interests of other values and, indeed, of freedom itself. For, without this, it was impossible to create the kind of association that they thought desirable. Consequently, it is assumed by these thinkers that the area of men's free action must be limited by law. But equally it is assumed, especially by such libertarians as Locke and Mill in England, and Constant and Tocqueville in France, that there ought to exist a certain minimum area of personal freedom which must on no account be violated; for if it is overstepped, the individual will find himself in an area too narrow for even that minimum development of his natural faculties which

[2] Helvétius made this point very clearly: "The free man is the man who is not in irons, nor imprisoned in a gaol, nor terrorized like a slave by the fear of punishment . . . it is not lack of freedom not to fly like an eagle or swim like a whale."

[3] The Marxist conception of social laws is, of course, the best-known version of this theory, but it forms a large element in some Christian and utilitarian, and in all socialist, doctrines.

[4] "A free man," said Hobbes, "is he that . . . is not hindered to do what he hath the will to do." Law is always a "fetter," even if it protects you from being bound in chains that are heavier than those of the law, say, some more repressive law or custom, or arbitrary despotism or chaos. Bentham says much the same.

alone makes it possible to pursue, and even to conceive, the various ends which men hold good or right or sacred. It follows that a frontier must be drawn between the area of private life and that of public authority. Where it is to be drawn is a matter of argument, indeed of haggling. Men are largely interdependent, and no man's activity is so completely private as never to obstruct the lives of others in any way. "Freedom for the pike is death for the minnows"; the liberty of some must depend on the restraint of others. "Freedom for an Oxford don," others have been known to add, "is a very different thing from freedom for an Egyptian peasant."

This proposition derives its force from something that is both true and important, but the phrase itself remains a piece of political claptrap. It is true that to offer political rights, or safeguards against intervention by the state, to men who are half-naked, illiterate, underfed, and diseased is to mock their condition; they need medical help or education before they can understand, or make use of, an increase in their freedom. What is freedom to those who cannot make use of it? Without adequate conditions for the use of freedom, what is the value of freedom? First things come first: there are situations, as a nineteenth-century Russian radical writer declared, in which boots are superior to the works of Shakespeare; individual freedom is not everyone's primary need. For freedom is not the mere absence of frustration of whatever kind; this would inflate the meaning of the word until it meant too much or too little. The Egyptian peasant needs clothes or medicine before, and more than, personal liberty, but the minimum freedom that he needs today, and the greater degree of freedom that he may need tomorrow, is not some species of freedom peculiar to him, but identical with that of professors, artists, and millionaires.

What troubles the consciences of Western liberals is not, I think, the belief that the freedom that men seek differs according to their social or economic conditions, but that the minority who possess it have gained it by exploiting, or, at least, averting their gaze from, the vast majority who do not. They believe, with good reason, that if individual liberty is an ultimate end for human beings, none should be deprived of it by others; least of all that some should enjoy it at the expense of others. Equality of liberty; not to treat others as I should not wish them to treat me; repayment of my debt to those who alone have made possible my liberty or prosperity or enlightenment; justice, in its simplest and most universal sense—these are the foundations of liberal morality. Liberty is not the only goal of men. I can, like the Russian critic Belinsky, say that if others are to be deprived of it—if my brothers are to remain in poverty, squalor, and chains—then I do not want it for myself, I reject it with both hands and infinitely prefer to share their fate. But nothing is gained by a confusion of terms. To avoid glaring inequality or widespread misery I am ready to sacrifice some, or all, of my freedom: I may do so willingly and freely: but it is freedom that I am giving up for the sake of justice or equality or the love of my fellow men. I should be guilt-stricken, and rightly so, if I were not, in some circumstances, ready to make this sacrifice. But a sacrifice is not an increase in what is being sacrificed, namely freedom, however great the moral need or the compensation for it. Everything is what it is: liberty is liberty, not equality or fairness or justice or culture, or human happiness or a quiet conscience. If the liberty of myself or my class or nation depends on the misery of a number of other human beings, the system which promotes this is unjust and immoral. But if I curtail or lose my freedom, in order to lessen the shame of such inequality, and do not thereby materially increase the individual liberty of others, an absolute loss of liberty occurs. This may be compensated for by a gain in justice or in happiness or in peace, but the loss remains, and it is a confusion of values to say that although my "liberal," individual freedom may go by the board, some other kind of freedom—"social" or "economic"—is increased. Yet it remains true that the freedom of some must at times be curtailed to secure the freedom of others. Upon what principle should this be done? If freedom is a sacred, untouchable value, there can be no such principle. One or other of these conflicting rules or principles must, at any rate in practice, yield: not always for reasons which can be clearly stated, let alone generalized into rules or universal maxims.

Still, a practical compromise has to be found.

Philosophers with an optimistic view of human nature and a belief in the possibility of harmonizing human interests, such as Locke or Adam Smith and, in some moods, Mill, believed that social harmony and progress were compatible with reserving a large area for private life over which neither the state nor any other authority must be allowed to trespass. Hobbes, and those who agreed with him, especially conservative or reactionary thinkers, argued that if men were to be prevented from destroying one another and making social life a jungle or a wilderness, greater safeguards must be instituted to keep them in their places; he wished correspondingly to increase the area of centralized control and decrease that of the individual. But both sides agreed that some portion of human existence must remain independent of the sphere of social control. To invade that preserve, however small, would be despotism. The most eloquent of all defenders of freedom and privacy, Benjamin Constant, who had not forgotten the Jacobin dictatorship, declared that at the very least the liberty of religion, opinion, expression, property, must be guaranteed against arbitrary invasion. Jefferson, Burke, Paine, Mill, compiled different catalogues of individual liberties, but the argument for keeping authority at bay is always substantially the same. We must preserve a minimum area of personal freedom if we are not to "degrade or deny our nature." We cannot remain absolutely free, and must give up some of our liberty to preserve the rest. But total self-surrender is self-defeating. What then must the minimum be? That which a man cannot give up without offending against the essence of his human nature. What is this essence? What are the standards which it entails? This has been, and perhaps always will be, a matter of infinite debate. But whatever the principle in terms of which the area of non-interference is to be drawn, whether it is that of natural law or natural rights, or of utility or the pronouncements of a categorical imperative, or the sanctity of the social contract, or any other concept with which men have sought to clarify and justify their convictions, liberty in this sense means liberty *from;* absence of interference beyond the shifting, but always recognizable, frontier. "The only freedom which deserves the name is that of pursuing our own good in our own way," said the most celebrated of its champions. If this is so, is compulsion ever justified? Mill had no doubt that it was. Since justice demands that all individuals be entitled to a minimum of freedom, all other individuals were of necessity to be restrained, if need be by force, from depriving anyone of it. Indeed, the whole function of law was the prevention of just such collisions: the state was reduced to what Lassalle contemptuously described as the functions of a night-watchman or traffic policeman.

What made the protection of individual liberty so sacred to Mill? In his famous essay he declares that, unless men are left to live as they wish "in the path which merely concerns themselves," civilization cannot advance; the truth will not, for lack of a free market in ideas, come to light; there will be no scope for spontaneity, originality, genius, for mental energy, for moral courage. Society will be crushed by the weight of "collective mediocrity." Whatever is rich and diversified will be crushed by the weight of custom, by men's constant tendency to conformity, which breeds only "withered capacities," "pinched and hidebound," "cramped and warped" human beings. "Pagan self-assertion is as worthy as Christian self-denial." "All the errors which a man is likely to commit against advice and warning are far outweighed by the evil of allowing others to constrain him to what they deem is good." The defence of liberty consists in the "negative" goal of warding off interference. To threaten a man with persecution unless he submits to a life in which he exercises no choices of his goals; to block before him every door but one, no matter how noble the prospect upon which it opens, or how benevolent the motives of those who arrange this, is to sin against the truth that he is a man, a being with a life of his own to live. This is liberty as it has been conceived by liberals in the modern world from the days of Erasmus (some would say of Occam) to our own. Every plea for civil liberties and individual rights, every protest against exploitation and humiliation, against the encroachment of public authority, or the mass hypnosis of custom or organized propaganda, springs from this individualistic, and much disputed, conception of man.

Three facts about this position may be noted. In the first place Mill confuses two distinct notions. One is that all coercion is, in so far as it frustrates human desires, bad as such, although it may have to be applied to prevent other, greater evils; while non-interference, which is the opposite of coercion, is good as such, although it is not the only good. This is the "negative" conception of liberty in its classical form. The other is that men should seek to discover the truth, or to develop a certain type of character of which Mill approved—fearless, original, imaginative, independent, non-conforming to the point of eccentricity, and so on—and that truth can be found, and such character can be bred, only in conditions of freedom. Both these are liberal views, but they are not identical, and the connexion between them is, at best, empirical. No one would argue that truth or freedom of self-expression could flourish where dogma crushes all thought. But the evidence of history tends to show (as, indeed, was argued by James Stephen in his formidable attack on Mill in his *Liberty, Equality, Fraternity*) that integrity, love of truth, and fiery individualism grow at least as often in severely disciplined communities among, for example, the puritan Calvinists of Scotland or New England, or under military discipline, as in more tolerant or indifferent societies; and if this is so, Mill's argument for liberty as a necessary condition for the growth of human genius falls to the ground. If his two goals proved incompatible, Mill would be faced with a cruel dilemma, quite apart from the further difficulties created by the inconsistency of his doctrines with strict utilitarianism, even in his own human version of it.[5]

In the second place, the doctrine is comparatively modern. There seems to be scarcely any discussion of individual liberty as a conscious political ideal (as

---

[5] This is but another illustration of the natural tendency of all but a very few thinkers to believe that all the things they hold good must be intimately connected, or at least compatible, with one another. The history of thought, like the history of nations, is strewn with examples of inconsistent, or at least disparate, elements artificially yoked together in a despotic system, or held together by the danger of some common enemy. In due course the danger passes, and conflicts between the allies arise, which often disrupt the system, sometimes to the great benefit of mankind.

opposed to its actual existence) in the ancient world. Condorcet had already remarked that the notion of individual rights was absent from the legal conceptions of the Romans and Greeks; this seems to hold equally of the Jewish, Chinese, and all other ancient civilizations that have since come to light.[6] The domination of this ideal has been the exception rather than the rule, even in the recent history of the West. Nor has liberty in this sense often formed a rallying cry for the great masses of mankind. The desire not to be impinged upon, to be left to oneself, has been a mark of high civilization both on the part of individuals and communities. The sense of privacy itself, of the area of personal relationships as something sacred in its own right, derives from a conception of freedom which, for all its religious roots, is scarcely older, in its developed state, than the Renaissance or the Reformation.[7] Yet its decline would mark the death of a civilization, of an entire moral outlook.

The third characteristic of this notion of liberty is of greater importance. It is that liberty in this sense is not incompatible with some kinds of autocracy, or at any rate with the absence of self-government. Liberty in this sense is principally concerned with the area of control, not with its source. Just as democracy may, in fact, deprive the individual citizen of a great many liberties which he might have in some other form of society, so it is perfectly conceivable that a liberal-minded despot would allow his subjects a large measure of personal freedom. The despot who leaves his subjects a wide area of liberty may be unjust, or encourage the wildest inequalities, care little for order, or virtue, or knowledge; but provided he does not curb their liberty, or at least curbs it less than many other régimes, he meets with Mill's specification.[8] Freedom in this sense is not, at any rate logically, connected with democracy or self-government. Self-government may, on the whole, provide a better guarantee of the preservation of civil liberties than other régimes, and has been defended as such by libertarians. But there is no necessary connexion between individual liberty and democratic rule. The answer to the question "Who governs me?" is logically distinct from the question "How far does government interfere with me?" It is in this difference that the great contrast between the two concepts of negative and positive liberty, in the end, consists.[9] For the "positive" sense of liberty comes to light if we try to answer the question, not "What am I free to do or be?," but "By whom am I ruled?" or "Who is to say what I am, and what I

---

[6] See the valuable discussion of this in Michel Villey, *Leçons d'histoire de la philosophie du droit,* who traces the embryo of the notion of subjective rights to Occam.

[7] Christian (and Jewish or Moslem) belief in the absolute authority of divine or natural laws, or in the equality of all men in the sight of God, is very different from belief in freedom to live as one prefers.

[8] Indeed, it is arguable that in the Prussia of Frederick the Great or in the Austria of Josef II, men of imagination, originality, and creative genius, and, indeed, minorities of all kinds, were less persecuted and felt the pressure, both of institutions and custom, less heavy upon them than in many an earlier or later democracy.

[9] "Negative liberty" is something the extent of which, in a given case, it is difficult to estimate. It might, prima facie, seem to depend simply on the power to choose between at any rate two alternatives. Nevertheless, not all choices are equally free, or free at all. If in a totalitarian state I betray my friend under threat of torture, perhaps even if I act from fear of losing my job, I can reasonably say that I did not act freely. Nevertheless, I did, of course, make a choice, and could, at any rate in theory, have chosen to be killed or tortured or imprisoned. The mere existence of alternatives is not, therefore, enough to make my action free (although it may be voluntary) in the normal sense of the word. The extent of my freedom seems to depend on (*a*) how many possibilities are open to me (although the method of counting these can never be more than impressionistic. Possibilities of action are not discrete entities like apples, which

am not, to be or do?" The connexion between democracy and individual liberty is a good deal more tenuous than it seemed to many advocates of both. The desire to be governed by myself, or at any rate to participate in the process by which my life is to be controlled, may be as deep a wish as that of a free area for action, and perhaps historically older. But it is not a desire for the same thing. So different is it, indeed, as to have led in the end to the great clash of ideologies that dominates our world. For it is this—the "positive" conception of liberty: not freedom from, but freedom to—to lead one prescribed form of life—which the adherents of the "negative" freedom notion represent as being, at times, no better than a specious disguise for brutal tyranny.

THE NOTION OF POSITIVE FREEDOM

The "positive" sense of the word "liberty" derives from the wish on the part of the individual to be his own master. I wish my life and decisions to depend on myself, not on external forces of whatever kind. I wish to be the instrument of my own, not of other men's, acts of will. I wish to be a subject, not an object; to be moved by reasons, by conscious purposes, which are my own, not by causes which affect me, as it were, from outside. I wish to be somebody, not nobody; a doer—deciding, not being decided for, self-directed and not acted upon by external nature or by other men as if I were a thing, or an animal, or a slave incapable of playing a human role, that is, of conceiving goals and policies of my own and realizing them. This is at least part of what I mean when I say that I am rational, and that it is my reason that distinguishes me as a human being from the rest of the world. I wish, above all, to be conscious of myself as a thinking, willing, active being, bearing responsibility for my choices and able to explain them by references to my own ideas and purposes. I feel free to the degree that I believe this to be true, and enslaved to the degree that I am made to realize that it is not.

The freedom which consists in being one's own master, and the freedom which consists in not being prevented from choosing as I do by other men, may, on the face of it, seem concepts at no great logical distance from each other—no more than

---

can be exhaustively enumerated); (*b*) how easy or difficult each of these possibilities is to actualize; (*c*) how important in my plan of life, given my character and circumstances, these possibilities are when compared with each other; (*d*) how far they are closed and opened by deliberate human acts; (*e*) what value not merely the agent, but the general sentiment of the society in which he lives, puts on the various possibilities. All these magnitudes must be "integrated," and a conclusion, necessarily never precise, or indisputable, drawn from this process. It may well be that there are many incommensurable kinds and degrees of freedom, and that they cannot be drawn up on any single scale of magnitude. Moreover, in the case of societies, we are faced by such (logically absurd) questions as "Would arrangement X increase the liberty of Mr. A more than it would that of Messrs. B, C, and D between them, added together?" The same difficulties arise in applying utilitarian criteria. Nevertheless, provided we do not demand precise measurement, we can give valid reasons for saying that the average subject of the King of Sweden is, on the whole, a good deal freer today than the average citizen of Spain or Albania. Total patterns of life must be compared directly as wholes, although the method by which we make the comparison, and the truth of the conclusions, are difficult or impossible to demonstrate. But the vagueness of the concepts, and the multiplicity of the criteria involved, is an attribute of the subject-matter itself, not of our imperfect methods of measurement, or incapacity for precise thought.

negative and positive ways of saying much the same thing. Yet the "positive" and "negative" notions of freedom historically developed in divergent directions not always by logically reputable steps, until, in the end, they came into direct conflict with each other.

One way of making this clear is in terms of the independent momentum which the, initially perhaps quite harmless, metaphor of self-mastery acquired. "I am my own master"; "I am slave to no man"; but may I not as Platonists or Hegelians tend to say be a slave to nature? Or to my own "unbridled" passions? Are these not so many species of the identical genus "slave"—some political or legal, others moral or spiritual? Have not men had the experience of liberating themselves from spiritual slavery, or slavery to nature, and do they not in the course of it become aware, on the one hand, of a self which dominates, and on the other, of something in them which is brought to heel? This dominant self is then variously identified with reason, with my "higher nature," with the self which calculates and aims at what will satisfy it in the long run, with my "real," or "ideal," or "autonomous" self, or with my self "at its best"; which is then contrasted with irrational impulse, uncontrolled desires, my "lower" nature, the pursuit of immediate pleasures, my "empirical" or "heteronomous" self, swept by every gust of desire and passion, needing to be rigidly disciplined if it is ever to rise to the full height of its "real" nature. Presently the two selves may be represented as divided by an even larger gap: the real self may be conceived as something wider than the individual (as the term is normally understood), as a social "whole" of which the individual is an element or aspect: a tribe, a race, a church, a state, the great society of the living and the dead and the yet unborn. This entity is then identified as being the "true" self which, by imposing its collective, or "organic," single will upon its recalcitrant "members," achieves its own, and therefore their, "higher" freedom. The perils of using organic metaphors to justify the coercion of some men by others in order to raise them to a "higher" level of freedom have often been pointed out. But what gives such plausibility as it has to this kind of language is that we recognize that it is possible, and at times justifiable, to coerce men in the name of some goal (let us say, justice or public health) which they would, if they were more enlightened, themselves pursue, but do not, because they are blind or ignorant or corrupt. This renders it easy for me to conceive of myself as coercing others for their own sake, in their, not my, interest. I am then claiming that I know what they truly need better than they know it themselves. What, at most, this entails is that they would not resist me if they were rational and as wise as I and understood their interests as I do. But I may go on to claim a good deal more than this. I may declare that they are actually aiming at what in their benighted state they consciously resist, because there exists within them an occult entity—their latent rational will, or their "true" purpose—and that this entity, although it is belied by all that they overtly feel and do and say, is their "real" self, of which the poor empirical self in space and time may know nothing or little; and that this inner spirit is the only self that deserves to have its wishes taken into account.[10] Once I take this view, I am in a position to

[10] "The ideal of true freedom is the maximum of power for all the members of human society alike to make the best of themselves," said T. H. Green in 1881. Apart from the confusion of freedom with equality, this entails that if a man chose some immediate pleasure—which (in whose view?) would not enable him to make the best of himself (what self?)—what he was exercising was not "true" freedom: and if deprived of it, would not lose anything that mattered. Green was a genuine liberal: but many a tyrant could use this formula to justify his worst acts of oppression.

ignore the actual wishes of men or societies, to bully, oppress, torture them in the name, and on behalf, of their "real" selves, in the secure knowledge that whatever is the true goal of man (happiness, fulfilment of duty, wisdom, a just society, self-fulfilment) must be identical with his freedom—the free choice of his "true," albeit often submerged and inarticulate, self.

This paradox has been often exposed. It is one thing to say that I know what is good for X, while he himself does not; and even to ignore his wishes for its—and his—sake; and a very different one to say that he has *eo ipso* chosen it, not indeed consciously, not as he seems in everyday life, but in his role as a rational self which his empirical self may not know—the "real" self which discerns the good, and cannot help choosing it once it is revealed. This monstrous impersonation, which consists in equating what X would choose if he were something he is not, or at least not yet, with what X actually seeks and chooses, is at the heart of all political theories of self-realization. It is one thing to say that I may be coerced for my own good which I am too blind to see: this may, on occasion, be for my benefit; indeed it may enlarge the scope of my liberty. It is another to say that if it is my good, then I am not being coerced, for I have willed it, whether I know this or not, and am free or "truly" free even while my poor earthly body and foolish mind bitterly reject it, and struggle against those who seek however benevolently to impose it, with the greatest desperation.

This magical transformation, or sleight of hand (for which William James so justly mocked the Hegelians), can no doubt be perpetrated just as easily with the "negative" concept of freedom, where the self that should not be interfered with is no longer the individual with his actual wishes and needs as they are normally conceived, but the "real" man within, identified with the pursuit of some ideal purpose not dreamed of by his empirical self. And, as in the case of the "positively" free self, this entity may be inflated into some super-personal entity—a state, a class, a nation, or the march of history itself, regarded as a more "real" subject of attributes than the empirical self. But the "positive" conception of freedom as self-mastery, with its suggestion of a man divided against himself, has, in fact, and as a matter of history, of doctrine and of practice, lent itself more easily to this splitting of personality into two: the transcendent, dominant controller, and the empirical bundle of desires and passions to be disciplined and brought to heel. It is this historical fact that has been influential. This demonstrates (if demonstration of so obvious a truth is needed) that conceptions of freedom directly derive from views of what constitutes a self, a person, a man. Enough manipulation with the definition of man, and freedom can be made to mean whatever the manipulator wishes. Recent history has made it only too clear that the issue is not merely academic. . . .

The Liberation of Women
Kate Millet

Kate Millet (1934-   ) is a professor, author, and feminist leader and is generally known as the "principal theoretician" of the woman's liberation movement. She wrote *Sexual Politics* (1970).

In introducing the term "sexual politics," one must first answer the inevitable question "Can the relationship between the sexes be viewed in a political light at all?" The answer depends on how one defines politics.[1] This essay does not define the political as that relatively narrow and exclusive world of meetings, chairmen, and parties. The term "politics" shall refer to power-structured relationships, arrangements whereby one group of persons is controlled by another. By way of parenthesis one might add that although an ideal politics might simply be conceived of as the arrangement of human life on agreeable and rational principles from whence the entire notion of power *over* others should be banished, one must confess that this is not what constitutes the political as we know it, and it is to this that we must address ourselves.

The following sketch, which might be described as "notes toward a theory of patriarchy," will attempt to prove that sex is a status category with political implications. Something of a pioneering effort, it must perforce be both tentative and imperfect. Because the intention is to provide an overall description, statements must be generalized, exceptions neglected, and subheadings overlapping and, to some degree, arbitrary as well.

The word "politics" is enlisted here when speaking of the sexes primarily because such a word is eminently useful in outlining the real nature of their relative status, historically and at the present. It is opportune, perhaps today even mandatory, that we develop a more relevant psychology and philosophy of power relationships beyond the simple conceptual framework provided by our traditional formal politics. Indeed, it may be imperative that we give some attention to defining a theory of politics which treats of power relationships on grounds less conventional than those to which we are accustomed.[2] I have therefore found it pertinent to define them on grounds of personal contact and interaction between members of well-defined and coherent groups: races, castes, classes, and sexes. For

Source: Sexual Politics (New York: Doubleday, 1969-1970), Ch. 2. Copyright © 1969, 1970 by Kate Millet. Reprinted by permission of Doubleday & Company, Inc.

[1] The American Heritage Dictionary's fourth definition is fairly approximate: "methods or tactics involved in managing a state or government." *American Heritage Dictionary* (New York: American Heritage and Houghton Mifflin, 1969). One might expand this to a set of stratagems designed to maintain a system. If one understands patriarchy to be an institution perpetuated by such techniques of control, one has a working definition of how politics is conceived in this essay.

[2] I am indebted here to Ronald V. Samson's *The Psychology of Power* (New York: Random House, 1968) for his intelligent investigation of the connection between formal power structures and the family and for his analysis of how power corrupts basic human relationships.

it is precisely because certain groups have no representation in a number of recognized political structures that their position tends to be so stable, their oppression so continuous.

In America, recent events have forced us to acknowledge at last that the relationship between the races is indeed a political one which involves the general control of one collectivity, defined by birth, over another collectivity, also defined by birth. Groups who rule by birthright are fast disappearing, yet there remains one ancient and universal scheme for the domination of one birth group by another—the scheme that prevails in the area of sex. The study of racism has convinced us that a truly political state of affairs operates between the races to perpetuate a series of oppressive circumstances. The subordinated group has inadequate redress through existing political institutions, and is deterred thereby from organizing into conventional political struggle and opposition.

Quite in the same manner, a disinterested examination of our system of sexual relationship must point out that the situation between the sexes now, and throughout history, is a case of that phenomenon Max Weber defined as *herrschaft*, a relationship of dominance and subordinance.[3] What goes largely unexamined, often even unacknowledged (yet is institutionalized nonetheless) in our social order, is the birthright priority whereby males rule females. Through this system a most ingenious form of "interior colonization" has been achieved. It is one which tends moreover to be sturdier than any form of segregation, and more rigorous than class stratification, more uniform, certainly more enduring. However muted its present appearance may be, sexual dominion obtains nevertheless as perhaps the most pervasive ideology of our culture and provides its most fundamental concept of power.

This is so because our society, like all other historical civilizations, is a patriarchy.[4] The fact is evident at once if one recalls that the military, industry, technology, universities, science, political office, and finance—in short, every avenue of power within the society, including the coercive force of the police, is entirely in male hands. As the essence of politics is power, such realization cannot fail to carry impact. What lingers of supernatural authority, the Deity, "His" ministry, together with the ethics and values, the philosophy and art of our culture—its very civilization—as T. S. Eliot once observed, is of male manufacture.

If one takes patriarchal government to be the institution whereby that half of the populace which is female is controlled by that half which is male, the principles of patriarchy appear to be two fold: male shall dominate female, elder male shall dominate younger. However, just as with any human institution, there is frequently

[3] "Domination in the quite general sense of power, i.e. the possibility of imposing one's will upon the behavior of other persons, can emerge in the most diverse forms." In this central passage of *Wirtschaft und Gesellschaft* Weber is particularly interested in two such forms: control through social authority ("patriarchal, magisterial, or princely") and control through economic force. In patriarchy as in other forms of domination "that control over economic goods, i.e. economic power, is a frequent, often purposively willed, consequence of domination as well as one of its most important instruments." Quoted from Max Rheinstein's and Edward Shil's translation of portions of *Wirtschaft und Gesellschaft* entitled *Max Weber on Law in Economy and Society* (New York: Simon and Schuster, 1967), pp. 323-24.

[4] No matriarchal societies are known to exist at present. Matrilineality, which may be, as some anthropologists have held, a residue or a transitional stage of matriarchy, does not constitute an exception to patriarchal rule, it simply channels the power held by males through female descent—, e.g. the Avunculate.

a distance between the real and the ideal; contradictions and exceptions do exist within the system. While patriarchy as an institution is a social constant so deeply entrenched as to run through all other political, social, or economic forms, whether of caste or class, feudality or bureaucracy, just as it pervades all major religions, it also exhibits great variety in history and locale. In democracies,[5] for example, females have often held no office or do so (as now) in such minuscule numbers as to be below even token representation. Aristocracy, on the other hand, with its emphasis upon the magic and dynastic properties of blood, may at times permit women to hold power. The principle of rule by elder males is violated even more frequently. Bearing in mind the variation and degree in patriarchy—as say between Saudi Arabia and Sweden, Indonesia and Red China—we also recognize our own form in the U.S. and Europe to be much altered and attenuated by the reforms described in the next chapter.

I. IDEOLOGICAL

Hannah Arendt[6] has observed that government is upheld by power supported either through consent or imposed through violence. Conditioning to an ideology amounts to the former. Sexual politics obtains consent through the "socialization" of both sexes to basic patriarchal polities with regard to temperament, role, and status. As to status, a pervasive assent to the prejudice of male superiority guarantees superior status in the male, inferior in the female. The first item, temperament, involves the formation of human personality along stereotyped lines of sex category ("masculine" and "feminine"), based on the needs and values of the dominant group and dictated by what its members cherish in themselves and find convenient in subordinates; aggression, intelligence, force, and efficacy in the male; passivity, ignorance, docility, "virtue," and ineffectuality in the female. This is complemented by a second factor, sex role, which decrees a consonant and highly elaborate code of conduct, gesture and attitude for each sex. In terms of activity, sex role assigns domestic service and attendance upon infants to the female, the rest of human achievement, interest, and ambition to the male. The limited role allotted the female tends to arrest her at the level of biological experience. Therefore, nearly all that can be described as distinctly human rather than animal activity (in their own way animals also give birth and care for their young) is largely reserved for the male. Of course, status again follows from such an assignment. Were one to analyze the three categories one might designate status as the political component, role as the sociological, and temperament as the psychological—yet their interdependence is unquestionable and they form a chain. Those awarded higher status tend to adopt roles of mastery, largely because they are first encouraged to develop temperaments of dominance. That this is true of caste and class as well is self-evident.

---

[5] Radical democracy would, of course, preclude patriarchy. One might find evidence of a general satisfaction with a less than perfect democracy in the fact that women have so rarely held power within modern "democracies."

[6] Hannah Arendt, "Speculations on Violence," *The New York Review of Books,* Vol. XII No. 4, February 27, 1969, p. 24.

II. BIOLOGICAL

Patriarchal religion, popular attitude, and to some degree, science as well[7] assumes these psycho-social distinctions to rest upon biological differences between the sexes, so that where culture is acknowledged as shaping behavior, it is said to do no more than cooperate with nature. Yet the temperamental distinctions created in patriarchy ("masculine" and "feminine" personality traits) do not appear to originate in human nature, those of role and status still less.

Not only is there insufficient evidence for the thesis that the present social distinctions of patriarchy (status, role, temperament) are physical in origin, but we are hardly in a position to assess the existing differentiations, since distinctions which we know to be culturally induced at present so outweigh them. Whatever the "real" differences between the sexes may be, we are not likely to know them until the sexes are treated differently, that is alike. And this is very far from being the case at present. Important new research not only suggests that the possibilities of innate temperamental differences seem more remote than ever, but even raises questions as to the validity and permanence of psycho-sexual identity. In doing so it gives fairly concrete positive evidence of the overwhelmingly *cultural* character of gender, i.e. personality structure in terms of sexual category.

What Stoller and other experts define as "core gender identity" is now thought to be established in the young by the age of eighteen months. This is how Stoller differentiates between sex and gender:

Dictionaries stress that the major connotation of sex is a biological one, as for example, in the phrases sexual relations or the male sex. In agreement with this, the word sex, in this work will refer to the male or female sex and the component biological parts that determine whether one is a male or a female; the word sexual will have connotations of anatomy and physiology. This obviously leaves tremendous areas of behavior, feelings, thoughts and fantasies that are related to the sexes and yet do not have primarily biological connotations. It is for some of these psychological phenomena that the term gender will be used: one can speak of the male sex or the female sex, but one can also talk about masculinity and femininity and not necessarily be implying anything about anatomy or physiology. Thus, while sex and gender seem to common sense inextricably bound together, one purpose of this study will be to confirm the fact that the two realms (sex and gender) are not inevitably bound in anything like a one-to-one relationship, but each may go into quite independent ways.[8]

In cases of genital malformation and consequent erroneous gender assignment at birth, studied at the California Gender Identity Center, the discovery was made that it is easier to change the sex of an adolescent male, whose biological identity turns out to be contrary to his gender assignment and conditioning—through surgery— than to undo the educational consequences of years, which have succeeded in making the subject temperamentally feminine in gesture, sense of self, personality and interests. Studies done in California under Stoller's direction offer proof that gender identity (I am a girl, I am a boy) is the primary identity any human being holds—the first as well as the most permanent and far-reaching. Stoller later makes

---

[7] The social, rather than the physical sciences are referred to here. Traditionally, medical science had often subscribed to such beliefs. This is no longer the case today, when the best medical research points to the conclusion that sexual stereotypes have no bases in biology.

[8] Robert J. Stoller, *Sex and Gender* (New York: Science House, 1968), from the preface, pp. viii-ix.

emphatic the distinction that sex is biological, gender psychological, and therefore cultural: "*Gender* is a term that has psychological or cultural rather than biological connotations. If the proper terms for sex are "male" and "female," the corresponding terms for gender are "masculine" and "feminine"; these latter may be quite independent of (biological) sex."[9] Indeed, so arbitrary is gender, that it may even be contrary to physiology: ". . . although the external genitalia (penis, testes, scrotum) contribute to the sense of maleness, no one of them is essential for it, not even all of them together. In the absence of complete evidence, I agree in general with Money, and the Hampsons who show in their large series of intersexed patients that gender role is determined by postnatal forces, regardless of the anatomy and physiology of the external genitalia."[10]

III. SOCIOLOGICAL

Patriarchy's chief institution is the family. It is both a mirror of and a connection with the larger society; a patriarchal unit within a patriarchal whole. Mediating between the individual and the social structure, the family effects control and conformity where political and other authorities are insufficient.[11] As the fundamental instrument and the foundation unit of patriarchal society the family and its roles are prototypical. Serving as an agent of the larger society, the family not only encourages its own members to adjust and conform, but acts as a unit in the government of the patriarchal state which rules its citizens through its family heads. Even in patriarchal societies where they are granted legal citizenship, women tend to be ruled through the family alone and have little or no formal relation to the state.[12]

As co-operation between the family and the larger society is essential, else both would fall apart, the fate of three patriarchal institutions, the family, society, and the state are interrelated. In most forms of patriarchy this has generally led to the granting of religious support in statements such as the Catholic precept that "the father is head of the family," or Judaism's delegation of quasi-priestly authority to the male parent. Secular governments today also confirm this, as in census practices of designating the male as head of household, taxation, passports, etc. Female heads of household tend to be regarded as undesirable; the phenomenon is a trait of poverty or misfortune. The Confucian prescription that the relationship between ruler and subject is parallel to that of father and children points to the essentially feudal character of the patriarchal family (and conversely, the familial character of feudalism) even in modern democracies.[13]

[9] *Ibid.*, p. 9.

[10] *Ibid.*, p. 48.

[11] In some of my remarks on the family I am indebted to Goode's short and concise analysis. See William J. Goode, *The Family* (Englewood Cliffs, New Jersey: Prentice-Hall, 1964).

[12] Family, society, and state are three separate but connected entities: women have a decreasing importance as one goes from the first to the third category. But as each of the three categories exists within or is influenced by the overall institution of patriarchy, I am concerned here less with differentiation than with pointing out a general similarity.

[13] J. K. Folsom makes a convincing argument as to the anomalous character of patriarchal family systems within democratic society. See Joseph K. Folsom *The Family and Democratic Society* (New York: John Wiley, 1934, 1943).

IV. CLASS

It is in the area of class that the castelike status of the female within patriarchy is most liable to confusion, for sexual status often operates in a superficially confusing way within the variable of class. In a society where status is dependent upon the economic, social, and educational circumstances of class, it is possible for certain females to appear to stand higher than some males. Yet not when one looks more closely at the subject. This is perhaps easier to see by means of analogy: a black doctor or lawyer has higher social status than a poor white sharecropper. But race, itself a caste system which subsumes class, persuades the latter citizen that he belongs to a higher order of life, just as it oppresses the black professional in spirit, whatever his material success may be. In much the same manner, a truck driver or butcher has always his "manhood" to fall back upon. Should this final vanity be offended, he may contemplate more violent methods. The literature of the past thirty years provides a staggering number of incidents in which the caste of virility triumphs over the social status of wealthy or even educated women. In literary contexts one has to deal here with wish-fulfillment. Incidents from life (bullying, obscene, or hostile remarks) are probably another sort of psychological gesture of ascendancy. Both convey more hope than reality, for class divisions are generally quite impervious to the hostility of individuals. And yet while the existence of class division is not seriously threatened by such expressions of enmity, the existence of sexual hierarchy has been re-affirmed and mobilized to "punish" the female quite effectively.

The function of class or ethnic mores in patriarchy is largely a matter of how overtly displayed or how loudly enunciated the general ethic of masculine supremacy allows itself to become. Here one is confronted by what appears to be a paradox: while in the lower social strata, the male is more likely to claim authority on the strength of his sex rank alone, he is actually obliged more often to share power with the women of his class who are economically productive; whereas in the middle and upper classes, there is less tendency to assert a blunt patriarchal dominance, as men who enjoy such status have more power in any case.[14]

It is generally accepted that Western patriarchy has been much softened by the concepts of courtly and romantic love. While this is certainly true, such influence has also been vastly overestimated. In comparison with the candor of "machismo" or oriental behavior, one realizes how much of a concession traditional chivalrous behavior represents—a sporting kind of reparation to allow the subordinate female certain means of saving face. While a palliative to the injustice of woman's social position, chivalry is also a technique for disguising it. One must acknowledge that the chivalrous stance is a game the master group plays in elevating its subject to pedestal level. Historians of courtly love stress the fact that the raptures of the poets had no effect upon the legal or economic standing of women, and very little upon their social status.[15] As the sociologist Hugo Beigel has observed, both the

[14] Goode, *op. cit.*, p. 74.
[15] This is the gist of Valency's summary of the situation before the troubadours, acknowledging that courtly love is an utter anomaly: "With regard to the social background, all that can be stated with confidence is that we know nothing of the objective relationships of men and women in the Middle Ages which might conceivably motivate the strain of love-poetry which the troubadours developed." Maurice Valency, *In Praise of Love* (New York: Macmillan, 1958), p. 5.

courtly and the romantic versions of love are "grants" which the male concedes out of his total powers.[16] Both have had the effect of obscuring the patriarchal character of Western culture and in their general tendency to attribute impossible virtues to women, have ended by confining them in a narrow and often remarkably conscribing sphere of behavior. It was a Victorian habit, for example, to insist the female assume the function of serving as the male's conscience and living the life of goodness he found tedious but felt someone ought to do anyway.

The concept of romantic love affords a means of emotional manipulation which the male is free to exploit, since love is the only circumstance in which the female is (ideologically) pardoned for sexual activity. And convictions of romantic love are convenient to both parties since this is often the only condition in which the female can overcome the far more powerful conditioning she has received toward sexual inhibition. Romantic love also obscures the realities of female status and the burden of economic dependency. As to "chivalry," such gallant gesture as still resides in the middle classes has degenerated to a tired ritualism, which scarcely serves to mask the status situation of the present.

Within patriarchy one must often deal with contradictions which are simply a matter of class style. David Riesman has noted that as the working class has been assimilated into the middle class, so have its sexual mores and attitudes. The fairly blatant male chauvinism which was once a province of the lower class or immigrant male has been absorbed and taken on a certain glamour through a number of contemporary figures, who have made it, and a certain number of other working-class male attitudes, part of a new, and at the moment, fashionable life style. So influential is this working-class ideal of brute virility (or more accurately, a literary and therefore middle-class version of it) become in our time that it may replace more discreet and "gentlemanly" attitudes of the past.[17]

One of the chief effects of class within patriarchy is to set one woman against another, in the past creating a lively antagonism between whore and matron, and in the present between career woman and housewife. One envies the other her "security" and prestige, while the envied yearns beyond the confines of respectability for what she takes to be the other's freedom, adventure, and contact with the great world. Through the multiple advantages of the double standard, the male participates in both worlds, empowered by his superior social and economic resources to play the estranged women against each other as rivals. One might also recognize subsidiary status categories among women: not only is virtue class, but beauty and age as well.

Perhaps, in the final analysis, it is possible to argue that women tend to transcend the usual class stratifications in patriarchy, for whatever the class of her birth and education, the female has fewer permanent class associations than does the male. Economic dependency renders her affiliations with any class a tangential, vicarious, and temporary matter. Aristotle observed that the only slave to whom a commoner might lay claim was his woman, and the service of an unpaid domestic

---

[16] Hugo Beigel, "Romantic Love," *The American Sociological Review*, Vol. 16, 1951, p. 331.

[17] Mailer and Miller occur to one in this connection, and Lawrence as well. One might trace Rojack's very existence as a fictional figure to the virility symbol of Jack London's Ernest Everhard and Tennessee William's Stanley Kowalski. That Rojack is also literate is nothing more than an elegant finish upon the furniture of his "manhood" solidly based in the hard oaken grain of his mastery over any and every "broad" he can better, bludgeon, or bugger.

still provides working-class males with a "cushion" against the buffets of the class system which incidentally provides them with some of the psychic luxuries of the leisure class.

V. ECONOMIC AND EDUCATIONAL

One of the most efficient branches of patriarchal government lies in the agency of its economic hold over its female subjects. In traditional patriarchy, women, as non-persons without legal standing, were permitted no actual economic existence as they could neither own nor earn in their own right. Since women have always worked in patriarchal societies, often at the most routine or strenuous tasks, what is at issue here is not labor but economic reward. In modern reformed patriarchal societies, women have certain economic rights, yet the "woman's work" in which some two thirds of the female population in most developed countries are engaged is work that is not paid for.[18] In a money economy where autonomy and prestige depend upon currency, this is a fact of great importance. In general, the position of women in patriarchy is a continuous function of their economic dependence. Just as their social position is vicarious and achieved (often on a temporary or marginal basis) though males, their relation to the economy is also typically vicarious or tangential.

Since education and economy are so closely related in the advanced nations, it is significant that the general level and style of higher education for women, particularly in their many remaining segregated institutions, is closer to that of Renaissance humanism than to the skills of mid-twentieth-century scientific and technological society. Traditionally patriarchy permitted occasional minimal literacy to women while higher education was closed to them. While modern patriarchies have, fairly recently, opened all educational levels to women,[19] the kind and quality of education is not the same for each sex. This difference is of course apparent in early socialization, but it persists and enters into higher education as well. Universities, once places of scholarship and the training of a few professionals, now also produce the personnel of a technocracy. This is not the case with regard to women. Their own colleges typically produce neither scholars nor professionals nor technocrats. Nor are they funded by government and corporations

[18] Sweden is an exception in considering housework a material service rendered and calculable in divorce suits, etc. Thirty-three to forty per cent of the female population have market employment in Western countries: this leaves up to two thirds out of the market labor force. In Sweden and the Soviet Union that figure is lower.

[19] We often forget how recent an event is higher education for women. In the U.S. it is barely one hundred years old; in many Western countries barely fifty. Oxford did not grant degrees to women on the same terms as to men until 1920. In Japan and a number of other countries universities have been open to women only in the period after World War II. There are still areas where higher education for women scarcely exists. Women do not have the same access to education as do men. The Princeton Report stated that "although at the high school level more girls than boys receive grades of 'A,' roughly 50% more boys than girls go to college." *The Princeton Report to the Alumni on Co-Education* (pamphlet), Princeton, N.J. 1968, p. 10. Most other authorities give the national ratio of college students as two males to one female. In a great many countries it is far lower.

as are male colleges and those co-educational colleges and universities whose primary function is the education of males.

   .   .   .

In keeping with the inferior sphere of culture to which women in patriarchy have always been restricted, the present encouragement of their "artistic" interests through study of the humanities is hardly more than an extension of the "accomplishments" they once cultivated in preparation for the marriage market. Achievement in the arts and humanities is reserved, now, as it has been historically, for males. Token representation, be it Susan Sontag's or Lady Murasaki's, does not vitiate this rule.

VI. FORCE

We are not accustomed to associate patriarchy with force. So perfect is its system of socialization, so complete the general assent to its values, so long and so universally has it prevailed in human society, that it scarcely seems to require violent implementation. Customarily, we view its brutalities in the past as exotic or "primitive" custom. Those of the present are regarded as the product of individual deviance, confined to pathological or exceptional behavior, and without general import. And yet, just as under other total ideologies (racism and colonialism are somewhat analogous in this respect) control in patriarchal society would be imperfect, even inoperable, unless it had the rule of force to rely upon, both in emergencies and as an ever-present instrument of intimidation.

Historically, most patriarchies have institutionalized force through their legal systems. For example, strict patriarchies such as that of Islam, have implemented the prohibition against illegitimacy or sexual autonomy with a death sentence. In Afghanistan and Saudi Arabia the adulteress is still stoned to death with a mullah presiding at the execution. Execution by stoning was once common practice through the Near East. It is still condoned in Sicily. Needless to say there was and is no penalty imposed upon the male corespondent. Save in recent times or exceptional cases, adultery was not generally recognized in males except as an offense one male might commit against another's property interest. . . .

   .   .   .

Excepting a social license to physical abuse among certain class and ethnic groups, force is diffuse and generalized in most contemporary patriarchies. Significantly, force itself is restricted to the male who alone is psychologically and technically equipped to perpetrate physical violence.[20] Where differences in physical strength have become immaterial through the use of arms, the female is rendered innocuous by her socialization. Before assault she is almost universally defenseless both by her physical and emotional training. Needless to say, this has the most far-reaching effects on the social and psychological behavior of both sexes.

. . . In rape, the emotions of aggression, hatred, contempt, and the desire to break or violate personality, take a form consummately appropriate to sexual politics. . . .

   .   .   .

[20] Vivid exceptions come to mind in the wars of liberation conducted by Vietnam, China, etc. But through most of history, women have been unarmed and forbidden to exhibit any defense of their own.

VII. ANTHROPOLOGICAL: MYTH AND RELIGION

Evidence from anthropology, religious and literary myth all attests to the politically expedient character of patriarchal convictions about women. One anthropologist refers to a consistent patriarchal strain of assumption that "woman's biological differences set her apart . . . she is essentially inferior," and since "human institutions grow from deep and primal anxieties and are shaped by irrational psychological mechanisms . . . socially organized attitudes toward women arise from basic tensions expressed by the male."[21] Under patriarchy the female did not herself develop the symbols by which she is described. As both the primitive and the civilized worlds are male worlds, the ideas which shaped culture in regard to the female were also of male design. The image of women as we know it is an image created by men and fashioned to suit their needs. These needs spring from a fear of the "otherness" of woman. Yet this notion itself presupposes that patriarchy has already been established and the male has already set himself as the human norm, the subject and referent to which the female is "other" or alien. Whatever its origin, the function of the male's sexual antipathy is to provide a means of control over a subordinate group and a rationale which justifies the inferior station of those in a lower order, "explaining" the oppression of their lives.

The feeling that woman's sexual functions are impure is both world-wide and persistent. One sees evidence of it everywhere in literature, in myth, in primitive and civilized life. It is striking how the notion persists today. The event of menstruation, for example, is a largely clandestine affair, and the psycho-social effect of the stigma attached must have great effect on the female ego. There is a large anthropological literature on menstrual taboo; the practice of isolating offenders in huts at the edge of the village occurs throughout the primitive world. . . .

Primitive peoples explain the phenomenon of the female's genitals in terms of a wound, sometimes reasoning that she was visited by a bird or snake and mutilated into her present condition. Once she was wounded, now she bleeds. Contemporary slang for the vagina is "gash." The Freudian description of the female genitals is in terms of a "castrated" condition. The uneasiness and disgust female genitals arouse in patriarchal societies is attested to through religious, cultural, and literary proscription. In preliterate groups fear is also a factor, as in the belief in a castrating *vagina dentata*. The penis, badge of the male's superior status in both preliterate and civilized patriarchies, is given the most crucial significance, the subject both of endless boasting and endless anxiety.

. . .

The Pandora myth is one of two important Western archetypes which condemn the female through her sexuality and explain her position as her well-deserved punishment for the primal sin under whose unfortunate consequences the race yet labors. Ethics have entered the scene, replacing the simplicities of ritual, taboo, and mana. The more sophisticated vehicle of myth also provides official explanations of sexual history. In Hesiod's tale, Zeus, a rancorous and arbitrary father figure, in sending Epimetheus evil in the form of female genitalia, is actually chastising him

[21] H. R. Hays, *The Dangerous Sex, the Myth of Feminine Evil* (New York: Putnam, 1964). Much of my summary in this section is indebted to Hays's useful assessment of cultural notions about the female.

for adult heterosexual knowledge and activity. In opening the vessel she brings (the vulva or hymen, Pandora's "box") the male satisfies his curiosity but sustains the discovery only by punishing himself at the hands of the father god with death and the assorted calamities of postlapsarian life. The patriarchal trait of male rivalry across age or status line, particularly those of powerful father and rival son, is present as well as the ubiquitous maligning of the female.

The myth of the Fall is a highly finished version of the same themes. As the central myth of the Judeo-Christian imagination and therefore of our immediate cultural heritage, it is well that we appraise and acknowledge the enormous power it still holds over us even in a rationalist era which has long ago given up literal belief in it while maintaining its emotional assent intact.[22] This mythic version of the female as the cause of human suffering, knowledge, and sin is still the foundation of sexual attitudes, for it represents the most crucial argument of the patriarchal tradition in the West.

The Israelites lived in a continual state of war with the fertility cults of their neighbors; these latter afforded sufficient attraction to be the source of constant defection, and the figure of Eve, like that of Pandora, has vestigial traces of a fertility goddess overthrown. There is some, probably unconscious, evidence of this in the Biblical account which announces, even before the narration of the fall has begun—"Adam called his wife's name Eve; because she was the mother of all living things." Due to the fact that the tale represents a compilation of different oral traditions, it provides two contradictory schemes for Eve's creation, one in which both sexes are created at the same time, and one in which Eve is fashioned later than Adam, an afterthought born from his rib, peremptory instance of the male's expropriation of the life force through a god who created the world without benefit of female assistance.

The tale of Adam and Eve is, among many other things, a narrative of how humanity invented sexual intercourse. Many such narratives exist in preliterate myth and folk tale. Most of them strike us now as delightfully funny stories of primal innocents who require a good deal of helpful instruction to figure it out. There are other major themes in the story: the loss of primeval simplicity, the arrival of death, and the first conscious experience of knowledge. All of them revolve about sex. Adam is forbidden to eat of the fruit of life or of the knowledge of good and evil, the warning states explicitly what should happen if he tastes of the latter: "in that day that thou eatest thereof thou shalt surely die." He eats but fails to die (at least in the story), from which one might infer that the serpent told the truth.

But at the moment when the pair eat of the forbidden tree they awake to their nakedness and feel shame. Sexuality is clearly involved, though the fable insists it is only tangential to a higher prohibition against disobeying orders in the matter of another and less controversial appetite—one for food. Róheim points out that the Hebrew verb for "eat" can also mean coitus. Everywhere in the Bible "knowing" is

---

[22] It is impossible to assess how deeply embedded in our consciousness is the Eden legend and how utterly its patterns are planted in our habits of thought. One comes across its tone and design in the most unlikely places, such as Antonioni's film *Blow-Up*, to name but one of many striking examples. The action of the film takes place in an idyllic garden, loaded with primal overtones largely sexual, where, prompted by a tempter with a phallic gun, the female again betrays the male to death. The photographer who witnesses the scene reacts as if he were being introduced both to the haggard knowledge of the primal scene and original sin at the same time.

synonymous with sexuality, and clearly a product of contact with the phallus, here in the fable objectified as a snake. To blame the evils and sorrows of life—loss of Eden and the rest—on sexuality, would all too logically implicate the male, and such implication is hardly the purpose of the story, designed as it is expressly in order to blame all this world's discomfort on the female. Therefore it is the female who is tempted first and "beguiled" by the penis, transformed into something else, a snake. Thus Adam has "beaten the rap" of sexual guilt, which appears to be why the sexual motive is so repressed in the Biblical account. Yet the very transparency of the serpent's universal phallic value shows how uneasy the mythic mind can be about its shifts. Accordingly, in her inferiority and vulnerability the woman takes and eats, simple carnal thing that she is, affected by flattery even in a reptile. Only after this does the male fall, and with him, humanity—for the fable has made him the racial type, whereas Eve is a mere sexual type and, according to tradition, either expendable or replaceable. And as the myth records the original sexual adventure, Adam was seduced by woman, who was seduced by a penis. "The woman whom thou gavest to be with me, she gave me of the fruit and I did eat" is the first man's defense. Seduced by the phallic snake, Eve is convicted for Adam's participation in sex.

Adam's curse is to toil in the "sweat of his brow," namely the labor the male associates with civilization. Eden was a fantasy world without either effort or activity, which the entrance of the female, and with her sexuality, has destroyed. Eve's sentence is far more political in nature and a brilliant "explanation" of her inferior status. "In sorrow thou shalt bring forth children. And thy desire shall be to thy husband. And he shall rule over thee." Again, as in the Pandora myth, a proprietary father figure is punishing his subjects for adult heterosexuality. It is easy to agree with Róheim's comment on the negative attitude the myth adopts toward sexuality: "Sexual maturity is regarded as a misfortune, something that has robbed mankind of happiness ... the explanation of how death came into the world."

What requires further emphasis is the responsibility of the female, a marginal creature, in bringing on this plague, and the justice of her suborned condition as dependent on her primary role in this original sin. The connection of woman, sex, and sin constitutes the fundamental pattern of western patriarchal thought thereafter.

VIII. PSYCHOLOGICAL

The aspects of patriarchy already described have each an effect upon the psychology of both sexes. Their principal result is the interiorization of patriarchal ideology. Status, temperament, and role are all value systems with endless psychological ramifications for each sex. Patriarchal marriage and the family with its ranks and division of labor play a large part in enforcing them. The male's superior economic position, the female's inferior one have also grave implications. The large quantity of guilt attached to sexuality in patriarchy is overwhelmingly placed upon the female, who is, culturally speaking, held to be the culpable or the more culpable party in nearly any sexual liaison, whatever the extenuating circumstances. A tendency toward the reification of the female makes her more often a sexual object than a person. This is particularly so when she is denied human rights through chattel status. Even where this has been partly amended the cumulative effect of religion and custom is still very powerful and has enormous psychological consequences. Woman is still denied sexual freedom and the biological control over her body through the cult of virginity, the double standard, the prescription against abortion, and in many places because contraception is physically or psychically unavailable to her.

.   .   .

When in any group of persons, the ego is subjected to such invidious versions of itself through social beliefs, ideology, and tradition, the effect is bound to be pernicious. This coupled with the persistent though frequently subtle denigration women encounter daily through personal contacts, the impressions gathered from the images and media about them, and the discrimination in matters of behavior, employment, and education which they endure, should make it no very special cause for surprise that women develop group characteristics common to those who suffer minority status and a marginal existence. A witty experiment by Philip Goldberg proves what everyone knows, that having internalized the disesteem in which they are held, women despise both themselves and each other.[23] This simple test consisted of asking women undergraduates to respond to the scholarship in an essay signed alternately by one John McKay and one Joan McKay. In making their assessments the students generally agreed that John was a remarkable thinker, Joan an unimpressive mind. Yet the articles were identical: the reaction was dependent on the sex of the supposed author.

As women in patriarchy are for the most part marginal citizens when they are citizens at all, their situation is like that of other minorities, here defined not as dependent upon numerical size of the group, but on its status. "A minority group is any group of people who because of their physical or cultural characteristics, are singled out from others in the society in which they live for differential and unequal treatment." Only a handful of sociologists have ever addressed themselves in any meaningful way to the minority status of women. And psychology has yet to produce relevant studies on the subject of ego damage to the female which might bear comparison to the excellent work done on the effects of racism on the minds of blacks and colonials. The remarkably small amount of modern research devoted to the psychological and social effects of masculine supremacy on the female and on the culture in general attests to the widespread ignorance or unconcern of a conservative social science which takes patriarchy to be both the status quo and the state of nature.

What little literature the social sciences afford us in this context confirms the presence in women of the expected traits of minority status: group self-hatred and self-rejection, a contempt both for herself and for her fellows—the result of that continual, however subtle, reiteration of her inferiority which she eventually accepts as a fact.[24] Another index of minority status is the fierceness with which all minority group members are judged. The double standard is applied not only in cases of sexual conduct but other contexts as well. In the relatively rare instances of female crime too: in many American states a woman convicted of crime is awarded

[23] Philip Goldberg, "Are Women Prejudiced Against Women?" *Transaction,* April 1968.
[24] My remarks on the minority status of women are summarized from all the articles listed, and I am particularly indebted to an accomplished critique of them in an unpublished draft by Professor Marlene Dixon, formerly of the University of Chicago's Department of Sociology and the Committee on Human Development, presently of McGill University.

a longer sentence.[25] Generally an accused woman acquires a notoriety out of proportion to her acts and due to sensational publicity she may be tried largely for her "sex life." But so effective is her conditioning toward passivity in patriarchy, woman is rarely extrovert enough in her maladjustment to enter upon criminality. Just as every minority member must either apologize for the excesses of a fellow or condemn him with a strident enthusiasm, women are characteristically harsh, ruthless and frightened in their censure of aberration among their numbers.

Perhaps patriarchy's greatest psychological weapon is simply its universality and longevity. A referent scarcely exists with which it might be contrasted or by which it might be confuted. While the same might be said of class, patriarchy has a still more tenacious or powerful hold through its successful habit of passing itself off as nature. Religion is also universal in human society and slavery was once nearly so; advocates of each were fond of arguing in terms of fatality, or irrevocable human "instinct"—even "biological origins." When a system of power is thoroughly in command, it has scarcely need to speak itself aloud; when its workings are exposed and questioned, it becomes not only subject to discussion, but even to change.

Suggested Readings

1. Adler, Mortimer J., *The Idea of Freedom,* 2 vols. (Garden City, N.Y.: Doubleday, 1958-1961).
2. Chafee, Z., *Free Speech in the United States* (Cambridge, Mass.: Harvard University Press, 1940).
3. Friedrich, Carl J. (ed.), *Liberty; Nomos IV* (New York: Atherton, 1962). An anthology devoted to Mill's essay "On Liberty."
4. MacCallum, Gerald C., Jr., "Negative and Positive Freedom," *Philosophical Review*, Vol. 76, No. 3 (July 1967), 312-333.
5. Muller, Herbert J., *Issues of Freedom: Paradoxes and Promises* (New York: Harper, 1960).

---

[25] See The Commonwealth v. Daniels, 37 L.W. 2064, Pennsylvania Supreme Court, 7/1/68 (reversing 36 L.W. 2004).

VIOLENCE

Violence is neither evil or good. Violence to us has become a necessity to survive.
—Eddie Eugene Bolden (former Black Panther, Omaha)

Someone asks YOU: Do you believe in violence?

YOU reply: Let's put it this way: I don't like it when other people do violence to me.

SHE: I'm not asking whether you like violence, done either to yourself or others, I want to know whether you think the use of violence is ever right.

YOU: Why, no. It's never right.

SHE: Oh. Then you're a pacifist, right?

YOU: No, I'm not. In my view, a pacifist is a person who thinks it's never right to use force, who remains passive no matter what anyone is doing to someone else, including injuring them. I'm not a pacifist, because I think it's OK to use force sometimes. It would be more accurate to call me a nonresistant in **Adin Ballou**'s [third essay in this section] sense. He thinks it's never right to use force to do evil in return for evil done to you, that it's never right to resist injury with injury.

SHE: But then you couldn't believe the use of violence is always wrong if you think it's OK to use force sometimes.

YOU: Sure, I can believe violence is always wrong. It's easy. It's as easy as believing being bad is always wrong. Violence is just another form of badness. To be violent is to be bad.

Using force isn't necessarily a form of badness. In fact, nothing can be done in the world without using force. Every human act is moving the body in some way, and that takes force.

SHE: So?

YOU: So, since some human acts are good, the use of force in those cases is good. That's why you can't equate force and violence.

SHE: Then sometimes the use of force is good and sometimes it's bad.

YOU: Right. When force is good, we call it benevolence; when force is bad, we call it violence.

SHE: How can you tell the difference between the two? How can you tell when there is violence? That seems pretty important to me.

YOU: I think it's important, too. And so do philosophers. **Newton Garver** [first essay in this section], for example, writes a whole essay just concentrating on what violence is, on trying to define violence.

SHE: How does he tell when the use of force is violence?

YOU: For him, you have to consider a person's rights. When his rights, such as the right to his body, or to make his own decisions, or to the product of his labor, are violated by the use of physical or psychological force, then force is violence.

SHE: I'm not sure I agree that violence is always bad. It seems to me that sometimes it's legitimate to use violence.

YOU: How can that be if violence is bad?

SHE: Because sometimes one bad thing isn't as bad as another bad thing, and because occasionally the situation in the world is such that a person is forced to choose doing either of two bad things. We don't always have the luxury of doing pure good. Sometimes doing good is doing what is least bad.

For example, a policeman may have to wound a person if he catches him trying to kill another person. Wounding him isn't a pure good, but it is better than letting him kill. And when a dictator has a powerful hold on a country and enslaves the people, and makes arbitrary, unjust decisions, and exploits them, then it seems legitimate for the people to violently overthrow him; at least it's legitimate if they really don't think he can be overthrown nonviolently.

YOU: Interesting that you should use that example. Here's another essay, this one by **Robert Audi** [second essay in this section] that tries to make a similar point. He thinks social violence can sometimes be justified if it is the only way to secure freedom, justice, and/or social welfare.

SHE: Do you agree with him and me?

YOU: No.

SHE: You're just being stubborn.

YOU: I don't think so. I said that force in itself may be good or bad, depending on whether it is benevolence or violence. If force is bad, then it's violence. But if your examples show anything, they simply show what I said earlier, namely, that in some circumstances force is good—even though, as you say, what you accomplish, as in social revolution, isn't always purely good. The word "violence" is often wrongly used in place of "force." Audi, I think, uses "violence" when he should be using "force" instead. When we try to make the use of unusual force legitimate, we are trying to show that it is benevolence; we are not trying to show that violence is legitimate and, consequently, good. Violence is always bad; I still say so.

SHE: Still—if benevolence, when it involves the use of force that injures someone, can't really be good, just a lesser bad than some other action, how can you say that violence, being the opposite of benevolence, is always bad?

YOU: I'm not sure I get your point.

SHE: Since benevolence isn't always good, and violence is the opposite of benevolence, then I don't see how violence is always bad.

YOU: Maybe you mean "isn't always *purely* good" or "*purely* bad."

SHE: Yes, I think so.

YOU: Since nothing in this world may be purely bad or purely good, maybe "better" is the key moral term rather than "good" and "bad." When we choose how to use our force, perhaps our standard should not be "Which act will result in good and which in bad?" but "Which act's results are better?" The better act is benevolence and the worse act is violence.

SHE: Maybe.

YOU: Incidentally, Reinhold Niebuhr has some interesting things to say about the morality of violence, particularly in relation to revolution. I suggest you read his essay. [See the next section.]

What Violence Is

Newton Garver

Newton Garver (1928-   ) teaches philosophy at the State University of New York, Buffalo. He has written a number of journal articles.

I

Most people deplore violence, many people embrace violence (perhaps reluctantly), and a few people renounce violence. But through all these postures there runs a certain obscurity, and it is never entirely clear just what violence is.

Those who deplore violence loudest and most publicly are usually identified with the status quo—school principals, businessmen, politicians, ministers. What they deplore is generally overt attacks on property or against the "good order of society." They rarely see violence in defense of the status quo in the same light as violence directed against it. At the time of the Watts riots in 1965 President Johnson urged Negroes to realize that nothing of any value can be won through violent means—an idea which may be true but which Johnson himself seemed to ignore in connection with the escalation of the Vietnam war he was simultaneously embarking upon. But the President [Johnson] is not the only one of us who deplores violence while at the same time perpetrating it, and a little more clarity about what exactly we deplore might help all around.

Those who renounce violence are equally hard to follow. Tolstoy, Gandhi, and Muste stand out among the advocates of nonviolence of the past century, and as one reads them it becomes clear that they do not all renounce exactly the same thing. There is much that is concrete and detailed in the writings of these men, but nonetheless it is not easy to avoid the impression that "nonviolence" is really just morality itself rather than a specific commitment to eschew a certain well-defined sort of behavior.

Those who embrace violence are in a much better position, for they stand ready to embrace whatever is "inevitable" or "necessary" in the circumstances, and hence the question of just where violence begins or leaves off does not arise for them. But if we want to know about the nature and varieties of violence, it does not help to be told that violence is unavoidable or that it is a necessary means to some end. There is a question about understanding violence before we come to adopt a posture toward it, and it is to that question we now turn.

II

What I want to do is to present a kind of typology of violence. I want, that is, to try to make clear what some of the different types and kinds and forms of violence

Source: The Nation, June 24, 1968, pp. 817-822. (Revised by author.) Reprinted by permission of the author.

are, and thereby to give a perspective of the richness of this topic. Unfortunately, I can't begin saying what the types of violence are without saying first what it is I'm giving you a typology of. So let's begin with a definition of violence.

What is violence? That is a typical philosophical question. The psychiatrists and the sociologists are interested in the questions: why is there violence? what causes violence? That's not my concern—at least not my professional concern nor my concern here. What I'm interested in is the old-fashioned philosophical question: What is the nature or essence of violence? We can make a good start etymologically. The word "violence" comes, of course, from the French, prior to that from the Latin, and you can find Greek roots if you're up to it—which I'm not. The Latin root of the word "violence" is a combination of two Latin words—the word "*vis*" (force) and the past participle "*latus*" of the word "*fero*" (to carry). The Latin word "*violare*" is itself a combination of these two words, and its present participle "*violans*" is a plausible source for the word "violence"—so that the word "violence," in its etymological origin, has the sense of to carry force at or toward. An interesting feature of the etymology is that the word "violation" comes from this very same source as the word "violence," which suggests to us the interesting idea that violence is somehow a violation of something: that carrying force against something constitutes in one way or another a violation of it.

The idea of force being connected with violence is a very powerful one. There is no question at all that in many contexts the word "force" is a synonym for the word "violence." This is particularly true if you talk about, for example, a violent blizzard: a violent blizzard is nothing but a blizzard with very great force. The same is true of a violent sea and other bits of violence in nature. It is simply some aspect of nature manifested to us with especially great force. But I don't want to talk about natural phenomena—certainly not meteorological phenomena. I want to talk instead about human phenomena. In human affairs violence cannot be equated with force.

One of the very first things to understand about violence in human affairs is that it is not the same thing as force. It is clear that force is often used on another person's body and there is no violence done. For example, if a man is drowning—thrashing around and apparently unable to save himself—and you use the standard Red Cross life-saving techniques, you will use force against his body although certainly you won't be doing any violence to him. You will, in fact, be saving his life instead. To think so rigidly of force and violence being identical with one another that you call this sort of life-saving an act of violence is to have lost sight entirely of the significance of the concept. Similarly, surgeons and dentists use force on our bodies without doing violence to us.

The idea of violence in human affairs is much more closely connected with the idea of violation than it is with the idea of force. What is fundamental about violence in human affairs is that a person is violated. Now that is a tough notion to explain. It is easy enough to understand how you can violate a moral rule or a parking regulation, but what in the world does it mean to talk about "violating a person"? That, I think, is a very important question, and because it can give a fresh perspective on what it means to be human it deserves fuller consideration than I can give it in this context. If it makes sense to talk about violating a person, that just is because a person has certain rights which are undeniably, indissolubly, connected with his being a person. The very idea of natural rights is controversial since it is redolent of Scholasticism, but I find myself forced to accept natural rights in order to understand the moral dimension of violence. One of the most fundamental rights a person has is a right to his body—to determine what his body does and what is done to his body—because without his body he wouldn't be a person anymore. The most common way a person ceases to exist is that his body stops functioning—a point which appeals especially forcefully if you think of a person as a living, growing thing rather than as something static or as a substance in the traditional sense. Apart from a body what is essential to one's being a person is dignity in something like the existentialist sense. The dignity of a person does not consist in his remaining prim and proper or dignified and unruffled, but rather in his making his own decisions. In this respect what is fundamental about a person is radically different from what is fundamental, for example, about a dog. I have a dog. I don't expect him to make decisions: When I tell him to sit or to stay I expect him just to do it, not to decide. And, indeed, the way I have treated my dog, which seems to be a good way to treat a dog, is to train him to respond in a more or less mechanical way to certain commands. Now that, it seems to me, is to give a dog a very good place in life, at least as we have arranged it. However, to treat a human being that way is an affront to his dignity as a human being, just because it is essential to a human being that he have a kind of dignity or "autonomy," as Kant put it.

The right to one's body and the right to autonomy are undoubtedly the most fundamental natural rights of persons, but there are subsidiary ones that deserve mention as part of the background for our discussion of violence. One of these stems from the right to autonomy. It is characteristic of human action to be purposive and to have results and consequences, and freedom therefore is normally conceived as involving not only the right to decide what to do but also the right to dispose of or cope with the consequences of one's action. One aspect of this right is the right to the product of one's labor, which has played an important role in the theory of both capitalism and communism. Both Marx and Locke, in two entirely different traditions as we think of it nowadays, have a labor theory of economic value: that the inherent value of something is determined by the amount of labor that is required to produce it. It is one of the ironies of intellectual history that the right of persons to the product of their labor constitutes the basis for both Locke's defense of private property and Marx's attack on it. If we follow this line of thought to the extent that we consider one's property as an extension of his person, the scope of the concept of violence becomes greatly enlarged, perhaps in harmony with popular thought on the subject, at least on the part of propertied persons; but one should always bear in mind that a person can reconcile himself much more readily to loss of property than he can to loss of life.

If we say that the results of what a person does belongs to him, we should have in mind not only this kind of labor theory of value but also the more or less natural and expectable consequences of a person's action. One of Jean-Paul Sartre's most interesting plays, *Altona,* develops this theme. In this play Sartre depicts a young man who does things that would normally have very serious consequences, probably his death. At one time he defies the Nazis, at another time the American Military Government that is occupying the country. On both occasions his father intervenes and cuts him off from the normal, expected consequences of his actions, consequences which anybody else would have suffered. Sartre shows what an awful impact it has upon this man, as a person, to have the consequences of his actions cut off in this way. In the end this victim of paternalism is one of Sartre's rather hideous characters, sequestered in a room in the center of his father's grand mansion having hallucinations of crabs and visions of expiation.

Here then is an indication of what is involved in talking about the violation of a person, and it seems to me that violence in human affairs comes down to violating persons. With that in mind, let me turn now to discussion of the different types and forms of violence. Violence can be usefully classified into four different kinds based on two criteria, whether the violence is personal or institutionalized and whether the violence is overt or a kind of covert or quiet violence.

III

Overt physical assault of one person on the body of another is the most obvious form of violence. Mugging, rape, and murder are the flagrant "crimes of violence," and when people speak of the danger of violence in the streets it is usually visions of these flagrant cases that float before their minds. I share the general concern over the rising rate of these crimes, but at the same time I deplore the tendency to cast our image of violence just in the mold of these flagrant cases. These are cases where an attack on a human body is also clearly an attack on a person and clearly illegal. We must not tie these characteristics in too tight a package, for some acts of violence are intended as a defense of law or a benefit to the person whose body is beaten—e.g. ordinary police activity (not "police brutality")[1] and the corporal punishment of children by parents and teachers. The humbler cases are violence too, although the fact that policemen, teachers, and parents have socially defined roles which they invoke when they resort to violence indicates that these cases have institutional aspects that overshadow the purely personal ones. These institutional overtones make a great deal of difference but they cannot erase that there is violence done. Of course not all cases are so clear: I leave to the reader to ponder whether all sex acts are acts of violence, or just how to distinguish in practical terms those that are from those that are not. Whenever you do something to another person's body without his consent you are attacking not just a physical entity—you are attacking a person. You are doing something by force, so the violence in this case is something that is easily visible, has long been recognized as violence, and is a case of overt, personal violence.

In cases of war, what one group tries to do to another group is what happens to individuals in cases of mugging and murder. The soldiers involved in a war are responsible for acts of violence against "the enemy," at least in the sense that the violence would not have occurred if the soldiers had refused to act. (Of course some other violence might have occurred. But in any case I do not wish to try to assess blame or lesser evils.) The Nuremberg trials after World War II attempted to establish that individual soldiers are responsible morally and legally too, but this attempt overlooked the extent to which the institutionalization of violence changes its moral dimension. On the one hand an individual soldier is not acting on his own initiative and responsibility, and with the enormous difficulty in obtaining reliable information and making a timely confrontation of government claims, not even

[1] A persuasive account of the extent to which law itself can be a form of violence, rather than an alternative to it, is to be found in E. Z. Friedenberg's essay "A Violent Country" in the *New York Review,* October 20, 1966.

U.S. Senators, let alone soldiers and private citizens, are in a good position to make the necessary judgments about the justice of a military engagement. On the other hand a group does not have a soul and cannot act except through the agency of individual men. Thus there is a real difficulty in assigning responsibility for such institutional violence. The other side of the violence, its object, is equally ambiguous, for "the enemy" are being attacked as an organized political force rather than as individuals, and yet since a group does not have a body any more than it has a soul "the enemy" is attacked by attacking the bodies of individual men (and women and children). Warfare, therefore, because it is an institutionalized form of violence, differs from murder in certain fundamental respects.

Riots are another form of institutionalized violence, although their warlike character was not widely recognized until the publication of the report of the President's National Advisory Commission on Civil Disorders (the "Riot" Commission). In a riot, as in a war, there are many instances of personal violence, and some persons maintain that the civil disorders are basically massive crime waves. But on the other hand there is also much of a warlike character. One of the characteristics of the Watts riot, as any will know who have read Robert Conot's very interesting book, *The Rivers of Blood, Years of Darkness,* is that in that riot the people who were supposed to be controlling the situation, the Los Angeles police and their various reinforcements, simply did not know basic facts about the community. In particular they did not know who was the person who could exercise a sort of leadership if the group were left alone and that person's hand was strengthened. One incident illustrates the sort of thing that happened. A Negro policeman was sent in plain clothes into the riot area and told to call back into the precinct whenever there was anything to report. He was told, furthermore, not to identify himself as a policeman under any conditions for fear of jeopardizing himself. At one point, he tried to intervene when some cops were picking on just altogether the wrong person and he ended up getting cursed and having his head bashed in by one of his fellow members of the Los Angeles police force. The police were in such a state that they couldn't even refrain from hitting a Negro policeman who was sent on a plain-clothes assignment into that area. In effect, the Los Angeles police and their various allies conducted what amounted to a kind of a war campaign. They acted like an army going out to occupy a foreign territory where they didn't know the people and didn't speak the language. The result was that their actions had the effect of breaking down whatever social structure there might have been. And the breakdown of the social structure then had the effect of releasing more and more overt violence. The military flavor of our urban disturbances has increased over the years, and 1967 saw the appearance not only of machine guns and automatic rifles but also of tanks and armored personnel carriers in Newark and Detroit, in what the Kerner Commission characterized as "indiscriminate and excessive use of force." For that reason the urban disorders that we've been having in recent summers are really a kind of institutionalized violence where there are two sides in combat with one another. It is quite different from a normal criminal situation where police act against individual miscreants.

Since these overt forms of violence are, on the whole, fairly easily recognized, let us go on to consider the other forms of violence, the quiet forms which do not necessarily involve any overt physical assault on anybody's person or property. There are both personal and institutional forms of quiet violence, and I would like to begin with a case of what we might call psychological violence, where individuals are involved as individuals and there are not social institutions responsible for the violation of persons that takes place. Consider the following news item:[2]

PHOENIX, Ariz., Feb. 6 (AP)—Linda Marie Ault killed herself, policemen said today, rather than make her dog Beauty pay for her night with a married man.

The police quoted her parents, Mr. and Mrs. Joseph Ault, as giving this account:

Linda failed to return home from a dance in Tempe Friday night. On Saturday she admitted she had spent the night with an Air Force lieutenant.

The Aults decided on a punishment that would "wake Linda up." They ordered her to shoot the dog she had owned about two years.

On Sunday, the Aults and Linda took the dog into the desert near their home. They had the girl dig a shallow grave. Then Mrs. Ault grasped the dog between her hands, and Mr. Ault gave his daughter a .22-caliber pistol and told her to shoot the dog.

Instead, the girl put the pistol to her right temple and shot herself.

The police said there were no charges that could be filed against the parents except possibly cruelty to animals.

Obviously, the reason there can be no charges is that the parents did no physical damage to Linda. But I think your reaction might be the same as mine—that they really did terrible violence to the girl by the way they behaved in this situation. Of course one must agree that Linda did violence to herself, but that is not the whole account of the violence in this case. The parents did far more violence to the girl than the lieutenant, and the father recognized that when he said to a detective, "I killed her. I killed her. It's just like I killed her myself." If we fail to recognize that there is really a kind of psychological violence that can be perpetrated on people, a real violation of their autonomy, their dignity, their right to determine things for themselves, their right to be humans rather than dogs, then we fail to realize the full dimension of what it is to do violence to one another.

One of the most obvious transition cases between overt personal violence and quiet personal violence is the case of a threat. Suppose a robber comes into a bank with a pistol, threatens to shoot one of the tellers, and walks out with money or a hostage or both. This is a case of armed robbery, and we rightly lump it together with cases of mugging and assault, morally and legally speaking, even if everybody emerges from the situation without any bruises or wounds. The reason is that there is a clear threat to do overt physical violence. By means of such a threat a person very often accomplishes what he might otherwise accomplish by actual overt violence. In this case the robber not only gets as much loot but he also accomplishes pretty much the same thing with respect to degrading the persons he is dealing with. A person who is threatened with being shot and then does something which he certainly would never otherwise do is degraded by losing his own autonomy as a person. We recognize that in law and morals: If a person who is threatened with a revolver takes money out of a safe and hands it to the robber we don't say that the person who has taken the money out of the safe has stolen it. We say that the person acted under compulsion, and hence the responsibility for what is done does not lie with him but with the person who threatened him.

It is very clear, and very important, that in cases where there is a threat of overt physical violence that we acknowledge that a person acting under that sort of a threat loses his autonomy. Of course, he needn't surrender his autonomy: he could

---

[2] *New York Times*, February 7, 1968.

just refuse to hand over the loot. There can be a great deal of dignity in such a refusal, and one of the messages of Sartre's moral philosophy, his existentialism, is that whenever you act other than with full responsibility yourself for your own actions that you are acting in bad faith. Now that is a very demanding philosophy, but it is one which puts a great deal of emphasis upon autonomy and dignity in human action and is not to be lightly dismissed. Nevertheless we do not expect that people will act with such uncompromising strength and dignity. To recognize that people can be broken down by threats and other psychological pressures, as well as by physical attack, and that to have acted under threat or duress is as good an excuse before the law as physical restraints—these recognitions constitute acknowledgement of the pertinence of the concept of psychological violence.

Psychological violence often involves manipulating people. It often involves degrading people. It often involves a kind of terrorism one way or another. Perhaps these forms that involve manipulation, degradation and terror are best presented in George Orwell's book, *1984*. In that book the hero is deathly afraid of being bitten by a rat. He never is bitten by the rat, but he is threatened with the rat and the threat is such as to break down his character in an extraordinary way. Here what might be called the phenomenology of psychological violence is presented in as convincing a form as I know.

Apart from these cases of terror and manipulation and degradation there are certain other forms of psychological violence. One of the most insidious is what might be called the "Freudian rebuff."[3] The Freudian rebuff works something like this. A person makes a comment on the Vietnam war or on civil rights or on some other current topic. The person he is talking to then says, "Well, you're just saying that because of your Oedipal relations with your father." The original speaker naturally objects, "Don't be silly. Of course I had a father and all that. But look at the facts." And then he starts bringing out the journals and newspapers and presents facts and statistics from them. "You must have a terrible Oedipal complex; you're getting so excited about this." And the person then says, "Look, I've had some fights with my father, but I'm not hung-up on him, I just have normal spats and affection. I've read the paper and I have an independent interest in the civil rights question. It has nothing to do with my relations with my father." To which the response is, "Well, your denial just proves how deep your Oedipal complex is." This type of Freudian rebuff has the effect of what John Henry Newman[4] called "poisoning the wells." It gives its victim just no ground to stand on. If he tries to stand on facts and statistics, they are discounted and his involvement is attributed to Freudian factors. If he tries to prove that he doesn't have the kind of psychological aberration in question, his very attempt to prove that he doesn't have it is taken to be evidence that he does. He can't get out of the predicament. It is like a quagmire in which the victim sinks deeper no matter which way he moves. So long as the proffered definition of the situation is imposed on him, a person has no way to turn: there is no possible sort of response that can extricate him from that charge laid upon him. To structure a situation against a person in such a manner does violence to him by depriving him of his dignity: no matter what he does there

---

[3] Of course this is an aspect of cocktail-party Freudianism rather than of psychoanalytic theory, and what Freud invented was not this little ploy but the concepts that were later distorted into it.

[4] In his famous debate with Charles Kingsley. See his *Apologia Pro Vita Sua*, conveniently available in a paperback edition, Garden City, Doubleday, 1956.

is no way at all, so long as he accepts the problem in the terms in which it is presented, for him to make a response that will allow him to emerge with honor.

Although this sort of cocktail-party Freudianism is not very serious in casual conversations where the definition of the situation can be challenged or the whole matter just shrugged off, it must be kept in mind that there are many forms of this ploy and that sometimes the whole life and character of a person may be involved. A classic literary and religious version is the dispute between Charles Kingsley and John Henry Newman in the 19th century, in which Kingsley challenged Newman's integrity and ended up losing his stature as a Protestant spokesman, and which is written up in fascinating detail in Newman's *Apologia*. A political variation is the Marxian rebuff where, of course, it is because of your class standing that you have such and such a view, and if you deny that the class standing is influencing you in that way your very denial shows how imbued you are with the class ideology. Between parent and child as well as between husband and wife there are variations of this ploy which turn around the identification (by one insistent party) of love with some particular action or other, so that the other party must either surrender his autonomy or acknowledge his faithlessness.

The cases where this sort of psychological violence are damaging are those where the person structuring the situation is in some position of special authority. Another form particularly virulent in urban schools—and probably suburban schools too—is the teacher's rebuff. An imaginative child does something out of the ordinary, and the teacher's response is that he is a discipline problem. It now becomes impossible for the child to get out of being a problem. If he tries to do something creative he will be getting out of line and thereby "confirm" that he is a discipline problem. If he stays in line he will be a scholastic problem, thereby "confirming" that he did not have potential for anything but mischief. The result is a kind of stunted person typical of schools in large urban areas, where it is common for a child to enter the public schools half a year behind according to standard tests. Such a child has undoubtedly been a discipline problem during this time and the teacher has spent her effort trying to solve the discipline problem and keep him from getting out of line—that is, from learning anything.[5]

This last variation of the psychological rebuff brings us to the fourth general category of violence, institutionalized quiet violence. The schools are an institution, and teachers are hired not so much to act on their own in the classroom as to fulfill a predetermined role. Violence done by the teacher in the classroom may therefore not be personal but institutional, done while acting as a faithful agent of the educational system. The idea of such institutional violence is a very important one.

A clearer example of quiet institutional violence might be a well established system of slavery or colonial oppression, or the life of contemporary American ghettos. Once established such a system may require relatively little overt violence to maintain it. It is legendary that Southerners used to boast, "We understand our nigras. They are happy here and wouldn't want any other kind of life,"—and there is no reason to doubt that many a Southerner, raised in the system and sheltered from the recurrent lynchings, believed it quite sincerely. In that sort of situation it

[5] Among the many works commenting on this aspect of public education, I have found those of Edgar Friedenberg and Paul Goodman most instructive. See Paul Goodman, *Compulsory Miseducation,* New York, Horizon, 1964; Edgar Z. Friedenberg, *The Vanishing Adolescent,* Boston, Beacon Press, 1959, and *Coming of Age in America,* New York, Knopf, 1963.

is possible for an institution to go along placidly, as we might say, with no overt disturbances and yet for that institution to be one that is terribly brutal and that does great harm to its victims and which, incidentally, at the same time brutalizes people who are on top, since they lose a certain measure of their human sensitivity.

There is more violence in the black ghettos than there is anywhere else in America—even when they are quiet. At the time of the Harlem riots in 1964 the Negro psychologist, Kenneth Clark, said that there was more ordinary, day-to-day violence in the life of the ghettos than there was in any day of those disturbances. I'm not sure exactly what he meant. The urban ghettos are places where there is a great deal of overt violence, much of it a kind of reaction to the frustrations of ghetto life. Fanon describes the similar phenomenon of the growth of violence within the oppressed community in the colonial situation in Algeria.[6] When people are suppressed by a colonial regime, when they lack the opportunities which they see other people, white people, around them enjoying, then they become frustrated and have great propensities to violence. The safest target for such angry, frustrated people are their own kind. The Algerians did their first violence to other Algerians, in part because it wasn't safe to do it to a Frenchman. And the same is largely true of the situation that has developed in our urban ghettos. It isn't safe for a person living in the ghettos, if he is feeling frustrated and at the point of explosion, to explode against somebody outside the ghetto; but he can do it to his kids, his wife, his brother and his neighbor, and society will tend to look the other way. So there is a good deal of overt violence in the black ghettos. Perhaps, that is what Clark meant.

But we also have to recognize that there is sometimes a kind of quiet violence in the very operation of the system. Bernard Lafayette, who has worked in urban areas for both the American Friends Service Committee and the Southern Christian Leadership Conference, speaks angrily of the violence of the status quo: "The real issue is that part of the 'good order of society' is the routine oppression and racism committed against millions of Americans every day. That is where the real violence is."[7] The fact that there is a black ghetto in most American cities which operates very like any system of slavery. Relatively little violence is needed to keep the institution going and yet the institution entails a real violation of the human beings involved, because they are systematically denied the options which are obviously open to the vast majority of the members of the society in which they live. A systematic denial of options is one way to deprive men of autonomy. If I systematically deprive a person of the options that are normal in our society, then he is no longer in a position to decide for himself what to do. Any institution which systematically robs certain people of rightful options generally available to others does violence to those people.

Perhaps denying options would not do violence to people if each individual person was an island unto himself and individuality were the full truth about human life. But it is not. We are social beings. Our whole sense of what we are is dependent on the fact that we live in society and have open to us socially determined options. I am now writing. As I write I make many choices about what to say, some having to do with whole paragraphs, some with single words, and some with punctuation. These choices are dependent upon a social institution, language. Unless I knew the

[6] Frantz Fanon. *The Wretched of the Earth*, New York, Grove Press, 1966.
[7] In *Soul Force*, February 15, 1968.

language, and unless there were a society of language speakers, I would have no options at all about what to say. The options opened to us by language are very important, but language is only one part of our society. There are many sorts of options which are open to us and important to us as individuals. It is how we act, how we choose with respect to socially defined options, that constitutes what we really are as human beings.

What we choose to do with respect to our socially defined options is much more important than which language or which system of property rights we inherit at birth—provided we have access to the options defined in the system. By suppressing options you deprive a person of the opportunity to be somebody because you deprive him of choices. The institutional form of quiet violence operates when people are deprived of choices in a systematic way by the very manner in which transactions normally take place, without any individual act being violent in itself or any individual decision being responsible for the system.

These, then, are the main types of violence that I see. By recognizing those types of violence we begin to get the whole question of violence into a much richer perspective than when we hear the Chief of Police deplore violence. Such a richer perspective is vitally necessary, because we cannot do anything about the violence in our society unless we can see it, and most of us do not see it very well. Conceptions and perceptions are closely dependent on one another, and perhaps having a better idea of what violence is will enable us to recognize more readily the many sorts of violence that surround our lives.

IV

In concluding I would like to call attention to two aspects of violence. The first is that the concept of violence is a moral concept, but not one of absolute condemnation. Very often psychologists and sociologists and other scientists and students of animal behavior avoid the word "violence" just become it does have a moral connotation. The word "aggression" is sometimes used instead in some of the literature in psychology, and it is prominent in the title of Konrad Lorenz's recent book on animal behavior and aggression.[8] They choose this word "aggression" because it lacks the moral connotations of the term "violence." I think it is important to recognize that the concept of violence is a moral concept, and that the moral elements come in through the fact that an act of violence is a violation of a person. I think that it is also important to recognize that the normal pattern of moral discourse allows for excuses and rationalization. We don't expect people never to do anything which is at all wrong: we allow for excuses.[9] Sartre's very hard line, that excuses undermine the dignity and moral strength of the person being excused, has not really won the day in law courts or in the general moral view; or perhaps what Sartre meant is that we should never allow ourselves excuses rather than that we should never allow them to others. When a person commits an act of

[8] A classic study in psychology is John Dollard *et al. Frustration and Aggression*, New Haven, Yale, 1939. See also A. Buss, *The Psychology of Aggression*, New York, Wiley, 1961; K. Lorenz, *On Aggression*, New York, Harcourt Brace, 1966.

[9] The late Prof. John L. Austin called the attention of moral philosophers to the importance of excuses in moral discourse. See "A Plea for Excuses," *Philosophical Papers,* London, Oxford University Press, 1961.

violence he is not necessarily to be condemned, though he does have some explaining to do. The fact that we would require an excuse from him, or some justification of his behavior, indicates that a person's doing an act of violence puts the burden of proof on him; but it doesn't suffice to show that the case has gone against him yet.

The second thing I want to say is that it is entirely clear to me that there are degrees of violence. All these various forms of violence are indeed violence, but if I simply say of an act or an institution that it is violent I have not yet said enough to give a clear evaluation of that act. I must also take account of how *much* violence it does to persons affected. Unfortunately this is easier said than done. It might at first be thought that overt violence is always worse than quiet violence, but that rule does not hold generally except in the case of murder; in fact, physical injury often heals more readily than psychological damage. It is more plausible to argue that institutional violence is always of greater harm than personal violence, but that obviously depends on the degree of violence on each side—which means that we must be able to judge the degree of violence in an act or an institution independent of the kind of violence involved. What we need is a scale for measuring degrees of violence, and we don't have one. Still there are degrees of violence, and it is possible to achieve considerable intersubjective agreement about comparisons of pairs of cases.

The Justification of Violence

Robert Audi

Robert Audi (1941–   ) teaches philosophy at the University of Texas. He was a Woodrow Wilson fellow and received an award for his article on violence from the Council for Philosophical Studies.

Violence is the physical attack upon, or the vigorous physical abuse of, or vigorous physical struggle against, a person or animal; or the highly vigorous psychological abuse of, or the sharp, caustic psychological attack upon, a person or animal; or the highly vigorous, or incendiary, or malicious and vigorous, destruction or damaging of property or potential property.

.   .   .

In discussing the justification of violence I shall be primarily concerned with the sorts of considerations relevant to deciding whether its use is morally justified. After outlining what some of these considerations are, I shall go on in the next section to show some of their implications for various important views, most of them well known, about the conditions under which violence is morally justified.

Source: "On the Meaning and Justification of Violence," in Jerome Shaffer (ed.), *Violence* (New York: David McKay Company, Inc., 1971). Copyright 1971 by Robert Audi. Reprinted by permission of the publishers.

The moral position I shall propose will be quite general. This should not be surprising: if I have been correct about how many ways there are in which people can do violence, then we should not ask about the justification of violence in the abstract; we must consider what kind of violence is in question, and this forces us to examine a very wide range of actions and activities. I shall be primarily concerned, however, with violence contemplated as a strategy for achieving social reform, particularly where the reform envisaged is regarded as the rectification of grave moral wrongs, and even where revolution is considered necessary to achieve this reform. At the present time, violence of this sort is perhaps more controversial than any other sort, though the question of the conditions, if any, under which one nation is justified in making war on another is also important and difficult. The position I shall take on the justification of violence will, I hope, provide a way of dealing with this latter question; but I shall not have space to address it explicitly. The question of the justification of violence in purely personal affairs is also an important one; but I shall only outline how my position would lead us to deal with the question.

In discussing the justification of violence as a strategy for achieving social reform, we must first recognize considerations of justice: as virtually everyone would grant, to say that a strategy, policy, or course of action would be unjust is to produce a moral consideration against it, one which is normally—and perhaps always—morally conclusive. It is equally clear that to say that something would be just is to produce a moral consideration in favor of it. . . .

In addition to considerations of justice we must also recognize, in discussing the justification of violence as a strategy for achieving social reform considerations of freedom: whether the use of violence would enhance or diminish human freedom. . . .

The third consideration relevant to the justification of violence as a strategy for achieving social reform, is what we may roughly call welfare: that some action or program of action increases human happiness, and especially that it reduces human suffering, is a consideration which is nearly always relevant to any moral assessment of it. . . .

.   .   .

. . . It is worth making at least a very rough distinction between personal and social violence: personal violence has nonpolitical motives and is perpetrated by a single person or small group of persons against another person or small group; social violence is violence by a group of people, almost always directed against the state or against another group of people, and usually perpetrated for political reasons. A person's shooting an acquaintance would usually be a paradigm of personal violence; a large riot resulting in extensive personal injury would be a paradigm of social violence. It seems somewhat unnatural to speak of violence done by one army to another as social violence, and it is probably better to call this simply military violence, though it is certainly social as opposed to personal. We also need to distinguish between violence to persons and violence to property or other inanimate things; and it is important to distinguish homicidal from nonhomicidal violence; and morally injurious violence—violence which violates someone's rights—from morally excusable violence, that is, violence which does not violate anyone's rights, as in the case of most violent athletic contests. Perhaps we should also distinguish hand-to-hand violence, as in the case of a fist fight, from violence "at a distance"—such as sniping, shelling, and bombing. There also seems to be an important difference between defensive and offensive violence, the former being violence undertaken on a reasonable belief that using it is necessary to protect one's moral rights, the latter being violence undertaken in order to subjugate someone or otherwise violate his moral rights. But this is a very difficult distinction to draw, nor do defensive and offensive violence seem to exhaust the possibilities of violence, since spontaneous violence might well be of neither kind.

What seems of greatest philosophical interest at present among the kinds of violence just mentioned is social violence, both to people and to property, homicidal and nonhomicidal, defensive and offensive, and whether hand-to-hand or done at a distance. In particular, I am concerned with the justifiability of such forms of violence in civil disobedience, in resistance, in revolution, and in attempts to achieve social progress that cannot be placed in any of these three categories. In discussing each case I shall appeal primarily to the three moral principles outlined above, and I shall proceed from arguing the inadequacy of various mistaken views about the justifiability of violence to some constructive suggestions about its use in civil disobedience, resistance, revolution, and social reform. Although the discussion will be focused on violence, what I have to say will have important application to questions concerning the justification of force as a strategy for achieving social reform and to various other moral questions concerning policies of social action.

This is not meant to suggest that the principles proposed have no application to the justification of personal violence; as moral principles of the most general sort, at least one of them should have an indirect bearing on any moral issue. But in a great many cases, particularly in deciding what moral obligations one individual has to another individual of his acquaintance, their bearing is very often only indirect: they may be appealed to in justifying the subsidiary moral principals which "govern" much of our conduct toward other individuals; but a great many of our typical obligations toward other individuals, for example, to do what we have promised to do, have their immediate basis in these more specific principles. To apply this to a case of personal violence, imagine a man who is contemplating beating his wife. My position does not imply that in deciding whether it would be right to do this he is free to appeal directly to the three general principles; as the wording of the principles suggests, they are intended to apply primarily to policies, strategies, practices, and other general prescriptions of conduct. Their rigorous application to the kind of case imagined would, I think, support the principle that (possibly with a few very special exceptions) we ought not to beat people. I would also hold, though I cannot argue for it here, that my principles would support both some form of the ordinary moral principles requiring truth-telling and promise-keeping, and the ordinary moral conviction that people in certain special relations to others, such as parents and children, acquire special obligations. None of this implies that it is never morally right to call ordinary moral principles into question; the point is simply that in deciding what is morally obligatory or permissible in our relations with other individuals, we cannot bypass moral principles ordinarily relevant to the kind of situation in question, though where two such principles conflict, we may in most cases appeal to one or more of the three general principles.

Let us take first the extreme view that no one is ever justified in using violence. The natural thing to say here is that if violence is necessary to stop a Hitler from carrying out his planned atrocities, then it should be used. Most people would find it hard to deny this, but advocates of nonviolence might well argue that in fact it is never necessary to use violence, even to stop a man like Hitler, particularly if nonviolent protests are used at the first signs of evil. Although I find this claim highly implausible, neither a philosopher nor anyone else can assess it, as applied to an actual case, without a thorough analysis of the facts regarding various societies. But what chiefly needs to be said here is that it is certainly conceivable that a man like Hitler might be stopped only through violence; and insofar as there is good reason to think that only violence can stop him, the use of at least some violence, especially nonhomicidal violence aimed at bringing about a coup or forcing the needed change in social policy, might obviously be justified by the moral principles to which I am appealing.

Another extreme position would be that violence is always justified if it is the most efficient means of throwing off oppression or rectifying some other form of injustice. This position seems almost as implausible as the first: clearly injustice and suffering created by the violence might substantially outweigh the burden of using a less efficient means of reform. Suppose that nonviolent protest could bring down an oppressive but unstable regime in a somewhat longer time than would be required by the use of violence. If it were evident that the violence would probably involve suffering and deaths, the nonviolent protest would almost certainly be preferable. Here it is important to mention something which seems both obvious and important, but which is much too rarely taken into account in discussions of violence and revolution: that there is simply no way to compare with any precision the moral "cost" of taking a man's life, especially an innocent man's life, with the moral value of reducing suffering or eliminating oppression or some other form of injustice. No doubt there is a level of atrocity at which almost anyone would say—and could justifiably say—that there is so much oppression, injustice, or suffering that if, in order to improve the situation substantially, we have to do something that might well take an innocent man's life we ought still to do it. To be sure, if it is a certainty that some innocent person must die, particularly if his identity is known, the situation becomes even more problematic and violence would be much more difficult—perhaps impossible—to justify. It seems clear that in deciding whether to use violence that might result in death, especially the death of someone not guilty of whatever wrong must justify the use of violence in the first place, we have to make every possible effort to find a nondeadly alternative; and we should be extremely careful not to exaggerate the moral outrage that requires rectification, particularly if we regard ourselves as the victims. But there is no simple way, perhaps no way at all, to answer the question how to weigh the taking of lives, especially of people innocent or largely innocent of the moral wrongs we want to rectify, against the moral gains we might make through their rectification. The principles of justice, maximization of freedom, and maximization of welfare suggest why this should be so; for how can we say how much injustice we do to a man in taking his life, or how much freedom or happiness we deprive him of? Given that the preservation of human life is of very great moral value on almost any moral outlook, and certainly on the principles proposed above, this is surely one of the most powerful arguments that can be brought against most of the typical uses of violence.

Two other views that deserve mention are (a) that violence of the sort we are concerned with—social violence done out of a genuinely moral desire to achieve social change—cannot be justified unless all channels of nonviolent protest have been exhausted, and (b) that violence is never justified in a democratic society.

Regarding (a), it is not clear that there usually *is* any definite number of channels of nonviolent protest, or what it takes to exhaust a channel of protest. Yet even assuming that there were a definite number and that we could exhaust them, this might take so long and allow so much moral wrong in the meantime that some degree of nonhomicidal violence, and especially violence to property, would be warranted if it could be reasonably argued to be necessary to rectifying the moral wrongs in question. If nonviolent means of eliminating oppressive curfews and arbitrary travel restrictions, or of providing a minority group with the rights of citizens, would take many years, whereas damaging a few nonresidential buildings could achieve the needed changes in a few months or a year, the latter course could perhaps be justified by the principles of justice, maximization of freedom, and maximization of welfare. This point depends, of course, not only on the view that violence is not "by definition" unjustifiable, but also on the view that certain kinds of damage to property constitute violence; yet I believe I have argued adequately for these views in defending my analysis of the concept of violence. I would not claim, however, that a situation of the sort envisaged here is probable; more important, I am certainly not denying that there is a strong prima facie obligation to try a reasonable amount of nonviolent protest before using violence, nor would I claim that we can usually be at all sure that social violence can be prevented from becoming homicidal. But even the minimal claims I have made suggest that we cannot reasonably hold that violence is never justified unless all channels of nonviolent protest have been exhausted.

Regarding (b), the thesis that social violence of the sort that concerns us is never justified in a democratic society, I would first want to say that much depends on what we mean by "democratic." If it means something like "such that political power lies in the hands of the people," then the thesis is surely false. For the majority of people in a society could be, and indeed at times have been, deceived into accepting or voting for measures whose injustice might in some cases be eradicable only by violent, though not necessarily homicidal, protest. If, on the other hand, "democratic" is used, as it often is nowadays, in such a way that a society is not considered democratic unless certain moral rights are guaranteed and the government has a certain minimum concern for the welfare of the citizens, then there is no clear answer to the question whether violence is ever justified in a democratic society. For it is not clear that the term "democratic," used this way, would ever apply to a society in which the three principles I am appealing to are seriously violated. In any case, the general position I want now to propose should enable us to deal with the issues concerning the justification of violence regardless of the kind of political system with respect to which they arise.

What I propose is that in deciding whether violence would be justified in a given case in which it is being considered as a means of correcting certain grave moral wrongs, we should ascertain its probable consequences for justice, freedom, and human welfare, and compare these with the probable consequences of the most promising nonviolent alternative(s) we can think of on careful reflection, choosing the course of action which satisfies, or comes closest to satisfying, the requirements of the principles of justice, maximization of freedom, and maximization of welfare. The restriction to cases in which violence is being considered as a means of correcting certain grave moral wrongs is important: these would have to be cases in which a serious attempt has been made, or at least considered, to solve the problem through legal or other nonviolent procedures; and they would usually be cases of serious injustice, such as deprivations of freedom, though certain other serious moral wrongs—such as a government's neglecting the welfare of its people—might sometimes justify the consideration of some forms of violence. It would certainly not do to say that, regardless of the moral grievance and regardless of whether nonviolent means have been tried, it is morally legitimate to consider using violence; and while I believe this sort of restriction would follow from the principles I am using, it seems best to include it at the outset in the interest of explicitness and brevity.

It is important to reemphasize my position that considerations of justice and freedom have priority over considerations of welfare. In comparing violent and nonviolent strategies of reform, our first concern should be to determine what would establish, or come closest to establishing, justice and the maximum freedom possible within the limits of justice. Secondarily, we should consider the consequences for welfare of adopting a violent as opposed to a nonviolent strategy; but these considerations could be decisive only where the more fundamental considerations weighed equally in favor of some violent and some nonviolent strategy, or perhaps, with the qualifications suggested earlier, where a huge gain in welfare is balanced against a minor injustice. Suppose that a group of young men who have vigorously protested the Vietnam War have very good evidence that records of their public protests are being kept by their draft boards and will be used unfairly against them, say in drafting them as a punitive measure. They might face the alternatives of violently breaking into the office and burning all its records or, on the other hand, taking the case to the courts. My point here would be that the most important consideration should be what is required by the principles of justice and freedom; and as I see it they would here require, assuming there is legal recourse for the grievance, that efforts be made to take the case to the courts: for the men to violate laws which the great majority of others respect and obey, often with considerable sacrifice, would be a prima facie violation of the requirement that benefits and burdens be distributed equally, and hence a prima facie injustice; and breaking into the office would be, prima facie, an unjustified violation of others' rights and an interference with their freedom to carry out their regular jobs. Even if it could be shown that all concerned would be happier if the men simply broke into the office and burned the records, this would not be a substantial consideration in favor of the violent alternative, and it is worth pointing out that the publicity which injustice receives from court proceedings is often an important step toward reform, even if the case is initially lost and sometimes when it is lost in the highest courts.

Let us now complicate the example by supposing that the men go to the very highest court and lose. What now should they do? Much depends on whether they lost the principle that punitive use of the draft is unjust or simply failed to win the point that their draft board was planning it. Suppose they lose the latter point. What then? For one thing, this may indicate some weakness in their evidence against their draft board; secondly, in many societies, nonviolent resistance would in this case be both the morally courageous course of action and most likely to arouse the conscience of people who might help. If, on the other hand, we suppose that the men's evidence against their draft board is of the sort a reasonable man would consider conclusive, but that they lost because their witnesses were afraid to testify, then the case becomes even more problematic. One consideration not yet mentioned would be the kind and degree of immorality of the war for which they were to be drafted; another would be what they might be able to do by some new nonviolent attempt to expose those who have perpetrated the injustice against them and their witnesses. There are other considerations, and I cannot now go into sufficient detail to try to settle the question, though perhaps enough has been said to suggest that the kind of limited violence envisaged here is not obviously impossible to justify under any circumstances whatever, even if it does appear that in a country like America today nonviolent protest would be morally preferable. The case would have been equally complicated had we supposed that, in the highest court of the land, the men had lost the principle that punitive use of the draft, especially against political dissenters, is unjust. Here we would have an even larger issue which might well warrant the consideration, though not necessarily the adoption, of revolution.

There are, of course, a number of difficulties confronting the view I propose regarding the justification of violence. I have already mentioned the impossibility of weighing with any precision the moral cost of taking a human life, especially an innocent life, against moral gains in justice, freedom, and welfare. But this is likely to be a serious problem for any plausible position on the justification of violence, and we can at least say that there is one kind of case in which some weighing might be possible: when the risks to human life of undertaking violence can be compared with the risks to it of abstaining from violence. Thus, if violence that would probably cost about a hundred lives could be shown necessary to save thousands, it would presumably be justified if it did not have certain other morally undesirable consequences such as the brutalization of a large number of people.

Secondly, there are profound difficulties in measuring justice or injustice, freedom or its curtailment, and happiness or suffering. It would be wrong to conclude, however, that there are not even rough standards which are in practice very useful. While the notions of equality and of a justified exception to the principle that men should be treated equally are vague, it is nonetheless clear that denying various civil liberties on grounds of color is not a justified inequality, whereas denying voting privileges to children is; and a great many injustices, particularly those serious enough to warrant the consideration of violence, are equally obvious. Moreover, even if we grant that there is an area of reasonable disagreement concerning a large number of freedoms, there is wide agreement on such fundamental freedoms as freedom of speech, freedom of worship, and freedom of personal movement; and these are the sorts of freedoms whose curtailment would be appealed to in most cases in which considerations of freedom might warrant the use of violence.

Finally, it is clear that there are rough indices of suffering and happiness which make possible at least judgments about the suffering or happiness of one person or group as compared to that of another or to their own suffering or happiness at different times: we can consider disease as opposed to physical well-being; psychological well-being (insofar as this can be measured without indulging any moral prejudice); poverty as opposed to comfortable income; observations and subjective reports of pain, tension, and malaise, as opposed to observations and subjective reports of zest, comfort, and satisfaction; and proportion of things done or submitted to that are wanted as opposed to unwanted.

Let me now comment briefly on the implications of my position for the use of violence in civil disobedience, resistance, revolution, and social reform. To begin with civil disobedience, one may reasonably question whether there is any kind of violence with which it is logically compatible. Certainly in the clear cases of civil disobedience the protest is both nonviolent and orderly; and if we think of civil disobedience as undertaken in protest against some particular law(s), but out of respect for law as an institution, one may well question whether violence could be a part of it. Suppose, however, that a group of students decided to block the pathway of some unarmed fellow students engaging in military drill and soon to go to war; and suppose the protesters were unarmed and planned not to use violence. If violence broke out but remained on the level of mild fisticuffs, with the protesters fighting only defensively, and if the protesters were willing to accept punishment if the courts demanded it, would we have to say that they had not succeeded in practicing civil disobedience? The answer to this question does not seem to be simply that they did not succeed, though it perhaps would be if, even without having planned to use violence, the protesters did initiate it. Civil disobedience requires that those practicing it be making a reasoned attempt to appeal to the conscience of others; they must not be attempting to impose their will on others through the use of force, which they would certainly be doing if violence were a calculated part of civil disobedience. On the other hand, if violence "spontaneously" breaks out, particularly where the protesters fight only defensively, it is entirely possible that we could speak of their having succeeded in committing civil disobedience. Perhaps we could say that in certain cases civil disobedience may be accompanied by violence, even on the part of those committing the disobedience, but the violence must not have been calculated; nor can a protest count as civil disobedience if the protesters respond to violence with substantially greater violence than is required for self-defense. If violence has any place in civil disobedience, then, it seems to be a very minor and restricted one.

The case with resistance is different, and what chiefly needs to be said here is that there is no moral justification for the use of large-scale social violence except where injustice or some other form of moral wrong is very serious and where nonviolent means of rectification have been carefully considered and, if possible, attempted. It seems reasonable to maintain that justice, maximization of freedom, and maximization of welfare should be the guiding principles; and they should be applied in the light of questions like the following: What are the chances of death and in how many cases? How many are likely to suffer violence, and what sort of violence would it be—bodily violence or violence to property? To what extent are those who use violence likely to be brutalized by it or come to use it indiscriminately, either at the time in question or at a later time? How much violence is likely to be evoked as a *response* to the violence being considered? Of those who may suffer violence, how many are guilty of creating or perpetuating the moral wrongs which might justify the violence, and how many are innocent or largely innocent in this respect? How effective will the contemplated violence be in rectifying the wrongs it is meant to reduce or remove? Is the immorality which might warrant violence getting worse or better, and what is the likelihood of dealing with it nonviolently in a reasonable length of time? Is violence to be definitely planned, or is it simply to be approved should certain circumstances arise?

Questions like these seem to be equally relevant to the justifiability of attempting a revolution. But since revolution almost necessarily requires very extensive violence, even greater care must be taken in attempting to justify it. The questions I suggest we ask in considering whether to use violence are very difficult; and it is not surprising that many of them have not been faced, much less answered, by advocates of violence. Yet it is only through rigorously pursuing these and similar questions that we can weigh the consequences for justice, freedom, and welfare, of using a violent as opposed to a nonviolent method of moral rectification, and decide whether the best course of action would be nonviolent protest within the law, civil disobedience, resistance, or revolution, which is likely to require widespread and deadly violence.

Regarding the use of violence to achieve social reforms that do not qualify as the correction of injustice—such as certain improvements in state services or in the material well-being of large groups of people—it seems reasonable to say that particularly where material well-being is already at a level representing a secure and not uncomfortable life, any appreciable violence to persons could not be justified. For even assuming that there is no legal or other nonviolent way of achieving the goal, violence would probably require injustice to someone, and I am supposing that the gains in happiness that might result would not outweigh the injustice done. Suppose that a highway, which was a mere convenience to a large number of people, would have to go through a place where some American Indians who had been living there for generations were determined to stay unless bodily ejected. If we assume that neither they nor the larger community has a clear right in the dispute, probably the state would not be justified in using violence (or even force) to remove them, even if the convenience to the community could be reasonably claimed to outweigh substantially the inconvenience to them. Of course, if the disparity between what the community stands to gain and what a few stand to lose in being forced, violently if necessary, to comply with the community's wishes, becomes very great, the issue becomes more complex and we may begin to ask how much convenience a small group has a *right* to deny to a much larger group, especially to the community as a whole. In this case the minority's insistence on what it wants could be unjust, since it could be an interference with the community's freedom to do what it has a right to do; but it still seems clear that, with perhaps very few exceptions, if gains in happiness which do not represent what anyone has a right to should require violence to persons, the violence should not be used. For surely it is reasonable to give considerations of justice very high priority over considerations of welfare, as I have already suggested in discussing possible conflicts among the three moral principles proposed; and doing violence to someone, at least violence of the sort relevant here, unless it can be shown to be required to rectify some serious injustice, is certainly doing him an injustice.

The Justification of Nonviolence
Adin Ballou

Adin Ballou (1803-1890) was closely associated with William Lloyd Garrison; they were both founding spirits of the New England Non-Resistance Society in 1838. He wrote *Christian Non-Resistance* in 1846.

THE TERM NON-RESISTANCE

The term non-resistance itself . . . demands attention. It requires very considerable qualifications. I use it as applicable *only* to the conduct of human beings towards human beings—not towards the inferior animals, inanimate things, or satanic influences. If an opponent, willing to make me appear ridiculous, should say—"You are a non-resistant, and therefore must be *passive* to all assailing beings, things and influences, to satan, man, beast, bird, serpent, insect, rocks, timbers, fires, floods, heat, cold and storm"—I should answer, *not so;* my non-resistance relates solely to conduct between human beings. This is an important limitation of the term. But I go further, and disclaim using the term to express *absolute passivity,* even towards *human* beings. I claim the right to offer the utmost *moral* resistance, not sinful, of which God has made me capable, to every manifestation of evil among mankind. Nay, I hold it my *duty* to offer such moral resistance. In this sense my very non-resistance becomes the highest kind of *resistance* to evil. This is another important qualification of the term. But I do not stop here. There is an uninjurious, benevolent *physical* force. There are cases in which it would not only be allowable, but in the highest degree commendable, to *restrain* human beings by this kind of force. Thus, maniacs, the insane, the delirious sick, ill natured children, the intellectually or *morally* non-compos mentis, the intoxicated and the violently passionate, are frequently disposed to perpetrate outrages and inflict injuries, either on themselves or others, which ought to be kindly and uninjuriously prevented by the muscular energy of their friends. And in cases where deadly violence is inflicted with deliberation and malice aforethought, one may nobly throw his body as a temporary barrier between the destroyer and his helpless victim, choosing to die in that position, rather than be a passive spectator. Thus another most important qualification is given to the term non-resistance. It is not non-resistance to animals and inanimate things, nor to satan, but only to human beings. Nor is it *moral* non-resistance to human beings, but chiefly physical. Nor is it physical non-resistance to all human beings, under all circumstances, but only so far as to abstain totally from the infliction of personal injury, as a means of resistance. It is simply non-resistance of injury with injury—evil with evil.

Will the opposer exclaim—"This is no non-resistance at all; the term is mischosen!" I answer. So said the old opposers of the Temperance Reformation, respecting the term "*total abstinence.*" They began by insisting that the term *must* be taken unqualifiedly, and pronounced total abstinence an *absurdity*. It was

Source: *Christian Non-Resistance* (1846).

replied—"we limit its application to the use of ardent spirits and intoxicating liquors." "Then you exclude these substances from the arts and from external applications, do you?" rejoined the opposers. "No," replied the advocates of the cause, "we mean *total abstinence* from the *internal* use—the *drinking* of those liquors." "But are they not sometimes necessary for medical purposes?" said the opposers, "and *then* may they not be taken internally?" "Certainly, with proper precautions," was the reply; "we mean by *total abstinence,* precisely *this* and no more, the entire disuse of all ardent spirits and intoxicating liquors, *as a beverage.*" "That," exclaimed the objectors (despairing of a reductio ad absurdum), "is *no total* abstinence *at all;* the term is mischosen!" Nevertheless, it was a most significant term. It had in it an almost talismanic power. It expressed better than any other just what was meant, and wrought a prodigious change in public opinion and practice. The term *non-resistance* is equally significant and talismanic. It signifies total abstinence from all resistance of injury with injury. It is thus far *non-resistance*—no farther.

The almost universal opinion and practice of mankind has been on the side of resistance of injury *with* injury. It has been held justifiable and *necessary,* for individuals and nations to inflict any amount of *injury* which would effectually resist a supposed greater injury. The consequence has been universal suspicion, defiance, armament, violence, torture and bloodshed. The earth has been rendered a vast slaughterfield—a theatre of reciprocal cruelty and vengeance—strewn with human skulls, reeking with human blood, resounding with human groans, and steeped with human tears. Men have become drunk with mutual revenge; and they who could inflict the greatest amount of injury, in pretended defence of life, honor, rights, property, institutions and laws, have been idolized as the heroes and rightful sovereigns of the world. Non-resistance explodes this horrible delusion; announces the impossibility of overcoming evil with evil; and, making its appeal directly to all the *injured* of the human race, enjoins on them, in the name of God, never more to *resist injury with injury;* assuring them that by adhering to the law of love under all provocations, and scrupulously suffering wrong, rather than inflicting it, they shall gloriously "overcome evil with good," and exterminate all their enemies by turning them into faithful friends. . . .

THE TERM INJURY

. . . I use this term in a somewhat peculiar sense, to signify any moral influence or physical force exerted by one human being upon another, the legitimate *effect* of which is to destroy or impair *life,* to destroy or impair the *physical faculties,* to destroy or impair the *intellectual powers,* to destroy, impair or pervert the *moral and religious sentiment,* or to destroy or impair the *absolute welfare,* all things considered, of the person on whom such influence or force is exerted; whether that person be innocent or guilty, harmless or offensive, injurious or uninjurious, sane or insane, compos mentis or non-compos, adult or infant. Some of the lexicographers define an *"injury"* to be "hurt, harm or mischief, *unjustly* done to a person"; thereby implying that any hurt, harm or mischief done to one who *deserves* nothing better or can be considered as justly liable to it, *is no injury at all.* I reject entirely every such qualification of the term. I hold an *injury* to be an *injury,* whether *deserved* or *undeserved,* whether intended or unintended, whether well meant or ill meant, determining the fact in accordance with the foregoing definition. But, says the inquirer—"what if it can be proved justifiable, by the law of God, to inflict personal injury in certain cases on the offensive and guilty?" Then, of course, it will be proved that non-resistance is a false doctrine. "What if it can be proved that the infliction of small injuries may prevent much greater evils?" Then it will be proved that we may do evil that good may come, which will forever keep the world just where it is. "What if it can be shown that the person who inflicts an injury honestly intended it for a benefit?" That will only prove him *honestly mistaken*, and so undeserving of blame. "What if a man inflicts death or any other injury, according to established human laws, but does it without malice, or revenge, or any malevolent intent?" Then he does an *anti-christian* act, without conscience as to its real nature. The act must be condemned; he must be credited for his motives; due allowance must be made for his misapprehension of duty; and light poured into his mind to superinduce a better conscience, that he may be brought to act the Christian part. But in no case must we lose sight of the inquiry, whether an *injury* has been done. And in determining this, we must not ask whether the recipient were guilty or innocent, whether the thing done were well or ill intended, whether it were done in a right or a wrong spirit. If it be in fact an *injury*, it is contrary to the doctrine of Christian non-resistance; and no person knowing it to be such can repeat it under any pretext whatsoever, without violating the law of God. This is the sense and signification of the terms *injury, injurer, injurious, &c.*, as used in these pages. The objector may here interpose critical queries, with a view to test the soundness of my definition. He may suppose that a man's leg, hand, or eye, is so diseased as to require amputation, in order to save his life. But such member is one of his physical faculties, which must not be destroyed or impaired, because that would be an *injury*. I answer. The diseased member is already lost. The question is not whether the friendly surgeon shall destroy or impair it; but only whether he shall amputate it, in order to preserve the life and remaining faculties. No *injury*, but an absolute *benefit* is proposed. This case is clear. But suppose the minister of the *law* is ordered to amputate a sound leg, hand or eye, as a punishment, or for an example to deter others from the commission of crime. This is absolute *injury*, done under good pretexts indeed, but on that account none the less an *injury*. Again; a child dangerously sick requires some medical application, very disagreeable, yet indispensable to his recovery, which can only be applied by physical force. Or an insane adult is in the same circumstances. Or a person infected with hydrophobia and subject to terrible paroxysms of the disease, needs to be confined; and yet for want of judgement, even in his intervals, refuses to be. Or a man subject to violent impulses of propensity or passion, rendering him dangerous to all around him when excited, needs to be excluded from general society, or otherwise watched and restrained by keepers, in order to prevent serious mischief to others; and yet he resents and resists all entreaties to submit to such restriction. Or a wicked man is exceedingly alarmed, disturbed and offended by a truthful exposure of his iniquitous proceedings, or by the faithful remonstrances and rebukes of some good man. Now in all such cases the *will* must be crossed, the personal freedom abridged, and the feelings pained. Must it not be an *injury* to coerce, restrain, expose and reprove such persons, however necessary to their and the public good, and however kindly executed? Is it not generally more intolerable to be *crossed* in one's *will*, and wounded in one's *feelings*, than to be beaten, maimed and otherwise maltreated? Answer. It is not man's imaginations, thoughts, and feelings, that determine what *is*, or *is not injurious* to him. Love itself may "heap coals of fire on a man's head." Truth may torment his mind. The most benevolent restraint may be painful to his feelings. He may be made, for a while, quite unhappy by crossing his evil will. He may prefer to be smitten and mutilated, rather than be exposed in his secret iniquities, or endure the faithful reproof of the upright. Such persons often prefer an *injury* to a benefit. They are not, for the time being, in a state of mind to understand and choose what is best for them. Therefore their wills, feelings and opinions are not the indices of their own *good*—much less that of others. Is it *good* for a capricious obstinate child to be indulged in opposing a necessary medical application? Is it *good* for an insane or delirious sick adult to have his own *will*, even to the commission of murder and self-destruction? Is it *good* for a man to have unlimited freedom, when he will almost certainly make it a curse to himself and others, by gross involuntary outrage, or uncontrollable passion? Is it *good* for a wicked man, under specious hypocritical disguises, to perpetrate the most atrocious mischief, unexposed and unreproved? These things are not good for mankind. On the contrary, it is good for them to be crossed, restrained, coerced and reproved, by all uninjurious moral and physical forces, which benevolence prompts and wisdom dictates. To cross their wills, and pain their feelings, by such means, under such circumstances, is not an *injury*, but a substantial *good*, to them and all who are connected with them. It may be said—"these things cannot be done *uninjuriously*. It would be impracticable." Cannot unreasonable children be nursed, delirious adults controlled, dangerously distempered people prevented from doing themselves and others harm, outrageous non-compos persons restrained, hypocrites exposed, and sinners reproved without *inflicting injury* on them! Then can nothing good be done without doing evil. Imperfection is indeed incidental to all human judgement and conduct; and therefore it is probable that some mistakes and some accidental injuries might happen. But the reason and common sense of mankind, once fairly pledged to the true principle of action, would seldom fail to discharge all these duties to general satisfaction. Still it may be asked: "What is to be done if uninjurious force should prove inadequate? May life be sacrificed, limbs broken, the flesh mangled, or any other injuries allowed in extreme cases?" Never. The principle of *non-injury* must be held inviolable. It is worth worlds, and must be preserved at all hazards. What cannot be done uninjuriously must be left undone. But these extreme cases are mostly imaginary. The truth is, that what cannot be done uninjuriously can scarcely ever be done at all. Or if done, had better have been let alone. Experience in the case of the insane has already proved that incomparably more can be done by *uninjurious* forces, scrupulously and judiciously employed, than by any admixtures of the injurious element. Presuming that my definition and use of the terms *injure, injury, injurer, injurious*, &c., cannot be misunderstood, I pass on.

THE TERM CHRISTIAN NON-RESISTANCE

Whence originated the term *Christian non-resistance*? Non-resistance comes from the injunction, "resist not evil," Matt. 5: 39. The words "*resist not*," being changed from the form of a *verb* to that of a substantive, give us *non-resistance*. This term is considered more strikingly significant than any other, of the *principle* involved, and the *duty* enjoined in our Saviour's precept. Hence its adoption and established use.

It is denominated *Christian* non-resistance, to distinguish it, as the genuine primitive doctrine, from mere *philosophical, sentimental* and *necessitous* non-resistance. Literally, then, *Christian non-resistance* is the original non-resistance taught and exemplified by Jesus Christ; the bearings, limitations and applications of which are to be learned from the Scriptures of the New Testament. And what are those bearings, limitations and applications? I have already given an imperfect view of them in the previous definitions. But I will be more explicit. What I aim at is to carry the obligations of non-resistance just as far and no farther than Jesus Christ has. It is easy to go beyond, or to fall short of his limits. Ultra radicals go beyond him. Ultra conservatives fall short of him. Even those of both these classes, who profess to abide implicitly by his teachings, construe and interpret his language so as to favor their respective errors. The ultra radicals seize on strong figurative, hyperbolic, or *intensive* forms of expression, and make him *seem* to mean *much more* than he *could have intended.* The ultra conservatives ingeniously fritter away and nullify the very essence of his precepts, in such a manner as to make him *seem* to mean *much less* than he *must have intended.* There is, however, a general rule for such cases, which can scarcely fail to expose the errors of both classes, in respect to any given text. It is this: "Consider the context; consider parallel texts; consider examples; consider the known spirit of Christianity." Any construction or interpretation of the recorded language of Christ, or of his apostles, in which all *these concur,* is sound. Any other is probably erroneous.

THE KEY TEXT OF NON-RESISTANCE

Now let us examine Matt. 5: 39. "I say unto you, resist not evil," &c. This single text, from which, as has been stated, the term non-resistance took its rise, if justly construed, furnishes a complete key to the true bearings, limitations and applications of the doctrine under discussion. This is precisely one of those precepts which may be easily made to mean *much more,* or *much less,* than its author intended. It is in the *intensive,* condensed form of expression, and can be understood only by a due regard to its context. What did the divine teacher mean by the word *"evil,"* and what by the word *"resist"*? There are several kinds of *evil.* 1. Pain, loss, damage, suffered from causes involving no moral agency, or *natural evil.* 2. Sin in general, or *moral evil.* 3. Temptations to sin, or *spiritual evil;* and 4. Personal wrong, insult, outrage, injury—or *personal evil.* Which of these kinds of evil does the context show to have been in our Saviour's mind when he said, *"resist not evil"*? Was he speaking of fires, floods, famine, disease, serpents, wild beasts, or any other mere *natural evil agents?* No. Then of course he does not prohibit our resisting *such evil.* Was he speaking of sin in general? No. Then of course he does not prohibit our resisting *such evil* by suitable means. Was he speaking of temptations addressed to our propensities and passions, enticing us to commit sin? No. Then of course he does not prohibit our resisting the *devil,* withstanding the *evil* suggestions of our own carnal mind, and suppressing our *evil* lusts. Was he speaking of *personal evil,* injury personally inflicted by man on man? Yes. "Ye have heard that it hath been said, an eye for an eye, and a tooth for a tooth; but I say unto you that ye resist not evil," i.e. personal outrage, insult, affront—*injury.* The word *"evil"* necessarily means, in this connexion, *personal injury,* or evil inflicted by human beings on human beings.

But what did Jesus mean by the words *"resist not"*? There are various kinds of *resistance,* which may be offered to personal injury, when threatened or actually inflicted. There is *passive* resistance—a dead silence, a sullen inertia, a complete muscular helplessness—an utter refusal to speak or move. Does the context show that Jesus contemplated, pro or con, any such resistance in his prohibition? No. There is an active righteous moral resistance—a meek firm remonstrance, rebuke, reproof, protestation. Does the connexion show that Jesus prohibits this kind of resistance? No. There is an active, firm, compound, moral and physical resistance, *uninjurious* to the evil doer, and only calculated to restrain him from deadly violence or extreme outrage. Was Jesus contemplating such modes of resisting personal injury? Does the context show that he intended to prohibit all resistance of evil by such means? No. There is a determined resistance of *personal injury* by means of *injury inflicted;* as when a man deliberately takes life to save life, destroys an assailant's eye to save an eye, inflicts a violent blow to prevent a violent blow; or, as when, in retaliation, he takes life for life, eye for eye, tooth for tooth, hand for hand, &c.; or, as when, by means of governmental agencies, he causes an injurious person to be punished by the infliction of some injury equivalent to the one he has inflicted or attempted. It was of such resistance as this, that our Saviour was speaking. It is such resistance as this, that he prohibits. His obvious doctrine is: *Resist not personal injury with personal injury....*

WHAT A CHRISTIAN NON-RESISTANT CANNOT CONSISTENTLY DO

1. He cannot kill, maim, or otherwise *absolutely injure* any human being, in personal self-defence, or for the sake of his family, or any thing he holds dear.

2. He cannot participate in any lawless conspiracy, mob, riotous assembly, or disorderly combination of individuals, to cause or countenance the commission of any such absolute personal injury.

3. He cannot be a member of any voluntary association, however orderly, respectable or allowable by law and general consent, *which declaratively* holds as *fundamental truth,* or claims as an essential right, or distinctly inculcates as sound doctrine, or approves as commendable in practice, *war, capital* punishment, or any other absolute personal injury.

4. He cannot be an *officer* or *private,* chaplain or retainer, in the army, navy, or militia of any nation, state, or chieftain.

5. He cannot be an officer, elector, agent, legal prosecutor, passive constituent, or approver of any government, as a sworn or otherwise pledged supporter thereof, whose civil constitution and fundamental laws, require, authorize, or tolerate war, slavery, capital punishment, or the infliction of any absolute personal injury.

6. He cannot be a member of any chartered corporation, or body politic, whose articles of compact oblige or authorize its official functionaries to resort for compulsory aid, in the conducting of its affairs, to a government of constitutional violence.

7. Finally, he cannot do any act, either in person or by proxy; nor abet or encourage any act in others; nor demand, petition for, request, advise or approve the doing of any act, by an individual, association or government, *which* act would

inflict, *threaten* to inflict, or *necessarily* cause to *be* inflicted *any absolute personal injury*, as herein before defined.

Such are the necessary bearings, limitations and applications of the doctrine of Christian non-resistance. Let the reader be careful not to misunderstand the positions laid down. The platform of principle and action has been carefully founded, and its essential peculiarities plainly delineated. Let it not be said that the doctrine goes against all religion, government, social organization, constitution, laws, order, rules and regulations. It goes against none of these things, *per se*. It goes for them, in the highest and best sense. It goes only against *such* religion, government, social organization, constitution, laws, order, rules, regulations and restraints, as are unequivocally contrary to the law of Christ; as sanction taking "life for life, eye for eye, tooth for tooth"; as are based on the assumption, that it is *right* to resist *injury with injury, evil with evil.*

THE CONCLUSION

But the Son of the Highest, the great self-sacrificing Non-Resistant, is our prophet, priest and king. Though the maddened inhabitants of the earth have so long turned a deaf ear to his voice, he shall yet be heard. He declares that *good* is the only antagonist of *evil*, which can conquer the deadly foe. Therefore he enjoins on his disciples the duty of resisting *evil only* with *good*. This is the sub-principle of Christian non-resistance. "Evil can be overcome only with *good*." Faith, then, in the inherent superiority of *good* over *evil*, truth over error, right over wrong, love over hatred, is the immediate moral basis of our doctrine. Accordingly we transfer all the faith we have been taught to cherish in *injury*, to *beneficence, kindness*, and *uninjurious treatment*, as the only all-sufficient enginery of war against *evil doers*. No longer seeking or expecting to put down evil with evil, we lift up the cross for an ensign, and surmountng it with the glorious banner of love, exult in the divine motto displayed on its immaculate folds. "RESIST NOT INJURY WITH INJURY." Let this in all future time be the specific rule of our conduct, the magnetic needle of our pathway across the troubled waters of human reform, till all men, all governments and all social institutions shall have been moulded into moral harmony with the grand comprehensive commandment of the living God "THOU SHALT LOVE THY NEIGHBOR AS THYSELF." Then shall *Love* (God by his sublimest name) "be all in all."

> The earth, so long a slaughter-field,
> Shall yet an Eden bloom;
> The tiger to the lamb shall yield,
> And War descend the tomb:
> For all shall feel the Saviour's love,
> Reflected from the cross—
> That love, that non-resistant love,
> Which triumphed on the cross.

Suggested Readings

1. Arendt, Hannah, "Violence," *The New York Review of Books,* February 27, 1969, p. 19.
2. Brown, Richard Maxwell, "The American Vigilante Tradition," in H. Graham and T. Gurr (eds.), *Violence in America* (New York: Bantam Books, 1969), pp. 144-219.
3. Fanon, Frantz, *The Wretched of the Earth* (New York: Grove Press, 1968), esp. Ch. 2.
4. Shaffer, Jerome (ed.), *Violence* (New York: McKay, 1971).
5. Smith, Bruce R., "The Politics of Protest: How Effective Is Violence?" in *Urban Riots: Violence and Social Change, Proceedings of the Academy of Political Science,* Vol. 29, No. 1 (July 1968), pp. 111-128.

REVOLUTION

Revolutions are not produced by the forces of the market economy alone; they require the belief in human power and in the possibility of vast material improvement, but they require also anger and the prospects of success.
—Eugene Kamenka

Common parlance suggests that the term "revolution" is applicable to almost any aspect of human culture. We speak of moral revolutions and of educational, scientific, industrial, religious, economic, youth, and political revolutions. Insofar as the term "revolution" has a single sense in all these applications, it conveys the idea of a sharp, extensive, fundamental change in the cultural area being described. In this section, the essays deal only with political revolution.

As we said in the introduction to this chapter, political revolution is an event that shifts the power relations in some social unit. However, this change, sharp, extensive, and fundamental as it may be, is not all there is to a political revolution. A shift in power relations occurs also in rebellions, insurrections, uprisings, *coup d'états, Putschs,* overthrows, and secessions. **Eugene Kamenka,** in this section's first essay, makes a persuasive case for distinguishing political revolution from these other kinds of political fluxes, which occur when there is a change merely of personnel who hold political power, as in many South

American turnovers. The change in personnel does not necessarily lead to a change in any other aspect of a social unit's culture; it may lead only to a change in whose nose is in the public trough or in whose command the armed forces reside. Contrast this with the Russian revolution where the replacement of a whole class in power led to vast economic, religious, and educational change; or to the American revolution where power passed from a monarchy to another group of men who changed the whole method and structure of governance; or the French revolution where the new power fostered a new set of human priorities—liberty, equality, fraternity; or to the English revolution where the new power laid the groundwork for the Industrial Revolution.

Kamenka sums up the contrast in the concept of "progress"; for him, the Western realist concept of "revolution" contains the concept of "progress," whereas the other kinds of political fluxes are simply cyclical turnovers. The outcome of the revolutionary effort does not have to be actual progress, but at least the aim of him who would be a revolutionary should be to seize power to improve his society's culture over the prerevolutionary culture. In this connection, we refer you to the components of an ideology that we outlined in the introduction to Chapter One, "The New Generation." Without improvement in mind, the seizure of power, as in insurrections, rebellions, *coup d'états*, and so on, appears to be simply a criminal activity, being without any point other than the forcible improvement of the insurrectionists' personal well-being.

The element of progress is central not only to characterizing the nature of revolution but also to justifying revolution. In this section's second essay, **Reinhold Niebuhr** argues that revolutions are justifiable despite the fact that they generally occur only with the use of violence. His argument is somewhat similar to Robert Audi's (essay in the previous section). It is interesting to note that both Niebuhr and Audi use the term "violence" rather than "force." We suggested in our introduction to the previous section ("Violence") that this is a mistake: one does not justify violence; one justifies the use of force; we have suggested that use of force when justified is not rightly called violence. However, whether the term "violence" or "force" is used, the concept of progress is central to the attempt to justify forcible (violent) revolution, because the element of progress implies that the revolutionary is trying to bring about a good end, such as the establishment of a just society, such as freedom for the members of the society, or such as improvement of the personal welfare of the citizens. The desirability of attaining such ends, goes the argument, outweighs the undesirability of many consequences that are predicted will flow from the use of force in consummating the revolution. Of special interest in Niebuhr's essay is his attempt to show that the maxims of personal morality do not *a priori* prove that the use of force in political revolutions is immoral.

Ernesto Che Guevara's and Wang Tao-ming's essays are of allied interest (Chapter Six); Guevara places a revolutionary burden on the Cuban political changeover; the new people in power have the obligation to bring progress by improving men's nature. They must replace the capitalist man with the socialist man, the latter being a moral improvement on the former. Wang details the moral improvement wrought in him by the revolutionary teachings of Mao Tse-tung.

The concept of progress figures as a part not only in the concept of revolution and revolution's justification but also in the concept of a "political prisoner." Angela Davis, George Jackson, and Huey Newton have been called political prisoners.

Many of their supporters and the persons themselves have denied that they are criminals. That there are people in prison who are there for political rather than for criminal reasons is not a strange notion. This appears to be certainly true of Vietnam, Greece, and Spain. That the United States has political prisoners is not illogical or unthinkable. Nor is it illogical or unthinkable for anyone who does not hold the same political beliefs as Angela Davis or Huey Newton.

Given two persons, each of whom has, say, made a physical attack on another person, how are we to distinguish one's act as a political act and the other's as a criminal act? If the aim of progress distinguishes revolution from insurrection, then the same aim should distinguish the revolutionary from the criminal. The revolutionary performs his act in order to improve the lot of people in his social unit, the criminal in order to improve solely his own lot.

It does not follow from the distinction, however, that the revolutionary should not be imprisoned or that once in prison he should be freed. That requires additional argument. Surely there are limits to what a person may do to others even in the pursuit of the most worthwhile goals. The inept or hopelessly out-of-step-with-the-times revolutionary who cannot be persuaded to desist from absurdly hopeless actions should be coerced to desist at least as a reproof to his ineptness or obtuseness. Perhaps the only reward the revolutionary should expect is success.

The concept of a political prisoner takes on a less doubtful application when applied to a person who has been imprisoned merely because he discussed or advocated revolution than when it is applied to someone who has performed some overt act to attain his revolutionary aims. However, the **Supreme Court** in the third essay in this section indicates that it is still controversial to maintain that one should not be imprisoned for merely discussing and advocating revolution. The late Chief Justice Carl Vinson, while acknowledging that he was upholding the conviction of men for their political beliefs, making the men political prisoners, justified his action on the ground that a country has a right and the power to protect itself from the "clear and present danger" that these men would in the future actually perform overt acts in accordance with their beliefs. The late Justice Hugo Black, on the contrary, dissented from this view in both the Dennis case and the Barenblatt case. The question, of course, is "What are the limits of revolutionary political activity that a society should tolerate?"

The Concept of a Political Revolution

Eugene Kamenka

Eugene Kamenka (1930-   ) is a professorial fellow at Australian National University. Among his books are *The Ethical Foundations of Marxism* (1962), *Marxism and Ethics* (1969), and *The Philosophy of Ludwig Feuerbach* (1970).

The twentieth century is and is not the era of revolutions. In the past six decades we have witnessed one upheaval after another; the momentous revolution in Russia and two or three revolutions in China, the rise of Kemal Pasha Atatürk, the collapse of the Austro-Hungarian Empire, the abortive attempts at revolution in Germany and Hungary, the seizure of power by Nazis and Fascists, the "revolution from above" in most of Eastern Europe, the collapse of the old regime in Egypt followed by revolutionary impulses throughout the Arab world, and, finally, the revolution in Cuba. In Latin America, the almost institutionalized cycle of revolutions and *coups d'état* remains unbreached; in the old colonial and neo-colonial territories of Asia, Africa, and the Pacific there have been momentous transfers of power, some peaceful, some more violent. The twentieth century, at first sight, seems the century of revolutions and instability *par excellence.*

Yet to many of us whose attitudes are shaped by conditions in the highly industrialized countries of the West, these revolutions and upheavals now seem to be *in* the twentieth century, but not *of* it. We write, as I myself have written, that the revolution in Russia was successful precisely because Russia under the Czar was not like modern England, or Norway, or Australia, or the United States; we tend to agree with Karl Kautsky in treating the Austro-Hungarian Empire as a grotesque survival from the past, notable not for its fall, but for its astonishing ability to totter on into the twentieth century. Consciously or unconsciously, sweepingly or cautiously, we liken the social struggles in Asia, Africa, and Latin America to the social struggles of eighteenth- and nineteenth-century Europe and not to the problems confronting advanced industrial societies in the modern age of technology. Communism, *the* revolutionary movement of our time, smacks to us of 1848; we see it and the revolutionary ideology in general, as the understandable, whether regrettable or commendable, ideology of backward nations. The aim of all this fuss is not really to change the course of development in the twentieth century, but to catch up with it.

The revolutions that seem to us in some sense not "of" the twentieth century are, of course, *political* revolutions—the only kind of revolutions I am concerned with in this paper. One can also speak of the industrial revolution, the scientific revolution, the computer revolution, the Freudian revolution, or, perhaps, of the

Source: Carl J. Friedrich (ed.), *Revolution, Nomas VIII* (New York: Atherton, 1966), pp. 122-135. Reprinted by permission of the publishers, Atherton Press, Inc. Copyright © 1966, Atherton Press, Inc., New York. All rights reserved.

annual revolution in female fashions. These revolutions are very much, *of* the twentieth century: indeed, the more men see such revolutions as part of the regular life of their country, the less prone they seem to be to turn to political revolutions for salvation. Viewed in terms of the historical development of Western society, which we see as now setting the fundamental economic objectives and values pursued in contemporary history, the twentieth century is notable not as the era that gave the world political revolutions, but as the era that successfully institutionalized society's passage from one nonpolitical, social or economic revolution to another.

What is a political revolution? When Aristotle spoke of revolutions, he used the term *metabole,* change, and where appropriate, *metabole kai stasis,* change and uprising. But what sort of change, and how important is the element of uprising or violence? Aristotle thought the change had to be one in the *type* of political organization, e.g., from monarchy to oligarchy, from oligarchy to democracy, and so on. Today, we are perhaps somewhat less confident than Aristotle was that the political changes that amount to a change in type, or in the *essence* of the social order, can so readily be detected among other changes; at the same time, we tend to pay even greater attention than he does to the ideology, the beliefs and habits, involved in the existence of a social order. As a preliminary approach to the problem of isolating and describing the meaning of the term "revolution," we might therefore suggest the following: Revolution is a sharp, sudden change in the social location of political power, expressing itself in the radical transformation of the process of government, of the official foundations of sovereignty or legitimacy and of the conception of the social order. Such transformations, it has usually been believed, could not normally occur without violence, but if they did, they would still, though bloodless, be revolutions. The concept of a sharp, sudden change is no doubt a relative concept; what appears to the participants as the slow, gradual evolution of a new style of life may, to later generations, seem a sudden and revolutionary change. At the same time, acknowledged revolutions are rarely sharp and sudden enough to take place at a clearly defined point in time, or to reveal themselves unequivocally as revolutions at the very moment of the formal transfer of power. The violent outburst that heralds the beginning of the revolution for the chronicler may be understandable only as the product of important, if less spectacular, social changes that preceded it; the task of distinguishing a revolutionary outbreak from a *coup d'état* or a rebellion may be impossible until we see how the new masters use their new-won power. But unless we confine the term "revolution" to the field of *convulsive* changes we shall find revolution everywhere, all the time.

The history of the term "revolution" as a political concept has been traced for us in a scholarly work by the German sociologist Eugen Rosenstock-Huessy.[1] The men of the Italian Renaissance had used "revolution" (*rivoluzioni*) to describe the motion of the planets under the iron laws of the celestial spheres. In transposing the term into the field of politics, they meant to recognize in the rise and fall of princes a superhuman, astral force—the revolving wheel of fortune that raised up one prince

---

[1] Eugen Rosenstock-Huessy, *Revolution als politischer Begriff in der Neuzeit* (Breslau: 1931). There is a short summary of Rosenstock's argument in Sigmund Neumann, "The International Civil War," *World Politics,* 1 (1948-9), pp. 333-350. For a brief but independent confirmation of some of Rosenstock's findings, see Arthur Hatto, "Revolution: An Enquiry into the Usefulness of an Historical Term," *Mind,* 58 (1949), pp. 495-517.

or government and threw down another. This concept of a revolution as a total, fundamental and *objective* transformation, as a natural catastrophe, Rosenstock-Huessy calls the *naturalistic* concept. It persisted, according to him, right up to the French Revolution. When the Duc de Liancourt informed Louis XVI of the storming of the Bastille, the King exclaimed, "But good God! That is a revolt!" "No, Sire," replied the Duc, *"c'est la révolution"*—meaning that this was a force of nature completely beyond human control.[2]

With the French Revolution, Rosenstock argues, a new concept of revolution, the *romantic* concept, comes to the fore. Revolution is now seen as the heroic, romantic deed, as the assertion of human subjectivity, of man as the master of history. Before the Revolution Voltaire and Condorcet had laid down the elements of this view; Robespierre became its spokesman; the barricades of 1848 and the Blanquist faction in the Paris Commune were its visible expression. But in reality, the romantic period in Europe was short-lived. By 1850 it had lost most of its force. In the Italian *Risorgimento,* the realist Cavour replaced the romantic Mazzini; Germany moved into the age of Bismarck; the Republican opposition in the France of the Second Empire falls under the sway of the Comtean positivist Gambetta.[3] We enter a new period in the history of the idea of revolution, the general trend of which is only confirmed by the defeat of the Paris Commune. It is the period of the *realist* concept of revolutions.

Rosenstock-Huessy is in the Hegelian tradition; he sees the realist phase as the dialectical negation and synthesis (*Aufhebung*) of the two previous phases. Revolution is no longer seen as an unpredictable result of superhuman forces; to that extent, naturalism is overcome. But revolutions are seen as dependent on objective conditions; they come when the time is ripe for them. To that extent, naturalism is preserved. Neither are revolutions the mere product of human will, they can occur only in a revolutionary situation. Thus, romanticism is overcome. But for the revolutionary situation to become effective, there must be a class ready to do its work, or a decided leadership able to recognize, articulate, and direct the revolutionary forces of the time. Thus, romanticism, the importance of subjectivity, is also preserved. It is because Karl Marx, the outstanding "realist," combined and yet transcended the naturalistic and the romantic views of revolution, that he and his disciples could claim to be neither the astrologers nor the poets of revolution, but its scientists.

The realist theory of revolutions has yet one more important component, which die-hard Hegelians, no doubt, might seek to interpret as the *Aufhebung* of cyclical repetition and lawless leaps into the future. This is the concept of progress. Revolutions were the milestones in humanity's inexorable march toward true freedom and true universality. Each revolution, Marx and Engels write in the

[2] Cited by Neumann, *op. cit.,* p. 336. The naturalistic concept of revolution retained the cyclical conception of astronomy and of Classical political philosophy; the term "revolution" was associated with a concept of restoration, of the wheel of fortune returning to its original mark. It is for this reason, as Hatto points out (*op. cit.,* p. 505), that Clarendon called the events in England in 1660 a "revolution," that is, a *return* to the rightful order of things. For the opposing party, 1688 was the return of restoration, occurring, as they were delighted to note, precisely one hundred years after the expulsion of the Papists from England. The year 1688 was thus their "revolution": the Glorious Revolution that marked the restoration of their fortunes.

[3] Cf. David Thomson, "Scientific Thought and Revolutionary Movements," *Impact of Science on Society,* VI (1955), pp. 23-24.

German Ideology, is the work of a particular class, but during the revolution it appears as the representative of the whole society; as we pass from aristocracy to *bourgeoisie* and from *bourgeoisie* to proletariat, we pass to an ever-broadening base of social power; each revolution is thus truly nearer universality than the last.

The ascription of responsibility in history is governed by much the same psychological mechanisms as the ascription of responsibility in morals and law. A revolution, like a street accident, results from the interaction of a number of factors, each of them necessary but not sufficient to produce the result. We are constantly tempted to pick out as *the* cause the factor that we consider unusual or improper, the factor that lies outside the normal range of our expectations. The young Marx, accustomed to think of governments and social structures as rigid, and greatly impressed with the comparatively recent consciousness of the far-reaching economic changes taking place in society, saw revolution as caused by these changes. By the turn of the century, there was a new generation of Anglo-American thinkers, accustomed to think of far-reaching economic changes as the norm of social life: To them, *the* cause of revolutions seemed the rigidity of governments, the lack of social mobility and political flexibility, repression, and administrative incompetence.[4]

Though the emphases differ, the position is basically the same. Revolution, says Marx, is the bursting of the integument by the repressed forces of economic and social development; revolution, say later sociologists as different as Ward, Ellwood, Pareto, and Brooks Adams,[5] is the conflict between advancing classes or groups or interests in a society and the rigid structure or elite that holds them back.

Karl Marx, who saw revolutions as the violent conflicts between classes, defined these classes as purely economic groups, whose behavior and attitude were determined by their relationship to the means of production. Contemporary sociologists have been very strongly aware not only of the difficulties of Marx's class position in general, but of its particular weakness in dealing with revolutions. The leaders of the French revolution, for the most part, were not merchants, but lawyers, notaries, and bailiffs—professional men. The Russian revolution in 1917 depended heavily for its success on the leadership of that very special noneconomic class, the intelligentsia, and on the fact that a significant number of peasants had been converted, for a period, into soldiers. In these circumstances, most modern writers on revolution have turned, consciously or unconsciously, to Max Weber's conception of class as composed of those who share the same chance in life (*Lebenschance*)—a definition that enables us to cope with intellectuals and, in

---

[4] Cf. the passage in L. F. Ward's *Pure Sociology* (p. 230): "Only the labile is truly stable, just as in the domain of living things only the plastic is enduring. For lability is not an exact synonym of instability, but embodies, besides, the idea of flexibility and susceptibility to change without destruction or loss. It is that quality in institutions which enables them to change and still persist, which converts their equilibrium into a moving equilibrium, and which makes possible their adaptation to both internal and external modification. . . . When a society makes for itself a procrustean bed, it is simply preparing the way for its own destruction by the on-moving agencies of social dynamics." Charles A. Ellwood puts the position even more strongly: the causes of revolution are the causes of social rigidity—the breakdown of those habits and institutions (free discussion, public criticism, etc.) that makes a government responsive to the need or demand for social transitions. See Ellwood, "A Psychological Theory of Revolutions," *American Journal of Sociology,* II (1905-6), p. 53.

[5] V. Pareto, *The Mind and Society,* Vols. III and IV, esp. pp. 2050-2059, 2170-2203, and 2227; Brooks Adams, *The Theory of Social Revolution, passim.*

certain circumstances, with racial or national conflicts and the politics of minorities.

The conception of revolution as connected with members of a Weberian class seeking to improve their life chance, throws into relief once more the role of social rigidity in the production of revolutions and the mitigating influence that we might expect from the existence of a fairly high degree of social mobility, or from the strong belief in its possibility. Members of a class may ascend as individuals; they may ascend collectively as the result of objective conditions; or they may seek the revolutionary path of destroying the privileges of an upper class and reducing its life chances until it ceases to exist as a separate class—normally in the belief that a gain in average life chances will result. Collective ascent as the result of objective conditions is usually slow, but it can be extremely significant. Few people would doubt that the gradual collective ascent of the working classes of Western Europe and North America between 1815 and 1914 did a very great deal indeed to contain and even discredit revolutionary forces and movements. The extent and significance of individual ascent is much more the subject of controversy; but again, one might reasonably assert that the significant chance of individual ascent offered by the assisted migration schemes in England from the 1860's to the 1880's played a marked role in averting the revolutionary situation, or at least the sustained atmosphere of revolt, that might have resulted from the agricultural depression.

An important allied point about revolution was first hinted at by Karl Marx in *Wage Labour and Capital*[6] and put quite decisively by Alexis de Tocqueville a few years later:

Revolutions are not always brought about by a gradual decline from bad to worse. Nations that have endured patiently and almost unconsciously the most overwhelming oppression often burst into rebellion against the yoke the moment it grows lighter. The regime which is destroyed by a revolution is almost always an improvement on its immediate predecessor. . . . Evils which are patiently endured when they seem inevitable become intolerable when once the idea of escape from them is suggested.[7]

The final sentence is the crucial one. Part of the difference between a revolutionary uprising and a rebellion is the difference in the beliefs and expectations of those involved; rebels seek the redress of grievances, the return to a former state of comparative justice or prosperity; it is amazing, when we look back, just how limited the demands of that Great Peasant Rebellion in Germany in 1525 actually were, and how ready its leaders were to accept the authority of princes and kings. Revolutionaries, on the other hand, have great expectations; they think in terms of a new order, of progress, of changing times that need changing systems of government. For nearly two thousand years, China witnessed civil wars, rebellions, secessions, and *coups d'état;* but until the European revolutions came, there had

[6] "A noticeable increase in wages presupposes a rapid growth in productive capital. The rapid growth of productive capital brings about an equally rapid growth of wealth, luxury, social wants, social enjoyments. Thus, although the enjoyments of the workers have risen, the social satisfaction that they give has fallen in comparison with the increased enjoyments of the capitalist, which are inaccessible to the worker, in comparison with the state of development of society in general." Marx and Engels, *Selected Works*, vol. 1 (Moscow: 1955), p. 94.

[7] Alexis de Tocqueville, *The Old Regime and the Revolution,* transl. by John Bonner (New York: 1856), p. 214.

been not one revolution in China. For revolutions, as Crane Brinton found,[8] require among other things an economically advancing society, the concept of progress, of the human ability to bring about fundamental social change, which seems, as far as we can tell, to be exclusively associated with the conception of a market economy. Rebellions and *coups d'état* occur everywhere; revolutions, it is fascinating to note, seem to have occurred only in *cities* and, until comparatively recently, in Western societies. The revolutions in other types of social structures, I shall argue, rest on the permeation of Western economy and ideology; they are revolutions by contact and imitation.

Revolutions are not produced by the forces of the market economy alone; they require the belief in human power and in the possibility of vast material improvement, but they require also anger and the prospects of success. They require, that is, the support of a significant section of people not normally given to revolt. This tends to occur when two requirements are fulfilled. First, there must have been a strong rise in people's expectations, such as an economically advancing society normally produces, which is suddenly vitiated by a sharp decline in satisfactions. As James C. Davies puts it, "Revolutions are most likely to occur when a prolonged period of economic and social development is followed by a short period of sharp reversal. People then subjectively fear that ground gained with great effort will be quite lost; their mood then becomes revolutionary."[9] Davies attempts to show that this was in fact what happened just before Dorr's (unsuccessful) nineteenth-century rebellion in Rhode Island in 1840-42, in the period preceding the Russian Revolution, and in postwar Egypt before the fall of Farouk. Revolutions, he concludes, do not take place in a society where there is the continued, unimpeded opportunity to satisfy new needs, new hopes and new expectations; neither do they take place in a society in which there are no hopes, no expectations, but only hardship and hunger as long as men can remember.

The second requirement is related to the need for prospects of success, but is often intimately connected with the economic reversal that satisfies the first requirement. In every revolution that I can think of, the state against which the revolutionaries fought had been strikingly weakened by financial failure, administrative incompetence, lack of self-confidence and, in a very high number of cases, by defeat in war.

This latter point should not surprise. For if revolutions are the milestones on the way to the development of an advanced industrialized economy, they are also bloody battles, desperate struggles against the authority and power of the previously existing state. As Borkenau puts it:

Every great revolution has destroyed the State apparatus which it found. After much vacillation and experimentation, every revolution has set another apparatus in its place, in most cases of quite a different character from the one destroyed; for the changes in the state order which a revolution produces are no less important than the changes in the social order. The revolutionary process itself is in the first instance a struggle for political power. And whatever may be the deeper driving-forces of a revolution, the struggle for the State always appears as its immediate content (!); indeed to such an extent that the transformation of the social order

---

[8] Crane Brinton, *Anatomy of Revolution*, rev. ed. (London: 1953), p. 277 ("Some tentative uniformities").

[9] James C. Davies, "Toward a Theory of Revolution," *American Sociological Review*, 27 (1962), p. 5.

often appears not as the goal of the revolution, but simply as means used by revolutionaries to conquer or to exercise power.[10]

Contemporary political thinkers molded in the background of Western democracy are extremely conscious, in recent years, of the ruthless internal logic of revolutions, of the fraudulence of their claim to transfer power to "the people." Most of us today would accept what Borkenau calls "the law of the twofold development of revolutions. They begin as anarchistic movements against the bureaucratic state organization, which they inevitably destroy; they continue by setting in its place another, in most cases stronger, bureaucratic organization, which suppresses all free mass movements."[11] The Thermidorian reaction seems to us no longer a possible danger that revolutions must avoid, but a necessary consequence of the very nature of the revolutionary ideology and the revolutionary struggle. So clear, and so apparently inevitable, is the centralizing, dictatorial trend of revolutions that for the first time in human history we actually find revolution cynically used as a *means* for welding together a diffuse society, for creating centralized authority and power.

It is tempting, in these circumstances, to merge into one concept the successful rebellion, the revolution, and the *coup d'état*. Peter Amann, in a recent paper,[12] tries to do just this. Revolution, as he defines it, "prevails when the State's monopoly of power is effectively challenged and persists until a monopoly of power is re-established."[13] This approach, he argues, avoids such traditional problems as that of distinguishing a revolution from a *coup d'état,* the uncertain differentiation between wars of independence, civil wars and revolutions, and the difficulty of deciding how much social change is necessary before a movement may be called a revolution. At the same time, the definition recognizes the possibility of suspended revolutions, where we have the prolonged co-existence of two antagonistic governmental power centers, e.g., the Army and the Government in the Weimar Republic or in the post-Peron Frondizi regime in Argentina.

Such simplifications are always attractive and, in a sense, they are not wrong. Words have no natural definitions; social events have no clearly manifest essential character. *Eadem sed aliter* is the motto of history and of nature. The distinctions we make, the connections and similarities we emphasize, are made for a purpose, an explanatory purpose. For some purposes, we may be interested only in the breakdown of the governmental monopoly of public power; for these purposes Amann's use of the word "revolution" may well be a useful shorthand. For other purposes—and they are the ones with which I and most students of revolution are concerned—it misses crucial distinctions. It is, I think, important to recognize the role of rising expectations and of ideology in revolutions, to be able to say that revolution is different from peasant uprisings and slave rebellions in respects crucial to understanding the process, and that there have been no revolutions in Asia and Africa until this century. To understand why this is so, we need a concept of revolution that is no doubt trickier to work with, but that has also far greater explanatory power, than the formalized concept that Amann proposes.

[10] F. Borkenau, "State and Revolution in the Paris Commune, the Russian Revolution, and the Spanish Civil War," in *Sociological Review*, 29 (1937), p. 41.
[11] *Ibid.*, p. 67.
[12] Peter Amann, "Revolution: A Redefinition," *Political Science Quarterly*, 77 (1962), pp. 36-53.
[13] *Ibid.*, p. 39.

We have noted the naked emergence, in the twentieth century, of the centralizing motif in revolutions—the open preoccupation with power that lends plausibility to Amann's suggested redefinition. But even here there is a crucial distinction between, say, the Indonesian Revolution on the one hand and the Old Chinese Triad movement to "overthrow the Ch'ing and restore the Ming" on the other.[14] Revolution has come to Asia because Europe has come to Asia; the change in power is no longer seen as a restoration, but as a leap forward, a leap forward into the universalized, industrialized society of the West. The Indonesian rebellion against the Dutch was utterly different from the Jewish rebellion against the Romans: it was not merely a movement of national liberation from foreign masters, but a struggle for *control* over political, social, and economic processes that were now recognized as the key to the future. In this sense, it seems to me, the movements of national liberation and the more or less peaceful transfers of power in Asian, African, and Pacific countries have to be seen not only as revolutions, but as *revolutions within the history of Europe,* the transfer of social power from one governing class to a new class. It is only because Asia, Africa, and the Pacific have entered the history of Europe that such true revolutions have become possible to them. It is because Turkey had entered the history of Europe that Kemal Pasha Atatürk's *coup d'état* aspired to become a revolution.

In the advanced, industrial countries of the West, on the other hand, one is inclined to say that the age of revolutions is over. As R. S. Parker put it recently: "If . . . we consider preindustrial societies where the population pressed hard on the means of subsistence, we invariably expect to find direct power relations playing a larger part in the distribution of material welfare. . . . Comparatively speaking, high average living standards and the economic and social mobility that go with them in a country like Australia conduce, other things being equal, to a general acceptance of the economic processes of bargaining and exchange, and reduced need for the exercise of power in arranging the allocation of material values."[15] For the first time in human history technological advance has become so great that society can, as Toynbee notes in his *Reconsiderations,*[16] support a vast proliferation of bureaucracy without a sharp decrease in the sub-bureaucratic standard of living; the cyclical law of the rebellion against bureaucratic rule no longer applies. At the same time, the ideology of the market has found its political counterpart in the procedures of representative government. While popular political control is no doubt as imperfect as the consumer control extolled by capitalist apologetics, it is nevertheless there. Representative government *has* produced, in conjunction with the radically "capitalized" society, a comparatively flexible, responsive social structure able to make the transitions for which revolution and uprising were needed in the past.

This is not to say that the present political structure of advanced industrial societies has no tendencies that might lead to rigidity, or that a sharp discrepancy

[14] The T'ai-p'ing T'ien-kuo rebellion of 1850-64 marks the transition; on the one hand, it drew on the traditions of southern separatism and hostility to the Ch'ing (the Manchus), on the other hand it drew from European missionary influence and the penetration of European trade a Messianic character that laid some of the groundwork for the revolutionary movement in China.

[15] R. S. Parker, "Power in Australia," a seminar paper delivered in the Institute of Advanced Studies, Australian National University, on October 8, 1962, and circulated to participants in the seminar on "The Sociology of Power," pp. 2-3.

[16] See Arnold Toynbee, *A Study of History*, vol. XII (London: 1961), esp. pp. 200-209.

between people's economic expectations and their economic satisfactions might not once more arise, producing a decidedly rebellious, revolutionary mood. But from the standpoint of the classical conception of revolutions, there will be fundamental differences in any such future situations. The concept of universality has been exhausted, for all practical purposes, in the attaining of representative government and reasonable economic affluence. The revolution of the future in advanced, democratic, industrialized society could only be a counterrevolution, a seizure of power by a group intent on re-establishing despotic rule and a status society. The intensification of military struggle or of population pressures on food resources could make such a possibility seem far more real than it does today; but they could hardly convert such a coup from its obvious place with Roman dictatorships to an affinity with the French, the Russian, or even the Chinese and Indonesian Revolutions.

In the Communist world, future revolutions in my sense of the word do not seem to us impossible. The Hungarian revolt was indeed part of a tradition that goes back to the French, Polish, and Russian Revolutions; it might even have ended, if successful, more happily than any of these. For the revolutionary in the Communist world the problem is the concentration of power in the hands of the modern state, the comparatively blurred nature of the class against which he is rebelling, and the fact that his revolution—unlike previous revolutions directed against idle aristocrats, absentee landlords, and broken-down bureaucracies—would be against a class playing a significant role in the process of production.

The problems of social theory will not be solved by any careful, preliminary analysis of concepts. The definition of revolution is not the beginning but the end of an inquiry into social upheaval, social change, and the translocation of power. There is not a right definition and a wrong definition, there are only fruitful distinctions and less fruitful distinctions, terms useful in one context and useless in another. In this paper I have tried to suggest that we should not abandon too readily the economic strand in the realist conception of revolutions. The Leninist emphasis on revolutionary theory as a manual for the seizure of power has led many contemporary sociologists to seek to treat revolution in static terms, as a situation in which the state monopoly of a power is being effectively challenged. This emphasizes the undoubted connections between revolutions, rebellions, civil wars, wars of liberation, and *coups d'état;* it is useful in deflating revolutionary pretensions about the elimination of power in human affairs and bringing out the centralizing tendencies inherent in bitter conflict. But this static, cross-sectional treatment of societies in the throes of conflict seems to me totally inadequate as a foundation for examining the causes and more general consequences of such conflicts, for understanding when and why they are likely to occur. For these purposes, we do need to distinguish between a *coup d'état* and a revolution, between the inauguration of a new dynasty and the inauguration of a new social order. The distinctions cannot be made sharply; social events run together, they vacillate between one category and another, they end where no one dreamed at the beginning they would end. Kemal Pasha's *coup d'état,* I have suggested, aspired, through its association with the Young Turks, to become a revolution; and for some purposes it may best be understood as such. The transfer of power in India, with its momentous revolutionary implications, has perhaps not succeeded in realizing them; one might easily query whether the India of 1963 is a new India in comparison with the India of 1938. Nevertheless, distinctions that can be blurred, or that can fail to be helpful in some situations, may still be vital to understanding the general picture. To do this, I have suggested, we need a *dynamic* concept of revolutions, a concept of political revolutions that sees them in their intimate relationship to the more general class of social revolutions of which they are part rather than to the allied classes of rebellions, uprisings, and wars.

Justice Through Revolution
Reinhold Niebuhr

Reinhold Niebuhr (1890-1971) was vice-president of the faculty of Union Theological Seminary. From 1928 until his death, he was professor of Christian ethics and philosophy of religion. After preparing for the ministry at Eden Theological Seminary in St. Louis, he studied at Yale University, taking his B.D. degree in 1914 and his M.A. in 1915. Then he became pastor of a struggling little church in Detroit. Among his books are *Leaves from the Notebooks of a Tamed Cynic* (1929), *Moral Man and Immoral Society* (1932), *Faith and History* (1949), *Christian Realism* (1952), and *The Self and the Dramas of History* (1955).

The disillusioning consequences of the World War [I], the inability of the nations to extricate themselves from the financial and defensive burdens which the war left them as an unholy legacy, the comparative failure of the peace machinery devised to prevent future conflicts, the world depression and the consequent misery and insecurity of millions of workers in every land, and finally the dramatic success of the Russian Revolution, all these factors have made the despised political philosophy of rebellious helots, the great promise and the great peril of the political life of the Western world. It no longer expresses merely the political conviction of advanced proletarians. Intellectuals show covert and overt sympathy toward it, and the business men use it as the bogey man with which to scare the timorous community and prevent it from granting significant concessions to the impatient and sullenly rebellious labor world. The breadth and the depth of the world depression have, moreover, tempted others beside proletarians to express a temper of catastrophism. If they do not share the proletarian hope, that salvation will come out of catastrophe, they are at least inclined to question the possibility of avoiding catastrophe by methods of gradual social change, and await the revolution in the ambivalence of hope and fear.

In spite of the more general consideration and sympathy which the prophecies of revolution receive in the middle-class community, the methods of revolution remain abhorrent to it. Violence and revolution are usually ruled out as permissible instruments of social change on *a priori* grounds. The middle classes and the

Source: *Moral Man and Immoral Society* (New York: Scribner's, 1932, 1960), Ch. 7. Reprinted by permission of Charles Scribner's Sons. Copyright 1932 Charles Scribner's Sons; renewal copyright © 1960 Reinhold Niebuhr.

rational moralists, who have a natural abhorrence of violence, may be right in their general thesis; but they are wrong in their assumption that violence is intrinsically immoral. Nothing is intrinsically immoral except ill-will and nothing intrinsically good except goodwill. We have previously examined proletarian motives and discovered that, while they are not altogether pure, they are as pure as the motives of collective man usually are; and are certainly not less moral than the motives of those who defend special privileges by more covert means of coercion than the proletarians are able to command.

Since it is very difficult to judge human motives, it is natural that, from an external perspective, the social consequences of an action or policy should be regarded as more adequate tests of its morality than the hidden motives. The good motive is judged by its social goal. Does it have the general welfare as its objective? When viewing a historic situation all moralists become pragmatists and utilitarians. Some general good, some *summum bonum,* "the greatest good of the greatest number" or "the most inclusive harmony of all vital capacities" is set up as the criterion of the morality of specific actions and each action is judged with reference to its relation to the ultimate goal. We have previously analysed the ultimate objectives of Marxian politics and have found them to be identical with the most rational possible social goal, that of equal justice.

The choice of instruments and immediate objectives which fall between motive and ultimate objective, raises issues which are pragmatic to such a degree that they may be said to be more political than they are ethical. The realm of politics is a twilight zone where ethical and technical issues meet. A political policy cannot be intrinsically evil if it can be proved to be an efficacious instrument for the achievement of a morally approved end. Neither can it be said to be wholly good merely because it seems to make for ultimately good consequences. Immediate consequences must be weighed against the ultimate consequences. The destruction of a life or the suppression of freedom result in the immediate destruction of moral values. Whether the ultimate good, which is hoped to be accomplished by this immediate destruction, justifies the sacrifice, is a question which depends upon many considerations for its answer. How great is the immediate and less inclusive value which is sacrificed for a more ultimate and more inclusive one? How certain is the attainment of the ultimate value? Is there any certainty that violence can establish equality or that an equality so established can be maintained? These are some of the pragmatic questions which suggest themselves. The questions are important but none of them can be dealt with adequately if it is assumed that any social policy, as violence for instance, is intrinsically immoral. The assumption that violence and revolution are intrinsically immoral rests upon two errors.

The one error is the belief that violence is a natural and inevitable expression of ill-will, and non-violence of good-will, and that violence is therefore intrinsically evil and non-violence intrinsically good. While such a proposition has a certain measure of validity, or at least of plausibility, it is certainly not universally valid. It is less valid in inter-group relations than in individual relations, if our assumption is correct that the achievement of harmony and justice between groups requires a measure of coercion, which is not necessary in the most intimate and the most imaginative individual relations. Once we admit the factor of coercion as ethically justified, though we concede that it is always morally dangerous, we cannot draw any absolute line of demarcation between violent and non-violent coercion. We may argue that the immediate consequences of violence are such that they frustrate the ultimate purpose by which it is justified. If that is true, it is certainly not self-evident; and violence can therefore not be ruled out on *a priori* grounds. It is all the more difficult to do this if we consider that the immediate consequences of violence cannot be differentiated as sharply from those of non-violence, as is sometimes supposed. The difference between them is not an absolute one, even though there may be important distinctions, which must be carefully weighed. Gandhi's boycott of British cotton results in the undernourishment of children in Manchester, and the blockade of the Allies in war-time caused the death of German children. It is impossible to coerce a group without damaging both life and property and without imperilling the interests of the innocent with those of the guilty. Those are factors which are involved in the intricacies of group relations; and they make it impossible to transfer an ethic of personal relations uncritically to the field of inter-group relations.

The second error by which violence comes to be regarded as unethical in intrinsic terms is due to an uncritical identification of traditionalised instrumental values with intrinsic moral values. Only goodwill is intrinsically good. But as soon as goodwill expresses itself in specific actions, it must be determined whether the right motive has chosen the right instruments for the attainment of its goal and whether the objective is a defensible one. For reason may err in guiding the righteous will in the choice of either means or ends. But there are certain specific actions and attitudes which are generally not judged in terms of their adequacy in achieving an approved social end. Experience has established them; and their traditionalised instrumental value is regarded as an intrinsic one. Respect for the life, the opinions and the interests of another is regarded as intrinsically good and violence to the fellowman's life, opinions and interests is prohibited. It is not only assumed that they will have the right ultimate consequences but that they are the natural and inevitable expression of goodwill. In purely personal relations these assumptions are quite generally justified. The moral will expresses itself unconsciously in terms of consideration for the life, the interests and the rights of others; and the consequences of such consideration may be presumed to be good. It is good to trust the neighbor, for it will prompt him to trustworthy action; it is good to respect his life because this respect helps to establish and preserve that general reverence for life upon which all morality rests; it is good not to coerce the opinions of the other because coercion does not change opinion or because it may give an undue advantage to the wrong opinion; it is good to tell the truth because truth-telling facilitates the sharing of experience which is basic to all social life. Such judgments as these may not be universally accepted, but they are the working capital of personal morality.

It is well to note that even in the comparatively simple problems of individual relationships there is no moral value which may be regarded as absolute. It may, in a given instant, have to be sacrificed to some other value. Every action resolves a certain competition between values, in which one value must be subordinated to another. This is necessary in a specific instance even though there may be an ultimate harmony of all high and legitimate moral values. Thus a physician who believes that the neighbor has a right to the truth as well as a right to his life, and that there is no ultimate conflict between the two rights, may nevertheless deny his patient the truth in a given instant, because in that instant the truth might imperil his life. In the same way, though believing that reverence for life is basic to all morality, he may have to make a choice between types of life, and sacrifice an unborn infant to save the life of a mother. A reflective morality is constantly under the necessity of reanalysing moral values which are regarded as intrinsically good and of judging them in instrumental terms. The more inclusive the ends which are held in view, the more the immediate consequences of an action cease to be the authoritative criteria of moral judgment. Since society must constantly deal with these inclusive ends, it always seems to capitulate to the dangerous principle that the end justifies the means. All morality really accepts that principle, but the fact is obscured by the assumption, frequently though not universally justified, that the character of immediate consequences guarantees the character of the ultimate end. A community may believe, as it usually does, that reverence for life is a basic moral attitude, and yet rob a criminal of his life in order to deter others from taking life. It may be wrong in doing this; but if it is, the error is not in taking the life but in following a policy which does not really deter others from murder. The question cannot be resolved on *a priori* grounds but only by observing the social consequences of various types of punishment. Society may believe that the preservation of freedom of opinion is a social good, not because liberty of thought is an inherent or natural right but because it is a basic condition of social progress. Yet in a given instance the principle of freedom may have to yield to the necessities of social cohesion, requiring a measure of coercion. If the state usually errs in throttling freedom, its error is in using an undue measure of coercion, in applying it prematurely before efforts to achieve solidarity by a mutual accommodation of interests have been exhausted, and in exploiting the resultant social solidarity for morally unapproved ends. On the question of the relative value of freedom and solidarity no final and authoritative answer can be given. Every answer will be relative to the social experience of particular individuals and groups, who have suffered from either anarchy or autocracy and tend to embrace the evils of the one in the effort to escape the perils of the other.

The differences between proletarian and middle-class morality are on the whole differences between men who regard themselves as primarily individuals and those who feel themselves primarily members of a social group. The latter will emphasise liberty, respect for individual life, the rights of property and the moral values of mutual trust and unselfishness. The former will emphasise loyalty to the group and the need of its solidarity, they will subject the rights of property to the total social welfare, will abrogate the values of freedom for the attainment of their most cherished social goal and will believe that conflicts of interest between groups can be resolved, not by accommodation but by struggle. The middle class tries to make the canons of individual morality authoritative for all social relations. It is shocked by the moral cynicism, the tendency toward violence and indifference toward individual freedom of the proletarian. Inasfar as this represents an honest effort to make the ideals of personal morality norms for the conduct of human groups, it is a legitimate moral attitude which must never be completely abandoned. Inasfar as it represents the illusions and deceptions of middle-class people, who never conform their own group conduct to their individual ideals, it deserves the cynical reaction of the proletarian. The illusory element must be admitted to be very large. The middle classes believe in freedom, but deny freedom when its exercise imperils their position in society; they profess a morality of love and unselfishness but do not achieve an unselfish group attitude toward a less privileged group; they claim to abhor violence and yet use it both in international conflict and in the social crises in which their interests are imperilled; they want mutuality of interest between classes rather than a class struggle but the mutuality must not be so complete as to destroy all their special privileges.

The proletarian on the other hand is not enough of an individual, in the attainments of his own cultural life and in the conditions of his social life, to be strongly moved by the canons of individual morality. He is most conscious of the reality of group behavior. He is not only more completely immersed in his own group than the more privileged classes, but he feels the effect of the behavior of other groups upon his life more definitely than do the members of privileged classes. His moral attitudes are determined by the moral behavior of groups rather than by the moral behavior of individuals. He discounts the latter not only because he is himself not an individual, as more privileged persons are, but because he has not found individual morality qualifying the dominant greed and lust to power of privileged groups to any appreciable degree. He has come to the conclusion that the hope of achieving a moral group life results in illusion. The conflict between proletarian and middle-class morality is thus a contest between hypocrisy and brutality, and between sentimentality and cynicism. The limitations of the one tend to accentuate the limitations of the other. The full import of that conflict is revealed in Trotsky's words: "As for us, we were never concerned with the Kantian priestly and vegetarian-Quaker prattle about the 'sacredness of human life.' We were revolutionaries in opposition and remain revolutionaries in power. To make the individual sacred we must destroy the social order which crucifies him and this problem can only be solved by blood and iron."

If a season of violence can establish a just social system and can create the possibilities of its preservation there is no purely ethical ground upon which violence and revolution can be ruled out. This could be done only upon the basis of purely anarchistic ethical and political presuppositions. Once we have made the fateful concession of ethics to politics, and accepted coercion as a necessary instrument of social cohesion, we can make no absolute distinctions between non-violent and violent types of coercion or between coercion used by governments and that which is used by revolutionaries. If such distinctions are made they must be justified in terms of the consequences in which they result. The real question is: what are the political possibilities of establishing justice through violence?

A certain system of power, based upon the force which inheres in property, and augmented by the political power of the state is set against the demands of the worker. Efforts to destroy the economic power by giving the worker the political power, inherent in the strength of his numbers, are frustrated by the use of the organs of education and propaganda in control of the dominant group, and the ignorance of a portion of the workers. Can the workers overthrow the existing power and come in control of both the apparatus of the state and organs of education so that they can establish an equalitarian world and educate a new generation which will maintain it? The realistic Marxians who have analysed this problem in terms of the comparative resources of power available on each side, do not give themselves to the romantic illusions current among certain classes of intellectuals, who think that a revolution is a fairly easy achievement. They know that the task is not easy, even though they believe the inexorable forces of history are gradually changing the proportion of power and making the ultimate victory of the worker possible. They believe that the increased centralisation of power and privilege will reduce the comparative strength of the privileged groups, that the increased misery of the workers, and of the lower middle classes, will augment their numbers and increase their revolutionary fervor and that international wars, in which capitalism inevitably involves the present social order, will finally reduce the prestige and the power of the national state sufficiently to make a transfer of power possible.

These catastrophic predictions, which in the true proletarian achieve the character of a religious hope and creed, have been neither proved nor disproved in any authoritative fashion by the history of industrial civilization. There is very strong evidence both for and against the possibility of their realisation.

Should the Advocacy of Revolution Be Legal?
The Supreme Court

One of the basic questions in the area of political freedom is "What classes of speech and publications ought to be protected by a society?" Historically, in the United States, the speeches that present "clear and present danger of action of a kind the state is empowered to prevent and punish have not been protected." This phrasing was first made in the Supreme Court by Justice Holmes in 1919. Although this test has been used since that time, the members of the Court have differed as to when a danger is "clear" or when it is "present" or when the evil sought to be prevented is circumstantial.

The first case reprinted below, called *The Dennis Case*, involved the conviction of eleven Communist Party leaders (of whom Dennis was one). The majority of the Court upheld the conviction for conspiracy under the Smith Act of 1940. Most of the judges agreed that the "clear and present danger" standard was to be used. The second case reprinted below, called *The Barenblatt Case*, involved the right of an individual, on the basis of the First Amendment, to remain silent about his own political views. Justice Hugo Black's dissenting opinion, defending Barenblatt's right to remain silent, is given here.

DENNIS CASE: VINSON AFFIRMING, BLACK DISSENTING*

Mr. Chief Justice Vinson:

Petitioners were indicted in July, 1948, for violation of the conspiracy provisions of the Smith Act, 54 Stat. 671, 18 U.S.C. (1946 ed.) § 11, during the period of April, 1945, to July, 1948. . . . A verdict of guilty as to all the petitioners was returned by the jury on October 14, 1949. The Court of Appeals affirmed the

* [*Dennis vs. United States, 341 U.S. 510 (1952).*—Eds.]

convictions. . . . We granted certiorari, . . . limited to the following two questions: (1) Whether either § 2 or § 3 of the Smith Act, inherently or as construed and applied in the instant case, violates the First Amendment and other provisions of the Bill of Rights; (2) whether either § 2 or § 3 of the Act, inherently or as construed and applied in the instant case, violates the First and Fifth Amendments because of indefiniteness.

Sections 2 and 3 of the Smith Act provide as follows:

Sec. 2

(a) It shall be unlawful for any person—

(1) to knowingly or willfully advocate, abet, advise, or teach the duty, necessity, desirability, or propriety of overthrowing or destroying any government in the United States by force or violence, or by the assassination of any officer of any such government;

(2) with the intent to cause the overthrow or destruction of any government in the United States, to print, publish, edit, issue, circulate, sell, distribute, or publicly display any written or printed matter advocating, advising, or teaching the duty, necessity, desirability, or propriety of overthrowing or destroying any government in the United States by force or violence;

(3) to organize or help to organize any society, group, or assembly of persons who teach, advocate, or encourage the overthrow or destruction of any government in the United States by force or violence; or to be or become a member of, or affiliate with any such society, group, or assembly of persons, knowing the purposes thereof.

(b) For the purposes of this section, the term "government in the United States" means the Government of the United States, the government of any State, Territory, or possession of the United States, the government of the District of Columbia, or the government of any political sub-division of any of them.

Sec. 3. It shall be unlawful for any person to attempt to commit, or to conspire to commit, any of the acts prohibited by the provisions of . . . this title.

The indictment charged the petitioners with wilfully and knowingly conspiring (1) to organize as the Communist Party of the United States of America a society, group and assembly of persons who teach and advocate the overthrow and destruction of the Government of the United States by force and violence, and (2) knowingly and wilfully to advocate and teach the duty and necessity of overthrowing and destroying the Government of the United States by force and violence. The indictment further alleged that § 2 of the Smith Act proscribes these acts and that any conspiracy to take such action is a violation of § 3 of the Act.

The trial of the case extended over nine months, six of which were devoted to the taking of evidence, resulting in a record of 16,000 pages. Our limited grant of the writ of certiorari has removed from our consideration any question as to the sufficiency of the evidence to support the jury's determination that petitioners are guilty of the offense charged. Whether on this record petitioners did in fact advocate the overthrow of the Government by force and violence is not before us, and we must base any discussion of this point upon the conclusions stated in the opinion of the Court of Appeals, which treated the issue in great detail. That court held that the record in this case amply supports the necessary finding of the jury that petitioners, the leaders of the Communist Party in this country, were unwilling to work within our framework of democracy, but intended to initiate a violent revolution whenever the propitious occasion appeared. Petitioners dispute the meaning to be drawn from the evidence, contending that the Marxist-Leninist doctrine they advocated taught that force and violence to achieve a Communist form of government in an existing democratic state would be necessary only because the ruling classes of that state would never permit the transformation to be accomplished peacefully, but would use force and violence to defeat any peaceful political and economic gain the Communists could achieve. But the Court of Appeals held that the record supports the following broad conclusions: By virtue of their control over the political apparatus of the Communist Political Association, petitioners were able to transform that organization into the Communist Party; that the policies of the Association were changed from peaceful cooperation with the United States and its economic and political structure to a policy which had existed before the United States and the Soviet Union were fighting a common enemy, namely, a policy which worked for the overthrow of the Government by force and violence; that the Communist Party is a highly disciplined organization, adept at infiltration into strategic positions, use of aliases, and double-meaning language; that the Party is rigidly controlled; that Communists, unlike other political parties, tolerate no dissension from the policy laid down by the guiding forces, but that the approved program is slavishly followed by the members of the Party; that the literature of the Party and the statements and activities of its leaders . . . advocate, and the general goal of the Party was, during the period in question, to achieve a successful overthrow of the existing order by force and violence.

. . . The structure and purpose of the statute demand the inclusion of intent as an element of the crime. Congress was concerned with those who advocate and organize for the overthrow of the Government. Certainly those who recruit and combine for the purpose of advocating overthrow intend to bring about that overthrow. We hold that the statute requires as an essential element of the crime proof of the intent of those who are charged with its violation to overthrow the Government by force and violence. . . .

Nor does the fact that there must be an investigation of a state of mind under this interpretation afford any basis for rejection of that meaning. A survey of Title 18 of the U.S. Code indicates that the vast majority of the crimes designated by that Title require, by express language, proof of the existence of a certain mental state in words such as "knowingly," "maliciously," "wilfully," "with the purpose of," "with intent to," or combinations or permutations of these and synonymous terms. The existence of a *mens rea* is the rule of, rather than the exception to, the principles of Anglo-American criminal jurisprudence. . . .

The obvious purpose of the statute is to protect existing Government, not from change by peaceable, lawful and constitutional means, but from change by violence, revolution and terrorism. That it is within the *power* of the Congress to protect the Government of the United States from armed rebellion is a proposition which requires little discussion. Whatever theoretical merit there may be to the argument that there is a "right" to rebellion against dictatorial governments is without force where the existing structure of the government provides for peaceful and orderly change. We reject any principle of governmental helplessness in the face of preparation for revolution, which principle, carried to its logical conclusion, must lead to anarchy. No one could conceive that it is not within the power of Congress to prohibit acts intended to overthrow the Government by force and violence. The question with which we are concerned here is not whether Congress has such *power*, but whether the *means* which it has employed conflict with the First and Fifth Amendments to the Constitution.

One of the bases for the contention that the means which Congress has employed are invalid takes the form of an attack on the face of the statute on the grounds that by its terms it prohibits academic discussion of the merits of Marxism-Leninism, that it stifles ideas and is contrary to all concepts of a free speech and a free press. . . .

The very language of the Smith Act negates the interpretation which petitioners would have us impose on that Act. It is directed at advocacy, not discussion. Thus, the trial judge properly charged the jury that they could not convict if they found that petitioners did "no more than pursue peaceful studies and discussions or teaching and advocacy in the realm of ideas." He further charged that it was not unlawful "to conduct in an American college and university a course explaining the philosophical theories set forth in the books which have been placed in evidence." Such a charge is in strict accord with the statutory language, and illustrates the meaning to be placed on those words. Congress did not intend to eradicate the free discussion of political theories, to destroy the traditional rights of Americans to discuss and evaluate ideas without fear of governmental sanction. Rather Congress was concerned with the very kind of activity in which the evidence showed these petitioners engaged.

. . . The basis of the First Amendment is the hypothesis that speech can rebut speech, propaganda will answer propaganda, free debate of ideas will result in the wisest governmental policies. It is for this reason that this Court has recognized the inherent value of free discourse. An analysis of the leading cases in this Court which have involved direct limitations on speech, however, will demonstrate that both the majority of the Court and the dissenters in particular cases have recognized that this is not an unlimited, unqualified right, but that the societal value of speech must, on occasion, be subordinated to other values and considerations. . . .

The rule we deduce from these cases is that where an offense is specified by a statute in nonspeech or nonpress terms, a conviction relying upon speech or press as evidence of violation may be sustained only when the speech or publication created a "clear and present danger" of attempting or accomplishing the prohibited crime, e.g., interference with enlistment. . . .

. . . Neither Justice Holmes nor Justice Brandeis ever envisioned that a shorthand phrase should be crystallized into a rigid rule to be applied inflexibly without regard to the circumstances of each case. Speech is not an absolute, above and beyond control by the legislature when its judgment, subject to review here, is that certain kinds of speech are so undesirable as to warrant criminal sanction. Nothing is more certain in modern society than the principle that there are no absolutes, that a name, a phrase, a standard has meaning only when associated with the considerations which gave birth to the nomenclature. . . . To those who would paralyze our Government in the face of impending threat by encasing it in a semantic straitjacket we must reply that all concepts are relative.

. . . In this case we are squarely presented with the application of the "clear and present danger" test, and must decide what that phrase imports. We first note that many of the cases in which this Court has reversed convictions by use of this or similar tests have been based on the fact that the interest which the State was attempting to protect was itself too insubstantial to warrant restriction of speech. . . . Overthrow of the Government by force and violence is certainly a substantial enough interest for the Government to limit speech. Indeed, this is the ultimate value of any society, for if a society cannot protect its very structure from armed internal attack, it must follow that no subordinate value can be protected. If, then, this interest may be protected, the literal problem which is presented is what has been meant by the use of the phrase "clear and present danger" of the utterances bringing about the evil within the power of Congress to punish.

. . . Obviously, the words cannot mean that before the Government may act, it must wait until the *putsch* is about to be executed, the plans have been laid and the signal is awaited. If Government is aware that a group aiming at its overthrow is attempting to indoctrinate its members and to commit them to a course whereby they will strike when the leaders feel the circumstances permit, action by the Government is required. The argument that there is no need for Government to concern itself, for Government is strong, it possesses ample powers to put down a rebellion, it may defeat the revolution with ease needs no answer. For that is not the question. Certainly an attempt to overthrow the Government by force, even though doomed from the outset because of inadequate numbers or power of the revolutionists, is a sufficient evil for Congress to prevent. The damage which such attempts create both physically and politically to a nation makes it impossible to measure the validity in terms of the probability of success, or the immediacy of a successful attempt. In the instant case the trial judge charged the jury that they could not convict unless they found that petitioners intended to overthrow the Government "as speedily as circumstances would permit." This does not mean, and could not properly mean, that they would not strike until there was certainty of success. What was meant was that the revolutionists would strike when they thought the time was ripe. We must therefore reject the contention that success or probability of success is the criterion.

. . . Chief Judge Learned Hand, writing for the majority below, interpreted the phrase as follows: "In each case [courts] must ask whether the gravity of the 'evil,' discounted by its improbability, justifies such invasion of free speech as is necessary to avoid the danger."

. . . We adopt this statement of the rule. As articulated by Chief Judge Hand, it is as succinct and inclusive as any other we might devise at this time. It takes into consideration those factors which we deem relevant, and relates their significances. More we cannot expect from words.

. . . Likewise, we are in accord with the court below, which affirmed the trial court's finding that the requisite danger existed. The mere fact that from the period 1945 to 1948 petitioners' activities did not result in an attempt to overthrow the Government by force and violence is of course no answer to the fact that there was a group that was ready to make the attempt. The formation by petitioners of such a highly organized conspiracy, with rigidly disciplined members subject to call when the leaders, these petitioners, felt that the time had come for action, coupled with the inflammable nature of world conditions, similar uprisings in other countries, and the touch-and-go nature of our relations with countries with whom petitioners were in the very least ideologically attuned, convince us that their convictions were justified on this score. And this analysis disposes of the contention that a conspiracy to advocate, as distinguished from the advocacy itself, cannot be constitutionally restrained, because it comprises only the preparation. It is the existence of the conspiracy which creates the danger. . . . If the ingredients of the reaction are present, we cannot bind the Government to wait until the catalyst is added.

... Although we have concluded that the finding that there was a sufficient danger to warrant the application of the statute was justified on the merits, there remains the problem of whether the trial judge's treatment of the issue was correct. He charged the jury, in relevant part, as follows: ...

If you are satisfied that the evidence established beyond a reasonable doubt that the defendants, or any of them, are guilty of a violation of the statute as I have interpreted it to you, I find as a matter of law that there is sufficient danger of a substantive evil that the Congress has a right to prevent to justify the application of the statute under the First Amendment of the Constitution.

This is a matter of law about which you have no concern. It is a finding on a matter of law which I deem essential to support my ruling that the case should be submitted to you to pass upon the guilt or innocence of the defendants. ...

It is thus clear that he reserved the question of the existence of the danger for his own determination, and the question becomes whether the issue is of such a nature that it should have been submitted to the jury.

... The argument that the action of the trial court is erroneous, in declaring as a matter of law that such violation shows sufficient danger to justify the punishment despite the First Amendment, rests on the theory that a jury must decide a question of the application of the First Amendment. We do not agree. ...

The question in this case is whether the statute which the legislature has enacted may be constitutionally applied. In other words, the Court must examine judicially the application of the statute to the particular situation, to ascertain if the Constitution prohibits the conviction. We hold that the statute may be applied where there is a "clear and present danger" of the substantive evil which the legislature had the right to prevent. Bearing, as it does, the marks of a "question of law," the issue is properly one for the judge to decide.

There remains to be discussed the question of vagueness—whether the statute as we have interpreted it is too vague, not sufficiently advising those who would speak of the limitations upon their activity. It is urged that such vagueness contravenes the First and Fifth Amendments. ...

We agree that the standard as defined is not a neat, mathematical formulary. Like all verbalizations it is subject to criticism on the score of indefiniteness. But petitioners themselves contend that the verbalization, "clear and present danger," is the proper standard. We see no difference from the standpoint of vagueness, whether the standard of "clear and present danger" is one contained in *haec verba* within the statute, or whether it is the judicial measure of constitutional applicability. We have shown the indeterminate standard the phrase necessarily connotes. We do not think we have rendered that standard any more indefinite by our attempt to sum up the factors which are included within its scope. We think it well serves to indicate to those who would advocate constitutionally prohibited conduct that there is a line beyond which they may not go—a line, which they, in full knowledge of what they intend and the circumstances in which their activity takes place, will well appreciate and understand. ...

We hold that § § 2(a) (1), 2(a) (3), and 3 of the Smith Act, do not inherently, or as construed or applied in the instant case, violate the First Amendment and other provisions of the Bill of Rights, or the First and Fifth Amendments because of indefiniteness. Petitioners intended to overthrow the Government of the United States as speedily as the circumstances would permit. Their conspiracy to organize the Communist Party and to teach and advocate the overthrow of the Government of the United States by force and violence created a "clear and present danger" of an attempt to overthrow the Government by force and violence. They were properly and constitutionally convicted for violation of the Smith Act. The Judgments of conviction are affirmed.

Mr. Justice Black, dissenting:

Here ... my basic disagreement with the Court is not as to how we should explain or reconcile what was said in prior decisions but springs from a fundamental difference in constitutional approach. Consequently, it would serve no useful purpose to state my position at length.

At the outset I want to emphasize what the crime involved in this case is, and what it is not. These petitioners were not charged with an attempt to overthrow the Government. They were not charged with overt acts of any kind designed to overthrow the Government. They were not even charged with saying anything or writing anything designed to overthrow the Government. The charge was that they agreed to assemble and to talk and publish certain ideas at a later date: The indictment is that they conspired to organize the Communist Party and to use speech or newspapers and other publications in the future to teach and advocate the forcible overthrow of the Government. No matter how it is worded, this is a virulent form of prior censorship of speech and press, which I believe the First Amendment forbids. I would hold § 3 of the Smith Act authorizing this prior restraint unconstitutional on its face and as applied.

But let us assume, contrary to all constitutional ideas of fair criminal procedure, that petitioners although not indicted for the crime of actual advocacy, may be punished for it. Even on this radical assumption, the other opinions in this case show that the only way to affirm these convictions is to repudiate directly or indirectly the established "clear and present danger" rule. This the Court does in a way which greatly restricts the protections afforded by the First Amendment. The opinions for affirmance indicate that the chief reason for jettisoning the rule is the expressed fear that advocacy of Communist doctrine endangers the safety of the Republic. Undoubtedly, a governmental policy of unfettered communication of ideas does entail dangers. To the Founders of this Nation, however, the benefits derived from free expression were worth the risk. They embodied this philosophy in the First Amendment's command that Congress "shall make no law . . . abridging the freedom of speech, or of the press. . . ." I have always believed that the First Amendment is the keystone of our Government, that the freedoms it guarantees provide the best insurance against destruction of all freedom. At least as to speech in the realm of public matters, I believe that the "clear and present danger" test does not "mark the furthermost constitutional boundaries of protected expression" but does "no more than recognize a minimum compulsion of the Bill of Rights." *Bridges v. California*, 314 U.S. 252. . . .

So long as this Court exercises the power of judicial review of legislation, I cannot agree that the First Amendment permits us to sustain laws suppressing freedom of speech and press on the basis of Congress' or our own notions of mere "reasonableness." Such a doctrine waters down the First Amendment so that it amounts to little more than an admonition to Congress. The Amendment as so construed is not likely to protect any but those "safe" or orthodox views which rarely need its protection. I must also express my objection to the holding because, as Mr. Justice Douglas' dissent shows, it sanctions the determination of a crucial issue of fact by the judge rather than by the jury. Nor can I let this opportunity pass without expressing my objection to the severely limited grant of certiorari in this case which precluded consideration here of at least two other reasons for reversing these convictions: (1) the record shows a discriminatory selection of the jury panel which prevented trial before a representative cross-section of the community; (2) the record shows that one member of the trial jury was violently hostile to petitioners before and during the trial.

Public opinion being what it now is, few will protest the conviction of these Communist petitioners. There is hope, however, that in calmer times, when present pressures, passions and fears subside, this or some later Court will restore the First Amendment liberties to the high preferred place where they belong in a free society.

BARENBLATT CASE: BLACK DISSENTING*

The Questions Infringe Upon the First Amendment. The First Amendment says in no equivocal language that Congress shall pass no law abridging freedom of speech, press, assembly or petition. The activities of this Committee, authorized by Congress, do precisely that, through exposure, obloquy and public scorn. See *Watkins* v. *United States*, 354 U.S. 178, 197-198. The Court does not really deny this fact but relies on a combination of three reasons for permitting the infringement: (A) The notion that despite the First Amendment's command Congress can abridge speech and association if this Court decides that the governmental interest in abridging speech is greater than an individual's interest in exercising that freedom. (B) the Government's right to "preserve itself," (C) the fact that the Committee is only after Communists or suspected Communists in this investigation.

First Amendment Freedoms and the Balancing Test. (A) I do not agree that laws directly abridging First Amendment freedoms can be justified by a congressional or judicial balancing process. There are, of course, cases suggesting that a law which primarily regulates conduct but which might also indirectly affect speech can be upheld if the effect on speech is minor in relation to the need for control of the conduct. With these cases I agree. Typical of them are *Cantwell* v. *Connecticut*, 310 U.S. 296, and *Schneider* v. *Irvington*, 308 U.S. 147. Both of these involved the right of a city to control its streets. In *Cantwell*, a man had been convicted of breach of the peace for playing a phonograph on the street. He defended on the ground that he was disseminating religious views and could not, therefore, be stopped. We upheld his defense, but in so doing we pointed out that the city did have substantial power over conduct on the streets even where this power might to some extent affect speech. A State, we said, might "by general and non-discriminatory legislation regulate the times, the places, and the manner of soliciting upon its

* [*Barenblatt vs. United States, 360 U.S. 109 (1959).*—Eds.]

streets and holding meetings thereon." 310 U.S., at 304. But even such laws governing conduct, we emphasized, must be tested, though only by a balancing process, if they indirectly affect ideas. On one side of the balance, we pointed out, is the interest of the United States in seeing that its fundamental law protecting freedom of communication is not abridged; on the other the obvious interest of the State to regulate conduct within its boundaries. In *Cantwell* we held that the need to control the streets could not justify the restriction made on speech. We stressed the fact that where a man had a right to be on a street, "he had a right peacefully to impart his views to others." 310 U.S., at 308. Similar views were expressed in *Schneider*, which concerned ordinances prohibiting the distribution of handbills to prevent littering. We forbade application of such ordinances when they affected literature designed to spread ideas. There were other ways, we said, to protect the city from littering which would not sacrifice the right of the people to be informed. In so holding, we, of course, found it necessary to "weigh the circumstances." 308 U.S., at 161. But we did not in *Schneider*, any more than in *Cantwell*, even remotely suggest that a law directly aimed at curtailing speech and political persuasion could be saved through a balancing process. Neither these cases, nor any others, can be read as allowing legislative bodies to pass laws abridging freedom of speech, press and association merely because of hostility to views peacefully expressed in a place where the speaker had a right to be. Rule XI, on its face and as here applied, since it attempts inquiry into beliefs, not action—ideas and associations, not conduct, does just that.

To apply the Court's balancing test under such circumstances is to read the First Amendment to say "Congress shall pass no law abridging freedom of speech, press, assembly and petition, unless Congress and the Supreme Court reach the joint conclusion that on balance the interests of the Government in stifling these freedoms is greater than the interest of the people in having them exercised." This is closely akin to the notion that neither the First Amendment nor any other provision of the Bill of Rights should be enforced unless the Court believes it is *reasonable* to do so. Not only does this violate the genius of our *written* Constitution, but it runs expressly counter to the injunction to Court and Congress made by Madison when he introduced the Bill of Rights. "If they [the first ten amendments] are incorporated into the Constitution, independent tribunals of justice will consider themselves in a peculiar manner the guardians of those rights; they will be an impenetrable bulwark against *every* assumption of power in the Legislative or Executive; they will be naturally led to resist *every* encroachment upon rights expressly stipulated for in the Constitution by the declaration of rights." Unless we return to this view of our judicial function, unless we once again accept the notion that the Bill of Rights means what it says and that this Court must enforce that meaning, I am of the opinion that our great charter of liberty will be more honored in the breach than in the observance.

The Right to Err Politically. But even assuming what I cannot assume, that some balancing is proper in this case, I feel that the Court after stating the test ignores it completely. At most it balances the right of the Government to preserve itself, against Barenblatt's right to refrain from revealing Communist affiliations. Such a balance, however, mistakes the factors to be weighed. In the first place, it completely leaves out the real interest in Barenblatt's silence, the interest of the people as a whole in being able to join organizations, advocate causes and make political "mistakes" without later being subjected to governmental penalties for having dared to think for themselves. It is this right, the right to err politically, which keeps us strong as a Nation. For no number of laws against communism can have as much effect as the personal conviction which comes from having heard its arguments and rejected them, or from having once accepted its tenets and later recognized their worthlessness. Instead, the obloquy which results from investigations such as this not only stifles "mistakes" but prevents all but the most courageous from hazarding any views which might at some later time become disfavored. This result, whose importance cannot be overestimated, is doubly crucial when it affects the universities, on which we must largely rely for the experimentation and development of new ideas essential to our country's welfare. It is these interests of society, rather than Barenblatt's own right to silence, which I think the Court should put on the balance against the demands of the Government, if any balancing process is to be tolerated. Instead they are not mentioned, while on the other side the demands of the Government are vastly overstated and called "self-preservation." It is admitted that this Committee can only seek information for the purpose of suggesting laws, and that Congress' power to make laws in the realm of speech and association is quite limited, even on the Court's test. Its interest in making such laws in the field of education, primarily a state function, is clearly narrower still. Yet the Court styles this attenuated interest self-preservation and allows it to overcome the need our country has to let us all think, speak, and associate politically as we like and without fear of reprisal. Such a result reduces "balancing" to a mere play on words and is completely inconsistent with the rules this Court has previously given for applying a "balancing test," where it is proper: "[T]he courts should be *astute* to examine the *effect* of the challenged legislation. Mere *legislative preferences or beliefs* ... may well support regulation directed at other personal activities, but be insufficient to justify such as diminishes the exercise of rights so vital to the maintenance of democratic institutions." *Schneider* v. *Irvington*, 308 U.S. 147, 161. (Italics supplied.)

Freedom and National Security. (B) Moreover, I cannot agree with the Court's notion that First Amendment freedoms must be abridged in order to "preserve" our country. That notion rests on the unarticulated premise that this Nation's security hangs upon its power to punish people because of what they think, speak or write about, or because of those with whom they associate for political purposes. The Government, in its brief, virtually admits this position when it speaks of the "communication of unlawful ideas." I challenge this premise, and deny that ideas can be proscribed under our Constitution. I agree that despotic governments cannot exist without stifling the voice of opposition to their oppressive practices. The First Amendment means to me, however, that the only constitutional way our Government can preserve itself is to leave its people the fullest possible freedom to praise, criticize or discuss, as they see fit, all governmental policies and to suggest, if they desire, that even its most fundamental postulates are bad and should be changed; "Therein lies the security of the Republic, the very foundation of constitutional government." On that premise this land was created, and on that premise it has grown to greatness. Our Constitution assumes that the common sense of the people and their attachment to our country will enable them, after free discussion, to withstand ideas that are wrong. To say that our patriotism must be protected against false ideas by means other than these is, I think, to make a baseless charge. Unless we can rely on these qualities—if, in short, we begin to punish speech—we cannot honestly proclaim ourselves to be a free Nation and we have lost what the Founders of this land risked their lives and their sacred honors to defend.

Outlawing the Communist Party. (C) The Court implies, however, that the ordinary rules and requirements of the Constitution do not apply because the Committee is merely after Communists and they do not constitute a political party but only a criminal gang. "[T]he long and widely accepted view," the Court says, is "that the tenets of the Communist Party include the ultimate overthrow of the Government of the United States by force and violence." This justifies the investigation undertaken. By accepting this charge and allowing it to support treatment of the Communist Party and its members which would violate the Constitution if applied to other groups, the Court, in effect, declares that Party outlawed. It has been only a few years since there was a practically unanimous feeling throughout the country and in our courts that this could not be done in our free land. Of course it has always been recognized that members of the Party who, either individually or in combination, commit acts in violation of valid laws can be prosecuted. But the Party as a whole and innocent members of it could not be attainted merely because it had some illegal aims and because some of its members were lawbreakers. Thus in *De Jonge* v. *Oregon*, 299 U. S. 353, 357, on stipulated facts that the Communist Party advocated criminal syndicalism—"crime, physical violence, sabotage or any unlawful acts or methods as a means of accomplishing or effecting industrial or political change or revolution"—a unanimous Court, speaking through Chief Justice Hughes, held that a Communist addressing a Communist rally could be found guilty of no offense so long as no violence or crime was urged at the meeting. The Court absolutely refused to concede that either De Jonge or the Communist Party forfeited the protections of the First and Fourteenth Amendments because one of the Party's purposes was to effect a violent change of government. See also *Herndon* v. *Lowry*, 301 U. S. 242.

Later, in 1948, when various bills were proposed in the House and Senate to handicap or outlaw the Communist Party, leaders of the Bar who had been asked to give their views rose up to contest the constitutionality of the measures. The late Charles Evans Hughes, Jr., questioned the validity under both the First and Fifth Amendments of one of these bills, which in effect outlawed the Party. The late John W. Davis attacked it as lacking an ascertainable standard of guilt under many of this Court's cases. And the Attorney General of the United States not only indicated that such a measure would be unconstitutional but declared it to be unwise even if valid. He buttressed his position by citing a statement by J. Edgar Hoover, Director of the Federal Bureau of Investigation, and the declaration of this Court in *West Virginia Board of Education* v. *Barnette*, 319 U.S. 624,642, that:

If there is any fixed star in our constitutional constellation, it is that no official, high or petty, can prescribe what shall be orthodox in politics, nationalism, religion, or other matters of opinion or force citizens to confess by word or act their faith therein.

Even the proponent of the bill disclaimed any aim to outlaw the Communist Party and pointed out the "disadvantages" of such a move by stating that "the Communist Party was illegal and outlawed in Russia when it took over control of the Soviet Union." Again, when the Attorney General testified on a proposal to bar the Communist Party from the ballot he said, "an organized group, whether you call it political or not, could hardly be barred from the ballot without jeopardizing the constitutional guarantees of all other political groups and parties."

All these statements indicate quite clearly that no matter how often or how quickly we repeat the claim that the Communist Party is not a political party, we cannot outlaw it, as a group, without endangering the liberty of all of us. The reason is not hard to find, for mixed among those aims of communism which are illegal are perfectly normal political and social goals. And muddled with its revolutionary tenets is a drive to achieve power through the ballot, if it can be done. These things necessarily make it a political party whatever other, illegal, aims it may have. Cf. *Gerende* v. *Board of Supervisors*, 341 U. S. 56. Significantly until recently the Communist Party was on the ballot in many States. When that was so, many Communists undoubtedly hoped to accomplish its lawful goals through support of Communist candidates. Even now some such may still remain. To attribute to them, and to those who have left the Party, the taint of the group is to ignore both our traditions that guilt like belief is "personal and not a matter of mere association" and the obvious fact that "men adhering to a political party or other organization notoriously do not subscribe unqualifiedly to all of its platforms or asserted principles." *Schneiderman* v. *United States*, 320 U. S. 118, 136. See also *Dennis* v. *United States*, 341 U. S. 494, 579, 581 (dissenting opinions).

No Group Is Safe. The fact is that once we allow any group which has some political aims or ideas to be driven from the ballot and from the battle for men's minds because some of its members are bad and some of its tenets are illegal, no group is safe. Today we deal with Communists or suspected Communists. In 1920, instead, the New York Assembly suspended duly elected legislators on the ground that, being Socialists, they were disloyal to the country's principles. In the 1830's the Masons were hunted as outlaws and subversives, and abolitionists were considered revolutionaries of the most dangerous kind in both North and South. Earlier still, at the time of the universally unlamented alien and sedition laws, Thomas Jefferson's party was attacked and its members were derisively called "Jacobins." Fisher Ames described the party as a "French faction" guilty of "subversion" and "officered, regimented and formed to subordination." Its members, he claimed, intended to "take arms against the laws as soon as they dare." History should teach us then, that in times of high emotional excitement minority parties and groups which advocate extremely unpopular social or governmental innovations will always be typed as criminal gangs and attempts will always be made to drive them out. It was knowledge of this fact, and of its great dangers, that caused the Founders of our land to enact the First Amendment as a guarantee that neither Congress nor the people would do anything to hinder or destroy the capacity of individuals and groups to seek converts and votes for any cause, however radical or unpalatable their principles might seem under the accepted notions of the time. Whatever the States were left free to do, the First Amendment sought to leave Congress devoid of any kind or quality of power to direct any type of national laws against the freedom of individuals to think what they please, advocate whatever policy they choose, and join with others to bring about the social, religious, political and governmental changes which seem best to them. Today's holding, in my judgment, marks another major step in the progressively increasing retreat from the safeguards of the First Amendment.

It is, sadly, no answer to say that this Court will not allow the trend to overwhelm us; that today's holding will be strictly confined to "Communists," as the Court's language implies. This decision can no more be contained than could the holding in *American Communications Assn.* v. *Douds*, 339 U. S. 382. In that case the Court sustained as an exercise of the commerce power an Act which required labor union officials to take an oath that they were not members of the Communist Party. The Court rejected the idea that the *Douds* holding meant that the Party and all its members could be attainted because of their Communist beliefs. It went to great lengths to explain that the Act held valid "touches only a relative handful of persons, leaving the great majority of persons of the identified affiliations and beliefs completely free from restraint." "[W]hile this Court sits," the Court proclaimed, no wholesale proscription of Communists or their Party can occur. 339 U. S., at 404, 410. I dissented and said:

Under such circumstances, restrictions imposed on proscribed groups are seldom static, even though the rate of expansion may not move in geometric progression from discrimination to arm-band to ghetto and worse. Thus I cannot regard the Court's holding as one which merely bars Communists from holding union office and nothing more. For its reasoning would apply just as forcibly to statutes barring Communists and their respective sympathizers from election to political office, mere membership in unions, and in fact from getting or holding any job whereby they could earn a living. 339 U. S., at 449.

My prediction was all too accurate. Today, Communists or suspected Communists have been denied an opportunity to work as government employees, lawyers, doctors, teachers, pharmacists, veterinarians, subway conductors, industrial workers and in just about any other job. See *Speiser* v. *Randall*, 357 U.S. 513, 531 (concurring opinion). Cf. *Barsky* v. *Board of Regents*, 347 U. S. 442, 456, 467, 472 (dissenting opinions). In today's holding they are singled out and, as a class, are subjected to inquisitions which the Court suggests would be unconstitutional but for the fact of "Communism." Nevertheless, this Court still sits!

Suggested Readings

1. Arendt, Hannah, *On Revolution* (New York: Viking, 1962).
2. Brinton, Crane, *The Anatomy of Revolution* (New York: Viking, 1962).
3. Friedrich, Carl J. (ed.), *Revolution* (New York: Atherton, 1964).
4. Laquer, Walter, "Revolution," *International Encyclopedia of the Social Sciences,* Vol. 8 (1968), pp. 501-507.
5. Lenin, V. I.. *State and Revolution* (London: Allen & Unwin, 1919).

FIVE

Up Against the Law, Citizen

The main supports of crime are idleness, law and authority; laws about property, laws about government, laws about penalties and misdemeanors; and authority, which takes upon itself to manufacture these laws and apply them."

—Peter Kropotkin

INTRODUCTION

One often hears it said that the best country is a nation of laws and not of men. That is, a country governed by men who are governed by law is more likely to have a just society than one governed by men who are not governed by law.

Monarchies and dictatorships are cited as examples of government by men who are not governed by law; monarchs and dictators have no legal limits on their power. Their sound judgments or absurd whims are equally sufficient bases for governmental decisions. In the United States, the Constitution was expressly framed to provide legal limits on the men who govern the country: the executives, the legislators, and the judges.

Although the long-range likelihood that there will be greater justice in a nation of laws than in a nation of men may be correct, the civil rights movement, the Vietnam War, and the Third World dissent against domestic colonialism have shown that to be a nation of laws may not be enough to guarantee a just society. The laws must also be just.

Of course, it is not enough to have just laws on the books. The people in a society must obey the just laws if the society is to be just. Although school desegregation is required by law, there are many communities and cities, north and south, that have not desegregated or that have given merely token obeisance to the law. Thus, even if a country's government is subject to law, and even if its laws are just, if a country's citizens do not obey the laws, then it is a country of men and not of laws.

When people do not obey just laws, society is justified in taking appropriate legal steps to enforce the laws. But what if a person who fails to obey the law does so not out of malicious intent but because he honestly believes the law is unjust? Since any law that has been passed in accordance with authorized procedures is "legal," it isn't possible to appeal to the law itself to challenge the law. It appears that one must appeal to extra-legal concepts and principles in order to challenge, or justify, the justness of a disputed law. It is a well-known fact that people often believe they are morally justified in disobeying a law because by moral standards they judge the law to be unjust. If laws are to be evaluated by moral standards, moral standards must supersede legal standards as a basis for our actions; therefore, a person who believes a law is unjust is morally obligated to disobey the law.

So far, we have spoken only of some of a nation's laws as possibly being unjust and have not challenged the rubric that a nation of laws is more likely to be just than a nation without laws. It is this rubric that anarchists challenge. In this chapter's last essay, **Peter Kropotkin** argues that a society without laws would be more just than one with laws. He claims that "Customs, absolutely essential to the very being of society, are, in the [legal] code, cleverly intermingled with usages imposed by the ruling caste, and both claim equal respect from the crowd. . . . Such was law; and it has maintained its two-fold character to this day. Its origin is the desire of the ruling class to give permanence to customs imposed by themselves for their own advantage."

For Kropotkin and other anarchists, laws, instead of being a source of justice, are the chief source of injustice because they are promulgated by the people in power who devise the laws in their own interest. Justice implies that no class or group of persons should use the state to serve their own interests at the expense of the rest of the citizens. But laws designed for special interests do not satisfy this minimum requirement of justice; therefore, laws are a source of injustice.

If one concedes that laws may be a source of injustice, he could still maintain against Kropotkin's view that instead of doing away with law we should devise governmental reform that will be more likely to insure passage of laws that do not favor one class over against another. This reform would seek a balance of powers in the state. If this seems as utopian as Kropotkin's confidence in moral customs, it could be argued, alternatively, that, because laws or customs can always be expected to favor some class over against others, the best course to take is to permit the existence of law in order to assure stability while disobeying the laws that are unjust.

We can imagine a counterargument. Although it is true that challenging a law by disobedience may force or hurry lawmakers and judges to change the law, still a society that continually uses this method to force legal reform may sacrifice order and stability. Repeated disobedience may lead either to anarchy (which Kropotkin favors) or repression. Granted, those who argue for stability often do so only to extend the life of unjust laws; still, we must be sensitive to the age-old conflict between the claims of order, on the one hand, and justice on the other. These considerations show us that we may have a prima-facie moral duty to obey the law; hence, if we have a moral duty to obey the law, we cannot have a moral duty to disobey the law, even if it is an unjust law, unless it can be shown that the duty to disobey an unjust law is higher than the duty to obey it.

Plato has Socrates argue in the *Crito,* this chapter's first essay, that we should never disobey the law. Several considerations to support this claim are given, but the following is an important argument to be extracted from the *Crito:* No man may do wrong. To harm anyone is to do a wrong. Disobeying a law (just or unjust) is harming the state (and eventually other citizens). Even if the law is unjust, disobeying an unjust law harms someone, and, so, wrongs someone. Therefore, disobeying the law is to do a wrong; hence, no man may disobey the law.

A counterargument, using Socrates' first premise but turning on an act of omission rather than commission, can be fashioned as follows: No man may do wrong (Socrates' first premise). To allow someone to be harmed (omission) is to do a wrong. If obeying a law (just or unjust) deters one from preventing harm, then he has done a wrong. Therefore, obeying a law is to do a wrong; hence, no man may obey the law.

Of course, what you will probably find objectionable in both of these arguments are their sweeping conclusions. You may think that the sound position is not to obey or disobey all laws but some only and that, further, there may be a way of disobeying that does not threaten stability. This is the position taken by **Rudolph H. Weingartner** in this chapter's second essay. He argues that there are some conditions under which we are morally justified in civilly disobeying a law. He defines "civil disobedience" as acting illegally, nonviolently, publicly, and conscientiously with intent to frustrate a law or laws of the government.

We are deeply immersed in international anarchy. International law has practically no deterrent effect on nations. International laws regarding war have been liberally disobeyed; unfortunately, they are infrequently civilly disobeyed. We have included Justice **Robert Jackson**'s Nuremberg trial statement as part of the third essay in this chapter to remind us that there are advocates of transnational laws. The Nuremberg trials of Nazi war criminals is a painful reminder to us: The My Lai incident in the Vietnam War has showed us that it isn't always other countries' wars that have spawned war criminals. The question that arose about the extent of "German guilt" arose in this country about the extent of our guilt. Who was guilty? Lieutenant William Calley alone? Our colonels and the generals in Vietnam? The generals in the Pentagon? The Secretary of Defense? The President and his panoply of advisers? Every United States citizen?

Using the Nuremberg Trials as a guideline to evaluate the My Lai affair seems necessary if we are not to be guilty of hypocrisy, unless it can be shown that we were in error in the Nuremberg Trials. Consider first the Nuremberg precedent for guilt at the lower level: The concept of individual responsibility prescribes that crimes are committed by individuals, not nations, and that individuals cannot "take refuge in superior orders." As to guilt at the highest level, which is where many Americans believe the real guilt for My Lai lies, notice the following definitions issued by the International Military Tribunal of 1945 (in the third essay of this chapter): (a) crimes against peace—planning a war of aggression; (b) war crimes—deportation of the civil population; (c) crimes against humanity—persecution on political grounds.

Despite the precedent of the Nuremberg Trials, many who hold the view that every President in office during the Vietnam War and all United States citizens are guilty of My Lai fail to note that the crimes for which the lower levels are guilty are different from the crimes for which the upper levels are guilty. An instance of the failure to make this distinction is found in a resolution that the Kansas legislative House passed: "Let the soul of our nation be blemished and not the life of a man [Calley] caught in the complex cobwebs of a combat assignment that we directly or indirectly foisted upon him." Lieutenant Calley was accused of deliberately killing Vietnam civilians; President Richard Nixon cannot be held responsible for that, though one might more plausibly accuse him and other Vietnam War presidents of waging a "war of aggression."

Consider the following argument against the claim that the highest governmental levels, and all the American people, are responsible for Lieutenant Calley's crime: Grant that Calley is responsible for Act *c*. To hold someone else, B, responsible for Act *c* requires that B and Calley share responsibility for Act *c*. To hold a person responsible for an act requires at least that (1) he be able to make moral distinctions; (2) be conscious of what he is doing, including intending to do what he did; and (3) be in control of himself, that is, not be coerced. Calley, having been present at the shooting, was conscious of what he was doing and apparently intended to do what he did do. But someone else, B, either a general in the Pentagon, the President of the United States, or merely some U.S. citizen, was not present at My Lai when the massacre occurred and, so, could not have been conscious of what was happening in the requisite sense. Since B does not fulfill the conditions for responsibility, he cannot be held responsible with Calley for the My Lai massacre.

It might be replied that although B cannot be held directly responsible for My Lai, he can be held indirectly responsible. To hold B indirectly responsible for Act *c* requires, of course, that B be held directly responsible for some Act *b*, and Act *b* must be related to Act *c* in such a way that Act *b* contributed to the occurrence of Act *c* in some requisite way.

We might outline a notion of indirect responsibility as follows, where a series of two or more direct responsibilities add up to an indirect responsibility.

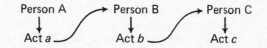

Neither Act *a* nor Act *b* can be related to Act *c* itself. To do that would make Act *c* a combination of two direct responsibilities, Act *a* and Act *b*, such as our beating Jones, me holding him while you hit him. Act *a* must be related in some way to Person B, and Act *b* must be related in some way to Person C. Thus, a general, B, ordering Calley and his unit into the field would be such a relationship.

So would the President, A, be related to the general, B, by ordering the general in Vietnam, who was to put Calley into the field, to put men into the field.

Once we start working on a notion of indirect responsibility, notice that neither A nor B can now be held indirectly responsible for the massacre at My Lai unless someone can show that they knew that Calley would be likely to do what he did or ordered him to do what he did—none of which seems to be the case. The President, A, may be responsible for waging a war of aggression without declaration and we, as citizens, may be responsible for insufficient protest or resistance to the war, but these acts are difficult to relate to Calley's My Lai acts in a way that makes the President or us either directly or indirectly responsible for what Calley did, though, of course, we and the President may be responsible for some other acts for which we and he should be condemned.

We cannot assume, however, that carrying on or supporting a war is always a crime. It is open to one to defend a country's political leaders, soldiers, and citizens by arguing that the war they sanctioned and supported was a just war—if there is such a thing as a just war. You probably believe that we were just in waging war against Nazi Germany, that our war was a just war, although one is given pause by Adin Ballou's vivid sentences:

It has been held justifiable and necessary, for individuals and nations to inflict any amount of injury which would effectually resist a supposed greater injury. . . . The earth has been rendered a vast slaughterfield—a theatre of reciprocal cruelty and vengeance—strewn with human skulls, reeking with human blood, resounding with human groans, and steeped with human tears.

Donald Wells (fourth essay of this chapter) raises some interesting questions about the concept of a "just war." Even if it were a legitimate concept at one time, he suggests it may be possible that the conditions of war have changed so drastically that it can never again be applied consistently.

Whether you are against all or only some wars, some people do conscientiously object to all wars, others to only some. Should society allow its citizens to refuse war service? The United States presently has a law that provides exemption for conscientious objectors, but it contains two limiting provisions that objectors strongly challenge. **Carl Cohen,** in the fifth essay in this chapter, examines the merits of these two provisions. The first provision requires that a person's objection to war be based on religious grounds; the second prevents a person from being classified as a conscientious objector unless he objects to all wars. Cohen considers the demerits of the religious-ground provision and in the last section of his essay states how the concept of the religious has been so extended as to accommodate a great many other grounds for conscientious objection. The second provision is highly relevant to Wells' discussion of just war because many young men and women believe that our war against Germany was just but that our war against the North Vietnamese is unjust. If the second provision were amended to allow selective conscientious objections, then a man could legally refuse to serve in the Vietnamese War even though he would have willingly served in World War II.

Controversy about a particular law, such as a law about conscientious objectors, is bound to lead one to gain a wider perspective on the law, to lead one to a philosophical examination of related issues in an effort to find support for his view on a particular law. **Roscoe Pound,** in this chapter's next-to-the-last essay, summarizes twelve views of the nature of law per se because he finds that ideas of what law is for lie embedded in views of what law is. Ideas of what law is for are important for Pound because he thinks they influence us to pass the laws we actually promulgate and are willing to enforce. Lying in back of a controversy about a particular law may be differing views of what law is for.

Pound traces the development of four different views of the purpose of law and relates them to the kinds of laws they helped foster. To give an immediate point to Pound's essay, you might try to determine to which of the four purposes of law he distinguishes you think a person subscribes who wants a narrow conscientious objector law.

That the purpose of law and particular laws are related becomes more evident if you consider that a particular law presumably can be evaluated on the basis of its being a functional (or dysfunctional) means to accomplish the purpose of law. If the end or purpose is good, then, on the assumption that the ends justify (or condemn) the means, the means to that end is (so far) good (or bad). Suppose, though, that Law_1 serves End_1 and that Law_2 serves End_2. Suppose, further, that Law_1 thwarts End_2 and that Law_2 thwarts End_1. Then Law_1 is (so far) bad, and likewise for Law_2. We must conclude that Law_1 is both good and bad and that Law_2 is both good and bad. But this is an absurd result; something cannot be both good and bad; therefore, one might conclude that it is not possible to judge the merits of a particular law on the basis of its serving or thwarting good ends.

However, we can formulate an argument in defense of Pound's position that the purpose of law can be used to evaluate a particular law. See what you think of it.

We get an absurd conclusion that a law is both good and bad when an argument contains an incompatibility. That incompatibility lies between End_1 and End_2. For example, Pound's third and fourth ends of law, that law is for maximizing free self-assertion and for maximizing the satisfaction of human wants, are not always compatible. Now, if two ends are incompatible, then their means will be incompatible. That is, if End_1 and End_2 are incompatible, then if $Means_1$ promotes End_1 it will thwart End_2. If two ends are incompatible, not both can be good. Therefore, supposing End_1 is good and End_2 is bad, $Means_1$ will be good because it promotes End_1, and it will also be good (hence, not also bad) because it thwarts End_2. $Means_1$ is not, then, both good and bad, but good and good. Thus, Pound's criterion is saved.

The Citizen and the Law

Plato

Plato (427/8-347/8 B.C.), one of the great Greek philosophers, has exerted more influence upon the development of Western philosophy than any other writer with the possible exception of his student, Aristotle. He established the Academy in Athens, the first of the major schools of ancient Greece. His works, written in dialogue form and featuring his teacher Socrates as the principal figure, have continued to be widely read, not only for their intellectual content but also for their literary merit. Among his writings of interest to the student of ethics are *Euthyphro, Apology, Crito, Phaedo, The Republic, Protagoras, Gorgias,* and *Philebus.*

CRITO. ... But, oh! my beloved Socrates, let me entreat you once more to take my advice and escape. For if you die I shall not only lose a friend who can never be replaced, but there is another evil: people who do not know you and me will believe that I might have saved you if I had been willing to give money, but that I did not care. Now, can there be a worse disgrace than this—that I should be thought to value money more than the life of a friend? For the many will not be persuaded that I wanted you to escape, and that you refused.

SOCRATES. But why, my dear Crito, should we care about the opinion of the many? Good men, and they are the only persons who are worth considering, will think of these things truly as they occurred.

CR. But you see, Socrates, that the opinion of the many must be regarded, for what is happening shows that they can do the greatest evil to any one who has lost their good opinion.

SOC. I only wish it were so, Crito; and that the many could do the greatest evil; for then they would also be able to do the greatest good—and what a fine thing this would be! But in reality they can do neither; for they cannot make a man either wise or foolish; and whatever they do is the result of chance.

CR. Well, I will not dispute with you; but please tell me, Socrates, whether you are not acting out of regard to me and your other friends: are you not afraid that if you escape from prison we may get into trouble with the informers for having stolen you away, and lose either the whole or a great part of our property; or that even a worse evil may happen to us? Now, if you fear on our account, be at ease; for in order to save you, we ought surely to run this, or even a greater risk; be persuaded, then, and do as I say.

SOC. Yes, Crito, that is one fear which you mention, but by no means the only one.

CR. Fear not—there are persons who are willing to get you out of prison at no great cost; and as for the informers, they are far from being exorbitant in their demands—a little money will satisfy them. My means, which are certainly ample,

Source: *The Apology,* in *The Dialogues of Plato,* Benjamin Jowett, trans. (3d ed.; London: The Macmillan Company, Ltd., 1892).

are at your service, and if you have a scruple about spending all mine, here are strangers who will give you the use of theirs; and one of them, Simmias the Theban, has brought a large sum of money for this very purpose; and Cebes and many others are prepared to spend their money in helping you to escape. I say, therefore, do not hesitate on our account, and do not say, as you did in the court, that you will have a difficulty in knowing what to do with yourself anywhere else. For men will love you in other places to which you may go, and not in Athens only; there are friends of mine in Thessaly, if you like to go to them, who will value and protect you, and no Thessalian will give you any trouble. Nor can I think that you are at all justified, Socrates, in betraying your own life when you might be saved; in acting thus you are playing into the hands of your enemies, who are hurrying on your destruction. And further I should say that you are deserting your own children; for you might bring them up and educate them; instead of which you go away and leave them, and they will have to take their chance; and if they do not meet with the usual fate of orphans, there will be small thanks to you. No man should bring children into the world who is unwilling to persevere to the end in their nurture and education. But you appear to be choosing the easier part, not the better and manlier, which would have been more becoming in one who professes to care for virtue in all his actions, like yourself. And indeed, I am ashamed not only of you, but of us who are your friends, when I reflect that the whole business will be attributed entirely to our want of courage. The trial need never have come on, or might have been managed differently; and this last act, or crowning folly, will seem to have occurred through our negligence and cowardice, who might have saved you, if you had been good for anything; and you might have saved yourself, for there was no difficulty at all. See now, Socrates, how sad and discreditable are the consequences, both to us and you. Make up your mind then, or rather have your mind already made up, for the time of deliberation is over, and there is only one thing to be done, which must be done this very night, and if we delay at all will be no longer practicable or possible; I beseech you therefore, Socrates, be persuaded by me, and do as I say.

SOC. Dear Crito, your zeal is invaluable, if a right one; but if wrong, the greater the zeal the greater the danger; and therefore we ought to consider whether I shall or shall not do as you say. For I am and always have been one of those natures who must be guided by reason, whatever the reason may be which upon reflection appears to me to be the best; and now that this chance has befallen me, I cannot repudiate my own words: the principles which I have hitherto honoured and revered I still honour, and unless we can at once find other and better principles, I am certain not to agree with you; no, not even if the power of the multitude could inflict many more imprisonments, confiscations, deaths, frightening us like children with hobgoblin terrors. What will be the fairest way of considering the question? Shall I return to your old argument about the opinions of men?—we are saying that some of them are to be regarded, and others not. Now were we right in maintaining this before I was condemned? And has the argument which was once good now proved to be talk for the sake of talking—mere childish nonsense? That is what I want to consider with your help, Crito: whether, under my present circumstances, the argument appears to be in any way different or not; and is to be allowed by me or disallowed. That argument, which, as I believe, is maintained by many persons of authority, was to the effect, as I was saying, that the opinions of some men are to be regarded, and of other men not to be regarded. Now you, Crito, are not going to die to-morrow—at least, there is no human probability of this—and therefore you are disinterested and not liable to be deceived by the circumstances in which you are placed. Tell me then, whether I am right in saying that some opinions, and the opinions of some men only, are to be valued, and that other opinions, and the opinions of other men, are not to be valuable. I ask you whether I was right in maintaining this?

CR. Certainly.

SOC. The good are to be regarded, and not the bad?

CR. Yes.

SOC. And the opinions of the wise are good, and the opinions of the unwise are evil?

CR. Certainly.

SOC. And what was said about another matter? Is the pupil who devotes himself to the practice of gymnastics supposed to attend to the praise and blame and opinion of every man, or of one man only—his physician or trainer, whoever he may be?

CR. Of one man only.

SOC. And he ought to fear the censure and welcome the praise of that one only, and not of the many?

CR. Clearly so.

SOC. And he ought to act and train, and eat and drink in the way which seems good to his single master who has understanding, rather than according to the opinion of all other men put together?

CR. True.

SOC. And if he disobeys and disregards the opinion and approval of the one, and regards the opinion of the many who have no understanding, will he not suffer evil?

CR. Certainly he will.

SOC. And what will the evil be, whither tending and what affecting, in the disobedient person?

CR. Clearly, affecting the body; that is what is destroyed by the evil.

SOC. Very good; and is not this true, Crito, of other things which we need not separately enumerate? In questions of just and unjust, fair and foul, good and evil, which are the subjects of our present consultation, ought we to follow the opinion of the many and to fear them; or the opinion of the one man who has understanding? ought we not to fear and reverence him more than all the rest of the world: and if we desert him shall we not destroy and injure that principle in us which may be assumed to be improved by justice and deteriorated by injustice;—there is such a principle?

CR. Certainly there is, Socrates.

SOC. Take a parallel instance:—if, acting under the advice of those who have no understanding, we destroy that which is improved by health and is deteriorated by disease, would life be worth having? And that which has been destroyed is—the body?

CR. Yes.

SOC. Could we live, having an evil and corrupted body?

CR. Certainly not.

SOC. And will life be worth having, if that higher part of man be destroyed, which is improved by justice and depraved by injustice? Do we suppose that principle, whatever it may be in man, which has to do with justice and injustice, to be inferior to the body?

CR. Certainly not.

SOC. More honourable than the body?

CR. Far more.

SOC. Then, my friend, we must not regard what the many say of us: but what he, the one man who has understanding of just and unjust, will say, and what the truth will say. And therefore you begin in error when you advise that we should regard the opinion of the many about just and unjust, good and evil, honourable and dishonourable,—"Well," some one will say, "but the many can kill us."

CR. Yes, Socrates; that will clearly be the answer.

SOC. And it is true: but still I find with surprise that the old argument is unshaken as ever. And I should like to know whether I may say the same of another proposition—that not life, but a good life, is to be chiefly valued?

CR. Yes, that also remains unshaken.

SOC. And a good life is equivalent to a just and honourable one—that holds also?

CR. Yes, it does.

SOC. From these premises I proceed to argue the question whether I ought or ought not to try and escape without the consent of the Athenians: and if I am clearly right in escaping, then I will make the attempt; but if not, I will abstain. The other considerations which you mention, of money and loss of character and the duty of educating one's children are, I fear, only the doctrines of the multitude, who would be as ready to restore people to life, if they were able, as they are to put them to death—and with as little reason. But now, since the argument has thus far prevailed, the only question which remains to be considered is, whether we shall do rightly either in escaping or in suffering others to aid in our escape and paying them in money and thanks, or whether in reality we shall not do rightly; and if the latter, then death or any other calamity which may ensue on my remaining here must not be allowed to enter into the calculation.

CR. I think that you are right, Socrates; how then shall we proceed?

SOC. Let us consider the matter together, and do you either refute me if you can, and I will be convinced; or else cease, my dear friend, from repeating to me that I ought to escape against the wishes of the Athenians: for I highly value your attempts to persuade me to do so, but I may not be persuaded against my own better judgment. And now please to consider my first position, and try how you can best answer me.

CR. I will.

SOC. Are we to say that we are never intentionally to do wrong, or that in one way we ought and in another we ought not to do wrong, or is doing wrong always evil and dishonourable, as I was just now saying, and as has been already acknowledged by us? Are all our former admissions which were made within a few days to be thrown away? And have we, at our age, been earnestly discoursing with one another all our life long only to discover that we are no better than children? Or, in spite of the opinion of the many, and in spite of consequences whether better or worse, shall we insist on the truth of what was then said, that injustice is always an evil and dishonour to him who acts unjustly? Shall we say so or not?

CR. Yes.

SOC. Then we must do no wrong?

CR. Certainly not.

SOC. Nor when injured injure in return, as the many imagine; for we must injure no one at all?

CR. Clearly not.

SOC. Again, Crito, may we do evil?

CR. Surely not, Socrates.

SOC. And what of doing evil in return for evil, which is the morality of the many—is that just or not?

CR. Not just.

SOC. For doing evil to another is the same as injuring him?

CR. Very true.

SOC. Then we ought not to retaliate or render evil for evil to any one, whatever evil we may have suffered from him. But I would have you consider, Crito, whether you really mean what you are saying. For this opinion has never been held, and never will be held, by any considerable number of persons; and those who are agreed and those who are not agreed upon this point have no common ground, and can only despise one another when they see how widely they differ. Tell me, then, whether you agree with and assent to my first principle, that neither injury nor retaliation nor warding off evil by evil is ever right. And shall that be the premiss of our argument? Or do you decline and dissent from this? For so I have ever thought, and continue to think; but, if you are of another opinion, let me hear what you have to say. If, however, you remain of the same mind as formerly, I will proceed to the next step.

CR. You may proceed, for I have not changed my mind.

SOC. Then I will go on to the next point, which may be put in the form of a question:—Ought a man to do what he admits to be right, or ought he to betray the right?

CR. He ought to do what he thinks right.

SOC. But if this is true, what is the application? In leaving the prison against the will of the Athenians, do I wrong any? or rather do I not wrong those whom I ought least to wrong? Do I not desert the principles which were acknowledged by us to be just—what do you say?

CR. I cannot tell, Socrates; for I do not know.

SOC. Then consider the matter in this way:—Imagine that I am about to play truant (you may call the proceeding by any name which you like), and the laws and the government come and interrogate me: "Tell us, Socrates," they say, "what are you about? are you not going by an act of yours to overturn us—the laws, and the whole state, as far as in you lies? Do you imagine that a state can subsist and not be overthrown, in which the decisions of law have no power, but are set aside and trampled upon by individuals?" What will be our answer, Crito, to these and the like words? Any one, and especially a rhetorician, will have a good deal to say on behalf of the law which requires a sentence to be carried out. He will argue that this law should not be set aside; and shall we reply, "Yes; but the state has injured us and given an unjust sentence." Suppose I say that?

CR. Very good, Socrates.

SOC. "And was that our agreement with you?" the law would answer; "or were you to abide by the sentence of the state?" And if I were to express my astonishment at their words, the law would probably add: "Answer, Socrates, instead of opening your eyes—you are in the habit of asking and answering questions. Tell us,—What complaint have you to make against us which justifies you in attempting to destroy us and the state? In the first place did we not bring you into existence? Your father married your mother by our aid and begat you. Say whether you have any objection to urge against those of us who regulate marriage?" None, I should reply. "Or against those of us who after birth regulate the nurture and education of children, in which you also were trained? Were not the laws, which have the charge of education, right in commanding your father to train you in music and gymnastic?" Right, I should reply. "Well then, since you were brought into the world and nurtured and educated by us, can you deny in the first place that you are our child and slave, as your fathers were before you? And if this is true you are not on equal terms with us; nor can you think that you have a right to do to us what we are doing to you. Would you have any right to strike or revile or do any other evil to your father or your master, if you had one, because you have been struck or reviled by him, or received some other evil at his hands?—you would not say this? And because we think right to destroy you, do you think that you have any right to destroy us in return, and your country as far as in you lies? Will you, O professor of true virtue, pretend that you are justified in this? Has a philosopher like you failed to discover that our country is more to be valued and higher and holier far than mother or father or any ancestor, and more to be regarded in the eyes of the gods and of men of understanding? Also to be soothed, and gently and reverently entreated when angry, even more than a father, and either to be persuaded, or if not persuaded, to be obeyed? And when we are punished by her, whether with imprisonment or stripes, the punishment is to be endured in silence; and if she leads us to wounds or death in battle, thither we follow as is right; neither may any one yield or retreat or leave his rank, but whether in battle or in a court of law, or in any other place, he must do what his city and his country order him; or he must change their view of what is just: and if he may do no violence to his father or mother, much less may he do violence to his country." What answer shall we make to this, Crito? Do the laws speak truly, or do they not?

CR. I think that they do.

SOC. Then the laws will say, "Consider, Socrates, if we are speaking truly that in your present attempt you are going to do us an injury. For, having brought you into the world, and nurtured and educated you, and given you and every other citizen a share in every good which we had to give, we further proclaim to any Athenian by the liberty which we allow him, that if he does not like us when he has become of age and has seen the ways of the city, and made our acquaintance, he may go where he pleases and take his goods with him. None of us laws will forbid him or interfere with him. Any one who does not like us and the city, and who wants to emigrate to a colony or to any other city, may go where he likes, retaining his property. But he who has experience of the manner in which we order justice and administer the state, and still remains, has entered into an implied contract that he will do as we command him. And he who disobeys us is, as we maintain, thrice wrong; first, because in disobeying us he is disobeying his parents; secondly, because we are the authors of his education; thirdly, because he has made an agreement with us that he will duly obey our commands; and he neither obeys them nor convinces us that our commands are unjust; and we do not rudely impose them, but give him the alternative of obeying or convincing us;—that is what we offer, and he does neither.

"These are the sort of accusations to which, as we were saying, you, Socrates, will be exposed if you accomplish your intentions; you, above all other Athenians." Suppose now I ask, why I rather than anybody else? they will justly retort upon me that I above all other men have acknowledged the agreement. "There is clear proof," they will say, "Socrates, that we and the city were not displeasing to you. Of all Athenians you have been the most constant resident in the city, which, as you never leave, you may be supposed to love. For you never went out of the city either to see the games, except once when you went to the Isthmus, or to any other place unless when you were on military service; nor did you travel as other men do. Nor had you any curiosity to know other states or their laws: your affections did not go beyond us and our state; we were your special favourites, and you acquiesced in our government of you; and here in this city you begat your children, which is a proof of your satisfaction. Moreover, you might in the course of the trial, if you had liked, have fixed the penalty at banishment; the state which refuses to let you go now would have let you go then. But you pretended that you preferred death to exile, and that you were not unwilling to die. And now you have forgotten these fine sentiments, and pay no respect to us the laws, of whom you are the destroyer; and are doing what only a miserable slave would do, running away and turning your back upon the compacts and agreements which you made as a citizen. And first of all answer this very question: Are we right in saying that you agreed to be governed according to us in deed, and not in word only? Is that true or not?" How shall we answer, Crito? Must we not assent?

CR. We cannot help it, Socrates.

SOC. Then will they not say: "You, Socrates, are breaking the covenants and agreements which you made with us at your leisure, not in any haste or under any compulsion or deception, but after you have had seventy years to think of them, during which time you were at liberty to leave the city, if we were not to your mind, or if our covenants appeared to you to be unfair. You had your choice, and might have gone either to Lacedaemon or Crete, both which states are often praised by you for their good government, or to some other Hellenic or foreign state. Whereas you, above all other Athenians, seemed to be so fond of the state, or, in other words, of us her laws (and who would care about a state which has no laws?), that you never stirred out of her; the halt, the blind, the maimed were not more stationary in her than you were. And now you run away and forsake your agreements. Not so, Socrates, if you will take our advice; do not make yourself ridiculous by escaping out of the city.

"For just consider, if you transgress and err in this sort of way, what good will you do either to yourself or to your friends? That your friends will be driven into exile and deprived of citizenship, or will lose their property, is tolerably certain; and you yourself, if you fly to one of the neighboring cities, as, for example, Thebes or Megara, both of which are well governed, will come to them as an enemy, Socrates, and their government will be against you, and all patriotic citizens will cast an evil eye upon you as a subverter of the laws, and you will confirm in the minds of the judges the justice of their own condemnation of you. For he who is a corrupter of the laws is more than likely to be a corrupter of the young and foolish portion of mankind. Will you then flee from well-ordered cities and virtuous men? and is existence worth having on these terms? Or will you go to them without shame, and talk to them, Socrates? And what will you say to them? What you say here about virtue and justice and institutions and laws being the best things among men? Would that be decent of you? Surely not. But if you go away from well-governed states to Crito's friends in Thessaly, where there is great disorder and licence, they will be charmed to hear the tale of your escape from prison, set off with ludicrous particulars of the manner in which you were wrapped in a goatskin or some other disguise, and metamorphosed as the manner is of runaways; but will there be no one to remind you that in your old age you were not ashamed to violate the most sacred laws from a miserable desire of a little more life? Perhaps not, if you keep them in a good temper; but if they are out of temper you will hear many degrading things; you will live, but how?—as the flatterer of all men, and the servant of all men; and doing what?—eating and drinking in Thessaly, having gone abroad in order that you may get a dinner. And where will be your fine sentiments about justice and virtue? Say that you wish to live for the sake of your children—you want to bring them up and educate them—will you take them into Thessaly and deprive them of Athenian citizenship? Is this the benefit which you will confer upon them? Or are you under the impression that they will be better cared for and educated here if you are still alive, although absent from them; for your friends will take care of them? Do you fancy that if you are an inhabitant of Thessaly they will take care of them, and if you are an inhabitant of the other world that they will not take care of them? Nay; but if they who call themselves friends are good for anything, they will—to be sure they will.

"Listen, then, Socrates, to us who have brought you up. Think not of life and children first, and of justice afterwards, but of justice first, that you may be justified before the princes of the world below. For neither will you nor any that belong to you be happier or holier or juster in this life, or happier in another, if you do as Crito bids. Now you depart in innocence, a sufferer and not a doer of evil; a victim, not of the laws but of men. But if you go forth, returning evil for evil, and injury for injury, breaking the covenants and agreements which you have made with us, and wronging those whom you ought least of all to wrong, that is to say, yourself, your friends, your country, and us, we shall be angry with you while you live, and our brethren, the laws of the world below, will receive you as an enemy; for they will know that you have done your best to destroy us. Listen, then, to us and not to Crito."

This, dear Crito, is the voice which I seem to hear murmuring in my ears, like the sound of the flute in the ears of the mystic; that voice, I say, is humming in my ears and prevents me from hearing any other. And I know that anything more which you may say will be in vain. Yet speak, if you have anything to say.

CR. I have nothing to say, Socrates.

SOC. Leave me then, Crito, to fulfil the will of God, and to follow whither he leads.

Justifying Civil Disobedience
Rudolph H. Weingartner[1]

Rudolph H. Weingartner (1927-   ) teaches philosophy at Vassar College. He has written on German philosophy, the philosophy of history, and other subjects.

I

In general, we ought to obey the law. Suppose I ask whether I should do *A* or *B;* if you then tell me that to do *A* is to break the law, surely this information must weigh on the side of *B* and count against *A*. It is not a conclusive reason for not doing *A*, for, as I shall suggest, the arguments designed to show that breaking the law is never justified are not successful. What the truth of this generalization does show, however, is that any breach of the law is in *need* of a justification, that it is not one of those matters—like telling the truth or being kind to children—that requires justification only under special circumstances.

This may be obvious in most cases of lawbreaking, but it seems not to be so obvious when it comes to civil disobedience. Indeed, so much passion has of late been aroused by the issue of civil disobedience that we are scarcely aware of the lack of clarity in our thinking about the subject. More than one commentator discussing the rioting and violence in the Watts district of Los Angeles in the summer of 1965 used the term "civil disobedience" in referring to events and actions to which it certainly does not apply. Before discussing its justification it would be well to consider what civil disobedience is.

Civil disobedience is, above all, disobedience. It is the violation of a command issued by an authority, such as a government, that has a claim to our obedience. When a number of people disobey a bank official who asks them to leave the bank and to cease immobilizing it by perpetually requesting coins to be changed into bills and bills into coins, it is not civil disobedience, unless a law is also broken. The law has a claim to our obedience; bank officials as such do not. Where a government is not directly confronted in an illegal act, there may be a strike, a boycott, harassment, or some other kind of pressure, but not civil disobedience. Nor is *legal* non-obedience of the law civil disobedience. Conscientious objectors are exempted

Source: Reprinted from the *Columbia Forum*, Vol. 9, No. 2 (Spring 1966). Copyright 1966 by the Trustees of Columbia University in the City of New York.

[1] I have learned much from the following: Hugo A. Bedau, "On Civil Disobedience," *Journal of Philosophy*, 58 (1961); Charles L. Black, Jr., "The Problem of the Compatibility of Civil Disobedience with American Institutions of Government," *Texas Law Review*, 43 (1965); Carl Cohen, "Essence and Ethics of Civil Disobedience," *The Nation*, 198 (1964); John Dickinson, "A Working Theory of Sovereignty II," *Political Science Quarterly*, 43 (1928); Morris Keeton, "The Morality of Civil Disobedience," *Texas Law Review*, 43 (1965); Harold Laski, *The State in Theory and Practice*, New York, 1935; Richard A. Wasserstrom, "The Obligation to Obey the Law," *UCLA Law Review*, 10 (1963).

from service in the armed forces, and Jehovah's Witnesses are permitted to refrain from saluting the flag. Neither group is engaged in civil disobedience.

Moreover, civil disobedience must be *civil* disobedience of a law. If those who disobey the law use violence in doing so, they are no longer practicing civil disobedience. For while the violence may overtly be aimed at private persons, it is at least implicitly directed against those charged with enforcing the law. But to that extent the act is no longer confined to the transgression of a particular law; instead it becomes a defiance of the authority that makes and enforces the laws. Violent disobedience is not simply a noisier kind of civil disobedience; it is rebellion.

This distinction is an important one. Rebellion or revolution, whether it is peaceful or violent, aims to modify the established order either by supplanting those who make and enforce the laws, or by changing the very processes of legislation and enforcement, or by doing both. The change sought is not simply a change in one or another law, but of the entire framework within which laws are made and carried out. Accordingly, insofar as Gandhi aimed at the elimination of British rule in India, he was a revolutionary, for civil disobedience aims at a particular law or governmental measure, and not at the state itself. An important though not infallible symbol of this distinction is that in the clearest cases of civil disobedience those engaged in it are willing to accept the punishment that is meted out to those who break the law in question. They use violence neither in disobeying the law nor in their reaction to arrest, trial, and the sentencing that may follow disobedience.

But surely, most people who disobey a law non-violently are not thereby practicing civil disobedience. A person may knowingly park in a no-parking zone hoping not to get caught and be ready, if not happy, to pay the fine if he is so unlucky as to be found out. Still, this does not make him a practitioner of civil disobedience. Whoever engages in civil disobedience commits an illegal act because he takes a law or governmental measure to be wrong; he seeks to protest and possibly to change a wrong done by the state, pitting what he takes to be right—that is to say moral—against what the state takes to be right—that is to say, at least legal. There is no type of law or governmental measure which is, by its nature, immune to civil disobedience; moreover, the *way* in which a law or measure might be found wanting must be left open. Some laws are protested because they are thought unjust; others because they are taken to transgress a divine commandment; some because they are thought to violate rights possessed by all men; still others because they are held to produce effects contrary to the common good. To say that the goal must be moral requires that the illegal act not be undertaken simply to gain an advantage for the actor. And because it is not always so clear what someone's purposes may be (including one's own), the willingness to accept punishment is a useful sign that the disobedience is not simply the means to a private end.

It does not follow from this that a Negro can never employ genuine civil disobedience in order to bring about civil rights for Negroes, or that his actions must be seen as self-seeking, however understandable—analogous, say, to a steel-worker's strike for higher wages. A Negro practitioner of civil disobedience will undoubtedly be better off if he succeeds in bringing about a change in the laws. But the question of purposes is not settled by such a consideration of effects. If an illegal act is performed in order to protest against a law for being unjust or contrary to the good of the community, then it is civil disobedience, even if justice or the common good is also to the advantage of the protester. What remains of fundamental importance for the identification of an act of civil disobedience and for its justification alike is that the purposes of the act be moral.

Finally, the activity of civil disobedience must be public. Simple evasion of the law, even when undertaken for the highest reasons of conscience, is not yet civil disobedience. The physician, for example, who quietly administers a fatal injection to an incurable patient in order to relieve great suffering evades a law but does not engage in civil disobedience. Even if the doctor is resigned to accepting punishment should he be found out, his act is not civil disobedience unless he intends his transgression to be publicly known. Civil disobedience *usually* involves an unwillingness to obey a law thought to be wrong, but it *always* constitutes a protest against a law or governmental measure. And a protest is more than the expression of a disagreement; it includes a desire for a change. As such, the evasion of a law makes no contribution to getting a law or policy revoked or modified. For an act of conscience to be also one of protest, it must at least potentially be able to persuade others. That the whole town knew of Thoreau's imprisonment was not adventitious: it was a part of his civil disobedience.

An act of civil disobedience, to sum up, is an illegal, non-violent, moral, and public protest against a law or governmental measure.

I want also to distinguish between two types of civil disobedience, *direct* and *indirect*, a difference that will have a bearing on the question of justification. In some cases of civil disobedience, the very law that is being protested against is the one disobeyed. It is direct civil disobedience when a law calls for the separate seating of whites and Negroes, and a person violates that very law because he thinks it is wrong. But in many instances, civil disobedience cannot take so straightforward a form. The suffragettes who fought for women's rights could not disobey the law that disenfranchised them. These militant ladies violated trespassing laws, statutes against disturbing the peace, and the like.

Clearly, indirect civil disobedience is the only kind that is possible when the wrong being protested is the *absence* of a law or a governmental measure. But often, too, indirect civil disobedience is the only possible form of disobedience when the protest is directed against a law or measure that *does* exist. The ordinary citizen, for example, cannot readily interfere with the testing of nuclear arms or the appropriation of money for war, so that the law or command to be disobeyed will have to be different from that being protested against. The connection between the object of protest and the measure violated may be close: the suffragettes disturbed the peace at political meetings of campaigners who did not support the proposal to give women the vote. At other times there is no intrinsic connection at all: Bertrand Russell was arrested for refusing to keep the peace as a protest against nuclear arms.

II

Society requires order for its existence. Throughout history this need has been affirmed with passion and pursued with singlemindedness. It is thus not surprising that many men have held that one is never justified in breaking a law and that civil disobedience is always wrong. On the other hand, in more than one reformation has the conscience of the individual been raised above the rules of institutions and the mores of society. Accordingly, we have been urged never to obey a law that we think is wrong. In this view civil disobedience is then always justified when directed against laws that conflict with one's convictions. I think both of these views are wrong and I shall furthermore argue that there cannot even be a general rule which serves to decide when civil disobedience is justified and when it is not.

Some have claimed that is is never morally right to disobey the law because morality simply consists in obedience to the laws. This is an ancient doctrine that tries to define what is right wholly in terms of what the laws say is right. And its refutation is equally old. Laws conflict at least from one period to another and from place to place; if rightness were constituted by what the laws dictate, then we are led to the weird conclusion that the same act can be both right and not right, or, whenever the law is silent, be neither right nor not right. Moreover, this logical identification of morality with law would make it meaningless nonsense to evaluate a law: to censure a law as unjust or to praise it as in accord with morality would have to be considered as unintelligible as criticizing squares for having right angles or praising them for having sides that are straight.

Then, it has been held that any law which fails to conform to the demands of morality is not truly a law. But surely this is an odd view of the nature of laws. It makes well-nigh irrelevant to their character as laws their creation and promulgation by a properly constituted legislature, their enforcement by a legitimate executive, and their application by an acknowledged judiciary. To define the legal in terms of the moral makes little more sense than to define the moral in terms of the legal.

Others have granted that morality and legality can and do diverge, but they nevertheless hold that one is never justified in disobeying a law, because of the difficulties of *determining* what is right. Their argument may be formulated in this way:

Societies differ greatly in the ways in which their laws are made. The law of the land may be the word of a single, unquestioned sovereign, or the product of assemblies in which all the people participate. Secular authorities create and interpret the laws in some societies; in others, a special priestly class reads the will of the gods. But no group of men that is rightly called a society is without a relatively stable method for answering the question, what does the law say with regard to this matter? It may be a difficult one to answer, but at least it is always possible to point to some social institutions whose job it is to answer it, and to standards, however crude, by which the adequacy of any answer can be measured.

The moral realm is not similarly favored. Individuals and groups, some more powerful than others, all have opinions as to what is right. While there may be much agreement, there is also conflict. Above all, there is no recognized authority to adjudicate moral disputes. No doubt, it is then argued, there are differences between what is right and what is legal, but there is no institution that determines whether what someone thinks to be wrong actually *is* wrong. Accordingly, no one is ever justified in disobeying a law on the grounds that the law is wrong, for who can say what is right?

Two replies can be made to this objection to civil disobedience. First, the lack of an institution for making moral decisions does not imply that there cannot be reasons—even conclusive reasons—in support of a moral claim. Whatever may be the conditions for definitiveness in moral judgment, the existence of special institutions is surely not a necessary one, however much their existence may help in securing agreement. And agreement is precisely what should not be expected. More often than not, the moral critic of the law proposes to apply to the law a higher, a finer, or a more advanced standard of morality than do the institutions that make and interpret the laws. In a democracy at least, these legal institutions can be expected to be quite close to the moral norm of the community, so that the critic is not likely to find pervasive assent to his views.

Second, the lack of an institution for determining what is right is not sufficient ground for failing to do what one thinks is right. For there is never an institution that dispenses the correct answer and secures everyone's agreement to boot. While not everything we do is as grave as civil disobedience, some acts we perform, such as begetting children or going off to war—acts that do not conflict with the law—are at least of equal gravity. Yet neither the lack of a sure method of decision nor the absence of agreement should or does stop us from acting. What one thinks is right does not always turn out to be so, but it would be strange advice never to do what one thinks is right simply because others do not agree or because one *might* be wrong.

This leads to a final group of arguments in support of the thesis that civil disobedience is never justified. These arguments claim, in various ways, that the social consequences of civil disobedience are always worse than those of obedience. "What if everybody did it?" is the question to which a fatal sting is attributed; and of course the prospect of a society in which no one obeys the law is frightening. But just what is the connection between one person's act of civil disobedience and the chaos of a lawless society? Surely it is evident that such an act does not actually bring about the commission of countless other breaches of law. Indeed, an act of civil disobedience may confirm more citizens in their legal rectitude than it induces to break laws. What causes what is a question of empirical fact, and observation simply fails to bear out the contention that *everyone* will do what *somebody* does. And if it is argued that the risk of violence, the suffering of punishment, and other such consequences of disobeying the law will always be worse than those of obedience to the law, I must reply that this is all too grandiose a claim about the way of the world. Whether the consequences of one act are better or worse than those of another is a matter of looking and seeing; to say that one type of act *must* be better than another, regardless of the circumstances, is not warranted by any general law about human behavior.

What now of the other side of the controversy? Have not the floodgates been opened to the view that whenever one thinks the law to be wrong, civil disobedience is justified? Laws ought to be obeyed, some have maintained, only when and if they are morally right. And who else but each person himself can judge the moral adequacy of the law? When he judges the law to be morally deficient, he is at least *justified* in disobeying it and possibly *obligated* to do so. It is even held that men who do not act on what they think is right give up their function as citizens; surely, it is argued, men give up their dignity as moral agents unless they themselves determine what they ought to do.

There is a nobility to this position which makes it an attractive one; nevertheless, I think that it is at best confused. First there is the matter of conscientiousness: I might take a law to be wrong on the basis of quick and superficial thought or I might come to this conclusion after prolonged reflection. I may be ignorant of the issues involved or I may have made a special study of them. The following sentence, accordingly, is not paradoxical, but merely expresses the complexity of moral judgments: "I think this law is morally wrong, but because you are more knowledgeable than I about its long-range effects, I concede that you may be right in saying that the law is good." If civil disobedience is justified when one thinks a law to be wrong, then surely it is justified only to the degree to which one is entitled to one's opinion.

Second, there is a vast difference between judging that a law is wrong and judging that one ought to disobey it. Even if I am correct in thinking that a particular law requires an act that is morally wrong (or the omission of one that is needed), it by no means just follows that I should disobey it. For many other considerations must enter into a decision to disobey a law, even after the question of the rightness of the law has been already settled. It is not self-contradictory to say that such and such a law is wrong, but that it ought to be obeyed. One is therefore not automatically justified in disobeying *any* law one thinks is wrong, much less in protesting publicly against it.

It has now been shown, I think, that the extreme positions on the justifiability of civil disobedience are difficult to maintain: civil disobedience is neither prohibited nor permitted by some perfectly general formula. Indeed, there is no simple way of dealing with the ethics of civil disobedience, for it can be demonstrated that there cannot even be a rule that serves to decide when civil disobedience is and when it is not justified.

Surely, one might contend, all those cases in which civil disobedience is justified share some characteristic, simple or complex, that the unjustifiable ones do not possess. And in a sense, this is indeed true. One may be justified in disobeying a law if, after one has conscientiously reflected on all the relevant factors, one has good evidence that a greater good is achieved by breaking than by obeying it. Correct or not, this rule is at least plausible; still, it will not serve to decide when one is justified in breaking a law. How much reflection is conscientious reflection? Which factors are relevant factors? How much evidence is good evidence? And which goods are greater than which? These questions are not simple ones and for none is the answer the same for all possible cases. (What is good enough evidence for breaking a date need not be good enough for breaking the engagement.)

We could agree to accept such a rule and cease asking which cases of civil disobedience are justified. But in exchange we inherit the new problem of finding out to which cases the rule applies. The gain is only apparent: the simplicity of a wholesale solution is illusory.

III

We are now left with the requirement that each case of civil disobedience must be examined on its own merits. The best that we can do is to spell out what some of the relevant considerations are which help to decide whether or not a case of civil disobedience is justified. It will be convenient to discuss these issues under five general headings, though I have no illusions that the list is exhaustive.

1. *The wrongness of the law.* Civil disobedience is justified to the degree to which the object of the protest is thought to be wrong. If the law or measure is not thought to be wrong at all, breaking it does not constitute civil disobedience; if it is thought to be wrong only in a trivial or minor way, its wrongness cannot outweigh either the general obligation we have to obey the law or the disadvantageous consequences of civil disobedience. If the wrong is thought to be grievous, civil disobedience may be more readily justified.

Two comments. It is assumed here, as it is throughout this essay, that, in principle, questions of right and wrong have answers, even if in fact we often fail to arrive at them. Such a view of morals as objective, however, does not require us to suppose that there are simple moral absolutes holding for all times and places. Rather, to hold that criteria in ethics are objective and to say that moral questions have answers is to assert above all that what is right or wrong is conceptually independent of what happens to be thought right or wrong—by a few people or even by all. (Just as the shape of the earth is independent of what it is thought to be at any time of place.) Accordingly, it cannot be enough that the law is *thought* to be wrong: the question as to whether it *is* wrong is relevant too.

Second, whether the case of civil disobedience is direct or indirect is relevant here. One's protest is, I think, more readily justified when it involves the breaking of a law that is thought to be wrong, rather than some other law. The reason is not complicated. In the case of indirect civil disobedience, the wrongness of the law serves as a reason for the *protest* against it. But in those cases of civil disobedience in which the law that is not obeyed is the same law against which the protest is made, the law's wrongness has an additional function as well. On the general grounds that one ought to do what is right and refrain from doing what is wrong, the wrongness of a law helps to justify *any* willing failure to obey it and since civil disobedience is not only protest but also disobedience, the wrongness of the law plays a dual role in the justification of direct civil disobedience.

2. *The purity and strength of the motive.* It is perfectly possible to believe a law to be wrong but to act against it for self-seeking reasons. "Of course it is a bad law," someone might think, "but I will protest against it because it reduces my income." If one is to be genuinely engaged in civil disobedience, the act of protest must be performed *because* a law is thought to be wrong; the motive must be moral. Yet, it may very well be true that there is no such thing as an unmixed motive; thus, if there is to be justified civil disobedience, it must at least be *relatively* free of an admixture of self-seeking motives. Not only the desire for personal gain counts against the justifiability of an act of civil disobedience; there are other, more subtle, temptations: the desire for fame or revenge, or for the grateful thanks from the underdog, or the anticipation of that special pleasure that may come from breaking the law. The purer and stronger the motive for setting right a wrong, the more readily a person is justified in performing an act of civil disobedience.

But not always when we ask whether an instance of civil disobedience is justified are we interested in whether some—or any—particular *person* was justified in doing what he did. Frequently, our concern in justifying civil disobedience is with the act as abstracted from the individuals who perform it. Motives, thus, have no place in the discussion; we ask only the other questions relevant to the justification of civil disobedience. But to ignore motives in this way is not tantamount to remaining neutral with regard to them. We are not asking whether an act of civil disobedience is justified on the supposition that the motive of the person who performs it either is or is not moral; on the contrary, as we reflect about the justifiability of an act of civil disobedience, we *assume* that it is done for moral reasons, that the person was not simply hired, for example. This is what we take as given as we go on to inquire whether the act can be justified with respect to the other considerations relevant to justifying civil disobedience.

3. *The foreseeable consequences of the act.* One's estimate of what the consequences of engaging in civil disobedience are likely to be in a particular case is

relevant to the justification of that case. To begin with, it makes a difference whether or not there is a likelihood of the act's being successful in bringing about the desired change. But there is no simple relation between probability of success and justification. If one's aim in the commission of an act of civil disobedience is fundamentally utilitarian, it will be harder to justify it, if the chances of success in bringing about the desired change are poor or absent than when they are excellent. Perhaps rebellion is called for, perhaps acquiescence. Still, if success in changing the law is more or less ruled out, there remains both the possibility of the creation of a moral climate *favorable* to future success, as well as the danger of public reaction *against* the very cause of the persons involved. And, depending upon the degree to which the law is thought to be wrong, one is justified in acting with greater or lesser expectations of success. On the other hand, if the person who engages in civil disobedience does so simply in order to manifest his belief that the law is wrong (however much he may *also* desire that the law be changed), the likelihood of the law's actually being changed is not a relevant consideration to the justifying of civil disobedience. In short, the relevance of success to the justification of an act of civil disobedience depends in part upon the *kind* of moral motive that plays a role in the performance of an act of civil disobedience.

Other consequences one must consider are what the risks may be that individuals and groups will in one or another way be harmed. It is more difficult to justify civil disobedience when the danger of violence is great, when not only those actually disobeying the law, but also officers of the government and innocent bystanders are likely to be hurt. Furthermore, the consequences for those who propose to engage in civil disobedience must be taken into consideration. If the punishment for breaking the law can be expected to be extremely severe, the commission of civil disobedience (always assuming other things to be equal) is less justified, for we do have duties to ourselves as well as to others. And from the consideration of these consequences for bystanders and actors follows a corollary that seems paradoxical. Still, it is true that where the agents of the state—the police and the judiciary—are cruel and punitive in the extreme, civil disobedience is not likely to be justified. In Nazi Germany of 1940, say, civil disobedience would have been pathetically inappropriate: a certain minimum level of civilization must be attained before civil disobedience can be justified; below it only evasion or rebellion—or acquiescence—are justifiable.

Finally, the more likely it is that the protest involved in civil disobedience can be confined to the law or measure thought to be wrong, the more readily can civil disobedience be justified. If there is in fact a clear danger that committing civil disobedience will spread to other laws, to lawlessness generally, or to a defiance of the state itself, then (again other things being equal) the justification of civil disobedience will be more difficult. For then what must be justifiable is not the single act of civil disobedience, but the lawlessness or revolution which is the likely consequence of that act. But the justification of this is a separate issue.

4. *The availability of alternative methods of reform.* It matters whether other techniques for modifying or revoking the law are available—for example, a cogent presentation at a public hearing. Civil disobedience is much more likely to be justified if the chances of change through legal means are remote.

Only an outline of what is involved in this question of alternative methods of reform can be included here. There are two broad classes of alternatives, the legal and the political; and in a society such as ours each has several modes. Both the federalist system and the system of common law provide more than one type of legal recourse in the case of a law thought to be wrong. And politically, the separation of the legislative and the executive functions alone means that there is more than one avenue of approach to the government, not to mention the many different techniques by means of which it can be subjected to pressure. Civil disobedience is more readily justified, the fewer alternative methods there are and the less likely it is that alternative methods will be successful.

It has been maintained that in a democracy, because there is always an alternative method and because success by legal or political methods is at least in principle always possible, civil disobedience is never justified. But this is surely false, for there are also the questions of probability and time. If the wrong is at all a serious one, the remote (in either sense) possibility of change is not enough reason for denying the justified use of civil disobedience. It was Harold Laski who pointed out the absurdity of claiming that "the duty of a minority whose values are denied is the simple one of becoming a majority." The existence of alternative methods of reform is relevant to the justification of civil disobedience, but by no means to the extent of removing its possibility.

5. *Conscientiousness and evidence.* Whether what one takes to be wrong is indeed wrong, whether innocent bystanders are likely to be hurt, whether the community will respond to the moral claims being made, whether alternative methods of reform are likely to be successful, these and other similar questions are susceptible to a great deal of reflection and investigation. When we act, we can only act on the basis of what we think to be right; but recall that we can take fewer or greater pains to determine whether what we think to be the case is indeed so. For each degree of gravity of an undertaking there is a degree of conscientiousness that is appropriate. It would be silly to require a full-length study of possible consequences to help us to decide whether we ought to *eat out* or stay at home. But civil disobedience is a serious business: it goes counter to the general obligation to obey the law and almost always there are serious dangers of undesirable consequences for others. There is, therefore, a particular obligation to act conscientiously: to reflect carefully about all the considerations relevant and to bring oneself into possession of the best possible evidence pertaining to the many claims that are involved in *any* act of civil disobedience.

There is no doubt in my mind that many actual cases of civil disobedience, past and present, were justified. The injustice of the laws protested against was great; the motives of those engaged in the civil disobedience were as free of self-regarding admixtures as is possible among men; the various consequences that may follow from publicly breaking the law in protest were thought about and taken into consideration; alternative methods of reform were considered and found wanting. But above all, what distinguishes such men as Thoreau and Gandhi is the thoughtful way in which they reflected about the nature and ramifications of their acts. It is sometimes forgotten that one is justified in doing what one thinks is right only to the degree to which one is conscientious in trying to determine what is right. And because of the complexity of the act and the gravity of its consequences, this last consideration is of particular importance in justifying civil disobedience.

War Crimes: The Nuremberg Trials

CHARTER OF THE INTERNATIONAL MILITARY TRIBUNAL

I.—Constitution of the International Military Tribunal

Article 1 In pursuance of the Agreement signed on the 8th August, 1945, by the Government of the United Kingdom of Great Britain and Northern Ireland, the Government of the United States of America, the Provisional Government of the French Republic and the Government of the Union of Soviet Socialist Republics, there shall be established an International Military Tribunal (hereinafter called 'the Tribunal') for the just and prompt trial and punishment of the major war criminals of the European Axis.

II.—Jurisdiction and General Principles

Article 6 The Tribunal established by the Agreement referred to in Article 1 hereof for the trial and punishment of the major war criminals of the European Axis countries shall have the power to try and punish persons who, acting in the interests of the European Axis countries, whether as individuals or as members of organisations, committed any of the following crimes.

The following acts, or any of them, *are crimes* coming within the jurisdiction of the Tribunal for which there shall be individual responsibility:—

(a) *Crimes against peace:* namely, planning, preparation, initiation or waging of *a war of aggression,* or a war in violation of international treaties, agreements or assurances, or participation in a common plan or conspiracy for the accomplishment of any of the foregoing:

(b) *War crimes:* namely, violations of the laws or customs of war. Such violations shall include, but not be limited to, murder, ill-treatment or deportation to slave labour or for any other purpose of civilian population of or in occupied territory, murder or ill-treatment of prisoners of war or persons on the seas, killing of hostages, plunder of public or private property, wanton destruction of cities, towns or villages, or devastation not justified by military necessity;

(c) *Crimes against humanity:* namely, murder, extermination, enslavement, deportation, and other inhumane acts committed *against any civilian population, before or during the war;* or *persecutions on political, racial or religious grounds* in execution of or in connection with any crime within the jurisdiction of the Tribunal, *whether or not in violation of the domestic law of the country where perpetrated.*

Leaders, organisers, instigators and accomplices participating in the formulation or execution of a common plan or conspiracy to commit any of the foregoing crimes are responsible for all acts performed by any persons in execution of such plan.

Source: *The Nuremberg Case*, by Robert H. Jackson. Copyright 1947 by Alfred A. Knopf, Inc. Reprinted by permission of the publisher.

Article 7 The official position of defendants, whether as Heads of State or responsible officials in Government Departments, shall not be considered as freeing them from responsibility or mitigating punishment.

Article 8 The fact that the Defendant acted pursuant to order of his government or of a superior shall not free him from responsibility, but may be considered in mitigation of punishment if the Tribunal determines that justice so requires.

OPENING STATEMENT FOR THE UNITED STATES OF AMERICA
by Justice Robert Jackson*

The Law of the Case
The end of the war and capture of these prisoners presented the victorious Allies with the question whether there is any legal responsibility of high-ranking men for acts which I have described. Must such wrongs either be ignored or redressed in hot blood? Is there no standard in the law for a deliberate and reasoned judgment on such conduct?

The Charter of this Tribunal evidences a faith that the law is not only to govern the conduct of little men, but that even rulers are, as Lord Chief Justice Coke put it to King James, "under God and the law." The United States believed that the law long has afforded standards by which a juridical hearing could be conducted to make sure that we punish only the right men and for the right reasons. Following the instructions of the late President Roosevelt and the decision of the Yalta Conference, President Truman directed representatives of the United States to formulate a proposed International Agreement, which was submitted during the San Francisco Conference to Foreign Ministers of the United Kingdom, the Soviet Union, and the Provisional Government of France. With many modifications, that proposal has become the Charter of this Tribunal.

But the Agreement which sets up the standards by which these prisoners are to be judged does not express the views of the signatory nations alone. Other nations with diverse but highly respected systems of jurisprudence also have signified adherence to it. These are Belgium, The Netherlands, Denmark, Norway, Czechoslovakia, Luxembourg, Poland, Greece, Yugoslavia, Ethiopia, Australia, Haiti, Honduras, Panama, and New Zealand. You judge, therefore, under an organic act which represents the wisdom, the sense of justice, and the will of nineteen governments, representing an overwhelming majority of all civilized people.

The Charter by which this Tribunal has its being embodies certain legal concepts which are inseparable from its jurisdiction and which must govern its decision. These, as I have said, also are conditions attached to the grant of any hearing to defendants. The validity of the provisions of the Charter is conclusive upon us all whether we have accepted the duty of judging or of prosecuting under it, as well as upon the defendants, who can point to no other law which gives them a right to be heard at all. My able and experienced colleagues believe, as do I, that it will

---

* [Robert H. Jackson (1892-1954) was an associate justice of the Supreme Court. While he was solicitor general of the United States, he argued more constitutional issues before the Supreme Court than any other lawyer in history. He was also the chief prosecutor for the United States at the Nuremburg trials. Among his books are *Dispassionate Justice, The Nuremburg Case,* and *The Supreme Court in the American System of Government*—Eds.]

contribute to the expedition and clarity of this trial if I expound briefly the application of the legal philosophy of the Charter to the facts I have recited.

While this declaration of the law by the Charter is final, it may be contended that the prisoners on trial are entitled to have it applied to their conduct only most charitably if at all. It may be said that this is new law, not authoritatively declared at the time they did the acts it condemns, and that this declaration of the law has taken them by surprise.

I cannot, of course, deny that these men are surprised that this is the law; they really are surprised that there is any such thing as law. These defendants did not rely on any law at all. Their program ignored and defied all law. That this is so will appear from many acts and statements, of which I cite but a few. In the Führer's speech to all military commanders on November 23, 1939, he reminded them that at the moment Germany had a pact with Russia, but declared, "Agreements are to be kept only as long as they serve a certain purpose." Later on in the same speech he announced, "A violation of the neutrality of Holland and Belgium will be of no importance." A Top Secret document, entitled "Warfare as a Problem of Organization," dispatched by the Chief of the High Command to all Commanders on April 19, 1938, declared that "the normal rules of war toward neutrals may be considered to apply on the basis whether operation of rules will create greater advantages or disadvantages for belligerents." And from the files of the the German Navy Staff, we have a "Memorandum on Intensified Naval War," dated October 15, 1939, which begins by stating a desire to comply with International Law. "However," it continues, "if decisive successes are expected from any measure considered as a war necessity, it must be carried through even if it is not in agreement with International Law." International Law, natural law, German law, any law at all was to these men simply a propaganda device to be invoked when it helped and to be ignored when it would condemn what they wanted to do. That men may be protected in relying upon the law at the time they act is the reason we find laws of retrospective operation unjust. But these men cannot bring themselves within the reason of the rule which in some systems of jurisprudence prohibits ex post facto laws. They cannot show that they ever relied upon International Law in any state or paid it the slightest regard.

The Third Count of the Indictment is based on the definition of war crimes contained in the Charter. I have outlined to you the systematic course of conduct toward civilian populations and combat forces which violates international conventions to which Germany was a party. Of the criminal nature of these acts at least, the defendants had, as we shall show, clear knowledge. Accordingly, they took pains to conceal their violations. It will appear that the defendants Keitel and Jodl were informed by official legal advisors that the orders to brand Russian prisoners of war, to shackle British prisoners of war, and to execute commando prisoners were clear violations of International Law. Nevertheless, these orders were put into effect. The same is true of orders issued for the assassination of General Giraud and General Weygand, which failed to be executed only because of a ruse on the part of Admiral Canaris, who was himself later executed for his part in the plot to take Hitler's life on July 20, 1944.

The Fourth Count of the Indictment is based on crimes against humanity. Chief among these are mass killings of countless human beings in cold blood. Does it take these men by surprise that murder is treated as a crime?

The First and Second Counts of the Indictment add to these crimes the crime of plotting and waging wars of aggression and wars in violation of nine treaties to which Germany was a party. There was a time, in fact I think the time of the first World War, when it could not have been said that war inciting or war making was a crime in law, however reprehensible in morals.

Of course, it was under the law of all civilized peoples a crime for one man with his bare knuckles to assault another. How did it come that multiplying this crime by a million, and adding firearms to bare knuckles, made a legally innocent act? The doctrine was that one could not be regarded as criminal for committing the usual violent acts in the conduct of legitimate warfare. The age of imperialistic expansion during the eighteenth and nineteenth centuries added the foul doctrine, contrary to the teaching of early Christian and International Law scholars such as Grotius, that all wars are to be regarded as legitimate wars. The sum of these two doctrines was to give war making a complete immunity from accountability to law.

This was intolerable for an age that called itself civilized. Plain people, with their earthy common sense, revolted at such fictions and legalisms so contrary to ethical principles and demanded checks on war immunity. Statesmen and international lawyers at first cautiously responded by adopting rules of warfare designed to make the conduct of war more civilized. The effort was to set legal limits to the violence that could be done to civilian populations and to combatants as well.

The common sense of men after the first World War demanded, however, that the law's condemnation of war reach deeper, and that the law condemn not merely uncivilized ways of waging war, but also the waging in any way of uncivilized wars—wars of aggression. The world's statesmen again went only as far as they were forced to go. Their efforts were timid and cautious and often less explicit than we might have hoped. But the 1920's did outlaw aggressive war.

The re-establishment of the principle that there are unjust wars and that unjust wars are illegal is traceable in many steps. One of the most significant is the Briand-Kellogg Pact of 1928, by which Germany, Italy, and Japan, in common with practically all the nations of the world, renounced war as an instrument of national policy, bound themselves to seek the settlement of disputes only by pacific means, and condemned recourse to war for the solution of international controversies. This pact altered the legal status of a war of aggression. As Mr. Stimson, the United States Secretary of State, put it in 1932, such a war "is no longer to be the source and subject of rights. It is no longer to be the principle around which the duties, the conduct, and the rights of nations revolve. It is an illegal thing. . . . By that very act, we have made obsolete many legal precedents and have given the legal profession the task of re-examining many of its codes and treaties."

The Geneva Protocol of 1924 for the Pacific Settlement of International Disputes, signed by the representatives of forty-eight governments, declared that "a war of aggression constitutes . . . an international crime." The Eighth Assembly of the League of Nations in 1927, on unanimous resolution of the representatives of forty-eight member nations, including Germany, declared that a war of aggression constitutes an international crime. At the Sixth Pan-American Conference of 1928, the twenty-one American Republics unanimously adopted a resolution stating that "war of aggression constitutes an international crime against the human species."

A failure of these Nazis to heed, or to understand the force and meaning of this evolution in the legal thought of the world is not a defense or a mitigation. If anything, it aggravates their offense and makes it the more mandatory that the law they have flouted be vindicated by juridical application to their lawless conduct.

Indeed, by their own law—had they heeded any law—these principles were binding on these defendants. Article 4 of the Weimar Constitution provided that "the generally accepted rules of International Law are to be considered as binding integral parts of the law of the German Reich." Can there be any doubt that the outlawry of aggressive war was one of the "generally accepted rules of International Law" in 1939?

Any resort to war—to any kind of a war—is a resort to means that are inherently criminal. War inevitably is a course of killings, assaults, deprivations of liberty, and destruction of property. An honestly defensive war is, of course, legal and saves those lawfully conducting it from criminality. But inherently criminal acts cannot be defended by showing that those who committed them were engaged in a war, when war itself is illegal. The very minimum legal consequence of the treaties making aggressive wars illegal is to strip those who incite or wage them of every defense the law ever gave, and to leave war-makers subject to judgment by the usually accepted principles of the law of crimes.

But if it be thought that the Charter, whose declarations concededly bind us all, does contain new law I still do not shrink from demanding its strict application by this Tribunal. The rule of law in the world, flouted by the lawlessness incited by these defendants, had to be restored at the cost to my country of over a million casualties, not to mention those of other nations. I cannot subscribe to the perverted reasoning that society may advance and strengthen the rule of law by the expenditure of morally innocent lives but that progress in the law may never be made at the price of morally guilty lives.

It is true, of course, that we have no judicial precedent for the Charter. But International Law is more than a scholarly collection of abstract and immutable principles. It is an outgrowth of treaties and agreements between nations and of accepted customs. Yet every custom has its origin in some single act, and every agreement has to be initiated by the action of some state. Unless we are prepared to abandon every principle of growth for International Law, we cannot deny that our own day has the right to institute customs and to conclude agreements that will themselves become sources of a newer and strengthened International Law. International Law is not capable of development by the normal processes of legislation for there is no continuing international legislative authority. Innovations and revisions in International Law are brought about by the action of governments designed to meet a change in circumstances. It grows, as did the Common Law, through decisions reached from time to time in adapting settled principles to new situations. The fact is that when the law evolves by the case method, as did the Common Law and as International Law must do if it is to advance at all, it advances at the expense of those who wrongly guessed the law and learned too late their error. The law, so far as International Law can be decreed, had been clearly pronounced when these acts took place. Hence, I am not disturbed by the lack of judicial precedent for the inquiry we propose to conduct.

The events I have earlier recited clearly fall within the standards of crimes, set out in the Charter, whose perpetrators this Tribunal is convened to judge and punish fittingly. The standards for war crimes and crimes against humanity are too familiar to need comment. There are, however, certain novel problems in applying other precepts of the Charter which I should call to your attention.

The Crime Against Peace

A basic provision of the Charter is that to plan, prepare, initiate, or wage a war of aggression, or a war in violation of international treaties, agreements, and assurances, or to conspire or participate in a common plan to do so is a crime.

It is perhaps a weakness in this Charter that it fails itself to define a war of aggression. Abstractly, the subject is full of difficulty and all kinds of troublesome hypothetical cases can be conjured up. It is a subject which, if the defense should be permitted to go afield beyond the very narrow charge in the Indictment, would prolong the trial and involve the Tribunal in insoluble political issues. But so far as the question can properly be involved in this case, the issue is one of no novelty and is one on which legal opinion has well crystallized.

One of the most authoritative sources of International Law on this subject is the Convention for the Definition of Aggression signed at London on July 3, 1933, by Rumania, Estonia, Latvia, Poland, Turkey, the Soviet Union, Persia, and Afghanistan. The subject has also been considered by international committees and by commentators whose views are entitled to the greatest respect. It had been little discussed prior to the first World War but has received much attention as International Law has evolved its outlawry of aggressive war. In the light of these materials of International Law, and so far as relevant to the evidence in this case, I suggest that an "aggressor" is generally held to be that state which is the first to commit any of the following actions:

(1) Declaration of war upon another State;

(2) Invasion by its armed forces, with or without a declaration of war, of the territory of another State;

(3) Attack by its land, naval, or air forces, with or without a declaration of war, on the territory, vessels, or aircraft of another State;

(4) Provision of support to armed bands formed in the territory of another State, or refusal, notwithstanding the request of the invaded State, to take in its own territory, all the measures in its power to deprive those bands of all assistance or protection.

And I further suggest that it is the general view that no political, military, economic, or other considerations shall serve as an excuse or justification for such actions; but exercise of the right of legitimate self-defense, that is to say, resistance to an act of aggression, or action to assist a state which has been subjected to aggression, shall not constitute a war of aggression.

It is upon such an understanding of the law that our evidence of a conspiracy to provoke and wage an aggressive war is prepared and presented. By this test each of the series of wars begun by these Nazi leaders was unambiguously aggressive.

It is important to the duration and scope of this trial that we bear in mind the difference between our charge that this war was one of aggression and a position that Germany had no grievances. We are not inquiring into the conditions which contributed to causing this war. They are for history to unravel. It is no part of our task to vindicate the European *status quo* as of 1933, or as of any other date. The United States does not desire to enter into discussion of the complicated pre-war currents of European politics, and it hopes this trial will not be protracted by their consideration. The remote causations avowed are too insincere and inconsistent, too complicated and doctrinaire to be the subject of profitable inquiry in this trial.

A familiar example is to be found in the "Lebensraum" slogan, which summarized the contention that Germany needed more living space as a justification for expansion. At the same time that the Nazis were demanding more space for the German people, they were demanding more German people to occupy space. Every known means to increase the birth rate, legitimate and illegitimate, was utilized. "Lebensraum" represented a vicious circle of demand—from neighbors more space, and from Germans more progeny. We do not need to investigate the verity of doctrines which led to constantly expanding circles of aggression. It is the plot and the act of aggression which we charge to be crimes.

Our position is that whatever grievances a nation may have, however objectionable it finds the *status quo,* aggressive warfare is an illegal means for settling those grievances or for altering those conditions. It may be that the Germany of the 1920's and 1930's faced desperate problems, problems that would have warranted the boldest measures short of war. All other methods—persuasion, propaganda, economic competition, diplomacy—were open to an aggrieved country, but aggressive warfare was outlawed. These defendants did make aggressive war, a war in violation of treaties. They did attack and invade their neighbors in order to effectuate a foreign policy which they knew could not be accomplished by measures short of war. And that is as far as we accuse or propose to inquire.

The Law of Individual Responsibility

The Charter also recognizes individual responsibility on the part of those who commit acts defined as crimes, or who incite others to do so, or who join a common plan with other persons, groups or organizations to bring about their commission. The principle of individual responsibility for piracy and brigandage, which have long been recognized as crimes punishable under International Law, is old and well established. That is what illegal warfare is. This principle of personal liability is a necessary as well as logical one if International Law is to render real help to the maintenance of peace. An International Law which operates only on states can be enforced only by war because the most practicable method of coercing a state is warfare. Those familiar with American history know that one of the compelling reasons for adoption of our Constitution was that the laws of the Confederation, which operated only on constituent states, were found ineffective to maintain order among them. The only answer to recalcitrance was impotence or war. Only sanctions which reach individuals can peacefully and effectively be enforced. Hence, the principle of the criminality of aggressive war is implemented by the Charter with the principle of personal responsibility.

Of course, the idea that a state, any more than a corporation, commits crimes is a fiction. Crimes always are committed only by persons. While it is quite proper to employ the fiction of responsibility of a state or corporation for the purpose of imposing a collective liability, it is quite intolerable to let such a legalism become the basis of personal immunity.

The Charter recognizes that one who has committed criminal acts may not take refuge in superior orders nor in the doctrine that his crimes were acts of states. These twin principles working together have heretofore resulted in immunity for practically everyone concerned in the really great crimes against peace and mankind. Those in lower ranks were protected against liability by the orders of their superiors. The superiors were protected because their orders were called acts of state. Under the Charter, no defense based on either of these doctrines can be

The "Just War" Justifies Too Much / 343

entertained. Modern civilization puts unlimited weapons of destruction in the hands of men. It cannot tolerate so vast an area of legal irresponsibility.

Even the German Military Code provides that:

If the execution of a military order in the course of duty violates the criminal law, then the superior officer giving the order will bear the sole responsibility therefor. However, the obeying subordinate will share the punishment of the participant: (1) if he has exceeded the order given to him, or (2) if it was within his knowledge that the order of his superior officer concerned an act by which it was intended to commit a civil or military crime or transgression. (Reichsgesetzblatt, 1926, No. 37, p. 278, Art. 47.)

Of course, we do not argue that the circumstances under which one commits an act should be disregarded in judging its legal effect. A conscripted private on a firing squad cannot expect to hold an inquest on the validity of the execution. The Charter implies common sense limits to liability just as it places common sense limits upon immunity. But none of these men before you acted in minor parts. Each of them was entrusted with broad discretion and exercised great power. Their responsibility is correspondingly great and may not be shifted to that fictional being, "the State," which cannot be produced for trial, cannot testify, and cannot be sentenced.

The Charter also recognizes a vicarious liability, which responsibility is recognized by most modern systems of law, for acts committed by others in carrying out a common plan or conspiracy to which a defendant has become a party. I need not discuss the familiar principles of such liability. Every day in the courts of countries associated in this prosecution, men are convicted for acts that they did not personally commit but for which they were held responsible because of membership in illegal combinations or plans or conspiracies.

The "Just War" Justifies Too Much
Donald Wells

Donald A. Wells (1917-   ) teaches philosophy at the University of Hawaii at Hilo. He is the author of *The War Myth* (1967).

"Justification" is not an unambiguous term. In the context of logical justification, the defense of a claim is a function of a given system, where consistency with axioms is a necessary, if not sufficient, criterion of proof. In normative discourse, however, justification takes on an honorific and emotion laden

Source: "How Much Can the 'Just War' Be Justified?" Revised and reprinted with permission of the author. The original article first appeared in *Journal of Philosophy*, Vol. 66, No. 23 (December 4, 1969).

aura. In addition to both consistency and truth claims, moral justification entails some notion of "rightness" or "goodness." The problem of the "Just War" is, in this latter sense, more than a matter of consistency with some given axioms, more than a question of the truth of some factual claims, more than a matter of what is permissible legally, and surely more than an exercise in the possible limits of an hypothetical ethics.

In a very ordinary sense of the term "justify" we commonly seek an explanation of why a war was waged in the first place. "Why did Athens war against Sparta?" is in this sense "justified" by giving the antecedent reasons prompting the declaration. But more has been involved than this in traditional dispute over the justice of some war. Commonly the dispute sounds more like the defense of an appellant before a judge, and the "justification" consists in part in showing that some acts of war were consistent with the legal rules under which we have agreed to operate. In a further sense, the justification of war is like the famous "justification of induction," and its resolution involves us in a metalinguistic search for some frame of reference that transcends both politics and morals.

More pertinently, however, the attempts to justify war constitute a recognition that the terms "just" and "war" are, if not contradictions, at least of doubtful conjunction. Since the kind of havoc which war entails is normally classed with immoral actions, the concept of the "just war" aims to show the circumstances under which it would be proper to perform otherwise immoral acts and to contribute to evil consequences. The first century of the Christian church, with its pacifist rejection of war altogether, did not produce any theorizers of the just war. While by the time Christianity was adopted as the official religion of the Roman Empire, war had lost its aura of absolute evil, and men now proposed conditions under which it would be appropriate to kill in war. While the post-Constantine church accepted war as a defensible method, it never quite lost its first-century suspicion that killing was still evil. Thus the defenses of the "just war" exhibited a friction or tension between the ethical ideal of non-killing and the political practice of killing in the service of the state.

In his essay "Politics as a Vocation" Max Weber distinguished these two basically contrary concerns. He formulated them in two maxims: (1) the ethics of ultimate ends, and (2) the ethics of responsibility. In the case of the first position the Christians act rightly and leave the outcome to God. The Christian commitment to the sacredness of human life led them to posit limits to the means a person can rightly perform in the support of any other end. The end of human life precluded, in this sense, the acceptance of any alternative end which might destroy this prior humanistic one. In the case of the second position, the politician or head of state accepts the survival of the state as the supreme goal, and he rejects, therefore, the idea that there are limits to permissible action. While he did not intend that the statesman be given carte blanche to do any act whatsoever, he did mean to grant to the statesman the right to perform absolutely any act needed to preserve the state. While Weber's essay suggests that the problem is basically one of ends versus means, this is surely not what differentiates the traditional or modern conflict between moralists and statesmen over the use of war. What is, for the Christian of the first century, the summum bonum of human life, is for the statesman of the Empire replaced by the summum bonum of national survival. The former could scarcely adopt a means that destroyed human life, while the latter could sacrifice human lives since he did not value them above the life of the state. Put in very simple terms, the problem of the just war became one of reconciling early Christian compunction with later political necessity.

Historically the medieval thesis of the just war was to set limits to the so-called "reasons of state" without at the same time denying that right of the state to survive, apparently at any cost. The just war criteria set hypothetical limits, but at no point was it intended to require states to surrender their sovereignty. In operation the criteria of the just war established the rules by which states ought to defend themselves. These rules aimed to curb excessively inhumane war practices, where they were not really needed, to reduce the number of reasons that could justify a war, to assure that the means of war bore some proportional relation to the ends of war, and generally to reduce the number of wars that actually occurred. There was no doubt in the Middle Ages that the concept functioned as a defense of national sovereignty, and of the right of nations to defend themselves by war in a basically lawless world. It made national survival feasible, while making international organization unlikely. If the rules for just wars seemed counsels of perfection, it was clear enough in practice that they set no serious limits to the aspiration of Princes.

Since the notion of the just war has been revived after nearly two centuries of silence on the issue, it is appropriate to look again at the general principles of the medieval position to determine whether, if they had a defense then, they have any defense now. The entire case for the medieval thinker rested, of course, on a concession which itself needs reassessment: namely, that war has a place in the moral scheme. Traditional questions about war were prudential, and the discussion centered on such questions as to time, place, and cause. Wars were presumed to be neutral means which could be given moral properties under the appropriate conditions. Wars were criticised, if at all, in practice rather than in principle. In this regard, medieval discussion of capital punishment shared common predicates. It wasn't the fact of killing that was the determinant, but rather the reasons given for the acts of killing that were decisive. How did the medieval thinker develop this notion?

THE CRITERIA OF SAINT THOMAS

In order for a war to be just three general conditions had to be met: (1) an authoritative sovereign must declare the war, (2) a just cause is required, and (3) the men who wage the war must have noble intentions and moderate means so that some good actually results. Furthermore, the good that results should be greater by some magnitude than the evil that must be produced by waging war. In the application of these criteria very few criticisms of war emerged, suggesting that Princes were remarkably wise and beneficent, or else that the criteria of the just war were too vague to be discriminating. In addition to the paucity of critique against wars, what protest there was came from persons not officially in government so that their objection was a kind of baying at the moon. George Fox, for example, challenged the wars of Cromwell, but then Fox was a pacifist who rejected all wars and could thus be dismissed as unrealistic. Franciscus de Victoria, a theological professor at the University of Salamanca in the 16th century, chastised his Spanish superiors for their wars against the American Indians.[1] University professors,

[1] Franciscus de Victoria, *On the Law of War*. Washington, D.C.: The Carnegie Institute, 1917. Section 22.

however, were no more influential in effecting changes in foreign policy in the 16th century than they appear to be now, and thus such remarks as these constituted a kind of irrelevant campus protest.

More recently, Joseph McKenna[2] has revived the just war doctrine with an expanded list of seven conditions. They are: (1) the war must be declared by the duly constituted authority, (2) the seriousness of the injury inflicted on the enemy must be proportional to the damage suffered by the virtuous, (3) the injury to the aggressor must be real and immediate, (4) there must be a reasonable chance of winning the war, (5) the use of war must be a last resort, (6) the participants must have right intentions, and (7) the means used must be moral. The problem before us is whether such criteria can be made applicable to modern war. To put this issue this way suggests that the methodology of war is a datum entailing its justice, and it insinuates that the weapons of war determine to some degree the morality of war. This brings us back to the medieval position that it is not so much a question of killing as it is the manner of the killing that really counts.

JUST WAR IS ONE DECLARED BY THE DULY CONSTITUTED AUTHORITY

For a theologian like Saint Augustine or Saint Thomas, who presumed some ameliorating influence from Christian prelates, such a criterion might be considered to constitute a limitation on careless heathen scoundrels. Since both worthy Saints accepted heathen Princes as duly constituted, it was not obvious how this influence was supposed to work. By the 16th century, however, with the proliferation of Princes, and the fading away of Christian prelates, a radically new situation had emerged. By this time the "reasons of state" as Machiavelli elaborated them, permitted every Prince to wage war whenever he deemed it fit. Since by the 18th century war had become the sport of kings, it was clear that authorities had no special claim to sensitivity or good sense.

The rise of nationalism made this first criterion undifferentiating. It became increasingly obvious that to grant to any Prince the privilege of judging his neighboring prelates posed an odd situation. Every Prince judged every other Prince and was in turn judged by them, and there appeared to be a kind of gentleman's agreement not to be too critical of each other. It was this anomaly that led Grotius and Victoria to insist that while only one side of a war should properly be considered to be just, in fact persons on both sides could, in good conscience, presume that they had justice on their respective sides. In the absence of any international judge, no one was in a position to assess the claims of the national judges.

If rulers were saints or scholars there might be some reason to suppose that their judgements on war were adequate, and that they would not declare war for scurrilous reasons. At least two obstacles lay in the way of such a likelihood occurring. In the first place, the permissible reasons for waging war were so inclusive that virtually any conceivable princely aim could get support. Even wars of vindictive justice were permitted. In the second place, there were no plausible

---

[2] "Ethics and War: A Catholic View." *American Political Science Review.* September, 1960. pp. 647-658.

reasons to suppose that secular leaders had intentions that would meet even minimal standards of humaneness. It is not necessary to have in mind leaders like Hitler, Mussolini, Tojo, or Thieu to see that this is so. There is nothing in the nature of the process by which leaders are selected to give assurance that the leaders of France, England, or America have moral insights that are even as good as the average, let alone sufficiently discerning to be used as the criteria for a just war. We do not imagine our Princes to be especially gifted in domestic policy. Why should we imagine that they are wise as Solomon in foreign affairs?

Even clerics have had a rather poor reputation for sound moral judgment. Witness, for example, the stand of Archbishop Groeber of Freiburg-im-Breisgau who rejected Christian pacifism for German Catholics on the grounds that Hitler was the duly constituted authority. Pope Pius XII was no more reassuring on this point when he rejected the right of conscientious objection for German Catholics at the time of the formation of NATO. This first criterion of the duly constituted authority seems, therefore, to serve no distinguishing function at all. Indeed it is so ambiguous that applied to the present conflict in Vietnam both Ho Chi Minh and Thieu would satisfy the condition since they have declared war, while the American part in the war would be unjust since no war declaration has been made by the duly constituted authority.

A JUST WAR USES MEANS PROPORTIONAL TO THE ENDS

Franciscus de Victoria (1480-1546) observed that if to retake a piece of territory would expose a people to "intolerable ills and heavy woes,"[3] then it would not be just to retake it. We must be sure, he continued, that the evils we commit in war do not exceed the evils we claim to be averting. This was appropriate general advice, but in the absence of any specific suggestions as to how to make such measurement of relative ills, it was not even a helpful counsel of perfection, let alone a practical guide in the concrete situation. How do we measure proportionality? This was the problem of the hedonic calculus on which Mill's system first foundered. Since Victoria granted to Princes the right to despoil innocent children, if military necessity required it, it ceased to be apparent what proportionality meant at all. When this was combined with an equal vagueness on what constituted military necessity, the net contribution amounted to zero.

In a recent paper on this issue Father John A. Connery[4] stated that the morality of the violence depends on the proportionality of this violence to that of the aggression. Here again, what is required is some calculus to make this measurement. The latitude with which conscientious persons have interpreted what is proportional as a response suggests, what was clear enough to Mill, that we possess neither the quantitative nor the qualitative yardstick for such a decision. Pope Pius XII believed that the annihilation of vast numbers of persons was impermissible. Did he then intend for nations to surrender if the only price for success was such annihilation? Since the Pope was not explicit on this matter, John Courtney Murray[5] assumed that the papal prohibition was a conditional one. It was merely

[3] Victoria, *op. cit.*, Sections 33, 37.
[4] "Morality and Nuclear Armament." In William J. Nagle (Ed.), *Morality and Modern Warfare.* Baltimore: Helicon, 1960. p. 92.
[5] *Morality and Modern War.* New York: The Council on Religion and International Affairs, 1959. p. 9.

that large numbers of persons ought not to be slaughtered needlessly. Such a view, however, makes Pope Pius XII appear like a fool, for either he did not mean what he appeared to be saying, or he had not thought through the implications of what he appeared to be saying.

Proportionality is a slippery term unless there is some measure. Herbert Hoover thought in 1939 that the aerial bombing of cities was beyond moral proportion, although he did urge the U.S. to build bombing planes to perform this banned action. Jacques Maritain also put bombing from the air in the category of an absolutely proscribed act.[6] But how is such a determination made? In the early period of World War II "saturation bombing" was considered to be too inhumane for the American citizens to accept. Our military practiced instead what was euphemistically called "precision bombing." But even here where measurement would seem most plausible, the distinction was empty. This was illustrated when the Air Force announced at the time of the first test shot of the Atlas missile, that a bomb that lands within fifty miles of its target is considered accurate.[7]

In the concept of proportionality the medieval theorist introduced a distinction that made no difference. It is all very well to insist that actions be proportional, but if there are no criteria for the determination of proportionality, then the advice is not even a helpful counsel of perfection, let alone a useful curb to military excesses. Here again history reports the vacuity of the criterion. In the days of the cross-bow it was deemed necessary to remind military men of proportionality in relation to the ends to be preserved. If this was needful then, what about proportionality in the use of guns, fragmentation bombs, germ and chemical weapons, and thermonuclear explosives. Since the ends to be preserved by the cross-bow are essentially the same as those to be preserved by the H-bomb, one would expect that if there could have been an excessive use of the bow, then modern weapons could have no proportional use at all.

During World War II the English writer, Vera Brittain, attacked both Britain and America for the bombing of civilians in her book, *Massacre by Bombing*. Here was an opportunity to see whether proportionality was still alive. Mrs. Brittain said that the bombing of civilians was not proportional to the threat or to the goal to be achieved. The Protestant journal, *The Christian Century*, editorialized in support of the bombing of civilians. The American Bar Association defeated a resolution calling for a condemnation of the bombing of civilians.[8] *The Saturday Evening Post* suggested that it was a sign of "instability" to question the need for the bombing of civilians. Orthodox clergy like the Reverend Carl McIntyre and the Reverend H. J. Ockenga called Mrs. Brittain's position "un-American and pro-Fascist." Can such positions be defended on the basis of proportionality? Whether they can or not, the fact is that they were not so defended.

Proportionality, in use, appears to have been a justification for increasing escalation, rather than a curb to ascending violence. John Courtney Murray, in an essay on "Morality and Modern War,"[9] defended the survival of American culture as well as of the American state on the grounds that it was without peer in any moral system. Furthermore, he saw Communism as a kind of Anti-Christ, so evil and so destructive of the values of his personal national outlook, that he defended

[6] "War and the Bombardment of Cities." *Commonweal*. September 2, 1938.
[7] Nagle, *op. cit.,* p. 107.
[8] *New York Times*. July 15, 1939. p. 3.
[9] Murray, *op. cit.,* p. 6.

any means necessary to their preservation. The possibility of the loss of the pure and noble Western capitalist, democratic, and Christian culture was so unpleasant to him that he was able to tolerate the intolerable, think the unthinkable, and admit a cosmic amount of human destruction as quite proportional to the ends and the threat. Is there, indeed, any measure for such an assessment? The medieval concern with misplaced sword-thrusts is qualitatively unrelated to the contemporary calculation with the mega-death of civilians. Unless some case could be made that the modern values are infinitely more worthy than medieval values, the immense increase in human destruction that our wars now involve make proportionality absolutely inapplicable.

In the medieval calculation, wars for religion were considered to be unsupportable. Waging wars for religious reasons, such as the goal of conversion to Christianity or of abolishing heathenism, was classed as simply disproportional to war's havoc. Part of the medieval rejection of religious war, at least in principle, rested on their objection to wars against ideas or abstractions. Such an antipathy may be supported from a variety of bases. Conversion to an idea is normally considered a function of education, not of war. The method of war is simply not suited to changing opinion. In addition, false opinion or even heretical doctrine is not so cosmic an evil that war could be considered the lesser of two so-called evils. Much of the modern just war theorizing presumes that wars for politics are proportionally defensible, and it would seem that the medieval reasons against wars for religion hold here with equal cogency. Our twentieth century wars to save democracy, freedom, or to banish fascism, communism, or socialism have failed signally to alter opinion or to establish new thinking on such generalities. War is, in this regard, not a form of debate or of mental persuasion. As a matter of fact persons live well under a variety of economic and political systems—communist, socialist, capitalist, monarchic, democratic, or republican, even fascist. They can equally live poorly under these same systems—the Jews in Germany, the Blacks in the United States, and the Orientals in Australia. Wars for ideology not only misunderstand the sources of human ills, but they are, in part because of this misunderstanding, all out of proportion. Even our most callous storm-trooper does not recommend the bomb on Selma, Little Rock, or Chicago, while some of our most sensitive leaders propose simple genocide on Vietnam for putative ideological reasons.

Consideration of the current discussion of what is called "rational nuclear armament" suggests that the criterion calling for just means or for proportionality in our actions of war is only a verbal genuflection. Dr. Kahn, famous for his ability to think the unthinkable, has recommended in the interests of proportionality that bombs be limited to the one-half megaton class. Since this is fifty times greater than the bomb dropped on Hiroshima proportionality has obviously become a rather loose term. This is the same conclusion we reach in the context of the language of "overkill" or "megakill." If we have enough bombs to kill every person in a country twice, or in effect twice as many bombs as we actually need to exterminate the population, then it makes no moral sense to speak of the reduction of bombs to the precise amount needed as illustrating any degree of humane or ethical proportion. To be sure there is a mathematical difference, and from the point of view of the military-educational-industrial complex there is a production difference. From the point of view of moral distinctions, however, there is no difference at all. The use of too much "firepower" is an economic waste, not a superfluity of immorality.

WAR MAY JUSTLY BE TAKEN ONLY AS A LAST RESORT

In conventional discourse the notion of a "last resort" presupposes some notion of "first resort." Thus, unless a nation could show that it had indeed exhausted first resorts, it would make no sense for that nation to claim any right to use the last resort. First resorts might be such alternatives as economic, social, or political boycott, negotiations through the U.N. or through some unilateral means, and, of course, surrender is a first resort. Now let us assume that the first resorts have all been attempted, and that there appear to be no non-violent alternatives nor any violent options less destructive than war. We would still need to show that the last resort of war ought to be taken in this case. To permit war as a last resort is not the same as requiring that the last resort be taken. To say that war is a last resort is not the same as granting the right to go to war. It is possible that the last resort that can morally be defended is the first resort that is taken. This is clearer in a case like that of the Nazi treatment of the Jews, than it is usually seen to be in actions of our own nation like our treatment of the Blacks or of the Vietnamese. Could the Germans have defended the statement: "Having exhausted every other resort to remove the threat of the Jews to Aryan supremacy, may we now as a last resort, open the gas chambers?"

What confuses the case in war is the presumption that war is a proper resort at all, while domestically we assume citizens deserve better treatment. Somehow we contemporaries have retained the legitimacy of the means of war in spite of the escalation of its instruments and the scope of its use. In domestic gas chambers, on the contrary, we draw the line at excess. Some American states still use gas chambers on offenders, but these same defenders of local gas chambers were offended by the German use of them. It was as if they were saying that gas chambers as methods are proper or proportional as a last resort, provided that they are not used too widely. Or that the use of gas chambers was an appropriate last resort provided that the offense was of a certain magnitude. If all the German Jews had been culpable by American standards of offenses that in America would have sent them to the gas chambers, then, the conjecture seems to be, it would have been a proper last resort for the German Nazis to administer Belsen, Buchenwald, and the rest.

Most contemporary defense of the just war doctrine bypasses an important decisional matter: is the expression "just war" different in kind from the expressions "just murder," "just torture," "just genocide," or even "just annihilation of innocents." Since the words "murder," "torture," and "genocide" are pejorative, and communicate a clear moral condemnation as to their practice, we surely need to show that "war" is not also this kind of pejorative term. If war were shown to be a kind of murder, would just war theorists now wish to speak of just murder? At least a part of the implication of the War Crimes Trials in Nuremberg was that if war did become murder or genocide then it could not be justified. Thus in some cases, at least, war could not be considered as even a viable or justifiable last resort.

In this day of massive retaliation and mega-kill, the justification of war as any resort at all requires a defense that medieval concepts are unable to support. If persons are of the value that medieval theology assigned to them, then the sheer scope and devastation of modern war makes it impossible to find another value so over-riding that an Hiroshima becomes the lesser of two evils, and that war becomes a proper resort at all. The military claim that Ben Tre was destroyed to save Ben Tre makes no sense in the language of resorts. That vacuous maxim "military necessity" has led us to endorse unbelievable slaughter on the inference that what is militarily necessary must be morally approvable. There has never been a clear explication of what is militarily necessary, and furthermore, there has been no argument to show that morality should take its cue from generals. Paul Ramsey, the distinguished Protestant advocate of the just war thesis, endorses the use of thermonuclear bombs on civilians if military necessity requires it.[10] Obviously the only way to answer his claim is that this is not too great a price to pay is to consult the living, but equally the only way for him to defend his thesis is for him to consult the dead.

Since the doctrine of the just war has become the verbal tool of military theologians or moral tacticians of war, no one seriously considers that surrender might be the most moral option, making it additionally clear that the discussants are speaking only for nations that win wars. Indeed, if the just war has any credence at all, there should be situations where the wise Prince surrenders rather than declare war. Politicians and military strategists argue from premises of national sovereignty and a proper power struggle, not from a concern with virtue, and is further reason why modern carnage turns out to be just. That there is a blind spot on this forbidden notion of surrender was illustrated by the spectacle in August, 1958, when the Senate of the United States voted 82 to 2 to deny government funds to any person or institution that proposes or actually conducts any study regarding the possible results of the surrender of the U.S. as an alternative to war. Since nations with arms are loth to succumb to their national neighbors, and moreover to do so over concern with whether first resorts still remain, about all the theory of last resort tells us is that war is a resort that nations are bound to take.

A JUST WAR MUST BE WAGED BY MEN WITH RIGHT INTENTIONS

This issue has a direct relation to the question of whether war is an appropriate resort, first or last. Both what we intend to do and what we intend to preserve are related to whether it can be said that our intentions in war were actually just. Vatican II spoke to this matter when it reported: "As long as the danger of war remains and there is no competent and sufficiently powerful authority at the international level, governments cannot be denied the right to legitimate defense once every means of peaceful settlement has been exhausted."[11] But are there no limits on any governments. Isn't it conceivable that Nazi Germany did not deserve to survive, any more than the government of Thieu in South Vietnam? Is the preservation of the state so incontrovertibly significant that the resort to war to save it is always an act of right intention?

Much of the medieval controversy over intentionality revolved around the doctrine of the "double-effect." A just belligerent intended only as much killing as was proportional to the threat, and he was responsible only for the deaths he

[10] "Just War and Reasons of State." In Robert W. Tucker, *Just War and Vatican Council II: A Critique.* New York: The Council on Religion and International Affairs, 1966. pp. 68f.

[11] *Pastoral Constitution on the Church in the Modern World.* Part II, Chapter V. National Catholic Welfare Conference, 1966.

intended to cause. It was, of course, assumed that he did not intend to kill non-combatants. That this was the ideal, not always implemented in practice, was borne out by the concessions of men from Saint Thomas to Victoria that military necessity might justify even the despoiling of innocents. Still the medieval concern with the death of the by-stander was one that could be implemented. Their weapons made such a concern practical. Although an archer might shoot his arrow into the air and not be too clear as to where it landed, he was not in doubt as to whether he was aiming it at combatants. He might miss a small barn, but he did hit the right city. Modern weapons make such a concern with the innocents inoperable and unfeasible. In addition, the fact that so many non-combatants are killed in modern war, a number commonly exceeding that of the soldiers, suggests that something is awry. Instead of proper regret for the scope of modern weapons of destruction on the civilians, contemporaries have theorized that the class of non-combatants is now a null class. The limited war of the past has been replaced by the total war of the present—total in the sense that military necessity now justifies the death of all without exception. The medieval man might pardonably weep for the accidentally slain civilians, but modern man cannot afford to weep since he knows that he intends the death of every person slain.

This problem of unwanted or unintended death has always been an harassing one. In 1076 at a Council in Winchester, England, the cases were considered of men who had fought with William the Conqueror at the Battle of Hastings. Many of the soldiers were troubled by the memory of the men they had slain, and in the case of archers, with the thought that they had slain some unknowingly. Archers were assigned the penance of daily prayers for the rest of their lives for the unknown deaths they may have caused. No comparable clerical or council concern has emerged in the twentieth century. Now when our weapons make our intentions to no avail, we cling to the weapons and adjust our intentions to our moral yardstick. If military necessity now requires the mega-death of civilians, then modern theorists will show that such intended deaths are consistent with the doctrine of right intentions. If medieval men suffered pangs of guilt for ricocheting arrows, modern men exhibit no comparable concern for Dresden, Tokyo, Hiroshima, Nagasaki, or Ben Tre. When we realize, in addition, that "double-effect" is not something that plays a role in military tactics or political strategy, it is apparent that moral concerns at this point are rather ivory tower ephemera.

A further problem with intentionality is that of showing that the means of war are appropriate even for those persons considered to be fair game because they are combatants. Nowhere has the ingenuity of man been more exercised then in the enterprise of developing "humane" ways to exterminate his fellows. In 1041 the Bishop of Arles and the Abbot of Cluny established the "truce of God" which limited the times when war could properly be carried out. Initially, war was permitted only between Monday morning and Wednesday evening, and holy days could further delimit this range. The "peace of God" decreed at the Council of Narbonne in 1054 limited the kinds of persons who could properly be attacked. By the sixteenth century Pierino Belli[12] while urging that war remain a conflict only of armed soldiers concluded that the rules of the "peaces" may safely be ignored.

In every age the attempt was made anew to proscribe some war weapons even against combatants. William Paley eschewed poison and assassination.[13] J. G.

[12] Pierino Belli, *A Treatise on Military Matters.* Oxford: Clarendon Press, 1936. p. 81.
[13] William Paley, *Moral Philosophy, Volume IV.* London: C. and J. Rivington, 1825. p. 531.

Fichte considered the use of snipers to be "downright illegal."[14] Pope Pius XII added his anathema against poison gas.[15] By the time Hitler declaimed against attack from the air as too inhumane to be tolerated,[16] it should have occurred to all that this discussion left something to be desired. The Hague Declarations of 1899 and 1907 made "prohibited" the discharge of projectiles from the air, the use of asphyxiating gases, expanding bullets, contact mines, and torpedoes which remain dangerous after they have missed their mark.[17] Little remained for soldiers to do save to joust in the knightly fashion of the middle ages. The absurdity of such an exercise was sharpened by the remarks of a doctor to the Berlin Military Medical Society in 1885 on the discovery of a high-speed, non-expanding bullet. "I welcome the new bullet with great joy and believe that if it were generally adopted by international consent, all humanity would have cause to rejoice."[18] He called this new type bullet "humane." Haven't we lost something of the medieval sense of humane intentions if we can talk seriously in this fashion? Yet the mandate against expanding bullets so impressed Hiram Maxim (1840-1916) that he considered his machine gun to be "the greatest life-saving instrument ever invented."[19]

Serious discussion among just war theorists today about the limits of just intention rarely begin until thermonuclear weapons. The whole range of "lesser" evils has been reconciled into the moral scheme. Only new tools of destruction pose any problem. Thus Richard J. Krickus[20] believed that chemical bombs were moral while biological bombs were not. Part of his reasoning rested on the thesis that control was more possible with the former than with the latter, but also that there has been a long religious-psychic association between germs and evil. Still napalm, anti-personnel shrapnel, and expanding bullets posed no moral dilemmas.

The Gas Chamber has been a disturbing symbol in modern times of a possible limit to how man can justly treat his fellows. Since we in America use gas chambers for domestic offenders, it must have been something other than the tool itself that led to the War Crimes Trials against the Nazis. Perhaps it was that the Germans gassed the wrong persons. Would the deed have been palatable if they had killed only soldiers, and had left the women, children, and civilian men alone? Was it that the Nazis killed the Jews for the wrong reasons? If the Nazis were being exterminated in Belsen would there be no moral problem? Is there a way to calculate that the death of twenty civilians poses a different moral problem from the death of twenty soldiers? Is it worse to kill twenty children than to kill twenty adults? Perhaps there is no way to calculate the relative horrors in these alternatives, but it is precisely this kind of question that the just war theorists must answer.

Our problem here is one of calculating the relative evil of war with the relative evil of any alternative. And surely part of the relevant variables include the magnitude of the weapons, and the scope of their application to various persons normally considered to be innocent or at least non-combatant. Since it is unlikely that the values now claimed to be the justification for war are any better, let alone

[14] J. G. Fichte, *The Science of Rights.* Philadelphia: J. B. Lippincott, 1869. p. 484.
[15] "C'est une Vive Satisfaction." September 14, 1939.
[16] Adolf Hitler, *My New Order.* New York: Reynal and Hitchcock, 1941. p. 951.
[17] Carnegie Endowment for International Peace. Pamphlets 1-22.
[18] I. S. Bloch, *The Future of War.* New York: Doubleday, 1902. p. 150.
[19] Hiram Maxim, *Defenseless America.* New York: Hearst, 1915. p. 83.
[20] Richard J. Krickus, "On the Morality of Chemical/Biological War." *Journal of Conflict Resolution.* June, 1965. pp. 200-210.

any different, from those in the Middle Ages, the increased destruction of war must surely be germane to the question whether war as a means can be made just at all any more. If in the middle ages some wars were conceivably less tragic than the alternatives, although live illustrations would be hard to find, modern wars are so ghastly and so much more destructive of the humane virtues than the alternatives, that to justify war now seems to justify too much.

CONCLUSION

We are back to our starting point and the problem, as yet unpersuasively resolved, is to show that war is a potentially moral means at all. While we know the legal distinction between killing done by private citizens (called murder) and the killing done by soldiers in the name of the state (called war) and the killing done by the state to its criminals (called capital punishment), the moral indictment against taking life once applied equally to every instance. Surely it made no difference to the person slain what the circumstances of his death were, or by what name the deed was called. "Thou shalt not kill" once had an absolute ring to it. Since human life was the supreme value, taking it was a supreme disvalue, and extenuating circumstances did not alter this assessment. Furthermore, the question of self-defense posed an apparent dilemma to the matter of human life. If each person has a right to self-defense, at the price of the death of the opponent, hasn't there occurred a radical reorganization of relative values? Or isn't it rather that self-defense, while a ubiquitous political right renowned in oratory, is not a moral right at all. Nor, doubtless, is the supposed right of national defense any more rooted in moral axioms. In fact, for rather evident reasons national survival is less important than personal survival. The former can be revived should it be thought a good idea, while dead citizens are irrevocably gone.

What has not yet been demonstrated by the just war theorist is the radical distinction he draws between killing in war and killing under any other circumstance. The following illustration is not resolved by any just war dogmas yet devised. Suppose we are the Aryans, genuinely confronted by "mongrelization" by the Jews, and we approach our problem with the concepts and axioms of the medieval theologian. Our problem is that of the "just pogrom." Aryans may, of course, exterminate the Jews provided that the duly constituted leader declares the pogrom. Furthermore, the "death camps" need to be administered with means proportional to the threat, taking special care not to kill non-Jews. With this minimum presumption the citizens may kill the Jews if the Prince commands it with reasons as good as outlined. Cultural defense, like national defense, once granted as a supreme good, will allow all the gas chambers needed to preserve it. This is what military necessity justifies. The citizens would, in addition, be expected to implement the State Department policy of the "containment of Judaism" and to seek to rid by every means creeping Jews from the world. With no more intellectual effort than the just war theory requires we would be able to conduct the pogrom in accordance of the "laws of pogroms." Our means would naturally be humane gas chambers and sanitary ovens. With pure hearts we could march to Armageddon, with "just war" or "just pogrom" emblazoned on our banners. But isn't this to justify too much?

There are several presuppositions in conventional just war theory that make any resolution, short of ultimate annihilation under a mushroom-shaped cloud, unlikely.

(1) Given a world of sovereign nation states, and without any adjudicating power, and given that such nations deserve to survive ultimately and unquestionably, then no moral doctrine can take away the right of states to do whatever is needful for their continuation.

(2) Given war as a proper method, at worst neutral in quality and at best endowed with virtue, then no moral doctrine can attack war because it contains both the weapons and the deeds that destroy human life. It would be comparable to condemning the surgeon and his scalpel since there is a risk that the patient may die. Obviously the analogy is not quite appropriate here since the successful soldier kills his "patient," while the successful surgeon saves his patient.

(3) Given that the state is more important than the individual, indeed, that the state is more important than an infinite number of individuals, mere human death will never be a significant argument against war.

But, if this much be "given" then what is left for just war theory to adjudicate? Generally, it will be able to resolve what the medieval theorists claimed, namely:

(1) It can resolve that the war was properly announced.

(2) It can assess reasons, other than national defense, for their appropriateness. It must, of course, be recognized that national defense is the only reason theorists give any more, and thus there really isn't any assessment called for.

(3) It can determine that the means are proportional to the end of national defense. But unless it is clearly stated how long it is proper to wage a war, how great a human price it is proper to pay, what subsidiary losses in property, culture, or manner of living it is moral to suffer,—this is, what "military necessity" consists of—then there really isn't anything save an hypothetical exercise in casuistry that can engage the effort of the just war spokesman.

With these limitations, discussion of the just war can raise merely questions of consistency within the set of given axioms, and engage in a kind of aesthetic or psychological exercise in sensitivity. In the context of the presuppositions with which theories of the just war must operate, the "just war" justifies too much.

Conscientious Objection

Carl Cohen

Carl Cohen (1931-   ) is a professor of philosophy at the University of Michigan. He is the editor of *Communism, Fascism, and Democracy* (1962) and the author of *Democracy* (1971) and *Civil Disobedience* (1971).

Conscientious objection deserves more reflective attention than it generally gets; I want to help correct this deficiency. My object is not to urge that anyone be, or not be, a conscientious objector; I am not wise enough for that. Rather, I hope to make conscientious objection more deeply and more accurately understood. With such understanding, those who contemplate conscientious objection for themselves can (given an awareness of their own beliefs) act more consistently and more intelligently, while those who witness conscientious objection by others can better appreciate the essential nature of that conduct. A fuller understanding of conscientious objection has a further practical consequence of immediate importance. It exposes two grave injustices imposed by the rules governing conscientious objection presently in force in our system of military conscription, and may lead to their correction.

I

The provision of a special category for conscientious objectors is a *device* of the body politic. Recognizing that there are certain kinds of laws which may command the performance of acts that a significant minority cannot perform in good conscience, the community provides a special mechanism which permits that minority to be released from the requirement that those acts be performed, normally on the condition that some alternative acts rendering equal service to the community be performed in their stead. Conscientious objection may be viewed as a legal pressure valve, deliberately devised to relieve the tension between deeply held moral convictions and the demands of the law, when that tension becomes extreme. How great must the pressure be before the valve will open? That must depend upon the judgment of the legislators and administrators of the community in which the device is employed; in most cases, their aim is to avoid a situation in which some respected and law-abiding citizens are forced to choose between deliberate disobedience of the law in question and (if obedient) excruciating moral anguish. The sound principle which underlies conscientious objection is that, in framing its laws, the community should avoid creating situations in which any of its respected members are necessarily faced with an intolerable moral dilemma.

Provision for conscientious objection is a mark of considerable sophistication in

Source: Ethics, Vol. 78, No. 4 (August 1968), 269-279. Reprinted by permission of The University of Chicago Press (the publisher) and the author. © 1968 by The University of Chicago. *"Post script"* was added by the author specifically for this reprinting.

a political community. It indicates that there is a general awareness, in that community, of the depth of moral disagreements, and it is a concrete exhibition of the community's disposition to tolerate such disagreements when they are genuine and profound. It is, at the same time, an implicit recognition by the community that obedience to certain of its own laws might be held, by good and reasonable men, to be a moral evil. One does not encounter provisions for conscientious objection in the Code of Hammurabi or other primitive legal systems; their presence is a sign of political refinement and community self-restraint.

Almost invariably, conscientious objection is thought of in the context of military conscription, and that is the context in which I shall discuss it too. But it is worth noting that this is not the only sphere in which it is applicable, and the same (or similar) devices could be instituted more widely in the law than is presently the case. Wherever civic action comes (or is likely to come) into direct conflict with genuine and powerful moral scruples held by some, provision for lawful exemption, or lawful alternatives to specific compliance, might be made. For example, if the religious convictions of some group require that their children be taught by persons who cannot be certified as teachers under state law, exception to the certifying procedures, or to the universal requirement of certification, might be permitted on grounds of conscience. Again, those who cannot swear in good conscience are permitted, in our courts, to affirm that what they say is the truth, rather than being forced to take an oath to that effect. Other situations in which conscientious objection would be appropriate might be thought of. While I do not wish to defend here the embodiment of conscientious objection provisions in legislation in any particular sphere outside that of military conscription, I do submit that this kind of device has, wherever it is employed, at least two very attractive features to recommend it:

(a) It permits conscientious citizens who may hold unusual views to live in accord with their principles, and to apply their scruples to affairs of great consequence to them, without great cost to the state. In this way, the state can practice as well as profess its concern for the well-being of individual citizens and small minorities (even when eccentric) as well as its concern for the general welfare. Not only the few are thus protected, but also the many, in knowing that, were they someday to find themselves in a like case, the same opportunity for lawful relief will be open to them.

(b) By permitting such conscientious objection, the community can protect and honor variety—in manner, moral conviction, style of life. That variety not only adds richness and interest to the life of the whole but may prove essential to the long life of the community. This is so because that long life depends upon the ability of the community and its elements to adapt themselves to a planetary environment that changes ever more rapidly. When, as presently, it is uncertain what set of self-governing principles will prove most useful in helping subcommunities to adjust and survive in that changing environment, the preservation of a wide range of moral schemes within the larger community is an intelligent and humane form of political life insurance.

Wherever conscientious objection provisions are in force—whether in the context of military conscription or some other affair in which legal compulsion creates grave moral problems—the application of those provisions to particular cases will always be a delicate matter. In determining the applicability of such provisions to an individual who seeks the formal status of conscientious objector, the issue to be decided is *not* "Is the conscientious objector right?" in some objective sense. On the principles the legislators have employed, it is clear that the answer to that question is sure to be negative. Rather, what must be determined in applying such provisions is whether the objector is truly conscientious—that is, right in a fundamentally *subjective* sense. If a man truly thinks that he ought never to participate in making war, then, whether objectively right or wrong in that belief, he is *subjectively* right not to do so. When a man does what he honestly and deeply believes he ought not to do, we think him unprincipled and a hypocrite. The conscientious objector, who will not tolerate that hypocrisy in himself, and will defy his community rather than be untrue to himself, deserves honor and respect that far—even though we may think his conduct objectively wrong.

II

Section 6 (j) of the Military Selective Service Act of 1967 reads:

Nothing contained in this title shall be construed to require any person to be subject to combatant training and service in the armed forces of the United States who, by reason of religious training and belief, is conscientiously opposed to participation in war in any form. As used in this subsection, the term "religious training and belief" does not include essentially political, sociological, or philosophical views, or a merely personal moral code. . . .

This provision, while exhibiting some of that sophistication and restraint previously alluded to, is nevertheless seriously unjust in two important respects:

1. It opens the possibility of conscientious objection *only to those who profess religious beliefs of certain kinds,* and thereby discriminates improperly on the basis of religious belief.

2. It opens the possibility of conscientious objection *only to those who (on religious grounds) conscientiously oppose participation in war in any form,* and thereby discriminates improperly among beliefs on the basis of their content, or (more exactly) on the basis of the scope of the principle endorsed.

I shall explain each of these injustices more carefully in what follows; to do that clearly, however, I must first register three prefatory remarks.

1. One criticism of all conscientious objection provisions in military conscription statutes is that they officially condone cowardice. This complaint is as superficial as it is common. In the first place, it involves a misunderstanding of *what* is being permitted as an exception to the normal requirements of the law. Neither cowardice nor courage is at issue—only conscientiousness. In the second place, this criticism fails on the very criterion it seems to suppose. If courage is to be honored, it is well to remember that to apply for conscientious objector status when the nation is at war, or threatened by war, requires very great courage indeed. It is only a brave man who can stand up to the social pressures which every conscientious objector must face. Attacks upon his character (and perhaps that of his family as well), damage to his reputation and very probably to his career, abuse of every sort from those who think him unpatriotic at best and treasonous at worst—all these, as well as the serious doubts and misgivings of his friends and relations, must make his position a very difficult one. It is a stance that only a man of high moral courage can maintain. Probably there are many who, if they were fully conscientious, would have been conscientious objectors had they not lacked the necessary courage.

2. Two different kinds of conscientious objection need to be distinguished. The first, wholly lawful, is that already described. (Within this kind, the law actually provides for two categories of objectors: those who cannot conscientiously accept combatant status but who will serve in the armed forces, and those who cannot conscientiously serve in the armed forces at all. For my present purpose I lump these together as lawful conscientious objectors.) The second kind takes the form of deliberate disobedience to the conscription laws. One may conscientiously believe himself obliged, out of regard for higher moral principles, to refuse to co-operate with the state in any way in its war-making activities and therefore believe himself obliged not to comply with the regulations it imposes, even those permitting special release for conscientious objectors. This second form of conscientious objection, therefore, takes the form of civil disobedience—perhaps a refusal to register for the draft or, perhaps, after registering, to make it clear that he is not hiding, the objector may deliberately refuse to comply with any further commands pertaining to military conscription. Rightly or wrongly, such a disobedient argues that to apply for conscientious objector status within the law is to assist in the state's immoral activity by admitting in some measure the propriety of that law or the state's right to enact it. Conscientiously unable to make that admission, he feels morally obliged to refuse to co-operate and therefore defies the law outright. Many complex problems, moral and political, are raised by such civil disobedience, problems that I have discussed elsewhere and cannot enter here.[1] I would not wish to foreclose the possibility that even such disobedient conscientious objection may under some circumstances be justifiable, but my present purpose is to examine conscientious objection of the first type, which is entirely within the law, and to explain why it is a category that ought to be expanded in important ways.

3. Does a man have the *right* to claim the status of conscientious objector? The answer to this question depends, of course, upon what kind of right is being asked about. If one is asking whether there is a *moral* right to conscientious objection, I am not sure of the answer. The claim to such a moral right would be based upon whatever moral principles or scheme of moral values one adopts or discovers. Many moral systems do provide for such a right; great philosophers and jurisprudents have often viewed conscientious objection as a moral right; and the Supreme Court of the United States has suggested a similar view in holding that "in the domain of conscience there is a moral power higher than the state." But whether every moral system should specify or defend such a right is an issue I do not seek to resolve here. If the point of the question is to determine whether there is a *legal* right to conscientious objection, the answer will depend upon the laws (and their interpretations) in some given political community. One's legal rights extend as far as the laws provide. In the United States, at present, one has a legal right to the status of conscientious objector if he falls into certain categories and can establish to the satisfaction of the appropriate governmental agency that he does so qualify. But there is still a third sense in which one may ask about a right to conscientious objection. One may claim a *constitutional* right to it when the laws provide it for some, and that legally qualified group is distinguished from the rest on grounds which the more fundamental principles of the community do not permit. Then we may say, not that there is a constitutional right to conscientious objection in

---

[1] Carl Cohen, "The Ethics of Civil Disobedience," *Nation* (March 16, 1964).

general, but that, given a constitutional commitment to the equality of citizens before the law, and to the wrongfulness of discrimination on the basis of religious or moral beliefs, if conscientious objection is available to some—whether by right, or because its provision is believed to be wise policy, or both—others may have a constitutional right not to be denied that opportunity because of the content of their beliefs. That is the shape of the second argument I shall present. Whether any specific document—say, the Constitution of the United States—does technically require the expansion of the category of conscientious objection may presently be a moot point. But when we understand by "constitution" the set of larger principles under which the community lives and operates, the constitutional right of Americans to an expansion of the category of conscientious objection becomes virtually undeniable.

III

In order to qualify as a conscientious objector to military (or combatant) service in the United States today, one must show that his conscientious objection is grounded in "religious training and belief." Although some effort is made in the statute itself to clarify this phrase by specifying what it does not include— "essentially political, sociological, or philosophical views, or a merely personal moral code"—its precise force remains unclear.

This unclarity is not relieved by the recent change effected in the law on this matter. Formerly (in the Universal Military Training and Service Act, which the present law replaces), the same key phrase in question was elaborated with the following statement: "Religious training and belief in this connection means an individual's belief in a relation to a Supreme Being involving duties superior to those arising from any human relation." This "Supreme Being" clause, now removed, gave rise to much litigation, finally receiving from the U.S. Supreme Court, in 1965, a rather liberal interpretation.[2] The court there held that "within that phrase would come all sincere religious beliefs which are based upon a power or being, or upon a faith, to which all else is subordinate or upon which all else is ultimately dependent." To determine the presence of such a belief, the Court then concluded that "the test of belief 'in a relation to a Supreme Being' [is] whether a given belief that is sincere and meaningful occupies a place in the life of its possessor parallel to that filled by the orthodox belief in God of one who clearly qualifies for the exemption." Now that the "Supreme Being" clause to which this ruling of the Court specifically pertains, has been eliminated, one cannot be certain how the law will be interpreted and applied. It appears that it was the intent of Congress, in eliminating that clause, to restrict more narrowly the varieties of conscientious objection permissible under the law, by rendering the Seeger decision no longer applicable.

We are now left with little to go on but that little is ominous. Under the present act only those "who, by reason of religious training and belief" are conscientious objectors may be recognized as such by the law. Of course, religious training and belief may take a great many forms, but it is reasonable to suppose that selective service boards in this country will continue to interpret this restriction very much

[2] *U.S. v. Seeger*, 380 U.S. 163.

as they have in recent years. For most Americans an honest interpretation of religious belief is one that, at the least, entails a belief in God. Most men are quite prepared to allow that belief in God is itself a fuzzy matter, and subject to a range of permissible differences, but would insist that, without some such conviction, a man's principles could hardly be called "religious" beliefs. Therefore, he who denies the existence of God, or who states that his moral principles are not based upon any relation to a Supreme Being, or supernatural force, is most unlikely to be granted the status of lawful conscientious objector. Even if such a person were to claim (as he may not wish to do) that his conscientious objection is religiously grounded, that claim will almost certainly be denied and his views classified as "philosophical, or a merely personal moral code." In a word, some form of *theism*, however described or diluted, must be the foundation of conscientious objection if that conscientiousness is to be honored, and therefore only theists may now qualify as conscientious objectors.

This seems clearly to violate the First Amendment of the Constitution of the United States which specifically prohibits Congress from making any law "respecting an establishment of religion." But whatever technical, legal interpretation be given to the First Amendment, it is surely a principle central to the life of our national community—and one of which we are very proud—that the acceptance of any specific belief or set of beliefs, in religion or about religious matters, not be a requirement for enjoying the protections or privileges that the law extends to citizens. Yet it is precisely that kind of requirement which is imposed by the Military Selective Service Act of 1967. Put it another way: we Americans hold that no preference before the law shall be given to anyone because of his religious beliefs, but our present law governing conscientious objection does give marked preference to theists over atheists (and probably agnostics).

This is gravely unjust. Some persons who conscientiously object to participation in war in any form are atheists. The fact that they are atheists does not show them to be any less conscientious in their objection. Indeed, it is precisely their conscientious adherence to moral principles which causes them, when asked if their objection is grounded in religious belief, to answer truthfully that it is not. Were they hypocritical enough to lie about the source of their convictions they might qualify, but the very conscientiousness of which legal provisions aim to take cognizance must disclose a fact about their beliefs which renders those provisions inapplicable.

Why is this requirement of theistic foundation imposed? If outright religious bigotry be discounted, two other possible reasons might be given. First (the defender of the theistic qualification might argue), if this were not a condition of conscientious objection, the authorities would lose control of the situation; anyone might claim to be a conscientious objector, and there would be no way to stem the tide of claimants. But this is a very bad argument. Restricting conscientious objection to theists does not greatly narrow the field; in contemporary America the overwhelming majority (*Time* magazine once reported 98 per cent) may reasonably claim some theistic training or belief. If anyone would be qualified to claim the status of conscientious objection after the elimination of that requirement, almost the same universal qualification is in effect now. And even if the possible number of objectors were to rise sharply (which it surely would not), that fact has no bearing whatever upon the issue of the justice of imposing theistic belief as a qualification for such objection. We might as justly require brown eyes instead; that would cut out a greater number and be no less relevant to the real question, which is the genuineness of the conscientious motivation.

The second, and probably the main line of defense for those who support the theistic qualification, is the claim that religious training and belief *is* relevant to conscientiousness. "We are interested in conscientiousness only," they might agree, "but we know that only those who do believe that it is their relation to a Supreme Being which imposes overriding duties can be truly conscientious. The requirement that conscientiousness be based upon religious training or belief is therefore a control on the legitimacy of claims; when that requirement is not met we can be sure that the claim of conscientiousness is not legitimate." As an argument, this one is as bad as the other, but it is even less worthy of respect because it harbors a covert but fundamental religious prejudice unbecoming in civilized men. On the one hand, no one denies that persons with theistic training and beliefs are often not conscientious and that is clearly evidenced by the fact that we do not treat the exhibition of those beliefs as conclusive evidence of conscientiousness. When a theist claims to be a conscientious objector, we proceed to examine him, and his claim, in the effort to determine if he really does believe that warlike conduct is always immoral and really does manifest that belief in his daily life. On the other hand, it does not require much experience in the world to know that one may exhibit the highest level of personal integrity, and the utmost of conscientiousness, and still not believe in the existence of any God. To suppose that the absence of theistic conviction is, *ipso facto*, proof of guile or unreliability is to display the crudest sort of religious bigotry. Again, the legal provision in question should be devised to determine who is a genuinely *conscientious* objector, that is, who honestly and deeply believes (whatever his grounds for that belief) that it would be morally wrongful for him to participate in war.

Unfortunately, that is very far from the present state of affairs. Even the most liberal interpretation of the present statute is restricted, by its wording, to a broadening of the conception of *religious* belief. Every applicant for conscientious objector status must file a selective service form on which he will be asked, specifically, whether his conscientious objection is grounded in religious training and belief. If he replies in full candor that his conscientious beliefs do not have a religious foundation (and probably even if he claims a religious foundation but also honestly states that he does not believe in a Supreme Being), he will disqualify himself for classification as a conscientious objector. Put bluntly, the truthful atheist is punished for his views on religious matters.

The same cruel persecution was remarked by John Stuart Mill, in noting the penalties inflicted by English law, in the mid-nineteenth century, upon persons who did not conform to the mass in their religious beliefs. Even refusal of redress in the courts was then possible for one who did not believe in God. This happens, Mill points out,

in virtue of the legal doctrine, that no person can be allowed to give evidence in a court of Justice, who does not profess belief in a God (any god is sufficient) and in a future state; which is equivalent to declaring such persons to be outlaws, excluded from the protection of tribunals; who may not only be robbed or assaulted with impunity, if no one but themselves, or persons of similar opinions, be present, but anyone else may be robbed or assaulted with impunity, if the proof of the fact depends on their evidence. The assumption on which this is grounded is that the oath is worthless, of a person who does not believe in a future state; a proposition which betokens much ignorance of history in those who assent to it (since it is historically true that a

*large proportion of infidels in all ages have been persons of distinguished integrity and honor);
and would be maintained by no one who has the smallest conception how many of the persons
in greatest repute with the world, both for virtues and for attainments, are well known, at least
to their intimates, to be unbelievers. The rule, besides, is suicidal, and cuts away its own
foundation. Under pretense that atheists must be liars, it admits the testimony of all atheists
who are willing to lie, and rejects only those who brave the obloquy of publicly confessing a
detested creed rather than affirm a falsehood. A rule thus self-convicted of absurdity so far as
regards its professed purpose, can be kept in force only as a badge of hatred, a relic of
persecution; a persecution, too, having the peculiarity, that the qualification for undergoing it,
is the being clearly proved not to deserve it.*[3]

The American conscientious objector of the present day, whose conscientiousness,
although genuine, is not founded upon any religious belief, is in precisely the same
case. He, too, suffers under a persecution "having the peculiarity, that the
qualification for undergoing it, is the being clearly proved not to deserve it."

IV

A second and equally serious failing in the operation of our present rules governing
conscientious objection arises from the requirement that, to qualify as a
conscientious objector, one must be "conscientiously opposed to participation in
war in any form." The consequence of this requirement is that persons who might,
in good conscience, fight for their country under some circumstances, but who
cannot, as a matter of conscience, participate in a *specific* war, are disqualified. Our
present laws do not recognize what is not only possible but frequently
actual—deeply conscientious objection to a particular war. I contend that this is a
grave mistake, for two reasons:

(a) It violates both the spirit of our constitution and the spirit of the device of
conscientious objection itself and is, therefore, *unjust*.

(b) It creates deep moral perplexity and anxiety among many citizens and forces
all citizens to blunt their moral judgments rather than to refine and deepen them. It
is, therefore, a requirement that is profoundly *unwise*.

I shall elaborate upon these two reasons in turn.

(a) Recall that by conscientious objection we mean simply objection that is
based truly and deeply upon moral convictions. In saying that a person is a genuine
conscientious objector, we say nothing about the objective correctness or
incorrectness of his judgments but only that he has made them reflectively and
honestly and is prepared to stand by them. What is "conscience," after all, but our
blanket name for the personal governing principles to which a man is ultimately
committed? We honor those who "obey their conscience," and we call it a moral
(sometimes even religious) duty to do so. We revile those who knowingly do not do
so.

Now what form may such principles of conscience take? They may take the
form of universal prohibition: For example, "Never, under any circumstances, fight
or kill another human being"; or "Any participation in any war is always wrong."
They may also take the form of universal positive demands: For example, "Always
defend your country, whether she be right or wrong"; or "Always obey the Ten

[3] John Stuart Mill, *On Liberty*, Chap. ii.

Commandments no matter who or what may suffer in consequence." Such directives, whether put negatively ("*Never* do . . .") or positively ("*Always* do . . ."), are alike in being absolute and universal, and that is one kind of principle that a man may believe governs him. Whether he is objectively right or wrong in adhering absolutely to these principles, he may do so, being scrupulous and conscientious in guiding his conduct by them. But no sensible person will deny that he whose principles take another form, less sweeping or general in their scope, may also be truly conscientious. Suppose a man accepts the following principle: "Every citizen of a democracy has a duty to defend his country, and to fight for it, but his obligation to kill other human beings at its command is cancelled when the country's cause is unjust, or its warlike conduct inappropriate"; or, "Killing or torturing other human beings may sometimes be justified by the most desperate needs of national self-defense, but such acts are morally wrong when done to preserve national influence or expand national power." These also are principles in which a man may deeply believe, and he may adhere to them unfailingly in governing his conduct. The key point is that, whether right or wrong in adopting these more limited principles, he may adopt them conscientiously and obey them scrupulously. Acting on such principles, he may then conclude that he cannot in good conscience participate in a given war—say, the present war in Vietnam—and he is then as truly and rightly considered a conscientious objector as one who objects because he is opposed to war in any form.

The requirement that the conscientious objector must be opposed to war in *any* form creates a serious *constitutional* injustice. For its consequence is discrimination among persons, regarding their qualification for a certain legal protection, on the basis of the *content* of their moral beliefs. The fundamental objective of conscientious objection provisions is to provide lawful release for those who cannot comply with certain kinds of commands in good conscience. *But conscientiousness cannot depend upon the content of the principle that one is conscientiously applying.* This requirement (of opposition to *all* war) does impose a certain content as a condition of qualification; it therefore distinguishes among citizens purely on the basis of what moral principles they happen to hold. It discriminates baldly and unfairly in favor of those with principles of sweeping generality and against those whose principles are more refined or more limited.

I conclude that, if it is right to excuse a man from combatant status, or from service in the armed forces, on grounds of conscientious objection, that treatment cannot be justly limited to those whose objection is to war in any form but must, in all fairness, be extended to those who object, *conscientiously*, to a particular war as well.

(b) Not only as a matter of justice, but also as a matter of wisdom, we ought to respect, and to recognize in law, the conscientiousness of one who objects to a particular war, or a particular kind of war. The world being as confusing as it is, and human affairs as complex as they are, principles of the form "*Always* do . . ." or "*Never* do . . ." are almost sure to lead to error through oversimplification; while principles of a more limited scope, while also uncertain, have a far better chance of approximating the truth, if there is one. We do well, therefore, to credit the conscientious man with limited principles, rather than to discredit him because his principles are limited.

Such limitation, after all, is the normal product of rational reflection and analysis. We do not find fault with the criminal law because it punishes some forms of violence but excuses other forms of violence resorted to in self-defense. We do not say: "If the law were really moral it would punish *all* violence or none at all." We think sweeping generalizations of that sort naïve, crude, inadequate to deal with the complexity of human activity. We are right in this. We give no special advantages to those who advocate such sweeping legal rules, and indeed we are likely to think such advocates to be slightly unbalanced. Similarly, in matters of national conduct, we do not say to another country—for example, Great Britain—that to be moral, or to be conscientious, it must fight whenever offended, or to forego all resort to war. We honor the British for their battles against the Kaiser, and the Third Reich, but condemn their imperialistic wars under King George III, their naval war of 1812, and their recent military adventures in Suez. So others may look at us, and so we may look at ourselves.

The same reasonableness, and willingness to make essential discriminations, must be employed in appraising the character and conduct of individuals. It is absurd to demand of individuals, before allowing that their acts may be truly conscientious, that the principles they employ be of *universal* scope. It is foolish to insist that the judgments of individuals be sweeping, when the laws, nations, and individuals we most respect are always making careful distinctions in the application of moral principles.

Note that those who refuse to allow conscientious objection to a particular war (but permit it to *all* war) admit the competence of the individual to judge the morality of a *means* (war, killing, etc.) but do not admit his competence to judge the morality of an *end* (dictatorship, democracy, national power, etc.) To put this more exactly, while they may think the conscientious objector gravely mistaken in his judgments, they are prepared to honor the conscientiousness of those judgments when expressed about means, but not when expressed about ends. Therefore, when reflecting about the conduct of his country, whatever one's principles are regarding the means his country may employ, he is obliged (on their view) to apply them without regard to the objectives sought. He is not permitted effectively to ask or to answer, with reference to his nation's acts, "Is this means justified by this end?" He is permitted to say "I *never* kill," and (If he says that truly) he will be excused. But if he says with honest candor, "I would kill for my country under *some* circumstances, but not under *these* circumstances," his plea, because it is qualified, will go unheard. Let him once admit that he will kill, and it must then be presumed that he is not able to judge where or when it is appropriate for him to do so in matters of national concern.

Even if the reasons given for this presumption were good, it would be important to recognize the unhappy consequences of proceeding as we do. By compelling the citizen to accept or reject certain means (that is, war) in the sphere of his own nation's conduct, *without exception,* we punish, in effect, his effort to draw morally essential discriminations. We refuse any citizen the opportunity to weigh ends and means together, as one must if ever he is to make refined and sensitive moral judgments, whether of his own acts or of another's. This refusal invites, sometimes forces, that very disparity of ends and means which is so disastrous in social affairs, and which we so vehemently and rightly condemn in the conduct of other nations. This narrow conception of conscientiousness, which obliges the citizen to approve or disapprove of means without attention to the purposes they are means for, seriously disrupts our moral thinking in the one sphere in which that disruption is most likely to be catastrophic—the acts of nations in matters of war and peace.

I do not claim here that all conscientious objection, or all conscientious objection to a particular war, is objectively right or justifiable; I am not sure how that objective rightness (or wrongness) is to be determined. But I do insist that conscientious objection to a particular war may be *as* right and *as* justifiable as the conscientious objection we now permit. Moreover, since conscientious objection of the more limited sort involves the reflective consideration of means *and* ends, it is more likely, rather than less likely, to be the outcome of an intelligent and reliable moral judgment. Weighing the objectives of national policy as well as the instruments of it may render a man's conduct *more* moral; surely it is not likely to render it *less* so. And in any event, the opportunity to weigh ends as well as means certainly does not keep the objector from being fully and profoundly conscientious.

Why has conscientious objection to a specific war been refused a hearing? I cannot be certain what the actual considerations motivating that refusal have been, but the reasons commonly given for it do not stand up on careful examination.

(1) *To permit conscientious objection to a particular war would be to commit national suicide. War is a matter of life or death for the nation; if individual citizens were permitted to object on grounds of personal convictions, the danger to all would be too great to tolerate.*

This objection derives superficial plausibility from the truth that war is sometimes a matter of national life or death; when at war a nation is in great danger. But the claim that permitting conscientious objection to a given war will significantly increase that danger cannot be substantiated and is almost certainly false. When a nation goes to war, for whatever cause, the vast majority of its citizens rally to its flag. The number who have refused to fight on grounds of conscience has historically been very small; even if the category of conscientious objectors were widened as I propose, there is every reason to believe that the number who would openly hold their nation to be morally wrong would constitute no significant threat to national safety. Even the present war in Vietnam—for which there is more moral repugnance and articulate objection than for any previous war in American history—would bring forth only a small minority who, when called to serve, would refuse on grounds of conscience. This objection grossly underestimates the passion of our citizens (and that of the citizens of most countries) for their national welfare, and their general readiness to respond, particularly in times of crisis, to the requests of their elected leaders.

From a strictly military point of view, moreover, the elimination from the armed services of those who believe that a particular war is wrong would be a measure increasing safety, not risk. If fighting in that war offends against their deepest moral principles, such objectors would make poor soldiers. The number of persons involved is not likely to shake national security one way or the other, but if degree of military risk is the chief consideration, that risk is likely to be lowest if the prosecution of such a war in no way depends upon would-be conscientious objectors.

(2) *To permit conscientious objection to a particular war (even if doing so does not increase risk) is wholly unreasonable because it gives too much authority to the individual. In a law-governed community individual citizens cannot be allowed to*

decide for themselves whether fighting in a given war is or is not in accord with their moral principles.

This objection is profoundly mistaken, but it is commonly voiced, and even more commonly given tacit or indirect support. Why is it so widely believed that it is somehow wrong or improper to recognize in each citizen the right to decide for himself whether his nation's cause (or conduct) is just? In part it is an irrational consequence of blind love for fatherland, and unreasoned deference to those in authority. But where this objection is given some rational support, it usually takes the form of one or more of three principles, often unclearly formulated, each of which is itself mistaken, though possessing a germ of truth.

(a) *Once the majority (or its instrument) has spoken, the nation acts; the individual citizen may not refuse to go along with these decisions and acts.*
There is some truth here. The citizen does have an obligation to abide by the decisions of the body politic, especially in a democracy where he had at least a right to participate in making those decisions. But it is not necessarily the case that this obligation to go along with the lawful decisions of his community overrides *all other* obligations he may have. He *may* have a yet more compelling obligation to refuse to abide by the decision of the majority if, after careful reflection, he concludes that it calls for conduct which to him is morally intolerable.

(b) *The conflict of moral obligation with national loyalty does not arise in this country. Conscientious objection to a particular war is unnecessary in a country which is never wrong, and never acts immorally.*
This supposition, that Americans (or the citizens of one's own nation, whichever it may be) are made of nobler, finer stuff than the rest of humanity, and that somehow our national acts exhibit a purity and integrity that cannot reasonably be questioned, is terribly naïve; because it blinds us to the serious mistakes we do make on occasion and hinders our efforts to correct them, it is also extremely dangerous.

(c) *Our nation may, on rare occasion, act wrongly, perhaps immorally. But it is never within the competence of an individual citizen to determine that error, or to guide his conduct on the basis of such a finding, in opposition to his lawful government.*
If not individuals, who then may detect our moral wrongs—the gods alone? Individual citizens not only may but must pass judgment upon the acts of their government. There is too much likelihood that they will be strongly biased in favor of their own, that they will give every benefit of doubt or interpretation to their leaders, and where a wrong is evident, that they will judge too leniently. But judge they must. Of course no man is competent to decide such questions for another, or for all, and here lies the apparent plausibility of this third principle. When the community must act, and must judge its own acts, no single citizen may presume to act or judge for it. But if, in spite of all the considerations of loyalty and private interest which must dispose him to side with his government, the individual citizen is constrained to conclude that it is behaving with gross immorality, it is surely his duty to act in accord with that judgment, recognizing that he speaks only for himself, and that he may be in error.

The danger, in short, lies not in giving too much authority to the individual but in giving him too little. In matters of deep moral principle nobody can relieve the individual of his responsibility to exercise his moral judgment; all that the state can do is make it harder or easier for him to act in accord with that judgment. Present provisions for conscientious objectors are commendable insofar as they do ease that task for some; it remains to recognize in law the truly conscientious objection of others.

(3) *To permit conscientious objection to a particular war (even if it were clearly just to do so) is simply not practical. To give each citizen the privilege of opting out when the situation becomes dangerous or critical is to invite chaos.*

The plausibility of this objection depends wholly upon the supposition that being a conscientious objector to a particular war is merely a matter of "opting out." This is not so. Whoever claims to be a conscientious objector must make specific application for that status, must undergo intense, thorough examination by the classifying agency. He must show convincingly, through his own testimony and that of his teachers or associates, that the moral scruples he professes are in fact part of his conscientiously held position. The status of conscientious objector is very far indeed from being a matter of simple option; it will be allowed only after a serious claim has been carefully documented and its truth solidly established.

Making such determinations, by Selective Service boards or equivalent agencies, will involve the expenditure of some time and energy. There may be some additional administrative complexities, and some small additional expense. But the trouble and expense are insignificant when contrasted with the moral good this policy would accomplish. Even were that resulting expense and inconvenience great (which is very unlikely) considerations of justice would oblige us to undertake the effort to identify conscientious objectors without discriminating as to the sweep or content of their moral views.

(4) *If conscientious objection to a particular war were permissible, the difficulty of determining the legitimacy of any particular application for that status would be so great as to encourage fakery. In consequence, many would simply lie their way out of military service.*

These predictions are very probably false, and they are based upon an assumption that is certainly false. The assumption is that, because moral matters are at issue, it is practically impossible to determine the legitimacy of a claim of conscientious objection. In reality, however, although the claims made are *about* moral views of which the truth is difficult to determine, the claims themselves are plainly factual, and can be thoroughly scrutinized and carefully tested. What has to be decided by the classifying agency is not the correctness of the moral convictions of the applicant but the objective truth or falsity of his claim that those are his convictions, and that the case at hand is a legitimate and necessary application of them. Even the objective facts about the war (insofar as these can be determined) are not the basic issue but rather the objector's conscientiously determined understanding of those facts.

On such matters it is practically impossible to lie so consistently and convincingly as to deceive an experienced board of examiners. Under present regulations, the danger of fakery is practically nil; were conscientiousness to be understood in the larger and more just way that I propose, the number of conscientious objectors might increase somewhat, but the danger of fakery need not increase at all. The social pressure inevitably applied against every conscientious objector would effectively keep the devious and the cowardly from even seeking that avenue of escape from military service.

Finally, even if it were true that with an enlarged conception of conscientious objection a few were to escape military service by deception who otherwise would not be able to do so, that is a price that can be paid by a society whose first concern is the humanity and justice of its laws. In the criminal courts we apply rules of evidence and procedure which may result in some who are guilty being acquitted, and we do so recognizing this consequence because such rules are essential for the protection of the innocent. To achieve that protection it is necessary that we develop considerable self-restraint in the trial of all persons accused of crime, and it is altogether right and a tribute to our society that we do this. In the context of military conscription, although the issue is not guilt or punishment, the same circumspection is called for. If we are obliged to raise an army by conscripting young citizens, we ought to apply rules and procedures which (although conceivably usable by very artful liars for selfish advantage) are designed to insure the protection and equal treatment of *all* those whose objections are genuinely conscientious.

The objections to the practicality and desirability of legislation permitting conscientious objection to a particular war are all very weak, and the reasons for its enactment are compelling. There is yet another consideration, however, beyond those already discussed, which weighs heavily in support of this proposed policy. Formally adopted, it would serve as a safety device, not simply for individuals but for the nation as a whole. War is so grave a matter, so thoroughly awful, that every nation needs, and ought to cultivate, the conscientious reflection of its individual citizens upon national conduct having such frightful consequences. Legislation which makes it possible for citizens, in their private capacities, to refuse participation in what honestly appears to them to be recklessness or irresponsibility on the part of their government could become a very wholesome restraint upon the impetuosity of some political leaders. Where there is the possibility that such conscientious objection may be widespread, it may even help to prevent grave international crimes by honorably motivated but narrow-minded or irrational leaders.

That is the really crushing answer to those who say: "If we permit conscientious objection to a particular war, so many may refuse to fight as to endanger the nation." The danger is nil if the nation's cause is just; its citizens will not fail it in time of crisis. But if large masses of citizens cannot conscientiously pursue the nation's course, at least through killing or force of arms, that may be the best of reasons for not engaging in that war, even at the cost of some temporary national loss of face.

Leo Tolstoy wrote, in *The Kingdom of God Is Within You* (1893):

In early Christian times a soldier, Theodore, told the authorities that being a Christian he could not bear arms, and when he was executed for this the responsible authorities quite sincerely regarded him as a madman and far from trying to conceal such an occurrence, exposed him to public scorn at the execution. But now when cases of refusals of military service occur more and more frequently, these cases are no longer regarded by the authorities as madness, but as a very dangerous awakening from madness, and the governments, far from holding such cases up to public scorn, carefully conceal them, knowing that the salvation of men from humiliation, enslavement and ignorance, will come about not by revolutions, trade-unions, peace-congresses, and books, but in the simplest way—by each man who is called upon to share in the infliction of violence on his fellow men and on himself, asking in perplexity: "But why should I do this?"

A national policy of permitting conscientious objection to military conscription in a given war would be not only eminently just and entirely practical but exceedingly wise. A nation allowing itself to be restrained by such considerations, tempered in its acts by the conscientious concerns of its individual citizens, acquires thereby a deeper and more long-lasting power than any military force can provide.

V. POSTSCRIPT

In the several years since the first four sections of this essay were written, conscientious objection has become a focus of attention in the United States as never before, chiefly because of the prolonged American military involvement in a distant and unpopular war. Legislative provisions for conscientious objectors have remained unchanged; but in the courts controversy over the injustices discussed above has been intense, and important developments have taken place. Juridical disputes concerning the two central issues exhibit forcefully the interweaving of the legal and the moral, of governmental policy and philosophical argument.

The first issue concerns the statutory requirement that conscientious objection to participation in war—to be officially recognized—must be "by reason of religious training and belief." This demand seems clearly to discriminate unjustly, as well as unconstitutionally, among truly conscientious persons, permitting special considera- tion for those with religious training and belief, while denying that consideration for those whose conscientious principles have non-religious foundations. Sensitive to this injustice, the Supreme Court of the United States has much mitigated it, through a series of recent decisions.

In 1965, in the case of *U.S.* v. *Seeger* [380 U.S. 163] the test for determining whether the applicant's beliefs were "religious" (within the meaning of Section 6 (j) of the Military Selective Service Act of 1967) had been formulated so as to include beliefs not normally called religious. Said the Court then: "A sincere and meaningful belief which occupies in the life of the possessor a place parallel to that filled by the God of those admittedly qualifying for the exemption comes within the statutory definition."

The scope of the term "religious" was thus greatly extended, although technically the demand for "religious training and belief" remained intact. A bolder step was taken in 1970, however, which virtually nullified the requirement of religious foundation for conscientious objection. In the case of *Welsh* v. *U.S.* [398 U.S. 333] the Supreme Court held that "very few registrants are fully aware of the broad scope of the word 'religious' as used in Sec. 6 (j)" of the statute, and that therefore even a registrant's statement that his beliefs are nonreligious (Welsh had crossed out the word "religious" in his application, and later characterized his beliefs as having been formed "by reading in the fields of history and sociology") is not sufficient to disqualify him. It being agreed that Welsh held his beliefs with the strength of more traditional religious convictions, the Court held him clearly entitled to a conscientious objection exemption. Properly understood, the statute exempts from military service (said the Court) "all those whose consciences, spurred by deeply held moral, ethical, or religious beliefs, would give them no rest or peace if they allowed themselves to become a part of an instrument of war."

Does this decision fly in the face of the specific exclusion, in the statute, of "essentially political, sociological, or philosophical views, or a merely personal moral code"? Definitely not, said the Court; for although the conscientious scruples of both Seeger and Welsh undeniably had a political dimension, views having that dimension cannot, on that ground alone, be held excluded from those conscientious by reason of religious training and belief. Once the Selective Service System has determined, under the standards set out in the Welsh and Seeger cases, that the registrant is a "religious" conscientious objector, it follows that his views *cannot* be "essentially political, etc."

This is the present state of the law, and the standards of the Welsh decision have been applied in a series of recent cases.[4] Typical of these is a recent case [*U.S.* v. *Coffey,* 9th Cir., 3 SSLR 3182, 1970] in which the Federal Court concluded:

It is of course obvious from the Form 150 that Coffey's beliefs were religious in no ordinary sense of the word. But the test of religion for purposes of Sec. 6(j) is no ordinary test. It is now settled that to entitle him to conscientious objection status, a registrant's beliefs "need not be confined in either source or content to traditional or parochial concepts of religion." It is sufficient that "an individual deeply and sincerely holds beliefs which are purely ethical or moral in source and content but which nevertheless impose upon him a duty of conscience to refrain from participation in any war at any time." [Internal references are to Welsh v. U.S.]

The second large issue concerns the statutory requirement that the registrant's conscientious principles preclude his participation *in any war at any time*. May he qualify as a conscientious objector although morally precluded from participation only in some wars, or a particular war? The latter position (defended as an ideal in Section IV above) has been rejected by the Supreme Court in the cases of *Gillette* v. *U.S.* and *Negre* v. *Larsen et al.* [401 U.S. 437, 1971].

The stage for these decisions had been set by the case of *U.S.* v. *Sisson* [294 F. Supp. 511, 1969; 399 U.S. 267, 1970] in which a Federal District Court had clearly supported the position of one selective conscientious objector. The First Amendment's protection of the free exercise of religion, and the Fifth Amendment's protection of due process, that lower court decided, "prohibit the application of the 1967 Draft Act to Sisson to require him to render combat service in Vietnam" because the magnitude of Sisson's interest, as a "sincerely conscientious man" in not killing in the Vietnam conflict outweighs the country's present need for him to be so employed.[5] The Supreme Court dismissed the Government's direct appeal of this decision for technical reasons, but on the same day agreed to hear the Gillette and Negre cases, specifically in order to reach the larger issue here at stake. Selective pacifism thus won a temporary foothold.

That foothold was lost when the Supreme Court held, in the Gillette and Negre cases, that the statutory requirement that conscientious objection, to qualify for exemption, must be to *all* wars, *is* within the constitutional power of Congress to impose. The effort to legitimize the status of the conscientious objector to a particular war, under the existing statute, failed badly.

[4] *Christiansen* v. *Laird,* D. Minn., 3 SSLR (Selective Service Law Reporter) 3831, 1971; *U.S.* v. *Calderaro,* D. Ore., 3 SSLR 3827, 1971; *U.S.* v. *Velen,* 7th Cir., 3 SSLR 3757, 1971.

[5] Also embedded in that decision was the judgment that Sec. 6 (j) of the statute "unconstitutionally discriminates against atheists, agnostics, and men, like Sisson, who, whether they be religious or not, are motivated in their objection to the draft by profound moral beliefs which constitute the central convictions of their beings"—in that this discrimination violates the First Amendment's prohibition of the establishment of religion. But this passage bore chiefly on the matter of religious foundations, not that of selective pacifism.

This important decision, written by Justice Marshall for an 8-1 majority of the Court, is of both philosophical and legal interest. The argument in its defense is in three parts, the first dealing with the interpretation of the statute, the second and third dealing with alleged violations of the Constitution entailed by Section 6 (j) of that statute. Regarding interpretation, the Court was surely correct in holding that the intention of the statute, clear both from its wording and from an examination of its legislative history, is to grant exemption only to those conscientious objectors to participation in all wars. The focal language of Section 6 (j) is "conscientiously opposed to participation in war in any form." There may be alternative readings of this wording; but on a straightforward meaning: "that conscientious scruples relating to war and military service must amount to conscientious opposition to participation personally in any war and all wars."

The remaining questions with which the Court dealt concerned the petitioners' arguments that the statute, construed to cover only objection to *all* wars, violates these clauses of the First Amendment which provide that "Congress shall make no law respecting an establishment of religion, or prohibiting the free exercise thereof. . . ." Petitioners argued that their religious convictions oblige them to distinguish between just and unjust wars, and forbid only their participation in the latter. They cannot morally object to all wars, and must morally object to some, they contend, if they are to remain obedient to the overriding imperatives of their conscientious religious principles.

But, replied the Court, the constitutional prohibition of the "establishment of religion" is intended to safeguard against any governmental *favoritism* in support of religion or particular religions. It prohibits statutory provisions designed to advantage any persons by reason of their religious affiliations. It demands, in effect, that laws be neutral with respect to religious affiliation—and against that neutrality the statute in question does not offend. It does not do so, they argued, because the crucial exempting clauses focus on individual conscientious belief—objection to all wars—and not adherence to any sect or extraneous theological viewpoint. The general purposes of provisions for conscientious objection have "nothing to do with a design to foster or favor any sect, religion, or cluster of religions." Not only in general are the purposes underlying conscientious objection neutral and secular, but specifically (they held) the reasons for limiting the exemption to objectors to all wars are neutral and valid. Chief among those reasons, as reviewed in the Court's opinion, are these: the difficulty of distinguishing between conscientious moral dissent to a particular war and ordinary political dissent; the danger that the more articulate and the better educated might be unduly favored by the need to draw this distinction; the difficulty of weeding out spurious claims and hence of applying the exemption fairly; and the need to protect the integrity of democratic decision-making against claims to individual non-compliance. However weighty these considerations are thought to be, their clear secularity and theological impartiality cannot be said (the Court concluded) to reflect a religious preference. The Court did not conclude that the justifications offered for the present form of the exemption are compelling, or that Congress would have acted irrationally or unreasonably if it had decided to exempt those who object to particular wars. Its conclusion was simply that there *are* arguments in support of the line Congress has drawn which are neutral with respect to religion, and that having such reasons for its statute, this act of Congress does not violate the establishment of religion clause. Considerations of feasibility and fairness which (however wise) lie behind the insistence that exempting conscientious objection be to war in any form are, the

Court said, "without question properly congnizable by Congress. In light of these valid concerns, we conclude that it is supportable for Congress to have decided that the objector to all war—to all killing in war—has a claim that is distinct enough and intense enough to justify special status, while the objector to a particular war does not."

Finally, the Court rejected the claim that that distinction violates the clause safeguarding the free exercise of religion. Of course religious convictions may at times call for actions which collide with the laws. No one supposes that under the rubric "free exercise of religion" any duty imposed by law may be avoided by a conscientious believer who is convinced that that duty offends against his religion. The question, then, is whether there are governmental interests of a kind and weight sufficient to justify the unfortunate impact of the conscription laws upon those who conscientiously object to particular wars. The Court held that there are. The issue of free exercise is distinct from that of the establishment of religion, but the fact that secular, neutral considerations underlie Congressional action is relevant in both cases similarly. Although the conscription laws in question treat particular and general conscientious objectors differently, they "are not designed to interfere with any religious ritual or practice, and do not work a penalty against any theological position." The burdens born by the objector to particular wars, the Court therefore concluded, are "strictly justified" by substantial government interests, and broadly justified by the need to procure military manpower, pursuant to the constitutional power of Congress to raise and support armies.

Selective conscientious objection has been flatly rejected, for the present, by the highest court in the land; but the grounds of that rejection ought to be kept in mind. The statute is clear in denying conscientious objector status to those who object only to some wars and not to all; the Court held that such a statute does not violate the establishment of religion and free exercise clauses of the First Amendment. The further claim, that that distinction works an invidious discrimination in violation of the principle of *equal protection of the laws* (of the Fifth Amendment) was rejected by the Court in a footnote, on the ground that if there are neutral, secular reasons justifying the line Congress has drawn, and those reasons suffice to show that the establishment clause has not been violated, "it follows as a more general matter that the line is neither arbitrary nor invidious." But *does* that follow? The fact that the reasons marshalled in support of the distinction are neutral with respect to the several religious sects does not of itself show that the reasons are reasons good enough to justify a distinction between kinds of conscientious objectors, once conscientious objection in general is admitted as a proper ground for exemption. What is shown by the Gillette and Negre cases is that the defense of selective conscientious objection, through recourse to the religious clauses of the First Amendment, is quite unlikely to succeed. Other constitutional resources are not yet fully exhausted.

More fundamentally, these judicial analyses—in focussing not upon the wisdom of the distinctions Congress has drawn, but upon their apparent reasonableness, and the right of Congress to draw them—show that it is probably in the legislature, not the courts, where the battle for selective conscientious objection must ultimately be fought. If, in the end, one were compelled to admit that a conscientious objector clause in its present universal form is not strictly unconstitutional, he may yet insist (as I have, in Section IV, above) that it is painfully unfair, and certainly unwise. Alternative formulations of such clauses are both feasible and desirable; that is what the people's representatives, in the halls of the legislature, must be brought to see.

Philosophical Theories of Law

Roscoe Pound

Roscoe Pound (1870-1964) taught law at Harvard University. He is the author of many books, including *An Introduction to the Philosophy of Law.*

Making or finding law, call it which you will, presupposes a mental picture of what one is doing and of why he is doing it. Hence the nature of law has been the chief battleground of jurisprudence since the Greek philosophers began to argue as to the basis of the law's authority. But the end of law has been debated more in politics than in jurisprudence. In the stage of equity and natural law the prevailing theory of the nature of law seemed to answer the question as to its end. In the maturity of law the law was thought of as something self-sufficient, to be judged by an ideal form of itself, and as something which could not be made, or, if it could be made, was to be made sparingly. The idea of natural rights seemed to explain incidentally what law was for and to show that there ought to be as little of it as possible, since it was a restraint upon liberty and even the least of such restraint demanded affirmative justification. Thus apart from mere systematic and formal improvement the theory of lawmaking in the maturity of law was negative. It told us chiefly how we should not legislate and upon what subjects we should refrain from lawmaking. Having no positive theory of creative lawmaking, the last century was little conscious of requiring or holding a theory as to the end of law. But in fact it held such a theory and held it strongly.

As ideas of what law is for are so largely implicit in ideas of what law is, a brief survey of ideas of the nature of law from this standpoint will be useful. No less than twelve conceptions of what law is may be distinguished.

First, we may put the idea of a divinely ordained rule or set of rules for human action, as for example, the Mosaic law, or Hammurabi's code, handed him ready made by the sun god, or Manu, dictated to the sages by Manu's son Bhrigu in Manu's presence and by his direction.

Second, there is an idea of law as a tradition of the old customs which have proved acceptable to the gods and hence point the way in which man may walk with safety. For primitive man, surrounded by what seem vengeful and capricious powers of nature, is in continual fear of giving offense to these powers and thus bringing down their wrath upon himself and his fellows. The general security requires that men do only those things and do them only in the way which long custom has shown at least not displeasing to the gods. Law is the traditional or recorded body of precepts in which that custom is preserved and expressed. Whenever we find a body of primitive law possessed as a class tradition by a political oligarchy it is likely to be thought of in this way, just as a body of like tradition in the custody of a priesthood is certain to be thought of as divinely revealed.

Source: An Introduction to the Philosophy of Law (New Haven, Conn.: Yale University Press, 1954). Copyright © 1922, 1954 by Yale University Press. Reprinted by permission of the publisher.

A third and closely related idea conceives the law as the recorded wisdom of the wise men of old who had learned the safe course or the divinely approved course for human conduct. When a traditional custom of decision and custom of action has been reduced to writing in a primitive code it is likely to be thought of in this way, and Demosthenes in the fourth century B.C. could describe the law of Athens in these terms.

Fourth, law may be conceived as a philosophically discovered system of principles which express the nature of things, to which, therefore, man ought to conform his conduct. Such was the idea of the Roman jurisconsult, grafted, it is true, on the second and third ideas and on a political theory of law as the command of the Roman people, but reconciled with them by conceiving of tradition and recorded wisdom and command of the people as mere declarations or reflections of the philosophically ascertained principles, to be measured and shaped and interpreted and eked out thereby. In the hands of philosophers the foregoing conception often takes another form so that, fifth, law is looked upon as a body of ascertainments and declarations of an eternal and immutable moral code.

Sixth, there is an idea of law as a body of agreements of men in politically organized society as to their relations with each other. This is a democratic version of the identification of law with rules of law and hence with the enactments and decrees of the city-state which is discussed in the Platonic *Minos*. Not unnaturally Demosthenes suggests it to an Athenian jury. Very likely in such a theory a philosophical idea would support the political idea and the inherent moral obligation of a promise would be invoked to show why men should keep the agreements made in their popular assemblies.

Seventh, law has been thought of as a reflection of the divine reason governing the universe; a reflection of that part which determines the "ought" addressed by that reason to human beings as moral entities, in distinction from the "must" which it addresses to the rest of creation. Such was the conception of Thomas Aquinas, which had great currency down to the seventeenth century and has had much influence ever since.

Eighth, law has been conceived as a body of commands of the sovereign authority in a politically organized society as to how men should conduct themselves therein, resting ultimately on whatever basis was held to be behind the authority of that sovereign. So thought the Roman jurists of the Republic and of the classical period with respect to positive law. And as the emperor had the sovereignty of the Roman people devolved upon him, the *Institutes* of Justinian could lay down that the will of the emperor had the force of a law. Such a mode of thought was congenial to the lawyers who were active in support of royal authority in the centralizing French monarchy of the sixteenth and seventeenth centuries and through them passed into public law. It seemed to fit the circumstances of parliamentary supremacy in England after 1688 and became the orthodox English juristic theory. Also it could be made to fit a political theory of popular sovereignty in which the people were thought of as succeeding to the sovereignty of parliament at the American Revolution or of the French king at the French Revolution.

A ninth idea of law takes it to be a system of precepts discovered by human experience whereby the individual human will may realize the most complete freedom possible consistently with the like freedom of will of others. This idea, held in one form or another by the historical school, divided the allegiance of jurists with the theory of law as command of the sovereign during almost the whole of the past century. It assumed that the human experience by which legal principles were discovered was determined in some inevitable way. It was not a matter of conscious human endeavor. The process was determined by the unfolding of an idea of right and justice or an idea of liberty which was realizing itself in human administration of justice, or by the operation of biological or psychological laws or of race characters, whose necessary result was the system of law of the time and people in question.

Again, tenth, men have thought of law as a system of principles, discovered philosophically and developed in detail by juristic writing and judicial decision, whereby the external life of man is measured by reason, or in another phase, whereby the will of the individual in action is harmonized with those of his fellow men. This mode of thought appeared in the nineteenth century after the natural-law theory in the form in which it had prevailed for two centuries had been abandoned and philosophy was called upon to provide a critique for systematic arrangement and development of details.

Eleventh, law has been thought of as a body or system of rules imposed on men in society by the dominant class for the time being in furtherance, conscious or unconscious, of its own interest. This economic interpretation of law takes many forms. In an idealistic form it thinks of the inevitable unfolding of an economic idea. In a mechanical sociological form it thinks of class struggle or a struggle for existence in terms of economics, and of law as the result of the operation of forces or laws involved in or determining such struggles. In a positivist-analytical form it thinks of law as the command of the sovereign, but of that command as determined in its economic content by the will of the dominant social class, determined in turn by its own interest. All of these forms belong to transition from the stability of the maturity of law to a new period of growth. When the idea of the self-sufficiency of law gives way and men seek to relate jurisprudence to the other social sciences, the relation to economics challenges attention at once. Moreover in a time of copious legislation the enacted rule is easily taken as the type of legal precept and an attempt to frame a theory of legislative lawmaking is taken to give an account of all law.

Finally, twelfth, there is an idea of law as made up of the dictates of economic or social laws with respect to the conduct of men in society, discovered by observation, expressed in precepts worked out through human experience of what would work and what not in the administration of justice. This type of theory likewise belongs to the end of the nineteenth century, when men had begun to look for physical or biological bases, discoverable by observation, in place of metaphysical bases, discoverable by philosophical reflection. Another form finds some ultimate social fact by observation and develops the logical implications of that fact much after the manner of the metaphysical jurist. This again results from the tendency in recent years to unify the social sciences and consequent attention to sociological theories.

Digression is worth while in order to note that each of the foregoing theories of law was in the first instance an attempt at a rational explanation of the law of the time and place or of some striking element therein. Thus, when the law has been growing through juristic activity, a philosophical theory of law, as declaratory of philosophically ascertainable principles, has obtained. When and where the growing point of law has been in legislation, a political theory of law as the command of the sovereign has prevailed. When the law has been assimilating the results of a prior period of growth, a historical theory of law as something found by experience, or a metaphysical theory of law as an idea of right or of liberty realizing in social and legal development, has tended to be dominant. For jurists and philosophers do not make these theories as simple matters of logic by inexorable development of philosophical fundamentals. Having something to explain or to expound, they endeavor to understand it and to state it rationally and in so doing work out a theory of what it is. The theory necessarily reflects the institution which it was devised to rationalize, even though stated universally. It is an attempt to state the law or the legal institution of the time and place in universal terms. Its real utility is likely to be in its enabling us to understand that body of law or that institution and to perceive what the men of the time were seeking to do with them or to make of them. Accordingly analysis of these theories is one way of getting at the ends for which men have been striving through the legal order.

What common elements may we find in the foregoing twelve pictures of what law is? For one thing, each shows us a picture of some ultimate basis, beyond reach of the individual human will, that stands fast in the whirl of change of which life is made up. This steadfast ultimate basis may be thought of as the divine pleasure or will or reason, revealed immediately or mediately through a divinely ordained immutable moral code. It may be put in the form of some ultimate metaphysical datum which is so given us that we may rest in it forever. It may be portrayed as certain ultimate laws which inexorably determine the phenomena of human conduct. Or it may be described in terms of some authoritative will for the time and place, to which the wills of others are subjected, that will deriving its authority ultimately and absolutely in some one of the preceding forms, so that what it does is by and large in no wise a matter of chance. This fixed and stable starting point is usually the feature upon which the chief emphasis is placed. Next we shall find in all theories of the nature of law a picture of a determinate and mechanically absolute mode of proceeding from the fixed and absolute starting point. The details may come from this starting point through divine revelation or a settled authoritative tradition or record, or an inevitable and infallible philosophical or logical method, or an authoritative political machinery, or a scientific system of observation, or historically verifiable ideas which are logically demonstrable to be implications of the fundamental metaphysically given datum. Third, we shall see in these theories a picture of a system of ordering human conduct and adjusting human relations resting upon the ultimate basis and derived therefrom by the absolute process. In other words, they all picture, not merely an ordering of human conduct and adjustment of human relations, which we have actually given, but something more which we should like to have, namely, a doing of these things in a fixed, absolutely predetermined way, excluding all merely individual feelings or desires of those by whom the ordering and adjustment are carried out. Thus in these subconscious picturings of the end of law it seems to be conceived as existing to satisfy a paramount social want of general security. Certainly the nineteenth-century jurist had this conception. But is this because the function of law is limited to satisfaction of that one want, or is it because that want has been most conspicuous among those which men have sought to satisfy through law, and because the ordering of human conduct by the force of politically organized society has been adapted chiefly to satisfying that one want in the social order of the past?

Today a newer and broader idea of security is appearing in a time when the world seems no longer to afford boundless opportunities, which men only need freedom to realize, in order to be assured of their reasonable expectations. So long as there are opportunities everywhere for freely exerting one's will in pursuit of what he takes to be the goods of existence, security is taken to mean a regime of ordered competition of free wills in which acquisitive competitive self-assertion is made to operate with the least friction and waste. But when and where such an ordered struggle for existence does not leave opportunities at hand for everyone, and where especially the conquest of physical nature has enormously increased the area of human wants and expectations without corresponding increase in the means of satisfying them, equality no longer means equality of opportunity. Security no longer means simply that men are to be secure in freely taking advantage of opportunities abounding around them. Men begin to assert claims to an equality of satisfaction of expectations which liberty in itself does not afford them. Quest of an ideal relation among men leads to thinking in terms of an achieved ideal relation rather than of means of achieving it. Instead of thinking of men as ideally free to achieve it, we begin to think of them as ideally already in that relation. Hence security is to be security from what may stand between them and that relation, and keeps many far from finding themselves in it. The ideal of a world in which all men are to find themselves secure in that sense may be called the humanitarian ideal. Such an ideal is increasingly affecting the law throughout the world.

If we turn to ideas which have obtained in conscious thinking about the end of law, we may recognize three which have held the ground successively in legal history and a fourth which is beginning to assert itself. The first and simplest idea is that law exists in order to keep the peace in a given society; to keep the peace at all events and at any price. This is the conception of what may be called the stage of primitive law. It puts satisfaction of the social want of general security, stated in its lowest terms, as the purpose of the legal order. So far as the law goes, other individual or social wants are ignored or are sacrificed to this one. Accordingly the law is made up of tariffs of exact compositions for every detailed injury instead of principles of exact reparation, of devices to induce or coerce submission of controversies to adjudication instead of sanctions, of regulation of self-help and self-redress instead of a general prohibition thereof, and of mechanical modes of trial which at any rate do not admit of argument instead of rational modes of trial involving debate and hence dispute and so tending to defeat the purpose of the legal order. In a society organized on the basis of kinship, in which the greater number of social wants were taken care of by the kin-organizations, there are two sources of friction: the clash of kin-interests, leading to controversies of one kindred with another, and the kinless man, for whom no kin-organization is responsible, who also has no kin-organization to stand behind him in asserting his claims. Peace between kindreds and peace between clansmen and the growing mass of nongentile population is the unsatisfied social want to which politically organized society must address itself. The system of organized kindreds gradually breaks down. Groups of kinsmen cease to be the fundamental social units. Kin-organization is replaced by political organization as the primary agency of social control. The legal unit comes to be the free citizen or the free man. In this transition regulation of self-redress and prevention of private war among those who have no strong clan-organizations to control them or respond for them are demanded by the general security. The means of satisfying these social wants are found in a legal order conceived solely in terms of keeping the peace.

Greek philosophers came to conceive of the general security in broader terms and to think of the end of the legal order as preservation of the social *status quo*.

They came to think of maintaining the general security mediately through the security of social institutions. They thought of law as a device to keep each man in his appointed groove in society and thus prevent friction with his fellows. The virtue on which they insisted was *sophrosyne*, knowing the limits which nature fixes for human conduct and keeping within them. The vice which they denounced was *hybris*, willful bound-breaking—willful transgression of the socially appointed bounds. This mode of thinking follows the substitution of the city-state political organization of society for the kin-organization. The organized kindreds were still powerful. An aristocracy of the kin-organized and kin-conscious, on the one hand, and a mass of those who had lost or severed their ties of kinship or had come from without, on the other hand, were in continual struggle for social and political mastery. Also the politically ambitious individual and the masterful aristocrat were continually threatening the none-too-stable political organization through which the general security got a precarious protection. The chief social want, which no other social institution could satisfy, was the security of social institutions generally. In the form of maintenance of the social *status quo* this became the Greek and thence the Roman and medieval conception of the end of law.

Transition from the idea of law as a device to keep the peace to the idea of law as a device to maintain the social *status quo* may be seen in the proposition of Heraclitus, that men should fight for their laws as for the walls of their city. In Plato the idea of maintaining the social order through the law is fully developed. The actual social order was by no means what it should be. Men were to be reclassified and everyone assigned to the class for which he was best fitted. But when the classification and the assignment had been made the law was to keep him there. It was not a device to set him free that he might find his own level by free competition with his fellows and free experiment with his natural powers. It was a device to prevent such disturbances of the social order by holding each individual to his appointed place. As Plato puts it, the shoemaker is to be only a shoemaker and not a pilot also; the farmer is to be only a farmer and not a judge as well; the soldier is to be only a soldier and not a man of business besides; and if a universal genius who through wisdom can be everything and do everything comes to the ideal city-state, he is to be required to move on. Aristotle puts the same idea in another way, asserting that justice is a condition in which each keeps within his appointed sphere; that we first take account of relations of inequality, treating individuals according to their worth, and then secondarily of relations of equality in the classes into which their worth requires them to be assigned. When St. Paul exhorted wives to obey their husbands, and servants to obey their masters, and thus everyone to exert himself to do his duty in the class where the social order had put him, he expressed this Greek conception of the end of law.

Roman lawyers made the Greek philosophical conception into a juristic theory. For the famous three precepts to which the law is reduced in Justinian's *Institutes* come to this: Everyone is to live honorably; he is to "preserve moral worth in his own person" by conforming to the conventions of the social order. Everyone is to respect the personality of others; he is not to interfere with those interests and powers of action, conceded to others by the social order, which make up their legal personality. Everyone is to render to everyone else his own; he is to respect the acquired rights of others. The social system has defined certain things as belonging to each individual. Justice is defined in the *Institutes* as the set and constant purpose of giving him these things. It consists in rendering them to him and in not interfering with his having and using them within the defined limits. This is a legal development of the Greek idea of harmoniously maintaining the social *status quo*. The later eastern empire carried it to the extreme. Stability was to be secured by rigidly keeping everyone to his trade or calling and his descendents were to follow him therein. Thus the harmony of society and the social order would not be disturbed by individual ambition.

In the Middle Ages the primitive idea of law as designed only to keep the peace came back with Germanic law. But the study of Roman law presently taught the Roman version of the Greek conception, and the legal order was thought of once more as an orderly maintenance of the social *status quo*. This conception answered to the needs of medieval society, in which men had found relief from anarchy and violence in relations of service and protection and a social organization which classified men in terms of such relations and required them to be held to their functions as so determined. Where the Greeks thought of a stationary society corrected from time to time with reference to its nature or ideal, the Middle Ages thought of a stationary society resting upon authority and determined by custom or tradition. To each, law was a system of precepts existing to maintain this stationary society as it was.

In the feudal social order reciprocal duties involved in relations established by tradition and taken to rest on authority were the significant legal institutions. With the gradual disintegration of this order and the growing importance of the individual in a society engaged in discovery, colonization, and trade, to secure the claims of individuals to assert themselves freely in the new fields of human activity which were opening on every side became a more pressing social want than to maintain the social institutions by which the system of reciprocal duties was enforced and the relations involving those duties were preserved. Men did not so much desire that others perform for them the duties owing in some relation as that others keep hands off while they achieved what they might for themselves in a world that continually afforded new opportunities to the active and the daring. The demand was no longer that men be kept in their appointed grooves. Friction and waste were apprehended, not from men getting out of these grooves, but from attempts to hold them there by means devised to meet the needs of a different social order whereby they were made to chafe under arbitrary restraint and their powers were not utilized in the discovery and exploitation of the resources of nature, to which human powers were to be devoted in the succeeding centuries. Accordingly the end of law comes to be conceived as a making possible of the maximum of individual free self-assertion.

Transition to the newer way of thinking may be seen in the Spanish jurist-theologians of the sixteenth century. Their juristic theory was one of natural limits of activity in the relations of individuals with each other, that is, of limits to human action which expressed the rational ideal of man as a moral creature and were imposed upon men by reason. This theory differs significantly from the idea of antiquity, although it goes by the old name. The Greeks thought of a system of limiting men's activities in order that each might be kept in the place for which he was best fitted by nature—the place in which he might realize an ideal form of his capacities—and thus to preserve the social order as it stands or as it shall stand after a rearrangement. The sixteenth-century jurists of the Counter-Reformation held that men's activities were naturally limited, and hence that positive law might and should limit them in the interest of other men's activities, because all men have freedom of will and ability to direct themselves to conscious ends. Where Aristotle thought of inequalities arising from the different worth of individual men and their different capacities for the things which the social order called for, these jurists thought of a natural (i.e., ideal) equality, involved in the like freedom of will and the like power of conscious employment of one's faculties inherent in all men. Hence law did not exist to maintain the social *status quo* with all its arbitrary restraints on the will and on employment of individual powers; it existed rather to maintain the natural equality which often was threatened or impaired by the traditional restrictions on individual activity. Since this natural equality was conceived positively as an ideal equality in opportunity to do things, it could easily pass into a conception of free individual self-assertion as the thing sought, and of the legal order as existing to make possible the maximum thereof in a world abounding in undiscovered resources, undeveloped lands, and unharnessed natural forces. The latter idea took form in the seventeenth century and prevailed for two centuries thereafter, culminating in the juristic thought of the last century.

Law as a securing of natural equality became law as a securing of natural rights. The nature of man was expressed by certain qualities possessed by him as a moral, rational creature. The limitations on human activity, of which the Spanish jurist-theologians had written, got their warrant from the inherent moral qualities of men which made it right for them to have certain things and do certain things. These were their natural rights and the law existed simply to protect and give effect to these rights. There was to be no restraint for any other purpose. Except as they were to be compelled to respect the rights of others, which the natural man or ideal man would do without compulsion as a matter of reason, men were to be left free. In the nineteenth century this mode of thought takes a metaphysical turn. The ultimate thing for juristic purposes is the individual consciousness. The social problem is to reconcile conflicting free wills of conscious individuals independently asserting their wills in the varying activities of life. The natural equality becomes an equality in freedom of will. Kant rationalized the law in these terms as a system of principles or universal rules, to be applied to the human action, whereby the free will of the actor may coexist along with the free will of everyone else. Hegel rationalized the law in these terms as a system of principles wherein and whereby the idea of liberty was realizing in human experience. Bentham rationalized it as a body of rules, laid down and enforced by the state's authority, whereby the maximum of happiness, conceived in terms of free self-assertion, was secured to each individual. Its end was to make possible the maximum of free individual action consistent with general free individual action. Spencer rationalized it as a body of rules, formulating the "government of the living by the dead," whereby men sought to promote the liberty of each limited only by the like liberty of all. In any of these ways of putting it, the end of law is to secure the greatest possible general individual self-assertion; to let men do freely everything they may consistently with a like free doing of everything they may by their fellow men. This is indeed a philosophy of law for discoverers and colonizers and pioneers and traders and entrepreneurs and captains of industry. Until the world became crowded, it served well to eliminate friction and to promote the widest discovery and utilization of the natural resources of human existence.

Looking back at the history of this conception, which has governed theories of the end of law for some two hundred and fifty years, we may note that it has been put to three uses. It has been used as a means of clearing away the restraints upon free economic activity which accumulated during the Middle Ages as incidents of the system of relational duties and as expressions of the idea of holding men to their place in a static social order. This negative side played an important part in the English legislative reform movement in the last century. The English utilitarians insisted upon removal of all restrictions upon individual free action beyond those necessary for securing like freedom on the part of others. This, they said, was the end of legislation. Again it has been used as a constructive idea, as in the seventeenth and eighteenth centuries, when a commercial law which gave effect to what men did as they willed it, which looked at intention and not at form, which interpreted the general security in terms of the security of transactions and sought to effectuate the will of individuals to bring about legal results, was developed out of Roman law and the custom of merchants through juristic theories of natural law. Finally it was used as a stabilizing idea, as in the latter part of the nineteenth century, when men proved that law was an evil, even if a necessary evil, that there should be as little law made as possible, since all law involved restraint upon free exertion of the will, and hence that jurist and legislator should be content to leave things legal as they are and allow the individual "to work out in freedom his own happiness or misery" on that basis.

When this last stage in the development of the idea of law as existing to promote or permit the maximum of free individual self-assertion had been reached, the juristic possibilities of the conception had been exhausted. There were no more continents to discover. Natural resources had been discovered and exploited and the need was for conservation of what remained available. The forces of nature had been harnessed to human use. Industrial development had reached large proportions, and organization and division of labor in our economic order had gone so far that anyone who would could no longer go forth freely and do anything which a restless imagination and daring ambition suggested to him as a means of gain. Although lawyers went on repeating the old formula, the law began to move in another direction. The freedom of the owner of property to do upon it whatever he liked, so long as he did not overstep his limits or endanger the public health or safety, began to be restricted. Nay, the law began to make men act affirmatively upon their property in fashions which it dictated, where the general health was endangered by nonaction. The power to make contracts began to be limited where industrial conditions made abstract freedom of contract defeat rather than advance full individual human life. The power of the owner to dispose freely of his property began to be limited in order to safeguard the security of the social institutions of marriage and the family. Freedom of appropriating *res nullius* and of using *res communes* came to be abridged in order to conserve the natural resources of society. Freedom of engaging in lawful callings came to be restricted, and an elaborate process of education and examination to be imposed upon those who would engage in them, lest there be injury to the public health, safety, or morals. A regime in which anyone might freely set up a corporation to engage in a public service, or freely compete in such service, was superseded by one of legal exemption of existing public utilities from destructive competition. In a crowded world, whose resources had been exploited, a system of promoting the maximum of individual self-assertion had come to produce more friction than it relieved and to further rather than to eliminate waste.

At the end of the last and the beginning of the present century, a new way of thinking grew up. Jurists began to think in terms of human wants or desires or expectations rather than of human wills. They began to think that what they had to do was not simply to equalize or harmonize wills, but, if not to equalize. at least to harmonize the satisfaction of wants. They began to weigh or balance and reconcile claims or wants or desires or expectations, as formerly they had balanced or reconciled wills. They began to think of the end of law, not as a maximum of self-assertion, but as a maximum satisfaction of wants. Hence for a time they thought of the problem of ethics, of jurisprudence, and of politics as chiefly one of valuing; as a problem of finding criteria of the relative value of interests. In jurisprudence and politics they saw that we must add practical problems of the possibility of making interests effective through governmental action, judicial or administrative. But the first question was one of the wants to be recognized—of the interests to be recognized and secured. Having inventoried the wants or claims or interests which are asserting and for which legal security is sought, we were to value them, select those to be recognized, determine the limits within which they were to be given effect in view of other recognized interests, and ascertain how far we might give them effect by law in view of the inherent limitations upon effective legal action. This mode of thinking may be seen, concealed under different terminologies, in more than one type of jurist in the present century.

Three elements contributed to shift the basis of theories as to the end of law from wills to wants, from a reconciling or harmonizing of wills to a reconciling or harmonizing of wants. The most important part was played by psychology which undermined the foundation of the metaphysical will philosophy of law. Through the movement for unification of the social sciences, economics also played an important part, especially indirectly through the attempts at economic interpretation of legal history, reinforcing psychology by showing the extent to which law had been shaped by the pressure of economic wants. Also the differentiation of society, involved in industrial organization, was no mean factor, when classes came to exist in which claims to a minimum human existence, under the standards of the given civilization, became more pressing than claims to self-assertion. Attention was turned from the nature of law to its purpose, and a functional attitude, a tendency to measure legal rules and doctrines and institutions by the extent to which they further or achieve the ends for which law exists, began to replace the older method of judging law by criteria drawn from itself. In this respect the thought of the present is more like that of the seventeenth and eighteenth centuries than that of the nineteenth century. French writers have described this phenomenon as a "revival of juridical idealism." But in truth the social utilitarianism of today and the natural-law philosophy of the seventeenth and eighteenth centuries have only this in common: Each has its attention fixed upon phenomena of growth; each seeks to direct and further conscious improvement of the law.

In its earlier form social-utilitarianism, in common with all nineteenth-century philosophies of law, was too absolute. Its teleological theory was to show us what actually and necessarily took place in lawmaking rather than what we were seeking to bring about. Its service to the philosophy of law was in compelling us to give over the ambiguous term "right" and to distinguish between the claims or wants or demands, existing independently of law, the legally recognized or delimited claims or wants or demands, and the legal institutions, which broadly go by the name of legal rights, whereby the claims when recognized and delimited are secured. Also it first made clear how much the task of the lawmaker is one of compromise. To the law-of-nature school, lawmaking was but an absolute development of absolute principles. A complete logical development of the content implicit in each natural right would give a body of law adequate to every time and place. It is true an idea of compromise did lurk behind the theory of the metaphysical jurists in the nineteenth century. But they sought an absolute harmonizing rather than a working compromise for the time and place. Conflicting individual wills were to be reconciled absolutely by a formula which had ultimate and universal authority. When we think of law as existing to secure social interests, so far as they may be secured through an ordering of men and of human relations through the machinery of organized political society, it becomes apparent that we may reach a practicable system of compromises of conflicting human desires here and now, by means of a mental picture of giving effect to as much as we can, without believing that we have a perfect solution for all time and for every place. As the Neo-Kantians put it, we may formulate the social ideal of the time and place and try juristic problems thereby without believing ourselves competent to lay out a social and political and legal chart for all time. As the Neo-Hegelians put it, we may discover and formulate the jural postulates of the civilization of the time and place without assuming that those postulates are a complete and final picture of ultimate law, by which it must be measured for all time.

Social utilitarianism has stood in need of correction both from psychology and from sociology. It must be recognized that lawmaking and adjudication are not in fact determined precisely by a weighing of interest. In practice the pressure of wants, demands, desires will warp the actual compromises made by the legal system this way or that. In order to maintain the general security we endeavor in every way to minimize this warping. But one needs only to look below the surface of the law anywhere at any time to see it going on, even if covered up by mechanical devices to make the process appear an absolute one and the result a predetermined one. We may not expect that the compromises made and enforced by the legal order will always and infallibly give effect to any picture we may make of the nature or ends of the process of making and enforcing them. Yet there will be less of this subconscious warping if we have a clear picture before us of what we are seeking to do and to what end, and if we build in the image thereof so far as we consciously build and shape the law.

Difficulties arise chiefly in connection with criteria of value. If we say that interests are to be catalogued or inventoried, that they are then to be valued, that those which are found to be of requisite value are to be recognized legally and given effect within limits determined by the valuation, so far as inherent difficulties in effective legal securing of interests will permit, the question arises at once. How shall we do this work of valuing? Philosophers have devoted much ingenuity to the discovery of some method of getting at the intrinsic importance of various interests, so that an absolute formula may be reached in accordance wherewith it may be assured that the weightier interests intrinsically shall prevail. But I am skeptical as to the possibility of an absolute judgment. We are confronted at this point by a fundamental question of social and political philosophy. I do not believe the jurist has to do more than recognize the problem and perceive that it is presented to him as one of securing all social interests so far as he may, of maintaining a balance or harmony among them that is compatible with the securing of all of them. The last century preferred the general security. The present century has shown many signs of preferring the individual moral and social life. I doubt whether such preferences can maintain themselves.

Social utilitarians would say, weigh the several interests in terms of the end of law. But have we any given to us absolutely? Is the end of law anything less than to do whatever may be achieved thereby to satisfy human desires? Are the limits any other than those imposed by the tools with which we work, whereby we may lose more than we gain, if we attempt to apply them in certain situations? If so, there is always a possibility of improved tools. The Greek philosopher who said that the only possible subjects of lawsuit were "insult, injury, and homicide" was as dogmatic as Herbert Spencer, who conceived of sanitary laws and housing laws in our large cities as quite outside the domain of the legal order. Better legal machinery extends the field of legal effectiveness as better machinery has extended the field of industrial effectiveness. I do not mean that the law should interfere as of course in every human relation and in every situation where someone chances to think a social want may be satisfied thereby. Experience has shown abundantly how futile legal machinery may be in its attempts to secure certain kinds of interests. What I do say is, that if in any field of human conduct or in any human relation the law, with such machinery as it has, may satisfy a social want without a disproportionate sacrifice of other claims, there is no eternal limitation inherent in the nature of things, there are no bounds imposed at creation to stand in the way of its doing so.

Let us apply some of the other theories which have been current recently. The Neo-Hegelians say: Try the claims in terms of civilization, in terms of the development of human powers to the most of which they are capable—the most complete human mastery of nature, both human nature and external nature. The Neo-Kantians say: Try them in terms of a community of free-willing men as the social ideal. Duguit says: Try them in terms of social interdependence and social function. Do they promote or do they impede social interdependence through similarity of interest and division of labor? In these formulas do we really get away from the problem of a balance compatible with maintaining all the interests, with responding to all the wants and claims and expectations, which are involved in civilized social existence?

For the purpose of understanding the law of today I am content with a picture of satisfying as much of the whole body of human wants as we may with the least sacrifice. I am content to think of law as a social institution to satisfy social wants—the claims and demands and expectations involved in the existence of civilized society—by giving effect to as much as we may with the least sacrifice, so far as such wants may be satisfied or such claims given effect by an ordering of human conduct through politically organized society. For present purposes I am content to see in legal history the record of a continually wider recognizing and satisfying of human wants or claims or desires through social control; a more embracing and more effective securing of social interests; a continually more complete and effective elimination of waste and precluding of friction in human enjoyment of the goods of existence—in short, a continually more efficacious social engineering.

Anarchism
Peter Kropotkin

Peter Kropotkin (1842-1921) was a Russian revolutionary anarchist who escaped
from prison in Russia and lived mainly in England. He wrote extensive defenses of
anarchism. After the Russian Revolution, he returned to Russia but was greatly
disturbed by the "law and authority" that he saw developing there.

I

"When ignorance reigns in society and disorder in the minds of men, laws are
multiplied, legislation is expected to do everything, and each fresh law being a fresh
miscalculation, men are continually led to demand from it what can proceed only
from themselves, from their own education and their own morality." It is no
revolutionist who says this, not even a reformer. It is the jurist, Dalloy, author of
the collection of French law known as *Répertoire de la Législation*. And yet,
though these lines were written by a man who was himself a maker and admirer of
law, they perfectly represent the abnormal condition of our society.

In existing States a fresh law is looked upon as a remedy for evil. Instead of
themselves altering what is bad, people begin by demanding a *law* to alter it. If the
road between two villages is impassable, the peasant says:--"There should be a law
about parish roads." If a park-keeper takes advantage of the want of spirit in those
who follow him with servile observance and insults one of them, the insulted man
says, "There should be a law to enjoin more politeness upon park-keepers." If there
is stagnation in agriculture or commerce, the husbandman, cattle-breeder, or corn
speculator argues, "it is protective legislation that we require." Down to the old
clothesman there is not one who does not demand a law to protect his own little
trade. If the employer lowers wages or increases the hours of labor, the politician in
embryo exclaims, "We must have a law to put all that to rights." In short, a law
everywhere and for everything! A law about fashions, a law about mad dogs, a law
about virtue, a law to put a stop to all the vices and all the evils which result from
human indolence and cowardice.

We are so perverted by an education which from infancy seeks to kill in us the
spirit of revolt, and to develop that of submission to authority; we are so perverted
by this existence under the ferrule of a law, which regulates every event in life--our
birth, our education, our development, our love, our friendship--that, if this state
of things continues, we shall lose all initiative, all habit of thinking for ourselves.
Our society seems no longer able to understand that it is possible to exist otherwise
than under the reign of law, elaborated by a representative government and
administered by a handful of rulers. And even when it has gone so far as to
emancipate itself from the thralldom, its first care has been to reconstitute it
immediately. "The Year I of Liberty" has never lasted more than a day, for after

Source: Law and Authority (London: Freedom Press, 1866). Abridged.

proclaiming it men put themselves the very next morning under the yoke of law and authority.

Indeed, for some thousands of years, those who govern us have done nothing but ring the changes upon "Respect for law, obedience to authority." This is the moral atmosphere in which parents bring up their children, and school only serves to confirm the impression. Cleverly assorted scraps of spurious science are inculcated upon the children to prove necessity of law; obedience to the law is made a religion; moral goodness and the law of the masters are fused into one and the same divinity. The historical hero of the schoolroom is the man who obeys the law, and defends it against rebels.

Later when we enter upon public life, society and literature, impressing us day by day and hour by hour as the water-drop hollows the stone, continue to inculcate the same prejudice. Books of history, of political science, of social economy, are stuffed with this respect for law. Even the physical sciences have been pressed into the service by introducing artificial modes of expression, borrowed from theology and arbitrary power, into knowledge which is purely the result of observation. Thus our intelligence is successfully befogged, and always to maintain our respect for law. The same work is done by newspapers. They have not an article which does not preach respect for law, even where the third page proves every day the imbecility of that law, and shows how it is dragged through every variety of mud and filth by those charged with its administration. Servility before the law has become a virtue, and I doubt if there was ever even a revolutionist who did not begin in his youth as the defender of law against what are generally called "abuses," although these last are inevitable consequences of the law itself. . . .

To understand this [worship of law], we must transport ourselves in imagination into the eighteenth century. Our hearts must have ached at the story of the atrocities committed by the all-powerful nobles of that time upon the men and women of the people before we can understand what must have been the magic influence upon the peasant's mind of the words, "Equality before the law, obedience to the law without distinction of birth or fortune." He who until then had been treated more cruelly than a beast, he who had never had any rights, he who had never obtained justice against the most revolting actions on the part of a noble, unless in revenge he killed him and was hanged—he saw himself recognized by this maxim, at least in theory, at least with regard to his personal rights, as the equal of his lord. Whatever this law might be, it promised to affect lord and peasant alike: it proclaimed the equality of rich and poor before the judge. The promise was a lie, and today we know it; but at that period it was an advance, a homage to justice, as hypocrisy is a homage rendered to truth. This is the reason that when the saviors of the menaced middle class (the Robespierres and the Dantons) took their stand upon the writings of the Rousseaus and the Voltaires, and proclaimed "respect for law, the same for every man," the people accepted the compromise; for their revolutionary impetus had already spent its force in the contest with a foe whose ranks drew closer day by day; they bowed their neck beneath the yoke of law to save themselves from the arbitrary power of their lords.

The middle class has ever since continued to make the most of this maxim, which with another principle, that of representative government, sums up the whole philosophy of the bourgeois age, the nineteenth century. It has preached this doctrine in its schools, it has propagated it in its writings, it has moulded its art and science to the same purpose, it has thrust its beliefs into every hole and corner—like a pious Englishwoman, who slips tracts under the door—and it has done all this so successfully that today we behold the issue in the detestable fact that men who long for freedom begin the attempt to obtain it by entreating their masters to be kind enough to protect them by modifying the laws which these masters themselves have created!

But times and tempers are changed. Rebels are everywhere to be found who no longer wish to obey the law without knowing whence it comes, what are its uses, and whither arises the obligation to submit to it, and the reverence with which it is encompassed. The rebels of our day are criticizing the very foundations of society which have hitherto been held sacred, and first and foremost amongst them that fetish, law.

The critics analyze the sources of law, and find there either a god, product of the terrors of the savage, and stupid, paltry and malicious as the priests who vouch for its supernatural origin, or else, bloodshed, conquest by fire and sword. They study the characteristics of law, and instead of perpetual growth corresponding to that of the human race, they find its distinctive traits to be immobility, a tendency to crystallize what should be modified and developed day by day. They ask how law has been maintained, and in its service they see the atrocities of Byzantinism, the cruelties of the Inquisition, the tortures of the Middle Ages, living flesh torn by the lash of the executioner, chains, clubs, axes, the gloomy dungeons of prisons, agony, curses and tears. In our own days they see, as before, the axe, the cord, the rifle, the prison; on the one hand, the brutalized prisoner, reduced to the condition of a caged beast by the debasement of his whole moral being, and on the other, the judge, stripped of every feeling which does honor to human nature, living like a visionary in a world of legal fictions, revelling in the infliction of imprisonment and death, without even suspecting, in the cold malignity of his madness, the abyss of degradation into which he has himself fallen before the eyes of those whom he condemns.

They see a race of law-makers legislating without knowing what their laws are about; today voting a law on the sanitation of towns, without the faintest notion of hygiene, tomorrow making regulations for the armament of troops, without so much as understanding a gun; making laws about teaching and education without ever having given a lesson of any sort, or even an honest education to their own children; legislating at random in all directions, but never forgetting the penalties to be meted out to ragamuffins, the prison and the galleys, which are to be the portion of men a thousand times less immoral than these legislators themselves.

Finally, they see the jailer on the way to lose all human feeling, the detective trained as a blood-hound, the police spy despising himself; "informing," metamorphosed into a virtue; corruption, erected into a system; all the vices, all the evil qualities of mankind countenanced and cultivated to insure the triumph of law.

All this we see, and, therefore, instead of inanely repeating the old formula, "Respect the law," we say, "Despise law and all its attributes!" In place of the cowardly phrase, "Obey the law," our cry is "Revolt against all laws!"

Only compare the misdeeds accomplished in the name of each law with the good it has been able to effect, and weigh carefully both good and evil, and you will see if we are right.

II

Relatively speaking, law is a product of modern times. For ages and ages mankind lived without any written law, even that graved in symbols upon the entrance stones of a temple. During that period, human relations were simply regulated by customs, habits and usages, made sacred by constant repetition, and acquired by each person in childhood, exactly as he learned how to obtain his food by hunting, cattle-rearing or agriculture.

All human societies have passed through this primitive phase, and to this day a large proportion of mankind have no written law. Every tribe has its own manners and customs; customary law, as the jurists say. It has social habits, and that suffices to maintain the cordial relations between the inhabitants of the village, the members of the tribe or community. . . .

Two distinctly marked currents of custom are revealed by analysis of the usages of primitive people.

As man does not live in a solitary state, habits and feelings develop within him which are useful for the preservation of society and the propagation of the race. Without social feelings and usages, life in common would have been absolutely impossible. It is not law which has established them; they are anterior to all law. Neither is it religion which has ordained them; they are anterior to all religions. They are found amongst all animals living in society. They are spontaneously developed by the very nature of things, like those habits in animals which men call instinct. They spring from a process of evolution, which is useful, and, indeed, necessary, to keep society together in the struggle it is forced to maintain for existence. Savages end by no longer eating one another because they find it in the long run more advantageous to devote themselves to some sort of cultivation than to enjoy the pleasure of feasting upon the flesh of an aged relative once a year. Many travelers have depicted the manners of absolutely independent tribes, where laws and chiefs are unknown, but where the members of the tribe have given up stabbing one another in every dispute, because the habit of living in society has ended by developing certain feelings of fraternity and oneness of interest, and they prefer appealing to a third person to settle their differences. The hospitality of primitive peoples, respect for human life, the sense of reciprocal obligation, compassion for the weak, courage, extending even to the sacrifice of self for others which is first learnt for the sake of children and friends, and later for that of members of the same community—all these qualities are developed in man anterior to all law, independently of all religion, as in the case of the social animals. Such feelings and practices are the inevitable results of social life. Without being, as say priests and metaphysicians, inherent in man, such qualities are the consequence of life in common.

But side by side with these customs, necessary to the life of societies and the preservation of the race, other desires, other passions, and therefore other habits and customs, are evolved in human association. The desire to dominate others and impose one's will upon them; the desire to seize upon the products of the labor of a neighboring tribe; the desire to surround oneself with comforts without producing anything, while slaves provide their master with the means of procuring every sort of pleasure and luxury—these selfish, personal desires give rise to another current of habits and customs. The priest and the warrior, the charlatan who makes a profit out of superstition, and after freeing himself from the fear of the devil cultivates it in others; and the bully, who procures the invasion and pillage of his neighbors that he may return laden with booty and followed by slaves. These two, hand in hand have succeeded in imposing upon primitive society customs advantageous to both of them, but tending to perpetuate their domination of the masses. Profiting by the indolence, the fears, the inertia of the crowd, and thanks to the continual repetition of the same acts, they have permanently established customs which have become a solid basis for their own domination.

For this purpose, they would have made use, in the first place, of that tendency to run in a groove, so highly developed in mankind. In children and all savages it attains striking proportions, and it may also be observed in animals. Man, when he is at all superstitious, is always afraid to introduce any sort of change into existing conditions; he generally venerates what is ancient. "Our fathers did so and so; they got on pretty well; they brought you up; they were not unhappy; do the same!" the old say to the young every time the latter wish to alter things. The unknown frightens them, they prefer to cling to the past even when that past represents poverty, oppression and slavery.

It may even be said that the more miserable a man is, the more he dreads every sort of change, lest it may make him more wretched still. Some ray of hope, a few scraps of comfort, must penetrate his gloomy abode before he can begin to desire better things, to criticize the old ways of living, and prepare to imperil them for the sake of bringing about a change. So long as he is not imbued with hope, so long as he is not freed from the tutelage of those who utilize his superstition and his fears, he prefers remaining in his former position. If the young desire any change, the old raise a cry of alarm against the innovators. Some savages would rather die than transgress the customs of their country because they have been told from childhood that the least infraction of established routine would bring ill-luck and ruin the whole tribe. Even in the present day, what numbers of politicians, economists, and would-be revolutionists act under the same impression, and cling to a vanishing past. How many care only to seek for precedents. How many fiery innovators are mere copyists of bygone revolutions.

The spirit of routine, originating in superstition, indolence, and cowardice, has in all times been the mainstay of oppression. In primitive human societies it was cleverly turned to account by priests and military chiefs. They perpetuated customs useful only to themselves, and succeeded in imposing them on the whole tribe. So long as this conservative spirit could be exploited so as to assure the chief in his encroachments upon individual liberty, so long as the only inequalities between men were the work of nature, and these were not increased a hundred-fold by the concentration of power and wealth, there was no need for law and the formidable paraphernalia of tribunals and ever-augmenting penalties to enforce it.

But as society became more and more divided into two hostile classes, one seeking to establish its domination, the other struggling to escape, the strife began. Now the conqueror was in a hurry to secure the results of his actions in a permanent form, he tried to place them beyond question, to make them holy and venerable by every means in his power. Law made its appearance under the sanction of the priest, and the warrior's club was placed at its service. Its office was to render immutable such customs as were to the advantage of the dominant minority. Military authority undertook to ensure obedience. This new function was a fresh guarantee to the power of the warrior; now he had not only mere brute force at his service; he was the defender of law.

If law, however, presented nothing but a collection of prescriptions serviceable to rulers, it would find some difficulty in insuring acceptance and obedience. Well, the legislators confounded in one code the two currents of custom of which we have just been speaking, the maxims which represent principles of morality and social union wrought out as a result of life in common, and the mandates which are meant to ensure external existence to inequality. Customs, absolutely essential to the very being of society, are, in the code, cleverly intermingled with usages imposed by the ruling caste, and both claim equal respect from the crowd. "Do not kill," says the code, and hastens to add, "And pay tithes to the priest." "Do not steal," says the code, and immediately after, "He who refuses to pay taxes, shall have his hand struck off."

Such was law; and it has maintained its two-fold character to this day. Its origin is the desire of the ruling class to give permanence to customs imposed by themselves for their own advantage. Its character is the skillful commingling of customs useful to society, customs which have no need of law to insure respect, with other customs useful only to rulers, injurious to the mass of the people, and maintained only by the fear of punishment.

Like individual capital, which was born of fraud and violence, and developed under the auspices of authority, law has no title to the respect of men. Born of violence and superstition, and established in the interests of consumer, priest and rich exploiter, it must be utterly destroyed on the day when the people desire to break their chains. . . .

III

. . . The great [French] Revolution began the demolition of this framework of law, bequeathed to us by feudalism and royalty. But after having demolished some portions of the ancient edifice, the Revolution delivered over the power of law-making to the bourgeoisie, who, in their turn, began to raise a fresh framework of laws intended to maintain and perpetuate middle-class domination among the masses. Their parliament makes laws right and left, and mountains of law accumulate with frightful rapidity. But what *are* all these laws at bottom?

The major portion have but one object—to protect private property, i.e., wealth acquired by the exploitations of man by man. Their aim is to open out to capital fresh fields for exploitation, and to sanction the new forms which that exploitation continually assumes, as capital swallows up another branch of human activity, railways, telegraphs, electric light, chemical industries, the expression of man's thought in literature and science, etc. The object of the rest of these laws is fundamentally the same. They exist to keep up the machinery of government which serves to secure to capital the exploitation and monopoly of the wealth produced. Magistrature, police, army, public instruction, finance, all serve one God—capital; all have but one object—to facilitate the exploitation of the worker by the capitalist. Analyze all the laws passed and you will find nothing but this.

The protection of the person, which is put forward as the true mission of law, occupies an imperceptible space among them, for, in existing society, assaults upon the person directly dictated by hatred and brutality tend to disappear. Nowadays, if anyone is murdered, it is generally for the sake of robbing him; rarely because of personal vengeance. But if this class of crimes and misdemeanors is continually diminishing, we certainly do not owe the change to legislation. It is due to the growth of humanitarianism in our societies, to our increasingly social habits rather than to the prescriptions of our laws. Repeal tomorrow every law dealing with the protection of the person, and tomorrow stop all proceedings for assault, and the number of attempts dictated by personal vengeance and by brutality would not be augmented by one single instance.

It will perhaps be objected that during the last fifty years, a good many liberal laws have been enacted. But, if these laws are analyzed, it will be discovered that this liberal legislation consists in the repeal of the laws bequeathed to us by the barbarism of preceding centuries. Every liberal law, every radical program, may be summed up in these words—abolition of laws grown irksome to the middle-class itself, and return and extension to all citizens of liberties enjoyed by the townships of the twelfth century. The abolition of capital punishment, trial by jury for all "crimes" (there was a more liberal jury in the twelfth century), the election of magistrates, the right of bringing public officials to trial, the abolition of standing armies, free instruction, etc., everything that is pointed out as an invention of modern liberalism, is but a return to the freedom which existed before church and king had laid hands upon every manifestation of human life.

Thus the protection of exploitation directly by laws on property, and indirectly by the maintenance of the State is both the spirit and the substance of our modern codes, and the one function of our costly legislative machinery. But it is time we gave up being satisfied with mere phrases, and learned to appreciate their real significance. The law, which on its first appearance presented itself as a compendium of customs useful for the preservation of society, is now perceived to be nothing but an instrument for the maintenance of exploitation and the domination of the toiling masses by rich idlers. At the present day its civilizing mission is *nil*; it has but one object—to bolster up exploitation.

This is what is told us by history as to the development of law. Is it in virtue of this history that we are called upon to respect it? Certainly not. It has no more title to respect than capital, the fruit of pillage. And the first duty of the revolution will be to make a bonfire of all existing laws as it will of all titles to property.

IV

The millions of laws which exist for the regulation of humanity appear upon investigation to be divided into three principal categories: protection of property, protection of persons, protection of government. And by analyzing each of these three categories, we arrive at the same logical and necessary conclusion: *the uselessness and hurtfulness of law.*

Socialists know what is meant by protection of property. Laws on property are not made to guarantee either to the individual or to society the enjoyment of the produce of their own labor. On the contrary, they are made to rob the producer of a part of what he has created, and to secure to certain other people that portion of the produce which they have stolen either from the producer or from society as a whole. When, for example, the law establishes Mr. So-and-So's right to a house, it is not establishing his right to a cottage he has built for himself, or to a house he has erected with the help of some of his friends. In that case no one would have disputed his right. On the contrary, the law is establishing his right to a house which is *not* the product of his labor; first of all because he has had it built for him by others to whom he has not paid the full value of their work, and next because that house represents a social value which he could not have produced for himself. The law is establishing his right to what belongs to everybody in general and to nobody in particular. The same house built in the midst of Siberia would not have the value it possesses in a large town, and, as we know, that value arises from the labor of something like fifty generations of men who have built the town, beautified it, supplied it with water and gas, fine promenades, colleges, theatres, shops, railways and roads leading in all directions. Thus, by recognizing the right of Mr. So-and-So to a particular house in Paris, London or Rouen, the law is unjustly appropriating to him a certain portion of the produce of the labor of mankind in general. And it is precisely because this appropriation and all other forms of property bearing the same character are a crying injustice, that a whole arsenal of laws and a whole army of soldiers, policemen and judges are needed to maintain it against the good sense and just feeling inherent in humanity.

Half our laws—the civil code in each country—serves no other purpose than to maintain this appropriation, this monopoly for the benefit of certain individuals against the whole of mankind. Three-fourths of the causes decided by the tribunals are nothing but quarrels between monopolists—two robbers disputing over their booty. And a great many of our criminal laws have the same object in view, their end being to keep the workman in a subordinate position towards his employer, and thus afford security for exploitation.

As for guaranteeing the product of his labor to the producer, there are no laws which even attempt such a thing. It is so simple and natural, so much a part of the manners and customs of mankind, that law has not given it so much as a thought. Open brigandage, sword in hand, is no feature of our age. Neither does one workman ever come and dispute the produce of his labor with another. If they have a misunderstanding they settle it by calling in a third person, without having recourse to law. The only person who exacts from another what that other has produced, is the proprietor, who comes in and deducts the lion's share. As for humanity in general, it everywhere respects the right of each to what he has created, without the interposition of any special laws.

As all the laws about property which make up thick volumes of codes and are the delight of our lawyers have no other object than to protect the unjust appropriation of human labor by certain monopolists, there is no reason for their existence, and, on the day of the revolution, social revolutionists are thoroughly determined to put an end to them. Indeed, a bonfire might be made with perfect justice of all laws bearing upon the so-called "rights of property," all title-deeds, all registers, in a word, of all that is in any way connected with an institution which will soon be looked upon as a blot in the history of humanity, as humiliating as the slavery and serfdom of past ages.

The remarks just made upon laws concerning property are quite as applicable to the second category of laws; those for the maintenance of government, i.e., constitutional law.

It again is a complete arsenal of laws, decrees, ordinances, orders in council, and what not, all serving to protect the diverse forms of representative government, delegated or usurped, beneath which humanity is writhing. We know very well—anarchists have often enough pointed out in their perpetual criticism of the various forms of government—that the mission of all governments, monarchical, constitutional, or republican, is to protect and maintain by force the privileges of the classes in possession, the aristocracy, clergy and traders. A good third of our laws—and each country possesses some tens of thousands of them—the fundamental laws on taxes, excise duties, the organization of ministerial departments and their offices, of the army, the police, the church, etc., have no other end than to maintain, patch up, and develop the administrative machine. And this machine in its turn serves almost entirely to protect the privileges of the possessing classes. Analyze all these laws, observe them in action day by day, and you will discover that not one is worth preserving.

About such laws there can be no two opinions. Not only anarchists, but more or less revolutionary radicals also, are agreed that the only use to be made of laws concerning the organization of government is to fling them into the fire.

The third category of law still remains to be considered; that relating to the protection of the person and the detection and prevention of "crime." This is the most important because most prejudices attach to it; because, if law enjoys a certain amount of consideration, it is in consequence of the belief that this species of law is absolutely indispensable to the maintenance of security in our societies. These are laws developed from the nucleus of customs useful to human communities, which have been turned to account by rulers to sancitfy their own domination. The authority of the chiefs of tribes, or rich families in towns, and of the king, depended upon their judicial functions, and even down to the present day, whenever the necessity of government is spoken of, its function as supreme judge is the thing implied. "Without a government men would tear one another to pieces," argues the village orator. "The ultimate end of all government is to secure twelve honest jurymen to every accused person," said Burke.

Well, in spite of all the prejudices existing on this subject, it is quite time that anarchists should boldly declare this cateogry of laws as useless and injurious as the preceding ones.

First of all, as to so-called "crimes"—assaults upon persons—it is well known that two-thirds, and often as many as three-fourths, of such "crimes" are instigated by the desire to obtain possession of someone's wealth. This immense class of so-called "crimes and misdemeanors" will disappear on the day on which private property ceases to exist. "But," it will be said, "there will always be brutes who will attempt the lives of their fellow citizens, who will lay their hands to a knife in every quarrel, and revenge the slightest offense by murder, if there are no laws to restrain and punishments to withhold them." This refrain is repeated every time the right of society to *punish* is called in question.

Yet there is one fact concerning this head which at the present time is thoroughly established; the severity of punishment does not diminish the amount of crime. Hang, and, if you like, quarter murderers, and the number of murders will not decrease by one. On the other hand, abolish the penalty of death, and there will not be one murder more; there will be fewer. Statistics prove it. But if the harvest is good, and bread cheap, and the weather fine, the number of murders immediately decreases. This again is proved by statistics. The amount of crime always augments and diminishes in proportion to the price of provisions and the state of the weather. Not that all murders are actuated by hunger. That is not the case. But when the harvest is good, and provisions are at an obtainable price, and when the sun shines, men, lighter-hearted and less miserable than usual, do not give way to gloomy passions, do not from trivial motives plunge a knife into the bosom of a fellow creature.

Moreover, it is also a well known fact that the fear of punishment has never stopped a single murderer. He who kills his neighbor from revenge or misery does not reason much about consequences; and there have been few murderers who were not firmly convinced that they should escape prosecution.

Without speaking of a society in which a man will receive a better education, in which the development of all his faculties, and the possibility of exercising them, will procure him so many enjoyments that he will not seek to poison them by remorse—even in our society, even with those sad products of misery whom we see today in the public houses of great cities—on the day when no punishment is inflicted upon murderers, the number of murders will not be augmented by a single case. And it is extremely probable that it will be, on the contrary, diminished by all those cases which are due at present to habitual criminals, who have been brutalized in prisons.

We are continually being told of the benefits conferred by law, and the beneficial effect of penalties, but have the speakers ever attempted to strike a balance between the benefits attributed to laws and penalties, and the degrading effect of these penalities upon humanity? Only calculate all the evil passions awakened in mankind by the atrocious punishments formerly inflicted in our streets! Man is the cruelest animal upon earth. And who has pampered and developed the cruel instincts unknown, even among monkeys, if it is not the king, the judge, and the priests, armed with law, who caused flesh to be torn off in strips, boiling pitch to be poured into wounds, limbs to be dislocated, bones to be crushed, men to be sawn asunder to maintain their authority? Only estimate the torrent of depravity let loose in human society by the "informing" which is countenanced by judges, and paid in hard cash by governments, under pretext of assisting in the discovery of "crime." Only go into jails and study what man becomes when he is deprived of freedom and shut up with other depraved beings, steeped in the vice and corruption which oozes from the very walls of our existing prisons. Only remember that the more these prisons are reformed, the more detestable they become. Our model modern penitentiaries are a hundred-fold more abominable than the dungeons of the middle ages. Finally, consider what corruption, what depravity of mind is kept up among men by the idea of obedience, the very essence of law; of chastisement; of authority having the right to punish, to judge irrespective of our conscience and the esteem of our friends; of the necessity for executioners, jailers, and informers—in a word, by all the attributes of law and authority. Consider all this, and you will assuredly agree with us in saying that a law inflicting penalties is an abomination which should cease to exist.

Peoples without political organization, and therefore less depraved than ourselves, have perfectly understood that the man who is called "criminal" is simply unfortunate; that the remedy is not to flog him, to chain him up, or to kill him on the scaffold or in prison, but to help him by the most brotherly care, by treatment based on equality, by the usages of life among honest men. In the next revolution we hope that this cry will go forth:

"Burn the guillotines; demolish the prisons; drive away the judges, policemen and informers—the impurest race upon the face of the earth; treat as a brother the man who has been led by passion to do ill to his fellow; above all, take from the ignoble products of middle-class idleness the possibility of displaying their vices in attractive colors; and be sure that but few crimes will mar our society."

The main supports of crime are idleness, law and authority; laws about property, laws about government, laws about penalties and misdemeanors; and authority, which takes upon itself to manufacture these laws and to apply them.

No more laws! No more judges! Liberty, equality, and practical human sympathy are the only effectual barriers we can oppose to the anti-social instincts of certain among us.

Suggested Readings

1. Bedau, Hugo (ed.), *Civil Disobedience* (New York: Pegasus, 1969).
2. Friedman, W., *Legal Theory*, 4th ed. (London: Stevens and Sons, 1960).
3. Mayer, Peter (ed.), *The Pacifist Conscience* (Chicago: Henry Regnery, 1966).
4. Ramsey, Paul, *War and the Christian Conscience* (Durham, N.C.: Duke University Press, 1961).
5. Wasserstrom, Richard, "The Relevance of Nuremberg," *Philosophy and Public Affairs,* Vol. 1, No. 1 (Fall 1971), 15-30.
6. Wasserstrom, Richard (ed.), *War and Morality* (Belmont, Calif.: Wadsworth, 1971).

Third World Liberation

My idea of philosophy is that if it is not relevant to human problems, if it does not tell us how we can go about eradicating some of the misery in this world, then it is not worth the name of philosophy. I think that Socrates made a very profound statement when he asserted that the raison d'être *of philosophy is to teach us proper living.*

—Angela Davis

INTRODUCTION

The Third World consists of the people of Africa, Asia, and Latin America. They are the people of color: black, yellow, and brown. The other two worlds are the white people of Europe and North America. The emergence of the Third World is one of the most important political changes occurring in our time. For the student of history, the political, social, and economic shifts are evidence of Third World people's aspirations to free themselves of domination by Europe and North America. The rise of nationalism that overthrew Spanish and Portuguese empires in Latin America during the nineteenth century has been matched in our own century with the creation of new nations in Africa, the dissolution of the British Empire in Asia, and the wars of liberation.

Colonialism of the old order, the actual direction of people by a colonial government, and the newer economic colonialism of the "have" nations have been characterized frequently enough to be relatively common knowledge even to casual observers of the international scene. The detection of colonialism has become sufficiently refined in students and victims of politics to enable them to spot its presence within the borders of the United States. And many Third World people here have come to see their relationship to whites as one of colonials. They see themselves playing as much a subsidiary political, economic, and social role in the United States as black, yellow, and brown people played in African, Asian, and Latin American colonial societies.

The political, economic, and social consequences of colonialism, foreign and domestic, their detection, and the changes that have to be made to rid ourselves of them are familiar enough. What is not so well known is how philosophy relates to colonialism, foreign and domestic.

In surveying the writings of Third World authors, we have been struck by a recurring theme: the extent to which the white world has practiced cultural colonialism. Europe and the United States have exported cultural missionaries with their soldiers and business agents. Imperialists generally feel as confident of their cultural and philosophical superiority as of their military and financial superiority. Along with their destruction of native government and trade comes their annihilation of native culture. Hence, it is natural that colonized people try to think their way through to cultural independence before, during, and after their struggle for political and economic independence.

In a racist society, the out-race (those discriminated against) is made to feel inferior. The survival of personal dignity and a feeling of human worth can be regained by out-race people in either of two ways: First, by personal effort, an individual can try to make himself sufficiently useful to the in-race to gain its approval; in-race approval is a substitute for the out-race individual's self-approval, although it is a poor one, for the in-race approves merely to obtain its own ends. Second, by group effort, out-race people can create a culture and ideology that affirms independently of in-race attitudes their human worth. The second route is superior to the first because instead of leaving the individual to battle for himself, it provides him with a philosophical mutual aid society. Collective strength is superior to individual effort.

The next couple of decades should see some exciting philosophical contributions developing out of Third World consciousness. The essays in this chapter preview some of the concepts on which we can expect Third World philosophers to concentrate and elaborate. The concepts are familiar in the philosophical literature, both classical and contemporary: freedom, oppression, discipline, identity, individualism, sacrifice, dialectic, contradiction, and so on. In treating these concepts, the philosophical literature of Third World thinkers reflects the agony, anger, and urgency absent from much of recent professional philosophical literature.

AT HOME

The rules of the *Black Panther Party* (first essay of this section) exhibit the categorical, simple, militant, and Puritanical ethics of a minority race striving for self-determination and survival. Out-races' cultural welfare and philosophical confidence are as dependent on militant, organized power as the in-races' are, particularly if they have been colonials for a long time. There are serious, mutual dependencies between might and right. You will notice the same demanding morals when you read Che Guevara's essay in the next section. You might anticipate the effect that the need for such moral rules will have on the philosophical discussion of ethics by turning your thoughts back to Chapter Three, "Morality: Old and New," particularly the section on rules and situations.

George D. Kelsey (second essay of this section) digs deeply into the concept of racism by bringing philosophical and theological concepts to bear on it rather than the usual psychological and social analyses. Racism is essentially a metaphysical issue, an issue about being; Kelsey says, "Racial alienation stands alone among the forms of human conflict as the one form of collective hostility founded in the question of human being as such." Philosophical discussions of racism will increase as white people are increasingly called upon to root it out of themselves. We have not as yet attained the philosophical sophistication about human nature that Third World philosophizing about racism should help us acquire.

Linda La Rue's discussion of racism (third essay of this section) takes a more concrete turn than Kelsey's. She discusses racial oppression in the context of women's liberation. For the white women liberationists who believe that they have personal experience similar to that of Third World people who experience racism, La Rue takes strong exception. She distinguishes sharply between the oppression imposed by racists and the suppression imposed by male chauvinists. To aid your approach to this distinction, we suggest you carefully read or reread Kate Millet's essay in Chapter Four, in the section entitled "Freedom."

Relating La Rue's definition of the "oppressed" (persons "unreasonably burdened, unjustly, severely, rigorously, cruelly and harshly fettered by white authority") to **Lerone Bennett**'s essay (fourth essay in this section) may give you a keener appreciation of the link he attempts to make between the white man's and the black man's freedom. He says, "My argument here is the very simple one that the depth of racism is a measure of the unfreedom in the white community." White Americans' complacent belief that they are free, acquired by the docile repetition of phrases from the Declaration of Independence, will be shaken by such Third World probes into the concept of freedom.

Achieving cultural identity is stressed by both **Octavio Paz** and **Hilario H. Contreras.** Paz (next-to-last essay of this section) eloquently states the problems facing a person who is trying to find his identity when he has origins in one culture but is forced to find his place in another culture. Paz shows how the search for personal identity by the *pachucos* was a collective effort. Contreras (last essay of this section) says the case is the same for the Chicanos. Both authors reveal how profoundly social we human animals are. And both characterize the Mexican culture and the North American culture, contrast them, and, particularly Contreras, show how the cultural tug-of-war in which a Third World person is caught generates identity crises. You may be especially struck by Contreras's lament for one kind of hyphenated American, the Anglo-American; Contreras says, "The tragedy of the Anglo-American's *lack* of identity is final, while the Chicano's *loss* of cultural identity is only temporary. What was lost can be regained." And, of course, what one *lacks* is something one never had.

There is a considerable literature and a complex of concepts around the concept of identity. For more on this topic, we refer you to the next chapter. In its introduction, we set out and relate something of that complex of concepts.

Black Panther Rules

CENTRAL HEADQUARTERS: OAKLAND, CALIFORNIA

Every member of the BLACK PANTHER PARTY throughout this country of racist America must abide by these rules as functional members of this party. CENTRAL COMMITTEE members, CENTRAL STAFFS, and LOCAL STAFFS, including all captains subordinate to either national, state, and local leadership of the BLACK PANTHER PARTY will enforce these rules. Length of suspension or other disciplinary action necessary for violation of these rules will depend on national decisions by national, state or state area, and local committees and staffs where said rule or rules of the BLACK PANTHER PARTY WERE VIOLATED.

Every member of the party must know these verbatim by heart. And apply them daily. Each member must report any violation of these rules to their leadership or they are counter-revolutionary and are also subjected to suspension by the BLACK PANTHER PARTY.

The Rules Are

1.   No party member can have narcotics or weed in his possession while doing party work.

2.   Any party member found shooting narcotics will be expelled from this party.

3.   No party member can be DRUNK while doing daily party work.

4.   No party member will violate rules relating to office work, general meetings of the BLACK PANTHER PARTY, and meetings of the BLACK PANTHER PARTY ANYWHERE.

5.   No party member will USE, POINT, or FIRE a weapon of any kind unnecessarily or accidentally at anyone.

6.   No party member can join any other army force other than the BLACK LIBERATION ARMY.

7.   No party member can have a weapon in his possession while DRUNK or loaded off narcotics or weed.

8.   No party member will commit any crimes against other party members or BLACK people at all, and cannot steal or take from the people, not even a needle or a piece of thread.

9.   When arrested BLACK PANTHER MEMBERS will give only name, address, and will sign nothing. Legal first aid must be understood by all Party members.

10.   The Ten Point Program and platform of the BLACK PANTHER PARTY must be known and understood by each Party member.

11.   Party Communications must be National and Local.

12.   The 10-10-10-program should be known by all members and also understood by all members.

Source: The Black Panther, Sunday, April 6, 1969, p. 21.

13. All Finance officers will operate under the jurisdiction of the Ministry of Finance.

14. Each person will submit a report of daily work.

15. Each Sub-Section Leader, Section Leader, Lieutenant, and Captain must submit Daily reports of work.

16. All Panthers must learn to operate and service weapons correctly.

17. All Leadership personnel who expel a member must submit this information to the Editor of the Newspaper, so that it will be published in the paper and will be known by all chapters and branches.

18. Political Education Classes are mandatory for general membership.

19. Only office personnel assigned to respective offices each day should be there. All others are to sell papers and do Political work out in the community, including Captains, Section Leaders, etc.

20. COMMUNICATIONS—all chapters must submit weekly reports in writing to the National Headquarters.

21. All Branches must implement First Aid and/or Medical Cadres.

22. All Chapters, Branches, and components of the BLACK PANTHER PARTY must submit a monthly Financial Report to the Ministry of Finance, and also the Central Committee.

23. Everyone in a leadership position must read no less than two hours per day to keep abreast of the changing political situation.

24. No chapter or branch shall accept grants, poverty funds, money or any other aid from any government agency without contacting the National Headquarters.

25. All chapters must adhere to the policy and the ideology laid down by the CENTRAL COMMITTEE of the BLACK PANTHER PARTY.

26. All Branches must submit weekly reports in writing to their respective Chapters.

8 Points of Attention

(1) Speak politely.

(2) Pay fairly for what you buy.

(3) Return everything you borrow.

(4) Pay for anything you damage.

(5) Do not hit or swear at people.

(6) Do not damage property or crops of the poor, oppressed masses.

(7) Do not take liberties with women.

(8) If we ever have to take captives do not ill-treat them.

3 Main Rules of Discipline

(1) Obey orders in all your actions.

(2) Do not take a single needle or a piece of thread from the poor and oppressed masses.

(3) Turn in everything captured from the attacking enemy.

Racism as Idolatry

George D. Kelsey

George D. Kelsey (1910-   ) is an American theologian. He received his Ph.D. at
Yale University and now teaches at Drew University Theological School. Among his
books are *Racism and the Christian Understanding of Man* (1965).

Racism is a faith. It is a form of idolatry. It is an abortive search for meaning. In its
early modern beginnings, racism was a justificatory device. It did not emerge as a
faith. It arose as an ideological justification for the constellations of political and
economic power which were expressed in colonialism and slavery. But gradually the
idea of the superior race was heightened and deepened in meaning and value so that
it pointed beyond the historical structures of relation, in which it emerged, to
human existence itself. The alleged superior race became and now persists as a
center of value and an object of devotion. Multitudes of men gain their sense of the
"power of being" from their membership in the superior race. Accordingly, the
most deprived white man, culturally and economically, is able to think of himself as
"better'n any nigger."

The purpose of this book [from which this essay is taken] is to provide a
Christian criticism of racism as a faith system in all of its facets and tendencies. By
and large, Christians have failed to recognize racism as an idolatrous faith, even
though it poses the problem of idolatry among Christians in a way that no other
tendency does. Racism is especially problematical not only because of the peculiar
nature of the racist faith, but because it is a "Trojan horse" within organized
Christianity and Christian civic communities.

The procedure which is followed in this book is that of correlating the questions
implied in the racist situation with the relevant answers of the Christian message.
The search for meaning is first pursued from the side of racism. This is followed by
the elaboration of Christian answers which are related to the situation. The use of
the expression "the Christian . . ." in this book is done in full acknowledgment that
a particular theological point of view is represented.

The Christian faith is brought into dialogue with racism for two reasons.
First, I am convinced that Christian faith provides authentic answers to the
questions which racism poses but to which racism is able to provide only false
answers. Second, racism is a phenomenon of modern Christian civilization. By and
large, the people who have been the racists of the modern world have also been
Christians or the heirs of Christian civilization. Among large numbers of Christians,
racism has been the other faith or one of the other faiths.

The phrase "in-race" refers to the race of the speaker who makes the racist
pronouncements or the actor who implements racist aims. The "out-race" is the
ethnic group which is vilified, discriminated against, segregated, exterminated, or is

Source: Racism and the Christian Understanding of Man (New York: Scribner's, 1965),
pp. 19-30, 36-38, 86, 114. Copyright © 1965 George D. Kelsey. Reprinted by permission of
Charles Scribner's Sons.

to be exterminated in the great "eschatological event." The terms "aggressive racism" or "imperialistic racism" are used to describe white racism or racism in power. Black racism or Black Muslimism is referred to as "counter-racism" because it arises as a racist answer to white "imperialistic racism."

Racism has the character of faith in both its imperialistic and counter-racist forms, but an important distinction between the two must be noted. Imperialistic racism is full-bodied. It can walk on its feet and strike with its fists because its spirit permeates the institutions of power. A race as such lacks centeredness. The racist faith must therefore find its life through the use of political, military, economic, and cultural institutions. White men control the political, military, economic, and cultural institutions. Black men do not. Racism among the former is accordingly imperialistic and aggressive. They are able to project and implement concrete programs of political action while the Black Muslims must substitute eschatology for political action. Black Muslimism is racism out of power.

This difference is important to the analysis found in this book. The form of racism is a naturalistic ontology, but its vital principle is the will to power expressed in a political plan of action. Since Black Muslimism lacks power, it is not full-bodied racism. It lacks feet to walk on and fists with which to strike. The spirit is present; the hope is compelling; but the will to power cannot find the institutions of power through which it can express itself. The result of this distinction for this book is the fact that Black Muslimism provides no illustrative material for the study of racism in its most important facet—the plan of political action.

RACISM—MODERN PHENOMENON

Racism is a modern phenomenon. It is a product of modern world conditions. It is a system of meaning and value that could only have arisen out of the peculiar conjunction of modern ideas and values with the political, economic, and technological realities of colonialism and slavery. Various forms of groupism appeared on the stage of history prior to the modern period, but none of them was racist.[1] In the late 1880's, the French racist philosopher Vacher de Lapouge wrote, "I am convinced that in the next century millions will cut each other's throats because of one or two degrees more or less of cephalic index."[2] In this statement, Lapouge gave a strictly modern reason for the mutual slaughter of men.

It is often said that racism has been a perennial problem in human history. But those who make this claim employ the concept of race erroneously. They loosely identify the idea of race with tribal, territorial, national, religious, and cultural groups. It is true that ethnocentrism—the belief in the unique value and rightness of one's own group—is universal as well as perennial. But ethnocentrism does not always take the form of racism.

While the late medieval and early modern Church granted the right of conquest

[1] The Hindu caste system of India is frequently identified with the caste practices of modern racism because it maintains itself primarily by direct blood relationship. But the Indian caste order is not based on color or physical characteristics in the sense that its objective is "purity of blood." The aim of the caste order is to preserve the sacred style of life. Sacred duties and ritualistic requirements are correlated with status and rank, and the community is accordingly preserved.

[2] Quoted in Ruth Benedict, *Race: Science and Politics* (rev. ed.; New York, 1947), p. 3.

and enslavement of the heathen, it nevertheless imposed a responsibility with that right. In the fifteenth century Nicholas V. issued a papal bull authorizing the Portuguese "to attack, subject, and reduce to perpetual slavery the Saracens, pagans, and other enemies of Christ southward of Cape Bojador and Non, including all the coast of Guinea."[3] The condition attached to this authorization was that the captives must be converted to Christianity, and conversion must be followed by manumission. About a century after the bull of Nicholas V, a memorial of the Archbishop of Valencia was issued to Philip III of Spain. This memorial reaffirms the "Christian justification for conquest and enslavement," but it also reflects a new motive. The memorial explicitly affirms the economic motive in addition to that of conversion to Christianity as a justification for slavery.

... *Your majesty may, without any scruple of conscience, make slaves of all the Moriscos and may put them into your own galleys or mines, or sell them to strangers. And as to their children they may be all sold at good rates here in Spain, which will be so far from being a punishment, that it will be a mercy to them; since by that means they will all become Christians. ... By the holy execution of which piece of Justice, a great sum of money will flow into your majesty's treasury.*[4]

Since men are never willing to justify their behavior on the simple claim that might makes right or that their conduct satisfies their interests and desires, a new justification for colonialism and slavery was necessary. A ready-made explanation was at hand. The conquered and enslaved people were dark-skinned. The conquerors were white. Since the white people possessed a superior economic and military technology and were therefore able to conquer and enslave the people of color, it was a simple matter to explain the superiority of the cultural apparatus in terms of a superior human endowment. In other words, the exploiters read from right to left—from a cultural effect to a natural or congenital cause. Thus modern racism emerged as a sort of afterthought, a by-product of the ideological justification of European political and economic power arrangements over colored peoples—the justification of a set of advantages that medieval religious sanctions could no longer sustain.

For this reason, and because racial hostility is most potently manifest on the political and economic planes, many observers mistakenly assume that racism is nothing more than a device by which political, economic, and cultural interests are defended and expanded. Although racism did have its beginnings in a particular constellation of political and economic events in the early modern world, it has developed into an independent phenomenon, possessing meaning and value in itself and giving character to all the institutions of some societies. The cultural phenomenon that made its appearance in modern history as a form of self-justification and a defense of political and economic interests eventually became a complete system of meaning, value, and loyalty.

The fact that racism exists alongside other faiths does not make it any less a faith. Rather, this fact is testimony to the reality of polytheism in the modern age. In its maturity, racism is not a mere ideology that a political demagogue may be expected to affirm or deny, depending upon the political situation in which he finds himself. Racism is a search for meaning. The devotee of the racist faith is as

---

[3] Quoted in Ina Corinne Brown, *Race Relations in a Democracy* (New York, 1949), p. 41.
[4] *Ibid.*, p. 42.

certainly seeking self-identity in his acts of self-exaltation and his self-deifying pronouncements as he is seeking to nullify the selfhood of members of out-races by acts of deprivation and words of vilification.

HUMAN ALIENATION PURELY AND SIMPLY

It is this faith character of racism which makes it the final and complete form of human alienation. Racism is human alienation purely and simply; it is the prototype of all human alienation. It is the one form of human conflict that divides human beings as human beings. That which the racist glorifies in himself is his being. And that which he scorns and rejects in members of out-races is precisely their human being. Although the racist line of demarcation and hostility inevitably finds expression through the institutions of society, it is not primarily a cultural, political, or economic boundary. Rather, it is a boundary of estrangement in the order of human being as such.

Accordingly, the basic racist affirmation of superiority, on the one hand, and inferiority, on the other, is not an empirical generalization as is commonly supposed. Rather, it is an affirmation concerning the fundamental nature of human beings. It is a declaration of faith that is neither supported nor weakened by any objective body of fact. Racism is an expression of the will to believe. The fundamental racist affirmation is that the in-race is glorious and pure as to its being, and out-races are defective and depraved as to their being. Any statement the racist makes concerning the cultural and political achievement, or potential, of the in-race or the out-races is based on this prior judgment concerning human being.

The claim of the racist that he studies the facts of history and arrives inductively at his generalizations is contradicted by his consistently negative response to contrasting situations. For example, when the racist asserts that Negroes cannot learn to operate complicated machinery or that all Jews are dishonest, instances to the contrary do not disturb his confidence in the truth of these generalizations. His confidence is not disturbed because his assertions are not empirical generalizations. The "facts" which the racist claims to be reading from Negro and Jewish character and behavior are in reality "faith" facts. Declarations of faith do not need to be proved from evidences in the objective world of facts. They do not need to be proved because the devotee of a faith is convinced that his faith assertions are reflections of the fundamental order of reality.

Thus when the racist sees Negroes actually operating complicated machinery he dismisses the meaning of what he sees by pointing out that these particular Negroes are "different." He believes that the place of the Negro is fixed in the fundamental order of reality: his status is not a matter of the accidents of history. And when the racist sees Jews who are honest by every objectively discernible standard available, he is still convinced that Jews are dishonest because the honesty of the Jew is Jewish honesty. To the anti-Semitic consciousness, the honesty of the Jew is not the same as the honesty of the Christian or non-Jew. The honesty of the Jew inheres in the Jewish being. Even the virtue of the Jew is therefore vice because it is his because it inheres in defective being.

The claim that racism is human alienation purely and simply may be clarified by comparing racial alienation with other forms of human conflict. All other forms of collective hostility are expressions of conflict over some value or interest that exists *between* men. Human groups contend with each other because they cannot agree on the appropriate relationship each has to some value or values. For example, capital and labor struggle over the definition of their respective shares in the distribution of income from a product or a service. They also contend over their respective rights to power of decision in certain areas of economic process. The nations compete and contend against each other for land, minerals, markets, spheres of influence, and political hegemony. Organized religious bodies struggle with each other over the issues of who possesses the truth, of the proper means for its communication, and of the right to propagate it. Racial alienation stands alone among the forms of human conflict as the one form of collective hostility founded in the question of human being as such. A particular conflict among races may involve political or economic interests, but it is not the political or economic interests that make the conflict racial. The conflict is racial because of the racist faith present in the society involved. Numerous political and economic conflicts occur in one and the same society, but they have a racial character only when two or more racially related groups of that society are in contention. Furthermore, racial antipathy exists and persists in the hearts of men who have no contact whatsoever with the objects of their hostility. A popular saying in many suburbs and small towns of America is, "We do not have the problem because we do not have any of them here." The damaging nature of this claim to the very people who utter it is completely overlooked. It means that if any of *them* do show up, we are ready spiritually and politically to send them reeling back where they came from.

CHRISTIAN RACISM IMPLIES A PEJORATIVE JUDGMENT CONCERNING THE ACTION OF GOD

Since racism assumes some segments of humanity to be defective in essential being, and since for Christians all being is from the hand of God, racism alone among the idolatries calls into question the divine creative action. The central claim of the racist is fundamentally a proposition concerning the nature of creation and the action of God rather than a doctrine concerning the nature of man. By implication, one part of the primary racist affirmation is the idea that God has made a creative error in bringing out-races into being. For Christians, the only possible theological alternative to the implication that God has made a creative error is the doctrine that out-races are the victims of a double fall. If the doctrine of the Demiurge had triumphed in Christianity, a third theological ground for explaining the existence of out-races would be available. But in the Gnostic controversies of the early Church the concept of the Demiurge was relegated to the limbo of heresy. In accounting for the origin of out-races, the Black Muslims enjoy a decided advantage over Christian racists. The creation mythology of the Black Muslims contains a Demiurge as the creator of the white man.

While Christian racists never appeal to the notion of the Demiurge to account for the nature of the existence of out-races, the doctrine of a second fall is explicitly enunciated in some naïve and obscurantist circles. The usual form of this theological proposition is the assertion that God himself has condemned Negroes to be "the hewers of the wood and drawers of the water now henceforth and forever" under the curse of Ham. A variation of the doctrine is the notion that Negroes are the descendants of Cain's union with an ape whom Cain, the first criminal, saw fit to marry "in the land of Nod."[5] This means that while the Negro shares the universal condemnation of the human race in Adam, he also bears the added condemnation of God in a special, racial fall. Since no promise of renewal and redemption is ever correlated with this second, special, racial fall, the Negro is a permanent victim of history and ultimately without hope. Whether the defectiveness in the humanity of out-races be an implication of the nature of creation or an explicit affirmation concerning a special, racial fall, the conclusion cannot be avoided that the action of God is the primary point of reference for Christian racists.

THE FAITH CHARACTER OF RACISM

As a doctrine concerning the fundamental nature of human beings and a way of life elaborated on that doctrine, racism is a faith. H. Richard Niebuhr defines faith as "trust in that which gives value to the self," on the one hand; and on the other, "it is loyalty to what the self values."[6] It is in this sense that we speak of the racist faith.

In the experience of faith, the devotee has a double relation to the object of faith. He trusts in it as the source of his personal value, and at the same time he is loyal to the object of his faith for the value it possesses independent of himself. Niebuhr illustrates this double relation in the life of the patriot whose faith is nationalism. The experience of the racist corresponds to that of the patriot, with the difference that the racist deifies his own being rather than an objective historic structure. The racist relies on the race as the source of his personal value. His life has meaning and worth because it is a part of the racial context. It fits into and merges with a valuable whole, the race. As the value-center, the race is the source of value, and it is at the same time the object of value. No questions can be raised about the rightness or wrongness of the race; it is the value-center which throws light on all other value. Criminals, degenerates, and even enemies have worth and goodness if they are members of the in-race. They have a goodness and worth which is not found in the most noble character of members of out-races, for goodness and worth are only secondarily qualities of behavior and character. Primarily they are qualities of being. Goodness and worth inhere in being that is worthy. If noble character inheres in a racially defective being, that person of noble character is nonetheless depraved, for the nobility he has achieved inheres in his unalterably corrupt humanity.

When the racist is also a Christian, which is often the case in America, he is frequently a polytheist. Historically, in polytheistic faiths, various gods have controlled various spheres of authority. Thus a Christian racist may think he lives under the requirements of the God of biblical faith in most areas of his life, but whenever matters of race impinge on his life, in every area so affected, the idol of race determines his attitude, decision, and action.

Polytheistic faith has been nowhere more evident than in that sizable group of

[5] The idea of a racial fall is also ascribed to the Jews. It is the view, held by some Christians, that since the Jews are the chosen people, God has punished them and will continue to punish them until they acknowledge the Messiah. Thus the persecutions of Jews by Christians are preordained.

[6] H. Richard Niebuhr, *Radical Monotheism and Western Culture* (New York, 1960), p. 16.

Christians who take the position that racial traditions and practices in America are in no sense a religious matter. These people assert that the whole field of race relations is an area with which religion has nothing to do. When pressed for a positive statement of the matter, they say that segregationist racial practices are merely amoral expressions of private preference. They completely overlook the fact that race relations are structured as a system which is not only enforced by the social mores but by institutional policy over all the country, and in some sections of the country, by law and public policy as well. The judgment that race relations involve amoral forms of behavior means in effect that interracial attitudes and practices are beyond the reach of Christian moral ideas and norms. The presence of polytheism among the adherents of the greatest monotheistic religion is not shocking in view of the insights of that very religion concerning original sin. The Old Testament provides ample historical evidence of man's continuous effort to restrict the Covenant of the Lord so that he may pursue certain interests and values as he sees fit. The prophetic tradition makes it equally clear that the only alternative to the worship of and obedience to the Lord God Jehovah is devotion to the Baals of the Canaanites.

It is an anomaly that morally concerned Christian leaders have rarely understood racism for what it really is. For a long time racist ideas and practices were viewed by morally sensitive Christians as nothing more than expressions of cultural lag and as products of ignorance. Since racial hostility is one of the forms of human conflict, many Christians have sought to understand racism wholly in terms of political, economic, and cultural factors. They have not seen the faith character of racist devotion and commitment, nor that racial antipathy is conflict in the order of humanity. A probable explanation of this peculiar state of affairs is that modern Christianity and Christian civilization have domesticated racism so thoroughly that most Christians stand too close to assess it properly.

THE MEANING OF RACISM

The faith character of racism may be fully disclosed by an analysis of its various facets. In her *Race: Science and Politics,* Ruth Benedict defines racism as

the dogma that one ethnic group is condemned by Nature to hereditary inferiority and another group is destined to hereditary superiority. It is the dogma that the hope of civilization depends upon eliminating some races and keeping others pure. It is the dogma that one race has carried progress throughout human history and can alone ensure future progress. [7]

From this definition, it may be seen first of all that racism is a form of naturalism. Man owes his existence to nature and nature controls his destiny. Nature has condemned inferior races and blessed the superior race. This means that the fundamental thing about a man is his body, specifically his genetic structure. Mental and spiritual qualities depend upon the natural quality, and are, in fact, but expressions of it.

This naturalistic view of man is diametrically opposed to the biblical doctrine of the creation of man in the image of God; it is also opposed to the main tendencies in the development of Western philosophy. One of the great anomalies of our time

[7] Benedict, *op. cit.,* p. 98.

is the fact that the racist ideology has taken so firm a grasp upon the heirs of both traditions, and has emerged in the modern world which is precisely that world wherein philosophy and theology broke their esoteric bonds, and became widely available, at least in their main ideas, through popular education.

It must be observed that not all people who understand man naturalistically in the context of race relations subscribe to the naturalistic doctrine in general. Some Christians would be horrified to discover that they really believe in a naturalistic view of man when race relations call for decision and action. If told that this is the case, they will vigorously deny it. Many of them are quite orthodox in their theology and even literalistic in their approach to the Bible. In the abstract, they constantly repeat the phrase that God has created all men in His own image. In the abstract, they believe that the essence of man is spirit. But when they actually view the races in relation to each other, or make social and political decisions concerning race, they bring judgments to bear upon the situation which clearly indicate their belief that the races are poles apart in the order of humanity and that the ground of the great human differences lies in the genes.

The fact that racist claims are affirmations concerning the fundamental nature of humanity, rather than empirical generalizations as they are popularly thought to be, may be made more evident by a few illustrations. During the last war, General J. L. DeWitt was in charge of the evacuation of naturalized Japanese from California. General DeWitt made the following statement concerning Japanese Americans: "A Jap's a Jap. . . . It makes no difference whether he is an American citizen or not. . . . I don't want any of them here. . . . They are a dangerous element. . . . There is no way to determine their loyalty."[8] In another statement, General DeWitt made it unqualifiedly clear that the element which he regarded as evil within the Japanese character is incorrigible because it is rooted in the genetic structure. "The Japanese race is an enemy race and while many second and third generation Japanese born on United States soil, possessed of United States citizenship, have been 'Americanized' the racial strains are undiluted."[9]

KNOWLEDGE OF THE SELF IN ANTITHETICAL RELATION TO THE OTHER

The racist consciousness operates in what Martin Buber has called "the World of It."[10] The World of It is the world of objects and things. In this world there is a single center of consciousness. This single subject, the "I," experiences, arranges, and appropriates. It does not enter into relationship with other, different beings. It experiences human beings racially different from itself only as "the other," as antithetical to the self in the order of humanity. The "I" self "knows" itself as pure being while it "knows" the other as depraved being. The "I" self does not enter into communion with the other, for the other is not known as "Thou." The other is first, last, and always "It." The other is an object to be used, manipulated, or eliminated. But since the other in fact belongs to the order of human being, and not

[8] U.S. Army, Western Defense Command and Fourth Army, Final Report, Japanese Evacuation from the West Coast, 1942 (Washington, D.C., Government Printing Office, 1943), p. 34; quoted in Charles Abrams, *Forbidden Neighbors* (New York, 1955), p. 41.
[9] *Ibid.*
[10] Martin Buber, *I and Thou*, trans. Ronald Gregor Smith (New York, 1937).

merely to the animal kingdom, the relation of the self to the other is on a different plane than the relation of the self to the worlds of animality and nature. The self is aware that the other is in some sense a center of consciousness. The fact that the other in some way belongs on the same plane with the self will not down. The radical contrast between the self and the other can therefore be expressed only in polar terms. The racist consciousness knows itself in contrast, in polarity with and opposition to the racially contemptible object. This means that in the racial context, the racist cannot know himself until he first knows the other. The racist is completely dependent upon the antithetical correlation. When the other is properly experienced, appropriated, and arranged, the racist consciousness can know itself as the other pole in a structure of human contrasts.

The idea that the Negro appears in the anti-Negro consciousness as a contrast conception was ably presented by Lewis Copeland about a generation ago, but very little has been made of this notion in the literature of race relations. Copeland found the social opposition between Negroes and whites so sharp as to give rise to a conceptual dichotomy "somewhat analogous to that between God and the devil in popular religion."[11] And just as in popular religion the contrast between God and the devil introduces a dichotomy which is conceived as running through the whole universe, dividing both the natural world and the social order, the counterconcepts of the racist consciousness "form the basis for the interpretation of human nature and society."[12]

The idea of the contrast conception as a basic constituent of the racist self-consciousness seems to have originated with Erich Voegelin. In his *Rasse und Staat,* Voegelin develops the thesis that Judaism in Christian Germany is a counterconception. Likewise, Jean-Paul Sartre, writing on French anti-Semitism, designates the Jew as a contrast conception. When the anti-Semite speaks of Jewish avarice, says Sartre, he means there is a "Jewish" avarice, an avarice determined by that synthetic whole, the Jewish person. This avarice is different from Christian avarice. It is not the universal, human trait of avarice, but an avarice which emerges from a unique synthesis, the Jewish being.

In popular thought in America, black and white have become conceptual opposites.

The black man and his appurtenances stand at the antithesis of the character and properties of the white man. The conception makes of the Negro a counter-race. The black race serves as a foil for the white race, by which the character of the latter is made all the more impressive.[13]

The antipodal positions of the two races are often verbalized in the phrase "the opposite race." In its fullest meaning, the word "opposite" is a reference to more than the extremes of color. It suggests the two opposites of human being. An examination of the counter-racist consciousness discloses the same element. Eric Lincoln writes:

To a great extent the Muslims define their movement by negative contrast to their most important audiences; Negroes, Jews, the orthodox Moslems in America and the hated whites.

[11] Lewis C. Copeland, "The Negro as a Contrast Conception," in Edgar T. Thompson, ed., *Race Relations and the Race Problem* (Durham, N.C., 1939), p. 152.
[12] *Ibid.*
[13] Copeland, *op. cit.*, p. 153.

They assert their strength and purity by castigating the weakness and depravity they claim to see among these strangers.[14]

To the Black Muslim, knowledge of the self has its corollary in "the truth about the white man."[15] The Black Muslim therefore cannot "know" himself until he first "knows" the white man. Knowledge of "the truth about the white man" produces knowledge of the self as the opposite in the order of human being.

THE CHRISTIAN DOCTRINE OF EQUALITY

The Christian doctrine of equality is an affirmation of faith. It is not a perception of sight. It is an affirmation of faith because it relates solely to the action of God, and not to the achievements of men or to any intrinsic quality which men may possess. Men are equal because God has created them in His own image and called them to sonship. The Christian doctrine of equality does not draw at all upon measurements of talent and merit. It is a doctrine concerning the creative gift of God.

There is ample evidence in history that men are unequal in knowledge, skill, power, and cultural achievements in general. Most of life is organized and proceeds on the assumption of these inequalities. Men of sight, rather than faith, are obviously much more impressed and influenced by historically conditioned and structured inequalities than by any doctrines of equality, philosophical or theological. But the conviction that men are equal in some fundamental sense has not been destroyed in the West, despite the ideological claims to the contrary or widespread practices that belie the idea. The Western democracies have developed a relatively high degree of political equalitarianism at the very moment in history when disproportions of power, wealth, knowledge, and skill are great and numerous as never before. An important influence in this development has been Christian teaching concerning man.

When Christian faith speaks of equality, it refers to the action and purpose of God. God has created all men in His own image and called all men to the same destiny. The decision as to whether or not men are equal cannot be made by looking at men; he who would decide must look at God. God alone is the source of human dignity. All men are equal because God has bestowed upon all the very same dignity. He has created them in His own image and herein lies their dignity. Human dignity is not an achievement, nor is it an intrinsic quality; it is a gift, a bestowal. Christian faith asserts that men are equally human; all are creatures and all are potentially spiritual sons of God. Variations in the talents and skills of culture rest upon this fundamental humanness.

Thus Christian faith affirms the unity of mankind. The idea of the unity of mankind is another way of expressing the essential likeness of man. Modern science supports the claim of biblical faith that mankind is a unity, but it is not upon empirical evidence that the biblical conviction is based. The conviction of faith is independent of all scientific results because creation stands above the historical and empirical planes.

[14] Eric Lincoln, *The Black Muslims in America* (Boston, 1961), p. 135.
[15] *Ibid.*, p. 190.

The religious belief in the unity of the human race through the Creation, in and for the Divine image, is completely independent of all biological, palaeontological, scientific results. The story of Adam in Genesis expresses, in historical form, it is true, a fact which in itself is super-empirical and super-historical; the biological genealogical question has very little to do with belief in the unity of the creation. . . . The unity of the divine creation of man lies upon a quite different plane. Humanity is not necessarily a unity from a zoological point of view; it may indeed be composed of different species of differing origin or it may not. It is, however, beyond all doubt a unity, a humanitas, "through" the humanum, its one origin and its one destiny in God's creative Word and plan of salvation, spiritually given to man by God himself.[16]

It is upon the foundation of the equal humanness of men that democratic rights are established. The American Declaration of Independence asserts that "all men are created equal." This proposition was never intended to mean that all men are equal in capacity, knowledge, and skill. Yet it does have concrete political significance. It means that there are some rights that belong to persons as persons, as creatures of God. These rights are said to be inalienable for the very reason that they belong to every person as a person. They can no more be transferred from one person to another than personhood itself can be transferred. And to deny these rights is identical with denying the reality of the person. Inalienable rights are primal. They exist prior to the performance of any function, and are the foundation upon which all secondary and derived rights are elaborated. The rights of the individual as man are primary and unique. All particularized rights are secondary and derived. They derive from the social organization of life and belong to persons only in the exercise of their particular technical, professional, and institutional functions.

Not only does the idea of equal human dignity place the stress on the likeness and unity of mankind and thus constitute the foundation for all assessment of human rights; it also combines harmoniously with unlikeness and inequality. The essential rights of the individual are primary and universal; but individual rights combine harmoniously with derived and differentiated rights relating to historic function because individuality and community are equally original in God's creative act. Man is the covenant-partner of God and of man from the creation. But each man is also created a unique being, with his own individuality. Thus equal dignity and likeness are united with individuality and unlikeness in the Christian doctrine of creation.

The Christian doctrine of individuality and unlikeness is radically opposed to racist particularism. In the Christian idea, individuality means unlikeness and inequality in community. But in the racist idea, individuality does not exist: the individual is made faceless in a homogenized collectivity. Unlikeness and inequality are alleged to be characteristics of racial collectivities rather than individuals. While even the racist is obliged to admit the reality of inequality and unlikeness within races, it is only the alleged inequalities between races that have significance for him. Christian faith knows of unlikeness and inequality only as between individuals. But since individuality is always related to community which is also original in God's plan for man, inequality and equality are harmoniously combined.

The Christian conception of equality is inseparable from the idea of person in community. The two elements of equality and inequality, of equal dignity and different function, are both fully expressed. They are brought together in the

---

[16] Emil Brunner, *Man in Revolt,* trans. Olive Wyon (London, 1939), p. 333.

Christian idea of communion. The fact that men are different from each other means that they are dependent on each other. In a Christian community, men will to serve each other in their mutual dependence. The one recognizes his dependence upon the other, no matter how lowly the occupation of the other may be in the eyes of the world. There are so many respects in which one man may be superior or inferior to another that there is probably no man who is superior or inferior to another in every respect. The unity of mankind is made the more manifest by the inequalities which have their basis in individuality.

The Christian idea of the unity of mankind finds concrete expression in societies of mutual cooperation and helpfulness. Differences of function create of necessity variations in status and role in institutional structures. But the roles and statuses in these institutions are assigned on the strength of real individual differences. They are not, as in racism, based upon hostile power arrangements, upon the results of previous discriminations, or upon invidious comparisons that falsify the nature of man as a creature of God.

DESEGREGATION AND INTEGRATION

In the field of race relations, American society is in a state of flux. Within the last decade, social change in this field has reached revolutionary proportions. Since American society is, and has been to a great degree, a color-caste society, the terms "desegregation" and "integration" are now in constant use. These terms belong together, but they do not mean the same thing. Desegregation refers to a process—the elimination of compulsory segregation. Desegregation may be voluntary or involuntary. It is voluntary when those who administer and make the policies of an institution freely decide to change its policy from one of racial exclusivism to one of racial inclusivism. It is involuntary when law, judicial decision, or public pressure requires such a change. Integration refers to a realized condition of community, involving mutuality, reciprocity, and respect among persons. Integration is voluntary and spiritual. The two terms belong together because in a racially segregated society, by and large, people of different racial groups lack the simple conditions and experience of togetherness upon which integration can exist without the prior process of desegregation.

Desegregation is referred to as a prior process because the mere "mixing" of the races is not integration. There is much desegregation in the United States outside the South but little integration. Integration requires more of persons than the mere removal of the external barriers and distances that separate them. But the transition from a segregated to an integrated society cannot be made without the process of removing the external barriers. The simple experiences of doing things together, such as working, playing, learning, etc., provide the foundation upon which genuine community can grow.

A society may be referred to as integrated when it has become a community of persons.

In the deepest sense, integration has taken place only when those of another race or class are accepted as full and equal partners in a common task. It is based on mutual respect and on a sense of the dignity and worth of the human person.[17]

[17] Maston, *op. cit.*, p. 63.

An integrated society is one in which there is both a sense of and a will toward the common good. The common good is received through and communicated by persons. This means that an integrated society is one in which the individual person comes alive. It is not really the group which accepts or respects another group; it is, rather, a community of persons who accept and respect each other. In such a society, all definitions of function and opportunity presuppose the equal dignity of persons. Men are thus able in defining tasks to focus on those qualities of the individual person which are really related to performance; namely talent, training, knowledge, and skill. Extraneous issues, such as the question, "Who is your mother?" do not enter into the decision as to whether a man shall be permitted to study law in the state university. His admission to the law school rests on such criteria as his individual character, ability, and the quality of his prelegal training. And these are precisely the same criteria which every other person must individually meet in the society.

An integrated society in no sense reduces the individual. It is the one society in which a person can at all times be a person. In racially segregated society, parochialism and prideful separation are normative values. Lest some people fail to interiorize these values, they are forced by law and custom to "keep step" in their external behavior. Thus a white man is required by law to relate to a Negro as a white man; he is not permitted to relate to him as a creature of God or as a religiously committed person. Obviously, the same law regulates the goings, comings, and doings of the Negro, except that it specifies that he remain "outside" or "beneath," in all matters pertaining to the larger society. To dare to act in a legally segregated society as a member of a more universal community of love than a racial community can provide is often to court imprisonment. An integrated society is, on the contrary, a community in which persons have become persons. They remain persons in all their relationships, for even professional and technical functions are exercised by persons.

The objection may rightly be raised that an authentic community of persons does not exist anywhere on a large scale; and accordingly, a truly integrated society, with or without a history of racial alienation, is an ideal. But to say this is not to dismiss such a society as a human and Christian requirement. Man never fully achieves any of his ideals that have the quality of the transcendent, but they are nevertheless incumbent upon him. In truth, an authentic community of persons would be a society of pure persons in which "the good of society and the good of each person would be one and the same good."[18] Although such a society is never fully realized, nevertheless it can be in process of realization if its ideal of the common good is informed and urged by that which transcends itself.

A society is integrated and is a genuine community of persons when it exists under God in fact. The community of persons is found in the common bond of the Spirit. The common good of society escapes every form of particularism—racial, class, religious, or otherwise—because the center of meaning and value transcends the society.

[18] Jacques Maritain, *The Person and the Common Good* (New York, 1947), p. 50.

The Black Movement and Women's Liberation

Linda La Rue

Linda Jo La Rue was a graduate student in political science at Purdue University. She was one of twenty-four students to be awarded the coveted Marshall fellowship for study in England in 1969. She plans to do further study at Cornell University in Asian and Third World studies.

Let us first discuss what common literature addresses as the "common oppression" of blacks and women. This is a tasty abstraction designed purposely or inadvertently to draw validity and seriousness to the women's movement through a universality of plight. Every movement worth its "revolutionary salt" makes these headliner generalities about "common oppression" with others—but let us state unequivocally that, with few exceptions, the American white woman has had a better opportunity to live a free and fulfilling life, both mentally and physically, than any other group in the United States, with the exception of her white husband. Thus, any attempt to analogize black oppression with the plight of the American white woman has the validity of comparing the neck of a hanging man with the hands of an amateur mountain climber with rope burns.

"Common oppression" is fine for rhetoric, but it does not reflect the actual distance between the oppression of the black man and woman who are unemployed, and the "oppression" of the American white woman who is "sick and tired" of *Playboy* fold-outs, or Christian Dior lowering hemlines or adding ruffles, or of Miss Clairol telling her that blondes have more fun.

Is there any logical comparison between the oppression of the black woman on welfare who has difficulty feeding her children and the discontent of the suburban mother who has the luxury to protest the washing of the dishes on which her family's full meal was consumed.

The surge of "common oppression" rhetoric and propaganda may lure the unsuspecting into an intellectual alliance with the goals of women's liberation, but it is not a wise alliance. It is not that women ought not to be liberated from the shackles of their present unfulfillment, but the depth, the extent, the intensity, the importance—indeed, the suffering and depravity of the *real* oppression blacks have experienced—can only be minimized in an alliance with women who heretofore suffered little more than boredom, genteel repression, and dishpan hands.

For all the similarities and analogies drawn between the liberation of women and the liberation of blacks, the point remains that when white women received their voting rights, most blacks, male and female, were systematically disenfranchised and had been that way since Reconstruction. And even in 1970 [year this essay was written], when women's right of franchise is rarely questioned, it is still a less than common occurrence for blacks to vote in some areas of the South.

Source: The Black Scholar, May 1970, pp. 36-42. Reprinted by permission.

Tasteless analogies like abortion for oppressed middle class and poor women idealistically assert that all women have the right to decide if and when they want children, and thus fail to catch the flavor of the actual circumstances. Actual circumstances boil down to middle class women deciding when it is convenient to have children, while poor women decide the prudence of bringing into a world of already scarce resources, another mouth to feed. Neither their motives nor their objectives are the same. But current literature leads one to lumping the decisions of these two women under one generalization, when in fact the difference between the plights of these two women is as clear as the difference between being hungry and out of work, and skipping lunch and taking a day off.

If we are realistically candid with ourselves, and accept the fact that despite our beloved rhetoric of Pan-Africanism, our vision of third world liberation, and perhaps our dreams of a world state of multi-racial humanism, most blacks and a good many who generally exempt themselves from categories, still want the proverbial "piece of cake." American values are difficult to discard for, unlike what more militant "brothers" would have us believe, Americanism does not end with the adoption of Afro hairstyles on pregnant women covered in long African robes.

.   .   .

The study of many developing areas and countries reflects at least an attempt to allow freedom of education and opportunity to women. Yet, black Americans have not adopted developing area's "new role" paradigm, but rather the Puritan-American status of "home and babies," which is advocated by the capitalist Muslims. This reflects either ingrained Americanism or the lack of the simplest imagination.

Several weeks ago, women's lib advocates demanded that a local women's magazine be "manned" by a woman editor. Other segments of the women's movement have carried on a smaller campaign in industry and business.

If white women have heretofore remained silent while white men maintained the better position and monopolized the opportunities by excluding blacks, can we really expect that white women, when put in direct competition for employment, will be any more open-minded than their male counterparts when it comes to the hiring of black males and females in the same positions for which they are competing? From the standpoint of previous American social interaction, it does not seem logical that white females will not be tempted to take advantage of the fact that they are white, in an economy that favors whites. It is entirely possible that women's liberation has developed a sudden attachment to the black liberation movement as a ploy to share the attention that it has taken blacks 400 years to generate. In short, it can be argued that women's liberation not only attached itself to the black movement, but did so with only marginal concern for black women and black liberation, and functional concern for the rights of white women.

The industrial demands of two world wars temporarily offset the racial limitations to mobility and allowed the possibility of blacks entering industry, as an important labor force, to be actualized. Similarly, women have benefited from an expanded science and industrialization. Their biological limitation, successfully curbed by the pill and by automation, which makes stressing physical labor more the exception than the rule, has created an impressively large and available labor force of women.

The black labor force, never fully employed and always representing a substantial percentage of the unemployed in the American economy, will now be driven into greater unemployment as white women converge at every level on an already dwindling job market.

Ideally, we chanced to think of women's liberation as a promising beginning of the "oppressed rising everywhere" in the typically Marxian fashion that many blacks seem drawn to. Instead, the spectre of racism and inadequate education, job discrimination, and even greater unequal opportunity will be, more than ever before, a function of neither maleness nor femaleness, but blackness.

This discussion has been primarily to ward off any unintelligent alliance of black people with white women in this new liberation movement. Rhetoric and anathema hurled at the right industrial complex, idealism which speaks of a final humanism, and denunciations of the system which makes competition a fact of life, do not mean that women's liberation has as its goal anyone else's liberation except its own.

It is time that definitions be made clear. Blacks are *oppressed*, and that means unreasonably burdened, unjustly, severely, rigorously, cruelly and harshly fettered by white authority. White women, on the other hand, are only *suppressed*, and that means checked, restrained, excluded from conscious and overt activity. And there is a difference.

For some, the dangers of an unintelligent alliance with women's liberation will suggest female suppression as the only way to protect against a new economic threat. For others, a greater answer is needed, and required, before women's liberation can be seen in perspective.

To say that black women must be freed before the black movement can attain full revolutionary consciousness, is meaningless because of its malleability. To say that black women must be freed from the unsatisfactory male-female role relationship which we adopted from whites as the paradigm of the good family, has more meaning because it indicates the incompatibility of white role models with the goal of black liberation. If there is anything to be learned from the current women's lib agitation, it is that roles are not ascribed and inherent, but adopted and interchangeable in every respect except pregnancy, breastfeeding and the system generally employed to bring the two former into existence.

Role integration, which I will elaborate upon as the goal and the strength of the black family, is substantially different from the role "usurpation" of men by women. The fact that the roles of man and woman are deemed in American society as natural and divine, leads to false ego attachments to these roles. During slavery and following Reconstruction, black men felt inferior for a great number of reasons, among them that they were unable to work in positions comparable to the ones to which black women were assigned. With these positions often went fringe benefits of extra food, clothes, and perhaps elementary reading and writing skills. Black women were in turn jealous of white women, and felt inadequate and inferior because paraded in front of them constantly was the white woman of luxury who had no need for work, who could, as Sojourner Truth pointed out, "be helped into carriages, and lifted over ditches, and . . . have the best place everywhere."

The resulting "respect" for women and the acceptance of the dominating role for men, encouraged the myth of the immutability of these roles. The term "matriarchy" Frazier employed and Moynihan exploited, was used to indicate a dastardly unnatural role alteration which could be blamed for inequality of opportunity, discrimination in hiring and sundry other ills. It was as if "matriarchy" was transgression of divine law or natural law, and thus would be punished until the proper hierarchy of man over woman was restored.

Black people have an obligation, as do white women, to recognize that the designation of "mother-head" and "father-head" does not imply inferiority of one and the superiority of the other. They are merely arbitrary role distinctions which vary from culture to culture and circumstance to circumstance.

Thus to quip, as it has been popularly done, that the only place in the black movement for black women, is prone, is actually supporting a white role ideal, and it is neither a compliment to men or women to advocate such sexual capitalism or sexual colonialism.

It seems incongruous that the black movement has sanctioned the revolutionary involvement of women in the Algerian revolution, even though its revolutionary circumstances modified and often alternated the common role models, but have been duped into hating even their own slave grandmothers who, in not so admirable yet equally frightening and demanding circumstances, also modified and altered the common role models of the black family. Fanon wrote in glorious terms about this role change:

The unveiled Algerian woman, who assumed an increasingly important place in revolutionary action, developed her personality, discovered the exalting realm of responsibility. . . . This woman who, in the avenues of Algiers or of Constantine, would carry the grenades or the submachine gun charges, the woman who tomorrow would be outraged, violated, tortured, could not put herself back into her former state of mind and relive her behavior of the past. . . . [1]

Can it not be said that in slavery black women assumed an increasingly important place in the survival action and thus developed their personalities and sense of responsibility? And after being outraged, violated and tortured, could she be expected to put herself back into her former state of mind and relive her behavior of the past?

The crux of this argument is essentially that blacks, since slavery and through their entire existence in America, have also been living in revolutionary circumstances and under revolutionary pressures. Simply because the black liberation struggle has taken 400 years to come to fruition does not mean that it is not every bit as dangerous or psychologically exhausting as the Algerian struggle. Any revolution calls upon the best in both its men and women. This is why Moynihan's statements that "matriarchy" is a root *cause* of black problems is as unfounded as it is inane. He does not recognize the liberation struggle and the demands that it has made on the black family.

How unfortunate that blacks and whites have allowed the most trying and bitter experience in the history of black people to be interpreted as the beginning of an "unashamed plot" to usurp the very manhood of black men. But the myth was perpetuated, and thus what brought the alternation of roles in Algeria was distorted and systematically employed to separate black men and women in America.

Black women take kindness for weakness. Leave them the least little opening and they will put you on the cross. . . . It would be like trying to pamper a cobra. . . . [2]

[1] Frantz Fanon, *A Dying Colonialism,* New York: Grove Press, 1965, p. 107.
[2] Eldridge Cleaver, *Soul on Ice,* New York: McGraw-Hill, 1968, p. 158.

Unless we realize how thoroughly the American value of male superiority and female inferiority has permeated our relationships with each other, we can never appreciate the role it plays in perpetuating racism and keeping black people divided.

Most, but not all, American relationships are based on some type of "exclusive competition of the superior, and the exclusive competition of the inferior." This means essentially that the poor, the uneducated, the deprived and the minorities of the aforementioned groups, compete among themselves for the same scarce resources and inferior opportunities, while the privileged, middle-class, educated, and select white minorities, compete with each other for rather plentiful resources and superior opportunities for prestige and power. Competition among groups is rare, due to the fact that elements who qualify are almost invariably absorbed to some extent (note the black middle-class) by the group to which they seek entry. We may well understand that there is only one equal relationship between man and woman, black and white, in America, and this equality is based on whether or not you can force your way into qualifying for the same resources.

But instead of attempting to modify this competitive definition within the black movement, many black males have affirmed it as a way of maintaining the closure of male monopolization of scarce benefits and making the "dominion of males" impenetrable to black females. This is, of course, very much the American way of exploitation.

The order of logic which makes it possible to pronounce, as did Dr. Robert Staples, that "black women cannot be free qua women until all blacks attain their liberation,"[3] maintains, whether purposely or not, that black women will be able to separate their femaleness from their blackness and thus they would be able to be free as blacks, if not free as woman; or, that male freedom ought to come first; or, finally, that the freedom of black women and men, and the freedom of black people as a whole, are not one and the same.

Only with the concept of role integration can we hope to rise above the petty demarcations of human freedom that America is noted for, and that are unfortunately inherent in Dr. Staples' remark. Role integration is the realization that:

- ego attachments to particular activities or traits must be abolished as a method of determining malehood and femalehood; that instead, ego attachments must be distributed to a wider variety of tasks and traits in order to weaken the power of one activity in determining self-worth, and

- the flexibility of a people in effecting role alternation and role integration has been an historically proven asset to the survival of any people—witness Israel, China and Algeria.

Thus, the unwitting adoption and the knowing perpetuation of this American value reflects three inter-related situations:

- black people's growing sense of security and well-being, and their failure to recognize the expanse of black problems;

- black people's over-identification with the dominant group, even though the survival of blacks in America is not assured, and

- black people's belief in the myth of "matriarchy" and their subsequent rejection of role integration as unnatural and unnecessary.

[3] Robert Staples, "The Myth of the Black Matriarchy," *The Black Scholar*, Jan.-Feb. 1970, p. 16.

If white radical thought has called upon the strength of all women to take a position of responsibility and power, can blacks afford to relegate black women to "home and babies" while white women reinforce the status quo?

The cry of black women's liberation is a cry against chaining a very much needed labor force and agitating force to a role that once belonged to impotent, apolitical white women. Blacks speak lovingly of the vanguard and the importance of women in the struggle, and yet fail to recognize that women have been assigned a new place, based on white ascribed characteristics of women, rather than on their actual potential. The black movement needs its women in a position of struggle, not prone. The struggle blacks face is not taking place between knives and forks, at the washboard, or in the diaper pail. It is taking place on the labor market, at the polls, in government, in the protection of black communities, in local neighborhood power struggles, in housing and in education.

Can blacks afford to be so unobservant of current events as to send their women to fight a non-existent battle in a dishpan?

Even now, the black adoption of the white values of women has begun to show its effects on black women in distinctive ways. The black liberation movement has created a politicized, unliberated copy of white womanhood. Black women who participated in the struggle have failed to recognize, for the most part, the unique contradiction between renunciation of capitalistic competition and the acceptance of sexual colonialism. The failure of the black movement to resolve and deal with this dilemma has perpetuated the following attitudes in American politicized black women:

• The belief in the myth of matriarchy. The black woman has been made to feel ashamed of her strength, and so to redeem herself she has adopted from whites the belief that superiority and dominance by the male is the most "natural" and "normal" relationship. She consequently believes that black women ought to be suppressed in order to attain that "natural balance."

• Because the white woman's role has been held up as an example to all black women, many black women feel inadequate and so ardently compete in "femininity" with white females for black males' attention. She further competes with black females in an attempt to be the "blackest and the most feminine," thereby, the more superior to her fellow black sisters in appealing to black politicized men. She competes also with the apolitical black female in an attempt to keep black males from "regressing" back to females whom she feels have had more "practice" in the traditional role of white women than has she.

• Finally, she emphasizes the traditional roles of women, such as housekeeping, children, supportive roles, and self-maintenance, but she politicizes these roles by calling them the role of black women. She then adopts the attitude that her job and her life is to have more children which can be used in the vanguard of the black struggle.

Black women, as the song "Black Pearl" relates, have been put up where they belong, but by American standards. Is it so inconceivable that the American value of respect and human relationships is distorted? It has taken the birth of women's liberation to bring the black movement back to its senses.

The black woman is demanding a new set of female definitions and a recognition of herself as a citizen, companion and confidant, not a matriarchal villain or a step stool baby-maker. Role integration advocates the complementary recognition of man and woman, not the competitive recognition of the same.

The recent, unabated controversy over the use of birth control in the black community is of grave importance here. Black people, even the "most liberated of mind," are still infused with ascribed inferiority of females and the natural superiority of males. These same values foster the idea of "good blood" in children. If, indeed there can be any black liberation, it must start with the recognition of contradictions like the following.

It gives a great many black males pride to speak, as Dr. Robert Staples does, of "... the role of the black woman in the black liberation struggle is an important one and cannot be forgotten. From her womb have come the revolutionary warriors of our time."[4]

How many potential revolutionary warriors stand abandoned in orphanages while blacks rhetorize disdain for birth control as a "trick of the man" to halt the growth of black population? Why are there not more revolutionary couples adopting black children? Could it be that the American concept of bastard, which is equivalent to inferior in our society, reflects black anglo-saxonism? Do blacks, like whites, discriminate against black babies because they do not represent "our own personal" image? Or do blacks, like the most racist of whites, require that a child be of their own blood before they can love that child or feed it? Does the vanguard, of which Dr. Staples so reverently speaks, recognize the existence of the term "bastard"?

Someone once suggested that the word "bastard" be deleted from the values of black people. Would it not be more revolutionary for blacks to advocate a five-year moratorium on black births until every black baby in an American orphanage was adopted by one or more black parents? Then blacks could really have a valid reason for continuing to give birth. Children would mean more than simply a role for black women to play, or fuel for the legendary vanguard. Indeed, blacks would be able to tap the potential of the existing children and could sensibly add more potential to the black struggle for liberation. To do this would be to do something no other civilization, modern of course, has ever done, and blacks would be allowing every black child to have a home and not just a plot in some understaffed children's penal farm.

What makes a healthy black baby in an orphanage different from "our own flesh and blood"? Except for the American value of inferiority-superiority, and the concept of "bastard" that accompanies it, there is nothing "wrong" with the orphaned child save what white society has taught us to perceive.

We can conclude that black women's liberation and black men's liberation is what we mean when we speak of the liberation of black people. I maintain that the true liberation of black people depends on their rejection of the inferiority of women, the rejection of competition as the only viable relationship between men, and their re-affirmation of respect for general human potential in whatever form man, child or woman, it is conceived.

[4] *Ibid.*

The Meaning of the Black Revolution

Lerone Bennett, Jr.

Lerone Bennett, jr. (1928-) is senior editor of *Ebony* magazine. His numerous works on the Negro in America include *Before the Mayflower: A History of the Negro in America, 1619-1966* (3d ed., 1966), *The Negro Mood* (1964), and *Confrontation: Black and White* (1965).

If white men come forward now to claim their own freedom and individuality, America will become the America that was dreamed.

There has never been a free people, a free country, a real democracy on the face of this earth. In a city of some 300,000 slaves and 90,000 so-called free men, Plato sat down and praised freedom in exquisitely elegant phrases.

In a colony of 500,000 slaves and thousands of white indentured servants, Thomas Jefferson, a wealthy slaveowner, sat down and wrote the memorable words of the Declaration of Independence.

In a country with 10 million second-class citizens and millions on millions of poverty-stricken whites, Woodrow Wilson segregated the toilets in Washington, D.C., and went forth to make the world safe for democracy.

There has never been a free people, a free country, a real democracy in the recorded history of man.

The great masses of men have always lived in suburbs of hell.

The great masses of men and almost all women have always been anvils for the hammers of the few.

We have gathered therefore to talk about a subject which has no past, insofar as mankind is concerned, and which can have no future, unless it is visualized and made concrete in the body of mankind. And it seems to me that one forfeits the right to talk about freedom unless one is prepared to face that fact and to do something about it.

Almost 200 years ago at a time of revolutionary turbulence not unlike the present, Tom Paine held that unpalatable truth up to the unseeing eyes of his contemporaries. "Freedom," he said, "hath been hunted around the Globe ... O! receive the fugitive, and prepare in time an asylum for mankind." Today, after a thousand evasions, after a thousand proclamations and manifestoes, freedom is still a fugitive—in America as well as in Russia, in Portugal as well as in Angola, in England as well as in Rhodesia, in Boston as well as in Mississippi.

We live in a world where two-thirds of the people are hungry.

We live in a world where most of the peoples are diseased and illiterate.

In such a world, who has the effrontery—who has the gall—to praise the state of freedom?

The whole problem of freedom in the white and nonwhite worlds must be placed first in this larger context, for henceforth it will be impossible to speak of freedom in terms of the concerns of the tiny minority of men who live in Europe and North America. We must note, moreover, that freedom in Western Europe and North America is abstract, negative and largely illusory. And even in these areas, millions live on the edge of despair, and millions more are slaves to their skin or to their omnivorous machines.

It will be my argument here that the truth of freedom in the world is the truth of the truly disinherited. And by that I mean that the state of freedom is most accurately reflected in the lives of the men on the bottom. The men on the top and the men in the middle can remain ignorant of what they do and of what they are. But the men on the bottom experience the truth of society irremediably. They are the truth of every society. In them, we can see what we are, and what we have become. In the mirror of their eyes, we can measure the depth of our alienation from freedom and from man.

To be even more explicit and to bring the matter closer to home, I intend to maintain here that racism is the best index of the failure of American society to create a human and equitable society *for white people.* My argument here is the very simple one that the depth of facism is a measure of the unfreedom in the white community. And from that premise, we can conclude that black men are not free because white men are not free. And by all this we must understand that when the Emancipation Proclamation finally comes it will be most of all an emancipation of white people from the fears and frailties that cruelly twist and goad their lives.

Before pursuing that argument, let us pause for a moment and examine the meaning and implications of the word that everybody praises and few people live. As we all know, freedom lends itself to numerous interpretations. In the white Western world, it is usually defined negatively as "freedom from." This definition finds its truth in certain abstract liberties: freedom of speech, freedom of association, *et cetera.* To define freedom thusly, and to stop there, is, in my opinion, a perversion of freedom, for freedom also means "freedom to." And this positive definition finds its truth in concrete possibilities created in the social field in the right to work, in the right to eat, in the right to shelter, in the right to be.

There is still another definition of freedom, a psychological one, which stresses the act of willing or choosing. And this definition, in turn, is linked to a fourth one which contends that man—by his ability to rise above or transcend a situation, any situation, by his ability to say No—is the measure and the meaning of freedom in the world.

In my opinion, no definition of freedom is adequate in today's world which does not embrace all these meanings—freedom from, freedom to transcendence—in a concrete context linked to conditions that open or close real possibilities to concrete men in their social and historical situation. Such a definition would recognize the existentialist truth that man *is* freedom and would recognize that the alienation of the world from freedom is a measure of its alienation from man and the possibilities of man. It would also recognize the truth that man has not yet been created and that the creation of man—black man as well as white man—awaits the winning of real, concrete freedom for all men.

Here and there, across the great wastelands of time, little knots of men have glimpsed the terrifying possibilities of that paradox. I think particularly of African village democracy and other free forms developed by American Indians and other communal groups. But these groups were hemmed in by material limitations and it was left to Western Europe to free man from feudal restrictions and to hoist high the standards of individuality and personal autonomy. But Europe, in its lunge toward freedom, made three fatal errors. First of all, and most important of all, Europe experienced its newfound freedom as the untrammelled exercise of the ego. And in pursuit of the goal of possessive individualism it drew a circle around itself, excluding and enslaving three-fourths of mankind.

Second, out of sheer terror, Europe cut freedom into two parts, separating man into positive and negative poles, the mind and the body, reason and emotion, sex and the soul. Refusing to recognize the full force of freedom, which manifests itself in sex as well as in prayer, Europe facilitated that manic process by which men project their rejected freedom onto the scapegoats and outcasts of society.

In the third place, Europe refused to admit the full logic of its own idea. With few exceptions, Europeans and the sons of Europeans found it difficult to extend the idea of freedom to poor whites and impossible to extend it to nonwhites. In Europe and in the extensions of Europe, freedom became a function of the skin and of property.

Despite the huge achievements of European technology and science, European freedom, beautiful as it was, was not freedom. Or better still: it was not yet freedom. Having freed man from arbitrary restraints, Europe stopped halfway, leaving man tied to the chains of caste, class and passion. Having expelled man from his tribal and feudal Eden, Europe retreated, in terror, from Nietzsche's lucid question:

"Not free from what, but free for what?"

America inherited Europe's immense achievements and its immense failures—and extended both. The history of America, like the history of Europe, has been a history of a magnificent evasion of the multiple meanings of freedom. The most obvious example of that failure is the black American. But the failure to integrate black people into the American community is only a part of our culture's general inability to create a just and human environment.

Despite our alleged affluence, 30 to 40 million Americans, many of them white, live in abject poverty, and millions more live lives of harrowing economic insecurity.

Despite our extraordinary mechanical ability, which cannot be praised so highly, we have failed to create a truly human community. Machines are more real here than human beings—and vastly more important. In a society of machines, by machines and for machines, we are increasingly powerless, and a nihilistic individualism has made conformists—and cowards—of us all. Dehumanized, depersonalized, distracted by bread and television, we have almost lost sight of man. Mystified by an ethic which confuses the verb to be with the verb to have, we try to staunch the running wound of our lives by adding layers and layers of mechanical band-aids. We lack passion, we lack purpose, and we decide nothing. The great alternatives are formulated by others, and in our name and without our assent men, women, and little children are killed in poverty-stricken countries. Increasingly irresponsible as our choices become fewer, and as the world becomes more threatening, we whirl around and in a materialistic inferno between collective madness and collective self-destruction.

And we are afraid.

We are afraid of our neighbors, of Negroes, of Chinese, of Communists, of four-letter words, sex . . . —we are afraid, in a word, of ourselves.

Because we fear ourselves and others, because we are dominated by machines and things, because we are not in control of our destiny, we are neither happy nor free.

"If one probes beneath the chrome-plated surface," Senator J. W. Fulbright says, "he comes inescapably to the conclusion that the American people by and large are not happy . . . . I believe . . . that America's trouble is basically one of aimlessness at home and frustration abroad."

As you have probably guessed by now, I believe America's trouble is at a deeper level. The problem, in my opinion, is structural, that is, institutional. We have not created a single community here. We have not even created a single community for white people. Men tell me that white people ought to love black people. But it is clear to me that white people don't love each other, not to speak of the fact that an incredibly large number of white Americans don't love themselves.

Racism in America is a reflection of this structural problem. As I have said elsewhere, we misunderstand racism completely if we do not see it as a confused and alienated protest against a suffocating reality. On the level of power, racism is used by men to effect magical solutions of the unresolved social problems in the white community. On a personal level, particularly among lower-income and middle-income whites, racism is an avenue of flight, a cry for help from desperate men stifling in the prisons of their skins. Viewed in this perspective, racism is a flight from freedom, a flight from the self, a flight from the intolerable burdens of being a man in a mechanized world.

There is considerable evidence that America's stress on possessive individualism induces exaggerated anxieties which are displaced onto the area of race relations. The fear of failure, the fear of competitors, the fear of losing status, of not living in the right neighborhood, of not having the right friends or the right gadgets: these fears weigh heavily on the minds of millions of Americans and lead to a search for avenues of escape. And so the factory worker or the poor farmer who finds himself at a dead end with a nagging wife, a problem child and a past-due bill uses the black man as a screen to hide himself from himself and from an intolerable reality.

To adapt the perceptive words of Richard Wright, social discontent assumes many guises, and the social commentator who focuses on the police blotter misses the real clues to contemporary reality. By this I mean that it is possible to know, *before it happens*, that certain forms of violence will occur. It can be known, *before it happens*, that a native-born American, educated, healthy, with a pretty wife, a split-level house and two cars, with all the abstract liberties *but devoid of basic human satisfactions*, will seize upon a powerless black man and derive deep feelings of pleasure from hacking him to death with a chain. "But," as Wright said, "To know that a seemingly normal, ordinary American is capable of such brutality implies making a judgment about the nature and quality of our everyday American experiences which most Americans simply cannot do, FOR, TO ADMIT THAT OUR INDIVIDUAL EXPERIENCES ARE OF SO LOW A QUALITY . . . AS TO PRECLUDE THE DEEP, ORGANIC SATISFACTIONS NECESSARY FOR CIVILIZED, PEACEFUL LIVING, IS TO CONDEMN THE SYSTEM THAT PROVIDES THOSE EXPERIENCES."

The real question in America is how we build a society in which apparently normal people do not need scapegoats or whipping boys to build their egos and to maintain their dignity?

How can we build a society that will enhance freedom and integrity and obviate the need for racism?

First of all, we have to condemn the system.

And we have to condemn the system in the name of that America, of that Commonwealth of Silence, which was written, which was promised, and which has never existed. I am suggesting here that we must initiate a sustained dialogue on the foundations of our society. And we must demand the right to subject every institution to the claims of freedom.

Let me say immediately that I don't have all the answers. The only thing I know is that everything must be rethought again. We need a new definition of work embracing any act of value that a man brings to society and a new definition of politics embracing the full and effective participation of all men in formulating the alternatives and choosing between the alternatives of the political, economic and social decisions that affect their lives. We also need a new definition of sex which would free women for equal roles in the church, in labor unions, in the professions and every other institution of our society. I often say to my wife that women, not Negroes, are the most brainwashed people in the Western world. Of course, in this regard, I am very much like Thomas Jefferson. I want women to have absolute freedom everywhere right now—but I hope that the revolution starts with somebody else's wife.

But wherever the revolution starts, I am prepared to welcome it, for I believe that the future of freedom in America is dependent upon the formulation of a broader definition of freedom and of man and of woman than our society is based upon. And it seems to me that it is necessary to set liberty in the context of equality with the understanding that every individual is entitled to the space and the chance to fulfill himself, which is only another way of saying that every individual is entitled to the instruments that will permit him to go to the boundaries of himself.

This, I believe, is a precondition for black and white freedom in America. For if we want black men and white men to cooperate, we must create conditions that will make it possible for them to cooperate. In other words, we must change the conditions that lead white men to see black men as threats to their homes, to their jobs, to their masculinity. And to do this we must modify the situation of the white man from top to bottom. For to demand that white men give up their irrational responses to black reality is to demand that a situation which requires irrational responses be abolished.

We must conceive and organize in this country programs that will make it impossible for one man to profit by another man's falls.

We must conceive and organize in this community, and in every other community, programs that will relieve the economic pressures on all men so that some men will not find it to their short-term economic interest to keep other men down.

In other words, we must take the profit out of bigotry.

The first steps in this direction would be a guaranteed annual income, the extension of Medicare to all citizens, the elimination of regressive taxes, and housing and educational subsidies to lower- and middle-income groups.

Ultimately, however, such an effort would require a reevaluation of our dominant myths, including the myth of possessive individuality, which is the greatest single obstacle to individuality, and the myth of property, which is the greatest single obstacle to the free enjoyment of property by all men.

Let there be no misunderstanding here: I am not saying that property in itself is evil—what I'm saying is that property masquerading as God is the major roadblock to freedom in the world today. Men need a certain amount of property to validate themselves and their freedom, but freedom becomes unfreedom and life loses its meaning when property becomes an inhuman idol, when anything and everything is sacrificed to an abstract Thing.

There was an interesting article on this subject in the New York Post which I would like to quote at some length. The article referred to the summer marches by Dr. Martin Luther King, Jr., and his supporters through the Gage Park area of Chicago. Pete Hamill visited the neighborhood and wrote the following words:

"This was the way the Hollywood hustlers used to put their cardboard America together, in a time more innocent than ours.

"Children played in the streets, or burbled from baby carriages. Young boys mowed lawns which still smelled sweetly from the morning rains. Housewives pushed strollers to the grocery stores, or drove the family cars to the supermarkets. A man on vacation nailed a brass numeral to his front door. A lot of people seemed to be polishing automobiles with an almost reverent devotion. Gage Park on Monday afternoon seemed as innocuous as anyplace where Doris Day had ever lived on film.

"But underneath, past the front doors of those two-story houses, in the secret places behind those lawns and those automobiles and those smiling children, Gage Park was like a tray of summer worms. By the time the thing that is crawling through Gage Park has hooked its last inhabitant, that neighborhood is almost certainly going to murder someone. It is going to murder someone because of the accident of color. It is going to murder someone over the combination of wood, metal and concrete which the inhabitants fondly describe as their property."

The same animal is crawling through the Gage Parks of Boston and New York and California. And if we don't confront it soon, an unspeakably horrible disaster is going to happen here. It's going to happen because our churches and schools have not taught people that no thing is higher than man. It's going to happen because our civilization has not yet learned that men are important, whether they own property or not.

To a great extent, racism in America is grounded on the whole sick syndrome surrounding real estate, status, greed, and human pettiness. If we are serious about freedom, we are going to have to come to grips with that syndrome.

We hear a great deal about freedom and property, but we must have the courage to say that words cannot be prostituted with impunity. Freedom is a fine word, but it has its boundaries. Men who say the community is free when it is enslaved, men who say the sky is black when it is blue, are debasing reality and preparing the way for tyranny.

We can respect freedom only when it is intended for freedom. A freedom that denies freedom must be denied in the name of freedom. For to be free is not to have the power to do anything you want to do. I am oppressed if I am denied the right of free movement, but I am not oppressed if I am denied the right to deny my neighbor freedom of movement.

Beyond all that, we must note that the idea of one-class, one-kind neighborhoods is in and of itself a clear and present danger to American democracy. The standardized neighborhoods, the standardized house, the standardized minds and the standardized fears which stretch from one end of America to another is a denial of the movement of life which advances by integrating differences. As Chardin has said: "Joy lies not in exclusiveness and isolation, but in variety, which is the reservoir of experience and emotion." On the other hand, uniformity, sameness, standardization make for cultural stagnation and, as sure as night follows day, regimentation and eventually neo-Fascism.

In order to deal with the anti-democratic ideas, which have made deep inroads in American life, we must make revolutionary changes at every level of our lives. We confront, in a word, the need for not a law here or a law there but for a vital change in the whole spirit of our civilization.

.   .   .

This is an important moment in the history of the Commonwealth. There stretch out before us now two roads and two roads only. America must now become America or something else, a Fourth Reich perhaps or a Fourth Reich of the spirit. To put the matter bluntly—we must become what we say we are or give in to the secret dream that blights our hearts.

Let us rejoice that it has come to this.

Now that freedom is dangerous, perhaps men will stop prostituting it. Now that freedom is exploding in broad open daylight in the streets of America and Vietnam perhaps we will be able to recognize her true friends.

As individuals, we are called upon to make a creative response to this challenge by assuming our own freedom and validating it in social acts designed to create spaces in which the seeds of freedom can grow.

In a very real sense, the struggle in America is a struggle to free white Americans or, to be quite precise, it is a struggle to put them in the presence of their freedom. And it seems to me that it is the duty of this convocation to send abroad the good news that one can be free, even in Boston or Chicago or New York.

Freedom isn't something you can buy on the installment plan. It is not a gift, from anybody—it is a priceless possession that must be reclaimed and rewon every day. As Silone has said: "One can be free, even under a dictatorship. All you have to do is to struggle against it." He who thinks with his own head and acts with his own heart is free. He who is not afraid of his neighbors is free. He who struggles for what he believes in is a free man. On the other hand: If you live in the richest Boston suburb and if you are lazy, timid, conformist, you are not free, but a slave.

Because men deny the tiny bit of psychological freedom at their disposal, it is necessary to awaken them by social movements in which wills confront each other. This is the meaning of the Black Revolution, which is inviting us to become ourselves by going to the limits of ourselves. This revolution defines the state of freedom in America today, and it tells us that freedom has no future in America if the black man does not have a future in freedom.

More than 100 years ago, Walt Whitman told Ralph Waldo Emerson: "Master, I am a man who has perfect faith. But Master, we have not come through centuries, caste, heroism, fables, to halt in this land today."

The spirit of Walt Whitman is marching today in the Harlems of our mind. Men and women made in Whitman's image are saying to us: "Fellow Americans, we have perfect faith. But Fellow Americans, we have not come through slavery, segregation, degradation, blood, cotton, roaches, rats, to halt in this land today."

Black Americans, by daring to claim their freedom, are daring us to claim our own.

And the movement which expresses that thrust will continue despite the recent revelations of the depth and extent of racism in America. Whatever the problems, whatever the setbacks, whatever the dangers, oppression must be rejected at any cost. For, as [W. E. B.] Du Bois said, the price of freedom is always less than the cost of oppression.

In the Black Revolution, America comes hard up against a new fact: *the color of the world has changed.* And with that change, a terrifying freedom has become the burden of all men, especially those men who were tyrannized for so long by the arbitrary limitations of their skin. If white men come forward now to claim their own freedom and individuality, if they abandon their trenches and come out into the open, America will become the America that was dreamed.

This is the real meaning of the Black Revolution, which is a desperate attempt to place before our freedom the burning alternatives history is offering us.

Walt Whitman said:

"We have not come through centuries, caste, fables, to halt in this land today."

Black Americans are saying:

"We have not come through slavery, segregation, degradation to halt in this land today."

And the question now is:

What do you say?

On Being Mexican in America
Octavio Paz

Octavio Paz (1914-   ), a Mexican writer, is the author of *The Labyrinth of Solitude* (1961).

All of us, at some moment, have had a vision of our existence as something unique, untransferable and very precious. This revelation almost always takes place during adolescence. Self-discovery is above all the realization that we are alone: it is the opening of an impalpable, transparent wall—that of our consciousness—between the world and ourselves. It is true that we sense our aloneness almost as soon as we are born, but children and adults can transcend their solitude and forget themselves

Source: "The Pachuco and Other Extremes," *Labyrinth of Solitude: Life and Thought in Mexico* (New York: Grove Press, 1961), pp. 9-28. Reprinted by permission of Grove Press, Inc. Translated by Lysander Kemp. Copyright © 1961 by Grove Press, Inc.

in games or work. The adolescent, however, vacillates between infancy and youth, halting for a moment before the infinite richness of the world. He is astonished at the fact of his being, and this astonishment leads to reflection: as he leans over the river of his consciousness, he asks himself if the face that appears there, disfigured by the water, is his own. The singularity of his being, which is pure sensation in children, becomes a problem and a question.

Much the same thing happens to nations and peoples at a certain critical moment in their development. They ask themselves: What are we, and how can we fulfill our obligations to ourselves as we are?

Something of the same sort characterizes the Mexicans you see in the streets. They have lived in the city for many years, wearing the same clothes and speaking the same language as the other inhabitants, and they feel ashamed of their origin; yet no one would mistake them for authentic North Americans. I refuse to believe that physical features are as important as is commonly thought. What distinguishes them, I think, is their furtive, restless air: they act like persons who are wearing disguises, who are afraid of a stranger's look because it could strip them and leave them stark naked. When you talk with them, you observe that their sensibilities are like a pendulum, but a pendulum that has lost its reason and swings violently and erratically back and forth. This spititual condition, or lack of a spirit, has given birth to a type known as the *pachuco*. The *pachucos* are youths, for the most part of Mexican origin, who form gangs in Southern cities; they can be identified by their language and behavior as well as by the clothing they affect. They are instinctive rebels, and North American racism has vented its wrath on them more than once. But the *pachucos* do not attempt to vindicate their race or the nationality of their forebears. Their attitude reveals an obstinate, almost fanatical will-to-be, but this will affirms nothing specific except their determination—it is an ambiguous one, as we will see—not to be like those around them. The *pachuco* does not want to become a Mexican again; at the same time he does not want to blend into the life of North America. His whole being is sheer negative impulse, a tangle of contradictions, an enigma. Even his very name is enigmatic: *pachuco*, a word of uncertain derivation, saying nothing and saying everything. It is a strange word with no definite meaning; or, to be more exact, it is charged like all popular creations with a diversity of meanings. Whether we like it or not, these persons are Mexicans, are one of the extremes at which the Mexican can arrive.

The *pachuco* tries to enter North America society in secret and daring ways, but he impedes his own efforts. Having been cut off from his traditional culture, he asserts himself for a moment as a solitary and challenging figure. He denies both the society from which he originated and that of North America. When he thrusts himself outward, it is not to unite with what surrounds him but rather to defy it. This is a suicidal gesture, because the *pachuco* does not affirm or defend anything except his exasperated will-to-be. He is not divulging his most intimate feelings: he is revealing an ulcer, exhibiting a wound. A wound that is also a grotesque, capricious, barbaric adornment. A wound that laughs at itself and decks itself out for the hunt. The *pachuco* is the prey of society, but instead of hiding he adorns himself to attract the hunter's attention. Persecution redeems him and breaks his solitude: his salvation depends on his becoming part of the very society he appears to deny. Solitude and sin, communion and health become synonymous terms. . . .

This is not the moment to analyze our profound sense of solitude, which alternatively affirms and denies itself in melancholy and rejoicing, silence and sheer noise, gratuitous crimes and religious fervor. Man is alone everywhere. But the solitude of the Mexican, under the great stone night of the high plateau that is still inhabited by insatiable gods, is very different from that of the North American, who wanders in an abstract world of machines, fellow citizens and moral precepts. In the Valley of Mexico man feels himself suspended between heaven and earth, and he oscillates between contrary powers and forces, and petrified eyes, and devouring mouths. Reality—that is, the world that surrounds us—exists by itself here, has a life of its own, and was not invented by man as it was in the United States. The Mexican feels himself to have been torn from the womb of this reality, which is both creative and destructive. both Mother and Tomb. He has forgotten the word that ties him to all those forces through which life manifests itself. Therefore he shouts or keeps silent, stabs or prays, or falls asleep for a hundred years.

. . . Our solitude has the same roots as religious feelings. It is a form of orphanhood, an obscure awareness that we have been torn from the All, and an ardent search: a flight and a return, an effort to re-establish the bonds that unite us with the universe.

Nothing could be further from this feeling than the solitude of the North American. In the United States man does not feel that he has been torn from the center of creation and suspended between hostile forces. He has built his own world and it is built in his own image: it is his mirror. But now he cannot recognize himself in his inhuman objects, nor in his fellows. His creations, like those of an inept sorcerer, no longer obey him. He is alone among his works, lost—to use the phrase by José Gorostiza—in a "wilderness of mirrors."

.   .   .

When I arrived in the United States I was surprised above all by the self-assurance and confidence of the people, by their apparent happiness and apparent adjustment to the world around them. This satisfaction does not stifle criticism, however, and the criticism is valuable and forthright, of a sort not often heard in the countries to the south, where long periods of dictatorship have made us more cautious about expressing our points of view. But it is a criticism that respects the existing systems and never touches the roots. I thought of Ortega y Gasset's distinction between uses and abuses, in his definition of the "revolutionary spirit." The revolutionary is always a radical, that is, he is trying to correct the uses themselves rather than the mere abuses of them. Almost all the criticisms I heard from the lips of North Americans were of the reformist variety: they left the social or cultural structures intact and were only intended to limit or improve this or that procedure. It seemed to me then, and it still does, that the United States is a society that wants to realize its ideals, has no wish to exchange them for others, and is confident of surviving, no matter how dark the future may appear. I am not interested in discussing whether this attitude is justified by reason and reality; I simply want to point out that it exists. It is true that this faith in the natural goodness of life, or in its infinite wealth of possibilities, cannot be found in recent North American literature, which prefers to depict a much more somber world; but I found it in the actions, the words and even the faces of almost everyone I met. . . .[1]

On the other hand, I heard a good deal of talk about American realism and also about American ingenuousness, qualities that would seem to be mutually exclusive. To us a realist is always a pessimist. And an ingenuous person would not remain so for very long if he truly contemplated life realistically. Would it not be more accurate to say that the North American wants to use reality rather than to know it? In some matters—death, for example—he not only has no desire to understand it, he obviously avoids the very idea. I met some elderly ladies who still had illusions and were making plans for the future as if it were inexhaustible. Thus they refuted Nietzsche's statement condemning women to an early onset of skepticism because "men have ideals but women only have illusions." American realism, then, is of a very special kind, and American ingenuousness does not exclude dissimulation and even hypocrisy. When hypocrisy is a character trait it also affects one's thinking, because it consists in the negation of all the aspects of reality that one finds disagreeable, irrational or repugnant.

In contrast, one of the most notable traits of the Mexican's character is his willingness to contemplate horror: he is even familiar and complacent in his dealings with it. The bloody Christs in our village churches, the macabre humor in some of our newspaper headlines, our wakes, the custom of eating skull-shaped cakes and candies on the Day of the Dead, are habits inherited from the Indians and the Spaniards and are now an inseparable part of our being. Our cult of death is also a cult of life, in the same way that love is a hunger for life and a longing for death. Our fondness for self-destruction derives not only from our masochistic tendencies but also from a certain variety of religious emotion.

And our differences do not end there. The North Americans are credulous and we are believers; they love fairy tales and detective stories and we love myths and legends. The Mexican tells lies because he delights in fantasy, or because he is desperate, or because he wants to rise above the sordid facts of his life; the North American does not tell lies, but he substitutes social truth for the real truth, which is always disagreeable. We get drunk in order to confess; they get drunk in order to forget. They are optimists and we are nihilists—except that our nihilism is not intellectual but instinctive, and therefore irrefutable. We are suspicious and they are trusting. We are sorrowful and sarcastic and they are happy and full of jokes. North Americans want to understand and we want to contemplate. They are activists and we are quietists; we enjoy our wounds and they enjoy their inventions. They believe in hygiene, health, work and contentment, but perhaps they have never experienced true joy, which is an intoxication, a whirlwind. In the hubbub of a fiesta night our voices explode into brilliant lights, and life and death mingle together, while their vitality becomes a fixed smile that denies old age and death but that changes life to motionless stone.

What is the origin of such contradictory attitudes? It seems to me that North Americans consider the world to be something that can be perfected, and that we

[1] These lines were written before the public was clearly cognizant of the danger of universal annihilation made possible by nuclear weapons. Since then the North Americans have lost their optimism but not their confidence, a confidence based on resignation and obstinacy. The truth is that although many people talk about the danger, secretly no one believes—no one wants to believe—that it is real and immediate.

consider it to be something that can be redeemed. Like their Puritan ancestors, we believe that sin and death constitute the ultimate basis of human nature, but with the difference that the Puritan identifies purity with health. Therefore he believes in the purifying effects of asceticism, and the consequences are his cult of work for work's sake, his serious approach to life, and his conviction that the body does not exist or at least cannot lose—or find—itself in another body. Every contact is a contamination. Foreign races, ideas, customs, and bodies carry within themselves the germs of perdition and impurity. Social hygiene complements that of the soul and the body. Mexicans, however, both ancient and modern, believe in communion and fiestas: there is no health without contact. Tlazolteotl, the Aztec goddess of filth and fecundity, of earthly and human moods, was also the goddess of steam baths, sexual love and confession. And we have not changed very much, for Catholicism is also communion.

These two attitudes are irreconcilable, I believe, and, in their present form, insufficient. . . .

The North American system only wants to consider the positive aspects of reality. Men and women are subjected from childhood to an inexorable process of adaptation; certain principles, contained in brief formulas, are endlessly repeated by the press, the radio, the churches and the schools, and by those kindly, sinister beings, the North American mothers and wives. A person imprisoned by these schemes is like a plant in a flowerpot too small for it: he cannot grow or mature. This sort of conspiracy cannot help but provoke violent individual rebellions. Spontaneity avenges itself in a thousand subtle or terrible ways. The mask that replaces the dramatic mobility of the human face is benevolent and courteous but empty of emotion, and its set smile is almost lugubrious: it shows the extent to which intimacy can be devastated by the arid victory of principles over instincts. The sadism underlying almost all types of relationships in contemporary North American life is perhaps nothing more than a way of escaping the petrifaction imposed by that doctrine of aseptic moral purity. The same is true of the new religions and sects, and the liberating drunkenness that opens the doors of "life." It is astonishing what a destructive and almost physiological meaning this word has acquired: to live means to commit excesses, break the rules, go to the limit (of what?), experiment with sensations. The act of love is an "experience" (and therefore unilateral and frustrating). But it is not to my purpose to describe these reactions. It is enough to say that all of them, like their Mexican opposites, seem to me to reveal our mutual inability to reconcile ourselves to the flux of life.

A study of the great myths concerning the origin of man and the meaning of our presence on earth reveals that every culture—in the sense of a complex of values created and shared in common—stems from the conviction that man the intruder has broken or violated the order of the universe. He has inflicted a wound on the compact flesh of the world, and chaos, which is the ancient and, so to speak, *natural* condition of life, can emerge again from this aperture. The return of "ancient Original Disorder" is a menace that has obsessed every consciousness in every period of history. Hölderlin expresses in several different poems his dread of the great empty mouth of chaos with its fatal seduction for man and the universe:

. . . if, beyond the straight way,
The captive Elements and the ancient
Laws of the Earth break loose

> *Like maddened horses. And then a desire to return*
> *To chaos rises incessantly. There is much*
> *To defend, and the faithful are much needed. . . .*[2]

The faithful are much needed because there is *much to defend.* Man collaborates actively in defending universal order, which is always being threatened by chaos. And when it collapses he must create a new one, this time his own. But exile, expiation and penitence should proceed from the reconciliation of man with the universe. Neither the Mexican nor the North American has achieved this reconciliation. What is even more serious, I am afraid we have lost our sense of the very meaning of all human activity, which is to assure the operation of an order in which knowledge and innocence, man and nature are in harmony. If the solitude of the Mexican is like a stagnant pool, that of the North American is like a mirror. We have ceased to be springs of living water.

The Chicanos Search for Identity

Hilario H. Contreras

Hilario H. Contreras has written about the Chicanos and their search for identity.

The most human faculty of man is the awareness of his existence as a distinct person who exists in the continuum of the past, the present and the future and who, with a sense of self-determination, plans and shapes his own fate.

Self-awareness is the most immediate of our experiences; it can't be compared with any other experience, and, because it can't be experienced except from the one single vantage point of subjectivity, it is quite elusive. And yet, it is the most fundamental fact of our life. Paradoxically, one becomes keenly aware of one's self in the morbid states of depersonalization, when a person suddenly feels strange to himself an experience well known to many members of minority groups in Anglo-American society. Only when the feeling of identity is disrupted do we become aware of its existence.

We realize that it is the same person who played on the floor as an infant, was praised, loved, and also scolded by his parents, who quarreled with his brothers and sisters, who went to school, who chose an occupation or profession, who married and had children. This feeling of *continuity in an emotionally undisturbed person* is not interrupted and starts quite early in life. Beyond this there is no memory because remembering presupposes the existence of an *ego* which has the feeling of some kind—no matter how vague—of identity.

The preservation of an undisturbed feeling of identity depends on a

---

[2] *Reif sind, in Feuer getaucht. . . .*

Source: Con Safos, Vol. 2, No. 5.

continuously progressive, integrative process during the distinct phases of personality development: infancy, early childhood, adolescence, early adulthood and adulthood, each characterized by biologically determined changes in the person's physical, emotional, and intellectual capacities.

Each new phase of development is considered an identity-crisis requiring new integrative tasks to include the changing libidinal forces and the *changing expectations of the environment* upon the growing individual into a harmonious unit which is perceived as a distinct *self*.

In adolescence such an identity-crisis is very noticeable: a yet emotionally unprepared ego has to cope with the impact of the biologically reinforced sexual impulses that are symptomatic of puberty. Suddenly a mature body, almost overnight, is entrusted to an inexperienced ego. At the same time, the adolescent is confronted with an environment which considers him almost an adult. And has new expectations of him. From lack of experience, the adolescent feels most insecure.

Such transitory identity-crises during the process of ego maturation are easily overcome *under stable external conditions* to be found only in countries with old civilizations. In the United States of America, on the other hand, cultural traditions, in a strict sense, do not exist. The only behavioral demands American society makes on the individual citizen is conformity to the life pattern of the Anglo majority. And it is exactly at this point when the identity-crises of members of minority groups have been provoked.

The constant influx of foreign-born parents has been a consistent feature of the American scene, a factor that has been recognized by such anthropologists as Margaret Mead as a particular danger to psychological maturation. Second-generation children, especially among European immigrants, can't take their parents as models of accepted *Anglo behavior*. They must experiment by trying to imitate their Anglo peers who, in the majority of cases, hesitate to accept them completely and never let them forget that *your parents speak English with a foreign accent!*

In the case of Chicanos we can't speak of immigrants, because historically speaking, it is the Anglos who have immigrated into the states of Texas, New Mexico, Colorado, Arizona and California. And instead of *adjusting* to the prevalent indio-hispano civilization, they colonized the native population and treated them as *racially inferior and second-class citizens*. As a consequence of that shameless confiscation of the American Southwest by the Anglo immigrants, *the personal and racial identity of the Chicano,* during the last century, has been seriously and constantly threatened.

The Chicano child does not have to wait for the advent of puberty to undergo the ordinary identity-crisis caused by sudden physical maturation without emotional preparedness. His ego identity is already threatened when he enters elementary school where the English language is compulsory and where he is given to understand that Spanish is a *foreign, un-American* idiom which he must forget in order to think, talk and behave like an Anglo-American, in order to be—not accepted, but rather—*tolerated* by his Anglo teachers and fellow-pupils. Thus, at the age of six, the Chicano child is precipitated into the worst identity-crisis that can happen to a person at such an early age. The impact of the crudely condescending attitude of Anglo teachers on the helpless Chicano child can be of traumatic intensity and become the cause of a life-long, severe identity-crisis with all its psychological complications resulting in *dropping-out* at a pre-puberty age, in delinquency, and drug-addiction, and all the other symptoms of emotional insecurity.

In order to understand the magnitude of the average Chicano's loss of identity, one must compare the characteristics of the centuries-old Mexican civilization with those of Anglo-American society. I intentionally use the term *society* because the United States of America confuses the instruments of civilization with civilization itself. A people may possess all the gadgets of civilization such as banks, industrial enterprise, newspapers, radio, television, washing machines and garbage disposals and yet remain uncivilized; whereas so-called primitive peoples, such as many American and Mexican Indian tribes and certain *backward* Oriental peoples, might have none of these gadgets and yet be highly civilized. The Chicano, whose identity has been continually threatened, instinctively recognizes the Anglo society's lack of genuine civilization, not to speak of a lack of *culture*—culture which is an exaltation of the human spirit, *la alma*, the soul of a people.

Anglo-American society, or shall we say, the American Way of Life, is based on a soulless philosophy which may be called *economism;* it interprets the purpose of human life in terms of the production, acquisition and distribution of wealth. The French economist, Michel Chevalier (1806-1879), who visited the United States early in the 19th century, said that "American society has the morale of an army on the march"; the morale of the looter. The German economist, Theodor Luddecke, defined *Americanism* as "the economic instinct raised in all departments of private and public life to its highest power." Whenever the United States has undertaken to *help* underdeveloped peoples, it never has concerned itself with beauty, intellect or spiritual values, but it has concerned itself with better material living conditions. This is called the pursuit of happiness. And, although the Anglo immigrants conquered and occupied and industrialized all the land between the Atlantic and the Pacific oceans, they have not found happiness.

The Chicano, who does not conceive of *culture* as the pursuit of material happiness, noticed quite early that the center of the Anglo-American's life was an empty waste similar to the continental wilderness he had so greedily colonized. Of a real *inner* life, despite the often exaggerated religious and sociological enthusiasm, the Anglo possesses only a ready-made cliché. Most of his science, art and sophisticated amusement came straight from Europe. The best American writers always dreamed of something America did not offer. They often died abroad of severed roots, or remained to suffer and blaspheme. The American mass-man never found happiness and began to confuse it with *fun.* Although the great Mexican poet and thinker, Octavio Paz, speaks of the *Labyrinth of Solitude* in the Mexican psyche, he is well aware of the psyche, he is well aware of the psychological loneliness of the average Anglo-American who, more and more, manifests this in psycho-neurotic symptoms. The purely materialistic ambition of the *pioneer* survives in contemporary Anglo thinking: "Better a new continent—or a new planet—to conquer and colonize than an empty mind to fill!"

The tragedy of the Anglo-American's *lack* of identity is final, while the Chicano's *loss* of cultural identity is only temporary. What was lost can be regained. When we speak of the *cultural heritage* of the Chicano, we should think mainly in psychological terms. The Mexican, in contrast to the Anglo, has always been what the social psychologist, David Riesman, calls an *inner-directed* person.

According to Riesman, the inner-directed person is one who possesses a well-defined stable internal organization of principles and values which govern his behavior. This gives such a person a relative independence from the changing attitudes and expectations of others. It goes hand-in-hand with a feeling of identity, as with a person who takes himself for granted and is not disturbed by constant doubts about his goals, values and internal problems, and is not constantly occupied in comparing himself to others. Such a person's attention can be fully absorbed by goals and strivings toward causes which lie outside of him; he can afford the luxury of healthy extroversion, devotion to things beyond his personal concerns. He can successfully incorporate and integrate *traditional cultural values* with his own individual propensities. He does not need to be preoccupied with the ways of a good life; these were given to him through identifications with parents and peers, each corresponding to his chronological and emotional age. He acquired them during a relatively undisturbed process of mental growth.

The so-called *other-directed* person is typified by the modern Anglo-American. He is constantly challenged to make adjustments; in fact, his life is spent in finding his place; he can never accept himself as he is; he does not know who he is, since his self was never crystallized. Because he remains a problem to himself, he must constantly watch others. All his cues come from outside. He has none of his own. He is always on the go, always searching without ever knowing what he is after. His energies are absorbed by *the continuous, never-ending problem of adjustment,* because no adjustment he makes is supposed to last for long in the restless Anglo society. Because of his social mobility, he continuously changes his jobs, his occupation, his marriages and his social environment. He depends more than the inner-directed person on chance and opportunities. Because his life does not follow a design which is the expression of a *traditional value system* modified by his unique self, there is less continuity in his self-awareness. Today he is this and tomorrow something else, not only in his occupation but in his own personality.

The arduous job of adjusting to an ever-changing human environment consumes all of his energies. Consequently, there is little left for creativity, for solid relationships, for devotion to causes that lie outside of himself. *His principal occupation is to get along with others.* Neurotic or psychotic disintegration of personality is only one of the outcomes of this constant unsuccessful struggle to find a balance between a lacking identity and a changing environment. This is the reason why the other-directed Anglo is not capable of cultivating cultural values, and, even less, of identifying with a distinct cultural group. All he is able to identify with are the colorless masses whose sole purpose of life is the amassing of wealth for the mere sake of doing so. In Anglo-American society the human individual is reduced to a cog in the social machinery. For such a society the uniqueness of the individual is useless; hence, it prefers to deal with him in terms of a *social role* and not in terms of the development of a *distinct* personality with the capacity to realize unique potentialities.

The instinctive protest of the Chicano against such a society is caused by its emphasis on *adjustment* and utility instead of creativity, the polor opposite of adjustment. To be creative means to produce something which is not yet in existence; adjustment means to accept and to conform with what is already here.

The Chicano knows that the nearer man comes to acquiring wealth, the more he undermines the foundations of a meaningful existence in which materialistic goals are not ultimate aims *but only means by which he can remain human.* Therefore, in order to regain and retain his cultural identity, the Chicano protests not only against exposing his children to teachers who believe that the English language and the white race are God's gift to the world, but chiefly against an *other-directed* society whose members have no identity of their own and will never be able to acquire one unless they realize that the human spirit, *la alma*, alone creates culture. The *primitive* Indian's distrust of the white man's machines and his computerized society stems from an ancient, inherently instinctual truth that happiness does not come from the possession of things, but from self-knowledge, from realizing the union of the individual self with the cosmic self. Or, as Jesus said to the Pharises: "The kingdom of heaven cometh not with observation . . . It is neither here, nor there; for behold, the kingdom of heaven is *with you* . . . !"

Modern psychology would express this by speaking of an *integrated personality*, of a person who knows his real identity that embraces everything created and uncreated. Man as a spiritual being goes beyond organized religion, beyond dogma and creeds. Although the Chicano knows that the body has to be fed, housed and clothed, he feels his identity with the spirit and declares with pride: *Por mi raza habla el espiritu!**

Suggested Readings

1. Cleaver, E., *Soul on Ice* (London: Jonathan Cape, 1969).
2. Foner, Philip S. (ed.), *The Black Panthers Speak* (Philadelphia: Lippincott, 1970).
3. Hanke, L., *Aristotle and the American Indians* (London: Hollis & Carter, 1959).
4. Leiden, Carl, and Schmitt, Karl M. *The Politics of Violence* (Englewood Cliffs, N.J.: Prentice-Hall, 1968).
5. McEvoy, James, and Miller, Abraham (eds.), *Black Power and Student Rebellion* (Belmont, Calif.: Wadsworth, 1969).
6. Mason, Philip, *Race Relations* (Oxford: University Press, 1970).

ABROAD

As the Third World struggles toward cultural and philosophical identity, its philosophy must bear the features of an ideology, because people do not struggle effectively if they have empty, aimless minds. Men must have their goals, values, and world outlook spelled out in a philosophical framework in order to weld

* [My spirit is expressed through my race.—Eds.]

themselves into an effective communal unity. Both **Ernesto Che Guevara** and **Mao Tse-tung** have made important ideological statements. They are aptly described by Kwame Nkrumah's line: "circumstances can be changed by revolution and revolutions are brought about by men, by men who think as men of action and act as men of thought." Both Guevara and Mao have treated the concept of the consummated revolution, neither being satisfied with mere political overthrow; both tried to construct a new society from which new men would emerge. Guevara tries, in this essay, to philosophize his way into a new concept of man and into how a revolution can bring him into existence. According to Guevara, "The road is long and in part unknown; we are aware of our limitations. We will make the twenty-first-century man; we ourselves. We will be tempered in daily actions, creating a new human being with a new technology."

You will be struck by the **Chinese essays** (last six essays of this section) because the authors set out in amazingly confessional detail just exactly how they try to temper themselves by their daily actions; the concreteness of Chinese thought on this topic will be a useful complement to Josiah Royce's somewhat more abstract essay in the second section of the next chapter. Perhaps you will see that philosophy can be as practical an instrument in building a life as any material tool is in making a violin.

The New Man

Ernesto Che Guevara

Ernesto Che Guevara (1927-1967) was a leader in the Cuban Communist Movement. Among his writings are *Che Guevara Speaks, Complete Bolivian Diaries of Che Guevara and Other Captured Documents, On Vietnam and World Revolution, Socialism and Man,* and *Venceremos.*

Dear Comrade:

I am finishing these notes while traveling through Africa, moved by the desire to keep my promise, although after some delay. I should like to do so by dealing with the topic that appears in the title. I believe it might be of interest to Uruguayan readers.

It is common to hear how capitalist spokesmen use as an argument in the ideological struggle against socialism the assertion that such a social system, or the period of building socialism upon which we have embarked, is characterized by the extinction of the individual for the sake of the state. I will make no attempt to refute this assertion on a merely theoretical basis, but will instead establish the facts of the Cuban experience and add commentaries of a general nature. I shall first

Source: Letter to Carlos Quijano, editor-publisher of the Uruguayan weekly *Marcha*; written early in 1965; published in Cuba as "El Socialismo y el Hombre en Cuba" (Havana: Ediciones R.); official government translation by Margarita Zimmerman.

broadly sketch the history of our revolutionary struggle both before and after taking of power.

As we know, the exact date of the beginning of the revolutionary actions which were to culminate on January 1, 1959, was July 26, 1953. A group of men led by Fidel Castro attacked the Moncada military garrison in the province of Oriente, in the early hours of the morning of that day. The attack was a failure. The failure became a disaster and the survivors were imprisoned, only to begin the revolutionary struggle all over again, once they were amnestied.

During this process, which contained only the first seeds of socialism, man was a basic factor. Man—individualized, specific, named—was trusted and the triumph or failure of the task entrusted to him depended on his capacity for action.

Then came the stage of guerrilla warfare. It was carried out in two different environments: the people, an as yet unawakened mass that had to be mobilized, and its vanguard, the guerrilla, the thrusting engine of mobilization, the generator of revolutionary awareness and militant enthusiasm. This vanguard was the catalyst which created the subjective condition necessary for victory. The individual was also the basic factor in the guerrilla, in the framework of the gradual proletarianization of our thinking, in the revolution taking place in our habits and in our minds. Each and every one of the Sierra Maestra fighters who achieved a high rank in the revolutionary forces has to his credit a list of noteworthy deeds. It was on the basis of such deeds that they earned their rank.

It was the first heroic period in which men strove to earn posts of greater responsibility, of greater danger, with the fulfillment of their duty as the only satisfaction. In our revolutionary educational work we often return to this instructive topic. The man of the future could be glimpsed in the attitude of our fighters.

At other times of our history there have been repetitions of this utter devotion to the revolutionary cause. During the October Crisis and at the time of the hurricane Flora, we witnessed deeds of exceptional valor and self-sacrifice carried out by an entire people. One of our fundamental tasks from the ideological standpoint is to find the way to perpetuate such heroic attitudes in everyday life.

The revolutionary government was established in 1959 with the participation of several members of the "sell-out" bourgeoisie. The presence of the rebel army constituted the guarantee of power as the fundamental factor of strength.

Serious contradictions arose which were solved in the first instance in February 1959, when Fidel Castro assumed the leadership of the government in the post of Prime Minister. This process culminated in July of the same year with the resignation of President Urrutia in the face of mass pressure.

With clearly defined features, there now appeared in the history of the Cuban Revolution a personage which will systematically repeat itself: the masses.

This multifacetic being is not, as it is claimed, the sum total of elements of the same category (and moreover, reduced to the same category by the system imposed upon them) and which acts as a tame herd. It is true that the mass follows its leaders, especially Fidel Castro, without hesitation, but the degree to which he has earned such confidence is due precisely to the consummate interpretation of the people's desires and aspirations, and to the sincere struggle to keep the promises made.

The mass participated in the agrarian reform and in the difficult undertaking of the management of the state enterprises; it underwent the heroic experience of

Playa Girón; it was tempered in the struggle against the groups of bandits armed by the CIA; during the October Crisis it lived one of the most important definitions of modern times, and today it continues the work to build socialism.

Looking at things from a superficial standpoint, it might seem that those who speak of the submission of the individual to the state are right; with incomparable enthusiasm and discipline, the mass carries out the tasks set by the government whatever their nature: economic, cultural, defense, sports, etc. The initiative generally comes from Fidel or the high command of the revolution: it is explained to the people, who make it their own. At times local experiences are taken up by the party and the government and are thereby generalized, following the same procedure.

However, the state at times makes mistakes. When this occurs, the collective enthusiasm diminishes palpably as a result of a quantitative diminishing that takes place in each of the elements that make up the collective, and work becomes paralyzed until it finally shrinks to insignificant proportions; this is the time to rectify.

This was what happened in March 1962 in the presence of the sectarian policy imposed on the party by Anibal Escalante.

This mechanism is obviously not sufficient to ensure a sequence of sensible measures; what is missing is a more structured relationship with the mass. We must improve this connection in the years to come, but for now, in the case of the initiatives arising on the top levels of government, we are using the almost intuitive method of keeping our ears open to the general reactions in the face of the problems that are posed.

Fidel is a past master at this; his particular mode of integration with the people can only be appreciated by seeing him in action. In the big public meetings one can observe something like the dialogue of two tuning forks whose vibrations summon forth new vibrations each in the other. Fidel and the mass begin to vibrate in a dialogue of growing intensity which reaches its culminating point in an abrupt ending crowned by our victorious battle cry.

What is hard to understand for anyone who has not lived the revolutionary experience is that close dialectical unity which exists between the individual and the mass, in which both are interrelated, and the mass, as a whole composed of individuals, is in turn interrelated with the leader.

Under capitalism certain phenomena of this nature can be observed with the appearance on the scene of politicians capable of mobilizing the public, but if it is not an authentic social movement, in which case it is not completely accurate to speak of capitalism, the movement will have the same life span as its promoter or until the rigors of capitalist society put an end to popular illusions. Under capitalism man is guided by a cold ordinance which is usually beyond his comprehension. The alienated human individual is bound to society as a whole by an invisible umbilical cord: the law of value. It acts upon all facets of his life, shaping his road and his destiny.

The laws of capitalism, invisible and blind for most people, act upon the individual without his awareness. He sees only the broadness of horizon that appears infinite. Capitalist propaganda presents it in just this way, and attempts to use the Rockefeller case (true or not) as a lesson in the prospects for success. The misery that must be accumulated for such an example to arise and the sum total of baseness contributing to the formation of a fortune of such magnitude do not appear in the picture, and the popular forces are not always able to make these concepts clear. (It would be fitting at this point to study how the workers of the imperialist countries gradually lose their international class spirit under the influence of a certain complicity in the exploitation of the dependent countries and how this fact at the same time wears away the militant spirit of the masses within their own national context, but this topic is outside the framework of the present note.)

In any case we can see the obstacle course which may apparently be overcome by an individual with the necessary qualities to arrive at the finish line. The reward is glimpsed in the distance and the road is solitary. Furthermore, it is a race of wolves: He who arrives does so only at the expense of the failure of others.

I shall now attempt to define the individual, the actor in this strange and moving drama that is the building of socialism, in his twofold existence as a unique being and a member of the community.

I believe that the simplest approach is to recognize his unmade quality: he is an unfinished product. The flaws of the past are translated into the present in the individual consciousness and constant efforts must be made to eradicate them. The process is twofold: On the one hand society acts upon the individual by means of direct and indirect education, while on the other hand the individual undergoes a conscious phase of self-education.

The new society in process of formation has to compete very hard with the past. This makes itself felt not only in the individual consciousness, weighed down by the residues of an education and an upbringing systematically oriented toward the isolation of the individual, but also by the very nature of this transition period, with the persistence of commodity relations. The commodity is the economic cell of capitalist society: As long as it exists, its effects will make themselves felt in the organization of production and therefore in man's consciousness.

Marx's scheme conceived of the transition period as the result of the explosive transformation of the capitalist system torn apart by its inner contradictions: Subsequent reality has shown how some countries, the weak limbs, detach themselves from the imperialist tree, a phenomenon foreseen by Lenin. In those countries capitalism has developed sufficiently to make its effects felt upon the people in one way or another, but it is not its own inner contradictions that explode the system after exhausting all of its possibilities. The struggle for liberation against an external oppressor, the misery which has its origin in foreign causes, such as war, whose consequences make the privileged classes fall upon the exploited, the liberation movements aimed at overthrowing neocolonial regimes, are the customary factors in this process. Conscious action does the rest.

In these countries there still has not been achieved a complete education for the work of society, and wealth is far from being within the reach of the masses through the simple process of appropriation. Underdevelopment and the customary flight of capital to "civilized" countries make impossible a rapid change without sacrifices. There still remains a long stretch to be covered in the building of the economic base, and the temptation to follow the beaten paths of material interest as the lever of speedy development is very great.

There is a danger of not seeing the forest because of the trees. Pursuing the chimera of achieving socialism with the aid of the blunted weapons left to us by capitalism (the commodity as the economic cell, profitability and individual material interest as levers, etc.), it is possible to come to a blind alley. And the arrival there comes about after covering a long distance where there are many crossroads and where it is difficult to realize just when the wrong turn was taken. Meanwhile, the adapted economic base has undermined the development of consciousness. To build communism, a new man must be created simultaneously with the material base.

That is why it is so important to choose correctly the instrument of mass mobilization. That instrument must be fundamentally of a moral character, without forgetting the correct use of material incentives, especially those of a social nature.

As I already said, in moments of extreme danger it is easy to activate moral incentives: To maintain their effectiveness, it is necessary to develop a consciousness in which values acquire new categories. Society as a whole must become a huge school.

The broad characteristics of the phenomenon are similar to the process of formation of capitalist consciousness in the system's first stage. Capitalism resorts to force, but it also educates people in the system. Direct propaganda is carried out by those who are entrusted with the task of explaining the inevitability of a class regime, whether it be of divine origin or due to the imposition of nature as a mechanical entity. This placates the masses, who see themselves oppressed by an evil against which it is not possible to struggle.

This is followed by hope, which differentiates capitalism from the previous caste regimes that offered no way out. For some the caste formula continues in force: The obedient are rewarded by the *post mortem* arrival in other wonderful worlds where the good are requited, and the old tradition is continued. For others, innovation: The division in classes is a matter of fate, but individuals can leave the class to which they belong through work, initiative, etc. This process, and that of self-education for success, must be deeply hypocritical: It is the interested demonstration that a lie is true.

In our case, direct education acquires much greater importance. Explanations are convenient because they are genuine; subterfuges are not needed. It is carried out through the State's educational apparatus in the form of general, technical, and ideological culture, by means of bodies such as the Ministry of Education and the party's information apparatus. Education takes among the masses, and the new attitude that is praised tends to become habit; the mass gradually takes it over and exerts pressure on those who have still not become educated. This is the indirect way of educating the masses, as powerful as the other, structured, one.

But the process is a conscious one: The individual receives the impact of the new social power and perceives that he is not completely adequate to it. Under the influence of the pressure implied in indirect education, he tries to adjust to a situation that he feels to be just and whose lack of development has kept him from doing so thus far. He is educating himself.

We can see the new man who begins to emerge in this period of the building of socialism. His image is as yet unfinished. In fact it will never be finished, since the process advances parallel to the development of new economic forms. Discounting those whose lack of education makes them tend toward the solitary road, toward the satisfaction of their ambitions, there are others who, even within this new picture of over-all advances, tend to march in isolation from the accompanying mass. What is important is that people become more aware every day of the need to incorporate themselves into society and of their own importance as motors of that society.

The institutionality of the Revolution has still not been achieved. We are seeking something new that will allow a perfect identification between the government and the community as a whole, adapted to the special conditions of the building of socialism and avoiding to the utmost the commonplaces of bourgeois democracy transplanted to the society in formation (such as legislative houses, for example). Some experiments have been carried out with the aim of gradually creating the institutionalization of the Revolution, but without too much hurry. We have been greatly restrained by the fear that any formal aspect might make us lose sight of the ultimate and most important revolutionary aspiration: to see man freed from alienation.

Notwithstanding the lack of institutions, which must be overcome gradually, the masses now make history as a conscious aggregate of individuals who struggle for the same cause. In spite of the apparent standardization of man in socialism, he is more complete; his possibilities for expressing himself and making himself heard in the social apparatus are infinitely greater, in spite of the lack of a perfect mechanism to do so.

It is still necessary to accentuate his conscious, individual and collective, participation in all the mechanisms of direction and production and associate it with the idea of the need for technical and ideological education, so that the individual will realize that these processes are closely interdependent and their advances are parallel. He will thus achieve total awareness of his social being, which is equivalent to his full realization as a human being, having broken the chains of alienation.

This will be translated concretely into the reappropriation of his nature through freed work and the expression of his own human condition in culture and art.

In order for it to develop in culture, work must acquire a new condition; man as commodity ceases to exist, and a system is established that grants a quota for the fulfillment of social duty. The means of production belong to society, and the machine is only the front line where duty is performed. Man begins to free his thought from the bothersome fact that presupposed the need to satisfy his animal needs by working. He begins to see himself portrayed in his work and to understand its human magnitude through the created object, through the work carried out. This no longer involves leaving a part of his being in the form of labor power sold, which no longer belongs to him; rather it signifies an emanation from himself, a contribution to the life of society in which he is reflected, the fulfillment of his social duty.

We are doing everything possible to give work this new category of social duty and to join it to the development of technology, on the one hand, which will provide the conditions for greater freedom, and to voluntary work on the other, based on the Marxist concept that man truly achieves his full human condition when he produces without being compelled by the physical necessity of selling himself as a commodity.

It is clear that work still has coercive aspects, even when it is voluntary: Man has still not transformed all the coercion surrounding him into conditioned reflexes of a social nature, and in many cases he still produces under the pressure of the environment (Fidel calls this moral compulsion). He is still to achieve complete spiritual recreation in the presence of his own work, without the direct pressure of the social environment but bound to it by new habits. That will be communism.

The change in consciousness does not come about automatically, just as it does not come about automatically in the economy. The variations are slow and not rhythmic; there are periods of acceleration, others are measured and some even involve a retreat.

We must also consider, as we have pointed out previously, that we are not before a pure transition period such as that envisioned by Marx in the "Critique of the Gotha Program," but rather a new phase not foreseen by him: the first period in the transition to communism or in the building of socialism.

Elements of capitalism are present within this process, which takes place in the midst of violent class struggle. These elements obscure the complete understanding of the essence of the process.

If to this be added the scholasticism that has held back the development of Marxist philosophy and impeded the systematic treatment of the period, whose political economy has still not been developed, we must agree that we are still in diapers. We must study all the primordial features of the period before elaborating a more far-reaching economic and political theory.

The resulting theory will necessarily give preeminence to the two pillars of socialist construction: the formation of the new human being and the development of technology. We still have a great deal to accomplish in both aspects, but the delay is less justifiable as far as the conception of technology as the basis is concerned: Here, it is not a matter of advancing blindly, but rather of following for a sizable stretch the road opened up by the most advanced countries of the world. This is why Fidel harps so insistently on the necessity of the technological and scientific formation of all of our people and especially of the vanguard.

The error of mechanical realism has not appeared (in Cuba), but rather the contrary. This is so because of the lack of understanding of the need to create a new human being who will represent neither nineteenth-century ideas nor those of our decadent and morbid century. It is the twenty-first-century man whom we must create, although this is still a subjective and unsystematic aspiration. This is precisely one of the basic points of our studies and work; to the extent that we make concrete achievements on a theoretical base or vice versa, that we come to broad theoretical conclusions on the basis of our concrete studies, we will have made a valuable contribution to Marxism-Leninism, to the cause of mankind.

I should now like to explain the role played by the personality, the man as the individual who leads the masses that make history. This is our experience, and not a recipe.

Fidel gave impulse to the Revolution in its first years, he has always given it leadership and set the tone, but there is a good group of revolutionaries developing in the same direction as Fidel and a large mass that follows its leaders because it has faith in them. It has faith in them because these leaders have known how to interpret the longings of the masses.

It is not a question of how many kilograms of meat are eaten or how many times a year someone may go on holiday to the seashore or how many pretty imported things can be bought with present wages. It is rather that the individual feels greater fulfillment, that he has greater inner wealth and many more responsibilities. In our country the individual knows that the glorious period in which it has fallen to him to live is one of sacrifice; he is familiar with sacrifice.

The first came to know it in the Sierra Maestra and wherever there was fighting;

later we have known it in all Cuba. Cuba is the vanguard of America and must make sacrifices because it occupies the advance position, because it points out to the Latin American masses the road to full freedom.

Within the country, the leaders have to fulfill their vanguard role; and it must be said with complete sincerity that in a true revolution, to which you give yourself completely without any thought for material retribution, the task of the vanguard revolutionary is both magnificent and anguishing.

Let me say, with the risk of appearing ridiculous, that the true revolutionary is guided by strong feelings of love. It is impossible to think of an authentic revolutionary without this quality. This is perhaps one of the great dramas of a leader; he must combine an impassioned spirit with a cold mind and make painful decisions without flinching. Our vanguard revolutionaries must idealize their love for the people, for the most hallowed causes, and make it one and indivisible. They cannot descend, with small doses of daily affection, to the terrain where ordinary men put their love into practice.

The leaders of the Revolution have children who do not learn to call their father with their first faltering words; they have wives who must be part of the general sacrifice of their lives to carry the Revolution to its destination; their friends are strictly limited to their comrades in revolution. There is no life outside the Revolution.

In these conditions the revolutionary leaders must have a large dose of humanity, a large dose of a sense of justice and truth, to avoid falling into dogmatic extremes, into cold scholasticism, into isolation from the masses. They must struggle every day so that their love of living humanity is transformed into concrete deeds, into acts that will serve as an example, as a mobilizing factor.

The revolutionary, ideological motor of the Revolution within his party is consumed by this uninterrupted activity that ends only with death, unless construction be achieved on a worldwide scale. If his revolutionary eagerness becomes dulled when the most urgent tasks are carried on on a local scale, and if he forgets about proletarian internationalism, the revolution that he leads ceases to be a driving force and it sinks into a comfortable drowsiness which is taken advantage of by imperialism, our irreconcilable enemy, to gain ground. Proletarian internationalism is a duty, but it is also a revolutionary need. This is how we educate our people.

That immense multitude is ordering itself; its order responds to an awareness of the need for order; it is no longer a dispersed force, divisible in thousands of fractions shot into space like the fragments of a grenade, trying by any and all means, in a fierce struggle with their equals, to achieve a position that would give them support in the face of an uncertain future.

We know that we have sacrifices ahead of us and that we must pay a price for the heroic fact of constituting a vanguard as a nation. We, the leaders, know that we must pay a price for having the right to say that we are at the head of the people that is at the head of America.

Each and every one of us punctually pays his share of sacrifice, aware of being rewarded by the satisfaction of fulfilling our duty, aware of advancing with everyone toward the new human being who is to be glimpsed on the horizon.

Allow me to attempt to come to some conclusions:

We socialists are more free because we are more fulfilled: We are more fulfilled because we are more free.

The skeleton of our complete freedom is formed, but it lacks the protein substance and the draperies. We will create them.

Our freedom and its daily sustenance are the color of blood and swollen with sacrifice.

Our sacrifice is a conscious one: It is in payment for the freedom we are building.

The road is long and in part unknown; we are aware of our limitations. We will make the twenty-first-century man; we ourselves.

We will be tempered in daily actions, creating a new human being with a new technology.

The personality plays the role of mobilization and leadership in so far as it incarnates the highest virtues and aspirations of the people and does not become detoured.

The road is opened up by the vanguard group, the best among the good, the party.

The basic raw material of our work is the youth: In it we place our hopes and we are preparing it to take the banner from our hands.

If this faltering letter has made some things clear, it will have fulfilled my purpose in sending it.

Accept our ritual greetings, as a handshake or an "Ave María Purísima."

Patria o muerte

CHINESE COMMUNISM

Let a Hundred Flowers Blossom

Mao Tse-tung

Mao Tse-tung (1893-   ) is Chairman of the Communist Party of the Peoples' Republic of China and the leader of some 800 million Chinese. His numerous writings include *New Democracy* (1944), *The Fight for a New China* (1945), and *Quotations from Chairman Mao Tse-tung* (1966).

"Let a hundred flowers blossom, let a hundred schools of thought contend" and "long-term coexistence and mutual supervision"—how did these slogans come to be put forward? They were put forward in the light of China's specific conditions, on the basis of the recognition that various kinds of contradictions still exist in socialist society, and in response to the country's urgent need to speed up its economic and cultural development. Letting a hundred flowers blossom and a hundred schools of thought contend is the policy for promoting the progress of the arts and the sciences and a flourishing socialist culture in our land. Different forms and styles in art should develop freely and different schools in science should contend freely. We think that it is harmful to the growth of art and science if administrative measures are used to impose one particular style of art or school of thought and to ban another. Questions of right and wrong in the arts and sciences should be settled through free discussion in artistic and scientific circles and through practical work in these fields. They should not be settled in summary fashion. A period of trial is often needed to determine whether something is right or wrong. Throughout history, new and correct things have often failed at the outset to win recognition from the majority of people and have had to develop by twists and turns in struggle. Often correct and good things have first been regarded not as fragrant flowers but as poisonous weeds. Copernicus' theory of the solar system and Darwin's theory of evolution were once dismissed as erroneous and had to win through over bitter opposition. Chinese history offers many similar examples. In a socialist society, conditions for the growth of the new are radically different from and far superior to those in the old society. Nevertheless, it still often happens that new, rising forces are held back and rational proposals constricted. Moreover, the growth of new things may be hindered in the absence of deliberate suppression simply through lack of discernment. It is therefore necessary to be careful about questions of right and wrong in the arts and sciences, to

Source: *Quotations from Chairman Mao* (Peking: Foreign Languages Press, 1966).

encourage free discussion and avoid hasty conclusions. We believe that such an attitude can help to ensure a relatively smooth development of the arts and sciences.

People may ask, since Marxism is accepted as the guiding ideology by the majority of the people in our country, can it be criticized? Certainly it can. Marxism is scientific truth and fears no criticism. If it did, and if it could be overthrown by criticism, it would be worthless. In fact, aren't the idealists criticizing Marxism every day and in every way? Aren't those who harbour bourgeois and petty-bourgeois ideas and do not wish to change—aren't they also criticizing Marxism in every way? Marxists should not be afraid of criticism from any quarter. Quite the contrary, they need to temper and develop themselves and win new positions in the teeth of criticism and in the storm and stress of struggle. Fighting against wrong ideas is like being vaccinated—a man develops greater immunity from disease as a result of vaccination. Plants raised in hot-houses are unlikely to be sturdy. Carrying out the policy of letting a hundred flowers blossom and a hundred schools of thought contend will not weaken but strengthen the leading position of Marxism in the ideological field.

What should our policy be towards non-Marxist ideas? As far as unmistakable counter-revolutionaries and saboteurs of the socialist cause are concerned, the matter is easy: we simply deprive them of their freedom of speech. But incorrect ideas among the people are quite a different matter. Will it do to ban such ideas and deny them any opportunity for expression? Certainly not. It is not only futile but very harmful to use summary methods in dealing with ideological questions among the people, with questions concerned with man's mental world. You may ban the expression of wrong ideas, but the ideas will still be there. On the other hand, if correct ideas are pampered in hot-houses without being exposed to the elements or immunized from disease, they will not win out against erroneous ones. Therefore, it is only by employing the method of discussion, criticism and reasoning that we can really foster correct ideas and overcome wrong ones, and that we can really settle issues.

Combat Liberalism
*Mao Tse-tung**

We stand for active ideological struggle because it is the weapon for ensuring unity within the Party and the revolutionary organizations in the interest of our fight. Every Communist and revolutionary should take up this weapon.

But liberalism rejects ideological struggle and stands for unprincipled peace, thus

Source: Five Articles by Chairman Mao Tse-tung (Peking: Foreign Languages Press, 1968). Presented September 7, 1937.

* For headnote, see page 448.

giving rise to a decadent, philistine attitude and bringing about political degeneration in certain units and individuals in the Party and the revolutionary organizations.

Liberalism manifests itself in various ways.

To let things slide for the sake of peace and friendship when a person has clearly gone wrong, and refrain from principled argument because he is an old acquaintance, a fellow townsman, a schoolmate, a close friend, a loved one, an old colleague or old subordinate. Or to touch on the matter lightly instead of going into it thoroughly, so as to keep on good terms. The result is that both the organization and the individual are harmed. This is one type of liberalism.

To indulge in irresponsible criticism in private instead of actively putting forward one's suggestions to the organization. To say nothing to people to their faces but to gossip behind their backs or to say nothing at a meeting but to gossip afterwards. To show no regard at all for the principles of collective life but to follow one's own inclination. This is a second type.

To let things drift if they do not affect one personally; to say as little as possible while knowing perfectly well what is wrong, to be worldly wise and play safe and seek only to avoid blame. This is a third type.

Not to obey orders but to give pride of place to one's own opinions. To demand special consideration from the organization but to reject its discipline. This is a fourth type.

To indulge in personal attacks, pick quarrels, vent personal spite or seek revenge instead of entering into an argument and struggling against incorrect views for the sake of unity or progress or getting the work done properly. This is a fifth type.

To hear incorrect views without rebutting them and even to hear counter-revolutionary remarks without reporting them, but instead to take them calmly as if nothing had happened. This is a sixth type.

To be among the masses and fail to conduct propaganda and agitation or speak at meetings or conduct investigations and inquiries among them, and instead to be indifferent to them and show no concern for their well-being, forgetting that one is a Communist and behaving as if one were an ordinary non-Communist. This is a seventh type.

To see someone harming the interests of the masses and yet not feel indignant, or dissuade or stop him or reason with him, but to allow him to continue. This is an eighth type.

To work half-heartedly without a definite plan or direction; to work perfunctorily and muddle along—"So long as one remains a monk, one goes on tolling the bell." This is a ninth type.

To regard oneself as having rendered great service to the revolution, to pride oneself on being a veteran, to disdain minor assignments while being quite unequal to major tasks, to be slipshod in work and slack in study. This is a tenth type.

To be aware of one's own mistakes and yet make no attempt to correct them, taking a liberal attitude towards oneself. This is an eleventh type.

We could name more. But these eleven are the principal types.

They are all manifestations of liberalism.

Liberalism is extremely harmful in a revolutionary collective. It is a corrosive which eats away unity, undermines cohesion, causes apathy and creates dissension. It robs the revolutionary ranks of compact organization and strict discipline, prevents policies from being carried through and alienates the Party organizations from the masses which the Party leads. It is an extremely bad tendency.

Liberalism stems from petty-bourgeois selfishness; it places personal interests first and the interests of the revolution second; and this gives rise to ideological, political and organizational liberalism.

People who are liberals look upon the principles of Marxism as abstract dogma. They approve of Marxism, but are not prepared to practise it or to practise it in full; they are not prepared to replace their liberalism by Marxism. These people have their Marxism, but they have their liberalism as well—they talk Marxism but practise liberalism; they apply Marxism to others but liberalism to themselves. They keep both kinds of goods in stock and find a use for each. This is how the minds of certain people work.

Liberalism is a manifestation of opportunism and conflicts fundamentally with Marxism. It is negative and objectively has the effect of helping the enemy; that is why the enemy welcomes its preservation in our midst. Such being its nature, there should be no place for it in the ranks of the revolution.

We must use Marxism, which is positive in spirit, to overcome liberalism, which is negative. A Communist should have largeness of mind and he should be staunch and active, looking upon the interests of the revolution as his very life and subordinating his personal interests to those of the revolution; always and everywhere he should adhere to principle and wage a tireless struggle against all incorrect ideas and actions, so as to consolidate the collective life of the Party and strengthen the ties between the Party and the masses; he should be more concerned about the Party and the masses than about any individual, and more concerned about others than about himself. Only thus can he be considered a Communist.

To Remold My World Outlook with Mao Tse-tung's Thought
Wang Tao-ming

Wang Tao-ming is a deputy political instructor in a People's Liberation Army unit.

Under the guidance of the Party and with the help of my comrades, I have been studying and applying Chairman Mao's works in a practical way in order to remould my ideology and as a result I have made some progress in class consciousness and theoretical understanding of revolution in the last few years. Following are some of

Source: *Mao Tse-tung's Thought Is the Invincible Weapon* (Peking: Foreign Languages Press, 1968).

my experiences in remoulding my thinking by studying and applying Chairman Mao's "Three Good Old Articles" and other articles in a positive way.

THERE IS NO "BORN RED"

I did not understand the importance of ideological remoulding before enlisting and was just not interested in the idea. I thought, "Our generation studies in the schools run by the Party, reads the books published in the new society, receives the Party's education from childhood and grows up with the song *The East Is Red* on the lips and the Young Pioneer's tie around the neck. Our thinking has been revolutionary since childhood. Because I am of a poor peasant family and my father is a revolutionary cadre, I have absorbed no undesirable ideas and there is no need for me to undergo any remoulding. I am a 'born red' youth and a 'born' revolutionary successor. My taking the revolutionary road is not in question at all." So when my father told me to work hard on Chairman Mao's works and remould my thinking earnestly or I would commit errors and would degenerate, I thought what he said was exaggerated to scare me.

But it was only after Chairman Mao issued the call "Learn from Comrade Lei Feng"[1] that I really and truly realized the importance of ideological remoulding and began conscientiously to remould myself with Mao Tse-tung's thought. I came to see that the reason why Comrade Lei Feng could perform great deeds in everyday life and become a communist fighter lies basically in the fact that by studying and applying Chairman Mao's works in a vital way, he understood the significance of life, knew whom he should serve and formed the world outlook of serving the people whole-heartedly. . . .

With the idea of making revolution for the world's people strongly in my mind, I set higher demands on myself and plunge into my work with greater enthusiasm. In daily life, I struggle hard against any manifestation of selfishness in me and sometimes while I am eating my meal I will ask myself whether I really put others before myself. While practising bayonet fighting last year, some comrades thought this method of fighting amounted to very little in modern warfare. I organized my comrades to study Chairman Mao's teachings on people's war and built up our belief in the importance of bayonet fighting. We arrived at the conclusion that "we can defeat atom bombs by bayonet fighting." We are ready at any time to support the revolutionary struggles of the people of the world.

. . . Mao Tse-tung's thought is the unsetting red sun in my heart and I will forever consider myself a seedling which cannot do without the sunshine even for a single moment.

[1] Lei Feng was a squad leader in a transportation company of the P.L.A. stationed in Shenyang. He worked very hard on Chairman Mao's works and put special emphasis on applying what he had learnt. As a result he attained a high political consciousness, a firm proletarian stand and the noble quality of serving the people whole-heartedly. He received distinction three times for meritorious service and was cited as a model Communist Youth Leaguer. He joined the Party in November 1960 and died in August 1962 while performing his duty. Chairman Mao wrote the inscription "Learn from Comrade Lei Feng!"

With this realization, I have been more conscientious in dealing with problems. For instance, when I go out on business and return late the cooks often want to prepare a special meal for me. But I insist on having just what is left. The cooks know that I like onions and often want to give me some. But I refuse to accept any. It is out of their concern for me that they want to do these things. But if I accept these favours, I will put myself in a privileged position and become different from the masses. Another example, when some comrades have made some progress and say that this is due to my help, I will strictly examine myself to see whether I have given too much prominence to my personal role in the work and will organize the core members to talk with these comrades so that they will not only tell their ideological problems to me but also to the leader of the Party Group and other Party members. It will never do to overemphasize one's own role in work and seek to win personal fame.

Chairman Mao has said:

Even if we achieve gigantic successes in our work, there is no reason whatsoever to feel conceited and arrogant. Modesty helps one to go forward, whereas conceit makes one lag behind. This is a truth we must always bear in mind.

He has also said, "It is not hard for one to do a bit of good. What is hard is to do good all one's life and never do anything bad. . . ." He teaches us to engage in arduous struggle for decades on end. I think that I have made some progress in studying Chairman Mao's works. Nevertheless I should not try to live on what I have achieved for the rest of my life. The road of revolution and the road of life still stretch out a long way ahead. As long as I am alive, I will go on making revolution, remoulding myself, and studying and applying Chairman Mao's works in a living way. I'll follow Mao Tse-tung's thought and be a revolutionary all my life. To persons with heads full of bourgeois individualism, achievements and honours are signboards painted in golden letters, are "capital" with which to gain personal position and comfort and at that point they come to the dead end of progress. But proletarian fighters never rest content because of achievements and honours. In their view, achievements and honours are a kind of encouragement and stimulant, prompting them to achieve still greater successes for the Party, setting new tasks for them, and setting still higher demands for revolutionizing their ideology; they are the point of departure for new progress.

In Memory of Norman Bethune
Mao Tse-tung*

Comrade Norman Bethune, a member of the Communist Party of Canada, was around fifty when he was sent by the Communist Parties of Canada and the United States to China; he made light of travelling thousands of miles to help us in our War of Resistance Against Japan. He arrived in Yenan in the spring of last year, went to work in the Wutai Mountains, and to our great sorrow died a martyr at his post. What kind of spirit is this that makes a foreigner selflessly adopt the cause of the Chinese people's liberation as his own? It is the spirit of internationalism, the spirit of communism, from which every Chinese Communist must learn. Leninism teaches that the world revolution can only succeed if the proletariat of the capitalist countries supports the struggle for liberation of the colonial and semi-colonial peoples and if the proletariat of the colonies and semi-colonies supports that of the proletariat of the capitalist countries. Comrade Bethune put this Leninist line into practice. We Chinese Communists must also follow this line in our practice. We must unite with the proletariat of all the capitalist countries, with the proletariat of Japan, Britain, the United States, Germany, Italy and all other capitalist countries, before it is possible to overthrow imperialism, to liberate our nation and people, and to liberate the other nations and peoples of the world. This is our internationalism, the internationalism with which we oppose both narrow nationalism and narrow patriotism.

Comrade Bethune's spirit, his utter devotion to others without any thought of self, was shown in his boundless sense of responsibility in his work and his boundless warmheartedness towards all comrades and the people. Every Communist must learn from him. There are not a few people who are irresponsible in their work, preferring the light to the heavy, shoving the heavy loads on to others and choosing the easy ones for themselves. At every turn they think of themselves before others. When they make some small contribution, they swell with pride and brag about it for fear that others will not know. They feel no warmth towards comrades and the people but are cold, indifferent and apathetic. In fact such people are not Communists, or at least cannot be counted as true Communists. No one who returned from the front failed to express admiration for Bethune whenever his name was mentioned, and none remained unmoved by his spirit. In the Shansi-Chahar-Hopei border area, no soldier or civilian was unmoved who had been treated by Dr. Bethune or had seen how he worked. Every Communist must learn this true communist spirit from Comrade Bethune.

Comrade Bethune was a doctor, the art of healing was his profession and he was constantly perfecting his skill, which stood very high in the Eighth Route Army's medical service. His example is an excellent lesson for those people who wish to

Source: Five Articles by Chairman Mao Tse-tung. (Peking: Foreign Languages Press, 1968). Presented December 21, 1939.

* For headnote, see page 448.

change their work the moment they see something different and for those who despise technical work as of no consequence or as promising no future.

Comrade Bethune and I met only once. Afterwards he wrote me many letters. But I was busy, and I wrote him only one letter and do not even know if he ever received it. I am deeply grieved over his death. Now we are all commemorating him, which shows how profoundly his spirit inspires everyone. We must all learn the spirit of absolute selflessness from him. With this spirit everyone can be very useful to the people. A man's ability may be great or small, but if he has this spirit, he is already noble-minded and pure, a man of moral integrity and above vulgar interests, a man who is of value to the people.

On Contradiction
Mao Tse-tung*

When we understand the universality and the particularity of contradiction, we must proceed to study the problem of the identity and struggle of the aspects of a contradiction.

Identity, unity, coincidence, interpenetration, interpermeation, interdependence (or mutual dependence for existence), interconnection or mutual co-operation—all these different terms mean the same thing and refer to the following two points: first, the existence of each of the two aspects of a contradiction in the process of the development of a thing presupposes the existence of the other aspect, and both aspects coexist in a single entity; second, in given conditions, each of the two contradictory aspects transforms itself into its opposite. This is the meaning of identity.

Lenin said:

Dialectics *is the teaching which shows how* opposites *can be and how they happen to be (how they become)* identical—*under what conditions they are identical, transforming themselves into one another—why the human mind should take these opposites not as dead, rigid, but as living, conditional, mobile, transforming themselves into one another.*

What does this passage mean?

The contradictory aspects in every process exclude each other, struggle with each other and are in opposition to each other. Without exception, they are contained in the process of development of all things and in all human thought. A simple process contains only a single pair of opposites, while a complex process contains more. And in turn, the pairs of opposites are in contradiction to one another. That is how all things in the objective world and all human thought are constituted and how they are set in motion.

Source: *Four Essays on Philosophy* (Peking: Foreign Languages Press, 1968), pp. 60-67.

* For headnote, see page 448.

This being so, there is an utter lack of identity or unity. How then can one speak of identity or unity?

The fact is that no contradictory aspect can exist in isolation. Without its opposite aspect, each loses the condition for its existence. Just think, can any one contradictory aspect of a thing or of a concept in the human mind exist independently? Without life, there would be no death; without death, there would be no life. Without "above," there would be no "below"; without "below," there would be no "above." Without misfortune, there would be no good fortune; without good fortune, there would be no misfortune. Without facility, there would be no difficulty; without difficulty, there would be no facility. Without landlords, there would be no tenant-peasants; without tenant-peasants, there would be no landlords. Without the bourgeoisie, there would be no proletariat; without the proletariat, there would be no bourgeoisie. Without imperialist oppression of nations, there would be no colonies or semi-colonies; without colonies or semi-colonies, there would be no imperialist oppression of nations. It is so with all opposites; in given conditions, on the one hand they are opposed to each other, and on the other they are interconnected, interpenetrating, interpermeating and interdependent, and this character is described as identity. In given conditions, all contradictory aspects possess the character of non-identity and hence are described as being in contradiction. But they also possess the character of identity and hence are interconnected. This is what Lenin means when he says that dialectics studies "how *opposites* can be . . . *identical*." How then can they be identical? Because each is the condition for the other's existence. This is the first meaning of identity.

But is it enough to say merely that each of the contradictory aspects is the condition for the other's existence, that there is identity between them and that consequently they can coexist in a single entity? No, it is not. The matter does not end with their dependence on each other for their existence; what is more important is their transformation into each other. That is to say, in given conditions, each of the contradictory aspects within a thing transforms itself into its opposite, changes its position to that of its opposite. This is the second meaning of the identity of contradiction.

Why is there identity here, too? You see, by means of revolution the proletariat, at one time the ruled, is transformed into the ruler, while the bourgeoisie, the erstwhile ruler, is transformed into the ruled and changes its position to that originally occupied by its opposite. . . .

.   .   .

Our state is a people's democratic dictatorship led by the working class and based on the worker-peasant alliance. What is this dictatorship for? Its first function is to suppress the reactionary classes and elements and those exploiters in our country who range themselves against the socialist revolution, to suppress all those who try to wreck our socialist construction, or in other words, to resolve the internal contradictions between ourselves and the enemy. For instance, to arrest, try and sentence certain counter-revolutionaries, and to deprive landlords and bureaucrat-capitalists of their right to vote and their freedom of speech for a specified period of time—all this comes within the scope of our dictatorship. To maintain public order and safeguard the interests of the people, it is likewise necessary to exercise dictatorship over embezzlers, swindlers, arsonists, murderers, criminal gangs and other scoundrels who seriously disrupt public order. The second function of this dictatorship is to protect our country from subversion and possible aggression by external enemies. In that event, it is the task of this dictatorship to resolve the external contradiction between ourselves and the enemy. The aim of this dictatorship is to protect all our people so that they can devote themselves to peaceful labour and build China into a socialist country with a modern industry, agriculture, science and culture. Who is to exercise this dictatorship? Naturally, the working class and the entire people under its leadership. Dictatorship does not apply within the ranks of the people. The people cannot exercise dictatorship over themselves, nor must one section of the people oppress another. Law-breaking elements among the people will be punished according to law, but this is different in principle from the exercise of dictatorship to suppress enemies of the people. What applies among the people is democratic centralism. Our Constitution lays it down that citizens of the People's Republic of China enjoy freedom of speech, of the press, assembly, association, procession, demonstration, religious belief, and so on. Our Constitution also provides that the organs of state must practise democratic centralism, that they must rely on the masses and that their personnel must serve the people. Our socialist democracy is democracy in the broadest sense such as is not to be found in any capitalist country. Our dictatorship is the people's democratic dictatorship led by the working class and based on the worker-peasant alliance. That is to say, democracy operates within the ranks of the people, while the working class, uniting with all others enjoying civil rights, and in the first place with the peasantry, enforces dictatorship over the reactionary classes and elements and all those who resist socialist transformation and oppose socialist construction. By civil rights, we mean, politically, the rights of freedom and democracy.

But this freedom is freedom with leadership and this democracy is democracy under centralized guidance, not anarchy. Anarchy does not accord with the interests or wishes of the people.

. . . They ask for a two-party system as in the West, with one party in office and the other out of office. But this so-called two-party system is nothing but a device for maintaining the dictatorship of the bourgeoisie; it can never guarantee freedom to the working people. As a matter of fact, freedom and democracy do not exist in the abstract, only in the concrete. In a society rent by class struggle, if there is freedom for the exploiting classes to exploit the working people, there is no freedom for the working people not to be exploited, and if there is democracy for the bourgeoisie, there is no democracy for the proletariat and other working people. The legal existence of the Communist Party is tolerated in some capitalist countries, but only to the extent that it does not endanger the fundamental interests of the bourgeoisie; it is not tolerated beyond that. Those who demand freedom and democracy in the abstract regard democracy as an end and not a means. Democracy sometimes seems to be an end, but it is in fact only a means. Marxism teaches us that democracy is part of the superstructure and belongs to the category of politics. That is to say, in the last analysis, it serves the economic base. The same is true of freedom. Both democracy and freedom are relative, not absolute, and they come into being and develop in specific historical conditions. Within the ranks of the people, democracy is correlative with centralism, and freedom with discipline. They are the two opposites of a single entity, contradictory as well as united, and we should not one-sidedly emphasize one to the denial of the other. Within the ranks of the people, we cannot do without freedom, nor can we do without discipline; we cannot do without democracy, nor can we do without centralism. This unity of democracy and centralism, of freedom and discipline, constitutes our democratic centralism. Under this system, the people enjoy extensive democracy and freedom, but at the same time they have to keep within the bounds of socialist discipline. All this is well understood by the broad masses of the people.

In advocating freedom with leadership and democracy under centralized guidance, we in no way mean that coercive measures should be taken to settle ideological questions or questions involving the distinction between right and wrong among the people. All attempts to use administrative orders or coercive measures to settle ideological questions or questions of right and wrong are not only ineffective but harmful. We cannot abolish religion by administrative decree or force people not to believe in it. We cannot compel people to give up idealism, any more than we can force them to believe in Marxism. The only way to settle questions of an ideological nature or controversial issues among the people is by the democratic method, the method of discussion, or criticism, of persuasion and education, and not by the method of coercion or repression. To be able to carry on their production and studies effectively and to arrange their lives properly, the people want their government and those in charge of production and of cultural and educational organizations to issue appropriate orders of an obligatory nature. It is common sense that the maintenance of public order would be impossible without such administrative regulations. Administrative orders and the method of persuasion and education complement each other in resolving contradictions among the people. Even administrative regulations for the maintenance of public order must be accompanied by persuasion and education, for in many cases regulations alone will not work.

How I Used Chairman Mao's Scientific Thinking
Yao Shih-chang

Yao Shih-chang is Chairman of the Revolutionary Committee of the Tuanchieh Production Brigade, Nanwang Commune, Penglai County, Shantung Province.

I am a peasant. I was born in a poor-peasant family and I'm now 47 years old. I had four years of school as a child. In addition to studying Chairman Mao's "three constantly read articles," I have also repeatedly studied Chairman Mao's brilliant philosophical works to arm myself with dialectical materialism and I've made scientific experiments to increase peanut production. In the course of doing this I got rid of the metaphysics in my thinking and overcame various kinds of

Source: Peking Review, November 13, 1970.

interference and obstacles. As a result, our brigade has gradually raised the average per-*mu* yield of peanuts from some 200 *jin* to 450 *jin*. The highest is more than 800 *jin* per *mu*. Practice has made me understand profoundly that Chairman Mao's brilliant philosophical thinking is a beacon guiding our scientific experiments.

TURNING FAILURE INTO SUCCESS

Most of our brigade's fields is in hilly areas and we cultivate more than 4,800 *mu*, of which 2,000 are grown to peanuts. Before we set up the agricultural producers' co-operative, the average per-*mu* yield of peanuts was only 150 *jin*. Although yield was raised after that, it was still low. I was very worried about this and always considered finding a way to raise output. I had begun tackling this problem in 1953. At that time I didn't put Mao Tse-tung Thought in command and my experiments failed because I had no idea of dialectical materialism and didn't have a clear orientation.

When we started sowing one year we were hit by drought. There wasn't enough moisture in the soil, and there was no guarantee all the seeds would sprout into seedlings. I'd heard that the Tsaolintien Production Team used the method of digging deep furrows and covering them with only a thin layer of soil in order to make all the seedlings come up and grow well. I got our brigade to use their method. Though it had been effective in Tsaolintien, it didn't work in our brigade and output dropped that autumn.

This saddened me and a fierce struggle took place in my mind. At the time, the leadership had asked me to sum up our experience and draw lessons from it. With this problem in mind, I conscientiously studied Chairman Mao's brilliant works *On Contradiction* and *On Practice*. Chairman Mao teaches: "Only those who are subjective, one-sided and superficial in their approach to problems will smugly issue orders or directives the moment they arrive on the scene, without considering the circumstances, without viewing things in their totality (their history and their present state as a whole) and without getting to the essence of things (their nature and the internal relations between one thing and another). Such people are bound to trip and fall."

Chairman Mao's teaching opened my mind and immediately enlightened me greatly. I found that I had made the metaphysical error of imitating others without considering the concrete circumstances. The Tsaolintien Production Team's land is level and fertile. So the people there plant peanuts in rows widely apart. Their method of lightly-covered deep furrows guarantees all the seedlings coming up and growing well. Our brigade is situated in valleys and the soil cover is thin. So we plant peanuts closely with the distance between rows narrow. When we dug deep furrows the soil fell in and buried the seeds. In effect, we were digging deep and covering deep. Though we had good intentions, the result was bad and output fell. Chairman Mao's philosophical thinking helped me find the cause of our failure. My subjective concept did not conform to objective reality. Speaking of knowledge of the objective world, I was still in a blind and passive position.

Chairman Mao teaches: "If a man wants to succeed in his work, that is, to achieve the anticipated results, he must bring his ideas into correspondence with the laws of the objective external world; if they do not correspond, he will fail in his practice. After he fails, he draws his lessons, corrects his ideas to make them correspond to the laws of the external world, and can thus turn failure into success." In accordance with this teaching of Chairman Mao's, I made up my mind to use Chairman Mao's philosophical thinking in continuing the scientific experiment to increase the peanut yield and to turn failure into success.

IN TRANSFORMING THE OBJECTIVE WORLD, ONE SHOULD ALSO TRANSFORM THE SUBJECTIVE WORLD

I was determined to find the law of the growth of peanuts so as to blaze a new trail in increasing yields. How to do it? I thought about it day in and day out, but for a long time I wasn't able to get at the essence of it. What was I to do? I opened my copy of *On Practice* and studied it word for word and sentence by sentence. Chairman Mao teaches: "Whoever wants to know a thing has no way of doing so except by coming into contact with it, that is, by living (practising) in its environment. . . . If you want knowledge, you must take part in the practice of changing reality. If you want to know the taste of a pear, you must change the pear by eating it yourself." From then on, I was determined to find the law of the growth of peanuts through practice.

Having found the laws governing the growth of peanuts, I applied them in carrying out repeated experiments to increase the yield. To do this, it was essential to get the best out of the first pair of branches. Shallow sowing was preferable, because sowing of seeds deep in the soil would affect the bearing of pods by that first pair of branches which grew round the base. But the area of our production brigade was stricken by drought almost every spring, which left the soil dry. Moreover, the large, oil-rich seeds took a long time to sprout. Shallow sowing would cause the seeds to dry up easily, and this meant not all the seedlings would sprout and increasing the yield would be impossible. Not knowing how to solve this problem worried us very much.

With this problem in mind, I studied Chairman Mao's *On Contradiction* and finally got the answer. Chairman Mao teaches: "In studying any corollary process in which there are two or more contradictions we must devote every effort to finding its principal contradiction. Once this principal contradiction is grasped, all problems can be readily solved." Chairman Mao's teaching enlightened me. I pondered: If we want to increase the peanut yield, we must first of all ensure the full sprouting of the seedlings, without which a high yield would be out of the question. Therefore, the principal contradiction at the time was to ensure the growth of all the seedlings, and the method of resolving this contradiction was deep sowing. Having solved this question, the problem of the first pair of branches buried deep in the soil, which affected the bearing of the pods, came to the fore. Formerly a secondary contradiction, it now became the principal contradiction.

How to solve this contradiction? Again I turned to Chairman Mao's works for instruction. In *On Contradiction*, Chairman Mao points out: "It [materialist dialectics] holds that external causes are the condition of change and internal causes are the basis of change, and that external causes become operative through internal causes." I made an analysis: The first pair of branches blossomed early and luxuriantly, with a big potential for increasing the yield. But deep sowing was unfavourable to the growth of the first pair of branches, which meant that their potential could not be fully used. This, I realized, was because of the restriction by the external causes. Following Chairman Mao's teaching, I tried to find a solution to this problem through practice.

ADVANCING CONTINUOUSLY IN THE COURSE OF RESOLVING CONTRADICTIONS

Popularization of this method in our production brigade has, to the joy of everybody, resulted in a big boost in the peanut yield. I deeply realize that it is Chairman Mao's brilliant philosophical thinking that has helped unravel the mystery of raising the yield. Mao Tse-tung Thought is the beacon guiding our scientific research: as long as we follow Chairman Mao's teachings and act according to his instructions, we shall always be victorious. In accordance with Chairman Mao's teaching that "man has constantly to sum up experience and go on discovering, inventing, creating and advancing," I carried on with my experiments and succeeded in constantly raising the peanut yield.

Contradictions are bound to crop up continuously, and we advance continuously in the course of resolving them. In 1967, our area was hit by the worst drought in decades, resulting in a big decrease in output. I felt badly that we couldn't sell large quantities of peanuts to the state. The following year saw another long dry spell. Determined to fight the drought, we worked hard to water the peanut plots. However, most of our peanuts were grown on poor hilly land with only a thin layer of soil. After we watered the plants, the temperature of the soil rose when the sun shone on it, with the result that many pods of the large peanuts formed in the early stage began to rot.

This was a new contradiction which had to be solved. In the light of the truth that contradictory things transform themselves into each other, I set about creating conditions for resolving it. With the help of our technical team, we built row after row of ridges for growing peanuts, and we watered the furrows between the ridges. This prevented rotting. But by building ridges we had increased the distance between the rows, with a corresponding decrease in the total number of clusters on each *mu* of land. The result was that the yield still could not be raised.

At that point, we interplanted large and small peanuts, growing the small peanuts in the furrows because they were better able to resist water-logging and took less time to grow. So we succeeded in working out a method of preventing the pods of the large peanuts from rotting and at the same time not reducing the total number of clusters grown on each *mu*. After experimenting on the small plots, we gathered from each *mu* more than 400 *jin* of large peanuts and over 200 *jin* of small peanuts. Thus we found a new way to conquer both drought and water-logging and get a high and stable yield of peanuts.

From practice I realize that in farming we always have to deal with contradictions, and through scientific experiment we create conditions to make the contradictions transform in the direction beneficial to mankind's cause of revolution and construction. Objective things are always developing; there will always be contradictions and there is no end to scientific experiment.

462 / Third World Liberation

Suggested Readings

1. Fann, K. T., and Hodges, Donald C. (eds.), *Readings in U.S. Imperialism* (Boston: Porter Sargent, 1971).
2. Fanon, Frantz, *The Wretched of the Earth*, (New York: Grove Press, 1965).
3. Lavan, George, *Che Guevara Speaks,* (New York: Grove Press, 1967).
4. Marquard, L., *The Peoples and Policies of South Africa,* 2d ed. (New York: Oxford University Press, 1960).
5. Nkrumah, Kwame, *Consciencism* (New York: Modern Reader Paperbacks, 1964).
6. North, Robert C., *Chinese Communism* (New York: McGraw-Hill, 1970).

In Search of Self and Identity

But I did not stop to consider what the soul was, or if I did stop, I imagined that it was something extremely rare and subtle like a wind, a flame, or an ether, which was spread throughout my grosser parts.

—René Descartes

INTRODUCTION

FOOL: What is it which everything that ever was, is, or will be has, yet which nothing that ever was, is, or will be has in common with anything else?
KING: I know thee for a fool for certain, if thou knowest not the answer to that riddle.
FOOL: Nay, but I know it.
KING: If thou knowest it, why do you ask me?
FOOL: But to see if Kings may be Fools!
KING: Well, then, since that would be 'gainst all sense, 'tis necessary that you answer it.
FOOL: (Aside—The King may be no fool, but I'll wager he would be a Fool.) Self-identity.
KING: That was, is, and will be the obvious answer, for if it were not, then Kings would be Fools and Fools Kings, and I would have your head, Fool, before allowing this kingdom to be blast against all Nature. I would have self-identity to be a monarchical principle.
FOOL: I yield, Sire; I know thee for my King, for thou art the King of Fools.

The fool and the king have said they are self-identical. Let us take it that each thing is identical with itself. And now we may ask, as so many before have asked, "What is it about myself that is self-identical?"

Before we consider this metaphysical question about the self, it will be instructive to lay some groundwork by considering some metaphysical questions about things in general.

1. *Individuation.* Is there more than one thing in the universe? It seems obvious that there is, for if we get past the number "one" in counting things, then there must be more than one thing. A student sits at his desk with a piece of paper in front

of him. He hears a song coming from his radio as he inhales the smoke from his cigar and tastes the flavor. If we consider the paper, the song, and the flavor of the cigar, there are at least three things, three individuals. Individuation is the process of dividing the world into a number of things.

Counting is the process of putting individuals and numerals in a one-to-one relationship. Each individual is to be assigned one and only one numeral. The piece of paper is assigned the numeral "one," the song "two," the cigar flavor "three," and so forth. Counting depends on individuating. Then what is the criterion for individuating, for deciding that something is an individual and may be assigned a numeral? Why is it that when one looks at the piece of paper he decides it is a separate thing, not, for example, merged with the song? Because a piece of paper is one kind of thing and a song is another; they are different kinds. Difference is the basis for individuating. And what about counting things of the same kind, for example, two pieces of paper? A person counts two things because there is difference; perhaps they have different colors or perhaps different relations, one being to the left of the typewriter and the other to the right.

2. *Unity*. When one looks at the piece of paper or listens to the song, he assigns the piece of paper one number, not, for example, two. The same for the song. They are one although they are many; the paper has many areas, the song has many notes. How does one decide that there is a single piece of paper and a single song? There is one piece of paper because it is all of one piece. If he cuts it, then there are two pieces; lifting one of them does not lift the other. Physical connections of the fibers holds the many areas together and makes them one thing. However, this will not do as a way of explaining the unity of a song. The song has an early part and a late part. Why does a person count the song as one thing rather than two things? Not because they are connected by fibers. Think of a class of schoolchildren. Why should a person count the class of children as one thing, even though there are many children?

In counting the contents of the universe we must be able to see individuals as one thing, and we have seen that different kinds of things have different principles of unity. The unity of pieces of paper is achieved by different means than the unity of songs; musical notes are not held together by fibers.

3. *Identity*. Suppose that at one time a person counts N number of things in the universe and at another time counts M number of things. How many of the Ms were Ns? Generally we recognize individuals as being numerically the same at one time as at another time. Hence, we say they maintain their identity through time, even though many of the individuals have changed. The student has now typed on that piece of paper; this time the song is played with a piano instead of a guitar.

What criteria do we use to decide that the piece of paper with the writing on it is identical with the piece of paper that did not have writing on it? We said before that we use differences to individuate and to count things as distinct individuals. Now there is a difference between the paper at one time and at a later time; by the criterion of difference, they should be counted as numerically distinct rather than as numerically identical. Clearly, in order to say things keep their identity through time, we shall have to say that some changes do not alter identity.

Which changes don't alter identity? Suppose the student burns the paper so that it changes into ash. Are the paper and the ash to be counted as one identical thing despite having such radically different properties? One cannot burn songs, although he can burn printed notations of songs; so a song's principle of identity through time must be considered independently from that of a piece of paper. Suppose that we use exactly the same notes that are in the song and rearrange them? Do we have the identical song, or should we say that now there are two songs rather than one?

4. *Creation and destruction.* Some changes are so drastic that we say a thing cannot hold its identity. For most people, burning the piece of paper would be such a change; they would say the piece of paper was destroyed. It is out of existence; it is not something we count anymore.

Some changes are so drastic that we say something exists that we never counted before. Thus, we may say that rearranging the notes of a song creates a new song. It has come into existence.

Now we are ready to consider the self in terms of these concepts—individuation, unity, identity, creation, and destruction.

SELF AND SUBSTANCE

If you do not yet feel the need for a metaphysical investigation of the concept of self, perhaps you are blissfully unaware that many writers have made it the prime victim of our modern, perilous social conditions. They have said we are empty, dehumanized, depersonalized, full of dread, anxious, and full of despair. This news is bound to reach you sooner or later, so we hope to prepare you for the worst!

Our first essay is by René **Descartes** because he made the topic of self of prime importance in Western philosophy and cultural consciousness. Notice the elaborate, earnest, deeply felt doubts about all he had learned at the university. Adrift on a sea of doubt, the one anchorage he finds is in the self; the one thing he cannot doubt is that he exists. He makes a key remark about the self: "But I do not yet know clearly enough what I am, I who am certain that I am." From this statement, Descartes can be interpreted as an existentialist, emphasizing the primacy of the self's existence over the self's whatness or nature. Descartes' first knowledge is that he knows he exists (which is why he might be interpreted as an existentialist); his second knowledge will be of what he is, of his essence.

Another reason Descartes is of special interest to us is because he stood within two overlapping phases of thought. One phase we shall call "theological" and the other "humanistic." The theological phase relates to the concept of the self because it introduces special difficulties about counting. How many human selves are there in the universe? How do we individuate selves? According to

Christian theology, a person is a dual entity consisting of a body and a soul. In counting human selves, which are we to count? The body or the soul?

In counting human selves, we probably count people; and the way we count people, as in a crowd at a rally, is to count the number of human bodies present. In short, we use the body as a principle for individuating selves. If we do in fact individuate by bodies, we are not very good Christians—for a Christian, it is the soul that is the important member of the pair. One reason that it is important is, of course, that Christian doctrine claims man to be immortal. However, the body is obviously destructible; it loses its continuity and, hence, its identity through time. So, the immortal person cannot be identified with his body; he must be identified with something that is not destructible, which, for a dualist, must be the soul, because that is the only candidate for immortality he has left after denying that a person is the body.

Descartes was a devout Christian, or so he professed, and stood in the theological phase because he maintained the dual-substance view of man, one of man's parts being the immortal soul. But Descartes also stands in the humanistic phase because he honestly faced the metaphysical questions about the soul self. Suppose that the self's existence is assured. What is the self? What is its nature, its essence? The kind of thing it is, as we saw earlier, will have important bearings on the criteria for individuation, unity, identity, creation, and destruction. If the self is a soul, and the soul is not a body—not "a wind, a flame, or an ether," as Descartes imagined in unreflective moments—then we cannot use physical criteria to individuate or identify souls. How do we count souls? We cannot answer that question until we know what kind of a thing the soul is, until we discover the nature of souls.

Descartes took a modern turn toward the humanistic phase by the way he characterized the soul. Although he did say that the soul was a mental substance, he gave it empirical content by saying that he was a "thing which thinks. What is a thing which thinks? It is a thing which doubts, understands, conceives, affirms, denies, wills, refuses, which also imagines and feels."

This brings us to a crucial point in trying to understand the metaphysics of the self. Notice that Descartes says the soul is a "thing." It is a thing that does something. It is a "thing which thinks." He does not say the soul *is* (identical to) thinking. Obviously the soul is conceived by Descartes as an object, analogous to a ball, for example. The ball is not just rolling, any more than the soul is just thinking. There is a *soul* thinking, as there is a *ball* rolling. The concept of an object is deeply rooted in our common-sense thinking. Descartes is moving in the groove here. Commonsensical or not, we can raise an interesting question that suggests a criticism of Descartes' position. Can we have any knowledge of the nature of this soul thing or substance apart from our understanding of its doings (its thinking, doubting, denying, imagining, and so forth)? A positive answer to this question will not be satisfactory if it does not enable us to say how we individuate souls or account for their unity, their identity through time, or their creation and destruction or their immortality.

The author of the second essay in this section, **David Hume,** gave a negative answer to this question and effectively erased the theological phase. He took Descartes' humanistic phase seriously. He tried to make direct acquaintance with the self as a thing by introspecting. However, what he found was not anything he could label a "self thing" or "soul thing"; all he found were thoughts, doubts, and so on. "For my part, when I enter most intimately into what I call *myself,* I always stumble on some particular perception or other, of heat or cold, light or shade, love or hatred, pain or pleasure. I never can catch *myself* at any time without a perception, and never can observe anything but the perception." Hume finds, then, no way to talk about the self's individuation or identity other than in terms of thinking, perceiving, feeling, and so forth. If there is a self, it is not something over and above experience itself; hence, it must be identical to each thought itself or must be constructed out of the series of thoughts. The first alternative would leave one with as many selves as there are thoughts; this is an extreme form of individuation that seems to vary too much from our usual individuation practice to be acceptable. The alternative is to specify ways of constructing a self from the series of thoughts. Individuation of selves, following this alternative, does not seem particularly difficult, because two series with different thoughts give a way of individuating each of the two series, hence, of individuating each of the two selves constructed from the two series. To provide for the unity of the series, a way of relating the thoughts to each other must be found; of course, it cannot be done by relating each thought to *oneself* because one cannot assume a "oneself" that stands outside the series, the "oneself" being the series itself. As to how one can provide for the self's continuity or identity through time, we leave you to glean that from Hume's essay, the bulk of it directed at that question. Since a series may be finite (have a beginning and an end), the creation and destruction of selves is easily accounted for.

In the third essay in this section, **John Koller** gives an account of Samkhya yoga that provides another alternative to Descartes' common-sense view of the self. The Hindu Samkhya philosophers are, like Descartes, dualists; they distinguish between object and subject. Their terms for it are *prakriti* and *purusha*, the former being the objective world and the latter the subjective component. But a major difference between Descartes and the Samkhya philosophers is that whereas Descartes takes thinking, willing, imagining, and feeling to be aspects of the subjective self, Samkhya places them in the objective world; they are part of *prakriti*, to which the empirical self belongs; it is the empirical self that psychologists study; it is caught up in the world of causality, an account of which is given in the part of Koller's essay labeled "Causality." Once these psychological features are seen to be alien to the real subjective component of the world, they are no longer useful for individuating the subjective component; when the individuating tools are gone, we can count only a single, ultimate subject in the world, and that is *purusha.*

Samkhya Yoga is the goal we must achieve to rid ourselves of the kind of ignorance about the self to which Descartes fell prey. The empirical self is a false self; it is caught up in *prakriti's* transformations; identification with this false, empirical Cartesian self is the source of pain and agony. Once we rid ourselves of this ignorance and recognize that our pure consciousness is a manifestation of *purusha*, our wordly troubles will drop from us. Koller lists eight disciplinary aids to help us achieve *yoga.*

Aren't these speculations about the self as sweet as honey? And as necessary as bread?

The Self as Substance
René Descartes

René Descartes (1595-1658) was the first outstanding French philosopher and the father of modern philosophy. He was educated at the Jesuit college of La Fleche, where he first developed his interest in mathematics, and at the University of Poitiers, from which he received a law degree. Although he spent some time traveling and as a mercenary in a foreign army, he eventually returned to study and to do scientific research. His most important writings include *Discourse on the Method of Properly Guiding the Reason in the Search for Truth in the Sciences* (1637), *Meditations on First Philosophy in Which the Existence of God and the Distinction Between Mind and Body Are Demonstrated* (1641), *Principles of Philosophy* (1644), and *The Passions of the Soul* (1649).

MEDITATION I: OF THE THINGS WHICH MAY BE BROUGHT WITHIN THE SPHERE OF THE DOUBTFUL

It is now some years since I detected how many were the false beliefs that I had from my earliest youth admitted as true, and how doubtful was everything I had since constructed on this basis; and from that time I was convinced that I must once for all seriously undertake to rid myself of all the opinions which I had formerly accepted, and commence to build anew from the foundation, if I wanted to establish any firm and permanent structure in the sciences. But as this enterprise appeared to be a very great one, I waited until I had attained an age so mature that I could not hope that at any later date I should be better fitted to execute my design. This reason caused me to delay so long that I should feel that I was doing wrong were I to occupy in deliberation the time that yet remains to me for action. Today, then, since very opportunely for the plan I have in view I have delivered my mind from every care [and am happily agitated by no passions] and since I have procured for myself an assured leisure in a peaceable retirement, I shall at last seriously and freely address myself to the general upheaval of all my former opinions.

Now for this object it is not necessary that I should show that all of these are false—I shall perhaps never arrive at this end. But inasmuch as reason already persuades me that I ought no less carefully to withhold my assent from matters which are not entirely certain and indubitable than from those which appear to me manifestly to be false, if I am able to find in each one some reason to doubt, this will suffice to justify my rejecting the whole. And for that end it will not be requisite that I should examine each in particular, which would be an endless undertaking; for owing to the fact that the destruction of the foundations of necessity brings with it the downfall of the rest of the edifice, I shall only in the first place attack those principles upon which all my former opinions rested.

Source: The Philosophical Works of Descartes, trans. E. S. Haldane and G. R. T. Ross (New York: Cambridge University Press, 1911), pp. 69-80. Reprinted by permission of the publisher.

All that up to the present time I have accepted as most true and certain I have learned either from the senses or through the senses; but it is sometimes proved to me that these senses are deceptive, and it is wiser not to trust entirely to any thing by which we have once been deceived.

But it may be that although the senses sometimes deceive us concerning things which are hardly perceptible, or very far away, there are yet many others to be met with as to which we cannot reasonably have any doubt, although we recognise them by their means. For example, there is the fact that I am here, seated by the fire, attired in a dressing gown, having this paper in my hands and other similar matters. And how could I deny that these hands and this body are mine, were it not perhaps that I compare myself to certain persons, devoid of sense, whose cerebella are so troubled and clouded by the violent vapours of black bile, that they constantly assure us that they think they are kings when they are really quite poor, or that they are clothed in purple when they are really without covering, or who imagine that they have an earthenware head or are nothing but pumpkins or are made of glass. But they are mad, and I should not be any the less insane were I to follow examples so extravagant.

At the same time I must remember that I am a man, and that consequently I am in the habit of sleeping, and in my dreams representing to myself the same things or sometimes even less probable things, than do those who are insane in their waking moments. How often has it happened to me that in the night I dreamt that I found myself in this particular place, that I was dressed and seated near the fire, whilst in reality I was lying undressed in bed! At this moment it does indeed seem to me that it is with eyes awake that I am looking at this paper; that this head which I move is not asleep, that it is deliberately and of set purpose that I extend my hand and perceive it; what happens in sleep does not appear so clear nor so distinct as does all this. But in thinking over this I remind myself that on many occasions I have in sleep been deceived by similar illusions, and in dwelling carefully on this reflection I see so manifestly that there are no certain indications by which we may clearly distinguish wakefulness from sleep that I am lost in astonishment. And my astonishment is such that it is almost capable of persuading me that I now dream.

Now let us assume that we are asleep and that all these particulars, e.g. that we open our eyes, shake our head, extend our hands, and so on, are but false delusions; and let us reflect that possibly neither our hands nor our whole body are such as they appear to us to be. At the same time we must at least confess that the things which are represented to us in sleep are like painted representations which can only have been formed as the counterparts of something real and true, and that in this way those general things at least, i.e. eyes, a head, hands, and a whole body, are not imaginary things, but things really existent. For, as a matter of fact, painters, even when they study with the greatest skill to represent sirens and satyrs by forms the most strange and extraordinary, cannot give them natures which are entirely new, but merely make a certain medley of the members of different animals; or if their imagination is extravagant enough to invent something so novel that nothing similar has ever before been seen, and that their work represents a thing purely fictitious and absolutely false, it is certain all the same that the colours of which this is composed are necessarily real. And for the same reason, although these general things, to wit, [a body], eyes, a head, hands, and such like, may be imaginary, we are bound at the same time to confess that there are at least some other objects yet more simple and more universal, which are real and true; and of these just in the same way as with certain real colours, all these images of things which dwell in our thoughts, whether true and real or false and fantastic, are formed.

To such a class of things pertains corporeal nature in general, and its extension, the figure of extended things, their quantity or magnitude and number, as also the place in which they are, the time which measures their duration, and so on.

That is possibly why our reasoning is not unjust when we conclude from this that Physics, Astronomy, Medicine and all other sciences which have as their end the consideration of composite things, are very dubious and uncertain; but that Arithmetic, Geometry and other sciences of that kind which only treat of things that are very simple and very general, without taking great trouble to ascertain whether they are actually existent or not, contain some measure of certainty and an element of the indubitable. For whether I am awake or asleep, two and three together always form five, and the square can never have more than four sides, and it does not seem possible that truths so clear and apparent can be suspected of any falsity [or uncertainty].

Nevertheless I have long had fixed in my mind the belief that an all-powerful God existed by whom I have been created such as I am. But how do I know that He has not brought it to pass that there is no earth, no heaven, no extended body, no magnitude, no place, and that nevertheless [I possess the perceptions of all these things and that] they seem to me to exist just exactly as I now see them? And, besides, as I sometimes imagine that others deceive themselves in the things which they think they know best, how do I know that I am not deceived every time that I add two and three, or count the sides of a square, or judge of things yet simpler, if anything simpler can be imagined? But possibly God has not desired that I should be thus deceived, for He is said to be supremely good. If, however, it is contrary to His goodness to have made me such that I constantly deceive myself, it would also appear to be contrary to His goodness to permit me to be sometimes deceived, and nevertheless I cannot doubt that He does permit this.

There may indeed be those who would prefer to deny the existence of a God so powerful, rather than believe that all other things are uncertain. But let us not oppose them for the present, and grant that all there is here said of a God is a fable; nevertheless in whatever way they suppose that I have arrived at the state of being that I have reached—whether they attribute it to fate or to accident, or make out that it is by a continual succession of antecedents, or by some other method—since to err and deceive oneself is a defect, it is clear that the greater will be the probability of my being so imperfect as to deceive myself ever, as is the Author to whom they assign my origin the less powerful. To these reasons I have certainly nothing to reply, but at the end I feel constrained to confess that there is nothing in all that I formerly believed to be true, of which I cannot in some measure doubt, and that not merely through want of thought or through levity, but for reasons which are very powerful and maturely considered; so that henceforth I ought not the less carefully to refrain from giving credence to these opinions than to that which is manifestly false, if I desire to arrive at any certainty [in the sciences].

But it is not sufficient to have made these remarks, we must also be careful to keep them in mind. For these ancient and commonly held opinions still revert frequently to my mind, long and familiar custom having given them the right to occupy my mind against my inclination and rendered them almost masters of my belief; nor will I ever lose the habit of deferring to them or of placing my confidence in them, so long as I consider them as they really are, i.e. opinions in some measure doubtful, as I have just shown, and at the same time highly probable, so that there is much more reason to believe in than to deny them. That is why I consider that I shall not be acting amiss, if, taking of set purpose a contrary belief, I allow myself to be deceived, and for a certain time pretend that all these opinions are entirely false and imaginary, until at last, having thus balanced my former prejudices with my latter [so that they cannot divert my opinions more to one side than to the other], my judgment will no longer be dominated by bad usage or turned away from the right knowledge of the truth. For I am assured that there can be neither peril nor error in this course, and that I cannot at present yield too much to distrust, since I am not considering the question of action, but only of knowledge.

I shall then suppose, not that God who is supremely good and the fountain of truth, but some evil genius not less powerful than deceitful, has employed his whole energies in deceiving me; I shall consider that the heavens, the earth, colours, figures, sound, and all other external things are nought but the illusions and dreams of which this genius has availed himself in order to lay traps for my credulity; I shall consider myself as having no hands, no eyes, no flesh, no blood, nor any senses, yet falsely believing myself to possess all these things; I shall remain obstinately attached to this idea, and if by this means it is not in my power to arrive at the knowledge of any truth, I may at least do what is in my power [i.e. suspend my judgment], and with firm purpose avoid giving credence to any false thing, or being imposed upon by this arch deceiver, however powerful and deceptive he may be. But this task is a laborious one, and insensibly a certain lassitude leads me into the course of my ordinary life. And just as a captive who in sleep enjoys an imaginary liberty, when he begins to suspect that his liberty is but a dream, fears to awaken, and conspires with these agreeable illusions that the deception may be prolonged, so insensibly of my own accord I fall back into my former opinions, and I dread awakening from this slumber, lest the laborious wakefulness which would follow the tranquillity of this repose should have to be spent not in daylight, but in the excessive darkness of the difficulties which have just been discussed.

MEDITATION II: OF THE NATURE OF THE HUMAN MIND; AND THAT IT IS MORE EASILY KNOWN THAN THE BODY

The Meditation of yesterday filled my mind with so many doubts that it is no longer in my power to forget them. And yet I do not see in what manner I can resolve them; and, just as if I had all of a sudden fallen into very deep water, I am so disconcerted that I can neither make certain of setting my feet on the bottom, nor can I swim and so support myself on the surface. I shall nevertheless make an effort and follow anew the same path as that on which I yesterday entered, i.e. I shall proceed by setting aside all that in which the least doubt could be supposed to exist, just as if I had discovered that it was absolutely false; and I shall ever follow in this road until I have met with something which is certain, or at least, if I can do nothing else, until I have learned for certain that there is nothing in the world that is certain. Archimedes, in order that he might draw the terrestrial globe out of its place, and transport it elsewhere, demanded only that one point should be fixed and immovable; in the same way I shall have the right to conceive high hopes if I am happy enough to discover one thing only which is certain and indubitable.

I suppose, then, that all the things that I see are false; I persuade myself that nothing has ever existed of all that my fallacious memory represents to me. I consider that I possess no senses; I imagine that body, figure, extension, movement and place are but the fictions of my mind. What, then, can be esteemed as true? Perhaps nothing at all, unless that there is nothing in the world that is certain.

But how can I know there is not something different from those things that I have just considered, of which one cannot have the slightest doubt? Is there not some God, or some other being by whatever name we call it, who puts these reflections into my mind? That is not necessary, for is it not possible that I am capable of producing them myself? I myself, am I not at least something? But I have already denied that I had senses and body. Yet I hesitate, for what follows from that? Am I so dependent on body and senses that I cannot exist without these? But I was persuaded that there was nothing in all the world, that there was no heaven, no earth, that there were no minds, nor any bodies: was I not then likewise persuaded that I did not exist? Not at all; of a surety I myself did exist since I persuaded myself of something [or merely because I thought of something]. But there is some deceiver or other, very powerful and very cunning, who ever employs his ingenuity in deceiving me. Then without doubt I exist also if he deceives me, and let him deceive me as much as he will, he can never cause me to be nothing so long as I think that I am something. So that after having reflected well and carefully examined all things, we must come to the definite conclusion that this proposition: I am, I exist, is necessarily true each time that I pronounce it, or that I mentally conceive it.

But I do not yet know clearly enough what I am, I who am certain that I am; and hence I must be careful to see that I do not imprudently take some other object in place of myself, and thus that I do not go astray in respect of this knowledge that I hold to be the most certain and most evident of all that I have formerly learned. That is why I shall now consider anew what I believed myself to be before I embarked upon these last reflections; and of my former opinions I shall withdraw all that might even in a small degree be invalidated by the reasons which I have just brought forward, in order that there may be nothing at all left beyond what is absolutely certain and indubitable.

What then did I formerly believe myself to be? Undoubtedly I believed myself to be a man. But what is a man? Shall I say a reasonable animal? Certainly not, for then I should have to inquire what an animal is, and what is reasonable; and thus from a single question I should insensibly fall into an infinitude of others more difficult; and I should not wish to waste the little time and leisure remaining to me in trying to unravel subtleties like these. But I shall rather stop here to consider the thoughts which of themselves spring up in my mind, and which were not inspired by anything beyond my own nature alone when I applied myself to the consideration of my being. In the first place, then, I considered myself as having a face, hands, arms, and all that system of members composed of bones and flesh as seen in a corpse which I designated by the name of body. In addition to this I considered that I was nourished, that I walked, that I felt, and that I thought, and I referred all these actions to the soul: but I did not stop to consider what the soul was, or if I did stop, I imagined that it was something extremely rare and subtle like a wind, a flame, or an ether, which was spread throughout my grosser parts. As to body I had no manner of doubt about its nature, but thought I had a very clear knowledge of it; and if I had desired to explain it according to the notions that I had then formed of it, I should have described it thus: By the body I understand all that which can be defined by a certain figure: something which can be confined in a certain place, and which can fill a given space in such a way that every other body will be excluded from it; which can be perceived either by touch, or by sight, or by hearing, or by taste, or by smell: which can be moved in many ways, not, in truth, by itself, but by something which is foreign to it, by which it is touched [and from which it receives impressions] : for to have the power of self-movement, as also of feeling or of thinking, I did not consider to appertain to the nature of body: on the contrary, I was rather astonished to find that faculties similar to them existed in some bodies.

But what am I, now that I suppose that there is a certain genius which is extremely powerful, and, if I may say so, malicious, who employs all his powers in deceiving me? Can I affirm that I possess the least of all those things which I have just said pertain to the nature of body? I pause to consider, I revolve all these things in my mind, and I find none of which I can say that it pertains to me. It would be tedious to stop to enumerate them. Let us pass to the attributes of soul and see if there is any one which is in me? What of nutrition or walking [the first mentioned]? But if it is so that I have no body it is also true that I can neither walk nor take nourishment. Another attribute is sensation. But one cannot feel without body, and besides I have thought I perceived many things during sleep that I recognised in my waking moments as not having been experienced at all. What of thinking? I find here that thought is an attribute that belongs to me; it alone cannot be separated from me. I am, I exist, that is certain. But how often? Just when I think; for it might possibly be the case if I ceased entirely to think, that I should likewise cease altogether to exist. I do not now admit anything which is not necessarily true: to speak accurately I am not more than a thing which thinks, that is to say a mind or a soul, or an understanding, or a reason, which are terms whose significance was formerly unknown to me. I am, however, a real thing and really exist; but what thing? I have answered: a thing which thinks.

And what more? I shall exercise my imagination [in order to see if I am not something more]. I am not a collection of members which we call the human body: I am not a subtle air distributed through these members, I am not a wind, a fire, a vapour, a breath, nor anything at all which I can imagine or conceive; because I have assumed that all these were nothing. Without changing that supposition I find that I only leave myself certain of the fact that I am somewhat. But perhaps it is true that these same things which I supposed were non-existent because they are unknown to me, are really not different from the self which I know. I am not sure about this, I shall not dispute about it now; I can only give judgment on things that are known to me. I know that I exist, and I inquire what I am, I whom I know to exist. But it is very certain that the knowledge of my existence taken in its precise significance does not depend on things whose existence is not yet known to me; consequently it does not depend on those which I can feign in imagination. And indeed the very term *feign* in imagination[1] proves to me my error, for I really do this if I imagine myself a something, since to imagine is nothing else than to contemplate the figure or image of a corporeal thing. But I already know for certain that I am, and that it may be that all these images, and, speaking generally, all things that relate to the nature of body are nothing but dreams [and chimeras]. For

---

[1] Or 'form an image' (effingo).

this reason I see clearly that I have as little reason to say, "I shall stimulate my imagination in order to know more distinctly what I am," than if I were to say, "I am now awake, and I perceive somewhat that is real and true: but because I do not yet perceive it distinctly enough, I shall go to sleep of express purpose, so that my dreams may represent the perception with greatest truth and evidence." And, thus, I know for certain that nothing of all that I can understand by means of my imagination belongs to this knowledge which I have of myself, and that it is necessary to recall the mind from this mode of thought with the utmost diligence in order that it may be able to know its own nature with perfect distinctness.

But what then am I? A thing which thinks. What is a thing which thinks? It is a thing which doubts, understands, [conceives], affirms, denies, wills, refuses, which also imagines and feels.

Certainly it is no small matter if all these things pertain to my nature. But why should they not so pertain? Am I not that being who now doubts nearly everything, who nevertheless understands certain things, who affirms that one only is true, who denies all the others, who desires to know more, is averse from being deceived, who imagines many things, sometimes indeed despite his will, and who perceives many likewise, as by the intervention of the bodily organs? Is there nothing in all this which is as true as it is certain that I exist, even though I should always sleep and though he who has given me being employed all his ingenuity in deceiving me? Is there likewise anyone of these attributes which can be distinguished from my thought, or which might be said to be separated from myself? For it is so evident of itself that it is I who doubts, who understands and who desires, that there is no reason here to add anything to explain it. And I have certainly the power of imagining likewise; for although it may happen (as I formerly supposed) that none of the things which I imagine are true, nevertheless this power of imagining does not cease to be really in use, and it forms part of my thought. Finally, I am the same who feels, that is to say, who perceives certain things, as by the organs of sense, since in truth I see light, I hear noise, I feel heat. But it will be said that these phenomena are false and that I am dreaming. Let it be so; still it is at least quite certain that it seems to me that I see light, that I hear noise and that I feel heat. That cannot be false; properly speaking it is what is in me called feeling; and used in this precise sense that is no other thing than thinking.

From this time I begin to know what I am with a little more clearness and distinction than before; but nevertheless it still seems to me, and I cannot prevent myself from thinking, that corporeal things, whose images are framed by thought, which are tested by the senses, are much more distinctly known than that obscure part of me which does not come under the imagination. Although really it is very strange to say that I know and understand more distinctly these things whose existence seems to me dubious, which are unknown to me, and which do not belong to me, than others of the truth of which I am convinced, which are known to me and which pertain to my real nature, in a word, than myself. But I see clearly how the case stands: my mind loves to wander and cannot yet suffer itself to be retained within the just limits of truth. Very good, let us once more give it the freest rein, so that, when afterwards we seize the proper occasion for pulling up, it may the more easily be regulated and controlled.

Let us begin by considering the commonest matters, those which we believe to be the most distinctly comprehended, to wit, the bodies which we touch and see; not indeed bodies in general, for these general ideas are usually a little more confused, but let us consider one body in particular. Let us take, for example, this piece of wax: it has been taken quite freshly from the hive, and it has not yet lost the sweetness of the honey which it contains; it still retains somewhat of the odour of the flowers from which it has been culled; its colour, its figure, its size are apparent; it is hard, cold, easily handled, and if you strike it with the finger, it will emit a sound. Finally all the things which are requisite to cause us distinctly to recognise a body, are met with in it. But notice that while I speak and approach the fire what remained of the taste is exhaled, the smell evaporates, the colour alters, the figure is destroyed, the size increases, it becomes liquid, it heats, scarcely can one handle it, and when one strikes it, no sound is emitted. Does the same wax remain after this change? We must confess that it remains; none would judge otherwise. What then did I know so distinctly in this piece of wax? It could certainly be nothing of all that the senses brought to my notice, since all these things which fall under taste, smell, sight, touch, and hearing are found to be changed, and yet the same wax remains.

Perhaps it was what I now think, viz. that this wax was not that sweetness of honey, nor that agreeable scent of flowers, nor that particular whiteness, nor that figure, nor that sound, but simply a body which a little while before appeared to me as perceptible under these forms, and which is now perceptible under others. But what, precisely, is it that I imagine when I form such conceptions? Let us attentively consider this, and, abstracting from all that does not belong to the wax, let us see what remains. Certainly nothing remains excepting a certain extended thing which is flexible and movable. But what is the meaning of flexible and movable? Is it not that I imagine that this piece of wax being round is capable of becoming square and of passing from a square to a triangular figure? No, certainly it is not that, since I imagine it admits of an infinitude of similar changes, and I nevertheless do not know how to compass the infinitude by my imagination, and consequently this conception which I have of the wax is not brought about by the faculty of imagination. What now is this extension? Is it not also unknown? For it becomes greater when the wax is melted, greater when it is boiled, and greater still when the heat increases; and I should not conceive [clearly] according to truth what wax is, if I did not think that even this piece that we are considering is capable of receiving more variations in extension than I have ever imagined. We must then grant that I could not even understand through the imagination what this piece of wax in particular is, for as to wax in general it is yet clearer. But what is this piece of wax which cannot be understood excepting by the [understanding or] mind? It is certainly the same that I see, touch, imagine, and finally it is the same which I have always believed it to be from the beginning. But what must particularly be observed is that its perception is neither an act of vision, nor of touch, nor of imagination, and has never been such although it may have appeared formerly to be so, but only an intuition of the mind, which may be imperfect and confused as it was formerly, or clear and distinct as it is at present, according as my attention is more or less directed to the elements which are found in it, and of which it is composed.

Yet in the meantime I am greatly astonished when I consider [the great feebleness of mind] and its proneness to fall [insensibly] into error; for although without giving expression to my thoughts I consider all this in my own mind, words often impede me and I am almost deceived by the terms of ordinary language. For we say that we see the same wax, if it is present, and not that we simply judge that it is the same from its having the same colour and figure. From this I should conclude that I knew the wax by means of vision and not simply by the intuition of the mind; unless by chance I remember that, when looking from a window and saying I see men who pass in the street, I really do not see them, but infer that what I see is men, just as I say that I see wax. And yet what do I see from the window but hats and coats which may cover automatic machines? Yet I judge these to be men. And similarly solely by the faculty of judgment which rests in my mind, I comprehend that which I believed I saw with my eyes.

A man who makes it his aim to raise his knowledge above the common should be ashamed to derive the occasion for doubting from the forms of speech invented by the vulgar; I prefer to pass on and consider whether I had a more evident and perfect conception of what the wax was when I first perceived it, and when I believed I knew it by means of the external senses or at least by the common sense[2] as it is called, that is to say by the imaginative faculty, or whether my present conception is clearer now that I have most carefully examined what it is, and in what way it can be known. It would certainly be absurd to doubt as to this. For what was there in this first perception which was distinct? What was there which might not as well have been perceived by any of the animals? But when I distinguish the wax from its external forms, and when, just as if I had taken from it its vestments, I consider it quite naked, it is certain that although some error may still be found in my judgment, I can nevertheless not perceive it thus without a human mind.

But finally what shall I say of this mind, that is, of myself, for up to this point I do not admit in myself anything but mind? What then, I who seem to perceive this piece of wax so distinctly, do I not know myself, not only with much more truth and certainty, but also with much more distinctness and clearness? For if I judge that the wax is or exists from the fact that I see it, it certainly follows much more clearly that I am or that I exist myself from the fact that I see it. For it may be that what I see is not really wax, it may also be that I do not possess eyes with which to see anything; but it cannot be that when I see, or (for I no longer take account of the distinction) when I think I see, that I myself who think am nought. So if I judge that the wax exists from the fact that I touch it, the same thing will follow, to wit, that I am; and if I judge that my imagination, or some other cause, whatever it is, persuades me that the wax exists, I shall still conclude the same. And what I have here remarked of wax may be applied to all other things which are external to me [and which are met with outside me]. And further, if the [notion or] perception of wax has seemed to me clearer and more distinct, not only after the sight or the touch, but also after many other causes have rendered it quite manifest to me, with how much more [evidence] and distinctness must it be said that I now know myself, since all the reasons which contribute to the knowledge of wax, or any other body whatever, are yet better proofs of the nature of my mind! And there are so many other things in the mind itself which may contribute to the elucidation of its nature, that those which depend on body such as these just mentioned, hardly merit being taken into account.

But finally here I am, having insensibly reverted to the point I desired, for, since it is now manifest to me that even bodies are not properly speaking known by the senses or by the faculty of imagination, but by the understanding only, and since

---

[2] *Sensus communis.*

they are not known from the fact that they are seen or touched, but only because they are understood, I see clearly that there is nothing which is easier for me to know than my mind. But because it is difficult to rid oneself so promptly of an opinion to which one was accustomed for so long, it will be well that I should halt a little at this point, so that by the length of my meditation I may more deeply imprint on my memory this new knowledge.

There Is No Substantial Self
David Hume

David Hume (1711-1776), an outstanding British empiricist, not only wrote upon philosophical subjects but also became famous as a historian. Among his major works are *A Treatise of Human Nature* (1739-1740), *Essays, Moral and Political* (1741-1742), and *The History of England* (1754-1762).

There are some philosophers who imagine we are every moment intimately conscious of what we call our Self; that we feel its existence and its continuance in existence; and are certain, beyond the evidence of a demonstration, both of its perfect identity and simplicity. The strongest sensation, the most violent passion, say they, instead of distracting us from this view, only fix it the more intensely, and make us consider their influence on *self* either by their pain or pleasure. To attempt a farther proof of this were to weaken its evidence; since no proof can be derived from any fact, of which we are so intimately conscious; nor is there any thing, of which we can be certain, if we doubt of this.

Unluckily all these positive assertions are contrary to that very experience, which is pleaded for them, nor have we any idea of *self*, after the manner it is here explained. For from what impression could this idea be derived? This question it is impossible to answer without a manifest contradiction and absurdity; and yet it is a question, which must necessarily be answered, if we would have the idea of self pass for clear and intelligible. It must be some one impression, that gives rise to every real idea. But self or person is not any one impression, but that to which our several impressions and ideas are supposed to have a reference. If any impression gives rise to the idea of self, that impression must continue invariably the same, through the whole course of our lives; since self is supposed to exist after that manner. But there is no impression constant and invariable. Pain and pleasure, grief and joy, passions and sensations succeed each other, and never all exist at the same time. It cannot, therefore, be from any of these impressions, or from any other, that the idea of self is derived; and consequently there is no such idea.

But farther, what must become of all our particular perceptions upon this hypothesis? All these are different, and distinguishable, and separable from each

Source: A Treatise of Human Nature, Book I, Part 4 (London, 1739).

other, and may be separately considered, and may exist separately, and have no need of any thing to support their existence. After what manner, therefore, do they belong to self; and how are they connected with it? For my part, when I enter most intimately into what I call *myself*, I always stumble on some particular perception or other, of heat or cold, light or shade, love or hatred, pain or pleasure. I never can catch *myself* at any time without a perception, and never can observe any thing but the perception. When my perceptions are removed for any time, as by sound sleep; so long am I insensible of *myself*, and may truly be said not to exist. And were all my perceptions removed by death, and could I neither think, nor feel, nor see, nor love, nor hate after the dissolution of my body, I should be entirely annihilated, nor do I conceive what is farther requisite to make me a perfect non-entity. If any one upon serious and unprejudiced reflexion, thinks he has a different notion of *himself*, I must confess I can reason no longer with him. All I can allow him is, that he may be in the right as well as I, and that we are essentially different in this particular. He may, perhaps, perceive something simple and continued, which he calls *himself*; though I am certain there is no such principle in me.

But setting aside some metaphysicians of this kind, I may venture to affirm of the rest of mankind, that they are nothing but a bundle or collection of different perceptions, which succeed each other with an inconceivable rapidity, and are in a perpetual flux and movement. Our eyes cannot turn in their sockets without varying our perceptions. Our thought is still more variable than our sight; and all our other senses and faculties contribute to this change; nor is there any single power of the soul, which remains unalterably the same, perhaps for one moment. The mind is a kind of theatre, where several perceptions successively make their appearance; pass, re-pass, glide away, and mingle in an infinite variety of postures and situations. There is properly no *simplicity* in it at one time, nor *identity* in different; whatever natural propension we may have to imagine that simplicity and identity. The comparison of the theatre must not mislead us. They are the successive perceptions only, that constitute the mind; nor have we the most distant notion of the place, where these scenes are represented, or of the materials, of which it is composed.

What then gives us so great a propension to ascribe an identity to these successive perceptions, and to suppose ourselves possest of an invariable and uninterrupted existence through the whole course of our lives? . . .

We have a distinct idea of an object, that remains invariable and uninterrupted through a supposed variation of time; and this idea we call that of *identity* or *sameness*. We have also a distinct idea of several different objects existing in succession, and connected together by a close relation; and this to an accurate view affords as perfect a notion of *diversity*, as if there was no manner of relation among the objects. But though these two ideas of identity, and a succession of related objects be in themselves perfectly distinct, and even contrary, yet it is certain, that in our common way of thinking they are generally confounded with each other. That action of the imagination, by which we consider the uninterrupted and invariable object, and that by which we reflect on the succession of related objects, are almost the same to the feeling, nor is there much more effort of thought required in the latter case than in the former. The relation facilitates the transition of the mind from one object to another, and renders its passage as smooth as if it contemplated one continued object. This resemblance is the cause of the confusion and mistake, and makes us substitute the notion of identity, instead of that of related objects. However at one instant we may consider the related succession as variable or interrupted, we are sure the next to ascribe to it a perfect identity, and regard it as invariable and uninterrupted. Our propensity to this mistake is so great from the resemblance above-mentioned, that we fall into it before we are aware; and though we incessantly correct ourselves by reflexion, and return to a more accurate method of thinking, yet we cannot long sustain our philosophy, or take off this biass from the imagination. Our last resource is to yield to it, and boldly assert that these different related objects are in effect the same, however interrupted and variable. In order to justify to ourselves this absurdity, we often feign some new and unintelligible principle, that connects the objects together, and prevents their interruption or variation. Thus we feign the continued existence of the perceptions of our senses, to remove the interruption; and run into the notion of a *soul*, and *self*, and *substance*, to disguise the variation. But we may farther observe, that where we do not give rise to such a fiction, our propension to confound identity with relation is so great, that we are apt to imagine[1] something unknown and mysterious, connecting the parts, beside their relation; and this I take to be the case with regard to the identity we ascribe to plants and vegetables. And even when this does not take place, we still feel a propensity to confound these ideas, though we are not able fully to satisfy ourselves in that particular, nor find any thing invariable and uninterrupted to justify our notion of identity.

Thus the controversy concerning identity is not merely a dispute of words. For when we attribute identity, in an improper sense, to variable or interrupted objects, our mistake is not confined to the expression, but is commonly attended with a fiction, either of something invariable and uninterrupted, or of something mysterious and inexplicable, or at least with a propensity to such fictions. . . .

We now proceed to explain the nature of *personal identity*, which has become so great a question in philosophy, especially of late years in *England*, where all the abstruser sciences are studied with a peculiar ardour and application. . . .

It is evident, that the identity, which we attribute to the human mind, however perfect we may imagine it to be, is not able to run the several different perceptions into one, and make them lose their characters of distinction and difference, which are essential to them. It is still true, that every distinct perception, which enters into the composition of the mind, is a distinct existence, and is different, and distinguishable, and separable from every other perception, either contemporary or successive. But, as, notwithstanding this distinction and separability, we suppose the whole train of perceptions to be united by identity, a question naturally arises concerning this relation of identity; whether it be something that really binds our several perceptions together, or only associates their ideas in the imagination. That is, in other words, whether in pronouncing concerning the identity of a person, we observe some real bond among his perceptions, or only feel one among the ideas we form of them. This question we might easily decide, if we would recollect what has been already proved at large, that the understanding never observes any real connexion among objects, and that even the union of cause and effect, when strictly examined, resolves itself into a customary association of ideas. For from thence it evidently follows, that identity is nothing really belonging to these

---

[1] If the reader is desirous to see how a great genius may be influenced by these seemingly trivial principles of the imagination, as well as the mere vulgar, let him read my Lord Shaftsbury's reasonings concerning the uniting principle of the universe, and the identity of plants and animals. See his *Moralists:* or, *Philosophical Rhapsody.*

different perceptions, and uniting them together; but is merely a quality, which we attribute to them, because of the union of their ideas in the imagination, when we reflect upon them. Now the only qualities, which can give ideas an union in the imagination, are these three relations above-mentioned. These are the uniting principles in the ideal world, and without them every distinct object is separable by the mind, and may be separately considered, and appears not to have any more connexion with any other object, than if disjoined by the greatest difference and remoteness. It is, therefore, on some of these three relations of resemblance, contiguity and causation, that identity depends; and as the very essence of these relations consists in their producing an easy transition of ideas; it follows, that our notions of personal identity, proceed entirely from the smooth and uninterrupted progress of the thought along a train of connected ideas, according to the principles above-explained.

The only question, therefore, which remains, is, by what relations this uninterrupted progress of our thought is produced, when we consider the successive existence of a mind or thinking person. And here it is evident we must confine ourselves to resemblance and causation, and must drop contiguity, which has little or no influence in the present case.

To begin with *resemblance;* suppose we could see clearly into the breast of another, and observe that succession of perceptions, which constitutes his mind or thinking principle, and suppose that he always preserves the memory of a considerable part of past perceptions; it is evident that nothing could more contribute to the bestowing a relation on this succession amidst all its variations. For what is the memory but a faculty, by which we raise up the images of past perceptions? And as an image necessarily resembles its object, must not the frequent placing of these resembling perceptions in the chain of thought, convey the imagination more easily from one link to another, and make the whole seem like the continuance of one object? In this particular, then, the memory not only discovers the identity, but also contributes to its production, by producing the relation of resemblance among the perceptions. The case is the same whether we consider ourselves or others.

As to *causation;* we may observe, that the true idea of the human mind, is to consider it as a system of different perceptions or different existences, which are linked together by the relation of cause and effect, and mutually produce, destroy, influence, and modify each other. Our impressions give rise to their correspondent ideas; and these ideas in their turn produce other impressions. One thought chases another, and draws after it a third, by which it is expelled in its turn. In this respect, I cannot compare the soul more properly to anything than to a republic or commonwealth, in which the several members are united by the reciprocal ties of government and subordination, and give rise to other persons, who propagate the same republic in the incessant changes of its parts. And as the same individual republic may not only change its members, but also its laws and constitutions; in like manner the same person may vary his character and disposition, as well as his impressions and ideas, without losing his identity. Whatever changes he endures, his several parts are still connected by the relation of causation. And in this view our identity with regard to the passions serves to corroborate that with regard to the imagination, by the making our distant perceptions influence each other, and by giving us a present concern for our past or future pains or pleasures.

As memory alone acquaints us with the continuance and extent of this succession of perceptions, it is to be considered, upon that account chiefly, as the source of personal identity. Had we no memory, we never should have any notion of causation, nor consequently of that chain of causes and effects, which constitute our self or person. But having once acquired this notion of causation from the memory, we can extend the same chain of causes, and consequently the identity of our persons beyond our memory, and can comprehend times, and circumstances, and actions, which we have entirely forgot, but suppose in general to have existed. For how few of our past actions are there, of which we have any memory? Who can tell me, for instance, what were his thoughts and actions on the first of *January* 1715, the 11th of *March* 1719, and the 3d of *August* 1733? Or will he affirm, because he has entirely forgot the incidents of these days, that the present self is not the same person with the self of that time; and by that means overturn all the most established notions of personal identity? In this view, therefore, memory does not so much *produce* as *discover* personal identity, by shewing us the relation of cause and effect among our different perceptions. It will be incumbent on those, who affirm that memory produces entirely our personal identity, to give a reason why we can thus extend our identity beyond our memory.

The whole of this doctrine leads us to a conclusion, which is of great importance in the present affair, *viz.*, that all the nice and subtile questions concerning personal identity can never possibly be decided.

Self-discipline and Yoga
John Koller

John Koller (1932-   ) is professor of philosophy at Rensselaer Polytechnic Institute. In addition to *Oriental Philosophies,* he has authored several articles in scholarly journals and has given numerous lectures. Presently he is completing a book on the philosophy of Mao Tse-tung.

Focusing attention on ordinary human knowledge and the ordinary world known by such knowledge, the Samkhya philosophers argue that the entire world that can be experienced is fundamentally of the same nature. That is to say, desires, feelings, intelligence, etc., are not basically different from colors, sounds, odors, etc., all of which are fundamentally like sticks and stones. But all of this—the world that can, in principle, be experienced—is of the nature of object (or potential object), or not-self, as opposed to the Self that is always experiencer, that is ultimately and finally Subject. It would seem that the ultimate Subject is of a different nature and order than the world, since what is ultimate Subject can never become object, and what is object cannot be ultimate Subject. The difference between Self and the world is fundamentally the difference between subject and object.

Source: Oriental Philosophies (New York: Scribner's, 1970), pp. 52-63. Reprinted by permission of Charles Scribner's Sons. Copyright © 1970 Charles Scribner's Sons.

The starting point for any analysis of the world and the self must be the experience of the self and the world one has available for analysis. This experience reveals the existence of a knowing self in a changing world. Nothing is more obvious than that we and the world around us are changing. It is with this obvious fact that the Samkhya philosophers begin, and from which they derive the conclusion that all experience and all that is experienced is fundamentally of the same nature, though basically different from the ultimate experiencing subject.

CAUSALITY

The orderliness and regularity of the experienced world cannot be dismissed as the result of chance. Changes are caused. Whatever is or will be, is or will be due to various causes. The first important consequence of this is that human knowledge that comes to be must be caused. It is the effect of some prior cause. But since causality is unintelligible unless the dominant features of the effect be derived from the cause, it follows that the effect must be essentially like the cause. Therefore, our knowledge must be essentially like the world that is known. Since knowledge is the result of ordering experiences, the nature of experience must be basically the same as the world. Hence the claim that experience and the experienceable are fundamentally the same.

The analysis of causality provides the main reasons for the claims made about the world and the self by Samkhya. The theory of causality adopted is called *satkaryavada,* which means that the effect preexists in the cause. Now if it is admitted that nothing can occur without a cause and also that every effect has prior existence in the cause, it follows that in an important sense the effect does not provide any new reality, for it is simply a matter of making explicit what already existed implicitly.

The Samkhya theory of the nature of causation is summed up by Ishvara Krishna when he says: "The effect is existent (pre-existent): (1) because what is non-existent cannot be produced; (2) because there is a definite relation of the cause with the effect; (3) because all is not possible; (4) because the efficient can do only that for which it is efficient; (5) because the effect is of the same essence as the cause."[1]

The reason for claiming that effects exist is that the reality of the effect can be denied only upon denial of the cause, as a cause is a cause only to the extent it produces its effects. Therefore if there are no real effects then there are no real causes. Furthermore, the effect is as real as the cause, for the effect is simply a transformation of the cause. If one were to deny the existence of both cause and effect one would be forced to deny the whole starting point of one's analysis, which would make all the conclusions contradictory. Consequently, the existence of effects cannot be denied.

The claim that the effect is of the same essence as the cause is crucially important to Samkhya, for it is the main support of the claim that all objective reality is ultimately of the same nature, the connection being that all of objective reality is simply the result of various transformations of some one ultimate stuff.

To see the force of the Samkhya argument here it is helpful to consider some of

[1] *Samkhya-Karika,* IX.

the objections that might be raised against this theory of causation. It might be objected that the effect is a new whole different from the constituent parts, and not simply a transformation of them. Evidence is provided for this objection by the fact that no effect can be known before it is produced. But if it were essentially the same as its cause it could be known by knowing the cause prior to the production of the effect. According to Samkhya this objection is not valid, for it makes no sense to say that a whole is different from its material cause. Take the case of a table. The pieces of wood, which are the material cause of the table when arranged in a certain way, are not different from the table. If it were different, one could perceive the table independently of its parts. But this is clearly impossible. And to argue that the effect and the cause are independent and separate because they are perceived as separate and independent is to beg the question. The Samkhya claim is that perceiving an effect is simply perceiving the cause in transformation. To go on from this to say, "and therefore seeing the effect is seeing a new entity," is not to present an objection at all, but to beg the question.

Another objection that might be raised is that if Samkhya is right in maintaining that causality is simply a matter of transformation and not the production of something new, then the activity of the agent, or efficient cause, would be unnecessary, for the effect was already in existence. But if the effect preexisted, then no efficient cause is required to bring the effect into existence. This objection is addressed by considering the assumption that the effect does not preexist in the cause. If the effect did not preexist in the cause, the causality would be the bringing into existence of something out of nothing. (Hence the claim, "What is non-existent cannot be produced.") If we look at some non-existent things, such as square circles, it will be discovered that no amount of exertion can bring them into existence. To claim that what is can be caused by what is not is not to provide an alternative view of causation but to deny causality completely. Furthermore, if you do not admit that the effect preexists, then you have to say that it does not exist until it is caused. This is tantamount to saying that the non-existent effect belongs to the cause. But since the effect does not exist there is really nothing to belong to the cause, for a relation of belonging is possible only between existing things. Thus, if the effect can be said to belong to the cause it must be admitted that it preexists in the cause. But then what of the objection that in this case no cause is needed? The answer is that the agent or efficient cause simply manifests or makes explicit what was implicit and unmanifest, and does not create something new.

Another reply to the objection that cause and effect are distinct entities is that the preexistence of the effect can be seen from the fact that nothing can be gotten out of a cause which was not in the cause. For example, curd is gotten from milk because it preexisted in the milk. It cannot be gotten from water or oil because it did not preexist in them. If it were not the case that the effect preexisted in the cause it would be possible for any effect to proceed from any cause. But this is obviously not the case; for example, you cannot produce iron from water.

Now if it is the case that only certain causes can produce certain effects, then obviously some causes are potent with respect to some effects, but not with respect to others. But this shows that the effect preexists in the cause; otherwise it would make no sense to say that a cause is potent with respect to a given effect. The reason is that the potent cause of an effect has some power related to the effect, and without the preexistence of the effect there is nothing for the power to be related to, and then it makes no sense to talk about potent causes or potentiality.

Another objection that might be raised is that to talk about manifestation and transformation is to smuggle the notion of causality, in the sense of production of new events and objects, back into the picture in disguised form. This is answered by showing that the nature of transformation has nothing to do with the cessation of preexisting attributes nor with the coming-to-be of a pre-non-existent attribute. Rather, transformation means the manifestation of an attribute or characteristic implicitly present in the substance, and alternatively, the relapse of the manifested attribute into the unmanifest condition.

To clinch the case, the Samkhya philosopher argues that the very concept of causal possibility requires the preexistence of the effect in the cause. Non-being, the non-existent, requires no cause. So if the effect were non-existent at any time there would be no question of locating its cause. But it does make sense to talk about the possibility of effects which do not yet exist and to try to determine what will cause these effects to come into existence. This, however, makes sense only upon the assumption that the effect preexists in some sense, for that which is absolutely non-existent has no possibility of coming into existence.

The foregoing are all arguments essentially designed to support the claim that causes and effects are essentially the same. Cause is here being considered in the sense of material cause—the stuff out of which something comes to be. No effect can exist in a place different from its material cause. Hence cause and effect are numerically the same. An example given of the essential sameness of cause and effect is the tortoise going in and out of his shell. The spread-out tortoise is the effect, the contracted tortoise, the cause (and vice versa). But this does not involve the production of something new. Another example is a piece of gold which can be pressed into many shapes and pieces. But changing its shape does not make the effect something totally new. The flower made of gold is basically gold, as is the tree that is made of gold; the difference involves only name and form, and not the stuff out of which they are made.

Having established that the causality that must be assumed to exist in order to make sense out of human experience is of the nature of *satkaryavada* (meaning that the effect necessarily preexists in the cause), the Samkhya philosophers proceed to argue that this implies some one ultimate principle, which as a result of its transformations is experienced in its effects as the objective world. This claim follows once one admits that the present world exists as the result of previous changes and that change is not the production of something radically new. If this is admitted, then in order to avoid ultimate infinite regress it must be admitted that there is some one ultimate material cause, which in its various transformations or manifestations constitutes the world of experience. From this it follows that the entire world of experience is of the same fundamental nature as this ultimate material cause, for everything is basically only a transformation of this first cause. In this way Samkhya comes to the conclusion that the entire experiencable world is of the nature of *prakriti*, which is the name given to the ultimate causal principle.

This conclusion brings to the fore another question, however. How does the pluralistic world of experience derive, through a series of transformations, from this basic reality called *prakriti*? Obviously, if there are no effects except those that preexisted in the cause, then all of the effects that constitute the experienced world must have preexisted in *prakriti*. Consequently, *prakriti* itself must be composed of different tendencies, or characteristics. Accordingly, *Samkhya* posits various tendencies: *sattva*, which is the tendency responsible for the self-manifestation and self-maintenance of *prakriti; rajas,* the tendency of motion and action; and *tamas,* the tendency of inertia. From the psychological standpoint, *sattva, rajas,* and *tamas* are the principles responsible for pleasure, pain, and indifference, respectively. By various combinations of these differing principles it is possible to account for the evolution of the whole world. The varying proportions of these embodied principles account for all the diversity found in the world.

But what caused the evolution of *prakriti*? If the world is looked at as evolving it is implied that there was a logical time when the principles constituting *prakriti* were in a quiet state of equilibrium. If this is the case, it is necessary to suppose another principle of reality in the world, a principle responsible for disturbing the equilibrium of the tendencies, and thereby setting in motion the evolution of *prakriti.* This second reality is called *purusha.* and it is considered to be of the nature of pure consciousness, being ultimate Subject. It is, in fact, the Samkhya version of the Upanishadic *Atman* or *Brahman.*

It is the existence of *purusha* that accounts for the evolution of *prakriti.* It is not that *purusha* actually has anything to do with *prakriti,* but simply because of the existence and presence of *purusha*, the equilibrium of *prakriti* is upset and the evolutionary process begins.

A summation of the arguments given for the existence of *purusha* is given by Ishvara Krishna as follows: "(a) Because all composite objects are for another's use, (b) because there must be absence of the three attributes and other properties, (c) because there must be control, (d) because there must be someone to experience, and (e) because there is a tendency toward 'isolation' or final beatitude, therefore, the *purusha* must be there."[2]

Arguments (a) and (b) rest on the premises that (1) all experienced objects consist of parts, these parts being ordered in such a way as to serve the purposes of other objects or beings so that the whole of nature hangs together as an ordered whole, and (2) unless there is that which is not composed of parts for the sake of which those things composed of parts exist we are caught in an infinite regress. The conclusion is that the world of *prakriti,* which is the world of objects, exists for the sake of another, proving the existence of a principle other than *prakriti.* This principle is *purusha.*

Argument (c) assumes that material objects, the objects constituting the world of *prakriti,* could not work together, each being directed to its proper end, unless there be some principle of intelligence guiding this world. The conclusion is that *purusha* must exist in order that the world be ordered as it is.

Argument (d) claims that from the psychological point of view all the objects of the world are of the nature of pleasure, pain, or indifference. But pleasure and pain cannot exist without an experiencer. The conclusion is that the world of *prakriti,* must exist for some experiencer, and therefore *purusha* as the principle of experiencer must exist.

Argument (e) claims that *purusha* must exist because of the desire of the individual to transcend himself. In an ordered universe it couldn't happen that the universal tendency toward the infinite—toward self-realization—would be self-frustrating. Consequently, the *purusha* must be there to be realized, since it is being sought.

But aside from arguments, the existence of *purusha* is put beyond question or doubt by the experience of those who have transcended the world of *prakriti.*

---

[2] *Samkhya-Karika,* XVII.

That *purusha* is regarded as being independent of *prakriti* is clear from the claim that "from the repeated study of the truth, there results that wisdom, 'I do not exist [as *prakriti*] , naught is mine, I am not [*prakriti*] ,' which leaves no residue to be known, is pure, being free from ignorance, and is absolute."[3]

But if *purusha* is independent of *prakriti*, are not the questions of how they are related, and how the empirical self can realize the *purusha* within, even more enigmatic than ever? The clue to the reply is contained in the above quotation according to which it is wisdom that releases the *purusha* from *prakriti*. If the *purusha* were *really* caught up in the *prakriti* and constrained by it, then to say that the *purusha* is completely different from and independent of *prakriti* would be nonsensical. But the Samkhya view is that the relation between *prakriti* and *purusha* has its basis in ignorance. In this ignorance a tragic mistake is made, and *purusha* is confused with *prakriti*.

In order to explain how an illusory connection between *purusha* and *prakriti* can cause the real evolution of *prakriti* it is necessary to see how the mere existence and presence of *purusha* affects *prakriti*. Imagine that *purusha* were a shining light and *prakriti* a pool of water reflecting the light. Without *purusha* doing anything more than shining by its own light, the reflection in *prakriti* reflects on itself. But this is not the true light of *purusha;* it is a reflection in *prakriti* and therefore essentially of the nature of *prakriti*. Now in this reflection, which is the reflection of *purusha* in *prakriti, purusha* is lost sight of, and *prakriti* is taken to be the ultimate reality. Due to this mistake, the illumination of the empirical self which enables a person to see, hear, feel, think, desire, etc., is not recognized to proceed from the great light that is *purusha*. Consequently, as *prakriti* continues to evolve, *purusha* is not discriminated from *prakriti* but is identified with the evolutes of *prakriti*.

The order of evolution of *prakriti* sketched in the Samkhya philosophy regards the first illumination of *prakriti* by *purusha* as *Buddhi,* or *Mahat*—the "great one." This reflection becoming aware of itself is the "I-Maker" (*ahamkara*) responsible for individuation in nature. From these evolutes proceed the mind and the organs of sensation as well as the organs of actions and the essences of the things that are sensed and acted upon. Finally the gross objects of the world evolved. In this way the origin of all of experienced reality is accounted for by Samkhya.

SELF-DISCIPLINE

The preceding account of the nature of the empirical self and world, and their relation to the *purusha,* or ultimate Self, provides a rational basis for the techniques of discipline known as *yoga.* The practice of *yoga* is required to achieve the wisdom whereby the ignorance wherein the *purusha* is confused with *prakriti* is alleviated and the essential nature of the Self as *purusha* is realized.

The basic question of *yoga* is, How can that wisdom be achieved wherein the *purusha,* pure subject, recognizes itself for what it is; simply the spectator of *prakriti,* not actually a part of it or connected to it? When this wisdom is achieved there is no longer suffering, for the *purusha* is no longer mistakenly attached to the changing and suffering *prakriti.* Consequently, the afflictions of *prakriti* have nothing to do with *purusha,* and cannot cause suffering.

How the relationship between *purusha* and *prakriti* results in suffering, as

---

[3] *Samkhya-Karika,* LXIV.

explained by Samkhya, can be pictured by imagining a person in a room surrounded by audio-visual devices. These devices lead the person to identify himself with a person being picked up out of the sea, wafted to the peak of a jagged cliff high over the water, and plummeted down to be dashed against the rocks below. Time after time the process is repeated; each time the broken pieces are fused together again and the process commenced anew. For the person who has mistaken this image for himself there is the pain and suffering of a thousand horrible deaths. Nothing could be more wonderful than to escape this horrible fate. But when the person realizes that he has identified himself with a self created out of film and sound he recognizes that nothing that happens to that self has anything to do with him and he is free of the suffering with which he had identified himself. The point is that the person was really free from suffering all of the time, but ignorance prevented this realization. It was neither the audio-visual material in itself nor the person himself that caused the suffering. It was the mistaken identification of the one with the other that led to suffering. In an analogous way, neither *purusha* nor *prakriti* themselves are capable of suffering, but a wrong identification of *purusha* with *prakriti* leads to suffering. To overcome the suffering of the self something must be done to remove the ignorance leading to the mistaken identification of the pure Self with the not-Self.

To this end the *Yoga* aphorisms of Patanjali prescribes *yoga,* or self-discipline. The first four aphorisms indicate the nature and purpose of *yoga:* "Now the exposition of *yoga. Yoga* is the restriction of the fluctuations of the mind-stuff (*citta*). Then the Seer [that is, the Self] abides in himself. At other times it [the Self] takes the same forms as the fluctuations [of mind-stuff] ."[4]

What is here called "mind-stuff" corresponds to what in Samkhya is called the *Buddhi,* or *Mahat,* the "great one." The fluctuations or movements in *Buddhi,* or mind-stuff, lead to the identification with these fluctuations which are due to the not-Self, or *prakriti.* When the changes or fluctuations of the mind-stuff cease there is no foundation for the mistaken identification of *purusha* with *prakriti* and the independence of *purusha* is realized. But when the fluctuations occur they are mistaken for the real Self, the *purusha.* It is as though the light of *purusha* is caught by the rippling dirtied waters of the pool and is therefore regarded as changing and dirty. When the pool is calmed and the dirt allowed to settle, the light is no longer obscured. Accordingly, the important feature of *yoga* is the disciplining and controlling of the mind-stuff.

The eight aids to *yoga* indicate that since the mind-stuff has already identified with the ego, the mind, the senses, and bases of action, one restricts the fluctuations through self-discipline, by bringing under control the other aspects of *prakriti* that have evolved as empirical self—the habits, desires, physical self, etc.

The eight aids to the achievement of the goal of *yoga* are listed as: (1) abstinence from injury, falsehood, theft, incontinence, and the acceptance of gifts; (2) cleanliness, contentment, self-castigation, study, and devotion to the Ishvara; (3) stable and easy posture, accompanied by the relaxation of effort, or by a state of balance; (4) restraint of breath; (5) withdrawal of the senses; (6) not allowing the mind-stuff to wander; (7) focusing the mind-stuff, or contemplation; (8) concentration, wherein the object of contemplation is transcended and duality destroyed.[5]

---

[4] *Yoga Sutras of Patanjali,* I, 1-4, trans. by James Haughton Woods, *Harvard Oriental Series,* XVII (Cambridge: Harvard University Press, 1914).

[5] *Yoga Sutras,* II, III.

The first five aids are indirect or preliminary steps in that they prepare the empirical self for the discipline of the mind-stuff that is taken up in the last three steps. Essentially, the discipline of *yoga* is a matter of bringing under control the various evolutes of *prakriti* as shaped by mind-stuff, the reflected *purusha.* It is thus really the reverse process of the evolution of *prakriti;* the involution of *prakriti* back to the stage where the original mistake took place. When this occurs the *purusha* will no longer be regarded as constrained by matter and the Self will be realized in its pure subjectivity.

The explanation of the relation between the empirical and the ultimate by Samkhya, and the nature of the mistake causing bondage and suffering which is to be remedied by the discipline of *yoga,* is nicely summed up in an old and favorite Indian story. The story deals with a little tiger raised by wild goats who mistook himself for a goat and had to be instructed by a master and provided with the right kinds of experience in order to realize his true nature—that of a tiger.

The tiger's mother had died giving birth, and the infant was left all alone in the world. Fortunately, the goats were compassionate and adopted the little fellow, teaching him how to eat grass with his pointed teeth and how to bleat like they did. Time passed and the tiger assumed that he was just like the rest of the band of goats. But one day an old male tiger came upon this little band of goats. They all fled in terror, except for the tiger-goat, now about half-grown, who for some unknown reason felt no fear. As the savage jungle beast approached, the cub began to feel self-conscious and uncomfortable. To cover his self-consciousness he began to bleat a bit and nibble some grass. The old tiger roared at the little one in amazement and anger, asking him what he thought he was doing eating grass and bleating like a goat. But the little one was too embarrassed by all this to answer, and continued to nibble grass. Thoroughly outraged by this behavior, the jungle tiger grabbed him by the scruff of his neck and carried him to a nearby pool. Holding him over the water he told him to look at himself. "Is that the pot face of a tiger or the long face of a goat?" he roared.

The cub was still too frightened to answer, so the old tiger carried him to his cave, and thrust a huge chunk of juicy, red, raw meat between his jaws. As the juices trickled into his stomach the cub began to feel a new strength and a new power. No longer mistaking himself for a goat the little tiger lashed his tail from side to side and roared like the tiger he was. He had achieved Tiger-realization! He no longer took himself to be what he appeared to be in his ignorance, but realized his true nature, which had nothing to do with the world of goats.

THE IDEAL SELF

. . . karmic insight emerges in the situation of one who is driven by anxiety and suffering, who seeks self-awareness, and who is grappling in a highly personal way with the fragmented, enslaving lives which he has lived, is living, and hopes to escape.

—*Herbert Fingarette*

Given that each person regards his own fate and fortunes with some interest (sometimes neurotic, occasionally pathological), no discussion of the self can pretend to have touched the important bases unless it examines the influence that self-evaluation has on our conception of the self. That this influence extends to metaphysical conceptions of the self is no exception. This is made clear in both **Josiah Royce**'s and Herbert Fingarette's essays in this section.

Royce has a nice feel for popular conceptions of the self. He points out that common sense wavers between conceiving the self as the whole bodily organism, as an incorporeal entity, and as a combination of them, the dual combination generally holding the day. This metaphysical dualism about the nature of man is traced by Royce to a dual moral evaluation of the self. Each of us recognizes a baser side and a nobler side to ourselves. The baser side is tied to the natural, fleshly self, with the nobler side tied to an ideal, spiritual self. According to Royce's historical assessment, it was Plato and Christianity that tied this dual moral evaluation of the self to a metaphysical claim: "The higher Self is originally not myself at all, but the Spirit warring against the Flesh. This spirit is essentially from God. It comes *into* the man like Aristotle's Creative Nous. . . ." Royce claims, further, that this dualism of a higher, outer, nobler self and a lower, inner, baser self has factual support drawn from our ordinary experience of the good outside influences that emanate from our parents, teachers, counselors, and friends.

Apart from the origin of the two selves, the question that confronts anyone who entertains this morally based dualism is Which is my self? Supposedly each of us is a unique, single self. When we count selves, we count ourselves as one; but a dualism of higher and lower selves forces us to count two selves, to find a way of unifying the two aspects into a single self, or to take Royce's option (Samkhya's option also) to designate one of them as our "True Self" and the other as a "False" or apparent self.

According to Royce, "the true individual Self of any man gets its final expression in some form of consciousness different from that which we men now possess." This different form of consciousness would be aware of the universe as a whole, and as morally ordered, where each Self gets its significance or meaning articulated within a system of contrasting and cooperating lives. For Royce, the self must be defined in moral terms; it cannot be properly conceived in a detached, nonmoral, metaphysical way. The vision of our "True Self" is a vision of ourselves systematically embedded in a morally saturated "Absolute."

Royce thinks, in part, that we must conceive the self in moral terms because the nature of the self is not something discovered by careful metaphysical or scientific scrutiny; the self is not a found object that has been cast up by an indifferent nature. The self is something we make. In making ourselves with deliberate forethought and in fitting ourselves to other selves, we, as moral creatures, fashion a moral model to guide us. This Ideal moral model is the vision of what we wish our self to become; thus, the nature of the higher self, even if attained only partially, is soaked with moral properties. Each higher "True Self" is an Ideal entity fashioned by each of us to fit into an ideal pattern whose extent is the entire universe, including other selves and Nature. Our true self takes on a meaning, a significance, because of its place in that ideal pattern. Royce says, perhaps metaphorically, that the Self is not a Thing but a Meaning embodied in a conscious life. We might analogize to language: a word takes on meaning because it has a particular place in a sentence; that sentence in turn is embedded in a paragraph; change the paragraph and the significance of the sentence is altered.

Essentially, according to Royce's conception, it is up to each of us, in creating ourselves, to individuate, unify, and identify ourselves. Individuation is accomplished by making ourselves unique. We take on a unique moral task and thereby give ourselves a unique meaning and value in the total scheme of things. We unify ourselves by integrating the various fragmentary aspects of our experience; we make them count toward an ethical mission in conjunction with other selves. (On this, we suggest you read or reread Hilario H. Contreras's essay in the first section of Chapter Six.) We keep our identity through time by supplying a continuity of memory of the past and commitment for the future. Royce says, "one *ought to be able* to select from all the universe a certain portion of remembered and expected, of conceived and of intended life as that of his own true and individual Self." We create the self when we determine not to accept the "capricious and shifting" self of common sense but to shape our own self on the pattern of an Ideal self; "you will know that you are a Self precisely in so far as you intend to accomplish God's will by becoming one."

Herbert Fingarette's essay covers three topics, each of them interestingly relatable to Royce's views. First, Fingarette reinforces Royce's characterization of the fragmentariness of our experience in that Fingarette reminds us of the dual selves many people construct, sometimes due to the gap they feel between their waking life and their life of dreams and fantasy. Fingarette also remarks on the similarity of the fragmentary man depicted by Freud and that found in the Tibetan *Book of the Dead*.

Second, Fingarette bolsters Royce's insistence upon fitting the self into a larger moral scheme of the universe. He shows how the Hindu and Buddhist thinkers "stretch" the self beyond our usual mapping by the doctrine of karma and reincarnation. "My present life is only one of a set of lives. These lives are in certain respects entirely separate: their social, geographic, and physical characters may be quite unrelated to one another. Yet they form an interdependent series by virtue of a peculiar continuity: *karma*, or action." Further supporting Royce, Fingarette points out, "This karmic continuity is a psychomoral one. . . . The karmic law is much closer to the old Greek notion of cosmic justice."

Third, Fingarette perhaps helps soften the rigid resistance you may feel toward Royce's rather florid and expansive notion of men's place in the Absolute. If your attitudes have been curbed by our modern technological approach to the world, perhaps Fingarette's point that "the special fate of modern man [is] that he has a 'choice' of spiritual visions" will free your imagination enough to enjoy overrunning those curbs.

The Self as an Ethical Ideal
Josiah Royce

Josiah Royce (1855-1916) taught philosophy at Harvard University. Some of his more important works are *The Religious Aspect of Philosophy* (1885), *The Spirit of Modern Philosophy* (1892), *The Conception of God* (1897), *Studies of Good and Evil* (1898), *The World and the Individual* (1900-1901), *The Conception of Immortality* (1900), *Outlines of Psychology* (1903), *The Philosophy of Loyalty* (1908), *The Sources of Religious Insight* (1912), and *Lectures on Modern Idealism* (1919).

Each person is separately unique and also a part of the whole. It is believed in India that the way to recognize this unique self and realize 'dharma,' is through knowledge. "When we know the highest ideal of freedom which a man has, we know his 'dharma,' the essence of his nature, the real meaning of his self." This freedom is attained through giving up possessions and through a perfect love in which a man joys to love others. . . .

CONFLICTING, POPULAR VIEWS OF THE SELF

. . . Now as we know Man, he first of all appears to us as a being whose inner life is that of an individual Self. The Self of each man apparently has had an origin in time, and a development such as makes it dependent, for its contents and its character, upon natural conditions. In its turn, our self-consciousness, when once it has developed, furnishes to us the sort of insight by means of which we may hope for a comprehension of some of the mysteries of Nature. Any deeper criticism of our hypothesis about Nature must therefore depend upon a more exact account of what we mean by the human Self. We must know how we are able, both to conceive this Self as in any sense the outcome of the processes of Nature, and to apply our view of the Self to an explanation of Nature.

My next task must therefore be to state, in outline, a theory of the human Self.

Source: The World and the Individual (New York: Macmillan, 1900-1901).

What a man means by himself is notoriously a question to which common sense gives various and ambiguous answers. That by the Self one means a real being, common sense indeed insists. But the nature of this real being forms the topic of the greatest vacillation in all popular metaphysics. The most frequently mentioned doubt is that as to whether the Self is, or at least essentially includes, the bodily organism, or whether the Self is essentially an incorporeal entity. But this is but a single instance of the doubts and hesitancies of the popular doctrine concerning the Ego. And this indefiniteness of customary opinion regarding our problem most of all appears in the practical aspect of the current notions of the Self. If we ask, What is the value of the Self, and what do we gain by cultivating, by knowing, by observing, and by satisfying the Self?—common sense gives contradictory answers which at once show that the very idea of what the Self is, is subject to the most momentous changes as we alter our point of view.

The Independent Self. Ask the teacher of the people about the value and dignity of the Self at a moment when he is insisting upon the significance and the rights of individuality, and upon the duty of conscious reasonableness, and of moral independence. He will reply, perhaps, in the terms that Burns has made so familiar. "The man of independent mind" knows, asserts, expresses, preserves, glorifies the true Self, the moral individual. And the Self which he thus makes central in his moral world is an essentially honorable Self, the determiner of all true values, the despiser of mere externals, the freeman to whom fortune is nothing compared with inner dignity. When one views the moral Self thus, one conceives that the root of all evil and of all baseness must always lie without and beyond the Self. The Self sins not through self-assertion but through self-abandonment. The lost soul is the man who is the slave of fortune. Pleasure, worldly honor, external good,—these may harm the Self, just because they are foreign to its true independence. The ideal lies where the Stoics sought it, in casting off the external bondage. For such a view, every man's Self, if you could only get at the heart of it, and get it to express itself, would appear as essentially good. What corrupts and enchains men is not their innermost selfhood, but the power of an external world of temptations. To assert the true Self, is to be saved.

The Dependent Self. But even more familiar than this ethical individualism, which so often thrills the hearts of noble youth, and which inspires so many to heroism, is another ancient and, as its history shows, profoundly religious doctrine. This latter doctrine equally appeals to the moral common sense of mankind; it is crystallized, so to speak, in some of the most familiar of our customary phrases; it inspires numerous effective moral appeals; it comes to us with all the weight of the authority of the faith of the fathers. This view is that the Self of man is precisely that which in its original nature is evil, so that it is just our salvation which must to us come from without, and be won through self-abnegation. "By grace ye are saved, and that *not* of yourselves." Self-denial is, for this view, the cardinal virtue. Self-consciousness is even a vice. A man ought to think little of himself, and much of God, of the world, and of his own external business. The central evil of our life is selfishness. Virtue is definable as altruism, *i.e.* as forgetting ourselves in the thought of others. The best eulogy that one can make over the grave of the departed saint is: "He had no thought of Self; he served, he sacrificed himself; he gave himself as an offering for the good of mankind; he lived for others; he never even observed his own virtues; he forsook himself; he asked for nothing but bondage to his duty." And George Eliot sings in praise of the "scorn for miserable aims that end in Self."

The Dual Self. Now the opposition just suggested between two views of the value of Self, is so familiar that common sense not only uses these apparently conflicting phrases, but has its own lore regarding various devices by which they are to be reconciled. A man has, as we sometimes learn, two Selves,—the inner and the outer, the nobler and the baser. There is the natural man, who is by his very essence evil; and the spiritual man, who is by nature good. It is to the natural man that the advice about self-abnegation is given; it is to the spiritual Self that the well-known words of Burns make their stirring appeal. The fleshly Self is the root of all evil. The spiritual Self belongs, by origin and by destiny, to a higher realm.

This dualistic way of stating the case, and of attempting to solve the practical problem here at issue, would be more nearly final were it not that in the very effort to carry it out to its consequences, the former ambiguity only arises afresh, in a slightly altered form. The higher Self, the deeper spiritual nature, the individuality which ought to be, to whom does it originally belong? To the man who finally wins a consciousness that this has become to him his true Self? Or does this higher Self come, as Aristotle said of the Nous, $\theta\acute{v}\rho a\theta\epsilon\nu$, from without, into the natural man? Does it create for him or in him a new selfhood, so that before the higher selfhood appears in this man, it exists perhaps merely as the intent of God to save this man, or as a selfhood embodied in other men, the teachers, inspirers, guides, of the man who is to be thus brought to the possession of the higher Self in his own person? This question may indeed at first appear an idle subtlety. But as a fact, both common sense and religion, both the teacher's art and the inner consciousness of those who have in any sense passed from death unto life, give this question a very living and practical significance. Our models and our inspirations, the mysterious grace that saves us and the visible social order that moulds us,—these lie at first without the Self. Yet they in such wise determine whatever is best about us that we are all accustomed to nourish the higher selfhood by means of what we find as no creation of the original Self, but as the free gift of the world. And the two doctrines which, in European history, have most insisted upon the duality of our higher and our lower selfhood, viz. the ethical teaching of Plato and the Gospel of the Christian Church, have agreed in insisting that the higher Self is a resultant of influences which belong to the eternal world, and which the individual man himself is powerless to initiate. In Plato's account of the process of the soul's release from its own lower nature, the eternal Ideas appear as the supernatural source of truth and of goodness. In the mythical state of preëxistence, the Ideas guided the soul by their visible presence; and the soul's higher nature meant nothing but the contemplation of their uncreated perfection. In this foreign authority the soul found all that was good. And in the present life our higher nature means only our memory of the former presence of the all-powerful truth. This memory guides our awakening reason, controls our irrational passions, binds the lower Self with the might of the eternal, and conducts us back towards that renewed and direct intercourse with the ideal world wherein consists our only higher Selfhood. Christianity, in all its essential teachings, has emphasized a similar source and meaning in speaking of the higher Self. The Divine Spirit enters a man in ways that its own wisdom predetermines, and without the work of God in preparing and accomplishing the plan of salvation, in revealing the truth to man by outward means, and in preparing the heart within for the reception of the truth, the nobler Self of each man not only is unable to win control of the baser Self, but never could come effectively to exist at all. In this sense, then, it is not I who win salvation, but it is God who works in me. The higher Self is originally not myself at all, but the Spirit warring against the Flesh. This spirit is essentially from God. It comes *into* the man like Aristotle's Creative Nous, and is precisely so much of a man as is not his own, but God's.

Factual Source of Dualism. Now this well-known ambiguity of the traditional doctrines concerning the source and meaning of the higher Self in man, is not, as some have unwisely maintained, a mere consequence of theological and philosophical speculation. On the contrary, it is an expression, in terms of faith, of empirical facts about the Self which common sense everywhere recognizes. The same problems, in other formulations, exist in Hindoo philosophy as well as in Plato's; and they are recognized by Buddhism as well as by Christianity. Every watchful parent, and every conscientious teacher, is perfectly well acquainted with facts that illustrate the doctrines of saving grace and of the apparently external source of the higher selfhood, in case of every plastic child. We all of us know, or ought to recognize, how powerless we are, or should have been, to win any higher selfhood, unless influences from without,—whether you know them as mother love, or conceive them as the promptings of the divine Spirit, or view them as the influences of friends and of country,—have brought into us a truth and an ideality that is in no ordinary sense our own private creation. And every man who knows what the wiser humility is, has sometime said: "Of myself I am nothing. It is the truth alone that, coming from without, works in me."

Dualism and the Loss of Unity. But if you lay aside the problem as to the source of the higher Self, and consider merely the supposed duality of the lower and the higher Self as a given fact, have you in that case even begun to solve the problem as to what the Self of a man actually is? For the Self was to be something unique and individual. But the account here in question makes of it something disintegrated and internally manifold, and threatens to cause the name Self to mean, in case of every individual, a mere general term, applicable to various groups of different facts. For by the same principle whereby you distinguish the lower and the higher Self of a man, you might distinguish, and upon occasion, even in common life, do distinguish, many various selves, all clustered together in what we call the life of a single individual.

For if we are internally in any sense more than one Self, then we consist not merely of the lower and the higher self, but have, in some sense, as many selves as we have decidedly various offices, duties, types of training and of intellectual activity, or momentous variations of mood and condition. Of the man who is once seriously ill, common sense often says that he is no longer himself. If you ask, who then is he, if not himself, you may get the answer that he is another, a deeply changed, a strange Self. And if the change has at all the character of a mental derangement, common sense, ever since the savage stage of our social life, has been disposed to conceive the alteration in question as the appearance of an actually foreign and other Self, a new and invading individuality, which the superstitious view as a possession of the man's body by an evil spirit. Such instances are extreme;

but health furnishes to us similar, if less unhappy variations, with whose mystery the popular imagination is constantly busy. Deep emotional experiences give the sense of a new or of a wavering selfhood. There are many people, of a fine social sensibility, who are conscious of a strong tendency to assume, temporarily, the behavior, the moods, and in a measure, both the bearing and the accent, both the customs and the opinions of people in whose company they spend any considerable time. I have known amongst such people those who were oppressed by a sense of insincerity in consequence of their own social plasticity. "I almost seem to have no true Self at all," such a sensitive person may say. "I am involuntarily compelled to change my whole attitude towards the most important things whenever I change my company. I find myself helplessly thinking and believing and speaking as the present company want me to do. I feel humiliated by my own lack of moral independence. But I cannot help this fickleness. And the saddest is that I do not know where my true Self lies, or what one amongst all these various selves is the genuine one."

Now such confessions stand again for rather extreme types of variability of the mere sense of selfhood. Yet the experiences of which such less stable souls complain, exist in various degrees in many of us who are merely not sensitive enough, or perhaps not reflective enough, to notice our own actual variations of self-consciousness. I have known very obstinate men, who were full of a consciousness of their own independence and absolute stability of will and character. Yet, as a fact, they were people of very various and complex selfhood, who were, far more than they themselves supposed, the slaves of circumstances and of social influences. Only they regarded themselves as both independent and resolutely fixed in their individuality, merely because their one type of reaction in presence of any other man's opinion was to disagree with that opinion, and their one way of asserting their independence was to insist that their neighbors were wrong, while their fixed device for preserving their independence was to refuse to do whatever external authority desired them to do. But now such resolute opponents of their fellows are as much without a fixed and rational conscious principle of selfhood as their brothers, the self-accused slaves of the passing social situation. For it is as fickle to disagree with everybody as to agree with everybody. And the man who always opposes is as much the slave of external fortune as the man who always agrees. . . .

But enough of familiar illustrations of how the mere sense of selfhood may vary, or of how its outer and inner expression may seem dual or multiple. What these facts give us, is not any decision as to the true nature of the Self, but some specification of our problem, and some explanation of the reason why common sense is so uncertain about how to define the true unity of the Self. . . .

THEORIES OF UNITY

The Empirical Concept of Self. Such considerations ought once for all to give pause to those who have regarded the problem of the true nature of the Self as a matter of direct inner knowledge, or as something to be settled by an appeal to the plain man. But of course these considerations merely indicate a problem, and are by no means decisive as against any metaphysical view which insists upon a true and deeper unity of Selfhood at the basis of all these variations of the apparent Self.

But wherein shall our own metaphysical doctrine seek for guidance in this world of complexities?

I reply, The concept of the human Self, like the concept of Nature, comes to us, first, as an empirical concept, founded upon a certain class of experiences. But like the concept of Nature, the concept of the human Self tends far to outrun any directly observable present facts of human experience, and to assume forms which define the Self as having a nature and destiny which no man directly observes or as yet can himself verify. If we consider first the empirical basis of the conception of the Self, and then the motives which lead us beyond our direct experience in our efforts to interpret the Self, we find, as a result of a general survey, three different kinds of conceptions of what it is that one means or ought to mean by the term Self as applied to the individual man. Each of these sorts of conception of the human Self is once more capable of a wide range of variation. Each can be used as a basis of different and, on occasion, of conflicting notions of what the Self is. But the three have their strong contrasts with one another, and each lays stress upon its own aspect of the facts.

First then, there is the more directly empirical way of conceiving the Self. In this sense, by a man's Self, you mean a certain totality of facts, viewed as more or less immediately given, and as distinguished from the rest of the world of Being. These facts may be predominantly corporeal facts, such as not only the man himself but also his neighbors may observe and comment upon. In this sense my countenance and my physical deeds, my body and my clothing,—all these may be regarded as more or less a part of myself. My neighbor so views them. I may and very generally do so view them myself. If you changed or wholly removed such facts, my view of what I am would unquestionably alter. For to my neighbor as to myself, I am this man with these acts, this body, this presence. I cannot see these facts as my neighbor does, nor can he take my view of them. But we all regard such facts, not only as belonging to the Self, but as constituting, in a measure, what we regard as the Self of the present life. In addition to the external or corporeal Self of the phenomenal world, there is the equally empirical and phenomenal Self of the inner life, the series of states of consciousness, the feelings, thoughts, desires, memories, emotions, moods. These, again, both my neighbor and myself regard as belonging to me, and as going to make up what I am. To be sure, within this inner empirical Self, we all make distinctions, now so freely illustrated, between what does and what does not essentially belong to the Self. When a man tells me a piece of interesting news, or expounds to me his opinions, I naturally regard the ideas which then arise in my mind as his and not as mine. I have to reflect in order to observe the somewhat recondite fact that the ideas which he seems to convey to me are in one sense ideas of my own, aroused in me according to laws of association. On the other hand, when I think alone by myself, the ideas which occur to me seem to be primarily mine. I have to reflect in order to remember how largely they have been derived from books, from nature, or from conversation, and how little I can call originally my own. And everywhere in the inner life, as it flits by, I observe a constantly shifting play of what I distinguish as more truly myself, from what I regard as relatively foreign. This feeling or purpose, this mood or this choice, is my own. That other emotion or idea is alien to me. It belongs to another. I do not recognize it as mine. The distinctions, thus empirically made, have no one rational principle. They are often founded upon the most arbitrary and unstable motives. The vacillation of common sense regarding the Self is endlessly repeated in my own inner life. I am constantly sure that there exists a Self, and that there I am, present to my own consciousness as the one whose experiences all these are, and who set myself over against the foreign non-Ego at every moment. But in distinguishing my empirical non-Ego from the Ego, I follow no stateable rule in my inner life from moment to moment. I even voluntarily play with the distinctions of Self and not-Self, dramatically address myself as if I were another, criticise and condemn myself, and upon occasion observe myself in a relatively impersonal fashion, as if I were a wholly alien personality. On the other hand, there are countless automatic processes that alter or that diminish the immediately given distinctions between Ego and non-Ego. The lover in Locksley Hall somewhat unobservantly tells us how:

> Love took up the harp of life, and smote on all the chords with might;
> Smote the chord of Self that trembling, passed in music out of sight.

The lover admits that in the state which he thus describes, the Self, if invisible in the inner experience, was still able, most decidedly, to make itself heard. And, as a fact, one may well question whether, in view of what the lover in Locksley Hall tells us, the Self of this lover ever passed beyond his own range of vision at all, or was in the least out of sight. But the happy emotional confusion of self-consciousness here in question is familiar indeed to all who know joyous emotion. And in the sadder emotions one also has endless varieties in the intensity, clearness, and outlines which in our empirical consciousness characterize, from moment to moment, the relations of Self and not-Self.

But one may now ask, still dwelling upon the empirical Self, what manner of unity is left, in the midst of all these variations, as the unity that the concept of the Self can still be said to possess in our ordinary experience? And by what marks is the Self to be distinguished from the rest of the world? I reply, by pointing out a fact of central importance for the whole understanding of the empirical Ego. The variations of our experience and of our opinion concerning the empirical Self are countless in number. And no purely rational principle guides us in defining the Self from moment to moment in the world of common sense, or in distinguishing it from the not-Self. But there still does remain *one psychological principle* running through all these countless facts, and explaining, in general, both why they vary, and why yet we always suppose, despite the chaos of experiences, that the Self of our inner and outer life preserves a genuine, although to us hidden unity. This psychological principle is the simple one that, in us men, the distinction between Self and not-Self has a predominantly *Social origin,* and implies a more or less obviously present contrast between what we at any moment view as the life of another person, a fellow-being, or, as you may for short in general call him, an Alter, and the life, which, by contrast with that of the Alter, is just then viewed as the life of the present Ego. To state the case more briefly, I affirm that our empirical self-consciousness, from moment to moment, depends upon a series of contrast-effects, whose psychological origin lies in our literal social life, and whose continuance in our present conscious life, whenever we are alone, is due to habit, to our memory of literal social relations, and to an imaginative idealization of these relations. Herein lies a large part of the explanation of those ambiguities of common sense upon which I have so far insisted.

. . . Here there is time only for a brief indication of what I mean by this theory of the empirical Ego, of its unity in variety, and of its distinction from the world of the non-Ego.

Nobody amongst us men comes to self-consciousness, so far as I know, except under the persistent influence of his social fellows. A child in the earlier stages of his social development,—say from the end of the first to the beginning of the fifth year of life,—shows you, as you observe him, a process of the development of self-consciousness in which, at every stage, the Self of the child grows and forms itself through Imitation, and through functions that cluster about the Imitation of others, and that are secondary thereto. In consequence, the child is in general conscious of what expresses the life of somebody else, before he is conscious of himself. And his self-consciousness, as it grows, feeds upon social models, so that at every stage of his awakening life his consciousness of the Alter is a step in advance of his consciousness of the Ego. His playmates, his nurse, or mother, or the workmen whose occupations he sees, and whose power fascinates him, appeal to his imitativeness, and set him the copies for his activities. He learns his little arts, and as he does so, he contrasts his own deeds with those of his models, and of other children. Now contrast is, in our conscious life, the mother of clearness. What the child does instinctively, and without comparison with the deeds of others, may never come to his clear consciousness as his own deed at all. What he learns imitatively, and then reproduces, perhaps in joyous obstinacy, as an act that enables him to display himself over against others,—this constitutes the beginning of his self-conscious life. And in general, thenceforth, social situations, social emotions, the process of peering into the contents of other minds during the child's questioning period, the conflicts of childish sport, the social devices for winning approval,—in brief, the whole life of social harmony and rivalry,—all these things mean an endless series of contrasts between two sets of contents, which retain, amidst all their varieties, *one* psychologically important character. Upon this character the empirical unity and the general continuity of our adult self-consciousness depend.

In any literal social situation, namely, one is aware of ideas, designs, interests, beliefs, or judgments, whose expression is observed in the form of acts, words, looks, and the like, belonging to the perceived organisms of one's fellow-men. In strong contrast, both in the way in which they appear in the field of our sense-perceptions, and in the current interests and feelings with which they are accompanied and blended, are the acts, words, and other expressions, of our own organism, together with the ideas, designs, and beliefs which accompany these acts. Now these two contrasting masses of mental contents simply constitute the Alter and the Ego, the neighbor and the Self, of any empirical instant of our literal social life together. That these sets of contents stand in strong contrast to each other is, for the first, a mere fact of sense and of feeling. One does not reason about this fact from instant to instant. One finds it so. Nor does one appeal to any intuition of an ultimate or of a spiritual Ego, in order to observe the presented fact that my neighbor's words, as he speaks to me, do not sound or feel as my words do when I speak to him, and that the ideas which my neighbor's words at once bring to my consciousness, stand in a strong and presented contrast to the ideas which receive expression in my words as I reply to him. Alter and Ego, in such cases, are found as facts of our direct observation. Were no difference observed between the contents which constitute the observed presence of my neighbor, and the contents which constitute my own life in the same moment, then my sense of my neighbor's presence, and my idea of myself, would blend in my consciousness, and there would be so far neither Alter nor Ego observed.

. . . The Alter, viewed as a mass of experienced facts,—the words, looks, and deeds and ideas of other people,—differentiates and integrates into all that I call my experience of mankind; the Ego, centred about the relatively constant organic sensations, but receiving its type of unity especially through the social contrast-effects, stands as that totality of inner and outer experience which I recognize as my own, just because it sharply differs from my experience of any of the rest of mankind, and stands in a certain permanent sort of contrast thereto.

In origin, then, the empirical Ego is secondary to our social experience. In literal social life, the Ego is always known as in contrast to the Alter. And while the permanent character of our organic sensations aids us in identifying the empirical Ego, this character becomes of importance mainly because hereby we find ourselves always in a certain inwardly observable type of contrast to the whole of our social world.

Now what literal social life thus trains us to observe, the inner psychological processes of memory and imagination enable us indefinitely to extend and to diversify. The child soon carries over his plays into more or less ideal realms, lives in the company of imaginary persons, and thus, idealizing his social relations, idealizes also the type of his self-consciousness. In my inner life, I in the end learn ideally to repeat, to vary, to reorganize, and to epitomize in countless ways, the situations which I first learned to observe and estimate in literal social relations. Hereby the contrast between Ego and Alter, no longer confined to the relations between my literal neighbor and myself, can be refined into the conscious contrasts between present and past Self, between my self-critical and my naïve Self, between my higher and lower Self, or between my Conscience and my impulses. My reflective life, as it empirically occurs in me from moment to moment, is a sort of abstract and epitome of my whole social life, viewed as to those aspects which I find peculiarly significant. And thus my experience of myself gets a certain provisional unity. But never do I observe my Self as any single and unambiguous fact of consciousness.

The empirical Ego has now been, in outline, characterized. The source of its endless varieties has been sketched. Its unity has been found to be not, in our present form of existence, a fact that gets anywhere fully presented, as a rationally determined whole of life or of meaning. The empirical unity of the Ego depends merely upon a certain continuity of our social and of our inner life of experience and memory. The most stable feature about the empirical Ego, is that *sort of contrast in which it stands to the social world, literal and ideal, in which we live.* But precisely as here upon earth we have no abiding city, just so, in our present human form of consciousness, the Self is never presented except as a more or less imperfectly organized series of experiences, whose contrast with those of all other men fascinates us intensely, but whose final meaning can simply never be expressed in the type of experience which we men now have at our disposal. Were our life not hid in an infinitely richer and more significant life behind the veil, we who have once observed the essential fragmentariness of the empirical Ego would indeed have parted with our hope of a true Selfhood.

The Substance Concept of Self. The second type of the conceptions of the Ego consists of all those views which regard the Self as in some metaphysical sense a real being, without defining the true Being of this Self in strictly idealistic terms. Such conceptions of the human Self as an entity are numerous in the history of philosophy.... For the moment I may exemplify them by mentioning as their most familiar examples, those views which conceive the human Self as, in some realistic sense, a distinct and independent entity. For such views the true Self is often essentially a Substance. Its individuality means that in essence it is separable, not only from the body, but from other souls. It preserves its unity despite the chaos of our experiences, just because in itself, and apart from all experience, it *is* One. It lies at the basis of our psychical life; and it must be sharply distinguished from the series of the states of consciousness, and even from their empirical organization. It is the source of all the order of our mental life; and all our self-consciousness is a more or less imperfect indication of its nature.

Such realistic views are well known to you. And you also know now why, without showing the least disrespect to their historical dignity, I can and must simply decline to follow them into their details in these lectures. They are all founded upon the realistic conception of Being. They must therefore all fall with that conception. Their true spirit indeed is often of far deeper moment than their mere letter. What doctrines of Soul-Substance have often meant to express, namely, a respect for human individuality, and an appreciation of its eternal worth in the life of the Universe, our own theory of the human individual will erelong develope in its own fashion. But taken literally, the doctrine that beneath or behind our conscious life there is a permanent substance, itself never either presented or presentable in consciousness, but real, and real in such wise that its Being is independent of any knowledge that from without refers to it,—this whole doctrine, I say, simply perishes, for the purposes of our argument, together with Realism, and only its revised and purified inner meaning can reappear, in quite another guise, in the world of Idealism. Whatever the Self is, it is not a Thing. It is not, in Aristotle's or in Descartes' sense, a Substance. It is not a realistic entity of any type. Whether we men ever rightly come to know it or not, it exists only as somewhere known, and as a part of the fulfilment of meaning in the divine life. . . .

The Ethical Concept of Self. Well, there remains the third type of conception of the Self, namely, the strictly idealistic type. And precisely this type it was that I exemplified before, when I spoke of the way in which the Self has been distinguished, even by common sense, into a higher and a lower, a nobler and a baser Self. As stated in ordinary fashion, such concepts, as we saw, remain crude, and lead to frequent inconsistency. Revised with reference to the demands of our Idealism, the concept of the Self will assume a form which will reduce to unity these apparent inconsistencies of ethical common sense, and will also escape from bondage to those empirical complexities forced upon us by the Ego of the passing moment. We shall then see that the concept of the individual Self is, in its higher forms, in large measure an essentially Ethical Conception. And the third type of conceptions of the Ego consists of definitions which have always laid stress upon just this aspect. From this point of view, the Self is not a Thing, but a Meaning embodied in a conscious life. Its individuality, in case of any human being, implies the essential uniqueness of this life. Its unity, transcending as it does what we ever find presented in our present type of consciousness, implies that the true individual

Self of any man gets its final expression in some form of consciousness different from that which we men now possess. The empirical variety, complexity, ambiguity, and inconsistency of our present consciousness of the Self, is to be explained as due to the fact that, in the moral order of the universe, no individual Self is or can be isolated, or in any sense sundered from other Selves, or from the whole realm of the inner life of Nature itself. Consequently, even what is most individual about the Self never appears except in the closest connection with what transcends both the meaning and the life of the finite individual. Now, in our present form of conscious existence, we catch mere glimpses of the true meaning of the individual Self, as this meaning gets expressed in our deeds and in our ideals, and we also obtain equally fragmentary glimpses of the way in which this Self is linked to the lives of its fellows, or is dependent for its expression upon its relations to Nature, or is subject to the general moral order of the universe. These various transient flashes of insight constitute our present type of human experience. And it is their variety, their manifoldness, and their fragmentariness, which together are responsible for all those inconsistencies in our accounts of the Self,—inconsistencies which our present discussion has been illustrating. But if you want to free yourself from hopeless bondage to such inconsistencies, you must look, not to some realistic conception of a Soul-Substance, but to some deeper account of the ethical meaning of our present life than we have yet formulated. And from this point of view we get a notion of Selfhood and of individuality which may be summarized at the present stage much as follows.

. . . Any instant of finite consciousness partially embodies a purpose, and so possesses its own Internal Meaning. Any such instant of finite consciousness also seeks, however, for other expression, for other objects, than are now present to just that instant, and so possesses what we have called its External Meaning. Our Idealism has depended, from the first, upon the thesis that the Internal and the External meaning of any finite process of experience are dependent each upon the other, so that if the whole meaning and intent of any finite instant of life is fully developed, and perfectly embodied, this Whole Meaning of the instant becomes identical with the Universe, with the Absolute, with the life of God. Even now, whatever you are or seek, the implied whole meaning of even your blindest striving is identical with the entire expression of the divine Will. And it is in this aspect of the world that we have found the unity of Being. On the other hand, as we have also seen, this unity of the world-life is no simple unity, such as the mystic sought. It is an infinitely complex unity. And of this complexity, of this wealth of life that the complete expression of even your most transient and finite glimpses of meaning implies, the foregoing facts about the Self are merely instances. If you are in company with a friend, the whole meaning of your thoughts and of your interests while you speak with him, not only requires for its complete expression his inner life as well as yours, and not only requires the genuine and conscious unity of his life and of yours by virtue of the ties of your friendship; but this same meaning also demands that, despite this unity of your life as friends,—yes, even because of this unity, your friend and yourself shall remain also contrasted lives, whose unity includes and presupposes your variety as these two friends. For a friendship is not a simple unity of conscious life, but the unity of two conscious lives each of which contrasts itself with the other, and feels in the other's relative independence the fulfilment of its own purpose. And just so, when your meaning is not friendly but hostile, and when you stand in presence of your opponent, your rival, your enemy, your finite conscious meaning still implies, even in the midst of all its confused illusions, the demand that the very life of your enemy shall exist as the expression of your hostile intent to hold him as your real enemy, while nevertheless this life of his, other than your present conscious experience, and linked with your experience through the ties of meaning, is contrasted with your own life as the life that yours opposes and in so far seeks either to win over to your purposes, or to annul. Finite love and finite hate, and human experience of life in any form, always imply, therefore, that the will now present, but imperfectly expressed, in this passing instant, is genuinely expressed through other conscious life that, from the Absolute point of view, is at once in conscious unity with this instant's purpose, and also in conscious contrast with this instant's purpose.

Primarily then, the contrast of Self and not-Self comes to us as the contrast between the Internal and the External meaning of this present moment's purpose. In the narrowest sense, the Self is just your own present imperfectly expressed pulsation of meaning and purpose,—this striving, this love, this hate, this hope, this fear, this inquiry, this inner speech of the instant's will, this thought, this deed, this desire,—in brief, this idea taken as an Internal Meaning. In the widest sense, the not-Self is all the rest of the divine whole of conscious life,—the Other, the outer World of expressed meaning taken as in contrast with what, just at this instant of our human form of consciousness, is observed, and, relatively speaking, possessed. Any finite idea is so far a Self; and I can, if you please, contrast my present Self with my past or my future Self, with yesterday's hopes or with to-morrow's deeds, quite as genuinely as with your inner life or with the whole society of which I am a member, or with the whole life of which our experience of Nature is a hint, or, finally, with the life of God in its entirety. In every such case, I take account of a true contrast between Self and not-Self. All such contrasts have a common character, namely, that in them an imperfectly expressed will is set over against its own richer expression, while stress is laid upon the fact,—a perfectly genuine fact of Being,—the fact that the whole expression always retains, and does not merely absorb or transmute, the very contrast between the finite Self and its desired or presupposed Other,—its world of External Meanings. But if you ask how many such contrasts can be made, I reply, An infinite number. In countless ways can the Self of this instant's glimpse of conscious meaning be set into contrast with the not-Self, whose content may be the life of past and future, of friends and of enemies, of the social order and of Nature, of finite life in general, and of God's life in its wholeness.

But if the contrast of Self and not-Self can thus be defined with an infinite variety of emphasis, the unity of each of the two, Self and not-Self, can be emphasized in an equally infinite number of ways, whose depth and whose extent of meaning will vary with the range of life of which one takes account, and with the sort of contrast between Self and not-Self which one leaves still prominent over against the unity. Thus, in the familiar case of our ordinary social self-consciousness, I first view a certain realm of past and future experience as so bound up with the internal meaning of this instant's conscious experience, that I call this temporal whole of life the life of my own human Self, while I contrast this private existence of mine with that of my friends, my opponents, or of my other fellows, or with that of human society in general. . . . What will remain, after such an examination of the Self of common sense, will be the really deep and important persuasion that he *ought to possess* or to create for himself, despite this chaos, some one principle, some finally significant contrast, whereby he should be able, with an united and permanent meaning, to identify that portion of the world's life which is to be, in the larger sense, his own, and whereby he should become able to contrast with this, his larger Self, all the rest of the world of life.

And now this very consideration, this fact that one *ought to be able* to select from all the universe a certain portion of remembered and expected, of conceived and of intended life as that of his own true and individual Self, and that one ought to contrast with this whole of life, with this one's larger or truer individuality, the life of all other individual Selves, and the life of the Absolute in its wholeness,—this consideration, I say, shows us at once the sense in which the Self is an Ethical Category. At this instant, as I have said, you can indeed identify the Self, if you please, with just the instant's passing glimpse of Internal Meaning; and in that case you can call all else the not-Self. To do this is to leave the Self a mere thrill of transient life,—a fragment whose deeper meaning is wholly external to itself. But you can, and in general you do, first identify a remembered past, and an intended future, with the Self whose individuality is just now hinted to you; and this enlarged self of memory and purpose you then oppose to a not-Self whose content is first the world of your fellow-men, and then the world of Nature and of the absolute in its wholeness. Now what justification have you for this view of your larger Self? Apart from the capricious and shifting views of common sense, you can have, I reply, but one justification, namely this: You regard this present moment's life and striving as a glimpse of a certain task now assigned to you, the task of your life as friend, as worker, as loyal citizen, or in general as man, *i.e.* as one of God's expressions in human form. You conceive that, however far you might proceed towards the fulfilment of this task, however rich this individual life of yours might become, it would always remain, despite its unity with the world-life, in some true sense contrasted with the lives of your fellows, and with the life of God, just as now you stand in contrast to both. While your whole meaning is now, and will always remain one with the entire life of God, you conceive that this whole meaning expresses itself in the form of an articulate system of contrasting and coöperating lives, of which one, namely your own individual life, is more closely linked, in purpose, in task, in meaning, with the life of this instant, than is the life of any other individual. Or as you can say: "... And in the manifold lives that the world in its unity embodies, there is one, and only one, whose task is here hinted to me as my task, my life-plan,—an ideal whose expression needs indeed the coöperation of countless other Selves, of a social order, of Nature, and of the whole universe, but whose individual significance remains contrasted with all other individual significance. If this is my task, if this is what my past life has meant, if this is what my future is to fulfil, if it is in this way that I do God's work, if my true relation to the Absolute is only to be won through the realization of this life-plan, and through the accomplishment of this unique task, then indeed I am a Self, and a Self who is nobody else, just precisely in so far as my life has this purpose and no other. *By this meaning of my life-plan, by this possession of an ideal, by this Intent always to remain another than my fellows despite my divinely planned unity with them,—by this, and not by the possession of any Soul-Substance, I am defined and created a Self.*"

Such, I say, will be your confession, if once you come to define the Self in the only genuine terms,—namely, in ethical terms. If once you choose this definition, then the endless empirical varieties of self-consciousness, and the caprices of common sense, will not confuse you. You will know that since now we see through a glass darkly, you cannot expect at present to experience your human selfhood in any one consistent and final expression. But, too, you will know that you are a Self precisely in so far as you intend to accomplish God's will by becoming one; and that you are an individual precisely in so far as you purpose to do your Father's business in unique fashion, so that in this instant shall begin a work that can be finished only in eternity,—a work that, however closely bound up it may be with all the rest of the divine life, still remains in its expression distinguishable from all this other life. You will indeed recognize that at every moment you receive from without, and from other Selves, the very experiences that give your Selfhood a chance to possess its meaning. You will know that of yourself alone you would be nothing. You will also know that as co-worker with your fellows, and as servant of God, you have a destiny of which our present life gives us but the dimmest hint.

Karma and the Inner Self

Herbert Fingarette

Herbert Fingarette (1921-   ) teaches philosophy at the University of California, Santa Barbara. Among his books are *The Self in Transformation* (1963), *On Responsibility* (1968), and *Self-deception* (1969).

The doctrine of karma, whether we accept it or not, poses profound questions about the structure, transformation, and transcendence of the Self. It raises in new ways general questions of ontology. We may be parochial and dismiss the doctrine, especially its theses on reincarnation, as obvious superstition. Or we may recall that it was not any self-evident spiritual superficiality but the historical accident of official Christian opposition which stamped it out as an important Greek and Roman doctrine, a doctrine profoundly meaningful to a Plato as well as to the masses. Perhaps more significant, it has remained, from the first millennium B.C. until the present, an almost universal belief in the East, even among most of the highly trained and Western-educated contemporary thinkers. As one Western student of the subject quite properly says,

A theory which has been embraced by so large a part of mankind, of many races and religions, and has commended itself to some of the most profound thinkers of all time, cannot be lightly dismissed.[1]

In any case, an investigation of the doctrine will force us to examine from a fresh perspective both the nature of the self and the ontological question, What is Reality?

Source: *The Self in Transformation* (New York: Basic Books, 1963), Part 2, Ch. 5, pp. 171-181, 224-237. Copyright © 1963 by Basic Books, Inc., Publishers, New York.

[1] Moore, G. F., *Metempsychosis*, Harvard University Press, Cambridge, 1914, p. 67.

Certainly we can avoid some irrelevant psychological hurdles if it be stressed at once that, in our discussion of karma and reincarnation, we will not have jumped into an antiscientific position, nor will we be treating reincarnation as "pseudo" or as "super" science. The real issues are philosophical. They have nothing to do with amassing reports of *wunderkinder*, Indian yogis, or the periodic newspaper sensationalisms exploiting fakes or unfortunates claiming inexplicable knowledge of past events. These "marvels" are as philosophically uninteresting to us as it turns out that they are to the great prophets of karma.

The assumption in this chapter is that joining a fresh examination of karmic doctrine to an examination of certain aspects of psychoanalytic therapy will throw a new light on therapy, on the meaning of the karmic doctrine, and on certain of our major philosophical and cultural commitments. The task of the reader in such a discussion is to see what the evidence and the argument say rather than to read into the words the Westerner's stock interpretation of "esoteric" doctrines.

I: SOME SUGGESTIVE ILLUSTRATIONS

Let us set the stage by introducing illustrative material out of two contexts, one the ancient East, the other the contemporary West.

We are told in the Tibetan *Book of the Dead* that, upon entering a womb (for a new birth):

If [about] to be born as a male, the feeling of itself being a male dawneth upon the Knower, and a feeling of intense hatred towards the father and of jealousy and attraction towards the mother is begotten. If [about] to be born as a female, the feeling of itself being a female dawneth upon the Knower, and a feeling of intense hatred towards the mother and of intense attraction and fondness towards the father is begotten. [2]

An early Indian sutra states:

Finally, as the time of [the human being's] death approaches he sees a bright light, and being unaccustomed to it at the time of his death he is perplexed and confused. He sees all sorts of things such as are seen in dreams, because his mind is confused. He sees his [future] father and mother making love, and seeing them a thought arises in him. If he is going to be reborn as a man he sees himself making love with his mother and being hindered by his father; or if he is going to be reborn as a woman, he sees himself hindered by his mother. It is at that moment that the Intermediate Existence is destroyed and life and consciousness arise and causality begins once more to work. It is like the imprint made by a die; the die is destroyed, but the pattern has been imprinted. [3]

It takes little effort to "transpose" such passages into the analogous psychoanalytic language; indeed they can be read as poetic accounts of the nature and import of the Oedipal phase in individual maturation. The "birth" of a unified self and personality, the profound "imprint" which this Oedipal birth into selfhood places upon the fundamental character of the person, the "womb" or dreamlike "Intermediate Existence" of the infantile, pre-Oedipal period, the beginning of life,

---

[2] Evans-Wentz, W. Y., *The Tibetan Book of the Dead*, Oxford University Press, New York, 1927, p. 179.

[3] *Saddharma-smrtyupasthana Sutra*, Chap. XXXIV, in *Buddhist Texts*, Conze, E., Philosophical Library, New York, 1954, p. 283.

consciousness, and "causality" on the new level of a psyche now essentially complete and integrated, the central role of intrafamilial sexuality, aggression, and anxiety in this process at its crisis all these need only be mentioned once the juxtaposition is made. It will be no great surprise after this to learn that, according to the detailed Tibetan accounts, the "Intermediate Existence" before "entering the womb in order to be born" is a complex one, an existence fraught with openly id-like experiences, an existence which has a definite genetic continuity, however, with the eventual "birth" and with the specific spiritual nature of the being which thus comes to life.

In such discussion of birth and rebirth, the three driving forces which must be overcome in the inner man are, of course, Anger, Lust, and Stupidity.[4] These are mentioned in varying terminologies, but nowhere can we mistake the broad intention. These three "cravings" at the root of all suffering are remarkably reminiscent of certain basic psychoanalytic conceptions. I refer to libidinal drive and aggressive drive and to the neurotic self-deception or psychotic delusions which are the generic consequences of unsublimated libido and aggression. The anxiety which prevails is vividly expressed in images of monstrous horrors and cataclysms, terror-inspiring precipices. ("Fear these not . . . O nobly-born, they are not really precipices; they are Anger, Lust, and Stupidity."[5])

A teacher has a frustrating, unsuccessful day in class. He knows that there have been successful days, that things cannot always go well. Nevertheless, he feels resentful, guilty, shameful, and impotent. That night, asleep, he dreams. He is addressing a class, teaching them of the wonderful nature and powers of the Sun. It is evident that he is not merely teaching about the Sun's great power, he is in that very act the transmitter of that power, its medium, the agent and offspring of the Sun. He is—an anxiety-fraught pun—the son. The students, however, have difficulty appreciating the magnificence of the whole subject, the wonder of the Sun's power.

The dream may be looked at as an obvious reaction to the frustration and impotence felt during the day. It is a fantasy of omnipotence lived out in a manic dream world, with only the nagging tag ends of frustration caused by an unforgivably dense group of students. But the dream is not only a reaction to the day's events. For both dream and the preceding day's events are expressions of a more enduring, underlying fantasy. The day-feelings of guilt and impotence are in substantial part the natural psychomoral consequences of archaic unconscious fantasies of pride and omnipotence. The dream is then understood as a particular plastic manifestation during sleep of an enduring, unconscious "drama" operating continuously day and night. The night-dream, as Freud said, is simply a special form of expression of a deep, unconscious wish.

Let us "stretch" our language a bit. We may say that the teacher in question lives a secret "life," a colorful, quasimythological life, a life aimed at glorious domination over others while acting as the protected agent of the All-Powerful. Garbed in twentieth-century attire, the dream-teacher is a twentieth-century Sun-priest. This secret life has, as we have noted, an intimate relation to his public life. Yet the teacher does not know of its existence as a continuous life; he directly encounters it erratically, only in the form of isolated dreams. He forgets even these,

---

[4] Evans-Wentz, W. Y., *op. cit.,* p. 162.
[5] *Loc. cit.*

or he ignores them. Immediately the dream ceases and he awakes, that life is "alien" to him, "unreal."

There is, then, an "occult" influence upon the teacher's "real" (waking and conscious) life. It is not a fantastic occultism to say that the teacher lives two lives: in secret he is a sun-priest intoxicated with his powers; in public, he lives a life in which he tastes the bitter moral fruits of his pride: he is no longer a glorious and charismatic preacher but a prosaic, impotent teacher. With insight, the teacher himself might come to experience fully and acknowledge consciously the reality of both his lives.

I spoke of "stretching" our language to truth; the language just used is quite simple and direct, it would be recognizable as a quite natural description of the situation if we had not previously "stretched" our language into the more technical terminology of "fantasy," "unconscious wish," and similar psychoanalytic conceptions which have themselves only relatively recently come to feel familiar rather than "stretched."

Let us put aside for the moment, then, such technical terms as "fantasy" (which the dream is) and "unconscious fantasy" (which the dream represents in a distorted way). Let us put aside for the moment the notion of reality in the physical, biological, or even psychological senses of systematic theory or historical reportage. Instead let us focus upon the teacher's *experience*, the meaning and character of life *as lived*, as perceived, apprehended, prehended—but not as conceived, observed by the outsider, or theorized about. Then we may say, based on his own reports and our inferences, that his secret sun-priest life is among the important realities intimately affecting his life as teacher, though he does not know that it is or why it is.

The psychologist, and the dreamer himself, may do well for *some* purposes to distinguish between "fantasy" and "reality." The dreamer, however, as the psychoanalyst knows, must in another sense of these terms experience the *reality* of his secret life if he is ever to be liberated from his bewildered and unknowing bondage to it. For him to label it facilely as "fantasy" is to dismiss it; here is the seed of neurosis. To confuse it with public, waking, conscious life is to be psychotic. The person who, on the one hand, can live through this secret life, perceive it as real, and explore it with complete seriousness and who, on the other hand, does not confuse it with the structure of public, waking reality—he is the one who moves in the dimension of normality-creativity.

II: THE DOCTRINE OF KARMA

With these introductory comments and illustrations as background, it is now appropriate to review briefly but more systematically the doctrine of karma and reincarnation as traditionally expounded.

Although familiar to the ancient Greek world, and stressed in Orphic, Pythagorean, and Platonic teachings, the most elaborate and sophisticated forms of karmic doctrine known to us are to be found in Upanishadic and Buddhist texts. Avoiding the many specific differences among the sects, the general notion of reincarnation may be sketched along the following lines. My present life is only one of a set of lives. These lives are in certain respects entirely separate: their social, geographic, and physical characters may be quite unrelated to one another. Yet they form an interdependent series by virtue of a peculiar continuity: *karma,* "action." This karmic continuity is a psychomoral one. In Christian terms: "Whatsoever a man soweth that shall he reap"—if not in this life, then in some other one. In Upanishadic and Buddhist language:

As a man acts, so does he become. . . .
As a man's desire is, so is his destiny.[6]

Beings, O monks, are responsible for their deeds.
Their actions mould them and are their parents. . . .[7]

The deeds of this life, and the impressions
they leave behind, follow [the dying man].[8]

This continuity is not ordinarily known to us. We are—or ordinarily appear to ourselves to be—tossed at random into a world of haphazard delights and miseries, the latter preponderant as is evident to those who will but look. We are alive only insofar as we strive and struggle, and hence these lives are at their root generative of dissatisfaction, of suffering. The more one strives and struggles in the usual way, the tighter one's chains become. There is no evading spiritual cause and effect: what does not ripen in one life will ripen in another. This is the law of karma, of action and its consequences.

In the West, we tend to think of heaven and hell as analogues to our penological practices: the punishment is physical discomfort and psychic isolation (prison) regardless of the specific nature of the criminal act. The karmic law is much closer to the old Greek notion of cosmic justice, or to the notion of "poetic justice." The punishment exactly fits the crime. But poetic justice must operate within a life, if not this one, then another one. It cannot be realized if life terminates in an essentially static heaven or hell. It is utterly alien to the idea of nondiscriminating spiritual awards (hell fire regardless of the individual's specific crime, amorphous heavenly joy regardless of the specific virtues of the individual).

Karmic law is not the edict of an All-Powerful Disciplinarian, not an expression of will accompanied by the threat of sanctions. It purports to be factual description: Somehow or other, things do eventually "balance out" in the moral realm; each moral action produces, eventually, its quite specific moral reaction. And our constant strivings are constantly producing new "karma" as well as bringing past karma to fruition; the weary round of births and deaths is perpetuated.

In the course of spiritual progress toward freedom from the round of births and rebirths one eventually achieves the power of remembering past lives. One then sees their connection with the present life. The ordinary person can neither remember nor understand: "And what happened to you in your mother's womb, all that you have quite forgotten."[9] The greater the spiritual progress, the greater the ability and the easier the task. Knowledge of one's former lives is one of the "five kinds of superknowledge."[10] In achieving this "superknowledge," one is concurrently

[6] *Brihadaranyaka Upanishad,* IV, iv, 5, in *The Upanishads,* Prabhavananda & Manchester, F., Mentor, New York, 1957, p. 109.
[7] Percheron, M., *Buddha and Buddhism,* Harper & Bros., New York, 1957, p. 66. (Anguttara-Nikaya.)
[8] *Brihadaranyaka Upanishad,* IV, iv, 2. (Mentor, p. 108.)
[9] *Saddharmapundarika,* V, 70, in *Buddhist Texts,* p. 125.
[10] *Ibid.,* V, 71, p. 125.

achieving liberation from the karmic bonds. As in psychoanalysis, this knowledge is not the goal, but it is a distinctive ingredient in the achievement of freedom. Spiritual knowledge and spiritual freedom are born as one. (Compare Lao-tse, II: "Being and Non-being grow out of one another."[11])

Siwek has expressed the view that the doctrine of reincarnation is morally enervating: for not only are we assured of an indefinite number of lives in which to rectify our ways, but the widespread desire to keep on living on earth is a powerful motive to "sin" *in order* to assure rebirth.[12]

This view is understandable as "external," a result of seeing the words of the doctrine rather than its meaning as it functions in the appropriate context. From this "external" standpoint there have also been defenses of the karmic doctrine. Such late nineteenth-century metaphysicians as McTaggart and Moore have argued that the doctrine of reincarnation is more just and humane than, e.g., the Christian doctrine.[13,14] Karma, after all, faces one only with deserts proportionate to one's acts, not with eternal damnation for the finite acts of a relatively brief life. The door to reform is never absolutely cut off by karma as it is by Christianity. Such legalistic arguments pro and con, while of some interest in other contexts, divert one from the spiritual core of the karmic doctrine.

The doctrine of reincarnation does not receive its spiritual impulse and quality from theoretical discussion. I have tried to set the stage for detailed analysis by suggesting that karmic insight emerges in the situation of one who is driven by anxiety and suffering, who seeks self-awareness, and who is grappling in a highly personal and direct way with the fragmented, enslaving lives which he has lived, is living, and hopes to escape. For one who is not urgently concerned with suffering and illusion, who does not feel despair and the need for illumination, the doctrine of reincarnation is indeed a devilish snare. Although it has other meanings too, the Christian way can at least be used to *threaten* the ignorant with future massive suffering, thus acting, it is hoped, as a spur to the regenerative processes. But the way of reincarnation must begin where there is already an awareness of present suffering and enslavement. Life *is* suffering: This was the first of the Buddha's Four Noble Truths and the generative postulate of his teaching.

My karma is the body of all my deeds and thoughts as viewed from the moral perspective, all of them seeds guaranteed to bear their proper sorts of fruit. But we must ask who is the person represented by "my"? The reference here is to the unity which transcends the various phenomenal selves. The Buddhists, in contrast with Upanishadic orthodoxy, deny that this unity is to be identified with anything like a substantial soul. All, however, recognize that we are dealing with two different orders of existence, the phenomenal and noumenal, the latter being characterized either as Atman, Purusha, or Self, or as nonego, the Emptiness which is full, Nirvana.

Even in this first sketch of the karmic doctrine, we must pause to note parallels with the more detailed version of psychoanalysis.

[11] Lao-tse, *Tao Te Ching,* II, in *The Way and Its Power,* Waley, A., The Macmillan Co., New York, 1934, p. 143.

[12] Siwek, Paul, S. J., *La Réincarnation des Esprits,* Desclée, De Brovwer et Cie., Paris, 1942, II, 2.

[13] McTaggart, J. Mc. E., *Some Dogmas of Religion,* Edward Arnold, London, 1906, pp. 127-139.

[14] Moore, G. F., *op. cit.,* p. 69.

We become responsible agents when we can face the moral continuity of the familiar, conscious self with other strange, "alien" psychic entities—our "other selves." We should perhaps speak of an "identity" with other selves rather than a "continuity." For we must accept responsibility for the "acts" of these other selves; we must see these acts as *ours*. As Freud said of our dream lives, they are not only in me but act "from out of me as well."[15]

Yet identity is, in another way, too strong a term. There is a genuine difference between, say, the infantile, archaic (unconscious) mother-hater and the adult, humane, and filial (conscious) self, between the primitive, fantastic brother-murderer and the sophisticated fair-minded business competitor, between the archaic sun-priest and the teacher. Indeed, it is the assumption that there *is* a *genuinely* civilized self which is the prerequisite for classical psychoanalysis as a therapy. The adult, realistic self is the "therapeutic" *sine qua non* of the therapist. The hope in the psychotherapy of the neurotic is that his neurotic guilt is engendered by a "self" which *is* in a profound sense alien to his adult, civilized, realistic self. "For whosoever hath, to him shall be given. . . ." Insight only helps those who already have a realistic ego.

The psychoanalytic quest for autonomy reveals the Self in greater depth; it reveals it as a *community* of selves. The genuinely startling thing in this quest is not simply the discovery that these other, archaic selves exist, nor even that they have an impact in the present. What startles is the detailed analysis of the peculiarly close, subtle, and complex texture of the threads which weave these other selves and the adult conscious self into a single great pattern.

It is a special, startling kind of intimacy with which we deal. It calls for me to recognize that I suffer, whether I will or no, for the deeds of those other selves. It is an intimacy which, when encountered, makes it self-evident that I must assume responsibility for the acts and thoughts of those other persons as if they were I. Finally and paradoxically, in the morally clear vision which thus occurs, there emerges, as in a montage, a new Self, a Self free of bondage to the old deeds of the old selves. For it is a Self which sees and therefore sees through the old illusions which passed for reality. Yet this Self is the Seer who is not seen, the Hearer not heard. It is a no-self.

. . . . .

VIII: THE ONTOLOGICAL STATUS OF REINCARNATION

The question which now re-emerges with additional force is this: if the spiritual sources of reincarnationist doctrine lie so close to the kind of experience touched by psychoanalysis, why is the matter formulated in terms of *bodily* lives in past and future? In part we have answered this in an earlier section of this chapter. The complicated disruption of time perception caused by uprushes of the unconscious, the "living" quality of the new perceptions, their combined "alienness" and yet "belongingness"—all these and more lend themselves wonderfully to expression, at least as "metaphor," in reincarnationist language. But to leave the doctrine as an elaborate metaphor is to fail to learn a fundamental philosophical and existential lesson. For I want to show that whereas it may be viewed as metaphor, it need not be. And to see it as *not* metaphor is to achieve a form of self-liberation.

[15] Freud, S., "Moral Responsibility for Dreams," in *CP*, V, p. 156.

Let us return to Freud. Among the key ideas which enabled Freud to continue his early explorations was the idea of "psychic reality." This is related to his conception of "the omnipotence of thought." Freud showed that the unconscious mind takes the "thought" for the deed; or, even more correctly, in the unconscious, the thought *is* the deed. To wish death is, for the unconscious mind, already to have killed. Freud was here restating in his own language one of the revolutionary and characteristic insights of Jesus as well as of the Far Eastern traditions.

You have heard how it used to be said, Do not commit adultery. But I tell you, anyone who even looks with lust at a woman has committed adultery with her already in his heart.[16]

And the Dhammapada opens:

All that we are is the result of what we have thought: it is founded on our thoughts, it is made up of our thoughts.[17]

Freud, too, took seriously the *entire* inner life, and he postulated that it is all meaningfully interconnected. This postulate of "psychic determinism" is, as I have in effect argued, closely related to the doctrine of karma: no psychic event is a psychic accident: it grew out of its specific seed and bears its specific fruit.

Now such a doctrine emphasizes the importance, the reality and the vitality of the unconscious life. How does it come to be, then, that the psychoanalyst should interpret his discoveries as finally "debunking" visions, prophesy, devils, gods, and reincarnation?

The usual answer would be that the psychoanalyst now sees the true causes for these beliefs. He understands that they are "superstitions," quasi-physicalistic or "para"-physicalistic interpretations of what are really "psychological" phenomena. How else would we understand the charge that these are, for example, "merely" projections of subjective experiences.

This way of putting the matter stems from Freud's having taken a stand at the very beginning of his inquiry which prejudiced the issue. Freud, quite naturally, took the stand of science, technology, the modern West: he oriented himself fundamentally toward the public world, toward reliably interpretable theory when cast in a logically consistent and predictive form. Physical space-time, and the concept of history as rooted in these, frame not only the commonsense Weltanschauung of technological man, they establish the framework of reality for Freud, too. This is a legitimate orientation; it has profound uses. But for Freud it was more than a useful orientation; it was for him, as for most Westerners regardless of professed beliefs, the ultimate orientation.

When Freud discovered the world of inner life and its remarkable degree of autonomy from the social and physical environment at any moment, he was forced to attribute to this nonlogical, nonphysical world a secondary kind of reality—it was "psychological," "subjective," "fantasy," unless reinterpreted in terms of some logical scheme tied to physical space-time events. At least this was his way of looking at it when theoretical and philosophical description was in question. In daily practice, Freud was precisely the man, as I have said, who systematically grasped the *reality* of this realm.

[16] *Matt.* 5:27-28, Moffatt translation.
[17] Dhammapada, Chap. I in *The Wisdom of China and India.*

Freud was not alone. All of us in the West are so in bondage to the public, physical orientation that we can only allow ourselves to come to terms with the "inner" world (where it deviates from the physical) by indirection; we do so on various levels of awareness through art, play, or dream, conscious fantasy, neurosis, or psychosis. The limping metaphor "inner" serves to mark how we have crippled ourselves, cut ourselves off from the "outer" world, even in the language we use.

In those cultures which are not so fascinated by the public, the logical, and the physical, it is easier and more common to consider another mode of existence as reality. It is the world of the human being, the drama of men in their relations to each other and to nature, which plays the central role.

In such societies the physical-causal aspect of the world is as vague, shadowy, and crudely understood as is the dream-world in the West. In the modern West, the dream and the hallucination are still perceived by most persons as isolated, largely meaningless eruptions. For those who belong to nontechnological cultures, however, quite the reverse holds: it is the physical object—as physical—which, although recognized, is isolated, meaningless, unconnected with other events. No objects or events are firmly located in a clear structure of physical space-time and causality. Even when the rudiments of operating a Western Machine are learned by someone from a nontechnological culture, the machine and its operation are still located by him in the larger structure of a world moved by persons and motives. He is, to the technician, a perversely superstitious and unteachable savage or peasant. In the nontechnological culture, the meaningful world, the real world, the world that binds together, is the highly elaborated and familiar world of human drama, of myth, ritual, dream, hallucination, and daily ritualized work. All these are bound in an essentially *dramatic* unity rather than a technological one.

It is a great discovery of the major civilizations that the person is a plurality-in-unity. The modern Westerner assigns the unity to the body (the reality) and assigns the multi-personal aspects of self, the appearances, to the mind, the psychic, the subjective. By contrast, the Easterner postulates a psychic-spiritual unity, and is quite at ease associating the multiplicity of many selves, the appearances, to a multiplicity of bodily lives. Thus, for each culture, what is familiar, sensitively elaborated, and fundamental is seen as the realm of unity; what is obscure, eccentric, and less important is seen as the realm of plurality, of appearances, illusion, maya, fantasy. East and West show an exact reversal of emphasis and conceptualization.

We must not suppose, however, that the Chinese, for example, were unskilled in the study of numbers, of the physical heavens, or of nature; far from it. The Chinese did have "empirical" achievements. But, as Granet stresses in his study of Chinese thought, the important thing to note is that "the history of Chinese thought is remarkable for the independence which philosophic wisdom manages to maintain in regard to what we call science."[18] "In place of a *Science* having knowledge of the World for its object, the Chinese conceived an *Etiquette* of life which they supposed sufficiently potent to institute a total Order."[19]

In getting at the inner meaning of the classic conceptions held by Chinese thinkers we must keep reminding ourselves that

[18] Granet, M., *La Pensée Chinoise,* La Renaissance du Livre, Paris, 1934, p. 23. (Author's translation.)
[19] *Ibid.,* p. 24.

When they speak and when they write, the Chinese seek by means of stylized gestures, vocal or other, to shape and to suggest forms of conduct. Their thinkers do not have any other pretentions. They are perfectly satisfied with a traditional system of symbols which are more powerful in orienting action than they are congenial to the formation of concepts, theories, or dogmas.[20]

When a psychiatrist told a Chinese that Harry Stack Sullivan's psychiatry was based on a study of interpersonal relationships, the Chinese asked with surprise, "What other kind are there?"[21]

Whatever the scholastic superstructure, it is vital to remember that the Chinese conception of the universe "proceeds directly from mythic conceptions."[22] Traditional Eastern empirical knowledge was instrumental to spiritual demands and categories and to quite limited, practical purposes of a military or agricultural kind. The point of doing astronomy, for example, was not to develop elaborate logical-experimental theories; it was to cast better horoscopes, to adjust oneself to the Tao of the Universe.

The categories of time and history have quite different import in the East than in the West. Percheron concludes that the people of India have had an "indifference for historical dating" and, in their legends, no more respect "for geographical extent than for the duration of time or unity of aspect."[23]

Lily Abegg in her study of the mind of East Asia provides support for this point as well as insight into it.

When the East Asian surveys his history, he does not actually look backwards; it is the eternal present that he contemplates. We therefore do wrong when we say, for example, that an East Asian "looks back" towards his "ancient sages," for this is a term derived from Western concepts of time and historical development. He just regards them as if they were still living.

East Asians have a well-developed sense of history, inasmuch as the past remains alive and is ever-present to them. Thanks to their great powers of memory their historical knowledge is extremely rich. They have, however, little sense of chronological sequence in history and of the causal relationships between successive happenings; in this sense they are "history-less."[24]

We must take such perspectives into account in interpreting the karmic doctrine as it is understood by those indigenous to the Eastern cultures. When they speak of different bodies and different lives, we must inquire whether it is the moral-psychological-mythic "implications" of their statements which primarily concern them or the physical-historical ones. We cannot, of course, expect a clear and sharp *avoidance* of physical-historical comments since this aspect of the world, as we have said, is not clearly distinguished from the dramatic aspect in the first place. One cannot *consistently* avoid something of whose existence one is not consistently aware. Bits of what we Westerners would call naïve physicalistic reasoning occur occasionally in the classic texts on reincarnation. What we must do, however, is to look to the preponderance of evidence, argument, applications, and origins. We must see in what framework these are presented and toward what they point.

[20] *Ibid.*, p. 31.
[21] Weakland, J. H., "The Organization of Action in Chinese Culture," *Psychiatry* 13:361-370 (1950).
[22] Granet, M., *op. cit.*, p. 22.
[23] Percheron, M., *op. cit.*, p. 183.
[24] Abegg, L., *The Mind of East Asia*, Thames & Hudson, London, 1952, p. 310.

We might take as our watchword here the amply supported statement of Lord Raglan that "only the smallest fraction of the human race has ever acquired the habit of taking an objective view of the past."[25] And we might add that this "smallest fraction" belongs almost entirely to the cluster of subcultures having their roots in postmedieval Western Europe.

Typically, where the belief in reincarnation is held, there is no serious concern with historical documentation of the series of former lives. If such a remarkable process as transmigration referred to physical time, it is surely simple to see that historical documentation would be relevant. Yet it is the case that although the belief is nearly universal in India *even today,* there is still no serious concern on the part of spiritual leaders with providing or checking physical or historical proof. Why not? These aspects of the matter are sensed to be and are stated to be trivial and irrelevant to the main point of karmic doctrine. If anyone should find what appears to be a case confirmatory of the doctrine as taken in a physicalistic-historical sense, that is interesting. But it is no cause for special joy or increased confidence. Should anyone find disconfirmatory physical or historical evidence, it is ignored. This strongly suggests that the content of the belief, its meaning for the believer, has little or nothing to do with what *we* Westerners mean by physical or historical events as such.

When we of the modern West say, "Jones was alive in 1867," we mean clearly to indicate that our statement is logically tied to propositions about certain physical space-time events, to geographical space and to calendar time. We have an elaborate historiography as well as laboratory science with which to confirm many such statements. Physical time is a beautifully elaborated, solid structure, ever dominating our thoughts. "Subjective time," with all its comparable richness of structure, remains for us the "leftover," the residual, obscure, formless penumbra of our time-consciousness. But just as a few ancient Chinese showed remarkable, though limited, ability to elaborate physical, logical, and mathematical distinctions, so a few Westerners have achieved remarkable discriminations with regard to subjective time. The West can offer the "stream of consciousness" writers to match the Chinese "Dialecticians."

I am not emasculating the reincarnation doctrine by cutting out its physical implications. I am trying to preserve it whole. My aim here is to keep the Western mind from reading an alien, physical-historical meaning *into* it. I am not "psychologizing" it; I am "de-technologizing" it. I want to present it as a reality, not a metaphor.

The late David Roberts wrote:

From a naturalistic perspective, the language of vision in literature, philosophy and religion, tells us something interesting about the imaginary worlds which human wishes and needs have spun; but only scientific language is accurately geared to the structure of reality. From a theistic perspective, the language of drama and of personal relationships—struggle and triumph, anxiety and fellowship, guilt and forgiveness—will be regarded as fundamental.[26]

Which language reveals Reality? Which *is* "fundamental"? For those inseparably wedded to the physicalistic orientation, to orient oneself toward the dramatic

[25] Raglan, F. R., *The Hero,* Vintage Books, New York, 1956, p. 3.
[26] Roberts, D. E., *Psychotherapy and a Christian View of Man,* Charles Scribner's Sons, New York, 1950, p. 87.

world is a "flight from reality." For those of a more flexible cast of mind (a less question-begging mind?), we may consider such a reorientation as a "shifting of the index-pointer of reality."[27] Chuang-tse's anecdote about the butterfly takes on a more general and profound meaning when we see that his words *wu hua* may also be taken to mean "the ontological transformation of things" as well as "metempsychosis."[28] Where shall we set the "index-pointer of reality"? Things will work out meaningfully, though differently, *either* way.

"Reality" is, as a metaphysical term, an honorific, not a descriptive, term. We call "real" the world as viewed from our preferred orientation. Even could we in principle deduce ("explain") the world of the dramatic from a sufficiently full physicalistic account of the world, this would not settle the issue. For we can, contrariwise, make sense of the physical world in terms of a dramatic account of the world. The truth is that this latter goal has been realized, whereas the former is as yet a moot program. For we have a variety of elaborate and satisfactory accounts of the significance of the physical world within the basic framework of mythic and dramatic images. That there is variety, and that the accounts are not all logically consistent with one another, is irrelevant. The criteria of validity for dramatic unity do not include internal logical coherence, laboratory verification, or consistency with other such accounts. It is such differences in criteria which objectively distinguish the scientific from the dramatic orientation. But to insist that one or another of these orientations is the *reality*-orientation is to express fundamental cultural or personal leanings, and it is not to provide any further information.

Ultimately the question is: Which way do we choose to grasp the world: in dramatic, human images, or in logical-physical-causal conceptions? Each world is "secondary" for the other. For the world of science, the dramatic is, roughly speaking, "subjective"; the imagin*ative* is a portrayal of the imagin*ary*. But for those whose fundamental stance is in the dramatic world, the physical is, so to say, illusion. It is an obstacle which must be seen *through* when it is not a conceptual device to be used.

Whitehead argued that John Locke had misled the rest of us by so stressing scientific abstractions that "we have mistaken our abstraction for concrete realities."[29] The conception of the universe framed in terms of such high abstractions is, says Whitehead, "quite unbelievable."[30] But Wyndham Lewis, in turn critical of Whitehead's critique, has commented bitterly on this modern, condescending anti-Lockianism. Lewis asks

Who has mistaken, or mistook the very practical and useful abstractions of Science for "concrete reality" or for truth?

It is he, Dr. Whitehead, who has believed in this "dull," "meaningless" picture, quite naïvely, no doubt. And now with a gesture of enfranchisement and discovery, he announces that it is "quite unbelievable." But of course it is unbelievable. It has always been unbelievable. But, from certain aspects, and if kept in its own province, it can be extremely useful. So why not let its "dullness" and evident unreality alone, and allow it to go on doing its work?[31] [Emphases in original]

[27] Firth, R., "Elements of Social Organization," in *Reader in Comparative Religion*, Lessa, W. A., and Vogt, E. Z., eds., Row, Peterson & Co., Evanston, 1958, p. 128.

[28] Chuang-tse, Book II. (Author's translation.)

[29] Whitehead, A. N., *Science and the Modern World*, New American Library, New York, 1948, p. 56.

[30] *Loc. cit.*

[31] Lewis, W., *op. cit.*, pp. 199-200.

It is unfortunate that our slavery to the physical-causal mode of thought is so great that many attempts to assign "ontological primacy" to the human, the dramatic realities, are beset by charges of mystification, obscurantist irrationalism, even—ironically—antihumanism. It is ironic that the directly graspable world of human beings in dramatic conflict, the world which has been familiar to humankind since the beginnings of the race—all this we now find dark, obstreperous, esoteric, even silly or boring. The *human* world in the West has become peripheral and surreptitious, an "underground" world.

The things I thought were real are shadows, and the real are what I thought were private shadows. 32

I know quite well that a discussion such as the present one, if it succeeds at all, can make a person intellectually open to the view that the world of the spirit is "real"; but it cannot bring the conviction that counts. These are not, at bottom, matters of disputation but of the gesture of life, of "forms of life." One cannot accept a new reality-orientation through the medium of a generalized analysis. The response to life is always concrete, dense with meaning.

Until now I have simplified the alternatives to two: the physical orientation and the dramatic. There is, of course, a spectrum of orientations which merge one into another. Even among the "dramatic" orientations classified in the most wholesale terms we have significant choice. The Judaeo-Christian apprehends life on earth as a unique cosmic event, a coming out of nothing, a staking of all on the one chance, and, finally, a reaping of eternal reward or punishment. The Far Eastern image is of a multitude of interconnected lives, a slow and arduous struggle toward spiritual enlightenment. The physicalistic image is of a cosmically meaningless life, beginning and ending in nothingness. None of these views is intrinsically more sentimental or hard-boiled than another. Each can, in its own way, both liberate and burden; and each can be used sentimentally—whether by the infantile optimist or the defensive cynic.

Although we must be specific in life and follow one way or another, there is a sense in which these are no longer mutually exclusive alternatives. It is true each image of man's fate must be taken—when it is taken—as absolute and universal. But, for twentieth-century man, there is no one particular orientation which we must take, indeed no one which is adequate. We can no longer be parochial. The absoluteness of each perspective has validity only as and when a commitment to an orientation is made; and what is suggested by "absolute" can only be precisely interpreted within an orientation. When an orientation is not taken, the claims generated by it are not valid. For the validity of such images comes in their operation. In particular it comes when they function as the central, dominating, organizing images of a man's life. Let such an image cease to dominate a man's life and, as a *spiritual* conception, it ceases to be. The validity or invalidity of such a vision is not like the truth or falsity of a proposition in science; it is like winning or losing a race. But if a man does not enter the race, he can neither be said to win or to lose. So there is no question of the validity of a basic orientation to the world for one who is not at the time committed to that orientation. It is not a question of true or false but of increments of Being. True and false take their meaning *within* the orientation selected.

32 Eliot, T. S., "The Family Reunion," in *The Complete Poems and Plays,* Harcourt, Brace & Co., New York, 1952, p. 276.

If we are guided by the scientific orientation to the universe, of course we cannot validly introduce the illogical, the antimathematical. But an analogous prohibition holds true of the Christian conception or the Buddhist: in neither can we properly introduce that which is respectively either anti-Christian or anti-Buddhist. The question is not how to introduce what is alien in spirit into any of these, visions of life. It is, rather, when and how to shift from one great vision to another so as to maximize our total vision, to deepen it, to build it in many dimensions, to render what was opaque into that which is never transparent but increasingly translucent.

What each conception, each vision demands is that it be the genuine organizing and generative seed, that its integrity be respected and enhanced, that it receive the utter commitment which guarantees the dominance of its spirit and excludes that which is alien to its spirit. We cannot toy with the idea of reincarnation as an intellectual or cultural curiosity having a certain piquant and quaint validity and still discover its power and its worth. Nor can we, along Christian lines, only half suppose that on this moment everything rests and still discover the life of which such a conception is the seed. Nor can we fiddle with mechanical gadgets or read a syndicated newspaper column on science and then expect to experience anything but a variant of our previous mythology expressed in a pseudo-scientific lingo.

It is the special fate of modern man that he has a "choice" of spiritual visions. The paradox is that although each requires complete commitment for complete validity, we can today generate a context in which we see that no one of them is the sole vision. Thus we must learn to be naïve but undogmatic. That is, we must take the vision as it comes and trust ourselves to it, naïvely, as reality. Yet we must retain an openness to experience such that the dark shadows deep within one vision are the mute, stubborn messengers waiting to lead us to a new light and a new vision.

At first one lives with one vision for years before there is readiness for another. After the accumulation of experience and of acquaintance with more than one of these ways of seeing, the movement from one organizing view to another can come more rapidly. This shifting of visions is not then any the less a matter of genuine and deep commitment. It is not a sampling or tasting, not an eclecticism. For one calls upon a vision with a life, one's own, behind it. One earns a vision by living it, not merely thinking about it. Eventually, however, when several such lives have been lived, one can shift from life to life more often and more easily, from vision to vision more freely.

Here a Buddhist image helps. We are told that there are degrees of enlightenment and, further, that with the higher forms of enlightenment, the enlightened one can move from realm to realm, from world to world, from dharma to dharma, with ease; yet he is at home in each. The Buddha uses doctrine; he is not a slave to it. Doctrine is the ferry, and the enlightened one knows there are many ferries which travel to the farther shore. But when he is ferrying, he is skillful, wholehearted, and at one with his craft.

We know also that, even in Buddhist terms, the very Buddhas and Bodhisattvas have their special or favorite powers and realms. We must not ignore the fact that in this last analysis, commitment to a specific orientation outweighs catholicity of imagery. One may be a sensitive and seasoned traveler, at ease in many places, but one must have a home. Still, we can be intimate with those we visit, and while we may be only travelers and guests in some domains, there are our hosts who are truly at home. Home is always home for someone; but there is no Absolute Home in general. And reality is a favored base of operations, a favored place from which to greet the world, not an Absolute Place in general. With all its discovery of relativism, the West has been fundamentally absolutist and therefore parochial: we claim to tolerate other visions than the logical and technological; we explain them, praise them, enjoy them; and, gently, skillfully, appreciatively, do we not, too often, betray them?

SELF AND OTHERS

People are becoming more aware of their isolation even while they continue to worship the rugged individualist who needs no one. The self-sufficient man is casting about for a community to call his own. The glittering generalities and mythologies of American society no longer satisfy the need and desire to belong.

—Vine Deloria

Perhaps no concept related to the self has had a wider currency recently than alienation. The search for community as an escape from alienation (isolation) is a serious and pervasive one today, particularly among young people. In this section, we have included three essays that stress the relation of the individual self to other selves.

Alienation is the deprivation of psychosocial relations with others. This can occur when we are ignored, avoided, or imprisoned. These are deliberate, alienating postures. We can suffer alienation also because the society in which we live is psychosocially impoverished, when its fabric is so thin that it provides few opportunities for relating to others. Suburban society has been described as one of the impoverished social arrangements.

Alienation is a human condition of concern to many because the self by its very nature has needs or wants and because among these needs are ones that can be satisfied only by such relations as love, friendship, caring, and cooperation. In the first essay in this section, **Edward Tolman** outlines a theory of the nature of the self and its different kinds of needs. Tolman's essay is particularly interesting because he claims that an overemphasis on any one of the five kinds of needs he lists produces a particular kind of society. The society becomes structured in such a way that it tends to provide only the particular psychosocial relations that satisfy the needs being overemphasized. For example, the Christian era spawned the "spiritual man" and structured society in such a way that it satisfied the superego needs, but the society disintegrated because it alienated men from the relations that would satisfy their id and ego needs.

The second essay in this section is **Karl Marx's** famous, foundational essay on alienation. For Marx, too, alienation is an unwanted human condition because it runs athwart man's essential nature. Marx does not confine alienation to the deprivation of relations between man and man; he points out that man may also be alienated from his products, from himself, and from his species life. He tries to show how the concept of private property is the "expression" of these four kinds of alienation.

A person feels alienated from his product when he realizes a disparity in his own and his product's value. In a capitalist economy, the product increases in value while his own value decreases. This value disparity leads him to see his product as alien to him because it has power that is independent of him. Because the product is alien and because his own work activity is embedded in the object, he also comes to realize that his own activity is alien to him. He works not because it is a fulfillment of his essential nature but because he is forced to work; work becomes merely a means to bodily survival, an externally imposed activity.

The worker's alienation from his product and from his own activity is closely tied to the alienation from his species life. Man is the only entity that has a species life, because he is the only creature that is conscious of himself. He is conscious of himself in that "his own life is an object for him." Every kind of thing in the world has an essence; that is what makes it that kind of thing and what makes it differ from other kinds of things. The essence of a chair is different from the essence of a book or of an elephant or of a human. Man, in being his own object, is aware of his own essence. Hence, he is aware of himself as a species, for this essence is what defines the species man.

For Marx, the essence or nature of man, what makes him different from other kinds of things, is that he is capable of free, conscious activity. He literally objectifies his own essence by freely making objects, intellectual and material; he can contemplate himself when he contemplates the objects he has made; in those objects he has deposited himself, provided that he sees them as his own. But this is precisely what he cannot do if he is alienated from his products and his own activity. Thus, his alienation from his species life follows from his alienation from the objects he has produced and from his own activity. When alienated from his own activity, he is, as we saw, forced to work; being forced to work, he no longer works freely according to his essence, and this alienates him from his species life. Since each man qua species bears the same essence, essence being universal in men, when a man is alienated from his own essence or species life, he is, thereby, also alienated from other men who bear that same essence. In this alienated condition, the worker is divorced from and loses his own reality (his product, his activity, his essence). By consenting to his alienated condition, the worker creates his own domination in that someone else comes to possess that from which the worker has been alienated. This dominating possessor is the one who holds private property. Alienation has been shown, Marx believes, to be the expression of private property. If Marx's analysis is correct, quite obviously, man's alienated condition cannot be relieved until private property disappears.

When we treated Josiah Royce in the introduction to the previous section, we pointed out that it is possible to consider the self as something that we make rather than something that is given us already completed. Part of this making involves relating to other selves and to nature. Because our relations to other selves include moral relations, Royce insisted that we conceive the self in moral terms. Clearly, if making the self involves relating to others (in short, setting up a society), then, in deciding what kind of a self we want to be, we have to decide what kind of a society we want. In making a society, we make ourselves. **Vine Deloria**, in this section's last essay, considers two forms of individualism: the typical American rugged individualism and the Indian form of individualism. Because, according to DeLoria, Indian society is structured differently from American society, the kinds of self it is possible to make with them differs. The tribe is a social unit that is absent from American society. His argument is intended to show that the current cultural trends in the West betoken a shift in our conception of the self and that the Indian social organization by tribes is well suited to nurturing the kind of self that is appropriate to the changing cultural trends. You will find that much of what he says supports Marx's analysis, though couched in less abstract terms.

Of related interest to the topic in this section are the articles by Paz, Contreras, Guevara, and Wang in Chapter Six, as well as Satre in Chapter Eight.

The Kinds of Men

Edward Tolman

Edward C. Tolman (1886-1959) was a well-known psychologist, who taught at the University of California, Berkeley. Among his books are *Purposive Behavior in Animals and Men* (1932), *Comparative Psychology* (1934), and *Drives Toward War* (1942).

There has come a frenzy in the tides of men. Social forces whose power we have not understood or, if we have understood, we have been helpless to control, have sucked us into a dark whirlpool. What, as psychologists, ought, or can, we say at such a time? The concepts of motivation, attitude, personality—these seem about all that we psychologists have to offer. And it must be confessed they do sound awfully barren, jejune, and too much a matter of mere individual behavior to be very heartening in the face of the all-powerful social currents which are sweeping us today. Yet we psychologists still have, I believe, the task and the duty of seeing how far just such concepts can help us.

Source: Journal of Social Psychology, S.P.S.S.I. Bulletin, Vol. 13 (1941), 205-218. Reprinted by permission of The Journal Press.

I

Consider the motives leading to war. Human beings both like war and hate and recoil from it. Under some conditions they do more of the former and under others more of the latter. Psychology and the other social sciences proceed to record these facts. And at first consideration it would seem that this is all that as mere sciences they can do. Thus, the Good, the *Summum Bonum,* to the psychologist, or to other social scientists, would seem to be merely that which the majority of the people want. And war is something which people both want and don't want or—perhaps better put—something which at a given time, some individuals and some groups want and which at the same time, or at other times, other individuals and other groups hate. A psychologist can, it would seem, merely count noses and, if in the long run, more noses seem to love the stench of war, it would seem that he can but conclude that wars always will be and must be.

But my contention is going to be that psychology as a study of motivation and personality structure does not really have to end with a mere counting of noses. Motivation is not so simple and atomistic an affair as is thus implied. We do not love and hate war as mere individuals but as components of larger groups with whom we have identified. Any analysis of war or of other large-scale social phenomena requires, then, an investigation of this matter of the individual's relation to a group and the motives emphasized by that group.

To adopt, then, this sociological point of view, human motives can and must, I believe, be reëvaluated into four different types of socially oriented subclasses, which, for lack of better names, I shall call respectively: the *id wants,* the *ego wants,* the *superego wants,* and the *enlarged ego wants.* Let me hasten to add, however, that I am not here proposing these terms *id, ego* and *superego* in precisely their original psychoanalytical meanings. The psychoanalytical meanings will, however, I hope, help to suggest my meanings.

Consider, first, the *id wants.* Here I would group all the fundamental biological demands such as those for food, water, air, shelter, absence of pain, and sex. These are to be conceived as going off relatively independently of one another and as constituting by themselves a mere congeries of simultaneous or successive demands.

Consider, next, the *ego wants.* These I would conceive, in contrast, as built up through early training, and by virtue of the social mores to which the individual is subjected, upon the id wants. They differ from the id wants in that they are directed towards the self as a persisting whole. They are the prestige wants, the wants for personal strength and ability, and for personal domination. And normally they are ancillary to the id wants, for it is obvious that these goals of prestige, ability, and dominance will, generally speaking and in the long run, serve as means towards the better achievement of the id goals. That is, normally—in say, the young child—prestige, ability, and dominance seems to be primarily ways of obtaining better id goals. The child who stands out from his mates and who has especial strength and ability is one who tends to be better treated both by siblings and parents and hence gets better food and more love and less pain. It must be noted, however, that such a greater consummation of the id wants, at least in adults, need not always result from the attainment of the ego goals. Sometimes an "abnormal" social set-up may develop such that the ego goals of prestige and dominance result, not in the fulfillment, but in the crucifying of the id wants. The prestige of the religieux of the middle ages required sexual abstinence, fasting and, in general, the denial of the flesh rather than any enhanced satisfaction of the flesh.

Consider, next, the *superego wants*. These are, in a sense, just the opposite of the ego wants. A strongly developed superego demands that the individual submerge himself in the group—the family, the school, the political party, the gang, the economic class, the nation, the entire human race, or whatever it may be—with which he has identified. The superego wants are the selfless wants. But nevertheless, here, as also in the case of the ego wants, the normal result is an attainment of a greater satisfaction of the id wants. The superego, normally, is thus also ancillary to the id. The child who develops a strong set of superego demands, who always tends to submerge his own prestige and dominance and his id satisfactions in those of the group, is also a child who may tend in the long run to be protected and secure—one whose fundamental id needs will tend to be looked after by its parents or in later life by parent-surrogates. But again, in some social set-ups, this consummation of id wants as a result of the attainment of the superego goals does not result. In some social situations as, for example, in war the "good" individual—the "good" private in the ranks—is brought thereby not to the satisfaction of his id wants but to their wholesale crucifixion. The result as far as the id is concerned is not more life but death.

Further, it must again be stressed that not only the superego wants and the ego wants tend thus, on occasion, to conflict with the id wants out of which they both arise and relative to which they are normally both ancillary but they also almost invariably and inevitably conflict one with the other. The ego wants demand that the individual have prestige, that he stand out from the group. The superego wants demand just the opposite—that the individual submerge himself in the group and renounce his individual prestige.

Finally, let us turn to what I am calling the *enlarged ego wants*. By the enlarged ego I refer to a further feature involved in an individual's adherence to and identification with a group. He who identifies with a group not only tends to develop a strong superego in the sense of being ready to sacrifice many of his id wants and his primary ego wants for the welfare of that group, but also acquires a compensating enlarged ego. This enlarged ego he equates with the group. The successes and failures of the latter become *his* successes and failures. And when there are successes these come in large measure to compensate for and assuage the privations demanded of his primary ego and of his id. Thus, for example, we are told that the feudal serf compensated vicariously not only in the glory and prestige of his lord but also in the latter's superior food, drink, and shelter.

Let me sum up, now, this account of the four classes of wants and their interrelationships by eight statements, as follows:

(1) A congeries of biologically determined id wants is fundamental and the original source of all wants. (2) The primary ego wants, i.e., those for prestige and dominance of the self, are built up upon the id wants and tend in a "normal" childhood and in a "healthy" social order to lead to increased satisfaction of the id wants. (3) In some set-ups, however, this may not occur. In some social orders the achievement of the ego satisfaction may actually lead to the denial, rather than to the fulfillment, of the id wants and yet the ego wants may continue in control to a surprising degree. (4) The superego wants for submission to, and the approval of, the group also are originally built up upon the id wants. The subservient child or party member or patriot is in a normal and "healthy" family or political party or

nation rewarded therefor. (5) But here again such an outcome does not always materialize. In some set-ups of the social order the achievement of the superego wants of submission and docility may result in the sacrifice of most or, in the extreme case, even of all the id satisfactions; and yet these superego wants continue in control. (6) It appears, further, that not only may the ego wants and the superego wants conflict with the id wants to which they are normally ancillary but they may also, and almost inevitably do, conflict with one another. For, obviously, not all the members of the group can simultaneously belong to the élite. If one is to submit to the group, one cannot usually also dominate the group. (7) Further, there develops through the identification with the group an expanded or enlarged ego. This enlarged ego has as its goal the prestige and success of the group with which the individual has identified. (8) Finally, such satisfactions of the enlarged ego can often come to compensate in large measure for the deprivation of most of the primary ego wants and of many of the id wants.

II

My thesis from here on is going to be that the above classification of motives becomes a practical and useful frame of reference not only for describing and comparing the motivational structures of different individuals but also for comparing the motivational structures of different social orders.

And as a fundamental step in the application of the above analysis to social orders I shall invoke the descriptive evaluations of Western society presented by Drucker in an article in *Harpers* and in a recent book, both entitled *The End of Economic Man* [1, 2].

Drucker contends that since Christianity, western Europe has been dominated successively by some three or four "ideas" or concepts as to the best way in which individual happiness and welfare can be obtained. Each of these concepts, which I shall call myths, has held up a certain type of man—a certain way of life—as the ideal and has assumed that, if this ideal can be achieved, individual happiness and welfare will result. One of the last of these myths—the one which has just begun to lose its force for the masses in this country and which has already, according to Drucker, lost practically all of its force for the masses in Europe (except in Russia)—is the myth of the Economic Man. It is the myth which is held by both capitalists and socialists. It is the myth that the economic satisfactions are the only important ones and that, if these can be universally achieved, either through free competition as predicated by the protagonists of capitalism or through social ownership of the tools of production as predicated by the protagonists of socialism, then all the other good things of human life—that is, human welfare and human happiness in general—will also inevitably result. To quote:

Every organized society is built upon a concept of the nature of man and of his function and place in society. Whatever its truth as a picture of human nature, this concept always gives a true picture of the nature of the society which recognizes and identifies itself with it. It symbolizes the fundamental tenets and beliefs of society by showing the sphere of human activity which it regards as socially decisive and supreme. The concept of man as an "economic animal" is the true symbol of the societies of bourgeois capitalism and of Marxist socialism, which see in the free exercise of man's economic activity the means toward the realization of their aims. Economic satisfactions alone appear socially important and relevant. Economic position, economic privileges, and economic rights are those for which man works. For these he wages war, and for these he is prepared to die. All others seem mere hypocrisy, snobbism, or romantic nonsense [2, p. 45].

But prior to this myth of Economic Man there have dominated since Christianity two other concepts which Drucker designates, respectively, as the idea, i.e., the myth, of Spiritual Man, and the idea or myth of Intellectual Man. And, finally, there is now just appearing or there has already appeared in the fascist countries the myth of Heroic Man.

My thesis is, now, that each of these successive myths is really equivalent to a set of propositions concerning the relative importance to be allotted to the satisfaction of id wants, ego wants, superego wants, and enlarged ego wants.

Consider, first, the myth of Spiritual Man and the Christian era which attempted to live by it. This, I hold, was a myth and an era in which the primary importance of the superego values was predicated. Christianity was a society which officially and for the average man preached the prime importance of loyalty and self-sacrifice. But these are the superego values. If each person obeyed the Golden Rule, turned the other cheek, and loved his neighbor as himself, and submerged himself for the glory of God, then individual happiness and welfare, it was asserted, must accrue to all.

But such a truly Christian society could not be maintained indefinitely. The attempt to make such a way of life the rule for all produced a type of social order which was necessarily unstable. For it meant the constant suppression of id wants and of primary ego wants. Also it was inevitable that in the élite the primary ego wants should expand at the expense of the publicly preached superego wants. But any society in which some wants are too suppressed and in which the élite obviously lead a different psychological life from that constantly preached by them to the masses is bound sooner or later to break down. The impingement of any new technological or external social force which suggests some new way, some new possibility, of life will lead to the myth's downfall. In late Christian society the masses were continually tempted to indulge, and the leaders actually did indulge, the sins of gluttony and self-indulgence, on the one hand, and those of personal pride, vainglory, on the other. That is, they constantly fell into the temptation of satisfying their ids and their primary egos. Hence with the fall of Constantinople and the spread of the wisdom of the ancients, Christian society was all ready to accept a new way of life. The ego demands could be gainsaid no longer and the intelligentsia and the upper classes grasped at the new possibilities for satisfying their primary egos.

Philosophy and the arts once again flourished. The Renaissance and Reformation came and with them a new myth—that of Intellectual Man. This new myth was that of the prime importance of ego wants. But once again the resulting society was unstable. For the fulfillment of the ego wants was possible only among the intellectually and artistically favored and the economically secure. It was not a way of life which could be experienced by all classes; and so the Renaissance in its turn was ready to fall as soon as internal or external forces suggested still another possibility of life.

And in this case the new way came from within. For, in the course of the Renaissance, Intellectual Man gave birth to science and laid the beginnings of the industrial revolution. And the industrial revolution brought it about that a relatively widespread and deepened satisfaction of id wants was made possible. The id no longer had to be sacrificed either to the superego as in Christianity or to the ego as in the Renaissance and the Reformation, but could at last come into its own and with this coming into its own there appeared the new myth of Economic Man. Industry, thrift, private investment could now, it was felt, bring material welfare to all. That is, the myth declared that as soon as all should have enough food, shelter, and sex and each man obeyed his own "enlightened self-interest"—that is, as soon as the id was not abandoned but it and the primary ego worked together—then all would live happily forever after. Whether it was that the prince would marry the beggar maid and thus make possible the satisfaction of her id wants, or the noble lord would marry the daughter of an American industrialist and make possible once again the satisfaction of his lordship's id wants, or whether you and I and the next man would all join in a Socialist Utopia by sleeping in a joint house, eating from a joint kitchen and giving free rein to our love for the other sex, freed from distorting notions of property rights, the myth was the same. It was the myth that the id wants and the primary ego wants built upon them are enough.

But, as Drucker has argued, this myth is one which has now also already lost its force or is fast losing it. But why? Its goals are now technologically possible. Enough material production could now, at least in America, be achieved so that, if goods were properly distributed, beggar maids could all become, or better, be born, princesses, noble lords could all find rich wives, and all of us could communistically share food, drink, and sex, flatter our respective egos and have plenty left to go around.

But western Europe has abandoned or is abandoning this goal just as the last steps towards its final consummation seemed about to be realized. There must, then, have been some fundamental weakness inherent in this myth also. And that weakness was, as I see it, that in modern society the attempt to satisfy the id wants and the primary ego wants left the superego wants and the enlarged ego wants almost wholly neglected. The ruling classes because of their strong primary and restricted class egos would not give up their perquisites so that the ids and primary egos of the masses could be equally satisfied. The two hundred families put their own interests first as did also the French labor leaders, and France went under at the first blow of foreign invasion. Id wants and primary ego wants had been preached so strongly at the expense of the superego goals of loyalty and self-sacrifice that coöperative action became impossible. And human beings crave to be loyal and to perform self-sacrifices just as much as they crave food, drink, sex, and individual prestige.

Democratic Italy and Germany, and after them, Spain, Norway, Holland, Belgium, and France all collapsed for fundamentally the same reasons. All were ready for the appearance of strong men—dictators, i.e., father surrogates—relative to whom the superego wants could again find satisfaction. The myth of Heroic Man came into its own. This myth differs from that of Economic Man in that it reinstates once again the importance of self-sacrifice, submission to the group. The Id satisfactions are not, however, completely denied (as they were in early Christianity) largely, of course, because of our present greater technological sufficiency. They are, however, to be kept at a low level. The common man will have a job and security even though his level of subsistence will be reduced. But, more importantly, he is once again assured that his sacrifices are for the sake of some larger whole. Once again he that loseth all is promised all. Furthermore, this time he is promised it not in some merely future life, as in Christianity, but here and now in the success, the glory, and the prestige of his earthly group. His enlarged ego as well as his superego is to be rewarded superabundantly. He is to be an integral part of some all-conquering super race which shall gloriously survive on this earth. This, of course, is a horrible doctrine to those of us who are outside the conquering group, but it is a glorious and heartening one to those who are among the chosen.

III

What, then, of the future? Will the myth of Heroic Man also go under? Yes, I assert that it will.[1] It cannot persist for two reasons: The first reason is that it requires ever-continuing group successes. The private in the ranks will not continually forego most of his id satisfactions and all of his primary ego satisfactions unless he be continually compensated by the ever-renewed success of the larger group—i.e., unless the satisfactions of his enlarged ego continuously make up to him for the deprivations of his id and of his primary ego. Hence when the group as a whole fails of new successes, either because the other opposing groups do not finally go under or they do go under and hence there are no new fields to conquer, there is bound to be internal collapse. The frustration of their ids and of their primary egos suffered by the masses will lead to aggression against the élite who have deprived them.

And the second reason why this myth of the Heroic Man cannot persist forever is that in this case also the élite do not, and in fact cannot, practice what they preach. They do not and cannot suffer the same id deprivations and primary ego deprivations which they impose upon the masses. Neither do they, or can they, practice quite the same intensity of subordination to the group—i.e., quite the same intensity of superego satisfactions which they preach to the masses. Perhaps the original leaders—the Hitlers and the Mussolinis—do and can work permanently for the success of the group. The Hitlers and the Mussolinis are, however, peculiar. They are driven by childhood and adolescent inferiorities. They can compensate only by the successes of the groups with which they have identified. But the second generation of leaders, who are now being trained, will not be so driven. They will not have started from nothing. They will have been early adopted into the élite. And the greater primary id satisfactions and primary ego satisfactions possible to the élite will sooner or later corrupt them. They will come to think not in terms of the group but in terms solely of their primary selves and of their narrow class.

Granted then that Fascism will sooner or later break down—that the myth of Heroic Man is doomed—can we predict what the new myth, which will follow it, must be? Perhaps we cannot. Perhaps there *is* nothing in the bare logic of events to tell us what shall and must succeed. Two relatively immediate possibilities seem to me, however, possible. On the one hand, all we may perhaps expect is another Dark Ages—a complete breakdown in civilization as thus far known—a future some such as that depicted in H. G. Wells' *Things to Come*. On the other hand, there is a second possibility which, if certain forces which we can now descry in our midst are strong enough, can and will come. I wish to suggest this latter possibility.

[1] Drucker himself emphasizes that the myth of Heroic Man is but a straw at which the masses have grasped while waiting for some new and more abundant myth to appear.

IV

The forces which, as I see it, will bring this second result are the forces resulting this time, not from an industrial revolution, but from a psychological revolution—the revolution in which Freud is the outstanding name. If these forces are strong enough, then the new myth will be that of Harmonious Man or, if I dare say it, of Psychological Man.

The social order which adopted this myth of Psychological Man would be one in which all four sets of wants—the id wants, the primary ego wants, the superego wants, and the enlarged ego wants—would all be brought into harmony with one another and all granted reasonable amounts of satisfaction in both the masses and the élite. Both the common man and the leader would be consciously aware of all their needs. Particularly the leaders would be made conscious of what it was all about. They, the more intelligent, the more trainable, would be taught to be constantly on the lookout that their primary ego wants and their enlarged ego wants did not run away with their superego needs. They would be taught always and in some measure to submerge and sacrifice themselves for the good of the group.

The id demands of all could be satisfied because of modern technology. In fact, even one of the most economically conservative among us admitted it would now be possible to provide a car in every garage and a chicken in every pot. The difficulty to date has been that of distribution. But this difficulty, as I believe and as Drucker suggests, will disappear when we no longer have the myth that the id wants and the primary ego wants are solely important. These latter will tend to be rewarded once we have become less focused upon them. If the leaders but shift their emphasis from the id to the rational and coöperative whole—if we can but imbue our children, not with the goal of getting rich, but with that of being rational and internally and externally coöperative human beings—the problem of the distribution of material goods will no longer be a problem but a straightforward task upon which leaders and led will naturally coöperate.

The primary ego satisfactions of the masses will also have to be satisfied. That is, each common man, however humble his abilities, must be given some feeling of his own individual success and some degree of resulting primary prestige. But this, I believe, will be possible with the development and spread of the modern psychology of abilities and traits. Clinics, vocational guidance centers, schools, even institutions for the feeble-minded are already accomplishing wonders in this direction. Pleasure, success, prestige in doing some task well is, I am confident, a possible goal for everyone. When we no longer preach that the individual must be better than everybody else in all things, but preach, rather, the goal of internal coöperation of his own wants and abilities, then prestige will come to each not from being better than all others but in being the very best that he himself can be.

The superego satisfactions of sacrifice also will be provided for both the masses and the élite by all sorts of vocational groups and place groups in which the individual can immerse himself and relative to which he will be willing to give up some of his primary ego demands. But, and here we come back again to the question of war, these larger groups must (and will) finally stop not at a nation, a class, a race, whose final and all-consuming competition is with the other nations, classes, races, but with the idea of humanity as a whole with which the individual must identify.

That is, our enlarged ego satisfactions will also have to be satisfied, but these satisfactions will have to come primarily in our identification with humanity and not from our identification solely with mere narrower groups as such. We must not preach American against Germans, against Europeans, against Asiatics, against Africans, but all humanity against nature, against disease and misery and ignorance—against battle, murder, and sudden death. Our violent aggressions—our wars—will then occur not between one group and another but between the whole of humanity and hostile nature.

V

But you will ask, finally, how are we to implement any such Utopia? How are we, as social psychologists, to make our desire for it actually bring it about, I know but one answer—*education*. And by education I mean what goes on in the nursery school and in the home, in secondary schools and in colleges, in trades unions and in chambers of commerce, in CCC camps and in our selective military training camps, in our churches and in the market place, in pressure groups and in Congress. In all these institutions we must have everlasting teaching and propaganda always in the direction of the harmonious balancing in all classes of the id satisfactions, the ego satisfactions, the superego satisfactions, and the enlarged ego satisfactions.

Our present society is going under. The myth of Economic Man has disappeared or is just disappearing. The myth of Heroic Man has come. But it also is going to disappear. And we here in America have perhaps still time to combat this myth of Heroic Man, not through adopting it ourselves—that will be our ever-constant danger—but only if (now that technology has been solved) we see to it that this technology be used not merely in the name of America and the American way of life but in the name of a human, a psychologically informed, way of life. Then our aggressions which we shall still have and shall still enjoy will take themselves out not against our fellow men but against disease and starvation and maladjustment. We shall fight primarily not against the Nazis and the Hitlers abroad but always and simultaneously here at home against the myth which they symbolize.

Aggression, which is a combination of id and ego drives, will not disappear. But the sort of aggression which ends in violence (and which, as Professor Stratton has pointed out,[2] is the only sort of aggression which we really want to get rid of) will disappear because, whatever our narrower groups, we will also all be members of a larger total human community and the enemy of that latter group will be nature and not other human beings.

Finally, it is obvious that if this education for the new order, that is, for Psychological Man, is really ever going to prevail, it can do so only if there also appears some corresponding new emotional dynamic behind it—some new religion to push and to force it. And this new religion will have to be as strong as the religion of simple nationalism that is behind the myth of Heroic Man or the simple Protestant religion of enlightened self-interest and direct communication with God that was behind the early myth of Economic Man. But where is such a new religion—such a new set of symbols and slogans to be found—that will emotionally put across our education for Psychological Man? I confess that I do not at present

[2] George M. Stratton. *Science News Letter,* July 27, 1940, pp. 54 f.

clearly descry any such a religion. I feel, however, that it will have to be some combination and balancing and adding together of the old religions. It must be a nationalism, but a nationalism which declares that one's own nation is better when other nations are also strong. It must be a religion of individual salvation, but one in which the salvation of the other fellow is just as necessary as one's own salvation. It must be a religion of self-sacrifice, but one in which self-sacrifice brings butter and guns (if the latter must be) not merely to ourselves but to others also.

VI

This would be my Utopia, and the sermon I would try to preach, though Utopias and sermons are, I realize, inexcusable in such a company as this. But our fellow human beings today all over the world are giving up their lives in the name of new loyalties. And, if we psychologists here in America don't preach our own sermons, we shall be caught by theirs. If we don't say our say, not merely as to how to detect and measure and tabulate social change, but as to what good social changes would be, then we shall deserve no better fate than the one which otherwise undoubtedly lies in store for us. America will have to be not only a surviving America, but also a New America. For, if it be not a New America, it will not survive.

REFERENCES

[1] *Drucker, P. F., "The end of economic man in Europe,"* Harp. Mo., *178 (1939), 561-570.*
[2] *Drucker, P. F.,* The end of economic man, *New York: Day, 1939.*

Alienated Man

Karl Marx

Karl Marx (1818-1883), together with Friedrich Engels, collaborated on *The Communist Manifesto* (1848) and wrote *Das Kapital* (1867-1888). Marx is the most important single figure in the development of the modern communist philosophy. Marx rebelled against the Hegelian philosophy and said "the most important task of the philosopher is not to know the world but to change it."

We have proceeded from the premises of political economy. We have accepted its language and its laws. We presupposed private property, the separation of labor, capital and land, and of wages, profit of capital and rent of land—likewise division of labor, competition, the concept of exchange-value, etc. On the basis of political

Source: Economic and Philosophic Manuscripts of 1844, translated by Martin Milligan (Moscow: Progress Publishers, 1959).

economy itself, in its own words, we have shown that the worker sinks to the level of a commodity and becomes indeed the most wretched of commodities; that the wretchedness of the worker is in inverse proportion to the power and magnitude of his production; that the necessary result of competition is the accumulation of capital in a few hands, and thus the restoration of monopoly in a more terrible form; and that finally the distinction between capitalist and land rentier, like that between the tiller of the soil and the factory worker, disappears and that the whole of society must fall apart into the two classes—the property *owners* and the propertyless *workers*.

Political economy starts with the fact of private property, but it does not explain it to us. It expresses in general, abstract formulas the *material* process through which private property actually passes, and these formulas it then takes for *laws*. It does not *comprehend* these laws, i.e., it does not demonstrate how they arise from the very nature of private property. Political economy does not disclose the source of the division between labor and capital, and between capital and land. When, for example, it defines the relationship of wages to profit, it takes the interest of the capitalists to be the ultimate cause, i.e., it takes for granted what it is supposed to explain. Similarly, competition comes in everywhere. It is explained from external circumstances. As to how far these external and apparently accidental circumstances are but the expression of a necessary course of development, political economy teaches us nothing. We have seen how exchange itself appears to it as an accidental fact. The only wheels which political economy sets in motion are *greed* and the war *amongst the greedy—competition.*

Precisely because political economy does not grasp the way the movement is connected, it was possible to oppose, for instance, the doctrine of competition to the doctrine of monopoly, the doctrine of the freedom of the crafts to the doctrine of the guild, the doctrine of the division of landed property to the doctrine of the big estate—for competition, freedom of the crafts and the division of landed property were explained and comprehended only as accidental, premeditated and violent consequences of monopoly, of the guild system, and of feudal property, not as their necessary, inevitable and natural consequences.

Now, therefore, we have to grasp the essential connection between private property, greed, and the separation of labor, capital and landed property; between exchange and competition, value and the devaluation of men, monopoly and competition, etc.—the connection between this whole estrangement and the *money* system.

Do not let us go back to a fictitious primordial condition as the political economist does, when he tries to explain. Such a primordial condition explains nothing; it merely pushes the question away into a gray nebulous distance. It assumes in the form of a fact, of an event, what the economist is supposed to deduce—namely, the necessary relationship between two things—between, for example, division of labor and exchange. Theology in the same way explains the origin of evil by the fall of man; that is, it assumes as a fact, in historical form, what has to be explained.

We proceed from an economic fact *of the present.*

The worker becomes all the poorer the more wealth he produces, the more his production increases in power and size. The worker becomes an ever cheaper commodity the more commodities he creates. With the *increasing value* of the world of things proceeds in direct proportion the *devaluation* of the world of men.

Labor produces not only commodities: it produces itself and the worker as a *commodity*—and this in the same general proportion in which it produces commodities.

This fact expresses merely that the object which labor produces—labor's product—confronts it as *something alien,* as a *power independent* of the producer. The product of labor is labor which has been embodied in an object, which has become material: it is the *objectifications* of labor. Labor's realization is its objectification. In the sphere of political economy this realization of labor appears as *loss of realization* for the workers; objectification as *loss of the object* and *bondage to it;* appropriation as *estrangement,* as *alienation.*

So much does labor's realization appear as loss of realization that the worker loses realization to the point of starving to death. So much does objectification appear as loss of the object that the worker is robbed of the objects most necessary not only for his life but for his work. Indeed, labor itself becomes an object which he can obtain only with the greatest effort and with the most irregular interruptions. So much does the appropriation of the object appear as estrangement that the more objects the worker produces the less he can possess and the more he falls under the sway of his product, capital.

All these consequences result from the fact that the worker is related to the *product of his labor* as to an *alien* object. For on this premise it is clear that the more the worker spends himself, the more powerful becomes the alien world of objects which he creates over and against himself, the poorer he himself—his inner world—becomes, the less belongs to him as his own. It is the same in religion. The more man puts into God, the less he retains in himself. The worker puts his life into the object; but now his life no longer belongs to him but to the object. Hence, the greater this activity, the greater is the worker's lack of objects. Whatever the product of his labor is, he is not. Therefore the greater this product, the less is he himself. The *alienation* of the worker in his product means not only that this labor becomes an object, an *external existence,* but that it exists *outside him,* independently, as something alien to him, and that it becomes a power on its own confronting him. It means that the life which he has conferred on the object confronts him as something hostile and alien.

Let us now look more closely at the *objectification,* at the production of the worker; and in it at the *estrangement,* the *loss* of the object, of his product.

The worker can create nothing without *nature,* without the *sensuous external world.* It is the material on which his labor is realized, in which it is active, from which and by means of which it produces.

But just as nature provides labor with the *means of life* in the sense that labor cannot *live* without objects on which to operate, on the other hand, it also provides the *means of life* in the more restricted sense, i.e., the means for the physical subsistence of the *worker* himself.

Thus the more the worker by his labor *appropriates* the external world, hence sensuous nature, the more he deprives himself of *means of life* in a double manner: first, in that the sensuous external world more and more ceases to be an object belonging to his labor—to be his labor's *means of life;* and secondly, in that it more and more ceases to be *means of life* in the immediate sense, means for the physical subsistence of the worker.

In both respects, therefore, the worker becomes a slave of his object, first, in that he receives an *object of labor,* i.e., in that he receives *work;* and secondly, in that he receives *means of subsistence.* Therefore, it enables him to exist, first, as a *worker;* and, second as a *physical subject.* The height of this bondage is that it is only as a *worker* that he continues to maintain himself as a *physical subject,* and that it is only as a *physical subject* that he is a *worker.*

(The laws of political economy express the estrangement of the worker in his object thus: the more the worker produces, the less he has to consume; the more values he creates, the more valueless, the more unworthy he becomes; the better formed his product, the more deformed becomes the worker; the more civilized his object, the more barbarous becomes the worker; the more powerful labor becomes, the more powerless becomes the worker; the more ingenious labor becomes, the less ingenious becomes the worker and the more he becomes nature's bondsman.)

Political economy conceals the estrangement inherent in the nature of labor by not considering the direct relationship between the worker (labor) *and production.* It is true that labor produces for the rich wonderful things—but for the worker it produces privation. It produces palaces—but for the worker, hovels. It produces beauty—but for the worker, deformity. It replaces labor by machines, but it throws a section of the workers back to a barbarous type of labor, and it turns the other workers into machines. It produces intelligence—but for the worker stupidity, cretinism.

The direct relationship of labor to its products is the relationship of the worker to the objects of his production. The relationship of the man of means to the objects of production and to production itself is only a *consequence* of this first relationship—and confirms it. We shall consider this other aspect later.

When we ask, then, what is the essential relationship of labor we are asking about the relationship of the *worker* to production.

Till now we have been considering the estrangement, the alienation of the worker only in one of its aspects, i.e., the worker's *relationship to the products of his labor.* But the estrangement is manifested not only in the result but in the *act of production,* within the *producing activity,* itself. How could the worker come to face the product of his activity as a stranger, were it not that in the very act of production he was estranging himself from himself? The product is after all but the summary of the activity, of production. If then the product of labor is alienation, production itself must be active alienation, the alienation of activity, the activity of alienation. In the estrangement of the object of labor is merely summarized the estrangement, the alienation, in the activity of labor itself.

What, then, constitutes the alienation of labor?

First, the fact that labor is *external* to the worker, i.e., it does not belong to his essential being; that in his work, therefore, he does not affirm himself but denies himself, does not feel content but unhappy, does not develop freely his physical and mental energy but mortifies his body and ruins his mind. The worker therefore only feels himself outside his work, and in his work feels outside himself. He is at home when he is not working, and when he is working he is not at home. His labor is therefore not voluntary, but coerced; it is *forced labor.* It is therefore not the satisfaction of a need; it is merely a *means* to satisfy needs external to it. Its alien character emerges clearly in the fact that as soon as no physical or other compulsion exists, labor is shunned like the plague. External labor, labor in which man alienates himself, is a labor of self-sacrifice, of mortification. Lastly, the external character of labor for the worker appears in the fact that it is not his own, but someone else's, that it does not belong to him, that in it he belongs, not to himself, but to another. Just as in religion the spontaneous activity of the human imagination, of the human brain and the human heart, operates independently of the individual—that is, operates on him as an alien, divine or diabolical activity—so is the worker's activity not his spontaneous activity. It belongs to another; it is the loss of his self.

As a result, therefore, man (the worker) only feels himself freely active in his animal functions—eating, drinking, procreating, or at most in his dwelling and in dressing-up, etc.; and in his human functions he no longer feels himself to be anything but an animal. What is animal becomes human and what is human becomes animal.

Certainly eating, drinking, procreating, etc., are also genuinely human functions. But abstractly taken, separated from the sphere of all other human activity and turned into sole and ultimate ends, they are animal functions.

We have considered the act of estranging practical human activity, labor, in two of its aspects. (1) The relation of the worker to the *product of labor* as an alien object exercising power over him. This relation is at the same time the relation to the sensuous external world, to the objects of nature, as an alien world inimically opposed to him. (2) The relation of labor to the *act of production* within the *labor* process. This relation is the relation of the worker to his own activity as an alien activity not belonging to him; it is activity as suffering, strength as weakness, begetting as emasculating, the worker's *own* physical and mental energy, his personal life indeed, what is life but activity?—as an activity which is turned against him, independent of him and not belonging to him. Here we have *self-estrangement,* as previously we had estrangement of the *thing.*

We have still a third aspect of *estranged labor* to deduce from the two already considered.

Man is a species being, not only because in practice and in theory he adopts the species as his object (his own as well as those of other things), but—and this is only another way of expressing it—also because he treats himself as the actual, living species; because he treats himself as a *universal* and therefore a free being.

The life of the species, both in man and in animals, consists physically in the fact that man (like the animal) lives on inorganic nature; and the more universal man is compared with an animal, the more universal is the sphere of inorganic nature on which he lives. Just as plants, animals, stones, air, light, etc., constitute theoretically a part of human consciousness, partly as objects of natural science, partly as objects of art—his spiritual inorganic nature, spiritual nourishment which he must first prepare to make palatable and digestible—so also in the realm of practice they constitute a part of human life and human activity. Physically man lives only on these products of nature, whether they appear in the form of food, heating, clothes, a dwelling, etc. The universality of man appears in practice precisely in the universality which makes all nature his *inorganic* body—both inasmuch as nature is (1) his direct means of life, and (2) the material, the object, and the instrument of his life activity. Nature is man's *inorganic body*—nature, that is, in so far as it is not itself the human body. Man *lives* on nature—means that nature is his *body,* with which he must remain in continuous interchange if he is not to die. That man's physical and spiritual life is linked to nature means simply that nature is linked to itself, for man is a part of nature.

In estranging from man (1) nature, and (2) himself, his own active functions, his life activity, estranged labor estranges the *species* from man. It changes for him the *life of the species* into a means of individual life. First it estranges the life of the species and individual life, and secondly it makes individual life in its abstract form the purpose of the life of the species, likewise in its abstract and estranged form.

Indeed, labor, *life-activity, productive life* itself, appears in the first place merely as a *means* of satisfying a need—the need to maintain physical existence. Yet the productive life is the life of the species. It is life-engendering life. The whole character of a species—its species character—is contained in the character of its life activity; and free, conscious activity is man's species character. Life itself appears only as a *means to life.*

The animal is immediately one with its life activity. It does not distinguish itself from it. It is *its life activity.* Man makes his life activity itself the object of his will and of his consciousness. He has conscious life activity. It is not a determination with which he directly merges. Conscious life activity distinguishes man immediately from animal life activity. It is just because of this that he is a species being. Or rather, it is only because he is a species being that he is a conscious being, i.e., that his own life is an object for him. Only because of that is his activity free activity. Estranged labor reverses this relationship, so that it is just because man is a conscious being that he makes his life activity, his *essential* being, a mere means to his *existence.*

In creating a *world of objects* by his practical activity, in *his work upon* inorganic nature, man proves himself a conscious species being, i.e., as a being that treats the species as its own essential being, or that treats itself as a species being. Admittedly animals also produce. They build themselves nests, dwellings, like the bees, beavers, ants, etc. But an animal only produces what it immediately needs for itself or its young. It produces one-sidedly, whilst man produces universally. It produces only under the dominion of immediate physical need, whilst man produces even when he is free from physical need and only truly produces in freedom therefrom. An animal produces only itself, whilst man reproduces the whole of nature. An animal's product belongs immediately to its physical body, whilst man freely confronts his product. An animal forms things in accordance with the standard and the need of the species to which it belongs, whilst man knows how to produce in accordance with the standard of every species, and knows how to apply everywhere the inherent standard to the object. Man therefore also forms things in accordance with the laws of beauty.

It is just in his work upon the objective world, therefore, that man first really proves himself to be a *species being.* This production is his active species life. Through and because of this production, nature appears as *his* work and his reality. The object of labor is, therefore, the *objectification of man's species life:* for he duplicates himself not only, as in consciousness, intellectually, but also actively, in reality, and therefore he contemplates himself in a world that he has created. In tearing away from man the object of his production, therefore, estranged labor tears from him his *species life,* his real objectivity as a member of the species and transforms his advantage over animals into the disadvantage that his inorganic body, nature, is taken away from him.

Similarly, in degrading spontaneous, free, activity, to a means, estranged labor makes man's species life a means to his physical existence.

The consciousness which man has of his species is thus transformed by estrangement in such a way that species life becomes for him a means.

Estranged labor turns thus:

(3) *Man's species being,* both nature and his spiritual species property, into a being *alien* to him, into a *means* to his *individual existence.* It estranges from man his own body, as well as external nature and his spiritual essence, his *human* being.

(4) An immediate consequence of the fact that man is estranged from the product of his labor, from his life activity, from his species being is the *estrangement of man* from *man.* When man confronts himself, he confronts the *other* man. What applies to a man's relation to his work, to the product of his labor and to himself, also holds of a man's relation to the other man, and to the other man's labor and object of labor.

In fact, the proposition that man's species nature is estranged from him means that one man is estranged from the other, as each of them is from man's essential nature.

The estrangement of man, and in fact every relationship in which man stands to himself, is first realized and expressed in the relationship in which a man stands to other men.

Hence within the relationship of estranged labor each man views the other in accordance with the standard and the relationship in which he finds himself as a worker.

We took our departure from a fact of political economy—the estrangement of the worker and his production. We have formulated this fact in conceptual terms as *estranged, alienated* labor. We have analyzed this concept—hence analyzing merely a fact of political economy.

Let us now see, further, how the concept of estranged, alienated labor must express and present itself in real life.

If the product of labor is alien to me, if it confronts me as an alien power, to whom, then, does it belong?

If my own activity does not belong to me, if it is an alien, a coerced activity, to whom, then, does it belong?

To a being *other* than myself.

Who is this being?

The *gods?* To be sure, in the earliest times the principal production (for example, the building of temples, etc., in Egypt, India and Mexico) appears to be in the service of the gods, and the product belongs to the gods. However, the gods on their own were never the lords of labor. No more was *nature.* And what a contradiction it would be if, the more man subjugated nature by his labor and the more the miracles of the gods were rendered superfluous by the miracles of industry, the more man were to renounce the joy of production and the enjoyment of the product in favor of these powers.

The *alien* being, to whom labor and the product of labor belongs, in whose service labor is done and for whose benefit the product of labor is provided, can only be *man* himself.

If the product of labor does not belong to the worker, if it confronts him as an alien power, then this can only be because it belongs to some *other man than the worker.* If the worker's activity is a torment to him, to another it must be *delight* and his life's joy. Not the gods, not nature, but only man himself can be this alien power over man.

We must bear in mind the previous proposition that man's relation to himself only becomes for him *objective* and *actual* through his relation to the other man. Thus, if the product of his labor, his labor *objectified,* is for him an *alien,* hostile, powerful object independent of him, then his position towards it is such that someone else is master of this object, someone who is alien, hostile, powerful, and independent of him. If his own activity is to him related as an unfree activity, then he is related to it as an activity performed in the service, under the dominion, the coercion, and the yoke of another man.

Every self-estrangement of man, from himself and from nature, appears in the relation in which he places himself and nature to men other than and differentiated from himself. For this reason religious self-estrangement necessarily appears in the relationship of the layman to the priest, or again to a mediator, etc., since we are here dealing with the intellectual world. In the real practical world self-estrangement can only become manifest through the real practical relationship to other men. The medium through which estrangement takes place is itself *practical.* Thus through estranged labor man not only creates his relationship to the object and to the act of production as to men that are alien and hostile to him; he also creates the relationship in which other men stand to his production and to his product, and the relationship in which he stands to these other men. Just as he creates his own production as the loss of his reality, as his punishment; his own product as a loss, as a product not belonging to him; so he creates the domination of the person who does not produce over production and over the product. Just as he estranges his own activity from himself, so he confers to the stranger an activity which is not his own.

We have until now only considered this relationship from the standpoint of the worker and later we shall be considering it also from the standpoint of the non-worker.

Through *estranged, alienated labor,* then, the worker produces the relationship to this labor of a man alien to labor and standing outside it. The relationship of the worker to labor creates the relation to it of the capitalist (or whatever one chooses to call the master of labor). *Private property* is thus the product, the result, the necessary consequence, of *alienated labor,* of the external relation of the worker to nature and to himself.

Private property thus results by analysis from the concept of *alienated labor,* i.e., of *alienated man,* of estranged labor, of estranged life, of *estranged* man.

True, it is as a result of the *movement of private property* that we have obtained the concept of *alienated labor (of alienated life)* from political economy. But on analysis of this concept it becomes clear that though private property appears to be the source, the cause of alienated labor, it is rather its consequence, just as the gods are *originally* not the cause but the effect of man's intellectual confusion. Later this relationship becomes reciprocal.

Only at the last culmination of the development of private property does this, its secret, appear again, namely, that on the one hand it is the *product* of alienated labor, and that on the other it is the *means* by which labor alienates itself, the *realization of this alienation.*

This exposition immediately sheds light on various hitherto unsolved conflicts.

(1) Political economy starts from labor as the real soul of production; yet to labor it gives nothing, and to private property everything. Confronting this contradiction, Proudhon has decided in favor of labor against private property. We understand, however, that this apparent contradiction is the contradiction of *estranged labor* with itself, and that political economy has merely formulated the laws of estranged labor.

We also understand, therefore, that *wages* and *private property* are identical: since the product, as the object of labor, pays for labor itself, therefore the wage is but a necessary consequence of labor's estrangement. After all, in the wage of labor, labor does not appear as an end in itself but as the servant of the wage. We shall develop this point later, and meanwhile will only derive some conclusions.

An enforced increase of wages (disregarding all other difficulties, including the fact that it would only be by force, too, that higher wages, being an anomaly, could be maintained) would therefore be nothing but *better payment for the slave,* and would not win either for the worker or for labor their human status and dignity.

Indeed, even the *equality of wages* demanded by Proudhon only transforms the relationship of the present-day worker to his labor into the relationship of all men to labor. Society is then conceived as an abstract capitalist.

Wages are a direct consequence of estranged labor, and estranged labor is the direct cause of private property. The downfall of the one must involve the downfall of the other.

(2) From the relationship of estranged labor to private property it follows further that the emancipation of society from private property, etc., from servitude, is expressed in the *political* form of the *emancipation of the workers;* not that *their* emancipation alone is at stake, but because the emancipation of the workers contains universal human emancipation—and it contains this, because the whole of human servitude is involved in the relation of the worker to production, and every relation of servitude is but a modification and consequence of this relation.

Just as we have derived the concept of *private property* from the concept of *estranged, alienated labor* by *analysis,* so we can develop every *category* of political economy with the help of these two factors; and we shall find again in each category, e.g., trade, competition, capital, money, only a *definite* and *developed expression* of these first elements.

Before considering this aspect, however, let us try to solve two problems.

(1) To define the general *nature of private property,* as it has arisen as a result of estranged labor, in its relation to *truly human* and *social property.*

(2) We have accepted the *estrangement of labor,* its *alienation,* as a fact, and we have analyzed this fact. How, we now ask, does *man* come to *alienate,* to estrange, his *labor?* How is this estrangement rooted in the nature of human development? We have already gone a long way to the solution of this problem by *transforming* the question of the *origin of private property* into the question of the relation of *alienated labor* to the course of humanity's development. For when one speaks of *private property,* one thinks of dealing with something external to man. When one speaks of labor, one is directly dealing with man himself. This new formulation of the question already contains its solution.

As to (1): The general nature of private property and its relation to truly human property.

Alienated labor has resolved itself for us into two elements which mutually condition one another, or which are but different expressions of one and the same relationship. *Appropriation* appears as *estrangement,* as *alienation;* and *alienation* appears as *appropriation, estrangement* as true introduction into society.

We have considered the one side—*alienated* labor in relation to the *worker* himself, i.e., the *relation of alienated labor to itself.* The *property relation of the non-worker to the worker and to labor* we have found as the product, the necessary outcome of this relationship. *Private property*, as the material, summary expression of alienated labor, embraces both relations—the *relation of the worker to work and to the product of his labor and to the non-worker,* and the relation of the *non-worker to the worker and to the product of his labor.*

Having seen that in relation to the worker who *appropriates* nature by means of his labor, this appropriation appears as estrangement, his own spontaneous activity as activity for another and as activity of another, vitality as a sacrifice of life, production of the object as loss of the object to an alien power, to an *alien* person—we shall now consider the relation to the worker, to labor and its object of this person who is *alien,* to labor and the worker.

First it has to be noted that everything which appears in the worker as an *activity of alienation, of estrangement*, appears in the non-worker as a *state of alienation, of estrangement.*

Secondly, that the worker's *real, practical attitude* in production and to the product (as a state of mind) appears in the non-worker confronting him as a *theoretical* attitude.

Thirdly, the non-worker does everything against the worker which the worker does against himself; but he does not do against himself what he does against the worker.

Let us look more closely at these three relations.

[At this point the first manuscript breaks off unfinished.]

The Indian Tribe and the Self
Vine Deloria

Vine Deloria (1934-) is a writer on American Indian affairs. He is the author of *Custer Died for Your Sins* (1969) and *We Talk; You Listen* (1971).

There are a great many things happening today that can be related to ideas, movements, and events in Indian country—so many that it is staggering to contemplate them. American society is unconsciously going Indian. Moods, attitudes, and values are changing. People are becoming more aware of their isolation even while they continue to worship the rugged individualist who needs no one. The self-sufficient man is casting about for a community to call his own. The glittering generalities and mythologies of American society no longer satisfy the need and desire to belong.

Trying to communicate is an insurmountable task, however, since one cannot

Source: We Talk, You Listen (New York: Macmillan, 1970), pp. 10-14, 123-127, 135-137, 169-179. Reprinted by permission of The Macmillan Company. Copyright © 1970 by Vine Deloria, Jr.

skip readily from a tribal way of life to the conceptual world of the non-tribal person. The non-tribal person thinks in a linear sequence, in which A is the foundation for B, and C always follows. The view and meaning of the total event is rarely understood by the non-tribal person, although he may receive more objective information concerning any specific element of the situation. Non-tribals can measure the distance to the moon with unerring accuracy, but the moon remains an impersonal object to them without personal relationships that would support or illuminate their innermost feelings.

Tribal society is of such a nature that one must experience it from the inside. It is holistic, and logical analysis will only return you to your starting premise none the wiser for the trip. Being inside a tribal universe is so comfortable and reasonable that it acts like a narcotic. When you are forced outside the tribal context you become alienated, irritable, and lonely. In desperation you long to return to the tribe if only to preserve your sanity. While a majority of Indian people today live in the cities, a substantial number make long weekend trips back to their reservations to spend precious hours in their own land with their people.

The best method of communicating Indian values is to find points at which issues appear to be related. Because tribal society is integrated toward a center and non-Indian society is oriented toward linear development, the process might be compared to describing a circle surrounded with tangent lines. The points at which the lines touch the circumference of the circle are the issues and ideas that can be shared by Indians and other groups. There are a great many points at which tangents occur, and they may be considered as windows through which Indians and non-Indians can glimpse each other. Once this structural device is used and understood, non-Indians, using a tribal point of view, can better understand themselves and their relationship to Indian people.

The problem is complicated by the speed of modern communications media. It floods us with news that is news because it is reported as news. Thus, if we take a linear viewpoint of the world, the sequence of spectacular events creates the impression that the world is going either up- or downhill. Events become noted more for their supportive or threatening aspects than for their reality, since they fall into line and do not themselves contain any means of interpretation. When we are unable to absorb the events reported to us by the media, we begin to force interpretations of what the world really means on the basis of what we have been taught rather than what we have experienced.

Indian people are just as subject to the deluge of information as are other people. In the last decade most reservations have come within the reach of television and computers. In many ways Indian people are just as directed by the electric nature of our universe as any other group. But the tribal viewpoint simply absorbs what is reported to it and immediately integrates it into the experience of the group. In many areas whites are regarded as a temporary aspect of tribal life and there is unshakable belief that the tribe will survive the domination of the white man and once again rule the continent. Indians soak up the world like a blotter and continue almost untouched by events. The more that happens, the better the tribe seems to function and the stronger it appears to get. Of all the groups in the modern world Indians are best able to cope with the modern situation. To the non-Indian world, it does not appear that Indians are capable of anything. The flexibility of the tribal viewpoint enables Indians to meet devastating situations and survive. But this flexibility is seen by non-Indians as incompetency, so that as the non-Indian struggles in solitude and despair he curses the Indian for not coveting the same disaster.

In 1969, non-Indians began to rediscover Indians. Everyone hailed us as their natural allies in the ancient struggle they were waging with the "bad guys." Conservatives embraced us because we didn't act uppity, refused to move into their neighborhoods, and didn't march in *their* streets. Liberals loved us because we were the most oppressed of all the peoples who had been oppressed, and besides we generally voted Democratic.

Blacks loved us because we objected to the policies of the Department of the Interior (we would probably object if we had set the damn thing up ourselves) which indicated to them that we were another group to count on for the coming revolution. I attended one conference last fall at which a number of raging militants held forth, giving their views on the upcoming revolt of the masses. In a fever pitch they described the battle of Armageddon in which the "pigs" would be vanquished and the meek would inherit the earth (or a reasonable facsimile thereof). When asked if he supported the overthrow of the establishment, an old Sioux replied, "not until we get paid for the Black Hills." Needless to say, revolutionaries have not been impressed with the Indian fervor for radical change.

Hippies proudly showed us their beads and, with a knowing smile, bid us hello in the Navajo they had learned while passing through Arizona the previous summer. We watched and wondered as they paraded by in buckskin and feathers, anxiously playing a role they could not comprehend. When the Indians of the Bay area occupied Alcatraz, the hippies descended on the island in droves, nervously scanning the horizon for a vision of man in his pristine natural state. When they found that the tribesmen had the same organizational problems as any other group might have, they left in disappointment, disillusioned with "Indianism" that had existed only in their imaginations.

For nearly a year, the various minority and power groups have tried to get Indians to relate to the social crisis that plagues the land. Churches have expended enormous sums creating "task forces" of hand-picked Indians to inform them on the national scope of Indian problems. They have been disappointed when Indians didn't immediately embrace violence as a technique for progress. Government agencies have tried to understand Indians in an urban context that no longer has validity for even the most stalwart urbanite. Conservationists have sought out Indians for their mystical knowledge of the use of land. It has been an exciting year.

There is no doubt in my mind that a major crisis exists. I believe, however, that it is deeper and more profound than racism, violence, and economic deprivation. American society is undergoing a total replacement of its philosophical concepts. Words are being emptied of old meanings and new values are coming in to fill the vacuum. Racial antagonisms, inflation, ecological destruction, and power groups are all symptoms of the emergence of a new world view of man and his society. Today thought patterns are shifting from the traditional emphasis on the solitary individual to as yet unrelated definitions of man as a member of a specific group.

This is an extremely difficult transition for any society to make. Rather than face the situation head-on, people have preferred to consider social problems as manifestations of a gap between certain elements of the national community. The most blatant example of this attitude is to speak of the "generation gap." Other times it is categorized as a racial problem—the white racist power structure against the pure and peace-loving minority groups. We know that this is false. In those programs where blacks have dominated they have been as racist against Indians as they claim whites have been against them. Behind every movement is the undeniable emergence of the group as a group. Until conceptions of the nature of mass society are enlarged and accepted by the majority of people there will be little peace in this society.

But one cannot go skipping from group to group checking out movements and ideas to see if everything will come out all right. A better way of understanding events would be to find the similarities of structure that exist. Generalizations on this basis, if the necessary philosophical distinctions are maintained, would be most helpful. It would appear to me that modern society has two alternatives at this point. American people are being pushed into new social forms because of the complex nature of modern communications and transportation, and the competing forms are neotribalism and neofeudalism. The contest of the future is between a return to the castle or the tipi.

The difference between the castle and the tipi is immense, yet there are such great similarities that it is difficult to distinguish between them. Each offers social identity and economic security within a definite communal system. But the leveling process of the tribal form prevents the hereditary control over a social pyramid, and the feudalistic form has the efficiency to create and control technology. Both are needed if we are to rule machines instead of submit to them.

Many people can and will support the return of the castle. We have already experienced Camelot and the universal longing for its return. The massive corporate organizations have driven us well into the era of neofeudalism. But the continual failure of the total economic system to support the population and the corporations speaks of the necessity to reorient social goals more in line with a tribal-communal life style. Tribalism can only be presented in mosaic form. And there is a certain novelty in this approach. No single idea inevitably leads to another. The total impact of tribalism is thus not dependent upon acceptance of a single thesis. If events and ideas do not strike one immediately, time does not erode them but serves to shed further light on the problem.

After viewing social problems from a number of angles, I can see but one conclusion: America needs a new religion. Nearly every event and movement today shows signs of fulfilling this role, but none has the centered approach that would permit it to dig its roots in and survive. I am not advocating a return to Christianity. That "religion" has had two thousand years of bloodshed and hypocrisy and has failed to do anything more than help turn men into machines. We are probably entering an era in which religious sensitivity is expressed in rigorous adherence to the valus of racial and ethnic groups—secularization of religious feelings in political action.

If my conclusion is correct, then it is necessary to outline the Indian point of view as a contribution to the discussion of the problem. Further generalizations about how we are all alike—all people—are useless today. Definite points of view, new logic, and different goals define us. All we can do is try to communicate what we feel our group means to itself and how we relate to other groups. Understanding each other as distinct peoples is the most important thing.

As to the point of view, there really is a difference. A man was explaining his war experiences to his son one day. "There we were, surrounded by thousands of the enemy. Bullets were whizzing around our heads. Our water was gone. We had no food and our ammunition was running out. Suddenly, in the distance, we heard the welcome sound—of war whoops."

THE NEW INDIVIDUALISM

We have two antithetical ideas of the individual in today's society. One stems directly from the ideas held in the founding days of the Republic. At that time people assumed that a person, given free will and the right to exercise it, would generally make the correct decisions for himself and for his community. The voting franchise was thus considered to be the best method of arriving at a determination of the desires of the community at large, since any decisions made would be the result of the conscious and intelligent decisions of a number of responsible people.

This concept was more than optimistic. We have seen in practice that each person makes decisions according to his own good and hopes that somehow society will arrive at a wise and just decision in its deliberations. Unless a political movement is triggered by a charismatic political leader, society generally limps along postponing fundamental decisions because a majority of people want small adjustments and not major changes in their lives.

One theory of individualism has risen in recent years and is best characterized by the saying "do your thing." It indicates a complete freedom of movement for the individual person without regard to social goals and political movements. The remarkable thing is that the latter form of individualism has proven to be catalytic, whereas the more traditional understanding of the individual has produced stagnation and inability to comprehend mass movements.

Indians have always been the utmost individualists, but American society has failed to absorb them in its mainstream and there has been a continual warfare between the Indian tribes and the rest of society over this question. Yet the extreme individualism of the Indian has made it appear as if he would be suited above all to enter into the American social and political system. People are stunned to find that Indians totally reject American political ideology and concepts of equality, all the while being unable to reach any kind of conclusion within their own tribes as to programs and policies.

The vital difference between Indians in their individualism and the traditional individualism of Anglo-Saxon America is that the two understandings of man are built on entirely different premises. White America speaks of individualism on an economic basis. Indians speak of individualism on a social basis. While the rest of America is devoted to private property, Indians prefer to hold their lands in tribal estate, sharing the resources in common with each other. Where Americans conform to social norms of behavior and set up strata for social recognition, Indians have a free-flowing concept of social prestige that acts as a leveling device against the building of social pyramids.

Thus the two kinds of individualism are diametrically opposed to each other, and it would appear impossible to reconcile one with the other. Where the rich are admired in white society, they are not particularly welcome in Indian society. The success in economic wars is not nearly as important for Indians as it is for whites, since the sociability of individuals with each other acts as a binding tie in Indian society.

It is thus very important to understand the advent of the hippie and his subsequent influence on American life styles. The hippie, like the Indian, does not depend upon economic competition for his identity. He is more relaxed, more sociable, less worried about material goods, and more concerned with creating a community of others who share his interests and values. Youth of today fall into all grades of commitment to the new life style. Broadway shows reflect the new mode of life, books and magazines and underground newspapers chronicle it, and popular music spreads it abroad like a raging forest fire. Clothing and hair styles are creeping forward into age groups that formerly rejected out of hand a change in values.

The important thing about the hippie, and one thing that has certainly been missed by older commentators, is that the release from economic competition has created the necessity to derive a new identity based on other than economic criteria. Thus some of the most active and enthusiastic people in the new movement have been children of affluent homes that have not had to face economic competition. Born into the good life, they have been at a loss for identity since early childhood, and they have been the first generation that has been able to examine itself purely on the basis of feelings and experiences.

Older people have been horrified because their children have rejected out of hand the riches and power that they have spent so much time accumulating. They grew up in the Depression, where a lack of economic power meant relegation to a long line of unemployed, broken, status-less people. Thus the older generation promptly sought and in many cases achieved a position of economic power in which they could express their identity as a person without suffering the demeaning indignity of being another man in a long line or another number in an endless list of numbers.

The generation gap is more than an age difference in many ways. It reflects a difference in views of the world. The younger generation sees the world as inhabited by persons who must in some way relate to each other. The older generation understands the world as an economic jungle where, without allies, the individual is crushed by forces beyond his control. If the world of economic reality is destroyed, then the older generation will lose identities that it has struggled all its life to achieve. If there is continued economic definition of man, then the younger generation will feel hopelessly trapped with identities it does not accept or understand.

The ideological basis of society is thus shifting every year as the older generation dies off and the younger generation becomes more radical in its search for itself.

When competition becomes freed from its economic foundation, as it has been in the Indian tribes, then life takes on a whole new aspect. Status depends upon the manner in which a person contributes to his community. Knowledge for knowledge's sake becomes an irrelevant assertion, because it does not directly contribute to the elevation of people within the group. It becomes much more important that a person be wise and enter into the decisions of the group than that he know a great number of facts. Science is the handmaiden of economics because it creates tools by which men can climb the economic ladder, but it is useless in a noneconomic society because it is an abstraction of life.

Eliminating economic competition from a society thus creates a change of great dimensions. Wisdom with respect to the immediate situation is much more valuable than is the ability to consume and dispense great gobs of knowledge. Depth rather than breadth characterizes the tribal society. In the younger generation we can already see a rabid devouring of esoteric works in search of wisdom, and their poetry reflects a more sophisticated understanding of life than does the work of previous generations. Dylan's poetry, for example, caricatures the procedures by which the older generation operates, warning the youth that this is ephemeral and perhaps a charade that may fascinate but also entrap.

The outrageous clothing worn by young people emphasizes the "beautiful" aspect of their lives. It corresponds in many ways to Indian war-bonnet vanity and the desire to demonstrate acceptance by the group and honored status. It is no accident that many hippies wear beads and buckskin, because these combine simplicity of economic origin with advertisement of personal worth. Beads are extraneous to clothing, yet they become an integral part of personality.

The contemporary movement toward communes also emphasizes tribalistic life and is not competitive in economic terms. The concept of massing great stores of wealth runs counter to the demand that a person be respected in his group because of what he is. For that reason Charlie Manson's charisma was much more important than his ability to provide an economic base for his "family." As communes gather, the standard of living is defined by the group and not by outside forces. Thus communes can exist because they provide an understanding of togetherness which then defines economic reality. The older generation views it differently, feeling that economic considerations come first and neighborhoods form on that basis. Thus the suburbs are settled according to economic ability to provide and not sociability of people. Families are isolated in the suburbs because all they have in common is a bank balance of a certain size and the ability to keep it replenished.

．　　　．　　　．

The tribal-communal way of life, devoid of economic competition, views land as the most vital part of man's existence. It is THEIRS. It supports them, tells them where they live, and defines for them HOW they live. Land does not have the simple sentimentality of purple mountains majesty or the artificial coloring of slides taken by tourists. It is more than a passing fancy to be visited on a vacation and forgotten. Rather it provides a center of the universe for the group that lives on it. As such, the people who hold land in this way always have a home to go to. Their identity is secure. They live with it and do not abstract themselves from it and live off it.

．　　　．　　　．

The result of the new individualism is that groups are formed that have experiences in common. Status is gained according to personal recognition by others of the trueness of the individual. Consistency of viewpoint is the hallmark of the new individualism, yet the world view held by younger peoples is so comprehensive that it often appears contradictory to people of the older generation who think in rigid categories of interest.

The Woodstock Nation is thus the result of a feeling of humanity shared by a substantial number of people. In a sense it did represent a gathering of the tribes in the same way that the old Sioux nation, in the days before the white men came, met every year near Bear Butte in northwestern South Dakota, to visit, exchange presents, and renew the existence of the tribe. Many people have downgraded the youth because there have not been a series of Woodstocks each greater than the previous one. But this would degrade the very basis for meeting in concert.

Identity derived from economic status will probably be with us to some degree for a great while. It serves as a means of distinguishing between people and in turn promotes economic growth necessary to keep society operating. That is, it is not all bad and has proven useful to all Americans in a number of ways. The real problem is that we have passed the point of no return with respect to economics. Machines and computers are now so efficient that they are eliminating the ability and opportunity of most people to compete economically. Whether we like it or not we have undertaken to remove ourselves from the economic equation that was designed to support American society.

Already conservatives are talking about the guaranteed annual income, and the major part of American industry is on subsidy or economic existence guaranteed by government support. Without the ability or necessity to compete economically as a means of distinguishing between individuals, society must necessarily change to another form of identity-formation. This is what the younger generation has largely done and it happens to coincide with tribalistic forms already present in Indian tribes. Thus social movement, after four centuries of economic determinism, is reverting to pre-Columbian expressions, although modified by contemporary technology.

With machines producing an overabundance of wealth, the primary task of people will be to consume what is produced, lest the system break apart by overproduction. Agriculture already has broken apart, with large areas held out of production, and the result has been the breakdown of rural society. Suicides range higher in those rural areas where affluence and support appears to be greatest, because the people have not yet adjusted to the vacuum created by the absence of economic competition. Thus Iowa, one of the richest farm states, has had a consistently high suicide rate for a state with an apparently stable rural population.

We can look forward to a tremendous drive for social reform in spite of ourselves. Already graduates of prestige colleges and universities are going into social service programs instead of business. Public-interest law firms are on the increase. Free universities are rising everywhere. The separate disciplines of former days are being torn out of the institutions that entrapped them and thrust into the street. The university as the "marketplace of ideas" has become an absurdity, but off-campus the ideas flow with increasing vigor and insight. Even the conservation movement is gearing up to demand a reevaluation of land use for the benefit of all of society instead of the profit of a few people.

Whether we like it or not, the movement is steadily in one direction. The best that we can do is to open up as many options as possible so that the polarization of groups and group values does not freeze movements into violent confrontations. This would mean dropping traditional ideas and getting behind them to discover what we think we have been trying to do. Persecution of one group for smoking pot while another group destroys itself via nicotine and alcohol is a refusal to face reality. Subsidization of large farms while quibbling over pennies in food stamps is ridiculous. Authorizing supersonic transport planes while cutting education budgets is absurd.

. . .

The "do-your-thing" doctrine of youth presents the ultimate challenge to American society, for it challenges society to expand its conception of the individual beyond the field of economics. It creates criteria by which a total sense of person and humanity can be defined. "Doing-your-thing" speaks of what a man IS, not what he HAS. In this type of change Indians are far ahead of the rest of society and may be steadily pulling away from the rest of the pack. Hence the absurdity of studies on how to bring Indians into the mainstream when the mainstream is coming to the tribe.

.   .   .

Suggested Readings

1. Broad, C. D., *The Mind and Its Place in Nature* (London: Routledge & Kegan Paul, 1925).
2. Chatterjee, S. C., and Datta, D. M., *An Introduction to Indian Philosophy* (Calcutta: Calcutta University Press, 1955).
3. Deloria, Vine, *Custer Died for Your Sins* (New York: Macmillan, 1969).
4. Frondizi, Risierei, *The Nature of the Self* (New Haven, Conn.: Yale University Press, 1953).
5. Hiriyana, M., *Outlines of Indian Philosophy* (London: Allen & Unwin, 1964).
6. James, William, *Principles of Psychology* (New York: Longmans, Green, 1890).
7. Mead, George H., *Mind, Self, and Society* (Chicago: University of Chicago Press, 1934).
8. Penelhum, T., "Hume on Personal Identity," *The Philosophical Review*, Vol. 64, No. 4 (October 1955), 571-589.
9. Quinton, Anthony M., "The Soul," *Journal of Philosophy*, Vol. 59, No. 15 (July 19, 1962), 393-409.
10. Radhakrishnan, S., *Indian Philosophy* (London: Allen & Unwin, 1964).
11. Radhakrishnan, S., and Raju, P. T. (eds.), *The Concept of a Man: A Study in Comparative Philosophy* (London: Allen & Unwin, 1969).

Man and Nature: Metaphysical Ecology

If nature is not a prison and earth a shoddy way station, we must find the faith and force to affirm its metabolism as our own—or rather our own as part of it. . . . . Without losing our sense of the great human destiny and without intellectual surrender, we must affirm that the world is a being, a part of our own body.

—Paul Shepard

INTRODUCTION

In this chapter, our essays deal with the problematic relation of man and nature. In the first section, "The Nature of Nature," our essays reveal how the problem has marred our portrait of science; in the second section, "The Nature of Man," the essays focus on how the problem has nagged ethical theory.

Today more than ever we are aware of ecology. Environmental disasters such as air and water pollution, oil spills, vanishing wildernesses, and species extinction have awakened man to nature and to his relation to it. It should be recalled, however, that theoreticians have never stopped worrying about ecology because no one has made a satisfactory theoretical statement about the relation between man and nature. Ecology is nothing new to philosophers because they are mindful of past theoretical disasters. After reading the essays in these two sections, you will see that ecological togetherness continually faces the threat of metaphysical divorce.

THE NATURE OF NATURE

Paul Shepard, in this section's first essay, presses hard for the oneness of the universe, the interconnectedness of everything. He derides the frenetic attempt to prove that man is unique and apart from nature. This is done with, in his terms, a "mass of pseudo distinctions" that spotlight the facts that only men have language and culture, are capable of love, possess consciousness, make history, and are capable of being awed by the supernatural. Shepard stresses both the biological continuity and the common character of man and other natural denizens. He sees our passion for separateness and uniqueness as the fount of modern man's hostility and fear of the natural, which have made us conquerors and despoilers of nature. If hostility is to be turned into love and fear into companionship, he recommends recovering our sense of oneness with nature.

While many would applaud the direction of Shepard's thinking, there is a theoretical difficulty that we must acknowledge. We might start by asking, How many universes are there? It won't do to answer, One, that's the very meaning of *uni*verse. And it won't do because there are many things that are one, a point we could gain cheaply by a linguistic trick: we could talk of a unichicken, a unitable, a unimarble, and so forth. Just as it is obvious that there are many unichickens, unitables, and unimarbles, it is also obvious that there may be many universes.

This forces us to consider what a universe is. Let us say that a universe is (1) a whole that either has or doesn't have parts and (2) a whole that is not itself a part of any other whole. Let us concede that our universe does have parts, being a complex universe. This notion of a universe leads us to say that if there is one and only one universe, then anything that exists is a part of a complex whole, and everything that is a part is a part of the same whole.

The operative question now is, Under what conditions would we be willing to say of anything that it is a part of the same whole as some other part? We can conjecture two conditions, a static one and a dynamic one. The static condition requires that two parts belong to the same whole if and only if they share at least one property. The dynamic condition requires that two parts belong to the same whole if and only if one has been acted on by the other directly, or indirectly through an intervening series of direct actions.

Consider, first, the static requirement and how a popular theory of man on that requirement leads us to conclude that there are two universes, not one. Man, in a popular view, has both a mind and a body. In Descartes' formulation of this (see his essay, first one in Chapter Seven), he notes that the nature of mind is that it thinks but is not spatial, whereas matter is spatial but does not think. Mental substance and material substance share no properties. Not sharing any properties, according to the static universe requirement, these two substances cannot be parts of the same whole; therefore, there is not one universe, but two universes. This frustrates Shepard's good intentions about relating us to nature.

Because we almost invariably identify man's essence with his mind, we usually exalt the mind; our mind is what makes us unique. Matter is usually identified as nature, and it is what natural science studies and hopes to understand by discovering the laws that govern matter's behavior. Man and nature, in the static view, constitute two universes.

Consider also the dynamic requirement and how our popular moral notions again lead us to conclude that there are two universes, not one. Our understanding of nature is ideally expressed in laws, preferably mathematical laws. These laws formulate regular relations between natural events, often stated as causal relations and causal laws. Two parts belong to the same universe, then, according to the dynamic condition, if one of them has been causally acted on by the other.

If every event in the universe is a natural event, then every event involving a part must directly or indirectly have been acted on by some other event involving some other part. But if this were so, then there would be no acts of free will. An act of free will must be one that has not been caused by some other act; thus, by escaping the dynamic requirement, whatever entity acts freely cannot be part of nature.

In this section's second essay, **R. G. Collingwood** points out that some ancient Greeks, unlike Descartes, did not see mind and matter as bequeathing us two universes. For them the whole universe was saturated with mind; the universe was alive, and life was a sign of the presence of mind; in addition, they inferred from the orderliness of the universe that it had an intelligence. The ancient Greeks conceived the universe on the analogy of an organism. Post-Renaissance thinkers conceived nature on the analogy of a machine. But if man is not a machine by reason of having a mind, a dual universe is again deposited in philosophers' hands. There were several "idealist" attempts to dissolve the dualism by arguing that nature is a product of mind. Collingwood thinks the idealist solution is unsatisfactory and sketches a modern way of reconceiving the universe as a unity on the analogy of history.

The last essay in this section is by **Alfred Whitehead**; he proposes a return to the organism model. His essay brilliantly interprets the Romantic poets as articulate rebels against the metaphysical mistake of confusing abstractions for reality. Abstractions have accounted for the machine analogy. This is a mistake with unfortunate consequences. In the West, according to Whitehead, "A scientific realism, based on mechanism, is conjoined with an unwavering belief in the world of men and of the higher animals as being composed of self-determining organisms. This radical inconsistency at the basis of modern thought accounts for much that is half-hearted and wavering in our civilization. . . . The only way of mitigating mechanism is by the discovery that it is not mechanism."

The Ecology of the Cosmos
Paul Shepard

Paul Shepard (1925-   ) teaches at Williams College. He is co-editor of *The Subversive Science: Essays Toward an Ecology of Man* (1969) and author of *Man in the Landscape* (1967). In addition, he has contributed to various journals, including *Bioscience, Perspectives in Biology and Medicine*, and *Landscape*.

Ecology is sometimes characterized as the study of a natural "web of life." It would follow that man is somewhere in the web or that he in fact manipulates its strands, exemplifying what Thomas Huxley called "man's place in nature." But the image of a web is too meager and simple for the reality. A web is flat and finished and has the mortal frailty of the individual spider. Although elastic, it has insufficient depth. However solid to the touch of the spider, for us it fails to denote the *eikos*—the habitation—and to suggest the enduring integration of the primitive Greek domicile with its sacred hearth, bonding the earth to all aspects of society.

Ecology deals with organisms in an environment and with the processes that link organism and place. But ecology as such cannot be studied, only organisms, earth, air, and sea can be studied. It is not a discipline: there is no body of thought and technique which frames an ecology of man.[1] It must be therefore a scope or a way of seeing. Such a *perspective* on the human situation is very old and has been part of philosophy and art for thousands of years. It badly needs attention and revival.

Man is in the world and his ecology is the nature of that *inness*. He is in the world as in a room, and in transience, as in the belly of a tiger or in love. What does he do there in nature? What does nature do there *in him*? What is the nature of the transaction? Biology tells us that the transaction is always circular, always a mutual feedback. Human ecology cannot be limited strictly to biological concepts, but it cannot ignore them. It cannot even transcend them. It emerges from biological reality and grows from the fact of interconnection as a general principle of life. It must take a long view of human life and nature as they form a mesh or pattern going beyond historical time and beyond the conceptual bounds of other humane studies. As a natural history of what it means to be human, ecology might proceed the same way one would define a stomach, for example, by attention to its nervous and circulatory connections as well as its entrance, exit, and muscular walls.

Many educated people today believe that only what is unique to the individual is important or creative, and turn away from talk of populations and species as they would from talk of the masses. I once knew a director of a wealthy conservation foundation who had misgivings about the approach of ecology to urgent

Source: The Subversive Science (Boston: Houghton Mifflin, 1969). Copyright © 1969 by Paul Shepard and Daniel McKinley. Reprinted by permission of the publisher, Houghton Mifflin Company. Original title of the selection was "Ecology and Man—a Viewpoint."

[1] There is a branch of sociology called Human Ecology, but it is mostly about urban geography.

environmental problems in America because its concepts of communities and systems seemed to discount the individual. Communities to him suggested only followers, gray masses without the tradition of the individual. He looked instead—or in reaction—to the profit motive and capitalistic formulas, in terms of efficiency, investment, and production. It seemed to me that he had missed a singular opportunity. He had shied from the very aspect of the world now beginning to interest industry, business, and technology as the biological basis of their—and our—affluence, and which his foundation could have shown to be the ultimate basis of all economics.

Individual man *has* his particular integrity, to be sure. Oak trees, even mountains, have selves or integrities too (a poor word for my meaning, but it will have to do). To our knowledge, those other forms are not troubled by seeing themselves in more than one way, as man is. In one aspect the self is an arrangement of organs, feelings, and thoughts—a "me"—surrounded by a hard body boundary: skin, clothes, and insular habits. This idea needs no defense. It is conferred on us by the whole history of our civilization. Its virtue is verified by our affluence. The alternative is a self as a center of organization, constantly drawing on and influencing the surroundings, whose skin and behavior are soft zones contacting the world instead of excluding it. Both views are real and their reciprocity significant. We need them both to have a healthy social and human maturity.

The second view—that of relatedness of the self—has been given short shrift. Attitudes toward ourselves do not change easily. The conventional image of a man, like that of the heraldic lion, is iconographic; its outlines are stylized to fit the fixed curves of our vision. We are hidden from ourselves by habits of perception. Because we learn to talk at the same time we learn to think, our language, for example, encourages us to see ourselves—or a plant or animal—as an isolated sack, a thing, a contained self. Ecological thinking, on the other hand, requires a kind of vision across boundaries. The epidermis of the skin is ecologically like a pond surface or a forest soil, not a shell so much as a delicate interpenetration. It reveals the self ennobled and extended rather than threatened as part of the landscape and the ecosystem, because the beauty and complexity of nature are continuous with ourselves.

And so ecology as applied to man faces the task of renewing a balanced view where now there is man-centeredness, even pathology of isolation and fear. It implies that we must find room in "our" world for all plants and animals, even for their otherness and their opposition. It further implies exploration and openness across an inner boundary—an ego boundary—and appreciative understanding of the animal in ourselves which our heritage of Platonism, Christian morbidity, duality, and mechanism have long held repellent and degrading. The older counter-currents—relics of pagan myth, the universal application of Christian compassion, philosophical naturalism, nature romanticism and pantheism—have been swept away, leaving only odd bits of wreckage. Now we find ourselves in a deteriorating environment which breeds aggressiveness and hostility toward ourselves and our world.

How simple our relationship to nature would be if we only had to choose between protecting our natural home and destroying it. Most of our efforts to provide for the natural in our philosophy have failed—run aground on their own determination to work out a peace at arm's length. Our harsh reaction against the peaceable kingdom of sentimental romanticism was evoked partly by the tone of its dulcet façade but also by the disillusion to which it led. Natural dependence and contingency suggest togetherness and emotional surrender to mass behavior and other lowest common denominators. The environmentalists matching culture and geography provoke outrage for their over-simple theories of cause and effect, against the sciences which sponsor them and even against a natural world in which the theories may or may not be true. Our historical disappointment in the nature of nature has created a cold climate for ecologists who assert once again that we are limited and obligated. Somehow they must manage in spite of the chill to reach the centers of humanism and technology, to convey there a sense of our place in a universal vascular system without depriving us of our self-esteem and confidence.

Their message is not, after all, all bad news. Our natural affiliations define and illumine freedom instead of denying it. They demonstrate it better than any dialectic. Being more enduring than we individuals, ecological patterns—spatial distributions, symbioses, the streams of energy and matter and communication—create among individuals the tensions and polarities so different from dichotomy and separateness. The responses, or what theologians call "the sensibilities" of creatures (including ourselves) to such arrangements grow in part from a healthy union of the two kinds of self already mentioned, one emphasizing integrity, the other relatedness. But it goes beyond that to something better known to 12th century Europeans or Paleolithic hunters than to ourselves. If nature is not a prison and earth a shoddy way-station, we must find the faith and force to affirm its metabolism as our own—or rather, our own as part of it. To do so means nothing less than a shift in our whole frame of reference and our attitude towards life itself, a wider perception of the landscape as a creative, harmonious being where relationships of things are as real as the things. Without losing our sense of a great human destiny and without intellectual surrender, we must affirm that the world is a being, a part of our own body.[2]

Such a being may be called an ecosystem or simply a forest or landscape. Its members are engaged in a kind of choreography of materials and energy and information, the creation of order and organization. [Analogy to corporate organization here is misleading, for the distinction between social (one species) and ecological (many species) is fundamental.] The pond is an example. Its ecology includes all events: the conversion of sunlight to food and the food-chains within and around it, man drinking, bathing, fishing, plowing the slopes of the watershed, drawing a picture of it, and formulating theories about the world based on what he sees in the pond. He and all the other organisms at and in the pond act upon one another, engage the earth and atmosphere, and are linked to other ponds by a network of connections like the threads of protoplasm connecting cells in living tissues.

The elegance of such systems and delicacy of equilibrium are the outcome of a long evolution of interdependence. Even society, mind and culture are parts of that evolution. There is an essential relationship between them and the natural habitat: that is, between the emergence of higher primates and flowering plants, pollinating insects, seeds, humus, and arboreal life. It is unlikely that a man-like creature could arise by any other means than a long arboreal sojourn following and followed by a time of terrestriality. The fruit's complex construction and the mammalian brain are

[2] See Alan Watts, "The World Is Your Body," in *The Book on the Taboo Against Knowing Who You Are* (New York: Pantheon Books, 1966).

twin offspring of the maturing earth, impossible, even meaningless, without the deepening soil and the mutual development of savannas and their faunas in the last geological epoch. Internal complexity, as the mind of a primate, is an extension of natural complexity, measured by the variety of plants and animals and the variety of nerve cells—organic extensions of each other.

The exuberance of kinds as the setting in which a good mind could evolve (to deal with a complex world) was not only a past condition. Man did not arrive in the world as though disembarking from a train in the city. He continues to arrive, somewhat like the birth of art, a train in Roger Fry's definition, passing through many stations, none of which is wholly left behind. This idea of natural complexity as a counterpart to human intricacy is central to an ecology of man. The creation of order, of which man is an example, is realized also in the number of species and habitats, an abundance of landscapes lush and poor. Even deserts and tundras increase the planetary opulence. Curiously, only man and possibly a few birds can appreciate this opulence, being the world's travelers. Reduction of this variegation would, by extention then, be an amputation of man. To convert all "wastes"—all deserts, estuaries, tundras, ice-fields, marshes, steppes and moors—into cultivated fields and cities would impoverish rather than enrich life esthetically as well as ecologically. By esthetically, I do not mean that weasel term connoting the pleasure of baubles. We have diverted ourselves with litter-bug campaigns and greenbelts in the name of esthetics while the fabric of our very environment is unravelling. In the name of conservation, too, such things are done, so that conservation becomes ambiguous. Nature is a fundamental "resource" to be sustained for our own well-being. But it loses in the translation into usable energy and commodities. Ecology may testify as often against our uses of the world, even against conservation techniques of control and management for sustained yield, as it does for them. Although ecology may be treated as a science, its greater and overriding wisdom is universal.

That wisdom can be approached mathematically, chemically, or it can be danced or told as a myth. It has been embodied in widely scattered economically different cultures. It is manifest, for example, among pre-Classical Greeks, in Navajo religion and social orientation, in Romantic poetry of the 18th and 19th centuries, in Chinese landscape painting of the 11th century, in current Whiteheadian philosophy, in Zen Buddhism, in the world view of the cult of the Cretan Great Mother, in the ceremonials of Bushman hunters, and in the medieval Christian metaphysics of light. What is common among all of them is a deep sense of engagement with the landscape, with profound connections to surroundings and to natural processes central to all life.

It is difficult in our language even to describe that sense. English becomes imprecise or mystical—and therefore suspicious—as it struggles with "process" thought. Its noun and verb organization shapes a divided world of static doers separate from the doing. It belongs to an idiom of social hierarchy in which all nature is made to mimic man. The living world is perceived in that idiom as an upright ladder, a "great chain of being," an image which seems at first ecological but is basically rigid, linear, condescending, lacking humility and love of otherness.

We are all familiar from childhood with its classifications of everything on a scale from the lowest to the highest: inanimate matter/vegetative life/lower animals/ higher animals/men/angels/gods. It ranks animals themselves in categories of increasing good: the vicious and lowly parasites, pathogens and predators/the filthy decay and scavenging organisms/indifferent wild or merely useless forms/good time creatures/and virtuous beasts domesticated for human service. It shadows the great man-centered political scheme upon the world, derived from the ordered ascendency from parishioners to clerics to bishops to cardinals to popes, or in a secular form from criminals to proletarians to aldermen to mayors to senators to presidents.

And so is nature pigeonholed. The sardonic phrase, "the place of nature in man's world," offers, tongue-in-cheek, a clever footing for confronting a world made in man's image and conforming to words. It satirizes the prevailing philosophy of anti-nature and human omniscience. It is possible because of an attitude which—like ecology—has ancient roots, and whose modern form was shaped when Aquinas reconciled Aristotelian homocentrism with Judeo-Christian dogma. In a later setting of machine technology, puritanical capitalism, and an urban ethos it carves its own version of reality into the landscape like a schoolboy initialing a tree. For such a philosophy nothing in nature has inherent merit. As one professor recently put it, "The only reason anything is done on this earth is for people. Did the rivers, winds, animals, rocks, or dust ever consider my wishes or needs? Surely, we do all our acts in an earthly environment, but I have never had a tree, valley, mountain or flower thank me for preserving it."[3] This view carries great force, epitomized in history by Bacon, Descartes, Hegel, Hobbes, and Marx.

Some other post-Renaissance thinkers are wrongly accused of undermining our assurance of natural order. The theories of the heliocentric solar system, of biological evolution, and of the unconscious mind are held to have deprived the universe of the beneficence and purpose to which man was a special heir and to have evoked feelings of separation, of antipathy towards a meaningless existence in a neutral cosmos. Modern despair, the arts of anxiety, the politics of pathological individualism and predatory socialism were not, however, the result of Copernicus, Darwin and Freud. If man was not the center of the universe, was not created by a single stroke of Providence, and is not ruled solely by rational intelligence, it does not follow therefore that nature is defective where we thought it perfect. The astronomer, biologist and psychiatrist each achieved for mankind corrections in sensibility. Each showed the interpenetration of human life and the universe to be richer and more mysterious than had been thought.

Darwin's theory of evolution has been crucial to ecology. Indeed, it might have helped rather than aggravated the growing sense of human alienation had its interpreters emphasized predation and competition less (and, for this reason, one is tempted to add, had Thomas Huxley, Herbert Spencer, Samuel Butler and G. B. Shaw had less to say about it). Its bases of universal kinship and common bonds of function, experience and value among organisms were obscured by pre-existing ideas of animal depravity. Evolutionary theory was exploited to justify the worst in men and was misused in defense of social and economic injustice. Nor was it better used by humanitarians. They opposed the degradation of men in the service of industrial progress, the slaughter of American Indians, and child labor, because each treated men "like animals." That is to say, men were not animals, and the temper of social reform was to find good only in attributes separating men from animals. Kindness both towards and among animals was still a rare idea in the 19th century, so that using men as animals could mean only cruelty.

[3] Clare A. Gunn in *Landscape Architecture*, July 1966, p. 260.

Since Thomas Huxley's day the nonanimal forces have developed a more subtle dictum to the effect that, "Man may be an animal, but he is more than an animal, too!" The *more* is really what is important. This appealing aphorism is a kind of anesthetic. The truth is that we are ignorant of what it is like or what it means to be any other kind of creature than we are. If we are unable to truly define the animal's experience of life or "being an animal" how can we isolate our animal part?

The rejection of animality is a rejection of nature as a whole. As a teacher, I see students develop in their humanities studies a proper distrust of science and technology. What concerns me is that the stigma spreads to the natural world itself. C. P. Snow's *Two Cultures*, setting the sciences against the humanities, can be misunderstood as placing nature against art. The idea that the current destruction of people and environment is scientific and would be corrected by more communication with the arts neglects the hatred for this world carried by our whole culture. Yet science as it is now taught does not promote a respect for nature. Western civilization breeds no more ecology in Western science than in Western philosophy. Snow's two cultures cannot explain the antithesis that splits the world, nor is the division ideological, economic or political in the strict sense. The antidote he proposes is roughly equivalent to a liberal education, the traditional prescription for making broad and well-rounded men. Unfortunately, there is little even in the liberal education of ecology-and-man. Nature is usually synonymous with either natural resources or scenery, the great stereotypes in the minds of middle class, college-educated Americans.

One might suppose that the study of biology would mitigate the humanistic— largely literary—confusion between materialism and a concern for nature. But biology made the mistake at the end of the 17th century of adopting a *modus operandi* or life style from physics, in which the question why was not to be asked, only the question how. Biology succumbed to its own image as an esoteric prologue to technics and encouraged the whole society to mistrust naturalists. When scholars realized what the sciences were about it is not surprising that they threw out the babies with the bathwater: the information content and naturalistic lore with the rest of it. This is the setting in which academia and intellectual America undertook the single-minded pursuit of human uniqueness, and uncovered a great mass of pseudo distinctions such as language, tradition, culture, love, consciousness, history and awe of the supernatural. Only men were found to be capable of escape from predictability, determinism, environmental control, instincts and other mechanisms which "imprison" other life. Even biologists, such as Julian Huxley, announced that the purpose of the world was to produce man, whose social evolution excused him forever from biological evolution. Such a view incorporated three important presumptions: that nature is a power structure shaped after human political hierarchies; that man has a monopoly of immortal souls; and omnipotence will come through technology. It seems to me that all of these foster a failure of responsible behavior in what Paul Sears calls "the living landscape" except within the limits of immediate self-interest.

What ecology must communicate to the humanities—indeed, as a humanity—is that such an image of the world and the society so conceived is incomplete. There is overwhelming evidence of likeness, from molecular to mental, between men and animals. But the dispersal of this information is not necessarily a solution. The Two Culture idea that the problem is an information bottleneck is only partly true; advances in biochemistry, genetics, ethology, paleoanthropology, comparative physiology and psychobiology are not self-evidently unifying. They need a unifying principle not found in any of them, a wisdom in the sense that Walter B. Cannon used the word in his book *Wisdom of the Body*,[4] about the community of self-regulating systems within the organism. If the ecological extension of that perspective is correct, societies and ecosystems as well as cells have a physiology, and insight into it is built into organisms, including man. What was intuitively apparent last year—whether aesthetically or romantically—is a find of this year's inductive analysis. It seems apparent to me that there is an ecological instinct which probes deeper and more comprehensively than science, and which anticipates every scientific confirmation of the natural history of man.

.   .   .

The humanness of ecology is that the dilemma of our emerging world ecological crises (overpopulation, environmental pollution, etc.) is at least in part a matter of values and ideas. It does not divide men as much by their trades as by the complex of personality and experience shaping their feelings towards other people and the world at large. I have mentioned the disillusion generated by the collapse of unsound nature philosophies. The anti-nature position today is often associated with the focusing of general fears and hostilities on the natural world. It can be seen in the behavior of control-obsessed engineers, corporation people selling consumption itself, academic superhumanists and media professionals fixated on political and economic crisis; neurotics working out psychic problems in the realm of power over men or nature, artistic symbol-manipulators disgusted by anything organic. It includes many normal, earnest people who are unconsciously defending themselves or their families against a vaguely threatening universe. The dangerous eruption of humanity in a deteriorating environment does not show itself as such in the daily experience of most people, but is felt as general tension and anxiety. We feel the pressure of events not as direct causes but more like omens. A kind of madness arises from the prevailing nature-conquering, nature-hating and self- and world-denial. Although in many ways most Americans live comfortable, satiated lives, there is a nameless frustration born of an increasing nullity. The aseptic home and society are progressively cut off from direct organic sources of health and increasingly isolated from the means of altering the course of events. Success, where its price is the misuse of landscapes, the deterioration of air and water and the loss of wild things, becomes a pointless glut, experience one-sided, time on our hands an unlocalized ache.

The unrest can be exploited to perpetuate itself. One familiar prescription for our sick society and its loss of environmental equilibrium is an increase in the intangible Good Things: more Culture, more Security and more Escape from pressures and tempo.

.   .   .

To come back to those Good Things: the need for culture, security and escape are just near enough to the truth to take us in. But the real cultural deficiency is the absence of a true *cultus* with its significant ceremony, relevant mythical cosmos, and artifacts. The real failure in security is the disappearance from our personal lives of the small human group as the functional unit of society and the web of other creatures, domestic and wild, which are part of our humanity. As for escape, the idea of simple remission and avoidance fails to provide for the value of solitude,

[4] Walter B. Cannon, *Wisdom of the Body* (New York: W. W. Norton, 1932).

to integrate leisure and natural encounter. Instead of these, what are foisted on the puzzled and troubled soul as Culture, Security and Escape are more art museums, more psychiatry, and more automobiles.

The ideological status of ecology is that of a resistance movement. Its Rachel Carsons and Aldo Leopolds are subversive (as Sears recently called ecology itself[5]). They challenge the public or private right to pollute the environment, to systematically destroy predatory animals, to spread chemical pesticides indiscriminately, to meddle chemically with food and water, to appropriate without hindrance space and surface for technological and military ends; they oppose the uninhibited growth of human populations, some forms of "aid" to "underdeveloped" peoples, the needless addition of radioactivity to the landscape, the extinction of species of plants and animals, the domestication of all wild places, large-scale manipulation of the atmosphere or the sea, and most other purely engineering solutions to problems of and intrusions into the organic world.

Truly ecological thinking need not be incompatible with our place and time. It does have an element of humility which is foreign to our thought, which moves us to silent wonder and glad affirmation. But it offers an essential factor, like a necessary vitamin, to all our engineering and social planning, to our poetry and our understanding. There is only one ecology, not a human ecology on one hand and another for the subhuman. No one school or theory or project or agency controls it. For us it means seeing the world mosaic from the human vantage without being man-fanatic. We must use it to confront the great philosophical problems of man—transience, meaning, and limitation—without fear. Affirmation of its own organic essence will be the ultimate test of the human mind.

[5] Paul B. Sears, "Ecology—a subversive subject," *BioScience*, Vol. 14, No. 7 (July 1964), p. 11.

The Idea of Nature

R. G. Collingwood

Robin George Collingwood (1889-1943) was an English philosopher. He spent all his working life at Oxford, first as an undergraduate, then as a fellow of Pembroke College, and finally as professor of metaphysics. In addition to his achievements in philosophy, he was an authority on archaeology and on the history of Roman Britain. Among his books are *Essay on Philosophical Method* (1933) and *The Idea of History* (1943).

1. SCIENCE AND PHILOSOPHY

In the history of European thought there have been three periods of constructive cosmological thinking; three periods, that is to say, when the idea of nature has come into the focus of thought, become the subject of intense and protracted reflection, and consequently acquired new characteristics which in their turn have given a new aspect to the detailed science of nature that has been based upon it.

To say that the detailed science of nature is "based" upon the idea of nature does not imply that the idea of nature in general, the idea of nature as a whole, is worked out first, in abstraction from any detailed study of natural fact, and that when this abstract idea of nature is complete people go on to erect upon it a superstructure of detailed natural science. What it implies is not a temporal relation but a logical one. Here, as often, the temporal relation inverts the logical one. In natural science, as in economics or morals or law, people begin with the details. They begin by tackling individual problems as they arise. Only when this detail has accumulated to a considerable amount do they reflect upon the work they have been doing and discover that they have been doing it in a methodical way, according to principles of which hitherto they have not been conscious.

But the temporal priority of detailed work to reflection on the principles implied in it must not be exaggerated. It would be an exaggeration, for example, to think that a "period" of detailed work in natural science, or any other field of thought or action, a "period" lasting for a half century or even for half a decade, is followed by a "period" of reflection on the principles which logically underlie it. Such a contrast between "periods" of non-philosophical thinking and subsequent "periods" of philosophizing is perhaps what Hegel meant to assert in his famous lament, at the end of the Preface to the *Philosophie des Rechts*: "When philosophy paints its grey in grey, a form of life has aged; and grey in grey does not enable us to make it young again, but only to know it. The owl of Minerva begins to fly only at the coming of dusk." If that was what Hegel meant, he made a mistake; and a mistake which Marx only turned upside down and did not correct when he wrote that "philosophy hitherto has confined itself to interpreting the world: the point,

Source: The Idea of Nature (Oxford: Clarendon, 1945), pp. 1-19. By permission of the Clarendon Press, Oxford.

however, is to change it" (*Theses on Feuerbach*, xi). The complaint against philosophy is borrowed, in the very same words, from Hegel; only what Hegel represents as a necessary feature of all philosophy Marx represents as a defect to which philosophy was subject until he, Marx, revolutionized it.

In fact, the detailed work seldom goes on for any length of time without reflection intervening. And this reflection reacts upon the detailed work; for when people become conscious of the principles upon which they have been thinking or acting they become conscious of something which in these thoughts and actions they have been trying, though unconsciously, to do: namely to work out in detail the logical implications of those principles. To strong minds this new consciousness gives a new strength, namely a new firmness in their approach to the detailed problems. To weak minds it adds a new temptation, the temptation to that kind of pedantry which consists in remembering the principle and forgetting the special features of the problem to which it is applied.

. . .

2. THE GREEK VIEW OF NATURE

Greek natural science was based on the principle that the world of nature is saturated or permeated by mind. Greek thinkers regarded the presence of mind in nature as the source of that regularity or orderliness in the natural world whose presence made a science of nature possible. The world of nature they regarded as a world of bodies in motion. The motions in themselves, according to Greek ideas, were due to vitality or "soul"; but motion in itself is one thing, they believed, and orderliness another. They conceived mind, in all its manifestations, whether in human affairs or elsewhere, as a ruler, a dominating or regulating element, imposing order first upon itself and then upon everything belonging to it, primarily its own body and secondarily that body's environment.

Since the world of nature is a world not only of ceaseless motion and therefore alive, but also a world of orderly or regular motion, they accordingly said that the world of nature is not only alive but intelligent; not only a vast animal with a "soul" or life of its own, but a rational animal with a "mind" of its own. The life and intelligence of creatures inhabiting the earth's surface and the regions adjacent to it, they argued, represent a specialized local organization of this all-pervading vitality and rationality, so that a plant or animal, according to their ideas, participates in its own degree psychically in the life-process of the world's "soul" and intellectually in the activity of the world's "mind," no lesss than it participates materially in the physical organization of the world's "body."

That vegetables and animals are physically akin to the earth is a belief shared by ourselves with the Greeks; but the notion of a psychical and intellectual kinship is strange to us, and constitutes a difficulty in the way of our understanding the relics of Greek natural science which we find in their literature.

3. THE RENAISSANCE VIEW OF NATURE

The second of the three cosmological movements mentioned at the beginning of this chapter took place in the sixteenth and seventeenth centuries. I propose to designate its view of nature by the name of "Renaissance" cosmology. The name is not a good one, because the word "Renaissance" is applied to an earlier phase in the history of thought, beginning in Italy with the humanism of the fourteenth century and continuing, in the same country, with the Platonic and Aristotelian cosmologies of that century and the fifteenth. The cosmology I have now to describe was in principle a reaction against these and might, perhaps, be more accurately called "post-Renaissance"; but this is a clumsy term.

. . .

The Renaissance view of nature began to take shape as antithetical to the Greek view in the work of Copernicus (1473-1543), Telesio (1508-88), and Bruno (1548-1600). The central point of this antithesis was the denial that the world of nature, the world studied by physical science, is an organism, and the assertion that it is devoid both of intelligence and of life. It is therefore incapable of ordering its own movements in a rational manner, and indeed incapable of moving itself at all. The movements which it exhibits, and which the physicist investigates, are imposed upon it from without, and their regularity is due to "laws of nature" likewise imposed from without. Instead of being an organism, the natural world is a machine: a machine in the literal and proper sense of the word, an arrangement of bodily parts designed and put together and set going for a definite purpose by an intelligent mind outside itself. The Renaissance thinkers, like the Greeks, saw in the orderliness of the natural world an expression of intelligence: but for the Greeks this intelligence was nature's own intelligence, for the Renaissance thinkers it was the intelligence of something other than nature: the divine creator and ruler of nature. This distinction is the key to all the main differences between Greek and Renaissance natural science.

Each of these cosmological movements was followed by a movement in which the focus of interest shifted from nature to mind. In the history of Greek thought this shift took place with Socrates. Whereas previous thinkers had not neglected ethics, politics, or even logic and the theory of knowledge, they had concentrated their main effort of thought upon the theory of nature. Socrates reversed this emphasis and concentrated his thought on ethics and logic; and from his time onwards, although the theory of nature was by no means forgotten even by Plato, who did far more work on that subject than is generally realized, the theory of mind predominated, and the theory of nature took the second place.

This Greek theory of mind in Socrates and his successors was intimately connected with and conditioned by the results already obtained in the theory of nature. The mind that was studied by Socrates, Plato, and Aristotle was always first and foremost mind *in* nature, the mind in the body and of the body, manifesting itself by its control of the body; and when these philosophers found themselves obliged to recognize mind as transcending body, they stated this discovery in a way that shows unmistakably how paradoxical it seemed to them and how remote from the habitual or (as we sometimes say) "instinctive" ways of thinking. Socrates in Plato's dialogues over and over again expects to be met with incredulity and misunderstanding when he sets out to assert that rational soul or mind operates independently of the body: either when he is discussing the theory of knowledge and contrasts the bodily mind of appetite and sense with the pure intellectual apprehension of the forms which is effected by the rational soul's wholly independent and self-contained activity without any help from the body, or when he is expounding the doctrine of immortality and asserting that the rational soul enjoys an eternal life unaffected by the birth or death of the body belonging to it.

The same tone is found in Aristotle, who treats it as a matter of course that the "soul" should be defined as the entelechy of an organic body—that is, the self-maintaining activity of an organism—but speaks as one expounding mysterious and difficult doctrine when he says that the intellect or reason, νοῦς, although in some sense it is a part of the "soul," possesses no bodily organ and is not acted upon, as sense is, by its proper objects (*De Anima* 429ª15 seqq.) so that it is nothing apart from its activity of thinking (ibid. 21-2) and is "separable" from the body (ibid. 429ᵇ5). All this shows what from a general knowledge of pre-Socratic physics we should expect: that Greek thinkers in general take it for granted that mind belongs essentially to body and lives with it in the closest union, and that when they are confronted with reasons for thinking this union partial, occasional, or precarious, they are puzzled to know how this can be.

In Renaissance thought this state of things is precisely reversed. For Descartes body is one substance and mind is another. Each works independently of the other according to its own laws. Just as the fundamental axiom of Greek thought about mind is its immanence in body, so the fundamental axiom of Descartes is its transcendence. Descartes knows very well that transcendence must not be pushed to the point of dualism; the two things must be connected somehow; but cosmologically he can find no connexion short of God, and in the individual human being he is driven to the desperate expedient, justly ridiculed by Spinoza, of finding it in the pineal gland, which he thinks must be the organ of union between body and soul because, as an anatomist, he can find no other function for it.

Even Spinoza, with his insistence on the unity of substance, is in no better case; for thought and extension are in his philosophy two utterly distinct attributes of this one substance, and each, as an attribute, completely transcends the other. Hence, when in the eighteenth century the centre of gravity in philosophical thought swung over from the theory of nature to the theory of mind, Berkeley being the critical point here as Socrates was for the Greeks, the problem of nature inevitably stated itself in this form: how can mind have any connexion with something utterly alien to itself, something essentially mechanical and non-mental, namely nature? This was the question, at bottom the only question, concerning nature which exercised the great philosophers of mind, Berkeley, Hume, Kant, Hegel. In every case their answer was at bottom the same: namely, that mind makes nature; nature is, so to speak, a by-product of the autonomous and self-existing activity of mind.

I shall discuss this idealistic view of nature more fully hereafter; all I wish to make clear at this point is that there are two things which it never meant. It never meant that nature is in itself mental, made of the stuff of mind; on the contrary, it set out from the assumption that nature is radically non-mental or mechanical, and never went back on that assumption, but always maintained that nature is essentially alien to mind, mind's other or opposite. Secondly it never meant that nature is an illusion or dream of mind, something non-existent; on the contrary, it always maintained that nature really is what it seems to be: it is the work of mind and not existing in its own right, but a work really produced and, because really produced, really existing.

The Greek view of nature as an intelligent organism was based on an analogy: an analogy between the world of nature and the individual human being, who begins by finding certain characteristics in himself as an individual, and goes on to think of nature as possessed of similar characteristics. By the work of his own self-consciousness he comes to think of himself as a body whose parts are in constant rhythmic motion, these motions being delicately adjusted to each other so as to preserve the vitality of the whole: and at the same time he finds himself to be a mind directing the activity of this body in accordance with its own desires. The world of nature as a whole is then explained as a macrocosm analogous to this microcosm.

The Renaissance view of nature as a machine is equally analogical in its origin, but it presupposes a quite different order of ideas. First, it is based on the Christian idea of a creative and omnipotent God. Secondly, it is based on the human experience of designing and constructing machines. The Greeks and Romans were not machine-users, except to a very small extent: their catapults and water-clocks were not a prominent enough feature of their life to affect the way in which they conceived the relation between themselves and the world. But by the sixteenth century the Industrial Revolution was well on the way. The printing-press and the windmill, the lever, the pump, and the pulley, the clock and the wheel-barrow, and a host of machines in use among miners and engineers were established features of daily life. Everyone understood the nature of a machine, and the experiences of making and using such things had become part of the general consciousness of European man. It was an easy step to the proposition: as a clockmaker or millwright is to a clock or mill, so is God to Nature.

4. THE MODERN VIEW OF NATURE

The modern view of Nature owes something both to Greek and to Renaissance cosmology, but it differs from each in fundamental ways. To describe the differences with precision is not easy, because the movement is still young and has not yet had the time to ripen its ideas for systematic statement. We are confronted not so much with a new cosmology as with a large number of new cosmological experiments, all very disconcerting if looked at from the Renaissance point of view, and all to some extent animated by what we can recognize as a single spirit; but to define this spirit is very difficult. We can, however, describe the kind of experience on which it is based, and so indicate the starting-point of this movement.

Modern cosmology, like its predecessors, is based on an analogy. What is new about it is that the analogy is a new one. As Greek natural science was based on the analogy between the macrocosm nature and the microcosm man, as man is revealed to himself in his own self-consciousness; as Renaissance natural science was based on the analogy between nature as God's handiwork and the machines that are the handiwork of man (the same *Analogy* which in the eighteenth century was to become the presupposition of Joseph Butler's masterpiece); so the modern view of nature, which first begins to find expression towards the end of the eighteenth century and ever since then has been gathering weight and establishing itself more securely down to the present day, is based on the analogy between the processes of the natural world as studied by natural scientists and the vicissitudes of human affairs as studied by historians.

Like the Renaissance analogy, this could only begin to operate when certain conditions were fulfilled. Renaissance cosmology, as I have pointed out, arose from a widespread familiarity with the making and handling of machines. The sixteenth century was the time when this familiarity had been achieved. Modern cosmology could only have arisen from a widespread familiarity with historical studies, and in particular with historical studies of the kind which placed the conception of process, change, development in the centre of their picture and recognized it as the fundamental category of historical thought. This kind of history appeared for the first time about the middle of the eighteenth century.[1] Bury finds it first in Turgot (*Discours sur l'histoire universelle*, 1750) and Voltaire (*Le Siècle de Louis XIV*, 1751). It was developed in the *Encyclopédie* (1751-65), and thereafter became a commonplace. Transposed during the next half-century into terms of natural science, the idea of "progress" became (as in Erasmus Darwin, *Zoonomia*, 1794-8, and Lamarck, *Philosophie zoologique*, 1809) the idea which in another half-century was to become famous as that of "evolution."

In its narrowest sense, evolution means the doctrine especially associated with the name of Charles Darwin, though not first expounded by him, that the species of living organisms are not a fixed repertory of permanent types, but begin to exist and cease to exist in time. But this doctrine is only one expression of a tendency which may work, and has in fact worked, in a much wider field: the tendency to resolve the very ancient dualism between changing and unchanging elements in the world of nature by maintaining that what had hitherto been regarded as unchanging was itself in reality subject to change. When this tendency works unchecked, and the conception of unchanging elements in nature is completely eradicated, the result may be called "radical evolutionism": a doctrine which hardly arrived at maturity until the twentieth century, and was first systematically expounded by Bergson.

The origin of this tendency, which can be traced at work in various fields of natural science for more than a hundred years before Bergson, must be sought in the historical movement of the late eighteenth century, and its further development in the growth of the same movement in the nineteenth.

The concept of evolution, as those who witnessed its detailed application by Darwin to the field of biology knew, marked a crisis of the first importance in the history of human thought. But the earliest attempts at a philosophical exposition of the concept, notably Herbert Spencer's, were amateurish and inconclusive; and the criticism which they justly provoked led not so much to a closer inquiry into the concept itself as to a belief that no such inquiry was worth making.

The question at issue was a very far-reaching one: under what conditions is knowledge possible? For the Greeks it had been an axiom that nothing is knowable unless it is unchanging. The world of nature, again according to the Greeks, is a world of continual and all-pervading change. It might seem to follow that a science of nature is impossible. But Renaissance cosmology had avoided this conclusion by a *distinguo*. The world of nature as it appears to our senses was admitted to be unknowable; but it was argued that behind this world of so-called "secondary qualities" there lay other things, the true objects of natural science, knowable because unchanging. First, there was the "substance" or "matter," itself not subject to change, whose changing arrangements and dispositions were the realities whose appearances to our sensibility took the shape of secondary qualities. Secondly, there were the "laws" according to which these arrangements and dispositions changed. These two things, matter and natural law, were then unchanging objects of natural science.

[1] J. B. Bury, *The Idea of Progress* (1924), ch. VII.

What is the relation between the "matter" which was regarded as the substrate of the changes in the perceptible natural world and the "laws" according to which those changes took place? Without at all fully discussing this question, I will venture to suggest that they represent the same thing said twice over. The motive for asserting either of them arises from the supposed need for an unchanging and therefore, according to the time-honoured axiom, knowable something behind the changing and therefore unknowable show of nature as we perceive it through our senses.

This changeless something was sought in two directions at once, or (if you will) described in two vocabularies at once. First it was sought by stripping away from nature-as-we-perceive-it whatever is obviously changeable, so as to leave a residue in the shape of a natural world now at last knowable because exempt from change; secondly, it was sought by looking for unchanging relations between the changeables. Alternatively, you may say that the unchangeable something was described first in the vocabulary of "materialism," as by the early Ionians and secondly in the vocabulary of "idealism," as by the Pythagoreans; where "materialism" means the attempt to understand things by asking what they are made of, and "idealism" the attempt to understand things by asking what "A is made of B" means: that is, what "form" has been imposed on it to differentiate it from that out of which it is made.

If the required "changeless something" can be found in one of these quests, or described in one of these vocabularies, the other becomes unnecessary. Hence "materialism" and "idealism," which in the seventeenth century existed peacefully side by side, revealed themselves gradually in the eighteenth century as rivals. . . . The question was: How are we to find a changeless and therefore knowable something in, or behind, or somehow belonging to, the flux of nature-as-we-perceive-it? In modern or evolutionary natural science, this question does not arise, and the controversy between "materialism" and "idealism," as two answers to it, no longer has any meaning.

This controversy became meaningless because its presuppositions had undergone a revolutionary change by the beginning of the nineteenth century. By then historians had trained themselves to think, and had found themselves able to think scientifically, about a world of constantly changing human affairs in which there was no unchanging substrate behind the changes, and no unchanging laws according to which the changes took place. History had by now established itself as a science, that is, a progressive inquiry in which conclusions are solidly and demonstratively established. It had thus been proved by experiment that scientific knowledge was possible concerning objects that were constantly changing. Once more, the self-consciousness of man, in this case the corporate self-consciousness of man, his historical consciousness of his own corporate doings, provided a clue to his thoughts about nature. The historical conception of scientifically knowable change or process was applied, under the name of evolution, to the natural world.

5. CONSEQUENCES OF THIS VIEW

This new conception of nature, the evolutionary conception based on the analogy of history, has certain characteristics which follow necessarily from the central idea on which it is based. It may be useful to mention a few of them.

i. *Change no longer cyclical, but progressive.* The first to which I will refer is that change takes on, in the mind of the natural scientist, a new character. Greek, Renaissance, and modern thinkers have all agreed that everything in the world of nature, as we perceive it, is in a state of continuous change. But Greek thinkers regarded these natural changes as at bottom always cyclical. A change from a state α to a state β, they thought, is always one part of a process which completes itself by a return from state β to state α. When they found themselves forced to recognize the existence of a change that was not cyclical because it admitted of no such return, e.g. in the change from youth to age in an animal or vegetable organism, they regarded it as a mutilated fragment of a change which, had it been complete, would have been cyclical; and the thing which exhibited it, whether animal or vegetable or anything else, they regarded as defective for that very reason, as not exhibiting in its changes that cyclic pattern which ideally all change ought to show. Alternatively, it was often possible to regard a non-cyclical change not as incomplete in itself but as incompletely known; as a rate of cyclical change where for some reason we could perceive only one part of the revolution. This tendency to conceive change as at bottom, or when it is able to realize and exhibit its proper nature *qua* change, not progressive (where by progress I mean a change always leading to something new, with no necessary implication of betterment) but cyclical, was characteristic of the Greek mind throughout its history. I will quote only one striking example of it: the doctrine which haunts Greek cosmology from the Ionians to Aristotle, that the total movement of the world-organism, the movement from which all other movements in the natural world are derived, is a uniform rotation.

Modern thought reverses this state of things. Dominated by the idea of progress or development, which is derived from the principle that history never repeats itself, it regards the world of nature as a second world in which nothing is repeated, a second world of progress characterized, no less than that of history, by the constant emergence of new things. Change is at bottom progressive. Changes that appear to be cyclical are not really cyclical. It is always possible to explain them as cyclical in appearance only, and in reality progressive, in either of two ways: subjectively, by saying that what have been taken for identicals are only similars, or objectively, by saying (to speak metaphorically) that what has been taken for a rotary or circular movement is in fact a spiral movement, one in which the radius is constantly changing or the centre constantly displaced, or both.

ii. *Nature no longer mechanical.* A negative result of introducing the idea of evolution into natural science was the abandonment of the mechanical conception of nature.

It is impossible to describe one and the same thing in the same breath as a machine and as developing or evolving. Something which is developing may build itself machines, but it cannot be a machine. On the evolutionary theory, therefore, there may be machines in nature, but nature cannot itself be a machine, and cannot be either described as a whole or completely described as to any of its parts in mechanical terms.

A machine is essentially a finished product or closed system. Until it is finished it is not a machine. While it is being built it is not functioning as a machine; it cannot do that until it is complete; therefore it can never develop, for developing means working at becoming what as yet one is not (as, for example, a kitten works at growing into a cat), and a machine in an unfinished state cannot work at anything. The only kind of change which a machine can produce in itself by its functioning is breaking down or wearing out. This is not a case of development, because it is not an acquisition of any new functions, it is only a loss of old ones. Thus a steamship in working order can do all the things a broken-down one can do and others besides. A machine may bring about a kind of development in that on which it works, as a grain elevator may build a heap of grain; but if the machine is to go on working this development must be cancelled in the next phase (e.g. the heap must be cleared away), and a cycle of phases substituted for the development.

iii. *Teleology reintroduced.* A positive corollary of this negative result is the reintroduction into natural science of an idea which the mechanical view of nature had banished: the idea of teleology. If the world of nature is a machine or a collection of machines, everything that happens in it is due to "efficient causes," not in the Aristotelian sense of that Aristotelian phrase but in the mechanistic sense, as denoting impact, attraction, repulsion, and so on. It is only when we discuss the relation of the machine to its maker that "final causes" begin to appear. If nature is regarded as a machine, then teleology or final causation, with the attendant idea of "nisus" or effort on the part of nature or something in nature towards the realization of something not yet existing, must be ruled out of natural science altogether; its proper application is to the sphere of mind; to apply it to nature is to confuse the characteristics of these two radically different things.

This negation of teleology in mechanistic natural science may undergo a qualification more apparent than real by contending, as Spinoza did in fact contend, that everything in nature makes an effort to maintain itself in its own being ("in suo esse perseverare conatur," *Ethics*, iii, prop. 6). This is only a quasi-teleology, because the *conatus* of which Spinoza writes is not directed towards the realization of anything not yet existing. Under a form of words which seems to assert the reality and universality of effort, the very essence of effort is in fact denied.

For an evolutionary science of nature, the *esse* of anything in nature is its *fieri;* and a science of that kind must therefore replace Spinoza's proposition by the proposition that everything in nature tries to persevere in its own becoming: to continue the process of development in which, so far as it exists at all, it is already engaged. And this contradicts what Spinoza meant to say; for the "being" of a thing, in Spinoza, means what it now is; and a thing engaged in a process of development is engaged in ceasing to be what it now is, e.g. a kitten, to become what it now is not, e.g. a cat.

iv. *Substance resolved into function.* The principle that the *esse* of a thing is its *fieri* requires a somewhat extensive reform in the vocabulary of natural science, such that all words and phrases descriptive of substance or structure shall be replaced by words and phrases descriptive of function. A mechanistic science of nature will already possess a considerable vocabulary of functional terms, but these will always be accompanied by another vocabulary of structural terms. In any machine structure is one thing, function another; for a machine has to be constructed before it can be set in motion.

In order to make a bearing you choose a piece of steel having a certain degree of hardness, and before it can function as a bearing you work it to a certain shape. Its size, shape, weight, hardness, and so forth are structural properties independent of its acting in this particular machine, or in any other machine, as a bearing or indeed as anything else. They remain the same whether or not the machine to which it belongs is in motion or at rest. Further, these structural properties belonging to a given part of a given machine, are the foundation and pre-requisite of its functional properties. Unless the piece of steel has the right shape, hardness, &c., it will not serve as a bearing.

If nature is a machine, therefore, the various motions of its parts will be motions of things which have structural properties of their own independent of these motions and serving as their indispensable prerequisites. To sum this up: in a machine, and therefore in nature if nature is mechanical, structure and function are distinct, and function presupposes structure.

In the world of human ·affairs as known to the historian there is no such distinction and *a fortiori* no such priority. Structure is resolvable into function. There is no harm in historians talking about the structure of feudal society or of capitalist industry or of the Greek city state, but the reason why there is no harm in it is because they know that these so-called structures are really complexes of function, kinds of ways in which human beings behave; and that when we say that, for example, the British constitution exists, what we mean is that certain people are behaving in a certain kind of way.

On an evolutionary view of nature a logically constructed natural science will follow the example of history and resolve the structures with which it is concerned into function. Nature will be understood as consisting of processes, and the existence of any special kind of thing in nature will be understood as meaning that processes of a special kind are going on there. Thus "hardness" in steel will be understood, as in fact it is by modern physicists, not as the name for a structural property of the steel independent of, and presupposed by, any special way in which the steel may behave, but as the name for a way in which it behaves: for example, the name for a rapid movement of the particles composing it, whereby these violently bombard anything that is brought into what is called "contact" with the steel, that is, within range of the bombardment.

v. *Minimum space and minimum time.* This resolution of structure into function has important consequences for the detail of natural science. Since the conception of any kind of natural substance is resolved into the conception of some kind of natural function; and since these functions are still conceived by natural scientists in the way in which they have been conceived ever since the dawn of Greek thought, namely, as movements; and since any movement occupies space and takes time; it follows that a given kind of natural substance can exist, according to the doctrines of an evolutionary natural science, only in an appropriate amount of space and during an appropriate amount of time. Let us take these two qualifications separately.

(*a*) *The principle of minimum space.* An evolutionary natural science will maintain that a given kind of natural substance can exist only in an appropriate amount of space. It is not infinitely divisible. There is a smallest possible quantity of it; and if that quantity is divided the parts are not specimens of that kind of substance.

This is the doctrine propounded by John Dalton early in the nineteenth century, and now universally accepted. It is called atomism, but it differs no less from the doctrine of the Greek atomists than it does from the homoeomerism of Anaxagoras. Anaxagoras held that specific natural substances were made up of particles homogeneous with themselves, and any such idea as this is in obvious conflict with Daltonian chemistry, according to which water, for example, is made up not of water but of oxygen and hydrogen, two gases. The Democritean atomism which we know from Epicurus and Lucretius, however, differs from Daltonian atomism quite as profoundly; for the Greek atoms were indivisible particles of undifferentiated matter, whereas Dalton's atoms (until Rutherford began to split them) were indivisible particles of this or that kind of matter, hydrogen or carbon or lead.

Dalton divided natural substances into two classes: those made up of "molecules" like water, and those made up of "atoms," like hydrogen. In each case the particle, molecule or atoms, was the smallest quantity of that substance which could exist: but not for the same reason. The molecule of water was the smallest possible amount of water because the only parts into which it could be divided were particles not of water but of oxygen and hydrogen. The atom of oxygen was the smallest possible amount of oxygen not because it was divisible into parts which were not oxygen but because it was not divisible at all.

This conception of a physically indivisible "atom" was not new. It was a fossilized relic of ancient Greek physics, anachronistically surviving in an alien environment, the evolutionary science of the nineteenth century. The fertile part of Daltonism was not the idea of the "atom" but the idea of the "molecule": not the Anaxagorean idea of particles homogeneous with that which they go to make up, but the thoroughly modern idea that particles having determinate special qualities of their own could make up bodies having quite different special qualities. This idea is nowhere to be found in the Greeks. The theory of the "four elements" in Empedocles is no anticipation of it; for according to that theory the elements earth, air, fire, and water preserve their special qualities in the compounds formed of them, so that these compounds are, as to their own special qualities, in part earthy, in part airy, and so forth.

Indeed, the Daltonian "atom" did not survive the nineteenth century. Before that century was over J. J. Thomson and others resolved the Daltonian dualism between the "atom" and the "molecule" and brought the theory of the atom into line with the theory of the molecule. This was done by maintaining that, just as the "molecule" of water was made up of parts which taken separately were not water but something else, namely oxygen and hydrogen, so the "atom" of oxygen was made up of parts which taken separately were not oxygen but something else, namely, electricity.

(*b*) *The principle of minimum time.* An evolutionary science of nature will maintain that a natural substance takes time to exist; an appropriate amount of time, different kinds of substance taking each its own specific amount. For each specific substance there is a specific time-lapse during which it can exist; in a shorter time-lapse it cannot exist, because the specific function or process whose occurrence is what we mean when we speak of the specific substance as existing cannot occur in so short a time.

If the suggestion made above was correct, that evolutionary natural science is based on analogy with historical science, and if history is the study of human affairs, human affairs should present us with analogies for this principle, just as they present us with analogies for the principle of minimum space in, for example, the fact that a given type of human activity involves as a minimum a certain number of human beings: that it takes two to make a quarrel, three to make a case of jealousy, four or five (if Plato is right, *Republic*, 369D) to make a civil society, and so on.

And these analogies in human affairs for the principle of minimum time should have been commonplaces long before that principle began to affect the work of natural scientists.

Nature Rehumanized
Alfred Whitehead

Alfred North Whitehead (1861-1947) was one of the most eminent mathematicians and philosophers of our time. With Bertrand Russell, he wrote *Principia Mathematica* (1910-1913), a work that opened up vast new fields in logic and mathematics. His extensive contributions to philosophy are no less notable.

My last lecture described the influence upon the eighteenth century of the narrow and efficient scheme of scientific concepts which it had inherited from its predecessor. That scheme was the product of a mentality which found the Augustinian theology extremely congenial. The Protestant Calvinism and the Catholic Jansenism exhibited man as helpless to co-operate with Irresistible Grace: the contemporary scheme of science exhibited man as helpless to co-operate with the irresistible mechanism of nature. The mechanism of God and the mechanism of matter were the monstrous issues of limited metaphysics and clear logical intellect. Also the seventeenth century had genius, and cleared the world of muddled thought. The eighteenth century continued the work of clearance, with ruthless efficiency. The scientific scheme has lasted longer than the theological scheme. Mankind soon lost interest in Irresistible Grace; but it quickly appreciated the competent engineering which was due to science. Also in the first quarter of the eighteenth century, George Berkeley launched his philosophical criticism against the whole basis of the system. He failed to disturb the dominant current of thought. In my last lecture I developed a parallel line of argument, which would lead to a system of thought basing nature upon the concept of organism, and not upon the concept of matter. In the present lecture, I propose in the first place to consider how the concrete educated thought of men has viewed this opposition of mechanism and organism. It is in literature that the concrete outlook of humanity receives its expression. Accordingly it is to literature that we must look, particularly in its more concrete forms, namely in poetry and in drama, if we hope to discover the inward thoughts of a generation.

We quickly find that the Western peoples exhibit on a colossal scale a peculiarity which is popularly supposed to be more especially characteristic of the Chinese.

Source: Science and the Modern World (New York: Macmillan, 1925), pp. 75-81, 83-86, 87-89, 91-94. Reprinted with permission of The Macmillan Company. Copyright 1925 by The Macmillan Company, renewed 1953 by Evelyn Whitehead.

Surprise is often expressed that a Chinaman can be of two religions, a Confucian for some occasions and a Buddhist for other occasions. Whether this is true of China I do not know; nor do I know whether, if true, these two attitudes are really inconsistent. But there can be no doubt that an analogous fact is true of the West, and that the two attitudes involved are inconsistent. A scientific realism, based on mechanism, in conjoined with an unwavering belief in the world of men and of the higher animals as being composed of self-determining organisms. This radical inconsistency at the basis of modern thought accounts for much that is half-hearted and wavering in our civilisation. It would be going too far to say that it distracts thought. It enfeebles it, by reason of the inconsistency lurking in the background. After all, the men of the Middle Ages were in pursuit of an excellency of which we have nearly forgotten the existence. They set before themselves the idea of the attainment of a harmony of the understanding. We are content with superficial orderings from diverse arbitrary starting points. For instance, the enterprises produced by the individualistic energy of the European peoples presuppose physical actions directed to final causes. But the science which is employed in their development is based on a philosophy which asserts that physical causation is supreme, and which disjoins the physical cause from the final end. It is not popular to dwell on the absolute contradiction here involved. It is the fact, however you gloze it over with phrases. Of course, we find in the eighteenth century Paley's famous argument, that mechanism presupposes a God who is the author of nature. But even before Paley put the argument into its final form, Hume had written the retort, that the God whom you will find will be the sort of God who makes that mechanism. In other words, that mechanism can, at most, presuppose a mechanic, and not merely *a* mechanic but *its* mechanic. The only way of mitigating mechanism is by the discovery that it is not mechanism.

When we leave apologetic theology, and come to ordinary literature, we find, as we might expect, that the scientific outlook is in general simply ignored. So far as the mass of literature is concerned, science might never have been heard of. Until recently nearly all writers have been soaked in classical and renaissance literature. For the most part, neither philosophy nor science interested them, and their minds were trained to ignore them.

There are exceptions to this sweeping statement; and, even if we confine ourselves to English literature, they concern some of the greatest names; also the indirect influence of science has been considerable.

A side light on this distracting inconsistency in modern thought is obtained by examining some of those great serious poems in English literature, whose general scale gives them a didactic character. The relevant poems are Milton's *Paradise Lost*, Pope's *Essay on Man*, Wordsworth's *Excursion*, Tennyson's *In Memoriam*. Milton, though he is writing after the Restoration, voices the theological aspect of the earlier portion of his century, untouched by the influence of the scientific materialism. Pope's poem represents the effect on popular thought of the intervening sixty years which includes the first period of assured triumph for the scientific movement. Wordsworth in his whole being expresses a conscious reaction against the mentality of the eighteenth century. This mentality means nothing else than the acceptance of the scientific ideas at their full face value. Wordsworth was not bothered by any intellectual antagonism. What moved him was a moral repulsion. He felt that something had been left out, and that what had been left out comprised everything that was most important. Tennyson is the mouthpiece of the attempts of the waning romantic movement in the second quarter of the nineteenth century to come to terms with science. By this time the two elements in modern thought had disclosed their fundamental divergence by their jarring interpretations of the course of nature and the life of man. Tennyson stands in this poem as the perfect example of the distraction which I have already mentioned. There are opposing visions of the world, and both of them command his assent by appeals to ultimate intuitions from which there seems no escape. Tennyson goes to the heart of the difficulty. It is the problem of mechanism which appalls him,

"The stars," she whispers, "blindly run on."

This line states starkly the whole philosophic problem implicit in the poem. Each molecule blindly runs. The human body is a collection of molecules. Therefore, the human body is a collection of molecules. Therefore, the human body blindly runs, and therefore there can be no individual responsibility for the actions of the body. If you once accept that the molecule is definitely determined to be what it is, independently of any determination by reason of the total organism of the body, and if you further admit that the blind run is settled by the general mechanical laws, there can be no escape from this conclusion. But mental experiences are derivative from the actions of the body, including of course its internal behaviour. Accordingly, the sole function of the mind is to have at least some of its experiences settled for it, and to add such others as may be open to it independently of the body's motions, internal and external.

There are then two possible theories as to the mind. You can either deny that it can supply for itself any experiences other than those provided for it by the body, or you can admit them.

If you refuse to admit the additional experiences, then all individual responsibility is swept away. If you do admit them, then a human being may be responsible for the state of his mind though he has no responsibility for the actions of his body. The enfeeblement of thought in the modern world is illustrated by the way in which this plain issue is avoided in Tennyson's poem. There is something kept in the background, a skeleton in the cupboard. He touches on almost every religious and scientific problem, but carefully avoids more than a passing allusion to this one.

This very problem was in full debate at the date of the poem. John Stuart Mill was maintaining his doctrine of determinism. In this doctrine volitions are determined by motives, and motives are expressible in terms of antecedent conditions including states of mind as well as states of the body.

It is obvious that this doctrine affords no escape from the dilemma presented by a thoroughgoing mechanism. For if the volition affects the state of the body, then the molecules in the body do not blindly run. If the volition does not affect the state of the body, the mind is still left in its uncomfortable position.

Mill's doctrine is generally accepted, especially among scientists, as though in some way it allowed you to accept the extreme doctrine of materialistic mechanism, and yet mitigated its unbelievable consequences. It does nothing of the sort. Either the bodily molecules blindly run, or they do not. If they do blindly run, the mental states are irrelevant in discussing the bodily actions.

I have stated the arguments concisely, because in truth the issue is a very simple one. Prolonged discussion is merely a source of confusion. The question as to the metaphysical status of molecules does not come in. The statement that they are mere formulae has no bearing on the argument. For presumably the formulae mean something. If they mean nothing, the whole mechanical doctrine is likewise without meaning, and the question drops. But if the formulae mean anything, the argument applies to exactly what they do mean. The traditional way of evading the difficulty—other than the simple way of ignoring it—is to have recourse to some form of what is now termed "vitalism." This doctrine is really a compromise. It allows a free run to mechanism throughout the whole of inanimate nature, and holds that the mechanism is partially mitigated within living bodies. I feel that this theory is an unsatisfactory compromise. The gap between living and dead matter is too vague and problematical to bear the weight of such an arbitrary assumption, which involves an essential dualism somewhere.

The doctrine which I am maintaining is that the whole concept of materialism only applies to very abstract entities, the products of logical discernment. The concrete enduring entities are organisms, so that the plan of the *whole* influences the very characters of the various subordinate organisms which enter into it. In the case of an animal, the mental states enter into the plan of the total organism and thus modify the plans of the successive subordinate organisms until the ultimate smallest organisms, such as electrons, are reached. Thus an electron within a living body is different from an electron outside it, by reason of the plan of the body. The electron blindly runs either within or without the body; but it runs within the body in accordance with its character within the body; that is to say, in accordance with the general plan of the body, and this plan includes the mental state. But the principle of modification is perfectly general throughout nature, and represents no property peculiar to living bodies. In subsequent lectures it will be explained that this doctrine involves the abandonment of the traditional scientific materialism, and the substitution of an alternative doctrine of organism.

I shall not discuss Mill's determinism, as it lies outside the scheme of these lectures. The foregoing discussion has been directed to secure that either determinism or free will shall have some relevance, unhampered by the difficulties introduced by materialistic mechanism, or by the compromise of vitalism. I would term the doctrine of these lectures, the theory of *organic mechanism*. In this theory, the molecules may blindly run in accordance with the general laws, but the molecules differ in their intrinsic characters according to the general organic plans of the situations in which they find themselves.

The discrepancy between the materialistic mechanism of science and the moral intuitions, which are presupposed in the concrete affairs of life, only gradually assumed its true importance as the centuries advanced. The different tones of the successive epochs to which the poems, already mentioned, belong are curiously reflected in their opening passages. Milton ends his introduction with the prayer,

> *That to the height of this great argument*
> *I may assert eternal Providence,*
> *And justify the ways of God to men.*

To judge from many modern writers on Milton, we might imagine that the *Paradise Lost* and the *Paradise Regained* were written as a series of experiments in blank verse. This was certainly not Milton's view of his work. To "justify the ways of God to men" was very much his main object. He recurs to the same idea in the *Samson Agonistes,*

> Just are the ways of God
> and justifiable to men.

We note the assured volume of confidence, untroubled by the coming scientific avalanche. The actual date of the publication of the *Paradise Lost* lies just beyond the epoch to which it belongs. It is the swan-song of a passing world of untroubled certitude.

A comparison between Pope's *Essay on Man* and the *Paradise Lost* exhibits the change of tone in English thought in the fifty or sixty years which separate the age of Milton from the age of Pope. Milton addresses his poem to God, Pope's poem is addressed to Lord Bolingbroke,

> Awake, my St. John! leave all meaner things
> To low ambition and the pride of kings.
> Let us (since life can little more supply
> Than just to look about us and to die)
> Expatiate free o'er all this scene of man;
> A mighty maze! but not without a plan.

Compare the jaunty assurance of Pope,

> A mighty maze! but not without a plan.

with Milton's

> Just are the ways of God
> And justifiable to men.

But the real point to notice is that Pope as well as Milton was untroubled by the great perplexity which haunts the modern world. The clue which Milton followed was to dwell on the ways of God in dealings with man. Two generations later we find Pope equally confident that the enlightened methods of modern science provided a plan adequate as a map of the "mighty maze."

Wordsworth's *Excursion* is the next English poem on the same subject. A prose preface tells us that it is a fragment of a larger projected work, described as "A philosophical poem containing views of Man, Nature, and Society."

Very characteristically the poem begins with the line,

> 'Twas summer, and the sun had mounted high.

Thus the romantic reaction started neither with God nor with Lord Bolingbroke, but with nature. We are here witnessing a conscious reaction against the whole tone of the eighteenth century. That century approached nature with the abstract analysis of science, whereas Wordsworth opposes to the scientific abstractions his full concrete experience.

.   .   .

Wordsworth was passionately absorbed in nature. It has been said of Spinoza, that he was drunk with God. It is equally true that Wordsworth was drunk with nature. But he was a thoughtful, well-read man, with philosophical interests, and sane even to the point of prosiness. In addition, he was a genius. He weakens his evidence by his dislike of science. We all remember his scorn of the poor man whom he somewhat hastily accuses of peeping and botanising on his mother's grave. Passage after passage could be quoted from him, expressing this repulsion. In this respect, his characteristic thought can be summed up in his phrase, "We murder to dissect."

In this latter passage, he discloses the intellectual basis of his criticism of science. He alleges against science its absorption in abstractions. His consistent theme is that the important facts of nature elude the scientific method. It is important therefore to ask, what Wordsworth found in nature that failed to receive expression in science. I ask this question in the interest of science itself; for one main position in these lectures is a protest against the idea that the abstractions of science are irreformable and unalterable. Now it is emphatically not the case that Wordsworth hands over inorganic matter to the mercy of science, and concentrates on the faith that in the living organism there is some element that science cannot analyse. Of course he recognises, what no one doubts, that in some sense living things are different from lifeless things. But that is not his main point. It is the brooding presence of the hills which haunts him. His theme is nature *in solido*, that is to say, he dwells on that mysterious presence of surrounding things, which imposes itself on any separate element that we set up as an individual for its own sake. He always grasps the whole of nature as involved in the tonality of the particular instance. That is why he laughs with the daffodils, and finds in the primrose thoughts "too deep for tears."

Wordsworth's greatest poem is, by far, the first book of *The Prelude*. It is pervaded by this sense of the haunting presences of nature. A series of magnificent passages, too long for quotation, express this idea. Of course, Wordsworth is a poet writing a poem, and is not concerned with dry philosophical statements. But it would hardly be possible to express more clearly a feeling for nature, as exhibiting entwined prehensive unities, each suffused with modal presences of others:

> Ye Presences of Nature in the sky
> And on the earth! Ye Visions of the hills!
> And Souls of lonely places! can I think
> A vulgar hope was yours when ye employed
> Such ministry, when ye through many a year
> Haunting me thus among my boyish sports,
> On caves and trees, upon the woods and hills,
> Impressed upon all forms the characters
> Of danger or desire; and thus did make
> The surface of the universal earth,
> With triumph and delight, with hope and fear,
> Work like a sea? . . .

In thus citing Wordsworth, the point which I wish to make is that we forget how strained and paradoxical is the view of nature which modern science imposes on our thoughts. Wordsworth, to the height of genius, expresses the concrete facts of our apprehension, facts which are distorted in the scientific analysis. Is it not possible that the standardised concepts of science are only valid within narrow limitations, perhaps too narrow for science itself?

Shelley's attitude to science was at the opposite pole to that of Wordsworth. He loved it, and is never tired of expressing in poetry the thoughts which it suggests. It symbolises to him joy, and peace, and illumination. What the hills were to the youth of Wordsworth, a chemical laboratory was to Shelley. It is unfortunate that Shelley's literary critics have, in this respect, so little of Shelley in their own mentality. They tend to treat as a casual oddity of Shelley's nature what was, in fact, part of the main structure of his mind, permeating his poetry through and through. If Shelley had been born a hundred years later, the twentieth century would have seen a Newton among chemists.

For the sake of estimating the value of Shelley's evidence it is important to realise this absorption of his mind in scientific ideas. It can be illustrated by lyric after lyric. I will choose one poem only, the fourth act of his *Prometheus Unbound*. The Earth and the Moon converse together in the language of accurate science. Physical experiments guide his imagery. For example, the Earth's exclamation,

> *The vaporous exultation not to be confined!*

is the poetic transcript of "the expansive force of gases," as it is termed in books on science. Again, take the Earth's stanza,

> *I spin beneath my pyramid of night,*
> *Which points into the heavens,—dreaming delight,*
> *Murmuring victorious joy in my enchanted sleep;*
> *As a youth lulled in love-dreams faintly sighing,*
> *Under the shadow of his beauty lying,*
> *Which round his rest a watch of light and warmth doth*
> *keep.*

This stanza could only have been written by someone with a definite geometrical diagram before his inward eye—a diagram which it has often been my business to demonstrate to mathematical classes. As evidence, note especially the last line which gives poetical imagery to the light surrounding night's pyramid. This idea could not occur to anyone without the diagram. But the whole poem and other poems are permeated with touches of this kind.

Now the poet, so sympathetic with science, so absorbed in its ideas, can simply make nothing of the doctrine of secondary qualities which is fundamental to its concepts. For Shelley nature retains its beauty and its colour. Shelley's nature is in its essence a nature of organisms, functioning with the full content of our perceptual experience. We are so used to ignoring the implication of orthodox scientific doctrine, that it is difficult to make evident the criticism upon it which is thereby implied. If anybody could have treated it seriously, Shelley would have done so.

Furthermore Shelley is entirely at one with Wordsworth as to the interfusing of the Presence in nature. Here is the opening stanza of his poem entitled *Mont Blanc:*

> *The everlasting universe of Things*
> *Flows through the Mind, and rolls its rapid waves,*
> *Now dark—now glittering—now reflecting gloom—*
> *Now lending splendour, where from secret springs*
> *The source of human thought its tribute brings*

> *Of waters,—with a sound but half its own,*
> *Such as a feeble brook will oft assume*
> *In the wild woods, among the Mountains lone,*
> *Where waterfalls around it leap for ever,*
> *Where woods and winds contend, and a vast river*
> *Over its rocks ceaselessly bursts and raves.*

Shelley has written these lines with explicit reference to some form of idealism, Kantian or Berkeleyan or Platonic. But however you construe him, he is here an emphatic witness to a prehensive unification as constituting the very being of nature.

Berkeley, Wordsworth, Shelley are representative of the intuitive refusal seriously to accept the abstract materialism of science.

The literature of the nineteenth century, especially its English poetic literature, is a witness to the discord between the aesthetic intuitions of mankind and the mechanism of science. Shelley brings vividly before us the elusiveness of the eternal objects of sense as they haunt the change which infects underlying organisms. Wordsworth is the poet of nature as being the field of enduring permanences carrying within themselves a message of tremendous significance. The eternal objects are also there for him,

> *The light that never was, on sea or land.*

Both Shelley and Wordsworth emphatically bear witness that nature cannot be divorced from its aesthetic values; and that these values arise from the cumulation, in some sense, of the brooding presence of the whole on to its various parts. Thus we gain from the poets the doctrine that a philosophy of nature must concern itself at least with these six notions: change, value, eternal objects, endurance, organism, interfusion.

We see that the literary romantic movement at the beginning of the nineteenth century, just as much as Berkeley's philosophical idealistic movement a hundred years earlier, refused to be confined within the materialistic concepts of the orthodox scientific theory. We know also that when in these lectures we come to the twentieth century, we shall find a movement in science itself to reorganise its concepts, driven thereto by its own intrinsic development.

It is, however, impossible to proceed until we have settled whether this refashioning of ideas is to be carried out on an objectivist basis or on a subjectivist basis. By a subjectivist basis I mean the belief that the nature of our immediate experience is the outcome of the perceptive peculiarities of the subject enjoying the experience. In other words, I mean that for this theory what is perceived is not a partial vision of a complex of things generally independent of that act of cognition; but that it merely is the expression of the individual peculiarities of the cognitive act. Accordingly what is common to the multiplicity of cognitive acts is the ratiocination connected with them. Thus, though there is a common world of thought associated with our sense-perceptions, there is no common world to think about. What we do think about is a common conceptual world applying indifferently to our individual experiences which are strictly personal to ourselves. Such a conceptual world will ultimately find its complete expression in the equations of applied mathematics. This is the extreme subjectivist position. There is of course the half-way house of those who believe that our perceptual experience does tell us of a common objective world; but that the things perceived are merely the outcome for us of this world, and are not *in themselves* elements in the common world itself.

Also there is the objectivist position. This creed is that the actual elements perceived by our senses are *in themselves* the elements of a common world; and that this world is a complex of things, including indeed our acts of cognition, but transcending them. According to this point of view the things experienced are to be distinguished from our knowledge of them. So far as there is dependence, the *things* pave the way for the *cognition*, rather than *vice versa*. But the point is that the actual things experienced enter into a common world which transcends knowledge, though it includes knowledge. The intermediate subjectivists would hold that the things experienced only indirectly enter into the common world by reason of their dependence on the subject who is cognising. The objectivist holds that the things experienced and the cognisant subject enter into the common world on equal terms. In these lectures I am giving the outline of what I consider to be the essentials of an objectivist philosophy adapted to the requirement of science and to the concrete experience of mankind. . . .

In the past, the objectivist position has been distorted by the supposed necessity of accepting the classical scientific materialism, with its doctrine of simple location. This has necessitated the doctrine of secondary and primary qualities. Thus the secondary qualities, such as the sense-objects, are dealt with on subjectivist principles. This is a half-hearted position which falls an easy prey to subjectivist criticism.

If we are to include the secondary qualities in the common world, a very drastic reorganisation of our fundamental concept is necessary. It is an evident fact of experience that our apprehensions of the external world depend absolutely on the occurrences within the human body. By playing appropriate tricks on the body a man can be got to perceive, or not to perceive, almost anything. Some people express themselves as though bodies, brains, and nerves were the only real things in an entirely imaginary world. In other words, they treat bodies on objective principles, and the rest of the world on subjectivist principles. This will not do; especially, when we remember that it is the experimenter's perception of another person's body which is in question as evidence.

But we have to admit that the body is the organism whose states regulate our cognisance of the world. The unity of the perceptual field therefore must be a unity of bodily experience. In being aware of the bodily experience, we must thereby be aware of aspects of the whole spatio-temporal world as mirrored within the bodily life. This is the solution of the problem which I gave in my last lecture. I will not repeat myself now, except to remind you that my theory involves the entire abandonment of the notion that simple location is the primary way in which things are involved in space-time. In a certain sense, everything is everywhere at all times. For every location involves an aspect of itself in every other location. Thus every spatio-temporal standpoint mirrors the world.

If you try to imagine this doctrine in terms of our conventional views of space and time, which presuppose simple location, it is a great paradox. But if you think of it in terms of our naïve experience, it is a mere transcript of the obvious facts. You are in a certain place perceiving things. Your perception takes place where you are, and is entirely dependent on how your body is functioning. But this functioning of the body in one place, exhibits for your cognisance an aspect of the distance environment, fading away into the general knowledge that there are things beyond. If this cognisance conveys knowledge of a transcendent world, it must be because the event which is the bodily life unifies in itself aspects of the universe.

This is a doctrine extremely consonant with the vivid expression of personal experience which we find in the nature-poetry of imaginative writers such as Wordsworth or Shelley. The brooding, immediate presences of things are an obsession to Wordsworth. What the theory does do is to edge cognitive mentality away from being the necessary sub-stratum of the unity of experience. That unity is now placed in the unity of an event. Accompanying this unity, there may or there may not be cognition.

At this point we come back to the great question which was posed before us by our examination of the evidence afforded by the poetic insight of Wordsworth and Shelley. This single question has expanded into a group of questions. What are enduring things, as distinguished from the eternal objects, such as colour and shape? How are they possible? What is their status and meaning in the universe? It comes to this: What is the status of the enduring stability of the order of nature? There is the summary answer, which refers nature to some greater reality standing behind it. This reality occurs in the history of thought under many names, The Absolute, Brahma, The Order of Heaven, God. The delineation of final metaphysical truth is no part of this lecture. My point is that any summary conclusion jumping from our conviction of the existence of such an order of nature to the easy assumption that there is an ultimate reality which, in some unexplained way, is to be appealed to for the removal of perplexity, constitutes the great refusal of rationality to assert its rights. We have to search whether nature does not in its very being show itself as self-explanatory. By this I mean, that the sheer statement, of what things are, may contain elements explanatory of why things are. Such elements may be expected to refer to depths beyond anything which we can grasp with a clear apprehension. In a sense, all explanation must end in an ultimate arbitrariness. My demand is, that the ultimate arbitrariness of matter of fact from which our formulation starts should disclose the same general principles of reality, which we dimly discern as stretching away into regions beyond our explicit powers of discernment. Nature exhibits itself as exemplifying a philosophy of the evolution of organisms subject to determinate conditions. Examples of such conditions are the dimensions of space, the laws of nature, the determinate enduring entities, such as atoms and electrons, which exemplify these laws. But the very nature of these entities, the very nature of their spatiality and temporality, should exhibit the arbitrariness of these conditions as the outcome of a wider evolution beyond nature itself, and within which nature is but a limited mode.

One all-pervasive fact, inherent in the very character of what is real, is the transition of things, the passage one to another. This passage is not a mere linear procession of discrete entities. However we fix a determinate entity, there is always a narrower determination of something which is presupposed in our first choice. Also there is always a wider determination into which our first choice fades by transition beyond itself. The general aspect of nature is that of evolutionary expansiveness. These unities, which I call events, are the emergence into actuality of something. How are we to characterise the something which thus emerges? The name *"event,"* given to such a unity, draws attention to the inherent transitoriness, combined with the actual unity. But this abstract word cannot be sufficient to characterise what the fact of the reality of an event is in itself. A moment's thought shows us that no one idea can in itself be sufficient. For every idea which finds its significance in each event must represent something which contributes to what realisation is in itself. Thus no one word can be adequate. But conversely, nothing must be left out. Remembering the poetic rendering of our concrete experience, we see at once that the element of value, of being valuable, of having value, of being an end in itself, of being something which is for its own sake, must not be omitted in any account of an event as the most concrete actual something. "Value" is the word I use for the intrinsic reality of an event. Value is an element which permeates through and through the poetic view of nature. We have only to transfer to the very texture of realisation in itself that value which we recognise so readily in terms of human life. This is the secret of Wordsworth's worship of nature. Realisation therefore is in itself the attainment of value. But there is no such thing as mere value. Value is the outcome of limitation. The definite finite entity is the selected mode which is the shaping of attainment; apart from such shaping into individual matter of fact there is no attainment. The mere fusion of all that there is would be the nonentity of indefiniteness. The salvation of reality is its obstinate, irreducible, matter-of-fact entities, which are limited to be no other than themselves. Neither science, nor art, nor creative action can tear itself away from obstinate, irreducible, limited facts. The endurance of things has its significance in the self-retention of that which imposes itself as a definite attainment for its own sake. That which endures is limited, obstructive, intolerant, infecting its environment with its own aspects. But it is not self-sufficient. The aspects of all things enter into its very nature. It is only itself as drawing together into its own limitation the larger whole in which it finds itself. Conversely it is only itself by lending its aspects to this same environment in which it finds itself. The problem of evolution is the development of enduring harmonies of enduring shapes of value, which merge into higher attainments of things beyond themselves. Aesthetic attainment is interwoven in the texture of realisation. The endurance of an entity represents the attainment of a limited aesthetic success, though if we look beyond it to its external effects, it may represent an aesthetic failure. Even within itself, it may represent the conflict between a lower success and a higher failure. The conflict is the presage of disruption.

The further discussion of the nature of enduring objects and of the conditions they require will be relevant to the consideration of the doctrine of evolution which dominated the latter half of the nineteenth century. The point which in this lecture I have endeavoured to make clear is that the nature-poetry of the romantic revival was a protest on behalf of the organic view of nature, and also a protest against the exclusion of value from the essence of matter of fact. In this aspect of it, the romantic movement may be conceived as a revival of Berkeley's protest which had been launched a hundred years earlier. The romantic reaction was a protest on behalf of value.

THE NATURE OF MAN

Immanuel Kant, in the first essay in this section, accepts the aim of natural science and law that we sketched in the introduction to the previous section; he also affirms that free will is a necessary condition for being able to praise or blame someone for his actions; for Kant, free will is a necessary condition for the possibility of morals. But these ideas of natural science and morals appear to be in conflict, events in nature being governed by causal laws while willed events escape them. How can man both be an object of science and a moral agent? Kant solves this conflict by distinguishing the sensible nature of man, that aspect of him that we can observe through our senses (science), from his intelligible nature, that aspect of man that we can grasp only through our "Reason" (morals). Kant says, "Our problem was this only: whether freedom and natural necessity can exist without conflict in one and the same action; and this we have sufficiently answered. [They can.] We have shown that since freedom may stand in relation to a quite different kind of conditions from those of natural necessity, the law of the latter does not affect the former, and that both may exist, independently of one another and without interfering with each other." Notice that Kant saves the possibility of morals at a cost that Paul Shepard (first essay in this chapter) deplores; Kant has "solved" himself into two universes. Despite Shepard's plea, we seem to be caught between two sets of alternatives, neither of which is very palatable. Either we give up morals to inherit one universe or we embrace two universes to save morals.

Baron Holbach's essay (second in this section) is a paradigm example of just how far pure mechanism can carry our issue. Holbach has contempt for anyone who holds the view that man has free will. He grants that there is the illusion that we have free will, but that it is due entirely to our ignorance. Holbach is direct. "Man is being purely physical; in whatever manner he is considered, he is connected to universal nature, and submitted to the necessary and immutable laws that she imposes on all the beings she contains, according to their peculiar essences." Notice that Holbach's physicalism yields him a single universe. And how are we to account for human actions that some attribute to will? "The will . . . is a modification of the brain, by which it is disposed to action, or prepared to give play to the organs." The brain, as we all know, is physical.

Arthur Campbell's essay (third in this section) argues that man has free will, and specifies the conditions of free will: An agent's free action must be self-caused, solely self-caused, and be a choice of alternatives. In a very interesting argument, he claims that the one experience we all have in which we find these "freedom" conditions satisfied is when we resist temptation. We call to your attention, particularly, his distinction between two selves: one of them makes the decision and the other, "as formed character" (formed by parents, desires, influences, companions), "determines not the decision but the situation within which the decision takes place." Confusing the two selves leads thinkers to an antifreedom determinism. This distinction between selves is a move similar to Kant's distinction between the sensible and intelligible agent, and, once again, Shepard's single universe seems out of reach.

The section's last essay is by **Jean-Paul Sartre**, who, like Royce (essay in second section of Chapter Seven), contends that man makes himself. He makes his own essence; his essence is not something given to him by nature. Thus, Sartre appears to join the company of dualists, which is not a happy turn when we consider that man's freedom and essence are bought at the price of anguish, forlornness, and despair, three notions that Sartre explains very clearly in this celebrated essay.

Freedom and the Necessity of Nature
Immanuel Kant*

That everything which happens has a cause, is a law of nature. Since the causality of this cause, that is, the *action* of the cause, is antecedent in time to the effect which has *ensued* upon it, it cannot itself have always existed, but must have *happened,* and *among the appearances* must have a cause by which it in turn is determined. Consequently, all events are empirically determined in an order of nature. Only in virtue of this law can appearances constitute a *nature* and become objects of experience. This law is a law of the understanding, from which no departure can be permitted, and from which no appearance may be exempted. To allow such exemption would be to set an appearance outside all possible experience, to distinguish it from all objects of possible experience, and so to make of it a mere thought-entity, a phantom of the brain.

. . .

Let us apply this to experience. Man is one of the appearances of the sensible world, and in so far one of the natural causes the causality of which must stand under empirical laws. Like all other things in nature, he must have an empirical character. This character we come to know through the powers and faculties which he reveals in his actions. In lifeless, or merely animal, nature we find no ground for thinking that any faculty is conditioned otherwise than in a merely sensible manner. Man, however, who knows all the rest of nature solely through the senses, knows himself also through pure apperception; and this, indeed, in acts and inner determinations which he cannot regard as impressions of the senses. He is thus to himself, on the one hand, phenomenon, and on the other hand, in respect of certain

Source: Critique of Pure Reason, trans. Norman K. Smith (New York: St. Martin's Press, 1929), pp. 469-479. By permission of St. Martin's Press, The Macmillan Company of Canada and Macmillan London and Basingstoke.

*For headnote, see page 137.

faculties the action of which cannot be ascribed to the receptivity of sensibility, a purely intelligible object. We entitle these faculties understanding and reason. The latter, in particular, we distinguish in a quite peculiar and especial way from all empirically conditioned powers. For it views its objects exclusively in the light of ideas, and in accordance with them determines the understanding, which then proceeds to make an empirical use of its own similarly pure concepts.

That our reason has causality, or that we at least represent it to ourselves as having causality, is evident from the *imperatives* which in all matters of conduct we impose as rules upon our active powers. *"Ought"* expresses a kind of necessity and of connection with grounds which is found nowhere else in the whole of nature. The understanding can know in nature only what is, what has been, or what will be. We cannot say that anything in nature *ought to be* other than what in all these time-relations it actually is. When we have the course of nature alone in view, *"ought"* has no meaning whatsoever. It is just as absurd to ask what ought to happen in the natural world as to ask what properties a circle ought to have. All that we are justified in asking is: what happens in nature? what are the properties of the circle?

Now, in view of these considerations, let us take our stand, and regard it as at least possible for reason to have causality with respect to appearances. Reason though it be, it must none the less exhibit an empirical character. For every cause presupposes a rule according to which certain appearances follow as effects; and every rule requires uniformity in the effects. This uniformity is, indeed, that upon which the concept of cause (as a faculty) is based, and so far as it must be exhibited by mere appearances may be named the empirical character of the cause. This character is permanent, but its effects, according to variation in the concomitant and in part limiting conditions, appear in changeable forms.

Thus the will of every man has an empirical character, which is nothing but a certain causality of his reason, so far as that causality exhibits, in its effects in the [field of] appearance, a rule from which we may gather what, in their kind and degrees, are the actions of reason and the grounds thereof, and so may form an estimate concerning the subjective principles of his will. Since this empirical character must itself be discovered from the appearances which are its effect and from the rule to which experience shows them to conform, it follows that all the actions of men in the [field of] appearance are determined in conformity with the order of nature, by their empirical character and by the other causes which cooperate with that character; and if we could exhaustively investigate all the appearances of men's wills, there would not be found a single human action which we could not predict with certainty, and recognise as proceeding necessarily from its antecedent conditions. So far, then, as regards this empirical character there is no freedom; and yet it is only in the light of this character that man can be studied—if, that is to say, we are simply *observing*, and in the manner of anthropology seeking to institute a physiological investigation into the motive causes of his actions.

But when we consider these actions in their relation to reason—I do not mean speculative reason, by which we endeavour *to explain* their coming into being, but reason in so far as it is itself the cause *producing* them—if, that is to say, we compare them with [the standards of] reason in its *practical* bearing, we find a rule and order altogether different from the order of nature. For it may be that all that *has happened* in the course of nature, and in accordance with its empirical grounds must inevitably have happened, *ought not to have happened*. Sometimes, however, we find, or at least believe that we find, that the ideas of reason have in actual fact proved their causality in respect of the actions of men, as appearances; and that these actions have taken place, not because they were determined by empirical causes, but because they were determined by grounds of reason.

Granted, then, that reason may be asserted to have causality in respect of appearance, its action can still be said to be free, even although its empirical character (as a mode of sense) is completely and necessarily determined in all its detail.[1] . . . Pure reason, as a purely intelligible faculty, is not subject to the form of time, nor consequently to the conditions of succession in time. The causality of reason in its intelligible character does not, in producing an effect, *arise* or begin to be at a certain time. For in that case it would itself be subject to the natural law of appearances, in accordance with which causal series are determined in time; and its causality would then be nature, not freedom. Thus all that we are justified in saying is that, if reason can have causality in respect of appearances, it is a faculty *through* which the sensible condition of an empirical series of effects first begins. For the condition which lies in reason is not sensible, and therefore does not itself begin to be. And thus what we failed to find in any empirical series is disclosed as being possible, namely, that the condition of a successive series of events may itself be empirically unconditioned. For here the condition is *outside* the series of appearances (in the intelligible), and therefore is not subject to any sensible condition, and to no time-determination through an antecedent cause.

The same cause does, indeed, in another relation, belong to the series of appearances. Man is himself an appearance. His will has an empirical character, which is the empirical cause of all his actions. There is no condition determining man in accordance with this character which is not contained in the series of natural effects, or which is not subject to their law—the law according to which there can be no empirically unconditioned causality of that which happens in time. Therefore no given action (since it can be perceived only as appearance) can begin absolutely of itself. But of pure reason we cannot say that the state wherein the will is determined is preceded and itself determined by some other state. For since reason is not itself an appearance, and is not subject to any conditions of sensibility, it follows that even as regards its causality there is in it no time-sequence, and that the dynamical law of nature, which determines succession in time in accordance with rules, is not applicable to it.

Reason is the abiding condition of all those actions of the will under [the guise of] which man appears. Before ever they have happened, they are one and all predetermined in the empirical character. In respect of the intelligible character, of which the empirical character is the sensible schema, there can be no *before* and *after*; every action, irrespective of its relation in time to other appearances, is the immediate effect of the intelligible character of pure reason. Reason therefore acts freely; it is not dynamically determined in the chain of natural causes through

[1] The real morality of actions, their merit or guilt, even that of our own conduct, thus remains entirely hidden from us. Our imputations can refer only to the empirical character. How much of this character is ascribable to the pure effect of freedom, how much to mere nature, that is, to faults of temperament for which there is no responsibility, or to its happy constitution (*merito fortunae*), can never be determined; and upon it therefore no perfectly just judgments can be passed.

either outer or inner grounds antecedent in time. This freedom ought not, therefore, to be conceived only negatively as independence of empirical conditions. The faculty of reason, so regarded, would cease to be a cause of appearances. It must also be described in positive terms, as the power of originating a series of events. In reason itself nothing begins; as unconditioned condition of every voluntary act, it admits of no conditions antecedent to itself in time. Its effect has, indeed, a beginning in the series of appearances, but never in this series an absolutely first beginning.

In order to illustrate this regulative principle of reason by an example of its empirical employment—not, however, to confirm it, for it is useless to endeavour to prove transcendental propositions by examples—let us take a voluntary action, for example, a malicious lie by which a certain confusion has been caused in society. First of all, we endeavour to discover the motives to which it has been due, and then, secondly, in the light of these, we proceed to determine how far the action and its consequences can be imputed to the offender. As regards the first question, we trace the empirical character of the action to its sources, finding these in defective education, bad company, in part also in the viciousness of a natural disposition insensitive to shame, in levity and thoughtlessness, not neglecting to take into account also the occasional causes that may have intervened. We proceed in this enquiry just as we should in ascertaining for a given natural effect the series of its determining causes. But although we believe that the action is thus determined, we none the less blame the agent, not indeed on account of his unhappy disposition, nor on account of the circumstances that have influenced him, nor even on account of his previous way of life; for we presuppose that we can leave out of consideration what this way of life may have been, that we can regard the past series of conditions as not having occurred and the act as being completely unconditioned by any preceding state, just as if the agent in and by himself began in this action an entirely new series of consequences. Our blame is based on a law of reason whereby we regard reason as a cause that irrespective of all the above-mentioned empirical conditions could have determined, and ought to have determined, the agent to act otherwise. This causality of reason we do not regard as only a co-operating agency, but as complete in itself, even when the sensuous impulses do not favour but are directly opposed to it; the action is ascribed to the agent's intelligible character; in the moment when he utters the lie, the guilt is entirely his. Reason, irrespective of all empirical conditions of the act, is completely free, and the lie is entirely due to its default.

Such imputation clearly shows that we consider reason to be unaffected by these sensible influences, and not liable to alteration. Its appearances—the modes in which it manifests itself in its effects—do alter; but in itself [so we consider] there is no preceding state determining the state that follows. That is to say, it does not belong to the series of sensible conditions which render appearances necessary in accordance with laws of nature. Reason is present in all the actions of men at all times and under all circumstances, and is always the same; but it is not itself in time, and does not fall into any new state in which it was not before. In respect to new states, it is *determining*, not *determinable*. We may not, therefore, ask why reason has not determined *itself* differently, but only why it has not through its causality determined the *appearances* differently. . . .

Thus in our judgements in regard to the causality of free actions, we can get as far as the intelligible cause, but not beyond it. We can know that it is free, that is, that it is determined independently of sensibility, and that in this way it may be the sensibly unconditioned condition of appearances. But to explain why in the given circumstances the intelligible character should give just these appearances and this empirical character transcends all the powers of our reason, indeed all its rights of questioning, just as if we were to ask why the transcendental object of our outer sensible intuition gives intuition in *space* only and not some other mode of intuition. But the problem which we have to solve does not require us to raise any such questions. Our problem was this only: whether freedom and natural necessity can exist without conflict on one and the same action; and this we have sufficiently answered. We have shown that since freedom may stand in relation to a quite different kind of conditions from those of natural necessity, the law of the latter does not affect the former, and that both may exist, independently of one another and without interfering with each other.

The Natural Determinism of Man
Baron Holbach

Baron Holbach (1723-1789) was the most outspoken materialist during the Enlightenment. In addition to contributing to Diderot's *Encyclopedia*, he wrote *The System of Nature* (1770) and *Good Sense* (1772).

Man is a being purely physical; in whatever manner he is considered, he is connected to universal nature, and submitted to the necessary and immutable laws that she imposes on all the beings she contains, according to their peculiar essences or to the respective properties with which, without consulting them, she endows each particular species. Man's life is a line that nature commands him to describe upon the surface of the earth, without his ever being able to swerve from it, even for an instant. He is born without his own consent; his organization does in nowise depend upon himself; his ideas come to him involuntarily; his habits are in the power of those who cause him to contract them; he is unceasingly modified by causes, whether visible or concealed, over which he has no control, which necessarily regulate his mode of existence, give the hue to his way of thinking, and determine his manner of acting. He is good or bad, happy or miserable, wise or foolish, reasonable or irrational, without his will being for any thing in these various states. Nevertheless, in despite of the shackles by which he is bound, it is pretended he is a free agent, or that independent of the causes by which he is moved, he determines his own will, and regulates his own condition.

However slender the foundation of this opinion, of which every thing ought to point out to him the error, it is current at this day and passes for an incontestable

Source: The System of Nature, Vol. 1, Chapter 11, H. D. Robinson, trans. (1853).

truth with a great number of people, otherwise extremely enlightened; it is the basis of religion, which, supposing relations between man and the unknown being she has placed above nature, has been incapable of imagining how man could either merit reward or deserve punishment from this being, if he was not a free agent. Society has been believed interested in this system; because an idea has gone abroad, that if all the actions of man were to be contemplated as necessary, the right of punishing those who injure their associates would no longer exist. At length human vanity accommodated itself to a hypothesis which, unquestionably, appears to distinguish man from all other physical beings, by assigning to him the special privilege of a total independence of all other causes, but of which a very little reflection would have shown him the impossibility.

As a part subordinate to the great whole, man is obliged to experience its influence. To be a free agent, it were needful that each individual was of greater strength than the entire of nature; or that he was out of this nature, who, always in action herself, obliges all the beings she embraces to act, and to concur to her general motion. . . .

The will . . . is a modification of the brain, by which it is disposed to action, or prepared to give play to the organs. This will is necessarily determined by the qualities, good or bad, agreeable or painful, of the object or the motive that acts upon [man's] senses, or of which the idea remains with him, and is resuscitated by his memory. In consequence, he acts necessarily, his action is the result of the impulse he receives either from the motive, from the object, or from the idea which has modified his brain, or disposed his will. When he does not act according to this impulse, it is because there comes some new cause, some new motive, some new idea, which modifies his brain in a different manner, gives him a new impulse, determines his will in another way, by which the action of the former impulse is suspended: thus, the sight of an agreeable object, or its idea, determines his will to set him in action to procure it; but if a new object or a new idea more powerfully attracts him, it gives a new direction to his will, annihilates the effect of the former, and prevents the action by which it was to be procured. This is the mode in which reflection, experience, reason, necessarily arrests or suspends the action of man's will: without this he would of necessity have followed the anterior impulse which carried him towards a then desirable object. In all this he always acts according to necessary laws, from which he has no means of emancipating himself.

If when tormented with violent thirst, he figures to himself an idea, or really perceives a fountain, whose limpid streams might cool his feverish want, is he sufficient master of himself to desire or not to desire the object competent to satisfy so lively a want? It will no doubt be conceded, that it is impossible he should not be desirous to satisfy it; but it will be said—if at this moment it is announced to him that the water he so ardently desires is poisoned, he will, notwithstanding his vehement thirst, abstain from drinking it: and it has, therefore, been falsely concluded that he is a free agent. The fact, however, is that the motive in either case is exactly the same: his own conservation. The same necessity that determined him to drink before he knew the water was deleterious, upon this new discovery equally determined him not to drink; the desire of conserving himself either annihilates or responds the former impulse; the second motive becomes stronger than the preceding, that is, the fear of death, or the desire of preserving himself, necessarily prevails over the painful sensation caused by his eagerness to drink: but, it will be said, if the thirst is very parching, an inconsiderate man without regarding the danger will risk swallowing the water. Nothing is gained by this remark: in this case, the anterior impulse only regains the ascendency; he is persuaded that life may possibly be longer preserved, or that he shall derive a greater good by drinking the poisoned water than by enduring the torment, which, to his mind, threatens instant dissolution: thus the first becomes the strongest and necessarily urges him on to action. Nevertheless, in either case, whether he partakes of the water, or whether he does not, the two actions will be equally necessary; they will be the effect of that motive which finds itself most puissant; which consequently acts in the most coercive manner upon his will.

This example will serve to explain the whole phenomena of the human will. This will, or rather the brain, finds itself in the same situation as a bowl, which, although it has received an impulse that drives it forward in a straight line, is deranged in its course whenever a force superior to the first obliges it to change its direction. The man who drinks the poisoned water appears a madman; but the actions of fools are as necessary as those of the most prudent individuals. The motives that determine the voluptuary and the debauchee to risk their health, are as powerful, and their actions are as necessary, as those which decide the wise man to manage his. But, it will be insisted, the debauchee may be prevailed on to change his conduct: this does not imply that he is a free agent; but that motives may be found sufficiently powerful to annihilate the effect of those that previously acted upon him; then these new motives determine his will to the new mode of conduct he may adopt as necessarily as the former did to the old mode. . . .

Choice by no means proves the free agency of man: he only deliberates when he does not yet know which to choose of the many objects that move him, he is then in an embarrassment, which does not terminate until his will is decided by the greater advantage he believes he shall find in the object he chooses, or the action he undertakes. From whence it may be seen, that choice is necessary, because he would not determine for an object, or for an action, if he did not believe that he should find in it some direct advantage. That man should have free agency it were needful that he should be able to will or choose without motive, or that he could prevent motives coercing his will. Action always being the effect of his will once determined, and as his will cannot be determined but by a motive which is not in his own power, it follows that he is never the master of the determination of his own peculiar will; that consequently he never acts as a free agent. It has been believed that man was a free agent because he had a will with the power of choosing; but attention has not been paid to the fact that even his will is moved by causes independent of himself; is owing to that which is inherent in his own organization, or which belongs to the nature of the beings acting on him.[1] Is he the master of willing not to withdraw his hand from the fire when he fears it will be burnt? Or has he the power to take away from fire the property which makes him fear it? Is he the master of not choosing a dish of meat, which he knows to be

---

[1] Man passes a great portion of his life without even willing. His will depends on the motive by which he is determined. If he were to render an exact account of every thing he does in the course of each day—from rising in the morning to lying down at night—he would find that not one of his actions have been in the least voluntary; that they have been mechanical, habitual, determined by causes he was not able to foresee; to which he was either obliged to yield, or with which he was allured to acquiesce: he would discover, that all the motives of his labours, of his amusements, of his discourses, of his thoughts, have been necessary; that they have evidently either seduced him or drawn him along.

agreeable, or analogous to his palate; of not preferring it to that which he knows to be disagreeable or dangerous? It is always according to his sensations, to his own peculiar experience, or to his suppositions, that he judges of things, either well or ill; but whatever may be his judgment, it depends necessarily on his mode of feeling, whether habitual or accidental, and the qualities he finds in the causes that move him, which exist in spite of himself. . . .

In despite of these proofs of the want of free agency in man, so clear to unprejudiced minds, it will, perhaps, be insisted upon with no small feeling of triumph, that if it be proposed to any one, to move or not to move his hand, an action in the number of those called *indifferent*, he evidently appears to be the master of choosing; from which it is concluded that evidence has been offered of his free agency. The reply is, this example is perfectly simple; man in performing some action which he is resolved on doing, does not by any means prove his free agency: the very desire of displaying this quality, excited by the dispute, becomes a necessary motive, which decides his will either for the one or the other of these actions: what deludes him in this instance, or that which persuades him he is a free agent at this moment, is, that he does not discern the true motive which sets him in action, namely, the desire of convincing his opponent: if in the heat of the dispute he insists and asks, "Am I not the master of throwing myself out of the window?" I shall answer him, no; that whilst he preserves his reason there is no probability that the desire of proving his free agency, will become a motive sufficiently powerful to make him sacrifice his life to the attempt: if, notwithstanding this, to prove he is a free agent, he should actually precipitate himself from the window, it would not be a sufficient warranty to conclude he acted freely, but rather that it was the violence of his temperament which spurred him on to his folly. Madness is a state, that depends upon the heat of the blood, not upon the will. A fanatic or a hero, braves death as necessarily as a more phlegmatic man or a coward flies from it.[2] . . .

To be undeceived on the system of his free agency, man has simply to recur to the motive by which his will is determined; he will always find this motive is out of his own control. It is said: that in consequence of an idea to which the mind gives birth, man acts freely if he encounters no obstacle. But the question is, what gives birth to this idea in his brain? was he the master either to prevent it from presenting itself, or from renewing itself in his brain? Does not this idea depend either upon objects that strike him exteriorly and in despite of himself, or upon causes, that without his knowledge, act within himself and modify his brain? Can he prevent his eyes, cast without design upon any object whatever, from giving him an idea of this object, and from moving his brain? He is not more master of the obstacles; they are the necessary effects of either interior or exterior causes, which always act according to their given properties. A man insults a coward, this necessarily irritates him against his insulter, but his will cannot vanquish the obstacle that cowardice places to the object of his desire, because his natural conformation, which does not

[2] There is, in point of fact, no difference between the man that is cast out of the window by another, and the man who throws himself out of it, except that the impulse in the first instance comes immediately from without, whilst that which determines the fall in the second case, springs from within his own peculiar machine, having its more remote case also exterior. When Mucius Scaevola held his hand in the fire, he was as much acting under the influence of necessity (caused by interior motives) that urged him to this strange action, as if his arm had been held by strong men: pride, despair, the desire of braving his enemy, a wish to astonish him, an anxiety to intimidate him, etc., were the invisible chains that held his hand bound to the fire. . . .

depend upon himself, prevents his having courage. In this case, the coward is insulted in despite of himself; and against his will is obliged patiently to brook the insult he has received.

The partisans of the system of free agency appear ever to have confounded constraint with necessity. Man believes he acts as a free agent, every time he does not see any thing that places obstacles to his actions; he does not perceive that the motive which causes him to will, is always necessary and independent of himself. A prisoner loaded with chains is compelled to remain in prison; but he is not a free agent in the desire to emancipate himself; his chains prevent him from acting, but they do not prevent him from willing; he would save himself if they would loose his fetters; but he would not save himself as a free agent; fear or the idea of punishment would be sufficient motives for his action.

Man may, therefore, cease to be restrained, without, for that reason, becoming a free agent: in whatever manner he acts, he will act necessarily, according to motives by which he shall be determined. He may be compared to a heavy body that finds itself arrested in its descent by any obstacle what ever: take away this obstacle, it will gravitate or continue to fall; but who shall say this dense body is free to fall or not? Is not its descent the necessary effect of its own specific gravity? The virtuous Socrates submitted to the laws of his country, although they were unjust; and though the doors of his jail were left open to him, he would not save himself; but in this he did not act as a free agent; the invisible chains of opinion, the secret love of decorum, the inward respect for the laws, even when they were iniquitous, the fear of tarnishing his glory, kept him in his prison; they were motives sufficiently powerful with this enthusiast for virtue, to induce him to wait death with tranquility; it was not in his power to save himself, because he could find no potential motive to bring him to depart, even for an instant, from those principles to which his mind was accustomed.

Man, it is said, frequently acts against his inclination, from whence it is falsely concluded he is a free agent; but when he appears to act contrary to his inclination, he is always determined to it by some motive sufficiently efficacious to vanquish this inclination. A sick man, with a view to his cure, arrives at conquering his repugnance to the most disgusting remedies: the fear of pain, or the dread of death, then becomes necessary motives; consequently this sick man cannot be said to act freely.

When it is said, that man is not a free agent, it is not pretended to compare him to a body moved by a simple impulsive cause: he contains within himself causes inherent to his existence; he is moved by an interior organ, which has its own peculiar laws, and is itself necessarily determined in consequence of ideas formed from perceptions resulting from sensations which it receives from exterior objects. As the mechanism of these sensations, of these perceptions, and the manner they engrave ideas on the brain of man, are not known to him; because he is unable to unravel all these motions; because he cannot perceive the chain of operations in his soul, or the motive principle that acts within him, he supposes himself a free agent; which, literally translated, signifies, that he moves himself by himself; that he determines himself without cause: when he rather ought to say, that he is ignorant how or for why he acts in the manner he does. It is true the soul enjoys an activity peculiar to itself: but it is equally certain that this activity would never be displayed, if some motive or some cause did not put it in a condition to exercise itself: at least it will not be pretended that the soul is able either to love or to hate without being moved, without knowing the objects, without having some idea of their qualities. Gunpowder has unquestionably a particular activity, but this activity will never display itself, unless fire be applied to it; this, however, immediately sets it in motion.

It is the great complication of motion in man, it is the variety of his action, it is the multiplicity of causes that move him, whether simultaneously or in continual succession, that persuades him he is a free agent: if all his motions were simple, if the causes that move him did not confound themselves with each other, if they were distinct, if his machine were less complicated, he would perceive that all his actions were necessary, because he would be enabled to recur instantly to the cause that made him act. A man who should be always obliged to go towards the west, would always go on that side; but he would feel that, in so going, he was not a free agent: if he had another sense, as his actions or his motion, augmented by a sixth, would be still more varied and much more complicated, he would believe himself still more a free agent than he does with his five senses.

It is, then, for want of recurring to the causes that move him; for want of being able to analyze, from not being competent to decompose the complicated motion of his machine, that man believes himself a free agent: it is only upon his own ignorance that he founds the profound yet deceitful notion he has of his free agency; that he builds those opinions which he brings forward as a striking proof of his pretended freedom of action. If, for a short time, each man was willing to examine his own peculiar actions, search out their true motives to discover their concatenation, he would remain convinced that the sentiment he has of his natural free agency, is a chimera that must speedily be destroyed by experience. . . .

Man either sees or believes he sees much more distinctly the necessary relation of effects with their causes in natural philosophy than in the human heart: at least he sees in the former sensible causes constantly produce sensible effects, ever the same, when the circumstances are alike. After this he hesitates not to look upon physical effects as necessary; whilst he refuses to acknowledge necessity in the acts of the human will: these he has, without any just foundation, attributed to a motive-power that acts independently by its own peculiar energy, which is capable of modifying itself without the concurrence of exterior causes, and which is distinguished from all material or physical beings. Agriculture is founded upon the assurance, afforded by experience, that the earth, cultivated and sown in a certain manner, when it has otherwise the requisite qualities, will furnish grain, fruit and flowers, either necessary for subsistence or pleasing to the senses. If things were considered without prejudice, it would be perceived, that in morals, education is nothing more than *the agriculture of the mind*: that, like the earth, by reason of its natural disposition, of the culture bestowed upon it, of the seeds with which it is sown, of the seasons, more or less favourable that conduct it to maturity, we may be assured that the soul will produce either virtue or vice—*moral fruit*, that will be either salubrious for man or baneful to society. *Morals* is the science of the relations that subsist between the minds, the wills, and the actions of men, in the same manner that geometry is the science of the relations that are found between bodies. Morals would be a chimera and would have no certain principles, if it was not founded upon the knowledge of the motives which must necessarily have an influence upon the human will, and which must necessarily determine the actions of human beings . . . .

In spite of the gratuitous ideas which man has formed to himself on his pretended free agency; in defiance of the illusions of this supposed intimate sense, which, maugre his experience, persuades him that he is master of his will; all his institutions are really founded upon necessity: on this, as on a variety of other occasions, practice throws aside speculation. Indeed, if it was not believed that certain motives embraced the power requisite to determine the will of man, to arrest the progress of his passions; to direct them towards an end, to modify him, of what use would be the faculty of speech? What benefit could arise from education, from legislation, from morals, even from religion itself? What does education achieve, save give the first impulse to the human will; make man contract habits; oblige him to persist in them; furnish him with motives, whether true or false, to act after a given manner? When the father either menaces his son with punishment, or promises him a reward, is he not convinced these things will act upon his will? What does legislation attempt except it be to present to the citizens of a state those motives which are supposed necessary to determine them to perform some actions that are considered worthy; to abstain from committing others that are looked upon as unworthy? What is the object of morals, if it be not to show man that his interest exacts he should suppress the momentary ebullition of his passions, with a view to promote a more certain happiness, a more lasting well-being, than can possibly result from the gratification of his transitory desires? Does not the religion of all countries suppose the human race, together with the entire of nature, submitted to the irresistible will of a necessary being who regulates their condition after the eternal laws of immutable wisdom? Is it not this divine being who chooses and who rejects? The anathemas fulminated by religion, the promises it holds forth, are they not founded upon the idea of the effects these chimeras will necessarily produce upon ignorant and timid people? Is not man brought into existence by this kind Divinity without his own knowledge? Is he not obliged to play a part against his will? Does not either his happiness or his misery depend on the part he plays?[3]

Education, then, is only necessity shown to children: legislation, is necessity shown to the members of the body politic: morals, is the necessity of the relations subsisting between men, shown to reasonable beings: in short, man grants necessity in every thing for which he believes he has certain unerring experience: that of which he does not comprehend the necessary connexion of causes with their effects he styles probability: he would not act as he does, if he was not convinced, or, at least, if he did not presume that certain effects will necessarily follow his actions. . . .

From all that has been advanced in this chapter, it results, that in no one moment of his existence is man a free agent. He is not the architect of his own conformation, which he holds from nature; he has no control over his own ideas, or

[3] Every religion is evidently founded upon fatalism. Among the Greeks they supposed men were punished for their *necessary* faults—as may be seen in Orestes, in Œdipus, etc., who only committed crimes predicted by the oracles. Christians have made vain efforts to justify God Almighty in throwing the faults of men on their *free will*, which is opposed to *Predestination*, another name for *fatalism*. However, their system of *Grace* will by no means obviate the difficulty, for God gives grace only to those whom he pleases. In all countries religion has no other foundation than the fatal decrees of an irresistible being who arbitrarily decides the fate of his creatures. All theological hypotheses turn upon this point; and yet those theologians who regard the system of fatalism as false or dangerous, do not see that the Fall of Angels, Original Sin, Predestination, the System of Grace, the small number of the Elect, etc., incontestably prove that religion is a true system of fatalism.

over the modification of his brain; these are due to causes, that, in despite of him, and without his own knowledge, unceasingly act upon him; he is not the master of not loving or coveting that which he finds amiable or desirable; he is not capable of refusing to deliberate, when he is uncertain of the effects certain objects will produce upon him; he cannot avoid choosing that which he believes will be most advantageous to him; in the moment when his will is determined by his choice he is not competent to act otherwise than he does. In what instance, then, is he the master of his own actions? In what moment is he a free agent?[4]

That which a man is about to do, is always a consequence of that which he has been—of that which he is—of that which he has done up to the moment of the action: his total and actual existence, considered under all its possible circumstances, contains the sum of all the motives to the action he is about to commit; this is a principle the truth of which no thinking being will be able to refuse accrediting: his life is a series of necessary moments; his conduct, whether good or bad, virtuous or vicious, useful or prejudicial, either to himself or to others, is a concatenation of action, as necessary as all the moments of his existence. To *live* is to exist in a necessary mode during the points of that duration which succeed each other necessarily; *to will* is to acquiesce or not in remaining such as he is; *to be free* is to yield to the necessary motives he carries within himself.

If he understood the play of his organs, if he was able to recall to himself all the impulsions they have received, all the modifications they have undergone, all the effects they have produced, he would perceive that all his actions are submitted to that *fatality*, which regulates his own particular system, as it does the entire system of the universe: no one effect in him, any more than in nature, produces itself by *chance;* this . . . is a word void of sense. All that passes in him; all that is done by him; as well as all that happens in nature, or that is attributed to her, is derived from necessary causes, which act according to necessary laws, and which produce necessary effects from whence necessarily flow others.

Fatality is the eternal, the immutable, the necessary order, established in nature; or the indispensable connexion of causes, that act, with the effects they operate. Conforming to this order, heavy bodies fall; light bodies rise; that which is analogous in matter reciprocally attracts; that which is heterogeneous mutually repels; man congregates himself in society, modifies each his fellow; becomes either virtuous or wicked; either contributes to his mutual happiness, or reciprocates his misery; either loves his neighbour, or hates his companion necessarily, according to the manner in which the one acts upon the other. From whence it may be seen,

---

[4] The question of *Free Will* may be reduced to this:—Liberty, or Free Will, cannot be associated with any known functions of the soul; for the soul, at the moment in which it acts, deliberates, or wills, cannot act, deliberate, or will otherwise than it does, because a thing cannot exist and not exist at the same time. Now, it is my will, such as it is, that makes me deliberate; my deliberation, that makes me choose; my choice that makes me act; my determination that makes me execute that which my deliberation has made me choose, and I have only deliberated because I have had motives which rendered it impossible for me not to be willing to deliberate. Thus liberty is not found either in the will, in the deliberation, in the choice, or in the action. Theologians must not, therefore, connect liberty with these operations of the soul, otherwise there will be a contradiction of ideas. If the soul is not free when it wills, deliberates, chooses, or acts, will theologians tell us when it can exercise its liberty?

It is evident that the system of liberty, or free will, has been invented to exonerate God from the evil that is done in this world. But is it not from God man received this liberty? Is it not from God he received the faculty of choosing evil and rejecting the good? If so, God created him with a determination to sin, else liberty is essential to man and independent of God.

that the same necessity which regulates the physical, also regulates the moral world, in which every thing is in consequence submitted to fatality. Man, in running over, frequently without his own knowledge, often in despite of himself, the route which nature has marked out for him, resembles a swimmer who is obliged to follow the current that carries him along: he believes himself a free agent, because he sometimes consents, sometimes does not consent, to glide with the stream, which, notwithstanding, always hurries him forward; he believes himself the master of his condition, because he is obliged to use his arms under the fear of sinking . . . .

The false ideas he has formed to himself upon free agency, are in general thus founded: there are certain events which he judges *necessary*; either because he sees that they are effects constantly and invariably linked to certain causes, which nothing seems to prevent; or because he believes he has discovered the chain of causes and effects that is put in play to produce those events: whilst he contemplates as *contingent* other events of whose causes he is ignorant, and with whose mode of acting he is unacquainted: but in nature, where every thing is connected by one common bond, there exists no effect without a cause. In the moral as well as in the physical world, every thing that happens is a necessary consequence of causes, either visible or concealed, which are of necessity obliged to act after their peculiar essences. *In man, free agency is nothing more than necessity contained within himself.*

The Natural Freedom of Man
C. Arthur Campbell

C. Arthur Campbell (1897-   ) is a professor emeritus at the University of Glasgow. He is the author of *Scepticism and Construction* (1939) and *Selfhood and Godhood* (1957).

The problem of free will gets its urgency for the ordinary educated man by reason of its close connection with the conception of moral responsibility. When we regard a man as morally responsible for an act, we regard him as a legitimate object of moral praise or blame in respect of it. But it seems plain that a man cannot be a legitimate object of moral praise or blame for an act unless in willing the act he is in some important sense a "free" agent. Evidently free will in some sense, therefore, is a precondition of moral responsibility. Without doubt it is the realisation that any threat to freedom is thus a threat to moral responsibility—with all that that implies—combined with the knowledge that there are a variety of considerations, philosophic, scientific, and theological, tending to place freedom in jeopardy, that gives to the problem of free will its perennial and universal appeal. And it is therefore in close connection with the question of the conditions of moral

Source: In Defence of Free Will (New York: Humanities Press, 1938). Reprinted by permission of Humanities Press, Inc. and George Allen & Unwin Ltd., publishers.

responsibility that any discussion of the problem must proceed, if it is not to be academic in the worst sense of the term.

We raise the question at once, therefore, what are the conditions, in respect of freedom, which must attach to an act in order to make it a morally responsible act? It seems to me that the fundamental conditions are two. . . .

The first condition is the universally recognised one that the act must be *self*-caused, *self*-determined. But it is important to accept this condition in its full rigour. The agent must be not merely *a* cause but the *sole* cause of that for which he is deemed morally responsible. If entities other than the self have also a causal influence upon an act, then that act is not one for which we can say without qualification that the *self* is morally responsible. If in respect of it we hold the self responsible at all, it can only be for some feature of the act—assuming the possibility of disengaging such a feature—of which the self *is* the sole cause. I do not see how this conclusion can be evaded. But it has awkward implications which have led not a few people to abandon the notion of individual moral responsibility altogether.

The first condition, however, is quite clearly not sufficient. It is possible to conceive an act of which the agent is the sole cause, but which is at the same time an act *necessitated* by the agent's nature. . . . In the case of such an act, where the agent could not do otherwise than he did, we must all agree, I think, that it would be inept to say that he *ought* to have done otherwise and is thus morally blameworthy, or *ought not* to have done otherwise and is thus morally praiseworthy. It is perfectly true that we do sometimes hold a person morally responsible for an act, even when we believe that he, being what he now is, virtually could not do otherwise. But underlying that judgement is always the assumption that the person has *come* to be what he now is in virtue of past acts of will in which he *was* confronted by real alternatives, by genuinely open possibilities: and, strictly speaking, it is in respect of these *past* acts of his that we praise or blame the agent *now*. For ultimate analysis, the agent's power of alternative action would seem to be an inexpugnable condition of his liability to moral praise or blame, i.e. of his moral responsibility.

We may lay down, therefore, that an act is a "free" act in the sense required for moral responsibility only if the agent (a) is the sole cause of the act; and (b) could exert his causality in alternative ways. . . . The doctrine which demands, and asserts, the fulfilment of both conditions is the doctrine we call "Libertarianism." . . .

And now, the conditions of free will being defined in these general terms, we have to ask whether human beings are in fact capable of performing free acts; and if so, where precisely such acts are to be found. In order to prepare the way for an answer, it is desirable, I think, that we should get clear at once about the significance of a certain very familiar, but none the less formidable, criticism of free will which . . . the Libertarian has to meet. This is the criticism which bases itself upon the facts of heredity on the one hand and of environment on the other. I may briefly summarise the criticism as follows.

Every historic self has an hereditary nature consisting of a group of inborn propensities, in range more or less common to the race, but specific to the individual in their respective strengths. With this equipment the self just *happens* to be born. Strictly speaking, it antedates the existence of the self proper, i.e. the existence of the self-conscious subject, and it is itself the effect of a series of causes leading back to indefinitely remote antiquity. It follows, therefore, that any of the self's choices that manifests the influence of his hereditary nature is not a choice of which *he*, the actual historic self, is the sole cause. The choice is determined, at least in part, by factors external to the self. The same thing holds good of "environment." Every self is born and bred in a particular physical and social environment, not of his own choosing, which plays upon him in innumerable ways, encouraging this propensity, discouraging that, and so on. Clearly any of the self's choices that manifests the influence of environmental factors is likewise a choice which is determined, at least in part, by factors external to the self. But if we thus grant, as seems inevitable, that heredity and environment are external influences, where shall we find a choice in the whole history of a self that is not subject to external influence? Surely we must admit that every particular act of choice bears the marks of the agent's hereditary nature and environmental nurture; in which case a free act, in the sense of an act determined solely by the self, must be dismissed as a mere chimaera. . . .

The externality of these influences is taken for granted in our reflective practical judgements upon persons. On those occasions when we are in real earnest about giving a critical and considered estimate of a man's moral caliber—as, e.g. in any serious biographical study—we impose upon ourselves as a matter of course the duty of enquiring with scrupulous care into his hereditary propensities and environmental circumstances, with a view to discovering how far his conduct is influenced by these factors. And having traced these influences, we certainly do not regard the result as having no bearing on the question of the man's moral responsibility for his conduct. On the contrary, the very purpose of the enquiry is to enable us, by due appreciation of the *external* influences that affect his conduct, to gain as accurate a view as possible of that which can justly be attributed to the man's own *self*-determination. The allowances that we all of us do in practice make for hereditary and environmental influences in passing judgement on our fellows would be meaningless if we did not suppose these influences to be in a real sense "external" to the self. . . .

We know now that condition (a) is not fulfilled by any act in respect of which inheritance or environment exerts a causal influence. For that type of influence has been shown to be in a real sense external to the self. The free act of which we are in search has therefore got to be one into which influences of this kind do not enter at all. . . .

. . . Our reflective practical judgements on persons, while fully recognising the externality of the influence of heredity and environment, do nevertheless presuppose throughout that there is *something* in conduct which is genuinely self-determined; something which the agent contributes solely on his own initiative, unaffected by external influences; something for which, accordingly, he may justly be held morally responsible. That conviction may, of course, be a false one. But the fact of its wide-spread existence can hardly be without significance for our problem.

Let us proceed, then, by following up this clue. Let us ask, why do human beings so obstinately persist in believing that there is an indissoluble core of purely *self*-originated activity which even heredity and environment are powerless to affect? There can be little doubt, I think, of the answer in general terms. They do so, at bottom, because they feel certain of the existence of such activity from their immediate practical experience of themselves. Nor can there be in the end much doubt, I think, in what function of the self that activity is to be located. There seems to me to be one, and only one, function of the self with respect to which the agent can even pretend to have an assurance of that absolute self-origination which is here at issue. But to render precise the nature of that function is obviously of quite paramount importance: and we can do so, I think, only by way of a somewhat thorough analysis—which I now propose to attempt—of the experiential situation in which it occurs, *viz*. the situation of "moral temptation."

It is characteristic of that situation that in it I am aware of an end A which I believe to be morally right, and also of an end B, incompatible with A, towards which, in virtue of that system of conative dispositions which constitutes my "character" as so far formed, I entertain a strong desire. There may be, and perhaps must be, desiring elements in my nature which are directed to A also. But what gives to the situation its specific character as one of moral temptation is that the urge of our desiring nature towards the right end, A, is felt to be *relatively* weak. We are sure that if our desiring nature is permitted to issue directly in action, it is end B that we shall choose. That is what is meant by saying, as William James does, that end B is "in the line of least resistance" relatively to our conative dispositions. The expression is, of course, a metaphorical one, but it serves to describe, graphically enough, a situation of which we all have frequent experience, *viz*. where we recognise a specific end as that towards which the "set" of our desiring nature most strongly inclines us, and which we shall indubitably choose if no inhibiting factor intervenes.

But inhibiting factors, we should most of us say, *may* intervene: and that in two totally different ways which it is vital to distinguish clearly. The inhibiting factor may be of the nature of another desire (or aversion), which operates by changing the balance of the desiring situation. Though at one stage I desire B, which I believe to be wrong, more strongly than I desire A, which I believe to be right, it may happen that before action is taken I become aware of certain hitherto undiscerned consequences of A which I strongly desire, and the result may be that now not B but A presents itself to me as the end in the line of least resistance. Moral temptation is here overcome by the simple process of ceasing to be a moral temptation.

That is one way, and probably by far the commoner way, in which an inhibiting factor intervenes. But it is certainly not regarded by the self who is confronted by moral temptation as the *only* way. In such situations we all believe, rightly or wrongly, that even although B *continues* to be in the line of least resistance, even although, in other words, the situation remains one with the characteristic marks of moral temptation, we *can* nevertheless align ourselves with A. We can do so, we believe, because we have the power to introduce a new energy, to make what we call an "effort of will," whereby we are able to act contrary to the felt balance of mere desire, and to achieve the higher end despite the fact that it continues to be in the line of greater resistance relatively to our desiring nature. The self in practice believes that it has this power; and believes, moreover, that the decision rests solely with its self, here and now, whether this power be exerted or not.

Now the objective validity or otherwise of this belief is not at the moment in question. I am here merely pointing to its existence as a psychological fact. No amount of introspective analysis, so far as I can see, even tends to disprove that we do as a matter of fact believe, in situations of moral temptation, that it rests with our self absolutely to decide whether we exert the effort of will which will enable us to rise to duty, or whether we shall allow our desiring nature to take its course.

I have now to point out, further, how this act of moral decision, at least in the significance which it has for the agent himself, fulfils in full the two conditions which we found it necessary to lay down at the beginning for the kind of "free" act which moral responsibility presupposes.

For obviously it is, in the first place, an act which the agent believes he could perform in alternative ways. He believes that it is genuinely open to him to put forth effort—in varying degrees, if the situation admits of that—or withhold it altogether. And when he *has* decided—in whatever way—he remains convinced that these alternative courses were really open to him.

It is perhaps a little less obvious, but, I think, equally certain, that the agent believes the second condition to be fulfilled likewise, i.e. that the act of decision is determined *solely* by his self. It appears less obvious, because we all realise that formed character has a great deal to do with the choices that we make; and formed character is, without a doubt, partly dependent on the external factors of heredity and environment. But is is crucial here that we should not misunderstand the precise nature of the influence which formed character brings to bear upon the choices that constitute conduct. No one denies that it determines, at least largely, what things we desire, and again how greatly we desire them. It may thus fairly be said to determine the felt balance of desires in the situation of moral temptation. But all that that amounts to is that formed character prescribes the nature of the situation *within* which the act of moral decision takes place. It does not in the least follow that it has any influence whatsoever in determining the act of decision itself—the decision as to whether we shall exert effort or take the easy course of following the bent of our desiring nature: take, that is to say, the course which, in virtue of the determining influence of our character as so far formed, we feel to be in the line of least resistance.

When one appreciates this, one is perhaps better prepared to recognise the fact that the agent himself in the situation of moral temptation does not, and indeed could not, regard his formed character as having any influence whatever upon his act of decision as such. For the very nature of that decision, as it presents itself to him, is as to whether he will or will not permit his formed character to dictate his action. In other words, the agent distinguishes sharply between the self which makes the decision, and the self which, as formed character, determines not the decision but the situation within which the decision takes place. Rightly or wrongly, the agent believes that through his act of decision he can oppose and transcend his own formed character in the interest of duty. We are therefore obliged to say, I think, that the agent *cannot* regard his formed character as in any sense a determinant of the act of decision as such. The act is felt to be a genuinely creative act, originated by the self *ad hoc*, and by the self alone. . . .

Now in considering the claim to truth of this belief of our practical consciousness, we should begin by noting that the onus of proof rests upon the critic who rejects this belief. Until cogent evidence to the contrary is adduced, we are entitled to put our trust in a belief which is so deeply embedded in our experience as practical beings as to be, I venture to say, ineradicable from it. Anyone who doubts whether it is ineradicable may be invited to think himself imaginatively into a situation of moral temptation as we have above described it, and then to ask himself whether in that situation he finds it possible to *disbelieve* that his act of decision has the characteristics in question. I have no misgivings about the answer. It is possible to disbelieve only when we are thinking abstractly about the situation; not when we are living through it, either actually or in imagination. This fact certainly establishes a strong *prima facie* presumption in favour of the Libertarian position. Nevertheless I agree that we shall have to weigh carefully several criticisms of high authority before we can feel justified in asserting free will as an ultimate and unqualified truth. . . .

I shall begin with one which, though it is a simple matter to show its irrelevance to the Libertarian doctrine as I have stated it, is so extremely popular that it cannot safely be ignored.

The charge made is that the Libertarian view is incompatible with the *predictability* of human conduct. For we do make rough predictions of people's conduct, on the basis of what we know of their character, every day of our lives, and there can be no doubt that the practice, within certain limits, is amply justified by results. Indeed if it were not so, social life would be reduced to sheer chaos. The close relationship between character and conduct which prediction postulates really seems to be about as certain as anything can be. But the Libertarian view, it is urged, by ascribing to the self a mysterious power of decision uncontrolled by character, and capable of issuing in acts inconsistent with character, denies that continuity between character and conduct upon which prediction depends. If Libertarianism is true, prediction is impossible. But prediction *is* possible, therefore Libertarianism is untrue.

My answer is that the Libertarian view is perfectly compatible with prediction within certain limits, and that there is no empirical evidence at all that prediction is in fact possible beyond these limits. The following considerations will, I think, make the point abundantly clear.

1. There is no question, on our view, of a free will that can will just anything at all. The range of possible choices is limited by the agent's character in every case; for nothing can be an object of possible choice which is not suggested by either the agent's desires or his moral ideals, and these depend on "character" for us just as much as for our opponents. We have, indeed, explicitly recognised at an earlier state that character determines the situation within which the act of moral decision takes place, although not the act of moral decision itself. This consideration obviously furnishes a broad basis for at least approximate predictions.

2. There is *one* experiential situation, and *one only*, on our view, in which there is any possibility of the act of will not being in accordance with character; *viz*. the situation in which the course which formed character prescribes is a course in conflict with the agent's moral ideal: in other words, the situation of moral temptation. Now this is a situation of comparative rarity. Yet with respect to all other situations in life we are in full agreement with those who hold that conduct is the response of the agent's formed character to the given situation. Why should it not be so? There could be no reason, on our view any more than on another, for the agent even to consider deviating from the course which his formed character prescribes and he most strongly desires, *unless* that course is believed by him to be incompatible with what is right.

3. Even within that one situation which is relevant to free will, our view can still recognise a certain basis for prediction. In that situation our character as so far formed prescribes a course opposed to duty, and an effort of will is required if we are to deviate from that course. But of course we are all aware that a greater effort of will is required in proportion to the degree in which we have to transcend our formed character in order to will the right. Such action is, as we say, "harder." But

if action is "harder" in proportion as it involves deviation from formed character, it seems reasonable to suppose that, on the whole, action will be of rarer occurrence in that same proportion: though perhaps we may not say that at any level of deviation it becomes flatly impossible. It follows that even with respect to situations of moral temptation we may usefully employ our knowledge of the agent's character as a clue to prediction. It will be a clue of limited, but of by no means negligible, value. It will warrant us in predicting, e.g., of a person who has become enslaved to alcohol, that he is unlikely, even if fully aware of the moral evil of such slavery, to be successful immediately and completely in throwing off its shackles. Predictions of this kind we all make often enough in practice. And there seems no reason at all why a Libertarian doctrine should wish to question their validity.

Now when these three considerations are borne in mind, it becomes quite clear that the doctrine we are defending is compatible with a very substantial measure of predictability indeed. And I submit that there is not a jot of empirical evidence that any larger measure than this obtains in fact.

Let us pass on then to consider a much more interesting and, I think, more plausible criticism. It is constantly objected against the Libertarian doctrine that it is fundamentally *unintelligible*. Libertarianism holds that the act of moral decision is the *self's* act, and yet insists at the same time that it is not influenced by any of those determinate features in the self's nature which go to constitute its "character." But, it is asked, do not these two propositions contradict one another? Surely a *self*-determination which is determination by something other than the self's *character* is a contradiction in terms? What meaning is there in the conception of a "self" in abstraction from its "character"? If you really wish to maintain, it is urged, that the act of decision is not determined by the self's character, you ought to admit frankly that it is not determined by the *self* at all. But in that case, of course, you will not be advocating a freedom which lends any kind of support to moral responsibility; indeed very much the reverse.

Now this criticism, and all of its kind, seem to me to be the product of a simple, but extraordinarily pervasive, error: the error of confining one's self to the categories of the external observer in dealing with the actions of human agents. Let me explain.

It is perfectly true that the stand-point of the external observer, which we are obliged to adopt in dealing with physical processes, does not furnish us with even a glimmering of a notion of what can be meant by an entity which acts causally and yet not through any of the determinate features of its character. So far as we confine ourselves to external observation, I agree that this notion must seem to us pure nonsense. But then we are *not* obliged to confine ourselves to external observation in dealing with the human agent. Here, though here alone, we have the inestimable advantage of being able to apprehend operations from the *inside*, from the stand-point of *living* experience. But if we do adopt this internal stand-point—surely a proper stand-point, and one which we should be only too glad to adopt if we could in the case of other entities—the situation is entirely changed. We find that we not merely can, but constantly do, attach meaning to a causation which is the self's causation but is yet not exercised by the self's character. We have seen as much already in our analysis of the situation of moral temptation. When confronted by such a situation, we saw, we are certain that it lies with our *self* to decide whether we shall let our character as so far formed dictate our action or whether we shall by effort oppose its dictates and rise to duty. We are certain, in other words, that the act is *not* determined by our *character*, while we remain equally certain that the act *is* determined by our *self*.

Or look, for a further illustration . . . to the experience of effortful willing itself, where the act of decision has found expression in the will to rise to duty. In such an experience we are certain that it is our self which makes the effort. But we are equally certain that the effort does not flow from that system of conative dispositions which we call our formed character; for the very function that the effort has for us is to enable us to act against the "line of least resistance," i.e. to act in a way *contrary* to that to which our formed character inclines us.

I conclude, therefore, that those who find the Libertarian doctrine of the self's causality in moral decision inherently unintelligible find it so simply because they restrict themselves, quite arbitrarily, to an inadequate stand-point: a stand-point from which, indeed, a genuinely creative activity, if it existed, never *could* be apprehended.

The Existential Man

Jean-Paul Sartre

Jean-Paul Sartre (1905-   ), French existentialist, was professor of philosophy at Lycée Condorcet from 1935 to 1942. A successful playwright and novelist as well as a philosopher, Sartre has given up teaching to devote his time to writing. His major works include *Being and Nothingness* (1943) and *Existentialism and Humanism* (1946).

What is meant by the term *existentialism?*

Most people who use the word would be rather embarrassed if they had to explain it, since, now that the word is all the rage, even the work of a musician or painter is being called existentialist. . . . It seems that for want of an advance-guard doctrine analogous to surrealism, the kind of people who are eager for scandal and flurry turn to this philosophy which in other respects does not at all serve their purposes in this sphere.

Actually, it is the least scandalous, the most austere of doctrines. It is intended strictly for specialists and philosophers. Yet it can be defined easily. What complicates matters is that there are two kinds of existentialists; first, those who are Christian, among whom I would include Jaspers and Gabriel Marcel, both Catholic; and on the other hand, the atheistic existentialists, among whom I class Heidegger, and then the French existentialists and myself. What they have in common is that they think that existence precedes essence, or, if you prefer, that subjectivity must be the starting point.

Source: Existentialism, translated by Bernard Frechtman (New York: Philosophical Library, Inc., 1947). Reprinted by permission of the Philosophical Library, Inc.

Just what does that mean? Let us consider some object that is manufactured, for example, a book or a paper-cutter: here is an object which has been made by an artisan whose inspiration came from a concept. He referred to the concept of what a paper-cutter is and likewise to a known method of production, which is part of the concept, something which is, by and large, a routine. Thus, the paper-cutter is at once an object produced in a certain way and, on the other hand, one having a specific use; and one cannot postulate a man who produces a paper-cutter but does not know what it is used for. Therefore, let us say that, for the paper-cutter, essence—that is, the ensemble of both the production routines and the properties which enable it to be both produced and defined—precedes existence. Thus, the presence of the paper-cutter or book in front of me is determined. Therefore, we have here a technical view of the world whereby it can be said that production precedes existence.

When we conceive God as the Creator, He is generally thought of as a superior sort of artisan. Whatever doctrine we may be considering, whether one like that of Descartes or that of Leibnitz, we always grant that will more or less follows understanding or, at the very least, accompanies it, and that when God creates He knows exactly what He is creating. Thus, the concept of man in the mind of God is comparable to the concept of paper-cutter in the mind of the manufacturer, and, following certain techniques and a conception, God produces man, just as the artisan, following a definition and a technique, makes a paper-cutter. Thus, the individual man is the realization of a certain concept in the divine intelligence.

In the eighteenth century, the atheism of the *philosophes* discarded the idea of God, but not so much for the notion that essence precedes existence. To a certain extent, this idea is found everywhere; we find it in Diderot, in Voltaire, and even in Kant. Man has a human nature; this human nature, which is the concept of the human, is found in all men, which means that each man is a particular example of a universal concept, man. In Kant, the result of this universality is that the wild-man, the natural man, as well as the bourgeois, are circumscribed by the same definition and have the same basic qualities. Thus, here too the essence of man precedes the historical existence that we find in nature.

Atheistic existentialism, which I represent, is more coherent. It states that if God does not exist, there is at least one being in whom existence precedes essence, a being who exists before he can be defined by any concept, and that this being is man, or, as Heidegger says, human reality. What is meant here by saying that existence precedes essence? It means that, first of all, man exists, turns up, appears on the scene, and, only afterwards, defines himself. If man, as the existentialist conceives him, is indefinable, it is because at first he is nothing. Only afterward will he be something, and he himself will have made what he will be. Thus, there is no human nature, since there is no God to conceive it. Not only is man what he conceives himself to be, but he is also only what he wills himself to be after this thrust toward existence.

Man is nothing else but what he makes of himself. Such is the first principle of existentialism. It is also what is called subjectivity, the name we are labeled with when charges are brought against us. But what do we mean by this, if not that man has a greater dignity than a stone or table? For we mean that man first exists, that is, that man first of all is the being in the future. Man is at the start a plan which is aware of itself, rather than a patch of moss, a piece of garbage, or a cauliflower; nothing exists prior to this plan; there is nothing in heaven; man will be what he will have planned to be. Not what he will want to be. Because by the word "will" we generally mean a conscious decision, which is subsequent to what we have already made of ourselves. I may want to belong to a political party, write a book, get married; but all that is only a manifestation of an earlier, more spontaneous choice that is called "will." But if existence really does precede essence, man is responsible for what he is. Thus, existentialism's first move is to make every man aware of what he is and to make the full responsibility of his existence rest on him. And when we say that a man is responsible for himself, we do not only mean that he is responsible for his own individuality, but that he is responsible for all men.

The word subjectivism has two meanings, and our opponents play on the two. Subjectivism means, on the one hand, that an individual chooses and makes himself; and, on the other, that it is impossible for man to transcend human subjectivity. The second of these is the essential meaning of existentialism. When we say that man chooses his own self, we mean that every one of us does likewise; but we also mean by that that in making this choice he also chooses all men. In fact, in creating the man that we want to be, there is not a single one of our acts which does not at the same time create an image of man as we think he ought to be. To choose to be this or that is to affirm at the same time the value of what we choose, because we can never choose evil. We always choose the good, and nothing can be good for us without being good for all.

If, on the other hand, existence precedes essence, and if we grant that we exist and fashion our image at one and the same time, the image is valid for everybody and for our whole age. Thus, our responsibility is much greater than we might have supposed, because it involves all mankind. If I am a workingman and choose to join a Christian trade-union rather than be a communist, and if by being a member I want to show that the best thing for man is resignation, that the kingdom of man is not of this world, I am not only involving my own case—I want to be resigned for everyone. As a result, my action has involved all humanity. To take a more individual matter, if I want to marry, to have children; even if this marriage depends solely on my own circumstances or passion or wish, I am involving all humanity in monogamy and not merely myself. Therefore, I am responsible for myself and for everyone else. I am creating a certain image of man of my own choosing. In choosing myself, I choose man.

This helps us understand what the actual content is of such rather grandiloquent words as anguish, forlornness, despair. As you will see, it's all quite simple.

First, what is meant by anguish? The existentialists say at once that man is anguish. What that means is this: the man who involves himself and who realizes that he is not only the person he chooses to be, but also a law-maker who is, at the same time, choosing all mankind as well as himself, cannot help escape the feeling of his total and deep responsibility. Of course, there are many people who are not anxious; but we claim that they are hiding their anxiety, that they are fleeing from it. Certainly, many people believe that when they do something, they themselves are the only ones involved, and when someone says to them, "What if everyone acted that way?" they shrug their shoulders and answer, "Everyone doesn't act that way." But really, one should always ask himself, "What would happen if everybody looked at things that way?" There is no escaping this disturbing thought except by a kind of double-dealing. A man who lies and makes excuses for himself by saying "not everybody does that," is someone with an uneasy conscience, because the act of lying implies that a universal value is conferred upon the lie.

Anguish is evident even when it conceals itself. This is the anguish that Kierkegaard called the anguish of Abraham. You know the story: an angel has ordered Abraham to sacrifice his son; if it really were an angel who has come and said, "You are Abraham, you shall sacrifice your son," everything would be all right. But everyone might first wonder, "Is it really an angel, and am I really Abraham? What proof do I have?" . . .

Now, I'm not being singled out as an Abraham, and yet at every moment I'm obliged to perform exemplary acts. For every man, everything happens as if all mankind had its eyes fixed on him and were guiding itself by what he does. And every man ought to say to himself, "Am I really the kind of man who has the right to act in such a way that humanity might guide itself by my actions?" And if he does not say that to himself, he is masking his anguish.

There is no question here of the kind of anguish which would lead to quietism, to inaction. It is a matter of a simple sort of anguish that anybody who has had responsibilities is familiar with. For example, when a military officer takes the responsibility for an attack and sends a certain number of men to death, he chooses to do so, and in the main he alone makes the choice. Doubtless, orders come from above, but they are too broad; he interprets them, and on this interpretation depend the lives of ten or fourteen or twenty men. In making a decision he cannot help having a certain anguish. All leaders know this anguish. That doesn't keep them from acting; on the contrary, it is the very condition of their action. For it implies that they envisage a number of possibilities, and when they choose one, they realize that it has value only because it is chosen. We shall see that this kind of anguish, which is the kind that existentialism describes, is explained, in addition, by a direct responsibility to the other men whom it involves. It is not a curtain separating us from action, but is part of action itself.

When we speak of forlornness, a term Heidegger was fond of, we mean only that God does not exist and that we have to face all the consequences of this. The existentialist is strongly opposed to a certain kind of secular ethics which would like to abolish God with the least possible expense. About 1880, some French teachers tried to set up a secular ethics which went something like this: God is a useless and costly hypothesis; we are discarding it; but meanwhile, in order for there to be an ethics, a society, a civilization, it is essential that certain values be taken seriously and that they be considered as having an *a priori* existence. It must be obligatory, *a priori*, to be honest, not to lie, not to beat your wife, to have children, etc., etc. So we're going to try a little device which will make it possible to show that values exist all the same, inscribed in a heaven of ideas, though otherwise God does not exist. In other words—and this, I believe, is the tendency of everything called reformism in France—nothing will be changed if God does not exist. We shall find ourselves with the same norms of honesty, progress, and humanism, and we shall have made of God an outdated hypothesis which will peacefully die off by itself.

The existentialist, on the contrary, thinks it very distressing that God does not exist, because all possibility of finding values in a heaven of ideas disappears along with Him; there can be no longer an *a priori* Good, since there is no infinite and perfect consciousness to think it. Nowhere is it written that the Good exists, that we must be honest, that we must not lie; because the fact is we are on a plane where there are only men. Dostoievsky said, "If God didn't exist, everything would be possible." That is the very starting point of existentialism. Indeed, everything is permissible if God does not exist, and as a result man is forlorn, because neither within him nor without does he find anything to cling to. He can't start making excuses for himself.

If existence really does precede essence, there is no explaining things away by reference to a fixed and given human nature. In other words, there is no determinism, man is free, man is freedom. On the other hand, if God does not exist, we find no values or commands to turn to which legitimize our conduct. So, in the bright realm of values, we have no excuse behind us, no justification before us. We are alone, with no excuses.

That is the idea I shall try to convey when I say that man is condemned to be free. Condemned, because he did not create himself, yet, in other respects is free; because, once thrown into the world, he is responsible for everything he does. The existentialist does not believe in the power of passion. He will never agree that a sweeping passion is a ravaging torrent which fatally leads a man to certain acts and is therefore an excuse. He thinks that man is responsible for his passion.

The existentialist does not think that man is going to help himself by finding in the world some omen by which to orient himself. Because he thinks that man will interpret the omen to suit himself. Therefore, he thinks that man, with no support and no aid, is condemned every moment to invent man. Ponge, in a very fine article, has said, "Man is the future of man." That's exactly it. But if it is taken to mean that this future is recorded in heaven, that God sees it, then it is false, because it would really no longer be a future. If it is taken to mean that, whatever a man may be, there is a future to be forged, a virgin future before him, then this remark is sound. But then we are forlorn.

To give you an example which will enable you to understand forlornness better, I shall cite the case of one of my students who came to see me under the following circumstances: his father was on bad terms with his mother, and, moreover, was inclined to be a collaborationist; his older brother had been killed in the German offensive of 1940, and the young man, with somewhat immature but generous feelings, wanted to avenge him. His mother lived alone with him, very much upset by the half-treason of her husband and the death of her older son; the boy was her only consolation.

The boy was faced with the choice of leaving for England and joining the Free French Forces—that is, leaving his mother behind—or remaining with his mother and helping her to carry on. He was fully aware that the woman lived only for him and that his going-off—and perhaps his death—would plunge her into despair. He was also aware that every act that he did for his mother's sake was a sure thing, in the sense that it was helping her to carry on, whereas every effort he made toward going off and fighting was an uncertain move which might run aground and prove completely useless; for example, on his way to England he might, while passing through Spain, be detained indefinitely in a Spanish camp; he might reach England or Algiers and be stuck in an office at a desk job. As a result, he was faced with two very different kinds of action: one, concrete, immediate, but concerning only one individual; the other concerned an incomparably vaster group, a national collectivity, but for that very reason was dubious, and might be interrupted en route. And, at the same time, he was wavering between two kinds of ethics. On the one hand, an ethics of sympathy, of personal devotion; on the other, a broader ethics, but one whose efficacy was more dubious. He had to choose between the two.

Who could help him choose? Christian doctrine? No. Christian doctrine says, "Be charitable, love your neighbor, take the more rugged path, etc., etc." But which is the more rugged path? Whom should he love as a brother? The fighting man or his mother? Which does the greater good, the vague act of fighting in a group, or the concrete one of helping a particular human being to go on living? Who can decide *a priori*? Nobody. No book of ethics can tell him. The Kantian ethics says, "Never treat any person as a means, but as an end." Very well, if I stay with my mother, I'll treat her as an end and not as a means; but by virtue of this very fact, I'm running the risk of treating the people around me who are fighting, as means; and, conversely, if I go to join those who are fighting, I'll be treating them as an end, and, by doing that, I run the risk of treating my mother as a means.

If values are vague, and if they are always too broad for the concrete and specific case that we are considering, the only thing left for us is to trust our instincts. That's what this young man tried to do; and when I saw him, he said, "In the end, feeling is what counts. I ought to choose whichever pushes me in one direction. If I feel that I love my mother enough to sacrifice everything else for her—my desire for vengeance, for action, for adventure—then I'll stay with her. If, on the contrary, I feel that my love for my mother isn't enough, I'll leave."

But how is the value of a feeling determined. What gives his feeling for his mother value? Precisely the fact that he remained with her. I may say that I like so-and-so well enough to sacrifice a certain amount of money for him, but I may say so only if I've done it. I may say, "I love my mother well enough to remain with her" if I have remained with her. The only way to determine the value of this affection is, precisely, to perform an act which confirms and defines it. But, since I require this affection to justify my act, I find myself caught in a vicious circle. . . .

As for despair, the term has a very simple meaning. It means that we shall confine ourselves to reckoning only with what depends upon our will, or on the ensemble of probabilities which make our action possible. When we want something, we always have to reckon with probabilities. I may be counting on the arrival of a friend. The friend is coming by rail or street-car; this supposes that the train will arrive on schedule, or that the street-car will not jump the track. I am left in the realm of possibility; but possibilities are to be reckoned with only to the point where my action comports with the ensemble of these possibilities, and no further. The moment the possibilities I am considering are not rigorously involved by my action, I ought to disengage myself from them, because no God, no scheme, can adapt the world and its possibilities to my will. When Descartes said, "Conquer yourself rather than the world," he meant essentially the same thing.

The Marxists to whom I have spoken reply, "You can rely on the support of others in your action, which obviously has certain limits because you're not going to live forever. That means: rely on both what others are doing elsewhere to help you, in China, in Russia, and what they will do later on, after your death, to carry on the action and lead it to its fulfillment, which will be the revolution. You even *have* to rely upon that, otherwise you're immoral." I reply at once that I will always rely on fellow fighters insofar as these comrades are involved with me in a common struggle, in the unity of a party or a group in which I can more or less make my weight felt; that is, one whose ranks I am in as a fighter and whose movements I am aware of at every moment. In such a situation, relying on the unity and will of the party is exactly like counting on the fact that the train will arrive on time or that the car won't jump the track. But, given that man is free and that there is no human nature for me to depend on, I cannot count on men whom I do not know by relying on human goodness or man's concern for the good of society. I don't know what will become of the Russian revolution; I may make an example of it to the extent that at the present time it is apparent that the proletariat plays a part in Russia that it plays in no other nation. But I can't swear that this will inevitably lead to a triumph of the proletariat. I've got to limit myself to what I see.

Given that men are free, and that tomorrow they will freely decide what man will be, I cannot be sure that, after my death, fellow fighters will carry on my work to bring it to its maximum perfection. Tomorrow, after my death, some men may decide to set up Fascism, and the others may be cowardly and muddled enough to let them do it. Fascism will then be the human reality, so much the worse for us.

Actually, things will be as man will have decided they are to be. Does that mean that I should abandon myself to quietism? No. First, I should involve myself; then, act on the old saw, "Nothing ventured, nothing gained." Nor does it mean that I shouldn't belong to a party, but rather that I shall have no illusions and shall do what I can. For example, suppose I ask myself, "Will socialization, as such, ever come about?" I know nothing about it. All I know is that I'm going to do everything in my power to bring it about. Beyond that, I can't count on anything. Quietism is the attitude of people who say, "Let others do what I can't do." The doctrine I am presenting is the very opposite of quietism, since it declares, "There is no reality except in action." Moreover, it goes further, since it adds, "Man is nothing else than his plan; he exists only to the extent that he fulfills himself; he is, therefore, nothing else than the ensemble of his acts, nothing else than his life."

Suggested Readings

1. Ayer, A. J., "Freedom and Necessity," in *Philosophical Essays* (London: Macmillan & Co., Ltd., 1954), pp. 271-284.
2. Campbell, C. A., "Is 'Free Will' a Pseudo-Problem?" *Mind*, Vol. 60 (1951), 446-465.
3. Darrow, Clarence, *Plea in Defense of Loeb and Leopold* (Gerard, Kan.: Little Blue Books, 1926), pp. 40-43.
4. Desan, Wilfrid, *The Tragic Finale* (New York: Harper, 1960).
5. Lehrer, Keith, "Can We Know That We Have Free Will by Introspection?" *Journal of Philosophy*, Vol. 57 (1960), 145-157.
6. Wood, Ledger. "The Free-Will Controversy," *Philosophy*, Vol. 16 (1941), 396-397.

NINE

Philosophy and Theological Thought

Do we not smell the divine putrefaction?—for even Gods putrefy! God is dead! God remains dead! And we have killed him! How shall we console ourselves, the most murderous of all murderers?

—Friedrich Nietzsche

INTRODUCTION

Why is there such a thing as religion at all? What accounts for its longevity? And why does it even seem to be gaining ground in an age that is enlightened compared with former times? More particularly, why are Eastern religions being adopted in the West by growing numbers of people? Is it because God is dead in the West and gods are alive in the East?

But what have gods to do with religion? Would a set of doctrines or attitudes or a posture be religious if it excluded gods? It doesn't seem possible to answer these last two questions without first defining what religion is. And after all these years and all the unsatisfactory attempts at definition, it seems we must either regard the definers as ill-equipped for their job or suspect that not everything that has been called a religion is really a religion. This would account for the failure of definitions to capture the essence of every "religion." Or perhaps we should acknowledge that there is no specific set of characteristics that every religion has in common, there being only a family resemblance between them, religions bearing only a set of overlapping characteristics. Buddhism and Christianity do not share the characteristic of requiring a God for their religion, but they do have the overlapping characteristic of being concerned with men's sufferings. Very generally, but not very helpfully, every so-called religion is concerned about man's fate and in each the history of the cosmos is regarded to be intimately linked with man's fate.

Without pretense of finality, and starting with man, we will state, first, a traditional division of his faculties; and then we will isolate some of man's concerns that grow from the way that those faculties are affected by the cosmos, at least as they are claimed to be affected by some religious thinkers.

CONTEMPORARY

Man's faculties have in many traditions been divided into the cognitive, the affective, and the conative. Insofar as we strive to cognize (to know) the cosmos, its complexity and immensity in space and time defy, according to many religions, complete understanding. If man's fate is affected by the cosmos and if we lack complete understanding of the cosmos, we cannot avoid mysteries. If we wish to live with the hope of a good fate in the face of these mysteries, many advise us to put our faith in a religion that espouses the existence of a benevolent, all-powerful, all-knowing deity. This is one reason why people associate religion with belief in the existence of a god or gods with these properties. And if God were dead, would religion still reassure us, give us hope against our suffering, or find a means of burying our sins in an infinite body of holy goodness? **William Hamilton** addresses himself to these questions in this section's second essay.

Insofar as we have feelings (affective faculties), none of us has escaped nor expects to escape physical and mental suffering while he lives. Suffering seems unavoidable in the present cosmos. Once again, the cosmos' nature and history dictate part of man's fate. Again, if we prefer to live with hope yet face unavoidable suffering, religion may help us cope with this state by promising us a life that extends beyond our life span on earth: If we had an immortal soul, and if there were after bodily death a lodgment for our immortal soul devoid of suffering, wouldn't we live with renewed hope, anticipating an eternity in a heavenly cosmos? Not if our capacity for faith were weakened and if the existence of a heavenly cosmos seemed like a fairy tale told by a wishbone breaker. Then religion fails us, doesn't it? Perhaps that kind of religion, typical of the West, fails us, but there are other religions. In this section's first essay, **Jacob Needleman** points out that Eastern religions take a different approach to suffering. Instead of acknowledging the unavoidable grip of suffering, they advise abandoning the affective animal self and urge transformation to a higher self, one not bedeviled by our "partying" desires that bequeath us painful spiritual hangovers the morning after. Further, gurus know this transformation is difficult and they are prepared to help us learn such techniques of transformation as yoga. Religion may call us to a nobler self. In this connection Koller's, Royce's, and Fingarette's essays in Chapter Seven will be instructive.

Insofar as we strive to act (conative faculties) in the world, we are imperfect. We often do harm; we often act wrongly. This is not always because we lack knowledge but sometimes because we have an ill will. This is one of the central tenets of many Christian sects, that man is by nature evil, by nature he has a propensity to sin. Because it is inherent in man's nature to sin, evil acts are unavoidable. If we accept this diagnosis of man and suppose further that sin does not go unpunished in our cosmos and that this has an unwanted dampening effect on our zest for life, some would welcome a religious solution that restores that zest to us. This solution might come with assurance of the existence of a loving, merciful, forgiving deity who takes all one's sins upon Himself. But for those caught in a daily crush of evil and who need and seek immediate relief, such as the black community, revolution appears to be a more promising source of hope than a forgiving deity. In this section's third essay, **Major Jones** emphasizes a need for a theology of hope because he recognizes the conflict of revolution, its violence and killing, with a Christian ethic that enjoins us to love our neighbor rather than to destroy him. There is unfinished but urgent business there. Theologians' work is never done.

The Spiritual Revolution
Jacob Needleman

Jacob Needleman (1934-   ) teaches philosophy and comparative religion at San Francisco State College. His recent book, *The New Religions* (1970), is a report and analysis of the "spiritual revolution" among the new generation. He is also author of *Being-in-the-World* (1963), a critical study of existential psychoanalysis.

SUSPICIONS

I came to San Francisco in 1962, quite sure that I understood the place of religion in the history and psychology of man. Having been trained as a philosopher at the best New England universities, I was able to speak sympathetically about the depths of man's "religious imagination" while retaining what I felt was a "cold and critical eye" toward his need to deny his mortal nature as a creature of the earth. At the same time, some practical experience as a clinical psychologist had confirmed my belief that contemporary psychology in all its forms addressed itself only to a very small portion of the human psyche and that even there its "successes" were much smaller than it pretended them to be.

I had cast my lot with the existentialists. Man's real burden was an unlimited psychological freedom bound in some mysterious and ironic way to the limitations

Source: The New Religions (New York: Doubleday, 1970), pp. 1-21. Copyright © 1970 by Jacob Needleman. Reprinted by permission of Doubleday and Company, Inc.

of the body, death and the Other. Religion, at its deepest level as in the Old Testament and the Gospels was a demonstration of this freedom shared by all men, the freedom to choose oneself with passionate intensity against a universe that reason showed was indifferent and blind. As for modern religious forms, they had degenerated in an effort to take away all responsibility from man, to separate him from the truths of the body, to comfort him with fables, and to rob him of his ultimate possibility: action in the world.

My courses in philosophy and in the history of Western religion were explorations into these themes. I agreed with Bultmann and others of the New Theologians that once the mythology was excised from the Western Bible, it could be read as an overpowering emotional statement of the existentialist insight that man is alone and unique, his tragic greatness consisting in the fact that he can make no echo in the universe. Such words as immortality, higher life, faith or righteousness applied to the moment, *now,* and were a call for man to accept his total mortality and in accepting it to find his own destiny *in* himself and *for* himself. In reading these ideas into our Bible, I felt an immense sense of relief. I had never been entirely comfortable thinking of Jesus, Moses, St. Paul and others as irrelevant—or worse.

With the sole exception of Zen Buddhism, the religions of the East were anathema to me, as was what I confidently labeled "mysticism." All this talk about "merging into the All"! destroying the self! when man's essential task was to affirm and preserve his self and to increase his individuality. And all this talk about ineffable experiences, incomprehensible truths, going beyond the ordinary mind— that rankled. I was very suspicious of anyone who claimed to know something but was unable to express it. In sum, I thought of mysticism as simply bad poetry: the poetry of men too weak to accept the joys and sufferings of our earthly nature.

No one was more ready than I to denounce the natural-scientific view of man as reductionistic. But if science had reduced man to less than he was, the religions of the East inflated man to more than he was. Besides, wasn't there something "unholy" about these so-called holy men of the East? What had religion or spirituality to do with such things as *energy, psychological power, consciousness, astral bodies* and God knows what else? There was something demonic about all that. Life was too short to bother with this spiritual circus of the Hindus or Tibetans. The antidote was a good reading of Ecclesiastes or Isaiah, against which this Eastern lust for extraordinary powers showed itself for what it was: yet another pathetic attempt to escape the human condition.

THE LOSS OF THE COSMIC

I am no historian, but perhaps my point will come across more clearly if we recall that for the most part what we know as American religion has emanated directly from modern Europe. We are really very far in time, and perhaps in practice as well, from the Christianity of the early fathers and the medieval monastic communities, and from the Judaism of the great rabbinic followings in the Middle East and Islamic Spain. In Europe the scientific revolution destroyed the idea of a sacramental universe, and religion became a matter between man and God; science took care of the cosmos—and very quickly erased all concepts of mind and intelligent purpose from it. Only in the Eastern Orthodox Church does the idea still live that nature and the universe itself is involved in man's religious life and in his quest for self-perfection.

By eliminating the cosmos from man's relationship to God, the European came to emphasize more and more the ethical and even legal aspect of religion. Religious life became a matter of belief or performance; the question of man's *ableness* to believe or act faded into the background because his dependency upon the universe with all its forces and purposes was no longer taken into account. It was taken for granted that man had the *power* to be righteous; the only question was whether he had the goodness. Along with this, the idea of religious *training* receded; man needed only to be told or persuaded and he could then either act well or wait intelligently for the grace of God.

A WIDER SENSE OF PSYCHOLOGY

In any event, during my years of teaching philosophy I witnessed at close hand the birth of the hippie movement, the flower children, the drug scene and everything that went with it. I was quite convinced that the drugs led nowhere and I still am convinced of that; but what I underestimated was the sincerity of these young people with regard to the religions of the East. ... I see now that conventional psychological analysis of this interest is really of secondary importance, especially as the religious systems we shall be dealing with contain their own psychodynamic categories which in many cases strike much deeper, in my opinion, than those formulated by twentieth-century Europeans like Freud, Jung or Heidegger.

I am sure it would make many of us less uncomfortable if we could subject this interest in the new religions to a comprehensive psychological study. It can be done; I myself was doing it for several years. But even apart from the fact that—as will become apparent—our modern idea of psychology is seriously challenged by these new teachings, we should miss the whole point if such analysis were a main concern of ours. These teachings resonate with something in people which is utterly untouched by everything else in our society, something which "makes no sense" from one point of view, but which makes the most essential and urgent sense in the world from another point of view.

The reader who wishes to fit these new teachings into familiar psychological, sociological or literary categories is, I am afraid, in for some bad moments. I recall one winter afternoon several years ago in New York discussing Jewish mystical communities with the great scholar Abraham Heschel at a time when he was working on the translation of a particular Hasidic text. He pounded his finger on a stack of manuscript in front of him and quoted something he had just translated: "God is not nice, He is not an uncle. God is an earthquake." Many of those we shall be quoting, the young as well as the older, the hippies as well as the established members of the community, including some highly articulate and urbane people, have been struck by just such an earthquake. We shall often find, if we have the patience and the sensitivity, that they are speaking from a very particular "place" in themselves. We may even find—as I found to my own surprise—that they are speaking *to* a similar "place" in ourselves.

Not long ago I discussed some of my findings with a very large group of interested psychiatrists and clinicians at the Langley-Porter Neuropsychiatric Institute in San Francisco. I am sure there were many reasons why they came to hear about the new religions. Certainly one of these reasons was that so many of their younger patients are deeply involved in the literature of this "spiritual explosion." But in their questions and in the discussions I had with them afterward, they made it clear to me that their motives were not only professional. They themselves were searching for ways to come in touch with something deeper in themselves, something of which, they felt, modern psychology was largely ignorant. Like many of us, they saw very little for themselves in the Judaism and Christianity of our society; indeed, from their professional perspective they judged much of contemporary religion as psychologically harmful. Was there something in the religions of the East, they asked, which could really call forth those human depths and heights which neither psychology nor Western religion seemed able to reach? If so, how, they wanted to know, could they come in touch with it? The directness and clarity of their questions brought me up short once again. Not only had I underestimated the sincerity of the younger followers of the new teachings, I had seriously underestimated the hunger in these people—trained, intelligent professionals who had staked their careers on the European psychological view of man—for a new sort of psychology and a new way of searching for the purpose and sense of their existence.

I trust that many others whose view of man has been similarly influenced by modern psychology can find in this book a basis for deciding if there is anything in the new religions worth exploring further. But, equally important, the presentations in this book may serve in similar fashion for those who have not turned away from our established religions, but who wish to deepen their understanding of the metaphysical and psychological basis of all religion. For, as will be quite apparent, the new religions pose absolutely no threat to the old—unless the reassessment of man's inward potential and psychological fallibility is understood as a threat.

Inasmuch as the condition of a society, its hopes and aspirations, are reflected in the condition of its religion, it is America and the West as a whole which stand to benefit from this "invasion from the East," and not just our religious forms. When our younger people rebel against our institutions, they are rebelling against our hopes both for ourselves and for them. If we wish to understand their hopes and the nature of the world they seek to live in, we must understand something about these new religions.

THE AGONIES OF RELIGIOUS "RELEVANCE"

What, then, have they found, these followers of the new religious teachings? It is possible that a serious look at them and at the people involved in them, will change our whole idea of religion.

Who will deny that some such change is necessary? When God was recently pronounced dead it was not because people were no longer asking fundamental questions about life and death, human identity, suffering, and meaninglessness. On the contrary. Never before have men been more desperate about these questions.

True, our established religions are alive to this desperation. They are in agony because of it. We see them twisting and turning, seeking to change form without altering their essence. They wish to become *relevant* to the times, for the times are torturing us all.

But how are they, how is religion, to do this? We are tortured—agreed. The scientific world-view, recently so full of hope, has left men stranded in a flood of forces and events they do not understand, far less control. Psychiatry has lost its messianic aura, and therapists themselves are among the most tormented by the times. In the social sciences, there exists a brilliant gloom of unconnected theories and shattered predictions. Biology and medicine promise revolutionary discoveries and procedures, but meanwhile we suffer and die as before; and our doctors are as frightened as we.

And we cling violently to forms of life which, perhaps, were not even meaningful to us in quieter times.

So, when religion, in the name of relevance, seeks to adjust itself to the times, the question is bound to arise: is the leader being led? As church and synagogue turn to psychiatry, the scientific world-view, or social action, are they not turning toward what has failed and is failing? And has not the very failure of these non-religious enterprises shifted the common mind back to a renewed interest in the religious?

Men turn to religion and find, to their ultimate dismay, that religion turns to them, to their sciences, their ideas of action and accomplishment, and their language. This is what is known as secularization: the effort by religion to be "relevant," to "solve" human problems, to make men "*happy*."

How, one asks, could this aim be wrong? Should religion strive to be irrelevant, out of touch? Should it try to make men *un*happy? And in any case, by rigidly maintaining the purity of its traditional forms does it not simply become spinsterish and, finally, extinct? Who needs the dull sentiment of antique languages and meaningless rituals? Who needs a system of moral behavior which no one can or will follow?

Certainly, such questions require that we keep an open mind toward anything new which could refresh our understanding of the religious process. We want to know: what do these Eastern teachings say about man's existential situation, his place in the universe, his relationship to God? What do they promise? What do they demand? What sorts of people do they attract and what have these people experienced? Who are the leaders, what manner of people are they? We shall try not only to understand their doctrines, but to get a feel of their activity.

THE SENSE OF ASIAN TEACHINGS

Most of these teachings are sourced in Asia. Therefore, if we wish to know what they have brought to America, we have to begin by understanding something about Eastern religion.

Almost all the religions of Asia have one thing in common: "self-centeredness." Their goal is always release from suffering, *my* suffering as well as the suffering of humanity. Their cosmology and metaphysics, their imperatives to act morally or to serve God, are almost always instrumental toward this goal. What is true or good is what helps me out of my suffering; what is false or evil is what locks me in it. The well-known Buddhist simile expresses this exactly: the human situation is that of a man who has been struck in the chest by a poisoned arrow. He does not waste time trying to discover who shot it or why; he is not interested in learning what the arrow is made of. He wishes only to get it out of his chest so that he will not die.

What is this suffering? And how is this goal any different from the contemporary Western effort to make men happy, which we have just characterized as "secularization"? The answer to this question involves an idea that is markedly alien to our modern minds: *the satisfaction of desire is not happiness.*

Because human desires are so multiform and contradictory, the satisfaction of one is always at the expense of another. And even if it were possible to satisfy all our desires, it would still be a contradictory and chaotic satisfaction corresponding to the contradictory and chaotic condition of the desires themselves. Contradictory satisfaction is what we call inner conflict, and the modern man experiences inner conflict as suffering.

In religious literature the desires—physical as well as emotional and mental, the wishes, hopes, fears, and so forth—are often symbolized by animals. It is as though within man there were a thousand animals each seeking its own food and comfort. Some of these animals are, moreover, the very food that the others seek. *What is called "pleasure" or satisfaction is the feeding of one or another of these animals.*

Thus, in this view, man's suffering is based on the mistake of identifying his whole self with these animals as they appear in him and make their wants known by howling for their food. No sooner is one fed than another appears, hungrier than ever, and sometimes hungry for the very food that has just been given his predecessor—and is therefore no longer available. By identifying himself with these animals, man forfeits the possibility of inner unity and wholeness, a possibility which represents another level of existence for him.

In these traditions, this level is variously spoken of as "higher" or "deeper" or "inner." It is that level from which consciousness can control and care for the animals in a way that corresponds to their true needs as part of a whole. In its function as master, this level of consciousness is spoken of as a special force; as guardian it is called knowledge; as action in the world it is known as love or service. It is *able, conscious,* and *beneficent:* i.e., "divine."

According to Eastern psychology, there is something in man which he squanders by understanding himself to be no more than these animals, a sort of energy or life which he ignorantly gives to them, and which they really do not need or use. To turn that energy to its proper use, to direct it toward the work of integration and awareness is one of the primal functions of religious discipline. But it is much, much harder to do than one thinks, for there is always an animal in man, a kind of monkey, perhaps, which imitates the real work and which wants to *feel* whole rather than *be* whole.

In this perspective, religion becomes "secularized" when its main concern is more to feed than to control the animals—that is, when its concern is primarily with the external conditions of human life. In this sense what we ordinarily call happiness is the exact opposite of what the Eastern traditions understand by release from suffering.

In Eastern thought these animals, these desires, are much more various than we might suspect. Physical desires—for ordinary food and drink, warmth, sexual gratification, etc.—comprise only a small fraction of the total. Some others are: the desire for praise and recognition, the wish to be superior, the fear of pain, the desire for security, the wish to control others, the desire to be desired, the desire to express oneself, the fear of the unknown, etc., etc. The list is very long, and relatively few religions become secularized in the sense of seeking to gratify only the basic physical desires. The difficulty is that certain non-physical desires are identified and officially sanctioned as corresponding to the inner or divine in man, whereas in reality they are merely "animals" on a level with all the others.

When this happens all the other animals go hungry, and when they are hungry enough they go crazy.

Religions have, for example, existed for the sole purpose of allaying man's fear of the unknown. This often takes the form of scholastic or highly rationalistic and doctrinaire systems of belief and explanation. Some anthropologists and religionists have even theorized that this is the fundamental purpose of religion at all times. Of course, from the perspective we are now presenting, this view is superficial.

Closely related to this, religions have existed for the purpose of making man feel secure and "cared for." At present this is a very popular form of religion and a very popular view of the function of all religion. Modern psychology gives this view of religion its blessing because, in our age, it has "officially sanctioned" the desire for recognition and "love" as the real inner spring of the human psyche. This has been done by labeling this desire a "need."

Later in the book we shall explore this general idea at greater length. The main point here is that the central thrust of Eastern religion is toward the *transformation of desire*, not satisfaction of desires. At its purest, it is a radical and constant movement inward, into the "self." Thus, the contemporary idea of "relevance"—which by and large has to do with the satisfaction of certain desires, or the allaying of certain fears—is antagonistic to the sense of Eastern religion. And thus the revolution in religion that is brewing among these new teachings in America is one that may run directly counter to the direction of contemporary religious reform.

No one can say that this "inward turn" is not also central to the Judaeo-Christian tradition, but it is also certainly true that this dimension of Western religion has been overlaid or neglected. Therefore, in looking at these new teachings we will want to know what light they can throw on our own traditions. Perhaps the East has to come West in this way for the West to rediscover the sense of its own religion.

WHY NOW? WHY HERE?

It is, in any case, this "inward turn" which has drawn so many Americans to these new religious teachings. What has happened to our culture and to our religions to make this inward turn so necessary? If we can begin to answer this question, we shall see something of the significance of this whole movement.

Here we immediately face an interesting difficulty. It is easy enough to argue that technology, affluence, the routinization of religion, and the like have stifled a deep longing in man, a "dark" side of his nature which is now welling forth to claim its own. From there, it is but one step to our "approving" of these new teachings because they satisfy an "irrational" need in the psyche of all men. We might even go so far as to argue that we must transform our view of reality by liberating our inherent attunement with the magical and by abandoning what has been called the "myth of objective consciousness." This has been done, and brilliantly, by Theodore Roszak in his book, *The Making of a Counter Culture.*

But to take this approach is, in the last analysis, to confess that we really do not wish to be serious about religion. It means that we have relied upon modern psychology or sociology to tell us what our possibilities are and which of them are not being realized in our society. Or, it means relying on our own feelings of frustration to tell us what reality should be like, or upon our responses to literature and art, themselves produced by men like us.

THE INCLUSION OF THE MIND

The terribly embarrassing thing about the great religions of the world is that *they* pass judgment on *us*, and that the moment we begin to pass judgment upon them without having submitted to their instruction, there is a real question whether we can understand them at all. Even to put the matter like this is already to have come upon one of the most striking ways in which the new teachings may change our contemporary concept of religion. To put it succinctly: they bring the idea that our mind and the power of thought itself is wretchedly inept without exposure to a spiritual discipline.

The exclusion of the mind from the religious process is one of the central characteristics of our religious forms. It was not always so, but by and large it is so now. We may be willing to grant religion the power to move us and stir us to the "depths" of our emotions, but we reserve the autonomy of our reasoning for ourselves. If we wish to train our minds, we know where to go, and it is not to religion.

Our popular religious forms long ago acquiesced to this. They spoke of human depravity, sin, faithlessness, immorality—but not so much of stupidity, illusion and bad thinking. It is true that Christianity and Judaism are essentially religions of the will, but the intellect was always understood as in the service of the will. Today, however, they, the will and the intellect, are tacitly recognized as separate.

Not so for the Eastern religions. Returning for a moment to our metaphor of the animals as symbols of human desires, the Eastern religions tell us that each animal has its own practical intelligence which operates only to procure its "food," namely the satisfaction of desire. Thus, when we are at the mercy of these animals our intelligence is also at their mercy. And as they are interested in pleasure and not in truth, so our minds inevitably follow the line of pleasure and attraction. Logic is a whore serving anyone who can pay the price.

The "inward turn" of the Eastern religions may thus be understood in part as the effort to include the mind in the process of psychological regeneration. "Who are *they* to train *my* mind!" one might say. Quite a legitimate question, but the problem is how are we to find out *who* "they" are? What in ourselves or in others do *we* trust to ascertain the truth: do we know? are we sure? That is the question which immediately comes back at us from the Eastern religions, and which used to come back at man from the Judaeo-Christian tradition.

To put the point another way, the established religions of the day tend to emphasize choice and action. But under the Eastern diagnosis of the human condition, choice without intellectual freedom is only impulse, the impulse of the animal. We might agree with that, but not with the added stipulation that we lack intellectual freedom outside of a spiritual discipline. In short, the Eastern religions tell us, as did Plato, that we are chained by our subjectivity. It is therefore quite wrong to see even our most ecstatic bursts of subjective feeling as a step toward spiritual regeneration in the Eastern sense.

Here I must hasten to say that when I speak of "our" religions, I am speaking of church and synagogue, not of what takes place in Western monasteries or convents. At the same time, it is also indicative of our idea of religion that monasticism is by and large considered on the fringe, as secondary to church religion. Of course, this is a complete reversal of the historical relationship between church and monastery, where the latter was the source of life of the former. Today, most of us tend to think of monks and nuns as a bit odd, rather than as holy people.

THE RETURN OF THE PRACTICAL

Which brings us to the second main point about our contemporary religious forms, namely, the absence in them of practical technique, method and discipline. Various rituals, prayers, services and the like no longer function as part of the mechanics of the religious process, but mainly as an emotional "lift," something to help us return to our ordinary life feeling better, psychologically more secure. In this way they help us to preserve the quality of the life we lead, rather than transform it.

This general forgetting of the instrumental nature of religious forms is in a way really quite bizarre. It is as though millions of people suffering from a painful disease were to gather together to hear someone read a textbook of medical treatment in which the means necessary to cure their disease were carefully spelled out. It is as though they were all to take great comfort in that book and in what they heard, going through their lives knowing that their disease could be cured, quoting passages to their friends, preaching the wonders of this great book, and returning to their congregation from time to time to hear more of the inspiring diagnosis and treatment read to them. Meanwhile, of course, the disease worsens and they eventually die of it, smiling in grateful hope as on their deathbed someone reads to them yet another passage from the text. Perhaps for some a troubling thought crosses their minds as their eyes close for the last time: "Haven't I forgotten something? Something important? Haven't I forgotten actually to undergo treatment?"

It is impossible to say when this forgetting of the fundamentally instrumental nature of religious forms began in the West. But obviously the general clergy—priests, ministers and rabbis—forgot it quite as much as their congregations. No wonder the young became disillusioned with religion. They heard exhortations, commandments, prescriptions by the basketful, but nobody was telling them *how to be able* to follow them. I do not say they formulated it this way to themselves, but they—and not only they—saw the absurd discrepancy between the ideal preached in their churches and the actual behavior of men, behavior which seemed reinforced rather than seriously challenged by religion.

The Eastern teachings which are attracting so much interest in this country have by and large preserved this instrumental aspect of religion. That is why they come to us with such things as meditation techniques, physical and psychological exercises, and why they tend to emphasize the necessity of a *guru,* or master. It takes no great research to discover that practical psychological methods were always a central part of Christianity and Judaism, and that they still exist in monastic settings or, for example, among certain communities such as the Jewish Hasidim. The point is only that this aspect of religion has been forgotten by almost all other Westerners.

It is only because it was forgotten that Judaism and Christianity were so shaken by psychoanalysis and various other movements in modern psychology. Compared, for example, to the early Christian diagnosis of the inner human condition, Freud's "exposé" of the nature of human motivation is a very weak tea indeed. For one thing—and this is the very least of it—he retained his trust in the power of reason, his own, and observation, also his own, to arrive at the truth about human psychology. But for the early Christians, and for several of the most interesting teachings, the power of thinking and observing clearly is a quality only of a higher state of consciousness, and not something that man is able to rely on without work in a spiritual discipline.

The main point here, however, is that because the instrumental nature of religious forms was forgotten, the science of psychology suddenly appeared as something *new*. Such an absurdity could only arise on the basis of a total misunderstanding or ignorance of the history of Judaeo-Christian thought and practice. One need only glance again at the writings of Augustine, Eckhardt, the Eastern Orthodox Fathers, or the great rabbis to confirm this point.

THE MODERN UNDERESTIMATION OF MAN

Modern psychology did indeed bring one thing that was new, namely an underestimation of human possibility. Which brings us to our third point about the nature of contemporary religion.

There is really a tremendous irony at this point. Because religion forgot the instrumental function of its forms, these forms changed to accommodate the ordinary desires of men—as we pointed out in discussing the idea of "secularization." As a result of this forgetting and this change of form, religion was no longer able to effect the essential improvement of human life. Observing this, various "original thinkers" immediately concluded that religion was a fraud and began to produce, by the dozens, their own methods for improving human life. For they quite accurately saw that what men were getting out of religion (religion which was no longer instrumental) could be gotten faster without all the rituals, "mumbo jumbo," metaphysics, and so forth, all of which originally formed part of the instrumentality of the Judaic and Christian *Way*, but whose essential function nobody seemed really to understand. To return for a moment to a medical metaphor, it was as though patients and doctors began to insist that medicine taste good and make one *feel* rather than *be* well, and as though certain clever benefactors of mankind discovered that this could be done more effectively by removing from the medicines precisely those ingredients which had genuine therapeutic properties.

What modern psychology offered as an improvement of human life was precisely that quality of life which drove men originally to the instrumentalities of religion, the only addition being the conviction that this was the highest quality of life one could realistically expect. Religion was dismissed as an illusion—and indeed the religion which psychologists dismissed was perhaps illusory because it had forgotten its practical function and had lost its instrumental forms. Thus psychology became much more efficient than religion which, pursuing the same goals as this new science, found itself hampered by "outworn" beliefs and rituals. Modern psychology began to lead religion. The destruction of religious forms proceeded at an accelerated pace, and the underestimation of human possibility became fixed in our society.

It is only partially true that this estimation of man was based on a premature acceptance of human limitation, itself based on a mistaken extrapolation from the failure of non-instrumental religion. To be sure, there were some thinkers, not in the majority, who claimed that all man could ever hope for was the illusion of freedom, the partial gratification of instinctual desires and a more or less tolerable, though meaningless, existence between oblivions. The freedom, immortality, higher consciousness and inner unity spoken of by religions was to them a romantic dream. At least they tried to some degree to avoid replacing this so-called romantic dream with a naïve belief in their own innate, fully developed powers.

Not so the majority of psychologists. They coupled their underestimation of man's possibilities with an emphatic overestimation of man's and their own actual psychological condition. Simply to mention one example, Freud's whole theory of dreams, parapraxes and neurotic symptomology is based on the assumption that there is a basic unity of purpose underlying all human behavior, and that everything man does is an expression, though unconscious, of this instinctual unity. Since it is precisely this unity which many of the Eastern religions call into question, from their perspective it is Freud's assumption which is the romantic dream. He once said, "Man has always known he possessed spirit; I had to show him he was also an animal." Unfortunately, he settled for only *one* animal, whereas the fundamental religious diagnosis of man is that he is an entire menagerie.

Blithely accepting the "tough-minded" scientific view that there are no purposes in the external world, psychoanalysis substituted the rather sentimental belief that there is nothing but purpose and intention in the psychic world. At least the positivists made a clean sweep of all purpose, inner and outer, and after them one could much more clearly see the dust bowl of modern thought for what it was.

Coupled with this assumption that everything in one's psychic life had "meaning," was the psychologists' belief that they were able to ascertain this meaning, to control their own feelings toward the patient, and to communicate the truth to the patient in a way that could be effective—all this being the general sort of thing which a spiritual master does, but toward an aim entirely different than "mental health" and only after he himself has submitted his life (including his mind) to the instrumental rigors of a spiritual path.

One obvious aspect of the modern, Western concept of religion was its picture of a "holy" man. He was nicer, kinder, gentler, more moral, perhaps, than other men—but more intelligent? more perceptive? emotionally stronger? psychologically more balanced? more creative? more unified? Were not these "*secular*" properties of men? Again, it is the Eastern religions with their practical methods involving work with the body, the attention, the intellect and memory, the training of the emotions, which has begun to supplant this simplistic picture of holiness. Till now, it has been entirely possible for many of us to be surprised if not slightly offended by the idea that Jesus Christ had a mind as well as a heart, and to be genuinely astonished that almost all of the enduring art in the world has been produced by men with obvious religious ties.

Summing up, there are three ways in which Western, and particularly American, religions are vulnerable to correction by the religions of the East: exclusion of the mind, the absence of religious techniques and methods, and the underestimation of human possibility. One could cite still more ways in which our religious forms have moved away from their original direction, but these, perhaps, are enough to have exposed as well some of the conditions of our American culture which make it ripe for this invasion from the East.

.   .   .

God Is Dead

William Hamilton

William Hamilton (1924-   ) teaches theology at Portland State University and has written much about the death of God. He is the author of *The Christian Man* (1956), *Modern Reader's Guide to the Gospels* (1958), *The New Essence of Christianity* (1961), and *Radical Theology and the Death of God* (1966).

Have you ever heard of the madman who on a bright morning lighted a lantern and ran to the market place calling out unceasingly: "I seek God! I seek God!"—As there were many people standing about who did not believe in God, he caused a great deal of amusement. Why! is he lost? said one. Has he strayed away like a child? said another. Or does he keep himself hidden? Is he afraid of us? Has he taken a sea-voyage? Has he emigrated?—the people cried out laughingly, all in a hubbub. The insane man jumped into their midst and transfixed them with his glances. "Where is God gone?" he called out. "I mean to tell you! We have killed him—you and I! We are all his murderers! . . .

"Do we not smell the divine putrefaction?—for even Gods putrefy! God is dead! God remains dead! And we have killed him! How shall we console ourselves, the most murderous of all murderers? . . . Is not the magnitude of this deed too great for us? Shall we not ourselves have to become Gods, merely to seem worthy of it? There was a greater event—and on account of it, all who are born after us belong to a higher history than any history hitherto!"—Here the madman was silent and looked again at his hearers: they also were silent and looked at him in surprise. At last he threw his lantern on the ground, so it broke in pieces and was extinguished. "I come too early," he then said, "I am not yet at the right time. This prodigious event is still on its way, and is traveling—it has not yet reached men's ears. . . ."

These wild and lovely words, written by Friedrich Nietzsche toward the close of the last century, have recently broken loose from the obscurity of lecture, textbook and monograph, into the incomprehending world of cocktail party, newsmagazine with intellectual pretensions and television. Why? What has happened? Is there really an event properly called "the death of God?" Or is the current chatter enveloping the phrase simply another of the many non-events afflicting our time?

Source: "The Death of God," *Playboy*, Vol. 13, No. 8 (August 1966). Reprinted by permission of the author.

No. The death of God *has* happened. To those of us with gods, and to those without. To the indifferent, the cynical and the fanatical. God is dead, whatever that means. To some, this is an event of terror, warranting tears and the writing of requiems. In the above passage, Nietzsche seems to reflect some of this cosmic horror. But to others, the event is one of great liberation and joy; an event not keeping one from something, but making something newly possible, in this case the Christian faith. In another connection, Nietzsche knew this joy as well.

In fact, we . . . feel ourselves irradiated as by a new dawn by the report that the "old God is dead"; our hearts overflow with gratitude, astonishment, presentiment and expectation. At last the horizon seems open once more, granting even that it is not bright; our ships can at last put out to sea in face of every danger; every hazard is again permitted to the discerner; the sea, our sea, again lies open before us; perhaps never before did such an "open sea" exist.

I am a Christian theologian by profession; I have recently been involved in the death-of-God fuss, and I am, as well, committed to the death of God as a theological and human event.

The affirmation of the death of God is Christian in two senses. It is, for the most part, made by Christian theologians. (Not entirely, however, and a dialog between Christians and Jews around this idea is coming into being that seems most promising and exciting.) And it is made by us in order to affirm the possibility of thinking and living as Christians. To say "death of God," then, is somehow to move toward and not away from Christianity. Thus it should be clear that we theologians are not trying to reduce the Christian faith to a bland and noncontroversial minimum so that it can be accepted by scientists, rationalists and freethinkers. We are not particularly anxious about relevance or communication. It is not because we long to slip something into the mind of "modern man" that we do what we do. It is because something has happened to us, and because we suspect that it may have happened to others, that we are talking about the death of God.

But let's move beyond introductory matters. Just what does the phrase "death of God" mean as we "radical" theologians use it? And how is this related to other possible and historical uses of the phrase? The best way to start this answer is to indicate that there are perhaps ten possible meanings for the phrase "death of God" in use today:

1. It might mean that there is no God and that there never has been. This position is traditional atheism of the old-fashioned kind, and it does seem hard to see how it could be combined, except very unstably, with Christianity or any of the Western religions.

2. It might mean that there once was a God to whom adoration, praise and trust were appropriate, possible and even necessary, but that there is now no such God. This is the position of the death-of-God or radical theology. It is an atheist position, but with a difference. If there was a God, and if there now isn't, it should be possible to indicate why this change took place, when it took place and who was responsible for it. I will be returning to questions like this.

3. It might mean that the idea of God and the word of God itself both are in need of radical reformulation. Perhaps totally new words are needed; perhaps a decent silence about God should be observed; but ultimately, a new treatment of the idea and the word can be expected, however unexpected and surprising it may turn out to be.

4. It might mean that our traditional liturgical and theological language needs a thorough overhaul; the reality abides, but classical modes of thought and forms of language may well have had it.

5. It might mean that the Christian story is no longer a saving or healing story. It may manage to stay on as merely illuminating or instructing or guiding, but it no longer performs its classical functions of salvation or redemption. In this new form, it might help us cope with the demons, but it cannot abolish them.

6. It might mean that certain concepts of God, often in the past confused with the classical Christian doctrine of God, must be destroyed: for example, God as problem solver, absolute power, necessary being, the object of ultimate concern.

7. It might mean that men do not today experience God except as hidden, absent, silent. We live, so to speak, in the time of the death of God, though that time will doubtless pass.

8. It might mean that the gods men make, in their thought and action (false gods or idols, in other words), must always die so that the true object of thought and action, the true God, might emerge, come to life, be born anew.

9. It might have a mystical meaning: God must die in the world so that he can be born in us. In many forms of mysticism the death of Jesus on the cross is the time of that worldly death. This is a medieval idea that influenced Martin Luther, and it is probably this complex of ideas that lies behind the German chorale *God Himself Is Dead* that may well be the historical source for our modern use of "death of God."

10. Finally, it might mean that our language about God is always inadequate and imperfect.

I want to go back to the second meaning of the phrase. If there was once a God and there is now not one, when did this change take place? There are a number of paths toward an answer. In one sense, God is always dying, giving himself to the world and to men, as in the fall of the primitive sky gods into animism. In a more decisive sense for Christians, the coming and the death of Jesus (the Incarnation, to use the technical term) stand for a kind of death of God. Here God, Christians have always said, takes on sin and suffering. Can it not also be said that God takes on mortality, that the coming of Jesus is the beginning of the death of God, and that because of this coming, men no longer need gods in the old religious sense? The New Testament perhaps comes closest to this in the saying, "He who abides in love abides in God."

But the "when" question has to be answered not only in terms of Jesus, but in terms of the nineteenth century. If Jesus makes the death of God a possible experience for men, the nineteenth century lives that reality and instructs us to do the same. A whole series of themes in the nineteenth century deals, directly or indirectly, with the collapse of God into the world, and thus with the death of God. Goethe and the romantics spoke of the movement from transcendence to nature, and even Protestants were invited by some of their spokesmen at the beginning of the century to fling themselves on the bosom of nature in order to recapture a lost divinity. William Blake is singing mysteriously of the death of the transcendent God at the close of the eighteenth century, and in the French Revolution itself we can perceive the close connection between regicide and deicide. Hegel, as early as 1807, speaks elliptically of God's death, and the left-wing Hegelians like Strauss and Feuerbach make it much clearer—the attributes of God must be transmuted into concrete human values. Karl Marx's own Marxism is in one sense an attempt to recover for the human community the values previously ascribed to God.

Ibsen and Strindberg knew the death of God, as did Victorian England. George Eliot found God and immortality impossible, duty alone irresistible, while the young Matthew Arnold's *Dover Beach* sang a song for a whole generation.

The Sea of Faith
Was once, too, at the full and round earth's shore
Lay like the folds of a bright girdle furl'd.
But now I only hear
Its melancholy, long, withdrawing roar,
Retreating, to the breath
Of the night-wind, down the vast edges drear
And naked shingles of the world.

And on our side of the Atlantic, Hawthorne rather quietly, and Melville with unforgettable force laid the God of the Puritan tradition to rest. Perhaps the most unforgettable image of the dying God in our language is that of Ahab finally fixing his harpoon in Moby Dick's side, as the two of them sink together, both of them God, both of them evil.

Cryptically, but not entirely falsely, in Europe and America between the French Revolution and the start of World War One, the Christian God is dying. The coming and death of Jesus makes God's death possible; the nineteenth century makes it real. And today, it is our turn to understand and to accept.

Thus, "When did it happen?" gets a three-part answer. In one sense with Jesus and the cross. In another sense in the Europe and America of the last century. In a final sense, today, just now. Just what is there about our time that has led us to see and to grasp this event?

Every man must answer for himself the question "What is the special quality of your experience of the death of God?" In one sense, I don't think one can or should try to persuade anyone else of the reality of the death of God. When I talk or write about it, I don't try to place a new thing into another's head, I try to remind him of what he already knows. If there is no answer, no recognition, I can be of no further use to him except as an example of the way he should not go. For me, the death of God is not a consequence of a simple experience like the discovery of, say, the scientific method that automatically rules out God. It is an emotional event, in the guts. It is made up of a number of things, modest in themselves, but overwhelming when taken together. It is for me partly the disappearance of the idea of God as a meeter of needs and a solver of problems. For much of its history, classical Christianity felt that while men, by their own hands, could solve many of the problems of life, there was always a dimension where man was powerless and which had to be ascribed to God. In this sense the longing for God was said to be common to all. Our hearts are restless, Saint Augustine said, until they come to rest in God. Today we must say some hearts are and some hearts aren't. Men may not need God, just as they may not need a single ultimate loyalty. Needs and problems are for the world to meet, and if it cannot meet them, nothing else can. This is one strand in the experience of the death of God for me.

Another has to do with the problem of suffering. If for you there is nothing special about the twentieth century's experience of suffering, then this line of argument will not persuade. There has always been unmerited suffering in the world, and it has always been a problem for the heart and the head to hold to the reality of suffering and to the goodness and power of God at the same time. It has always been hard, I am saying, and now it is impossible; for the terrible burden of suffering our time has witnessed can be ascribed to God only by turning him into a monster. The problem of Job, of Ivan Karamazov, of Albert Camus has fallen on our heads. It was *Christians* who did the work at Auschwitz, and their God became impossible after they had finished. Ernest Hemingway, whom we do not ordinarily think of as having been moved by these problems, has a touching scene on this point in *For Whom the Bell Tolls*: Anselmo is speaking to Jordan about his hopes when the war is over.

"But if I live later, I will try to live in such a way, doing no harm to any one, that it will be forgiven."

"By whom?"

"Who knows? Since we do not have God here any more, neither His Son nor the Holy Ghost, who forgives? I do not know."

"You have not God any more?"

"No. Man. Certainly not. If there were God, never would He have permitted what I have seen with my eyes. Let them have God."

"They claim Him."

"Clearly I miss Him, having been brought up in religion. But now a man must be responsible to himself."

"Then it is thyself who will forgive thee for killing."

"I believe so," Anselmo said.

Let me put this in another way. The death of God means two closely related things: that some of the human experiences to which men have traditionally given the name of God must be redescribed and renamed, and also that some of those experiences are no longer ours. For example, religious men have often pointed to experiences of dependence, awe, reverence, wonder, mystery, tragedy as signs of the incalculable and mysterious character of life, saying of these experiences taken together, "Something like this is what we mean by God." There are, of course, such things about us, and the only point I wish to make here is that one needn't give any of them the name of God. They are real facts of our life, we have human sciences and arts to clarify them, and they point to mystery and wonder, but not to God.

But a second thing is just as true. There are experiences that men have had in the past and which they have traditionally understood as pointing to God that are simply not available to us in the same way today. Take the experiences of dependence, especially in the presence of nature. Listen to a research biologist or a doctor or a physicist or a space scientist talk about his work. He is talking about mastery, control and power; not about a sense of his smallness before the universe.

Perhaps death can also become a sacred event in our time of the death of God. Not, of course, our experience of our own death, but at least the experience of its coming, of mortality, and a facing up to death, our own and others, so as to befriend it and deprive it of its ability to hurt and surprise us. What meaning would "sacred" have if we tried to say that death may become a way to a godless form of the sacred today?

Some examples might make this point a bit less bewildering. In the Gettysburg Address, Lincoln was offering what seems to me a moving example of death as a human, godless form of the sacred. He said, you'll recall, that they had met to dedicate a portion of the battlefield. Then he went on:

But, in a larger sense, we cannot dedicate—we cannot consecrate—we cannot hallow—this ground.

You might have expected him to make the pious point here and to say that we mortals cannot consecrate anything because that is God's prerogative alone. But he didn't say that:

The brave men, living and dead, who struggled here, have consecrated it, far above our poor power to add or detract.

Not just the "right" side, but all those who fought, are the consecrators. Suffering and dying men, he suggests, have the power to make holy or sacred what was ordinary and profane before.

It would be easy to find a contemporary example of sex as a sacred event. Such a view is common rhetoric in our modern sentimental panegyrics to sex, both Christian and secular. So I would rather turn to another source, to Puritan New England, as a matter of fact. This is from Nathaniel Hawthorne's *The Scarlet Letter*, and Dimmesdale is speaking to Hester about their adulterous love.

"We are not, Hester, the worst sinners in the world. There is one worse than even the polluted priest! That old Man's revenge has been blacker than my sin. [He is referring to Chillingworth's diabolical attack on him.] He has violated, in cold blood, the sanctity of a human heart. Thou and I, Hester, never did so!"

"Never, never," whispered she. "What we did had a consecration of its own. We felt it so! We said so to each other! Hast thou forgotten it?"

Here is not only sex, but nonmarital sex, and in the heart of Puritanism, affirmed as a form of the sacred. Along such lines as these, I think, a conception of the sacred without God might be worked out.

I want to raise one final question about the idea of the death of God. If God is dead, as we say, what do we put in his place? What does the work in this godless Christian vision that God used to do in the classical tradition? Have we, it might be asked, taken the full measure of the terrible cry of Ivan Karamazov, If there is no God, then everything is permitted? Are people really strong enough to lose not only the fear of hell and the consolations of the next life, but also the reality of God?

There are two answers or two forms of the same answer, to the question about the replacement of God. In one sense the answer must be "the human community" and in another sense it must be "Jesus." Let us distinguish between two kinds of meaning or function classically ascribed to God. If by God you mean the means by which forgiveness is mediated, or consolation in time of sorrow or despair, or judge of my arrogance and my idolatry—then we say that these functions, as central for us as they ever were in classical Christianity, must be taken over by the human community. We must learn to forgive each other with the radical unconditioned grace men used to ascribe to God. (Recall the touching words between Anselmo and Jordan quoted above.) We must learn to comfort each other, and we must learn to judge, check and rebuke one another in the communities within which we are wounded and in which we are healed. If these things cannot now be done by the human communities in the world, then these communities must be altered until they can perform these tasks and whatever others, once ascribed to God, that need to be done in this new context. In this sense the death of God leads to politics, to social change, and even to the foolishness of utopias.

But it would be misleading to pass over to what we are calling the human community every task once given to God. There is another kind of meaning attached to the classical idea of God that needs another kind of surrogate. If by God you mean the focus of obedience, the object of trust and loyalty, the meaning I give to love, my center, my meaning—then these meanings are given not to men in general but to Jesus, the *man*, in his life, his way with others and his death. We death-of-God theologians thus stake out a claim to be able to make it as Christians not merely because we speak of the death of the Christian God, but because we see as the center of the Christian faith a relation of obedience and trust directed to Jesus. Something like this is placed on the lips of Uncle Nikolai by Boris Pasternak in *Doctor Zhivago:*

As I was saying, one must be true to Christ. I'll explain. What you don't understand is that it is possible to be an atheist, it is possible not to know whether God exists, or why, and yet believe that man does not live in a state of nature but in history, and that history as we know it now began with Christ, and that Christ's gospel is its foundation. Now what is history? It is the centuries of systematic explorations of the riddle of death, with a view to overcoming death. That's why people discover mathematical infinity and electromagnetic waves, that's why they write symphonies. Now, you can't advance in this direction without a certain faith. You can't make such discoveries without spiritual equipment. And the basic elements of this equipment are in the Gospels. What are they? To begin with, love of one's neighbor, which is the supreme form of vital energy. Once it fills the heart of man it has to overflow and spend itself. And then the two basic ideals of modern man—without them he is unthinkable—the idea of free personality and the idea of life as sacrifice.

The human community in general—not as it is, but as it might be altered to become—and that particular instance of the human community, Jesus of Nazareth, thus take over the work, the action, the deeds, once ascribed to the Christian God. Thus the death of God is the least abstract event one can imagine. It moves straight into politics, revolutionary change, and the tragedies and delights of this world.

At the start of this article, the question was posed whether the death of God might be a non-event, fashioned by nothing more substantial than the eager and empty publicity mills of our day. We radical theologians have found, I think, that it is something more. It is a real event; it is a joyous event; it is a liberating event, removing everything that might stand between man and the relief of suffering, man and the love of his neighbor. It is a real event making possible a Christian form of faith for many today. It is even making possible church and ministry in our world.

The Black Theology of Hope
Major Jones

Major J. Jones (1920-   ) is president-director of Gammon Theological Seminary and is active in numerous academic, church, and community organizations.

The current development in the movement toward black awareness has been characterized by a kind of learned hope that presses its adherents, as Christians, to acknowledge the ontological priority of a kind of future mode of black being which has not revealed itself in the fullness of maturity. This fact has already been indicated above. However, it should be made clearer that this hope is currently at the very heart of the mood of black existence.

This is made more true because this hope is akin to the black revolution, whether violent or nonviolent, and it also seeks to make itself known to the nonblack world. Further, hope and revolution are sometimes fused concepts for black people for the simple reason that so many black people do not feel that the two concepts can be separated in a complex, inflexible, fixed, and unchangeable social structure such as ours. Meaningful change is so hard to come by that many have about lost faith in a hope unrelated to violence, revolution, or extreme social pressure.

.   .   .

Above all, it must be said that a black theology of hope, based on the black awareness movement, is not theological in a Moltmann or a Bloch sense of a theology of hope. This is so because the traditional language of theology is not very intelligible to the man in the street, and especially to the current black man of hope. An intelligible black theology of hope has been almost nonexistent, and yet for some time now black Christians have needed to take a look at the problems that might confront any attempts to develop an adequate theology of hope. This is not surprising when we recall that for too long white theologians have been producing systems in which the alien virtues of harmony, order, and stability have been stressed.

It may well be that black people have come to a time when, if the black theologian is to speak to their current conditions, he must at least develop a theology of hope that will embrace in some sense the concept of revolution in its fullest implications. Harvey Cox has seen this problem, which is faced not only by the black Christian in America, but by all Christians. He contends that "we are trying to live in a period of revolution without a theology of revolution. The development of such a theology should be the first item on the theological agenda today."[1] But the average Christian, black or white, might well venture the question of just why do we need a theology of revolution. For many minds such a thought is

Source: *Black Awareness: A Theology of Hope* (Nashville: Abingdon, 1971), pp. 87-106. Copyright © 1971 by Abingdon Press. Used by permission.

[1] Harvey Cox, *The Secular City* (New York: Macmillan, 1965), p. 107.

a terrifying mixture of categories or a confusion of horizons. Indeed, they ask, how can we define a theology of revolution as a theology related to an earthly eschatological hope within the context of our present society?

Within the black community, especially outside the church, there is too little time for the reflective type of theologizing of the past. We have come to a point where there is a tendency to fuse the concepts of hope and revolution. For the average black man in the ghetto, for any theology to be meaningful it must speak to only those factors or actions which are going to help him realize a better day within his lifetime; he would insist that the only time he has is now. In this light, then, there is a very practical reason for the urgent need for a theology of hope that is closely related to revolution. Without such hope, it would seem, the black churchman will be at a total loss about what to do with the concept of revolution for a long time to come. It may be that this is the reason there is such a cry against the black church, the black college, and many other black institutions—they simply have not found adequate words to articulate what they think of the future. It may well be because, as has been said, they have not seen hope as a viable possibility without revolutionary actions that are totally alien to their present mode of thought. Indeed, did the black theologians really mean it when they asserted with Eldridge Cleaver: "We shall have our manhood. We shall have it or the earth will be leveled by our efforts to gain it"?[2] One is moved to ask of them whether they are at one with Hannah Arendt in her book *On Revolution*, when she predicts that even though mankind has the good sense to set aside war as an international political instrument, revolutions will continue into the foreseeable future to make this a century of revolution. Then she says that "in the contests which divide the world today, and in which so much is at stake, those will probably win who understand revolution."[3] Black Christians must at least understand revolution, not with the intent to win a political revolution as such, but rather because, if it takes place, they cannot escape accepting or acquiring some responsibility for its outcome. The stakes are always high in revolutionary times—the future of mankind, the scale of justice, the quality of freedom; and ultimately there is at stake the shape of society beyond revolution. Indeed, the ultimate concern of the Christian, black or white, does not lie outside these secular interests; it rather relates to the problem of finding a formative expression through them. No matter what the context, the religious relationship between man and God does run alongside the relationship of both to the world. The commandment to love God has no substance at all apart from love of neighbor. Love of neighbor is always at stake in a revolution.

Though the church is to a large degree responsible for the revolutionary consciousness that is emerging around the world today, the people who seem now to be talking revolution, especially in the black community, are largely nontheological in their views. Thus, their view of revolution has very little of the content of a theology of hope. And yet in many ways, whether violent or nonviolent, a theology of hope must be related to a theology of revolution.

In the chapter "The Revolutionary West," in his book *Christianity in World History*, A. T. Van Leeuwen ascribes the revolutionary impulse in the West to the revolutionizing impact of the gospel of the coming kingdom of God.[4] Indirectly the

---

[2] Produced by the Committee of Theological Prospectus, June 13, 1969, at the Interdenominational Theological Center, Atlanta, Georgia.

[3] Hannah Arendt, *On Revolution* (New York: Viking Press, 1963), p. 8.

[4] Arend Th. Van Leeuwen, *Christianity in World History*, trans. by H. H. Hoskins (New York: Scribner's, 1966). p. 344.

church has sponsored the revolutionary process by preaching a message that sets things in motion by stirring up the imagination, arousing new expectations, and stimulating a crusading zeal to translate hopes—whose realization some would postpone for heaven above—into the social structures of this world. The simple fact of preaching the gospel is itself like putting sticks of explosives into the social structure. The church is indeed responsible for having planted the seed within the beloved structures that it, at the same time, had no desire to explode, since its own privileges were beholden to them. The church has too long preached a gospel of revolution without meaning to do so, and, more than that, without knowing clearly what it was talking about when it mentioned some of the revolutionary themes of the Bible and the Christian faith.

A theology of revolution is made all the more urgent by the additional fact that the Christian churches must repent of the inglorious role they have played in most modern revolutionary situations. While the gospel they preached pointed the way to hope for the future, the institutions they built impeded its coming. The white church and the black church have, at times, been at one in proclaiming a revolutionary gospel of equality. Neither one, however, has fully adhered to the reality in the area of race relations. If they had, both now would be more deeply engaged in the black liberation struggles of our time. Hope and revolution must be brought into some kind of understandable relationship.

When we speak specifically of the black church and a theology of hope, we must take a hard look at what revolution means for the black community, for this is where the issue is in such sharp current focus.

First of all, it must be understood that there is a sharp distinction between rebellion and revolution. The aim of a rebellion is to restore what has been lost; the aim of revolution is to create something new. The vision of the radically new, inherent in revolution, is what links revolutionary action to eschatological hope. Revolution is a relevant concept within the context of the black community.

Second, when revolution is mentioned in the black community, it is not confined, and many times not even related, to current theological expressions of hope; it is rather an expression related only to despair and hopelessness. This is why revolution should now be related to a theology of hope, lest we end up with despair and hopelessness.

.   .   .

The newer theologians who are impressed with the language of hope speak of God as "the absolute future," and at times one is led to feel that there is nothing man can do, that the pressure of the future brings creation out of nothing, making for a kind of inexhaustible source of innovation in the world. But when we talk of revolution within the context of the present world, Christians are confronted with several options. First, a Christian can be relevant to the revolution as a mere cheerleader for it. Second, the Christian can become engaged to a limited degree, setting limits beyond which he will not go. Third, no matter how a Christian may relate to a revolution, he must recognize that revolution in the modern world may mean possible violence, and violence means killing. However, if there were no danger of killing, one could never exclude the possibility that after the revolution, the newly structured society might become a new status quo, as in the case of Cuba. Often the Christian has no choice; he must either take sides and fight for an evil and oppressive regime, or take sides with what he feels to be a potentially better political or social order. Indeed, when a Christian wants to enter the political arena at all, he must cope with the possibility of a breakdown of peace or of politics and the ultimate possibility that violence, which means killing, will ensue—and he will be a part. It would seem that there can be no theology of revolution unless it comes to grips with the question of whether it is at all possible to extend a theological or an ethical justification for killing.

The black or white Christian theologians who attempt to construct a theology of revolution must face the ultimate risk of whether violence can produce enough good to justify the means. Without exception, any theology of revolution has to face the question whether under any condition, circumstances, or occasion it could ever support theologically or ethically the act of killing a neighbor. For when one enters the political arena, especially the revolutionary political arena, in any way at all, he must cope with the possibility that violence will ensue. Whether the call for revolution be a first or a last resort, the question the black Christian faces, in relation to violence, is whether he can, as a Christian, kill another person. Does killing ever become right in any war, even a "just" war? Whether the killing is intentional or unintentional, the problem is the same for the Christian. Even in contextual or situational ethics, if one is committed to act under the mandate of love for neighbor, the necessity of killing another person is problematic for the Christian. If one is committed to the love of neighbor, then it would seem impossible to reconcile the act of killing the neighbor that one is committed to love. Indeed, is it ever possible to kill a person one is committed by God to love? Is it at all possible for one to give adherence to the concept of the sacredness of persons, and at the same time will the destruction of a person? It would seem that it is impossible for the Christian to answer such questions in the affirmative.

Within this context there has been no attempt to deal with conditions that may, under certain circumstances, make killing necessary. Granted that some wars or revolutions may be just and even necessary. When such action becomes necessary, and the Christian feels that he must not or cannot remain neutral, he must at that point adopt what Paul Ricoeur has called the "ethics of distress,"[5] admitting to himself and to God that his actions beyond this point are not Christian. Such a stance would, it seems, prevent all impossible attempts to construct blanket theological justifications for so much that is wrong with war in general and killing in particular. Violence is necessarily contrary to love.

Indeed, to a black theologian, what is troubling is not that the opinions of Christians, black or white, are changing, or that their opinions are shaped by the current problems of a time—on the contrary, this is as it should be. What is more troubling is that too many Christians conform to the trend of the moment without introducing into it anything specifically Christian. Their ethical convictions are too often determined by their social milieu, not by faith in Christian revelation; they too often lack the uniqueness that ought to be more expressive of their religious faith. Thus, theologies, especially the newer expressions, tend too often to become mere mechanical exercises that justify the positions adopted on grounds that are absolutely not Christian. Much of what is now called theological justification for revolution would bespeak such a trend. Currently black churchmen and black theologians increasingly are finding it hard to resist offering theological justification for views akin to the black racism current within much of the black community.

[5] See Ricoeur's *History and Truth* (Evanston: Northwestern University Press, 1965), p. 243. Martin E. Marty concurs with this view in *The Search for a Usable Future* (New York: Harper, 1969), p. 115.

This is not to say that some counter-racism is probably not needed in the black community; it is rather to contend that black theology should not extend justification for it. Yet it is strange how far theologians will go in their attempt to be all things to all kinds of people.

One finds it hard to disagree that

the humane principle of revolution is this way: the slave revolts against his master. He denies him as a master, but not as a man. For his protest is directed against the master's refusal to treat him as a man. As master and slave, neither is a true man and neither can relate to the other in a humane way. If the denial of the master were total, the slave's revolt would bring nothing new into the world but would exchange the roles of inhumanity. The humane revolution, however, is not out to turn slaves into masters but to abolish the whole master-slave relationship so that in the future men will be able to treat one another as men. If the revolution loses sight of this goal, it becomes nihilistic and forfeits its fascination.[6]

In addition to this interesting exposition of Albert Camus's concept of a humane principle of revolution, Moltmann further contends that under certain conditions the use of revolutionary violence can be justified by humane goals. However, he is not too sure that such justification can be assured, and so he concludes that unless it is possible and assured, "revolutionary violence cannot be made meaningful or appropriate. Unless every possible means is put to use, the revolutionary future is not worth committing oneself to."[7] However, one wonders if black theology can embrace Moltmann's position when he advises that "people must be able to combine what they desire with what is objectively possible and what they can subjectively accomplish."[8]

Indeed, if a revolution can be this rational and if the aims can be preconceived, then one wonders if some more rational approach cannot be found than a violent revolution. It would seem that Moltmann is nearer right when he reminds us that

if the revolutionary goal is a more fully realized humanity, then revolutionaries cannot afford to be inhuman during the so-called transitional period. Already, on the way, we must directly begin with the future and make life truly human during the transitional period. . . .

It follows, therefore, that a revolution of the present for the benefit of a better and more humane future must not mold itself after the strategies of the world to be overthrown. Only with great restraint can revolutionaries enter the diabolical circle of violence and counter-violence if they are ever to conquer and abolish it as a whole. . . . How are we to bring about the kingdom of non-violent brotherhood with the help of violent action?[9]

These words of Moltmann cannot be read without recalling the teachings of Martin Luther King, Jr., for it was he who, perhaps more than many people who talk of revolution today, thought and acted out of a deep dimension of truth which was not dependent on political power and the rules of its games. Too many people could not accept this fact—that his frame of reference was theological, and he was, to a great extent, immune from anxiety and the seduction of political power. Precisely for that reason alone he became more and more in disfavor, and a greater

---

[6] Jürgen Moltmann, *Religion, Revolution and the Future*, p. 142.
[7] *Ibid.*, p. 143.
[8] *Ibid.*, p. 144.
[9] *Ibid.*

threat to people in positions of great power than even the prophets of violence themselves. In a very real sense, the true revolutionary must not allow the law of the opposition to prescribe his own course of action or response, otherwise he cannot become a part of the new humanity. Any means may be appropriate, but they must be different and better than those of the opposition if they would bewilder the opposition.

It is not the thesis of this book to assess the need or the lack of a need for revolution, whether violent or nonviolent. There has been little attempt to discuss whether the present social or political systems of the world can or cannot be altered without violence. My main concern has been over the trend of modern theologians to attempt to extend theological or ethical justifications for violent revolution, thus further confusing persons into believing that they are being Christian when indeed they are not. Colin Morris, in his book *Unyoung, Uncolored, Unpoor*, has made a cogent plea for such an unconditional justification, so it might be helpful to assess his basic thesis within this context. He contends that "Christians have both the right and the responsibility to take part in revolution," be it violent or nonviolent in nature. He is right in his assertion that

we weep with pride in the story of Dietrich Bonhoeffer's triumphant death at the hands of the Flossenberg hangman, and pore over his last writings with an eagerness that could not be greater had he handed them out personally to us from the other side of the Beyond. But we scurry quickly away from the tougher truth that he was a justly condemned accessory to murder. Hitler, the main target of the plot, indeed survived Stauffenberg's bomb, but others in that map room were destroyed, some of them honorable soldiers. If only Bonhoeffer had lived, we lament, to tell us more about the line of thought sketched out in the startling epigrams of Letters and Papers from Prison. I, for one, believe that his explanation of the theology behind the bomb plot might have more to say to our time. The new theology for which the Church is searching may be hidden in that violent deed of Bonhoeffer's which misfired and not in his musings about God without religion. Any Christian, tasting the sulphur which hangs in the air of our time, could wish for a theology of violence from the pen of a great theologian who dared to strike and paid for his temerity with his life. [10]

In his further contention, Dr. Morris talks about the timing of the Christian's action as being problematic because he has to delay long enough to make sure that the extent of the evil justifies the radical action. The problem is, how long should one delay doing what one feels that he has to do? Hitler should have been cut down sooner, and the six million Jews would have been spared, and the world would not have suffered so greatly at his hands. This is rightly a concern of the Christian. 'Bonhoeffer, Stauffenberg, and the rest indeed died to rid the world of a fount of evil. Yet if they had struck ten years earlier, before the smoke and the gas chambers had blackened the sky and Europe's cities were aflame, who knows how history might have been changed?" [11]

One might well accept the actions of Bonhoeffer, one might have agreed with those who plotted Hitler's death, one might also have accepted the fact that Hitler was indeed a "fount of evil"; but to say that even such a great theologian as Bonhoeffer was acting like a Christian is a much deeper question and a much more serious problem. Indeed, it would seem that maybe had he lived he would have

[10] Colin Morris, *Unyoung, Uncolored, Unpoor* (Nashville: Abingdon Press, 1969), p. 24.
[11] *Ibid.*, p. 25.

admitted that when the group gathered to plot Hitler's death they were not attempting to find theological justification for their actions, because there could be none. But they were honest Christians fully realizing that they were acting without any theological or ethical justification; and had they survived they would have been in need of deep forgiveness for actions that they might well have admitted were not Christian. But nevertheless, theirs were actions which they thought needed to be taken. Are there not times when Christian man

has not to decide simply between right and wrong and between good and evil, but between right and right and between wrong and wrong. . . . Precisely in this respect responsible action is a free venture; it is not justified by any law; it is performed without any claim to a valid self-justification, and therefore also without any claim to an ultimate valid knowledge of good and evil. Good, as what is responsible, is performed in ignorance of good and in the surrender to God of the deed which has become necessary and which is nevertheless, or for that very reason, free. [12]

It matters not how frustrating the situation may become, it would seem that any lasting solution must be found, especially for the black man, in some approach other than violence, for violence is the very language of the enemy, and against violence he seems to have an adequate response that would assure all rational thinkers that liberation cannot come by the way of violence.

This is not to withdraw from those actions which are necessary to counter the evils of racism, and this is not to rule out the fact that some of these actions may even be violent. It is just to argue that any actions against the enemy should further the cause of freedom, rather than restrict it.

So the concern here is not with a lack of action, it is rather that actions be seen rationally and honestly for what they are and not justified for what they are not. Thus, an "ethics of distress" is more honest to both self and God. And the lack of success, while engaging in actions that are ill advised, will not commit God to failures for which he may or may not be totally responsible.

Paul Ricoeur, in his book *History and Truth,* has described the violent moment as a time when an ethics of distress is invoked, and such an ethics would suggest that conditions are such that remedies cannot be justified theologically. His contention is that such honesty is better than an ethics or a theology which anticipates the legitimacy either of killing or of a pure passivism and the victim role. There are times, one must agree, when conventional ethical norms cannot be applied, especially in the black community. Indeed, there are situations in which one must do what one must do and then say one's prayers.

The current problem facing the black community is one of change, which will make life bearable for many black people in white America. For the oppressed and for those who appear now to have no hope, there seems to be no way except to embrace violence as a means of social change. To tell them it is futile and that it will bring no real change is an impossible position. They have tried other ways.

They saw the way of nonviolence suffer a bitter blow in the death of Dr. King. They also recall that Stokely Carmichael and H. Rap Brown both were once adherents to the nonviolent way of protest. In later years, they contended on many occasions that nonviolent protest was always met with violence from the white

[12] Dietrich Bonhoeffer, *Ethics,* ed. by Eberhard Bethge and trans. by N. H. Smith (New York: Macmillan, 1955), p. 249.

community, which resisted any change whatsoever. Intellectual guerrilla warfare, properly located spokesmen for change, the government, the police forces, all have failed in their support of any great and meaningful change for the vast majority of the black community.

The one question that faces the black community is still whether there are yet more effective nonviolent means for perfecting social change. There are many who still think that all the means have not been exhausted. Vincent Harding contends that massive nonviolent means have not been fully tried, and his is still a strong voice for further exploration of nonviolent means of protest for social change. But there are others, for instance the Black Panthers, who have come to feel that there is no hope short of violent revolution for changing current social structures; it is for them that hope is needed. But, while black Christian radicalism, even if it takes love seriously, forbids participation in violence of any kind, it cannot ever give counsel to the oppressed to be submissive and accepting. Too often in history Christians have betrayed their faith by preaching resignation to the oppressed without giving due attention to the oppressor.

Adherents of the way of nonviolence, whether it be conceived as a methodology or as a way of life, root their actions in a strong Christian belief that one should absorb hatred and transform it through love, that one should endure rather than inflict violence. This basic faith in the nonviolent way leads to two approaches. First, centering on persons, the proponents of nonviolence contend that nonviolence cannot be an external attitude; it must be internalized. It is in being himself at peace that a person becomes peaceful; it is in living by the law and mandate of love that a person becomes capable of manifesting that love; it is through the practice of it in one's personal life that nonviolence spreads to others. Second, it must be recalled that the whole problem of nonviolence comes down to two conclusions: (a) the state must be divested of its instruments of violence, and (b) for their part, proponents of nonviolence must respond to other people's use of violence by nonviolent actions—sacrifice, noncooperation, civil disobedience, etc. Nonviolence has not been tried on a wide scale since Gandhi. No hope for the future, whether with or without violence, can adequately speak to the black community unless it takes seriously the oppressed people's contentions against the oppressors.

On the assumption that the Christian cannot choose the way of violence, the ethics of revolutionary involvement is particularly problematic for those who advocate a nonviolent approach. Especially is it so if they do not believe that military action solves as much as it purports to achieve, and if they further contend that a man does not have a right to arrogate to himself the decision concerning who should live and who should die. The Christian who gives adherence to violence always must run the risk that violence will demand the end to the potentiality of another person, a person who may himself have been able to contribute to the world's good. The black Christian cannot propose to live by any other standard than those ethical principles, or the unconditional mandate of love, if he lives by any principle at all. It would seem that no ethical frame of reference which makes the development rather than the destruction of the person one of its central concerns can adhere to any concept of violent revolution. When the black Christian thinks otherwise, then he must embrace an ethics of distress, admitting that he has passed beyond Christian action. However, for nonviolence, as a method or as a way of life, to work, it would have to be adopted with the belief that: (1) a government can maintain itself without ever using violence against its citizens; (2) there is such a thing as a "just state" that would be sufficient unto itself; (3) the structures of society are still flexible enough for there to be a deep moral ethos that makes society receptive.

Few people of the black community would now accept such a basic presupposition. Most black people with whom one talks are more ready to believe that most levels of white society are ready for what Lerone Bennett calls "confrontation"[13] between the races, and that the majority of the black people know this will mean violence against the black community. Thus, there seems to be little hope for the black man ever retrogressing to the way of nonviolence as a means of protest or revolution.

There is no suggestion in this context that violence should be the methodology now adopted; it is rather to suggest that the "black mood" has created a new man who is through with humiliation, and he is seeking rescue through whatever means necessary, even revolution. This type of revolution is not, and cannot be, a strategy consciously devised. It will grow out of the deep, instinctive expression of human being denied individuality. Such expressions of revolution, violent or nonviolent, can be liberating. Or as Lerone Bennett puts it: "The boundary of freedom is man's power to say 'No!' and whoever refuses to say 'No' involves himself tragically in his own degradation."[14] From all levels of the black community there will increasingly come the answer "No!" to any type of degrading actions on the part of the white community.

The basic thesis of this book is that such a "No!" does not have to be violent if it is a collective "No!" and if it comes from the lips of a liberated people who really mean "No!" Such an ethos is collecting within the black community; it is the "now" and the "not-yet" facet of the hope that is inherent in the black awareness movement.

The hope within the black awareness movement is theological, because it is, as one can conceive it, under God. . . .

TRADITIONAL

For this section of the chapter, we have selected essays that deal with the existence of God. Perhaps you have noticed how convenient God is as an instrument for dealing with man's fate in the cosmos. Theologians' reliance on God is understandable. Theology and philosophy cross paths on the question of God's

[13] Lerone Bennett, *Confrontation: Black and White* (Baltimore: Penguin Books, 1966). See also Bennett's *Negro Mood*, p. 95.

[14] *Ibid.,* p. 256

existence because philosophers typically demand that arguments be given for beliefs. And theologians feel the need to meet the philosophers on their own ground; in this section, St. Anselm, St. Thomas Aquinas, and William Paley provide us with arguments for the existence of God.

The argument from **St. Anselm** (first essay in this section), recently the subject of a large number of articles in the philosophical journals, is very short yet elusive for the student, who too frequently casually dismisses it. We urge you to give the argument considerable thought. The best way to do this is to frame a refutation of it and then let one of your friends, the class, or your mentor show you why you have not got a refutation after all. Ironically, your refutation is likely to be embarrassingly longer than Anselm's argument.

St. Thomas Aquinas (second essay) recognized that some people do not accept Christianity because they lack faith. One can't give people faith as one would give them instruction; and it doesn't do much good to exhort or threaten them; and spellbinding generally has only a short-term effect. The most one can do is prepare the unbeliever, and take away the obstacles that have stunted the flower of faith. One of these obstacles could be rational doubt that the object of faith and worship exists. It may seem to the unbeliever that belief in the existence of God is a rag of mythological nonsense woven by the imagination of the insecure and frightened who need reassurance in a wicked world. If so, then the churchman who feels it his duty to help as many unbelievers to salvation as he can will formulate arguments that rationally prove the existence of God. This duty calls for churchmen to become philosophers, to supplement the "revealed truth" with philosophic reason.

William Hamilton has remarked that his son, who has become a technological man, does not feel the same awe that Hamilton felt as a youth when he looked into the sky. This feeling of awe has been called natural piety. The emotional experience of fully realizing the incredible complexity of the world may be so overwhelming that our breast fills with it and our mind says to our heart, "Yes, this is the religious experience." This natural piety may increase with an increase in knowledge; the natural piety of men took a sharp leap after Isaac Newton's great works were published, because they yielded additional knowledge and evidence of the universe's incredible order, an order marvelously matching the universe's incredible complexity. **William Paley**, in the third essay of this section, uses a watch as an example of designed order. That in itself would not seem relevant to a proof of God's existence, but it becomes pregnant with relevance if one is able to show that the universe has an order similar to the watch. That was precisely what people believed Newton had shown. Until then, the premise about nature's order was relatively weak; Newton gave it muscle. The divines praised Newton because he showed them that the glory of physics rests in its theological service. A vast structure of natural theology was erected on the basis of the strengthened design argument, neatly presented here by Paley.

There are many experiences and considerations that lead men to a belief in the existence of God. The arguments for God's existence are probably the least influential of all the causes of that belief. Similarly, the refutation of the arguments for the existence of God probably play less of a role in causing men to doubt God's existence than their suffering does. It is difficult for a person who has suffered deeply to reconcile the suffering with the existence of a good, all-powerful, omniscient God. If such a God exists, then there should be no evil in the world. There is evil in the world; therefore, there is no such God. In the last essay in this chapter, **John Hick** tries to reconcile the presence of evil and the existence of the typical Christian deity. Parenthetically, Hick's essay could profitably be related to the last chapter, "Flight from Meaninglessness."

The Ontological Argument
St. Anselm

St. Anselm (1033-1109) was made Archbishop of Canterbury in 1093. Anselm's name will forever be associated with the ontological argument for the existence of God. During his years in the abbey, he wrote two works for which he is best known: *The Monologium* and *The Proslogium*.

Truly there is a God, although the fool hath said in his heart, There is no God.

And so, Lord, do thou, who dost give understanding to faith, give me, so far as thou knowest it to be profitable, to understand that thou art as we believe; and that thou art that which we believe. And, indeed, we believe that thou art a being than which nothing greater can be conceived. Or is there no such nature, since the fool hath said in his heart, there is no God? (Psalms xiv. 1). But, at any rate, this very fool, when he hears of this being of which I speak—a being than which nothing greater can be conceived—understands what he hears, and what he understands is in his understanding; although he does not understand it to exist.

For, it is one thing for an object to be in the understanding, and another to understand that the object exists. When a painter first conceives of what he will afterwards perform, he has it in his understanding, but he does not yet understand it to be, because he has not yet performed it. But after he has made the painting, he both has it in his understanding and he understands that it exists, because he has made it.

Hence, even the fool is convinced that something exists in the understanding, at least, than which nothing greater can be conceived. For, when he hears of this, he understands it. And whatever is understood, exists in the understanding. And assuredly that, than which nothing greater can be conceived, cannot exist in the understanding alone. For, suppose it exists in the understanding alone: then it can be conceived to exist in reality; which is greater.

Therefore, if that, than which nothing greater can be conceived, exists in the understanding alone, the very being, than which nothing greater can be conceived, is one, than which a greater can be conceived. But obviously this is impossible.

Source: St. Anselm: Basic Writings, trans. S. N. Deane, with Intro. by Charles Hartshorne (La Salle, Ill.: Open Court, 1961). Reprinted by permission of The Open Court Publishing Co., La Salle, Illinois.

Hence, there is no doubt that there exists a being, than that which nothing greater can be conceived, and it exists both in the understanding and in reality.

God cannot be conceived not to exist—God is that, than which nothing greater can be conceived.—That which can be conceived not to exist is not God.

And it assuredly exists so truly, that it cannot be conceived not to exist. For, it is possible to conceive of a being which cannot be conceived not to exist; and this is greater than one which can be conceived not to exist. Hence, if that, than which nothing greater can be conceived, can be conceived not to exist, it is not that, than which nothing greater can be conceived. But this is an irreconcilable contradiction. There is, then, so truly a being than which nothing greater can be conceived to exist, that it cannot even be conceived not to exist; and this being thou art, O Lord, our God.

So truly, therefore, dost thou exist, O Lord, my God, that thou canst not be conceived not to exist; and rightly. For, if a mind could conceive of a being better than thee, the creature would rise above the Creator; and this is most absurd. And, indeed, whatever else there is, except thee alone, can be conceived not to exist. To thee alone, therefore, it belongs to exist more truly than all other beings, and hence in a higher degree than all others. For, whatever else exists does not exist so truly, and hence in a less degree it belongs to it to exist. Why, then, has the fool said in his heart, there is no God (Psalms xiv. 1), since it is so evident, to a rational mind, that thou dost exist in the highest degree of all? Why, except that he is dull and a fool?

How the fool has said in his heart what cannot be conceived.—A thing may be conceived in two ways: (1) when the word signifying it is conceived; (2) when the thing itself is understood. As far as the word goes, God can be conceived not to exist; in reality he cannot.

But how has the fool said in his heart what he could not conceive; or how is it that he could not conceive what he said in his heart? since it is the same to say in the heart, and to conceive.

But, if really, nay, since really, he both conceived, because he said in his heart; and did not say in his heart, because he could not conceive; there is more than one way in which a thing is said in the heart or conceived. For, in one sense, an object is conceived, when the word signifying it is conceived; and in another, when the very entity, which the object is, is understood.

In the former sense, then, God can be conceived not to exist; but in the latter, not at all. For no one who understands what fire and water are can conceive fire to be water, in accordance with the nature of the facts themselves, although this is possible according to the words. So, then, no one who understands what God is can conceive that God does not exist; although he says these words in his heart, either without any, or with some foreign signification. For God is that than which a greater cannot be conceived. And he who thoroughly understands this, assuredly understands that this being so truly exists, that not even in concept can it be non-existent. Therefore, he who understands that God so exists, cannot conceive that he does not exist.

I thank thee, gracious Lord, I thank thee; because what I formerly believed by thy bounty, I now so understand by thine illumination, that if I were unwilling to believe that thou dost exist, I should not be able not to understand this to be true.

Five Proofs of the Existence of God
St. Thomas Aquinas

St. Thomas Aquinas (1225-1274) devoted his life to the clarification of Christian doctrine and its integration with Aristotle's metaphysics. He was the greatest medieval Catholic philosopher and wrote more than a hundred volumes of philosophy.

WHETHER GOD EXISTS?

Objection 1. It seems that God does not exist; because if one of two contraries be infinite, the other would be altogether destroyed. But the name *God* means that He is infinite goodness. If, therefore, God existed, there would be no evil discoverable; but there is evil in the world. Therefore God does not exist.

Obj. 2. Further, it is superfluous to suppose that what can be accounted for by a few principles has been produced by many. But it seems that everything we see in the world can be accounted for by other principles, supposing God did not exist. For all natural things can be reduced to one principle, which is nature; and all voluntary things can be reduced to one principle, which is human reason, or will. Therefore there is no need to suppose God's existence.

On the contrary, It is said in the person of God: *I am who am* (Exod. iii. 14).

I answer that, The existence of God can be proved in five ways.

The first and more manifest way is the argument from motion. It is certain, and evident to our senses, that in the world some things are in motion. Now whatever is moved is moved by another, for nothing can be moved except it is in potentiality to that towards which it is moved; whereas a thing moves inasmuch as it is in act. For motion is nothing else than the reduction of something from potentiality to actuality. But nothing can be reduced from potentiality to actuality, except by something in a state of actuality. Thus that which is actually hot, as fire, makes wood, which is potentially hot, to be actually hot, and thereby moves and changes it. Now it is not possible that the same thing should be at once in actuality and potentiality in the same respect, but only in different respects. For what is actually hot cannot simultaneously be potentially hot; but it is simultaneously potentially cold. It is therefore impossible that in the same respect and in the same way a thing should be both mover and moved, *i.e.*, that it should move itself. Therefore, whatever is moved must be moved by another. If that by which it is moved be itself moved, then this also must needs be moved by another, and that by another again. But this cannot go on to infinity, because then there would be no first mover, and, consequently, no other mover, seeing that subsequent movers move only inasmuch as they are moved by the first mover; as the staff moves only because it is moved by the hand. Therefore it is necessary to arrive at a first mover, moved by no other; and this everyone understands to be God.

Source: Basic Writings of St. Thomas Aquinas, edited by Anton C. Pegis. Copyright 1945 by Random House, Inc. Reprinted by permission of the publisher and Ian Hislop, O.P., St. Dominic's Priory, London.

The second way is from the nature of efficient cause. In the world of sensible things we find there is an order of efficient causes. There is no case known (neither is it, indeed, possible) in which a thing is found to be the efficient cause of itself; for so it would be prior to itself, which is impossible. Now in efficient causes it is not possible to go on to infinity, because in all efficient causes following in order, the first is the cause of the intermediate cause, and the intermediate is the cause of the ultimate cause, whether the intermediate cause be several, or one only. Now to take away the cause is to take away the effect. Therefore, if there be no first cause among efficient causes, there will be no ultimate, nor any intermediate, cause. But if in efficient causes it is possible to go on to infinity, there will be no first efficient cause, neither will there be an ultimate effect, nor any intermediate efficient causes; all of which is plainly false. Therefore it is necessary to admit a first efficient cause, to which everyone gives the name of God.

The third way is taken from possibility and necessity, and runs thus. We find in nature things that are possible to be and not to be, since they are found to be generated, and to be corrupted, and consequently, it is possible for them to be and not to be. But it is impossible for these always to exist, for that which can not-be at some time is not. Therefore, if everything can not-be, then at one time there was nothing in existence. Now if this were true, even now there would be nothing in existence, because that which does not exist begins to exist only through something already existing. Therefore, if at one time nothing was in existence, it would have been impossible for anything to have begun to exist; and thus even now nothing would be in existence—which is absurd. Therefore, not all beings are merely possible, but there must exist something the existence of which is necessary. But every necessary thing either has its necessity caused by another, or not. Now it is impossible to go on to infinity in necessary things which have their necessity caused by another, as has been already proved in regard to efficient causes. Therefore we cannot but admit the existence of some being having of itself its own necessity, and not receiving it from another, but rather causing in others their necessity. This all men speak of as God.

The fourth way is taken from the gradation to be found in things. Among beings there are some more and some less good, true, noble, and the like. But *more* and *less* are predicated of different things according as they resemble in their different ways something which is the maximum, as a thing is said to be hotter according as it more nearly resembles that which is hottest; so that there is something which is truest, something best, something noblest, and, consequently, something which is most being, for those things that are greatest in truth are greatest in being, as it is written in [Aristotle's] *Metaphysics* ii. Now the maximum in any genus is the cause of all in that genus, as fire, which is the maximum of heat, is the cause of all hot things, as is said in the same book. Therefore there must also be something which is to all beings the cause of their being, goodness, and every other perfection; and this we call God.

The fifth way is taken from the governance of the world. We see that things which lack knowledge, such as natural bodies, act for an end, and this is evident from their acting always, or nearly always, in the same way, so as to obtain the best result. Hence it is plain that they achieve their end, not fortuitously, but designedly. Now whatever lacks knowledge cannot move towards an end, unless it be directed by some being endowed with knowledge and intelligence; as the arrow is directed by the archer. Therefore some intelligent being exists by whom all natural things are directed to their end: and this being we call God.

Reply Obj. 1. As Augustine says: *Since God is the highest good, He would not allow any evil to exist in His works; unless His omnipotence and goodness were such as to bring good even out of evil.* This is part of the infinite goodness of God, that He should allow evil to exist, and out of it produce good.

Reply Obj. 2. Since nature works for a determinate end under the direction of a higher agent, whatever is done by nature must be traced back to God as to its first cause. So likewise whatever is done voluntarily must be traced back to some higher cause other than human reason and will, since these can change and fail; for all things that are changeable and capable of defect must be traced back to an immovable and self-necessary first principle, as has been shown.

The Teleological Argument
William Paley

William Paley (1743-1806) wrote many apologetic works, including *Evidences of Christianity* (1794) and *Appearances of Nature* (1802).

STATEMENT OF THE ARGUMENT

In crossing a heath, suppose I pitched my foot against a *stone*, and were asked how the stone came to be there, I might possibly answer, that, for anything I knew to the contrary, it had lain their forever; nor would it, perhaps, be very easy to show the absurdity of this answer. But suppose I found a *watch* upon the ground, and it should be inquired how the watch happened to be in that place, I should hardly think of the answer which I had before given—that, for anything I knew, the watch might have always been there. Yet why should not this answer serve for the watch as well as for the stone? why is it not as admissible in the second case as in the first? For this reason, and for no other, viz., that, when we come to inspect the watch, we perceive (what we could not discover in the stone) that its several parts are framed and put together for a purpose, e.g. that they are so formed and adjusted as to produce motion, and that motion so regulated as to point out the hour of the day; that, if the different parts had been differently shaped from what they are, if a different size from what they are, or placed after any other manner, or in any other order than that in which they are placed, either no motion at all would have been carried on in the machine, or none which would have answered the use that is now served by it. To reckon up a few of the plainest of these parts, and of their offices, all tending to one result:—We see a cylindrical box containing a coiled elastic spring, which, by its endeavor to relax itself, turns round the box. We next observe a flexible chain (artificially wrought for the sake of flexure) communicating the action of the spring from the box to the fusee. We then find a series of wheels, the teeth of which catch in, and apply to, each other, conducting the motion from the

Source: Natural Theology (1802).

fusee to the balance, and from the balance to the pointer, and at the same time, by the size and shape of those wheels, so regulating that motion as to terminate in causing an index, by an equable and measured progression, to pass over a given space in a given time. We take notice that the wheels are made of brass, in order to keep them from rust; the springs of steel, no other metal being so elastic; that over the face of the watch there is placed a glass, a material employed in no other part of the work, but in the room of which, if there had been any other than a transparent substance, the hour could not be seen without opening the case. This mechanism being observed (it requires indeed an examination of the instrument, and perhaps some previous knowledge of the subject, to perceive and understand it; but being once, as we have said, observed and understood), the inference, we think, is inevitable, that the watch must have had a maker; that there must have existed, at some time, and at some place or other, an artificer or artificers who formed it for the purpose which we find it actually to answer; who comprehended its construction, and designed its use.

I. Nor would it, I apprehend, weaken the conclusion, that we had never seen a watch made; that we had never known an artist capable of making one; that we were altogether incapable of executing such a piece of workmanship ourselves, or of understanding in what manner it was performed; all this being no more than what is true of some exquisite remains of ancient art, of some lost arts, and, to the generality of mankind, of the more curious productions of modern manufacture. Does one man in a million know how oval frames are turned? Ignorance of this kind exalts our opinion of the unseen and unknown artist's skill, if he be unseen and unknown, but raises no doubt in our minds of the existence and agency of such an artist, at some former time, and in some place or other. Nor can I perceive that it varies at all the inference, whether the question arise concerning a human agent, or concerning an agent of a different species, or an agent possessing, in some respect, a different nature.

II. Neither, secondly, would it invalidate our conclusion, that the watch sometimes went wrong, or that it seldom went exactly right. The purpose of the machinery, the design, and the designer, might be evident, and, in the case supposed, would be evident, in whatever way we accounted for the irregularity of the movement, or whether we could account for it or not. It is not necessary that a machine be perfect, in order to show with what design it was made; still less necessary, where the only question is, whether it were made with any design at all.

III. Nor, thirdly, would it bring any uncertainty into the argument, if there were a few parts of the watch, concerning which we could not discover, or had not yet discovered, in what manner they conduced to the general effect; or even some parts, concerning which we could not ascertain whether they conduced to that effect in any manner whatever. For, as to the first branch of the case, if by the loss, or disorder, or decay of the parts in question, the movement of the watch were found in fact to be stopped, or disturbed, or retarded, no doubt would remain in our minds as to the utility or intention of these parts, although we should be unable to investigate the manner according to which, or the connection by which, the ultimate effect depended upon their action or assistance; and the more complex is the machine, the more likely is this obscurity to arise. Then, as to the second thing supposed, namely, that there were parts which might be spared without prejudice to the movement of the watch, and that he had proved this by experiment, these superfluous parts, even if we were completely assured that they were such, would not vacate the reasoning which we had instituted concerning other parts. The indication of contrivance remained, with respect to them, nearly as it was before.

IV. Nor, fourthly, would any man in his senses think the existence of the watch, with its various machinery, accounted for, by being told that it was one out of possible combinations of material forms; that whatever he had found in the place where he found the watch, must have contained some internal configuration or other; and that this configuration might be the structure now exhibited, viz., of the works of a watch, as well as a different structure.

V. Nor, fifthly, would it yield his inquiry more satisfaction, to be answered, that there existed in things a principle of order, which had disposed the parts of the watch into their present form and situation. He never knew a watch made by the principle of order; nor can he even form to himself an idea of what is meant by a principle of order, distinct from the intelligence of the watchmaker.

VI. Sixthly, he would be surprised to hear that the mechanism of the watch was no proof of contrivance, only a motive to induce the mind to think so:

VII. And not less surprised to be informed, that the watch in his hand was nothing more than the result of the laws of *metallic* nature. It is a perversion of language to assign any law as the efficient, operative cause of anything. A law presupposes an agent; for it is only the mode according to which an agent proceeds; it implies a power; for it is the order according to which that power acts. Without this agent, without this power, which are both distinct from itself, the *law* does nothing, is nothing. The expression, "the law of metallic nature," may sound strange and harsh to a philosophic ear; but it seems quite as justifiable as some others which are more familiar to him such as "the law of vegetable nature," "the law of animal nature," or, indeed, as "the law of nature" in general, when assigned as the cause of phenomena in exclusion of agency and power, or when it is substituted into the place of these.

VIII. Neither, lastly, would our observer be driven out of his conclusion, or from his confidence in its truth, by being told that he knew nothing at all about the matter. He knows enough for his argument: he knows the utility of the end: he knows the subserviency and adaptation of the means to the end. These points being known, his ignorance of other points, his doubts concerning other points, affect not the certainty of his reasoning. The consciousness of knowing little need not beget a distrust of that which he does know. . . .

APPLICATION OF THE ARGUMENT

Every indication of contrivance, every manifestation of design, which existed in the watch, exist in the works of nature; with the difference, on the side of nature, of being greater and more, and that in a degree which exceeds all computation. I mean that the contrivances of nature surpass the contrivances of art, in the complexity, subtilty, and curiosity of the mechanism; and still more, if possible, do they go beyond them in number and variety; yet in a multitude of cases, are not less evidently mechanical, not less evidently contrivances, not less evidently accommodated to their end, or suited to their office, than are the most perfect productions of human ingenuity. . . .

Solutions to the Problem of Evil

John Hick

John Hick (1922-   ) is Lecturer in Divinity, Cambridge University. He was formerly Stuart professor of Christian philosophy at Princeton Theological Seminary. He received his M.A. degree from the University of Edinburgh and his D.Phil. from Oxford University. His works include *Faith and Knowledge* (1957), *Philosophy of Religion* (1963), *The Existence of God* (1964), and *Faith and the Philosophers* (1964).

To many, the most powerful positive objection to belief in God is the fact of evil. Probably for most agnostics it is the appalling depth and extent of human suffering, more than anything else, that makes the idea of a loving Creator seem so implausible and disposes them toward one or another of the various naturalistic theories of religion.

As a challenge to theism, the problem of evil has traditionally been posed in the form of a dilemma: if God is perfectly loving, he must wish to abolish evil; and if he is all-powerful, he must be able to abolish evil. But evil exists; therefore God cannot be both omnipotent and perfectly loving.

Certain solutions, which at once suggest themselves, have to be ruled out so far as the Judaic-Christian faith is concerned.

To say, for example (with contemporary Christian Science), that evil is an illusion of the human mind, is impossible within a religion based upon the stark realism of the Bible. Its pages faithfully reflect the characteristic mixture of good and evil in human experience. They record every kind of sorrow and suffering, every mode of man's inhumanity to man and of his painfully insecure existence in the world. There is no attempt to regard evil as anything but dark, menacingly ugly, heart-rending, and crushing. In the Christian scriptures, the climax of this history of evil is the crucifixion of Jesus, which is presented not only as a case of utterly unjust suffering, but as the violent and murderous rejection of God's Messiah. There can be no doubt, then, that for biblical faith, evil is unambiguously evil, and stands in direct opposition to God's will.

Again, to solve the problem of evil by means of the theory (sponsored, for example, by the Boston "Personalist" School)[1] of a finite deity who does the best he can with a material, intractable and co-eternal with himself, is to have abandoned the basic premise of Hebrew-Christian monotheism; for the theory amounts to rejecting belief in the infinity and sovereignty of God.

Indeed, any theory which would avoid the problem of the origin of evil by depicting it as an ultimate constituent of the universe, coordinate with good, has

Source: Philosophy of Religion (Englewood Cliffs, N.J.: Prentice-Hall, 1963), pp. 40-47. © 1963. Reprinted by permission of Prentice-Hall, Inc., Englewood Cliffs, New Jersey.

[1] Edgar Brightman's *A Philosophy of Religion* (Englewood Cliffs, N.J.: Prentice-Hall, Inc., 1940), Chaps. 8-10, is a classic exposition of one form of this view.

been repudiated in advance by the classic Christian teaching, first developed by Augustine, that evil represents the going wrong of something which in itself is good.[2] Augustine holds firmly to the Hebrew-Christian conviction that the universe is *good*—that is to say, it is the creation of a good God for a good purpose. He completely rejects the ancient prejudice, widespread in his day, that matter is evil. There are, according to Augustine, higher and lower, greater and lesser goods in immense abundance and variety; but everything which has being is good in its own way and degree, except in so far as it may have become spoiled or corrupted. Evil—whether it be an evil will, an instance of pain, or some disorder or decay in nature—has not been set there by God, but represents the distortion of something that is inherently valuable. Whatever exists is, as such, and in its proper place, good; evil is essentially parasitic upon good, being disorder and perversion in a fundamentally good creation. This understanding of evil as something negative means that it is not willed and created by God; but it does not mean (as some have supposed) that evil is unreal and can be disregarded. Clearly, the first effect of this doctrine is to accentuate even more the question of the origin of evil.

Theodicy,[3] as many modern Christian thinkers see it, is a modest enterprise, negative rather than positive in its conclusions. It does not claim to explain, nor to explain away, every instance of evil in human experience, but only to point to certain considerations which prevent the fact of evil (largely incomprehensible though it remains) from constituting a final and insuperable bar to rational belief in God.

In indicating these considerations it will be useful to follow the traditional division of the subject. There is the problem of *moral evil* or wickedness: why does an all-good and all-powerful God permit this? And there is the problem of the *non-moral evil* of suffering or pain, both physical and mental: why has an all-good and all-powerful God created a world in which this occurs?

Christian thought has always considered moral evil in its relation to human freedom and responsibility. To be a person is to be a finite center of freedom, a (relatively) free and self-directing agent responsible for one's own decisions. This involves being free to act wrongly as well as to act rightly. The idea of a person who can be infallibly guaranteed always to act rightly is self-contradictory. There can be no guarantee in advance that a genuinely free moral agent will never choose amiss. Consequently, the possibility of wrongdoing or sin is logically inseparable from the creation of finite persons, and to say that God should not have created beings who might sin amounts to saying that he should not have created people.

This thesis has been challenged in some recent philosophical discussions of the problem of evil, in which it is claimed that no contradiction is involved in saying that God might have made people who would be genuinely free and who could yet be guaranteed always to act rightly. A quotation from one of these discussions follows:

If there is no logical impossibility in a man's freely choosing the good on one, or on several occasions, there cannot be a logical impossibility in his freely choosing the good on every

---

[2] See Augustine's *Confessions*, Book VII, Chap. 12; *City of God*, Book XII, Chap. 3; *Enchiridion*, Chap. 4.

[3] The word "theodicy" from the Greek *theos* (God) and *dike* (righteous) means the justification of God's goodness in the face of the fact of evil.

occasion. God was not, then, faced with a choice between making innocent automata and making beings who, in acting freely, would sometimes go wrong: there was open to him the obviously better possibility of making beings who would act freely but always go right. Clearly, his failure to avail himself of this possibility is inconsistent with his being both omnipotent and wholly good.[4]

A reply to this argument is suggested in another recent contribution to the discussion.[5] If by a free action we mean an action which is not externally compelled but which flows from the nature of the agent as he reacts to the circumstances in which he finds himself, there is, indeed, no contradiction between our being free and our actions being "caused" (by our own nature) and therefore being in principle predictable. There is a contradiction, however, in saying that God is the cause of our acting as we do but that we are free beings in relation to God. There is, in other words, a contradiction in saying that God has made us so that we shall of necessity act in a certain way, and that we are genuinely independent persons in relation to him. If all our thoughts and actions are divinely predestined, however free and morally responsible we may seem to be to ourselves, we cannot be free and morally responsible in the sight of God, but must instead be his helpless puppets. Such "freedom" is like that of a patient acting out a series of posthypnotic suggestions; he appears, even to himself, to be free, but his volitions have actually been predetermined by another will, that of the hypnotist, in relation to whom the patient is not a free agent.

A different objector might raise the question of whether or not we deny God's omnipotence if we admit that he is unable to create persons who are free from the risks inherent in personal freedom. The answer that has always been given is that to create such beings is logically impossible. It is no limitation upon God's power that he cannot accomplish the logically impossible, since there is nothing here to accomplish, but only a meaningless conjunction of words[6]—in this case "person who is not a person." God is able to create beings of any and every conceivable kind; but creatures who lack moral freedom, however superior they might be to human beings in other respects, would not be what we mean by persons. They would constitute a different form of life which God might have brought into existence instead of persons. When we ask why God did not create such beings in place of persons, the traditional answer is that only persons could, in any meaningful sense, become "children of God," capable of entering into a personal relationship with their Creator by a free and uncompelled response to his love.

When we turn from the possibility of moral evil as a correlate of man's personal freedom to its actuality, we face something which must remain inexplicable even when it can be seen to be possible. For we can never provide a complete causal explanation of a free act; if we could, it would not be a free act. The origin of moral evil lies forever concealed within the mystery of human freedom.

[4] J. L. Mackie, "Evil and Omnipotence," *Mind* (April, 1955), p. 209. A similar point is made by Antony Flew in "Divine Omnipotence and Human Freedom," *New Essays in Philosophical Theology*. An important critical comment on these arguments is offered by Ninian Smart in "Omnipotence, Evil and Supermen," *Philosophy* (April, 1961), with replies by Flew (January, 1962) and Mackie (April, 1962).

[5] Flew, in *New Essays in Philosophical Theology*.

[6] As Aquinas said, ". . . nothing that implies a contradiction falls under the scope of God's omnipotence," *Summa Theologica*, Part I, Question 25, article 4.

The necessary connection between moral freedom and the possibility, now actualized, of sin throws light upon a great deal of the suffering which afflicts mankind. For an enormous amount of human pain arises either from the inhumanity or the culpable incompetence of mankind. This include such major scourges as poverty, oppression and persecution, war, and all the injustice, indignity, and inequity which occur even in the most advanced societies. These evils are manifestations of human sin. Even disease is fostered to an extent, the limits of which have not yet been determined by psychosomatic medicine, by moral and emotional factors seated both in the individual and in his social environment. To the extent that all of these evils stem from human failures and wrong decisions, their possibility is inherent in the creation of free persons inhabiting a world which presents them with real choices which are followed by real consequences.

We may now turn more directly to the problem of suffering. Even though the major bulk of actual human pain is traceable to man's misused freedom as a sole or part cause, there remain other sources of pain which are entirely independent of the human will, for example, earthquake, hurricane, storm, flood, drought, and blight. In practice, it is often impossible to trace a boundary between the suffering which results from human wickedness and folly and that which falls upon mankind from without. Both kinds of suffering are inextricably mingled together in human experience. For our present purpose, however, it is important to note that the latter category does exist and that it seems to be built into the very structure of our world. In response to it, theodicy, if it is wisely conducted, follows a negative path. It is not possible to show positively that each item of human pain serves the divine purpose of good; but, on the other hand, it does seem possible to show that the divine purpose as it is understood in Judaism and Christianity could not be forwarded in a world which was designed as a permanent hedonistic paradise.

An essential premise of this argument concerns the nature of the divine purpose in creating the world. The skeptic's assumption is that man is to be viewed as a completed creation and that God's purpose in making the world was to provide a suitable dwelling-place for this fully-formed creature. Since God is good and loving, the environment which he has created for human life to inhabit is naturally as pleasant and comfortable as possible. The problem is essentially similar to that of a man who builds a cage for some pet animal. Since our world, in fact, contains sources of hardship, inconvenience, and danger of innumerable kinds, the conclusion follows that this world cannot have been created by a perfectly benevolent and all-powerful deity.[7]

Christianity, however, has never supposed that God's purpose in the creation of the world was to construct a paradise whose inhabitants would experience a maximum of pleasure and a minimum of pain. The world is seen, instead, as a place of "soul-making" in which free beings grappling with the tasks and challenges of their existence in a common environment, may become "children of God" and "heirs of eternal life." A way of thinking theologically of God's continuing creative purpose for man was suggested by some of the early Hellenistic Fathers of the Christian Church, especially Irenaeus. Following hints from St. Paul, Irenaeus taught that man has been made as a person in the image of God but has not yet been brought as a free and responsible agent into the finite likeness of God, which

---

[7] This is the nature of David Hume's argument in his discussion of the problem of evil in his *Dialogues*, Part XI.

is revealed in Christ.[8] Our world, with all its rough edges, is the sphere in which this second and harder stage of the creative process is taking place.

This conception of the world (whether or not set in Irenaeus' theological framework) can be supported by the method of negative theodicy. Suppose, contrary to fact, that this world were a paradise from which all possibility of pain and suffering were excluded. The consequences would be very far-reaching. For example, no one could ever injure anyone else: the murderer's knife would turn to paper or his bullets to thin air; the bank safe, robbed of a million dollars, would miraculously become filled with another million dollars (without this device, on however large a scale, proving inflationary); fraud, deceit, conspiracy, and treason would somehow always leave the fabric of society undamaged. Again, no one would ever be injured by accident; the mountain-climber, steeplejack, or playing child falling from a height would float unharmed to the ground; the reckless driver would never meet with disaster. There would be no need to work, since no harm could result from avoiding work; there would be no call to be concerned for others in time of need or danger, for in such a world there could be no real needs or dangers.

To make possible this continual series of individual adjustments, nature would have to work by "special providences" instead of running according to general laws which men must learn to respect on penalty of pain of death. The laws of nature would have to be extremely flexible: sometimes gravity would operate, sometimes not; sometimes an object would be hard and solid, sometimes soft. There could be no sciences, for there would be no enduring world structure to investigate. In eliminating the problems and hardships of an objective environment, with its own laws, life would become like a dream in which, delightfully but aimlessly, we would float and drift at ease.

One can at least begin to imagine such a world. It is evident that our present ethical concepts would have no meaning in it. If, for example, the notion of harming someone is an essential element in the concept of a wrong action, in our hedonistic paradise there could be no wrong actions—nor any right actions in distinction from wrong. Courage and fortitude would have no point in an environment in which there is, by definition, no danger or difficulty. Generosity, kindness, the *agape* aspect of love, prudence, unselfishness, and all other ethical notions which presuppose life in a stable environment, could not even be formed. Consequently, such a world, however well it might promote pleasure, would be very ill adapted for the development of the moral qualities of human personality. In relation to this purpose it would be the worst of all possible worlds.

It would seem, then, that an environment intended to make possible the growth in free beings of the finest characteristics of personal life, must have a good deal in common with our present world. It must operate according to general and dependable laws; and it must involve real dangers, difficulties, problems, obstacles, and possibilities of pain, failure, sorrow, frustration, and defeat. If it did not contain the particular trials and perils which—subtracting man's own very considerable contribution—our world contains, it would have to contain others instead.

To realize this is not, by any means, to be in possession of a detailed theodicy. It is to understand that this world, with all its "heartaches and the thousand natural shocks that flesh is heir to," an environment so manifestly not designed for the

---

[8] See Irenaeus' *Against Heresies*, Book IV, Chaps. 37 and 38.

maximization of human pleasure and the minimization of human pain, may be rather well adapted to the quite different purpose of "soul-making." [9]

These considerations are related to theism as such. Specifically, Christian theism goes further in the light of the death of Christ, which is seen paradoxically both (as the murder of the divine Son) as the worst thing that has ever happened and (as the occasion of Man's salvation) as the best thing that has ever happened. As the supreme evil turned to supreme good, it provides the paradigm for the distinctively Christian reaction to evil. Viewed from the standpoint of Christian faith, evils do not cease to be evils; and certainly, in view of Christ's healing work, they cannot be said to have been sent by God. Yet, it has been the persistent claim of those seriously and wholeheartedly committed to Christian discipleship that tragedy, though truly tragic, may nevertheless be turned, through a man's reaction to it, from a cause of despair and alienation from God to a stage in the fulfillment of God's loving purpose for that individual. As the greatest of all evils, the crucifixion of Christ, was made the occasion of man's redemption, so good can be won from other evils. As Jesus saw his execution by the Romans as an experience which God desired him to accept, an experience which was to be brought within the sphere of the divine purpose and made to serve the divine ends, so the Christian response to calamity is to accept the adversities, pains, and afflictions which life brings, in order that they can be turned to a positive spiritual use. [10]

At this point, theodicy points forward in two ways to the subject of life after death.

First, although there are many striking instances of good being triumphantly brought out of evil through a man's or a woman's reaction to it, there are many other cases in which the opposite has happened. Sometimes obstacles breed strength of character, dangers evoke courage and unselfishness, and calamities produce patience and moral steadfastness. But sometimes they lead, instead, to resentment, fear, grasping selfishness, and disintegration of character. Therefore, it would seem that any divine purpose of soul-making which is at work in earthly history must continue beyond this life if it is ever to achieve more than a very partial and fragmentary success.

Second, if we ask whether the business of soul-making is worth all the toil and sorrow of human life, the Christian answer must be in terms of a future good which is great enough to justify all that has happened on the way to it.

---

[9] This brief discussion has been confined to the problem of human suffering. The large and intractable problem of animal pain is not taken up here. For a discussion of it, see, for example, Nels Ferré, *Evil and the Christian Faith* (New York: Harper & Row, Publishers, Inc., 1947), Chap. 7; and Austin Farrer, *Love Almighty and Ills Unlimited* (New York: Doubleday & Company, Inc., 1961), Chap. 5.

[10] This conception of providence is stated more fully in John Hick, *Faith and Knowledge* (Ithaca: Cornell University Press, 1957), Chap. 7, from which some sentences are incorporated in this paragraph.

Suggested Readings

Contemporary

1. Flew, A., and Macintyre, A. (eds.), *New Essays in Philosophical Theology* (New York: Macmillan, 1955).
2. Macquarrie, J., *Studies in Christian Existentialism* (London: SCM Press, 1966).
3. Ross, J. E., *Introduction to the Philosophy of Religion* (New York: Macmillan, 1969).
4. Watts, Alan, *The Spirit of Zen* (London: John Murray, 1936).

Traditional

1. Burrill, Donald (ed.), *The Cosmological Arguments* (New York: Doubleday, 1967). An anthology of supporters and critics.
2. Hick, John, *Evil and the God of Love* (New York: Harper, 1966).
3. Laird, John, *Mind and Deity* (New York: Philosophical Library, 1941), esp. Ch. 6.
4. Pike, Nelson, *God and Evil* (Englewood Cliffs, N.J.: Prentice-Hall, 1964).
5. Platinga, Alvin, *The Ontological Arguments* (New York: Doubleday, 1961).
6. Taylor, Richard, *Metaphysics* (Englewood Cliffs, N.J.: Prentice-Hall, 1963). Ch. 7 contains an able restatement of the cosmological argument for God's existence.

TEN

Flight from Meaninglessness

I see many people die because they judge that life is not worth living. I see others paradoxically getting killed for the ideas or illusions that give them a reason for living (what is called a reason for living is also an excellent reason for dying). I therefore conclude that the meaning of life is the most urgent of questions.

—*Albert Camus*

INTRODUCTION

In his book *The Varieties of Religious Experience*, William James uses a distinction he learned from Francis W. Newman: that between the once-born and the twice-born. The once-born are healthy minded, optimistic, cheerful, assured, without metaphysical doubts, confident of a harmonious, friendly world, and congenitally happy. James cites Walt Whitman as a supreme example of the once-born consciousness. He says, "In some individuals optimism may become quasipathological. The capacity for even a transient sadness or a momentary humility seems cut off from them as by a kind of congenital anaesthesia."

In their first life, the twice-born are dark thinkers, often in despair, pessimistic, appalled at life's transiency, metaphysically inclined, perceptive of the falsity of beguiling goods and successes, sensitive to the presence of evil, and persuaded of its pervasiveness. The twice-born cannot shuck this fearsome baggage without being born again to a new life. A religious conversion is often hailed as the end of an old life and the beginning of a new life, a rebirth that signals an awakening to the meaningfulness of life. The twice-born communicant is freshly launched again after his travail in the slough of despair.

Moods of pessimism and optimism are not to be confused with the feelings of depression and elation. Feelings are relatively momentary compared to the more permanent moods. Presumably, our moods are subject to rational manipulation. If we have no well-founded reason for pessimism, the mood should lift. The question "What is the meaning of life?" could be construed as a plea for a rational explanation of why life is worth living, a plea for a rational shield against the corrosive effects of the pessimistic mood that, when buttressed by a feeling of despair, may wear down the will to live. As a plea, the question about the meaning of life seems, as it seemed to Camus, to be the most important philosophical question we humans must wrestle with. It seems to be so, at least, to the twice-born before his second birth.

Perhaps some thinkers' congenital optimism might be blamed for the disdain they have for the question about life's meaningfulness, but that is not the sole reason. Some philosophers doubt that the question itself is meaningful. For many of them, mostly contemporary, the question is as nonsensical as, to use **John Wisdom**'s example in this chapter's first essay, "What is bigger than the largest thing in the world?" Not every set of words that is grammatically a sentence and ends with a question mark is answerable. Some questions cannot be answered, not because they are difficult, but because logically they cannot have an answer. A question that can have no answer can hardly be construed as a real question. Wisdom, however, suggests that because there are different kinds of answers to "What is the meaning of . . .?" there are different kinds of questions lying beneath the sentence form "What is the meaning of . . .?" He tells us the kind of question that "What is the meaning of life?" is and the kind that it is not and the kind of answer that can be given and the kind of answer that cannot be given. Wisdom's essay is a fitting propaedeutic to your reflections about "the meaning of life."

"What is the meaning of life?" has a passive feel to it. Its form suggests that an answer to it is something we find after a proper investigation, as if the answer were ready for the taking even before the question was asked. Contrast the passive form with a more active question: "What meaning can we give to life?" In the active form, the meaning of life depends upon us and our own efforts, individually and collectively, rather than upon a kindly or demonic cosmos. In the passive form, the moods of optimism or pessimism are justified, depending upon our conception of the cosmos. The twice-born may be a religious convert who loses his pessimism and gains his optimism because he has discovered the cosmos is in the good hands of a kindly patriarch and/or matriarch or of a whole family of gods. Of course, the discovery can go the other way, too, with pessimism as the pay-off. In the active form, the moods of optimism or pessimism may be justified, depending upon one's appraisal of the nature of man. If you think man is by nature selfish and that his nature is not alterable, then the likelihood of changing your fortunes and the world-line is too bleak to support the mood of optimism. On the other hand, confidence in yourself and the goodness of your fellow man would support an optimistic answer to the active question.

Albert Camus, in this section's second essay, represents the agnostic existentialist position on the meaning of life. His agnosticism leads him to say, "I don't know whether this world has a meaning that transcends it. But I know that I do not know that meaning and that it is impossible for me just now to know it." That is why he calls the world absurd. It is only in "this unintelligible and limited universe" that "Man's fate henceforth assumes its meaning." Although this absurd world guarantees no future, this has the advantage that it provides the opportunity for the existential man to be the inwardly free man. In an absurd world, one is free to become what he wishes. A life can have meaning even if the world does not. Thus Camus is an agnostic about the passive question but finds advantages for us when we come to answer the active form of the question about life's meaning. For Camus, the meaning of life is cast in terms of two existentialist values: the *revolt* against conformity and the absurd, and the *freedom* felt through existentially free choices. We refer you to Jean-Paul Sartre's essay in the last section of Chapter Eight for further elaboration on man's existential freedom.

Camus's outlook can be contrasted with a religious view of man's situation. Consider the Christian outlook, one designed to answer the passive form of our question: The Christian view of man's situation emerges from its account of the creation, purpose, direction, and destiny of the cosmos; we are all born into the same cosmic situation and are subject to all its vicissitudes and glories. In the Christian view, death is neither a basis for despair nor the ground of absurdity, because death is not the end of life but the beginning of its best phase, the phase during which one's immortal soul enters into contemplation and communion with God. Rebirth through a realization of God's plan, love, and care are possible on earth and allow escape from the melancholy attacks to which those who have not hitherto grasped the meaningfulness of life on earth are subject. Other religions present different cosmic pictures and characterizations of the human situation, but, for all their variety, they all aim at the generality that qualifies their answer to the question about life's meaning as being a philosophical answer.

It is the generality of an answer to the question "What is the meaning of life?" that makes it philosophical rather than psychological. For example, psychological counselling is tailormade for each person's special circumstance. Philosophical answers, on the other hand, are fitting regardless of the person or his personal conditions.

This importance of general applicability has usually been recognized by those who believe life has a meaning and who try to say what it is. This has led to talk of such things as the "human condition," the "human situation," "the place of man in the scheme of things," "the purpose of human existence," and "the destiny of man." Here there is no discussion of this man or that man (Manuel, Neil, Bess, or Luigi) but of "man." Whatever is said of "man" is said of you as well, for, being a man, you too have the "condition" or are in the "situation," even though, as a once-born type, you may not be aware of it.

One such condition to which all men are subject is death. Furthermore, humans are the only form of life conscious of their mortality. The universal concern with death makes it eligible for philosophical attention, and its concomitant *Angst* can be addressed in a philosophical theory of life's meaningfulness, or meaninglessness.

Neither Camus nor **K. E. M. Baier** accept the Christian or any other religious characterization of the human situation. Baier (fourth essay of this chapter) believes that the cosmic picture that science provides replaces the Christian picture; however, this need not give us cause for despair, because our lives can still have meaning in one sense of that term. Our lives can be made worthwhile without the Christian machinery. He suggests man's life can be made meaningful because we can give purpose to our lives through moral commitments and efforts. Baier achieves philosophical generality by giving a general *prescription* of how men are to make their lives worthwhile rather than by giving a general *description* of the human condition, or human situation, or human destiny.

Both Baier and **Kenneth Keniston** argue that there are grounds for an optimistic mood because we can give a positive answer to the active question "What meaning can we give to life?" Keniston (third essay of this chapter) notes that young students are deeply concerned about the meaning of life; and he characterizes their present situation and tries to say why that situation compels them to search for meaning as they do. He also tries to explain rationally why some people turn to drugs as a means of helping themselves to counter their present situation and to find meaning in life. For Keniston, "the question of drug use is, in the last analysis, not a medical issue, but an existential, philosphical and ethical issue. . . . It is a matter of how one chooses to live one's life, how one hopes to seek experience, where and how one searches for meaning."

John Hick's essay on the problem of evil, the last essay of the previous chapter, is related to the topic of life's meaning. An optimistic, positive answer to the passive form of the question is standard with Christian thinkers; however, the presence of evil in the world is a challenge to the Christian doctrine. How can we be optimistic if God permits evil? If he cannot prevent it, does not care, or is ignorant of it, the reassurance the Christian thinker tries to give our optimism fades like the dying man's memory of his mortal happiness.

The Meanings of the Questions of Life

John Wisdom

John Wisdom (1908-   ) taught philosophy at Cambridge University and presently teaches at the University of Oregon. He is the author of many works, including *Other Minds* (1952) and *Paradox and Discovery* (1968).

When one asks "What is the meaning of life?" one begins to wonder whether this large, hazy and bewildering question itself has any meaning. Some people indeed have said boldly that the question has no meaning. I believe this is a mistake. But it is a mistake which is not without excuse. And I hope that by examining the excuse we may begin to remedy the mistake, and so come to see that whether or not life has a meaning it is not senseless to enquire whether it has or not. First, then, what has led some people to think that the whole enquiry is senseless?

There is an old story which runs something like this: A child asked an old man

Source: Paradox and Discovery (Oxford: Basil Blackwell, 1968), pp. 38-42. Reprinted by permission of the publisher.

"What holds up the world? What holds up all things?" The old man answered "A giant." The child asked "And what holds up the giant? You must tell me what holds up the giant." The old man answered "An elephant." The child said, "And what holds up the elephant?" The old man answered "A tortoise." The child said "You still have not told me what holds up all things. For what holds up the tortoise?" The old man answered "Run away and don't ask me so many questions."

From this story we can see how it may happen that a question which looks very like sensible meaningful questions may turn out to be a senseless, meaningless one. Again and again when we ask "What supports this?" it is possible to give a sensible answer. For instance what supports the top-most card in a house of cards? The cards beneath it which are in their turn supported by the cards beneath them. What supports all the cards? The table. What supports the table? The floor and the earth. But the question "What supports all things, absolutely all things?" is different. It is absurd, it is senseless, like the question "What is bigger than the largest thing in the world?" And it is easy to see why the question "What supports all things?" is absurd. Whenever we ask, "What supports thing A or these things A, B, C?" then we can answer this question only by mentioning some thing other than the thing A or things A, B, C about which we are asked "What supports it or them?" We must if we are to answer the question mention something D other than those things which form the subject of our question, and we must say that this thing is what supports them. If we mean by the phrase "all things" absolutely all things which exist then obviously there is nothing outside that about which we are now asked "What supports all this?" Consequently any answer to the question will be self-contradictory just as any answer to the question "What is bigger than the biggest of all things?" must be self-contradictory. Such questions are absurd, or, if you like, silly and senseless.

In a like way again and again when we ask "What is the meaning of this?" we answer in terms of something other than this. For instance imagine that there has been a quarrel in the street. One man is hitting another man on the jaw. A policeman hurries up. "Now then" he says, "what is the meaning of all this?" He wants to know what led up to the quarrel, what caused it. It is no good saying to the policeman "It's a quarrel." He knows there is a quarrel. What he wants to know is what went before the quarrel, what led up to it. To answer him we must mention something other than the quarrel itself. Again suppose a man is driving a motor car and sees in front of him a road sign, perhaps a red flag, perhaps a skull and cross bones. "What does this mean?" he asks and when he asks this he wants to know what the sign points to. To answer we must mention something other than the sign itself, such as a dangerous corner in the road. Imagine a doctor sees an extraordinary rash on the face of his patient. He is astonished and murmurs to himself "What is the meaning of this?" He wants to know what caused the strange symptoms, or what they will lead to, or both. In any case in order to answer his question he must find something which went before or comes after and lies outside that about which he asks "What does this mean?" This need to look before or after in order to answer a question of the sort "What is the meaning of this?" is so common, so characteristic, a feature of such questions that it is natural to think that when it is impossible to answer such a question in this way then the question has no sense. Now what happens when we ask "What is the meaning of life?"

Perhaps someone here replies, the meaning, the significance of this present life, this life on earth, lies in a life hereafter, a life in heaven. All right. But imagine that some persistent enquirer asks, "But what I am asking is what is the meaning of all life, life here and life beyond, life now and life hereafter? What is the meaning of all things in earth and heaven?" Are we to say that this question is absurd because there cannot be anything beyond all things while at the same time any answer to "What is the meaning of all things?" must point to some thing beyond all things?

Imagine that we come into a theatre after a play has started and are obliged to leave before it ends. We may then be puzzled by the part of the play that we are able to see. We may ask "What does it mean?" In this case we want to know what went before and what came after in order to understand the part we saw. But sometimes even when we have seen and heard a play from the beginning to the end we are still puzzled and still ask what does the whole thing mean. In this case we are not asking what came before or what came after, we are not asking about anything outside the play itself. We are, if you like, asking a very different sort of question from that we usually put with the words "What does this mean?" But we are still asking a real question, we are still asking a question which has sense and is not absurd. For our words express a wish to grasp the character, the significance of the whole play. They are a confession that we have not yet done this and they are a request for help in doing it. Is the play a tragedy, a comedy or a tale told by an idiot? The pattern of it is so complex, so bewildering, our grasp of it still so inadequate, that we don't know what to say, still less whether to call it good or bad. But this question is not senseless.

In the same way when we ask "what is the meaning of all things?" we are not asking a senseless question. In this case, of course, we have not witnessed the whole play, we have only an idea in outline of what went before and what will come after that small part of history which we witness. But with the words "What is the meaning of it all?" we are trying to find the order in the drama of Time. The question may be beyond us. A child may be able to understand, to grasp a simple play and be unable to understand and grasp a play more complex and more subtle. We do not say on this account that when he asks of the larger more complex play "What does it mean?" then his question is senseless, nor even that it is senseless for him. He has asked and even answered such a question in simpler cases, he knows the sort of effort, the sort of movement of the mind which such a question calls for, and we do not say that a question is meaningless to him merely because he is not yet able to carry out quite successfully the movement of that sort which is needed in order to answer a complex question of that sort. We do not say that a question in mathematics which is at present rather beyond us is meaningless to us. We know the type of procedure it calls for and may make efforts which bring us nearer and nearer to an answer. We are able to find the meaning which lies not outside but within very complex but still limited wholes whether these are dramas of art or of real life. When we ask "What is the meaning of all things?" we are bewildered and have not that grasp of the order of things the desire for which we express when we ask that question. But this does not render the question senseless nor make it impossible for us to move towards an answer.

We must however remember that what one calls answering such a question is not giving an answer. I mean we cannot answer such a question in the form: "The meaning is this."

Such an idea about what form answering a question must take may lead to a new despair in which we feel we cannot do anything in the way of answering such a question as "What is the meaning in it all?" merely because we are not able to sum up our results in a phrase or formula.

When we ask what is the meaning of this play or this picture we cannot express the understanding which this question may lead to in the form of a list of just those things in the play or the picture which give it its meaning. No. The meaning eludes such a list. This does not mean that words quite fail us. They may yet help us provided that we do not expect of them more than they can do.

A person who is asked what he finds so hateful or so lovable in another may with words help himself and us in grasping what it is that so moves him. But he will only mislead us and himself if he pretends that his words are a complete account of all that there is in the matter.

It is the same when we ask what is it in all things that makes it all so good, so bad, so grand, so contemptible. We must not anticipate that the answer can be given in a word or in a neat list. But this does not mean that we can do nothing towards answering these questions nor even that words will not help us. Indeed surely the historians, the scientists, the prophets, the dramatists and the poets have said much which may help any man who asks himself: Is the drama of time meaningless as a tale told by an idiot? Or is it not meaningless? And if it is not meaningless is it a comedy or a tragedy, a triumph or a disaster, or is it a mixture in which sweet and bitter are for ever mixed?

The Absurdity of Human Existence

Albert Camus

Albert Camus (1913-1960), born in Algeria, became one of the foremost existential writers and won the Nobel prize in literature. Among his books are *The Stranger* (1942) and *The Fall* (1957).

ABSURDITY AND SUICIDE

There is but one truly serious philosophical problem, and that is suicide. Judging whether life is or is not worth living amounts to answering the fundamental question of philosophy. All the rest—whether or not the world has three dimensions, whether the mind has nine or twelve categories—comes afterwards. These are games; one must first answer. And if it is true, as Nietzsche claims, that a philosopher, to deserve our respect, must preach by example, you can appreciate the importance of that reply, for it will precede the definitive act. These are facts the heart can feel; yet they call for careful study before they become clear to the intellect.

If I ask myself how to judge that this question is more urgent than that, I reply that one judges by the actions it entails. I have never seen anyone die for the ontological argument. Galileo, who held a scientific truth of great importance, abjured it with the greatest of ease as soon as it endangered his life. In a certain sense, he did right.[1] That truth was not worth the stake. Whether the earth or the sun revolves around the other is a matter of profound indifference. To tell the truth, it is a futile question. On the other hand, I see many people die because they judge that life is not worth living. I see others paradoxically getting killed for the ideas or illusions that give them a reason for living (what is called a reason for living is also an excellent reason for dying). I therefore conclude that the meaning of life is the most urgent of questions. How to answer it? On all essential problems (I mean thereby those that run the risk of leading to death or those that intensify the passion of living) there are probably but two methods of thought: the method of La Palisse and the method of Don Quixote. Solely the balance between evidence and lyricism can allow us to achieve simultaneously emotion and lucidity. In a subject at once so humble and so heavy with emotion, the learned and classical dialectic must yield, one can see, to a more modest attitude of mind deriving at one and the same time from common sense and understanding.

Suicide has never been dealt with except as a social phenomenon. On the contrary, we are concerned here, at the outset, with the relationship between individual thought and suicide. An act like this is prepared within the silence of the heart, as is a great work of art. The man himself is ignorant of it. One evening he pulls the trigger or jumps. Of an apartment-building manager who had killed himself I was told that he had lost his daughter five years before, that he had changed greatly since, and that that experience had "undermined" him. A more exact word cannot be imagined. Beginning to think is beginning to be undermined. Society has but little connection with such beginnings. The worm is in man's heart. That is where it must be sought. One must follow and understand this fatal game that leads from lucidity in the face of existence to flight from light.

.   .   .

But if it is hard to fix the precise instant, the subtle step when the mind opted for death, it is easier to deduce from the act itself the consequences it implies. In a sense, and as in melodrama, killing yourself amounts to confessing. It is confessing that life is too much for you or that you do not understand it. Let's not go too far in such analogies, however, but rather return to everyday words. It is merely confessing that that "is not worth the trouble." Living, naturally, is never easy. You continue making the gestures commanded by existence for many reasons, the first of which is habit. Dying voluntarily implies that you have recognized, even instinctively, the ridiculous character of that habit, the absence of any profound reason for living, the insane character of that daily agitation, and the uselessness of suffering.

What, then, is that incalculable feeling that deprives the mind of the sleep necessary to life? A world that can be explained even with bad reasons is a familiar world. But, on the other hand, in a universe suddenly divested of illusions and lights, man feels an alien, a stranger. His exile is without remedy since he is deprived of the memory of a lost home or the hope of a promised land. This divorce between

---

[1] From the point of view of the relative value of truth. On the other hand, from the point of view of virile behavior, this scholar's fragility may well make us smile.

man and his life, the actor and his setting, is properly the feeling of absurdity. All healthy men having thought of their own suicide, it can be seen, without further explanation, that there is a direct connection between this feeling and the longing for death.

The subject of this essay is precisely this relationship between the absurd and suicide, the exact degree to which suicide is a solution to the absurd. The principle can be established that for a man who does not cheat, what he believes to be true must determine his action. Belief in the absurdity of existence must then dictate his conduct. It is legitimate to wonder, clearly and without false pathos, whether a conclusion of this importance requires forsaking as rapidly as possible an incomprehensible condition. I am speaking, of course, of men inclined to be in harmony with themselves.

Stated clearly, this problem may seem both simple and insoluble. But it is wrongly assumed that simple questions involve answers that are no less simple and that evidence implies evidence. A priori and reversing the terms of the problem, just as one does or does not kill oneself, it seems that there are but two philosophical solutions, either yes or no. This would be too easy. But allowance must be made for those who, without concluding, continue questioning. Here I am only slightly indulging in irony: this is the majority. I notice also that those who answer "no" act as if they thought "yes." As a matter of fact, if I accept the Nietzschean criterion, they think "yes" in one way or another. On the other hand, it often happens that those who commit suicide were assured of the meaning of life. These contradictions are constant. It may even be said that they have never been so keen as on this point where, on the contrary, logic seems so desirable. It is a commonplace to compare philosophical theories and the behavior of those who profess them. . . . Schopenhauer is often cited, as a fit subject for laughter, because he praised suicide while seated at a well-set table. This is no subject for joking. That way of not taking the tragic seriously is not so grievous, but it helps to judge a man.

In the face of such contradictions and obscurities must we conclude that there is no relationship between the opinion one has about life and the act one commits to leave it? Let us not exaggerate in this direction. In a man's attachment to life there is something stronger than all the ills in the world. The body's judgment is as good as the mind's, and the body shrinks from annihilation. We get into the habit of living before acquiring the habit of thinking. In that race which daily hastens us toward death, the body maintains its irreparable lead. In short, the essence of that contradiction lies in what I shall call the act of eluding because it is both less and more than diversion in the Pascalian sense. Eluding is the invariable game. The typical act of eluding, the fatal evasion that constitutes the third theme of this essay, is hope. Hope of another life one must "deserve" or trickery of those who live not for life itself but for some great idea that will transcend it, refine it, give it a meaning, and betray it.

.   .   .

ABSURDITY AND MEANING

All great deeds and all great thoughts have a ridiculous beginning. Great works are often born on a street-corner or in a restaurant's revolving door. So it is with absurdity. The absurd world more than others derives its nobility from that abject birth. In certain situations, replying "nothing" when asked what one is thinking about may be pretense in a man. Those who are loved are well aware of this. But if that reply is sincere, if it symbolizes that odd state of soul in which the void becomes eloquent, in which the chain of daily gestures is broken, in which the heart vainly seeks the link that will connect it again, then it is as it were the first sign of absurdity.

It happens that the stage sets collapse. Rising, streetcar, four hours in the office or the factory, meal, streetcar, four hours of work, meal, sleep, and Monday Tuesday Wednesday Thursday Friday and Saturday according to the same rhythm—this path is easily followed most of the time. But one day the "why" arises and everything begins in that weariness tinged with amazement. "Begins"—this is important. Weariness comes at the end of the acts of a mechanical life, but at the same time it inaugurates the impulse of consciousness. It awakens consciousness and provokes what follows. What follows is the gradual return into the chain or it is the definitive awakening. At the end of the awakening comes, in time, the consequence: suicide or recovery. In itself weariness has something sickening about it. Here, I must conclude that it is good. For everything begins with consciousness and nothing is worth anything except through it.

At the heart of all beauty lies something inhuman, and these hills, the softness of the sky, the outline of these trees at this very minute lose the illusory meaning with which we had clothed them, henceforth more remote than a lost paradise. The primitive hostility of the world rises up to face us across millennia. For a second we cease to understand it because for centuries we have understood in it solely the images and designs that we had attributed to it beforehand, because henceforth we lack the power to make use of that artifice. The world evades us because it becomes itself again. That stage scenery masked by habit becomes again what it is. It withdraws at a distance from us. Just as there are days when under the familiar face of a woman, we see as a stranger her we had loved months or years ago, perhaps we shall come even to desire what suddenly leaves us so alone. But the time has not yet come. Just one thing: that denseness and that strangeness of the world is the absurd.

Men, too, secrete the inhuman. At certain moments of lucidity, the mechanical aspect of their gestures, their meaningless pantomime makes silly everything that surrounds them. A man is talking on the telephone behind a glass partition; you cannot hear him, but you see his incomprehensible dumb show: you wonder why he is alive. This discomfort in the face of man's own inhumanity, this incalculable tumble before the image of what we are, this "nausea," as a writer of today calls it, is also the absurd. Likewise, the stranger who at certain seconds comes to meet us in a mirror, the familiar and yet alarming brother we encounter in our own photographs is also the absurd. . . .

I come at last to death and to the attitude we have toward it. On this point everything has been said and it is only proper to avoid pathos. Yet one will never be sufficiently surprised that everyone lives as if no one "knew." This is because in reality there is no experience of death. Properly speaking, nothing has been experienced but what has been lived and made conscious. Here, it is barely possible to speak of the experience of others' deaths. It is a substitute, an illusion, and it never quite convinces us. That melancholy convention cannot be persuasive. The horror comes in reality from the mathematical aspect of the event. If time frightens us, this is because it works out the problem and the solution comes afterward. All the pretty speeches about the soul will have their contrary convincingly proved, at least for a time. From this inert body on which a slap makes no mark the soul has disappeared. This elementary and definitive aspect of the adventure constitutes the absurd feeling. Under the fatal lighting of that destiny, its uselessness becomes evident. No code of ethics and no effort are justifiable *a priori* in the face of the cruel mathematics that command our condition. . . .

Understanding the world for a man is reducing it to the human, stamping it with his seal. The cat's universe is not the universe of the anthill. The truism "All thought is anthropomorphic" has no other meaning. Likewise, the mind that aims to understand reality can consider itself satisfied only by reducing it to terms of thought. If man realized that the universe like him can love and suffer, he would be reconciled. If thought discovered in the shimmering mirrors of phenomena eternal relations capable of summing them up and summing themselves up in a single principle, then would be seen an intellectual joy of which the myth of the blessed would be but a ridiculous imitation. That nostalgia for unity, that appetite for the absolute illustrates the essential impulse of the human drama. But the fact of that nostalgia's existence does not imply that it is to be immediately satisfied. . . .

With the exception of professional rationalists, today people despair of true knowledge. If the only significant history of human thought were to be written, it would have to be the history of its successive regrets and its impotences.

Of whom and of what indeed can I say: "I know that!" This heart within me I can feel, and I judge that it exists. This world I can touch, and I likewise judge that it exists. There ends all my knowledge, and the rest is construction. For if I try to seize this self of which I feel sure, if I try to define and to summarize it, it is nothing but water slipping through my fingers. I can sketch one by one all the aspects it is able to assume, all those likewise that have been attributed to it, this upbringing, this origin, this ardor or these silences, this nobility or this vileness. But aspects cannot be added up. This very heart which is mine will forever remain indefinable to me. Between the certainty I have of my existence and the content I try to give to that assurance, the gap will never be filled. Forever I shall be a stranger to myself. . . .

Hence the intelligence, too, tells me in its way that this world is absurd. . . . In this unintelligible and limited universe, man's fate henceforth assumes its meaning. A horde of irrationals has sprung up and surrounds him until his ultimate end. In his recovered and now studied lucidity, the feeling of the absurd becomes clear and definite. I said that the world is absurd, but I was too hasty. This world in itself is not reasonable, that is all that can be said. But what is absurd is the confrontation of this irrational and the wild longing for clarity whose call echoes in the human heart. The absurd depends as much on man as on the world. . . .

I don't know whether this world has a meaning that transcends it. But I know that I do not know that meaning and that it is impossible for me just now to know it. What can a meaning outside my condition mean to me? I can understand only in human terms. What I touch, what resists me—that is what I understand. And these two certainties—my appetite for the absolute and for unity and the impossibility of reducing this world to a rational and reasonable principle—I also know that I cannot reconcile them. What other truth can I admit without lying, without bringing in a hope I lack and which means nothing within the limits of my condition?

If I were a tree among trees, a cat among animals, this life would have a meaning, or rather this problem would not arise, for I should belong to this world. I should *be* this world to which I am now opposed by my whole consciousness and my whole insistence upon familiarity. This ridiculous reason is what sets me in opposition to all creation. I cannot cross it out with a stroke of the pen. What I believe to be true I must therefore preserve. What seems to me so obvious, even against me, I must support. And what constitutes the basis of that conflict, of that break between the world and my mind, but the awareness of it? If therefore I want to preserve it, I can through a constant awareness, ever revived, ever alert. This is what, for the moment, I must remember. . . .

Let us insist again on the method: it is a matter of persisting. At a certain point on his path the absurd man is tempted. History is not lacking in either religions or prophets, even without gods. He is asked to leap. All he can reply is that he doesn't fully understand, that it is not obvious. Indeed, he does not want to do anything but what he fully understands. He is assured that this is the sin of pride, but he does not understand the notion of sin; that perhaps hell is in store, but he has not enough imagination to visualize that strange future; that he is losing immortal life, but that seems to him an idle consideration. An attempt is made to get him to admit his guilt. He feels innocent. To tell the truth, that is all he feels—his irreparable innocence. This is what allows him everything. Hence, what he demands of himself is to live *solely* with what he knows, to accommodate himself to what is, and to bring in nothing that is not certain. He is told that nothing is. But this at least is a certainty. And it is with this that he is concerned: he wants to find out if it is possible to live *without appeal.* . . .

Before encountering the absurd, the everyday man lives with aims, a concern for the future or for justification (with regard to whom or what is not the question). He weighs his chances, he counts on "someday," his retirement or the labor of his sons. He still thinks that something in his life can be directed. In truth, he acts as if he were free, even if all the facts make a point of contradicting that liberty. But after the absurd, everything is upset. That idea that "I am," my way of acting as if everything has a meaning (even if, on occasion, I said that nothing has)—all that is given the lie in vertiginous fashion by the absurdity of a possible death. Thinking of the future, establishing aims for oneself, having preferences—all this presupposes a belief in freedom, even if one occasionally ascertains that one doesn't feel it. But at that moment I am well aware that that higher liberty, that freedom *to be,* which alone can serve as basis for a truth, does not exist. Death is there as the only reality. . . .

But at the same time the absurd man realizes that hitherto he was bound to that postulate of freedom on the illusion of which he was living. In a certain sense, that hampered him. To the extent to which he imagined a purpose to his life, he adapted himself to the demands of a purpose to be achieved and became the slave of his liberty. Thus I could not act otherwise than as the father (or the engineer or the leader of a nation, or the post-office subclerk) that I am preparing to be. . . .

The absurd enlightens me on this point: there is no future. Henceforth, this is the reason for my inner freedom. . . .

But what does life mean in such a universe? Nothing else for the moment but indifference to the future and a desire to use up everything that is given. Belief in the meaning of life always implies a scale of values, a choice, our preferences. Belief in the absurd, according to our definitions, teaches the contrary. But this is worth examining.

Knowing whether or not one can live *without appeal* is all that interests me. I do not want to get out of my depth. This aspect of life being given me, can I adapt myself to it? Now, faced with this particular concern, belief in the absurd is tantamount to substituting the quantity of experiences for the quality. If I convince myself that this life has no other aspect than that of the absurd, if I feel that its whole equilibrium depends on that perpetual opposition between my conscious revolt and the darkness in which it struggles, if I admit that my freedom has no meaning except in relation to its limited fate, then I must say that what counts is not the best of living but the most living. . . .

On the one hand the absurd teaches that all experiences are unimportant, and on the other it urges toward the greatest quantity of experiences. How, then, can one fail to do as so many of those men I was speaking of earlier—choose the form of life that brings us the most possible of that human matter, thereby introducing a scale of values that on the other hand one claims to reject?

But again it is the absurd and its contradictory life that teaches us. For the mistake is thinking that that quantity of experiences depends on the circumstances of our life when it depends solely on us. Here we have to be over-simple. To two men living the same number of years, the world always provides the same sum of experiences. It is up to us to be conscious of them. Being aware of one's life, one's revolt, one's freedom, and to the maximum, is living, and to the maximum. Where lucidity dominates, the scale of values becomes useless.

. . .

The gods had condemned Sisyphus to ceaselessly rolling a rock to the top of a mountain, whence the stone would fall back of its own weight. They had thought with some reason that there is no more dreadful punishment than futile and hopeless labor.

If one believes Homer, Sisyphus was the wisest and most prudent of mortals. According to another tradition, however, he was disposed to practice the profession of highwayman. I see no contradiction in this. Opinions differ as to the reasons why he became the futile laborer of the underworld. To begin with, he is accused of a certain levity in regard to the gods. He stole their secrets. Ægina, the daughter of Æsopus, was carried off by Jupiter. The father was shocked by that disappearance and complained to Sisyphus. He, who knew of the abduction, offered to tell about it on condition that Æsopus would give water to the citadel of Corinth. To the celestial thunderbolts he preferred the benediction of water. He was punished for this in the underworld. Homer tells us also that Sisyphus had put Death in chains. Pluto could not endure the sight of his deserted, silent empire. He dispatched the god of war, who liberated Death from the hands of her conqueror.

It is said also that Sisyphus, being near to death, rashly wanted to test his wife's love. He ordered her to cast his unburied body into the middle of the public square. Sisyphus woke up in the underworld. And there, annoyed by an obedience so contrary to human love, he obtained from Pluto permission to return to earth in order to chastise his wife. But when he had seen again the face of this world, enjoyed water and sun, warm stones and the sea, he no longer wanted to go back to the infernal darkness. Recalls, signs of anger, warnings were of no avail. Many years more he lived facing the curve of the gulf, the sparkling sea, and the smiles of earth. A decree of the gods was necessary. Mercury came and seized the impudent man by the collar and, snatching him from his joys, led him forcibly back to the underworld, where his rock was ready for him.

You have already grasped that Sisyphus is the absurd hero. He *is,* as much through his passions as through his torture. His scorn of the gods, his hatred of death, and his passion for life won him that unspeakable penalty in which the whole being is exerted toward accomplishing nothing. This is the price that must be paid for the passions of this earth. Nothing is told us about Sisyphus in the underworld. Myths are made for the imagination to breathe life into them. As for this myth, one sees merely the whole effort of a body straining to raise the huge stone, to roll it and push it up a slope a hundred times over; one sees the face screwed up, the cheek tight against the stone, the shoulder bracing the clay-covered mass, the foot wedging it, the fresh start with arms outstretched, the wholly human security of two earth-clotted hands. At the very end of his long effort measured by skyless space and time without depth, the purpose is achieved. Then Sisyphus watches the stone rush down in a few moments toward that lower world whence he will have to push it up again toward the summit. He goes back down to the plain.

It is during that return, that pause, that Sisyphus interests me. A face that toils so close to stones is already stone itself! I see that man going back down with a heavy yet measured step toward the torment of which he will never know the end. That hour like a breathing-space which returns as surely as his suffering, that is the hour of consciousness. At each of those moments when he leaves the heights and gradually sinks toward the lairs of the gods, he is superior to his fate. He is stronger than his rock.

If this myth is tragic, that is because its hero is conscious. Where would his torture be, indeed, if at every step the hope of succeeding upheld him? The workman of today works every day in his life at the same tasks, and this fate is no less absurd. But it is tragic only at the rare moments when it becomes conscious. Sisyphus, proletarian of the gods, powerless and rebellious, knows the whole extent of his wretched condition: it is what he thinks of during his descent. The lucidity that was to constitute his torture at the same time crowns his victory. There is no fate that cannot be surmounted by scorn.

If the descent is thus sometimes performed in sorrow, it can also take place in joy. This word is not too much. Again I fancy Sisyphus returning toward his rock, and the sorrow was in the beginning. When the images of earth cling too tightly to memory, when the call of happiness becomes too insistent, it happens that melancholy rises in man's heart: this is the rock's victory, this is the rock itself. The boundless grief is too heavy to bear. These are our nights of Gethsemane. But crushing truths perish from being acknowledged. Thus, Œdipus at the outset obeys fate without knowing it. But from the moment he knows, his tragedy begins. Yet at the same moment, blind and desperate, he realizes that the only bond linking him to the world is the cool hand of a girl. Then a tremendous remark rings out: "Despite so many ordeals, my advanced age and the nobility of my soul make me conclude that all is well." Sophocles' Œdipus, like Dostoevsky's Kirilov, thus gives the recipe for the absurd victory. Ancient wisdom confirms modern heroism.

One does not discover the absurd without being tempted to write a manual of happiness. "What! by such narrow ways—?" There is but one world, however. Happiness and the absurd are two sons of the same earth. They are inseparable. It would be a mistake to say that happiness necessarily springs from the absurd discovery. It happens as well that the feeling of the absurd springs from happiness. "I conclude that all is well," says Œdipus, and that remark is sacred. It echoes in the wild and limited universe of man. It teaches that all is not, has not been, exhausted. It drives out of this world a god who had come into it with dissatisfaction and a preference for futile sufferings. It makes of fate a human matter, which must be settled among men.

All Sisyphus' silent joy is contained therein. His fate belongs to him. His rock is his thing. Likewise, the absurd man, when he contemplates his torment, silences all the idols. In the universe suddenly restored to its silence, the myriad wondering little voices of the earth rise up. Unconscious, secret calls, invitations from all the faces, they are the necessary reverse and price of victory. There is no sun without shadow, and it is essential to know the night. The absurd man says yes and his effort will henceforth be unceasing. If there is a personal fate, there is no higher destiny, or at least there is but one which he concludes is inevitable and despicable. For the rest, he knows himself to be the master of his days. At that subtle moment when man glances backward over his life, Sisyphus returning toward his rock, in that slight pivoting he contemplates that series of unrelated actions which becomes his fate, created by him, combined under his memory's eye and soon sealed by his death. Thus, convinced of the wholly human origin of all that is human, a blind man eager to see who knows that the night has no end, he is still on the go. The rock is still rolling.

I leave Sisyphus at the foot of the mountain! One always finds one's burden again. But Sisyphus teaches the higher fidelity that negates the gods and raises rocks. He too concludes that all is well. This universe henceforth without a master seems to him neither sterile nor futile. Each atom of that stone, each mineral flake of that night-filled mountain, in itself forms a world. The struggle itself toward the heights is enough to fill a man's heart. One must imagine Sisyphus happy.

Drugs and the Meaning of Life
*Kenneth Keniston**

Student drug users are generally treated by the mass media as an alien wart upon the student body of America. The use of drugs to alter psychic states, associated in the public mind with the abuse of narcotics, conjures up images of moral lepers and Mafia members. These images, in turn, help prevent any real understanding of the actual meanings and functions of drug use among a small minority of today's students.

In the comments to follow, I will argue that student drug use is closely related to the dominant pressures on American students, and is but a *variant* of values that are

Source: "Drug Use and Student Values," paper presented to the National Association of Student Personnel Administrators, Washington, D.C., November 7-8, 1966. By permission of the author.

*For headnote, see page 13.

shared by many and perhaps most American undergraduates today. To be sure, only a small minority turn towards drugs; but the members of this minority group are but first-cousins to the more "normal" college student. In particular, the student drug-user shares with his non-drug-using classmates an active search for meaning through intense personal experience.

In order to understand the values shared by many American college students, we must begin by considering some of the pressures that affect today's students. With regard to drug use, two pressures are particularly important: the pressure toward cognitive professionalism, and the pressure toward psychological numbing.

COGNITIVE PROFESSIONALISM

The past two decades have seen a revolution in our expectations about college students. Rising standards of academic performance in primary and secondary schools, the "baby boom" of the war, the slowness with which major American universities have expanded their size—all have resulted in increasing selectivity by the admissions offices of the most prestigious American colleges and universities. Furthermore, once a student is admitted to college, higher admission standards have meant that more could be demanded of him; students who a generation ago would have done "A" work now find themselves doing only "C" work with the same effort. The sheer volume of required reading and writing has increased enormously; in addition, the quality of work expected has grown by leaps and bounds. Finally, for a growing number of young Americans, college is but a stepping stone to professional and graduate school after college; and as a result, consistent academic performance in college increasingly becomes a prerequisite for admission to a desirable business school, medical school, law school or graduate school.

Not only have academic pressures mounted in the past generation, but these pressures have become more and more cognitive. What matters, increasingly, to admissions committees and college graders is the kind of highly intellectual, abstracting, reasoning ability that enables a student to do well on college boards, graduate records and other admissions tests, and—once he is in college or graduate school—to turn out consistently high grades that will enable him to overcome the next academic hurdle. And while such intellectual and cognitive talents are highly rewarded, colleges increasingly frown upon emotional, affective, non-intellectual and passionate forms of expression. What is rewarded is the ability to delay, postpone and defer gratification in the interests of higher education tomorrow.

Thus, while the systematic quest for cognitive competence occupies much of the time and effort of the pre-professional student at today's selective colleges, this pursuit does little to inform the student about life's wider purposes. One of the peculiar characteristics of professional competence is that even when competence is attained, all of the other really important questions remain unanswered: what life is all about, what really matters, what to stand for, how much to stand for, what is meaningful, relevant and important, what is meaningless, valueless and false. Thus, for many students, the pursuit of professional competence must be supplemented by another, more private and less academic quest for the meaning of life. Academic efforts seem, to a large number of students, divorced from the really important "existential" and "ultimate" questions. In this way, the student's private search for meaning, significance and relevance are experienced as unconnected with or opposed to his public exertions for grades, academic success and professional competence. How students search for significance and relevance are experienced as unconnected with or opposed to his public exertions for grades, academic success and professional competence. How students search for significance and relevance of course varies enormously from individual to individual; but as I will later suggest, drug use seems—to a small group of students—a pathway to the pursuit of meaning.

STIMULUS FLOODING AND PSYCHOLOGICAL NUMBING

Every society contains pressures and demands which its members simply take for granted. Thus, the pressure for extremely high levels of cognitive efficiency seems to most of us a necessary and an even desirable aspect of modern society. Our response to the second social pressure I want to discuss is even more unreflective and automatic. This second pressure has to do with the sheer quantity, variety and intensity of external stimulation, imagery and excitation to which most Americans are subjected. For lack of a better label, I will term our condition one of increasing "stimulus flooding."

Most individuals in most societies have at some point in their lives had the experience of being so overcome by external stimulation and internal feelings that they gradually find themselves growing numb and unfeeling. Medical students, for example, commonly report that after their first and often intense reactions to the cadaver in the dissecting room, they simply "stop feeling anything" with regard to the object of their dissection. Or we have all had the experience of listening to so much good music, seeing so many fine paintings, being so overwhelmed by excellent cooking that we find ourselves simply unable to respond further to new stimuli. Similarly, at moments of extreme psychic pain and anguish, most individuals "go numb," no longer perceiving the full implications of a catastrophic situation or no longer experiencing the full range of their own feelings. This lowered responsiveness, which I will call "psychological numbing," seems causally related to the variety, persistence and intensity of psychological flooding. In a calm and tranquil field of vision, we notice the slightest motion. In a moving field, only the grossest of movements are apparent to us.

One of the conditions of life in any modern technological society is continual sensory, intellectual and emotional stimulation which produces or requires a high tendency towards psychological numbing. Some of you, I am sure, have had the experience of returning to urban American life from a calm and tranquil pastoral setting. Initially, we respond by being virtually overwhelmed with the clamor of people, sights, sounds, images and colors that demand our attention and our response. The beauty and the ugliness of the landscape continually strikes us; each of the millions of faces in our great cities has written on it the tragi-comic record of a unique life history; each sound evokes a resonant chord within us. Such periods, however, tend to be transient and fleeting; often they give way to a sense of numbness, of non-responsiveness, and of profound inattention to the very stimuli which earlier evoked so much in us. We settle in; we do not notice any more.

In all these respects, modern men confront the difficult problem of keeping "stimulation" from without to a manageable level, while at the same time protecting themselves against being overwhelmed by their own inner responses to the stimuli from the outer world. Defenses or barriers against both internal and external stimulation are, of course, essential in order for us to preserve our intactness and integrity as personalities. From earliest childhood, children develop thresholds of responsiveness and barriers against stimulation in order to protect themselves against being overwhelmed by inner or outer excitement. Similarly, in adulthood, comparable barriers, thresholds and defenses are necessary, especially when we find ourselves in situations of intense stimulation.

Thus, in at least a minority of Americans, the normal capacity to defend oneself against undue stimulation and inner excitation is exaggerated and automatized, so that it not only protects but walls off the individual from inner and outer experience. In such individuals, there develops an acute sense of being trapped in their own shells, unable to break through their defenses to make "contact" with experience or with other people, a sense of being excessively armored, separated from their own activities as by an invisible screen, estranged from their own feelings and from potentially emotion-arousing experiences in the world. Presumably most of us have had some inkling of this feeling of inner deadness and outer flatness, especially in times of great fatigue, let-down, or depression. The world seems cold and two-dimensional; food and life have lost their savor; our activities are merely "going through the motions"; our experiences lack vividness, three-dimensionality, and intensity. Above all, we feel trapped or shut in our own subjectivity.

Such feelings are, I believe, relatively common among college students, and particularly so at moments of intense stress, loss, depression, discouragement and gloom. It is at such times that the gap between the public pursuit of professional competence and the private search for meaning seems widest; it is also at these times that the chasm between individual and his own experience seems most unbridgable.

Each of the two pressures I have discussed—cognitive professionalism and stimulus flooding—evoke characteristic responses among today's American college students. The pressure for cognitive professional competence leads to a search for meaning in other areas of life; the feeling and fear of psychological numbing leads to a pursuit, even a cult, of experiences for its own sake. And the use and abuse of psychoactive drugs by students is closely related to these two themes in student values.

THE SEARCH FOR MEANING

Among today's self-conscious college students, the statement, "I'm having an identity crisis" has become a kind of verbal badge of honor, a notch in the gun, a scalp at the belt. But although the term "identity crisis" can be easily parodied and misused, it points to fundamental issues of adolescence in all societies that are particularly heightened in our own society. Since academic pursuits, on the whole, tell the student so little about life's ultimate purposes, students are turned back upon their own resources to answer questions like, "What does life mean? What kind of a person am I? Where am I going? Where do I come from? What really matters?"

Obviously, our society does not attempt to provide young Americans ready-made and neatly packaged answers to these questions. Rather, we expect that students will, in general, arrive at individual solutions to the riddles of life, and indeed, we sometimes deliberately design our educational systems so as to provoke and challenge students to profound replies. Yet at the same time, we insist that students occupy themselves with getting good grades and getting ahead in the academic world, pursuits that often seem to have relatively little to do with "ultimate" questions. Thus, students often feel obligated to turn away from their academic pursuits toward a private quest for identity or search for meaning.

To understand this search for meaning, we must recall that many of the traditional avenues to meaning and significance have dried up. Traditional religious faith is not, for most sophisticated undergraduates, a means of ascertaining the meaning of life: traditional religions often seem to students to be worn out, insincere, or superficial. Similarly, the great classic political ideologies, whether they be political liberalism, conservatism, marxism, or fascism, arouse relatively little interest among most undergraduates. Nor does the "American Way of Life," as epitomized by 100% Americanism and free enterprise, stir most students to enthusiasm, much less provide them with answers about life's ultimate purposes.

At the same time, many traditional campus activities have lost their centrality as guidelines for or rehearsal of life's ultimate purposes. There was a day, when the quest for popularity seemed to a great many undergraduates, a reflection of a broader philosophy on life in which the most important goal was to make friends, to be popular and to influence people. Today, the pursuit of popularity and social success is declining in importance, and even those who pursue friendship and social skills most avidly are likely to recognize their limitations as ultimate values. Upward mobility, another ancient American goal, has also lost much of its savor. More and more students arrive in college already "ahead in the world," from well-situated middle-class families, and not particularly worried about status and upward mobility. Nor does the old American dream of giving one's children "a better chance" make great sense of life to a generation that has been born and bred amid affluence, and that rarely imagines a society in which starvation, unemployment, or depression will be major possibilities.

One by one, then, many of the traditional sources of meaning have disappeared, at the very same time that academic life itself, because of its intense pressure and professional specialization, seems to many students increasingly irrelevant to their major existential concerns. Where, then, do students turn?

THE CULT OF EXPERIENCE

The cult of experience has often been discussed as a defining characteristic of American youth cultures. Central to this cult is a focus on the present—on today, on the here-and-now. Thus, rather than to defer gratification and enjoyment for a distant future, immediate pleasure and satisfaction are emphasized. Rather than reverence for the traditions of the past, experience in the present is stressed. Psychologically, then, such human qualities as control, planning, waiting, saving, and postponing on the one hand, and revering, recalling, remembering and respecting on the other, are equally deemphasized. In contrast, activity, adventure, responsiveness, genuineness, spontaneity and sentience are the new experiential values. Since neither the future nor the past can be assumed to hold life's meaning, the meaning of life must be sought within present experience, within the self, within its activity and responsiveness in the here-and-now.

The cult of experience has many variants and forms, most of them visible in one aspect or another on most American campuses. One such variant is what is often termed "student existentialism." At the more intellectually sophisticated campuses, this outlook manifests itself in an intense interest in existential writers like Sartre and Camus. But at a variety of other colleges, it is evident by student discussions of the importance of simple human commitments as contrasted with absolute values, and by a pervasively high estimation of such human qualities as authenticity, genuineness, sincerity and directness, which are contrasted with phoniness, inauthenticity, artificiality and hypocrisy. This student existentialism is humanistic rather than religious, and its most immediate goals are love, intimacy, directness, immediacy, empathy and sympathy for one's fellow man. Thus, what matters is interpersonal honesty, "really being yourself," and genuineness, and what is most unacceptable is fraudulence, "role playing," "playing games."

The same focus on simple human experiences in the present is seen in a variety of other student values. Consider, for example, the great growth in interest in the arts—music, poetry, sculpture, drama, the film as art. Or recall the importance to many students of nature—that is, of wilderness, of the rapidly disappearing natural beauty of this country. Sex, too, is related to the same theme; for sex is above all that human experience that seems to require directness and immediacy, and that cannot be forced. Similarly, the focus by many students on family life—their willingness to sacrifice other goals for the creation and maintenance of a good family and a "productive" relationship with their future wives—these too are variations on the same experiential theme.

DISAFFILIATION AND DRUGS

The two student values I have discussed—the search for meaning and the cult of experience—are intimately related to the pressures I have outlined earlier. The search for meaning is made more urgent by the amount of time and energy the average student must spend in pre-professional academic pursuits that often appear to him irrelevant to his basic concerns. And the cult of experience is intensified by the fear or feeling in many undergraduates that, instead of becoming more open to themselves and to experience, they are becoming increasingly numbed and closed off from all that is exciting and beautiful. Both of these values are, as well, related to the use and abuse of drugs by students. For such is the cultism and propaganda that surrounds drugs, especially the hallucinogens, that many students have come to feel the states induced by these drugs will automatically produce a revelation of life's meaning, or at least an experience which itself will be highly significant and illuminating. Similarly, to the undergraduate who feels himself unduly walled-off from experience, drugs like the hallucinogens and the amphetamines (which intensify and alter ordinary states of consciousness) may seem a chemical sledge hammer for breaking out of his shell.

Obviously, despite the congruence of drug use with important student values in American colleges, the vast majority of American students do not seek meaning and experience primarily via psychoactive compounds. There are other values in most students that conflict sharply with drug use—for example, a kind of "do-it-yourselfism" that strongly rejects "artificial" and "chemical" means of altering psychic states; a sense of social responsibility that enjoins the student against doing socially disapproved things like abusing drugs; and—perhaps most important—a legitimate fear of the possible bad effects of drug use. Social and geographic factors also contribute to the low incidence of drug use. On many campuses, drugs are simply not available; on other campuses, the prevalent value system (e.g., religious fundamentalism) is completely at odds with the use of psychoactive compounds. Thus, despite the presence of some values which are consistent with drug use, most students have other values that argue against drug use. It is only a minority who are persuaded to choose drugs as a primary means of searching for meaning.

I doubt that it is possible to present an exact portrait of *the* type of student who is likely to use and abuse drugs. My own experience with student drug-users convinces me that there are many different motives for drug use and abuse, and there are many different factors—psychological, sociological, cultural and situational—that determine whether one student will use drugs while another will not. But despite the diversity of student types who *may* become involved in drug use, there is, I believe, one type that is particularly prone to drug abuse. Students of this type have, I think, particularly few values that militate against drug use and particularly strong motivations that incline them toward drugs, especially the hallucinogens. I will call such students "disaffiliates."

Elsewhere I have attempted a more comprehensive description of disaffiliates or "alienated" students. Here I will merely summarize some of the factors that predispose these students toward drug abuse. The defining characteristic of the disaffiliate is his generalized rejection of prevalent American values, which he rejects largely on esthetic, cultural and "humanistic" grounds. Such students are rarely political activists, and they are rarely concerned with the issues of economic, social and political justice that agitate many of their classmates. For these students, the problem is not political or social, but esthetic: American society is ugly, trashy, cheap and commercial; it is dehumanizing; its middle-class values are seen as arbitrary, materialistic, narrow and hypocritical. Thus, those conventional values which deem experimentation with drugs—or experimentation of all kinds—illicit are strongly rejected by disaffiliates; for them, what matters is somehow to seek a way out of the "air conditioned nightmare" of American society.

A second characteristic of disaffiliates is a more or less intense feeling of estrangement from their own experience. Such students are highly aware of the masks, façades and defenses people erect to protect themselves; and not only do they criticize these "defenses" in others, but even more strongly in themselves. Any "defense" that might prevent awareness of inner life must be rooted out and destroyed; self-deception, lack of self-awareness and any "phoniness" with regard to oneself are cardinal sins. But despite their efforts to make contact with their "real" selves and to have "genuine" experiences, disaffiliates often feel separated from both self and others. They experience themselves as separated from both self and others by a gray opaque filter, by invisible screens and curtains, by protective shells and crusts that prevent them from the fullness of experience. They recriminate themselves for their lack of feeling expressiveness, spontaneity and genuineness. One such student described human relations as being like people trying to contact and touch each other through airtight space suits; another talked of a wax that was poured over all of his experience, preventing him from genuine contact with it. These feelings of estrangement are often accompanied by considerable depression and a strong sense of personal isolation. Indeed, depression, following the loss of an important relationship, is commonly found in the immediate background of the student who begins to abuse drugs. For the student with intensified feelings of estrangement from himself and others, drugs that promise to heighten experience seem a tempting way out of his shell.

A third relevant characteristic of disaffiliates is a fantasy of fusion and merger, which contrasts sharply with their current feelings of estrangement. In the background, many of these students have a concept of an almost mystical fusion with nature, with their own inner lives, or above all with other people—a kind of communication that requires no words, a kind of oneness with nature or the world that has characterized intense religious experience for centuries, a special kind of automatic oneness with another. For an undergraduate with an especial longing for oneness with others, the hallucinogens are especially tempting. For one characteristic of the drug experience is a weakening or breaking down of the boundaries of the self such that many individuals in fact report feelings of oneness, merger and fusion with others.

On several grounds, then, the disaffiliate is strongly attracted by drugs. Arguments based on traditional American values against drug use carry little weight for him; on the contrary, he values most in himself his own rebellion against such "middle-class" standards. His frequent feelings of estrangement from experience lead him to seek means of breaking through the walls, shells, filters and barriers that separate him from the world. And his fantasy of fusion disposes him to seek out chemical instruments that will increase his "oneness" with others. For such students, who are young, searching, uncommitted and anti-conventional, drug use is primarily a way of searching for meaning via the chemical intensification of personal experience.

DRUG USE AND STUDENT VALUES

In portraying one type of student who is predisposed toward the abuse of psychoactive compounds, and in relating drug use to more general student values, I do not mean to portray all American students as potential drug users, nor to decry the student values which may be interpreted to support drug use. On the contrary, I am convinced that the search for meaning through experience is an important and valid search, although I personally doubt that present experience is itself enough to provide "the meaning of life." Similarly, even those students who actively abuse drugs are seeking, I think, legitimate ends through unwise means. It will not do, therefore, to repudiate students who misuse drugs as moral lepers and "addicts" without trying to understand their motives for drug use, and the values and goals they pursue. These motives are rarely simply anti-social or "thrill-seeking." On the contrary, they almost always involve a legitimate (if misguided) search for ultimate meaning and contact with the world. In dealing with individual drug-users, then, we must attempt to provide the student with alternate routes to attain his valid goals. And since drug use is notoriously hazardous and uncertain, it should not prove impossible to suggest better avenues toward meaning and experience than drugs. Even Dick Alpert commented, in an earlier talk, that he considers the use of LSD a "crutch"; we must help our students to understand that this is so.

.   .   .

As for counseling student drug-users—potential and actual—I think it important to acknowledge that the question of drug use is, in the last analysis, not a medical issue, but an existential, philosophical and ethical issue. Student drug-users are, as a group, extremely knowledgeable about the possible bad effects of drug use; they can usually teach their counselors, deans and advisors a good deal about the potential bad side effects of drugs. They will argue—with considerable validity—that society does not prohibit the use of other psychoactive compounds (e.g., alcohol, tobacco) which in some ways are far more dangerous than many of the hallucinogens or amphetamines. In the last analysis, then, whether one chooses or not to use drugs, in full consciousness of their possible bad effects and the legal implications of drug use, becomes an existential rather than a medical decision. It is a matter of how one chooses to live one's life, how one hopes to seek experience, where and how one searches for meaning. To be sure, I doubt that we can hope to persuade students that drugs are ethically, humanly or existentially undesirable if they are not already persuaded. But I think we can at least help the student to confront the fact that in using drugs he is making a statement about how he wants to live his life. And we can, perhaps, in our own lives and by our own examples, suggest that moral courage, a critical awareness of the defects of our society, a capacity for intense experience and the ability to relate genuinely to other people are not the exclusive possessions of drug-users.

In the long run, then, those of us who are critical of student drug abuse must demonstrate to our students that there are better and more lasting ways to experience the fullness, the depth, the variety and the richness of life than that of ingesting psychoactive chemicals. It would be a pity, for example, to allow the advocates of LSD to take exclusive possession of the term "consciousness-expansion." Consciousness-expansion seems to me not the prerogative solely of psychoactive compounds, but of education in its fullest sense. The giants of our intellectual tradition were men who combined critical consciousness of their own societies with a capacity for experience and relatedness. And they were consciousness-expanders par excellence in their attempts to lead their fellows out of ignorance to a clearer perception of truth, beauty, and reality.

Thus, insofar as we can truly and honestly help our students to become educated in the fullest sense, we will be able to provide alternative routes to the pursuit of meaning, the quest for experience and the expansion of consciousness. Obviously, much of what passes for higher education in America fails to accomplish any of these high objectives. As long as it continues to fail, I suspect that drugs will continue to be a problem on our campuses and in our society.

The Meaning of Life: Christianity Versus Science

K. E. M. Baier

K. E. M. Baier (1917-   ) was president of the Australian Association of Philosophy in 1961. He now teaches philosophy at the University of Pittsburgh. He wrote *Moral Point of View* (1958).

Tolstoy, in his autobiographical work, "A Confession," reports how, when he was fifty and at the height of his literary success, he came to be obsessed by the fear that life was meaningless.

At first I experienced moments of perplexity and arrests of life, as though I did not know what to do or how to live; and I felt lost and became dejected. But this passed, and I went on living as before. Then these moments of perplexity began to recur oftener and oftener, and always in the same form. They were always expressed by the questions: What is it for? What does it lead to? At first it seemed to me that these were aimless and irrelevant questions. I thought that it was all well known, and that if I should ever wish to deal with the solution it would not cost me much effort; just at present I had no time for it, but when I wanted to, I should be able to find the answer. The questions however began to repeat themselves frequently, and to demand replies more and more insistently; and like drops of ink always falling on one place they ran together into one black blot.[1]

A Christian living in the Middle Ages would not have felt any serious doubts about Tolstoy's questions. To him it would have seemed quite certain that life had a meaning and quite clear what it was. The medieval Christian world picture assigned to man a highly significant, indeed the central part in the grand scheme of things. The universe was made for the express purpose of providing a stage on which to enact a drama starring Man in the title role.

To be exact, the world was created by God in the year 4004 B.C. Man was the last and the crown of this creation, made in the likeness of God, placed in the Garden of Eden on earth, the fixed centre of the universe, round which revolved the nine heavens of the sun, the moon, the planets and the fixed stars, producing as they revolved in their orbits the heavenly harmony of the spheres. And this gigantic universe was created for the enjoyment of man, who was originally put in control of it. Pain and death were unknown in paradise. But this state of bliss was not to last. Adam and Eve ate of the forbidden tree of knowledge, and life on this earth turned into a death-march through a vale of tears. Then, with the birth of Jesus, new hope came into the world. After He had died on the cross, it became at least

Source: "The Meaning of Life," Inaugural Lecture delivered at the Canberra University College (1957), pp. 3-29. Reprinted with permission of the author.

[1] Count Leo Tolstoy, "A Confession," reprinted in *A Confession, The Gospel in Brief, and What I Believe*, No. 229, The World's Classics (London: Geoffrey Cumberlege, 1940).

possible to wash away with the purifying water of baptism some of the effects of Original Sin and to achieve salvation. That is to say, on condition of obedience to the law of God, man could now enter heaven and regain the state of everlasting, deathless bliss, from which he had been excluded because of the sin of Adam and Eve.

To the medieval Christian the meaning of human life was therefore perfectly clear. The stretch on earth is only a short interlude, a temporary incarceration of the soul in the prison of the body, a brief trial and test, fated to end in death, the release from pain and suffering. What really matters, is the life after the death of the body. One's existence acquires meaning not by gaining what this life can offer but by saving one's immortal soul from death and eternal torture, by gaining eternal life and everlasting bliss.

The scientific world picture which has found ever more general acceptance from the beginning of the modern era onwards is in profound conflict with all this. At first, the Christian conception of the world was discovered to be erroneous in various important details. The Copernican theory showed up the earth as merely one of several planets revolving around the sun, and the sun itself was later seen to be merely one of many fixed stars each of which is itself the nucleus of a solar system similar to our own. Man, instead of occupying the centre of creation, proved to be merely the inhabitant of a celestial body no different from millions of others. Furthermore, geological investigations revealed that the universe was not created a few thousand years ago, but was probably millions of years old.

Disagreements over details of the world picture, however, are only superficial aspects of a much deeper conflict. The appropriateness of the whole Christian outlook is at issue. For Christianity, the world must be regarded as the "creation" of a kind of Superman, a person possessing all the human excellences to an infinite degree and none of the human weaknesses, Who has made man in His image, a feeble mortal, foolish copy of Himself. In creating the universe, God acts as a sort of playwright-cum-legislator-cum-judge-cum-executioner. In the capacity of playwright, He creates the historical world process, including man. He erects the stage and writes, in outline, the plot. He creates the *dramatis personae* and watches over them with the eye partly of a father, partly of the law. While on stage, the actors are free to extemporise, but if they infringe the divine commandments, they are later dealt with by their creator in His capacity of judge and executioner.

Within such a framework, the Christian attitudes towards the world are natural and sound: it is natural and sound to think that all is arranged for the best even if appearances belie it; to resign oneself cheerfully to one's lot; to be filled with awe and veneration in regard to anything and everything that happens; to want to fall on one's knees and worship and praise the Lord. These are wholly fitting attitudes within the framework of the world view just outlined. And this world view must have seemed wholly sound and acceptable because it offered the best explanation which was then available of all the observed phenomena of nature.

As the natural sciences developed, however, more and more things in the universe came to be explained without the assumption of a supernatural creator. Science, moreover, could explain them better, that is, more accurately and more reliably. The Christian hypothesis of a supernatural maker, whatever other needs it was capable of satisfying, was at any rate no longer indispensable for the purpose of explaining the existence or occurrence of anything. In fact, scientific explanations do not seem to leave any room for this hypothesis. The scientific approach demands that we look for a natural explanation of anything and everything. The scientific way of looking at and explaining things has yielded an immensely greater measure of understanding of, and control over, the universe than any other way. And when one looks at the world in this scientific way, there seems to be no room for a personal relationship between human beings and a supernatural perfect being ruling and guiding men. Hence many scientists and educated men have come to feel that the Christian attitudes towards the world and human existence are inappropriate. They have become convinced that the universe and human existence in it are without a purpose and therefore devoid of meaning.[2]

1. THE EXPLANATION OF THE UNIVERSE

Such beliefs are disheartening and unplausible. It is natural to keep looking for the error that must have crept into our arguments. And if an error has crept in, then it is most likely to have crept in with science. For before the rise of science, people did not entertain such melancholy beliefs, while the scientific world picture seems literally to force them on us.

There is one argument which seems to offer the desired way out. It runs somewhat as follows. Science and religion are not really in conflict. They are, on the contrary, mutually complementary, each doing an entirely different job. Science gives provisional, if precise, explanations of small parts of the universe, religion gives final and over-all, if comparatively vague, explanations of the universe as a whole. The objectionable conclusion, that human existence is devoid of meaning, follows only if we use scientific explanations where they do not apply, namely, where total explanations of the whole universe are concerned.[3]

After all, the argument continues, the scientific world picture is the inevitable outcome of rigid adherence to scientific method and explanation, but scientific, that is, causal explanations from their very nature are incapable of producing real illumination. They can at best tell us *how* things are or have come about, but never *why*. They are incapable of making the universe intelligible, comprehensible, meaningful to us. They represent the universe as meaningless, not because it *is* meaningless, but because scientific explanations are not designed to yield answers to investigations into the why and wherefore, into the meaning, purpose, or point of things. Scientific explanations (this argument continues) began, harmlessly enough, as partial and provisional explanations of the movement of material bodies, in particular the planets, within the general framework of the medieval world picture. Newton thought of the universe as a clock made, originally wound up, and occasionally set right by God. His laws of motion only revealed the ways in which the heavenly machinery worked. Explaining the movement of the planets by these laws was analogous to explaining the machinery of a watch. Such explanations showed *how* the thing worked, but not *what it was for* or *why* it existed. Just as the explanation of how a watch works can help our understanding of the watch only if, in addition, we assume that there is a watchmaker who has designed it for a purpose, made it, and wound it up, so the Newtonian explanation of the solar

[2] See e.g. Edwyn Bevan, *Christianity*, pp. 211-227. See also H. J. Paton, *The Modern Predicament* (London: George Allen and Unwin Ltd., 1955) pp. 103-116, 374.
[3] See for instance, L. E. Elliott-Binns, *The Development of English Theology in the Later Nineteenth Century* (London: Longmans, Green & Co., 1952) pp. 30-33.

system helps our understanding of it only on the similar assumption that there is some divine artificer who has designed and made this heavenly clockwork for some purpose, has wound it up, and perhaps even occasionally sets it right, when it is out of order.

Socrates, in the Phaedo, complained that only explanations of a thing showing the good or purpose for which it existed could offer a *real* explanation of it. He rejected the kind of explanation we now call "causal" as no more than mentioning "that without which a cause could not be a cause," that is, as merely a necessary condition, but not the *real* cause, the real explanation.[4] In other words, Socrates held that *all* things can be explained in two different ways: either by mentioning merely a necessary condition, or by giving the *real* cause. The former is not an elucidation of the explicandum, not really a help in understanding it, in grasping its "why" and "wherefore."

This Socratic view, however, is wrong. It is not the case that there are two kinds of explanation for everything, one partial, preliminary, and not really clarifying, the other full, final, and illuminating. The truth is that these two kinds of explanation are equally explanatory, equally illuminating, and equally full and final, but that they are appropriate for different kinds of explicanda.

When in an uninhabited forest we find what looks like houses, paved streets, temples, cooking utensils, and the like, it is no great risk to say that these things are the ruins of a deserted city, that is to say, of something man-made. In such a case, the appropriate explanation is teleological, that is, in terms of the purposes of the builders of that city. On the other hand, when a comet approaches the earth, it is similarly a safe bet that, unlike the city in the forest, it was not manufactured by intelligent creatures and that, therefore, a teleological explanation would be out of place, whereas a causal one is suitable.

It is easy to see that in some cases causal, and in others teleological, explanations are appropriate. A small satellite circling the earth may or may not have been made by man. We may never know which is the true explanation, but either hypothesis is equally explanatory. It would be wrong to say that only a teleological explanation can *really* explain it. Either explanation would yield complete clarity although, of course, only one can be true. Teleological explanation is only one of several that are possible.

It may indeed be strictly correct to say that the question *"Why* is there a satellite circling the earth?" can only be answered by a teleological explanation. It may be true that "Why?"-questions can really be used properly only in order to elicit *someone's reasons for* doing something. If this is so, it would explain our dissatisfaction with causal answers to "Why?"-questions. But even if it is so, it does not show that "Why is the satellite there?" *must be answered by a teleological explanation.* It shows only that either it must be so answered or it must not be asked. The question "Why have you stopped beating your wife?" can be answered only by a teleological explanation, but if you have never beaten her, it is an improper question. Similarly, if the satellite is not man-made, "Why is there a satellite?" is improper since it implies an origin it did not have. Natural science can indeed only tell us *how* things in nature have come about and not *why,* but this is so not because something else can tell us the *why* and *wherefore,* but because there is none.

---

[4] See "Phaedo" (*Five Dialogues* by Plato, Everyman's Library No. 456) para. 99, p. 189.

What, then, does all this amount to? Merely to the claim that scientific explanations are no worse than any other. All that has been shown is that all explanations suffer from the same defect: all involve a vicious infinite regress. In other words, no type of human explanation can help us to unravel the ultimate, unanswerable mystery. Christian ways of looking at things may not be able to render the world any more lucid than science can, but at least they do not pretend that there are no impenetrable mysteries. On the contrary, they point out untiringly that the claims of science to be able to elucidate everything are hollow. They remind us that science is not merely limited to the exploration of a tiny corner of the universe but that, however far our probing instruments may eventually reach, we can never even approach the answers to the last questions: "Why is there a world at all rather than nothing?" and "Why is the world such as it is and not different?" Here our finite human intellect bumps against its own boundary walls.

Is it true that scientific explanations involve an infinite vicious regress? Are scientific explanations really only provisional and incomplete? The crucial point will be this. Do *all* contingent truths call for explanation? Is the principle of sufficient reason sound? Can scientific explanations never come to a definite end? It will be seen that with a clear grasp of the nature and purpose of explanation we can answer these questions.[5]

Explaining something to someone is making him understand it. This involves bringing together in his mind two things, a model which is accepted as already simple and clear, and that which is to be explained, the explicandum, which is not so. Understanding the explicandum is seeing that it belongs to a range of things which could legitimately have been expected by anyone familiar with the model and with certain facts.

There are, however, two fundamentally different positions which a person may occupy relative to some explicandum. He may not be familiar with any model capable of leading him to expect the phenomenon to be explained. Most of us, for instance, are in that position in relation to the phenomena occurring in a good seance. With regard to other things people will differ. Someone who can play chess, already understands chess, already has such a model. Someone who has never seen a game of chess has not. He sees the moves on the board but he cannot understand, cannot follow, cannot make sense of what is happening. Explaining the game to him is giving him an explanation, is making him understand. He can understand or follow chess moves only if he can see them as conforming to a model of a chess game. In order to acquire such a model, he will, of course, need to know the constitutive rules of chess, that is, the permissible moves. But that is not all. He must know that a normal game of chess is a competition (not all games are) between two people, each trying to win, and he must know what it is to win at chess: to manoeuvre the opponent's king into a position of check-mate. Finally, he must acquire some knowledge of what is and what is not conducive to winning: the tactical rules or canons of the game.

A person who has been given such an explanation and who has mastered

[5] In what follows I have drawn heavily on the work of Ryle and Toulmin. See for instance G. Ryle, *The Concept of Mind* (London: Hutchinson's University Library, 1949) pp. 56-60 &c. and his article, "If, So, and Because," in *Philosophical Analysis* by Max Black, and S. E. Toulmin, *Introduction to the Philosophy of Science* (London: Hutchinson's University Library, 1953).

it—which may take quite a long time—has now reached understanding, in the sense of the ability to follow each move. A person cannot in that sense understand merely one single move of chess and no other. If he does not understand any other moves, we must say that he has not yet mastered the explanation, that he does not really understand the single move either. If he has mastered the explanation, then he understands all those moves which he can see as being in accordance with the model of the game inculcated in him during the explanation.

However, even though a person who has mastered such an explanation will understand many, perhaps most, moves of any game of chess he cares to watch, he will not necessarily understand them all, as some moves of a player may not be in accordance with his model of the game. White, let us say, at his fifteenth move, exposes his queen to capture by Black's knight. Though in accordance with the constitutive rules of the game, this move is nevertheless perplexing and calls for explanation, because it is not conducive to the achievement by White of what must be assumed to be his aim: to win the game. The queen is a much more valuable piece than the knight against which he is offering to exchange.

An onlooker who has mastered chess may fail to understand this move, be perplexed by it, and wish for an explanation. Of course he may fail to be perplexed, for if he is a very inexperienced player he may not *see* the disadvantageousness of the move. But there is such a need whether anyone sees it or not. The move *calls for* explanation because to anyone who knows the game it must appear to be incompatible with the model which we have learnt during the explanation of the game, and by reference to which we all explain and understand normal games.

However, the required explanation of White's 15th move is of a very different kind. What is needed now is not the acquisition of an explanatory model, but the removal of the real or apparent incompatibility between the player's move and the model of explanation he has already acquired. In such a case the perplexity can be removed only on the assumption that the incompatibility between the model and the game is merely apparent. As our model includes a presumed aim of both players, there are the following three possibilities: (a) White has made a mistake: he has overlooked the threat to his queen. In that case, the explanation is that White thought his move conducive to his end, but it was not. (b) Black has made a mistake: White set a trap for him. In that case, the explanation is that Black thought White's move was not conducive to White's end, but it was. (c) White is not pursuing the end which any chess player may be presumed to pursue: he is not trying to win his game. In that case, the explanation is that White has made a move which he knows is not conducive to the end of winning his game because, let us say, he wishes to please Black who is his boss.

Let us now set out the differences and similarities between the two types of understanding involved in these two kinds of explanation. I shall call the first kind "model" understanding and explaining, respectively, because both involve the use of a model by reference to which understanding and explaining is effected. The second kind I shall call "unvexing," because the need for this type of explanation and understanding arises only when there is a perplexity arising out of the incompatibility of the model and the facts to be explained.

To sum up. The question, "Why is there anything at all?" looks like a perfectly sensible question modelled on "Why does *this* exist?" or "How has *this* originated?" It looks like a question about the origin of a thing. However, it is not such a question, for the universe is not a thing, but the totality of things. There is therefore no reason to assume that the universe has an origin. The very assumption that it has is fraught with contradictions and absurdities. If, nevertheless, it were true that the universe has originated out of nothing, then this would not call either for an unvexing or a model explanation. It would not call for the latter, because there could be no model of it taken from another part of our experience, since there is nothing analogous in our experience to origination out of nothing. It would not call for the former, because there can be no perplexity due to the incompatibility of a well-established model. If, on the other hand, as is more probable, the universe has not originated at all, but is eternal, then the question why or how it has originated simply does not arise. There can then be no question about why anything at all exists, for it could not mean how or why the universe had originated, since ex hypothesi it has no origin. And what else could it mean?

Lastly, we must bear in mind that the hypothesis that the universe was made by God out of nothing only brings us back to the question who made God or how God originated. And if we do not find it repugnant to say that God is eternal, we cannot find it repugnant to say that the universe is eternal. The only difference is that we know for certain that the universe exists, while we have the greater difficulty in even making sense of the claim that God exists.

2. THE PURPOSE OF MAN'S EXISTENCE

Our conclusion in the previous section has been that science is in principle able to give complete and real explanations of every occurrence and thing in the universe. This has two important corollaries: (i) Acceptance of the scientific world picture cannot be *one's reason for* the belief that the universe is unintelligible and therefore meaningless, though coming to accept it, after having been taught the Christian world picture, may well have been, in the case of many individuals, *the only or the main cause* of their belief that the universe and human existence are meaningless. (ii) It is not in accordance with reason to reject this pessimistic belief on the grounds that scientific explanations are only provisional and incomplete and must be supplemented by religious ones.

In fact, it might be argued that the more clearly we understand the explanations given by science, the more we are driven to the conclusion that human life has no purpose and therefore no meaning. The science of astronomy teaches us that our earth was not specially created about 6,000 years ago, but evolved out of hot nebulae which previously had whirled aimlessly through space for countless ages. As they cooled, the sun and the planets formed. On one of these planets at a certain time the circumstances were propitious and life developed. But conditions will not remain favourable to life. When our solar system grows old, the sun will cool, our planet will be covered with ice, and all living creatures will eventually perish. Another theory has it that the sun will explode and that the heat generated will be so great that all organic life on earth will be destroyed. That is the comparatively short history and prospect of life on earth. Altogether it amounts to very little when compared with the endless history of the inanimate universe.

Biology teaches us that the species man was not specially created but is merely, in a long chain of evolutionary changes of forms of life, the last link, made in the likeness not of God but of nothing so much as an ape. The rest of the universe, whether animate or inanimate, instead of serving the ends of man, is at best indifferent, at worst savagely hostile. Evolution to whose operation the emergence of man is due is a ceaseless battle among members of different species, one species being gobbled up by another, only the fittest surviving. Far from being the gentlest and most highly moral, man is simply the creature best fitted to survive, the most efficient if not the most rapacious and insatiable killer. And in this unplanned, fortuitous, monstrous, savage world man is madly trying to snatch a few brief moments of joy, in the short intervals during which he is free from pain, sickness, persecution, war or famine until, finally, his life is snuffed out in death. Science has helped us to know and understand this world, but what purpose or meaning can it find in it?

Complaints such as these do not mean quite the same to everybody, but one thing, I think, they mean to most people is that science shows life to be meaningless, because life is without purpose. The medieval world picture provided life with a purpose, hence medieval Christians could believe that life had a meaning. The scientific account of the world takes away life's purpose and with it its meaning.

There are, however, two quite different senses of "purpose." Which one is meant? Has science deprived human life of purpose in both senses? And if not, is it a harmless sense, in which human existence has been robbed of purpose? Could human existence still have meaning if it did not have a purpose in that sense?

What are the two senses? In the first and basic sense, purpose is normally attributed only to persons or their behavior as in "Did you have a purpose in leaving the ignition on?" In the second sense, purpose is normally attributed only to things, as in "What is the purpose of that gadget you installed in the workshop?" The two uses are intimately connected. We cannot attribute a purpose to a thing without implying that someone did something, in the doing of which he had some purpose, namely, to bring about the thing with the purpose. Of course, *his* purpose is not identical with *its* purpose. In hiring labourers and engineers and buying materials and a site for a factory and the like, the entrepreneur's purpose, let us say, is to manufacture cars, but the purpose of cars is to serve as a means of transportation.

There are many things that a man may do, such as buying and selling, hiring labourers, ploughing, felling trees, and the like, which are foolish, pointless, silly, perhaps crazy, to do if one has no purpose in doing them. A man who does these things without a purpose is engaging in inane, futile pursuits. Lives crammed full with such activities devoid of purpose are pointless, futile, worthless. Such lives may indeed be dismissed as meaningless. But it should also be perfectly clear that acceptance of the scientific world picture does not force us to regard our lives as being without a purpose in this sense. Science has not only not robbed us of any purpose which we had before, but it has furnished us with enormously greater power to achieve these purposes. Instead of praying for rain or a good harvest or offspring, we now use ice pellets, artificial manure, or artificial insemination.

By contrast, having or not having a purpose, in the other sense, is value neutral. We do not think more or less highly of a thing for having or not having a purpose. "Having a purpose," in this sense, confers no kudos, "being purposeless" carries no stigma. A row of trees growing near a farm may or may not have a purpose: it may or may not be a windbreak, may or may not have been planted or deliberately left standing there in order to prevent the wind from sweeping across the fields. We do not in any way disparage the trees if we say they have no purpose, but have just grown that way. They are as beautiful, made of as good wood, as valuable, as if they had a purpose. And, of course, they break the wind just as well. The same is true of living creatures. We do not disparage a dog when we say that it has no purpose, is not a sheep dog or a watch dog or a rabbiting dog, but just a dog that hangs around the house and is fed by us.

Man is in a different category, however. To attribute to a human being a purpose in that sense is not neutral, let alone complimentary: it is offensive. It is degrading for a man to be regarded as merely serving a purpose. If, at a garden party, I ask a man in livery, "What is your purpose?" I am insulting him. I might as well have asked, "What are you *for?*" Such questions reduce him to the level of a gadget, a domestic animal, or perhaps a slave. I imply that *we* allot to *him* the tasks, the goals, the aims which he is to pursue; that *his* wishes and desires and aspirations and purposes are to count for little or nothing. We are treating him, in Kant's phrase, merely as a means to our ends, not as an end in himself.

The Christian and the scientific world pictures do indeed differ fundamentally on this point. The latter robs man of a purpose in this sense. It sees him as a being with no purpose allotted to him by anyone but himself. It robs him of any goal, purpose, or destiny appointed for him by any outside agency. The Christian world picture, on the other hand, sees man as a creature, a divine artifact, something halfway between a robot (manufactured) and an animal (alive), a homunculus, or perhaps Frankenstein, made in God's laboratory, with a purpose or task assigned him by his Maker.

However, lack of purpose in this sense does not in any way detract from the meaningfulness of life. I suspect that many who reject the scientific outlook because it involves the loss of purpose of life, and therefore meaning, are guilty of a confusion between the two senses of "purpose" just distinguished. They confusedly think that if the scientific world picture is true, then their lives must be futile because that picture implies that man has no purpose given him from without. But this is muddled thinking, for, as has already been shown, pointlessness is implied only by purposelessness in the other sense, which is not at all implied by the scientific picture of the world. These people mistakenly conclude that there can be no purpose *in* life because there is no purpose *of* life; that *men* cannot themselves adopt and achieve purposes because *man,* unlike a robot or a watchdog, is not a creature with a purpose.[6]

However, not all people taking this view are guilty of the above confusion. Some really hanker after a purpose of life in this sense. To some people the greatest attraction of the medieval world picture is the belief in an omnipotent, omniscient, and all-good Father, the view of themselves as His children who worship Him, of their proper attitude to what befalls them as submission, humility, resignation in His will, and what is often described as the "creaturely feeling."[7] All these are attitudes and feelings appropriate to a being that stands to another in the same sort of relation, though of course on a higher plane, in which a helpless child stands to his progenitor. Many regard the scientific picture of the world as cold, unsympathetic, unhomely, frightening, because it does not provide for any

[6] See e.g. "Is Life Worth Living?" B.B.C. Talk by the Rev. John Sutherland Bonnell in *Asking Them Questions,* Third Series, ed. by R. S. Wright (London: Geoffrey Cumberlege, 1950).

[7] See e.g. Rudolf Otto, *The Idea of the Holy,* pp. 9-11. See also C. A. Campbell, *On Selfhood and Godhood* (London: George Allen & Unwin Ltd., 1957) p. 246, and H. J. Paton, *The Modern Predicament,* pp. 69-71.

appropriate object of this creaturely attitude. There is nothing and no one in the world, as science depicts it, in which we can have faith or trust, on whose guidance we can rely, to whom we can turn for consolation, whom we can worship or submit to—except other human beings. This may be felt as a keen disappointment, because it shows that the meaning of life cannot lie in submission to His will, in acceptance of whatever may come, and in worship. But it does not imply that life can have *no* meaning. It merely implies that it must have a different meaning from that which it was thought to have. Just as it is a great shock for a child to find that he must stand on his own feet, that his father and mother no longer provide for him, so a person who has lost his faith in God must reconcile himself to the idea that he has to stand on his own feet, alone in the world except for whatever friends he may succeed in making.

Let us, however, for argument's sake, waive all these objections. There remains one fundamental hurdle which no form of Christianity can overcome: the fact that it demands of man a morally repugnant attitude towards the universe. It is now very widely held[8] that the basic element of the Christian religion is an attitude of worship towards a being supremely worthy of being worshipped and that it is religious feelings and experiences which apprise their owner of such a being and which inspire in him the knowledge or the feeling of complete dependence, awe, worship, mystery, and self-abasement. There is, in other words, a bi-polarity (the famous "I-Thou relationship") in which the object, "the wholly-other," is exalted whereas the subject is abased to the limit. Rudolf Otto has called this the "creature-feeling"[9] and he quotes as an expression of it, Abraham's words when venturing to plead for the men of Sodom: "Behold now, I have taken upon me to speak unto the Lord, which am but dust and ashes" (Gen. XVIII. 27). Christianity thus demands of men an attitude inconsistent with one of the presuppositions of morality: that man is not wholly dependent on something else, that man has free will, that man is in principle capable of responsibility. We have seen that the concept of grace is the Christian attempt to reconcile the claim of total dependence and the claim of individual responsibility (partial independence), and it is obvious that such attempts must fail. We may dismiss certain doctrines, such as the doctrine of original sin or the doctrine of eternal hellfire or the doctrine that there can be no salvation outside the Church as extravagant and peripheral, but we cannot reject the doctrine of total dependence without rejecting the characteristically Christian attitude as such.

3. THE MEANING OF LIFE

Perhaps some of you will have felt that I have been shirking the real problem. To many people the crux of the matter seems as follows. How can there be any meaning in our life if it ends in death? What meaning can there be in it that our inevitable death does not destroy? How can our existence be meaningful if there is no after-life in which perfect justice is meted out? How can life have any meaning if

---

[8] See e.g. the two series of Gifford Lectures most recently published: *The Modern Predicament* by H. J. Paton (London: George Allen & Unwin Ltd., 1955) pp. 69ff., and *On Selfhood and Godhood* by C. A. Campbell (London: George Allen & Unwin Ltd., 1957) pp. 231-250.

[9] Rudolf Otto, *The Idea of the Holy*, p. 9.

all it holds out to us are a few miserable earthly pleasures and even these to be enjoyed only rarely and for such a piteously short time?

I believe this is the point which exercises most people most deeply. Kirilov, in Dostoevsky's novel, *The Possessed,* claims, just before committing suicide, that as soon as we realize that there is no God, we cannot live any longer, we must put an end to our lives. One of the reasons which he gives is that when we discover that there is no paradise, we have nothing to live for.

". . . there was a day on earth, and in the middle of the earth were three crosses. One on the cross had such faith that He said to another, 'To-day thou shalt be with me in paradise.' The day came to an end, both died, and they went, but they found neither paradise nor resurrection. The saying did not come true. Listen: that man was the highest of all on earth. . . . There has never been any one like Him before or since, and never will be. . . And if that is so, if the laws of Nature did not spare even *Him,* and made even Him live in the midst of lies and die for a lie, then the whole planet is a lie and is based on a lie and a stupid mockery. So the very laws of the planet are a lie and a farce of the devil. What, then, is there to live for?"[10] And Tolstoy, too, was nearly driven to suicide when he came to doubt the existence of God and an after-life.[11] And this is true of many.

What, then, is it that inclines us to think that if life is to have a meaning, there would be an after-life? It is this. The Christian world view contains the following three propositions. The first is that since the Fall, God's curse of Adam and Eve, and the expulsion from Paradise, life on earth for mankind has not been worth while, but a vale of tears, one long chain of misery, suffering, unhappiness, and injustice. The second is that a perfect after-life is awaiting us after the death of the body. The third is that we can enter this perfect life only on certain conditions, among which is also the condition of enduring our earthly existence to its bitter end. In this way, our earthly existence which, in itself, would not (at least for many people if not all) be worth living, acquires meaning and significance: only if we endure it, can we gain admission to the realm of the blessed.

Our disappointment therefore arises out of these two propositions, that the earthly life is not worth living, and that there is another perfect life of eternal happiness and joy which we may enter upon if we satisfy certain conditions. We can regard our lives as meaningful, if we believe both. We cannot regard them as meaningful if we believe merely the first and not the second. It seems to me inevitable that people who are taught something of the history of science, will have serious doubts about the second. If they cannot overcome these, as many will be unable to do, then they must either accept the sad view that their life is meaningless or they must abandon the first proposition: that this earthly life is not worth living. They must find the meaning of their life in this earthly existence. But is this possible?

A moment's examination will show us that the Christian evaluation of our earthly life as worthless, which we accept in our moments of pessimism and dissatisfaction, is not one that we normally accept. Consider only the question of murder and suicide. On the Christian view, other things being equal, the most kindly thing to do would be for every one of us to kill as many of our friends and dear ones as still have the misfortune to be alive, and then to commit suicide

---

[10] Fyodor Dostoyevsky, *The Devils* (London: The Penguin Classics, 1953) pp. 613-614.
[11] Leo Tolstoy, *A Confession, The Gospel in Brief, and What I Believe,* The World's Classics, p. 24.

without delay, for every moment spent in this life is wasted. On the Christian view, God has not made it that easy for us. He has forbidden us to hasten others or ourselves into the next life. Our bodies are his private property and must be allowed to wear themselves out in the way decided by Him, however painful and horrible that may be. We are, as it were, driving a burning car. There is only one way out, to jump clear and let it hurtle to destruction. But the owner of the car has forbidden it on pain of eternal tortures worse than burning. And so we do better to burn to death inside.

On this view, murder is a less serious wrong than suicide. For murder can always be confessed and repented and therefore forgiven, suicide cannot—unless we allow the ingenious way out chosen by the heroine of Graham Greene's play, *The Living Room,* who swallows a slow but deadly poison and, while awaiting its taking effect, repents having taken it. Murder, on the other hand, is not so serious because, in the first place, it need not rob the victim of anything but the last lap of his march in the vale of tears, and, in the second place, it can always be forgiven. Hamlet, it will be remembered, refrains from killing his uncle during the latter's prayers because, as a true Christian, he believes that killing his uncle at that point, when the latter has purified his soul by repentance, would merely be doing him a good turn, for murder at such a time would simply despatch him to undeserved and everlasting happiness.

These views strike us as odd, to say the least. They are the logical consequence of the official medieval evaluation of this our earthly existence. If this life is not worth living, then taking it is not robbing the person concerned of much. The only thing wrong with it is the damage to God's property, which is the same both in the case of murder and suicide. We do not take this view at all. Our view, on the contrary, is that murder is the most serious wrong because it consists in taking away from some one else against his will his most precious possession, his life. For this reason, when a person suffering from an incurable disease asks to be killed, the mercy killing of such a person is regarded as a much less serious crime than murder because, in such a case, the killer is not robbing the other of a good against his will. Suicide is not regarded as a real crime at all, for we take the view that a person can do with his own possessions what he likes.

However, from the fact that these are our normal opinions, we can infer nothing about their truth. After all, we could easily be mistaken. Whether life is or is not worthwhile, is a value judgment. Perhaps all this is merely a matter of opinion or taste. Perhaps no objective answer can be given. Fortunately, we need not enter deeply into these difficult and controversial questions. It is quite easy to show that the medieval evaluation of earthly life is based on a misguided procedure.

Let us remind ourselves briefly of how we arrive at our value judgments. When we determine the merits of students, meals, tennis players, bulls, or bathing belles, we do so on the basis of some criteria and some standard or norm. Criteria and standards notoriously vary from field to field and even from case to case. But that does not mean that we have *no* idea about what are the appropriate criteria or standards to use. It would not be fitting to apply the criteria for judging bulls to the judgment of students or bathing belles. They score on quite different points. And even where the same criteria are appropriate as in the judgment of students enrolled in different schools and universities, the standards will vary from one institution to another. Pupils who would only just pass in one, would perhaps obtain honours in another. The higher the standard applied, the lower the marks, that is, the merit conceded to the candidate.

The same procedure is applicable also in the evaluation of a life. We examine it on the basis of certain criteria and standards. The medieval Christian view uses the criteria of the ordinary man: a life is judged by what the person concerned can get out of it: the balance of happiness over unhappiness, pleasure over pain, bliss over suffering. Our earthly life is judged not worth while because it contains much unhappiness, pain, and suffering, little happiness, pleasure, and bliss. The next life is judged worthwhile because it provides eternal bliss and no suffering.

I have so far only spoken of the worthwhileness, only of what a person can get out of a life. There are other kinds of appraisal. Clearly, we evaluate people's lives not merely from the point of view of what they yield to the persons that lead them, but also from that of other men on whom these lives have impinged. We judge a life more significant if the person has contributed to the happiness of others, whether directly by what he did for others, or by the plans, discoveries, inventions, and work he performed. Many lives that hold little in the way of pleasure or happiness for its owner are highly significant and valuable, deserve admiration and respect on account of the contributions made.

It is now quite clear that death is simply irrelevant. If life can be worthwhile at all, then it can be so even though it be short. And if it is not worthwhile at all, then an eternity of it is simply a nightmare. It may be sad that we have to leave this beautiful world, but it is so only if and because it is beautiful. And it is no less beautiful for coming to an end. I rather suspect that an eternity of it might make us less appreciative, and in the end it would be tedious.

It will perhaps be objected now that I have not really demonstrated that life has a meaning, but merely that it can be worthwhile or have value. It must be admitted that there is a perfectly natural interpretation of the question, "What is the meaning of life?" on which my view actually proves that life has no meaning. I mean the interpretation discussed in section 2 of this lecture, where I attempted to show that, if we accept the explanations of natural science, we cannot believe that living organisms have appeared on earth in accordance with the deliberate plan of some intelligent being. Hence, on this view, life cannot be said to have a purpose, in the sense in which man-made things have a purpose. Hence it cannot be said to have a meaning or significance in that sense.

However, this conclusion is innocuous. People are disconcerted by the thought that *life as such* has no meaning in that sense only because they very naturally think that it entails that no individual life can have meaning either. They naturally assume that *this* life or *that* can have meaning only if *life as such* has meaning. But it should by now be clear that your life and mine may or may not have meaning (in one sense) even if life as such has none (in the other). Of course, it follows from this that your life may have meaning while mine has not. The Christian view guarantees a meaning (in one sense) to every life, the scientific view does not (in any sense). By relating the question of the meaningfulness of life to the particular circumstances of an individual's existence, the scientific view leaves it an open question whether an individual's life has meaning or not. It is, however, clear that the latter is the important sense of "having a meaning." Christians, too, must feel that their life is wasted and meaningless if they have not achieved salvation. To know that even such lost lives have a meaning in another sense is no consolation to them. What matters is not that life should have a guaranteed meaning, whatever happens here or here-after, but that, by luck (Grace) or the right temperament and attitude (Faith) or a judicious life (Works) a person should make the most of his life.

"But here lies the rub," it will be said. "Surely, it makes all the difference whether there is an after-life. This is where morality comes in." It would be a mistake to believe that. Morality is not the meting out of punishment and reward. To be moral is to refrain from doing to others what, if they followed reason, they would not do to themselves, and to do for others what, if they followed reason, they would want to have done. It is, roughly speaking, to recognize that others, too, have a right to a worthwhile life. Being moral does not make one's own life worthwhile, it helps others to make theirs so.

CONCLUSION

I have tried to establish three points: (i) that scientific explanations render their explicanda as intelligible as pre-scientific explanations; they differ from the latter only in that, having testable implications and being more precisely formulated, their truth or falsity can be determined with a high degree of probability; (ii) that science does not rob human life of purpose, in the only sense that matters, but, on the contrary, renders many more of our purposes capable of realization; (iii) that common sense, the Christian world view, and the scientific approach agree on the criteria but differ on the standard to be employed in the evaluation of human lives; judging human lives by the standards of perfection, as Christians do, is unjustified; if we abandon this excessively high standard and replace it by an everyday one, we have no longer any reason for dismissing earthly existence as not worthwhile.

On the basis of these three points I have attempted to explain why so many people come to the conclusion that human existence is meaningless and to show that this conclusion is false. In my opinion, this pessimism rests on a combination of two beliefs, both partly true and partly false: the belief that the meaningfulness of life depends on the satisfaction of at least three conditions, and the belief that this universe satisfies none of them. The conditions are, first, that the universe is intelligible, second, that life has a purpose, and third, that all men's hopes and desires can ultimately be satisfied. It seemed to medieval Christians and it seems to many Christians to-day that Christianity offers a picture of the world which can meet these conditions. To many Christians and non-Christians alike it seems that the scientific world picture is incompatible with that of Christianity, therefore with the view that these three conditions are met, therefore with the view that life has a meaning. Hence they feel that they are confronted by the dilemma of accepting either a world picture incompatible with the discoveries of science or the view that life is meaningless.

I have attempted to show that the dilemma is unreal because life can be meaningful even if not all of these conditions are met. My main conclusion, therefore, is that acceptance of the scientific world picture provides no reason for saying that life is meaningless, but on the contrary every reason for saying that there are many lives which are meaningful and significant. My subsidiary conclusion is that one of the reasons frequently offered for retaining the Christian world picture, namely, that its acceptance gives us a guarantee of a meaning for human existence, is unsound. We can see that our lives can have a meaning even if we abandon it and adopt the scientific world picture instead. I have, moreover, mentioned several reasons for rejecting the Christian world picture: (i) the biblical explanations of the details of our universe are often simply false; (ii) the so-called explanations of the whole universe are incomprehensible or absurd; (iii) Christianity's low evaluation of earthly existence (which is the main cause of the belief in the meaninglessness of life) rests on the use of an unjustifiably high standard of judgment.

Suggested Readings

1. Britton, Karl, *Philosophy and the Meaning of Life* (Cambridge: Cambridge University Press, 1969).
2. Hepburn, R. W., "Questions About the Meaning of Life," *Journal of Religious Studies,* Vol. 1 (1967), 125-140.
3. Dilman, Ihlam, "Professor Hepburn on Meaning in Life," *Journal of Religious Studies,* Vol. 3 (1967), 547-554.
4. Flew, Antony, "Tolstoi and the Meaning of Life," *Ethics,* Vol. LXXIII (1963), 110-118.
5. Nielsen, Kai, "Linguistic Philosophy and the 'Meaning of Life,'" *Cross Currents* (Summer 1964), 313-334.
6. Taylor, Richard, *Good and Evil* (New York: Macmillan, 1970), Ch. 18.

Index

A

B

C

D

E

V

W

Y